COMMERCIAL TRANSACTIONS

A Survey of United States Law with International Perspective

By

Kristen David Adams

Stetson University College of Law
LeRoy Highbaugh, Sr. Chair in Faculty Research
2004–2006

AMERICAN CASEBOOK SERIES®

THOMSON

™

WEST

Mat #40346302

American Casebook Series and West Group are trademarks registered in the U.S. Patent and Trademark Office.

© 2007 Thomson/ West
          610 Opperman Drive
          P.O. Box 64526
          St. Paul, MN 55164–0526
          1–800–328–9352

Printed in the United States of America

ISBN–13: 978–0–314–15950–2
ISBN–10: 0–314–15950–9

TEXT IS PRINTED ON 10% POST
CONSUMER RECYCLED PAPER

Variation on a Theme by Rilke

A certain day became a presence to me;
there it was, confronting me – a sky, air, light:
a being. And before it started to descend
from the height of noon, it leaned over
and struck my shoulder as if with
the flat of a sword, granting me
honor and a task, The day's blow
rang out, metallic – or it was I, a bell awakened,
and what I heard was my whole self
saying and singing what it knew: I can.

By Denise Levertov, from *Breathing the Water*.

This book is dedicated to my father,

Lawrence C. Adams,

who has always believed I can.

Preface

I have enjoyed writing this book and hope students and professors alike will find it to be informative, interesting, and user-friendly.

I have endeavored to keep the book relatively concise, to make it possible to cover all 18 chapters within the space of a single-semester survey course. It is the nature of a survey course in Commercial Transactions to be less comprehensive than the sum of three courses in Sales, Leases & Licenses, Payment Systems, and Secured Transactions would be, and individual professors may desire to add material to reflect their own interests.

One highlight of the book is its inclusion of brief "International Perspectives" features discussing many of the major topics in this book from the point of view of another legal system. Although this brief material in no way substitutes for the extensive coverage of a course in international commercial law, I hope it will serve to enrich students' understanding of U.S. commercial law and encourage additional exploration of international and transnational law.

The book includes a dozen or so jurisprudential and social-justice short features, in which I have endeavored to provide brief, relatively simple sketches of important constructs such as the Coase Theorem and the concept of the Repeat Player, as well as to present social-justice concerns, including those relating to racial profiling in commerce and "unbanked" low-income people. It is my hope that students and professors will use these short features to build their legal vocabulary and to tie together many of the book's concepts at a theoretical level.

The book includes numerous graphic illustrations that endeavor to show how a complex commercial transaction unfolds.

I have included a mix of cases and problems. Most principal cases are followed by at least one note and one problem. My notes are somewhat lengthier, and somewhat fewer in number, than is common; my goal was to address the most important topics in sufficient detail to give students a thorough understanding of each concept presented. Each problem is based on a real case and is intended to give students an opportunity to apply the law presented in the principal text and preceding notes.

I have used no string citations in this textbook and very few footnotes. Instead, where appropriate, I have added marginal comments, questions, and cross-references, hoping that keeping them brief and somewhat conversational will encourage users of the book to explore the concepts they contain. I have also included line numbering and chapter-specific pagination such as 1-1 for the first page of Chapter 1, 2-1 for Chapter 2, and so forth, hoping that these devices will make it easier for students and professors to find material quickly.

Excerpts from cases, articles, and other sources are heavily edited, with most footnotes and internal citations omitted in the interest of brevity, clarity, and consistency with the main text. All excerpts are indented and appear in 9-point Century Schoolbook type, while the main text appears in 10-point type. Questions are marked with bullet points.

When time pressures or interests militate in favor of abbreviated coverage of a topic, reading the main text and omitting the excerpts should make it possible to cover the material quickly.

Throughout the text, the word "**Read**" appears in bold-face type, followed by a statutory citation. At each such point, the student should stop reading the textbook and turn to the statute I have cited. I have assumed each professor will select and assign a statutory supplement. Many fine supplements with varying content are available. At a minimum, I have assumed students will have access to the text and official comments to the Uniform Commercial Code, the United Nations Convention on Contracts for the International Sale of Goods, and major federal statutes such as the Truth in Lending Act and certain important provisions of the Bankruptcy Code. Where I have made reference to sources I expect to be difficult to locate – such as the Geneva Uniform Laws and the British Bills of Exchange Act, I have reproduced the relevant sections within the text itself. For items that are included in some statutory supplements but excluded from others – such as the United Nations Convention on International Bills of Exchange and International Promissory Notes – I have included a web address where the material can be found.

The index uses no subcategories; instead, it is presented in a simple alphabetical style. My intention in doing so was to make it possible for a beginning student to locate material on a topic such as a "financing statement" even if he or she does not yet know the concept is associated with Article 9 Secured Transactions. I also wanted to make it easy for a reader to see how a single concept – such as trade usage or good faith – shows up in many different contexts throughout the text.

I look forward to being of assistance and receiving feedback.

Kristen David Adams

Gulfport, Florida
August 2006

Acknowledgements

This project was made possible by the strong support of Dean Darby Dickerson and Stetson University College of Law, and the College of Law's Leroy Highbaugh, Sr. Chair in Faculty Research, which I held for the 2004-2005 and 2005-2006 academic years. I give my particular thanks to Dean Dickerson for her outstanding leadership by example, steadfast support, and stalwart encouragement of me throughout this lengthy process. You are a wonderful inspiration; thank you for helping me to realize this goal and many others.

Thank you very much to West Law School Publishing, especially Louis Higgins and Bonnie Karlen, for excellent support and willingness to respond to my many questions.

The College of Law community has been a tremendous resource. Among many others, I owe a particular debt of gratitude to my faculty colleagues and mentors Bradford Stone, Charles A. Dana Professor of Law Emeritus; Wm. Reece Smith, Jr., Distinguished Professorial Lecturer; and Peter F. Lake, Charles A. Dana Chair. I would also like to acknowledge the excellent counsel of Theresa J. Pulley Radwan, Associate Dean of Academics and Associate Professor of Law; Brooke J. Bowman, Assistant Professor of Legal Skills and Special Assistant to the Dean; Ellen S. Podgor, Associate Dean of Faculty Development & Distance Education and Professor of Law; Peter L. Fitzgerald, Professor of Law; and Marleen A. O'Connor, Professor of Law, who contributed their support and shared their ideas throughout this writing process in significant and very helpful ways. All errors, of course, are entirely mine.

I greatly appreciate the support of the College of Law's excellent library and the leadership of Dr. Madison M. Mosley and Professor Rebecca S. Trammell, each of whom served as Library Director during this project. Sally Waters, Head of Public Services, Reference Librarian, and Adjunct Professor; and Wanita Scroggs, International Law and Reference Librarian, have been particularly helpful with difficult research questions.

Stetson University College of Law is truly privileged to have a department of faculty support services of the highest caliber. While I completed this textbook, this department was led with skill and grace by two directors, Ms. Connie Evans, who retired in May 2006, and Ms. Louise Petren. I am grateful for the support of the whole team, and especially for the outstanding work of Ms. Shannon Mullins, now Coordinator of Faculty Support Services, and Ms. Valerie Dudley, Ms. Claudia Villari, Ms. Dianne Oeste, and Ms. Silvia Manzanero, who have had the principal day-to-day involvement with the manuscript. I am very thankful for their careful eye and diligence, commitment to excellence, creative flair, and tremendous patience with my editing.

I acknowledge with appreciation a number of fine research assistants, all current or former students of the College of Law: Susan Bolduc, Kelley Campoli, Irena Floras, Lisa Golden, Susan Gregory, Darnell Ingram, Tino Lisella, Jennifer McClean, John Meffert, Gavin Stewart, Alison Strange, and Jennifer Tanck. Thank you to each of you for your hard work.

I am fortunate to count my colleagues among my closest friends. In addition to the friends I have listed above, I would like to thank Susan Bennett, Bob Bickel, J.J. Brown, Christen Civiletto Carey, Bobbi Flowers, Leeanne Frazier, Cynthia Hawkins-León, Janice McClendon, Mark, Teresa, and Mackenzie Neil, Pam and Earl Smith, and Stephanie Shack for supporting and encouraging me throughout this process. Teazer and Jerrie Adams and Gunnar Adams Smith provided comfort and companionship for which I am thankful, as well.

My greatest personal thanks are to Clay, Kyle, and Rhett Adams, Larry Adams, and Jeff Smith, whose collective love and faith in me have sustained and encouraged me throughout this project and so many others.

I would also like to thank the following authors and copyright holders for permission to reprint portions of their work:

Peter Alces and David Frisch, Commercial Codification as Negotiation, 32 University of California at Davis Law Review 17 (1998). Reprinted with permission from the University of California at Davis Law Review.

Paul Augustine Usman Ali, The Law of Secured Finance: An International Survey of Security Interests over Personal Property (2002). Reprinted with permission from the author.

American Law Institute, Certificate of Incorporation. Reprinted with permission.

American Law Institute, Bylaws. Reprinted with permission.

American Law Institute and National Conference of Commissioners on Uniform State Laws, General Comment to the Uniform Commercial Code. Reprinted with permission.

Ian Ayres, Fair Driving: Gender and Race Discrimination in Retail Car Negotiations, 104 Harvard Law Review 817, 822-23, 825-26, 828, 834-36 (1991). Reprinted with permission from the Harvard Law Review.

Douglas G. Baird, Llewellyn's Heirs, 62 Louisiana Law Review 1287 (2002). Reprinted with permission from the Louisiana Law Review.

Richard Barnes, Distinguishing Sales and Leases: A Primer on the Scope and Purpose of UCC Article 2, 25 University of Memphis Law Review 873 (1995). Reprinted with permission from the University of Memphis Law Review.

Michael S. Barr, Microfinance and Financial Development, 26 Michigan Journal of International Law 271 (2004). Reprinted with permission from the Michigan Journal of International Law.

David Barru, How to Guarantee Contractor Performance on International Construction Projects: Comparing Surety Bonds with Bank Guarantees and Standby Letters of Credit, 37 George Washington International Law Review 51 (2005). Reprinted with permission from the George Washington International Law Review.

Thomas C. Baxter, Jr., The UCC Thrives in the Law of Commercial Payment, 28 Loyola of Los Angeles Law Review 113, 114-15 (1996). Reprinted with permission from the Loyola of Los Angeles Law Review.

Marion Benfield, Consumer Provisions in Revised Article 9, 74 Chi-Kent L. Rev. 1255 (1999). Reprinted with permission from Chicago-Kent College of Law.

Lisa Bernstein, Merchant Law in a Merchant Court: Rethinking the Code's Search for Immanent Business Norms, 144 University of Pennsylvania Law Review 1765 (1996). Reprinted with permission from the University of Pennsylvania Law Review and William S. Hein.

Lisa Bernstein, The Questionable Empirical Basis of Article 2's Incorporation Strategy: A Preliminary Study, 66 University of Chicago Law Review 710, 713 (1999). Reprinted with permission from the University of Chicago Law Review.

Richard Bethell-Jones, England, in Bank Security and Other Credit Enhancement Models: A Practical Guide on Security Devices Available to Banks in Thirty Countries Throughout the World, Winnibald E. Moojen and Mattieu Ph. Van Sint Truiden editions, First Edition, Klewer International Law 1995. Reprinted with permission from the Rights and Permissions Department, Wolters Kluwer Law & Business.

Robert F. Blomquist, The Proposed Uniform Law on International Bills of Exchange and Promissory Notes: A Discussion of Some Special and General Problems Reflected in the Form and Content, Choice of Law, and Judicial Interpretation of Articles, 9 California Western International Law Journal 30 (1979). Reprinted with permission from the California Western School of Law, Law Review, and International Law Journal.

F. H. Buckley, Machine Law, Green Bag (Summer 2003). Reprinted with permission.

Mark E. Budnitz, Payment Systems Update 2005: Substitute Checks, Remotely-Created Items, Payroll Cards, and Other New-Fangled Products, 59 Consumer Finance Law Quarterly Report 3 (2005). Reprinted with permission.
Mark E. Budnitz, The Revision of UCC Articles Three and Four: A Process Which Excluded Consumer Protection Requires Federal Action, 43 Mercer Law Review 827 (1992). Reprinted with permission.

Lech Choroszucha, Secured Transactions in Poland: Practicable Rules, Unworkable Monstrosities, and Pending Reforms, 17 Hastings International and Comparative Law Review 389. ©1989 by University of California, Hastings College of the Law. Reprinted from Hastings International and Comparative Law Review, Volume 17, Number 2, 389 (1993-1994).

R. H. Coase, The Problem of Social Cost, 3 The Journal of Law and Economics 1. Copyright 1960 by the University of Chicago. All rights reserved.

Ronald Cuming, Article 9 North of 49#: The Canadian PPS Acts and the Quebec Civil Code, 29 Loyola of Los Angeles Law Review 971 (1996). Reprinted with permission from the Loyola of Los Angeles Law Review.

Lynne L. Dallas, Law and Public Policy: A Socioeconomic Approach 247-48 (2005). Reprinted with permission from Carolina Academic Press.

Iwan Davies, The New Lex Mercatoria: International Interests in Mobile Equipment, 52 International and Comparative Law Quarterly 151 (2003). Reprinted with permission from the International and Comparative Law Quarterly.

Christina Knuz et al., Browse-Wrap Agreements: Validity of Implied Assent in Electronic Form Agreements, The Business Lawyer, Volume 59, No. 1, November 2003. Reprinted with permission from the American Bar Association.

Beth S. Desimone and Carrie A. O'Brien, Payroll Cards: Would You Like Your Pay With Those Fries, 9 North Carolina Banking Institute 35 (2005). Reprinted with permission from the North Carolina Banking Institute at the University of North Carolina School of Law, Chapel Hill.

Jurgen Dohm, Draft Uniform Law on International Bills of Exchange and International Promissory Notes, 21 American Journal of Comparative Law 474 (1973). Reprinted with permission from the American Journal of Comparative Law, the University of Michigan Law School.

Kurt Eggert, Held up in Due Course: Codification and the Victory of Form over Intent in Negotiable Instrument Law, 35 Creighton Law Review 363 (2002). Reprinted with permission. Copyright © 2002 by Creighton University.

Stephen Friedman, Text and Circumstance: Warranty Disclaimers in a World of Rolling Contracts, 46 Arizona Law Review 677, 704-05 (1972). Used with permission from the Arizona Law Review.

Marc Galanter, Why the "Haves" Come Out Ahead: Speculations on the Limits of Legal Change, Law and Society Review, 95 (1974). Reprinted with permission from Blackwell Publishing.

Geoffrey R. Gerdes, The Use of Checks and Other Noncash Payment Instruments in the United States, 360 Board of Governors of the Federal Reserve System 360, 365-369 (August 2002). Reprinted with permission.

Grant Gilmore, Article 9: What It Does for the Past, 26 Louisiana Law Review 285 (1965). Reprinted with permission from the Louisiana Law Review.

Grant Gilmore, On the Difficulties of Codifying Commercial Law, 57 Yale Law Journal 1341 (1948). Reprinted by permission of the Yale Law Journal Company and William S. Hein Company from The Yale Law Journal, Vol. 57, pages 1341-1359.

Grant Gilmore, The Commercial Doctrine of Good Faith Purchase, 63 Yale Law Journal 1057 (1954). Reprinted by permission of the Yale Law Journal Company and William S. Hein Company from The Yale Law Journal, Vol. 63, pages 1057-1122.

Gerold Herrmann, Background and Salient Features of the United Nations Convention on International Bills of Exchange and International Promissory Notes, 10 University of Pennsylvania Journal of International Business Law (1988). Reprinted with permission.

Robert Hillman, On-line Consumer Standard-Form Contracting Practices: A Survey and Discussion of Legal Implications, Cornell Law School Research Paper No. 05-012, 2. Reprinted with permission from Cornell Law School.

Robert A. Hillman, Standard-Form Contracting in the Electronic Age, 77 New York University Law Review 429 (2002). Reprinted with permission from New York University Law Review.

Sandra L. Hughes, Can Bank Tellers Tell? Legal Issues Related to Banks Reporting Financial Abuse of the Elderly, 58 Consumer Finance Law Quarterly Report 293 (2004). Reprinted with permission.

A. Brooke Iverby, Modeling UCC Drafting, 29 Loyola of Los Angeles Law Review 645 (1996). Reprinted with permission from Loyola of Los Angeles Law Review.

Thomas Jackson, Quest for Uncertainty: A Proposal for Flexible Resolution of Inherent Conflicts Between Article 2 and Article 9 of the Uniform Commercial Code, 87 Yale L.J. 907 (1977). Reprinted with permission from the Yale Law Journal.

Donald B. King, W.H. Knight, Jr., Calvin A. Kuenzel, and Bradford Stone, Commercial Transactions under the Uniform Commercial Code and Other Laws, 73 (5th ed., Lexis Nexis 1997). Reprinted with permission. Copyright 1997 Matthew Bender & Company, Inc., a member of the LexisNexis Group. All rights reserved.

Hans Kuhn, Multi-State and International Secured Transactions under Revised Article 9 of the Uniform Commercial Code, 40 Virginia Journal of International Law 1009 (2000). Reprinted with permission.

Richard LaCroix and Pamps Varangis, Using Warehouse Receipts in Developing and Transition Economies, 33 Finance & Development 36 (Sept. 1996). Reprinted with permission.

William Lawrence, Rolling Contracts Rolling over Contract Law, 41 San Diego Law Review 1099. Copyright 2004 San Diego Law Review. Reprinted with permission from the San Diego Law Review.

Lary Lawrence, What Would Be Wrong with a User-Friendly Code?: The Drafting of Revised Articles 3 and 4 of the Uniform Commercial Code, 26 Loyola of Los Angeles Law Review 659 and 670 (1993). Reprinted with permission from the Loyola of Los Angeles Law Review.

Denise Levertov, Breathing the Water. By Denise Levertov, from Breathing the Water, copyright © 1987 by Denise Levertov. Reprinted with permission from the New Directions Publishing Corp.

Jonathan Lipson, Remote Control: Revised Article 9 and the Negotiability of Information, 63 Ohio State Law Journal 1327 (2002). Reprinted with permission.

Jonathan Lipson, Secrets and Liens: The End of Notice in Commercial Finance Law, 21 Emory Bankruptcy Developments Journal 421 (2005). Reprinted with permission from Emory Bankruptcy Developments Journal, Emory University School of Law.

Joseph Lookofsky, Understanding the CISG in the USA (2d ed. 2002). Reprinted with permission from the Rights and Permissions Department, Wolters Kluwer Law & Business.

Ann Lousin, Proposed UCC 2-103 of the 2000 Version of the Revision of Article 2, 54 Southern Methodist University Law Review 913 (2001). Reprinted with permission from the SMU Law Review and the Southern Methodist University Dedman School of Law.

Ronald J. Mann, Credit Cards and Debit Cards in the United States and Japan, 55 Vanderbilt Law Review 1055 (2002). Reprinted by permission of the Vanderbilt Law Review.

Ronald J. Mann, Explaining the Pattern of Secured Credit, 110 Harvard Law Review 625 (1997). Reprinted with permission from the Harvard Law Review.

Ronald J. Mann, The Role of Secured Credit in Small-Business Lending, 86 Georgetown Law Journal 1 (1997). Reprinted with permission from the Georgetown Law Journal.

Julian B. McDonnell, Purposive Interpretation of the Uniform Commercial Code: Some Implications for Jurisprudence, 126 University of Pennsylvania Law Review 795, 797-99 (1978). Reprinted by permission of the University of Pennsylvania Law Review and William S. Hein Company from the University of Pennsylvania Law Review, Vol. 126, page 795 (1978).

David Mellinkoff, The Language of the Uniform Commercial Code, 77 Yale L.J. 185 (1967). Reprinted with permission of the Yale Law Journal.

Fred H. Miller, U.C.C. Articles 3, 4 and 4A: A Study in Process and Scope, 42 Ala. L. Rev. 405 (1991). Reprinted with permission of Alabama Law Review.

Charles Mooney, The Cape Town Convention: A New Era for Aircraft Financing. Published in Air & Space Lawyer, Volume 18, No. 1, Summer 2003. © 2003 by the American Bar Association. Reprinted with permission.

Gerald Nehra, chart from UCC Course with Professor Bradford Stone. Used with permission.

Nancy Paradis, If caller has an emergency, tell him to call 911. Reprinted with permission. Copyright St. Petersburg Times 2005.

Norman Penney, The Draft Convention on International Bills of Exchange and International Promissory Notes: Formal Requisites, 27 American Journal of Comparative

Law 515. Reprinted with permission from the American Journal of Comparative Law, the University of Michigan Law School.

William Prosser, The Assault Upon the Citadel (Strict Liability to the Consumer), 69 Yale Law Journal 1099 (1960). Reprinted with permission from the Yale Law Journal Company and William S. Hein Company from The Yale Law Journal, Vol. 69, pages 1099-1148.

Jeffrey J. Rachlinski, Standard-Form Contracting in the Electronic Age, 78 New York University Law Review 429. Reprinted with permission from the New York University Law Review. 77 N.Y.U. L. Rev. 429, 461-62, 464, 468 (2002).

Kenneth C. Randall and John C. Norris, A New Paradigm for International Business Transactions, 71 Washington University Law Quarterly 599. Reprinted with permission from Washington University Law Quarterly and authors.

Linda J. Rusch, A History and Perspective of Revised Article 2: The Never-Ending Saga of a Search for Balance, 52 Southern Methodist University Law Review 1683, 1689-1691 (1999). Originally appearing in 52 SMU Law Review 1683, 1689-91 (1999). Reprinted with permission from the SMU Law Review and the Southern Methodist University Dedman School of Law.

Steven Schwarcz, The Easy Case for the Priority of Secured Claims in Bankruptcy, 47 Duke Law Journal 425 (1997). Reprinted with permission.

Steven Schwarcz, The Impact on Securitization of Revised UCC Article 9, 74 Chi-Kent L. Rev. 947 (1999). Reprinted with permission from Chicago-Kent College of Law.

Alan Schwartz and Robert Scott, Commercial Transactions: Principles and Policies, 3-5 (2nd ed., West 1991). Reprinted with permission of West Publishing, Inc.

Robert Scott, The Rise and Fall of Article 2, 62 Louisiana Law Review 1009, 1012 (2002). Reprinted with permission from the Louisiana Law Review.

Robert E. Scott, The Truth About Secured Financing, 82 Cornell Law Review 1436 (1997). Reprinted with permission from the Cornell Law Review.

John Sebert, Remedies under Article Two of the Uniform Commercial Code: An Agenda for Review, 130 University of Pennsylvania Law Review 360, 364-366 (1981). Reprinted by permission of the University of Pennsylvania Law Review and William S. Hein Company from the University of Pennsylvania Law Review, Vol. 130, page 360 (1981).

Section of Business Law's Joint Task Force on Deposit Account Control Agreements, Initial Report of the Joint Task Force on Deposit Account Control Agreements. Published in the Business Lawyer, Volume 61, No. 2, February 2006. © 2006 by the American Bar Association. Reprinted with permission.

Robert Skilton, Some Comments on the Comments to the Uniform Commercial Code, 1966 Wisconsin Law Review 597 (1966). "Copyright 2005 by the Board of Regents of the University of Wisconsin System; Reprinted by permission of the Wisconsin Law Review."

John A. Spanogle, The UN Convention on International Bills and Notes: A Primer for Attorneys and International Bankers, 25 Uniform Commercial Code Law Journal (1992). Reprinted with permission.

Richard E. Speidel, Robert S. Summers, and James J. White, Commercial and Consumer Law: Teaching Materials, 12-14 (4th ed., West 1987). Reprinted with permission of West Publishing, Inc.

Anthony D. Taibi, Banking, Finance, and Community Economic Empowerment: Structural Economic Theory, Procedural Civil Rights, and Substantive Racial Justice, 107 Harvard Law Review 1463 (1994). Reprinted with permission from the Harvard Law Review.

Willem Vis, Forged Indorsements, 27 American Journal of Comparative Law 547 (1979). Reprinted with permission from the American Journal of Comparative Law.

Jack K. Walton, The Use of Checks and Other Noncash Payment Instruments in the United States, 360 Board of Governors of the Federal Reserve System 360, 365-369 (August 2002).

James Whitman, Commercial Law and the American Volk: A Note on Llewellyn's German Sources for the Uniform Commercial Code, 97 Yale Law Journal 156 (1987). Reprinted by permission of the Yale Law Journal Company and William S. Hein Company from the Yale Law Journal, Vol. 97, pages 156-175.

William J. Woodward, Contractual Choice of Law: Legislative Choice in an Era of Party Autonomy, 54 Southern Methodist University Law Review 697, 698-701 (2001). Reprinted with permission from the SMU Law Review and the Southern Methodist University Dedman School of Law.

A Guide to Regulation CC Compliance, Board of Governors of the Federal Reserve System. Reprinted with permission.

Check Clearing for the 21st Century Act, Board of Governors of the Federal Reserve System. Reprinted with permission.

UNCITRAL - September 2003 Draft Legislative Guide on Secured Transactions Report of the Secretary General. Reprinted with permission.

Summary of Contents

PREFACE v
ACKNOWLEDGEMENTS vii
TABLE OF CASES xxvii
TABLE OF STATUTES xxxv

PART I: INTRODUCTION

Chapter 1:   **Introducing Commercial Law** 1-1

     A.   Historical Context and the UCC 1-1
     B.   Sources of Modern Commercial Law 1-13
     C.   Overview of the UCC and Guide to Its Use 1-16
     D.   Article 1: The Baseline for the UCC 1-22

PART II: TRANSACTIONS IN GOODS

Chapter 2:   **Introducing Article 2** 2-2

     A.   The Scope of Article 2 2-2
     B.   The Article 2 Sales Contract 2-22

Chapter 3:   **Article 2 Property Interests** 3-1

     A.   Title to Goods under Article 2 3-1
     B.   Insurable Interests and Risk of Loss 3-9
     C.   Warranties of Title 3-20

Chapter 4:   **Warranties of Quality** 4-1

     A.   Express Warranties 4-1
     B.   Implied Warranties 4-10
     C.   Disclaimers, Notice, and Privity 4-25
     D.   Damages for Breach of Warranty 4-42

Chapter 5:   **Performance under Article 2** 5-1

     A.   The Obligation of Good Faith 5-1
     B.   Basic Obligations of Buyers and Sellers 5-9
     C.   Rejection and Revocation 5-19
     D.   Mending a Breach: Notice and Cure 5-32
     E.   Remedies 5-39

Chapter 6:   **Rights of Third Parties** 6-1

     A.   Void and Voidable Title 6-1
     B.   Entrustment 6-9
     C.   Article 6 Bulk Sales 6-17

PART III: PAYMENT SYSTEMS

Chapter 7:   **Introducing Articles 3 and 4**..7-2

    A.   Introduction to Payment Systems Law 7-2
    B.   The Scope of Articles 3 and 4 7-10
    C.   The Concept of Negotiability...7-17
    D.   Specialized Instruments 7-22
    E.   Stages in a Negotiable Instrument's Life....................................7-28

Chapter 8:   **Requirements for Negotiability**..8-1

    A.   The Requirement of a Writing..8-1
    B.   Signature Requirement 8-4
    C.   "Magic" Words of Negotiability 8-7
    D.   The "Unconditional" Requirement 8-10
    E.   Additional Promises and Negotiability.......................................8-18
    F.   The Requirement of a Sum Certain 8-22
    G.   The "Time Certain" Requirement..8-30

Chapter 9:   **Holders in Due Course**..9-1

    A.   The Concept of a Holder..9-1
    B.   Indorsement 9-4
    C.   Real and Personal Defenses...9-14
    D.   Proving Holder-in-Due-Course Status..9-22
    E.   Special Problems Involving Holders 9-41

Chapter 10:   **The Collection Process** 10-1

    A.   Introducing the Collection Process 10-1
    B.   Banks and Their Customers...10-31

Chapter 11:   **Liability under Articles 3 and 4** 11-1

    A.   Contract Liability under Articles 3 and 4 11-1
    B.   Warranty Liability under Articles 3 and 4 11-22
    C.   Tort Liability under Articles 3 and 4..11-30

Chapter 12:   **Credit Cards, Debit Cards, Electronic Payments, and**
                 Nonbank Systems 12-1

    A.   Credit Cards 12-1
    B.   Electronic Fund Transfers...12-22
    C.   Non-Bank Financial Services 12-40

PART IV: SECURED TRANSACTIONS

Chapter 13: **An Introduction to Article 9** 13-2

    A.   The Purpose and Scope of Article 9 13-2
    B.   Types of Collateral 13-21
    C.   Types of Creditors 13-29

Chapter 14: **The Rights of Debtors and Secured Parties Vis-à-vis One Another** 14-1

    A.   Creating a Security Interest 14-1
    B.   Attachment of a Security Interest 14-29

Chapter 15: **Perfection of Security Interests** 15-1

    A.   Perfection by Filing 15-1
    B.   Other Means of Perfection.. 15-37

Chapter 16: **Priorities Among Creditors** 16-1

    A.   Introduction to Priority 16-1
    B.   Priority Rules for Unperfected Interests.......................................16-6
    C.   Priority Rules Among Secured Creditors.................................... 16-10
    D.   Priority Rules When Collateral is Sold.. 16-24
    E.   Priority Rules for Lien Creditors... 16-33

Chapter 17: **Default** 17-1

    A.   The Right of Repossession..17-1
    B.   Sale or Other Disposition of the Collateral................................. 17-18
    C.   The Right of Redemption.. 17-39

PART V: DOCUMENTARY TRANSACTIONS

Chapter 18: **Documentary Sales** 18-1

    A.   An Introduction to Documentary Sales...18-1
    B.   Letters of Credit.. 18-12
    C.   Documents of Title 18-27

Table of Contents

PREFACE V

ACKNOWLEDGEMENTS vii

TABLE OF CASES xxvii

TABLE OF STATUTES xxxv

PART I: INTRODUCTION

Chapter 1:   **Introducing Commercial Law** 1-1

A.   Historical Context and the UCC 1-1
        The UCC: Its Origins and Authorship 1-1
        The Purpose and Philosophy of the UCC 1-5
        UCC Revisions and Nonuniform Enactment 1-8

B.   Sources of Modern Commercial Law 1-13
        International Commercial Law 1-15

C.   Overview of the UCC and Guide to Its Use 1-16
        The Articles' Relationship to One Another 1-18
        Recurring Themes in the Code 1-19
        Reading the Code 1-21

D.   Article 1: The Baseline for the UCC 1-22
        The Scope of Article 1 1-22
        Article 1's Lengthy Definitions 1-22
        Choice of Law under the Code 1-23

PART II: TRANSACTIONS IN GOODS

Chapter 2:   **Introducing Article 2** 2-2

A.   The Scope of Article 2 2-2
        Sales vs. Leases 2-2
        Goods vs. Services: The Major Tests 2-6
        Goods vs. Services: Computer Information 2-14
        Connecting "Sale" and "Goods" 2-16
        Merchants and Nonmerchants under Article 2 2-18
        International Perspective: The CISG's Scope 2-20

B.   The Article 2 Sales Contract 2-22
        Mutual Assent in Boilerplate Contracts 2-24
        International Perspective: Battle of the Forms 2-34
        Mutual Assent in Rolling Contracts 2-35
        Mutual Assent in Electronic Contracts 2-38
        The Parol Evidence Rule 2-42
        International Perspective: Parol Evidence 2-47
        The Statute of Frauds 2-47
        International Perspective: Oral Contracts 2-53
        The Proposed Revisions to Article 2 2-54

Chapter 3:   **Article 2 Property Interests**...3-1

    A.   Title to Goods under Article 2..3-1
            International Perspective: Passage of Title 3-8
    B.   Insurable Interests and Risk of Loss...3-9
            International Perspective: Risk of Loss 3-19
    C.   Warranties of Title...3-20
            International Perspective: Warranties of Title 3-25

Chapter 4:   **Warranties of Quality**...4-1

    A.   Express Warranties..4-1
            International Perspective: Warranties.......................................4-9
    B.   Implied Warranties...4-10
            Implied Warranty of Merchantability 4-11
            Fitness for a Particular Purpose 4-21
    C.   Disclaimers, Notice, and Privity...4-25
            Disclaimers 4-26
            International Perspective: Disclaimer 4-30
            Notice 4-31
            International Perspective: Notice 4-35
            Privity 4-36
            International Perspective: Privity 4-41
    D.   Damages for Breach of Warranty...4-42
            International Perspective: Remedies.......................................4-50

Chapter 5:   **Performance under Article 2**...5-1

    A.   The Obligation of Good Faith 5-1
            International Perspective: Good Faith 5-8
    B.   Basic Obligations of Buyers and Sellers.....................................5-9
            Installment Sales 5-10
            Single-Delivery Sales...5-16
            Acceptance 5-17
            International Perspective: Party Obligations 5-19
    C.   Rejection and Revocation..5-19
            Rejection 5-20
            Revocation...5-25
            International Perspective: Nonconformity 5-30
    D.   Mending a Breach: Notice and Cure..5-32
            International Perspective: Mending a Breach 5-39
    E.   Remedies...5-39
            Remedies Available to the Buyer..5-41
            Remedies Available to the Seller 5-47
            International Perspective: Remedies.......................................5-52

Chapter 6:   **Rights of Third Parties**...6-1

    A.   Void and Voidable Title...6-1
            International Perspective: Third Parties 6-9

  B. Entrustment...6-9
      International Perspective: Entrustment....................................6-17
  C. Article 6 Bulk Sales...6-17
      International Perspective: Bulk Sales.......................................6-23

PART III: PAYMENT SYSTEMS

Chapter 7: **Introducing Articles 3 and 4**..7-2

  A. Introduction to Payment Systems Law...................................7-2
      International Perspective: Payment Systems.............................7-7
      Payment Systems Law: U.S. Top Trading Partners...................7-10
  B. The Scope of Articles 3 and 4..7-10
      Merger and Conditional Payment...7-11
      An Introduction to Notes and Drafts.......................................7-14
      International Perspective: The CIBN's Scope...........................7-17
  C. The Concept of Negotiability..7-17
      Third-Party Rights in Goods...7-18
      Third-Party Rights in a Check..7-18
      Third-Party Rights in a Note..7-21
      Third Party Rights in an Assigned Debt..................................7-21
      International Perspective: Negotiability...................................7-22
  D. Specialized Instruments..7-22
  E. Stages in a Negotiable Instrument's Life...............................7-28
      International Perspective: Stages in the Life of a Negotiable
        Instrument...7-30

Chapter 8: **Requirements for Negotiability**...8-1

  A. The Requirement of a Writing...8-1
      International Perspective: What Is a Writing?..........................8-3
  B. Signature Requirement...8-4
      International Perspective: Signatures.......................................8-6
  C. "Magic" Words of Negotiability..8-7
      International Perspective: "Magic" Words................................8-8
  D. The "Unconditional" Requirement...8-10
      International Perspective: Unconditionality.............................8-17
  E. Additional Promises and Negotiability...................................8-18
      International Perspective: Additional Terms............................8-21
  F. The Requirement of a Sum Certain.......................................8-22
      International Perspective: A Sum Certain................................8-29
  G. The "Time Certain" Requirement..8-30
      International Perspective: Due Dates.......................................8-34

Chapter 9: **Holders in Due Course**...9-1

  A. The Concept of a Holder..9-1
      International Perspective: Holders...9-3

B.   Indorsement 9-4
     Signatures by Agents 9-11
     International Perspective: Indorsement 9-14
C.   Real and Personal Defenses..9-14
     International Perspective: Defenses 9-21
D.   Proving Holder-in-Due-Course Status...................................9-22
     When a Holder Gives Value..9-24
     Determining Whether the Item is Overdue 9-32
     Determining the Holder's Good or Bad Faith 9-33
     International Perspective: Protected Holders.........................9-40
E.   Special Problems Involving Holders 9-41
     The Doctrine of Close Connectedness..................................9-42
     The FTC Holder in Due Course Rule...................................9-48
     The FDIC and the *D'Oench* Doctrine...................................9-50
     Payees as Holders in Due Course 9-55
     The Shelter Doctrine 9-57
     International Perspective: Special Problems Involving Holders
        in Due Course..9-57

Chapter 10:   The Collection Process 10-1

A.   Introducing the Collection Process 10-1
     Relationship between Articles 3 and 4 10-1
     Electronic Presentment 10-2
     The Federal Reserve System 10-5
     Check Kiting..10-7
     Regulation CC..10-9
     The Midnight Rule and Midnight Deadline 10-14
     Acceptance and Final Payment... 10-15
     Notice of Dishonor 10-19
     Charge-Back.. 10-24
     Responsibilities of Collecting Banks 10-27
     Introduction to Check 21 10-28
     International Perspective: Notice of Dishonor 10-30
B.   Banks and Their Customers... 10-31
     A Bank's Right to Debit a Customer Account....................... 10-31
     Wrongful Dishonor.. 10-35
     Stop-Payment.. 10-40
     Stale Checks 10-48
     Legal Process 10-50
     Death or Incompetence of Customer.................................. 10-50
     The Bank-Statement Rule 10-55
     International Perspective: Forgery and Loss 10-61

Chapter 11:   Liability under Articles 3 and 4 11-1

A.   Contract Liability under Articles 3 and 4 11-1
     Primary and Secondary Liability..11-1
     Liability of Indorsers...11-3
     Accord and Satisfaction..11-7

Obligation of Drawee as Acceptor...11-9
Liability of Accommodation Parties 11-12
Articles 3 and 4 Statutes of Limitations.....................................11-19
International Perspective: Contract Liability 11-21

B.   Warranty Liability under Articles 3 and 4 11-22
Transfer Warranties...11-23
Presentment Warranties..11-24
Encoding and Retention Warranties 11-29
International Perspective: Warranty Liability 11-30

C.   Tort Liability under Articles 3 and 4..11-30
International Perspective: Tort Liability 11-40

**Chapter 12:   Credit Cards, Debit Cards, Electronic Payments, and
Nonbank Systems 12-1**

A.   Credit Cards 12-1
Consumers and Credit Cards 12-1
Unauthorized Use of Credit Cards...12-2
Credit-Card Dispute Resolution..12-10
Account Cancellation and Billing Errors 12-13
Merchants and Credit Cards 12-18
International Perspective: Credit Cards 12-20

B.   Electronic Fund Transfers...12-22
Automated Teller Machines..12-24
Wholesale Wire Transfers 12-31
International Perspective: Debit Cards......................................12-39

C.   Non-Bank Financial Services 12-40
EBT and Basic Banking 12-41
Community Development Institutions.......................................12-44
Payroll Cards...12-48
International Perspective: Access to Banking 12-51

PART IV: SECURED TRANSACTIONS

Chapter 13:   An Introduction to Article 9 13-2

A.   The Purpose and Scope of Article 9..13-2
Purpose of Article 9 and Basic Vocabulary...............................13-2
Scope of Article 9...13-8
Accounts and Rights to Payment..13-9
Consignments 13-10
Leases 13-12
Efficiency and Justice Concerns...13-17
International Perspective: Current Initiatives 13-19

B.   Types of Collateral 13-21
International Perspective: Types of Collateral..........................13-28

C.   Types of Creditors 13-29
International Perspective: Security Interests 13-32

Chapter 14:   **The Rights of Debtors and Secured Parties Vis-à-vis One Another**.. 14-1

A.   Creating a Security Interest 14-1
      Intent of the Parties...14-2
      Description of the Collateral 14-13
      After-Acquired Collateral 14-18
      Dragnet Clauses 14-23
      International Perspective: Secret Liens 14-27
B.   Attachment of a Security Interest 14-29
      International Perspective: Attachment......................... 14-35

Chapter 15:   **Perfection of Security Interests**................................... 15-1

A.   Perfection by Filing 15-1
      The Financing Statement..15-2
      Logistics of Filing and Errors in Filing 15-9
      Perfected Interests in Proceeds 15-14
      Responsibilities of the Filing Party 15-20
      Responsibilities of the Searching Party...................... 15-23
      When Filing is Required 15-28
      When Filing is Permissive... 15-30
      Compliance with Other Law... 15-31
      International Perspective: Filing 15-35
B.   Other Means of Perfection... 15-37
      Automatic Perfection for PMSI Creditors.................. 15-37
      Automatic Perfection for Some Accounts Receivable 15-42
      Perfection by Possession 15-44
      Perfection by Control.. 15-47
      Temporary Perfection.. 15-52
      International Perspective: The Availability of Other Means of Perfection.. 15-56

Chapter 16:   **Priorities Among Creditors**.. 16-1

A.   Introduction to Priority 16-1
B.   Priority Rules for Unperfected Interests....................16-6
      International Perspective: Enforcement of Interests that are Unperfected 16-9
C.   Priority Rules Among Secured Creditors.................... 16-10
      Future Advances 16-11
      International Perspective: Priority Rules 16-17
      Purchase-Money Security Interests............................ 16-17
D.   Priority Rules When Collateral is Sold....................... 16-24
      International Perspective: Sales of Collateral to Buyers in Ordinary Course of Business 16-30
E.   Priority Rules for Lien Creditors................................. 16-33
      International Perspective: Lienholders 16-39

Chapter 17: Default.. 17-1

    A.   The Right of Repossession...17-1

            Wrongful Repossession 17-3

            Breach of Peace.. 17-11

            International Perspective: Default.. 17-18

    B.   Sale or Other Disposition of the Collateral... 17-18

            Notice 17-18

            Commercial Reasonableness 17-21

            Exercise of Reasonable Care Toward the Collateral 17-32

            Retention of the Collateral 17-36

            International Perspective: A Reasonable Sale 17-39

    C.   The Right of Redemption.. 17-39

            International Perspective: The Rights of Creditors and Debtors

                  upon Default... 17-42

PART V: DOCUMENTARY TRANSACTIONS

Chapter 18:   **Documentary Sales** 18-1

    A.   An Introduction to Documentary Sales...18-1

            International Perspective: The Various Laws Affecting

                  Documentary Sales 18-10

    B.   Letters of Credit... 18-12

            The Doctrine of Strict Compliance.. 18-13

            The Independence Principle 18-22

            International Perspective: Letters of Credit... 18-25

    C.   Documents of Title 18-27

            International Perspective: Documents of Title 18-33

Table of Cases

The principal cases are in bold type. Cases cited or discussed in the text are in regular type. References are to pages. Cases cited in principal cases and within other quoted materials are not included.

Adams v. Peter Tramontin Motor Sales, Inc. 4-9

Addis v. Bernadin, Inc. 4-22

Adrian Tabin Corp. v. Climax Boutique, Inc. 6-22

Aetna Life and Casualty Co. v. Hampton State Bank 11-26

AG Services of America, Inc. v. Empfield 16-10

Agribank, FCB v. Whitlock...................... 11-14

Ajax Tool Works, Inc. v. Can-Eng. Manufacturing Ltd..................................4-31

Al's Auto Sales v. Moskowitz................... 16-28

Alioto v. United States............................. 10-23

Amberboy v. Societe de Banque Privee.....8-27

American Card Co. v. H.M.H. Co. 14-4

Amick v. Baugh... 11-16

Anthony Pools v. Sheehan 2-7

Arcanum National Bank v. Hessler...........9-47

Arvida Corp. v. A. J. Industries, Inc...........2-11

Asante Technologies, Inc. v. PMC-Sierra, Inc. 2-21

Asciolla v. Manter Oldsmobile-Pontiac 5-29

Asian International, Ltd. v. Merrill Lynch, Pierce, Fenner and Smith, Inc. 9-11

Atlas Auto Rental Corp. v. Weisberg........6-17

Atlas Thrift Co. v. Horan........................... 17-19

Banco Espanol de Credito v. State Street Bank and Trust Co...................................18-6

Bank of Chapmanville v. Workman....... 17-20

Bank of Cochin Ltd. v. Manufacturers Hanover Trust Co...................................18-1

Bank of New York v. Amoco Oil Co. 18-3

Bankers Trust Co. v. Litton Systems, Inc.9-17

Barnes v. Turner.. 15-27

Barnett v. London Assurance Corp. 3-7

Bartlett & Co. v. Merchants Co. 5-23

Barton v. Chemical Bank.......................... 14-34

Bartus v. Riccardi.......................................5-37

Battiste v. St. Thomas Diving Club, Inc. ..4-19

Baystate Drywall, Inc. v. Chicopee Savings Bank 14-8

Bazak International Corp. v. Mast Industries, Inc. 2-51

Benjamin v. Diamond............................... 16-15

Benton v. General Mobile Homes, Inc. 17-22

Beyene v. Irving Trust Co. 18-22

BII Finance Co, Ltd. v. U-States Forwarding Services Corp. **18-6**

Bisbey v. D.C. National Bank.................... 12-23

Black, Robertshaw, Frederick, Copple & Wright, P.C. v. United States 15-42

Blaisdell Lumber Co. v. Horton 12-9

Blake v. Woodford Bank and Trust Co... 10-19

Boma Manufacturing Ltd. v. Canadian Imperial Bank of Commerce........**11-40**

Bonebrake v. Cox 2-12

Booker v. Everhart..................................... 8-16

Bowen v. Young... 5-25

Boyles Brothers Drilling Co. v. Orion Industries, Ltd. 11-5

BP Oil International, Ltd. v. Empresa Estatal Petroleos de Ecuador............................. 3-20

Branch Banking & Trust Co. v. Gill.......... 9-33

Brandeis Machinery & Supply Co. v. Capitol Crane Rental, Inc................ **5-47**

Brannons Number Seven, Inc. v. Phelps . 11-4

Broadway National Bank v. Barton-Russell Corp... 12-20

Brodie Hotel Supply, Inc. v. United States 16-24

Bromley v. Bromley 17-40

Brown Machine v. Hercules, Inc. **2-26**

Bryson v. Bank of New York 12-12

Buffaloe v. Hart...................................... **2-48**

Bufkor, Inc. v. Star Jewelry Co., Inc. **13-11**

Campbell Leasing, Inc. v. Federal Deposit Insurance Corp. **9-51**

Capos v. Mid-America National Bank.... 17-34

Cargill, Inc. v. Stafford 5-47

Carlson v. Gleichsner 4-9

Carnwright v. Gray 8-35

Casco Bank & Trust Co. v. Cloutier 14-5

Caspi v. Microsoft Network, L.L.C. 2-39

Central Bank of Yemen v. Cardinal Financial Investments Corp................................... 9-41

Chartered Bank of London v. Chrysler Corp. 14-31

Chatfield v. Sherwin-Williams Co. 4-24

Chemical Bank v. Miller Yacht Sales..... 15-15
**Cherwell-Ralli, Inc. v. Rytman Grain
    Co., Inc.**.. 5-14
Chevron, U.S.A., Inc. v. Natural Resources
    Defense Council, Inc............................ 16-37
Chicago Prime Packers, Inc. v. Northam Food
    Trading Co. 3-20, 4-10
Chittenden Trust Co. v. Andre Noel Sports
    17-32
Chrysler Corp. v. Adamatic, Inc. 16-32
Chysky v. Drake Brothers Co. 4-41
**Citizens Bank and Trust v. Gibson
    Lumber Co.**.. 14-13
Citizens National Bank of Englewood v. Fort
    Lee Savings & Loan Association 9-35
Citizens National Bank v. Cockrell......... 16-21
Citizens Savings Bank v. Sac City State Bank
    17-8
City National Bank v. Unique Structures,
    Inc. 17-35
Clark v. Zaid, Inc..5-24
Claudia v. Olivieri Footwear Ltd.................2-54
Clayton v. Crossroads Equipment Co.
    17-4
Coca-Cola Bottling Works v. Lyons 4-41
Coffer v. Standard Brands, Inc. 4-8
**Coin-O-Matic Service Co. v. Rhode
    Island Hospital Trust Co.** 16-11
Colonial Dodge, Inc. v. Miller 5-26
Columbia Nitrogen Corp. v. Royster Co....2-46
Cosden Oil & Chemical Co. v. Karl O. Helm
    Aktiengesellsschaft..................................5-45
Counceller v. Ecenbarger, Inc. 15-47
Courtaulds North America, Inc. v. North
    Carolina National Bank 18-20
Courtesy Financial Services, Inc. v. Hughes
    ....9-50, 9-57
Courtin v. Sharp 3-18
Covington v. Penn Square National Bank
    11-35
Crick v. HSBS Bank USA 11-32
D'Oench, Duhme & Co. v. Federal Deposit
    Insurance Corp..9-51
Daigle v. Chaisson 11-18
Dale R. Horning Co., Inc. v. Falconer Glass
    Industries, Inc...2-31
Dalessio v. Kressler 10-48
Daniel v. Bank of Hayward 16-32
Danning v. Daylin, Inc..................................6-21
Davenport v. Chrysler Credit Corp......... 17-11
Davis v. Dillard National Bank 11-7
Decatur Cooperative Association v. Urban
   2-19
Delbrueck & Co. v. Manufacturers Hanover
    Trust Co. 12-31

DeLuca v. BancOhio National Bank, Inc.
    10-51
Demos v. Lyons.. 10-35
Desmond v. Federal Deposit Insurance Corp.
    9-53
**Dickerson v. Mountain View Equipment
    Co.**.. 4-11
District of Columbia v. Thomas Funding
    Corp... 15-28
**Draft Systems, Inc. v. Rimar
    Manufacturing, Inc.** 5-41
Dulces Luisi, S.A. de C.V. v. Seoul
    International Co. Ltd.................................5-8
Dunn v. General Equities........................... 17-7
Dunnigan v. First National Bank..... 10-40
Dura-Wood Treating Co. v. Century Forest
    Industries, Inc.. 5-43
Dutch Mill Gardens v. J.J. Grullemans &
    Sons..4-2
Duxbury v. Spex Feeds, Inc. 2-10
Dziurak v. Chase Manhattan Bank........ 10-48
Eachen v. Scott Housing Systems, Inc. 9-49
Emmons v. Burkett 17-19
Essex Construction Corp. v. Industrial Bank
    of Washington 10-24
Evans v. Taco Bell Corp.............................. 4-49
Evra Corp. v. Swiss Bank Corp......... 12-32
Eximin S.A. v. Textile and FootwearItalstyle
    Ferarri Inc. 3-25
Expeditors International v. Official Creditors
    Committee 14-9
F.A.D. Andrea, Inc. v. Dodge 5-15
Farmers & Merchants State Bank v. Teveldal
    15-8
Farmers & Merchants State Bank v. Western
    Bank... 9-36
Favors v. Yaffe 7-19
Federal Deposit Insurance Corp. v. Meyer
    9-20
Federal Discount Corp., Ltd. v. St. Pierre and
    St. Pierre 9-57
Feldman v. Citibank.................................... 12-29
Fercus, s.r.l. v. Mario Palazzo Co. 2-53
Ferri v. Sylvia 8-32
Fidelity National Bank v. Dade County. 18-22
First Federal Savings & Loan Association v.
    Gump & Ayers Real Estate, Inc........... 8-14
First Galesburg National Bank & Trust Co. v.
    Martin... 16-4
First National Bank in Harvey v. Colonial
    Bank.. 10-8, 10-16
**First National Bank of Alamosa v. Ford
    Motor Credit Co.**.............................. 11-9
First National Bank of Boston v. Fidelity
    Bank, National Association................... 10-2

First National Bank of Commerce v. Anderson Ford Lincoln-Mercury, Inc. 11-34

First National Bank v. DiDomenico 17-42

First National Bank v. Power Equipment Co. 8-17

First State Bank v. Clark...................... 8-11

First State Bank v. Hallet......................... 17-19

First United Bank v. Philmont Corp. 12-18

First Valley Bank v. First Savings & Loan Association of Central Indiana..............11-7

First Wyoming Bank v. Cabinet Craft Distributors... 10-17

Fithian v. Jamar 11-19

Flickinger v. Genesee Corp. 17-37

Flippo v. Mode O'Day Frock Shops of Hollywood...4-20

Flournoy v. First National Bank of Jeffersonville, Indiana 10-15

Ford & Vlahos v. ITT Commercial Finance Corp. 17-28

Ford Motor Credit Co. v. Jackson............ 17-28

Ford Motor Credit Co. v. Welch 17-20

Forest Park National Bank v. Martin Grinding & Machine Works 14-18

France v. Ford Motor Credit Co.............. 11-30

Franklin Grain & Supply Co. v. Ingram...5-18

Frederickson v. Hackney............................4-10

Frericks v. General Motors Corp. 4-40

Funding Consultants, Inc. v. Aetna Casualty and Surety Co...9-34

Garden Check Cashing Service, Inc. v. First National City Bank 10-45

Gearing v. Berkson......................................4-39

General Electric Capital Corp. v. Stelmach Construction Co. 17-23

Georgia Railroad Bank & Trust Co. v. First National Bank & Trust Co. of Augusta 10-4

Gillispie v. Great Atlantic and Pacific Tea Co. 4-17

Giminez v. Great Atlantic & Pacific Tea Co. 4-40

Girard Bank v. Mount Holly State Bank 11-24

Godfrey v. Gilsdorf......................................6-13

Grace Label, Inc. v. Kliff...........................2-21

Graves Motors, Inc. v. Docar Sales, Inc.......6-6

Gray v. American Express Co. 12-14

Great Lakes Higher Education Corp. v. Austin Bank of Chicago.......... 11-28, 11-34

Greater Buffalo Press, Inc. v. Federal Reserve Bank of New York 10-5

Green v. American Tobacco Co. 4-16

Greenberg v. Service Business Forms Industries, Inc.. 17-9

Grimm v. Prudence Mutual Casualty Co. ..3-6

Groover v. Peters... 11-3

Gross v. Powell...3-5

Gunning ex. rel. Gunning v. Small Feast Caterers, Inc...................................2-16

Hadley v. Baxendale............................... 12-35

Hale v. Ford Motor Credit Co. 17-8

Hammer v. Thompson 6-15

Hane v. Exten 11-4

Hanna v. First National Bank of Rochester 10-14

Harper v. K & W Trucking Co. 7-11, 7-28

Harris Truck & Trailer Sales v. Foote ... 17-12, 17-13

Hartford Life Insurance Co. v. Title Guarantee Co....................................... 11-6

Hauter v. Zogarts 4-25

Hayward v. Postma 3-17

Hedges v. Public Service Co. 2-18

Holly Hill Acres, Ltd. v. Charter Bank of Gainesville 9-1

Howse v. Crumb....................................... 2-50

IBP, Inc. v. Hady Enterprises, Inc..............5-8

IBP, Inc. v. Mercantile Bank of Topeka . 10-49

Impact Computers and Electronics, Inc. v. Bank of America, North America 11-27

In re 20th Century Enterprises, Inc........ 15-32

In re Ace Lumber Supply, Inc. 14-7

In re Amex-Protein Development Corp... 14-4, 14-8

In re ASI Reactivation, Inc....................... 16-15

In re Aspen Impressions, Inc. 13-12

In re Bell 16-2

In re Berge 2-3

In re Bollinger Corp............................... 14-2

In re Brawn 15-14

In re Cliff's Ridge Skiing Corp. 13-21

In re Copeland..15-45

In re Crosby 17-39

In re Daniels...16-18

In re Deico Electronics, Inc....................... 17-2

In re Estate of Balkus.....................8-34, 9-2

In re Estis. 17-2

In re Fort Dodge Roofing Co. 15-44

In re Frazier 15-9

In re Gary & Connie Jones Drugs, Inc. .. 14-22

In re George 8-23

In re Grabowski...................................15-11

In re Haas 16-35

In re Hardy...2-4

In re Hudgins 15-25

In re Hurst... 15-31

In re Information Exchange 15-29
In re International Plastics, Inc. .. 13-13, **13-16**
In re Kinderknecht 15-20
In re Kingsley 15-15
In re Laminated Veneers Co. Inc. 14-14
In re Legal Data Systems, Inc. 14-16
In re Lockovich **15-37**
In re Manuel 15-40
In re Marhoefer Packing Co., Inc. v. Robert
    Reiser & Co. 2-6
In re McCord 16-39
In re McDougall 15-15
In re Modafferi................................... 14-12
In re Newman 13-23
In re Norrell 15-40
In re Numeric Corp. 14-4
In re Pipes 15-14
In re Powers 2-4
In re Powers.................................... **13-14**
In re Psalto 15-31
In re Reliance Equities, Inc. 15-54
In re Ripley Oil Co. Inc. 13-26
In re Robert Bogetti & Sons.......................15-2
In re Robinson Brothers Drilling, Inc. 11-16
In re S&J Holding Corp.............................15-7
In re Schoenfeld.................................. 15-31
In re Schwinn Cycling and Fitness, Inc. 15-53
In re Shinault Lumber Products, Inc. 13-3
In re Spearing Tool & Manufacturing
    Co., Inc.................................... **15-24**
In re Tower Air, Inc. 15-16
In re Tri-County Materials, Inc. 15-43
In re United Thrift Stores 13-6
In re Valley Media 13-10
In re Value-Added Communications,
    Inc. **15-5**
In re Viscount Furniture Corp. 15-44
In re Zaleha...................... 13-13, **13-17**
In re Zwagerman 13-9
Inmi-Etti v. Aluisi....................................6-9
Intraworld Industries, Inc. v. Girard Trust
    Bank 18-1
Investment Service Co. v. Martin Bros.
    Container & Timber Products Corp. ...7-12
ITT Commercial Finance Corp. v. Bank of the
    West 15-26
ITT Diversified Credit Corporation v. First
    City Capital Corp................................ 16-14
Izraelewitz v. Manufacturers Hanover Trust
    Co. 12-10
J.R. Hale Contracting Co., Inc. v. United New
    Mexico Bank 17-11
James Baird Co. v. Gimbel Bros., Inc. 16-16
James Talcott, Inc. v. Franklin National
    Bank of Minneapolis 15-42

Jason's Foods, Inc. vs. Peter Eckrich &
    Sons, Inc................................... 3-9
Jefferson v. Jones 3-23
Jorgensen v. Pressnall 5-36
Jubas v. Sampsell 6-22
Judd v. Citibank................................ 12-28
Kashanchi v. Texas Commerce Medical Bank
    12-23
Kaw Valley State Bank & Trust Co. v. Riddle
    9-46
Kedzie and 103rd Currency Exchange, Inc. v.
    Hodge.................................... 9-18
Keen v. Modern Trailer Sales, Inc. 5-28
Keep Fresh Filters, Inc. v. Reguli...... **16-6**
Keith v. Buchanan.................... **4-3, 4-24**
Kenerson v. Federal Deposit Insurance
    Corp. **9-7**
Kerr Steamship Co., Inc. v. Chartered Bank
    of India, Australia, and China 7-27
Ketterer v. Armour & Co............................4-7
Kham & Nate's Shoes No. 2, Inc. v. First
    Bank of Whiting 16-15
Kirby v. First & Merchants National
    Bank **10-24**
Knox v. Phoenix Leasing, Inc. 13-30
Koerner & Lambert v. Allstate Insurance Co.
    9-29
Kruser v. Bank of America NT & SA...... 12-25
Lachs v. Fidelity & Casualty Co. 2-37
Lambert v. Barker 7-12
Langeveld v. L.R.Z.H. Corp. 11-14
Lankford v. Rogers Ford Sales **4-26**
Lasky v. Economy Grocery Stores............. 4-17
Laurel Bank & Trust Co. v. City National
    Bank of Connecticut 7-27, 9-30
Layne v. Bank One **17-32**
Lema v. Bank of America, North America
    10-27
Levondosky v. Marina Associates............. 2-17
Lewis Broadcasting Corp. v. Phoenix
    Broadcasting Partners **17-40**
Lewis Hubbard & Co. v. Morton..................7-4
Lewis v. Mobil Oil Corp. 4-33, 4-46
Lincoln National Bank and Trust Co. v.
    Peoples Trust Bank of Ft. Wayne
    ....**10-32**
Litton Industrial Automation Systems,
    Inc. v. Nationwide Power Corp....**16-34**
Littwiller Machine & Manufacturing, Inc. v.
    NPB Alpena Bank 14-32
Livingston v. Stevens 17-7
Locks v. North Towne National Bank of
    Rockford 7-14
Lory v. Parsoff...15-27

Lynnwood Sand and Gravel, Inc. v. Bank of
        Everett 9-23
Maddox v. Federal Deposit Insurance Corp.
        14-13
Major's Furniture Mart, Inc. v. Castle Credit
        Corp., Inc. 17-29
Mammoth Cave Production Credit
        Association. v. York 14-13
Marandola v. Marandola Mechanical, Inc.
       13-9
Marine Midland Bank, N.A. v. Price, Miller,
        Evans & Flowers...................................9-11
Marine Midland Banks–New York v.
        Graybar Electric Co., Inc. 9-30
Martco, Inc. v. Doran Chevrolet, Inc..........2-53
Maryott v. First National Bank of Eden,
        South Dakota... 10-35
**Mayberry v. Volkswagen of America,
        Inc.** **4-42**
MCC-Marble Ceramic Center, Inc. v.
        Ceramica Nuova D'Agostino, S.p.A. 2-47
McMahon Food Corp. v. Burger Dairy Co.
       11-8
Mennen v. J.P Morgan & Co., Inc. **18-23**
Menzel v. List 3-24
Mercanti v. Persson......................................3-12
Mercedes-Benz Credit Corp. v. Morgan....17-8
Meritor v. Duke... 10-45
Messing v. Bank of America..................... 11-37
Metropolitan National Bank v. United States
        16-33
Metzger v. Americredit Financial Services,
        Inc. 16-30
Middlesex Bank & Trust Co. v. Mark
        Equipment Corp. 18-20
Milroy Bank v. First National Bank....... 15-56
Miron v. Yonkers Raceway, Inc........... **5-21**
Moe v. John Deere Co. 17-9
Morgan County Feeders, Inc. v. McCormick
        13-23
Morgan Guaranty Trust Co. of New York v.
        American Savings and Loan Association
        10-17
Morgan v. Crawford 11-9
Morton Booth Co. v. Tiara Furniture, Inc.
        14-33
Motors Acceptance Corp. v. Rozier.............17-3
Multiplastics, Inc. v. Arch Industries, Inc.3-17
Munao v. Lagattuta 17-38
Nanakuli Paving & Rock Co. v. Shell Oil Co.
       2-46
National Bank of Commerce v. Morgan ...9-31
National Newark & Essex Bank v. Giordano
        10-44

National Savings and Trust Co. v. Park Corp.
        10-18
National State Bank v. Federal Reserve
        Bank of New York................................... 10-7
NBD Park Ridge Bank v. SRJ Enterprises,
        Inc... 14-18
Nelson v. Union Equity Co-operative
        Exchange 2-19
Neri v. Retail Marine Corp......................... 5-50
New Freedom Corp. v. Brown................... 3-23
New Jersey Steel Corp. v. Warburton 7-17,
        10-60
Newmark v. Gimbel's Inc. 2-9
Nisky v. Childs Co....................................... 2-12
Nolin Production Credit Association. v.
        Canmer Deposit Bank 14-14
Northpark National Bank v. Bankers Trust
        Co.. 10-4
Northshore Bank v. Palmer...................... 10-38
**Northwestern National Insurance Co. v.
        Maggio** **9-33**
Novack v. Cities Service Oil Co. 12-13
O'Connor's Administratrix v. Clark 6-15
Ognibene v. Citbank................................... 12-29
Olsen v. BBRG Massachusetts Restaurant,
        Inc.. 4-35
Oswald v. Allen... 2-50
Overton v. Tyler..................................**8-19**
Pain v. Packard 11-16
Palsgraf v. Long Island Railroad 12-38
**Paulman v. Gateway Venture Partners
        III, LPI**.................................**14-19**
Peacock v. Rhodes.....................................9-6
People's National Bank of Mora v. Boyer
        11-18
Peoples National Bank v. Weiner............ 15-13
Peoria Savings and Loan Association v.
        Jefferson Trust and Savings Bank...... 9-23
Perlmutter v. Beth David Hospital 2-7
Phelps v. McQuade 6-7
Plateq Corp. v. Machlett Laboratories, Inc.
        5-51
Plymale v. Upright.................................... 9-16
Pollin v. Mindy Manufacturing Co. 9-12
Porter v. Citibank, N.A. 12-27
Porter v. Wertz...................................**6-10**
Pride Hyundai, Inc. v. Chrysler Financial Co.,
        LLC 14-23, **14-25**
Pritchard v. Liggett & Myers Tobacco Co.
        .... 4-16, 4-34
ProCD, Inc. v. Zeidenberg 2-35
Province of Alberta Treasury Branches v. D
        & L Insulation.................................. 8-22
Prutch v. Ford Motor Co..............**4-32, 4-46**

Ratner v. Chemical Bank New York Trust
    Co. 12-1
Reed v. Anglo Scandinavian Corp. ... 6-19
Republic National Bank of Miami v. Johnson
    10-54
Rex Smith Propane, Inc. v. National Bank of
    Commerce 9-3
Richardson v. Girner 9-32
Robbins v. Alberto-Culver Co. 4-19
Roberts v. Agricredit Acceptance Corp.
    .... **9-15**
Robinson v. Glass...............................9-17
Roder Zelt und Hallenkonstrucktionen
    GmbH v. Rosedown Party Ltd. 3-8
Rogers v. Toni Home Permanent Co. 4-38
Rogers v. Zielinksi...............................4-29
Roos v. Aloi......................................2-52
Royal Bank of Canada v. 216200 Alberta Ltd.
    16-31
Ruden v. Citizens Bank & Trust Co. 17-20
Sabin Meyer Regional Sales Corp. v. Citizens
    Bank 10-15
Salisbury Livestock Co. v. Colorado Central
    Credit Union 17-17
Samson v. Riesing...............................4-20
Savings Banks Trust Co. v. Federal Reserve
    Bank of New York 11-26
Schaeffer v. United Bank & Trust Co. of
    Maryland 9-20
Schekter v. Michael...............................8-34
Schiavone & Sons, Inc. v. Securally Co., Inc.
   2-45
Schmitz-Werke GMBH & Co. v. Rockland
    Industries, Inc. 4-9
Schmode's, Inc. v. Wilkinson............. 17-36
Sears Consumer Financial Corp. v.
    Thunderbird Products 16-27
Security Pacific National Bank v. Chess ..9-12
Security Trust Co. v. O'Hair 9-16
Seely v. White Motor Co. 4-6
Sequoyah State Bank v. Union National
    Bank 10-45
Shaffer v. Victoria Station, Inc. 2-17
Sheridan Suzuki, Inc. v. Caruso Auto Sales,
    Inc. 6-14
Shurlow v. Bonthius...............................13-8
Siegel v. Western Union Telephone Co. . 12-36
Smith v. Olympic Bank 9-37
Society National Bank v. Kienzle.............12-5
Solomon v. American National Bank........11-8
Soto v. Sea-Road International, Inc.
    .... **18-29**
Southern Concrete Services, Inc. v.
    Mableton Concrete Services, Inc. 2-43

Spacemakers of America, Inc. v.
    Suntrust Bank...............................**10-55**
Spangler v. Holthusen 12-36
Specht v. Netscape Communications Corp.
   2-38
Spittlehouse v. Northshore Marine, Inc.
    .... **16-30**
St. Paul Fire and Marine Insurance Co.
    v. State Bank of Salem....................**9-25**
St. Paul Guardian Insurance Co. v.
    Neuromed Medical Systems & Support 3-8
Staff Service Associates, Inc. v. Midlantic
    National Bank 10-46
Stang v. Hertz Corp. 4-1
Stannish v. Community Bank of
    Homewood-Flossmoor....................**14-23**
State ex rel. Chan Siew Lai v. Powell 10-44
State National Bank of El Paso v. Farah
    Manufacturing Co., Inc. 8-20
State of Florida v. Family Bank of
    Hallandale, Inc. 8-13
Stone Machinery Co. v. Kessler 17-17
Sunbelt Savings, FSB Dallas, Texas v.
    Montross 9-54
Sunseri v. RKO-Stanley Warner
    Theatres, Inc. **3-21**
T. W. Oil, Inc. v. Consolidated Edison Co.
    .... **5-33**
Tanbro Fabrics Corp. v. Deering Milliken,
    Inc. 16-24
Task Enterprises, Inc. v. Pratt Adjustment
    Co. 17-41
Taylor v. Roeder 8-26
Tepper v. Citizens Federal Savings & Loan
    Association 11-1, 11-20
Texas Commerce Bank-Fort Worth, N.A. v.
    United States 16-34
The Hong Kong and Shanghai Banking
    Corp., Ltd. v. HFH USA Corp. 14-28,
    14-30
Thorn v. Adams 6-16
Thorp Commercial Corp. v. Northgate
    Industries, Inc. 14-2, 15-3
Thorp Finance Corp. v. Ken Hodgins & Sons
    15-41
Tony Thornton Auction Service, Inc. v.
    United States 15-25
Towers World Airways, Inc. v. PHH
    Aviation Systems, Inc.....................**12-2**
Transamerica Commercial Finance Corp. v.
    Naef.. 11-17
Transamerica Insurance Co. v. Long 7-25
Transamerica Insurance Co. v. Standard Oil
    Co. 12-7

Transcontinental Refrigeration Co. v. Figgins 5-39

Trinity Temple Charities, Inc. v. City of Louisville 6-5

Trust Co. Bank of Augusta v. Henderson 11-39

Trust Co. Bank v. Barrett Distributors, Inc. 2-34

Twin City Bank v. Isaacs 10-39

Underground Construction Co. v. Sanitary District of Chicago 12-36

Unico v. Owen 9-42

Union Bank v. Mobilla.............................. 11-28

Union National Bank of Pittsburgh v. Northwest Marine, Inc. 15-39

Union Planters Bank, National Association v. Rogers.. 10-61

United Milk Products Co. v. Lawndale National Bank of Chicago 7-16

United Road Machinery Co. v. Jasper 6-3

United Savings Association v. Timbers of Inwood Forest..17-2

United States Fidelity and Guaranty Co. v. Federal Reserve Bank 10-4

United States v. Dailey............................. 16-18

United States v. Farrington 8-16

Universal Bank v. McCafferty 12-6

Universal C.I.T. Credit Corp. v. Ingel........9-40

Universal CIT Credit Corp. v. Farmers Bank 15-17

USAA Investment Management Co. v. Federal Reserve Bank of Boston 10-13

Voest-Alpine Trading USA Corp. v. Bank of China 18-14

W&D Acquisition, LLC v. First Union National Bank 10-50

Wachovia Bank, N.A. v. Federal Reserve Bank of Richmond 11-26

Wachter v. Denver National Bank......... 12-23, 12-24

Wade v. Ford Motor Credit Co. 17-15

Wainwright Bank & Trust Co. v. Railroadmens Federal Savings & Loan Association... 17-31

Walker Bank & Trust Co. v. Jones.......... 12-10

Walker Ford Sales v. Gaither 4-30, 4-49

Wallick v. First State Bank of Farmington 10-36

Watson v. Cudney... 17-6

Webster v. Blue Ship Tea Room, Inc......... 4-21

Weinrich v. Hawley 17-7

Wells Fargo Bank, National Assn. v. Hartford National Bank and Trust Co. 10-20

Wesche v. Martin 9-13

Western Union Telephone Co. v. Martin 12-36

Whitmer v. Bell Telephone 2-14

Wildman Stores, Inc. v. Carlisle Distributing Co., Inc... 11-21

William F. Wilke, Inc. v. Cummins Diesel Engines, Inc.. 3-1

Williams v. Ford Motor Credit Co. 17-8

Williams v. Walker-Thomas Furniture Co. 5-4, 13-14

Wilson Trading Corp. v. Ferguson............. 4-28

Wilson v. Scampoli...................................... 5-35

Winter & Hirsch, Inc. v. Passarelli............ 9-38

Wood v. General Electric Co. 4-38

Wood v. Holiday Inns, Inc. 12-18

Woodworth v. The Richmond Indiana Venture 8-21

Wooster Products, Inc. v. Magna-Tek, Inc. 2-13

Worrell v. Barnes 2-9

Xerox Corp. v. Hawkes...................................2-4

Zapatha v. Dairy Mart, Inc..................... 5-1

Zappanti v. Berge Service Center.................4-6

Zinni v. One Township Line Corp. 6-23

Table of Statutes

11 USC
362...17-1
362 (d)...15-39
544...........................13-29, 13-30, 15-30, 15-38
544 (a)...16-4
544 (a) (1)...........15-21, 16-2, 16-3, 16-5, 16-33
551...16-4

15 USC
714...8-23
1601.......................................12-1, 12-22
1602 (m)...................................12-9, 12-10
1602 (o)...........................12-4, 12-9, 12-10
1603...12-2
1637 (b)......................................12-16
1643.....................................12-2, 12-4
1645...12-2
1666..12-14
1666i...12-10
1666i (a)....................................12-10
1693...12-22
1693a (6)....................................12-23
1693b (d) (2)................................12-44
1693f..12-22
1693g.................................12-22, 12-24
2301...4-44
2308...4-44
2310...4-44
2310 (d) (2)..................................4-44
2311 (b)......................................4-44

26 USC
6321...16-33
6323...16-33
6323 (f) (2) (B).............................16-35
6323 (h) (1).................................16-38
6622...16-33

49 USC
80101...18-6
89124...1-14

7 CFR
770.4 (b) (2).................................8-24

12 CFR
205..12-22
205.11......................................12-22
205.6.......................................12-22
229.10..10-9
229.12..10-9
229.13..10-9

229.31 (b)....................................10-14

16 CFR
433...9-48
433.2...9-48

UCC Section
1-102....................................1-1, 1-22
1-103.........1-8, 1-13, 1-14, 4-35, 4-37, 4-39, 6-1
1-103 (a)................................1-5, 5-46
1-201.......................1-22, 5-1, 16-20, 18-3
1-201 (b) (6)...............................18-27
1-201 (b) (9)....................6-9, 6-10, 16-24
1-201 (b) (15)...........................7-29, 9-1
1-201 (b) (16)..............................18-27
1-201 (b) (21)................................9-1
1-201 (b) (24)........................7-11, 8-22
1-201 (b) (35)...............................13-2
1-201 (b) (37).................8-5, 13-14, 13-15
1-201 (b) (42)..............................18-27
1-201 (b) (43)................................8-1
1-203......................2-2, 13-12, 15-32
1-204..6-10
1-205.......................................10-50
1-206..1-22
1-208..8-35
1-301..1-23
1-302...1-4
1-302 (b)....................................1-4
1-304....................5-1, 8-20, 11-26
1-305.......................................17-20
1-309................................8-20, 17-8
2-101..................................3-1, 3-3
2-102..............1-14, 1-16, 2-2, 2-6, 2-18
2-102 (a) (6)...............................2-15
2-103.................2-14, 2-15, 2-16, 2-21, 6-12
2-103 (1) (k)...............................2-14
2-104.......................................2-19
2-104 (1).................2-18, 2-19, 4-11, 6-16
2-105.......................2-6, 2-13, 2-14
2-105 (1)....................................2-6
2-106 (2)...........................3-4, 5-20
2-107.......................................2-13
2-201..............2-19, 2-47, 2-48, 2-52, 2-53
2-201 (2)..................2-48, 2-51, 2-52
2-201 (3)..................2-48, 2-50
2-202...............2-42, 2-43, 2-44, 2-45
2-202 (b)....................................2-45
2-206................................2-24, 2-26
2-207....2-24, 2-26, 2-29, 2-31, 2-32, 2-33, 2-34,
2-35
2-207 (1).............................2-30, 2-33

2-207 (2) 2-30, 2-31, 2-32, 2-33, 2-34
2-301 5-9
2-302 5-3
2-309 (3) 5-3
2-312 .... 3-20, 3-21, 3-22, 6-9, 11-27
2-312 (1) (a) 3-20
2-312 (2) 3-25
2-313 .... 4-1, 4-2, 4-6
2-313A 4-1
2-313B 4-1
2-314 .... 1-20, 2-8, 2-18, 2-19, 4-11, 6-16
2-314 (1) 4-11, 4-17
2-314 (2) 4-11, 4-15, 4-18
2-315 .... 2-9, 2-19, 4-21, 4-22
2-316 .... 1-20, 4-6, 4-11, 4-26, 4-29
2-316 (1) 4-26
2-316 (4) 4-28
2-318 .... 4-36, 4-37, 4-39
2-326 13-11
2-327 13-11
2-401 .... 3-1, 3-4, 3-18, 14-30, 14-31
2-401 (2) 3-5
2-403 .... 6-2, 6-3, 6-8, 6-13, 6-16, 7-18
2-403 (1) 6-1, 6-2
2-403 (1) (b) 10-46
2-403 (2) 6-9, 6-10, 6-13, 6-15, 16-27, 16-28
2-403 (3) 6-9
2-501 .... 3-9, 3-18, 14-32
2-507 (1) 5-9
2-508 .... 5-32, 5-35
2-509 .... 3-9, 14-32
2-509 (2) 3-9, 3-10
2-509 (2) (b) 3-11
2-510 .... 3-9, 3-18, 14-32
2-510 (1) 3-4
2-510 (3) 3-12
2-511 (1) 5-9
2-601 5-16
2-602 5-20
2-602 (1) 5-22
2-602 (3) 5-20
2-603 5-20
2-604 5-20
2-606 5-17
2-606 (1) 5-22
2-607 .... 3-25, 4-33, 4-35, 4-40, 5-17, 5-19
2-607 (2) 5-25
2-607 (3) 4-31, 4-35
2-607 (3) (a) 5-32
2-608 5-25
2-609 .... 5-13, 5-15
2-610 .... 5-13, 5-44, 5-45, 5-46
2-612 5-10
2-702 5-51
2-703 5-47

2-706 5-40
2-708 5-47
2-708 (1) 5-40
2-708 (2) 5-40
2-709 5-47
2-709 (1) (b) 5-51
2-711 .... 5-41, 5-47
2-711 (3) 5-20
2-712 .... 5-40, 5-44
2-712 (2) 5-40
2-713 .... 5-40, 5-45
2-713 (1) 5-40
2-713 (1) (a) 5-45
2-714 4-50
2-714 (1) 5-40
2-714 (2) 4-42
2-714 (3) 4-46
2-715 .... 4-46, 5-40, 5-52
2-715 (2) (a) 5-18
2-715 (b) 5-42
2-716 5-52
2-719 .... 4-28, 4-29
2-719 (2) 4-26
2-719 (3) 5-43
3-102 (a) 7-11
3-102 (c) 7-11
3-103 8-5
3-103 (a) (4) 7-14
3-103 (a) (5) 7-14
3-103 (a) (6) 9-33
3-103 (a) (7) 7-14
3-103 (a) (8) 7-14, 8-1, 8-5
3-103 (a) (12) 7-14, 8-1, 8-5
3-103 (a) (17) 11-13
3-104 ...... 1-20, 7-15, 7-17, 7-19, 7-23, 7-28, 8-1,
       8-3, 8-8, 8-12, 8-20
3-104 (a) 8-10, 8-26
3-104 (a) (1) 8-7, 9-6
3-104 (a) (2) 8-31
3-104 (a) (3) 8-18
3-104 (a) (3) (i) 8-20
3-104 (a) (3) (ii) 8-20
3-104 (c) 8-7
3-104 (d) 18-28
3-104 (e) 7-14
3-104 (f) 7-14, 7-22, 7-24
3-104 (g) 7-22, 7-23
3-104 (h) 7-22, 7-23
3-105 (a) 7-29, 9-1
3-105 (c) 9-1
3-106 8-10
3-106 (b) 8-20
3-106 (b) (ii) 8-13
3-106 (d) 9-48
3-107 8-22

3-108	8-31
3-108 (a)	8-34
3-109	8-7, 8-35
3-110	9-5
3-112	8-22, 8-26
3-114	8-28
3-115	10-53
3-116	11-15, 11-16
3-118	11-19, 11-20
3-118 (c)	9-28
3-201	7-19, 9-1
3-201 (b)	9-6
3-203 (a)	7-29, 9-1, 11-29
3-203 (b)	9-57
3-203 (c)	9-6
3-203 (d)	9-31
3-204 (a)	9-4, 11-3
3-204 (b)	9-4
3-205 (a)	9-4
3-205 (b)	9-4
3-205 (c)	9-4
3-205 (d)	11-16
3-206 (a)	9-4
3-206 (c)	9-4, 11-31
3-206 (e)	9-4
3-302	7-19, 9-40, 9-55
3-302 (a)	9-22, 9-33
3-302 (d)	9-31
3-302 (g)	9-48
3-303	9-24
3-303 (b)	9-27
3-304	9-32
3-304 (1)	9-27
3-305	9-14, 9-19
3-305 (2)	9-29
3-305 (a)	9-14
3-305 (b)	9-14
3-305 (d)	11-13, 11-17
3-307	11-32, 11-34
3-310	7-11, 7-12
3-311	11-7, 11-8
3-401	9-11
3-401 (b)	8-5
3-402	9-11, 9-12
3-402 (c)	9-12
3-404	11-36
3-404 (a)	11-35
3-404 (d)	11-35
3-406	10-45, 11-26
3-407	10-45
3-408	11-9
3-409	7-22
3-409 (a)	10-15
3-409 (d)	7-24
3-410	11-9
3-411	10-44
3-411 (c)	10-44
3-412	11-2, 11-21
3-413	11-9, 11-21
3-414	11-2, 11-21
3-414 (1)	10-26
3-414 (c)	11-2
3-414 (d)	11-2
3-414 (f)	10-48, 10-49, 11-2
3-415	11-3, 11-4, 11-21
3-415 (b)	11-5
3-415 (e)	10-48, 10-49
3-416	11-23, 11-30
3-417	11-24, 11-25, 11-26
3-417 (a)	11-24
3-417 (b) (2)	11-27
3-417 (d)	11-24
3-418	10-16, 10-17, 10-35
3-418 (d)	10-17
3-419	11-12
3-419 (a)	11-16
3-419 (b)	11-12, 11-16
3-419 (e)	11-16
3-420	11-30
3-420 (a)	1-20
3-501	11-7
3-501 (a)	7-29
3-502	11-5
3-503	10-19, 11-4
3-504	10-19
3-504 (b)	10-19, 11-4
3-505	10-19
3-601 (b)	11-3
3-603	11-7
3-605	11-13
3-605 (a)	11-13
3-605 (b)	11-13
3-605 (d)	11-13
4-101	10-2
4-102 (a)	10-2
4-103 (5)	10-22
4-103 (a)	10-2
4-103 (b)	10-2
4-103 (c)	10-2
4-104 (a) (10)	10-14, 10-50
4-105	10-6
4-109 (b)	10-17, 10-18
4-110	10-28
4-111	11-19
4-201 (a)	10-27
4-202	10-28
4-205	9-6
4-207	11-25
4-208	11-24, 11-26
4-208 (1)	9-27

4-208 (d) 11-24
4-209 .... 9-27, 11-29
4-210 10-28
4-210 (a) 9-24
4-210 (b) 9-24
4-211 9-24
4-213 (1) 10-3
4-214 .... 10-24, 10-27
4-215 .... 10-16, 10-17
4-215 (a) 10-15
4-215 (b) 10-16
4-301 10-14
4-302 10-14
4-303 .... 10-40, 10-50
4-303 (a) 10-50
4-401 .... 10-31, 10-34
4-401 (1) 11-25
4-401 (c) 10-31
4-402 .... 10-35, 10-42
4-403 .... 10-40, 10-42, 10-43, 10-44, 10-45
4-404 .... 10-48, 10-49
4-405 .... 10-34, 10-50
4-405 (b) 10-51
4-406 10-55
4-406 (d) (2) 10-61
4-407 10-42
5-101 18-12
5-102 18-4
5-102 (a) (11) 18-4
5-102 (a) (4) 18-4
5-103 18-10
5-103 (c) 18-12
5-103 (d) 18-22
5-104 18-5
5-106 18-5
5-107 .... 18-4, 18-5
5-108 .... 18-10, 18-13
5-108 (a) 18-13, 18-20
5-108 (b) 18-5
5-108 (e) 18-13
5-108 (f) (1) 18-22
5-108 (g) 18-13
6-103 (1) 6-18
6-104 6-18
6-105 6-19
6-105 (1) 6-18
6-105 (2) 6-18
6-107 6-19
6-107 (1) 6-18
7-101 18-27
7-102 (a) (1) 18-28
7-102 (a) (3) 18-28
7-102 (a) (4) 18-28
7-102 (a) (5) 18-28
7-102 (a) (9) 18-28

7-104 .... 18-27, 18-28
7-106 15-47
7-204 18-28
7-309 18-28
7-403 18-28
7-501 (a) 18-29
8-102 15-46
9-101 .... 13-5, 13-7, 13-8
9-102 14-30
9-102 (a) 13-21, 13-22
9-102 (a) (7) 14-1
9-102 (a) (12) 13-2
9-102 (a) (18) 15-14
9-102 (a) (20) 13-10
9-102 (a) (28) 15-20
9-102 (a) (41) 13-21, 15-34
9-102 (a) (64) 14-30
9-102 (a) (72) 13-2
9-103 16-17
9-103 (a) 16-17
9-103 (b) 13-30
9-103 (b) (1) 16-17
9-104 .... 13-24, 15-47
9-104 (d) (1) 13-9
9-105 (1) (g) 15-46
9-105 (1) (h) 14-4
9-105 (a) (9) 13-25
9-107 15-47
9-108 .... 14-1, 14-2, 15-2
9-108 (c) 14-16
9-109 .... 13-8, 13-10
9-109 (a) (1) 13-8
9-109 (a) (3) 13-9
9-109 (c) (1) 13-8, 16-34
9-109 (d) (1) 13-8
9-109 (d) (4) 13-9
9-109 (d) (6) 13-10
9-110 14-14
9-201 1-14
9-203 .... 1-20, 14-1, 14-9, 14-32, 15-37, 16-23
9-203 (1) 14-30
9-203 (1) (b) 14-4, 14-5, 14-6
9-203 (2) 1-14
9-203 (a) 14-29
9-203 (b) 14-29
9-203 (b) (3) 14-8
9-203 (f) 14-30
9-204 .... 15-4, 15-41, 16-39
9-204 (a) 14-18
9-204 (b) 14-18
9-207 (a) 17-3
9-301 (3) 16-35
9-302 15-40
9-304 15-46
9-304 (1) 15-46

9-305	15-46
9-307	16-27
9-307 (1)	16-32
9-307 (c)	15-36
9-308 (c)	15-1
9-309 (1)	15-37, 16-21
9-309 (2)	15-42
9-310	15-28
9-310 (a)	15-1
9-310 (b)	15-1
9-311	15-31
9-311 (a)	15-31
9-311 (a) (2)	15-31
9-311 (b)	15-31
9-312	16-20
9-312 (5)	16-11, 16-13
9-312 (a)	15-30, 15-44
9-312 (d)	16-22
9-312 (e)	15-52
9-312 (f)	15-52
9-312 (g)	15-52
9-312 (h)	15-52
9-313	15-28, 15-45, 15-47
9-313 (a)	15-44, 15-45
9-313 (c)	15-44
9-314	15-47
9-315	15-15
9-315 (a) (2)	15-15
9-315 (b) (2)	15-17
9-317	1-20, 16-33
9-317 (a) (2)	13-30
9-320	16-6, 16-24
9-320 (a)	15-15, 16-30
9-320 (b)	16-30
9-320 (e)	16-24, 16-27
9-322	1-20, 16-21
9-322 (a) (1)	16-10, 16-11
9-322 (a) (2)	16-6
9-322 (a) (3)	16-6
9-323	16-11
9-324	16-17, 16-23
9-324 (c)	16-18
9-324 (e)	16-18
9-333	16-33, 16-38
9-334	13-21
9-337	16-29, 16-30
9-402	15-4
9-403 (1)	15-13, 15-14
9-501 (a)	15-32
9-501 (a) (2)	15-32
9-502	15-2, 15-4, 15-10
9-502 (d)	14-30
9-503	15-20
9-504	14-1, 14-2, 15-2
9-505 (2)	17-37
9-505 (b)	13-8, 13-9
9-506	15-10
9-507	17-19
9-508 (a)	16-39
9-509	15-10
9-510 (c)	15-10
9-512	15-10
9-513	15-10
9-515	15-10
9-518	15-10
9-521	15-2
9-601	17-1
9-601 (g)	17-1
9-602	13-5, 17-21
9-609	17-1
9-609 (b) (2)	17-11
9-610	17-22
9-610 (a)	17-21
9-610 (b)	17-21
9-610 (c)	17-3
9-611	17-3, 17-18, 17-28
9-611 (c)	17-21
9-611 (d)	17-31
9-614	17-3
9-615	17-22, 17-29
9-615 (d)	17-29
9-615 (d) (1)	17-3
9-615 (e)	17-29
9-620 (a)	17-36
9-623	17-3, 17-39
9-624	17-21, 17-22
9-625	17-3, 17-22
9-625 (a)	17-3
9-625 (b)	17-3
9-626	17-20
9-627	17-21

COMMERCIAL TRANSACTIONS

**A Survey of United States Law
with International Perspective**

PART I: INTRODUCTION

Chapter 1:
Introducing Commercial Law

A. Historical Context and the UCC

This section will introduce the Uniform Commercial Code ("UCC" or "Code") as well as earlier efforts to unify the commercial law of the United States.

The UCC: Its Origins and Authorship

The Uniform Commercial Code (as well as this casebook) purports to address the subject of "commercial transactions," and yet neither "commercial" nor "transaction" is a defined term within the Code.

Read UCC Section 1-102. A commercial transaction, as that term is used in the UCC, is any matter that falls within one of the Code's ten substantive articles, which are discussed below in Part C.

The UCC is not a product of any legislature or official government body, but rather is the result of a long-term collaboration between the National Conference of Commissioners on Uniform State Laws (NCCUSL) and the American Law Institute (ALI), both of which are private organizations. Because of this unique pedigree, the UCC is not law until it is adopted by a state legislature. The ALI and NCCUSL came together on this project for the purpose of creating a uniform body of law to make commerce function more effectively, and to normalize expectations across jurisdictions so that a business in California, for example, can have some idea of what to expect while engaged in a transaction with a business in Florida.

The ALI and NCCUSL each have their own, distinct mission and means of selecting members. The purpose of the American Law Institute, as contained in its Certificate of Incorporation, is as follows:

> The particular business and objects of the society are educational, and are to promote the clarification and simplification of the law and its better adaptation to social needs, to secure the better administration of justice, and to encourage and carry on scholarly and scientific legal work.

Unless the context otherwise requires, subsequent references to the UCC include only the section number, rather than "UCC Section ____." Other statutes, such as the Truth in Lending Act, are introduced by full citations. All citations to Article 1 are to the 2001 Revised Version. The full text of the UCC (but not its official commentary) can be found online at www.law.cornell.edu/ucc/ucc.table.html.

Institute members, all of whom are lawyers, are elected by an
internal process. In addition, according to the Institute bylaws,
the following classes of persons are recognized as ex-officio
members:

> The Chief Justice of the United States and the Associate Justices
> of the Supreme Court of the United States . . . ; The chief judge of
> the highest court of each State, of the District of Columbia, and of
> Puerto Rico, Guam, the U.S. Virgin Islands, American Samoa, and
> the Northern Mariana Islands; Chief Judges of the United States
> Courts of Appeals; The Attorney General and the Solicitor General
> of the United States; The Presidents of the National Conference of
> Commissioners on Uniform State Laws, the American, National,
> and Federal Bar Associations, and the Bar Association of each
> State and of the District of Columbia, Puerto Rico, Guam, the U.S.
> Virgin Islands, American Samoa, and the Northern Mariana
> Islands; and the dean of each law school that is a member of the
> Association of American Law Schools and the President of that
> Association.

- How would each class of persons be valuable to the
  work of the Institute, which includes the Restatements
  of the Law and other projects in addition to the UCC?

The purpose of NCCUSL, as stated in its constitution, is as
follows:

> It is the purpose of the Conference to promote uniformity in the
> law among the several States on subjects as to which uniformity is
> desirable and practicable.

- For what kinds of subjects is uniformity "desirable and
  practicable"?

NCCUSL Commissioners are appointed by the states
independently of one another, and are typically chosen by the
Governors of each state. Each Commissioner must be a
member of the bar of some state, although the organization's
Constitution does not expressly require that Commissioners be
admitted to the bar of the state selecting them for service in the
Conference.

- What differences do you discern in the purpose and
  membership of each organization and how would you
  expect these differences to result in differing
  perspectives on the uniform law process?

- What are the advantages and disadvantages of a joint
  process?

The first official UCC text was published in 1952. The Code project was not, however, the first attempt at preparing a uniform body of commercial law in the United States. In fact, NCCUSL had been engaged in uniform-law efforts since 1892 and had produced a number of Uniform Acts prior to the UCC, some of which were very successful. The following list of Uniform Acts predating the UCC is from the General Comment of National Conference of Commissioners on Uniform State Laws and the American Law Institute, which immediately precedes the text of the Code, and is modified to list the UCC Article that is most comparable to each:

Pre-UCC Uniform Law	Year	Comparable UCC Article
Uniform Negotiable Instruments Law	1896	Article 3: Negotiable Instruments
Uniform Warehouse Receipts Act	1906	Article 7: Documents of Title
Uniform Sales Act	1906	Article 2: Sales
Uniform Bills of Lading Act	1909	Article 7: Documents of Title
Uniform Stock Transfer Act	1909	Article 8: Investment Securities
Uniform Conditional Sales Act	1918	Article 9: Secured Transactions
Uniform Trust Receipts Act	1933	Article 9: Secured Transactions

In describing the importance of these previous Uniform Acts, the General Comment continues as follows:

> Two of these acts were adopted in every American State, and the remaining acts have had wide acceptance. Each of them has become a segment of the statutory law relating to commercial transactions. It has been recognized for some years that these acts needed substantial revision to keep them in step with modern commercial practices and to integrate each of them with the others.

It was the goal of the UCC to provide the needed revisions and integration referenced in the General Comment. As you read the Official Comments to the Code throughout your study of this material, note the reference to any "Prior Statutory Provision" that precedes the commentary to many Code provisions. As these references show, many UCC provisions incorporate content from previous Uniform Acts.

The Official Comments are introduced in Part C of this Chapter.

William A. Schnader's article *A Short History of the Preparation and Enactment of the Uniform Commercial Code*, 22 U. Miami L. Rev. 1, 11 (1968), includes a chart showing when the Code was enacted in each state. Visit www.nccusl.org and select "Final Acts & Legislation" for an up-to-date listing of the version of each Article enacted in each state.

Even though the UCC was written by law professors, judges, and practicing lawyers, rather than legislators, *some version* of each article has been passed into law in all 50 states, except for Louisiana, which never adopted Article 2 because the state's French civil-code heritage militated in favor of a different treatment of the law of contracts. Thus, the UCC project has been a tremendous success. The qualification "some version" is meant to countenance the way in which some states have chosen nonuniform enactment of the Code, as well as the way in which the Code has changed over time, as the discussion below of revisions will demonstrate. In addition to numerous amendments of the original nine Articles, two new Articles, 2A and 4A, were added in 1987 and 1989, respectively. Because of these additions and changes, the Code *as enacted* varies somewhat from state to state.

Read 1-302. One important characteristic of the UCC is that many of its provisions are default terms; that is, parties can contract around many UCC standards if they so desire. Exceptions exist with regard to duties – like good faith, diligence, reasonableness, and care – that are deemed too important to be waived by private agreement. Even with regard to these exceptions, however, 1-302 (b) provides the parties with some means of defining their obligations within reasonable parameters.

Because the UCC addresses an area – commercial transactions – in which common law and custom, in addition to the uniform law described above, had historically played an important role, it is important to understand the relative roles of courts and legislatures in crafting this body of law. The following language from Grant Gilmore's article *On the Difficulties of Codifying Commercial Law*, 57 Yale L.J. 1341 (1948), provides insight into some of the relevant considerations:

> The principal objects of draftsmen of general commercial legislation – by which I mean legislation which is designed to clarify the law about business transactions rather than to change the habits of the business community – are to be accurate and not to be original. . . . But achievement of those modest goals is a task of considerable difficulty. The draftsman is called upon to build a coherent pattern out of the infinite variety of business customs and practices in an unstable and rapidly changing economy. The more detail and color he loads into his statute, the sooner it will begin to wither on the vine; if, on the other hand, he proceeds from generalization to abstraction, his statute will never be of much use or interest to anyone. *Id.* at 1341.

- What are some risks in drafting that Gilmore identifies?

As you continue to read this chapter and the entire textbook, you might look for ways in which the Code drafters attempted to strike the balance to which Gilmore referred, and you might assess their degree of success in doing so.

The Purpose and Philosophy of the UCC

This textbook is designed for a UCC survey course. Commercial law is a form of business law, and this book will demonstrate how each UCC Article covered shows up in common business transactions. Understanding the business context for the Code, as well as the drafters' philosophy of law, can help clarify why certain provisions are written as they are. Commercial-law scholars have been particularly interested in studying Professor Karl N. Llewellyn, who was the Code's Chief Reporter and principal architect.

Read 1-103 (a). This provision sets forth the underlying purpose of the Code. To contextualize this statement of purpose, consider the following excerpt from Professor Julian B. McDonnell's article *Purposive Interpretation of the Uniform Commercial Code: Some Implications for Jurisprudence*, 126 U. Pa. L. Rev. 795 (1978):

> Professor Karl Llewellyn and his colleagues . . . fashioned themselves jurisprudes. In significant respects, they produced a Code structured by the orientations of the jurisprudential movement known as American Legal Realism.

| Llewellyn is often described as one of the principal figures in the Realist movement. |

> Central to the Realist movement was a belief in the necessity for a "purposive interpretation" of legal institutions. The theory of purposive interpretation is rooted in the concept of law as a means to selected social ends – a method of social engineering. It seeks to define legal standards in terms of the purposes they are designed to implement. It denies that either statutory provisions or common-law doctrines can be adequately understood by reference to a standard of ordinary or plain usage. Thus, the Realists never tired of resurrecting Justice Holmes' famous declaration: "A word is not a crystal, transparent and unchanged, it is the skin of a living thought and may vary greatly in color and content according to the circumstances and the time in which it is used."

| This approach can be contrasted with Formalism, which Realism sought to supplant. Formalism is characterized by the idea of law as a science, with certain, immutable rules that were to be discovered, not invented, by judges hearing common-law cases. |

> In drafting the Uniform Commercial Code, they first delineated central "underlying purposes and policies" of the project as a whole. These are contained in section [1-103 (a)]. . . .

> These goals were not casually derived. They reflect the fact that the drafters thought of the Code as remedial legislation. The Code was drawn to avoid the complexity, obsolescence, and divergent interpretations which had plagued prior uniform laws in the commercial field. In an effort to assure that these objectives were not treated as a mere preamble, the drafters directed: "This Act

shall be liberally construed and applied to promote its underlying purposes and policies."

Second, and more particularly, the drafters sought to articulate the policy embodied in each provision of the Code. In so doing they acted more like judges justifying a decision than legislators declaring law by fiat. They defended this approach to drafting as necessary for the attainment of the Code's underlying remedial objectives. Thus, the Chief Reporter listed as his first principle of drafting technique: "The principle of the patent reason: Every provision should show its reason on its face. Every body of provisions should display on their face their organizing principle." Llewellyn explained this principle in terms of the demands of rationality and the central objectives of a uniform and adaptive commercial law. *Id.* at 797-799.

- From what you have read, how are Realism and Formalism different?

- Based on what you have read so far, how does the Code reflect the Realist philosophy?

As you read this textbook, keep Professor McDonnell's thesis in mind and see whether you can discern the policy reasons underlying the various rules you will study in this course. The following excerpt from Professor Douglas G. Baird's article *Llewellyn's Heirs*, 62 La. L. Rev. 1287 (2002), may assist in this task, as it provides some additional insight into what the UCC drafters' central policy considerations might have been:

> One of Llewellyn's great strengths lay in his understanding that commercial law must be shaped by the world in which it operates and the forces at work there. Llewellyn turned to the law merchant and focused on its rules, particularly those centered around norms that emerged in a well-functioning market. These norms imposed obligations that do not exist in the case of one-shot deals, but granted benefits as well. Llewellyn advanced an idea of good faith with a higher threshold than mere honesty in fact, but at the same time, he believed that those who met the heightened standard of good faith desired greater rights than a discrete rights-based approach would allow. . . .

> . . . [W]e should not forget Llewellyn's starting place. Commercial law begins with the law merchant at the fair, not with William Blackstone, the horse trader. Commercial law applies in the first instance to those who engage in value-maximizing exchanges that leave both parties better off. . . .

> Llewellyn's commercial law had modest ambitions. It sought to work within an existing landscape, rather than transform it (which it had no power to do) or pretend it did not exist. The problem is one of ensuring that commerce flourishes among honest merchants. The problems of fraud and corruption are best

---

Black's Law Dictionary defines "law merchant" as "[a] system of customary law that developed in Europe during the Middle Ages and regulated the dealings of mariners and merchants in all the commercial countries of the world until the 17th century" (7th ed. 1999). For a general discussion of the relationship between law and social norms, see Chapter 3, Part A. For a discussion of how game theory describes healthy, ongoing business relationships as involving "tit for tat" behavior, see Chapter 5, Part B. As this material shows, one-shot transactions may foster different behavior.

left to criminal sanctions and administrative regulation, and the challenge of ensuring that everyone receives a fair deal and pays a just price is one that we can realize only imperfectly. In law, as elsewhere, 95% is perfection. *Id.* at 1290, 1292.

- What are the risks and benefits of the decision to focus on honest merchants, leaving other bodies of law to deal with dishonesty?

Especially because the ALI and NCCUSL must rely on state legislatures to adopt their work, their joint decision to create a Code that incorporates business norms and the principles of the law merchant as well as earlier, successful uniform codes of law was not only a reasonable choice, but probably also made an appreciable difference in the long-term success of the Code project.

- Which organizations' practices are most influential in modern commerce?

- How might the values and practices of these organizations shape a contemporary version of the law merchant?

Note: In her article *Merchant Law in a Merchant Court: Rethinking the Code's Search for Immanent Business Norms,* 144 U. Pa. L. Rev. 1765 (1996), Professor Lisa Bernstein uses empirical research involving members of the National Grain and Feed Association to suggest that it may not ultimately be in a merchant's best interest for courts to apply business norms to disputes that have resulted in litigation. Professor Bernstein shows that members of the NGFA tend to apply relationship-preserving norms (RPNs) to their internal, informal dispute-resolution practices, but would prefer, as a group, that RPNs not be applied during litigation. In presenting this portion of her thesis, Professor Bernstein states as follows:

> Even when . . . RPNs are clear and well-developed, they may be quite different from the terms of transactors' written contracts, which contain the norms that transactors would want a third-party neutral to apply in a situation where they were unable to cooperatively resolve a dispute and viewed their relationship as being at an end-game stage. *Id.* at 1796.

- In your own words, what is Professor Bernstein's argument against the use of RPNs in litigation?

Understanding Professor Bernstein's thesis will be crucial to grasping the concepts presented in this book. Especially when you learn about (1) Article 2's generous "cure" provisions when nonconforming goods are delivered, (2) the evolution of the

End-game tactics and other aspects of game theory are further discussed in Chapter 5, Part B. The idea of litigation as an end-game tactic is famously associated with Professor Robert Ellickson's landmark book *Order Without Law* (1991). Professor Ellickson shows that one of the strongest social norms, particularly among members of small, close-knit groups, is the norm against involving the formal legal system in dispute resolution.

Each topic is covered in Chapter 5.

"perfect tender" doctrine to allow what might appear at first
blush to be less-than-perfect tender of purchased goods, and (3)
the Code's compensatory (rather than punitive) approach to
assessment of damages, consider the possibility that the parties
might have preferred a system of rules that is more focused on
liability and the allocation of blame than the relationship-
preserving system that is currently in place.

UCC Revisions and Nonuniform Enactment

That the Code may be revised when its drafters find a once-
correct rule no longer useful or determine that a former
enactment was ill-advised seems too obvious to merit further
discussion. In their article *Commercial Codification as
Negotiation*, 32 U.C. Davis L. Rev. 17 (1998), Professors Peter
Alces and David Frisch describe a less obvious reason for
revision:

> The UCC is, in substantial ways, carved out of its context, the
> contract law. Section 1-103 acknowledges and posits the fit
> between each of the articles of the Code and the rest of the
> universe of law apposite to commercial transactions within the
> scope of the UCC. There are numerous instances in which the
> Code, particularly Article 2, either cooperates with or conflicts
> with the complementary bodies of statutory and common law. The
> courts have generally been adept at sorting through the related
> legal sources and arriving at conclusions that do not compromise
> the integrity of the Code.
>
> Since the time of the Code's initial promulgation, the
> complementary statutory and common law have evolved in ways
> that test their fit with the Code. Indeed, one very good reason to
> revise an article of the Code is to appreciate that type of evolution
> and revisit the terms of the Code's relationship with the
> complementary law. Conceptions of privity, fraud, and agreement,
> for example, are too fundamental to the fabric of the law generally
> to imagine that they could remain static as transactional patterns
> evolve. Further, the Code was first promulgated during dynamic
> times in the development of our economy, and our appreciation of
> transactor rights not dealing at arms' length has since matured.
> What fit snugly into the statutory and common law world of the
> early 1960s fits less well now. Where the Code was once the
> primary place to vindicate individual consumer rights, for
> instance, there is now a panoply of consumer-protection laws. *Id.*
> at 44-45.

Some of these consumer-protection laws are listed in the Speidel, Summers & White excerpt below in Part B.

- Based on your studies to date in law school, how have
  "privity, fraud, and agreement" evolved within the last
  decade or so?

Understanding that there are several reasons for the UCC to
be revised, consider the description of the Code-revision process

in Fred H. Miller's article *Realism Not Idealism in Uniform Laws – Observations from the Revision of the UCC*, 39 S. Tex. L. Rev. 707 (1998). Professor Miller is a member of the American Law Institute and the Executive Director of the National Conference of Commissioners of Uniform State Laws. This excerpt also gives insight into the logistics of the ALI-NCCUSL collaboration on the Code project.

Any suggestion for a Code revision, whether generated by an article or a study, is considered by the PEB [Permanent Editorial Board of the Uniform Commercial Code] under the agreement between the ALI and the Conference. The PEB is a joint monitoring body composed of members of each organization. If approved, the proposal is then forwarded and approved, or not approved, by the Executive Committee of the National Conference and the Council of the American Law Institute. Only if approved by both organizations does the President of the Conference appoint a drafting committee of eight to twelve members of the two organizations. Thus, again there is a significant screening process that tends to validate the need for, and general details of, the work to come.

> The Executive Committee and the Council are the governing bodies of NCCUSL and the ALI, respectively.

Drafting committees generally meet two or three times during the year. The period for these meetings begins in September and concludes in April, about two and one half months before the annual meeting of the Conference at the end of July. Drafting-committee meetings extend from Friday to Sunday noon. In these meetings, members of the drafting committee discuss the provisions of the proposed law and then draft them in statutory form.

At the end of the year, the work of the drafting committee is presented to the annual meeting of the National Conference in late July, where it is discussed by the entire membership, and approved or revised. This must occur at least twice before the proposal can be promulgated as an addition to or revision of the Uniform Commercial Code. In the case of the Code, the proposal also must be presented to at least one annual meeting of the Institute for approval. Thus, each proposal to amend the Code receives input not only from the Commissioners and Institute members on the drafting committee, and usually from at least one meeting with an ALI "consultative" group, but also from the entire membership of each organization at one or more of their annual meetings.

> An ALI Members Consultative Group is comprised of members who are self-selected for their interest in, and expertise with regard to, a given project.

As well vetted as the work is through this process, the actual participation in the promulgation of a Code Article involves more. First, each drafting committee is usually served by a reporter, who is a legal expert in the subject and whose task it is to advise the drafting committee on the present state of the law, the problems that exist under that present law, what solutions have been suggested to resolve those issues, and then to draft in statutory form the policy and language decisions made by the drafting committee.

Second, under an arrangement with the American Bar Association, the ABA appoints an ABA advisor for every drafting project. The task of the ABA advisor is to present the successive drafts of the proposal to each interested constituency within the ABA, obtain their comments, and convey these to the drafting committee. It is not uncommon for one or more sections of the ABA to appoint their own advisor to the drafting committee in addition to the ABA advisor. Through this process in the case of the Code, the some 50,000 members of the ABA Business Law Section (and often members of other sections) are able to participate in the process of formulating a new Article to the Uniform Commercial Code, and a large amount of collective experience and wisdom is available to the drafting committee.

Finally, at the start of each drafting project, an initial task of the drafting committee is to identify those interests and groups that will operate under or be otherwise impacted by the statute, and that thus presumably can, and have an incentive to, contribute insight into its formulation. Once identified, the President of the National Conference, upon the advice of the drafting committee, will invite these interest groups to send observers to the meetings of the drafting committee to present the viewpoint of those constituencies as to what, if any, rules or changes in present law are desirable, and as to how the rules proposed by the drafting committee will operate in the context with which they are familiar. Other interests, groups, or individuals may attend (the meetings are not closed), and those that do not wish to attend are invited to comment by mail or in other ways, and normally a drafting committee will receive a significant amount of communication through this process. *Id.* at 713-716.

- What does each identified group add to the project?

- Which groups are most important to the success of the project?

The excerpt concludes with a reminder that the process does not end when the Code revision is complete:

Once an amendment to the Code is promulgated, it is not law. Rather each Commissioner is under a duty to cause his or her state legislature to consider the proposal. This often is facilitated by the work of a law-revision commission or committee of the state bar association that reviews the proposal for the changes it will make in the law of the state, the desirability of those changes, and to ascertain how the proposed amendment will fit with the other law of the state. If all goes well, within a short time the proposed law is universally and uniformly enacted by the jurisdictions represented in the National Conference. *Id.* at 716.

This last portion of the Miller excerpt raises an important concern with regard to any revision project. Because neither the ALI nor NCCUSL has any independent authority to make law, any revision faces the prospect that a certain number of

states may choose not to enact the revision, or not to enact
some portions of it. In his article *The Code Project Confronts
Fundamental Dilemmas*, 26 Loy. L.A. L. Rev. 683 (1993),
Professor Julian McDonnell takes this analysis a step further,
considering the fundamental challenge that federalism poses to
the UCC project as a whole:

> [The UCC] is a special – some might say weird – type of
> codification effort: a proposed uniform law to be adopted not by one
> Congress but by over fifty legislative bodies. As with our
> commercial law in general, this uniform-law approach confronts
> certain fundamental American dilemmas.

> * * *

> To state the obvious, this country is a big nation populated by
> diverse and often contentious people. Americans do not want
> everything to be run from the center. . . . We value our federal
> system that leaves some important measure of political power at
> the state level. Thus, our standing assumption has been that the
> law of contracts, sales, and secured transactions are matters to be
> dealt with at the state level by state legislators and state judges.

> At the same time, however, we realize that our prosperity was
> built on the American common market. Enterprises must be able
> to operate nationally, unhindered by widely variant or oppressive
> state measures. How are we to develop a unified, national law of
> commerce within the context of a federal system that leaves
> critical areas of policy formulation to fifty legislative bodies and
> courts of last resort? That is the dilemma of federalism.

> At one point in American history, lawyers confronted with an
> outpouring of statutory pronouncements and judicial opinions in
> the area of commercial law relied principally on the great
> commentators to order their legal universe. In commercial
> matters, the lawyer of 1893 looked to Justice Joseph Story,
> Theophilus Parsons, or Judah Benjamin to find the "correct" rule
> to govern a particular transaction or dispute. The uniform-laws
> movement did not arrive until the turn of the century. Later still,
> the Restatements were designed to deal with the same problem of
> federalism. As the reporter for the first Restatement of Contracts,
> Samuel W. Williston, wrote: "The prodigious material from which
> our law must be sought should be summarized as effectively and
> as soon as possible."

> * * *

> Ultimately, it will be the business community in the United States
> that will decide whether the uniform-laws approach to achieving
> uniformity is satisfactory. It is unlikely that the UCC will be
> entirely federalized. Instead, it is more likely that we will continue
> to rely on a variety of tools to grapple with the dilemma of
> federalism. The piece-by-piece enactment of federal measures
> when the UCC solution does not produce the best outcome is not

> Story was elected to the U.S. Supreme Court in 1811 at 32 and is best known for his opinion in the 1811 *Amistad* case. Parsons was a central figure in the Massachusetts and United States Constitutions. Benjamin was an attorney general, a Senate orator, and declined two nominations for the Supreme Court.

> The Speidel, Summers & White excerpt in Part B below mentions some of the federal law to which McDonnell alludes.

really a defeat for the Code. It merely confirms that the Code is a partial codification of our commercial law. *Id.* at 683-686.

- What does Professor McDonnell mean when he describes the UCC as a "partial codification of our commercial law?"

- Given this country's commitment to federalism, how can you explain the success of the UCC?

- From what you have read, how is the Code different from the ALI's Restatements of the Law?

Despite the great success of the Code project as a whole, controversy has surrounded recent revisions, with some commentators opining that the future of the ALI/NCCUSL collaboration on the UCC could be in jeopardy. In her article *A History and Perspective of Revised Article 2: The Never-Ending Saga of a Search for Balance*, 52 S.M.U. L. Rev. 1683 (1999), Professor Linda J. Rusch provides insight into the strengths and weaknesses of the revision process. Professor Rusch was formerly the Associate Reporter to the Drafting Committee charged with the most recent revisions to Article 2.

> The most often repeated objections in the literature about the revision process pose two concerns: (i) the influence of interest groups that may capture the process in the absence of countervailing, equally powerful interest groups; and (ii) non-uniform enactment or failure to enact a revision product. These two fears together lead to doubts about the policy choices made in the drafts as not serving the public interest. This issue of whether the drafts serve the public interest has frequently been at the core of concerns about how the revision process deals with consumer issues that tend to be controversial and difficult for drafting committees to address. The difficulty in addressing controversial issues in light of interest-group influence and the quest for uniform enactability has in some cases led to a politicization of positions with the accompanying threat to stop enactment unless the drafting committee chooses the position taken by the entity making the threat.

> * * *

> The literature about the revision process discusses the significant toll on human and fiscal capital that the process involves. The time and resource commitment to participation in the process makes it difficult to bring all affected constituencies to the table to consider a product in a timely manner and to achieve consensus. Even if consensus is achieved in the drafting process, that consensus is often illusory when the product reaches the states and other groups get involved. In addition, another criticism directed at the process is that the natural tendency to resist change to the status quo makes meaningful reform difficult,

---

> Section 1-103 (b) may assist you in answering this question.

> Consider these statements in light of Professor Miller's description of the various steps involved in the revision process.

necessarily resulting in a law that, in some participants' view, does not go far enough in addressing various issues.

* * *

On the compliment side, there are several benefits from the uniform-laws process. First, uniform law in and of itself facilitates commercial activity, providing relatively well-drafted statutes that allow interstate commerce to play by the same sets of rules across the country. While federal legislation would result in uniformity, some express concern about whether federal action would be able to accomplish that goal with the same degree of quality as a NCCUSL product.

* * *

Another benefit of the uniform-law process is the ability to gather expertise that may result in more informed decision makers and ultimately better law.

* * *

The openness of the process is also a significant benefit. NCCUSL has worked hard to open up the process so that those who have the time and the money to attend meetings may participate in the process. The drafts are widely circulated and available electronically. This wider net facilitates bringing more people to the table with a variety of experiences that informs the drafting committee regarding the merits and demerits of particular proposals for the drafts. *Id.* at 1689-1691.

- After reading the Miller and Rusch excerpts, is it your opinion that the UCC drafting process is more or less inclusive and transparent than the state and federal legislative process?

- Is the UCC drafting process more or less inclusive and transparent than it should be?

B. Sources of Modern Commercial Law

Read 1-103. Part (a) describes the Code's purpose; part (b) addresses its relationship to other law.

- Are parts (a) and (b) consistent with, or in conflict with, one another, in terms of whether the Code is to be narrowly or broadly construed?

> Comment 2 may help you to answer this question.

As 1-103 shows and as the Alces & Frisch excerpt in Part A illustrates, the UCC is not intended to be an exclusive statement of U.S. commercial law. Instead, the Code is to be understood as part of a larger domestic and international context.

The following excerpt from Richard E. Speidel, Robert S. Summers, and James J. White's book *Commercial and Consumer Law: Teaching Materials* (4th ed. 1987) introduces the variety of sources of domestic contemporary consumer law:

> Despite its seemingly wide sweep, the Code is far from comprehensive. There are some transactions it does not govern at all, and there are many aspects of many transactions to which its provisions might apply but will not, for various reasons.
>
> First and at the fore, the parties can generally make their own "law." As one authority has put it, "We are within that area of law where—to use an old-fashioned, pre-positivistic phrase—businessmen are free to make their own law. They do so expressly, through contract, implicitly through a course of dealing, collectively through custom and resultant business understanding." By agreement, then, the parties to a commercial deal can vary most of the provisions of the Code.
>
> Second, the Code itself, by its own terms, does not purport to control many important types of transactions that can fairly be called commercial. For example, it does not apply to sales of commercial realty nor to security interests therein. It does not apply to the formation, performance, and enforcement of insurance contracts. It does not apply to suretyship transactions (except where a surety is a party to a negotiable instrument). It does not encompass the law of bankruptcy. It does not govern legal tender.
>
> Third, the Code does not even purport to govern exhaustively all aspects of all transactions to which its provisions do apply. . . . Many of its provisions obviously can come into play only by virtue of some key event, e. g., "default," which may be defined by the terms of the agreement between the parties. Furthermore, resort to supplemental principles of law outside the Code will sometimes be necessary. See generally, UCC 1-103. . . . In addition, the Code has its own "gaps" – situations arising within the framework of the Code on specific aspects of which the Code is altogether silent.
>
> Fourth, there are state statutes, most of which are regulatory in nature, which either supplement or supersede Code provisions altogether. See, e. g., UCC 2-102, 9-201, and [9-203 (d)] for references to the possible existence of such statutes. Usury laws and so-called "Retail Installment Sales Acts" are outstanding examples. . . .
>
> Fifth, the Uniform Commercial Code is state law. This means that any valid and conflicting federal commercial law supersedes it. For example, the Federal Bills of Lading Act, . . . 49 USCA § 89124 (1964), rather than Article 7 of the Code ["Documents of Title"], applies to all interstate bills of lading transactions.

This truth, captured in 1-302, is discussed above in Part A.

Sureties who are parties to negotiable instruments are addressed in 3-419 and Chapter 11, Part A.

3-302 Comment 7 addresses the impact of Retail Installment Sales Acts on the law of negotiable instruments.

Sixth, there is a growing body of federal regulatory law that supplements commercial law at many points. For example, the federal Food and Drug Act imposes controls on the quality of goods sold and on the ways they are marketed. The Robinson-Patman Act operates to regulate the price of some goods. Federal statutes govern the creation of security interests in some types of collateral.
. . .

> The Food and Drug Act is found at 21 USC §§ 301 et seq., the Robinson-Patman Act is found at 15 USC §§ 13 et seq.

Seventh, this survey of non-Code sources of commercial law would not be complete without some reference to procedural law. Generally, commercial claims are litigated in accordance with the procedures applicable in any ordinary case. . . .

Finally, there are practices and attitudes of legal officials and of men of commerce which cannot really be captured in the language of any Code but which, nonetheless, have an inevitable impact on legal evolution. *Id.* at 12-14.

> The authors are referring to the existence of business norms. As Part A suggested, the Code incorporates many business norms. The authors of this excerpt assert that many such norms remain outside the UCC, but still affect its development.

- How will you determine whether a transaction is within the UCC?

International Commercial Law

A major feature of this textbook is its inclusion of international perspectives. These "perspectives" provide anecdotes that introduce the major international commercial law initiatives, as well as the domestic law of the United States' top trading partners. The United States Department of Commerce has identified the following countries as the country's top partners in international trade:

Canada	Malaysia
China	Mexico
France	South Korea
Germany	Taiwan
Japan	United Kingdom

Because this textbook is intended for use in a survey course, these anecdotes are limited in length and scope. It is hoped, however, that they will enrich your understanding of United States law and pique your interest in international commercial law.

The following chart introduces some major sources of uniform international commercial law, together with the UCC Article most analogous to each:

Sources of Uniform International Law	UCC Articles
United Nations Convention on Contracts for the International Sale of Goods (CISG)	UCC Article 2
UNIDROIT Convention on International Financial Leasing	UCC Article 2A
UNCITRAL Convention on International Bills of Exchange and Promissory Notes	UCC Articles 3 and 4
UNCITRAL Model Law on International Credit Transfers	UCC Article 4A
UNCITRAL Convention on Independent Bank Guarantees and Stand-By Letters of Credit	UCC Article 5
UNIDROIT Convention on International Interests in Mobile Equipment	UCC Article 9

UNIDROIT is the International Institute for the Unification of Private Law.

UNCITRAL is the United Nations Commission on International Trade Law.

Each source of international law will be discussed in conjunction with the UCC Article most similar to each. The first time each is introduced, a website is provided where it may be found if it is not in the statutory supplement your professor has chosen. As later discussion will show, the success of these uniform international acts has varied considerably. In areas (such as Article 2) in which one international initiative (the CISG) is dominant, our international discussions will be focused accordingly. In other areas (such as Articles 3 and 4) in which uniform international commercial law has enjoyed less success, this textbook will also provide domestic anecdotes from the countries listed above.

C. Overview of the UCC and Guide to Its Use

The eleven articles of the UCC are briefly described as follows:

I use the word "generally" because some Articles contain definitions and other specific provisions that trump the general provisions in Article 1.

Article 1 – General Provisions. As the name suggests, the provisions in Article 1 generally apply throughout the ten substantive Articles that follow. Although Part D of this chapter is the book's most concentrated treatment of Article 1, relevant provisions are discussed as needed, throughout the balance of the textbook. As Part D shows, Article 1 is primarily comprised of definitions and general terms that aid a reader in applying the Code's substantive provisions.

The term "transactions in goods," and the way in which this concept differs from "sales of goods," is discussed in Chapter 2, Part A.

Article 2 – Sales. Article 2, which is concerned with "transactions in goods" as that term is defined in 2-102, is covered in Chapters 2 through 6. Chapter 2 introduces Article 2 in general terms, providing guidance on differentiating an Article 2 sale from an Article 2A lease, and an Article 2 sale of goods from a common-law sale of services. In addition, Chapter 2 introduces the basic sales contract. Chapter 3 introduces the concept of title and addresses insurable interests, risk of loss, and warranties of title. Chapter 4 covers express and implied warranties of quality, disclaimers of warranties, and the way in which privity and notice affect a seller's liability for breach of warranty. Chapter 5 discusses the relative duties of a buyer and seller under the Article 2 sales contract, including the obligation of good faith, both parties' duties with regard to nonconforming goods, and the awarding of damages. Chapter 6 addresses the rights of third parties, including bona fide purchasers for value, in situations of void and voidable title.

Article 2A – Leases. Article 2A is mentioned briefly in Chapters 2 and 13, in illustrating the distinction between Article 2 sales and Article 2A leases. In addition, marginal notes throughout Chapters 2 through 6 alert the reader to the Article 2A analogue for many Article 2 provisions.

Article 3 – Negotiable Instruments. This material is sometimes called Commercial Paper. Together with Articles 4 and 4A, this body of law is also called Payment Systems. Negotiable Instruments law governs drafts (including checks) and promissory notes.

Article 4 – Bank Deposits and Collections. Article 4 is concerned with the bank-collection process. Articles 3 and 4 are covered together in Chapters 7 through 11. In Chapter 7, the text introduces the concept of negotiability, describes the identifying characteristics of drafts and promissory notes, and presents the three stages in the life of a negotiable instrument: issuance, transfer, and presentment. Chapter 8 presents the seven requirements for negotiability. Chapter 9 discusses holders and holders in due course, explaining the legal significance of indorsement as well as the distinction between real and personal defenses (and the significance of this distinction). Chapter 10 introduces the collection process and describes the bank-customer relationship. Chapter 11 discusses various ways in which the parties to a negotiable-instrument transaction can become liable in tort, in contract, or for breach of warranty. Chapter 12 presents two payment methods that fall outside the scope of the Uniform Commercial Code: credit cards and debit cards. Chapter 12 also addresses electronic funds transfers and non-bank financial services.

Article 4A – Funds Transfers. Article 4A, which addresses wholesale wire transfers, is covered briefly in Chapter 12.

Article 5 – Letters of Credit. Letters of credit are an extremely important means of payment in international trade. This mechanism makes it possible for a seller to secure payment from an unfamiliar purchaser who may be halfway across the world, by guaranteeing payment through a third party. Article 5 is introduced in Chapter 18.

Article 6 – Bulk Sales. Historically, the bulk sale was a potential means of defrauding creditors. A fraudfeasor might acquire inventory on unsecured credit, sell it, and abscond with the proceeds without paying for the goods, thus thwarting the creditors who sold him the inventory. Article 6 addressed this problem by requiring certain purchasers of goods through bulk sales to provide the seller's creditors with notice of the sale before it took place. Recognizing that the requirements of Article 6 were onerous to purchasers, substantial recent reform in this area has resulted in the repeal of Article 6 in most jurisdictions. Article 6 is briefly presented in Chapter 6.

Article 7 – Documents of Title. Article 7 is primarily concerned with the law of bailment. This body of law establishes a standard means of establishing rights in goods either in storage or being transported from one location to another. Article 7 is covered in Chapter 18.

Article 8 – Investment Securities. The Uniform Commercial Code, along with federal and other state law, provides part of the body of law relating to investment securities. There are only a few, incidental references to Article 8 in this textbook.

Article 9 – Secured Transactions. Article 9 is the primary source of law governing sales, loans, and other credit agreements made with collateral. Article 9 is covered in Chapters 13 through 17. Chapter 13 introduces the scope of Article 9, describes the various kinds of collateral that may support an Article 9 secured transaction, and discusses different kinds of secured and unsecured creditors. Chapter 14 presents the security agreement and other means by which a security interest may be created and may become "attached" to the collateral supporting the transaction. Chapter 15 introduces "perfection," presenting the significance of the concept as well as its mechanics. Chapter 16 explains how a court determines which creditors have priority over one another. Chapter 17 deals with default, explaining the rights of secured creditors when a debtor defaults, as well as describing the rights of repossession and redemption and the mechanics of post-default sales and other means of disposing of collateral.

The Articles' Relationship to One Another

The various Articles of the UCC work in connection with one another, frequently within the context of a single transaction.

Understanding these connections is crucial to a meaningful study of commercial law.

The following excerpt is taken from the General Comment of National Conference of Commissioners on Uniform State Laws and the American Law Institute, which immediately precedes the text of the Code. This excerpt provides some perspective on how the various Articles of the UCC fit together, as well as the way in which each topic represents some aspect of Commercial Transactions:

> The concept of the present Act is that "commercial transactions" is a single subject of the law, notwithstanding its many facets.

The referenced "Act" is, of course, the UCC.

> A single transaction may very well involve a contract for sale, followed by a sale, the giving of a check or draft for a part of the purchase price, and the acceptance of some form of security for the balance.

Articles 2, 3, and 9

> The check or draft may be negotiated and will ultimately pass through one or more banks for collection.

Article 4

> If the goods are shipped or stored, the subject matter of the sale may be covered by a bill of lading or warehouse receipt or both.

Article 7

> Or it may be that the entire transaction was made pursuant to a letter of credit either domestic or foreign.

Article 5

> Obviously, every phase of commerce involved is but a part of one transaction, namely, the sale of and payment for goods.

> If, instead of goods in the ordinary sense, the transaction involved stocks or bonds, some of the phases of the transaction would obviously be different. Others would be the same. In addition, there are certain additional formalities incident to the transfer of stocks and bonds from one owner to another.

Article 8

> This Act purports to deal with all the phases which may ordinarily arise in the handling of a commercial transaction, from start to finish.

Recurring Themes in the Code

As you study the UCC, you will notice certain, particularly important concepts that show up in various ways throughout the Code. One example is the Article 2 "bona fide purchaser for value," who turns up in Article 3 bearing the name of "holder in due course," in Article 7 as a "holder by due negotiation," and in Article 8 as a "protected purchaser."

One of the pleasant results of the Code's continuity of themes, coupled with its consistent attention to business realities and

preferences, is that students of commercial law often find
themselves able to intuit the correct result in one area of the
UCC, once they have become familiar with another. If one of
the tests of good law is for it to be intuitive and consistent with
societal norms, the Code's predictability may be one reason for
its success.

Another way to understand the Code, and to chart its recurring
themes, is to focus on the nature of the rules it contains rather
than their legal substance. The following excerpt from Alan
Schwartz and Robert Scott's book *Commercial Transactions:
Principles and Policies* (2d ed. 1991) provides two scholars'
perspective on the nature of the Uniform Commercial Code and
the rules that it contains.

> The rules of the Uniform Commercial Code may be classified into
> four categories:
>
> *1. Directives.* Some rules of the Code direct outcomes that may not
> be varied by individual agreements between the parties. For
> example, section [3-420 (a)] provides that "an instrument is
> converted when it is paid on a forged endorsement." Similarly,
> section [9-317] directs that "an unperfected security interest is
> subordinate to the rights of . . . a person who becomes a lien
> creditor." Generally speaking, mandatory rules are employed only
> when the need for certainty is high (such as in rules governing
> negotiable instruments), when freedom of contract between the
> bargaining parties would adversely affect the rights of a third
> party . . . or when unequal bargaining power is likely to exist.
>
> *2. Risk Allocations.* A second type of Code rule structures
> commercial transactions by outlining the allocation of risks that
> will govern if the parties make no contrary agreement. For
> example, under section 2-314 a seller is deemed to make an
> implied warranty that the goods sold are merchantable. Under
> section 2-316, however, the seller may modify or disclaim any
> warranty. Thus, although the Code initially allocates the risk of
> non-merchantable goods to sellers, a seller may alter this
> allocation by a contrary individual agreement that shifts the risk
> to the buyer.
>
> *3. Enabling Provisions.* The Code sets forth requirements which, if
> met, enable parties to achieve favorable commercial status. For
> example, if a promise to pay money is cast in certain streamlined
> form, the instrument containing the promise will be "negotiable"
> (see 3-104); "negotiable instruments" are sometimes desirable for
> persons to issue or possess. As another illustration, if a creditor
> casts a secured loan transaction in a specified form and gives
> appropriate public notice, he will have a high priority in the
> debtor's assets in the event of default. See 9-203, [9-317], [9-322].
> There are two principal reasons why enabling provisions reduce
> the costs commercial parties incur in doing business: first, they
> specify clearly what parties must do to achieve particular

The authors are alluding here to the provisions of 1-302, discussed in Part A, which allow parties to vary most Code provisions by agreement. This excerpt has been edited to reflect the numerical changes in the 1990 Revisions to Article 3 and the 2001 revisions to Article 9. Note that the text of these provisions changed somewhat in the revision process.

Rules of risk allocation are sometimes called "default rules."

As Chapter 7 shows, a non-negotiable instrument is neither void nor worthless, but it does lack certain desirable qualities associated with negotiability.

outcomes, and second, because the provisions require transactions to be cast in standard forms, they make it relatively easy for people to know what is being proposed to them or what other relevant parties have done.

4. Vague Admonitions. Code rules require the parties to obey directives or perform obligations "in good faith," in a "commercially reasonable" manner and without using "unconscionable" clauses. Although these terms cannot be defined precisely, their violation may create a cause of action in the aggrieved party. Consequently, the vague form in which the admonitions are cast works to delegate to the courts the function of making some commercial laws. Because a Code is involved, a judge rather than looking only at past decisional law in deciding a dispute, must also measure the parties' behavior in light of current commercial practices and Code mores to determine if they acted "reasonably," in "good faith," and "conscionably." *Id.* at 4-5.

- What kinds of rules should be directives as opposed to presumptions or risk allocations?

Regardless of whether you choose to organize your study of the Code by theme or by type of rule, it is helpful to look for common threads to make the material more memorable and meaningful.

Reading the Code

Reading the Code can present a challenge, as many students find it grammatically awkward and sometimes difficult to follow in both its logic and its sentence constructions. Consider the various aids located within the text of the Code itself. The General Comment that precedes the text of the UCC, which has already been quoted twice in this chapter, provides an overview of the Code and its history. In addition, Articles 2A, 3, 5, 6, and 8 are preceded by a Foreword or Prefatory Note, written in a conversational fashion, that gives insight into the drafters' priorities and intentions. Official comments provide the same function with regard to individual Code provisions. Although the comments are not part of the UCC text and are thus generally not enacted into law, they are a helpful research tool and a persuasive source regularly consulted by courts and litigants alike. In his article *Some Comments on the Comments to the Uniform Commercial Code*, 1966 Wis. L. Rev. 597 (1966), Professor Robert Skilton provides the following advice with regard to the use of the Code comments:

In some states, the revised Comments had not yet been drafted at the time of the Code's adoption. In others, it is highly doubtful that the Comments were laid before the legislators in the form of a committee report explaining the legislation which the legislators were asked to adopt.

* * *

Surely the Comments may be given at least as much weight as an able article or treatise construing the Code. It is equally clear that the Comments do not approach the weight of legislation; if the statutory provisions adopted by the legislature contradict or fail to support the Comments, the Comments must be rejected.

* * *

A thorough job construing the Code calls for using the Comments to make sure one has found the pertinent language of the statute, as a double-check on a tentative construction, and as a secondary aid where the language of the statute is ambiguous. *Id.* at 604.

- Based on this excerpt, how are the Code Comments similar to, and different from, legislative history?

Finally, the Code's liberal use of internal cross-references can be a significant help in directing readers to definitions and other, related Code provisions. Becoming comfortable with the UCC itself, rather than resorting to this book (or any other text) as a primary source for explanation is crucial for a commercial lawyer.

D. Article 1: The Baseline for the UCC

This section introduces the voluminous Article 1 definitions, choice of law under the Code, and the possibility that the parties to a transaction may depart from, or vary, the Code's provisions by agreement.

The Scope of Article 1

Read 1-102 and Comment 1. This section has already been introduced in Part A as the UCC's statement of scope. In addition, as 1-102 indicates, no transaction is governed by Article 1 unless it falls within the scope of one of the ten substantive Articles of the Code. Thus, there is no such thing as an Article 1 transaction.

Article 1's Lengthy Definitions

Skim 1-201 through 1-206. This book makes reference to the definitions contained in Article 1 whenever they are relevant to the immediate context. In the meantime, note that one of the principal reasons to consult Article 1 is for definitions of key terms. There are numerous defined terms under the Code, and Article 1 (especially 1-201), as well as the first several sections of each subsequent Article, contains a wealth of definitions.

Unless a more specific definition is presented within the text of each Article, Article 1's definitions apply throughout the Code. In case of conflict, however, a substantive Article's specific definitions trump the general Article 1 provisions, for purposes of that Article.

- How is "value" defined for purposes of Article 2? For purposes of Article 3?

- How is "holder" defined for purposes of Article 3? For purposes of Article 7?

Choice of Law under the Code

Read 1-301 and Comment 1. One of the most controversial revisions to Article 1 in 2001 was a new choice-of-law provision that allows the parties to most commercial-law contracts to choose to apply the law of any state to their transaction, regardless of whether the transaction had any connection to that state. Thus, a Kentucky buyer of goods and a Nevada seller could choose to apply the law of New York to their transaction, even if there was no independent reason why New York law might be applicable. The major limitation on this freedom is that 1-301 cannot be applied to deprive a buyer of the consumer-protection law that would otherwise apply to him or her.

In *Is the Proposed UCC Choice of Law Provision Unconstitutional?*, 73 Temp. L. Rev. 1159 (2000), Professor Richard K. Greenstein expressed his concern with the proposed revision.

- Can the parties choose to apply the UCC to a sale of services that is not otherwise covered by the Code?

In his article *Contractual Choice of Law: Legislative Choice in an Era of Party Autonomy*, 54 S.M.U. L. Rev. 697 (2001), Professor William J. Woodward, Jr., explores the importance of the revision:

> [H]istory is replete with examples of State governments exercising their legal authority in unique ways. Texas, for example, established itself as a debtors' haven by creating generous debtors' exemptions from execution on judgments. Its history includes substantial migration of debtors from the Northeast attempting to avoid their debts. Florida has more recently done much the same thing by creating a regime of debtors' exemptions widely perceived to be unfair by those to whom the money has been owed. In the less distant past, California attracted families by offering a very high quality public education, Delaware has become the choice for incorporating many businesses, and New York may be the jurisdiction of choice for litigating commercial-law cases.
>
> Indeed, the perceived importance of state sovereignty and federalism is linked to the idea that one state might, through enlightened legislation or judicial decisions, create a more

hospitable regime for its inhabitants and thereby create for them benefits not presently available to citizens of other states. Obviously, in its traditional form in the United States, creating hospitable or inhospitable environments is the business of State governments. An individual's desire for different limits on creditor remedies, a different public school structure, different tax statutes, or other different rules traditionally calls for political action or physical relocation.

Since at least the 1930s, however, individual choice has played a slightly larger role in determining the legal regime that would apply to some of one's activities. Since that time, individual parties to contracts have had limited power to choose from among the different governing laws that might arguably apply to their contract. The development of this power was controversial well before that; but, recently, this limited power to select applicable law has been relatively uncontroversial.

When contracting parties or the subjects of their contracts are located in different states, it is not obvious which law ought to govern their relations. Uncertainty about applicable law creates commercial problems of predictability for those who draft contracts. To reduce that uncertainty, courts began giving parties limited power to choose from among the legal systems that the adjudicating court might have chosen in the absence of party choice. Since courts selected applicable law based on the "contacts" contending legal systems had with the contract, it naturally followed that parties could choose only from among those states.

Recently, driven by international models and by the rhetoric of party autonomy, there has developed a movement to substantially alter this established approach by deleting the limitation that parties can choose only the "related" law that an adjudicating court might otherwise have chosen in the absence of party choice. This movement started slowly, first being limited to large contracts by sophisticated parties where substantial money was at risk. . . .

> This act, called UCITA, is discussed in Chapter 2, Part A, and has been adopted in only two jurisdictions.

The movement took a giant step when the National Conference of Commissioners on Uniform State Laws promulgated the Uniform Computer Information and Transactions Act. Animated by ideas that high-tech contracts really had no situs, proponents of this proposed statute asserted that an analysis based on pre-existing State "interests" was inappropriate. The idea takes another big step in a pending proposal for Article 1 of the UCC that parties to commercial contracts – large and small – should be able to choose the law of any State regardless of that State's interest in, or connection with, the parties or their contract. These changes are important because, by permitting parties to choose law, whether or not "related" to the contract, the proposals may affect at a core level the very notion that States have "interest" in (and control or "jurisdiction" over) contracts that affect their residents or the property within their borders. *Id.* at 698-701.

- What are the benefits and risks of the new choice-of-law rule?

- What option is available to states that disapprove of the new rule?

Chapter Conclusion: As you leave this chapter, stop to make sure that you are comfortable with the Code on a superficial level. You should have a sense of the philosophy and purpose of the Code, the historical context in which it was written, and its relationship with other bodies of commercial law, both domestically and internationally. You should also have a basic understanding of the subject of each of the UCC's ten substantive articles, an approach in mind for navigating the Code's text, and an idea of how Article 1 assists in this process.

PART II:
TRANSACTIONS IN GOODS

Chapter 2 begins the six-chapter section of this textbook on UCC Article 2, Transactions in Goods. Chapter 2 is primarily concerned with the scope of Article 2 and the basic Article 2 sales contract. The two most important scope issues are the distinctions between sales and leases, and between goods and services. The second portion of Chapter 2, addressing the sales contract, includes materials presented in some first-year courses on contracts. These concepts, which include special problems in mutual assent, together with the parol evidence rule and the statute of frauds, set the stage for later chapters' coverage of warranties, disclaimers, and remedies.

Chapter 3 covers title and other Article 2 property interests. Understanding when title to goods passes is important when a dispute arises regarding risk of loss or insurable interest. Article 2's warranty of title, the final subject in Chapter 3, sets up an important distinction between Articles 2 and 3: the way in which the Code treats a good-faith purchaser of stolen goods, as opposed to a good-faith purchaser of a stolen negotiable instrument. This theme is continued in Chapter 6.

Chapter 4 covers Article 2 warranties of quality, which generate considerable litigation. This chapter presents express and implied warranties of quality, as well as disclaimers of implied warranties. Chapter 4 also shows how privity and notice affect a plaintiff's ability to bring suit for breach of warranty. The chapter closes with a discussion of damages. Understanding how warranty damages differ from the damages for breach of contract discussed in Chapter 5 can help an attorney pursue a client's best interest.

Chapter 5 discusses performance of an Article 2 sales contract. This chapter covers a seller's obligation to deliver conforming goods and to allow a buyer to inspect the goods, as well as a buyer's obligation to accept and pay for conforming goods. These materials explore acceptance, rejection, and revocation of acceptance, as well as the distinction between a single-delivery sale and an installment contract. The materials on cure and remedies demonstrate the options available when either party (or both parties) fail to meet their Article 2 obligations.

Chapter 6 covers the rights of good-faith purchasers and other third parties. These materials discuss the difference between void and voidable title, showing how this distinction affects a purchaser's legal rights and obligations. This chapter also discusses entrustment, comparing the rights and obligations of

two innocent parties: a "true owner" whose property has been
wrongfully sold, and a "bona-fide purchaser" who has
unknowingly purchased the property. The chapter closes with
a discussion of Article 6, which was formulated to protect
creditors against a certain kind of fraudulent sale but has been
repealed in most jurisdictions. This short section shows how
Article 9 now provides protections once supplied by Article 6.

> Unless otherwise
> indicated, all
> references to Article
> 2 are to the pre-2003
> version enacted in
> most states.

Chapter 2:
Introducing Article 2

A. The Scope of Article 2

This chapter begins with the scope of Article 2. The second
section introduces the Article 2 sales contract, with a focus on
mutual assent and other issues regarding the creation and
enforceability of sales contracts.

Sales vs. Leases

> The analogue to
> 2-102 for leases is
> 2A-102.

Read 2-102, which sets the scope of Article 2. **Also read
1-203 and its commentary**, which distinguishes a secured
sale from a lease. The former transactions are subject to
Articles 2 and 9, which are discussed in this textbook; the latter
are subject to Article 2A, which is covered only in the marginal
notes by way of analogy to Article 2.

- What is the common theme among the factors
  enumerated in 1-203; i.e., what did the drafters deem
  most (and least) important in differentiating a sale
  from a lease of goods?

> This issue is briefly
> introduced here and
> further explored in
> Chapter 13, Part A.

Professor Richard Barnes explains why the distinction between
Article 2 sales and Article 2A leases is legally significant, in
*Distinguishing Sales and Leases: A Primer on the Scope and
Purpose of UCC Article 2A*, 25 U. Mem. L. Rev. 873 (1995):

> One day a farmer/client walks into his attorney's office with a
> hand full of papers and says: "I need to know whether the
> irrigation equipment I bought last year was leased or purchased."
> The lawyer's eyes begin to glaze over as she tries to recall her
> commercial-law class. In part to fill the empty air between them
> while she is thinking she asks, "Why do you want to know?"
> Farmer replies, "Well, I am behind on my payments, and the
> company said that, because the equipment is on lease, they can
> come out and take it back if I miss a payment. Can they do that?"
>
> Without realizing it, the lawyer may have asked the crucial
> question. How we view or characterize our commercial
> transactions depends largely on the purpose we are pursuing. In

this case, the farmer needs to know about the right to repossess claimed by the seller/lessor/secured party. His purpose is to determine whether that claim is justified. The right to repossess exists if there was a secured transaction and a default. The right also exists if it was a lease, but it is called a right to "retake possession" after default. The right does not exist if it was a sale and no security interest was reserved because there is no similar right to retake the equipment on default after a sale. *Id.* at 873-874.

> Repossession is covered in Chapter 17, Part A. The Article 2A right to retake possession is found in 2A-525.

This excerpt highlights a characteristic that is common to secured sales and leases: the right to repossess.

- Based on what you know so far, how are leases and secured sales different from one another?

In *In re Berge*, 32 B.R. 370, 36 U.C.C. Rep. Serv. 1717 (B.R. W.D. Wisc. 1983), the court considered the following facts in determining whether a transaction was a "true lease" as opposed to a disguised secured sale.

> About a year prior to their filing a Chapter 11 petition, the [farmers who are the] debtors in this case entered into three separate equipment leases with Baldwin-United Leasing Company. Under these leases, the [debtor-]lessees have the option of purchasing the subject equipment (irrigation machinery and grain bins with dryers) for its "fair-market value" as of the date of expiration of each lease. The lessees have the obligation of maintaining, repairing, and insuring the equipment, and also must return all the equipment in good condition at their own expense at the conclusion of the term of the lease. *Id.* at 370-371.

In finding questions of fact precluded summary judgment, the court held as follows:

> [T]he true character of the option and its effect must be carefully considered. If the option is for a nominal price, it will be a clear index of an intention to transfer ownership by virtue of the lease agreement. If the exercise of the option is for a price which is not on its face nominal, the option must be scrutinized to determine whether the economic circumstances contemplated at the time the contract was signed were such that the exercise of the option was understood or calculated to be virtually certain as a matter of rational business judgment and, therefore, a significant part of the contract rights bargained for.

> Note that the court will look to the economic realities at the time of leasing.

> In the present case, although the option is available only upon the payment of the appraised fair-market value at the termination of the lease term, if that term extends beyond the anticipated useful life of the equipment it would be clear that all incidents of ownership contemplated at the time the lease agreement was entered into would have been conveyed under the terms of the original agreement since there would be virtually no residual

value in the property.   An appraisal for fair-market value, especially if minimal, would not change the fact that all the anticipated incidents of ownership would have been conveyed to the lessee under the lease agreement. In addition, if the fair-market value of the property contemplated at the end of the lease term was less than the cost of reassembly and transport of the equipment to the lessor as required by the terms of the lease agreement, it could be demonstrated that parties contemplated that the exercise of the option would be an economic benefit to the lessee of such magnitude that it was a portion of the price bargained for at the time the lease agreement was entered into, in exchange for which all incidents of ownership would be conveyed. In such a case, the exercise of the option would be virtually "compelled" or the "only sensible course," and the consideration *ipso facto* nominal. *Id.* at 372-374.

- Based on this excerpt, what is "nominal" consideration?

Note 1: Before Article 2A was promulgated in 1987, some courts applied Article 2 to lease transactions by analogy. One such example is *Xerox Corp. v. Hawkes*, 124 N.H. 610, 475 A.2d 7 (1984). In that case, the Supreme Court of New Hampshire applied Article 2's warranty and disclaimer provisions to a transaction involving a leased photocopier. The *Xerox* opinion is a useful source for treatises and other cases advocating a similar approach.

The Official Comment to 2A-101 may assist you in answering this question.

- What, if any, precedential value do cases like *Xerox* have in jurisdictions that have adopted Article 2A?

Note 2: As the court held in *In re Powers*, 138 B.R. 916 (C.D. Ill. 1992), the nature of the putative lessor's business may be a relevant consideration in determining whether a given transaction is a sale or a lease. A bank, for example, that does not commonly lease equipment, might be deemed to have sold the equipment simply due to the unlikelihood of its being an equipment lessor, where the facts are otherwise close.

Note 3: In *In re Hardy*, 146 B.R. 206, 20 U.C.C. Rep. Serv. 2d 1345 (B.R. N.D. Ill. 1992), the court addressed a litigant's contention that a $1 purchase option was not nominal consideration, but instead represented an accurate measure of the goods' worth. That case involved leases of beepers, and the putative lessor testified as follows: "[T]he fair-market value of a 20-month-old beeper was approximately $1 because beeper technology advances at a rapid pace, the market for beepers is dynamic, and . . . the typical beeper will break down approximately once per year." Because the putative lessee had failed to present evidence to support its bare assertion that the beepers were worth approximately $25 and the evidence showed the putative lease period had not wholly exhausted the goods' useful life, the court concluded the parties had entered into a true lease. The court explained its holding as follows:

> Both parties agree that a 20-month-old beeper is not tossed on the trash heap. Instead, an old beeper can be refurbished and resold or relet. Thus, the old beeper would have value [to the lessor]. If the [lessee] chose not to exercise the one-dollar option purchase at the end of the lease period, the [lessee] would be returning beepers to the lessor that have significant value in the real world. *Id.* at 210.

- Following this case, is there any purchase-option price that can be deemed conclusively and absolutely nominal?

Problem: Marhoefer Packing Co. negotiated with Robert Reiser & Co. for the acquisition of a Vemag Model 3007-1 Continuous Sausage Stuffer. The transaction was governed by a document entitled, "Lease Agreement." This agreement required Marhoefer to make 48 monthly payments of $665, with the first 9 payments (approximately $6000) to be paid upon execution of the lease. The other terms and conditions were as follows:

---

1. Any State or local taxes and/or excises are for the account of the Buyer.

2. The equipment shall at all times be located at

Marhoefer Packing Co., Inc.
1500 North Elm & 13th Street
Muncie, Indiana

and shall not be removed from said location without the written consent of Robert Reiser & Co. The equipment can only be used in conjunction with the manufacture of meat or similar products unless written consent is given by Robert Reiser & Co.

3. The equipment will carry a ninety-day guarantee for workmanship and materials and shall be maintained and operated safely and carefully in conformity with the instructions issued by our operators and the maintenance manual. Service and repairs of the equipment after the ninety-day period will be subject to a reasonable and fair charge.

4. If, after due warning, our maintenance instructions should be violated repeatedly, Robert Reiser & Co. will have the right to cancel the lease contract on seven days notice and remove the said equipment. In that case, lease fees would be refunded pro rata.

---

5. It is mutually agreed that, in case of lessee, Marhoefer Packing Co., Inc., violating any of the above conditions, defaulting in the payment of any lease charge hereunder, or if lessee shall become bankrupt, make or execute any assignment, or become party to any instrument or proceedings for the benefit of its creditors, Robert Reiser & Co. shall have the right at any time without trespass, to enter upon the premises and remove the aforesaid equipment, and if removed, lessee agrees to pay Robert Reiser & Co. the total lease fees, including all installments due or to become due for the full unexpired term of this lease agreement and including the cost for removal of the equipment and counsel fees incurred in collecting sums due hereunder.

6. It is agreed that the equipment shall remain personal property of Robert Reiser & Co. and retain its character as such no matter in what manner affixed or attached to the premises.

In a letter accompanying the lease, Reiser added two option provisions to the agreement. The first provided that, at the end of the four-year term, Marhoefer could purchase the stuffer for $9,968.00. In the alternative, it could elect to renew the lease for an additional four years at an annual rate of $2,990.00, payable in advance. At the conclusion of the second four-year term, Marhoefer would be allowed to purchase the stuffer for one dollar.

- Do these facts describe a lease of goods or a secured sale?

Based on *Marhoefer Packing Co., Inc. v. Robert Reiser & Co., Inc.*, 674 F.2d 1139, 1140-1141 (1982).

Goods vs. Services: The Major Tests

> The Article 2A equivalent is 2A-103 (n).

Read 2-105 (1), which defines "goods." Whereas the distinction between sales and leases affects which of two similar Articles – 2 or 2A – applies to a transaction, the distinction between goods and services determines whether a transaction is within the UCC at all. Contracts for goods are covered by Article 2; contracts for services are typically governed by state common law.

- Note that 2-102 refers, not to "sales of goods," but to "transactions in goods." Why did the drafters not use the simpler term "sales"?

> 2-501 provides a clue, but you may prefer to consult a legal dictionary to understand this concept fully. The analogue to 2-501 for leases is 2A-218.

- What is "identification to the contract," as the term is used in 2-105?

- What are "things in action"?

1
2
3
4
5
6
7
8
9
10
11
12
13
14
15
16
17
18
19
20
21
22
23
24
25
26
27
28
29
30
31
32
33
34
35
36
37
38
39
40
41
42
43
44
45
46
50
51
52
53

In the pre-UCC case of *Perlmutter v. Beth David Hospital*, 308 N.Y. 100, 123 N.E.2d 792 (1954), the court considered whether a hospital's supplying of blood to a patient during a transfusion constituted a "sale" of blood. In finding no sale of goods and thus declining to apply the Code's implied warranties of quality, the court held as follows:

> Concepts of purchase and sale cannot separately be attached to the healing materials – such as medicines, drugs, or, indeed, blood – supplied by the hospital for a price as part of the medical services it offers. That the property or title to certain items of medical material may be transferred, so to speak, from the hospital to the patient during the course of medical treatment does not serve to make each such transaction a sale. . . . *Id.* at 104.

> * * *

> . . . The supplying of blood by the hospital was entirely subordinate to its paramount function of furnishing trained personnel and specialized facilities in an endeavor to restore plaintiff's health. It was not for blood – or iodine or bandages – for which plaintiff bargained, but the wherewithal of the hospital staff, and the availability of hospital facilities to provide whatever medical treatment was considered advisable. *Id.* at 106.

- ▪ Would the analysis be different if the medical procedure involved a prosthetic device?

Not all cases fit neatly into the single category of goods or services. In the following case, the court considers three approaches to whether Article 2 should apply to a transaction involving both goods and services. Locate each test and make sure you understand the differences in each approach.

Anthony Pools v. Sheehan,
295 Md. 285, 455 A.2d 434, 35 U.C.C. Rep. Serv. 408 (1983).

Rodowsky, Judge.

Plaintiffs, John B. Sheehan and his wife, Pilar E. Sheehan, of Potomac Woods, Maryland, sued Anthony Pools, a division of Anthony Industries, Inc., in the Circuit Court for Montgomery County. Mr. Sheehan sustained bodily injuries when he fell from the side of the diving board of the plaintiffs' new, backyard swimming pool. The swimming pool had been designed and built by Anthony. Anthony also designed and manufactured the diving board, which it installed as part of the swimming-pool transaction.

. . . On August 21, 1976, the plaintiffs entertained at a pool party. Sheehan testified that he had not previously used the diving board. He said that on that evening he emerged from swimming in the pool, stepped up onto the diving board, and, while walking toward the pool-end of the diving board, slipped and fell from the right side of the diving

board and struck the coping of the pool. . . . [S]kid-resistant material
built into the surface of the top of the diving board did not extend to the
very edge of the board on each side. It stopped approximately one inch
short of each edge. This condition, it was claimed, breached an implied
warranty of merchantability. . . .

Anthony contends that the Sheehans' swimming pool is not "goods,"
[and that the UCC warranties are therefore inapplicable].

* * *

In the subject contract, Anthony's obligations included pool layout,
structural engineering, obtaining construction permits, excavation, use
of engineered steel reinforcing throughout the pool structure, guniting
the pool structure, finishing the pool interior with hand troweled,
waterproof plaster, installation both of a six-inch band of water-line tile
and of coping, and installation of a filter, a pump, a skimmer, and a
specified model of six-foot diving board. . . .

The subject contract presents a mixed or hybrid transaction. It is in
part a contract for the rendering of services and in part a contract for
the sale of goods.

* * *

G. Wallach, *The Law of Sales Under the Uniform Commercial Code*
(1981), § 11.05 [3] at 11-28, describes the current state of the law
concerning implied warranties in hybrid transactions to be as follows:
The general pre-Code approach to this issue was to examine the
transaction to see whether the goods aspect or the service aspect of the
transaction predominated. If the service aspect predominated, no
warranties of quality were imposed in the transaction, not even if the
defect or complaint related to the goods that were involved rather than
to the services. This mechanical approach remains the most popular
method of resolving the issue.

* * *

Here, Anthony undertook the construction of an in-ground, steel-
reinforced, gunite swimming pool with hand-finished plaster surfacing,
tile trim, and coping. The Sheehans were not buying steel rods, or
gunite, or plaster, or tiles. The predominant factor, the thrust, the
purpose of the contract was the furnishing of labor and service by
Anthony, while the sale of the diving board was incidental to the
construction of the pool itself. The question thus resolves itself into
whether the predominant-purpose test . . . should be applied to
determine whether the sale of the diving board, included in the
Anthony-Sheehans transaction, carries an implied warranty of
merchantability under § 2-314.

* * *

A number of commentators have advocated a more policy-oriented
approach to determining whether warranties of quality and fitness are
implied with respect to goods sold as part of a hybrid transaction in

---

Implied warranties of quality are covered in Chapter 4, Part B.

This approach is often called the "predominant purpose" test.

which service predominates.   To support their position, these commentators in general emphasize loss shifting, risk distribution, consumer reliance, and difficulties in the proof of negligence.   These concepts underlie strict liability in tort.

> How do the concepts listed as supporting the "policy-oriented" approach also underlie strict liability in tort?

A leading case applying a policy approach in this problem area is *Newmark v. Gimbel's Inc.*, 54 N.J. 585, 258 A.2d 697 (1969). There, the patron of a beauty parlor sued for injury to her hair and scalp allegedly resulting from a lotion used in giving her a permanent wave. Because the transaction was viewed as the rendering of a service, the trial court had ruled that there could be no warranty liability. The intermediate appellate court's reversal was affirmed by the Supreme Court of New Jersey which reasoned in part as follows:

> The transaction, in our judgment, is a hybrid partaking of incidents of a sale and a service. It is really partly the rendering of service, and partly the supplying of goods for a consideration. Accordingly, we agree with the Appellate Division that an implied warranty of fitness of the products used in giving the permanent wave exists with no less force than it would have in the case of a simple sale. Obviously, in permanent-wave operations, the product is taken into consideration in fixing the price of the service. The no-separate-charge argument puts excessive emphasis on form and downgrades the overall substance of the transaction. If the beauty-parlor operator bought and applied the permanent-wave solution to her own hair and suffered injury thereby, her action in warranty or strict liability in tort against the manufacturer-seller of the product clearly would be maintainable because the basic transaction would have arisen from a conventional type of sale. It does not accord with logic to deny a similar right to a patron against the beauty-parlor operator or the manufacturer when the purchase and sale were made in anticipation of, and for the purpose of use of, the product on the patron who would be charged for its use. Common sense demands that such patron be deemed a customer as to both manufacturer and beauty parlor operator.

> The salon had claimed that, since the cost of the lotion was not clearly separated from the cost of its application to the patron's hair, no sale of goods was involved.

> What remedies might the salon have against the manufacturer, and how might this consideration affect the court's analysis?

The court was careful to limit its holding to commercial transactions, as opposed to those predominately involving professional services.

* * *

A warranty of fitness for particular purpose under § 2-315 of the UCC was implied in *Worrell v. Barnes*, 87 Nev. 204, 484 P.2d 573 (1971). In that case, a contractor was engaged to do some carpentry work and to connect various appliances in the plaintiff's home to an existing liquefied-petroleum-gas system. The appliances were not supplied by the contractor. Suit was for damage to the plaintiff's home resulting from a fire. The plaintiff produced evidence that the fire was caused by a defective fitting installed by the contractor which had allowed propane to escape. . . .

1 W. Hawkland, *Uniform Commercial Code Series* (1982), § 2-102:04, at Art. 2, p. 12 has suggested what might be called a "gravamen" test in light of the decision in *Worrell*. He writes:

> This is sometimes called the "gravamen of the complaint" test.

Unless uniformity would be impaired thereby, it might be more
sensible and facilitate administration, at least in this grey area, to
abandon the "predominant factor" test and focus instead on
whether the gravamen of the action involves goods or services. For
example, in *Worrell v. Barnes*, if the gas escaped because of a
defective fitting or connector, the case might be characterized as
one involving the sale of goods. On the other hand, if the gas
escaped because of poor work by Barnes the case might be
characterized as one involving services, outside the scope of the
UCC.

* * *

The gravamen test of Dean Hawkland suggests the vehicle for
satisfying the legislative policy. Accordingly, we hold that where, as
part of a commercial transaction, consumer goods are sold which retain
their character as consumer goods after completion of the performance
promised to the consumer, and where monetary loss or personal injury
is claimed to have resulted from a defect in the consumer goods, the
provisions of the Maryland UCC dealing with implied warranties apply
to the consumer goods, even if the transaction is predominately one for
the rendering of consumer services.

* * *

Thus, the diving board which Anthony sold to the Sheehans as part of
the swimming pool construction contract carried an implied warranty
of merchantability under CL § 2-314.

  ▪ Are you convinced by the *Newmark* court's reasoning,
     or does the more concrete *Anthony Pools* analysis have
     greater appeal?

Note 1: *Duxbury v. Spex Feeds, Inc.*, 681 N.W.2d 380, 54
U.C.C. Rep. Serv. 2d 58 (Minn. App. 2004), provides guidance
in applying the "predominant purpose" test referenced – but
not applied – by the *Anthony Pools* court. *Duxbury* involved a
lawsuit by four farmers, all members of the Duxbury family,
against Spex Feeds, Inc., which supplied their farm with hog
feed. The farmers' sows experienced veterinary issues which,
the Duxburys believed, were traceable to toxins in the feed.
The suit alleged Spex Feeds, Inc. did not act reasonably in
seeking to ensure the feed was free from toxins. In deciding the
farmers' claim, the court considered the following facts:

> Spex manufactured the feed by grinding grain-bank corn and
> mixing in soybean meal, medicines, and nutritional supplements.
> The feed additives and supplements made up approximately 12 to
> 14 percent of the feed. The Duxburys were charged for all
> components of the feed except the corn. They also were charged a
> fee for the grinding, mixing, and delivery of the feed. *Id.* at 384.

The court concluded as follows regarding this issue:

> [To determine whether the UCC governs this transaction], we
> examine whether the predominant factor in the transaction is the
> transfer of goods or the provision of services. Relevant factors
> include the language of the contract, the business of the supplier,
> and the "intrinsic worth" of the goods involved. In practice, courts
> generally rely on the relative costs of the services and the goods.
> . . .
>
> . . . Spex is in the business of selling animal feed and feed
> supplements. Spex transferred a finished good, animal feed, to the
> Duxburys for a price. According to the receipts generated by Spex,
> the Duxburys were billed approximately $74 per ton for feed
> additives and supplements but only $8.50 per ton for the
> preparation and transport of the feed. Based on these facts, the
> predominant factor in the parties' transaction was the transfer of
> goods. We, therefore, conclude that the transaction was a sale. *Id.*
> at 386-387.

- Would the *Anthony Pools* holding have been different
  if it had engaged in a similar analysis of these same
  factors?

Note 2: In *Arvida Corp. v. A. J. Industries, Inc.*, 370 So. 2d
809, 26 U.C.C. Rep. Serv. 664 (Fla. 4th Dist. App. 1979), a real-
estate developer sued Porcelite, the company it hired to repair
bathroom fixtures in one of its developments, alleging breach of
contract and breach of warranty. The following excerpt shows
how the *Arvida* court concluded the repair work did not
implicate Article 2.

> Under careful enough examination, some parts or materials can
> nearly always be found that were used in making repairs, and
> these parts or materials could be held to qualify that transaction
> as a "sale of goods." This requires saying that the services are
> incidental to the goods used, regardless of whether the cost of the
> "goods" and the importance of the "goods" were small compared to
> the labor in making the repairs. This is hardly commendable
> detective work in uncovering the truly guilty party because it
> simply obliterates the distinction between sales of goods and sales
> of services.
>
> Since "services" includes lawyering and doctoring and other
> professions, the introduction of implied warranties in service
> transactions would impose standards on human beings, rather
> than on their artifacts. Conceivably all sorts of personal
> performances for hire could be subjected to judicial testing as to
> whether they met the implied warranty of "merchantability" or
> whatever else it is that is impliedly warranted.
>
> No doubt seals, caulking, screws, nuts, bolts, or pipe were used in
> its efforts at repair by Porcelite, but if there ever was a repair as

distinct from a sale of goods, it would be repairs of the bathroom
equipment that had been installed as fixtures in Arvida's
buildings when Porcelite came into the story. It does not make
sense to say that Porcelite was hired to sell Arvida seals, caulking,
screws, and whatever else it used in attempting repairs. *Id.* at
810-811.

- Why not apply warranty law to professional services?

- What body of law currently addresses these issues?

Note 3: *Bonebrake v. Cox*, 499 F.2d 951, 14 U.C.C. Rep. Serv.
1318 (8th Cir. 1974), is a seminal case in developing the
"predominant purpose" test. *Bonebrake* involved the sale of
bowling equipment and can be seen as the flip side of *Arvida*.
While *Arvida* shows the presence of goods in a transaction
dominated by services is not dispositive as to the applicability
of Article 2, *Bonebrake* makes the same point with regard to
the provision of services in what is predominantly a contract for
goods. The following portion of the *Bonebrake* opinion, citing R.
Nordstrom, *Handbook of the Law of Sales* 40, 44 (1970), is
illustrative:

> [Goods] are not the less "goods" within the definition of the [UCC]
> because service may play a role in their ultimate use. The Code
> contains no such exception. "Services . . . always play an
> important role in the use of goods, whether it is the service of
> transforming the raw materials into some usable product or the
> service of distributing the usable product to a point where it can
> easily be obtained by the consumer. The [Article 2] definition [of
> goods] should not be used to deny Code application simply because
> an added service is required to inject or apply the product." In
> short, the fact that the contract "involved substantial amounts of
> labor" does not remove it from inclusion under the Code. *Id.* at
> 958-959.

- After reading about the *Arvida* and *Bonebrake* cases,
  what is the distinction between goods and services,
  insofar as the "predominant purpose" test is
  concerned?

Problem 1: In the pre-UCC case of *Nisky v. Childs Co.*, 103
N.J.L. 464, 135 A. 805 (N.J. 1927), the court considered a
dispute between a restaurant and a patron who had eaten a
fried-oyster dish that made her ill. In finding the meal-
purchase transaction was not a sale of goods, the court held as
follows:

> The authorities . . . recognize that, while the food served
> constitutes, of course, an essential part [of the meal transaction],
> yet serving it cannot be regarded as a sale of goods, and this we
> think the common understanding. A customer at an eating place

seeks not to make a purchase but to be served with food to such reasonable extent as his present needs require. With the service go a place, more or less attractive, in which to eat it, a table, dishes, linen, silver, waiters, and sometimes music as an accompaniment, all tending to render more agreeable and palatable that which he eats. The food he obtains is then and there consumed; he does not eat the portion he can comfortably devour and place the remainder in his pockets or other receptacle, to be stored away for future needs. So one who purchases a steamship ticket, or one who registers at a hotel, does not conceive the transaction as a sale of goods when, as part of his passage in the one case, and as a guest in the other, he is supplied with meals; nor does one who enters a restaurant to be supplied with a meal or any portion thereof so regard the supplying of his food. This attitude of the public mind is indicated by the familiar signs, "Meals served here," "Dinners served here," and the like. *Id.* at 467-468.

> In modern understanding, does the customer have the right to take uneaten food home if he or she so chooses? How, if at all, should this consideration affect the court's analysis?

- Is this result consistent with 2-105 and 2-107?

- Is the reference to food served by common carriers and innkeepers an appropriate analogy to food served in a restaurant?

Problem 2: *Wooster Products, Inc. v. Magna-Tek, Inc.*, 52 U.C.C. Rep. Serv. 2d 602 (Ohio App. 9th Dist. 1990), involved a dispute arising from Magna-Tek's sale of equipment and technology to Wooster Products, Inc., an entity constructing a videotape-manufacturing business in India. In determining whether the transaction was to be governed by Article 2, the court considered the following information regarding the parties' contract:

[The] agreement purported to sell for $2.1 million:

(a) All plant machinery and equipment necessary or useful in the production of 1/2' videotape in India;

(b) All technology and expertise necessary or useful in operating said plant machinery and equipment so as to achieve the results desired, namely; the manufacture, sale, and distribution of quality videotape.

(c) Two of [Magna-Tek's] three principals will attend the manufacturing site in India from the date the plant and machinery are on site until the production of 1/2' videotape is running smoothly producing tapes which are compatible with all videotape systems [and] which tapes are of high quality.

(d) Training of [Wooster] Products' stateside and Indian personnel, on site, necessary to the proper operation and maintenance of the plant and machinery, testing procedures, quality maintenance, fault finding, and remedy. . . .

. . . The equipment was priced at $1.6 million and the technology was priced at $500,000. Baker, president of Magna-Tek, testified that Magna-Tek did not own the equipment, but that it merely assembled the equipment that the Acme Group of Companies shipped to its facility. *Id.* at 605.

In answering this question, you may wish to review the material contained in Note 1.

- Applying the *Duxbury* court's approach, how would you analyze the applicability of Article 2 to this transaction?

Problem 3: In *Whitmer v. Bell Telephone*, 361 Pa. Super. 282, 522 A.2d 584 (1987), the court considered a suit by Shirley Whitmer, who claimed she suffered personal injury when attempting to use a pay telephone in a K-Mart store. As she lifted the receiver, the metal cord connecting it to the wall unit broke and hit her in the mouth. She sued, claiming a breach of Article 2's implied warranty of merchantability. Bell Telephone, the owner of the unit, claimed the transaction involved no sale of goods, and the court agreed.

- From this brief vignette, is the court's holding consistent with *Anthony Pools*? *Newmark*?

- If there is a sale of goods in this case, what good was sold?

- Is the good being sold the same good that harmed the plaintiff?

- The court considered theories of bailment, lease, and sale. Which best describes Ms. Whitmer's use of the phone?

- Should the court's holding turn on whether the plaintiff had deposited coins in the telephone at the time of the injury, creating a contractual relationship with the defendant?

Goods vs. Services: Computer Information

Read current 2-105 and revised 2-103 (1) (k) and Comment 7.

Revised 2-103 excludes "information" from Article 2. Current 2-105 provides no guidance as to whether information should be included within Article 2, although most courts have assumed it is within the Article's purview. As Comment 7 suggests, the primary purpose of this change is to exclude computer information.

Professor Ann Lousin summarizes revised 2-103, as it relates to computer information, in the following excerpt from *Proposed UCC 2-103 of the 2000 Version of the Revision of Article 2*, 54 S.M.U. L. Rev. 913 (2001):

> 1. If [a] copy of [a] computer program is contained in goods that are sold or leased to a remote buyer or lessee, proposed Article 2 applies to both the copy and the computer program.

What would be an example of a computer program contained in goods?

> 2. However, point 1 is not true if the "goods" involved are a "computer" or "computer peripheral." Proposed Section 2-102 (a) (6) defines "computer." There is apparently no statutory definition of "computer peripheral." The report says, "The test for application of this Article is never satisfied, however, if the goods themselves are a computer or computer peripheral." Can this mean that a computer – a machine, hardware – is not within Article 2? Surely not, but the text and report are confusing here.

> 3. Also, point 1 is not true if "giving the buyer or lessee of the goods access to or use of the program is ordinarily a substantial purpose" of this type of goods transaction. The report indicates that the source of this exception is UCITA, Sec. 103 (b) (1) and that the only difference from UCITA is the substitution of "substantial" for "material." The report suggests "more than merely nontrivial" as a definition of "substantial."

What would be an example of this phenomenon?

UCITA is discussed in the text following this excerpt.

> Subsection (c) of proposed Section 2-103 completes the section's treatment of computer-related matters that may or may not fall within the scope of proposed Article 2. It addresses a "transaction that includes computer information and goods." Under subsection (c), as far as the "goods" are concerned, the parties may not agree to "alter a result" otherwise required by the proposed Article. This prohibition extends to a "copy of a computer program constituting goods." *Id.* at 918-919.

In your own words, what is the purpose of subsection (c)?

- Do the drafters' distinctions make sense?

The Lousin excerpt mentions UCITA, the Uniform Computer Information Transactions Act. UCITA was originally an ALI/NCCUSL collaboration like the UCC. The Act originated out of the drafters' assumption that computer information was sufficiently different from other goods typically covered by Article 2 to require a separate law of its own. The intent was to remove computer information from Article 2, to be governed instead by UCITA. However, UCITA was so controversial that the ALI withdrew its support of the Act. UCITA was perceived as anti-consumer, and only two states – Maryland and Virginia – have enacted it.

The text of UCITA can be found through NCCUSL's online archive at www.law.upenn.edu/bll/ulc/ulc_frame.htm.

- What body of law will cover computer information, if revised Article 2 is widely adopted and UCITA is not?

While state legislatures debate the future of revised Article 2, courts may continue to apply current Article 2 to computer information.

- What are the risks and benefits of continuing to apply current Article 2 to computer information?

As the Lousin excerpt suggests, revised 2-103 has been criticized as imperfectly articulating the line between goods and information. In *Amending the Uniform Commercial Code: Will a Change in Scope Alter the Concept of Goods?*, 82 Wash. U. L.Q. 275 (2004), Abby Hardwick suggests that the "predominant purpose" test should be used to determine whether a transaction involving computer information implicates Article 2.

- Based on what you have read, how similar to, or different from, revised 2-103 is Ms. Hardwick's proposed approach?

Connecting "Sale" and "Goods"

The following case analyzes both whether a sale has occurred and whether the transaction involved goods, rather than services. The opinion addresses whether a good includes its container and whether receipt of a "free" item can be deemed a sale.

> After reading the court's opinion, make sure you understand why the word "free" is in quotation marks.

Gunning ex. rel. Gunning v. Small Feast Caterers, Inc.,
4 Misc. 3d 209, 777 N.Y.S.2d 268,
53 U.C.C. Rep. Serv. 2d 502 (2004).

Herbert Kramer, J.

A glass of water allegedly exploded in a patron's hand in one of our local Brooklyn restaurants: Can recovery be had against the restaurant as the "seller" of this glass under theories of strict products liability and implied warranties of fitness? . . .

Defendants Small Feast Caterers, the restaurant at which the plaintiff dined, and Stoelzle-Oberglas, USA, an importer/distributor of items for restaurant tabletops including glasses, move for summary judgment . . . to dismiss the complaint and cross-claims.

The complaint alleges three theories of recovery: Express warranty, implied warranty, and strict products liability. The restaurant argues that it is not liable for the harm caused by the allegedly defective glass because it was not and is not in the "business of selling" the water or the water glasses it provides to its patrons.

Although there are no New York cases directly on point, this Court has found a decision in the United States District Court for the District of New Jersey that is legally and factually indistinguishable from our own. *Levondosky v. Marina Associates,* 731 F. Supp. 1210 (D.N.J. 1990). In *Levondosky,* a cocktail waitress in a gambling casino gave the plaintiff an alcoholic beverage free of charge while he was gambling. The plaintiff allegedly swallowed glass chips that had broken off the rim of the glass and sued under theories of express and implied warranty and strict products liability. The *Levondosky* Court, making its determination under New Jersey statutes identical to our own, reasoned as follows: The theories of implied warranty and strict liability are essentially identical juridically. With respect to implied warranty, the question is whether a "sale" occurred since the alcoholic beverage, like the glass of water in our case, was provided free of charge and the [implied warranty] statute requires a service "for value" of food or drink.

> After reading the materials on implied warranty in Chapter 4, Part B, make sure you know why this statement regarding strict liability is true.

In *Levondosky,* as here, defendant was offering a complimentary drink to its patrons, but was not doing so out of any sense of charity or hospitality. This glass of water was offered as an indispensable part of the meal that was sold to the patron. Moreover, here, as in *Levondosky,* the defendant served water on a regular basis as part of its business. In fact it would be difficult to imagine, except in times of severe drought, a restaurant that did not provide water to its patrons along with their meals. As to the question of value, even if we were to give this term a very restrictive meaning, it is reasonable to presume that the cost of providing this drink was built into the bill.

> Note the court's first step, finding that provision of a "free" item constitutes a sale for value. In so doing, note the court's broad construction of the concept of "service for value."

The second inquiry is whether the defendant gave an implied warranty as to the glass as well as to the drink in it. [The plaintiff] was the ultimate consumer of the drink, but the glass remained the property of the defendant. In *Shaffer v. Victoria Station, Inc.,* 91 Wash.2d 295, 588 P.2d 233 (1978), the Supreme Court of Washington was faced with a similar situation. In that case, plaintiff ordered a glass of wine and the glass broke in his hand, causing permanent injury. The state of Washington adopted the identical provision from the Uniform Commercial Code regarding implied warranties as did the state of New Jersey. In the opinion of the Supreme Court of Washington, when the Uniform Commercial Code states, "the serving for value of food or drink to be consumed either on the premises or elsewhere is a sale" and that such food and drink must be "adequately contained, packaged, and labeled as the agreement may require," it covers entirely the situation [when a glass causes injury] . . . The drink sold includes the wine and the container, both of which must be fit for the ordinary purpose for which used."

> Note the court's second step, finding that the good being sold included the container in which it was delivered, even though the container did not become the property of the buyer.

This Court finds that New York statute is identical to that of the Washington and New Jersey statutes and it adopts the *Levondosky* analysis, holding that the defendant restaurant impliedly warranted that the water it served to the plaintiff was fit for consumption. If the container that held the water was defective, then the water was not fit for consumption, and consequently plaintiff's claim under the theory of implied warranty is viable.

[The sections relating to strict liability in tort, a cause of action commonly raised in suits brought under Article 2's warranty provisions, and express warranty have been omitted.]

- Can *Levondosky* be distinguished from *Gunning*?

- Is the restaurant the lessor of the glass under Article 2A?

Problem: In *Hedges v. Public Service Co.*, 396 N.E.2d 933, 27 U.C.C. Rep. Serv. 945 (Ind. App. 1979), the court considered a suit brought against a supplier of electricity based upon the personal injuries the plaintiffs suffered after they came into contact with Public Service Co.'s high-voltage wires. In finding Article 2 did not govern the transaction, the court held as follows:

> It is necessary for goods to be (1) a thing; (2) existing; and (3) movable, with (2) and (3) existing simultaneously. We are of the opinion that electricity qualifies in each respect.
>
> * * *
>
> The high-voltage electricity with which the Hedges came into contact was not the good [PSC] was intending to sell or the Hedges were intending to buy. While the delivery of 135 volts of electricity[, the normal voltage delivered to a home or business,] can be considered the sale of a . . . good, the tragic escape of 7200 volts from the transmission wire, through the ladder, and into the bodies of these men is not a transaction in goods intended to be covered by the Uniform Commercial Code. *Id.* at 936.

- Is the result in *Gunning* consistent with this portion of *Hedges*?

- Is *Hedges* consistent with *Whitmer*, covered in Problem 3?

Merchants and Nonmerchants under Article 2

Read 2-102, 2-104 (1) and Comments 1 and 2, and 2-314.

The Article 2A equivalents are 2A-102 and 2A-103 (2), respectively. Article 2A adopts the 2-104 (1) definition of merchant, as well.

A common mistake is to assume Article 2 applies only to transactions involving merchants. Some provisions apply only to merchants, but those that do, expressly so state. Otherwise, Article 2 applies equally to merchants and nonmerchants. For a defense of the UCC's special rules for merchants, see John F. Dolan, *The Merchant Class of Article 2: Farmers, Doctors, and Others*, 1977 Wash. U. L. Q. 1. For an argument that the merchant rules did not reflect generally accepted commercial norms, but were Llewellyn's own invention, see Ingrid

Michelsen Hillinger, *The Article 2 Merchant Rules: Karl Llewellyn's Attempt to Achieve The Good, The True, The Beautiful in Commercial Law*, 73 Geo. L.J. 1141 (1985).

- From whose point of view — that of the putative merchant or the other party to the transaction — does the Code define merchant status?

- For the purposes of 2-104 (1), is a skilled businessperson who does not regularly deal in goods a merchant?

- For the purposes of 2-314, is this person a merchant?

- **Read 2-314, 2-315, and 2-201**, and compare their applicability to merchants and nonmerchants alike.

> 2-314 and 2-315 are covered in Chapter 4, Part B. The Article 2A analogues of 2-314, 2-315, and 2-201 are 2A-212, 2A-213, and 2A-201, respectively.

Whether an individual is a merchant is often relatively easy and straightforward to determine. Farmers present some of the more interesting questions in this area. The case and problem that follow use the definition of "merchant" in 2-104 to address whether the "merchant's exception" to the statute of frauds, discussed later in this chapter, applies to farmers.

Decatur Cooperative Association v. Urban, 219 Kan. 171, 547 P.2d 323, 18 U.C.C. Rep. Serv. 1160 (1976), addressed a lawsuit by a grain cooperative seeking to enforce an oral wheat-sale contract against a farmer. In concluding the farmer was not a merchant for purposes of the statute of frauds, the court held as follows:

> The concept of professionalism is heavy in determining who is a merchant under the statute. The writers of the official UCC Comment virtually equate professionals with merchants — the casual or inexperienced buyer or seller is not to be held to the standard set for the professional in business. The defined term "between merchants," used in the exception proviso to the statute of frauds, contemplates the knowledge and skill of professionals on each side of the transaction. The transaction in question here was the sale of wheat. Appellee as a farmer undoubtedly had special knowledge or skill in raising wheat, but we do not think this factor, coupled with annual sales of a wheat crop and purchases of seed wheat, qualified him as a merchant in that field. . . . [A]ppellee has sold only the products he raised. There is no indication any of these sales were other than cash sales to local grain elevators, where conceivably an expertise reaching professional status could be said to be involved. *Id*. at 176-177.

> The comment referenced here is UCC 2-104, Comment 1.

Problem: *Nelson v. Union Equity Co-operative Exchange*, 548 S.W.2d 352, 21 U.C.C. Rep. Serv. 1 (Tex. 1977), addressed whether a farmer is a merchant within the context of an

alleged breach of a grain-futures contract. The following are
the facts the court considered in holding that farmer Nelson
was a merchant:

> [Nelson] is a lifelong Oklahoma resident and owns 1,200 acres of
> land near Mangum, Oklahoma. He grazes cattle on this land and
> has grown cotton and wheat there since at least 1967. He does not
> consume the crops he raises, but sells them for his livelihood. He
> brings in one wheat crop a year, and he has sold that crop
> annually since 1967.

> Nelson is knowledgeable about the business of growing and selling
> crops, and he has made it his usual practice since 1967 to
> determine the best price obtainable for his crops. He stays abreast
> of the current market prices by listening to the market reports on
> the radio every day and by telephoning various grain dealers to
> get the current wheat-price quotations. *Id.* at 355.

- How would you argue for and against Nelson's
  merchant status, applying *Decatur Cooperative
  Association*?

- Do you agree with the following statement in the
  dissent?

> The unfortunate result of the majority decision is not only that
> every farmer in Texas is held to be a "merchant," but every
> individual who from time to time buys or sells significant
> household or personal items, house trailers, boats, or automobiles
> also becomes a "merchant." *Id.* at 360.

- If so, do you believe the majority reached the right
  result?

- If not, how would you distinguish Farmer Nelson from
  the sellers referenced by the dissenting judge?

The CISG is
translated into 6
official texts for the
6 official languages
of the United
Nations: English,
French, Spanish,
Russian, Chinese, &
Arabic. The text of
the CISG and
resources for
applying it are found
at www.cisg.
law.pace.edu.

International Perspective: The CISG's Scope

As Chapter 1 indicated, each section of this book includes an
"International Perspective" focusing on one or more topics
covered in that section, from the point of view of another legal
system.   As later chapters show, there is only limited
international consensus at this time in the fields of negotiable
instruments and secured transactions; for transactions in
goods, however, the United Nations Convention on Contracts
for the International Sale of Goods ("CISG") will dominate our
international discussions.   By some accounts, approximately
two-thirds of world trade is governed by the CISG.   The

following list shows which of the United States' top ten trading partners are, like the U.S., parties to the CISG:

Country	CISG Party?
Canada	Yes
China	Yes
France	Yes
Germany	Yes
Japan	No
Malaysia	No
Mexico	Yes
South Korea	Yes
Taiwan	No
United Kingdom	No

> For an article discussing the United Kingdom's refusal to become a party to the CISG, see Angelo Forte, *The United Nations Convention on Contracts for the International Sale of Goods: Reason and Unreason in the United Kingdom*, 26 U. Balt. L. Rev. 51 (1997).

Read CISG Article 2 and Article 3 (2). Like UCC Article 2, the CISG applies only to sales, not to leases, and only to goods, not to services. Unlike UCC Article 2, most provisions of which apply to *all* sales of goods, the CISG does not govern sales to consumers.

> Reading the recitals preceding the text of the CISG, together with UCC 1-102, may assist you in answering this question.

- What is the stated purpose of the CISG, as compared with the UCC, and how might this distinction have influenced the decision to include consumer transactions in the UCC, but exclude them from the CISG?

- "Goods" is a defined term under both the UCC and the CISG. Compare UCC 2-103 with CISG Article 2. What differences do you see in the definitions?

Problem: Read CISG Article 1. Does the CISG apply to a contract between a California printer and an Iowa manufacturer to produce trading cards bearing the likeness of pop star Britney Spears, to be sold in Mexico?

Based on *Grace Label, Inc. v. Kliff*, 355 F. Supp. 2d 965 (S. D. Iowa 2005).

Read CISG Article 6. When a contract is otherwise within the scope of the CISG, the parties can choose to opt out. However, they must choose their contractual language carefully to achieve the desired result. In *Asante Technologies, Inc. v. PMC-Sierra, Inc.*, 164 F. Supp. 2d 1142 (N.D. Cal. 2001), the court held it would be improvident for parties wishing to opt out of the CISG to specify that their contract would apply "the law of British Columbia," because "it is undisputed that the CISG is the [international] law of British Columbia." The court counseled that "selection of a particular choice of law" in the contract, however, "such as the California Commercial Code or the Uniform Commercial Code, *could* amount to implied exclusion of the CISG."

- In your own words, what distinction is the court making?

Read CISG Article 3 (1) and 3 (2). These provisions govern mixed contracts involving both goods and services.

- How are parts (1) and (2) distinct from one another, with regard to the transactions they govern?

- To which of the UCC approaches to hybrid contracts discussed in these materials is the CISG analysis most similar?

B. The Article 2 Sales Contract

The following excerpt from Donald B. King, Calvin A. Kuenzel, Bradford Stone & W. H. Knight, Jr., *Commercial Transactions Under the Uniform Commercial Code and Other Laws* 73-74 (Matthew Bender & Co., Inc., 5th ed. 1997), is a typical Article 2 form sales contract illustrating many of the issues students should consider throughout their studies of this material. Cross-references indicate where the material is covered in this book.

General Contract for Sale of Goods

[Name of seller], of [address], agrees to sell and [name of buyer], of [address], agrees to buy_____ tons of [describe or identify goods] at $_____ per ton to be delivered by [name of seller] to [name of buyer] at [address] on or before [date]. In consideration of the premises—and of the mutual benefits to each party, it is further agreed as follows:

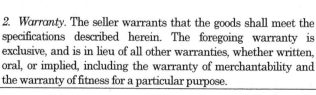

As Chapter 4, Part A indicates, terms of description may create a warranty.

1. Description. The goods which the seller shall deliver to the buyer and for which the buyer shall pay shall conform to the following specifications:

[here list specifications]

Warranties and disclaimers are covered in Chapter 4. After reading those materials, you might return to critique this language.

2. Warranty. The seller warrants that the goods shall meet the specifications described herein. The foregoing warranty is exclusive, and is in lieu of all other warranties, whether written, oral, or implied, including the warranty of merchantability and the warranty of fitness for a particular purpose.

3. *Delivery.* Delivery shall be on or before [date] and shall be to buyer at the seller's place of business. Seller agrees to furnish the facilities and at his cost to load the goods on trucks furnished by the buyer.

> The seller's delivery obligations are covered in Chapter 5, Part B.

4. *Packaging.* Buyer shall give the seller instructions for the packaging of the goods not less than 48 hours prior to the date of delivery, and the reasonable cost of such packaging shall be charged to the buyer.

5. *Title.* Title shall remain with the seller until delivery and actual receipt thereof by the buyer.

> Title is discussed in Chapter 3, Part A.

6. *Risk of loss.* Identification shall take place on the packaging of the goods, and the risk of loss shall pass on such identification.

> Risk of loss is discussed in Chapter 3, Part B.

7. *Price and time of payment.* The price of the goods shall be $_____ per ton, and shall be paid at the time of delivery and at the place of delivery in bank draft or cashier's check or certified check.

8. *Inspection.* Inspection shall be made by the buyer at the time and place of delivery.

9. *Claims.* Buyer's failure to give notice of any claim within _____ days from the date of delivery shall constitute an unqualified acceptance of the goods, and a waiver by the buyer of all claims with respect thereto.

> The relationship between inspection and acceptance is discussed in Chapter 5, Part B. The relationship between notice and acceptance is discussed in Chapter 5, Part D.

10. *Remedies.* Buyer's exclusive remedy and seller's limit of liability for any and all losses or damages resulting from defective goods or from any other cause shall be for the purchase price of the particular delivery with respect to which losses or damages are claimed plus any transportation charges actually paid by the buyer.

> Remedies are discussed in Chapter 5, Part E.

11. *Assignment and delegation.* Buyer may not assign its rights or delegate its performance hereunder without the prior written consent of the seller, and any attempted assignment or delegation without such consent shall be void.

12. *Choice of law.* This contract is to be construed according to the laws of, and under the Uniform Commercial Code as adopted by the State of _____.

> Recent changes to Article 1's provisions on choice of law are discussed in Chapter 1, Part D.

13. *Integration of contract.* This document constitutes the full understanding of the parties, and no terms, conditions, understandings, or agreement purporting to modify or vary the terms of this document shall be binding unless hereafter made in writing and signed by the party to be bound.

> Merger clauses, and their effect on the admissibility of parol evidence, are discussed in Part B of this chapter.

Signed and sealed in triplicate this____day of_____, _____.

Buyer _____

Seller _____

Instead of being expressed by a formal contract of sale such as the one above, mutual assent in a commercial transaction may be signaled by the exchange of standard-form documents such as a buyer's purchase order and a seller's invoice, or a seller's invoice and a buyer's confirmation. Mutual assent generally follows the rules of offer and acceptance that are covered in an

introductory course on contract law. A few nuances unique to   1
the Code are discussed in the remainder of this section.   2
                                                                       3
Mutual Assent in Boilerplate Contracts   4
                                                                       5
Read current and revised UCC 2-206 and 2-207.   6
                                                                       7
- Summarize the proposed revisions to each.   8
                                                                       9
The term "battle of the forms" describes a problem with mutual   10
assent that arises when parties exchange standard-form   11
documents – such as invoices and purchase orders or   12
confirmations – containing different fine print, and proceed   13
with the transaction without resolving the differences. For   14
example, a seller's invoice and a buyer's confirmation might   15
include the same price, quantity, and description of goods,   16
while the seller's fine print might mandate dispute resolution   17
in the Wisconsin court system and the buyer's might require   18
binding arbitration in New Mexico.   19
                                                                       20
Note that the parties in this example have reached some   21
modicum of agreement – if they had not, the transaction would   22
not proceed. They have reached agreement on the terms the   23
parties identified as most important during their negotiations: 24
price, quantity, and description of the goods.   Frequently,   25
however, disagreement later arises regarding a term in the fine   26
print, such as a forum-selection clause, and each party is likely   27
to believe the fine print contained in its own form – rather than   28
that of the other party – should control. The term "battle of the   29
forms" describes the law's attempt to determine which terms   30
govern the parties' contract.   A battle-of-the-forms problem   31
typically involves two questions: (1) "Is there a contract?" and   32
(2) "If so, what are its terms?"   33
                                                                       34
- Which portion of current UCC 2-207 addresses each   35
  question?   36
                                                                       37
- Which language in revised 2-206 and 2-207 addresses   38
  each question?   39
                                                                       40
To answer the first question, whether a contract has been   41
formed, a court will look to the document that purports to be   42
the acceptance of an offer. For example, if the buyer's purchase   43
order constitutes an offer to purchase goods, and the seller   44
responds by sending an invoice, the court will examine the   45
invoice to see if the seller has accepted the buyer's offer. This   46
time, we will assume the buyer's purchase order does not   50
address dispute resolution, and the seller's invoice calls for   51
                                                                       52
                                                                       53

arbitration in Indiana.   Thus, the purported acceptance contains an additional term not found in the offer.

If the document that purports to be an acceptance (1) shows a willingness to enter into the transaction, and (2) does not require that its own terms govern, it is in fact an acceptance, and a contract is therefore in existence. If, however, the document indicates the party is not yet willing to commit to the transaction, then no acceptance has occurred. In addition, if the document states that the party is unwilling to do business on terms other than its own, it is not an acceptance, but a counter-offer that must be accepted. Thus, in our example, the court will examine the invoice to see whether it contains a clause such as "Seller's terms must govern this sale." If not, and if the invoice is sufficiently certain and detailed to suggest contractual intent rather than mere preliminary negotiations, then the court will find an acceptance – and thus a contract, despite the additional term. The same analysis would be used to determine if a contract existed if the buyer's purchase order required dispute resolution through the Nevada court system, such that the terms were in direct conflict with one another.

If a court finds a contract, a second step determines which terms will govern. In other words, the court must determine whether the additional term in the seller's invoice becomes part of the parties' contract. To figure this out, a court will look to the offer. For nonmerchants, it is appropriate to assume that any *additional* terms the offeree has proposed are mere proposals that will not, in the absence of further agreement, be part of the contract. Between merchants, additional terms *do* become part of the contract – unless (1) the offeror objects to the addition of terms (either in advance or after seeing the additional terms) or (2) the additions materially alter the contract. Thus, in our example, if both parties are merchants, the court will look to the purchase order to see whether it includes a clause such as "Buyer's terms must govern this sale." If not, the court will review the facts to determine whether the buyer objected to the seller's terms after it received them. If it did not, the court would analyze whether the seller's proposed arbitration clause would materially alter the parties' agreement. If it would not, the term becomes part of the contract.

> *Different* terms (as opposed to *additional* terms) are discussed below at Note 2.

- How does your analysis change if one party is a nonmerchant?

- How does your analysis change if goods are shipped even though, according to 2-207 (1), no contract exists?

> 2-207 (3) may assist you in answering this question.

- The proposed revisions to 2-206 and 2-207 are intended to simplify the battle-of-the-forms analysis. Do these revisions appropriately balance considerations of fairness and clarity?

The following is a classic "battle of the forms" case. As you read the court's opinion, note there was no dispute as to whether a contract had been formed. Instead, the controversy centered on which document constituted the offer that the other party had accepted.

Brown Machine, Division of John Brown, Inc. v. Hercules, Inc.,
770 S.W.2d 416, 9 U.C.C. Rep. Serv. 2d 480
(Mo. App. E.D. 1989).

In early 1976, Brown Machine had sold appellant Hercules [, Inc.] a T-100 trim press. The trim press was a piece of equipment apparently used in manufacturing Cool Whip bowls. The initial sales negotiations between the two companies for the trim press began in October 1975. Bruce Boardman, an engineer at Hercules, asked Jim Ryan, Brown Machine's district sales manager, to send Hercules a quote for a trim press. On November 7, 1975, Brown Machine submitted its original proposal No. 51054 for the model T-100 trim press to Hercules. The proposal set out sixteen numbered paragraphs describing the machine to be sold. Attached to the proposal was a printed form of fifteen paragraphs in boilerplate style captioned "TERMS AND CONDITIONS OF SALE." The eighth paragraph provided as follows:

> 8. LIABILITY: The purchaser agrees to pay on behalf of BROWN all sums which BROWN becomes legally obligated to pay because of bodily injury or property damage caused by or resulting from the use or misuse of the IOS [item of sale], including reasonable attorneys fees and legal expenses. The purchaser agrees to indemnify and hold BROWN harmless from all actions, claims, or demands arising out of or in any way connected with the IOS, its operation, use or misuse, or the design construction or composition of any product made or handled by the IOS, including all such actions, claims, or demands based in whole or in part on the default or negligence of BROWN.

The term "boilerplate" was originally used to describe syndicated material supplied to newspapers in a plate form. Now, it is used to describe formulaic language.

Tim Wilson, Hercules' purchasing agent, reviewed the proposal submitted by Brown Machine. On January 7, 1976, he telephoned Jim Ryan at Brown Machine. Mr. Ryan's call report reflected that Hercules had prepared its purchase order No. 03361 in response to Brown Machine's proposal, but that Hercules had objected to the payment term requiring a twenty-percent deposit to be paid with the order. After talking with Mr. Fassett, Brown Machine's product manager, Mr. Ryan told Mr. Wilson that Brown Machine could not waive the deposit and that an invoice for payment would be forwarded to Hercules.

Watch how the facts unfold. Although the deposit term was controversial at the time of negotiations, this was not ultimately the source of litigation later. Instead, the liability term was the ultimate problem. This is not unusual; in fact, this is one of the common characteristics of battle of the forms cases. A term not originally focused upon, often buried in the fine print, can end up being crucial to a later dispute.

Mr. Fassett issued a work order that day giving the shop instructions concerning the trim-press equipment, followed by a written order the next day. The written order noted that "customer gave verbal P.O.

[purchase order] for this stock machine. Will issue revision when formal purchase order received."

On January 19, 1976, Brown Machine received Hercules' written purchase order No. 03361 dated January 6, 1976. The order was for a "Brown T-100 Trim press in accordance with Brown Machine quote # 51054. All specifications cited within quote except item # 6.1.1 which should read: 'Reverse trim' instead of 'Standard regular forward trim.'" In a blue box on the bottom left of the purchase-order form in bold print appeared "THIS ORDER EXPRESSLY LIMITS ACCEPTANCE TO THE TERMS STATED HEREIN, INCLUDING THOSE PRINTED ON THE REVERSE SIDE. ANY ADDITIONAL OR DIFFERENT TERMS PROPOSED BY THE SELLER ARE REJECTED UNLESS EXPRESSLY AGREED TO IN WRITING." The reverse side of Hercules' purchase order, captioned "TERMS AND CONDITIONS," contained sixteen boilerplate paragraphs, the last of which provided:

> 16. OTHER TERMS: No oral agreement or other understanding shall in any way modify this order, or the terms or the conditions hereof. Seller's action in (a) accepting this order, (b) delivering material, or (c) performing services called for hereunder shall constitute an acceptance of the above terms and conditions.

The purchase order contained no indemnity provision.

Brown Machine received two copies of the purchase order. One had been stamped "Vendor's Copy" at the bottom; the other was marked "ACKNOWLEDGMENT," with a space labeled "accepted by" for signature by Brown Machine. Brown Machine did not return this prepared acknowledgment to Hercules.

The next day, on January 20, 1976, Mr. Fassett issued his second machine order to the shop revising his description to reflect that Brown Machine had received Hercules' formal purchase order and that the machine was no longer inventoried as a Brown stock item. On January 21, 1976, Brown Machine sent Hercules an invoice requesting payment of $4,882.00, the twenty percent deposit for the trim press.

This process of taking an item out of inventory and setting it aside for a specific customer is known as identification of goods to a contract and is referenced above in Part A.

Rather than returning the acknowledgment of the purchase order prepared by Hercules, Mr. Fassett of Brown Machine sent Hercules an "ORDER ACKNOWLEDGEMENT" dated February 5, 1976. This letter stated as follows:

> Below in detail are the specifications covering the equipment ordered, and the equipment will be manufactured to meet these specifications. If these specifications and terms and conditions of sale are not in accordance with your understanding, please ADVISE US WITHIN SEVEN (7) DAYS OF RECEIPT OF THIS ACKNOWLEDGEMENT. If we do not hear from you within this period of time, we are proceeding with the construction of the equipment as per these specifications and terms as being agreed; and any changes occurring later may result in additional charges.
>
> *ONE T-100 TRIM PRESS AS FOLLOWS . . .*

The paragraphs following set out the same sixteen specifications contained in Brown Machine's original proposal. Paragraph 6.1.1 of the specifications again provided for "Standard-regular forward trim." Page four of the acknowledgment contained the same "TERMS AND CONDITIONS OF SALE" which had accompanied Brown Machine's earlier proposal of November 7, 1975, including paragraph eight on liability and indemnity. . . .

Note how the parties focused carefully on some provisions but not others.

Hercules responded with a letter on February 9, 1976, to Mr. Fassett that "This is to advise you that Provision 6.1 of your order acknowledgement dated 2/5/76 should read 'Reverse Trim' instead of 'Standard-regular forward trim.' All other specifications are correct." On February 16, 1976, Mr. Fassett confirmed the change in provision 6.1.1 and informed the shop that same day of the requested modification to be made.

Hercules never paid the twenty-percent deposit. Brown Machine sent Hercules an invoice dated April 14, 1976, requesting final payment of the total purchase price. Brown eventually shipped the trim press to Hercules, and Hercules paid the agreed-upon purchase price.

Sometime later, James Miller, an employee of Hercules, and his wife sued Brown Machine because of injuries he sustained while operating the trim press at Hercules' plant in Union, Missouri. Brown Machine demanded that Hercules defend the Miller lawsuit, but Hercules refused. Brown Machine eventually settled the Millers' lawsuit. Brown Machine later initiated this action against Hercules for indemnification of the settlement amount paid the Millers. Brown Machine claimed a condition of the original sales contract for the trim press required Hercules to indemnify Brown Machine for any claims arising from operation or misuse of the trim press.

* * *

The dispositive issue on appeal is whether the parties had agreed to an indemnification provision in their contract for the sale of the T-100 trim press.

Hercules' first point disputes Brown Machine's contention that its initial proposal on November 7, 1975, constitutes the offer and that Hercules verbally accepted the offer by the telephone call on January 7, 1976, followed by its written purchase order dated January 6, 1976, which Brown Machine received January 19, 1976.

* * *

What policy considerations support this general rule?

The general rule is that a price quotation is not an offer, but rather is an invitation to enter into negotiations or a mere suggestion to induce offers by others. However, price quotes, if detailed enough, can amount to an offer creating the power of acceptance; to do so, it must reasonably appear from the price quote that assent to the quote is all that is needed to ripen the offer into a contract.

In this case, Hercules could not have reasonably believed that Brown Machine's quotation was intended to be an offer, but rather an offer to enter into negotiations for the trim press. The cover letter accompanying the proposal mentioned that Brown Machine's sales representative would contact Hercules "to discuss this quote" and that the quotation was submitted for Hercules' "approval." The sale price as quoted also included the notation, "We have included a mechanical ejector because we understand this unit may be used for development of many items that would require this option. However, if you decide this is not necessary, $2,575.00 could be deducted from the above price for a total of $21,835.00." Most importantly, paragraph three of the terms and conditions of sale attached to the proposal expressly provided: "No order, sale, agreement for sale, accepted proposal, offer to sell and/or contract of sale shall be binding upon BROWN unless accepted by BROWN . . . on BROWN standard 'Order Acknowlegment' [sic] form." Thus, the quotation reasonably appeared to be an offer to enter into negotiations for the sale of a trim press with a mechanical ejector for $24,410.00. Brown's price quote was merely a proposal, not an offer, because of its provision that Hercules' acceptance was not binding upon Brown until Brown acknowledged the acceptance.

> In contracts terminology, what is the legal effect of the price quotation according to this court?

Even if we were to accept Brown Machine's characterization of its proposal as an offer, the quotation by its own terms and conditions expired thirty days after its issuance ("All quoted prices are subject to change without notice except those written proposals which shall expire without notice . . . thirty (30) calendar days from date issued . . ."). Hercules' written purchase order dated January 6, 1976, and their telephone conversation of January 7, 1976, were both well beyond the expiration of the quote. Thus, even if the quotation were construed as an offer, there was no timely acceptance.

If the acceptance of a price quotation, sufficiently detailed to constitute an offer, is not binding on the seller because the time within which it could have been accepted has lapsed, the purchase order, not the price quotation, is treated as the offer since the purchase order did not create an enforceable contract. Thus, we believe Hercules' purchase order constitutes the offer. As a general rule, orders are considered as offers to purchase.

The question then arises whether Brown Machine's acknowledgment containing the indemnity provision constitutes a counter-offer or an acceptance of Hercules' offer with additional or different terms. Section 400.2-207, RSMo 1986, which mirrors § 2-207 of the Uniform Commercial Code provides the workable rule of law addressing the problem of the discrepancies in the independently drafted documents exchanged between the two parties.

* * *

Under subsection (1) [of 2-207] an offeree's response to an offer operates as a valid acceptance of the offer even though it contains terms additional to, or different from, the terms of the offer unless the "acceptance is expressly made conditional" on the offeror's assent to the additional or different terms. Where the offeree's acceptance is made "expressly conditional" on the offeror's assent, the response operates not as an acceptance but as a counter-offer which must be accepted by the original offeror.

* * *

The general view held by the majority of states is that, to convert an acceptance to a counter offer under UCC § 2-207 (1), the conditional nature of the acceptance must be clearly expressed in a manner sufficient to notify the offeror that the offeree is unwilling to proceed with the transaction unless the additional or different terms are included in the contract. The conditional-assent provision has been construed narrowly to apply only to an acceptance which clearly shows that the offeree is unwilling to proceed absent assent to the additional or different terms.

We find nothing in Brown Machine's acknowledgment of February 5, 1976, which reflects its unwillingness to proceed unless it obtained Hercules' assent to the additional and different terms in Brown Machine's acknowledgment, that is, page four of the acknowledgment styled "TERMS AND CONDITIONS OF SALE" which contained the indemnity provision. Brown Machine's acknowledgment was not "expressly made conditional" on Hercules' assent to the additional or different terms as provided for under § 2-207 (1). Acceptance will be considered a counter-offer only if the acceptance is *expressly* made conditional on *assent* to the additional terms. We conclude Brown Machine's acknowledgment did not operate as a counter-offer within the scope of § 2-207 (1).

Having determined that Brown Machine's order acknowledgment is not a counter-offer, we believe that Brown Machine's acknowledgment operates as acceptance with additional or different terms from the offer, since the purchase order contained no indemnity provision. Under § 2-207 (2), additional terms become a part of the contract between merchants unless (a) the offer expressly limits acceptance to the terms of the offer; (b) they materially alter it; or (c) notification of objection to them has already been given or is given within a reasonable time after notice of them is given. Hercules' purchase order here expressly limited acceptance to the terms of its offer. Given such an express limitation, the additional terms, including the indemnification provision, failed to become part of the contract between the parties.

We can conclude Hercules intended the indemnity provision to become a part of the parties' contract only if Hercules, as offeror, expressly assented to the additional terms, and, thus, effectively waived its condition that acceptance be limited to the terms of its offer, the purchase order. . . .

The evidence does not establish that Hercules expressly assented to the additional terms contained in Brown Machine's order acknowledgment. Brown Machine's order acknowledgment of February 5, 1976, indicated that, "[i]f these specifications and terms and conditions of Sale are not in accordance with your understanding, please ADVISE US WITHIN SEVEN (7) DAYS OF RECEIPT OF THIS ACKNOWLEDGEMENT." Hercules replied by letter four days later advising Brown Machine that provision 6.1.1 should provide for reverse trim instead of standard regular forward trim, followed by "all other specifications are correct." Hercules' use of the term "specifications" is unambiguous and clearly refers only to the protocol for the machine's manufacture. Nothing in its response can be construed as express assent to Brown Machine's additional "terms and conditions of sale." Express assent under § 2-207 (2) cannot be presumed by silence or mere failure to object.

We believe it is clear as a matter of law that the indemnification clause cannot be held to be part of the contract agreed upon by the parties. The judgment of the trial court is reversed.

- Was the offer the purchase order, accepted by the acknowledgement, or was the offer the acknowledgement, accepted by performance when the machine was shipped?

- Would the analysis differ if the quotation were an offer?

- If revised 2-207 were applied, what would the result be?

Note 1: A battle of the forms can also arise when an oral contract is confirmed in writing. In such cases, there is no dispute as to whether a contract has been formed; instead, the only issue is whether the written confirmation adds to, or changes, the terms of the oral contract. *Dale R. Horning Co., Inc. v. Falconer Glass Industries, Inc.*, 730 F. Supp. 962, 11 U.C.C. Rep. Serv. 2d 536 (S.D. Ind. 1990), is a typical confirmation case.

In the summer of 1986, Architectural Glass & Metal worked as a subcontractor on a construction project whereby AGM was to install a glass "curtain wall" in a building. Time was of the essence, since the building could not be enclosed until the wall was in place. The project was to be complete by early October, and AGM was to be charged substantial penalties for any delays.

In early August, the president of AGM ordered ceramic-backed glass from Falconer Glass by telephone for the curtain wall. The parties discussed only price and quantity terms, as well as when the product would be delivered. There was no discussion of any limitation of warranties or damages. The following day, AGM sent an order form to confirm the transaction. Once again, limitations of warranties or damages were not mentioned. Falconer responded with a standard-form document containing 16 paragraphs of "fine print" on the reverse side, including a statement that replacement of any defective product would be the buyer's "exclusive and sole remedy." The form also specifically disclaimed liability for any "special, direct, indirect, incidental, or consequential damages."

In late September, Falconer timely delivered defective glass to   1
AGM. Because of time pressures, AGM temporarily installed   2
the glass, to meet the deadline for enclosure of the building.   3
AGM later removed and replaced the defective glass with   4
conforming glass, when it arrived.   AGM representatives   5
informed Falconer representatives on at least three occasions   6
that Falconer would be responsible for AGM's increased costs   7
due to the shipment of defective glass. On two occasions, the   8
Falconer representative simply did not object, but did not   9
affirmatively respond. On the other, a representative agreed   10
Falconer should be responsible, but added, "Take it easy on us."   11
                                                                                                    12
When AGM invoiced Falconer for the approximately $20,000 in   13
extra costs, Falconer refused to pay, citing the language on its   14
form.   Assume, in this industry, such limiting terms are   15
commonly included in contracts, but that suppliers usually   16
work with buyers to cover some – or even all – of the costs   17
associated with the delivery of a defective product. Further   18
assume AGM and Falconer have worked together previously,   19
have worked out similar quality issues in the past, and   20
Falconer knew AGM would be fined for delayed performance.   21
                                                                                                    22
Applying 2-207 to the written confirmation of an oral contract   23
can be confusing, since 2-207 (1) seems to suggest a   24
confirmation can act as a counter-offer. Many scholars suggest,   25
and the author of this textbook agrees, that a confirmation can   26
never act as a counter-offer to an oral contract that is correctly   27
so named, because by definition the contract has already been   28
formed.   Instead, the only issue is whether the confirmation   29
somehow changes the terms of the oral contract pursuant to   30
2-207 (2).   31
                                                                                                    32

   ▪   Does revised 2-207 address the issue of how to apply   33
        its terms to confirmations more clearly than the   34
        current version does?   35
                                                                                                    36

In applying 2-207 (2), the *Dale Horning* court found the central   37
issue to be whether the new term materially alters the prior   38
agreement. In addressing the issue, the court adopted a two-   39
component test, examining whether the term would surprise,   40
or cause hardship to, the other party. In deciding whether the   41
new element would be likely to catch the buyer unaware, the   42
court looked at evidence regarding the parties' course of   43
dealing, trade usage, and custom. Ultimately, the court found   44
the new term was not surprising.   45
                                                                                                    46

   ▪   Is the court's holding supported by the facts as related   50
        above?   51
                                                                                                    52
                                                                                                    53

However, the court did find the new term was likely to cause hardship, noting that AGM faced the possibility of thousands of dollars of liability for Falconer's error, and further noting that, after the parties had entered into a contract, Falconer attempted to shift this risk to AGM through the confirmation document. The court held this would not be permitted.

Note the language that concludes the court's opinion:

> [T]he best, and, in some instances, the only way to get a preferable term into a contract *is to actually propose the term and reach a meeting of the minds* on the issue. The Code did not completely abolish the concept of mutual assent. In this setting, for instance, if suppliers such as Falconer want to exclude consequential damages from all their contracts, they can simply adopt and enforce a policy that all sales representatives must inform the prospective buyer at the time of bidding that such damages will not be recoverable. On the other hand, if buyers such as AGM want to ensure that they can recover such extras without complex litigation, they can demand such provisions in all agreements. In both instances, counsel planning such action for the client would need to have an eye towards, among other things, the admissibility requirements for regularly recorded business records.

> This case also shows once again that a call to an attorney for preventive advice is often more cost-effective than the call made months or years later after the situation has become impenetrable and stubbornness has taken root. It also demonstrates that attorneys called upon to render such planning advice should probably do more than just draft fine-print boilerplate. Today's decision shows that the UCC requires more in this particular setting anyway. *Id.* at 970.

- How, if at all, should this language influence an attorney in drafting and negotiating contracts on behalf of future clients?

Note 2: Carefully read 2-207 (1) and (2). UCC 2-207 (1) refers to the possibility of *additional or different* terms being included in a document purporting to accept an offer. 2-207 (2), however, provides guidance only as to whether *additional* terms can become part of the parties' contract. Thus, the issue of whether *different* terms can become part of a contract through the battle of the forms is hotly disputed. Three alternatives exist:

1) The Knock-Out Rule: **Read 2-207, Comment 6.** Applying this approach, each party is presumed to object to the other's conflicting term, and thus neither term becomes part of the contract. If eliminating conflicting terms leaves gaps in the contract, the UCC may supply default terms.

> The term "blue-pencil" is commonly used to refer to editing.

2) The Blue-Pencil Rule: Courts applying this approach read 2-207 (2) as if it applies to *different* terms as well as *additional* ones.   This approach assumes the word "different" was inadvertently omitted from the text of 2-207 (2).

3)   The First-Shot Rule: This approach assumes that the exclusion of *different* terms from 2-207 (2) reflects the decision of the drafters that terms contradicting the offer should never be incorporated into a contract via fine print. Instead, the terms of the offer would always control the contract.

- Why does the inclusion of the "knock-out rule" in the commentary to 2-207 not guarantee its application?

- Does revised 2-207 clarify which test should be applied?

- Which option best meets 2-207's goals of clarity and fairness?

Problem: Barrett Distributors ordered from Venture Carpets on terms reflecting a discount for prompt payment. Venture shipped the carpet two weeks later and, a week later, mailed an invoice to Barrett reflecting different discount terms. Barrett responded, requesting the terms be changed to match its original order. When Venture refused, Barrett indicated it was rejecting the carpet, yet continued to maintain possession of it. Three months later, the carpet was destroyed by fire at Barrett's warehouse.   Assume liability turns on whether a contract was formed.

- Applying 2-207, who should prevail?

- What additional facts are required to complete your analysis?

Based on *Trust Co. Bank v. Barrett Distributors, Inc.*, 459 F. Supp. 959 (S.D. Ind. 1978).

International Perspective: Battle of the Forms

Read CISG Article 19.   Initially, the distinctions between Article 19 and UCC 2-207 are probably more apparent than the similarities.   While 2-207 clearly makes it possible for parties to enter a contract despite the existence of additional or different terms, Article 19 is sometimes described as a "mirror-image rule."   Upon   closer   observation,   some similarities emerge. Note particularly Article 19's discussion of the concepts of material alteration and notice, and compare these to UCC 2-207 as you answer the following questions:

- You have already learned that 2-207 cases involve two questions: (1) Has a contract been formed? (2) If so, what are the terms of the contract? Does Article 19 address each?

- The previous discussion of 2-207 has shown the controversy over whether *different* terms, as well as *additional* terms, can become part of a contract created by a battle of the forms. Does CISG Article 19 provide a clearer solution?

> For a comprehensive discussion of CISG Article 19's approach to *different* terms, see Pilar Perales Viscasillas, *Battle of the Forms and Burden of Proof: An Analysis of BGH 9 January 2002*, 6 V.J. 217 (2002).

Mutual Assent in Rolling Contracts

In addition to determining what terms govern a transaction memorialized by boilerplate forms with nonidentical terms, courts struggle to determine whether mutual assent can be shown when money is exchanged before complete contract terms are revealed. These exchanges are sometimes called "rolling contracts." Some of these mutual-assent issues arise in what are called "shrinkwrap" contracts. In *ProCD, Inc. v. Zeidenberg*, 86 F.3d 1447, 29 U.C.C. Rep. Serv. 2d 1109 (7th Cir. 1996), perhaps the best-known case on point, Judge Frank Easterbrook defined the term as follows:

> The "shrinkwrap license" gets its name from the fact that retail software packages are covered in plastic or cellophane "shrinkwrap," and some vendors . . . have written licenses that become effective as soon as the customer tears the wrapping from the package. *Id.* at 1449.

The following is an excerpt from the facts of that case:

> ProCD . . . has compiled information from more than 3,000 telephone directories into a computer database.
>
> * * *
>
> Matthew Zeidenberg bought a consumer package of [ProCD's product] SelectPhone . . . in 1994 from a retail outlet in Madison, Wisconsin, but decided to ignore the license. He formed Silken Mountain Web Services, Inc., to resell the information in the SelectPhone database. The [Silken Mountain] corporation makes the database available on the Internet to anyone willing to pay its price – which, needless to say, is less than ProCD charges its commercial customers. Zeidenberg has purchased two additional

SelectPhone packages, each with an updated version of the
database, and made the latest information available over the
World Wide Web, for a price, through his corporation. ProCD filed
this suit seeking an injunction against further dissemination that
exceeds the rights specified in the licenses (identical in each of the
three packages Zeidenberg purchased). *Id.* at 1449-1450.

In considering these facts, the court made the following
observations about contract formation in the modern
commercial environment:

> Vendors can put the entire terms of a contract on the outside of a
> box only by using microscopic type, removing other information
> that buyers might find more useful (such as what the software
> does, and on which computers it works), or both. The "Read Me"
> file included with most software, describing system requirements
> and potential incompatibilities, may be equivalent to ten pages of
> type; warranties and license restrictions take still more space.
> Notice on the outside, terms on the inside, and a right to return
> the software for a refund if the terms are unacceptable (a right
> that the license expressly extends), may be a means of doing
> business valuable to buyers and sellers alike.
>
> * * *
>
> Transactions in which the exchange of money precedes the
> communication of detailed terms are common. Consider the
> purchase of insurance. The buyer goes to an agent, who explains
> the essentials (amount of coverage, number of years) and remits
> the premium to the home office, which sends back a policy. . . . Or
> consider the purchase of an airline ticket. The traveler calls the
> carrier or an agent, is quoted a price, reserves a seat, pays, and
> gets a ticket, in that order. The ticket contains elaborate terms,
> which the traveler can reject by canceling the reservation. To use
> the ticket is to accept the terms, even terms that in retrospect are
> disadvantageous. Just so with a ticket to a concert. The back of
> the ticket states that the patron promises not to record the concert;
> to attend is to agree. A theater that detects a violation will
> confiscate the tape and escort the violator to the exit. One *could*
> arrange things so that every concertgoer signs this promise before
> forking over the money, but that cumbersome way of doing things
> not only would lengthen queues and raise prices but also would
> scotch the sale of tickets by phone or electronic data service. *Id.* at
> 1451.

- ▪ What options, other than rolling contracts, could
  address the court's concern with burdening commerce?

The court goes on to conclude that what it calls "money now,
terms later" contracts should be enforceable under Article 2:

> A vendor, as master of the offer, may invite acceptance by conduct,
> and may propose limitations on the kind of conduct that
> constitutes acceptance. A buyer may accept by performing the acts

For an alternative
analysis employing
2-207, see *Klocek v.
Gateway, Inc.*, 104 F.
Supp. 2d 1332 (D.
Kan. 2000).

the vendor proposes to treat as acceptance. And that is what happened. ProCD proposed a contract that a buyer would accept by *using* the software after having an opportunity to read the license at leisure. This Zeidenberg did. He had no choice, because the software splashed the license on the screen and would not let him proceed without indicating acceptance. So, although the district judge was right to say that a contract can be, and often is, formed simply by paying the price and walking out of the store, the UCC permits contracts to be formed in other ways. ProCD proposed such a different way, and without protest Zeidenberg agreed. Ours is not a case in which a consumer opens a package to find an insert saying "you owe us an extra $10,000," and the seller files suit to collect. Any buyer finding such a demand can prevent formation of the contract by returning the package, as can any consumer who concludes that the terms of the license make the software worth less than the purchase price. Nothing in the UCC requires a seller to maximize the buyer's net gains. *Id.* at 1452.

> What does this statement mean?

- What other arguments could you make on behalf of the buyer in the $10,000 hypothetical?

It can be tempting to think of complex contract-formation issues such as rolling contracts as a modern phenomenon, born of high technology. Cases like *Lachs v. Fidelity & Casualty Co.*, 306 N.Y. 357, 118 N.E.2d 555 (N.Y. 1954), however, show that similar issues have existed for some time, albeit in a slightly different context. In *Lachs*, the court addressed the enforceability of airline trip insurance purchased from a vending machine in an airport. After the decedent inserted 25 cents per $5,000 in trip insurance desired, the machine dispensed an application for insurance, consisting of one short paragraph. Upon completion of the application, the decedent pressed a button on the machine, which then dispensed the policy itself. In the policy, albeit obscured by the legend, "This Policy is Limited to Aircraft Accidents – Read it Carefully," appeared a clause limiting coverage to flights on a "Civilian Scheduled Airline." As a sign in the terminal indicated, decedent's flight was onboard a "Non Scheduled Airline" as defined by the Civil Aeronautics Act. In refusing to grant summary judgment in favor of the insurer, which claimed the flight was not covered by the policy's own terms, the court held as follows:

> The Civil Aeronautics Act of 1938 was the precursor to the Federal Aviation Act of 1958. A non-scheduled airline has no fixed operational timetable.

No doubt it is . . . a matter of business competition to sell insurance policies from automatic vending machines. It may save money to have a number of machines instead of a salesman. It may be wise because people hurrying to planes will not wait on a line to buy insurance. However, there must be a meeting of minds achieved between the applicant and the company through an application and signs and lettering, for while the applicant has a mind the machine has none and cannot answer questions. If the [insurance company] had paid for a living salesman, the decedent would not have purchased the insurance if it did not cover her trip, or she might have purchased it and changed her plane. So there must be additional care taken. While all this makes it more difficult for the insurance company, there is another side to the question. If the rule here was not made strict when machines are utilized, it would mean that in this large terminal all persons who put money into the machines there and then, thinking they were insured, went off on one of the ten so-called "non-scheduled air carriers," would have no insurance for their beneficiaries, and the company would be in receipt of contributions for which no service was ever rendered. *Id.* at 366.

To what contract-law concept is the court making reference here?

- How could the company address the mutual-assent concern?

The court's language echoes recent "rolling contract" cases, which have insisted on concrete evidence of mutual assent.

Mutual Assent in Electronic Contracts

"Clickwrap" and "browsewrap" are familiar terms in the field of electronic contracts. In *Standard-Form Contracting in the Electronic Age*, 77 N.Y.U. L. Rev. 429 (2002), Professors Robert Hillman and Jeffrey Rachlinski define the terms as follows:

In browsewrap contracts, Internet users, if they bother to look, will find a "terms or conditions" hyperlink somewhere on web pages that offer to sell goods and services. These contracts generally provide that using the site to purchase the goods or services offered (or just visiting the site) constitutes acceptance of the conditions contained therein. Clickwrap contracts require consumers to click through one or more steps that constitute the formation of an agreement. Software consumers encounter clickwrap contracts, for example, when installing new software on their personal computers. Installation processes typically include a step wherein the user must agree to the business's terms in order to complete installation. By clicking in all of the appropriate places, the user has formed the contract. *Id.* at 464.

- How would you argue for, and against, the proposition that clickwrap contracts are supported by mutual assent?

- How, if at all, would the arguments for browsewrap differ?

- How do browsewrap and clickwrap differ from shrinkwrap?

Specht v. Netscape Communications Corp., 306 F.3d 17, 48 U.C.C. Rep. Serv. 2d 761 (2d. Cir. 2002), illustrates a common principle: courts will not enforce browsewrap contracts that do

1
2
3
4
5
6
7
8
9
10
11
12
13
14
15
16
17
18
19
20
21
22
23
24
25
26
27
28
29
30
31
32
33
34
35
36
37
38
39
40
41
42
43
44
45
46
50
51
52
53

not evidence clear mutual assent.   In that case, the court
addressed Netscape's allegation that Mr. Specht and the others
in the plaintiff class seeking to escape Netscape's software-
license agreement had become bound to the terms of the
agreement by downloading Netscape's software. The license
agreement was not presented to the user via clickwrap, but
was available elsewhere on the site. Had the user scrolled
down the page, the link to the license agreement would have
become visible. In addressing this claim, the court held as
follows:

> Mutual manifestation of assent, whether by written or spoken
> word or by conduct, is the touchstone of contract. Although an
> onlooker observing the disputed transactions in this case would
> have seen each of the user plaintiffs click on the SmartDownload
> "Download" button, . . . a consumer's clicking on a download
> button does not communicate assent to contractual terms if the
> offer did not make clear to the consumer that clicking on the
> download button would signify assent to those terms. *Id.* at 29.

One should not assume browsewrap contracts will never be
enforced. As *Register.com, Inc. v. Verio, Inc.,* 356 F.3d 393 (2d
Cir. 2004), illustrates, these contracts may be enforced when
the court finds the user knew of the contract terms, despite the
browsewrap presentation.

- Are there good reasons to use a browsewrap format,
  despite the potential difficulty in proving mutual
  assent?

The article *Browse-Wrap Agreements: Validity of Implied
Assent in Electronic Form Agreements,* 59 Bus. Law. 279
(2003), suggests the following parameters for crafting an
enforceable browsewrap contract:

> (i) The user is provided with adequate notice of the existence of the
> proposed terms.

> (ii) The user has a meaningful opportunity to review the terms.

> (iii) The user is provided with adequate notice that taking a
> specified action manifests assent to the terms.

> (iv) The user takes the action specified in the latter notice. *Id.* at
> 281.

- How can a browsewrap contract satisfy each element?

Clickwrap contracts are more readily enforced than
browsewrap. In *Caspi v. Microsoft Network, L.L.C.,* 323 N.J.
Super. 118, 732 A.2d 528 (N.J. Super. App. Div. 1999), the

court enforced a contract created by clickwrap, despite the
argument that the forum-selection clause, which was the
subject of the dispute, was contained in "fine print." The
following excerpt gives some insight into the court's reasoning:

> The plaintiffs in this case were free to scroll through the various
> computer screens that presented the terms of their contracts
> before clicking their agreement. Also, it seems clear that there was
> nothing extraordinary about the size or placement of the forum-
> selection-clause text. By every indication we have, the clause was
> presented in exactly the same format as most other provisions of
> the contract. It was the first item in the last paragraph of the
> electronic document. We note that a few paragraphs in the
> contract were presented in upper-case typeface, presumably for
> emphasis, but most provisions, including the forum-selection
> clause, were presented in lower-case typeface. We discern nothing
> about the style or mode of presentation, or the placement of the
> provision, that can be taken as a basis for concluding that the
> forum-selection clause was proffered unfairly, or with a design to
> conceal or de-emphasize its provisions. To conclude that plaintiffs
> are not bound by that clause would be equivalent to holding that
> they were bound by no other clause either, since all provisions
> were identically presented. Plaintiffs must be taken to have
> known that they were entering into a contract; and no good
> purpose, consonant with the dictates of reasonable reliability in
> commerce, would be served by permitting them to disavow
> particular provisions or the contracts as a whole. *Id.* at 125-126.

- Based on your law-school studies to date, how does
  this holding comport with basic contract-law concepts
  such as unconscionability, the duty to read, and
  contracts of adhesion?

Robert Hillman and Jeffrey Rachlinksi suggest, in *Standard-
Form Contracting in the Electronic Age*, 77 N.Y.U. L. Rev. 429
(2002), that mutual assent in electronic commerce presents no
novel issues:

> As with their paper-world counterparts, e-consumers face an
> unavoidable set of realities when confronted with standard-form
> language. E-businesses present standard terms in a distinct take-
> it-or-leave-it fashion. The terms are also long, detailed, full of legal
> jargon, about remote risks, and one-sided. They include the usual
> litany of terms that are sometimes unenforceable in the paper
> world, such as arbitration provisions and limitations on remedies.
> Furthermore, e-consumers cannot negotiate because web pages
> and installation software do not allow for interaction with a live
> agent. E-consumers often cannot find answers to their questions
> about the terms. As with her paper-world counterpart, the e-
> consumer knows (or quickly recognizes) that reading through the
> boilerplate is unlikely to be of any benefit. Instead, she likely
> casually believes there is little risk to agreeing to standard terms.
> *Id.* at 468.

The authors conclude that the concept of "blanket assent," as defined by Karl Llewellyn, protects consumers in the electronic context as well as it does in the context of paper contracts. In the following excerpt, the authors define the term "blanket assent":

> "Blanket assent" is best understood to mean that, although consumers do not read standard terms, so long as their formal presentation and substance are reasonable, consumers comprehend the existence of the terms and agree to be bound to them. The purchaser of manufactured goods assumes the manufacturer has used appropriate parts and therefore impliedly agrees to their use even though painfully ignorant of the particulars. The law enforces the sale of goods with such parts, provided they are fit for their ordinary purpose, because the purchaser implicitly has agreed to delegate to the manufacturer the choice of parts. Similarly, the law appropriately holds that, by voluntarily agreeing to enter into the standard-form contract with full knowledge of the existence of standard terms, the consumer delegates to the business the duty of drafting reasonable standard terms that comprise the details of the parties' deal.

> The allusion here is to the implied warranty of merchantability found in 2-314 and covered in Chapter 4, Part B.

> Granted, the consumer would not necessarily have picked the particular terms that the business has selected. The concept of "blanket assent" comprehends the constraints of economic pressure and the consumer's lack of bargaining power. "Blanket assent" means only that, given the realities of mass-market contracting, the consumer chooses to enter a transaction that includes a package of reasonable, albeit mostly unfavorable to her, boilerplate terms. This conception of assent leaves to the courts the difficult task of drawing a line between permissible and impermissible pressure and terms. *Id.* at 461-462.

- How does the concept of "blanket assent" comport with the *Caspi* holding?

- How can contract terms be simultaneously "reasonable" and "mostly unfavorable" to a consumer?

Note: In *On-line Consumer Standard-Form Contracting Practices: A Survey and Discussion of Legal Implications*, Cornell Law School Research Paper No. 05-012, Professor Robert Hillman surveyed 92 contracts students and recorded their practices in reviewing standard-form contracts on-line. He reached the following conclusions:

> Few respondents read their e-standard forms beyond price and description of the goods "as a general matter." Further, beyond price and description, a large minority of respondents do not read their forms at all. However, more than a third of the respondents read their forms when the value of the contract is high and more than a third read when the vendor is unknown. Further, a small cadre of respondents read particular terms beyond price and

description, primarily warranties and product information
warnings. *Id.* at 2.

- Assuming the accuracy of Professor Hillman's data,
  does this information call into question the validity of
  electronic assent?

- Does it militate in favor of (or against) any of the
  approaches recommended by scholars or adopted by
  courts in this section?

The Parol Evidence Rule

> The Article 2A
> equivalent is 2A-
> 202.

Read 2-202, both in its current form and as revised.

- In your own words, what major changes have been
  proposed?

Mutual assent ensures the parties' agreement to a contract; the
parol evidence rule helps a court to determine the content of
the parties' agreement. Doing so may require a court to sort
through various writings and testimony regarding
conversations between the parties.

> Consult a legal
> dictionary as needed
> to answer this
> question.

- What does "parol" mean?

- Why should a court not simply require that all
  contract terms appear in a single written memorial of
  the contract?

2-202 governs the admission of parol evidence to construe a
written contract. As students may recall from an introductory
course on contracts, the UCC is more liberal than the common
law in addressing this issue.

- What guidance does 2-202 give for using parol
  evidence (1) to explain a contract, (2) to add terms to
  the contract, and (3) to contradict the written terms of
  the contract?

The following case shows how a court might analyze how
proffered parol evidence is to be used in deciding whether it will
be admitted.

1
2
3
4
5
6
7
8
9
10
11
12
13
14
15
16
17
18
19
20
21
22
23
24
25
26
27
28
29
30
31
32
33
34
35
36
37
38
39
40
41
42
43
44
45
46
50
51
52
53

Southern Concrete Services, Inc. v. Mableton Contractors, Inc.,
407 F. Supp. 581, 19 U.C.C. Rep. Serv. 79 (D.C. Ga. 1975).

Edenfield, Chief Judge.

In September 1972, the parties entered into a contract for the sale of concrete for use in the construction of the building foundation of a power plant near Carrollton, Georgia. The contract stipulated that plaintiff was to supply "approximately 70,000 cubic yards" of concrete from September 1, 1972, to June 15, 1973. The price to be paid for such concrete was $19.60 per cubic yard. The contract further stipulated that "No conditions which are not incorporated in this contract will be recognized." During the time period involved, defendant ordered only 12,542 cubic yards of concrete, that being the total amount needed by the defendant for its construction work. The plaintiff has brought this action to recover the profits lost by defendant's alleged breach and the costs plaintiff incurred in purchasing and delivering over $20,000 in raw materials to the jobsite.

> This is a merger clause, which signals that the parties intended the written document to be the final, complete expression of their agreement.

The defendant claims that the written contract must be interpreted both in light of the custom of the trade and in light of additional terms allegedly intended by the parties. Defendant contends that, under such custom and additional terms, it was understood that the quantity stipulated in the contract was not mandatory upon either of the parties and that both quantity and price were understood to be subject to renegotiation. It is this evidence of custom in the trade and of additional conditions allegedly agreed to by the parties that defendant seeks to introduce at trial.

In support of its position, defendant relies upon Georgia Code Ann. 109A-2-202, which provides that a written contract may be explained or supplemented "by a course of dealing or usage of trade" and by evidence of "consistent additional terms." This section was meant to liberalize the common-law parol evidence rule to allow evidence of agreements outside the contract, without a prerequisite finding that the contract was ambiguous. In addition, the section requires contracts to be interpreted in light of the commercial context in which they were written and not by the rules of legal construction.

The question then becomes what is meant by the term "explained or supplemented"; does defendant's evidence "explain" the contract or does it attempt to "contradict" it? The court will examine this question with regard to the trade usage issue first, and then deal with the "additional terms" question.

In the official comment to UCC 2-202, the draftsmen emphasize that contracts are to be interpreted with the assumption that the usages of trade "were taken for granted when the document was phrased. Unless carefully negated they have become an element of the meaning of the words used. . . ."

* * *

. . . Here, no prior dealings are alleged by either party; the contract by its terms does not intimate that the buyer would only be liable for concrete actually delivered, and the contract does not contain provisions granting one party special repricing rights. Instead, the contract sets out fairly specific quantity, price, and time specifications. To allow such specific contracts to be challenged by extrinsic evidence might jeopardize the certainty of the contractual duties which parties have a right to rely on. Certainly customs of the trade should be relevant to the interpretation of certain terms of a contract, and should be considered in determining what variation in specifications is considered acceptable, but this court does not believe that section 2-202 was meant to invite a frontal assault on the essential terms of a clear and explicit contract.

The type of evidence . . . which the defendant here undoubtedly wishes to introduce would probably show that very few contracts specifying quantity and price in a particular industry have been strictly enforced. While in some industries it may be virtually impossible to predict future needs under a contract, in other industries, such contracts may not be strictly adhered to for entirely different reasons. Lawsuits are costly, and they do not facilitate good business relations with customers. A party to a contract may very much prefer to work out a renegotiation of a contract rather than rest on its strict legal rights. Yet, the supplier or purchaser knows that he may resort to those enforceable contract rights if necessary. If the courts were to conclude that this reluctance to enforce legal rights resulted in an industry-wide waiver of such rights, then contracts would lose their utility as a means of assigning the risks of the market. The defendant here may be correct in its assertion that contracts for the sale of concrete are often subject to renegotiation, but that fact alone does not convince the court that the parties here did not contemplate placing on the buyer the risk of variation in quantity needs.

The court recognizes that all ambiguity as to the applicability of trade usage could be eliminated by a blanket condition that the express terms of the contract are in no way to be modified by custom, usage, or prior dealings. . . . This court, however, is reluctant to encourage the use of yet another standard boilerplate provision in commercial contracts. If such a clause is necessary to preserve the very essence of a contract, then the purposes of the Code will be quickly frustrated. Consideration of commercial custom is an important aid in the interpretation of the terms of a contract, but parties will have no choice but to foreclose the use of such an aid if the inevitable result of such consideration is to have explicit contracts negated by an evidentiary free-for-all.

Although the official comments suggest that parties which do not want trade usage to apply should so stipulate in the contract, that provision could not have been meant to allow the full-scale attack on the contract suggested here. The more reasonable approach is to assume that specifications as to quantity and price are intended to be observed by the parties and that the unilateral right to make a major departure from such specifications must be expressly agreed to in the written contract. That way, the courts will still be free to apply custom and trade usage in interpreting terms of the contract without raising apprehension in the commercial world as to the continued reliability of those contracts. Such an approach is consistent with the underlying

---

Margin notes:

> Consider the statements in this paragraph in light of the Bernstein excerpt in Chapter 1, Part A, regarding the application of Relationship-Preserving Norms during litigation.

> What role does the court's opinion envision for trade usage and custom?

> Note the court's attempt to balance precedential consistency with fairness in the case at bar.

purposes of the Uniform Commercial Code, which dictates that the express terms of a contract and trade usage shall be construed as consistent with each other only when such construction is reasonable. A construction which negates the express terms of the contract by allowing unilateral abandonment of its specifications is patently unreasonable.

The defendant also claims that section 2-202 allows the introduction of evidence of additional terms of the agreement between the parties. Those terms presumably called for price renegotiation and contained an understanding that the quantity quoted in the contract was intended only as an estimate. The court suspects, however, that the defendant is attempting to use section 2-202 (b) as merely an alternative vehicle to get in evidence as to trade usage. The defendant does not specify in its brief the terms of the alleged extrinsic agreement and does not indicate whether it was oral or written, prior or contemporaneous. Rather, the defendant merely tags its 2-202 (b) request on its trade usage claim as an apparent afterthought. But even if this court assumes that defendant will attempt to show additional terms of the contract, such evidence would be inadmissible. Section 2-202 requires that written contracts "not be contradicted" by evidence of agreements outside of the written contract, but that they may be explained or supplemented by evidence of "consistent additional terms" if the court finds the contract was not meant to be the complete statement of the agreement.

Whether or not the contract in issue was meant to be complete in itself, it is clear that the additional terms sought to be proved are not consistent with it. The type of evidence which may be admitted under subsection (b) deals with agreements covering matters not dealt with in the written contract. To admit evidence of an agreement which would contradict the express terms of the contract would clearly eviscerate the purpose of 2-202.

> Read this paragraph in light of the *Nanakuli* holding referenced in the note below.

The court is aware that at least one court has favored a broader construction of 2-202, holding that evidence of a contemporaneous oral agreement to provide up to 500 tons of steel was consistent with a written provision in the contract stipulating delivery of 500 tons. *Schiavone & Sons, Inc. v. Securally Co., Inc.*, 312 F. Supp. 801 (D. Conn. 1970). That court explained: "In making this determination, it must be borne in mind that to be inconsistent the terms must contradict or negate a term of the written agreement; and a term which has a lesser effect is deemed to be a consistent term." 312 F. Supp. 804. This court respectfully disagrees with the above reasoning; for the buyer who wished to obtain all 500 tons, and who had to cover his requirements elsewhere, the term "up to 500" tons was clearly inconsistent with the contract. Similarly, a hypothetical agreement between the instant parties that quantity and price terms were to be mere estimates is inconsistent with the written contract.

Finally, the contract at issue specified that conditions not incorporated in the contract would not be recognized. In contrast, in *Schiavone*, the court noted the absence of such a clause in finding the parol evidence admissible. The presence of such a clause here further convinces the court that the writing was intended to be the "complete and exclusive statement" of the terms of the agreement, Ga. Code Ann. § 109A-2-202 (b).

The court therefore concludes that the evidence sought to be introduced by the defendant is inadmissible at trial.

- How much weight does the *Southern Concrete Services, Inc.* court attach to the merger clause?

- Does the court ultimately conclude that the proffered evidence contradicts the written contract, or simply adds to it?

Note: *Columbia Nitrogen Corp. v. Royster Co.,* 451 F.2d 3, 9 U.C.C. Rep. Serv. 977 (4th Cir. 1971), addressed a contract for the sale of phosphate in light of the plunge in phosphate prices that occurred after the contract was executed. The purchaser, Columbia Nitrogen Corp., sought to introduce trade-usage evidence to show that quantity and price terms in phosphate contracts are commonly treated as "mere projections to be adjusted according to market forces." The seller, Royster Company, claimed this evidence should be excluded as a clear contradiction of the price term in the contract, which included no such language. In finding the trade-usage evidence should be considered, the court concluded such evidence was not inconsistent with the contractual price term. In so holding, the court was influenced by the fact that the contract did not expressly exclude trade-usage evidence:

> The contract is silent about adjusting prices and quantities to reflect a declining market. It neither permits nor prohibits adjustment, and this neutrality provides a fitting occasion for recourse to usage of trade . . . to supplement the contract and explain its terms. *Id.* at 9-10.

- Was the court disingenuous in claiming the evidence was being used to "supplement . . . and explain" the contract? Consider this question in light of *Nanakuli Paving & Rock Co. v. Shell Oil Co., Inc.,* 664 F.2d 772 (9th Cir. 1981), in which the court adopted what has become known as the "total negation" test, holding that "usage may be used to 'qualify' the agreement, which presumably means to 'cut down' express terms although not to negate them entirely."

- Does the *Nanakuli* holding more accurately address what the *Columbia Nitrogen Corp.* court was seeking to accomplish?

- What evidence will still be excluded, following these rulings?

- Should a drastic change in market price be sufficient to allow a party to seek relief from the contract price?

International Perspective: Parol Evidence

Read CISG Article 8 (3), which addresses parol evidence.

- Compare UCC 2-202 with CISG Article 8 (3). You have already examined the use of parol evidence under the CISG to add to, explain, or contradict the written terms of a contract. How does the CISG handle each class of parol evidence?

- How much weight will a merger clause be given in deciding whether parol evidence should be considered under CISG Article 8?

The court's opinion in *MCC-Marble Ceramic Center, Inc. v. Ceramica Nuova D'Agostino, S.p.A.*, 144 F.3d 1384 (11th Cir. 1998), includes the following guidance with regard to the parol evidence rule:

> [T]he parol evidence rule, contrary to its title, is a substantive rule of law, not a rule of evidence. The rule does not purport to exclude a particular type of evidence as an "untrustworthy or undesirable" way of proving a fact, but prevents a litigant from attempting to show the fact itself – the fact that the terms of the agreement are other than those in the writing. *Id.* at 1388-1389.

> The court also counsels against undue reliance on UCC caselaw when applying the CISG: "Courts applying the CISG cannot . . . upset the parties' reliance on the Convention by substituting familiar principles of domestic law when the Convention requires a different result." This is good general guidance in applying the CISG.

- What distinction is the court drawing in explaining what the function of the parol evidence rule is and is not?

The Statute of Frauds

Read current and revised 2-201, which is the UCC statute of frauds.

> The Article 2A analogue is 2A-201.

- In your own words, what major changes have been proposed?

The statute of frauds is an affirmative defense to contract enforcement. Once the plaintiff has made a prima facie case establishing the elements and breach of a contract, the defendant may avoid liability by showing the contract violates the statute of frauds and is therefore unenforceable.

■   What contracts fall within the UCC statute of frauds?

The statute of frauds is not intended to address actual fraud: other legal theories provide relief under those circumstances. Instead, the statute of frauds is intended to prevent fraud in certain kinds of oral contracts, by requiring written evidence of the contract, signed by the party against whom enforcement is sought.

■   **Read 2-201 Comment 1.** Is it correct to say that contracts implicating the statute of frauds are unenforceable unless they are in writing?

■   What is the purpose of the "merchant's exception" in 2-201 (2)?

■   What do the exceptions contained in 2-201 (3) have in common? Stated another way, why should these contracts be enforced despite the failure to satisfy the statute of frauds?

As the following case illustrates, courts are usually fairly lenient in finding the statute of frauds either has not been implicated or, if implicated, has been satisfied. As a general rule, courts prefer to determine these issues case-by-case based on real evidence of fraud rather than striking down contracts based upon a mere risk of fraud. A court strictly applying the statute of frauds might refuse to enforce an *entirely valid oral contract* simply because there is no written evidence of its existence.

Buffaloe v. Hart,
114 N.C. App. 52, 441 S.E.2d 172,
23 U.C.C. Rep. Serv. 2d 354 (1994).

[The initial portion of the court's opinion has been omitted, and the facts are paraphrased as follows:

Plaintiff Homer Buffaloe was a tobacco farmer in Franklin County, N.C., a rural area just outside what is commonly called the Research Triangle. He rented tobacco and tobacco barns from Lowell and Patricia Hart. These rental agreements were always oral, and the rent was generally paid in cash.

On October 20, 1988, Mr. Buffaloe paid Mr. and Mrs. Hart approximately $2,000 to rent the barns and approximately $1,000 to rent their allotment of tobacco. Then, several days later, the parties entered into negotiations for Mr. Buffaloe to purchase the barns. He offered $20,000 in four payments of $5,000 with no interest, and Mr. and Mrs. Hart accepted the offer with a handshake.

For an empirical study of the extent to which businesses actually complied with the statute of frauds a half-century ago, see *The Statute of Frauds and the Business Community: A Reappraisal in Light of Prevailing Practices,* 66 Yale L.J. 1038 (1956).

Many students are surprised by the notion of renting tobacco. Mr. Buffaloe is actually renting an *allotment* of tobacco: to protect the market, each farm was given an allotment representing the amount of tobacco that could be grown on the farm. Each farmer could grow the crop himself, or rent the allotment to another. Formerly, if a tenant rented a tobacco allotment, he or she was required to use that allotment to farm the owner's land. Today tobacco allotments can be freely traded, even across county lines.

Because Mr. Buffaloe was already renting the barns, he was in possession of them, so it was not necessary that they be moved from the Harts' land. He applied for a loan to pay for the barns, but his application was denied. After the loan fell through, he confirmed with the Harts that he still planned to purchase the barns. In addition, because he was not able to secure insurance for the barns, Mr. and Mrs. Hart purchased insurance, and he reimbursed them promptly.

Mr. Buffaloe then decided to sell the barns and placed a "for sale" ad in the Raleigh newspaper. Three individuals responded, and he received a down payment from each of them.

> Modern tobacco barns are much like trailers and can therefore be moved from place to place fairly easily.

Mrs. Hart contacted Mr. Buffaloe to "settle up" the purchase with her. He said it would take a couple of days for him to be able to do so, and also told her that he planned to sell the barns. Mrs. Hart assented to all of this.

On October 22 or 23, Mr. Buffaloe delivered to Mrs. Hart a check made payable to her for $5,000. She asked whether he needed a receipt, and he indicated that the cancelled check would be his receipt. Later, Mr. Hart decided that he did not want to sell the barns to Mr. Buffaloe. Instead, the Harts sold the barns directly to the same people with whom Mr. Buffaloe had been negotiating, and tore up the check.

Consider the court's opinion as to the legal effect of these facts:]

> Defendants [Mr. and Mrs. Hart] argue in their brief that the check delivered by plaintiff [Mr. Buffalo] to Mrs. Hart fails to meet the requirements of N.C.Gen.Stat. § 25-2-201 (1), commonly referred to as a statute of frauds, because the check "was not negotiated or endorsed by the Defendants and therefore the signature of the Defendants did not appear on the check." A check may constitute a writing sufficient to satisfy the requirements of Section 25-2-201 (1) provided it (1) contains a writing sufficient to indicate a contract of sale between the parties; (2) is signed by the party or his authorized agent against whom enforcement is sought; and (3) states a quantity.

> The only writing in this case is a personal check which, although specifying the quantity of "five barns" on the "for" line, addressed to Patricia Hart, signed by plaintiff, and containing an amount of $5,000.00, is not sufficient to satisfy Section 25-2-201. Defendants, the parties "against whom enforcement is sought," did not endorse the check, and therefore, their handwriting does not appear anywhere on the check. In fact, the name of defendant, Mr. Hart, is totally absent from the check. Therefore, because the requirement of Section 25-2-201 (1) that the writing be "signed by the party against whom enforcement is sought or by his authorized agent or broker" is absent from the check, the alleged oral contract between plaintiff and defendants is unenforceable under that section.

> Defendants further argue that the part-performance exception in Section 25-2-201 (3) (c) does not apply because ... "[t]here is no overt action of the Defendants in giving up possession of the

> Under the referenced subsection, a court may enforce a partially-performed oral contract without a written memorial.

tobacco barns," and "the delivery of the check by the Plaintiff to the Defendant, Patricia Hart, did not constitute partial payment of the contract because the check was never accepted legally by the Defendants." We disagree.

To qualify under Section 25-2-201 (3) (c), the seller must deliver the goods and have them accepted by the buyer. "Acceptance must be voluntary and unconditional" and may "be inferred from the buyer's conduct in taking physical possession of the goods or some part of them." *Howse v. Crumb*, 143 Colo. 90, 352 P.2d 285, 288 (Colo. 1960). The official comment to Section 25-2-201 explains that, for the buyer, he is required to deliver "something . . . that is accepted by the seller as such performance. Thus, part payment may be made by money or check, accepted by the seller." N.C.G.S. § 25-2-201 official cmt. Under this standard, Section 25-2-201 (3) (c) presents questions of fact, which are questions for the jury, on the issue of acceptance.

In this case, the evidence, in the light most favorable to plaintiff, establishes that plaintiff told several people about purchasing the barns, reimbursed defendants for insurance on the barns, paid for improvements, took possession, enlisted the aid of an auctioneer and the paper to sell the barns, and received deposits from three buyers on the barns. The evidence, in the light most favorable to plaintiff, also establishes that plaintiff delivered a check for $5,000.00 on 22 October 1989 to defendants, and the check was not returned to plaintiff until 26 October 1989. . . . [T]his evidence represents substantial relevant evidence that a reasonable mind might accept as adequate to support the conclusions reached by the jury that there was a "contract between the plaintiff, Homer Buffaloe, and the defendants," plaintiff "accept[ed] the tobacco barns under the terms and conditions of the contract," and defendants "accept[ed] a payment for the tobacco barns under the terms and conditions of the contract."

- Using the terminology of 2-201 (3), precisely what "part performance" did the court find in this case?

Note 1: While courts are flexible in addressing statute-of-frauds issues, *Oswald v. Allen*, 417 F.2d 43 (2d Cir. 1969), demonstrates that some limits remain. That case examined the "paper trail" between the owner and the prospective purchaser of a collection of Swiss coins. The court rejected the prospective purchaser's claim that the owner's reference to delivery arrangements, read in conjunction with a letter from the would-be purchaser written to confirm the sale, would satisfy the statute. The court acknowledged that modern law has relaxed the formality originally associated with the statute of frauds, but continued as follows:

This relaxation should be understood as directed toward the requirement that the memorandum contain all the material terms of the contract. It does not relax the requirement . . . that a

writing which establishes a contractual relationship be signed by
the party charged. . . .

The 1960 revision of the Statute of Frauds allowed material terms
such as price, delivery, and quality to be supplied by parol. It thus
removed the necessity for the careful piecing together of separate
writings to supply written evidence of each term. The piecing
together was to provide the terms of the contract – not the
contractual status itself. The [courts] have refused to extend the
doctrine of umbilical reference beyond its use . . . as a device for
supplying written evidence of material terms of a contractual
status to a use as a device for evidencing a defendant's assent to a
contractual status on terms in a writing supplied by a plaintiff. *Id.*
at 46.

- What distinction does the court draw between "the
terms of the contract" and "the contractual status
itself?"

> The difference between the two concepts is crucial in understanding the importance of the statute of frauds in modern law.

Note 2: One means of enforcing an oral contract despite the
existence of a statute-of-frauds barrier is the "merchant's
exception" in 2-201 (2).

- In your own words, what is the merchant's exception?

Bazak International Corp. v. Mast Industries, Inc., 73 N.Y.2d
113, 535 N.E.2d 633, 7 U.C.C. Rep. Serv. 2d 1380 (N.Y. 1989),
illustrates this exception. The facts are as follows:

On April 22, 1987, Karen Fedorko, marketing director of
defendant seller (Mast Industries), met with Tuvia Feldman,
[president of plaintiff buyer Bazak International], at Feldman's
office. Fedorko offered to sell Feldman certain textiles that Mast
was closing out, and the two negotiated all the terms of an oral
agreement except price. At a meeting the following day, Fedorko
and Feldman agreed on a price of $103,330. Fedorko told Feldman
that Bazak would receive written invoices for the goods the next
day and that the textiles would be delivered shortly. When no
invoices arrived, Feldman contacted Fedorko, who assured him
that everything was in order and that the invoices were on the
way. However, on April 30, 1987, Fedorko had Feldman come to
the New York City offices of Mast's parent company where,
following Fedorko's instructions, Feldman sent five purchase
orders by telecopier to Mast's Massachusetts office. That same
day, Feldman received written confirmation of Mast's receipt of
the orders. Mast made no objection to the terms set forth in the
telecopied purchase orders, but never delivered the textiles despite
Bazak's demands. *Id.* at 116.

In considering 2-201 (2), the court rejected the arguments (1)
that explicit words of confirmation are necessary to invoke the
merchant's exception and (2) that there should be a

presumption against application of the exception. Here, four
facts led the court to find 2-201 (2) was satisfied:

(1) The handwritten fax notation indicating the purchase
orders were being transmitted "in accordance with
presentation by Mast agent Karen Fedorko";

(2) The fact that the terms of the purchase orders were
highly specific as to quantity, description, price, and
payment terms;

(3) The fact that the dates on the purchase orders refer to
a transaction a week before; and

(4) The fact that Mast itself relayed Bazak's forms.

The court found these circumstances, considered together,
tended to prove confirmation of an existing contract through
the merchant's exception.

- Were the purchase orders "writings" that satisfy 2-201
(1)?

- Should the court consider parol evidence to determine
whether the purchase orders were sent to confirm an
oral contract?

Note 3: *Roos v. Aloi*, 127 Misc. 2d 864, 487 N.Y.S.2d 637, 41
U.C.C. Rep. Serv. 971 (N.Y. Sup. 1985), considered whether a
tape recording is a "writing" sufficient to satisfy the statute of
frauds. That case involved an alleged oral agreement between
the two shareholders of DJR, a close corporation that owned
and operated a retail card-and-gift shop in New York, by which
one shareholder agreed to sell all of his shares in the company
and the other agreed to purchase them. Consider the following
excerpt from the court's opinion:

> [O]n July 13, 1981, Roos and Aloi entered into an oral agreement
> wherein Roos agreed to sell his 50% stock interest in DJR to Aloi
> for the sum of $55,000.00, payable in 120 monthly installments.
> The terms of the oral agreement were set forth in a tape recording
> made by attorney William H. Kain at his office on July 13, 1981.
> At that time, the parties agreed that they would enter into a more
> formal written contract amplifying the terms of the oral
> agreement.
>
> . . . No written agreement with regard to the sale of stock by Roos
> to Aloi was consummated; no money was paid to Roos for the
> stock, and the stock was never delivered to Aloi. The Aloi cause of
> action, therefore, is based upon the oral agreement as formalized
> by the tape recording. *Id.* at 867.

Should this fact
affect the court's
holding?

With little discussion, the *Roos* court noted few cases address the issue and declined to extend the definition of "writing" to tape recordings.

- Is there a principled basis on which "writings" should exclude tape recordings?

- Is an e-mail a "writing" within the meaning of 2-201?

> Revised 2-201 and Comment 1 may assist you in answering this question.

Problem: *Martco, Inc. v. Doran Chevrolet, Inc.*, 632 S.W.2d 927, 33 U.C.C. Rep. Serv. 1619 (Tex. App. 5th Dist. 1982), considered a dispute between a Chevrolet dealership and a business that occasionally bought chassis to be constructed into custom trucks for a variety of uses. The dispute arose from the purchaser's alleged failure to pay for goods received. The court held that a writing entitled "Price Worksheet," which was on the dealership's stationery and signed by an authorized sales agent, was insufficient to satisfy the statute of frauds. In so holding, the court found as follows:

> The writing clearly contemplates a contract to be made in the future. The facts and circumstances surrounding these events merely confirm that the writing is not a confirmation of a pre-existing agreement, but constitutes an offer for an agreement that was not entered into until much later, if at all. Our inquiry is whether such a writing will satisfy the statute of frauds.

> * * *

> . . . Authorities in other jurisdictions uniformly . . . disqualify writings which contain "futuristic" language as not confirmatory of a contract already in existence. *Id.* at 928.

- Is the court's holding consistent with the Code?

International Perspective: Oral Contracts

Read CISG Articles 11 and 96.

CISG Article 11 takes a different approach from UCC 2-201 by eliminating the statute of frauds. This decision also has implications for the CISG's handling of parol evidence. *Fercus, S.R.L. v. Palazzo Co.*, 2000 WL 1118925 (S.D.N.Y. 2000), shows the relationship between these two concepts. As the *Fercus* court noted, the CISG applies only if a valid contract has been formed, and Article 4 of the CISG expressly leaves questions of contract validity to be determined by other law. Once the *Fercus* court found an oral contract had been formed, presumably under New York state common law, the court

> For a case, translated from its original German text, that discusses in significant detail how parties can accomplish a private "statute of frauds" requirement for themselves despite Article 11's provisions to the contrary, see Heidi Keschenat, *Case Translation: Supreme Court of Austria (Oberster Gerichtshof) 6 February 1996 10 ob 518/95*, 6 V.J. 153 (2002).

applied the CISG to determine no writing was necessary to
prove the existence of this oral contract, and instead permitted
the introduction of parol evidence to prove the agreement's
existence.   The following quote from *Claudia v. Olivieri
Footwear Ltd.*, 1998 WL 164824 (S.D.N.Y. 1998), clarifies the
relationship between parol evidence and the statute of frauds,
illustrating the CISG's approach to each:

> Unlike the UCC, under the CISG a contract need not be evidenced
> by a writing. According to the CISG, a contract "may be proved
> by any means . . ." and "any evidence that may bear on the issue of
> formation is admissible."   Such evidence may include oral
> statements made prior to a writing . . . Thus, contracts governed
> by the CISG are freed from the limits of the parol evidence rule
> and there is a wider spectrum of admissible evidence to consider in
> construing the terms of the parties' agreement. . . .
>
> Consequently, the standard UCC inquiry regarding whether a
> writing is partially or fully integrated has little meaning under the
> CISG, and courts are therefore less constrained by the "four
> corners of" the instrument in construing the terms of the contract.
> *Id.* at 5-6.

As a matter of review, make sure you know why the distinction between fully and partially integrated contracts is significant under the UCC.

The fact that Article 96 allows state parties to the Convention
to exclude themselves from Article 11 shows countries have
markedly different approaches to oral contracts, and also
demonstrates the drafters' concern that these differences not
impede the success of the CISG. In addition to the fact that
countries could "opt out" of Article 11 via Article 96, contracting
parties can require a writing.

- Insofar as Article 96 is concerned, does U.S. law
  (especially the statute of frauds) require that certain
  contracts for sale be (1) "concluded in" writing or,
  alternatively, (2) "evidenced by" writing?

- What is the difference?

The Proposed Revisions to Article 2

This chapter introduced several proposed changes to Article 2.
This revision process has generated strife that has caused some
to question the continuing utility and even the future of the
UCC. Much of the history of the revision project, including the
withdrawal of NCCUSL support for the July 1999 draft in the
summer of 2001, is chronicled in Professor Richard Speidel's
article *Revising UCC Article 2: A View from the Trenches*, 52
Hastings L.J. 607 (2001). At the same time, some have claimed
Article 2 is becoming less relevant. In *The Rise and Fall of*

Article 2, 62 La. L. Rev. 1009 (2002), Professor Robert Scott makes the following statements about the recent revisions to Article 2:

> I suggest that nobody but the participants has seemed to care for the simple reason that, to the rest of the commercial world, Article 2 has become largely irrelevant. What has happened? There is evidence that large numbers of commercial parties have opted out of the sales provisions of the Code. Private arbitration is used to enforce trade-association rules and standard-form terms that replace the default rules of Article 2. The opting out by commercial interests, extending over many years, would mean that the principal remaining function of Article 2 is to regulate mass-market sales transactions. *Id.* at 1012.

In *The Waning Importance of Revisions to UCC Article 2*, 78 Notre Dame L. Rev. 595 (2003), Professor Gregory Maggs expresses his position that electronic commerce has made much of what was formerly crucial in Article 2 – such as the statute of frauds – less relevant, and that federal and state law adequately address any new nuances, such that revisions to Article 2 are less important than many anticipated. Whatever the future of revised Article 2, students should be aware that the controversy surrounding the process may affect the future influence of the Code, as well as the ALI and NCCUSL.

Chapter Conclusion: As you leave this chapter, you should be able to distinguish a sale from a lease, and a sale of goods from a sale of services. You should be able to tell a merchant from a nonmerchant and should know when that distinction affects the application of the Code. You should also be comfortable with mutual assent, the battle of the forms, the parol evidence rule, and the statute of frauds.

Chapter 3:
Article 2 Property Interests

A. Title to Goods under Article 2

Knowing who owns the goods at each stage of an Article 2 sales transaction can be important when goods are lost, damaged, or destroyed, or when a party seeks to avoid the sales contract. This chapter examines title to goods under Article 2 and its relationship to risk of loss and insurable interest. This section discusses passage of title and introduces the relationship between the legal concept of "title" and the "title certificate" that often purports to represent title.

Read 2-401 and Comment 1. Also read the commentary to 2-101.

> The Article 2A equivalents of the two cited statutes are 2A-302 and 2A-101, respectively.

- Is "title" a defined term for the purposes of Article 2?

The following case introduces the UCC approach to title and shows how passage of title relates to risk of loss in a fact pattern involving the seller's delivery of nonconforming goods.

> Risk of loss is further discussed in Part B.

William F. Wilke, Inc. v. Cummins Diesel Engines, Inc.,
252 Md. 611, 250 A.2d 886, 6 U.C.C. Rep. Serv. 45 (Md. 1969).

Singley, Judge.

The dilemma which this controversy posed for the trial court was aptly put by Alexander Pope more than two centuries ago: "Be not the first by whom the new are try'd, Nor yet the last to lay the old aside." A resolution of the problem calls for a deep draft from Pope's Pierian spring.

> The reference here is to Alexander Pope's *Essays on Criticism.* In this context, the term "Pierian Spring" denotes a source of inspiration.

William F. Wilke, Inc., . . . is a mechanical contractor who was a subcontractor on a job involving the construction of certain facilities for the United States government at Aberdeen Proving Ground. The performance of the contract required, among other things, that Wilke supply and install an emergency diesel-powered generator in conformance with government specifications. After a discussion with representatives of Cummins Diesel Engines, Inc., . . . Wilke received a quotation from them dated July 14, 1965. On August 3, 1965, Wilke issued a purchase order for an emergency diesel generator "in strict compliance with plans and specifications . . . complete in all respects, including all required tests for the sum of Thirteen Thousand Three Hundred Dollars ($13,300). [FN3] . . ."

> Aberdeen Proving Ground has been a munitions-testing facility for the U.S. Army since 1917.

FN3. The parties agree that the stipulated price of $13,300 was the result of a mathematical error, and that the correct figure should have been $13,500.

After you finish reading the case, take another look at the fact that the job was progressing slowly, yet Cummins chose to deliver the generator early. How, if at all, should this fact enter into the court's reasoning?

The job progressed with agonizing slowness, and by August 1966 was only 50% complete. Although it was far too early to install the generator, Cummins was anxious to deliver it to the job site and did so on August 17, 1966. It was delivered by Cummins' truck, unloaded by Wilke's crane, and placed on a permanent base which had been prepared for it. At the time of delivery, the generator was lacking two starting batteries. When asked how Cummins' representative explained the absence of the batteries, Wilke's foreman at the job answered: "He said the batteries were not in the machine because he did not want us to start it or fool with it. His statement was, 'This is my baby until I start it and turn it over to you.'" This testimony was not challenged by Cummins. Also missing were the maintenance and operating instruction manuals that were included in the specifications.

On August 18, 1966, Cummins billed Wilke for $13,500, and on September 27, Wilke sent Cummins a check for $13,300, telling them that the remaining $200 would be paid after start-up and field tests.

The job continued to move at a snail's pace, and until the spring of 1967 the generator sat on its base enclosed in a housing intended to protect it from the weather since it was designed to operate out of doors. When Wilke started to hook up the generator, it was discovered that the water in its cooling system had frozen during the previous winter, and that the engine had been severely damaged.

Wilke notified Cummins of the damage, and Cummins, after an investigation, decided that repairs could not be made on the job site. The generator was picked up by Cummins and taken away to be repaired. There were no discussions between the parties as to the responsibility for the repairs prior to their completion. On June 9, Cummins sent Wilke a bill for $2,231.20 for the work and conditioned return of the generator on the payment of the bill. On June 19, Wilke instituted an action of replevin, and on that same day, Cummins sent Wilke a corrected bill in the amount of $2,798.27. The generator was returned to the job site where Cummins supervised the electrical installation, start-up and field tests. In April of 1968, the replevin action was tried without a jury by the Superior Court of Baltimore City which, on April 8, 1968, entered judgment absolute in favor of Cummins for the return of the property or, alternatively, for $2,798.27, one cent damages and costs. It is from this judgment that Wilke has appealed.

How does Cummins use the concept of title to make its argument? Although it is not expressly stated, what would you expect Wilke's counter-argument to be, insofar as title as concerned?

The court below concluded that "title did pass at the time of delivery of the machine; and that the tests which were to be made thereafter were not a condition to the passing of title" and that "the implication is that when someone in this kind of business (Cummins) is told that it is necessary that (the generator) be put into operation; these circumstances justify Cummins' conclusion that they have an implied order to repair . . . (which) carries with it the responsibility of payment for the repairs before the machine can be released from the custody of the repairman."

The Uniform Sales Act was repealed in favor of the UCC.

Wilke contends that this result and the reasons given in support of it could possibly have been a correct statement of the law under the Uniform Sales Act which was repealed in Maryland by Chapter 538 of

1
2
3
4
5
6
7
8
9
10
11
12
13
14
15
16
17
18
19
20
21
22
23
24
25
26
27
28
29
30
31
32
33
34
35
36
37
38
39
40
41
42
43
44
45
46
50
51
52
53

the Laws of 1963, but is at "cross purposes" with the Uniform Commercial Code, which has been in force in Maryland since February 1, 1964. Since we agree with this, we need not reach Wilke's allegation that the damage was caused by Cummins' negligence, or Cummins' contention that Wilke was responsible for the care of the generator and for the cost of repairs.

One of the more startling differences between the UCC and the Sales Act is the UCC's adoption of a flexible contractual approach instead of following the more rigid concept of title to which the Sales Act adhered.

The Official Comment to UCC 2-101, the first section in the Subtitle on Sales, puts it this way:

> This comment, and its placement following the first Code section in Article 2, should give you a clear sense of the changing importance of title under the UCC as compared to the Sales Act.

> The arrangement of the present Subtitle is in terms of contract for sale and the various steps of its performance. The legal consequences are stated as following directly from the contract and action taken under it without resorting to the idea of when property or title passed or was to pass as being the determining factor. The purpose is to avoid making practical issues between practical men turn upon the location of an intangible something, the passing of which no man can prove by evidence and to substitute for such abstractions proof of words and actions of a tangible character.

Hawkland, *A Transactional Guide to the Uniform Commercial Code* (1964), goes somewhat further:

> Make sure you follow the distinction between the "lump concept" and "narrow issue" approaches. Doing so is crucial to understanding the Code's approach to the concept of title.

> Under the UCC, the location of title is relatively unimportant, because the Code rejects the "lump-concept approach" of the common law and USA (Uniform Sales Act). At common law and under the USA, the approach was to decide under the specific facts of a case that the "title" was in the seller or the buyer, a "wide-premise decision," which then dictated the answers to many unrelated problems, such as risk of loss, liability for price as against mere damages, liability for taxes, standing to sue third party tortfeasors, and the like. A decision on title in one case was authority for a decision on title in another, even though the particular issues to be decided in the two cases were radically different.

> The UCC has adopted the policy of "narrow-issue" thinking. A number of specific rules govern the rights and duties of the buyer and seller, and often these provisions are not predicated upon ownership considerations. Under the UCC, the analysis of a sales problem does not start with a location of title, but with an analysis of the problem in terms of narrow issues and an ascertainment of whether or not the UCC contains specific provisions dealing with these issues. If it does, those rules govern the transaction, and title will play no part in its solution. If it does not, the title concept may still be employed. *Hawkland, supra,* 1.2401 at 143.

If we analyze the problem before us in terms of what Dean Hawkland calls the "narrow issues" and then ascertain how these are dealt with by the UCC, we come unerringly to the conclusion that, in the absence

of a delivery of conforming goods, the risk of damage remained with
Cummins, the seller, notwithstanding the delivery of the generator to
the job site, the receipt of payment from Wilke, and some eight months'
delay in start-up.

UCC 2-401 follows the contractual approach in providing that title
cannot pass prior to the identification of the goods to the contract; that
it will pass "in any manner and on any conditions explicitly agreed on
by the parties"; and in the absence of explicit agreement, that it will
pass "at the time and place at which the seller completes his
performance with reference to the physical delivery of the goods. . . ."

This is described in the Official Comment as the "step by step"
performance of the contract. *Hawkland, supra*, 1.3202 at 184 adds a
cautionary note:

> The seller does not fully perform his contract merely by getting
> goods to the right place at the right time, and thereafter making
> them available to the buyer. He must get "conforming" goods to
> the right place at the right time and properly tender them.

The narrow issue here is whether Cummins made a "delivery" of goods
which conformed to the contract. It will be recalled that Wilke's
purchase order specifically incorporated the government specifications,
which consisted of two and a half pages of single-spaced typescript
which detailed the field tests to be performed prior to acceptance by the
government. That these tests were not intended to be an empty ritual
can be indicated by a random selection of a few of them. The generator
was to be operated for eight hours at 75% of rated load; then operated
for eight hours at 100% of rated load; and finally operated for two hours
at 110% of rated load. Other provisions required an inspection of the
generator's components and the hourly recording of data during the
field tests. Further provisions set out an elaborate formula for the
development of a rebate should fuel consumption exceed certain
standards and described the tests to be made . . . to ascertain whether
radio interference had developed.

UCC 2-106 (2) provides that "Goods or conduct including any part of a
performance are 'conforming' or conform to the contract when they are
in accordance with the obligations under the contract." Non-conformity
cannot be viewed as a question of the quantity and quality of goods
alone, but of the performance of the totality of the seller's contractual
undertaking. 2-510 (1) reads, "[If] a tender or delivery of goods so fails
to conform to the contract as to give a right of rejection, the risk of their
loss remains on the seller until cure or acceptance" and the Official
Comment notes, "Under subsection (1) (of 2-510) the seller by his
individual action cannot shift the risk of loss to the buyer unless his
action conforms with all the conditions resting on him under the
contract."

How does this relate
to the rule stated in
statement 2-401 (4)?

Under the facts of this case, we have no difficulty in holding that the
delivery of the generator to the job site, while identifying the goods to
the contract, did not amount to a delivery of goods or the performance
of obligations conforming to the contract. It could not constitute such a
delivery and performance until the generator had been installed,

started up, and field tests completed to the satisfaction of the government. Until then, risk of loss remained with Cummins regardless of where title may have stood.

While it is conceivable that a negligent act could be postulated which would have made it possible to hold Wilke responsible for the cost of repairing the damage, such a course of conduct is absent here. The generator, when delivered, was completely enclosed and had been delivered in an inoperable condition so that no one could "start it or fool with it" until it was "turned over" to Wilke. On these facts, the judgment in Cummins' favor was clearly erroneous. Judgment reversed; Costs to be paid by appellee.

- How does a seller "complete his performance" under 2-401 (2)?

> 2-301, although not directly on point, may help you to answer this question.

- How does the UCC's shift away from a holistic focus on title mesh with UCC concepts – such as the analysis of whether a given transaction is a sale or a lease – that rely in some part on a determination of the incidents of ownership?

- What does this case suggest about the relationship between the concepts of title and risk of loss?

> This relationship is further developed in part B.

Note 1: *Gross v. Powell*, 181 N.W.2d 113 (1970), discusses passage of title within the context of tort liability and insurance coverage. On April 10, 1968, Leo Hendrickson executed a contract for the purchase of a 1962 Oldsmobile sedan from Proctor Motors, Inc. At the same time, Hendrickson delivered to Proctor a check for $600, the price on which the parties had agreed. In return, Proctor delivered the keys to Hendrickson, and he drove the car from the dealer's lot.

Hendrickson then delivered the car to his friend Robert H. Powell, requesting that Powell drive the car back to Hendrickson's hometown of Floodwood, while Hendrickson drove another car, his 1957 Oldsmobile. During the drive to Floodwood, Powell was involved in a collision that resulted in the death of one occupant of the other vehicle and serious injury to the other occupant. The 1962 Oldsmobile was destroyed in the collision.

Hendrickson had made arrangements with his hometown bank, the First State Bank of Floodwood, to deliver the car to the bank the following day for the purpose of using the vehicle to secure a loan to cover the check Hendrickson had previously written to Proctor. Because the vehicle was destroyed, he was unable to complete the loan transaction, and the check to Proctor was dishonored for insufficient funds. Proctor sued Hendrickson to recover the vehicle's price.

> Hendrickson had intended to set up a Purchase Money Security Interest in favor of the First State Bank of Floodwood. This concept is discussed in Chapter 13, Part C. The riskiness of his timing is obvious.

When the heirs of the deceased occupant of the other vehicle
sued Hendrickson and Powell for wrongful death, Powell
defended on the grounds that, since the check was dishonored,
title to the vehicle never passed to Hendrickson. He claimed
Proctor should be primarily liable, and that its insurance
company should defend and indemnify him for any judgment
against him.

The court rejected this argument, holding title passed to
Hendrickson no later than when the keys were delivered to
him and should not be affected by the subsequent dishonoring
of the check.

- Would it have been fair to hold the seller liable?

- What would sellers likely require from buyers as part
  of the sales transaction if they believed they could be
  responsible under facts such as these?

Note 2: *Grimm v. Prudence Mutual Casualty Co.*, 243 So. 2d
140, 8 U.C.C. Rep. Serv. 829 (Fla. 1971), another insurance-
coverage dispute, illustrates the concept of relativity of title.

Charles Grimm purchased a 1964 Cadillac automobile from a
Mr. Ash in January of 1967. He paid $1,500 by check and
financed the $1,000 balance through his bank. Mr. Ash
informed him that the Bank of Clearwater had a lien for $700
and agreed to extinguish this lien with a portion of the $1,500
check. It was further agreed that Ash would not receive the
last $1,000 until Grimm received clear title to the vehicle.
Grimm received possession of the vehicle and a bill of sale
reflecting the $700 lien.

Despite these promises, Ash never paid off the lien. Thus,
Grimm never received the title certificate. In addition, Grimm
later learned the lien was actually $2,800, rather than $700.
The Bank of Clearwater gave Grimm the option to assume the
debt or lose the car through repossession. Shortly thereafter,
the vehicle was stolen.

Prudence Mutual Casualty Company, which insured the
vehicle, refused to pay Grimm's claim, alleging a lack of
insurable interest. As part of its correspondence with Grimm
on this matter, Prudence refunded Grimm's premium.

Why was the refund necessary?

In considering these facts, the court held as follows:

What does this paragraph mean? See *Jefferson v. Jones*, cited in Part C, Note 1.

> The significance placed by the court below on Grimm's lack of a . . .
> title certificate was . . . misplaced. This Court has clearly stated
> that the absence of a . . . title certificate does not indicate the

absence of a valid title, but rather the absence of a marketable title.

Fla. Stat. 672.403 (1969) states that a purchaser of goods acquires all title which his transferor had or had power to transfer. In the case of . . . stolen cars . . . insured parties could not have any equitable interest therein since the transferors had no power to transfer. Their insurable interest, then, was their right to . . . possession against all but the rightful owner.

> Chapter 6, Part A examines when wrongdoers can (and cannot) convey good title.

* * *

[Similarly], there is no doubt but that Grimm had a right to possession of the automobile until such time as the bank's prior right cut his off. Nor is there any doubt but that Grimm had more than just an equitable interest in the automobile. He was not purchasing a stolen automobile, but rather an automobile with a larger lien than he had been aware of. Grimm was the legal owner of an automobile which was about to be repossessed. *Id.* at 142-143.

- Why does Grimm have a stronger case than the unknowing purchaser of a stolen vehicle?

Problem: On February 10, 1923, Joseph Barnett bought a Ford automobile in Chicago for $450. Later, he added accessories costing about $100. He used the car in Chicago until May 8, when he drove the vehicle to Seattle, arriving on May 22. He used the car in Seattle until it was stolen on August 22. On July 12, 1923, Barnett had purchased vehicle insurance from London Assurance Corporation. After the theft, he reported the loss to the insurer. In searching for the stolen Ford, the insurance company found another Ford with the same vehicle identification number in Mississippi. That Ford was in the possession of its rightful owner and was not the same vehicle Barnett had purchased and London Assurance had insured. Barnett's Ford was never found. Assuming Barnett's Ford was stolen property when Barnett purchased it, the insurance company refused to pay the claim. (Assume this assumption was correct and that Barnett had no idea he was purchasing a stolen vehicle.)

> Once you have read Chapter 6, Part B, you will have a clearer sense of why the company would not pay the claim.

- Why might the insurance company assume the vehicle was stolen property when Barnett purchased it?

> Use the *Grimm* holding in Note 2 to assist you in formulating an answer.

- As between the insurance company and the insured, who should prevail?

Based on *Barnett v. London Assurance Corp.*, 245 P. 3 (1926).

This case describes a source called "INCOTERMS," published by the International Chamber of Commerce with the stated goal "to provide a set of international rules for the interpretation of the most commonly used trade terms in foreign trade."

International Perspective: Passage of Title

Read CISG Article 4. The CISG does not address passage of title. Instead, as the cantonal court in Vaud, Switzerland held in *B. vs. O.* (No. 01 93 1308, May 17, 1994), passage of title is a matter of domestic law. German and Australian courts have interpreted the CISG the same way, holding that domestic law, not the CISG, will control the validity of a "reservation of title" clause agreed upon by the parties. *See Roder Zelt und Hallenkonstrucktionen GmbH v. Rosedown Party Ltd.* (No. 57 FCR 216, April 28, 1995), and *Unknown Parties* (No. 5 U 534/91, January 16, 1992). Under the CISG, risk of loss and passage of title are determined independently of one another. Consider the following excerpt from *St. Paul Guardian Insurance Co. v. Neuromed Medical Systems & Support GmbH*, 2002 WL 465312 (S.D.N.Y. 2002), in which the court considered a claim arising from damage to a mobile magnetic resonance imaging system ("MRI") during transit from Germany to the United States. The court describes the relationship between risk of loss and passage of title under the CISG, as follows:

> Pursuant to the CISG, "[t]he risk passes without taking into account who owns the goods. The passing of ownership is not regulated by the CISG according to Art. 4 (b)." Article 4 (b) provides that the Convention is not concerned with "the effect which the contract may have on the property in the goods sold." Moreover, according to Article 67 (1), the passage of risk and transfer of title need not occur at the same time, as the seller's retention of "documents controlling the disposition of the goods does not affect the passage of risk." *Id.* at 5.

- ▪ From what you have read about the relationship between risk of loss and passage of title under the UCC, is the CISG different?

Keep this short excerpt in mind as you begin the following section, in which you will learn more about the relationship between passage of title and risk of loss under the UCC. After you have completed section B, you may want to return to the *St. Paul* case to consider more comprehensively the similarities and differences between the UCC and CISG approaches to these concepts.

B. Insurable Interests and Risk of Loss

This section focuses on how title relates to other property-interest matters under Article 2.

Read 2-501.

- Which is first: passage of title or creation of an insurable interest?

Read 2-509 (both the current version and as revised) and 2-510.

- How does risk of loss depend on whether the contract is breached?

The following case illustrates the relationship between title, risk of loss, and insurable interest. Make sure you can articulate what "acknowledgment to the seller" means in current and revised 2-509 (2), respectively, as well as whether such acknowledgment took place in this case. Although the proposed revisions to 2-509 address the specific problem of statutory construction before the court, Posner's analysis will remain a worthwhile exposition of the relationship between these important topics, even if the revisions are adopted.

Jason's Foods, Inc. vs. Peter Eckrich & Sons, Inc.,
774 F.2d 214, 41 U.C.C. Rep. Serv. 1287 (7th Cir. 1985).

Posner, Circuit Judge.

Section 2-509 (2) of the Uniform Commercial Code . . . provides that, where "goods are held by a bailee to be delivered without being moved, the risk of loss passes to the buyer . . . (b) on acknowledgment by the bailee of the buyer's right to possession of the goods." We must decide whether acknowledgment to the *seller* complies with the statute. There are no reported cases on the question, either in Illinois or elsewhere.

* * *

On or about December 30, 1982, Jason's Foods contracted to sell 38,000 pounds of "St. Louis style" pork ribs to Peter Eckrich & Sons, delivery to be effected by a transfer of the ribs from Jason's account in an independent warehouse to Eckrich's account in the same warehouse – which is to say, without the ribs actually being moved. In its confirmation of the deal, Jason's notified Eckrich that the transfer in storage would be made between January 10 and January 14. On January 13, Jason's phoned the warehouse and requested that the ribs be transferred to Eckrich's account. A clerk at the warehouse noted the transfer on its books immediately, but did not mail a warehouse receipt until January 17 or January 18, and it was not till Eckrich received the

---

The Article 2A provisions on point are 2A-217 and 2A-218.

The Article 2A analogues are 2A-219 and 2A-220.

The *Wilke* decision in Part A alludes to this matter.

How does revised 2-509 (2) (b) endeavor to solve this problem?

Use of an Article 7 warehouse receipt is common under facts such as these. If "negotiable," this document of title represents ownership of the goods and can be sold or transferred while the goods stay in place. See 7-104, 7-201, and 7-202 for a general introduction to this kind of transaction, which is presented in Chapter 18. The concept of "negotiability" is explored at length in Chapter 7, Part C.

receipt on January 24 that it knew the transfer had taken place. But on
January 17, the ribs had been destroyed by a fire at the warehouse.
Jason's sued Eckrich for the price. If the risk of loss passed on January
13 when the ribs were transferred to Eckrich's account, or at least
before the fire, Jason's is entitled to recover the contract price;
otherwise not. The district judge ruled that the risk of loss did not pass
by then and therefore granted summary judgment for Eckrich.

Jason's argues that, when the warehouse transferred the ribs to
Eckrich's account, Jason's lost all rights over the ribs, and it should not
bear the risk of loss of goods it did not own or have any right to control.
Eckrich owned them, and Eckrich's insurance covered any ribs that it
owned; Jason's had no insurance and anyway, Jason's argues, it could
not insure what it no longer owned.

> How, if at all, should the availability of insurance coverage affect the court's decision?

* * *

Eckrich argues with great vigor that it cannot be made to bear the loss
of goods that it does not know it owns. But that is not so *outré* a
circumstance as it may sound. If you obtain property by inheritance,
you are quite likely to own it before you know you own it. And
Eckrich's position involves a comparable paradox: that Jason's
continued to bear the risk of loss of goods that it knew it no longer
owned. So the case cannot be decided by reference to what the parties
knew or did not know; and neither can it be decided, despite Jason's
urgings, on the basis of which party could have insured against the
loss. Both could have. Jason's had sufficient interest in the ribs until
the risk of loss shifted to Eckrich to insure the ribs until then. You do
not have to own goods to insure them; it is enough that you will suffer a
loss if they are lost or damaged, as of course Jason's would if the risk of
loss remained on it after it parted with title. Section 2-509 (2)
separates title from risk of loss. Title to the ribs passed to Eckrich
when the warehouse made the transfer on its books from Jason's
account to Eckrich's, but the risk of loss did not pass until the transfer
was "acknowledged."

> This is a good example of how a party's litigation strategy can be turned against it.

Thus, as is usually the case, insurability cannot be used to guide the
assignment of liability. (The costs of insurance might sometimes be
usable for this purpose, as we shall see, but not in this case.) Since
whoever will be liable for the loss can insure against it, the court must
determine who is liable before knowing who can insure, rather than
vice versa. If acknowledgment to the seller is enough to place the risk
of loss on the buyer, then Eckrich should have bought insurance
against any losses that occurred afterward. If acknowledgment to the
buyer is necessary (we need not decide whether acknowledgment to a
third party may ever suffice), Jason's should have bought insurance
against any losses occurring until then.

The suggestion that the acknowledgment contemplated by subsection
(b) can be to the seller seems very strange. What purpose would it
serve? When Jason's called up the warehouse and directed that the
transfer be made, it did not add: and by the way, acknowledge to me
when you make the transfer. Jason's assumed, correctly, that the
transfer was being made forthwith; and in fact there is no suggestion
that the warehouse clerk ever "acknowledged" the transfer to Jason's.

If the draftsmen of subsection (b) had meant the risk of loss to pass when the transfer was made, one would think they would have said so, and not complicated life by requiring "acknowledgment."

All this may seem a rather dry textual analysis, remote from the purposes of the Uniform Commercial Code, so let us shift now to the plane of policy. The Code sought to create a set of standard contract terms that would reflect in the generality of cases the preferences of contracting parties at the time of contract. One such preference is for assignments of liability – or, what amounts to the same thing, assignments of the risk of loss – that create incentives to minimize the adverse consequences of untoward events such as (in this case) a warehouse fire. There are two ways of minimizing such consequences. One is to make them less painful by insuring against them. Insurance does not prevent a loss – it merely spreads it – but in doing so it reduces (for those who are risk-averse) the disutility of the loss. So if one of the contracting parties can insure at lower cost than the other, this is an argument for placing the risk of loss on him, to give him an incentive to do so. But that as we have seen is not a factor in this case; either party could have insured (or have paid the warehouse to assume strict liability for loss or destruction of the goods, in which event the warehouse would have insured them), and so far as the record shows at equal cost.

> See Notes 2 and 3 following this case for a discussion of two concepts – social norms and the Coase theorem – that relate to this portion of this court's opinion.

The other method of minimizing the consequences of an unanticipated loss is through prevention of the loss. If one party is in a better position than the other to prevent it, this is a reason for placing the risk of loss on him, to give him an incentive to prevent it. It would be a reason for placing liability on a seller who still had possession of the goods, even though title had passed. But between the moment of transfer of title by Jason's and the moment of receipt of the warehouse receipt by Eckrich, neither party to the sale had effective control over the ribs. They were in a kind of limbo, until (to continue the Dantesque image) abruptly propelled into a hotter region. With Jason's having relinquished title and Eckrich not yet aware that it had acquired it, neither party had an effective power of control.

> In his landmark book *The Cost of Accidents: A Legal and Economic Analysis*, Guido Calabresi calls the person or entity in the best position to avoid the loss the "Cheapest Cost Avoider."

But this is not an argument for holding that the risk of loss shifted at the moment of transfer; it is just an argument for regarding the parties' positions as symmetrical from the standpoint of ability either to prevent or to shift losses. In such a case we have little to assist us besides the language of subsection (b) and its surrounding subsections and the UCC comments; but these materials do point pretty clearly to the conclusion that the risk of loss did not pass at the moment of transfer.

[Summary judgment for Eckrich was therefore affirmed.]

- Why does acknowledgment to a seller fail to satisfy 2-509 (2) (b)?

- What does this case add to your understanding about the relationship between title and risk of loss?

- What does this case suggest about the relationship between title and insurable interest?

Note 1: *Mercanti v. Persson*, 160 Conn. 468, 280 A.2d 137, 8 U.C.C. Rep. Serv. 969 (Conn. 1971), illustrates the relationship between risk of loss, trade usage or custom, and misrepresentation. That case involved a dispute between a boat builder and a yacht owner who had hired the builder to construct a ninety-two-foot mast. The owner furnished materials costing approximately $1,300, and the boat builder agreed to do the work for $4 an hour, totaling $4,558. The owner paid this amount, and construction was begun. Before the mast was completed and delivered to the owner, it was totally destroyed by fire at the builder's boat yard. The owner brought suit to recover the monies already paid to the builder, as well as monies representing his lost bookings of the yacht, which the builder knew would be used for fishing and boating parties. The builder defended on the grounds that he had not insured against the loss and claimed that, as a matter of custom and trade usage, the owner should have insured against the loss. The builder further claimed that the owner's delay in furnishing the materials should excuse the builder from liability in this case.

> What are the risks and benefits of permitting a party to defend successfully on the grounds that it has not insured against the loss?

As for the claim of delay, the court held as follows:

> The claim fails . . . because there is no finding that any date for the delivery of the hardware for the mast was included in the agreement between the parties. Consequently, the plaintiff's delay in making delivery could not be found to be a breach of the agreement. *Id.* at 473-474.

Thus, the builder was not able to take advantage of 2-510 (3)'s loss-shifting provisions, as referenced in the *Wilkes* case in Part A. The court held as follows with regard to the custom or trade usage claim:

> It is clear that if it was the custom or usage of the boat-building trade for the boat owner to assume the responsibility for insuring work in progress against risk of loss by fire, the risk of loss would be on the plaintiff in the absence of any inconsistent terms of the agreement, and there are none in the present case. There is, however, no finding as to any custom or usage in the boat-building trade of the sort claimed. Consequently, the agreement cannot be construed in the light of a custom or usage which has not been found to exist. *Id.* at 475.

> To answer this question, see 1-303 (c) and Comment 4 and *Nanakuli Paving & Rock Co. v. Shell Oil Co.*, 664 F.2d 772 (9th Cir. 1981), referenced in Chapter 2, Part B.

- Why should delay be relevant to risk of loss?

- What kind of evidence would prove an alleged trade usage?

Note 2: As the *Jason's Foods* opinion suggests, the UCC drafters endeavored to incorporate the best trade practices among contracting parties. The following excerpts explore whether Karl Llewellyn, principal architect of the Code, was successful in these efforts:

This discussion continues themes introduced in Chapter 1, Part A.

From James Whitman, *Commercial Law and the American Volk: A Note on Llewellyn's German Sources for the Uniform Commercial Code*, 97 Yale L.J. 156 (1987):

> Karl Llewellyn . . . gave the Code an often baffling jurisprudential framework: The UCC regularly refuses to supply substantive rules. Instead, with startling frequency, the Code directs courts to determine whether the parties in a given commercial dispute have acted "reasonably" or in accordance with "customs" and "usages of trade" that are nowhere specified or described in the Code itself. The Code's routine use of these vague directives has irritated some commentators and thrilled many others. *Id.* at 156.

- Is Llewellyn's approach as described by Whitman an improper delegation of responsibility, a way of keeping the Code current, both, or neither?

From Lisa Bernstein, *The Questionable Empirical Basis of Article 2's Incorporation Strategy: A Preliminary Study*, 66 U. Chi. L. Rev. 710 (1999):

Schnader was Pennsylvania's Attorney General in the early-to-mid-1930s and an unsuccessful Republican candidate for Governor.

> The Code was assumed to be based on a solid empirical foundation. William A. Schnader, a primary mover behind the Code project, chose Karl Llewellyn as Chief Reporter because not only was Professor Llewellyn a student of commercial law as it appeared in the law books, but he was the type of law professor who was never satisfied unless he knew exactly how commercial transactions were carried on in the marketplace. He insisted that the provisions of the Code should be drafted from the standpoint of what actually takes place from day to day in the commercial world rather than from the standpoint of what appeared in statutes and decisions.

> However, with the exception of seeking (and then ignoring) the opinions of merchants in hearings on the Code . . . , rigorous empirical research into what types of rules would actually be responsive to merchant concerns was never undertaken. While Llewellyn's defenders recognize that the lack of an empirical basis for the Code was inconsistent with his Realist and scientific approach to law as well as his often-expressed position that in drafting a commercial code attention should be paid to the wide basis of established commercial experience, . . . they are quick to point out that critics who have been suspicious of Llewellyn's alleged 'unscientific,' 'impressionistic,' or 'anecdotal' approach to facts have yet to point to any major factual assumptions of the Code that were misleading or inaccurate. Nor have suggestions been forthcoming as to specific empirical research that might have

The Code's Realist Orientation is discussed in Chapter 1, Part A.

been worth doing. [Others suggest] that the lack of solid empirical research led Code drafters to adopt provisions that are detrimental rather than accommodating to merchant concerns, and to a commercial law based on a deeply flawed understanding of merchant reality. *Id.* at 713.

- To what extent, if any, does the authority of the Code depend on its being reflective of actual commercial practices?

Note 3: In *Jason's Foods*, Judge Posner asserts that, "if one of the contracting parties can insure at lower cost than the other, this is an argument for placing the risk of loss on him, to give him an incentive to do so."

- Is this a fair means of assessing liability?

In considering this matter, review the following excerpt describing the work of Ronald Coase. The Coase Theorem, as it has become known, is the claim that the law's allocation of liability is often irrelevant because market forces will ensure entitlements and liabilities are allocated in the way that is most efficient.

From Ronald H. Coase, *The Problem of Social Cost*, 3 J.L. & Econ. 1 (1960):

This paper is concerned with those actions of business firms which have harmful effects on others. . . . *Id.* at 1.

* * *

A good example of the problem under discussion is afforded by the case of straying cattle which destroy crops growing on neighboring land. Let us suppose that a farmer and a cattle-raiser are operating on neighboring properties. Let us further suppose that, without any fencing between the properties, an increase in the size of the cattle-raiser's herd increases the total damage to the farmer's crops. . . .

To simplify the argument, . . . I shall assume that the annual cost of fencing the farmer's property is $9 and that the price of the crop is $1 per ton. Also, I assume that the relation between the number of cattle in the herd and the annual crop loss is as follows:

Number of steers in herd	Annual crop loss in tons	Crop loss per added steer in tons
1	1	1
2	3	2
3	6	3
4	10	4

Id. at 2.

First, Coase has the reader assume the cattle-raiser will be
liable for any crop damage:

> Given that the cattle-raiser is liable for the damage caused, the
> additional annual cost imposed on the cattle-raiser if he increased
> his herd from, say, two to three steers is $3 and in deciding on the
> size of the herd, he will take this into account along with his other
> costs. That is, he will not increase the size of the herd unless the
> value of the additional meat produced (assuming that the cattle-
> raiser slaughters the cattle) is greater than the additional costs
> that this will entail, including the value of the additional crops
> destroyed. . . . Given that the annual cost of fencing is $9, the
> cattle-raiser who wished to have a herd with four steers or more
> would pay for fencing to be erected and maintained, assuming
> that other means of attaining the same end would not do so more
> cheaply. When the fence is erected, the marginal cost due to the
> liability for damage becomes zero, except to the extent that an
> increase in the size of the herd necessitates a stronger and
> therefore more expensive fence because more steers are liable to
> lean against it at the same time. But, of course, it may be cheaper
> for the cattle-raiser not to fence and to pay for the damaged crops,
> as in my arithmetical example, with three or fewer steers. *Id.* at
> 2-3.

> * * *

> Assume initially that the value of the crop obtained from
> cultivating a given tract of land is $12 and that the cost incurred in
> cultivating this tract of land is $10, the net gain from cultivating
> the land being $2. I assume for purposes of simplicity that the
> farmer owns the land. Now assume that the cattle-raiser starts
> operations on the neighboring property [with one steer] and that
> the value of the crops damaged is $1. In this case $11 is obtained
> by the farmer from sale on the market and $1 is obtained from the
> cattle-raiser for damage suffered and the net gain remains $2.

> Now suppose that the cattle-raiser finds it profitable to increase
> the size of his herd [to two steers], even though the amount of
> damage rises to $3; which means that the value of the additional
> meat production is greater than the additional costs, including the
> additional $2 payment for damage. But the total payment for
> damage is now $3. The net gain to the farmer from cultivating the
> land is still $2. The cattle-raiser would be better off if the farmer
> would agree not to cultivate his land for any payment less than $3.
> The farmer would be agreeable to not cultivating the land for any
> payment greater than $2. There is clearly room for a mutually
> satisfactory bargain which would lead to the abandonment of
> cultivation. *Id.* at 3-4.

Thus, under this new set of facts, Coase argues it is more
profitable to society for the meat to be produced than for the
land to be cultivated, and he shows this result will be reached
through operation of market forces. This time, the law made
what might seem intuitively to be the "right" allocation of

Here, Coase returns to the initial set of facts which does not posit an annual profit or cost of farming. Thus, for this portion of the hypothetical fact pattern, those variables are undefined.

Why would the farmer be willing to make these payments? Make sure you can follow Coase's logic here.

rights and entitlements, because the cattle-raiser was required to pay for damage his cattle caused. One final example shows how Coase argued the market would reach an efficient result even if the law made the "wrong" initial allocation of rights and entitlements:

> The farmer would suffer increased damage to his crop as the size of the herd increased. Suppose that the size of the cattle-raiser's herd is three steers (and that this is the size of the herd that would be maintained if crop damage was not taken into account). Then the farmer would be willing to pay up to $3 if the cattle-raiser would reduce his herd to two steers, up to $5 if the herd were reduced to one steer and would pay up to $6 if cattle-raising was abandoned. The cattle-raiser would therefore receive $3 from the farmer if he kept two steers instead of three. This $3 foregone is therefore part of the cost incurred in keeping the third steer. Whether the $3 is a payment which the cattle-raiser has to make if he adds the third steer to his herd (which it would be if the cattle-raiser was liable to the farmer for damage caused to the crop) or whether it is a sum of money which he would have received if he did not keep a third steer (which it would be if the cattle-raiser was not liable to the farmer for damage caused to the crop) does not affect the final result. In both cases, $3 is part of the cost of adding a third steer, to be included along with the other costs. If the increase in the value of production in cattle-raising through increasing the size of the herd from two to three is greater than the additional costs that have to be incurred (including the $3 damage to crops), the size of the herd will be increased. Otherwise, it will not. The size of the herd will be the same whether the cattle raiser is liable for damage caused to the crop or not. *Id.* at 6.

- How does Coase believe the market will reach an efficient herd size regardless of which party bears the cost?

This formulation of the Coase theorem assumes there is no cost associated with seeking to reconcile this dispute, an assumption not reflective of real-world conditions. Coase addresses this criticism as follows:

> The argument has proceeded up to this point on the assumption that there were no costs involved in carrying out market transactions. This is, of course, a very unrealistic assumption. In order to carry out a market transaction, it is necessary to discover who it is that one wishes to deal with, to inform people that one wishes to deal and on what terms, to conduct negotiations leading up to a bargain, to draw up the contract, to undertake the inspection needed to make sure that the terms of the contract are being observed, and so on. These operations are often extremely costly, sufficiently costly at any rate to prevent many transactions that would be carried out in a world in which the pricing system worked without cost. *Id.* at 7.

- What transaction costs are associated with dispute resolution?

- When will a dispute be resolved despite the transaction costs?

- Other than efficiency, what factors might a legislature consider in determining how to allocate entitlements and liabilities as between the farmer and rancher?

Problem 1: On February 7, 1967, Buyer agreed to purchase a 30-foot Revel Craft Playmate Yacht from Seller for $10,000. This price included several options to be installed after Seller received the boat from its manufacturer. Seller was to deliver the boat to Buyer at some point in April. In early March, the boat arrived in Seller's showroom, and Buyer returned to sign a security agreement, coupled with a promissory note. In early April, before the boat was delivered to Buyer, a fire on Seller's premises destroyed the boat. Neither party had insured the craft. The relevant provisions of the security agreement are as follows:

> (7) Buyer will at all times keep the Goods in first-class order and repair, excepting any loss, damage, or destruction which is fully covered by proceeds of insurance;
>
> (8) Buyer will at all times keep the Goods fully insured against loss, damage, theft, and other risks, in such amounts and companies and under such policies . . . satisfactory to the secured party, which policies shall specifically provide that loss thereunder shall be payable to the secured party as its interest may appear.

- What is the effect of clauses 7 and 8 on the allocation of risk?

Based on *Hayward v. Postma*, 31 Mich. App. 720, 188 N.W.2d 31 (1971).

Problem 2: *Multiplastics, Inc. v. Arch Industries, Inc.*, 348 A.2d 618, 166 Conn. 280 (1974), explores the relationship between breach of contract and risk of loss. Arch Industries, Inc. and Multiplastics, Inc. entered into a contract whereby Multiplastics was to manufacture 40,000 pounds of brown polystyrene plastic pellets for nineteen cents per pound. These pellets were specially manufactured for Arch. Arch agreed to accept delivery of 1,000 pounds per day after production was completed. Arch confirmed its order with a document reading, "Make and hold for release. Confirmation." Within two weeks, Multiplastics had completed manufacture and contacted Arch,

requesting release so it could ship the pellets and clear its
warehouse for other work. Arch refused to accept delivery,
citing labor difficulties and its own vacation schedule. After it
had held the pellets more than forty days, Multiplastics
repeatedly contacted Arch seeking payment and delivery
instructions. Arch promised it would issue delivery orders, but
never did so. After Multiplastics had held the pellets for more
than seventy days, a fire in its warehouse destroyed the pellets.
Multiplastics' insurance did not cover the loss, and it brought
suit, seeking to recover the contract price from Arch.

- What should the result be under 2-510?

- Had title passed under 2-401?

- Who had an insurable interest under 2-501?

Problem 3: Llewellyn Sharp bred racehorses on a farm near
Lexington, Kentucky. James Courtin was an attorney in New
Orleans who owned several horses. Courtin had expressed an
interest in acquiring a colt sired by a stallion with the name,
"Devil Diver." To this end, Courtin asked two friends to attend
the 1956 Kentucky Derby to look for such a colt. Sharp claimed
that one of these friends, acting on Courtin's behalf, negotiated
a purchase price of $6,000; Courtin claimed the friends lacked
the authority to bind him to a contract of purchase, although he
admitted his friends recommended he purchase the horse. One
or two days after the visit, Courtin and Sharp spoke by
telephone; assume, as the court did, that the contract was
formed no later than this phone call.

After the call, but before Courtin had obtained possession of the
colt, it was found dead in its paddock, having gotten its head
stuck between two boards and, presumably upon being
spooked by a fly, having jerked its head abruptly and broken its
neck.

Sharp sought to recover the purchase price from Courtin, and
Courtin defended on the ground that neither title nor risk of
loss had passed to him at the time of the colt's death.

- What would be the result under Article 2?

- What facts would be most important to the court in
  determining the rights and obligations of both parties?

Based on *Courtin v. Sharp*, 280 F.2d 345 (5th Cir. 1960).

International Perspective: Risk of Loss

Read CISG Articles 66 through 70. Article 66 provides that, once the risk of loss has passed, the buyer must pay for the goods even if they never arrive. Article 67 shows that, in the absence of other agreement, the risk of loss will pass from buyer to seller when the goods are transferred to the buyer's carrier. Article 68 deals with goods that are sold while in transit. Article 69 applies when the buyer picks up the goods from the seller or a third party, rather than receiving them through shipment. Article 70 provides that fundamental breach on the part of the seller prevents the risk of loss from shifting to the buyer as it otherwise would.

Parties often incorporate terms such as "Free On Board" ("FOB") or "Cost, Insurance, and Freight" ("CIF") that describe their obligations with regard to risk of loss and insurance. You have been introduced to INCOTERMS (an acronym for "International Commercial Terms") in an earlier marginal note. "FOB" and "CIF" are defined in that source, as follows:

> "Free on Board" [with a named port of shipment] means that the seller delivers when the goods pass the ship's rail at the named port of shipment. This means that the buyer has to bear all costs and risks of loss of or damage to the goods from that point.
>
> "Cost, Insurance and Freight" [with a named port of destination] means that the seller delivers when the goods pass the ship's rail in the port of shipment.
>
> The seller must pay the costs and freight necessary to bring the goods to the named port of destination BUT the risk of loss of or damage to the goods, as well as any additional costs due to events occurring after the time of delivery, are transferred from the seller to the buyer. However, in CIF the seller also has to procure marine insurance against the buyer's risk of loss of or damage to the goods during the carriage.
>
> Consequently, the seller contracts for insurance and pays the insurance premium. The buyer should note that, under the CIF term, the seller is required to obtain insurance only on minimum cover. Should the buyer wish to have the protection of greater cover, he would either need to agree as much expressly with the seller or to make his own extra insurance arrangements.

- How would you expect the price to differ depending on whether goods are shipped FOB or CIF?

Read CISG Article 9 (2). That INCOTERMS are incorporated into the CISG through Article 9 (2) was confirmed

---

In Chapter 4 of *International Business Transactions: A Problem-Oriented Casebook* (West 2005), Ralph Folsom, Michael Wallace Gordon, John A. Spanogle, Jr. and Peter L. Fitzgerald provide an introduction to international contracts of sale. Problem 4.2 includes a useful introduction to INCOTERMS and their use. To learn more about INCOTERMS, see www.iccwbo.org/ index_incoterms.asp.

In support of this portion of its holding, the court cited the *St. Paul* decision referenced in the international materials in Part A.

in *BP Oil International, Ltd. v. Empresa Estatal Petroleos de Ecuador*, 332 F.3d 333 (5th Cir. 2003). As the court noted, "[e]ven if the use of INCOTERMS is not global, the fact that they are well known in international trade means that they are incorporated through Article 9 (2)."

Problem: Chicago Prime Packers, Inc. contracted with Northam Food Trading Company to sell 40,500 pounds (or 1,350 boxes) of pork ribs at a purchase price of $178,200.00. Chicago Prime was never in possession of the ribs, but arranged for them to be shipped from B&B Pullman Cold Storage, where its meat processor Brookfield Farms had stored the ribs. Brown Brothers Trucking Company, acting as the agent for Northam, picked up the ribs from B&B and delivered the ribs directly to Northam's customer Beacon Premium Meats. Thus, neither of the contracting parties was ever in physical possession of the ribs. Beacon subsequently complained to Northam that many of the ribs were, as noted by a United States Department of Agriculture Inspector, "putrid, green, [and] slimy." The USDA ordered that the entire shipment of ribs be condemned. Northam refused to pay for the ribs, and Chicago Prime sued for payment.

- When did the risk of loss pass to Northam?

Based on *Chicago Prime Packers, Inc. v. Northam Food Trading Co.*, 408 F.3d 894 (7th Cir. 2005).

C. Warranties of Title

The Article 2A equivalent is 2A-211. Note that the proposed revision to 2-312 switches the numbering of subparts (2) and (3). When you reach Chapter 4's discussion of warranties of quality, note the differences in how the two kinds of warranties are created and disclaimed.

This section discusses warranties of title under Article 2 and how they can be disclaimed. The seller owes the buyer an implied warranty of title, in addition to the contract-based duty to deliver conforming goods.

Read 2-312, both in its current version and as amended. This statute sets forth the Article 2 warranty of title.

- What language or circumstances would satisfy part (2)?

- How does part (3) reflect a balancing of responsibility?

- What does the new language in revised 2-312 (1) (a) add to the meaning and effect of the subsection?

The following case introduces the warranty of title, describing not only why the warranty exists, but also how it can be disclaimed.

Sunseri v. RKO-Stanley Warner Theatres, Inc.,
248 Pa. Super. 111, 374 A.2d 1342,
22 U.C.C. Rep. Serv. 41 (1977).

[RKO-Stanley Warner Theatres, Inc.] is the owner of the State Theatre building in Johnstown, Pennsylvania. Prior to July 1968, Francis Zatalava operated a bowling alley and billiard parlor in the basement of this building. Zatalava rented space from RKO and owned the recreational equipment himself, subject to a security interest in Trenton Trust Company. In July of 1968, the City of Johnstown closed Zatalava's business for failure to pay city taxes. Zatalava also owed back rent to RKO, which subsequently obtained an assignment of Trenton Trust's interest in Zatalava's equipment so that it could reach these assets.

In July of 1969, RKO sold the equipment to Samuel Pagano and . . . Michael Sunseri, who also leased the basement and ran the recreation center as partners. . . . Sunseri eventually bought out Pagano's interest in the business and became its sole owner. In April of 1971, Zatalava brought a replevin action against appellee and RKO to regain title to the equipment. In a non-jury proceeding, the court found that Zatalava had the paramount claim of ownership. [Sunseri] then instituted the action involved herein, claiming that RKO breached its warranty of title. . . .

The document which evidences the transaction between Pagano and Sunseri, as partners, and RKO is entitled "Bill of Sale" and provides, in pertinent part, as follows:

> (Seller) . . . does hereby sell, assign, convey, transfer, and deliver to Buyer any right, title, and interest Seller may have in the following goods and chattels. . . .
>
> It is expressly understood and agreed that the Seller shall in nowise be deemed or held to be obligated, liable, or accountable upon or under guaranties (sic) or warranties, in any manner or form including, but not limited to, the implied warranties of title, merchantability, fitness for use, or of quality.

The lower court found that, as a matter of law, the above-quoted language was insufficient to disclaim the warranty of title. We agree.

* * *

In the instant case, the bill of sale did not disclaim warranty of title in the "specific" language required by UCC 2-312. The provision for sale of "any right, title, and interest" is clearly not a positive warning or exclusion in regard to the status of title, and would be unlikely to offend or even catch the eye of an unsophisticated buyer. . . . The second relevant provision in the sale document, stating that "Seller shall in

Note the target of the intended protection.

nowise be deemed or held to be obligated, liable or accountable upon or under any guaranties (sic) or warranties" is similarly ineffective. It is couched in negative terminology, expressing what the seller will not be liable for rather than what the buyer is or is not receiving. The inadequacy of such a caveat is best illustrated by juxtaposing it with title disclaimer provisions suggested by authorities in the subject area. For example, 18 Am. Jur. Legal Forms 2d 253:825 (1974), provides: "Seller makes no warranty as to the title to the goods, and buyer assumes all risks of nonownership of the goods by seller." Another illustration is contained in Purdon's Pa. Forms, 12A P.S. 2-312, Form 2 (1970), which recommends the following language: "The seller does not warrant that he has any right to convey the title to the goods." Appellant's attempt to disclaim the warranty of title in its transaction with appellee was ineffective in that it failed to comply with the requirement, under the Uniform Commercial Code, that such a disclaimer be made in "specific language." The court below was thus not in error in deciding this issue as a matter of law and instructing the jury in conformance with its decision.

* * *

Appellant's [next] allegation is that the lower court erred in refusing to charge the jury that, as a matter of law, the circumstances surrounding the sale gave the buyer reason to know that no warranty of title was made. Appellant advanced two primary points in support of this claim: (1) Appellee was aware that the doors to the recreation center had been padlocked for an indefinite period of time subsequent to its operation by Zatalava and prior to appellee's purchase of the equipment; and (2) appellee knew that he had obtained possession and use of equipment that had a replacement value of approximately $50,000 at a cost of only $5,000. Appellant raised these matters at trial.

In his charge to the jury, the trial judge read section 2-312 and mentioned the substantial difference between the asserted value of the goods and the price paid by appellee. He then stated, "That alone is a fact you should consider, that there were troubles with title and that this plaintiff knew there were troubles with the title." This constituted the trial court's only mention of the point. Appellant did not, however, raise this issue in its post-verdict motions. It did not allege that the trial court erred in its charge on this point, or that the court charged inadequately or failed to charge thereon. This issue is thus not preserved for our review.

* * *

The judgment of the lower court is affirmed.

> The text of Comment 5 has been moved to Comment 6 in Revised Article 2.

- Would the outcome of the case have been different if this issue had been preserved for appeal? What is your instinct after reading 2-312, Comment 5?

- How should the contract language be changed to create an effective disclaimer?

Note: *Jefferson v. Jones*, 286 Md. 544, 408 A.2d 1036, 27 U.C.C. Rep. Serv. 1174 (1979), answers the question of whether a purchaser can recover from a seller when a third party challenges the purchaser's title in a way that requires the purchaser to expend money to defend his title, but the third-party claim ultimately fails.

Thomas N. Jefferson agreed to purchase a Honda motorcycle from Lawrence V. Jones in July 1975. Jefferson received possession of the motorcycle immediately, and Jones transferred the title certificate later, when the purchase price was fully paid. About two years later, Jefferson was asked by the police to produce proof of his ownership of the motorcycle, for reasons that are not clear. Jefferson produced the title certificate but, when the police found that the VIN in the certificate differed from that embossed on the frame of the cycle, the police seized the cycle. Jefferson proved he was the rightful owner of the motorcycle and sued Jones for breach of the warranty of title, seeking to recover the legal expenses he had incurred in retrieving the cycle. The court held in favor of Jefferson, noting as follows:

> Our holding here, that proof of a superior title is not necessary, does not mean . . . that all claims, no matter how unfounded, which may be made against the buyer's title should result in a breach of the warranty. "Good title" is usually taken to mean that the title which the seller gives to the buyer is 'free from reasonable doubt, that is, not only a valid title in fact, but (also) one that can again be sold to a reasonable purchaser or mortgaged to a person of reasonable prudence. As such, there is some point at which a third party's claim against the goods becomes so attenuated that we should not regard it as an interference against which the seller has warranted. All that a purchaser should expect from a seller of property is that he be protected from colorable claims against his title and not from all claims. Spurious title claims can be made by anyone at any time. *Id.* at 551.

> ***

> When we examine the facts of the case now before us, in light of the legal standard just mentioned, we conclude that, as a matter of law, there exists a warranty of title that has been breached here. An undisputed aspect of possessing good title is that a purchaser be "enable(d) . . . to hold the (property) in peace and, if he wishes to sell it, to be reasonably certain that no flaw will appear to disturb its market value." *New Freedom Corp. v. Brown*, 260 Md. 383, 389, 272 A.2d 401, 404 (1971). Whenever the title to personal property is evidenced by a document which is an aid to proving ownership, as is true in the case of motor vehicles, any substantial defect in that document necessarily creates a reasonable doubt as to that ownership. . . . In other words, a breach of the warranty of title occurs whenever a seller of a motor vehicle fails to provide his purchaser with adequate proof of ownership because of the

What would be an example of a spurious title claim?

reasonable doubts which faulty documentation raise as to the
validity of the buyer's title. *Jefferson* at 553-554.

- What does this case add to your understanding of the
   relationship between title and the title certificate?

Problem: *Menzel v. List*, 24 N.Y.2d. 91, 246 N.E.2d 742, 6
U.C.C. Rep. Serv. 330 (1969), contains several layers of parties
and presents questions as to the relevant measure of damages.
The following facts are excerpted from the court's opinion:

> In 1932, Mrs. Erna Menzel and her husband purchased a painting
> by Marc Chagall at an auction in Brussels, Belgium, for 3,800
> Belgian francs (then equivalent to about $150). When the
> Germans invaded Belgium in 1940, the Menzels fled and left their
> possessions, including the Chagall painting, in their apartment.
> They returned six years later and found that the painting had
> been removed by the German authorities and that a receipt for the
> painting had been left. The location of the painting between the
> time of its removal by the Germans in 1941 and 1955 is unknown.
> In 1955, Klaus Perls and his wife, the proprietors of a New York
> art gallery, purchased the Chagall from a Parisian art gallery for
> $2,800. The Perls knew nothing of the painting's previous history
> and made no inquiry concerning it, being content to rely on the
> reputability of the Paris gallery as to authenticity and title. In
> October 1955, the Perls sold the painting to Albert List for $4,000.
> However, in 1962, Mrs. Menzel noticed a reproduction of the
> Chagall in an art book accompanied by a statement that the
> painting was in Albert List's possession. She thereupon demanded
> the painting from him, but he refused to surrender it to her.
>
> Mrs. Menzel then instituted a replevin action against Mr. List and
> he, in turn, impleaded the Perls, alleging in his third-party
> complaint that they were liable to him for breach of an implied
> warranty of title. *Id.* at 93-94.

- Who should prevail?

The following excerpt describes the parties' arguments as to
damages. The value of the painting at the time of trial was
$22,500:

> The Perls contend that the only loss directly and naturally
> resulting, in the ordinary course of events, from their breach was
> List's loss of the purchase price. List, however, contends that that
> loss is the present market value of the painting, the value which
> he would have been able to obtain if the Perls had conveyed good
> title. *Id.* at 97.

- What is an appropriate measure of damages to
   compensate List if he is not permitted to keep the
   painting?

- Are you convinced by the following argument on behalf of List?

Clearly, List can only be put in the position he would have occupied if the contract had been kept by the Perls if he recovers the value of the painting at the time when, by the judgment in the main action, he was required to surrender the painting to Mrs. Menzel or pay her the present value of the painting. Had the warranty been fulfilled, i.e., had title been as warranted by the Perls, List would still have possession of a painting currently worth $22,500 and he could have realized that price at an auction or private sale. If List recovers only the purchase price plus interest, the effect is to put him in the same position he would have occupied if the sale had never been made. Manifestly, an injured buyer is not compensated when he recovers only so much as placed him in status quo ante since such a recovery implicitly denies that he had suffered any damage. . . . This measure of damages reflects what the buyer has actually lost and it awards to him only the loss which has directly and naturally resulted, in the ordinary course of events, from the seller's breach of warranty. *Id.* at 97-98.

> What is meant by the statement, "Such a recovery implicitly denies that he had suffered any damage"?

- What about the following argument on behalf of the Perls?

An objection raised by the Perls to this measure of damages is that it exposes the innocent seller to potentially ruinous liability where the article sold has substantially appreciated in value. . . . Mr. Perls [also] testified that to question a reputable dealer as to his title would be an "insult." *Id.* at 98.

International Perspective: Warranties of Title

Read Articles 41 through 43. Taken together, these provisions describe the CISG warranty of title, even though the CISG includes neither "warranty" nor "title" in the text of these Articles. Article 41 includes general provisions, while Article 42 is specifically applicable to industrial or intellectual property and addresses claims that a copyright, trademark, or patent has been infringed. Note that Article 42 (2) contains a shifting of responsibility that can be compared with 2-312 (2). Article 43 includes a notice requirement analogous to 2-607.

> For a comprehensive treatment of this subject, see Christian Rauda & Guillaume Etier, *Warranty for Intellectual Property Rights in the International Sale of Goods*, 4 Vindobona J. Intl. Comm. L. & Arb. 30 (2000).

Eximin S.A. v. Textile and Footwear Italstyle Ferarri Inc., No. 3912/90, decided on August 22, 1993 by the Supreme Court of Israel, provides an application of Article 42 (2) (a), under which the seller will be released from liability if the "buyer knew or could not have been unaware" that the transaction in question impinged upon the rights of a third party. In that case, the court considered a contract between an Israeli manufacturer

and a Belgian buyer that ordered "jeans boots" bearing a
symbol which was a trademark of Levi's. When the goods were
imported into the United States, U.S. Customs authorities
seized the boots because the symbol constituted a breach of the
Levi's trademark. Later, the parties reached a compromise:
the symbol was removed from the boots, which were then sold
on the United States market, albeit at a greatly reduced price.

When the Belgian buyer sued the Israeli manufacturer, the
court applied CISG Article 42 by analogy, since the contract
was actually governed by the 1964 Hague Sales Convention,
which preceded the CISG. Although the court found the buyer
"could not have been unaware" that the goods would impinge
upon the Levi's trademark, the court refused to place the loss
wholly on the buyer, but instead allocated the loss in equal
shares between the buyer and seller, based upon the court's
finding that both parties had acted in bad faith.

> The application of
> the concept of good
> faith under the
> CISG is further
> explored in Chapter
> 5, Part A.

- Is the court's decision consistent with Article 42?

- What are the risks and benefits of the court's decision
  to allocate the loss, rather than the buyer bearing the
  entire loss?

Chapter Conclusion: This chapter introduced the concept of
title, its relationship with the concepts of insurable interest and
risk of loss, and discussed warranties of title and how they can
be disclaimed. Before leaving this material, make sure you are
comfortable with each of these main concepts.

Chapter 4:
Warranties of Quality

A. Express Warranties

This section addresses express warranties created by affirmation, description, and sample.

Read 2-313, both in its current form and as revised. Also read proposed 2-313A and 2-313B.

> The Article 2A equivalent is 2A-210. Comment 1 to revised 2-313 and proposed 2-313A and 2-313B may assist you in answering this question.

- What changes to 2-313 have been proposed?

2-313 shows that neither intention nor any "magic words" are required to create a warranty. At common law, by contrast, no warranty was created unless the seller used specific words like "promise" or "affirm" in describing the goods. In the absence of specific words of warranty, the fallback position at common law was *caveat emptor*, or "buyer beware," which required the purchaser to make his or her own assessment of the goods being sold.

2-313 has two parts: first, some language or action must create the warranty. This requirement can be met by "any affirmation of fact or promise," "any description of the goods," or "any sample or warranty." Second, the language or action creating the warranty must become "part of the basis of the bargain." **Read Comment 3** and note the presumption that the warranty was part of the basis of the bargain, unless the seller can show otherwise.

> This is Comment 5 in Revised Article 2.

The case law shows how the seller can prove an express warranty was not part of the basis of the bargain. In *Stang v. Hertz Corp.*, 83 N.M. 217, 490 P.2d 475, 9 U.C.C. Rep. Serv. 794 (N.M. App. 1971), Sister Mary Assuanta Stang, as personal representative of the estate of another nun, attempted to recover damages on the basis of an express warranty contained in the rental agreement Hertz provided to a group of nuns. The agreement included a statement that "the vehicle was in good mechanical condition." The lawsuit also mentioned an alleged statement by a Hertz representative that "you have got good tires." When a tire blew out, the vehicle crashed. The accident killed the decedent, who was a passenger in the vehicle.

> Note that, since this transaction involved a lease rather than a sale of goods, this suit would now arise under the similar provisions of 2A-210, but was brought under 2-313 because Article 2A was not enacted until 1987.

- If the Hertz representative's statement had been made, and the rental agreement provided, before the car was rented, would they have been express warranties or just "puffing"?

This is Comment 9
in Revised Article 2.

Read Comment 7. Because the rental agreement was
provided, and the Hertz representative's statement was made,
after the vehicle had already been rented, and no evidence
suggested the nuns relied on the agreement or statement in
choosing to rent the vehicle, the court found no express
warranty.

- Is this result in accord with 2-313?

- What facts would have proven the nuns relied on the
  agreement and statement in choosing to rent the
  vehicle?

Read Comment 4. The language "the whole purpose of the
law of warranty is to determine what it is that the seller has in
essence agreed to sell" can become important when a seller
delivers a good – a suitcase, for example – of such shoddy
workmanship that it cannot keep garments clean and dry
during ordinary travel. In such a case, Comment 4 suggests
the seller may not be protected by a simple blanket disclaimer
of the kind presented in Part C of this chapter. Instead, if the
parties wish to agree to a lesser standard of quality than would
normally meet the most minimal standards of what it means
for something to be a suitcase, they must do so specifically.

Problem: J.J. Grullemans & Sons sued to recover the
purchase price of flower bulbs it had sold to Dutch Mill
Gardens. Dutch Mill Gardens declined to pay for the bulbs,
claiming a total failure of consideration and providing evidence
that the bulbs were "soft" and therefore would not sprout or
flower. The seller's order form used for the transaction
included the following language: "No warranty is given for the
results of planting, forcing, or flowering of any bulbs and roots."
The court allowed the seller to recover the full contract price.

- Can you explain the court's decision?

Based on *Dutch Mill Gardens v. J.J. Grullemans & Sons,* 238
S.W.2d 232 (Tex. Civ. App. 1951).

The following case provides guidance in determining when an
express warranty has been made, especially when
differentiating between a warranty and a statement of opinion.
The case also explains the requirement that the warranty be
"part of the basis of the bargain" and describes the burden of
proof in a warranty case.

Keith v. Buchanan,
173 Cal. App. 3d 13, 220 Cal. Rptr. 392,
42 U.C.C. Rep. Serv. 386 (1985).

Ochoa, J.

Plaintiff Brian Keith purchased a sailboat from defendants in November 1978 for a total purchase price of $75,610. Even though plaintiff belonged to the Waikiki Yacht Club, had attended a sailing school, had joined the Coast Guard Auxiliary, and had sailed on many yachts in order to ascertain his preferences, he had not previously owned a yacht. He attended a boat show in Long Beach[, California] during October 1978 and looked at a number of boats, speaking to sales representatives and obtaining advertising literature. In the literature, the sailboat which is the subject of this action, called an "Island Trader 41," was described as a seaworthy vessel. In one sales brochure, this vessel is described as "a picture of sure-footed seaworthiness." In another, it is called "a carefully well-equipped, and very seaworthy live-aboard vessel." Plaintiff testified he relied on representations in the sales brochures in regard to the purchase. Plaintiff and a sales representative also discussed plaintiff's desire for a boat which was ocean-going and would cruise long distances.

> With the motto, "America's Volunteer Lifesavers," the Coast Guard Auxiliary was established in 1939.

Plaintiff asked his friend, Buddy Ebsen, who was involved in a boat-building enterprise, to inspect the boat. Mr. Ebsen and one of his associates, both of whom had extensive experience with sailboats, observed the boat and advised plaintiff that the vessel would suit his stated needs. A deposit was paid on the boat, a purchase contract was entered into, and optional accessories for the boat were ordered. After delivery of the vessel, a dispute arose in regard to its seaworthiness.

Plaintiff filed the instant lawsuit alleging causes of action in breach of express warranty and breach of implied warranty. The trial court granted defendants' . . . motion for judgment at the close of plaintiff's case. . . .

* * *

In deciding whether a statement made by a seller constitutes an express warranty . . . , the court must deal with three fundamental issues. First, the court must determine whether the seller's statement constitutes an "affirmation of fact or promise" or "description of the goods" under California Uniform Commercial Code section 2313, subdivision (1) (a) or (b), or whether it is rather "merely the seller's opinion or commendation of the goods" under section 2313, subdivision (2). Second, assuming the court finds the language used susceptible to creation of a warranty, it must then be determined whether the statement was "part of the basis of the bargain." Third, the court must determine whether the warranty was breached.

A warranty relates to the title, character, quality, identity, or condition of the goods. The purpose of the law of warranty is to determine what it is that the seller has in essence agreed to sell. "Express warranties are chisels in the hands of buyers and sellers. With these tools, the parties to a sale sculpt a monument representing the goods. Having selected a stone, the buyer and seller may leave it almost bare, allowing considerable play in the qualities that fit its contours. Or the parties may chisel away inexactitudes until a well-defined shape emerges. The seller is bound to deliver, and the buyer to accept, goods that match the sculpted form." *Special Project: Article Two Warranties in Commercial Transactions, Express Warranties – Section 2-313* (1978-79) 64 Cornell L. Rev. 30.

. . . Recent decisions have evidenced a trend toward narrowing the scope of representations which are considered opinion, sometimes referred to as "puffing" or "sales talk," resulting in an expansion of the liability that flows from broad statements of manufacturers or retailers as to the quality of their products. Courts have liberally construed affirmations of quality made by sellers in favor of injured consumers. . . .

Courts in other states have struggled in efforts to create a formula for distinguishing between affirmations of fact, promises, or descriptions of goods on the one hand, and value, opinion, or commendation statements on the other. The code comment indicates that the basic question is: "What statements of the seller have in the circumstances and in objective judgment become part of the basis of the bargain?" The commentators indicated that the language of subsection (2) of the code section was included because "common experience discloses that some statements or predictions cannot fairly be viewed as entering into the bargain."

> This language is taken from UCC 2-313 Comment 8, which is Comment 10 in Revised Article 2.

Statements made by a seller during the course of negotiation over a contract are presumptively affirmations of fact unless it can be demonstrated that the buyer could only have reasonably considered the statement as a statement of the seller's opinion. Commentators have noted several factors which tend to indicate an opinion statement. These are (1) a lack of specificity in the statement made, (2) a statement that is made in an equivocal manner, or (3) a statement which reveals that the goods are experimental in nature.

> Why are statements revealing that the goods are experimental not express warranties?

It is clear that statements made by a manufacturer or retailer in an advertising brochure which is disseminated to the consuming public in order to induce sales can create express warranties. In the instant case, the vessel purchased was described in sales brochures as "a picture of sure-footed seaworthiness" and "a carefully well-equipped and very seaworthy vessel." The seller's representative was aware that appellant was looking for a vessel sufficient for long-distance ocean-going cruises. The statements in the brochure are specific and unequivocal in asserting that the vessel is seaworthy. Nothing in the negotiation indicates that the vessel is experimental in nature. In fact, one sales brochure assures prospective buyers that production of the vessel was commenced "after years of careful testing." The representations regarding seaworthiness made in sales brochures regarding the Island Trader 41 were affirmations of fact relating to the quality or condition of the vessel.

Under former provisions of law, a purchaser was required to prove that he or she acted in reliance upon representations made by the seller. California Uniform Commercial Code section 2313 indicates only that the seller's statements must become "part of the basis of the bargain." According to official comment 3 to this Uniform Commercial Code provision, "no particular reliance . . . need be shown in order to weave [the seller's affirmations of fact] into the fabric of the agreement. Rather, any fact which is to take such affirmations, once made, out of the agreement requires clear affirmative proof."

> Students often abbreviate "part of the basis of the bargain" to "the basis of the bargain." This paragraph illustrates the problem with doing so.

* * *

The shift in language clearly changes the degree to which it must be shown that the seller's representation affected the buyer's decision to enter into the agreement. A buyer need not show that he would not have entered into the agreement absent the warranty or even that it was a dominant factor inducing the agreement. . . .

* * *

. . . The buyer's actual knowledge of the true condition of the goods prior to the making of the contract may make it plain that the seller's statement was not relied upon as one of the inducements for the purchase, but the burden is on the seller to demonstrate such knowledge on the part of the buyer. Where the buyer inspects the goods before purchase, he may be deemed to have waived the seller's express warranties. But, an examination or inspection by the buyer of the goods does not necessarily discharge the seller from an express warranty if the defect was not actually discovered and waived.

Appellant's inspection of the boat by his own experts does not constitute a waiver of the express warranty of seaworthiness. Prior to the making of the contract, appellant had experienced boat builders observe the boat, but there was no testing of the vessel in the water. Such a warranty (seaworthiness) necessarily relates to the time when the vessel has been put to sea and has been shown to be reasonably fit and adequate in materials, construction, and equipment for its intended purposes.

In this case, appellant was aware of the representations regarding seaworthiness by the seller prior to contracting. He also had expressed to the seller's representative his desire for a long-distance ocean-going vessel. Although he had other experts inspect the vessel, the inspection was limited and would not have indicated whether or not the vessel was seaworthy. It is clear that the seller has not overcome the presumption that the representations regarding seaworthiness were part of the basis of this bargain.

[Discussion regarding the implied warranty of fitness for a particular purpose has been omitted.]

The trial court's judgment that no express warranty existed in this matter is reversed. . . . Since considerable contradictory evidence was elicited at trial relating to the asserted breach of warranty of seaworthiness of the subject vessel, and since the trial court made no finding in regard to that issue, the matter is remanded to the trial court for further proceedings consistent with this opinion.

- How could the statements in the sales brochure be altered to constitute "mere puffing"?

- **Read 2-316 and Comment 8.** Will the buyer's examination of goods relieve the seller of liability for an express warranty under a theory of waiver?

- How does the question of waiver relate to the issue of whether the express warranty is "part of the basis of the bargain"?

In Revised Article 2, this is Comment 7.

Note 1: Read 2-313 Comment 5. As this Comment shows, trade usage can affect whether an express warranty has been created. In *Zappanti v. Berge Service Center.*, 26 Ariz. App. 398, 19 U.C.C. Serv. 96 (1976), the court considered whether the fact that a sales agreement described a certain vehicle as a "1969 Volkswagen Dunebuggy" meant that all of the component parts of the vehicle were warranted to be from the 1969 model year. As the evidence showed, the vehicle included parts from earlier years. In finding no express warranty had been created as to the model year of the parts, the court considered the unusual nature of the vehicle, which was not a conventional, mass-produced Volkswagen automobile, but instead a reconstructed vehicle. Such vehicles, the court held, had no manufacturer-assigned model year. In addition, the court noted that the Department of Motor Vehicles, as a matter of course, used the year of reconstruction as the "year" of the vehicle for purposes of title issuance, without regard to the model year of any of the vehicle's component parts. In the absence of any evidence of contrary trade usage, the court held the buyer had no grounds for recovery under a theory of express warranty.

- For an ordinary vehicle, is a model year a statement of express warranty? Why or why not?

Note 2: As you will notice if you read the unexcerpted text of many cases in this chapter, plaintiffs often raise a warranty claim under the UCC together with a negligence or strict-liability claim under tort law. *Seely v. White Motor Co.*, 63 Cal. 2d 9, 403 P.2d 145, 45 Cal. Rptr. 17, 2 U.C.C. Rep. Serv. 915 (1965), describes the relationship between the two kinds of claims. That case involved a truck, purchased for heavy-duty hauling, that "bounced violently, an action known as galloping," for some eleven months, despite the manufacturer's attempted repairs on numerous occasions. One day, the brakes also failed, and the truck overturned. The purchaser was not injured, but sued to recover the money spent in repairing the truck, as well as damages related to the disruption that the

repeated problems had caused in his business. In considering
the purchaser's warranty claim, the court held as follows:

> The law of sales has been carefully articulated to govern the
> economic relations between suppliers and consumers of goods.
> The history of the doctrine of strict liability in tort indicates that it
> was designed, not to undermine the warranty provisions of the
> Sales Act or of the Uniform Commercial Code but, rather, to
> govern the distinct problem of physical injuries.

The reference here is
to the Uniform Sales
Act that pre-dated
the UCC.

> An important early step in the development of the law of products
> liability was the recognition of a manufacturer's liability in
> negligence to an ultimate consumer without privity of contract.
> About the same time, the courts began to hold manufacturers
> liable without negligence for personal injuries. Over a score of
> theories were developed to support liability, and the one that was
> generally accepted was borrowed from the law of sales warranty.
> ... Final recognition that "(t)he remedies of injured consumers
> ought not to be made to depend upon the intricacies of the law of
> sales" caused this court to abandon the fiction of warranty in favor
> of strict liability in tort. *Ketterer v. Armour & Co.*, 200 F. 322, 323
> (S.D.N.Y. 1912).

> * * *

> The distinction that the law has drawn between tort recovery for
> physical injuries and warranty recovery for economic loss is not
> arbitrary and does not rest on the "luck" of one plaintiff in having
> an accident causing physical injury. The distinction rests, rather,
> on an understanding of the nature of the responsibility a
> manufacturer must undertake in distributing his products. He
> can appropriately be held liable for physical injuries caused by
> defects by requiring his goods to match a standard of safety
> defined in terms of conditions that create unreasonable risks of
> harm. He cannot be held for the level of performance of his
> products in the consumer's business unless he agrees that the
> product was designed to meet the consumer's demands.   A
> consumer should not be charged at the will of the manufacturer
> with bearing the risk of physical injury when he buys a product on
> the market. He can, however, be fairly charged with the risk that
> the product will not match his economic expectations unless the
> manufacturer agrees that it will. Even in actions for negligence, a
> manufacturer's liability is limited to damages for physical injuries,
> and there is no recovery for economic loss alone. *Id.* at 15-18.

Many students
study the "economic
loss doctrine" in a
first-year torts class.

- After reading this excerpt, what guidance would you
   give to a client in choosing whether to bring suit under
   a theory of tort recovery or warranty liability?

- What are the differing purposes of contract law and
   tort law?

Problem 1: A clear glass jar of mixed nuts bore the following label:

> ```
> PLANTERS™
> Dry Roasted
> MIXED NUTS
> No oils or sugar used in processing.
> ```

- Would this language support an express-warranty suit by a plaintiff who was injured when he bit into an unshelled filbert contained in a handful of nuts he drew from the jar and ate?

Based on *Coffer v. Standard Brands, Inc.*, 30 N.C. App. 134, 226 S.E.2d 534, 20 U.C.C. Rep. Serv. 321 (1976).

Problem 2: Gwendolyn Adams visited the showroom of Peter Tramontin Motor Sales with her mother and uncle. A salesman showed her a new 1955 Pontiac automobile. The salesman stated, "This car is perfect for you; you couldn't buy a better car." In addition, the salesman stated that there would be a 90-day guarantee "in case anything went wrong."

The following paragraph describes Adams' experience with the car:

> [S]oon after receiving the car, she noticed the interior was dirty and she had trouble with the speedometer cable; three days later, she noticed a rumble in the rear of the car; two or three weeks after delivery, she found black smoke coming from the exhaust, the car stalled, and the motor missed; the door locks and tumblers were defective and had to be replaced; the dome light did not work, and the dashboard shook. She complained to defendant's service manager on each occasion, and he asked her to bring the car back for repair. She did so seven or eight times. Asked whether defendant had ever refused to take care of repairs, she replied, "They never said they weren't liable."

- Have any express warranties been created?

- Can the car dealership show the salesman's statements could not have been part of the basis of the bargain, since Ms. Adams brought relatives along when she selected the vehicle?

- If any express warranty has been made, has it been breached? Do you need any additional facts to answer this question?

Based on *Adams v. Peter Tramontin Motor Sales, Inc.*, 42 N.J. Super. 313, 317, 126 A.2d 358, 359 (1956).

Problem 3: Which of the following are statements of express warranty that a 1991 Lincoln automobile, sold as a used vehicle in 2003, would be without defects?

- The seller indicated the car was previously owned by a "little old lady" in Iowa.

- A document titled "Buyer's Guide," filled out by the seller, showed a checked "no" in the columns pertaining to the car's engine. By checking this box, the language of the form stated, the seller indicated the engine showed no sign of excessive oil consumption, exhibited no unusual noises, had no signs of a cracked block or head or blown head gasket, and did not miss or backfire.

- The seller indicated the car had been in his possession for sale for almost three years and stated he had occasionally used the car personally without problems.

- The seller told the buyer, who was a minor, that the car was a good vehicle, would last him through high school, was a reliable car, was in great condition, and the engine was rebuilt.

- The seller stated to the buyer, "If you can find anything wrong with the car, bring it back."

Based on *Carlson v. Gleichsner*, 694 N.W.2d 510 (Wis. App. 2005) (unpublished opinion).

=====

International Perspective: Warranties

Read CISG Article 35. As this Article shows, the CISG does not recognize a cause of action for breach of warranty in the same way that the UCC does. Instead, those factors that give rise to a warranty cause of action under the UCC become part of the factors to be considered in determining whether the seller has satisfied its duty to deliver conforming goods under the CISG. Although the terminology differs, it is possible to accomplish similar results under both bodies of law. In *Schmitz-Werke GMBH & Co. v. Rockland Industries, Inc.*, 37 Fed. Appx. 687 (4th Cir. 2002), in a dispute involving the quality of drapery-lining fabric, the court held that, "under

either the CISG or [the UCC], [the buyer] may prevail on a
claim that the fabric was unfit for the purpose for which it was
expressly warranted (transfer printing) by showing that when
the fabric was properly used for the purpose [the seller]
Rockland warranted, the results were shoddy." Another
example of the same phenomenon is *Chicago Prime Packers,
Inc. v. Northam Food Trading Co.*, 408 F.3d 894 (7th Cir.
2005). In this case, which was presented in Chapter 3, Part B,
the court cited sources stating that "the CISG's approach
'produces results which are comparable to the "warranty"
structure of the UCC.'"

- Based on what you have read about Article 35, what
  advice would you give to a purchaser of goods seeking
  to ensure "2-313-like" protection under the CISG?

B. Implied Warranties

This section includes the implied warranties of merchantability
and fitness for a particular purpose, both of which are
automatically present under certain circumstances, unless
disclaimed.

Frederickson v. Hackney, 159 Minn. 234, 198 N.W. 806 (1924),
involved a bull calf sold for the purpose of breeding and later
determined to be sterile. The animal cost $500, and the court
noted that "[t]he ancestry of the calf was such as to justify this
price, the assumption of both parties being . . . that he would be
a sure calf-getter when he obtained his maturity." "Plaintiff
was advised by [D]efendant to 'buy the bull and keep him' for
breeding purposes; that he would be a wonderful asset and
would put [Plaintiff] 'on the map.'" The plaintiff further
alleged, "He told me further of his blood lines, and what a great
record his relatives had made; . . . that his father was the
greatest living dairy bull; [and] that, if I would keep him, . . . he
would be a help to build up my breed." After finding as an
initial matter that the statements were just puffing, rather
than creating any express warranty, the court also held no
implied warranties had been created regarding the
reproductive capacities of the bull. In explaining its holding,
the court stated as follows:

> There can be no more appropriate occasion for the adoption of the
> rule of "caveat emptor" than the sale of an immature animal, the
> principal value of which depends upon its later being a breeder.
> *Id.* at 235.

This was a pre-UCC case. Now that you have read Part A of this chapter, would the court's ruling as to express warranty be the same under current law?

The court also described the relationship between express and implied warranties, as follows:

> Implied warranties ordinarily speak concerning the present and give assurance only as to qualities existing at the time being. They do not ordinarily speak of the future, nor of qualities later to be developed. That is the conventional field for express rather than implied warranty. *Id.* at 236.

After you have read the *Dickerson* case that follows, return to this excerpt and make sure you know whether this distinction remains valid today.

Implied Warranty of Merchantability

Read 2-314. The implied warranty of merchantability is the only warranty most consumers will ever need, as it covers every "ordinary use" of goods. Whether goods are fit for their ordinary purpose is a fact-specific inquiry. The implied warranty of fitness for a particular purpose comes into play only when goods are used for a specialized purpose.

The Article 2A equivalent is 2A-212.

Read 2-314, Comment 6. 2-314 (2) sets minimum standards for merchantability, but is not exhaustive. More rigorous standards, as part (3) shows, may be created by course of dealing or trade usage. As the name suggests, the implied warranty of merchantability applies only when goods are sold by a merchant. When the warranty applies, it will attach to a sale of goods automatically, unless disclaimed as directed by 2-316.

This is Comment 8 in Revised Article 2.

Disclaimers are discussed in Part C of this chapter.

- Compare the definitions of "merchant" in 2-314 (1) and 2-104 (1). Which standard is easier to satisfy?

The following case discusses the relationship between express and implied warranties and presents the implied warranty of merchantability as it relates to used goods. The case provides a working definition of the term "merchantable" and explains when a good's merchantability is assessed for purposes of the implied warranty.

Dickerson v. Mountain View Equipment Co.,
109 Idaho 711, 710 P.2d 621, 42 U.C.C. Rep. Serv. 114 (1985).

Walters, Chief Judge.

The events which led to this action are undisputed. In the spring of 1982, [Dan] Dickerson advised Mountain View [Equipment Company] that he needed to purchase a tractor for the spring planting season, which was from April 1 to May 15. He was shown two tractors with their engines, transmissions, and axles completely disassembled in the company's shop. The company assured Dickerson the tractors would be totally rebuilt. Dickerson paid $13,850 for one of the rebuilt tractors. He received a trade-in credit of $6,725 on his old tractor and paid the balance of $7,125. When he purchased the tractor, Dickerson received

a "Used Equipment Warranty." This warranty indicated the tractor
was sold under a "Mountain View Warranty." The Mountain View
Warranty stated:

> Machinery sold in this category will include a warranty of
> operation, service work, and parts performance . . . for 30 days
> from use date, and all repairs will be based 50-50 (customer to
> pay 50% of repair bill and Mountain View Equipment to pay 50%
> of repair bill). If the machine has a completely rebuilt engine or
> gearbox, the warranty will be 100% on these specified
> components for 90 days from use date.

Dickerson and the company agreed to modify the warranty. The
modified warranty provided: "Transmission & Differential to have a 90
day full warranty. MVE to put a 100% full warranty for 30 days from
date of delivery on major problems."

Mountain View delivered the tractor to Dickerson's farm on May 7,
1982. After Dickerson started the tractor and drove less than 200 feet,
the tractor "jumped out of gear." Dickerson called the company, and
Mountain View returned the tractor to the shop on the same day. The
company loaned Dickerson another tractor, but he testified it was too
small to pull any of his heavy planting equipment. He borrowed and
rented tractors during the week his tractor was being repaired. Using
the borrowed and rented tractors, Dickerson completed his spring
planting. After Mountain View had repaired a gear in the
transmission, the tractor was returned to Dickerson. Dickerson fueled
the tractor and attached a piece of field equipment, but the tractor's
hydraulic-power director would not function. Mountain View
attempted to fix the tractor in the field, but eventually had to take it
back to the shop. The tractor was again repaired and returned to
Dickerson. He operated the tractor for approximately ten hours
following the spring season. After the tractor had been repaired the
second time, Dickerson noted several problems in the tractor's steering,
throttle, right brake, and door. The engine was also leaking oil. While
still within the warranty period, Mountain View and Dickerson agreed
that the company would complete the necessary repairs after the fall
harvesting season. Dickerson used the tractor for approximately 190
hours in the fall. He used the tractor in fifth and sixth gear (light-load
situations) to pull a light twelve-foot disc. The agreed warranty work
was accomplished in January of 1983.

Dickerson next used the tractor during spring planting in late April
1983. The spring work was the most demanding on the tractor.
Dickerson used the tractor's third and fourth gears (heavy-load
situations) to pull a twenty-four-foot cultivator. He made two passes
pulling the cultivator, and the tractor broke down. Again, Mountain
View picked up the tractor and discovered that two teeth were sheared
off from the third gear wheel. Although the previous repairs had been
done by Mountain View under warranty, this time the company
charged Dickerson $1,732.29 before releasing the tractor. He paid the
charge and then instituted the small-claims action to recover this
amount.

> What are the strategic implications of his decision to pay first, then bring suit?

The district court found Mountain View's "Used Equipment Warranty" was an express warranty which attempted to disclaim any implied warranties. The court determined the disclaimer was ineffective. The court held the tractor was not merchantable; thus, Mountain View had breached an implied warranty of merchantability. The district court found that the gear was "more probably than not" defective at the time of sale and the string of breakdowns amply supported the finding that the company had breached its implied warranty of merchantability.

In a warranty cause of action, the burden is on the plaintiff to show the existence of a particular warranty, that the warranty was breached, and that damage was proximately caused by the alleged breach. More specifically, to recover for the breach of an implied warranty of merchantability, the plaintiff must prove: (1) the goods purchased were subject to an implied warranty of merchantability; (2) the goods did not comply with the warranty at the time of delivery; (3) the purchaser's damages were due to the unmerchantable nature of the goods; and (4) damages were suffered as a result of the breach of the warranty. Mountain View asserts the tractor was not subject to an implied warranty of merchantability for two reasons. First, the company suggests that any implied warranty of merchantability was limited or nonexistent because the tractor was sold as used equipment. Second, any warranty of merchantability had been superseded by the company's express warranty. Finally, the company asserts that if an implied warranty did exist, Dickerson failed to show the tractor was unmerchantable at the time of delivery. We will address these issues in turn.

. . . The implied warranty of merchantability is not intended to guarantee that the goods be the best or of the highest quality – the standard is measured by the generally acceptable quality under the description used in the contract.

Mountain View suggests that an implied warranty of merchantability was limited or nonexistent because the tractor was a used piece of equipment. Although at least one jurisdiction does not extend the implied warranty of merchantability to used goods, we note the majority of jurisdictions extend the warranty to used goods. The Code does not limit the merchantability warranty to new goods. . . . We hold that the implied warranty of merchantability recognized in section 28-2-314 applies to transactions of both new and used goods.

> Since UCC 2-314 Comment 3 (Comment 4 in Revised Article 2) clearly applies the implied warranty of merchantability to used goods, why is this not a settled question?

One distinction between new and used goods goes to the standard of merchantability applied to such goods. Generally, goods are merchantable when, at the least, they are fit for the ordinary purposes for which they are used. . . . [T]he new or used character of the tractor is a factor in determining its standard of merchantability. . . .

Mountain View also asserts that the express warranty embodied in its Used Equipment Warranty supersedes any implied warranty of merchantability. The company agrees with the district court's finding that the ninety-day coverage of the used-equipment warranty had expired when the tractor broke down in the spring of 1983. Accordingly, the company argues that the breakdown which constituted the alleged breach of the implied warranty occurred past

Read UCC 2-317.
In your own words,
explain the logic
behind rules (a), (b),
and (c).

the expiration of the ninety-day period. Mountain View directs our
attention to I.C. § 28-2-317, which discusses the cumulative effect of
multiple warranties. . . . Mountain View insists that the express
warranty coverage for ninety days supersedes the implied warranty of
merchantability and, consequently, any breakdown of the tractor past
the ninety-day period under an implied warranty of merchantability is
inconsistent and must fail. Mountain View argues that extending its
obligation to repair the tractor beyond the ninety-day warranty period
would be unreasonable and, thus, the express and cumulative
warranties are in conflict.

We believe Mountain View misconstrues the cumulative effect of an
implied warranty of merchantability and the express warranty. The
implied warranty of merchantability relates to the condition of goods at
the time of the delivery and does not extend into the future. "A breach
of warranty occurs when tender of delivery is made, except that where
a warranty *explicitly* extends to future performance of the goods and
discovery of the breach must await the time of such performance." I.C.
§ 28-2-725 (2). For warranty coverage to extend to future performance,
the warranty must be expressed. Because the Used Equipment
Warranty guaranteed the operation and parts performance of the
transmission for a full ninety days, such express warranty is congruous
with an implied warranty of merchantability. This analysis of the
merchantability warranty is consistent with its second element of proof
– that the goods were unmerchantable at the time of delivery.
Mountain View's express warranty did not supersede its implied
warranty of merchantability. . . .

This provision is in
Revised Article
2-725 (3) (c).

Does the contract-
interpretation
maxim of
"construction
against the drafter"
assist in your
analysis of this case?

* * *

We now turn to the . . . factors to be considered in determining the
appropriate standard of merchantability for the used tractor. The
company presented evidence that a new tractor would cost
approximately $40,000 in comparison to Dickerson's tractor purchased
for $13,850. It is significant to note that, although Dickerson paid only
35% of a new tractor's cost, his tractor was to receive the full ninety-day
warranty because of the rebuilt gearbox. Dickerson further testified
that he agreed to the ninety-day warranty under the assumption that
it would cover his initial use of the tractor during spring planting. He
testified that, "if the tractor held up during the spring work, I'd be more
than satisfied with the mechanical condition of the unit." The
warranty period would have covered the tractor during its period of
heaviest use. Because the tractor did not operate properly upon its
initial delivery, Dickerson was denied the opportunity to test the
tractor that first spring. Finally, the company's Used Equipment
Warranty also contained two other warranty categories. The first
indicated that the used equipment was sold "as is." The second
category only guaranteed the used equipment the first time it was
started in the field. Dickerson obviously received the most extensive
used equipment warranty offered by the company. Since Dickerson
received a full ninety-day warranty, it is reasonable to assume the
tractor would meet a higher standard of merchantability than one sold
under a thirty-day warranty.

In Sanford
Grossman's article
*The Informational
Role of Warranties
and Private
Disclosure About
Product Quality*, 24
J. L. & Econ. 461
(1981), he argues
that, because it is
"intuitively plausible
that a seller of a
high-quality item
can offer a better
warranty than can
be offered by a low-
quality seller," the
warranty offered
transmits to the
consumer
information about
the quality of the
goods that would
otherwise be costly
to gather and share.

* * *

1
2
3
4
5
6
7
8
9
10
11
12
13
14
15
16
17
18
19
20
21
22
23
24
25
26
27
28
29
30
31
32
33
34
35
36
37
38
39
40
41
42
43
44
45
46
50
51
52
53

Mountain View maintains that Dickerson failed to prove that the tractor was unmerchantable at the time of delivery. The company presented evidence that the gear could have been broken by "dumping the clutch" which would have subjected the transmission to a heavy torque load. The company also presented testimony that the gear in question was pitted and had wear marks on the leading edges of the gear teeth. The shop foreman testified that pitting and wear marks appear on a gear over time depending on the amount of stress placed on the gear. The foreman opined that the pitting on this particular gear may have occurred after the gear had been in service for approximately 1,000 to 5,000 hours. Dickerson testified unrebutted that he had only used the tractor for a total of 200 hours, of which 190 hours were used pulling light implements in the tractor's fifth and sixth gear. Dickerson did not have an opportunity to test the tractor the first spring, and the 190 hours of fall work were not equivalent to the heavy work normally occurring with spring planting. Although the shop foreman testified that the pitting would not directly result in the shearing of the teeth, he did indicate that it was the company's normal custom to replace a pitted gear. Dickerson asserted that the gear in question should have been replaced when the tractor was originally reassembled prior to delivery. He maintains that the pitting and wear marks on the gear indicates the gear's unmerchantability and should have been replaced.

> Note how both sides use the same fact — the pitted gear — to support their arguments.

Although the company presented testimony that the teeth of the gear were not sheared when the tractor was rebuilt, the question still remains whether the pitted and worn condition of the gear supported the court's finding that the tractor was unmerchantable. . . . Here, Mountain View's personnel estimated that pitting such as on the gear in question occurred with 1,000 to 5,000 hours of operation. Dickerson testified that he had only used the machine 200 hours. The company also presented testimony that a gear exhibiting wear marks and pitting such as the gear in question here should have been replaced when the tractor was originally rebuilt. . . .

We find that the record supports the district court's finding of a breach of an implied warranty of merchantability. Accordingly, we affirm the judgment of the district court.

- How should the fact that used goods are involved affect the court's analysis as to whether the implied warranty of merchantability has been satisfied?

Note 1: One controversial question is whether goods known to cause health risks should ever be deemed merchantable. This issue has arisen in litigation involving cigarettes, with varying results.

- **Read 2-314 (2)'s list of standards for merchantability.** Can you find a provision to support an argument that cigarettes are not merchantable?

Two cases decided within a year of one another illustrate the
range of outcomes. In *Green v. American Tobacco Co.*, 304 F.2d
70 (5th Cir. 1962), the court considered a claim by the estate of
Edwin Green, who died as a result of lung cancer allegedly
caused by smoking defendant American Tobacco Co.'s Lucky
Strike cigarettes. The estate claimed, among other theories,
breach of an implied warranty. In upholding the jury verdict
for the cigarette company, the court found the company lacked
the "superior opportunity to gain knowledge of the product and
to form a judgment of its fitness" that would be required under
this theory. The court described cigarettes as being goods
"heretofore thought by all to be wholesome or tolerable, but
which constantly expanding scientific research, thought, and
knowledge have now proved, or at least convinced many, to be
injurious."

Compare *Pritchard v. Liggett & Myers Tobacco Co.*, 295 F.2d
292 (3d Cir. 1961), in which the court considered similar facts
predicated upon the plaintiff's smoking of Chesterfield
cigarettes made by Liggett & Myers Tobacco Co. The plaintiff
sued under both an implied warranty of merchantability and
an implied warranty of fitness for a particular purpose. In
reversing the district court's dismissal of the warranty claims,
the court considered the following facts:

> After reading these facts and the materials on "fitness for a particular purpose," return to this note to explore how a claim could be made based upon such a theory.

As far back as July 16, 1934, an advertisement appeared in a
Pittsburgh newspaper claiming that, as to Chesterfields:

> "A good cigarette can cause no ills and cure no ailments, but
> it gives you a lot of pleasure, peace of mind, and comfort."

Later that month, it was said:

> "There is no purer cigarette made than Chesterfield."

Assurances also appeared in national magazines. After showing a
picture of Liggett & Myers Research Laboratories, this statement
follows:

> "The constant quality tests and advanced research in
> Chesterfield's modern laboratories are your guarantee that
> Chesterfields will always be much milder – the best cigarette
> for you to smoke."

On several occasions in 1953, advertisements similar to the
following appeared:

> "Chesterfield is Best for You."

* * *

One systematic and nationwide advertising campaign stands out in the record. . . . It appeared in a Pittsburgh newspaper, a national magazine, and was repeated on a national television program featuring Arthur Godfrey. Typical of the commercials he presented was the following:

> Arthur Godfrey was a popular television personality in the 1940s and 50s. Until he stopped smoking around 1953, Liggett & Myers Tobacco Co. was a major sponsor of his program.

> You hear stuff all the time about "cigarettes are harmful to you" this and that and the other thing.
>
> * * *
>
> Here's an ad, you've seen it in the papers – please read it when you get it. If you smoke it will make you feel better, really. Nose, throat, and accessory organs are not adversely affected by smoking Chesterfield. This is the first such report ever published about any cigarette. A responsible consulting organization has reported the results of a continuing study by a competent medical specialist and his staff on the effects of smoking Chesterfield cigarettes. *Id.* at 297.

- Could the *Pritchard* facts support an express-warranty claim?

- If so, what was warranted about Chesterfield cigarettes?

Note 2: Read 2-314 (1), focusing on the language "contract for their sale." A recurring question is whether the implied warranty of merchantability requires a fully-executed contract of sale. In *Lasky v. Economy Grocery Stores*, 319 Mass. 224, 65 N.E.2d 305 (1946), the court considered a suit by Mary Lasky, who was injured when a bottle of carbonated tonic exploded as she was taking it off the shelf with the intention of placing it in her shopping basket. In reversing the lower court's denial of directed verdict for the defendant grocery store on Ms. Lasky's warranty claim, the court held that "[p]ossession alone was not in these circumstances sufficient to pass title to the bottle. Title did not pass until the delivery became absolute upon the payment of the price to the cashier."

> *Lasky* was a pre-UCC case, and the facts therefore do not distinguish between an implied warranty of merchantability and an implied warranty of fitness for a particular purpose.

A contrary view is presented in *Gillispie v. Great Atlantic and Pacific Tea Co.*, 14 N.C. App. 1, 187 S.E.2d 441, 10 U.C.C. Rep. Serv. 754 (1972), in which the court addressed similar facts. Franklin Gillispie was injured when two of the Sprite bottles he was carrying in a carton in his left hand exploded, causing lacerations to his wrist. At the time of the injury, he was walking toward the checkout counter for the purpose of paying for the items. In reversing the lower court's directed verdict for the grocery store, the court held as follows:

Is this portion of the court's holding consistent with what you have learned about mutual assent in your study of contract law?

The presence of the drinks on the shelves in defendant's self-service store constituted an offer for sale and delivery at a stated price.   If plaintiff took the drinks into his possession with the intention of paying for them at the cashier's counter, there was no further act of delivery necessary on the part of the seller. All that remained was for plaintiff to pay for the drinks – an act delayed until he reached the cashier's counter primarily for the convenience of the seller.

* * *

Defendant calls attention to the custom in self-service stores which permits a customer to return goods to the shelf without liability if he changes his mind about a purchase before reaching the checkout counter. However, even a right to return delivered goods to the seller does not necessarily delay passage of the title until that right has expired. . . . [W]hen a purchaser in a self-service store changes his mind and returns to the shelf a product which he has picked up with the intention of buying, title is revested in the seller. However, as long as the purchaser has the product in his possession, intending to pay for it, he has title to the product. The seller's interest at that point is not "title" but a security interest to enforce payment. *Id.* at 6.

- Which approach better reflects consumer expectations?

- Should the fact that Franklin Gillispie was closer to consummating the sales transaction than Mary Lasky determine the outcome of these cases relative to one another?

Note 3: The *Dickerson* case involved used goods. Even when new goods are involved, the implied warranty of merchantability does not require excellent quality. 2-314 (2) makes this point by using language such as "pass without objection" and "fair average quality," rather than stronger positive language that might suggest superior quality. Refer back to the fact pattern in Part A, Problem 2, which involved Gwendolyn Adams. In finding the vehicle was merchantable, the *Adams* court held as follows:

The Pontiac here . . . was reasonably suitable for ordinary use, and was in fact used to meet plaintiff's daily needs. It possessed no remarkable defect; it was the average new car which one has come to expect in a mass-production era capable of producing over seven million automobiles a year. It was a car that required the usual "shakedown" period and relatively minor adjustments to put it in good working order. The motor had to be adjusted, loose elements tightened, the locks corrected, the dome light fixed, and a rumbling noise eliminated. All this was done. The record shows, as noted, that whatever repairs and adjustments had to be made were admittedly taken care of by defendant willingly and promptly. Whatever plaintiff's dissatisfaction with her new Pontiac (she describes it as a "non-vegetative member of the citrus family" – euphemistic longhand for what the trade bluntly calls a "lemon"), there is nothing in the record which spells out a breach of the implied warranty of merchantability. *Adams*, 42 N.J. Super. at 325.

■ Would the same analysis apply to a Rolls Royce automobile?

Note 4: The implied warranty of merchantability is a common cause of action in litigation involving food that is spoiled or contains a foreign body. In *Battiste v. St. Thomas Diving Club, Inc.*, 26 U.C.C. Rep. Serv. 324 (D.V.I. 1979), the court considered Gail and Lorne Battiste's consumption of fish and resultant ciguatera fish poisoning. The court described the state of the law as follows:

> Two distinct lines of authority exist for dealing with injuries suffered from a substance in food consumed in a restaurant, the "foreign-natural" test and the "reasonable expectations" test. . . . The rationale of the "foreign-natural" test is that "substances which are a natural part of the food served are not considered foreign matter or substances if inadvertently left therein. On this premise, it is reasoned that the presence of substances natural to the ingredients or finished product does not constitute breach of the vendor's implied warranty that the food is wholesome and fit for human consumption.
>
> . . . [T]he "reasonable expectations" test . . . holds that it is a question for the trier of fact whether a buyer could reasonably expect to find the substance in the food consumed. *Id.* at 326-327.

■ How would you analyze whether the marine microalgae made the fish unmerchantable under each test?

Note 5: Similar to the "reasonable expectations test" is the "reasonable foreseeability" test illustrated in *Robbins v. Alberto-Culver Co.*, 210 Kan. 147, 499 P.2d 1080, 11 U.C.C. Rep. Serv. 1 (1972). That case arose from the allergic reaction Beverly Robbins suffered when she applied Rinse Away, a dandruff-control product by Alberto-Culver Co., to her former mother-in-law's scalp. The evidence regarding the general safety of the product was as follows:

> [O]ver a period of some ten years, the company had received ninety-nine complaints, the last one in 1970, which averages out as two complaints per million bottles sold during that period of time; . . . [T]he complaints covered such problems as rash on head and ears, hair loss, breaking out of scalp, itching, skin trouble, allergic reaction, and swollen eyes; . . . . *Id.* at 154-155.

The Centers for Disease Control and Prevention provide the following definition: Ciguatera fish poisoning (or ciguatera) is an illness caused by eating fish that contain toxins produced by a marine microalgae. . . . People who have ciguatera may experience nausea, vomiting, and neurologic symptoms such as tingling fingers or toes. They also may find that cold things feel hot and hot things feel cold. Ciguatera has no cure. Symptoms usually go away in days or weeks but can last for years.

The court determined the company's liability should turn on "[w]hen the accumulation of complaints of allergic reaction up to the time of injury was sufficient for the defendant to have reasonably apprehended that its product would harm an appreciable class of people."

- At what point should the number of complaints put a company on notice that its product may be harmful?

According to the National Center for Environmental Health, 90% of brown recluse spider bites heal without serious incident. Is this fact relevant to the court's analysis?

Problem 1: Gladys Flippo sued Mode O'Day Frock Shops of Hollywood after she was bitten by a poisonous brown recluse spider concealed in slacks she tried on in, and subsequently purchased from, defendant's store. The pants were otherwise totally normal, and she laundered and wore them on a number of occasions after the purchase. Her lawsuit, which was unsuccessful, was based upon an alleged breach of the implied warranty of merchantability.

- Based on these facts, what is the greatest obstacle to her recovery?

Based on *Flippo v. Mode O'Day Frock Shops of Hollywood*, 248 Ark. 1, 449 S.W.2d 692, 7 U.C.C. Rep. Serv. 282 (1970).

Problem 2: Pearl Sampson purchased a meal consisting of turkey salad and a dessert at a fundraising luncheon put on by the Wauwatosa High School Band Mothers Association. The luncheon was organized to support the members of a local high-school band. Ms. Sampson subsequently became extremely ill with what was eventually diagnosed as salmonella. Leftover turkey salad was tested and found to be the source of the bacteria that made her ill.

- Does she have a cause of action for breach of the implied warranty of merchantability?

Based on *Samson v. Riesing*, 62 Wis. 2d. 698, 14 U.C.C. Rep. Serv. 618 (1974).

Battiste is discussed above in Note 4.

Problem 3: Apply the two tests in *Battiste* to the following facts.

On Saturday, April 25, 1959, about 1 p.m., [plaintiff Priscilla Webster] accompanied by her sister and her aunt, entered the Blue Ship Tea Room operated by the defendant. . . .

T-Wharf was the center of Boston's fishing industry in the late 1800s and early 1900s.

This restaurant, which the plaintiff characterized as "quaint," was located in Boston "on the third floor of an old building on T-Wharf which overlooks the ocean."

The plaintiff, who had been born and brought up in New England, ... ordered a cup of fish chowder. Presently, there was set before her "a small bowl of fish chowder." She had previously enjoyed a breakfast about 9 which had given her no difficulty. "The fish chowder contained haddock, potatoes, milk, water, and seasoning. The chowder was milky in color and not clear. The haddock and potatoes were in chunks." ... "She agitated it a little with the spoon and observed that it was a fairly full bowl. ... It was hot when she got it, but she did not tip it with her spoon because it was hot ... but stirred it in an up-and-under motion. She denied that she did this because she was looking for something, but it was rather because she wanted an even distribution of fish and potatoes." "She started to eat it, alternating between the chowder and crackers which were on the table with ... [some] rolls. She ate about 3 or 4 spoonfuls then stopped. She looked at the spoonfuls as she was eating. She saw equal parts of liquid, potato, and fish as she spooned it into her mouth. She did not see anything unusual about it. After 3 or 4 spoonfuls, she was aware that something had lodged in her throat because she couldn't swallow and couldn't clear her throat by gulping and she could feel it." This misadventure led to two esophagoscopies at the Massachusetts General Hospital, in the second of which, on April 27, 1959, a fish bone was found and removed. The sequence of events produced injury to the plaintiff which was not insubstantial.

- Should Ms. Webster prevail on the implied warranty of merchantability?

- What are the most important facts to be considered?

Based on *Webster v. Blue Ship Tea Room, Inc.*, 347 Mass. 421, 198 N.E.2d 309, 2 U.C.C. Rep. Serv. 161 (1964).

Fitness for a Particular Purpose

Read 2-315 and Comments 1 and 2. The implied warranty of fitness for a particular purpose can provide a remedy to a purchaser who has used the goods for something beyond their ordinary purpose. Comment 1 describes the state of mind and level of knowledge necessary to create this kind of warranty. The seller must have reason to know (1) the special use for which the goods are intended and (2) that the buyer is relying on the seller's expertise in selecting the goods. The implied warranty of merchantability has no such knowledge requirement; instead, the Code assumes the seller has knowledge that the goods will be used for ordinary purposes and also assumes the buyer relies on the merchant seller's advice with respect to the goods' suitability for ordinary purposes. Comment 2 describes the relationship between the two implied warranties of quality.

The Article 2A analogue is 2A-213.

- Must the seller be a merchant for 2-315 to apply?

- If not, to whom, other than a merchant, might 2-315 apply?

The result of the following case may surprise you. After you have read the case, consider how the seller could have avoided liability.

Addis v. Bernadin, Inc.,
226 Kan. 241, 597 P.2d 250, 27 U.C.C. Rep. Serv. 80 (1979)

Herd, Justice.

Appellee Sunset Products, a partnership managed by William Addis, of Wichita, Kansas, is engaged in the manufacture, bottling, and sale of salad dressing to the wholesale market. The dressing is bottled in gallon plastic jars and capped with a threaded lid which is usually sealed with a small plastic liner, known in the trade as "plastisol." Appellant Bernardin, Inc., an Indiana corporation, manufactures jar lids. . . . From time to time prior to August 1974, sales representatives from Bernardin contacted Sunset Products about selling it jar lids, with no luck. Finally, in August 1974, William Addis called Bernardin's sales representative, Larry Hooper, in Dallas, Texas, concerning the purchase of jar lids from Bernardin, Inc. The two men met in Addis' office in either August or September of 1974. Addis advised Hooper his company manufactured salad dressings which contained both vinegar and salt and any lids he purchased from Bernardin must be compatible with those contents. Addis also told Hooper he had been obtaining his jar lids from Dura Container and showed him an example saying he needed a similar product with a plastisol lining and a gold lacquer interior.

Addis called Hooper again in September 1974 to place the jar lid order. Addis requested white plastisol-lined lids with a gold lacquer interior. He believed the order of jar lids with a plastisol lining would be compatible with his product. Hooper advised Addis he would not recommend the jar lids for products containing vinegar and salt. Addis insisted he wanted lids exactly like those he had purchased from Dura. In spite of Bernardin's recommendation, he ordered 350,000 lids for delivery in early 1975. Hooper did not explain that the plastisol lining was only the seal on the lid and the incompatible part of the lid was the gold lacquer interior. This fact was never explained to Addis until the lawsuit was almost over. The delivery date was changed several times, and Sunset Products received its first shipment of Bernardin lids in May 1975.

Sunset Products very quickly began to receive complaints from disgruntled customers complaining of spoiled salad dressing. The company immediately picked up the jars of salad dressing and paid for the spoilage, which amounted to $115,000.00, according to Addis. . . .

* * *

Sunset Products brought suit against Bernardin for $750,000.00, which represented damages it had sustained as a result of the use of the incompatible lids. An examination of the pretrial order reveals plaintiff alleged Bernardin had been negligent in its dealings with Sunset Products and that Bernardin had breached an implied warranty of fitness. . . . The case was tried to the court and, after numerous stops and starts, the trial court found for Sunset Products in the amount of $95,891.08. Bernardin appeals.

* * *

Appellant maintains the pleadings and evidence do not support a judgment based on a finding of a breach of warranty of merchantability. An examination of the pretrial order reveals plaintiff contends defendant breached an "implied warranty of fitness." The order does not indicate whether the contention refers to goods which are "fit for the ordinary purposes for which such goods are used" under implied warranty of merchantability, or an implied warranty of fitness for a particular purpose. The trial court's findings of fact and conclusions of law state:

> It appears to the court that generally there is an implied warranty in K.S.A. 84-2-314 that arises through a course of dealing and usage in this trade, and that is generally that defendant company and others similarly situated converse and work with, as a part of their procedures, a purchaser to make sure that a lid is compatible with the products that the lids would be used on, and they warrant their merchandise in that regard. That warrant was breached by the defendant company.

Does this paragraph clarify which warranty is intended?

* * *

There is sufficient competent evidence to support the trial court's finding of a breach of implied warranty of fitness for a particular purpose. A buyer's recovery under K.S.A. 84-2-315 necessitates a showing of reliance on the seller's skill or judgment to select appropriate goods in conformity with the buyer's intended use of the goods. Here, although Addis insisted upon ordering white plastisol-lined lids with gold interiors that looked like the lids he had ordered from Dura Container, he did not realize he was ordering lids that would be incompatible with his product. He wanted lids like those he had purchased from Dura Container. When Hooper visited his office, Addis showed him the Dura lid that he had previously used. Those lids had been successfully utilized with his product, and he wished to duplicate his success with Bernardin's lids. Hooper, on the other hand, knew the type of highly acidic product the lids would be used with and failed to explain the difference between the type of lid Addis ordered and the type he thought he was ordering. He allowed Addis to place an order for a lid that was not like the Dura lid and was not suitable for his product, with only a recommendation against the order. It is clear the seller in this instance had superior knowledge and failed to properly caution the buyer. Addis relied on Hooper's knowledge of his product and of the type of lid he wanted, believing he was ordering the type of lid the two had previously examined. . . .

. . . The judgment of the trial court should be affirmed.

- How should Bernadin modify its business practices to prevent similar liability in the future?

- Would the goods in this case also violate the implied warranty of merchantability?

Note 1: *Keith v. Buchanan* was presented in Part A of this chapter. Return to that case for a review of its facts. In addition to his express-warranty claim, the plaintiff also claimed the seller breached the implied warranty of fitness for a particular purpose. The court rejected this claim, holding as follows, because it found the purchaser had not relied on the seller's expertise in selecting the boat:

> Appellant had extensive experience with sailboats at the time of the subject purchase, even though he had not previously owned such a vessel. He had developed precise specifications in regard to the type of boat he wanted to purchase. He looked at a number of different vessels, reviewed their advertising literature, and focused on the Island Trader 41 as the object of his intended purchase. He also had friends look at the boat before making the final decision to purchase. *Keith*, 173 Cal. App. 3d at 25-26.

The court affirmed the trial court's dismissal of this part of the case. As this case shows, a party may succeed on an implied warranty claim, but fail to prove a breach of express warranty – or vice versa.

- Could a claim for breach of the implied warranty of merchantability succeed on these facts?

Note 2: In *Chatfield v. Sherwin-Williams Co.*, 266 N.W.2d 171, 24 U.C.C. Rep. Serv. 285 (Minn. 1978), the court considered a lawsuit by a professional barn painter against a paint manufacturer based on theories of express warranty, implied warranty of merchantability, and implied warranty of fitness for a particular purpose. The plaintiff showed that, within one to four months of when the buildings were painted, the paint began to look chalky and fade. The plaintiff did not always use the paint as labeled, in that he did not always add the recommended amount of linseed oil. In addition, the paint he purchased was the manufacturer's "bottom of the line." The Minnesota Supreme Court affirmed the jury verdict for the plaintiff on all three counts. The court's holding was based in part on its finding that "the jury could infer from the fact that the fading was quite uniform that the presence or absence of linseed oil had no effect on the fading." This case tends to suggest three points: (1) "Ordinary use" need not be perfect

Linseed oil is used to bind paint.

use; instead, the manufacturer should expect consumers will not always use the goods exactly as labeled. (2) When the goods are not used as labeled, the plaintiff should attempt to show the goods would have exhibited the defect complained of even if they had been used as directed. (3) Even when the goods purchased are "the bottom of the line," the implied warranty of merchantability will impose minimal standards of quality.

- Now that you have learned about all three warranties of quality, how does the evidence to support each differ?

Problem: Identify all potential warranties in the following facts:

> [Defendants Rudy C. Zogarts and Miles Kimball Company] manufacture and sell the "Golfing Gizmo," a training device designed to help unskilled golfers improve their games. Defendants' catalogue states that the Gizmo is a "completely equipped backyard driving range."
>
> The Gizmo is a simple device consisting of two metal pegs, two cords – one elastic, one cotton – and a regulation golf ball. After the pegs are driven into the ground approximately 25 inches apart, the elastic cord is looped over them. The cotton cord, measuring 21 feet in length, ties to the middle of the elastic cord. The ball is attached to the end of the cotton cord. When the cords are extended, the Gizmo resembles the shape of a large letter "T," with the ball resting at the base.
>
> The user stands by the ball in order to hit his practice shots. The instructions state that, when hit correctly, the ball will fly out and spring back near the point of impact; if the ball returns to the left, it indicates a right-hander's "slice"; a shot returning to the right indicates a right-hander's "hook." If the ball is "topped," it does not return and must be retrieved by the player. The label on the shipping carton and the cover of the instruction booklet urge players to "drive the ball with full power" and further state: "COMPLETELY SAFE: BALL WILL NOT HIT PLAYER."

Based on *Hauter v. Zogarts*, 14 Cal. 3d 104, 534 P.2d 377, 120 Cal. Rptr. 681, 16 U.C.C. Rep. Serv. 938 (1975).

C. Disclaimers, Notice, and Privity

This section addresses disclaimers and warranty limitations, as well as the requirement of notice when a warranty is breached and the way in which privity affects the warranty-related rights of buyers and sellers.

Disclaimers

> The Article 2A equivalent is 2A-214.

Read 2-316, both in its current version and as amended.

- Which portion or portions relate to express warranties?

- Which portion or portions relate to implied warranties?

- What is the apparent policy reason for the proposed changes?

As 2-316 (1) shows, express warranties cannot be disclaimed. As for the disclaimer of implied warranties, the Code gives specific guidance in part (2) and also provides general language in part (3) (a) that will effectuate a blanket disclaimer.

- How can "words or conduct relevant to the creation of an express warranty" and "words or conduct tending to negate or limit warranty" be consistent with one another?

- What happens if the court cannot read the two as consistent?

- How are the standards for disclaiming implied warranties of merchantability and implied warranties of fitness for a particular purpose different from one another?

- Why do these differences make sense?

Read 2-719 (2). The following case shows how the Code's warranty-limitation provisions give parties the contractual freedom to fashion lesser standards than the UCC would require under the rubric of merchantability. As 2-719 (2) indicates, a warranty limitation will be struck down if the plaintiff is left with no meaningful remedy.

Lankford v. Rogers Ford Sales,
478 S.W.2d 248, 10 U.C.C. Rep. Serv. 777 (Tex. Civ. App. 1972).

Ramsey, Chief Justice.

[Buford B. Lankford, Jr.] purchased a new 1967 Thunderbird automobile on January 18, 1968, from the Defendant, Rogers Ford Sales, an authorized Ford dealer. The automobile was manufactured by the Defendant, Ford Motor Company. At the time of the purchase, Plaintiff received a written new-vehicle warranty. Soon after the purchase, many defects occurred, some of an exasperating nature (activating the safety flasher turned on the radio) and other defects rendering the vehicle unsuitable for use (power-steering defect). The details of the defects are not questioned, and the Plaintiff presented well-documented proof of the occurrences and circumstances. On May 19, 1969, Plaintiff filed this suit. Defects were repaired by Rogers when the breakdown occurred, and others were repaired by other dealers when breakdowns occurred out of town. In each instance, repairs were made to rectify the defects. The Plaintiff so testified, though at times it would take one to five attempts to make the repairs which would require returning the car to Rogers and leaving it for the repair work.

During approximately eighteen months, the car was in the shop for repairs some 45 days for about 50 different defects. Rogers' service personnel advised Plaintiff that this automobile developed more defects than would normally be expected in an automobile of this quality.

The gist of the controversy may be summarized in that Plaintiff alleges that the limited written warranty has failed in its essential purpose and therefore, the Plaintiff should then be entitled to rely on implied warranties of fitness and merchantability for relief. The Defendant Ford's contention is that the warranty furnished to Plaintiff was a limited written warranty whereby Ford was obligated to replace or repair any defective part without charge to the Plaintiff. That in so doing, Ford has performed in accordance with the warranty and should not be subjected to any claim in excess of that which it contractually undertook. Defendant Rogers, being the dealer and repair agency, asserts that the only warranty made on the vehicle was made by the manufacturer Ford and thus Rogers is not responsible for any warranty, but only for implementation of the warranty by repairs that have been performed. . . .

> This portion of the opinion brings to mind the issue of privity, covered later in this section.

The wording of the warranty is as follows:

> Basic Warranty
>
> Ford Motor Company warrants to the owner each part of this vehicle to be free under normal use and service from defects in material and workmanship for a period of 24 months from the date of original retail delivery or first use, or until it has been driven for 24,000 miles, whichever comes first.
>
> * * *
>
> All the warranties shall be fulfilled by the Selling Dealer (or if the owner is traveling or has become a resident of a different locality, by any authorized Ford or Lincoln-Mercury dealer) replacing with a genuine new Ford or Ford Authorized Reconditioned part, or repairing at his place of business, free of charge including related labor, any such defective part.
>
> * * *
>
> The warranties herein are expressly IN LIEU OF any other express or implied warranty, including any implied WARRANTY of MERCHANTABILITY or FITNESS, and of any other obligation on the part of the Company or the Selling Dealer.

> Applying the language of 2-316, has Ford successfully disclaimed both implied warranties of quality?

Plaintiff does not allege any fraud or misrepresentation either by Ford or Rogers in the selling of the automobile, nor is there any allegation of negligence or failure or refusal to repair when defects occurred.

Plaintiff's contention is that the Uniform Commercial Code, effective since September 1, 1967, affords a basis for relief to a purchaser when the limited warranty fails of its essential purpose.

Here the plaintiff makes reference to 2-719 (2).

* * *

. . . The parties in this suit consummated their transaction whereby the warrantor's liability was limited to repair or replacement. Plaintiff does not allege that the limitation is unconscionable, nor does he allege any fraudulent representation or over-reaching on the part of the manufacturer or dealer. We can only conclude that such limitation is therefore reasonable and acceptable and not violative of the provisions of the Uniform Commercial Code.

The only complaint made by Plaintiff is that the limited warranty has failed in its essential purpose, alleging, after repeated repairs, the automobile is still not of merchantable quality and as such breaches the Defendant's implied warranty of merchantability and fitness. . . . [I]t is important to note that the Plaintiff admits that on each and every occasion that a defect has occurred, the same has been repaired by a Ford dealer. Thus, there is no allegation of any repudiation of the limited warranty, nor any allegation of any willful failure or refusal to make the repairs needed nor any allegation of dilatory, careless or negligent compliance with the terms of the limited warranty. In the absence of such circumstances, we must conclude, as a matter of law, that the limited warranty has not failed in its essential purpose. The Defendants having complied with the provisions of the warranty as admitted by the Plaintiff himself, are thus entitled to assert its provisions in limitation of the remedies and liabilities expressed therein.

- What, if any, other theories might the plaintiff employ in seeking relief under the facts of this case?

Note 1: Read 2-316 (4) and 2-719 and Comment 1. *Wilson Trading Corp. v. Ferguson*, 23 N.Y. 2d 398, 244 N.E.2d 685 (1968), describes an important limitation on parties' ability to disclaim or limit warranty liability. In that case, the court addressed a dispute arising from the sale of yarn that was cut and knitted into sweaters, and then washed as a finished product. During the washing, the buyer found the yarn had "shaded." Shading is described as "a variation in color from piece to piece and within the pieces." The buyer declared the yarn to be unmerchantable and brought suit to recover the purchase price. In response, the defendant seller raised the following disclaimer language from the parties' contract:

2. No claims relating to excessive moisture content, short weight, count variations, twist, quality, or shade shall be allowed if made after weaving, knitting, or processing, or more than 10 days after receipt of shipment. . . . The buyer shall within 10 days of the receipt of the merchandise by himself or agent examine the merchandise for any and all defects.

* * *

4. This instrument constitutes the entire agreement between the parties, superseding all previous communications, oral or written, and no changes, amendments, or additions hereto will be recognized unless in writing signed by both seller and buyer or buyer's agent. It is expressly agreed that no representations or warranties, express or implied, have been or are made by the seller except as stated herein, and the seller makes no warranty, express or implied, as to the fitness for buyer's purposes of yarn purchased hereunder, seller's obligations, except as expressly stated herein, being limited to the delivery of good merchantable yarn of the description stated herein. *Id.* at 401.

The purchaser claimed the disclaimer should be deemed ineffective, because the defect could not have been discovered until after the yarn had been processed and washed. The court agreed, holding as follows:

> Parties to a contract are given broad latitude within which to fashion their own remedies for breach of contract. Nevertheless, it is clear from the official comments to section 2-719 of the Uniform Commercial Code that it is the very essence of a sales contract that at least minimum adequate remedies be available for its breach. . . .
>
> * * *
>
> . . . Section 2-719 [2] of the Uniform Commercial Code provides that the general remedy provisions of the code apply when "circumstances cause an exclusive or limited remedy to fail of its essential purpose." . . . Here, paragraph 2 of the contract bars all claims for shade and other specified defects made after knitting and processing. Its effect is to eliminate any remedy for shade defects not reasonably discoverable within the time limitation period. *Id.* at 403-404.

- What kinds of facts will prove failure of a contract remedy's essential purpose?

- Is it possible to square this holding with *Lankford*?

Note 2: Read 2-316 Comments 2 and 5. *Rogers v. Zielinksi,* 92 R.I. 479, 170 A.2d 294 (1961), illustrates the relationship between the parol evidence rule and warranties of quality. That case revolved around an alleged oral express warranty

Using language such as "$10 and other valuable considerations" is a common way of keeping the price paid private.

Is the trial court's holding a correct statement of the parol evidence rule?

covering a used Mercedes-Benz automobile. The evidence showed "a bill of sale signed by defendant . . . which recited the consideration of $10 and other valuable considerations, described the automobile, and contained a covenant as to title." The trial judge excluded testimony regarding the alleged oral express warranty, stating, "The contract is complete and regular on its face and no evidence may be accepted varying or adding to the terms of the contract." The purchaser argued the evidence should have been admitted because there was no evidence tending to show the contract was fully integrated, such that the evidence should be excluded. In agreeing with the purchaser, the Rhode Island Supreme Court held as follows:

> [T]he written agreement. . . did not contain even the contract price which was $3,600. It was the type of instrument which might well not contain warranties if there were such. There is no language in the bill of sale which would permit one to say that it necessarily represented the entire contract between the parties. *Id.* at 483-484.

The court also found it notable that the bill of sale did not include any disclaimer of warranties.

- ▪ After this case, what advice would you give an automotive dealership seeking to protect against employees' making unauthorized warranties?

Problem: Does the following language in a contract for the sale of an automobile effectively disclaim all warranties of quality?

> [T]o the extent allowed by law, THIS WARRANTY IS IN PLACE OF all other warranties, express or implied, including ANY IMPLIED WARRANTY OF MERCHANTABILITY or fitness. Under this warranty, repair or replacement of parts is the only remedy.

Based on *Walker Ford Sales v. Gaither*, 265 Ark. 275, 278, 578 S.W.2d 23, 25, 26 U.C.C. Rep. Serv. 335, 337 (1979).

International Perspective: Disclaimer

Read CISG Article 35. Because breach of warranty is not recognized as its own cause of action under the CISG, and especially because there are no implied warranties that attach unless otherwise disclaimed, no CISG provision governs the concept of disclaimer. Instead, under Article 35, the parties are bound by the terms of the transaction as negotiated.

In *Ajax Tool Works, Inc. v. Can-Eng. Manufacturing Ltd.*, No. 01 C 5938 (N.D. Ill. 2003), the court considered a dispute involving the quality of an industrial furnace. The court considered the seller's claim that its limited warranty disclaimed all implied warranties. In finding the seller had not effectively disclaimed such warranties, the court cited with approval the following language on this point:

> Under CISG, the presumption is that the goods are "fit for the purpose for which goods of the same description would ordinarily be used" and are "fit for any particular purpose expressly or impliedly made known to the seller at the time of the conclusion of the contract." However, this presumption is subject to an express agreement among the parties to the contrary. Under CISG, the only question is whether the disclaimer is a part of the agreement between the parties, arguably a tougher, yet ultimately fairer standard [than the UCC]. *Id.* at § IV.

Because there was no disclaimer in the parties' agreement, the court held the normal presumption of fitness would apply.

- How is the CISG standard "tougher, yet ultimately fairer"?

Notice

The material in this section is equally applicable to breach of warranty claims and to buyers' attempts to escape contract liability for nonconforming goods under the theories introduced in Chapter 5.

Read 2-607 (3), both in its current form and as revised.

> The Article 2A analogue is 2A-516 (3).

- What is the principal change that has been proposed?

2-607 (3) provides a major limitation on a buyer's ability to recover for breach of warranty. Even if the buyer can establish a breach, he or she can lose the right to bring suit by failing to give the seller notice.

Read Comment 4 for guidance regarding the timing of notice and the content of the notice that must be given. What is most important is that the seller not be prejudiced by the buyer's late notice, and that the notice be sufficient to inform the seller that problems exist with the goods.

The following case explains the purpose of the notice requirement and demonstrates the nature of the notice that is required.

Prutch v. Ford Motor Co.,
618 P.2d 657, 29 U.C.C. Rep. Serv. 1507 (Colo. 1980).

Per Curiam.

Petitioners Carl and Sam Prutch were plaintiffs below. They sued for alleged breaches of express and implied warranties arising out of their purchases of a tractor, plow, disc harrow, and hay baler. The defendants in the lawsuit were the Ford Motor Company, manufacturer of all four farm implements, and its dealer, Baldridge Implement Company, which had sold the equipment to the Prutches. [The Prutches, who were farmers, claimed the equipment was defective and had harmed their crops.]

The first trial ended in a mistrial. At the conclusion of the second trial, the jury rendered a verdict for $60,200 in favor of the plaintiffs against Ford. The jury, however, held Baldridge not liable.

Ford appealed. The court of appeals overturned the jury verdict and remanded the case for a third trial. The court of appeals ruled that the plaintiffs had the burden of proving . . . that the plaintiffs gave the manufacturer timely, direct notice of the claimed breach of warranty. We granted certiorari and now reverse the court of appeals' decision and reinstate the jury verdict.

* * *

Although the plaintiffs had promptly given Baldridge effective notice of the claimed breaches, and Baldridge in turn had immediately notified Ford, the court of appeals' opinion could be construed as holding that such indirect actual notice is insufficient and as requiring direct notice from ultimate consumer to remote manufacturer. We disagree. Our review of the purpose of the notice requirement, and of the evidence of actual notice in this case, leads us to conclude that the court of appeals erred in stating too stringent a notice requirement.

* * *

The plaintiffs, upon encountering problems with the newly-purchased equipment, immediately notified Baldridge, the seller. Baldridge, in turn, promptly advised Ford of the problem, and Ford dispatched a service representative who arrived to work on the equipment within a few days after it had been delivered. Surely formal notice communicated directly from the buyers to Ford could have accomplished no more.

In the law governing breach of warranty, the notice requirement serves three useful purposes. First, notice provides the seller a chance to correct any defect. Second, notice affords the seller an opportunity to prepare for negotiation and litigation. Third, notice provides the seller a safeguard against stale claims being asserted after it is too late for the manufacturer or seller to investigate them.

Here Ford received from its dealer prompt, actual notice of the machinery's malfunction and almost immediately had an opportunity to repair the equipment. In these circumstances, it is clear that the purposes of notice have been fulfilled. Indeed, it is highly unlikely that those purposes could have been more thoroughly or satisfactorily met by delivery of formal notice directly from the plaintiffs to the manufacturer.[FN6]

> FN6. UCC 2-607, Comment 4, makes clear that, where notice is given, no formal requisites must be met. It is sufficient if the notice lets "the seller know that the transaction is still troublesome and must be watched." A leading text states that "a scribbled note on a bit of toilet paper will do. . . ." White and Summers, *Uniform Commercial Code*, 11-9 at 347 (1972).

Must notice be given in writing?

The court of appeals noted a split of authority whether notice of a breach of warranty must be given to a remote manufacturer in all cases. Because such notice was given here, and because the answer may not be the same in all factual contexts, we do not pursue that question further. When, as here, the purposes of the notice requirement have been fully served by actual notice, the notice provision should not operate as a technical procedural barrier to deny claimants the opportunity to litigate the case on the merits.

[In the final sections of the opinion, which have been omitted, the court held Ford could reasonably be charged with the Prutches' crop damage as an element of consequential damages, because "[a] manufacturer knowing that its products will be used for crop production reasonably can be expected to foresee that defects in those products may cause crop losses." The court then went on to dismiss Ford's allegations of inconsistent verdicts between Ford and Baldridge, together with claimed evidentiary irregularities. The court therefore reversed the judgment of the appellate court and remanded the matter to the district court for reinstatement of the jury verdict.]

- Following this case, what general guidance would you give to a client to ensure it has complied with the notice requirement?

Note 1: In *Lewis v. Mobil Oil Corp.*, 438 F.2d 500, 8 U.C.C. Rep. Serv. 625 (8th Cir. 1971), the court considered whether the plaintiff, an operator of a sawmill using oil alleged to be ill-suited to the equipment, delayed too long in providing notice to the oil company of the trouble with the oil. The court found it reasonable that the plaintiff used the oil for a period of two and a half years, throughout which time there were signs of problems with the machinery caused by the oil. The court held as follows:

> Here there is not the slightest suggestion of bad faith on the part of the plaintiff. Furthermore, the evidence shows that, soon after using the [allegedly defective oil], plaintiff notified the Mobil dealer . . . that he wasn't sure if a proper oil was being supplied, and was constantly in touch . . . about his problems afterward. Mobil certainly had notice that "the transaction was still troublesome and must be watched." *Id.* at 509.

Thus, as this case shows, passage of time alone will not defeat a plaintiff's cause of action on notice grounds, when the evidence shows the parties were in touch regarding problems with the transaction.

- What advice would you give to a party in the position of the Mobil dealer, which has been notified of a potential problem with goods it sold?

Note 2: In *Pritchard v. Liggett & Myers Tobacco Co.*, 295 F.2d 292, 5 Fed. R. Serv. 2d 778 (3d Cir. 1961), the court allowed litigation regarding an injury allegedly caused by smoking cigarettes to proceed, even though the plaintiff had delayed more than ten months after his cancerous lung was removed before providing notice to the tobacco company that he believed its products had caused his injury. In finding the suit should proceed, the court held as follows:

> Plaintiff was a layman inexperienced in the scientific complications involved here that took many weeks of preparation and trial to unravel. There is no allegation or intimation that defendant has suffered any prejudice by not receiving notice sooner or in a different and more comprehensive form. The lack of prejudice is best manifested by the vigorous and thorough defense presented. *Id.* at 299.

Thus, the relative sophistication of the parties and the effect, if any, of late notice on the defendant's ability to prepare its case, may be relevant in determining whether notice is legally sufficient.

- What facts would show a defendant was prejudiced by late notice?

Problem 1: The *Seely* case was introduced in Part A, Note 2. In that case, the truck was purchased in October 1959 and immediately began to display the "galloping" problem referenced in the discussion of the case above. The purchaser worked with Southern Truck Sales, the dealer, which itself coordinated with White Motor Company, the manufacturer, for eleven months prior to the accident, in an unsuccessful effort to address the problem. After the accident, in September 1960, the plaintiff informed Southern that he would cease making payments on the truck.

- Based on these facts, when did the plaintiff provide notice to White?

- Was notice reasonable under the standards in 2-607 (3)?

Problem 2: Kyle Olsen ordered French fries as part of his meal at Joe's American Bar and Grill. When he bit into the third fry, he heard a "loud crunching noise" and "felt a powerful and immediate pain in his mouth." When he spit out the portion he had not yet swallowed, he saw part of his tooth, together with fragments of metal. He later learned he had fractured two teeth. He immediately called over the waitperson, who just as immediately notified the manager. At the manager's request, Olsen completed an accident report, which both he and the manager signed. At that time, the manager took away the metal fragments. Olsen asked for the ⟵ fragments before he left the restaurant, but the manager informed him they had already been discarded.

> What error did Olsen make?

- Did Olsen satisfy 2-607's notice requirement?

Based on *Olsen v. BBRG Massachusetts Restaurant, Inc.*, 2005 Mass. App. Div. 23, 52 U.C.C. Rep. Serv. 2d 792 (2005) (Mass. Mun. Ct. Boston A.D. Feb. 17, 2005).

International Perspective: Notice

Read CISG Articles 39, 40, and 44. The buyer's failure to give notice of an alleged nonconformity in the goods may release the seller from liability under the CISG as well as under the UCC. The CISG goes somewhat beyond the terms of the UCC, in that Article 44, which has no precise UCC analogue, expressly excuses a buyer's failure to give notice, if the buyer can show reasonable grounds for such failure. Although it may be possible to achieve a similar result under the UCC by application of the doctrine of promissory estoppel via 1-103, the Code does not expressly provide for this possibility. In addition, under Article 40, the CISG does not allow a seller to use the buyer's failure to give notice as a means of avoiding liability if the seller's superior knowledge and failure of disclosure prevented the buyer from discovering a nonconformity of which the seller knew or "could not have been unaware." Finally, revised 2-607 (3) arguably provides broader

protection for the buyer than the CISG, in allowing notice to
shield the seller from liability only if the buyer's failure to give
notice harmed the seller.

Other than CISG 39's "outside limit" of two years, which has no
equivalent in the UCC, no particular notice period is specified
in the Convention, so courts have been left to determine what a
reasonable notice period should be. In a Swiss case involving
unknown parties, numbered 11 95 123/357 and dated January
8, 1997, the Obergericht Kanton Luzern addressed a dispute
between a Swiss buyer of medical devices and an Italian seller.
The court indicated it believed a notice period of one month was
a good compromise between the more generous Anglo-
American and Dutch traditions which, according to the court,
frequently allow notice periods of several months, and the
stringent German standard, which imposes a limit of eight
days.

> This is the highest cantonal court in Lucerne, Switzerland.

- What are the benefits and burdens of bright-line notice
  rules as compared with more flexible standards?

- What are the benefits and burdens of long notice
  periods as compared with shorter ones?

Privity

> Comment 3 has been deleted from Revised Article 2. The Article 2A equivalent of 2-318 is 2A-216.

Read current and revised 2-318 and current Comment 3.

- What is the essence of the proposed changes?

Privity of contract is an important concept in determining who
can be liable to whom in a warranty action. Consider the
various parties who could be involved in a lawsuit based upon a
consumer's purchase of adulterated wine that he or she later
serves to dinner-party guests. Assume the wine was made in
Napa Valley, California, sold to stores through a national
distributor, and purchased in a retail wine boutique in New
York City. The following chart shows some of the litigation
possibilities, assuming the point at which the wine became
adulterated was in dispute.

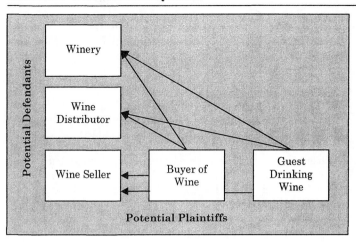

- Which parties are likely to be in a contractual relationship with one another?

There are two kinds of privity, but the Code addresses only one. "Vertical privity" addresses how far up the distribution chain warranty liability can go from the wine seller; in other words, can the buyer sue only the seller, or can he or she also sue the distributor or winery? The UCC does not address vertical privity. Instead, by application of 1-103, this matter is resolved by other state law.

"Horizontal privity" addresses how remote from the purchaser a cause of action can exist; in other words, can users who did not purchase the good bring suit under a warranty theory? 2-318 provides three alternatives to this matter, and states may choose any of the three.

- Do the alternatives flow from most liberal to most conservative, or vice versa?

- How does each alternative differ from the others?

- Most provisions of the UCC lack multiple alternatives. What were the likely reasons for the drafters' decision to do this?

- What are the benefits and risks of doing so?

The following case suggests why vertical privity should perhaps not be required in an action for breach of express warranty.

Rogers v. Toni Home Permanent Co.,
167 Ohio St. 244, 147 N.E.2d 612, 75 A.L.R.2d 103,
4 Ohio Op. 2d 291 (1958).

Zimmerman, Judge.

The precise question we are now required to determine is whether, in an action for damages brought by the ultimate purchaser of a product directly against its manufacturer and based on the claim that the ingredients of the product were advertised and represented by the manufacturer to such purchaser to be safe and harmless when devoted to their intended use, whereas in fact they were harmful and deleterious, such ultimate purchaser is restricted to prosecuting his action on the basis of negligence alone or whether he may proceed on the theory of an express warranty.

. . . [T]he Court of Common Pleas decided that plaintiff must proceed solely on the basis of negligence, whereas the Court of Appeals held that she might rely and proceed on the theory of express warranty.

In asking for a reversal of the judgment of the Court of Appeals, defendant places great reliance on the comparatively recent case of *Wood v. General Electric Co.*, 159 Ohio St. 273, 112 N.E.2d 8 (1953), wherein the second paragraph of the syllabus is as follows:

> Although a subpurchaser of an inherently dangerous article may recover from its manufacturer for negligence, in the making and furnishing of the article, causing harm to the subpurchaser or his property from a latent defect therein, no action may be maintained against a manufacturer for injury, based upon implied warranty of fitness of the article so furnished.

Such rule is based on the proposition that, to support an action grounded on an implied warranty, there must be contractual privity between the buyer who sues and the seller against whom the suit is brought.

It must be confessed that the prevailing view is that privity of contract is essential in an action based on a breach of an express or implied warranty, and that there is no privity between the manufacturer of an article and the ultimate purchaser thereof from a retailer, where the ultimate purchaser was in no way a party to the original sale.

However, there is a growing number of cases which, as an exception to the general rule, hold that as to foodstuffs and medicines, particularly when sold in cans, capped bottles, or sealed containers, a warranty of fitness for human consumption carries over from the manufacturer or producer to the ultimate consumer, regardless of privity of contract.

It would seem but logical to extend the rule last cited to cosmetics and other preparations, which are sold in sealed packages and are designed for application to the bodies of humans or animals.

* * *

Side note (left margin, upper): Here, the term "syllabus" is used to refer to the court's own outline of its holding. Like the West system of headnotes, the syllabus provides a useful reference, but is not itself part of the court's opinion. Thus, neither a West headnote nor a court's syllabus has the force of law.

Side note (left margin, lower): Why might it make sense to allow an exception for "foodstuffs and medicines . . . sold in . . . sealed containers"?

Occasions may arise when it is fitting and wholesome to discard legal concepts of the past to meet new conditions and practices of our changing and progressing civilization. Today, many manufacturers of merchandise, including the defendant herein, make extensive use of newspapers, periodicals, signboards, radio, and television to advertise their products. The worth, quality, and benefits of the products are described in glowing terms and in considerable detail, and the appeal is almost universally directed to the ultimate consumer. Many of these manufactured articles are shipped out in sealed containers by the manufacturer, and the retailers who dispense them to the ultimate consumers are but conduits or outlets through which the manufacturer distributes his goods. The consuming public ordinarily relies exclusively on the representations of the manufacturer in his advertisements. What sensible or sound reason then exists as to why, when the goods purchased by the ultimate consumer on the strength of the advertisements aimed squarely at him do not possess their described qualities and goodness and cause him harm, he should not be permitted to move against the manufacturer to recoup his loss? In our minds no good or valid reason exists for denying him that right. Surely under modern merchandising practices the manufacturer owes a very real obligation toward those who consume or use his products. The warranties made by the manufacturer in his advertisements and by the labels on his products are inducements to the ultimate consumers, and the manufacturer ought to be held to strict accountability to any consumer who buys the product in reliance on such representations and later suffers injury because the product proves to be defective or deleterious.

* * *

Judgment affirmed.

[The opinion of Judge Taft, who concurred in part, has been omitted.]

- **Read 1-103 Comment 1.** How did the Code drafters intend for their work to "meet new conditions and practices of our changing and progressing civilization"?

- How would this case be decided under revised 2-318?

Note 1: Some of the older privity cases illustrate a concept called "merger," which was founded on the legal fiction that, at marriage, a woman's legal identity was merged into that of her husband. The effect of the merger doctrine was that women became legally incapable of owning property or pursuing litigation based upon their own interests. Sometimes, this doctrine created bizarre results. In *Gearing v. Berkson*, 223 Mass. 257, 111 N.E. 785 (1916), the court considered a warranty claim arising from Katherine Gearing's purchase of pork chops for herself and her husband Percy, which subsequently made the two of them ill. Although Mrs. Gearing had purchased the chops, the court found no privity of contract between her and the grocery store, on the grounds that "the

only sale was that made to her husband through her as his
agent," and denied recovery to Mrs. Gearing.

Eighteen years later, the law had advanced somewhat. In
Giminez v. Great Atlantic & Pacific Tea Co., 264 N.Y. 390, 191
N.E. 27 (1934), the New York Court of Appeals rejected the
argument that had carried the day in *Gearing*. In *Giminez*, the
court found privity of contract did exist between Grace Giminez
and the grocery store where she purchased the crab meat that
ultimately made Grace and her husband Thomas ill. In
affirming judgment for Mrs. Giminez on her warranty claim,
the court held as follows: "[W]e take the law to be [that] where
the wife is the purchaser, the right of action is hers."

- What relationship exists between the merger doctrine
  and the contract defense of incapacity?

Note 2: Read 2-607, Comment 5. *Frericks v. General Motors
Corp.*, 278 Md. 304, 363 A.2d 460, 20 U.C.C. Rep. Serv. 371
(1976), shows the relationship between privity and notice. In
that case, the court considered a claim by John Joseph
Frericks, who was a passenger in a 1969 Opel Kadett
automobile driven by Ronald Baines. When Baines fell asleep,
the vehicle left the road and overturned. Frericks alleges he
was injured due to the failure of the locking system securing
the seat in which he was riding. He brought suit on a warranty
theory. General Motors claimed Frericks had failed to give
proper notice of his injuries. In rejecting this contention, the
court noted, as a preliminary matter, that Frericks would be
permitted to bring suit for the alleged breach of warranty as a
third-party beneficiary of General Motors' warranties to the
purchasers, in this case Mr. Baines' parents. The court found
that Frericks, as a third-party beneficiary, would not be
required to provide direct notice of his breach of warranty
claim.

> To test your understanding of 2-318, consider which of its three alternatives support such a statement.

Professor William Prosser's article *The Assault Upon the
Citadel: Strict Liability to the Consumer*, 69 Yale L. J. 1099
(1960), provides additional guidance on this topic:

> As between the immediate parties to the sale, [the notice
> requirement] is a sound commercial rule, designed to protect the
> seller against unduly delayed claims or damages. As applied to
> personal injuries, and notice to a remote seller, it becomes a booby-
> trap for the unwary. The injured consumer is seldom steeped in
> the business practice which justifies the rule, and at least until he
> has had legal advice it will not occur to him to give notice to one
> with whom he has had no dealings. *Id.* at 1130.

- What are the risks and benefits of exempting third parties from the notice requirement?

Problem 1: Bertha Chysky worked as a waitress. In return for her labor, she received a weekly salary, as well as lodging and meals. One day, her lunch included a piece of cake her employer had purchased from Drake Brothers Company. Assume this entity prepared and delivered the cake. When she bit into the cake, she discovered a nail had been baked in, in such a fashion that it was invisible from the surface. Her gums became infected and three of her teeth were removed.

- Does Ms. Chysky have a cause of action in warranty against her employer, against Drake Brothers Company, or against both?

Based on *Chysky v. Drake Brothers Co.*, 235 N.Y. 468, 139 N.E. 576, (1923).

Problem 2: Mrs. Lyons and Mrs. Jackson entered the Belen Drug Store in Belen, Mississippi, where Mrs. Jackson ordered and paid for two bottles of Coca-Cola. She gave one to Mrs. Lyons, and the women proceeded to drink the beverages. Inside Mrs. Lyons' bottle was some broken glass. She swallowed some and was injured. Assume the glass was introduced during the bottling process.

- Can Mrs. Lyons recover damages from Coca-Cola Bottling Works based upon an implied warranty of merchantability?

Based on *Coca-Cola Bottling Works v. Lyons*, 145 Miss. 876, 111 So. 305 (1927).

International Perspective: Privity

Read CISG Articles 4 and 35. The CISG provides no mechanism by which a user of goods who is not the buyer may assert claims against the seller. In addition, the CISG does not address whether the buyer, or another user of the goods, may assert claims against an entity other than the immediate seller of the goods.

- What law governs questions of privity in international sales?

D. Damages for Breach of Warranty

The Article 2A
equivalent is 2A-519
(4).

Read 2-714 (2) and Comment 2. This textbook addresses other Article 2 damages in Chapter 5. Warranty damages are dealt with separately here because they are different in some important ways from damages for delivery of nonconforming goods. The major difference is this: a buyer who chooses to sue for warranty damages has chosen to keep the goods and is seeking to recover for the loss suffered as a result of the goods' disappointing quality. By contrast, a buyer who sues for damages based on nonconformity may have rejected the goods or revoked acceptance of the goods and therefore may be seeking to recover the lost value of the entire contract. As 2-714 (2) states, the general measure of warranty damages is "the difference at the time and place of acceptance between the value of the goods accepted and the value they would have had if they had been as warranted, . . . unless special circumstances show proximate damages of a different amount." The "special circumstances" clause generates much discussion and litigation.

The Magnuson-Moss
Warranty Act, 15
USC §§ 2301 et seq.,
can be found online
at www.gpoaccess.
gov/uscode/index.
html.

The following case provides guidance in interpreting and applying the "special circumstances" language. The case also shows the relationship between UCC warranty claims and those brought pursuant to the federal Magnuson-Moss Warranty Act. Make sure you understand this relationship, as the Act can be a powerful tool for consumers.

Mayberry v. Volkswagen of America, Inc.,
278 Wis. 2d 39, 692 N.W.2d 226, 2005-1 Trade Cases P 74,710,
56 U.C.C. Rep. Serv. 2d 214, 2005 WI 13 (2005).

Jon P. Wilcox, J.

On October 14, 2000, the plaintiff, Jessica Mayberry, purchased a new 2001 galactic blue Volkswagen Jetta GLS from Van Dyn Hoven Imports in Appleton, Wisconsin. The cash price of the vehicle was $17,800. After sales tax, registration, title, and other fees, the price of the vehicle came to $18,526. However, according to Mayberry, the total purchase price of the vehicle came to $22,548 after adding finance charges. As part of the vehicle purchase, the manufacturer, Volkswagen, issued a two-year or 24,000 mile limited warranty for the Jetta. Under the terms of the written warranty, Volkswagen agreed to repair any manufacturer's defect in material or workmanship and replace defective parts free of charge for the warranty period. However, the warranty did not give Mayberry the right to a refund or replacement of the vehicle if it was defective.

Shortly after taking possession of the Jetta, Mayberry began experiencing problems with the vehicle. Service records from Van Dyn Hoven indicate that Mayberry brought the vehicle in for service on a number of occasions for various problems. The problems consisted of a broken armrest, intermittent illumination of the "check engine" light, and burning and leaking oil. The engine problems culminated in the replacement of a piston ring in the engine on November 29, 2001. On all occasions, the vehicle was inspected or repaired free of charge under the warranty. Thereafter, Mayberry attempted to revoke acceptance of the vehicle in writing. Volkswagen refused the revocation.

After you have read Chapter 5's materials on revocation of acceptance, return to this case and consider whether Mayberry can make a good-faith argument that she did so.

On June 3, 2002, Mayberry filed suit against Volkswagen under the federal Magnuson-Moss Warranty Act, 15 USC §§ 2301 et seq. (2000), . . . First, Mayberry alleged that Volkswagen breached its written warranty for the vehicle. Second, Mayberry contended that Volkswagen breached its implied warranty of merchantability under 15 USC §§ 2301 (7) & 2308. . . .

Subsequently, Mayberry traded in her Volkswagen for a 2003 Mazda Tribute at Mazda Knoxville. Mayberry received $15,100 as a trade-in allowance for the Jetta. The total purchase price of the Mazda Tribute was $24,149.32. At the time of the trade-in, the mileage on the Jetta was 32,737. On November 8, 2002, Mayberry amended her complaint to reflect the trade-in of the Jetta. As an affirmative defense to the amended complaint, Volkswagen alleged that Mayberry "suffered no damages as she received more than the full fair-market value for the vehicle which is the subject of the action, at the time of the trade in."

On February 18, 2003, Volkswagen moved for summary judgment on the ground that Mayberry did not suffer any damages as a result of the allegations set forth in her complaint. Specifically, Volkswagen argued that Mayberry was "unable to prove that she suffered any compensable damages" because "Mayberry traded in the vehicle for more than fair-market value." In addition, Volkswagen argued that Mayberry's extended use of the vehicle and subsequent trade-in for more than fair-market value invalidated her revocation of acceptance claim because she could not demonstrate that the value of the Jetta was substantially impaired.

In response to the summary judgment motion, Mayberry submitted the affidavit of Joseph Pennachio, her named expert and "retail vehicle-finance specialist." Mr. Pennachio opined that Mayberry did not receive fair-market value for her Jetta. He stated, based on the N.A.D.A. Official Used Car Guide, that the fair-market value of the vehicle at the time of the trade-in was $15,900 and that "[t]he Fair Market Value indicated, given the presumption of a private party transaction, would be $17,900." However, in a letter filed with the court on April 21, 2003, Mayberry conceded, "Mr. Joe Pennachio's report appears flawed. While Mr. Pennachio asserts the FMV of the vehicle at the time of sale was $15,900.00, it is true that the N.A.D.A. Official Used Car Guide states that the applicable FMV of this vehicle for trade-in is $14,200.00."

In addition, Mayberry herself filed an affidavit, stating:

> Based on the problems with the Jetta that I experienced, it is my opinion that I paid too much money for the vehicle. I believe that the Jetta was not worth the $18,526.00 I paid at the time I

purchased it, and at most was worth only $12,526.00 based on the problems I experienced.

. . . [The court found that] Mayberry failed to establish she suffered any damages for any breach of warranty. . . .

* * *

Thus, on May 28, 2003, the circuit court entered judgment in favor of Volkswagen, dismissing Mayberry's complaint in its entirety.

The court of appeals reversed, concluding that the circuit court utilized an incorrect standard for measuring damages and that genuine issues of material fact concerning damages existed. The court of appeals concluded that, under § 402.714 (2), the proper measure of damages for breach of warranty is the difference between the value of goods as accepted and the value as warranted at the time and place of acceptance. The court stated that the evidence demonstrated that the warranted value of the vehicle was $18,000 and that Mayberry's own testimony as to the actual value of the car was sufficient to survive summary judgment. The court of appeals also noted that Volkswagen might be entitled to an offset for the mileage Mayberry put on the vehicle under the "special circumstances" clause of Wis. Stat. § 402.714 (2). Therefore, the court of appeals reversed the circuit court order for summary judgment because the circuit court failed to apply the correct measure of damages in Wis. Stat. § 402.714 (2) and a genuine issue of material fact existed regarding damages insomuch as Mayberry had provided testimony as to the actual value of the vehicle and Volkswagen had "offered evidence suggesting 'proximate damages of a different amount.'"

[The court's analysis of the appropriate standard of review has been omitted.]

This is a breach of warranty action under the federal Magnuson-Moss Warranty Act, 15 USC §§ 2301 et seq. Mayberry filed suit under 15 USC § 2310 (d) (1), which allows a consumer to bring suit against a warrantor in any state for failure to comply with its obligations under a written warranty or implied warranty. Mayberry alleged that Volkswagen failed to comply with its written warranty. In addition, Mayberry claimed that Volkswagen breached its implied warranty under 15 USC §§ 2301 (7) & 2308. [FN9] Pursuant to 15 USC § 2310 (d) (1) (A) and 15 USC § 2311 (b) (1), state law governs the appropriate measure of damages for breach of warranty under the Magnuson-Moss Act.

> The "state law" to which reference is made is, of course, the UCC.

> FN9. Except where otherwise provided, the Magnuson-Moss Warranty Act requires application of state law governing written and implied warranties. From the consumer's perspective, the chief advantage of proceeding under the Magnuson-Moss Act for breach of limited warranty or breach of implied warranty is the availability of attorney fees to a prevailing consumer under 15 USC § 2310 (d) (2).

We begin by noting that we are not presented with any issue concerning whether Volkswagen actually breached any of its warranties in this case. Rather, the appeal concerns only the issue of what measure of damages is appropriate in this case. Thus, for purposes of this appeal, we will assume that Mayberry's allegations regarding Volkswagen's breach of warranties are true.

* * *

. . . Mayberry argues that we should follow the default rule for calculating damages as contained in § 402.714 (2). . . . Further, Mayberry asserts that the special-circumstances clause is applicable only where the standard method for calculating damages is insufficient to compensate the plaintiff for her loss or the goods in question are unique with no ready market. Mayberry states that Volkswagen is attempting to turn the special-circumstances clause on its head and use it to preclude her from any recovery. Mayberry notes that she presented a prima facie case of damages by presenting evidence of the value of the vehicle as warranted (its purchase price) and testified as to the actual value of the vehicle at the time and place of acceptance. Thus, the crux of the dispute before us is the interpretation of the "special circumstances" language contained in § 402.714 (2) and what effect, if any, a purchaser's use and subsequent resale of an allegedly defective vehicle has on her ability to recover damages.

* * *

The core of Volkswagen's argument is that special circumstances are present when an automobile purchaser uses the vehicle for an extended period of time, the manufacturer makes numerous repairs free of charge under its warranty, and the consumer later resells it for more than its fair-market value. According to Volkswagen, under these circumstances, damages should be calculated based on the actual value and fair-market value of the vehicle at the time of resale. . . .

* * *

[W]e have found no authority that stands for the proposition that the proper measure of damages under the Uniform Commercial Code is the difference between the market value and actual price of the defective product at the time and place of resale when the plaintiff alleges a breach of the manufacturer's written warranty and implied warranty of merchantability. Breach of contract remedies under the Uniform Commercial Code are designed to put the aggrieved party "in as good a position as if the other party had fully performed." Wis. Stat. § 401.106 (1). . . .

Mayberry has alleged that she suffered damages because her vehicle was defective when she accepted it and she did not receive a vehicle of the quality for which she paid. The fact that Mayberry later resold the vehicle for more than its fair-market value does not totally negate the fact that she did not receive the benefit of her bargain. While the amount of profit realized on the resale may be relevant to the issue of mitigation, construing the "special circumstances" clause of § 402.714 (2) to completely bar the plaintiff from maintaining a claim would

defeat the manifest purpose of the remedies under the Uniform
Commercial Code, which are to compensate the plaintiff for her direct
economic loss and place her in as good a position as if the seller had
fully performed.

Therefore, we hold that pursuant to Wis. Stat. § 402.714 (2), the
appropriate method for measuring damages in this case is the
difference between the warranted value of the vehicle in question and
its actual value at the time and place of acceptance. Further, we
conclude that Mayberry has established a prima facie case of damages
sufficient to survive summary judgment under this standard.

* * *

Because the circuit court applied an incorrect standard for measuring
damages, we affirm the decision of the court of appeals reversing the
circuit court's order of summary judgment.

[The concurring opinion has been omitted.]

- In what way is Volkswagen allegedly "attempting to
  turn the special-circumstances clause on its head"?

- In your own words, why does Volkswagen's argument
  fail?

Note 1: In *Lewis v. Mobil Oil Corp.*, 438 F.2d 500, 8 U.C.C.
Rep. Serv. 625, 8th Cir. 1971), introduced previously in Part C's
materials on Notice, the court addressed a lawsuit by a sawmill
operator against an oil company. The operator alleged that
Mobil's representative, who knew the operator was relying
upon Mobil to select suitable oil for his hydraulic system,
supplied improper oil, which caused his equipment to break
down repeatedly in a way that damaged his business. The
court allowed Lewis to recover his lost profits, holding that,

> [w]ith respect to breach of warranty, lost profits are held to be
> foreseeable if they are proximately caused by and are the natural
> result of the breath. Where a seller provides goods to a
> manufacturing enterprise with knowledge that they are to be used
> in the manufacturing process, it is reasonable to assume that he
> should know that defective goods will cause a disruption of
> production, and loss of profits is a natural consequence of such
> disruption. *Id.* at 510.

- **Read 2-714 (3) and 2-715.** Is the court's decision
  consistent with these provisions?

Note 2: *Prutch v. Ford Motor Co.*, 618 P.2d 657, 29 U.C.C.
Rep. Serv. 1507 (Colo. 1980) provides additional guidance as to
the recovery of consequential damages. The facts of the case
are set forth above in Part C's materials on Notice. In that

case, Ford tried to escape liability for the Prutches' crop damage by showing that it had no "prior actual knowledge" of the damage that would occur due to its defective products. In rejecting this argument, the court held that Ford "confuse[d] 'foreseeable' with 'actually foreseen.'" The court indicated requiring the damages be "actually foreseen" would be "excessively restrictive," and concluded that "[a] manufacturer knowing that its products will be used for crop production reasonably can be expected to foresee that defects in those products may cause crop losses."

- Which party bears the burden of proof as to consequential damages, and what kind of evidence is it expected to produce?

Note 3: In many cases in this chapter, the plaintiff's potential recovery was less than the parties' probable litigation costs. Scholars have explored the factors – economic and psychological – that might lead parties to litigate cases that do not appear to make economic sense. Much literature in this area stems from an article by Professor Marc Galanter, *Why the "Haves" Come Out Ahead: Speculations on the Limits of Legal Change*, 9 Law & Socy. Rev. 95 (1974). In this article, Professor Galanter introduces the concept of the "repeat player," showing the characteristics of the repeat player, how it plays the "litigation game," and how litigation favors the repeat player:

> We might divide our actors into those claimants who have only occasional recourse to the courts (one-shotters or OS) and repeat players (RP) who are engaged in many similar litigations over time. *Id.* at 97.

> * * *

> We would expect an RP to play the litigation game differently from an OS. Let us consider some of his advantages:

> (1) RPs, having done it before, have advance intelligence; they are able to structure the next transaction and build a record. It is the RP who writes the form contract, requires the security deposit, and the like.

> (2) RPs develop expertise and have ready access to specialists. They enjoy economies of scale and have low start-up costs for any case.

> (3) RPs have opportunities to develop facilitative informal relationships with institutional incumbents.

> (4) The RP must establish and maintain credibility as a combatant. His interest in his "bargaining reputation" serves

How does contract law respond to these advantages to level the playing field?

as a resource to establish "commitment" to his bargaining positions. With no bargaining reputation to maintain, the OS has more difficulty in convincingly committing himself in bargaining.

(5) RPs can play the odds. The larger the matter at issue looms for OS, the more likely he is to adopt a minimax strategy (minimize the probability of maximum loss). Assuming that the stakes are relatively smaller for RPs, they can adopt strategies calculated to maximize gain over a long series of cases, even where this involves the risk of maximum loss in some cases.

RPs can play for rules as well as immediate gains. First, it pays an RP to expend resources in influencing the making of the relevant rules by such methods as lobbying. (And his accumulated expertise enables him to do this persuasively.)

RPs can also play for rules in litigation itself, whereas an OS is unlikely to. That is, there is a difference in what they regard as a favorable outcome. Because his stakes in the immediate outcome are high and because by definition OS is unconcerned with the outcome of similar litigation in the future, OS will have little interest in that element of the outcome which might influence the disposition of the decision-marker next time around. For the RP, on the other hand, anything that will favorably influence the outcomes of future cases is a worthwhile result. *Id.* at 98-100.

Another concept that can be relevant in determining why some small lawsuits get litigated through several levels of appeal is the "nuisance suit." Robert Cooter and Thomas Ulen explore this concept in their book, *Law & Economics* (4th ed. Boston: Pearson/Addison Wesley 2004). If one party is able to litigate a dispute for less than the other, or will incur litigation costs later than the other, or will escape other costs (like delay to another project during the litigation), it might make sense to pursue a case to encourage the other party to settle the matter quickly. Cooter and Ulen provide the following model for computing a claim's value:

To file a complaint, the plaintiff must usually hire a lawyer and pay filing fees to the court. Filing a complaint creates a legal claim. To decide whether to initiate a suit, a rational plaintiff compares the cost of the complaint and the expected value of the legal claim. The expected value of the legal claim depends upon what the plaintiff thinks will occur after filing a complaint. . . . To decide whether to file a complaint, the rational plaintiff must attach probabilities and payoffs to these events. *Id.* at 392-393.

As Cooter & Ulen indicate, when trends show that successful plaintiffs are being awarded increasing damages, plaintiffs will tend to file more complaints because the expected value of plaintiffs' claims will be perceived as higher. Over time,

however, increasing damages for successful plaintiffs can have
a second effect, as well: defendants may wish to avoid
litigation, and thus avoid potential payment of claims, by
taking additional precautions to prevent the kinds of harms
that cause plaintiffs to file suit. For example, if plaintiffs have
been suing manufacturers – and winning – based upon claims
of defective products, the manufacturers might respond by
putting superior quality-control procedures in place to prevent
such defects in the future.

- Is a merchant or consumer more likely to be a repeat
  player?

- Is one more likely than the other to bring a nuisance
  suit?

- How can these dynamics interact to create litigation of
  some small-dollar matters through several levels of
  appeal?

Problem 1: What would be the proper measure of damages
under the following facts? (Your answer need not be numeric.)
Mr. and Mrs. Gaither purchased a 1974 Ford Thunderbird
automobile on July 13, 1974, from Walker Ford Sales. The car
was a "demo" model and had been driven 4,250 miles at the
time of purchase. They paid $1,400 down and signed a
promissory note for the balance of $4,900 plus interest. They
made payments of $2,900 on the note and refused to pay the
rest, citing a strong vibration at highway speeds, of which the
Gaithers claimed they had given Walker immediate notice.
The Gaithers further alleged that, despite the existence of a
"new car warranty" providing that the dealer "would repair or
replace, free of charge, any part except tires, found to be
defective in factory materials under normal use up to a
maximum of 12 months or 12,000 miles from the date of sale,"
the dealer refused to respond to their complaints about the
vehicle. Assume the court has found the dealer liable for
breach of an express warranty and the implied warranty of
merchantability.

Based on *Walker Ford Sales v. Gaither*, 265 Ark. 275, 578
S.W.2d 23, 26 U.C.C. Rep. Serv. 335 (1979).

Problem 2: What facts must a plaintiff prove to establish that
food prepared or served by an individual with Hepatitis A
violated the implied warranty of merchantability, and what
would the appropriate measure of damages be?

Based on *Evans v. Taco Bell Corp.*, 2005 WL 2333841 (D.N.H.
Sept. 23, 2005).

Note 5 in Part B
may assist you in
answering this
question.

International Perspective: Remedies

Read CISG Article 50. Because breach of warranty is not a separate cause of action under the CISG, damages based upon nonconformities that would be termed breaches of warranty under the UCC will be covered under Chapter 5 in the general discussion of CISG remedies. Article 50 is the closest equivalent to the UCC provisions for warranty damages, in that it allows a party to retain nonconforming goods and bring suit to recover damages based on the nonconformity.

- Does Article 50 include anything analogous to the "special circumstances" clause in 2-714?

Chapter Conclusion: As you leave this chapter, you should be able to identify express and implied warranties of quality. You should also be able to determine whether the seller has made an effective disclaimer of warranties and whether issues of privity or notice will bar the plaintiff's recovery. Finally, when a court has found a breach of warranty, you should have a sense of how damages will be computed.

1
2
3
4
5
6
7
8
9
10
11
12
13
14
15
16
17
18
19
20
21
22
23
24
25
26
27
28
29
30
31
32
33
34
35
36
37
38
39
40
41
42
43
44
45
46
50
51
52
53

Chapter 5:
Performance under Article 2

A. The Obligation of Good Faith

This section sets the context for the remainder of the chapter by describing the good-faith obligations that pervade Article 2.

> The concept of good faith is introduced in Chapter 1, Part C.

Read 1-304 and Comment 1. Bad faith is not its own cause of action, but describes a way of failing to perform other Article 2 duties.

- Recall 1-201's definition of good faith. How are "reasonable commercial standards of fair dealing" determined for a non-merchant?

> 1-201 Comment 20 may assist you in answering this question.

Read the following case, noting the relationship between bad faith and unconscionability. Attorneys sometimes join multiple causes of action without carefully analyzing whether the facts support each claim. After you have read this case, consider which facts are most relevant to unconscionability and which are most relevant to bad faith.

Zapatha v. Dairy Mart, Inc.,
381 Mass. 284, 408 N.E.2d 1370,
29 U.C.C. Rep. Serv. 1121 (1980).

Wilkins, Justice.

We are concerned here with the question whether Dairy Mart, Inc. lawfully undertook to terminate a franchise agreement under which [Bernard and Elaine Zapatha] operated a Dairy Mart store on Wilbraham Road in Springfield. The Zapathas brought this action seeking to enjoin the termination of the agreement, alleging that the contract provision purporting to authorize the termination of the franchise agreement without cause was unconscionable and that Dairy Mart's conduct was an unfair and deceptive act or practice in violation of G.L. c. 93A. The judge ruled that Dairy Mart did not act in good faith [and] that the termination provision was unconscionable.... We granted Dairy Mart's application for direct appellate review of a judgment that stated that Dairy Mart could terminate the agreement only for good cause and that the attempted termination was null and void. We reverse the judgments.

Mr. Zapatha is a high-school graduate who had attended college for one year and had also taken college evening courses in business administration and business law. From 1952 to May 1973, he was employed by a company engaged in the business of electroplating. He rose through the ranks to foreman and then to the position of operations manager, at one time being in charge of all metal finishing in the plant with 150 people working under him. In May 1973, he was

> After you have read the entire case, return to these facts. Are they relevant to good faith, unconscionability, both, or neither?

discharged and began looking for other opportunities, in particular a
business of his own. Several months later, he met with a representative
of Dairy Mart. Dairy Mart operates a chain of franchised "convenience"
stores. The Dairy Mart representative told Mr. Zapatha that working
for Dairy Mart was being in business for one's self and that such a
business was very stable and secure. Mr. Zapatha signed an
application to be considered for a franchise. In addition, he was
presented with a brochure entitled "Here's a Chance," which made
certain representations concerning the status of a franchise holder.
[FN3]

> FN3. It included the following statements: ". . . you'll have the
> opportunity to own and run your own business . . ."; "We want to
> be sure we're hooking up with the right person. A person who sees
> the opportunity in owning his own business . . . who requires the
> security that a multi-million-dollar parent company can offer him
> . . . who has the good judgment and business sense to take
> advantage of the unique independence that Dairy Mart offers its
> franchisees. . . . We're looking for a partner . . . who can take the
> tools we offer and build a life of security and comfort. . . ."

Dairy Mart approved Mr. Zapatha's application and offered him a store
in Agawam. On November 8, 1973, a representative of Dairy Mart
showed him a form of franchise agreement, entitled Limited Franchise
and License Agreement, asked him to read it, and explained that his
wife would have to sign the agreement as well.

. . . The termination provision [contained in the agreement] . . . allowed
either party, after twelve months, to terminate the agreement without
cause on ninety days' written notice. In the event of termination
initiated by it without cause, Dairy Mart agreed to repurchase the
saleable merchandise inventory at retail prices, less 20%.

After you have finished this case, return to these facts. If you were representing Dairy Mart in this contract-negotiation process, would you recommend that the process be handled differently next time? If so, why and how?

The Dairy Mart representative read and explained the termination
provision to Mr. Zapatha. Mr. Zapatha later testified that, while he
understood every word in the provision, he had interpreted it to mean
that Dairy Mart could terminate the agreement only for cause. The
Dairy Mart representative advised Mr. Zapatha to take the agreement
to an attorney and said, "I would prefer that you did." However, he also
told Mr. Zapatha that the terms of the contract were not negotiable.
The Zapathas signed the agreement without consulting an attorney.
When the Zapathas took charge of the Agawam store, a representative
of Dairy Mart worked with them to train them in Dairy Mart's
methods of operation.

In 1974, another store became available on Wilbraham Road in
Springfield, and the Zapathas elected to surrender the Agawam store.
They executed a new franchise agreement, on an identical printed
form, relating to the new location.

In November 1977, Dairy Mart presented a new and more detailed
form of "Independent Operator's Agreement" to the Zapathas for
execution. Some of the terms were less favorable to the store operator
than those of the earlier form of agreement. Mr. Zapatha told
representatives of Dairy Mart that he was content with the existing

contract and had decided not to sign the new agreement. On January 20, 1978, Dairy Mart gave written notice to the Zapathas that their contract was being terminated effective in ninety days. The termination notice stated that Dairy Mart "remains available to enter into discussions with you with respect to entering into a new Independent Operator's Agreement; however, there is no assurance that Dairy Mart will enter into a new Agreement with you, or even if entered into, what terms such Agreement will contain." The notice also indicated that Dairy Mart was prepared to purchase the Zapathas' saleable inventory.

The judge found that Dairy Mart terminated the agreement solely because the Zapathas refused to sign the new agreement. He further found that, but for this one act, Dairy Mart did not behave in an unconscionable manner, in bad faith, or in disregard of its representations. There is no evidence that the Zapathas undertook to discuss a compromise of the differences that led to the notice of termination.

[The portion of the opinion determining that Article 2 applies to the franchise agreement, at least by analogy, has been omitted.]

We consider first the plaintiffs' argument that the termination clause of the franchise agreement, authorizing Dairy Mart to terminate the agreement without cause, on ninety days' notice, was unconscionable by the standards expressed in G.L. c. 106, 2-302. . . . The issue is one of law for the court, and the test is to be made as of the time the contract was made. In measuring the unconscionability of the termination provision, the fact that the law imposes an obligation of good faith on Dairy Mart in its performance under the agreement should be weighed.

> The Article 2A equivalent to UCC 2-302 is 2A-108.

The official comment to 2-302 states that "(t)he basic test is whether, in the light of the general commercial background and the commercial needs of the particular trade or case, the clauses involved are so one-sided as to be unconscionable under the circumstances existing at the time of the making of the contract. . . . The principle is one of prevention of oppression and unfair surprise . . . and not of disturbance of allocation of risks because of superior bargaining power." Official Comment 1 to UCC 2-302. . . .

We start with a recognition that the Uniform Commercial Code itself implies that a contract provision allowing termination without cause is not per se unconscionable. Section 2-309 (3) provides that "(t)ermination of a contract by one party except on the happening of an agreed event requires that reasonable notification be received by the other party and an agreement dispensing with notification is invalid if its operation would be unconscionable." G.L. c. 106, 2-309. . . . This language implies that termination of a sales contract without agreed "cause" is authorized by the Code, provided reasonable notice is given. There is no suggestion that the ninety days' notice provided in the Dairy Mart franchise agreement was unreasonable.

> What additional language is proposed in Revised UCC 2-309 (3)?

We find no potential for unfair surprise to the Zapathas in the provision allowing termination without cause. We view the question of

unfair surprise as focused on the circumstances under which the
agreement was entered into. [FN13] The termination provision was
neither obscurely worded, nor buried in fine print in the contract. The
provision was specifically pointed out to Mr. Zapatha before it was
signed; Mr. Zapatha testified that he thought the provision was
"straightforward," and he declined the opportunity to take the
agreement to a lawyer for advice. The Zapathas had ample
opportunity to consider the agreement before they signed it.
Significantly, the subject of loss of employment was paramount in Mr.
Zapatha's mind. . . . We conclude that a person of Mr. Zapatha's
business experience and education should not have been surprised by
the termination provision and, if in fact he was, there was no element
of unfairness in the inclusion of that provision in the agreement.

> FN13. As we shall note subsequently, the concept of oppression
> deals with the substantive unfairness of the contract term. This
> two-part test for unconscionability involves determining whether
> there was "an absence of meaningful choice on the part of one of
> the parties, together with contract terms which are unreasonably
> favorable to the other party." *Williams v. Walker-Thomas
> Furniture Co.*, 350 F.2d 445, 449 (D.C. Cir. 1965). The inquiry
> involves a search for components of "procedural" and "substantive"
> unconscionability.

The *Williams* case provides the classic test for unconscionability.

We further conclude that there was no oppression in the inclusion of a
termination clause in the franchise agreement. We view the question
of oppression as directed to the substantive fairness to the parties of
permitting the termination provisions to operate as written. The
Zapathas took over a going business on premises provided by Dairy
Mart, using equipment furnished by Dairy Mart. As an investment,
the Zapathas had only to purchase the inventory of goods to be sold
but, as Dairy Mart concedes, on termination by it without cause Dairy
Mart was obliged to repurchase all the Zapathas' saleable merchandise
inventory, including items not purchased from Dairy Mart, at 80% of
its retail value. There was no potential for forfeiture or loss of
investment. . . . [The Zapathas] failed to sustain their burden of
showing that the agreement allocated the risks and benefits connected
with termination in an unreasonably disproportionate way and that
the termination provision was not reasonably related to legitimate
commercial needs of Dairy Mart. To find the termination clause
oppressive merely because it did not require cause for termination
would be to establish an unwarranted barrier to the use of termination
at will clauses in contracts in this Commonwealth, where each party
received the anticipated and bargained for consideration during the full
term of the agreement.

If Revised Article 2 is adopted, this definition will be found in UCC 1-201 (20).

We see no basis on the record for concluding that Dairy Mart did not
act in good faith, as that term is defined in the sales article ("honesty in
fact and the observance of reasonable commercial standards of fair
dealing in the trade"). G.L. c. 106, 2-103 (1) (b). There was no evidence
that Dairy Mart failed to observe reasonable commercial standards of
fair dealing in the trade in terminating the agreement. If there were
such standards, there was no evidence of what they were.

The question then is whether there was evidence warranting a finding that Dairy Mart was not honest "in fact." The judge concluded that the absence of any commercial purpose for the termination other than the Zapathas' refusal to sign a new franchise agreement violated Dairy Mart's obligation of good faith. Dairy Mart's right to terminate was clear, and it exercised that right for a reason it openly disclosed. The sole test of "honesty in fact" is whether the person was honest. We think that, whether or not termination according to the terms of the franchise agreement may have been arbitrary, it was not dishonest.

The judge concluded that bad faith was also manifested by Dairy Mart's introductory brochure, which made representations of "security, comfort, and independence." Although this brochure and Mr. Zapatha's mistaken understanding that Dairy Mart could terminate the agreement only for cause could not be relied on to vary the clear terms of the agreement, the introductory brochure is relevant to the question of good faith. However, although the brochure misstated a franchisee's status as the owner of his own business, it shows no lack of honesty in fact relating to the right of Dairy Mart to terminate the agreement. Furthermore, by the time the Zapathas executed the second agreement, and even the first agreement, they knew that they would operate the franchise, but that they would not own the assets used in the business (except the goods to be sold); that the franchise agreement could be terminated by them and, at least in some circumstances, by Dairy Mart; and that in fact the major investment of funds would be made by Dairy Mart. We conclude that the use of the brochure did not warrant a finding of an absence of "honesty in fact."

[The court then looked at franchise termination outside the UCC and reversed the lower court, finding no evidence of bad faith, unconscionable behavior, or other grounds to invalidate the termination clause.]

- How are bad faith and unconscionability distinguishable?

- Is either claim stronger than the other in this case?

Note: In *Fair Driving: Gender and Race Discrimination in Retail Car Negotiations*, 104 Harv. L. Rev. 817 (1991), Professor Ian Ayres presented the outcome of the following study:

> To test whether there is disparate treatment by car retailers on the basis of race or gender, pairs of consumers/testers (for example, a white male and a black female) used the same bargaining strategy in negotiating at new car dealerships. A white male tester was included in each pair of testers. The white male results provide a bench-mark against which to measure the disparate treatment of the non-"whitemale" tester. Three consumer pairs (black female and white male, black male and white male, and white female and white male) conducted approximately 180 tests at ninety Chicago dealerships.

Each tester followed a bargaining script designed to frame the bargaining in purely distributional terms: the only issue to be negotiated was the price. *Id.* at 822-823.

* * *

Testers were chosen to satisfy the following criteria for uniformity:

1. *Age*: All testers were twenty-four to twenty-eight years old.

2. *Education*: All testers had three or four years of college education.

3. *Dress*: All testers were dressed similarly during the negotiations. Testers wore casual "yuppie" sportswear: the men wore polo or buttondown shirts, slacks, and loafers; the women wore straight skirts, blouses, minimal make-up, and flats.

4. *Economic Class*: Testers volunteered that they could finance the car themselves.

5. *Occupation*: If asked by a salesperson, each tester said that he or she was a young urban professional (for example, a systems analyst for First Chicago Bank).

6. *Address*: If asked by the salesperson, each tester gave a fake name and an address for an upper-class, Chicago neighborhood (Streeterville).

7. *Attractiveness*: Applicants were subjectively ranked for average attractiveness.

The testers were trained for two days before visiting the dealerships. The training included not only memorizing the tester script, but also participating in mock negotiations designed to help testers gain confidence and learn how to negotiate and answer questions uniformly. The training emphasized uniformity in cadence and inflection of tester response. In addition to spoken uniformity, the study sought to achieve tester uniformity in non-verbal behavior. *Id.* at 825-826.

The results included the following:

Black female testers were asked to pay over three times the markup of white male testers, and black male testers were asked to pay over twice the white male markup. Moreover, race and gender discrimination were synergistic or "superadditive": the discrimination against the black female tester was greater than the combined discrimination against both the white female and the black male tester. *Id.* at 828-829.

* * *

Sellers asked black female testers more often [than white males] about their occupation, about financing, and whether they were married. Sellers asked black female testers less often whether they had been to other dealerships and whether they had offers from other dealers.

Sellers asked black male testers less often [than white males] if they would like to test drive the car, whether they had been to other dealerships, and whether they had offers from other dealers.

Sellers asked white female testers more often [than white males] whether they had been to other dealerships. Sellers asked white female testers less often what price they would be willing to pay. *Id.* at 834-835.

* * *

Salespeople tried to sell black female testers more often [than white males] on gas mileage, the color of the car, dependability, and comfort, and asked them more often to sign purchase orders.

Salespeople tried to sell white female testers more often [than white males] on gas mileage, the color of the car, and dependability.

With black male testers [as opposed to white males], salespeople more often offered the sticker price as the initial offer and forced the tester to elicit an initial offer from the seller. Salespeople asked black male testers to sign a purchase order less often. *Id.* at 835.

> What would be the purpose of requiring the buyer to sign a purchase order?

* * *

Instead of disclosing their cost information to black testers, the salespeople were more likely to dissemble and claim that they did not know the car's cost. *Id.* at 836.

- How does this study fit into a discussion of good faith? Specifically, is it "honest in fact" and "commercially reasonable" to conduct business in the fashion that Professor Ayres reports? If not, which factor fails and how?

Problem: IBP, Inc. is the world's largest producer of beef and prepares beef for exportation to a number of countries. Hady Enterprises, Inc. is an importer and exporter of frozen beef products. In November 1997, the Egyptian Government issued a decree regarding the packaging of all beef livers exported to Egypt during or after January 1998. Among other requirements, the decree mandated that the animals be prepared according to the Islamic rituals of "Halal" and be labeled to indicate the Halal rituals had been followed. Some other nations, including Russia, do not have the same requirements with regard to the preparation of beef livers. Thus, while beef livers prepared for the Egyptian market

would be suitable for sale in Russia, livers prepared for the
Russian market would not be acceptable for sale in Egypt.
Because of the stringent Halal requirements, Halal-prepared
livers are more expensive than others.

Hady Enterprises ordered more than one million beef livers
from IBP during a three-month period in 1998, falsely
indicating they were being purchased for the Russian market.
The livers were therefore not prepared according to Halal
requirements. Hady Enterprises representatives repackaged
the livers, changing the labels to state the meats were in
compliance with Halal and had been approved by the Islamic
American Society. Hady Enterprises intended to sell the livers
at the higher price Halal-prepared goods would garner, reaping
considerable profit from the sale.

After the livers arrived in Egypt, following an anonymous
complaint, the Egyptian General Authority for Export &
Import Control examined the livers, found them not to be in
compliance with the Halal decree, and ordered them to be
either exported or destroyed. The Egyptian government
thereafter issued a decree banning IBP from importing any
products into the country, causing considerable economic
detriment to IBP. The year prior to the ban, IBP sold about
twenty million pounds of beef livers in Egypt.

> After you have read
> Part E of this
> chapter, you might
> return to these facts
> and consider what
> kinds of damages
> would be most
> appropriate in this
> case.

- To say Hady Enterprises acted in bad faith seems an
  understatement. What causes of action would you
  expect to see joined with a bad faith/breach of contract
  claim by IBP?

Based on *IBP, Inc. v. Hady Enterprises, Inc.*, 267 F. Supp. 2d
1148, 51 U.C.C. Rep. Serv. 2d 950 (N.D. Fla. 2002).

International Perspective: Good Faith

Read CISG Article 7 (1).

- What differences do you discern between this standard
  and the UCC good-faith requirement?

The differences between the CISG "good faith" standard and
the UCC standard are not as great as may seem at first
appearance. Some sources have suggested that, in practice, the
Convention requires parties to act in good faith in much the
same way that the Code does. In the Mexican case of *Dulces
Luisi, S.A. de C.V. v. Seoul International Co. Ltd.*, No. M/115/97

(COMPROMEX Nov. 30, 1998), the court considered a dispute arising from the international sale of confections. The seller, a Mexican company, alleged the purchaser, a Korean company, had engaged in fraudulent behavior by misrepresenting its capacity to enter into a contract and misrepresenting Korean law regarding the labeling of sweets. In considering the dispute, the court held Article 7 (1) required the application of good faith as a basic principle underlying the formation of all contracts. The court specified, however, that it would not apply domestic-law standards of good faith, but instead would apply the standards developed in the market as a matter of international trade. This approach is consistent with the recommendation of John Felemegas, in his article *The United Nations Convention on Contracts for the International Sale of Goods: Article 7 and Uniform Interpretation*, contained in the book *Review of the Convention on Contracts for the International Sale of Goods (CISG) 2000-2001*, edited by Pace International Law Review. Felemegas suggests that, given the differing international conceptions of what good faith means, "the domestic experience of the concept is of limited practical value." The article provides an exhaustive survey of how good faith has been interpreted under various legal systems, as well as under the UCC and CISG.

- Why might conceptions of good faith vary significantly from one country to another?

B. Basic Obligations of Buyers and Sellers

This section shows how an Article 2 transaction proceeds when everything goes smoothly, explaining the basic obligations of buyers and sellers.

Read 2-301. The Code's basic intention is that a single-delivery contract be fulfilled by the seller's delivery of conforming goods and the buyer's acceptance of, and payment for, the goods. The seller's obligations are met through tender, which *Black's Law Dictionary* defines as "an unconditional offer to perform delivery of the goods." Simultaneous transfer of goods by the seller and payment by the buyer is the default assumption, but many contracts provide otherwise, with either delivery or payment to occur before the other.

> A single-delivery contract is to be distinguished from an installment-sales contract. As the materials in this section show, different performance standards apply to each.

Read Sections 2-507 (1) and 2-511 (1). These two provisions sound contradictory but are not. The plaintiff, whether the buyer or the seller, cannot successfully bring suit unless it can show it fulfilled its own obligation under the contract, while the

> Comment 1 to 2-507 provides a clue to how the two sections should be construed together.

other party was in breach. If neither side performed, neither may sue.

Installment Sales

Read 2-612 and Comments 5 and 6. Installment sales are covered by the substantial-performance doctrine, while single-delivery sales require perfect tender. The Code assumes the seller in an installment transaction has sufficient motivation to cure any defective performance such that a more stringent performance standard is unnecessary. Comment 6 reflects the Code's presumption that parties to an installment sale generally intend to continue doing business with one another despite small nonconformities in individual installments.

- When can a buyer reject an installment due to nonconformity?

- When must a buyer accept a nonconforming installment?

- When can a buyer cancel the entire contract due to a single nonconforming installment?

Read 2-612 and Comments 4 and 7. As Comment 4 shows, the Code allows parties to make more stringent performance requirements for themselves if they so choose. Thus, parties may agree that an installment sale will be governed by the perfect-tender rule instead of the doctrine of substantial performance. Parts 2 and 3 of 2-612 and Comment 7 show the interplay between the substantial-performance doctrine and the concept of cure introduced in Part D of this chapter.

The following two excerpts show two ways of conceptualizing an ongoing business relationship such as an installment contract, one based on trust and the other based on parties' expectations as to the logical consequences of misbehavior. Read both and consider which is closer to your own view of how business operates. The first excerpt is from Lynne L. Dallas, *Law and Public Policy: A Socioeconomic Approach* (Carolina Academic Press 2005), in which Professor Dallas examines the relationship between socioeconomics and trust. She describes three kinds of motivation for trust:

> *Normative*: The trustee is believed to intend to fulfill his contract because he is honest and has a strong sense of morality.

> *Affective*: The trustee is believed to intend to fulfill his contract because he cares about the trustor, likes the trustor, or views the

---

Comment 5 has been omitted from Revised Article 2. As Part D shows, the Perfect Tender Rule is softened considerably by the seller's right to cure a nonconforming tender.

trustor as someone in his group or someone with whom he identifies or empathizes.

Instrumental: The trustor is believed to intend to fulfill his contract because it is in his self-interest to do so. *Id.* at 247.

She describes why motivation matters in a business relationship:

[T]he motivations underlying transactions may play an important role in binding parties to contracts. For example, what are the consequences when the trustor's perception of the motivation of the trustee does not coincide with the trustee's actual motivation, and this state of affairs becomes apparent to the truster? What if the trustor believes the trustee to be motivated by normative or affective considerations, but later the trustor learns that the trustee is only motivated by self-interest? Or what if the trustee is motivated by normative or affective considerations and later learns that the trustor considers her to be motivated by self-interest only? The durability or strength of such relationships may be undermined.

> How could the circumstances described here undermine "the durability or strength" of a business relationship?

Moreover, many trust relationships are reciprocal. Most writers focus on simple trust relationships in which the trustor depends on the trustee. . . . In fact, few relationships exist in which the trustor is not also the trustee. Commercial relationships are examples of relationships characterized by reciprocity. Different motivations may underlie these relationships, which may have a bearing on their strength and longevity, as the following chart suggests. For example, if one party to the reciprocal relationship, party A, is motivated by affective considerations in fulfilling his side of the contract and the other party to the relationship, party B, is motivated by self-interest in fulfilling his part of the bargain, the relationship may be less durable than if the motivations of both parties are of the same type. *Id.* at 247-248.

THE TRUSTEE'S MOTIVATION	THE TRUSTOR'S MOTIVATION		
	Normative	**Affective**	**Instrumental**
Normative	Strong	Less Strong	Weak
Affective	Less Strong	Strong	Weak
Instrumental	Weak	Weak	Strong

> Make sure you can reason through Professor Dallas's thesis as summarized in this chart, also found on p. 248 of her book.

- On which motivation or motivations is the Code predicated?

> Review the materials on good faith in Part A and the materials in Chapter 1, Part A on the purpose and philosophy of the Code as needed.

Contrast the following excerpt from Robert Cooter & Thomas Ulen, *Law & Economics* (4th ed. Boston: Pearson/Addison Wesley 2004):

> The parties to long-run relations often rely upon informal devices, rather than enforceable rules, to secure cooperation. Thus, an overbearing partner may be brought back into line by a warning rather than a lawsuit. Or a businessman who oversteps the ethical boundaries of his profession may be chastened by gossip and ostracism. These informal devices usually operate within enduring relationships. Economists have studied how enduring relationships, as opposed to enforceable contracts, affect behavior. We will explain some of the central conclusions by using our example of the agency game. *Id.* at 225.

Cooter & Ulen describe what they call a "repeated game," terminology that may bring to mind Professor Marc Galanter's concept of the "repeat player" as described in Chapter 4. A repeated game is to be distinguished from a "one-shot game." In the repeated game described by Cooter & Ulen, a "principal" invests through an "agent" by placing certain funds under the agent's control to be invested for the principal's benefit, over a series of transactions. In any single transaction, or "round," the agent might be tempted to misbehave by appropriating the principal's funds. Because this is a repeated game involving several rounds, however, the principal can punish the agent for appropriation in any single round by refusing to invest with the agent during the next round. Likewise, the principal rewards appropriate action by the agent in any single round by continuing to invest with that agent in the next round. Cooter & Ulen refer to this cycle of "[r]ewarding cooperation and punishing appropriation" as "tit for tat." Thus, applying the principles of "tit for tat," in the "mid-game" segment of a repeated game, the agent will tend to cooperate with the principal, as doing so is in the agent's best interest. Conversely, if the parties had been participating in a one-shot game, the agent might choose to appropriate the principal's funds, because the principal would have no systemic means of retaliation.

> Remember that the previous excerpt challenges the validity of the unilateral-investment model. In the context of game theory, "appropriation" can be defined as the opposite of "cooperation" and consists of using the principal's investment for the agent's own purposes, instead of for the good of the enterprise.

When a long-term relationship comes to an end, a different dynamic emerges. If the parties know they are in the last round of a repeated game, Cooter & Ulen argue that these parties will act as though they are participating in a one-shot game. In other words, the agent might appropriate the principal's funds during this last round precisely because there will be no "next round" in which the principal could punish the agent for doing so. Thus, the agent might find its own immediate self-interest best served by appropriation.

- Does the Cooter & Ulen excerpt help to explain why litigation is sometimes referred to as a quintessential "endgame" tactic and why there is little litigation in intact relationships?

- Does this excerpt explain the differing performance standards for installment contracts and single-delivery contracts?

Richard Thaler's book *The Winner's Curse: Paradoxes and Anomalies of Economic Life* (Princeton University Press 1992), gives a competing vision of economic reality suggesting that a surprising number of people – approximately fifty percent, in one example – *do* cooperate in "one-shot games." He also found that forty to sixty percent of people contribute to "public goods" such as public radio, rather than choosing to "free-ride," even though they are not compelled to do so.

- How can you explain such seemingly irrational cooperation?

The Thaler research shows "cooperation does not fall to zero even in the last period of a multi-trial game when it is never selfishly rational to cooperate." Thaler suggests this result can be attributed to a societal "norm of cooperation."

- Is your explanation the same as Thaler's?

Read 2-610 and 2-609. If a party acts precipitously in cancelling an installment contract based on conduct by the other party that does not rise to the level of substantial impairment, the cancelling party may be liable for anticipatory repudiation. Therefore, in a close case, a party that believes the other party has breached – or will breach – the contract would be well-advised to seek assurance of performance as described in 2-609 before resorting to cancellation.

The following case illustrates anticipatory repudiation and substantial impairment in the context of an installment contract. In reading the case, pay attention to when a party should seek assurances before declaring a contract terminated by breach and, more generally, when one party has the right to demand assurances from the other.

Cherwell-Ralli, Inc. v. Rytman Grain Co., Inc.,
180 Conn. 714, 433 A.2d 984, 29 U.C.C. Rep. Serv. 513 (1980).

Peters, Justice.

The parties, on July 26, 1974, entered into an installment contract for the sale of Cherco Meal and C-R-T Meal on the basis of a memorandum executed by the Getkin Brokerage House. As modified, the contract called for shipments according to weekly instructions from the buyer, with payments to be made within ten days after delivery. Almost immediately, the buyer was behind in its payments, and these arrearages were often quite substantial. The seller repeatedly called these arrearages to the buyer's attention, but continued to make all shipments as requested by the buyer from July 29, 1974, to April 23, 1975.

By April 15, 1975, the buyer had become concerned that the seller might not complete performance of the contract, because the seller's plant might close and because the market price of the goods had come significantly to exceed the contract price. In a telephonic conversation between the buyer's president and the seller's president on that day, the buyer was assured by the seller that deliveries would continue if the buyer would make the payments for which it was obligated. Thereupon, the buyer sent the seller a check in the amount of $9,825.60 to cover shipments through March 31, 1975.

Several days later, on April 23, 1975, the buyer stopped payment on this check because he was told by a truck driver, not employed by the seller, that this shipment would be his last load. The trial court found that this was not a valid reason for stoppage of payment. Upon inquiry by the seller, the buyer restated his earlier concerns about future deliveries. Two letters, both dated April 28, 1975, describe the impasse between the parties: the seller again demanded payment, and the buyer, for the first time in writing, demanded adequate assurance of further deliveries. The buyer's demand for assurance was reiterated in its direct reply to the seller's demand for payment. The buyer, however, made no further payments, either to replace the stopped check or otherwise to pay for the nineteen accepted shipments for which balances were outstanding. The seller made no further deliveries after April 23, 1975, when it heard about the stopped check; the buyer never made specific requests for shipments after that date. Inability to deliver the goods forced the seller to close its plant, on May 2, 1975, because of stockpiling of excess material.

The trial court concluded, on the basis of these facts, that the party in breach was the buyer and not the seller. The court concluded that the seller was entitled to recover the final balance of $21,013.60, which both parties agreed to be due and owing. It concluded that the buyer could not prevail on its counterclaim because it had no reasonable grounds to doubt performance from the seller and had in fact received reasonable assurances. . . .

The buyer on this appeal challenges first the conclusion that the buyer's failure to pay "substantially impaired the value of the whole contract," so as to constitute "a breach of the whole contract," as is

---

If you represented the seller, how would you recommend that it respond to the buyer's delayed payments and the demand for assurances? What are the concerns to be balanced?

required by the applicable law governing installment contracts. What constitutes impairment of the value of the whole contract is a question of fact. The record below amply sustains the trial court's conclusion in this regard, particularly in light of the undenied and uncured stoppage of a check given to comply with the buyer's promise to reduce significantly the amount of its outstanding arrearages.

The buyer argues that the seller in an installment contract may never terminate a contract, despite repeated default in payment by the buyer, without first invoking the insecurity methodology of General Statutes 42a-2-609. That is not the law. If there is reasonable doubt about whether the buyer's default is substantial, the seller may be well advised to temporize by suspending further performance until it can ascertain whether the buyer is able to offer adequate assurance of future payments. But if the buyer's conduct is sufficiently egregious, such conduct will, in and of itself, constitute substantial impairment of the value of the whole contract and a present breach of the contract as a whole. . . .

> The Article 2A equivalent to UCC 2-609 is 2A-401 and the analogue to 2-610 is 2A-402.

The buyer's attack on the court's conclusions with respect to its counterclaim is equally unavailing. The buyer's principal argument is that the seller was obligated, on pain of default, to provide assurance of its further performance. The right to such assurance is premised on reasonable grounds for insecurity. Whether a buyer has reasonable grounds to be insecure is a question of fact. The trial court concluded that in this case the buyer's insecurity was not reasonable and we agree. A party to a sales contract may not suspend performance of its own for which it has "already received the agreed return." At all times, the buyer had received all of the goods which it had ordered. The buyer could not rely on its own nonpayments as a basis for its own insecurity. The presidents of the parties had exchanged adequate verbal assurances only eight days before the buyer itself again delayed its own performance on the basis of information that was facially unreliable. Contrary to the buyer's argument, subsequent events proved the buyer's fears to be incorrect, since the seller's plant closed due to a surplus rather than due to a shortage of materials.

- Why could the seller cancel the contract without first seeking assurance of performance under 2-609?

- Why did the seller's failure to respond to the buyer's request for assurance not constitute anticipatory repudiation?

Note: In the pre-UCC case of *F.A.D. Andrea, Inc. v. Dodge*, 15 F.2d 1003 (3d Cir. 1926), the court considered a dispute involving the sale of 20,000 radio cabinets. The defendant buyer ordered the cabinets from the plaintiff seller, and each order included the following language: "These cabinets to have best quality lacquer finish equal to our sample. The color must be identical with our sample." Some also included the additional language, "These cabinets to have best quality lacquer finish that will not change color or turn white."

After the cabinets were delivered to the defendant, which
added the radio sets and then sold them as completed units,
the defendant began to hear that some of the cabinets, perhaps
as many as one-third of the order, were developing white spots
and other blemishes. (This was apparently caused by a
mistake in the manufacturing process of which the plaintiff
was not aware.) The plaintiff refinished these cabinets upon
hearing of the complaints.

After this return-and-refinish process had continued for about
four months, the defendant sent word that it would consider
the contract to be cancelled because it had not received a
satisfactory response to its complaints, and defective cabinets
were still being produced. The plaintiff responded, insisting the
cancellation be withdrawn and declaring it would pursue the
account to collection if the full balance owed were not promptly
paid. The matter was not resolved, and litigation ensued.

The plaintiff's litigation theory was that the parties' contract
required only that the "bulk" of the goods comport with the
sample the defendant had submitted. The plaintiff thus
claimed the defendant could not avoid the contract unless "a
very large percentage" of the cabinets were nonconforming.
The trial court agreed and rendered judgment for the plaintiff.
In reversing, the Circuit Court of Appeals noted the contract
did not use the expression "bulk," and it thus appeared the
parties had agreed that all of the cabinets would conform to the
sample. The court concluded as follows:

> If the number of defective cabinets shipped to defendant by
> plaintiff was *material*, when all the facts and circumstances were
> considered, the bulk did not legally correspond with the sample,
> the defendant was justified in canceling the contract. . . .
> Materiality is the test that justifies cancellation, and not "a very
> large percentage"; for something less than "a very large
> percentage" might, under the circumstances, be material. *Id.* at
> 1006.

The court therefore reversed and remanded the case for a new
trial, since an improper standard had been applied in the lower
court.

- • When does delivery of nonconforming goods justify
  cancellation of an installment contract?

Single-Delivery Sales

Read 2-601 and Comment 1. The Perfect Tender Rule
applies to single-delivery contracts and, as the name suggests,
gives the buyer the right to reject goods that fall short of the

agreed standards in any way. This right cannot, however, be properly understood in isolation from the seller's right of cure, introduced in Section D. For current purposes, know that the name "Perfect Tender Rule" is something of a misnomer because the seller has the right to cure many nonconformities. In addition, the buyer does not always choose to reject nonconforming goods.

- If a buyer rejects goods, must it pay for them?

- Why might a buyer choose to accept nonconforming goods?

- A buyer can choose to accept some "commercial units" from a nonconforming delivery and reject others. Why must acceptance and rejection be made in commercial units?

> "Commercial unit" is defined in 2-105 (6) and will be 2-105 (5) in Revised Article 2. In Article 2A, the definition can be found in 2A-103 (1) (c) and will be in Revised 2A-103 (1) (b).

Acceptance

Read 2-606 and Comments 1 and 2. Comment 1 reiterates the buyer's duty to accept conforming goods. Acceptance does not automatically occur when the buyer receives possession of the goods. In addition, as Comment 2 shows, acceptance is not tied to the passage of title. Instead, acceptance is most commonly communicated by failing to make timely rejection. Also, acceptance generally will not occur until after the buyer has had a reasonable opportunity to inspect the goods, but it can occur when the buyer acts in a way that is inconsistent with the seller's ownership of the goods.

> The Article 2A equivalent is 2A-515.

- Will use of goods automatically signal acceptance?

Read 2-607. Acceptance triggers the buyer's obligation to pay for goods at the contract rate. Further, after acceptance, the buyer has a limited time to complain of any breach of contract, and the burden shifts to the buyer to prove the contract has been breached and to overcome the presumption that payment at the contract rate is due.

> The Article 2A equivalent is 2A-516.

- Why does the burden shift from the seller to the buyer, after acceptance, to prove the contract has been breached?

The following case introduces "forced acceptance," which will not preclude a buyer from seeking damages based upon harm caused by goods it would have rejected if given the option to do so.

Franklin Grain & Supply Co. v. Ingram,
44 Ill. App. 3d 740, 358 N.E. 2d 922, 3 Ill. Dec. 379,
21 U.C.C. Rep. Serv. 53 (1976).

Jones, Justice.

This was an action to recover the balance of the purchase price for approximately ten tons of nitrogenous fertilizer sold and delivered to the defendant by the plaintiff. The defendant counterclaimed, alleging that the plaintiff failed to deliver and spread the fertilizer at an agreed-upon time – or within such period of time as would permit the fertilizer to take effect on wheat planted by the defendant in the fall of 1973. The trial court held that the plaintiff was entitled to $408.50 as the balance on fertilizer delivered and spread and that the defendant was entitled to $2,936.25 as damages for reduction in yield of his wheat. The plaintiff appeals.

The evidence showed fertilizer was in short supply that year and the cost to suppliers was rising dramatically during this period.

On December 31, 1973, defendant called at the office of the plaintiff and asked to have ten tons of nitrogenous fertilizer spread on his wheat on that day. Plaintiff explained that this could not be done, apparently because their equipment was broken. Defendant then went ahead and purchased ten tons of nitrogenous fertilizer, paying $1,200 down and accepting a signed receipt which said:

> This is your receipt for a non-refundable payment of $1,200 for the purchase of ten (tons) of nitrogen for delivery in the month of January 1974, price to be adjusted on date of shipment.

The fertilizer was not spread until April 12, 1974. The defendant maintains that spreading the fertilizer this late was contrary to his agreement with the plaintiff and that, as a result, his yield was reduced, for which he is entitled to damages.

* * *

The trial court found that the delivery of the fertilizer on April 12 was too late to be effective upon the crop upon which it was spread. The defendant had paid in advance the sum of $1,200, and the receipt issued by plaintiff to defendant stated that the payment was "non-refundable." Thus, it is reasonable to conclude that the defendant believed he had no choice but to accept delivery on April 12. Failure to accept could mean forfeiture of payment. An acceptance under such circumstances may be categorized as compulsory and should not preclude defendant from seeking damages for late delivery and application despite the "acceptance."

* * *

Section 2-715 (2) (a) specifies that any consequential damages resulting from seller's breach includes:

> (A)ny loss resulting from general or particular requirements and needs of which the seller at the time of contracting had reason to

know and which could not reasonably be prevented by cover or otherwise.

> The plaintiff, being in the fertilizer business, would certainly have reason to know the requirements for timely application of fertilizer and the consequences of late delivery.

Accordingly, we find that the trial court properly awarded defendant consequential damages for what it found to be a late delivery.

- How does the "forced acceptance" affect the rights of the buyer as set forth in 2-607?

- What advice would you give the seller to ensure it does not find itself in a similar position with future deliveries?

International Perspective: Party Obligations

Read CISG Articles 30, 35, and 53. The basic obligations of sellers are set forth in Article 30, and the basic obligations of buyers are provided in Article 53. The standards for conformity are found in Article 35.

- Does the CISG recognize a distinction between installment contracts and single-delivery sales?

Read CISG Article 60. Instead of "acceptance," the CISG refers to "taking delivery," as defined in Article 60. As Part C shows, the buyer may refuse to take delivery of nonconforming goods or declare the contract avoided in the event of "fundamental breach."

C. Rejection and Revocation

This section discusses the rights of buyers and sellers after nonconforming goods are tendered. Rejection and revocation are self-help remedies. Thus, there is often no need to sue. Instead, the disappointed party can reject or revoke acceptance of the goods. Rightful rejection or revocation will relieve the buyer of the obligation to pay for the goods and allow recovery of any money already paid.

- Are rejection and revocation consistent with a warranty claim?

Rejection is a buyer's refusal to keep delivered goods, coupled with notification to the seller. Revocation is a refusal to keep delivered goods, communicated after acceptance has already taken place.

Rejection

Read 2-106 (2), which defines conforming goods. Rejection of goods pursuant to a single-delivery contract is permissible when the goods fail to conform to the Perfect Tender Rule. Rejection of goods pursuant to an installment contract is rightful when the goods fail to satisfy the doctrine of substantial performance introduced in the previous section.

The current Article 2A equivalent is 2A-103 (1) (d) and will be found in Revised 2A-103 (1) (c). Rejection is subject to the seller's right to cure as described in 2-508 and Part D of this chapter.

The Article 2A equivalents are 2A-509, 2A-510, 2A-511, and 2A-512.

Read 2-602, 2-603, and 2-604.

- Taken together, what guidance do these sections provide as to the buyer's responsibilities vis-à-vis rejected goods?

2-602 describes the manner and effect of rejection. 2-602 (3) raises the specter of wrongful-but-effective rejection.

- How does wrongful-but-effective rejection differ from rightful rejection?

- How does wrongful-but-effective rejection differ from ineffective rejection?

A buyer should give unequivocal notice of any intended rejection.

- Must notice of rejection be in writing?

The Article 2A analogue is 2A-522.

Read 2-711 (3), which shows why a buyer should not always be eager to surrender rejected goods, especially if the seller may be insolvent.

After you have read Chapters 13 through 17, consider how Article 2 and Article 9 security interests differ.

- What does it mean, within the context of 2-711 (3), to describe the buyer as having a "security interest"?

The following case illustrates rejection and the buyer's right to inspect delivered goods prior to acceptance. The case law applies four factors to determine whether a buyer was given a reasonable inspection period: (1) the difficulty of discovering a defect, (2) the terms of the contract, (3) the perishability of the goods, and (4) the parties' course of performance after sale and before rejection.

Miron v. Yonkers Raceway, Inc.,
400 F.2d 112, 5 U.C.C. Rep. Serv. 673 (2d Cir. 1968).

J. Joseph Smith, Circuit Judge.

Saul Finkelstein appeal[s] from a judgment of the District Court for the Southern District of New York rendering [him] liable to plaintiffs, [representatives of the estate of Gerard Miron, the Seller], for the purchase price of a horse and dismissing [his] counterclaims on the merits. The horse was sold to Finkelstein under a warranty that it was sound, but on the day after the sale, it was found to have a fractured bone in its leg, and Finkelstein demanded that the plaintiffs take it back. They refused to do so, and eventually sued . . . Finkelstein for the purchase price in the District Court. . . . Finkelstein counterclaimed for the expense of maintaining and caring for the horse. . . . [District] Judge Levet held that Finkelstein had accepted the horse and therefore bore the burden of proving a breach of warranty, and found that Finkelstein had failed to prove by a fair preponderance of the credible evidence that the horse was not sound at the time of sale. . . . We affirm.

In September 1965, plaintiffs entered the horse "Red Carpet" in an auction called the "Old Glory Horse Sale," sponsored by [Yonkers] Raceway, [Inc.] . . .

Plaintiffs delivered Red Carpet to Raceway on October 17, 1965; the auction of the horse took place early in the afternoon of October 19. At $17,000, there was a lull in the bidding, whereupon Murray Brown, plaintiffs' employee, took the microphone and said:

> This horse has won 2 of his last 3 starts. On September 24, he raced on a muddy track, big-stake race in Montreal . . . , beating Mr. Sea Song.
>
> Now, you know what Mr. Sea Song has done this year . . . he's a top free-for-all horse and this horse beat him racing a good trip, and this is just recently. He's as sound – as, as gutty a horse as you want to find anywhere. He'll race a good mile for you every time. He's got loads of heart, and you're way off on the price of this horse.

To review the express warranty concepts introduced in Chapter 4, you might consider which statements were express warranties, and which were merely puffing.

The bidding then resumed, and defendant Finkelstein submitted the highest bid, which was $32,000.

By about 3:00 p.m. that day, Raceway delivered possession of Red Carpet to Finkelstein . . . , and Finkelstein immediately had the horse transported to his barn at Roosevelt Raceway, Westbury, Long Island. The next morning, . . . the trainer for Finkelstein's horses took Red Carpet out of his stall and hitched him to a jog cart. He observed some swelling of the horse's left hind leg at that time and, when the horse was caused to walk and trot, it limped and favored its left hind leg. [The trainer] returned Red Carpet to the stall and summoned Dr. Bernard F. Brennan, a veterinarian, who found that Red Carpet's left hind leg was swollen, warm, and sensitive.

Finkelstein notified Raceway, at about 11:30 a.m. that day, October 20, that Red Carpet was lame and not sound, and that afternoon an official of Raceway notified Brown, at plaintiffs' stables, of Finkelstein's complaint. Finkelstein subsequently demanded, as we have said, that plaintiffs take back the horse because it was not sound, as warranted, but they have continued to refuse to accept its return. . . . Finkelstein has [not] paid plaintiffs any part of the purchase price for Red Carpet.

* * *

We affirm the judgment below on the breach-of-warranty issue, because we agree with the District Court that, under New York law, Finkelstein had the burden of proving a breach of warranty, and we find ample support in the record for the finding that Finkelstein did not carry that burden successfully.

* * *

The District Court based its determination that Finkelstein had the burden on New York Uniform Commercial Code § 2-607 (4), which provides: "The burden is on the buyer to establish any breach with respect to the goods accepted." The question thus is whether Finkelstein accepted the horse, and we turn for guidance to UCC § 2-606 (1). . . .

> How would you change the facts of this case to satisfy UCC 2-606 (1) (a) or (c)?

It has not been argued that Finkelstein accepted the horse under subsection (a). We doubt he could be said to have done any act inconsistent with the plaintiffs' ownership of the horse, within the meaning of subsection (c), but we need not decide the applicability of that subsection, for we think the trial judge was right in finding that Finkelstein failed to make an effective rejection of the horse under UCC § 2-602 (1), thereby accepting it under subsection (b). . . .

* * *

As the trial judge rightly pointed out, "The fact that the subject matter of the sale in this case was a live animal . . . bears on what is a reasonable time to inspect and reject." Finkelstein's own testimony showed that it is customary, when buying a racehorse, to have a veterinarian or trainer examine the horse's legs, and we agree that the existence of this custom is very important in determining whether there was a reasonable opportunity to inspect the horse. We gather from the record that the reason it is customary to examine a racehorse's legs at the time of sale is that a splint bone is rather easily fractured (there was testimony that a fracture could result from the horse kicking itself) and, although the judge made no specific findings as to this, we assume that is generally what he had in mind when he pointed out that "a live animal is more prone to rapid change in condition and to injury than is an inanimate object." As we have said, Finkelstein did not have the horse examined either at the place of sale or at his barn later the day of the sale. He thus passed up a reasonable opportunity to inspect Red Carpet.

Finkelstein having had a reasonable opportunity to inspect Red Carpet on the day of the sale, we have no problem with the finding that the attempted rejection on the next day did not come within a reasonable time. . . .

* * *

We conclude, then, that Finkelstein accepted the horse by failing to reject it within a reasonable time, and thus had the burden of proving any breach of warranty. As we have already said, we find ample support for the finding that he failed to prove a breach by a fair preponderance of the credible evidence.

[The court thus affirmed the decision of the lower court. The portion of the opinion relating to Raceway's alleged breach of contract has been omitted.]

- What is the role of custom in this case in determining a reasonable inspection period?

Note: In *Bartlett & Co. v. Merchants Co.*, 323 F.2d 501 (5th Cir. 1963), Judge John Minor Wisdom addressed third-party inspections of goods. That case involved a dispute over a barge shipment of corn that was, according to the parties' contract, to be of USDA No. 2 quality, meaning that it would "[w]eigh at least 54 lbs./bu and have less than 14% moisture, 2% cracked corn and foreign material, and 3% damaged kernels." When the barge was examined at the point of departure in Nebraska City, Nebraska, as the parties agreed, by a federally licensed grain inspector, the inspector certified the grain was of No. 2 quality. When the grain arrived at its destination in Guntersville, Alabama about twenty days later, it was found to be "overheating and musty," and the purchaser's representative called for a federal appeal grade inspection to be done. This inspection showed the corn to be partially No. 1 (or superior) grade, and partially "sample" grade, the designation given to corn not within the range of Grades No. 1 to 5, "or which contains stones and/or cinders; or which is musty, or sour, or heating, or hot; or which has any commercially objectionable foreign odor; or which is otherwise of distinctly low quality." The purchaser sued for breach of contract, and the court held the purchaser had no right, under the parties' contract, to reject the goods based upon any inspection at the point of destination.

Because the parties agreed to be bound by the weights and grades of the corn as determined at origin, the court remanded the action for a finding of whether the Nebraska City officer had acted with "fraud, bad faith, or such gross mistake as amounts to fraud." In the absence of such a finding, the court indicated, the inspection certificate would be conclusive. The court considered, among other evidence, "[t]he testimony of [the buyer's agent] that in the customary dealings in the trade,

Why does it make sense that this agreement would result in a price reduction?

lower prices are fixed on condition that there is no right to reject, on the basis of a destination inspection when the grain is inspected at origin." This case shows the parties can set binding standards for the conditions under which rejection can occur, and these negotiated standards can be important in setting the price of the goods.

- What is the strongest evidence that the corn did not degrade during shipment, but was improperly graded at departure?

Problem 1: Consider the following facts:

Arianna Clark desired to furnish her dining room and ordered from Zaid, Inc. (apparently from an illustrated catalog) four chairs, $792.00; a table, $497.00; a buffet, $515.00; and a hutch, $610.00. When the tax was added, the total due was $2,500.16. Miss Clark paid $900.16 when the order was given in May 1970, leaving a balance of $1,600.00. Zaid delivered the furniture on July 16, 1970, The same day, Miss Clark told Zaid flatly over the telephone that the furniture was severely damaged to the point of being entirely unacceptable and demanded that it take it back and call off the deal. Zaid refused and, in August, after it had inspected the furniture, offered to repair it. Miss Clark took the position that the furniture could not be restored to its pristine beauty and serve to glorify her home as she had expected, and reiterated her original demands. Almost immediately, Zaid sued Miss Clark for the $1,600 balance it claimed was due it, and Miss Clark counterclaimed for the $900.16 she had paid with the order. In September, employees of a linoleum company badly damaged the buffet while in the course of their work in the Clark apartment. Miss Clark complained to the linoleum company, and its insurer delivered to Miss Clark's counsel its draft to the order of Miss Clark and Zaid for $515.00, the full purchase price of the buffet, and took the buffet in order to salvage a part of the payment.

- Has Clark effectively rejected the goods?

Based on *Clark v. Zaid, Inc.*, 263 Md. 127, 282 A.2d 483, 9 U.C.C. Rep. Serv. 1014 (1971).

Problem 2: Mr. Young executed a contract on November 14, 1970, to purchase a two-bedroom mobile home from Mr. Bowen. Mr. Young specified a gas furnace, a 3 ½ ton air conditioner, an electric range, a two-door frost-free refrigerator, and a dishwasher, among other options. The home was to be delivered to him in South Carolina on November 30. Instead, he was notified on December 31 that the home had been delivered to Augusta, Georgia, and that he was responsible for making arrangements to have the home delivered to South Carolina, at his own expense. The moving cost was about $80.

When the contract was signed, Mr. Young paid a deposit of $1,000 and signed a promissory note for the balance.

When Mr. Young received the mobile home on January 4, it included an electric furnace and a 3-ton air conditioner, rather than the components he had specified. Between January 4 and January 21, he made numerous telephone calls to Mr. Bowen to complain, but received no reply. On January 21, he notified Mr. Bowen by telex that he had cancelled the contract. Because Mr. Young lacked sufficient funds to secure other housing for himself, he moved into the mobile home. He installed a gas furnace at a cost of $581 and, about a year later, spent almost $2,000 to move the mobile home to El Paso.

- Has Mr. Young effectively rejected the mobile home?

- If he has accepted the home, what causes of action, if any, can he still raise?

Based on *Bowen v. Young*, 507 S.W.2d 600, 14 U.C.C. Rep. Serv. 403 (Tex. Civ. App. 1974).

Revocation

Read 2-607 (2), 2-608 (both in its current form and as revised), and Comments 2 and 4. 2-608 and Comment 2 set forth the basic standard for revocation of acceptance. Comment 4 shows the interplay between revocation and notice. Revocation can be predicated upon the buyer's reasonable, but false, assumption that a defect would be cured or on the buyer's failure to discover a defect that was difficult to discover earlier. In theory, and according to the Code, revocation is permissible only when a buyer can prove a defect substantially impairs the value of the goods to the buyer. In practice, some courts employ a more liberal standard. Revocation must take place before any substantial change in the condition of the goods not caused by the defects – such as the natural deterioration of perishable goods.

The Article 2A analogues are 2A-516 (2) and 2A-217.

The following case explains the concept of "substantial impairment to the buyer." Take note of the facts on which the court relies to determine this particular buyer found his use of the vehicle in question substantially impaired.

Colonial Dodge, Inc. v. Miller,
420 Mich. 452, 362 N.W.2d 704, 40 U.C.C. Rep. Serv. 1 (1985).

Kavanagh, Justice.

This case requires the Court to decide whether the failure to include a spare tire with a new automobile can constitute a substantial impairment in the value of that automobile entitling the buyer to revoke his acceptance of the vehicle under M.S.A. § 19.2608.

We hold it may and reverse.

On April 19, 1976, defendant Clarence Miller ordered a 1976 Dodge Royal Monaco station wagon from plaintiff Colonial Dodge which included a heavy-duty trailer package with extra-wide tires.

On May 28, 1976, defendant picked up the wagon, drove it a short distance where he met his wife, and exchanged it for her car. Defendant drove that car to work while his wife returned home with the new station wagon. Shortly after arriving home, Mrs. Miller noticed that their new wagon did not have a spare tire. The following morning, defendant notified plaintiff that he insisted on having the tire he ordered immediately, but when told there was no spare tire then available, he informed the salesman for plaintiff that he would stop payment on the two checks that were tendered as the purchase price, and that the vehicle could be picked up from in front of his home. Defendant parked the car in front of his home, where it remained until the temporary ten-day registration sticker had expired, whereupon the car was towed by the St. Clair, [Michigan] police to a St. Clair dealership. Plaintiff had applied for license plates, registration, and title in defendant's name. Defendant refused the license plates when they were delivered to him.

> Stop payment is covered in 4-403 and Chapter 10, Part B.

According to plaintiff's witness, the spare tire was not included in the delivery of the vehicle due to a nation-wide shortage caused by a labor strike. Some months later, defendant was notified his tire was available.

Plaintiff sued defendant for the purchase price of the car. On January 13, 1981, the trial court entered a judgment for plaintiff, finding that defendant wrongfully revoked acceptance of the vehicle. The Court of Appeals decided that defendant never accepted the vehicle under M.S.A. § 19.2606 of the Uniform Commercial Code and reversed. On rehearing, the Court of Appeals, noting the trial court found the parties had agreed that there was a valid acceptance, affirmed the trial court's holding there was not a substantial impairment in value sufficient to authorize defendant to revoke acceptance of the automobile. . . .

> How would you argue for and against the proposition that defendant accepted the vehicle?

We are not persuaded that, had the matter been contested in the trial court, a finding of acceptance would be warranted on this record. However, since defendant did not submit the question to the trial judge, but in effect stipulated to acceptance, we will treat the matter as though there was acceptance.

We are satisfied defendant made a proper revocation under M.S.A. § 19.2608 (1) (b). . . .

Plaintiff argues the missing spare tire did not constitute a substantial impairment in the value of the automobile, within the meaning of M.S.A. § 19.2608 (1). Plaintiff claims a missing spare tire is a trivial defect, and a proper construction of this section of the UCC would not permit defendant to revoke under these circumstances. It maintains that since the spare tire is easy to replace and the cost of curing the nonconformity very small compared to the total contract price, there is no substantial impairment in value.

However, M.S.A. § 19.2608 (1) says "[t]he buyer may revoke his acceptance of a lot or commercial unit whose nonconformity substantially impairs its value *to him*. . ." (emphasis added). . . .

We cannot accept plaintiff's interpretation of M.S.A. § 19.2608 (1). In order to give effect to the statute, a buyer must show the nonconformity has a special devaluing effect on him and that the buyer's assessment of it is factually correct. In this case, the defendant's concern with safety is evidenced by the fact that he ordered the special package which included special tires. The defendant's occupation demanded that he travel extensively, sometimes in excess of 150 miles per day on Detroit freeways, and often in the early morning hours. Mr. Miller testified that he was afraid of a tire going flat on a Detroit freeway at 3 a.m. Without a spare, he testified, he would be helpless until morning business hours. The dangers attendant upon a stranded motorist are common knowledge, and Mr. Miller's fears are not unreasonable.

We hold that under the circumstances the failure to include the spare tire as ordered constituted a substantial impairment in value to Mr. Miller, and that he could properly revoke his acceptance under the UCC.

That defendant did not discover this nonconformity before he accepted the vehicle does not preclude his revocation. There was testimony that the space for the spare tire was under a fastened panel, concealed from view. This out-of-sight location satisfies the requirement of M.S.A. § 19.2608 (1) (b) that the nonconformity be difficult to discover.

M.S.A. § 19.2608 (2) requires that the seller be notified of the revocation of acceptance and that it occur within a reasonable time of the discovery of the nonconformity. Defendant notified plaintiff of his revocation the morning after the car was delivered to him. Notice was given within a reasonable time.

Plaintiff argues that defendant failed to effectively revoke acceptance because he neglected to sign over title to the car to plaintiff.

Defendant, however, had no duty to sign over title absent a request from plaintiff that he do so. Under M.S.A. § 19.2608 (3), "[a] buyer who so revokes has the same rights and duties with regard to the goods involved as if he had rejected them." And a buyer who has rejected goods in his possession "is under a duty . . . to hold them with reasonable care at the seller's disposition for a time sufficient to permit

the seller to remove them; but the buyer has no further obligations
with regard to the goods. . . ." M.S.A. § 19.2602 (2) (b) and (c).
Defendant's notice to plaintiff and holding of the car pending seller's
disposition was sufficient under the statute, at least in the absence of
evidence that defendant refused a request by the plaintiff to sign over
title.

Plaintiff contends defendant abandoned the vehicle, denying it any
opportunity to cure the nonconforming tender as prescribed in M.S.A.
§ 19.2508. We find that defendant's behavior did not prevent plaintiff
from curing the nonconformity. Defendant held the vehicle and gave
notice to the plaintiff in a proper fashion; he had no further duties.

Reversed.

[Dissenting opinions omitted.]

- To use the court's language, what facts establish a
  "special devaluing effect" to Mr. Miller?

- What facts establish that "the buyer's assessment of
  [the devaluing effect] is factually correct"?

Note 1: As *Keen v. Modern Trailer Sales, Inc.*, 40 Colo. App.
527, 578 P.2d 668 (1978), shows, continued use of a product
after revocation does not necessarily disprove substantial
impairment. Mr. and Mrs. Keen executed a contract for the
purchase of a mobile home from Modern Trailer Sales, Inc.
Prior to the execution of the contract, the Keens informed the
seller several times that they wished to purchase a three-
bedroom home that would be 14 feet by 70 feet in size. They
were assured several times that the home they had selected
was of the desired size. The salesperson knew the selected
home was shorter than 70 feet, but neglected to inform the
Keens of this fact. Likewise, the manufacturer's statement of
origin and the title application for the home incorrectly listed
the home's dimensions as 14 feet by 70 feet. In addition, the
written contract correctly specified the width of the home as 14
feet, but omitted the home's length.

> Based on the facts in this paragraph, what opinion have you formed of the seller's state of mind and how might this fact influence the proper outcome of the case?

Less than a month after the home was delivered to the Keens,
it drifted from its footings and, after Modern Trailer Sales
refused to address the problem, the Keens hired a third party,
who informed them for the first time that the length of the
home was actually 64 feet. The Keens complained, but the
seller once again failed to respond. The Keens then sought to
"rescind" their contract with Modern Trailer Sales. Treating
this as a request for revocation of acceptance, the trial court
denied the claim on the grounds that performance of the
contract was not substantially impaired by the nonconformity.
The appellate court reversed, finding a triable issue as to

> "Rescission" is often used imprecisely as a synonym for rejection or revocation. No cause of action for rescission exists under the Code.

whether the impairment was substantial. Citing 2-608, the court held as follows:

> This section creates a subjective test in the sense that the requirements of the particular buyer must be examined and deferred to. Yet, since the rationale of the substantial impairment requisite is to bar revocation for trivial defects or defects which may be easily corrected, the impairment of the buyer's requirements must be substantial in objective terms. *Id.* at 530.

The Keens lived in the mobile home during the litigation.

- What provision or provisions of the Code would you cite in support of their right to do so?

- Should the seller expect compensation for the buyers' continued residence in the home?

- On what basis can this case and *Bowen* be distinguished?

Note 2: *Asciolla v. Manter Oldsmobile-Pontiac, Inc.*, 117 N.H. 85, 370 A.2d 270, 21 U.C.C. Rep. Serv. 112 (1977), illustrates the "doctrine of shaken faith." Mr. Asciolla placed a special order for a 1973 Oldsmobile Delta 88 sedan from Manter Oldsmobile-Pontiac. This was his fourth car purchased from this particular dealership. The vehicle was delivered to the dealer a few months later and, following some initial servicing, delivered to Mr. Asciolla. He paid the purchase price in full at that time. The next day, Mr. and Mrs. Asciolla departed for a road trip of approximately 1,400 miles. During this three-day drive, they had no trouble with the car, except for a noise which Mr. Asciolla described as "sounding like a dry speedometer cable." The facts continue as follows, in the court's own words:

> The vehicle was parked outside during the plaintiff's stay in Wisconsin and received little use upon arrival, although the plaintiff started it up occasionally to warm the motor and keep the battery charged. On the evening of January 10, 1973, following an interval during which the Wisconsin temperature had dropped below zero, the plaintiff endeavored to start his new car. The vehicle, however, emitted a loud noise which stopped when it was shifted into gear. The car would move neither forward nor backward because the transmission would not respond to the gear lever. The car was towed to the nearest franchised Oldsmobile dealer, where the transmission was dismantled, the wheels removed, and an underbody inspection made. In the oil pan of the transmission were found deposits of ice, one of which was described to be half the size of a fist. Three inches of water were found in the truck wells. Considerable rust was found on the brake drums, prop shaft, exhaust pipe, and unpainted areas of the underbody. The transmission oil filter was also found to be covered

Did the Colonial Dodge *court find "the impairment of the buyer's requirements . . . substantial in objective terms"?*

with ice, and the forward clutch of the transmission at the pump hub had a split Teflon ring. The plaintiff testified that he was told that the car appeared to have been flooded or submerged. Upon receipt of this information, the plaintiff immediately informed Manter and the Oldsmobile Division of General Motors that he was not satisfied with the car and wanted it exchanged for a new one. The defendants refused to supply a new vehicle, but offered instead to either install a new transmission with a twelve-month warranty after installation or to extend the present warranties twelve months from the date of the repairs to the existing transmission performed by the Wisconsin dealership. *Id.* at 86-87.

> Do you think acceptance had occurred?

In finding Mr. Asciolla should be permitted to revoke acceptance of the vehicle, the court held as follows:

> Few items which are considered necessities occupy such a significant portion of an individual consumer's income as does a new automobile. Few purchases are made with more care and deliberation. The record indicates that the plaintiff was a particularly prudent and painstaking car buyer, and that he had indeed once before refused to accept an automobile from the defendants which merely had a dented fender which had been repaired. Within three weeks of the purchase of the car at issue in this case, he found it to be totally inoperable. He was informed by franchised representatives of the manufacturer that the car had been flooded or submerged. . . .
>
> Under these facts, we think it clear that plaintiff's confidence in the reliability and integrity of his new automobile was severely undermined. He had bargained for a new car, expecting to receive a vehicle upon whose dependability and safety he could comfortably rely. Instead he received a product which he understandably feared was what is known in popular parlance as "a lemon." [A] new automobile is more than the sum of its various components. It is the integrity of the vehicle as a whole which is the essence of the consumer's bargain. *Id.* at 89-90.

> After you have read the materials in Part D of this Chapter, make sure you understand why the seller was not permitted to cure the car's nonconformity.

- "Shaken faith" is a common Article 2 argument. Following *Asciolla,* to what situations should the doctrine be confined?

International Perspective: Nonconformity

Read CISG 25 and 49. When nonconformity rises to the level of what the Convention terms a "fundamental breach" of contract, the seller has the right to avoid the contract. In three separate cases involving unknown parties, German courts have provided guidance as to what does – and does not – constitute fundamental breach under the CISG.

- ▪ As you read about these cases, list the characteristics of fundamental breach you glean from them.

- ▪ If each case involved a single-delivery sale, would the UCC permit the buyer to reject the goods?

- ▪ What would be the result under the UCC if each case involved an installment-sales contract?

In case No. 5 U 15/93, decided on January 18, 1994, the Oberlandesgericht Frankfurt am Main held there is no fundamental breach if the buyer can make reasonable use of the goods, despite the nonconformity. That case involved shoes that were made from a different material than had been agreed upon by the parties, but could nevertheless be worn and used. Under these circumstances, the German court indicated damages could be awarded for nonconformity, but the purchaser could not cancel the contract.

This is the regional court of appeal in Frankfurt, Germany.

In an earlier case numbered 5 U 164/90, decided on September 17, 1991, the same court considered another contract involving shoes. That case involved a seller's breach of a contract under which the buyer was to have the exclusive right to distribute certain shoes to be designed by the buyer and produced by the seller. Instead, the seller contracted with another company to produce the shoes, and sold them without the buyer's consent at a trade fair. The court held that "a breach of a secondary obligation (like the exclusive distributorship here) under the contract may amount to a fundamental breach giving a right to avoid the contract if it so seriously jeopardizes the purpose of the contract that the aggrieved party has no more interest in it."

What does it mean that " the aggrieved party has no more interest in [the contract]"?

Finally, in a case decided July 3, 1992 and numbered 0 42/92, the Landgericht Heidelberg considered a dispute involving the purchase of eleven computer components from a Massachusetts seller by a German buyer. When the seller delivered only five components, the purchaser refused to pay, claiming the seller had fundamentally breached the contract. The court held this partial delivery was not a fundamental breach because the purpose of the parties' contract could be fulfilled by substitute goods from another source.

This is the district court in Heidelberg, Germany.

Initially, the differences between the UCC and CISG standards seem quite significant: the UCC allows rejection of goods in a single-delivery sale that are nonconforming in any way, while the CISG provides this right only in the case of "fundamental breach." When read in conjunction with the UCC's broad right to cure found in the next section, these differences are less significant. In *Interpretation, Gap-filling and Further*

Development of the UN Sales Convention, translated from the
German version found at   http://www.cisg-online.ch/cisg/
Schlechtriem-Symposium-Vischer.pdf (last updated July 27,
2004), Professor Peter Schlechtreim asserts that the remedies
available to a disappointed seller under the CISG, even under
circumstances amounting to less than a fundamental breach,
create a functional equivalent to the Code's Perfect Tender
Rule. He argues that, although the buyer is not permitted to
reject goods for a nonconformity short of fundamental breach,
the fact that the buyer may recover damages for such
nonconformity, as is shown in the last section of this chapter,
makes the buyer whole in a comparable fashion.

D. Mending a Breach: Notice and Cure

> The Article 2A equivalent is 2A-516.

Read current and revised 2-607 (3) (a), and review Chapter
4, Part C for a discussion of the disappointed party's obligation
to provide notice of an alleged breach. As those materials show,
a failure to give notice can cost the nonbreaching party its
ability to bring suit.

The previous section introduced the doctrine of shaken faith,
which limits a seller's right to cure a defect in performance.
The following section discusses the concept of cure. These
materials demonstrate the Code's strong preference for
relationship-mending conduct following the tender of
nonconforming goods.

> Both comments are new to the revised text. The Article 2A equivalent of 2-508 is 2A-513.

**Read current and revised 2-508 and revised Comments
3 and 4.**

- In your own words, what changes have been proposed?

Comment 3 shows the relationship between the seller's right to
cure and the pervasive Code obligation of good faith. Comment
4 explains the conditions under which cure is available.

The following case discusses the purpose of cure. One party
sought to punish the other for delivering nonconforming goods,
by refusing the proffered cure. Note the court's response to this
conduct, especially in contrast to what you might have learned
from studying tort law.

T. W. Oil, Inc. v. Consolidated Edison Co. of New York, Inc.,
57 N.Y.2d 574, 443 N.E.2d 932, 457 N.Y.S.2d 458,
36 A.L.R.4th 533, 35 U.C.C. Rep. Serv. 12 (1982).

Fuchsberg, J.

In January 1974, midst the fuel shortage produced by the oil embargo, plaintiff [T.W. Oil, Inc.] (then known as Joc Oil USA, Inc.) purchased a cargo of fuel oil whose sulfur content was represented to it as no greater than 1%. While the oil was still at sea en route to the United States in the tanker *M T Khamsin,* plaintiff received a certificate from the foreign refinery at which it had been processed, informing it that the sulfur content in fact was .52%. Thereafter, on January 24, the plaintiff entered into a written contract with the defendant (Con Ed) for the sale of this oil. The agreement was for delivery to take place between January 24 and January 30, payment being subject to a named independent testing agency's confirmation of quality and quantity. The contract, following a trade custom to round off specifications of sulfur content at, for instance, 1%, .5% or .3%, described that of the *Khamsin* oil as .5%. In the course of the negotiations, the plaintiff learned that Con Ed was then authorized to buy and burn oil with a sulfur content of up to 1% and would even mix oils containing more and less to maintain that figure.

> Should this fact be relevant to the court's holding?

When the vessel arrived on January 25, its cargo was discharged into Con Ed storage tanks in Bayonne, New Jersey. In due course, the independent testing people reported a sulfur content of .92%. On this basis, acting within a time frame whose reasonableness is not in question, on February 14 Con Ed rejected the shipment. Prompt negotiations to adjust the price failed; by February 20, plaintiff had offered a price reduction roughly responsive to the difference in sulfur reading, but Con Ed, though it could use the oil, rejected this proposition out of hand. It was insistent on paying no more than the latest prevailing price, which, in the volatile market that then existed, was some 25% below the level which prevailed when it agreed to buy the oil.

The very next day, February 21, plaintiff offered to cure the defect with a substitute shipment of conforming oil scheduled to arrive on the *S. S. Appollonian Victory* on February 28. Nevertheless, on February 22, the very day after the cure was proffered, Con Ed, adamant in its intention to avail itself of the intervening drop in prices, summarily rejected this proposal too. The two cargos were subsequently sold to third parties at the best price obtainable, first that of the *Appollonian* and, sometime later, after extraction from the tanks had been accomplished, that of the *Khamsin.*

There ensued this action for breach of contract, which. . . resulted in a nonjury decision for the plaintiff in the sum of $1,385,512.83, essentially the difference between the original contract price of $3,360,667.14 and the amount received by the plaintiff by way of resale of the *Khamsin* oil at what the court found as a matter of fact was a negotiated price which, under all the circumstances, was reasonably procured in the open market. To arrive at this result, the Trial Judge . . . decided as a matter of law that subdivision (2) of section 2-508 of the

Uniform Commercial Code was available to the plaintiff even if it had
no prior knowledge of the nonconformity. Finding that in fact plaintiff
had no such belief at the time of the delivery, that what turned out to
be a .92% sulfur content was "within the range of contemplation of
reasonable acceptability" to Con Ed, and that seasonable notice of an
intention to cure was given, the court went on to hold that plaintiff's
"reasonable and timely offer to cure" was improperly rejected. The
Appellate Division having unanimously affirmed the judgment entered
on this decision, the case is now here by our leave.

In support of its quest for reversal, the defendant now asserts that the
trial court erred . . . in failing to interpret subdivision (2) of section
2-508 of the Uniform Commercial Code to limit the availability of the
right to cure after date of performance to cases in which the seller
knowingly made a nonconforming tender. . . .

* * *

Section 2-508 may be conveniently divided between provisions for cure
offered when "the time for performance has not yet expired" (subd [1]),
a precode concept in this State and ones which, by newly introducing
the possibility of a seller obtaining "a further reasonable time to
substitute a conforming tender" (subd [2]), also permit cure beyond the
date set for performance. . . .

> How does whether UCC 2-508 (1) or (2) is applied affect the relevant standards?

Since we here confront circumstances in which the conforming tender
came after the time of performance, we focus on subdivision (2). On its
face, taking its conditions in the order in which they appear, for the
statute to apply (1) a buyer must have rejected a nonconforming
tender, (2) the seller must have had reasonable grounds to believe this
tender would be acceptable (with or without money allowance), and (3)
the seller must have "seasonably" notified the buyer of the intention to
substitute a conforming tender within a reasonable time.

In the present case, none of these presented a problem. The first one
was easily met, for it is unquestioned that, at .92%, the sulfur content
of the *Khamsin* oil did not conform to the .5% specified in the contract
and that it was rejected by Con Ed. The second, the reasonableness of
the seller's belief that the original tender would be acceptable, was
supported not only by unimpeached proof that the contract's .5% and
the refinery certificate's .52% were trade equivalents, but by testimony
that, by the time the contract was made, the plaintiff knew Con Ed
burned fuel with a content of up to 1%, so that, with appropriate price
adjustment, the *Khamsin* oil would have suited its needs even if, at
delivery, it was, to the plaintiff's surprise, to test out at .92%. Further,
the matter seems to have been put beyond dispute by the defendant's
readiness to take the oil at the reduced market price on February 20.
Surely, on such a record, the trial court cannot be faulted for having
found as a fact that the second condition, too, had been established.

As to the third, the conforming state of the *Appollonian* oil is
undisputed, the offer to tender it took place on February 21, only a day
after Con Ed finally had rejected the *Khamsin* delivery and the
Appollonian substitute then already was en route to the United States,
where it was expected in a week and did arrive on March 4, only four

days later than expected. Especially since Con Ed pleaded no prejudice (unless the drop in prices could be so regarded), it is almost impossible, given the flexibility of the Uniform Commercial Code definitions of "seasonable" and "reasonable," to quarrel with the finding that the remaining requirements of the statute also had been met.

Thus lacking the support of the statute's literal language, the defendant nonetheless would have us limit its application to cases in which a seller *knowingly* makes a nonconforming tender which it has reason to believe the buyer will accept. For this proposition, it relies almost entirely on a critique in Nordstrom, *Law of Sales* (§ 105), which rationalizes that, since a seller who believes its tender is conforming would have no reason to think in terms of a reduction in the price of the goods, to allow such a seller to cure after the time for performance had passed would make the statutory reference to a money allowance redundant. Nordstrom, interestingly enough, finds it useful to buttress this position by the somewhat dire prediction, though backed by no empirical or other confirmation, that, unless the right to cure is confined to those whose nonconforming tenders are knowing ones, the incentive of sellers to timely deliver will be undermined. To this it also adds the somewhat moralistic note that a seller who is mistaken as to the quality of its goods does not merit additional time. Curiously, recognizing that the few decisions extant on this subject have adopted a position opposed to the one for which it contends, Con Ed seeks to treat these as exceptions rather than exemplars of the rule.

* * *

[Prominent treatise authors and professors] White and Summers . . . put it well, and bluntly. Stressing that the code intended cure to be "a remedy which should be carefully cultivated and developed by the courts" because it "offers the possibility of conforming the law to reasonable expectations and of thwarting the chiseler who seeks to escape from a bad bargain," the authors conclude, as do we, that a seller should have recourse to the relief afforded by subdivision (2) of section 2-508 of the Uniform Commercial Code as long as it can establish that it had reasonable grounds, tested objectively, for its belief that the goods would be accepted.

[The court therefore affirmed the holding of the appellate division. The portion of the court's opinion relating to damages has been omitted.]

Note 1: *Wilson v. Scampoli*, 228 A.2d 848, 4 U.C.C. Rep. Serv. 178 (D.C. 1967) is often cited for its discussion of cure. Nick Scampoli purchased a television set on November 4, 1965, paying the total purchase price in cash. Two days later, the set was delivered to his home and plugged in to "cook out," allowing the set to magnetize itself and heat up the circuit to indicate the existence of any faulty wiring. The antennae were also adjusted at that time. When plugged in, the set did not function properly; instead, the picture had a "reddish tinge." Mr. Scampoli's daughter Mrs. Kolley complained to the deliveryperson, who indicated he could not resolve the issue,

but would ask a service representative to address her
complaint.

Two days later, a service representative spent about an hour
working on the set. At that time, he indicated he would need to
remove the chassis from its large wooden cabinet and take it to
the shop to determine the problem. Mrs. Kolley refused to
allow him to do so, insisting upon a new set instead. As an
alternative, she insisted upon a full refund of the purchase
price, but maintained she would keep the set. The seller
refused both demands, but remained willing to repair the set
or, if unable to do so, to replace the set. Mr. Scampoli brought
suit against the seller. In denying recovery to Mr. Scampoli,
the court held as follows:

> While [there is] no mandate to require the buyer to accept
> patchwork goods or substantially repaired articles in lieu of
> flawless merchandise, . . . minor repairs or reasonable
> adjustments are frequently the means by which an imperfect
> tender may be cured. . . . The seller . . .should be able to cure . . . in
> those cases in which he can do so without subjecting the buyer to
> any great inconvenience, risk, or loss.
>
> * * *
>
> . . . Removal of a television chassis for a short period of time in
> order to determine the cause of color malfunction and ascertain
> the extent of adjustment or correction needed to effect full
> operational efficiency presents no great inconvenience to the buyer
> In the instant case, [the seller's expert witness testified that this
> was not infrequently necessary with new televisions. . . The cause
> of the defect might have been minor and easily adjusted or it may
> have been substantial and required replacement by another new
> set – but the seller was never given an adequate opportunity to
> make a determination. *Id.* at 850.

- What facts do you think were most important to the
  court in determining the contract should not be
  avoided?

- Now that you have read these materials on cure, how
  would you paraphrase the Perfect Tender Rule?

- In practice, is the Perfect Tender Rule distinguishable
  from the Substantial Performance Doctrine?

Note 2: *Jorgensen v. Pressnall*, 274 Or. 285, 545 P.2d 1382, 18
U.C.C. Rep. Serv. 1206 (1976), shows the seller need not be
given an unlimited period of time to effectuate cure. In that
case, the court considered a dispute involving the purchase of a
mobile home delivered on November 1, 1972, with defects
including "water and air leaks, gaps in the 'tip-out,' as well as

A tip-out is a kind of
expansion room.

defective doors, cabinets, vents, and walls." Plaintiff purchasers Mr. and Mrs. Jorgensen provided prompt notice to the seller of these defects, and "a series of repair requests yielded no action except the appearance of workmen who were not prepared to make repairs." They hired an attorney, who negotiated for the seller to provide about thirty hours' worth of repairs that were unsatisfactory. The leaking problems continued, and new problems emerged in the course of the alleged repairs. On December 27, the Jorgensens notified the seller of their intent to revoke acceptance. The court found it was reasonable to revoke acceptance under these circumstances.

- If you were the attorney for Mr. and Mrs. Jorgensen, what steps would you take to ensure they reported the problems seasonably and acted reasonably in seeking to resolve the matter without allowing the dispute to drag on endlessly? In other words, when would you argue, "Enough is enough"?

Problem 1: Frank Riccardi visited a hearing-aid clinic and was advised to purchase an Acousticon Model A-660. He visited the office of Frank Bartus, a franchisee of Acousticon, and placed an order for an A-660. When he arrived to pick up the hearing-aid, he was told the model he ordered had been upgraded and improved, and was now called A-665. Accordingly, a model A-665 was delivered for his use. The hearing-aid was fitted to Mr. Riccardi, who complained about the noise associated with the device. Mr. Bartus responded that he would become accustomed to this characteristic of the unit. Mr. Riccardi used the hearing-aid for a total of approximately 15 hours. When he returned to the hearing-aid clinic, he was informed the model he had purchased was not the model he had been told to purchase. Thus, and complaining of headaches, he returned the hearing-aid to Mr. Bartus's office, where he was issued a receipt. Mr. Bartus offered to procure a Model A-660 for Mr. Riccardi, who neither accepted nor rejected the offer at that time. Upon hearing from Mr. Bartus of Mr. Riccardi's complaint, Acousticon contacted Mr. Riccardi directly, offering to supply either another A-665 or the older model A-660 he had ordered. Mr. Riccardi refused both offers and demanded a full refund.

- Should Riccardi be required to allow Bartus to cure?

Based on *Bartus v. Riccardi*, 55 Misc. 2d 3, 284 N.Y.S. 2d 222, 4 U.C.C. Rep. Serv. 845 (City Court, City of Utica, N.Y. 1967).

Problem 2: Everett Figgins was the owner and operator of the Big Sky Market in Manhattan, Montana. The market's

specialty was fresh meat, and various cuts were displayed in
refrigerated cases around the store. In the summer of 1975,
Figgins decided to replace these cases, and he met with a
representative of Transcontinental Refrigeration Company to
consider several alternatives. He choose the Model 3000 with
wood-grain sides and placed an order for two such cases. After
the order had been placed, Transcontinental contacted Figgins
to let him know the Model 3000 was not available in wood
grain and recommended substitution of a model called the MD.
According to the representative, the MD would "do the job."
The major difference between the models was that the Model
3000 employed a "gravity coil" system that did not circulate air
over the contents of the case, while the MD used three fans
that blew air over the case's contents.

Figgins received the MD cases and immediately noticed the
meat on display becoming dehydrated, dry, and discolored.
When he contacted Transamerica, he was told to make several
adjustments to the equipment, and he did so. The problem
continued and, despite Figgins' telephone calls and letters to
the company, no representative investigated the problem. The
company did send condensation pans to be filled with water
and placed inside the cases, but these did not alleviate the
problem. Several months later, Figgins removed the cases,
placing them in storage and replacing them with others from a
different company. He notified Transamerica that he
considered the contract cancelled.

At trial, a professor of thermodynamics testified the MD cases
were entirely unsuitable for Figgins' business, elaborating as
follows:

> [C]iting the American Society of Heating, Air Conditioning, and
> Refrigeration Data Guide, which he testified was a standard
> reference text, [the professor] stated that, while forced-air
> refrigeration [such as was used in the MD units] was suitable to
> preserve cured and wrapped delicatessen-type meats, the guide
> book very strongly recommended that circulating air coolers not be
> used with fresh meat because evaporation will cause the meat to
> "scorch or burn."

- What kinds of damages would you expect Figgins to
  seek?

- Assume the expert testimony was uncontroverted.
  Should Figgins be denied recovery because
  Transcontinental was not permitted to cure the
  nonconformity?

Based on *Transcontinental Refrigeration Co. v. Figgins*, 179 Mont. 12, 16, 585 P.2d 1301, 1304, 25 U.C.C. Rep. Serv. 458, 461 (1978).

International Perspective: Mending a Breach

Read CISG Articles 37 and 48. Like the UCC, the CISG provides that the right to cure may be exercised both before and after the time for performance has expired.

Read CISG Article 47. The CISG also contains another kind of "cure" provision with no equivalent in the UCC – Article 47's Nachfrist provision, which allows (but does not require) a buyer to allow a seller additional time in which to provide conforming goods. When a buyer chooses to do so, he or she normally may not engage any of the remedies provided under the CISG until the Nachfrist period has expired.

- Since the buyer is not required to provide additional time pursuant to Article 47, why would a buyer choose to do so?

> A careful reading of Article 49 may provide guidance in answering this question.

Although the UCC provides no analogous provision to Article 47, some commentators have suggested Article 47 is consistent with the general UCC policy promoting dispute resolution without unnecessary litigation. If the Nachfrist period expires without the seller's having remedied the nonconformities, the buyer may avoid the contract or invoke the other remedies presented in Part E of this chapter.

E. Remedies

Summarizing the Code's varied provisions on remedies is impossible in a survey textbook without significant simplification. The following excerpt from Professor John Sebert's article *Remedies under Article Two of the Uniform Commercial Code: An Agenda for Review*, 130 U. Pa. L. Rev. 360 (1981) provides an introduction, after which the balance of the chapter will focus on a few particularly important and common matters relating to remedies. Citations to Articles 2 and 2A have been added to this excerpt for ease of reference:

> A buyer's monetary remedies for a seller's breach depend initially on whether the buyer retains the goods. The buyer who does not keep the goods, either because the seller never delivers them or because the buyer effectively rejects them or revokes acceptance,

has two basic remedies. If the buyer in good faith covers by making a reasonable and timely purchase of substitute goods, [under 2-712 and 2A-2A-518] the buyer may recover damages from the seller measured by the excess of cover price over contract price.   Alternatively, [under 2-713 and 2A-519], the buyer's damages will be the difference between market price "at the time when the buyer learned of the breach" and contract price. Under either alternative, the buyer in addition may recover any incidental or consequential damages caused by the seller's breach [under 2-715 and 2A-520] together with payments already made to the seller [under 2-711 and 2A-508], but the buyer must credit the seller with expenses saved because of the breach [under 2-712 (2) and 2-713 (1), together with 2A-518 (2) and 2A-519 (1)]. On the other hand, the buyer may retain the goods, either out of choice or because she has accepted them and cannot revoke her acceptance. In this situation, the Code broadly permits the buyer to recover damages for any loss resulting from the seller's breach, [under 2-714 (1) and 2A-519 (3)] but the damage measure most frequently applied in this situation is the Code's version of the traditional measure of damages for breach of warranty—the difference between the value of the goods as warranted and their actual value at the time and place of acceptance [found in 2-714 (2) and 2A-519 (4)]. In addition, recovery of incidental and consequential damages is allowed [under 2-714 (3) and 2-715, together with 2A-519 and 2A-520]. Finally, in some circumstances the buyer may obtain the goods themselves through an action for specific performance or replevin [under 2-716 and 2A-521].

> Why is the seller's recovery of the price "the equivalent of specific performance at law"?

The remedies available to a seller upon a buyer's breach in many respects parallel the remedies provided for buyers. [Under 2-709 (1) and 2A-529 (1)], seller may recover the price, the equivalent of specific performance at law, in three situations: when the buyer has accepted the goods, when conforming goods have been lost or damaged after the risk of their loss has passed to the buyer, and when goods intended for the buyer cannot be resold at a reasonable price. The Code also provides the seller's equivalent of cover: [under 2-706 and 2A-527], if the seller makes a good faith and commercially reasonable resale, he may recover the excess of the unpaid contract price over the actual resale price, plus incidental damages but less expenses saved. Alternatively, [under 2-708 (1) and 2A-528 (1)], the seller's damages when the buyer does not accept or repudiates is the traditional market-value differential—the difference between the unpaid contract price and the market price at the time and place for tender. The seller has an additional and very significant remedy that has no analogue among buyers' remedies. [Under 2-708 (2) and 2A-528 (2), if] the market-value-differential damages are "inadequate to put the seller in as good a position as performance," the seller may recover the profit he would have made had the buyer fully performed, including reasonable overhead, together with costs incurred for performance and incidental damages, but less the payments or proceeds of resale. *Sebert,* 130 U. Pa. L. Rev. at 364-366.

- What questions would you ask a disappointed buyer who hired you as an attorney, to decide which remedy to pursue?

- What questions would you ask if you represented the seller?

Remedies Available to the Buyer

Read current and revised 2-711 and Comment 1. Revised 2-711 provides a more comprehensive and arguably clearer indexing of the buyer's remedies than the current provision does.

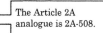
The Article 2A analogue is 2A-508.

- According to Comment 1, what is the relationship between the buyer's right to pursue remedies and the seller's right to cure?

The following case addresses the availability of consequential damages to an injured buyer, including unexpected manufacturing overages, lost profits, and interest paid on loans necessitated by the breach.

Draft Systems, Inc. v. Rimar Manufacturing, Inc.,
524 F. Supp. 1049, 32 U.C.C. Rep. Serv. 1493 (E.D. Pa. 1981).

John Morgan Davis, Senior District Judge.

Plaintiff Draft Systems is engaged in the business of manufacturing a type of dispensing unit used on beer kegs. This beer-dispensing unit consists essentially of two component parts – a double valve and a syphon tube. One component part, the syphon tube, which is approximately eighteen inches in length and made of graded nylon, was supplied by the defendant, Rimar Manufacturing, Inc. Throughout 1974, the plaintiff submitted purchase orders for various amounts of nylon 11 or nylon 2908L tubing to the defendant. In August 1975, the defendant filled the aforesaid orders by shipping the required amounts to the plaintiff. After the inspection of the amount of goods and specifications of the tubing, including a check of the accompanying documents which certified that the tubing was actually nylon 11, the plaintiff accepted the goods and began using them in its manufacturing process. Some months later, the plaintiff began receiving complaints from beer distributors that the dispensing mechanism was not functioning properly. It was later determined that the defendant forwarded a different grade of tubing, nylon 6, rather than the nylon 11 specified in the purchase orders and blueprints supplied by plaintiff.

Expert testimony established that, because of the higher liquid-absorption rate of nylon 6 tubing contrasted with the absorption rate of nylon 11, an excessive amount of beer was absorbed by the nylon 6 tubing. This excessive absorption caused the internal diameter of the tubing to expand, thus breaking the seal between the tubing and the metal portion of the dispensing unit to which the tubing was attached. It was theorized that, after carbon dioxide was pumped into the keg in order to force beer from it – i.e. drafting the beer – carbon dioxide entered the beer stream through the broken seal; this created a condition known as "wild beer" which was unfit for consumption.

The jury, by interrogatories, found that the defendant breached the express, and implied warranties of merchantability and fitness for a particular purpose which were incorporated into the contract. In its post-trial motions, defendant presents a myriad of claims for relief from the judgment against it. I now turn to these contentions.

> What precisely is the defendant's argument as to foreseeability and why does the court reject it?

Preliminarily, defendant vigorously contends that all items of consequential damages should be excluded from the verdict because the evidence is insufficient to support the jury award. More specifically, it asserts that the proof failed to demonstrate that defendant had any knowledge concerning the particular requirement of the contract that the nylon tubing supplied could not have a liquid absorption rate in excess of that of nylon 11. This argument, however, misconceives the nature of consequential damages.

* * *

. . . The defendant knew the nature of the plaintiff's business. The defendant knew that the nylon tubing was required as a component of the plaintiff's beer-dispensing system. It knew that the tubing would eventually be immersed within the beer. Furthermore, the company knew that nylon 6 did not have the same hydroscopic properties as nylon 11. It also knew that the plaintiff required nylon 11 for use in its product. In short, the defendant knew of all plaintiff's general and particular requirements except the precise demarcation in absorption rates which would render nylon 6 useless. But the plaintiff's specification of the particular grade of nylon coupled with the defendant's knowledge of the difference in the absorption properties of varying grades of nylon, put the defendant on notice of the particular quality of tubing which would be valuable to the buyer. Thus, the jury could properly find that the defendant had sufficient reason to know of the general and particular requirements of the plaintiff to thereby charge defendant with the consequential losses proximately following from the breach of warranty under section 2-715 (b).

* * *

Defendant also attacks various items of consequential damages which the jury found properly attributable to the breach of contract. Specifically, defendant contends that the awards of: (1) bank-interest charges in the amount of $120,420.05; (2) lost profits in the amount of $95,975.00; and (3) a percentage of the manufacturing costs reflecting overhead, were improper. These contentions are equally without merit.

* * *

Defendant . . . argues that . . . an award of interest on the loans obtained by the plaintiff to avoid financial disaster during the period of repair and replacement of the malfunctioning dispensing devices is not properly an item of consequential damages. . . . Where a seller provides defective goods to a manufacturer with knowledge that they are to be used in the manufacturing process, it is reasonable to assume that the consequent disruption of production will cause financial difficulties for the buyer, especially when the buyer is heavily dependent on one product for its financial success, as in the case at bar.

Accordingly, I cannot say as a matter of law that reasonable men in the position of the parties would not have foreseen the loss of bank-interest charges as a probable result of the breach. Defendant's second quarrel is with the jury's award of lost profits as an item of consequential damages. . . .

The failure to realize expected profits is a compensable loss resulting from a breach of contract. . . . The amount of damage suffered . . . may be determined in any reasonable manner, and proof with mathematical certainty is not required. . . . One traditional method is evidence of past profitability in an established business which furnishes a reasonable basis for estimating future profits.

In this case, the plaintiff's comptroller presented extensive testimony concerning the company's past profitability. The defendant meticulously cross-examined the witness on these figures. . . . In view of the proposition that the evaluation of damages is typically a question for the jury and the wealth of evidence presented at trial, I cannot conclude that the jury award was mere speculation. . . .

Defendant's final contention that the award of excess manufacturing costs attributable to manufacturing overhead is not recoverable is incorrect under the law of Pennsylvania. The manufacturing costs were expended to repair and replace the defective dispensing units. Additional time in operation of the plant was clearly required to remedy the breach, thus, manufacturing overhead attributable to that extra work is a proper item of damages.

. . . [T]he defendant's post-trial motions are denied.

- **Read 2-719 (3) and Comment 3.** How could Rimar limit its future liability for consequential damages?

Note 1: Read 2-712. *Dura-Wood Treating Co. v. Century Forest Industries, Inc.*, 675 F.2d 745, 33 U.C.C. Rep. Serv. 1201 (5th Cir. 1982), illustrates an interesting kind of cover and, in so doing, elucidates the policies underlying the concept of cover. Dura-Wood Treating Co., a manufacturer of cross-ties, sued another such manufacturer, Century Forest Industries, for its failure to deliver cross-ties pursuant to the parties' contract. The ties were to be re-sold to another company with which Dura-Wood did business. The cost of cross-ties had risen considerably during the pendency of the contract. When Century Forest notified Dura-Wood that it would be unable to perform, given the increased cost, Dura-Wood urged it on several occasions to supply the ties, but realized doing so was

futile and obtained price quotations from several other
suppliers. After doing so, Dura-Wood realized it could produce
the cross-ties internally for less money than it could purchase
them from other sources. It did so and brought suit to recover
the costs of cover.

Century Forest claimed Dura-Wood had used an unreasonable
means of cover and should not be permitted to recover the cost
of the substitute goods. In rejecting this argument, the court
held as follows:

> This Court acknowledges there is some language indicating the
> purchase of substitute goods should be "on the market." However,
> this language is explained by the Texas courts' interpretations of
> section 2-712. As Century Forest itself points out, the Texas courts
> have noted that one policy behind section 2-712 is a presumption
> "that the cost of cover will approximate the market price of the
> undelivered goods." Indeed, an appropriate cover has the effect of
> setting the market price so that an aggrieved buyer does not have
> to prove damages through more onerous means. However,
> actually purchasing the cover goods from another source is not the
> exclusive means of satisfying the presumption of section 2-712. In
> an appropriate situation, internally producing the substitute or
> cover goods can satisfy the recognized underlying presumptions of
> section 2-712.
>
> * * *
>
> The record demonstrates good faith on the part of Dura-Wood in
> choosing to cover by manufacturing the cross-ties internally. Dura-
> Wood took price quotations and ultimately determined it could
> produce the ties at a lower price. . . .
>
> Additionally, . . . Dura-Wood covered within a reasonable time and
> provided a reasonable substitute . . . . The record reveals Dura-
> Wood waited to cover in order to evaluate the market for cross-
> ties. There is evidence demonstrating the cross-tie market is
> volatile and subject to fluctuations. The price of cross-ties was high
> during the time Dura-Wood was evaluating the market.
> Consequently, Dura-Wood's waiting to determine whether a
> decrease in market price might occur was not unreasonable. In
> addition, Dura-Wood continued to urge performance, as
> contemplated by section 2-610 of the Tex. Bus. & Com. Code. The
> record also demonstrates the internally produced cover goods were
> commercially usable as reasonable substitutes for those due from
> Century Forest. *Id.* at 753-755.

Having allowed Dura-Wood to recover its cost of cover by
internal manufacture, the court refused to allow the company
also to recover lost potential profits. Dura-Wood had claimed,
citing a "lost volume" theory, that it should be able to recover
the profits it would have made if its manufacturing facilities

The quoted language
is from *Jon-T
Farms, Inc. v. Good
Pasture, Inc.*, 554
S.W.2d 743, 749
(Tex. Civ. App.-
Amarillo 1977).

had not been preparing the cross-ties to replace those Century Forest failed to deliver.

- Why can Dura-Wood not recover both sums?

Note 2: Read 2-610 and 2-713. *Cosden Oil & Chemical Co. v. Karl O. Helm Aktiengesellschaft,* 736 F.2d 1064, 38 U.C.C. Rep. Serv. 1645 (5th Cir. 1984), addresses a buyer's damages when a seller anticipatorily repudiates the contract and the buyer does not cover.   Karl O. Helm Aktiengesellsschaft, correctly anticipating a shortage of petrochemicals in 1979 due to political turmoil in Iran, decided to purchase a large quantity of polystyrene, a petroleum derivative.   Helm entered a contract with Cosden Oil & Chemical Co., which was to produce the product.   As Helm anticipated, the price of the product soared, and it became much more difficult to find, after the contract was negotiated.   Cosden shipped only a portion of the agreed-upon quantity and, after much delay, cancelled the contract.   Helm had paid for only a portion of the deliveries, and, when Cosden sued for the balance, Helm counter-claimed citing damages due to Cosden's failure to deliver the remainder of the goods.   Because of the skyrocketing price of polystyrene, it was important to determine, for purposes of the counterclaim, the price of polystyrene for the purpose of damages.   In considering this issue, the court held as follows:

> Article 2 of the Code has generally been hailed as a success for its comprehensiveness, its deference to mercantile reality, and its clarity. Nevertheless, certain aspects of the Code's overall scheme have proved troublesome in application. . . . The aggrieved buyer seeking damages for seller's anticipatory repudiation presents the most difficult interpretive problem. Section 2-713 describes the buyer's damages remedy. . . .

> Courts and commentators have identified three possible interpretations of the phrase [in 2-713 (1) (a)] "learned of the breach." If seller anticipatorily repudiates, buyer learns of the breach:

>> (1) When he learns of the repudiation;

>> (2) When he learns of the repudiation plus a commercially reasonable time; or

>> (3) When performance is due under the contract.

> * * *

> We do not doubt, and Texas law is clear, that market price at the time buyer learns of the breach is the appropriate measure of section 2-713 damages in cases where buyer learns of the breach at or after the time for performance. This will be the common case,

[Sidebar note, lines 9–11:] "Aktiengesellschaft" is a German word meaning "joint-stock company."

[Sidebar note, lines 34–36:] How does Revised UCC 2-713 address this ambiguity?

for which section 2-713 was designed. In the relatively rare case where seller anticipatorily repudiates and buyer does not cover, the specific provision for anticipatory-repudiation cases, section 2-610, authorizes the aggrieved party to await performance for a commercially reasonable time before resorting to his remedies of cover or damages.

In the anticipatory-repudiation context, the buyer's specific right to wait for a commercially reasonable time before choosing his remedy must be read together with the general-damages provision of section 2-713 to extend the time for measurement beyond when buyer learns of the breach.

* * *

. . . In light of the Code's persistent theme of commercial reasonableness, the prominence of cover as a remedy, and the time given an aggrieved buyer to await performance and to investigate cover before selecting his remedy, we agree with the district court that "learned of the breach" incorporates section 2-610's commercially reasonable time. *Id.* at 1071-1073.

This case illustrates how the provisions of the UCC must be read in conjunction with one another, even when doing so may give a counter-intuitive meaning to a provision that seemed clear.

- What would be the most reasonable interpretation of the phrase "learned of the breach," as a matter of common usage?

- **Read 1-103 (a) and Comment 1.** How does 1-103 (a) guide a court in a matter of interpretation?

Problem: Cargill, Inc. is a seller of grain. On July 23, 1973, Mr. Julsonnet, an agent of Cargill, telephoned Mr. Van Stafford, owner of Stafford Elevator, to discuss Cargill's interest in purchasing some wheat for resale. Stafford indicated he had 40,000 bushels on hand and might be interested in selling it. To that end, he asked Cargill to prepare a confirmation for his review. Julsonnet did so, but inadvertently mailed the document to a different entity, Stafford Brothers Elevator. Upon receiving the document, Stafford Brothers Elevator recognized the error and forwarded it to Stafford Elevator.

On July 31, Stafford Elevator telephoned Julsonnet to tell him the confirmation should include a protein premium. Julsonnet agreed to the change and promised to send a revised confirmation. In the same conversation, the parties agreed Stafford Elevator would sell, and Cargill would purchase, an additional 26,000 bushels of wheat. Confirmation of the additional sale was sent to the proper address, but

Make sure you follow the court's logic here.

confirmation of the contract change was inadvertently sent to
Stafford Brothers Elevator.

On August 21, having received the contract-change
confirmation through Stafford Brothers Elevator, Stafford
contacted Cargill to object to one provision of the confirmation,
which provided Cargill the option to cancel. Stafford expressed
his position that the contract was therefore void. On August 27
and September 6, Cargill urged Stafford to perform, and
Stafford refused. Cargill sought to recover from Stafford the
difference between the contract price and the price of wheat on
September 6. The price of wheat had risen considerably since
the end of July and reached its high point on August 21.
Stafford refused to pay, and Cargill sued.

- How should the buyer's damages be measured?
  Assume the buyer was unable to cover due to a lack of
  suitable goods.

Based on *Cargill, Inc. v. Stafford*, 553 F.2d 1222, 21 U.C.C.
Rep. Serv. 707 (10th Cir. 1977).

Remedies Available to the Seller

Read current and revised 2-703 and Comment 1. These
provisions summarize the remedies available to a seller. As
with 2-711, the revisions are meant to clarify and catalog the
many options.

- Using the language of Comment 1, will "the pursuit of
  one remedy bar [ ] another"?

Read 2-708 and 2-709. The following case discusses
wrongful-but-effective rejection of conforming goods, a concept
referenced in Part C. Note the difference in damages for
wrongful rejection and ineffective rejection.

*Brandeis Machinery & Supply Co., LLC v. Capitol Crane
Rental, Inc.,*
765 N.E.2d 173, 47 U.C.C. Rep. Serv. 2d 200 (Ind. App. 2002).

Vaidik, Judge.

Brandeis [Machinery & Supply Co.] and Capitol [Crane Rental, Inc.]
entered into a Lease Agreement on June 16, 1998. Under the lease,
Capitol rented a 35-ton Grove Model RT635C Rough Terrain Crane
from Brandeis for six months. The lease included an option for Capitol
to buy the Crane. When the first six months of the lease expired,
Capitol continued to rent the Crane for another six-month period on a
month-to-month basis.

Brandeis' lead salesman, Greg Henry, and Capitol's owner, Steve
Dotlich, executed a Cash Sales Contract on June 16, 1999. Under the
Contract, Capitol agreed to buy the Crane "as is – where is" for
$291,773.46. The Contract included the following provision:

> TERMS OF PAYMENT: Net 10 days from invoice date . . . .
> If not paid on due date, 2% per month service charge will be
> applied.

Brandeis' CEO signed the Contract to acknowledge approval of the
deal on June 22, 1999. Brandeis sent Capitol the invoice for the Crane
on June 29, 1999.

In late June of 1999, Maxim Crane Works, a national crane-rental
company, approached Dotlich about buying Capitol. After Maxim
asked to buy Capitol, Dotlich returned the Crane to the Brandeis lot.
About one week after Dotlich had returned the Crane, Henry, who had
dealt with Dotlich regarding the lease and the Contract, called Dotlich
to inquire about the returned Crane. During their telephone
conversation, Dotlich informed Henry that he "did not want to buy [the
Crane] any more." Dotlich also told Henry that he was selling his
business.

When Brandeis discovered that Dotlich had returned the Crane, the
Brandeis managers told Henry and the sales staff not to sell the Crane
because it belonged to Capitol and not to Brandeis. Additionally,
Brandeis marked the Crane with chalk to indicate that the Crane was
the property of Capitol and had already been sold to Capitol.

Before returning the Crane, Capitol repaired damage to the Crane.
Dotlich testified that the Crane's boom had been damaged around the
time that he signed the Contract, but he could not recall if the damage
occurred before or after he signed the Contract. Capitol bought parts
from Brandeis and repaired the Crane.

> How, if at all, would
> the parol-evidence
> rule affect the
> proper use of this
> testimony?

After Capitol returned the Crane to Brandeis, Brandeis expended
$9,794.86 to inspect the repairs made to the boom. Walter Ross,
Brandeis' Indianapolis Branch Manager, testified that the Crane was
inspected because he understood that Brandeis had reached "some
kind of resolution" with Capitol that Brandeis would prepare to resell
the Crane. He testified that the inspection of the Crane was performed
for the express purpose of selling the Crane to someone else.

At trial, Henry testified regarding Brandeis' customary business
practices. Henry stated that he was aware of more than one instance
when a customer had signed a contract with Brandeis, but decided to
cancel the contract before any money had changed hands. In these
cases, Brandeis cancelled the contracts and did not try to enforce the
sales. Henry explained that the reason for this practice was to avoid
upsetting and losing customers. Additionally, Henry testified that,
when dealing with Capitol and generally with all of Brandeis'
customers, a transaction was only considered final when payment was
made.

Following the trial, each side submitted post-trial briefs. In its brief, Brandeis contended that the appropriate damage award would include the purchase price of the Crane, which was $291,773.46, plus interest at the rate of 2% per month for late payment as provided for in the Contract. As of May 31, 2001, $159,302.38 had accumulated in late payment interest. Furthermore, Brandeis calculated the damage award to include the inspection fee of the Crane due to the damage sustained and repairs performed while in Capitol's care as an incidental cost. The costs for the inspection of the repairs were $9,794.86. Based on these numbers, Brandeis prayed for a damage award totaling $460,870.70.

In its brief, Capitol maintained that no damages should have been awarded. In the alternative, Capitol submitted that damages should be calculated by subtracting the fair-market value of the Crane from the Contract price of $291,773.46. Regarding the fair-market value of the Crane, Henry testified that, based on rates of depreciation, the Crane's fair-market value in June/July 1999 was between $270,000 and $275,000. Due to the difference, Capitol suggested using the median value of $272,500. The difference between the median fair-market value of $272,500 and the Contract price of $291,773.46 is a damage award of $19,273.46.

> In your own words, what is Capitol's theory supporting its claim that no damages should be awarded?

The trial court entered judgment in favor of Brandeis on June 21, 2001. The trial court ordered that "Brandeis Machinery & Supply Co., LLC, recover of and from the defendant, Capitol Crane Rentals, Inc., the sum of $29,067.00 with interest thereon from the date of judgment, as provided by law, plus costs of this action." This appeal ensued.

* * *

Brandeis asserts that the trial court erred by failing to include the full Contract price in the damage award. Specifically, Brandeis maintains that the damage award should have included the full Contract price of $291,773.46 because Capitol accepted the Crane before returning it, thereby justifying an action for the price under Indiana Code § 26-1-2-709. In addition, Brandeis contends that it was not obligated to hold the Crane for Capitol, it did not have a duty to resell the Crane, and the fact that Capitol was bought out by another business should not affect its right to recover the price of the Crane.

> How, if at all, does the notion of a "lost volume seller" come into play here? Note 1 following this case addresses the issue.

* * *

An action for the price is sustainable only if the buyer has accepted the goods. Acceptance is defined under the Indiana Code as "failure to make an effective rejection." Ind. Code § 26-1-2-606. A rejection of goods must be made "within a reasonable time after their delivery or tender. It is ineffective unless the buyer seasonably notifies the seller." Ind. Code § 26-1-2-602 (1). Therefore, an action for the price is a remedy for an ineffective rejection under Indiana Code § 26-1-2- 602 (1).

Rejection of goods by the buyer may be effective, but nonetheless wrongful. A wrongful rejection is a rejection of a conforming tender. Put differently, a rejection may be timely made and thus, effective, but wrongful in that conforming goods are rejected.

Damages for a wrongful rejection substantially differ from damages for an ineffective rejection. Indiana Code § 26-1-2-709 (3) provides that after a buyer has wrongfully rejected goods, a seller is not entitled to price but shall be awarded damages for nonacceptance under Indiana Code § 26-1-2-708. . . .

* * *

Because the trial court could have concluded that Capitol made a wrongful, yet effective rejection, Brandeis' action for the price must fail. Instead, the appropriate calculation of damages is the difference between the contract price and the market price at the time of delivery plus incidental damages. Therefore, we find that the trial court did not err when it declined to include the Contract price in the damage award.

[Discussion regarding the trial court's refusal to award services charges for late payment is omitted.]

- ▪ As a matter of policy, why do the differing damages for wrongful and ineffective rejection make sense?

Note 1: *Neri v. Retail Marine Corp.*, 30 N.Y.2d 393, 285 N.E.2d 311, 334 N.Y.S.2d 165, 10 U.C.C. Rep. Serv. 950 (1972), explains the concept of lost-volume sales. Anthony Neri contracted to purchase a new boat from Retail Marine Corp. for $12,587.40 to be delivered in four to six weeks and made a deposit of $40 at the time of contract. Shortly thereafter, Neri increased the deposit to $4,250 in return for Retail Marine's agreement to arrange for immediate delivery of the boat as a "firm sale." Six days after the deposit was increased, and after Retail Marine had already ordered – and received – the boat from the manufacturer, Neri's attorney sent a letter to Retail Marine seeking to rescind the sale on the grounds that Neri would shortly undergo surgery. Retail Marine refused to refund Neri's deposit, and Neri brought suit. Retail Marine counterclaimed, seeking the balance of the purchase price.

At trial, the evidence showed the boat was sold four months after it was delivered to another buyer, who paid the same price Neri had agreed to pay. Neri therefore argued Retail Marine had sustained no damages; Retail Marine responded that, but for Neri's breach of contract, it would have sold two boats, rather than one. Retail Marine's uncontroverted testimony showed that its profit on the sale would have been $2,579. In finding Retail Marine should be awarded its lost profit, the court held as follows:

> Closely parallel to the factual situation now before us is that hypothesized by Dean Hawkland as illustrative of the operation of the rules: "If a private party agrees to sell his automobile to a buyer for $2,000, a breach by the buyer would cause the seller no loss (except incidental damages, i.e., expense of a new sale) if the

seller was able to sell the automobile to another buyer for $2000. But the situation is different with dealers having an unlimited supply or standard-priced goods. Thus, if an automobile dealer agrees to sell a car to a buyer at the standard price of $2000, a breach by the buyer injures the dealer, even though he is able to sell the automobile to another for $2000. If the dealer has an inexhaustible supply of cars, the resale to replace the breaching buyer costs the dealer a sale, because, had the breaching buyer performed, the dealer would have made two sales instead of one. The buyer's breach, in such a case, depletes the dealer's sales to the extent of one, and the measure of damages should be the dealer's profit on one sale. . . ." (Hawkland, *Sales and Bulk Sales* (1958 ed.), pp. 153-154). *Neri*, 30 N.Y.2d at 399-400.

> What distinction does this excerpt recognize between private sellers and dealers?

- If the seller recovers lost profits, can it also recover incidental damages such as maintenance, storage, insurance, and financing costs incurred between the breach and second sale?

Note 2: In seeking damages under 2-709, a seller might claim the goods are unique or unusual. In *Plateq Corp. v. Machlett Laboratories, Inc.*, 189 Conn. 433, 456 A.2d 786, 35 U.C.C. Rep. Serv. 1162 (1983), the court considered a buyer's alleged wrongful refusal to accept delivery of specially-constructed steel tanks covered in lead. After finding the buyer had accepted the goods prior to its refusal to accept delivery of them, the court addressed the issue of damages. Because the goods could not be sold on the open market at a reasonable price, the court allowed the seller to use 2-709 (1) (b) to recover the contract price from the seller.

- As a practical matter, what steps should a seller take before manufacturing custom goods?

Note 3: Read current and revised 2-702. 2-702 provides the seller with a right of reclamation upon discovery of the buyer's insolvency. If the seller is successful in reclaiming the goods, it may not exercise any other remedial rights that would otherwise be available to it.

- What changes have been proposed?

- Why might a seller reclaim goods from an insolvent buyer rather than exercising other rights this section has presented?

International Perspective: Remedies

Read CISG Articles 45 and 61. These two articles are similar to UCC 2-711 and 2-703, in that they provide a roadmap of the remedies available to buyers and sellers, respectively, in the event of breach. In analyzing the similarities and differences between these CISG and UCC provisions, consider the following framework proposed by Joseph Lookofsky in *Understanding the CISG in the USA* (2d ed., Kluwer Law International 2004):

> It is convenient and, for present purposes, appropriate – to divide the various forms of CISG remedial relief into three basic categories: First comes *specific* relief, designed to compel the breaching promisor to perform his part of the bargain (deliver, pay, etc.) Next comes *substitutionary* relief, which requires the breaching party to pay (or return) an amount of money to compensate the loss suffered by the other party. The third major remedial heading is *avoidance,* i.e. the right of the promisee to "avoid" the contract and thus terminate (put an end to) the contractual relationship. *Id.* at 99-100.

Lookofsky notes that this way of classifying remedies will be familiar to civil-law-trained attorneys but may seem overly simplistic to those accustomed to a common-law system. He cautions, "[s]ince the Convention demands a uniform interpretation, and since blending domestic and international terminology can lead to confusion, American lawyers ought not try to press the CISG system into a domestic mould."

- Keeping in mind Lookofsky's warning, can you categorize some of the UCC's remedial provisions using his framework?

Read CISG Article 74. Like its Code counterpart 2-715, Article 74 requires that consequential damages have been foreseeable, even if not actually foreseen, when the contract was formed.

Read CISG Articles 28, 46, and 62 and compare UCC 2-716 and 2-709. U.S. attorneys may be surprised that specific performance is the primary CISG remedy. Because specific performance is not the primary remedy in the common-law tradition, Article 28 prevents parties from being required to give specific performance when their own country's domestic law would not require them to do so. Consider the following excerpt from Nayiri Boghossian's article, *A Comparative Study of Specific Performance Provisions in the United States*

Convention on Contracts for the International Sale of Goods 3-78, in *Review of Convention on Contracts for International Sale of Goods* (Kluwer Law International 1999):

> The rationale behind adopting [specific performance as the primary CISG remedy] is that the formation of a contract is reached with the consensus of both parties. Thus, each party is entitled to receive exactly what he contracted for.
>
> Another reason, which applies especially in international sales, is that buyers in certain countries cannot find the goods contracted for in local markets or any other accessible markets. Even when goods are available, it is difficult to substitute goods of the same quantity and quality as specified in the contract. Moreover, substitute goods only may be available for an unreasonable price or may not be available within the required time limit. In fact, this is exactly why a buyer will turn to the international market to procure the needed goods.
>
> Another argument set forth by proponents of specific performance is that granting damages requires time to assess and quantify the loss, which will result in additional expenses and delay for both parties. *Id.* at 21-22.

> Boghossian asserts that these concerns may be especially acute for parties from developing countries, and suggests their interests should be offered particular protection in the international market.

- What are the risks and benefits of awarding specific performance rather than money damages?

Chapter Conclusion: This chapter introduced the basic obligations of buyers and sellers, as well as the relevant standards for judging contractual performance and fashioning an appropriate remedy for breach. These materials should be useful in counseling a client who is filing suit – or being sued – under Article 2.

Chapter 6:
Rights of Third Parties

A. Void and Voidable Title

Read 1-103 and 2-403 (1). In a normal, undisputed sale of
goods, "good title" passes when a buyer with contractual
capacity and a seller with the power and right to convey title to
the goods in question participate in the transaction by mutual
assent. At the opposite end of the spectrum, "void title," or no
title at all, is passed in a transaction that the law deems so
tainted that neither the buyer nor the seller will be allowed to
enforce the contract. An example is the sale of stolen goods.
"Voidable title" occupies the middle ground between good title
and void title. Voidable title is passed in a sales transaction in
which one party engages in wrongdoing and the law has
determined that the other party, as the victim of the
wrongdoing, may choose either to enforce or to escape the sales
contract, at his or her election. The UCC does not indicate
when a transaction results in the passage of void or voidable
title, as opposed to good title. Thus, under 1-103, it is
appropriate to look to other state law to answer this question.

> The Article 2A analogues are 2A-304 and 2A-305.

Generally, "void" title results from extreme circumstances in
which the mutual assent of the parties is called strongly into
doubt or the seller is wholly without power to convey title to the
goods in question. Physical duress whereby one party
threatens the other at gunpoint is one situation in which most
jurisdictions will find the wrongdoer holds "void" title – that is,
no title at all – to any goods thus procured. Another example is
"fraud in the factum," which is fraud that prevents a party from
knowing he or she is signing a contract or, alternatively, from
knowing the essential terms of the contract he or she has
signed. One classic fact pattern illustrating void title involves a
party who is tricked into signing a contract while believing he
or she is signing a letter. This deceit is accomplished with a
contract carefully tucked into the letter by the fraudfeasor such
that the signer's pen strokes, unbeknownst to the signer, fall at
the contract's signature line. Theft, along the same lines,
creates void title in the thief, since no mutual assent to a theft
exists, by definition. The thief thus owns no title that it could
pass to any other party. In each of these circumstances,
neither the victimized party nor the wrongdoer could enforce
the exchange transaction; instead, the law deems the putative
contract a nullity.

Most other contract-law defenses a party might raise will, if
proven, result in voidable title, rather than void title. For
example, when a party shows he or she lacked contractual

capacity due to infancy or mental infirmity, the transaction is
generally voidable at the election of the incapacitated person.
Alternatively, if a formerly incapacitated person wishes to
enforce the contract once the incapacity has ended, he or she
can do so. The other party has no right to affirm or avoid the
contract, but is bound by the decision of the party holding the
defense.   Other voidable contracts are those that are
unconscionable, procured by undue influence, or marked by
actionable nondisclosure or misrepresentation. "Fraud in the
inducement," which is fraud as to some term of a contract, also
results in voidable title.

   ▪   Why should "fraud in the factum" result in void title,
       while "fraud in the inducement" creates voidable title?

> The concept of a "good-faith purchaser for value," which is sometimes called a "bona-fide purchaser" or "BFP," figures prominently in these materials. Chapter 9 introduces a character called a "holder in due course," who is the Article 3 equivalent of Article 2's BFP.

In addition, as Part B shows, voidable title is passed when the
owner of goods entrusts them to a merchant in goods of that
kind, who wrongfully sells them to an innocent third party.
Section 2-403 (1) provides that a party with voidable title has
the power to transfer good title to another party, so long as the
transferee is a "good-faith purchaser for value." As 2-403 (1)
subsections (a) through (d) show, this power may exist even
though the transferor has engaged in conduct that is objectively
wrongful.   Thus, in our example, the merchant acquires
voidable title but may pass good title to the innocent purchaser.

Students are often confused as to the differences between good
title, voidable title, and void title. A party that acquires goods
by wrongful conduct will not have "good title"; instead,
depending on the specific circumstances, it may have "void
title" or it may have "voidable title." The "true owner" from
whom the wrongdoer took or received the goods can recover the
goods while they are in the hands of the wrongdoer. Once the
goods have been transferred to a good-faith purchaser for value,
however, voidable title is "laundered" into good title, and thus
the good-faith purchaser can keep the goods if the wrongdoer
had voidable title, as opposed to void title. Thus, voidable title
is distinguishable from good title, which would have given the
transferor the right to the goods.   Voidable title is
distinguishable from void title, as well. Re-reading 2-403 (1),
carefully examine the first sentence: "A purchaser of goods
acquires all title which his transferor had or had power to
transfer. . . ." Thus, a purchaser of goods from a transferor with
void (as opposed to voidable) title acquires *no title at all*,
because the transferor had no title to give.

> Two common-law exceptions existed: (1) When the goods were sold on an open market, or (2) When the true owner engaged in bad or negligent conduct with regard to the goods.

2-403 softened the common law rule that a buyer could obtain
no greater rights than the seller. The general rule was that a
purchaser who bought goods from one who acted wrongfully in
acquiring or selling them bought nothing, regardless of

whether current law would hold that the seller had "voidable title" or "void title." Understanding the distinction between void and voidable title sets up an important distinction between Articles 2 and 3 that is introduced in Chapter 9. As those materials show, it is sometimes possible for an Article 3 holder in due course to obtain good title to a negotiable instrument procured from a thief, even though it is impossible for an Article 2 good-faith purchaser to obtain good title to stolen goods.

In reading the following case, note that the wrongdoer is not a party to the lawsuit. Instead, the suit is between two innocent parties – the original owner of the goods and a good-faith purchaser – while the wrongdoer, the intermediate seller who never paid for the goods, is either unavailable or judgment-proof. The court describes the policy reasons behind 2-403 and explains why bona-fide purchasers are often called "favorites of the law."

United Road Machinery Co. v. Jasper,
568 S.W.2d 242, 24 U.C.C. Rep. Serv. 610 (Ky. App. 1978).

White, Judge.

Appellant United Road Machinery Co. is a dealer in heavy road equipment, including truck scales. . . . Its supplier for such truck scales is Thurman Scale Company. . . . Appellant received a phone call on July 21, 1975, from James R. Durham, an officer of Consolidated Coal Co., seeking acquisition of truck scales for his coal-mining operation. A lease-purchase agreement was entered into by the parties at this time providing for monthly payments of $608 over a 24-month period with an option to purchase for one dollar consideration, exercisable at the termination of the lease. The designated scale was a Thurman portable-pitless scale, Model RS 5260-PFW-TPB, 50-ton capacity, serial number 75PT6126, valued at $13,133.

> Remember the discussion in Chapter 2, Part A, of the distinction between true leases and disguised sales. Which is this? The court provides a hint as to its own determination of this issue, later in the opinion.

Appellant subsequently notified its supplier, Thurman Scale Company, that Consolidated Coal would take possession of the scales from the supplier. Appellant paid for the machinery at that time. On July 28, 1975, Consolidated Coal obtained the scales without signing a contract with appellant at that time; rather, the contract papers were forwarded to Consolidated by appellant but never returned. The scales were taken to Consolidated's place of business in Laurel County[, Kentucky], where decking was added, increasing the value of the scales to approximately $16,000. Appellant has never received any consideration, either in rental payments or purchase price, on this equipment.

> On what theories might United Road machinery seek to recover, in the absence of a written contract?

On September 20, 1975, Consolidated Coal, through its agent and officer J. R. Durham, sold the truck scales to Kentucky Mobile Homes, whose president is Ethard Jasper, for a purchase price of $8,500. Before purchase, Ethard Jasper checked Laurel and Pulaski County[, Kentucky] records for any possible lien, mortgage, or other

> Should the price have put Jasper on notice of a potential problem with the sale? Note 1 may assist you in answering this question.

encumbrance on the property. Such search revealed no encumbrance of any kind. Ethard Jasper contends that Consolidated Coal appeared to have good title to the scales, and he further denies any knowledge of the dispute between appellant and Consolidated Coal.

The court's opinion provides no indication of any relationship between Ethard Jasper and Clyde Jasper.

On September 22, 1975, Kentucky Mobile Homes sold the truck scales to Clyde Jasper, individually, for $8,500 in cash. Before purchasing the equipment, Clyde Jasper also conducted a search of Laurel and Pulaski County records, which revealed no evidence of any lien, mortgage, or encumbrance on said machinery. Clyde Jasper also denies any knowledge of the dispute between appellant and Consolidated Coal Company or appellant and Kentucky Mobile Homes. The scales are presently in the possession of Clyde Jasper on his property in Pulaski County, Kentucky. . . .

Three possible situations exist under which appellees received possession of the scales, any one and/or all three of the possibilities conferring good title in appellees.

The first possibility is that Consolidated Coal Company had good title to the truck scales. Under both Common Law and the Uniform Commercial Code, a purchaser acquires all title the seller had or, if a limited interest is transferred, all title to the extent of that interest. Thus, if Consolidated Coal possessed good title to the truck scales, appellees in turn gained good title upon transfer.

The second possibility occurs if Consolidated Coal had voidable title. KRS 355.2-403 (1) provides: "A person with voidable title has power to transfer a good title to a good faith purchaser for value." Assuming that Consolidated Coal had voidable title, appellees, to obtain good title, must be found to be good-faith purchasers for value. . . . As the circuit court aptly put it: "A 'good-faith purchaser for value' can be defined as one who takes by purchase getting sufficient consideration to support a simple contract, and who is honest in the transaction of the purchase." It is the opinion of this court that appellees meet this criteria.

Concerning voidable title, KRS 355.2-403 (1) goes on to state that good title may be transferred under certain circumstances:

> When goods have been delivered under a transaction of purchase the purchaser has such power even though
>
> (a) the transferor was deceived as to the identity of the purchaser, or
>
> (b) the delivery was in exchange for a check which is later dishonored, or
>
> (c) it was agreed that the transaction was to be a "cash sale," or
>
> (d) the delivery was procured through fraud punishable as larcenous under the criminal law.

Assuming that Consolidated Coal's actions toward appellant fall within one of the four enumerated circumstances, a "transaction of purchase" is still requisite before the statute becomes operative allowing transfer of good title. Appellant argues that no transaction of purchase occurred, that the agreement between appellant and Consolidated Coal was not a purchase transaction but merely a lease, and that the law concerning landlord-tenant, and not the Uniform Commercial Code, governs. Therefore the concept of voidable title has no application in this case.

This court feels there was a "transaction of purchase" per the code definition. "The purpose, rather than the name given a contract by the parties controls, and the court will give effect to the real and dominant intention of the parties when definitely ascertained." *Trinity Temple Charities, Inc. v. City of Louisville*, 300 Ky. 172, 188 S.W.2d 91, 94 (1945).

Even if Consolidated Coal Company had no title in the truck scales to convey, this court finds appellant estopped from asserting his proper title against the appellees as bona-fide purchaser. The Common Law rule generally allowed a purchaser to obtain that title possessed by the seller and ". . . one who had no title could convey none." 67 Am. Jur.2d Sales § 259, at 394. Exceptions to the general rule were shaped by equity courts and under certain circumstances the true owner of the property was estopped from asserting title. The doctrine of estoppel was applied to circumstances where the seller possessed indicia of ownership sufficient to indicate to the purchaser that he had power to convey.

> Is this common-law estoppel exception recognized in UCC 2-403?

And it has been stated that no buyer was bound to assume that the seller with whom he dealt was a wrongdoer, and if the seller presented property the title to which was apparently valid and there were no circumstances disclosed which cast suspicion upon the title, the buyer might rightfully deal with him, and, paying full value of the same, acquire the rights of a purchaser in good faith.

In the present case, there was nothing to suggest that Consolidated Coal was not the owner of the scales. J. R. Durham in fact held himself out to be such owner. Furthermore, a search of county records revealed no encumbrances upon the machinery, and appellees had no knowledge of or reason to suspect a dispute between appellant and Consolidated Coal. Under these circumstances, appellees are found to be bona-fide purchasers in good faith.

Bona-fide purchasers are favorites of the law, and they should only be required to pay for another's negligence or mistake when the circumstances are so unusual as to justify a finding that they took unfair advantage of a transaction initiated by the complaining party.

It is unfortunate that (appellant was) defrauded. It is inequitable to require a blameless third party to pay for their mistake. Both parties being innocent, the loss must be borne by the party whose initial conduct puts it in the power of another to cause the loss.

For the foregoing reasons, the judgment is affirmed.

- The court's opinion brings to mind the concept of the cheapest cost avoider, presented in Chapter 3, Part B.

How could United Road Machinery have avoided this loss?

Note 1: *Graves Motors, Inc. v. Docar Sales, Inc.*, 414 F. Supp. 717, 20 U.C.C. Rep. Serv. 367 (E.D. La. 1976), shows the relationship between voidable title and payment with a check drawn on insufficient funds, the latter of which is further explored in Chapter 10, Part B. Graves Motors, Inc. sold five used cars to Park Auto Sales, which delivered a check in payment for the vehicles. After Park's check was returned due to insufficient funds, the parties agreed Park would convey to Graves a tractor-trailer truck worth at least $13,500 in return for Graves' forgiveness of Park's debt, which totaled about $9,100. Park was to maintain possession of the truck and use it to transport vehicles for Graves. Shortly thereafter, Park violated the agreement by delivering the truck to Docar Sales, Inc., from which it had purchased the truck, in return for Docar's forgiveness of the balance due on the truck, which Park had never paid. (As in the case of the transaction with Graves, Park had paid for the truck with a check drawn on insufficient funds.) Graves sought to recover the truck from Docar. Assume Park disappeared or was judgment-proof. In finding Docar should be permitted to keep the truck, the court held as follows:

> After you have read the materials in Chapter 7, Part C, make sure you know why both sellers would have been better served to have insisted that Park provide a cashier's check or certified personal check.

> Park, having been given a bill of sale and possession of the truck by Docar, had title, albeit one that was voidable because his check was dishonored. It could therefore transfer good title to a "good-faith purchaser for value." ...

> "Good faith" is defined by the Tennessee Code as "honesty in fact in the conduct or transaction concerned." Graves did not know that Park's title was voidable. To this extent therefore it was in subjective good faith. But honesty in fact means more than a mental belief that the seller has title. Graves knew that Park was sophisticated with respect to the value of automotive equipment, even though Park did not deal in trucks. It knew Park was in financial trouble, for Park had just given Graves three NSF checks. It had no reason to believe that Park would give equipment worth $13,500 or more to settle a debt of $9,100. And it let Park retain possession of the vehicle. *Id.* at 719.

- Could Graves have reasonably believed there was a good reason Park would exchange goods worth $13,500 for forgiveness of a $9,100 debt?

The court's opinion closes with a final, cryptic paragraph:

> There is a final equitable consideration that warrants mention, if only because Graves suggests the equity of its position; if Docar retains the truck, Graves is ultimately deprived of nothing. It had NSF checks; it took a truck and trailer in satisfaction of them; it is

no worse off than it was before its transaction with Shelton. But if Graves retains the truck, Docar will have suffered a true economic loss. *Id.* at 720.

- Is it possible to make sense of this paragraph?

Note 2: In *The Commercial Doctrine of Good Faith Purchase,* 63 Yale L.J. 1057 (1954), Professor Grant Gilmore described how concepts of good-faith purchase permeate the Code. He gathered examples from several UCC Articles, beginning with the following introduction:

> The triumph of the good-faith purchaser has been one of the most dramatic episodes in our legal history. In his several guises, he serves a commercial function: he is protected not because of his praiseworthy character, but to the end that commercial transactions may be engaged in without elaborate investigation of property rights and in reliance on the possession of property by one who offers it for sale or to secure a loan. Id.

> After you have completed this course, make sure you recognize each "guise" of the good-faith purchaser this book presents.

The paragraph closes with a word of caution:

> As the doctrine strikes roots in one or another field, the "good faith" component tends to atrophy, and the commercial purchaser is protected with little more than lip service paid to his "bona fides." *Id.*

- Why is it important that the "good faith" requirement remain and that the Code not simply protect all purchasers?

Note 3: *Phelps v. McQuade,* 220 N.Y. 232, 115 N.E. 441 (1917), involved the following facts:

> One Walter J. Gwynne falsely represented to the appellants that he was Baldwin J. Gwynne, a man of financial responsibility, residing at Cleveland, Ohio. Relying upon the truth of this statement, the appellants delivered to him upon credit a quantity of jewelry. Gwynne in turn sold it to the respondent, who bought it without notice, express or implied, of any defect in title, and for value. Learning of the deception practiced upon them, the appellants began an action in replevin to recover the goods. *Id.* at 234.

In addressing the replevin action, the court held as follows:

> Where the vendor of personal property intends to sell his goods to the person with whom he deals, then title passes, even though he be deceived as to that person's identity or responsibility. Otherwise it does not. It is purely a question of the vendor's intention.

The fact that the vendor deals with the person personally rather than by letter is immaterial, except in so far as it bears upon the question of intent.

Where the transaction is a personal one, the seller intends to transfer title to a person of credit, and he supposes the one standing before him to be that person. He is deceived. But in spite of that fact, his primary intention is to sell his goods to the person with whom he negotiates. Where the transaction is by letter, the vendor intends to deal with the person whose name is signed to the letter. He knows no one else. He supposes he is dealing with no one else. And while in both cases, other facts may be shown that would alter the rule, yet in their absence, in the first title passes; in the second it does not. *Id.* at 234-235.

The court concludes that the only relevant inquiry is whether the seller intended to do business with the person standing in front of him. This is true, the court finds, even if the seller thinks the person standing before him is someone else or has different characteristics, like wealth or trustworthiness.

- As between two innocent parties, the jeweler and the good-faith purchaser, who should bear the loss?

- **Read Section 2-403.** Is the "in person vs. by letter" distinction recognized in the Uniform Commercial Code?

Problem: Ms. Inmi-Etti, a native and resident of Nigeria, visiting her sister in the U.S. in 1981, decided to purchase a new Honda Prelude to take back with her. An acquaintance of the family, David Butler, offered to assist with the purchase. Ms. Inmi-Etti returned to Nigeria before the purchase was complete, before which time she paid the $200 deposit to the dealership, leaving the balance of $8,300 with her sister to finalize the purchase. The sister completed the transaction, and the car arrived. Butler drove it to the sister's house. Within a couple of weeks, the dealer sent the title certificate, in Ms. Inmi-Etti's name, to Butler. Butler came and took the car away, falsely representing to the sister that he was authorized to do so by Ms. Inmi-Etti.

Butler sought to sell the vehicle to a dealer, Pohanka Olds-GMC. Even though Butler had no title certificate in his name, the manager agreed to buy the vehicle for $7,200. The dealership gave him $2,000 on the spot, the rest to be paid when he produced the title certificate. The car remained on Pohanka's lot. Mr. Butler submitted a false affidavit of ownership to the Department of Motor Vehicles and was issued a certificate of title. He returned to Pohanka and claimed the

promised cash. In the meantime, Pohanka sold the car to Mr.
James Aluisi for $8,300.

- **Read 2-312.** Should Mr. Aluisi have questioned the
  dealer's authority to sell the goods?

- Did Mr. Butler ever have title to the car?

- As between Mr. Aluisi and Ms. Inmi-Etti, who should
  prevail?

Based on *Inmi-Etti v. Aluisi*, 492 A.2d 917, 40 U.C.C. Rep.
Serv. 1612 (Md. App. 1985).

International Perspective: Third Parties

Read CISG Article 4. As Article 4 (b) shows, the Convention
is not concerned with any effect the contract between a buyer
and seller might have on other parties' property interests.
Thus, whether a buyer who would qualify as a bona-fide
purchaser under the UCC can assert superior rights as against
a third-party who claims the seller had no right to sell the
goods is controlled by domestic law rather than the CISG. As
some scholars have asserted, one reason the CISG drafters
may have chosen not to address void and voidable title may be
the fact that the common-law and civil-law traditions vary
considerably in this area, such that harmonizing the various
approaches to the concept would be difficult. Because the CISG
does not address the issue, and because domestic law varies
widely, this is an area in which parties to an international sales
contract may face considerable uncertainty.

B. Entrustment

This material introduces the interplay between Article 2 and
bailment.

> The Article 2A analogues to 2-403 (2) and (3) are 2A-304 (2) and 2A-305 (2).

**Read 2-403 (2) and (3), 1-201 (b) (9) and Comment 9, and
1-204 and Comment 1.** As 2-403 (2) and (3) show, a party
who entrusts goods for repair, safekeeping, or other bailment to
a merchant dealing in goods of that kind may find it impossible
to recover those goods if the merchant wrongfully sells them to
a purchaser who qualifies as "a bona-fide purchaser for value."

- Against whom will the entrusting party have a cause of action?

- Why does 2-403 (2) use "power" to describe the actions of the wrongful seller, as opposed to "authority" or "right"?

1-201 (9) explains what it means for a purchaser to be a "buyer in ordinary course of business," and 1-204 provides guidance as to what "value" means in the context of a bona-fide purchaser for value.

> 2-403 Comment 2 may assist you in answering this question.

- What is the relationship between a "buyer in ordinary course of business" and a "bona-fide purchaser for value"?

- Why are pawnshop purchases excluded from 1-201 (9)?

- Under 1-204, does a purchaser of goods give value when he or she signs a contract promising to pay for the goods, or is value not given until payment is actually made?

The following case discusses entrustment and provides guidance as to whether a purchaser is a "buyer in ordinary course of business."

Porter v. Wertz,
68 A.D.2d 141, 416 N.Y.S 2d 254,
26 U.C.C. Rep. Serv. 876 (1979).

Birns, J.

[Samuel] Porter, the owner of a collection of artwork, bought the [disputed] Utrillo [painting] in 1969. During 1972 and 1973, he had a number of art transactions with one Harold Von Maker who used, among other names, that of Peter Wertz. [FN3] One of the transactions

> Childe Hassam, an American Impressionist, lived from 1859 to 1935.

was the sale by Porter to Von Maker in the spring of 1973 of a painting by Childe Hassam for $150,000, financed with a $50,000 deposit and 10 notes for $10,000 each. At about that time, Von Maker expressed an interest in the Utrillo. Porter permitted him to have it temporarily with the understanding that Von Maker would hang it in his (Von Maker's) home, pending Von Maker's decision whether to buy the painting. On a visit to Von Maker's home in Westchester[, New York] in May 1973, Porter saw the painting hanging there. In June 1973, lacking a decision from Von Maker, Porter sought its return, but was unable to reach Von Maker.

FN3. As will be seen, Peter Wertz was a real person, at least an acquaintance of Von Maker, who permitted Von Maker to use his name. Von Maker's true name was Harold Maker, presumably he was born in New Jersey. Apparently Maker added the prefix "Von" to his name to indicate nobility of birth.

The first note in connection with Von Maker's purchase of the Childe Hassam, due early July 1973, was returned dishonored, as were the balance of the notes. Porter commenced an investigation and found that he had not been dealing with Peter Wertz – but with another man named Von Maker. . . . [R]eports dated July 10 and July 17, 1973, disclosed that Von Maker was subject to judgments, that he had been sued many times, that he had an arrest record for possession of obscene literature, and for "false pretenses," as well as for "theft of checks," and had been convicted, among other crimes, of transmitting a forged cable in connection with a scheme to defraud the Chase Manhattan Bank and had been placed on probation for three years. Porter notified the FBI about his business transactions concerning the notes. He did not report that Von Maker had defrauded him of any painting, for, as will be shown, Porter did not know at this time that Von Maker had disposed of the Utrillo.

> As Chapter 10, Part A shows, dishonor occurs when an item is presented for payment and returned unpaid, reviving the underlying debt.

Porter did, however, have his attorney communicate with Von Maker's attorney. As a result, on August 13, 1973, a detailed agreement, drawn by the attorneys for Porter and Von Maker, the latter still using the name Peter Wertz, was executed. Under this agreement, the obligations of Von Maker to Porter concerning several paintings delivered by Porter to Von Maker (one of which was the Utrillo) were covered. In paragraph 11, Von Maker acknowledged that he had received the Utrillo from Porter together with a certain book on Utrillo, that both "belong to [Porter]," that the painting was on consignment with a client of Von Maker's, that within 90 days Von Maker would either return the painting and book or pay $30,000 therefor, and that, other than the option to purchase within said 90-day period, Von Maker had "no claim whatsoever to the Utrillo painting or Book."

> Consignment is addressed in Chapter 13, Part A.

Paragraph 13 provided that, in the event Von Maker failed to meet the obligations under paragraph 11, i.e., return the Utrillo and book within 90 days or pay for them, Porter would immediately be entitled to obtain possession of a painting by Cranach held in escrow by Von Maker's attorney, and have the right to sell that painting, apply the proceeds to the amount owing by Von Maker under paragraph 11, and Von Maker would pay any deficiency. Paragraph 13 provided further that "[t]he above is in addition to all [Porter's] other rights and remedies, which [Porter] expressly reserves to enforce the performance of [Von Maker's] obligations under this Agreement."

> It is not clear whether the reference here is to Lucas Cranach the Elder or Lucas Cranach the Younger. Both were German Northern Renaissance painters.

We note that the agreement did not state that receipt of the Cranach by Porter would be in full satisfaction of Porter's claim to the Utrillo and book. Title to the Utrillo and book remained in Porter, absent any payment by Von Maker of the agreed purchase price of $30,000. Indeed, no payment for the Utrillo was ever made by Von Maker.

At the very time that Von Maker was deceitfully assuring Porter he would return the Utrillo and book or pay $30,000, Von Maker had already disposed of this painting by using the real Peter Wertz to effect its sale for $20,000 to [Richard] Feigen [Gallery, Inc.]. Von Maker . . . had made the availability of the Utrillo known to Feigen. When Wertz,

at Von Maker's direction, appeared at the Feigen gallery with the
Utrillo, he was met by Feigen's employee, Mrs. Drew-Bear. She found a
buyer for the Utrillo in defendant [Irvin] Brenner. In effecting its
transfer to him, Feigen made a commission. Through a sale by
Brenner, the painting is now in Venezuela, South America. [Porter
now seeks to recover from Feigen based on the loss of the painting.]

We agree with the conclusion of the trial court that statutory estoppel
does not bar [Porter's] recovery [from Feigen].

The provisions of statutory estoppel are found in section 2-403 of the
Uniform Commercial Code. . . .

In order to determine whether the defense of statutory estoppel is
available to Feigen, we must begin by ascertaining whether Feigen fits
the definition of "a buyer in the ordinary course of business." Feigen
does not fit that definition, for two reasons. First, Wertz, from whom
Feigen bought the Utrillo, was not an art dealer – he was not "a person
in the business of selling goods of that kind." If anything, he was a
delicatessen employee. [FN6] Wertz never held himself out as a dealer.
. . . Second, Feigen was not "a person . . . in good faith" in the
transaction with Wertz. Section 2-103 (subd [1], par [b]) of the Uniform
Commercial Code defines "good faith" in the case of a merchant as
"honesty in fact and the observance of reasonable commercial
standards of fair dealing in the trade." Although this definition by its
terms embraces the "reasonable commercial standards of fair dealing
in the trade," it should not – and cannot – be interpreted to permit,
countenance or condone commercial standards of sharp trade practice
or indifference as to the "provenance," i.e., history of ownership or the
right to possess or sell an object d'art, such as is present in the case
before us.

> FN6. Wertz is described as a seller of caviar and other luxury food
> items (because of his association with a Madison Avenue gourmet
> grocery) and over whom the Trial Term observed, Von Maker
> "cast his hypnotic spell . . . and usurped his name, his signature,
> and his sacred honor."

* * *

We note that neither Ms. Drew-Bear nor her employer Feigen made
any investigation to determine the status of Wertz, i.e., whether he was
an art merchant, "a person in the business of selling goods of that
kind." Had Ms. Drew-Bear done so much as call either of the telephone
numbers Wertz had left, she would have learned that Wertz was
employed by a delicatessen and was not an art dealer. Nor did Ms.
Drew-Bear or Feigen make an effort to verify whether Wertz was the
owner or authorized by the owner to sell the painting he was offering.
Ms. Drew-Bear had available to her [an authoritative] volume on
Utrillo which included "Chateau de Lion-sur-Mer" [, the disputed
painting,] in its catalogue of the master's work. [FN8] Although this
knowledge alone might not have been enough to put Feigen on notice
that Wertz was not the true owner at the time of the transaction, it
could have raised a doubt as to Wertz' right of possession, calling for
further verification before the purchase by Feigen was consummated.

Margin notes:

The quoted language is from 1-201 (b) (9).

The quoted language is from 1-201 (b) (9).

Given the court's admonition against "sharp trade practice," how can a party pursue its own interests in good faith? Refer back to Chapter 5, Part A as needed to answer this question.

Thus, it appears that statutory estoppel provided by subdivision (2) of section 2-403 of the Uniform Commercial Code was not, as Trial Term correctly concluded, available as a defense to Feigen.

> FN8. Page 32 of that book clearly contained a reference to the fact that that painting, at least at the time of publication of the book in 1969, was in the collection of Mrs. Donald D. King of New York, supposedly the party from whom Porter obtained it.

[The portion of the court's opinion relating to what it termed "pre-Code estoppel" has been deleted. The court reversed the lower court's holding, reinstating the complaint and entering judgment for Porter against Feigen on liability, with damages to be determined upon remand.]

- • The court uses the term "statutory estoppel" to describe 2-403 (2). In this context, what does the term mean?

Note 1: Students often wonder about the relationship between a title certificate and the concept of title. The Nevada Supreme Court's analysis in *Godfrey v. Gilsdorf*, 86 Nev. 714, 476 P.2d 3, 8 U.C.C. Rep. Serv. 316 (1970), explains this relationship and connects these concepts with entrustment. Melvin Godfrey sought to recover his 1967 Toyota automobile from Gary Gilsdorf, an individual who bought the car from Auto Center, a used car dealer to which Godfrey had entrusted it for sale. In preparation for the vehicle's sale, Godfrey had removed its license plates and registration and delivered it to Auto Center. At that time, the vehicle was subject to a lien held by Commercial Credit Corporation.

Godfrey learned Auto Center had sold the car to Gilsdorf when he noticed it was no longer on the lot and inquired as to its whereabouts. Auto Center's representative notified Godfrey he would receive payment when Gilsdorf's check cleared the bank. Gilsdorf did not receive the certificate of title when he purchased the car, but was told Auto Center would mail the certificate to him directly. In the meantime, he was given a document entitled "Dealer's Report of Sale." Godfrey never received payment for the vehicle, Gilsdorf never received the title certificate, and Auto Center went out of business. Some time later, Godfrey paid off his debt to Commercial Credit Corporation on his former vehicle and received the certificate of title, after which he sought to recover his vehicle from Gilsdorf. The court held as follows, in refusing Godfrey's claim:

> The seller, Godfrey, plaintiff below and appellant here, insists that title to a motor vehicle can only be transferred in accordance with the motor-vehicle licensing-and-registration law, and not otherwise....

On the other hand, the buyer Gilsdorf, defendant below and respondent here, urges that the entrustment provisions of the Uniform Commercial Code create an estoppel against the seller to assert title to the car. Moreover, he argues that the buyer, in these circumstances, acquired the automobile free of the security interest of Commercial Credit Corporation. In persuasive fashion he presses the following. The seller entrusted his car to a merchant who deals in cars and, in the words of the UCC "gave him the power to transfer all rights of the entrustor to a buyer in the ordinary course of business." N.R.S. 104.2403 (2). Gilsdorf was a "buyer in the ordinary course of business." N.R.S. 104.1201 (9). He bought a used car from a person in the business of selling used cars, and bought it in good faith without knowledge of the ownership rights of a third party, Commercial Credit Corporation. He arranged immediate financing for the car and paid cash to the dealer. He inquired as to title and was assured by the dealer and by Allstate [Credit Corporation], who financed the purchase for him, that title would be taken care of by having the dealer send it to Allstate. He had the car registered in his name and paid for the license plates. Finally, the buyer stresses the fact that the seller set in motion the chain of events which led to the sale of the car and should bear the loss incurred from the misconduct of the dealer whom he selected. We turn to resolve these opposing views.

The licensing-and-registration provisions of the vehicle code are essentially police regulations, and strict compliance with them appears to be the prevailing view. The underlying policy and purpose of that regulatory scheme are best promoted by such a view. It does not follow, however, that those purposes are subverted by the application of an estoppel theory to a business transaction falling within the entrustment provisions of the UCC. . . .

* * *

In summary, we find . . . that Godfrey entrusted his car to a merchant who deals in cars. The merchant was empowered to transfer Godfrey's rights to a buyer in the ordinary course of business and did so. We conclude that the principle of estoppel precludes Godfrey from asserting his later-acquired title against Gilsdorf who purchased in good faith, for value and without notice of the then existing security interest of Commercial Credit Corporation. *Id.* at 717-719.

- How could Godfrey have avoided this loss?

> After you have studied the materials in Chapter 16 on priority, you will have a clearer understanding of why Gildorf's claim trumps that of Commercial Credit Corporation, which presumably loaned Godfrey the money to purchase the car and retained a purchase money security interest.

> This situation is an example of the way in which a state may choose to modify the UCC as enacted.

To understand this case fully, note that some states require a party to obtain a title certificate for title to exist. *See, e.g., Sheridan Suzuki, Inc. v. Caruso Auto Sales, Inc.*, 110 Misc. 2d 823 (1981) (in a case involving title to a motorcycle, citing 2113 (c) of the Vehicle and Traffic Law of New York and holding voidable title could not be established absent a title certificate). Thus, some states require that a party seeking to establish title obtain a title certificate as a *necessary* precondition; a title certificate, however, standing alone, may not be *sufficient* to allow a party to provide title to the goods, as the *Godfrey* case shows.

Note 2: Although *O'Connor's Administratrix v. Clark,* 170 Pa. 318, 32 A. 1029 (1895), predated the UCC by more than a half-century, its result is consistent with the Code. John O'Connor, the owner of a wagon, allowed George Tracy to use the wagon and to have painted on its side, "George Tracy, Piano Mover." When Tracy wrongfully sold the wagon to John Clark, falsely representing that the wagon was Tracy's to sell, O'Connor sought to recover the wagon from Clark.   In rejecting O'Connor's claim, the court held as follows, using the concept of apparent authority:

> While the soundness of the general rule of law that a vendee of personal property takes only such title or interest as his vendor has and is authorized to transfer cannot for a moment be doubted, it is not without its recognized exceptions. One of these is where the owner has so acted with reference to his property as to invest another with such evidence of ownership, or apparent authority to deal with and dispose of it, as is calculated to mislead, and does mislead, a good-faith purchaser for value. In such cases, the principle of estoppel applies, and declares that the apparent title or authority, for the existence of which the actual owner was responsible, shall be regarded as the real title or authority, at least so far as persons acting on the apparent title or authority, and parting with value, are concerned. Strictly speaking, this is merely a special application of the broad equitable rule that, where one of two innocent persons must suffer loss by reason of the fraud or deceit of another, the loss should fall upon him by whose act or omission the wrongdoer has been enabled to commit the fraud. Assuming, in this case, that a jury [should find that Clark] was misled into the belief that Tracy was the real owner, and he accordingly bought and paid him for the property, can there be any doubt, as between the real owner and the innocent purchaser, that the loss should fall upon the former, by whose act Tracy was enabled to thus fraudulently sell and receive the price of the property? We think not. *Id.* at 321-322.

- Which individual is a more sympathetic claimant: Melvin Godfrey or John O'Connor?

- How can the two cases be distinguished?

Note 3: *Hammer v. Thompson,* 35 Kan. App. 2d 165, 129 P.3d 609, 59 U.C.C. Rep. Serv. 2d 75 (2006), shows how a court may determine whether a seller is a "merchant who deals in goods of that kind" within the definition of 2-403 (2). The court noted the policy behind 2-403:

There are three general policies supporting the UCC entrustment provision. First, it protects the innocent buyer who believes the merchant has legal title to the goods because the goods are in the merchant's possession. Second, the entrustment provision is also based on the rationale that the entruster is in a better position than the innocent buyer to protect against the risk of the dishonesty of the dealer. Third, entrustment facilitates the flow of commerce when buyers in the ordinary course of business are involved. *Id.* at 184.

Acknowledging that 2-403 provides a more restrictive definition of the term "merchant" than 2-104 (1)'s general Article 2 definition does, the court indicated that only those merchants who sell or lease goods of the kind entrusted should be held to satisfy 2-403.

- Why does it make sense for 2-403 to employ a narrower definition of "merchant" than 2-104 (1) does?

- How does 2-403's definition of "merchant" compare with the definition contained in 2-314?

Problem 1: Debra Thorn asked her son-in-law Richard to take her late-model vehicle to Gateley's Fairway Motors, an automotive dealership, for repair. Vera Adams noticed the car on Gateley's lot, requested a test drive, and purchased the car from Gateley's. Adams did not ask, but assumed, that Gateley's was authorized to sell the vehicle, and she was never informed otherwise. When Ms. Thorn learned of the sale, she demanded that Ms. Adams return the vehicle. Ms. Adams not only refused, but brought suit requesting injunctive relief to require Ms. Thorn to surrender the vehicle's certificate of title, which Ms. Adams had not been able to secure due to the dispute. Ms. Thorn counterclaimed, demanding return of the car or payment of its fair-market value. The court found in favor of Ms. Adams.

- What remedies does Ms. Thorn have? Against whom?

- Was the court correct in finding Ms. Adams was a "buyer in ordinary course of business"?

Based on *Thorn v. Adams*, 125 Or. App. 257, 865 P.2d 417, 22 U.C.C. Rep. Serv. 2d 490 (1993).

Problem 2: Atlas Auto Rental, from time to time, sold off used automobiles that had been part of its rental stock and replaced them with new ones. On August 23, 1965, Herbert Schwartzman offered to purchase one such vehicle, a two-year-old Chevrolet station wagon, for $1,250 and tendered a check

for this amount. Because the check was not certified, Atlas
rejected the offer, but permitted Schwartzman to take the
vehicle on a test drive. Schwartzman disappeared with the
vehicle, leaving the check on the manager's desk. The check
was returned uncollected by the bank on which it was drawn,
due to insufficient funds. One week later, the vehicle was
traced to the premises of Eldorado Auto Wreckers, a licensed
junk dealer also licensed as a used-car seller. Its owner,
Edward Weisberg, had purchased the vehicle from
Schwartzman for $900. Schwartzman supplied Eldorado with
neither a bill of sale nor a registration certificate. Weisberg
sold the vehicle to a dealer the day he purchased it, for $1,200.

Certified checks are discussed in Chapter 7, Part D.

Atlas brought suit against Weisberg for conversion, seeking to
recover the value of the car. In response, Weisberg claimed he
had good title. Invoking the Code, he asserted that "he could
acquire good title from a merchant, or even from a thief."

- Based on these facts, who should prevail?

- Was Weisberg's statement correct as a matter of law?

Based on *Atlas Auto Rental Corp. v. Weisberg*, 281 N.Y.S.2d
400, 4 U.C.C. Rep. Serv. 572 (1967).

International Perspective: Entrustment

Read CISG Article 4. As Article 4 (b) shows, the Convention
does not address the effect of a contract between a buyer and a
seller on other parties' property interests. Thus, whether a true
owner can recover goods it entrusted to a merchant dealing in
such goods who wrongfully sold them to an innocent third
party, is controlled by domestic law.

C. Article 6 Bulk Sales

This section contains this book's only reference to this
increasingly obscure material and shows how reforms to UCC
Article 9 have contributed to the declining need for Article 6.

Article 6 was designed to protect unsecured creditors from a
specific kind of scam: companies in the business of selling
merchandise might suddenly close up shop and disappear
without repaying the creditors from whom they borrowed funds
to purchase their inventory. Unsecured creditors would suffer

"Unsecured" creditors are those whose rights to payment are not supported by any collateral that could be claimed in the event of default. Secured credit is the focus of Chapters 13-17. Unsecured creditors are particularly vulnerable to loss in the event of default.

a total loss of the unpaid balance because, due to their 1
unsecured status, they could not recover the merchandise and 2
apply its value to lessen the outstanding debt. 3

To prevent such losses, Article 6 provides that, when there is a 5
transfer of a major part of a seller's inventory outside the 6
normal course of business, the buyer of such merchandise must 7
prepare a schedule of the seller's creditors and send notice of 8
the proposed transfer at least ten days before it takes place. 9
Interestingly, the burden is placed on the buyer, not the seller, 10
even though the buyer normally has no relationship with the 11
seller's creditors. The consequence of failing to comply with the 12
Article 6 notice requirement is that the transfer is ineffective as 13
against any creditor who does not receive notice. Article 6 is, 14
however, just a notice provision – it does not require that the 15
buyer pay the creditors or apply the proceeds of the sale to any 16
creditor's benefit. Nevertheless, these requirements impose a 17
substantial burden that probably has had the effect of chilling 18
commerce because it provides creditors with a remedy against 19
a bona-fide purchaser for value, which is unusual outside the 20
context of void title as introduced in Part A. 21

Because Article 6 had become burdensome, and because 23
reforms to Article 9 have made it easier for creditors to obtain a 24
security interest should they choose to do so, in 1989 Article 6 25
was revised to give states the option of either repealing or 26
revising the Article. The drafters recommended that Article 6 27
be totally repealed, an approach described below as 28
"Alternative A," but proposed a set of revisions described below 29
as "Alternative B" for those states that did not wish to repeal 30
the Article altogether. 31

Read the Prefatory Note to Article 6, together with the 33
text of Alternative A. These materials describe the rationale 34
behind the drafters' recommendation that Article 6 be repealed. 35
As Chapter 1, Part A makes clear the UCC drafters have no 36
authority to make state legislatures follow their 37
recommendation. Instead, the ALI and NCCUSL can only 38
withdraw their support of the Article and recommend states do 39
the same. States can respond by adopting Alternative A or B 40
or by leaving prior Article 6 in place. 41

Read 6-103 (1), 6-104, 6-105 (1) and (2), and 6-107 (1). 43
Taken together, these provisions demonstrate how Article 6 is 44
to be applied in states that adopt the proposed revisions instead 45
of repealing the Article completely. 6-103 (1) provides guidance 46
on what kinds of sales implicate Article 6's notice requirements. 50
6-104 describes the general obligations of a buyer who 51
purchases goods through a bulk sale. 6-105 (1) and (2) 52
53

The drafters have
included a sample
notice in the text
that follows 6-105.

describes the kind of notice that a purchaser will be required to give to the creditors of the seller prior to a bulk sale.

Read Alternative B, 6-107. The most important recommended revision, for states that did not repeal Article 6, was to lessen the sanction for noncompliance: unlike prior Article 6, revised Article 6 stops short of making transfers ineffective as to those creditors who did not receive notice, but instead provides for the imposition of money damages. In addition, revised Article 6, unlike prior Article 6, provides exceptions whereby notice is not required for transfers worth less than $10,000 or more than $25,000,000.

- Why should relatively small transfers and very large transfers be exempted from the notice requirements of Article 6?

Read Alternative B, 6-105. In addition, Article 6 as originally drafted required a purchaser of goods pursuant to a bulk sale to provide individual notice to creditors. Revised Article 6 allows the buyer to file a general notice with the Secretary of State when more than 200 creditors are involved. The vast majority of jurisdictions have chosen to repeal Article 6, as recommended. A few have adopted the proposed revisions, and a few retain prior Article 6. For an up-to-date list of jurisdictions applying each approach, visit www.nccusl.org.

The following case, which applies prior Article 6, provides guidance as to what constitutes a "major part" of the seller's inventory, so as to invoke Article 6 in a jurisdiction where some version of the Article remains in effect. As the case shows, issues involving bulk sales often arise in the bankruptcy context, and specifically when the seller has filed for bankruptcy shortly after the bulk sale in question. The case also provides a general explanation of the purposes behind Article 6.

> The California legislature chose to use the term "substantial part" rather than "major part."

Reed v. Anglo Scandinavian Corp.,
298 F. Supp. 310, 6 U.C.C. Rep. Serv. 714 (E.D. Cal. 1969).

MacBride, Chief Judge.

This is an action under section 70e of the Bankruptcy Act by the trustee to avoid the bankrupt's prior transfer of property.

> The bankruptcy trustee's avoidance power is generally described in Title 11 § 544 of the Bankruptcy Code. The Bankruptcy Act was the predecessor to the Bankruptcy Code. The Bankruptcy Code is available online at www.gpoaccess.gov/uscode/index.html.

On May 7, 1967, Dorothy Penny Hansen (hereinafter the debtor), proprietor of Porter's Apparel and Ski Shop, sold an assortment of skis and ski boots to the defendant, Anglo Scandinavian Corporation. In the Fall of 1967, the debtor was adjudged bankrupt....

* * *

Plaintiff trustee here alleges that the sale of merchandise to defendant is void under the provisions of the California Commercial Code annulling certain bulk transfers. If the trustee can prove that this was a "bulk transfer," void under California law, he will prevail in this action.

California Commercial Code § 6105 provides that a "bulk transfer" is fraudulent and void against any creditor of the transferor unless the transferee gives the required statutory notice to creditors. A "bulk transfer" is "any transfer in bulk and not in the ordinary course of the transferor's business of a substantial part of the materials, supplies, merchandise, or other inventory . . . of an enterprise subject to this division." Cal. Com. Code § 6102 (1) (West 1964). Being a retail merchant, the debtor in this case was subject to the law.

A perusal of the memoranda and affidavits of the parties discloses that there is no genuine disagreement as to any fact necessary for plaintiff's recovery except what proportion of the total inventory was transferred. Plaintiff sets the percentage at "approximately 7.5 percent." Defendant offers to prove that the transfer was of "less than 5 percent" of the total inventory. The parties also disagree about what constitutes "a substantial part of the inventory of an enterprise" under the bulk-transfer law. Plaintiff argues that since, according to the debtor's testimony, the transfer was of about 50 percent of the ski boot inventory, it was a transfer of "a substantial part of the inventory." Defendant rejoins that the proper measure is the percentage of the whole inventory of the enterprise, not the percentage of the particular item transferred.

Surprisingly, there are few cases construing the words "substantial part of the inventory." It is indisputable, however, that to be "substantial" the proportion transferred need not be 50 percent or even close to 50 percent. The Uniform Commercial Code uses the words "major part." The California Commercial Code substituted the words "substantial part" to preserve prior California law. In California, as little as 6.3 percent, 15 percent, and 16 percent of the total inventory have been held to constitute a "substantial part" within the meaning of this section. The cases also illustrate that the proper gross measure is the entire inventory and not, as plaintiff suggests, the proportion of the specific item transferred. [FN7]

> FN7. Common sense also indicates that plaintiff's suggestion cannot be right. According to his view, if the debtor in this case had instead sold her entire supply of Chap Stick, worth say $20, that would be voidable as a bulk transfer even if the ski shop's total inventory was $100,000. The bulk-transfer law clearly does not contemplate such a result.

* * *

While it is true that the total value of the debtor's inventory at the time of transfer (and thus the exact percentage which was transferred) is still in dispute, that does not preclude summary judgment in this case.

In the first place, it is likely that there will never be a more accurate determination of the inventory. Secondly, I have concluded that even taking the defendant's estimate – less than 5 percent – the dollar amount of the transfer brings it within the meaning of the bulk-transfer law.

The major purpose of these bulk-transfer statutes is to afford the merchant's creditors an opportunity to satisfy their claims before the merchant can transfer his assets to a bona-fide purchaser and vanish with the proceeds of the sale. . . . Where the interests of creditors are involved, the dollar amount of the transfer is relevant in assessing the potential damage to creditors. Thus, in this case where the amount of the transfer, $5,489.64, is sufficient to prejudice the interests of creditors to a substantial degree, I hold that a sale in the vicinity of 5 percent of the total inventory is a transfer of "a substantial part of the inventory" and is subject to the bulk-transfer provisions. [FN11] Since there was no statutory notice given to creditors, the transfer is void under California law and voidable by the trustee in bankruptcy under section 70e of the Bankruptcy Act. . . .

> This portion of the court's holding would seem to call into question the UCC drafters' decision to recommend the repeal of Article 6. Which perspective do you find more persuasive?

FN11. Future business transactions will not be prejudiced by this holding if the transferor is on solid financial ground. The law does not prohibit any bulk transfers so long as the proper notice is given to creditors. That is not an inordinate burden.

> What steps will these creditors likely take upon receipt of notice of a pending Article 6 sale?

[The court therefore entered summary judgment for the bankruptcy trustee.]

- After reading this case, what advice would you give a client as to what sales trigger Article 6 where it remains in effect?

Note 1: In *Danning v. Daylin, Inc.*, 488 F.2d 185, 13 U.C.C. Rep. Serv. 691 (9th Cir. 1973), the court considered several arguments in the Article 6 context. That case involved a transaction by which two retail sales companies sought to exchange significant portions of their inventory with one another. Specifically, one company sought to exchange the inventory and fixtures of its sundries departments for the inventory and fixtures of the hardware and housewares departments of the other company. Daylin, Inc., the company that provided the hardware and housewares to the other, was subsequently adjudicated bankrupt, and several of its creditors sought to have the "inventory swap" avoided as an impermissible bulk sale of which they had received no notice. The court rejected, as an initial matter, Daylin's argument that it should no longer be considered a merchant within the ambit of Article 6 because, as the facts showed, it was no longer in the business of selling housewares and hardware. Daylin, Inc. also claimed the "inventory swap" should not be deemed a sale and should therefore fall outside the scope of Article 6. In rejecting this argument, the court noted the purpose of this Article:

The purpose of a bulk-transfer statute is to keep merchandise and inventory as a cushion available to satisfy the claims of creditors. Therefore, defendant argues, where there is merely a replacement of inventory and fixtures with another type of inventory and fixtures having equivalent value, there is no depletion of inventory, and existing creditors may not complain.

Article 6 requires, however, that creditors be allowed to police bulk sales, to make certain that the consideration paid in return is indeed equal in value to the inventory transferred. Daylin would have the transferor act as the "policeman" of his own sale.

The dangers of a bulk transfer – either fraud or mere inadequacy of consideration – can as easily occur with an exchange of assets as with a cash sale. When creditors have advance notice of a bulk sale, either for cash or assets, they can investigate before it is completed and then determine whether they should intervene. *Id.* at 188.

Finally, Daylin claimed "inventory swaps" are so common that they should be deemed "sales in the ordinary course of business" that fall outside Article 6 and therefore require no notice to the seller's creditors. The court rejected this argument, as well:

> This contention has been soundly rejected. In *Jubas v. Sampsell,* 185 F.2d 333 (9th Cir. 1950), a shoe store sold a quantity of [unmarketable] shoes at one dollar per pair to another dealer, then declared bankruptcy. The trustee successfully moved to set aside the transfer as fraudulent under California's bulk-sales act, despite the transferee's claim that "unloading" unmarketable shoes in that manner was a normal business practice. We held that "the ordinary course of business" contemplated only the day-to-day operation of a store, and not transfers of a significant portion of the inventory, no matter how usual a practice the transfer may have been.

The court also cited the *Reed* case that appears above, in support of this proposition.

> The plain meaning of the statute is that, when a storekeeper disposes of a substantial part of his stock in trade in bulk, and selling in bulk sales is not the usual and ordinary way in which he conducts his business from day to day, the sale falls within the statute. *Id.* at 334.

- Why does an "inventory swap" implicate Article 6?

Note 2: The liability of a buyer pursuant to an Article 6 bulk sale is not unlimited. Instead, as *Adrian Tabin Corp. v. Climax Boutique, Inc.,* 34 N.Y.2d 210, 313 N.E.2d 66, 14 U.C.C. Rep. Serv. 1196 (1974), shows, the buyer may rely on an affidavit provided by the seller as to the seller's financial security, especially if the buyer also conducts a separate inquiry of its own. Note the steps taken in this case:

At the closing, the transferor furnished a bill of sale, which was preserved by the transferee, containing a schedule of the property transferred, together with an affidavit averring that the business was "free and clear of any and all liens, mortgages, security interests, levies, debts, taxes, or other claims" and "that the Transferor is not indebted to anyone and has no creditors." In addition, before consummation of the sale, the transferee's attorney made a lien search, which disclosed no liens, and inquired of the transferor's attorney as to creditors and was assured that there were none. *Id.* at 212.

Under these circumstances, the court held the buyer should not be liable to creditors of the seller who sought to void the sale on the grounds that they had received no Article 6 notice of the transaction. The court's specific language was that "the Uniform Commercial Code imposes no duty of careful inquiry" upon the purchaser.

- Is this holding consistent with Revised Article 6?

- If Article 6 "imposes no duty of careful inquiry" on the purchaser, what kind of duty does it impose?

> 6-104 (1) and 6-107 (3) may assist you in answering this question.

> A careful reading of 6-102 (1) (a), (1) (c), and (1) (m) and the commentary to (1) (a) and (1) (c) may be of assistance in answering this question.

Problem: Should Article 6 be applied to the sale of a restaurant, cocktail lounge, and bar, together with a liquor license? Why or why not? Assume the seller owned and operated only this one restaurant.

Based on *Zinni v. One Township Line Corp.*, 36 Pa. D. & C.2d 297, 3 U.C.C. Rep. Serv. 305 (1965).

International Perspective: Bulk Sales

Read CISG Article 1 and Article 2. For purposes of the current analysis, Article 2 is most important for what it does not state: Article 2 does not in any way signify that bulk sales should be treated differently under the CISG from other sales. Therefore, if a sale falls within the scope of Article 1 and the CISG would otherwise apply – in other words, if the parties have not opted out of the CISG – the CISG will treat that sale like any other, even if it involves the sale of a major part of a merchant's inventory outside the ordinary course of business.

Chapter Conclusion: This chapter explored the interests of third parties in an Article 2 sales transaction. If the seller lacked the right to sell the goods, he or she may be capable of conveying only void or voidable title. If the seller has void title

– that is, no title at all – the buyer cannot obtain good title.
Voidable title, by contrast, becomes good title in the hands of a
bona-fide purchaser for value.   In addition, in those
jurisdictions in which some version of Article 6 remains in
force, a buyer of goods pursuant to a bulk sale has the
obligation to notify the seller's creditors before the sale takes
place.

1
2
3
4
5
6
7
8
9
10
11
12
13
14
15
16
17
18
19
20
21
22
23
24
25
26
27
28
29
30
31
32
33
34
35
36
37
38
39
40
41
42
43
44
45
46
50
51
52
53

PART III:
PAYMENT SYSTEMS

The following six chapters are concerned with the law of Payment Systems, an area of law governed by UCC Articles 3 and 4, together with other state and federal law. Because of the risk and inconvenience associated with carrying large sums of currency, much commerce is transacted using other forms of payment such as promissory notes and drafts such as checks. Chapter 7 discusses the characteristics of drafts and notes, showing examples of specialized varieties of each, and introduces the concept of negotiability, showing why an instrument's status as negotiable or nonnegotiable affects its marketability and value. Chapter 7 also explains the relationship between a negotiable instrument and the underlying transaction (such as a sale of goods) that prompted its issuance. The chapter closes with a discussion of issuance, transfer, and presentment, the three stages in the life of a negotiable instrument.

Chapter 8 presents the seven requirements for negotiability and the concept of negotiable instruments as "couriers without baggage" that each holder can evaluate at face value without time-consuming research. As this chapter shows, negotiable instruments must be signed writings with certain indicia of negotiability, containing unconditional language promising or ordering only the payment of a fixed sum of money at a time certain.

Chapter 9 builds upon the introductory material in Chapters 7 and 8 by describing different classes of persons who may have possession of a negotiable instrument: assignees, holders, and holders in due course. As these materials show, holders in due course have superior rights that enable them to take negotiable instruments free of certain defenses that bind assignees and other holders, thus protecting the marketplace and their own expectations. This chapter also shows how parties' indorsement (or failure to indorse) affects their rights and obligations vis-à-vis one another and with regard to the instrument.

Chapters 7 through 9 are primarily concerned with Article 3, with relatively few references to Article 4. Chapter 10 is the book's first comprehensive treatment of the bank-collection processes in Article 4. This chapter also explores the relationship between a bank and its customer, describing the rights and responsibilities of both with regard to the payment of items and the allocation of losses.

Chapter 11 presents the various ways in which parties can be
liable under Article 3 and Article 4 theories of contract liability,
tort liability, and breach of warranty. This chapter provides
guidance as to which theory of liability is most appropriate, and
which defendant or defendants most likely to bear the loss,
under a variety of different potential litigation scenarios.

Chapter 12 introduces several kinds of payments that fall
outside Articles 3 and 4, including payments by wholesale wire
transfer or with credit and debit cards. Chapter 12 also
discusses the payment options available to those who, for a
variety of reasons, conduct their financial transactions in
check-cashing institutions and other entities outside the
traditional banking system.

Chapter 7:
Introducing Articles 3 and 4

A. Introduction to Payment Systems Law

This chapter introduces terminology that may appear
antiquated, and some students may wonder whether this
material remains relevant in an age that sometimes seems to
be dominated by electronic payment systems. In considering
this issue, the following excerpt from Geoffrey R. Gerdes &
Jack K. Walton, II, *The Use of Checks and Other Noncash
Payment Instruments in the United States*, Fed. Reserve Bull.
360 (August 2002), may be useful:

> Over the past several decades, the payments industry has
> undergone significant change. New electronic payment
> instruments have been introduced, and the means for making
> electronic payments have become increasingly available for use in
> everyday commerce. Further, the adaptation of technology has
> driven down the costs of processing electronic payments relative to
> check payments. Partial statistics and anecdotal evidence suggest
> that consumers and businesses are increasingly using electronic
> payments. Nevertheless, the paper check continues to be the most
> commonly used type of noncash payment instrument in the U.S.
> economy. Checks' share in noncash payments has been declining,
> however, and recent evidence suggests that the total number of
> checks paid has been declining as well. *Id.* at 360.

> * * *

> Taken together, the data show that an estimated 32.8 billion
> checks were paid in the United States in 1979, 49.5 billion in 1995,
> and 42.5 billion in 2000. The exact year in which check use peaked
> is unknown, but it appears that the number paid began to decline
> sometime in the mid-1990s. By 2000, retail electronic payments
> had gained considerable ground. Nonetheless, checks remained

the predominant type of retail noncash payment. Checks also continued to account for a large proportion of the total value of retail noncash payments in 2000, though the real value of total checks paid had declined since 1979.

In the United States, most noncash payments are made using checks, credit cards, debit cards, and the electronic payment system called the automated clearinghouse (ACH) – collectively referred to as retail noncash payments. *Id.*

* * *

The share of checks written by consumers appears to have increased somewhat since the 1970s. According to the 2000 survey, consumers wrote about 58 percent of the sampled checks for which the payer could be classified, with business and government checks making up the rest. *Id.* at 367.

* * *

The number of retail electronic payments made in 1979 was small, accounting for about 15 percent of all retail noncash payments. Since then, the number made annually has grown at a high rate. Over the latter part of the period, the growth in electronic payments accelerated, nearly doubling between 1995 and 2000 and accounting for 40 percent of all retail noncash payments in 2000. Most of the growth was due to a dramatic increase in the number of debit-card payments. *Id.* at 368.

* * *

Compared with other industrialized economies – Japan, the European Monetary Union, the United Kingdom, and Canada – the number of noncash payments of any type per capita is considerably higher in the United States, as is the number of check payments per capita. The number of electronic payments per capita is also higher in the United States, though not substantially so. *Id.* at 369.

As the materials in this textbook show, electronic payment systems are governed by laws originally written with paper instruments in mind. Thus, in learning the law of electronic payment systems, it is important to understand the paper-based systems on which the law was built and to understand that these paper-based systems are still commonly used.

- What factors militate in favor of the development of electronic payment systems?

- Why might some users prefer a paper-based system?

Like Article 2, Articles 3 and 4 were intended to clarify and improve the existing body of law on point, but not to replace it entirely. Chapter 1, Part A made reference to the NIL, or Negotiable Instruments Law, a NCCUSL uniform enactment based on the English Bills of Exchange Act, dating back to 1896. Articles 3 and 4 were heavily influenced by the NIL. In addition, the NIL attempted to incorporate much of the law merchant. In *Lewis Hubbard & Co. v. Morton*, 80 W. Va. 137, 92 S.E. 252 (1917), the Supreme Court of Appeals of West Virginia characterized the NIL as follows:

> The law merchant is introduced in Chapter 1, Part A.

> The uniform negotiable instruments statute makes little alteration in the law of this state as it was understood to be at the time of the passage of the act, and in nearly all respects it is only declaratory of the general law merchant. *Id.* at 138.

> To delve back further than the NIL, see Frederick K. Beutel, *Colonial Sources of the Negotiable Instruments Law of the United States*, 34 Ill. L. Rev. 137 (1940).

Thus, it would seem logical that Articles 3 and 4, being based on the NIL, would also incorporate much of the law merchant and therefore generate relatively little controversy. Even so, Articles 3 and 4 have been criticized substantively and as being difficult to read. In *What Would Be Wrong with a User-Friendly Code? The Drafting of Revised Articles 3 and 4 of the Uniform Commercial Code*, 26 Loy. L.A. L. Rev. 659 (1993), Professor Lary Lawrence states that, "[d]espite the seeming simplicity of their subject matter, both the original Articles 3 and 4, as well as their 1990 versions, are probably the most inaccessible articles of the entire Uniform Commercial Code."

- Is there any reason why payment-systems law should be inherently less accessible than other bodies of commercial law such as sales, or is what Lawrence is describing just a result of poor drafting?

Lawrence suggests the problem with Articles 3 and 4 is that, "[l]ooking at the list of advisors and persons who attended the drafting meetings, it is apparent virtually all participants are either employed by banks, clearing houses or the Federal Reserve Bank." He continues,

> [b]ecause all the persons intimately involved in the project were so familiar with the terms, concepts, and operations of the law of negotiable instruments and bank collection, the level of discussion was far more concerned with the proposed substantive rules than with the manner of their expression. In addition, because the terminology was second nature to virtually all of the participants, it was difficult for them to look through the eyes of a lawyer or judge who is not as well versed in these areas. *Id.* at 670.

- What other constituent groups should have been included in the drafting process?

Professor Lawrence goes on to suggest that collaboration from those outside the banking industry might have made an important difference in the readability of the two Articles:

> [C]onsider a film written and directed by the same person. Although that person knows better than anyone what he or she intends to communicate, the writer-director may not have the perspective to ascertain whether the style and manner of expression of the ideas reaches filmgoers. The writer-director is too close to the subject matter. Every nuance has a meaning. These nuances are not visible to any but the most dedicated of fans. *Id.* at 670.

Because of the very difficulties that Lawrence describes, it may bear mentioning that these materials, in introducing the law of Payment Systems, must necessarily begin by defining some initial terms while leaving others for later explanation. Thus, the early materials in this section of the text make a good deal of reference to terms more fully explored in later chapters. Learning this material requires what filmmakers call "the willing suspension of disbelief," or the willingness to be somewhat disoriented until the concepts are fully introduced. Cross-references indicate where material briefly introduced in one chapter is explained more fully in another. After reading Chapters 7 through 12 once, it may make sense to review them as a whole to ensure the pieces have come into place such that your understanding is complete. The following excerpt from Thomas C. Baxter, Jr.'s article *The UCC Thrives in the Law of Commercial Payment*, 28 Loy. L.A. L. Rev. 113 (1994), provides a concise introduction to this body of law that may serve as a useful starting point:

> This article comes from Mr. Baxter's experience as Deputy General Counsel and Senior Vice President of the Federal Reserve Bank of New York.

> [P]ayment describes a concept, the commercial mechanism that people use either to discharge some underlying indebtedness or to transfer money from one place to another. Often a payment is associated with the acquisition of goods or services, but that is not always the case. A payment may be made by a party simply to transfer bank credit from one point to another; for example, from a demand-deposit account to a money-market mutual-fund account.

> A smoothly functioning payment system is essential to a safe and sound economy in a sophisticated economic system like we have in the United States. In some industrialized countries, the payment system is regarded as so important that it is operated by the government, and payments are effected by a governmental agency, such as the postal, telephone, and telegraph service. In the United States, the payment system is operated by a cooperative blend of public and private organizations. There are quasi-governmental organizations, like the Federal Reserve Banks and the Federal Home Loan Banks, and there are commercial banks, which are wholly private corporate entities.

Although the operation of the U.S. payment system is rightly seen as a collaborative mix of public and private elements, it is so important to our economy that it is closely watched and nurtured by governmental oversight and participation. One of the significant functions performed by the Federal Reserve System, in addition to its monetary policy making and bank-supervision functions, is to assure that the U.S. payment system remains safe and sound. The Federal Reserve has performed this particular function very well during its seventy-five-year history. The proof may be seen in the U.S. payment system, which boasts an efficiency and reliability that make it one of the more attractive aspects of the U.S. banking industry. It is also the backbone that supports our securities and financial markets, which are probably the most sophisticated in the world. A well-functioning financial system must have efficient and effective clearings and settlements.

To assure a safe and sound payment system, it is necessary to understand and control payment-system risk. Payment law is directly related to payment-system risk, and payment risk is uncontrollable if there is uncertainty in payment law. To understand and control the risk of any participant in the payment system, it is necessary to predict, with certainty, the participant's liability in various factual situations. *Id.* at 114-115.

- Based on what you have read so far, what is the scope and purpose of payment-systems law?

Chapter 2 described turmoil in the Article 2 revision process and introduced UCITA, an ALI/NCCUSL collaboration adopted in only two states. The American Law Institute and the National Conference of Commissioners on Uniform State Laws have experienced a setback in the Payment Systems context that is similar in some ways to the challenges they encountered in their treatment of UCITA. In *UCC Articles 3, 4, and 4A: A Study in Process and Scope*, 42 Ala. L. Rev. 405 (1991), Professor Fred H. Miller, who served on the drafting council for Articles 3, 4, and 4A, describes an ambitious eleven-year project called the "New Payments Code" that incorporated empirical studies of the banking industry and attempted to address, among other issues, significant matters of consumer protection. The project was terminated after much debate in 1985 and replaced with two more modest projects, which became the 1990 revisions to Articles 3, 4, and 4A.

The 1990 revisions that were finally adopted generated their own controversy, as the following excerpt from Professor A. Brooke Overby's article *Modeling UCC Drafting*, 29 Loy. L.A. L. Rev. 645 (1996), shows:

The wake left by the 1990 revisions to Articles 3 and 4 of the Uniform Commercial Code indicates that the UCC is

---

The Federal Reserve System is further discussed in Chapter 10, Part A.

All citations to Articles 3 and 4 in this textbook are to the 1990 version and incorporate the 2002 Amendments, which generally were intended to keep pace with advances in electronic-payments technology.

approaching, if not wholly immersed in, a midlife crisis. . . . The alleged pro-bank, anticonsumer bias of those revisions and their inefficient treatment of many payment-law issues have led not only to remonstrations on the substantive provisions of those articles, but also to demands for a critical reexamination of the entire process by which the UCC is drafted. The principal targets in this frontal assault are the UCC's sponsors – specifically the [ALI] and [NCCUSL] – and their perceived willingness to cater to powerful interest groups in the drafting process. Harsh edicts call for these institutions to reform the UCC drafting process, undergo significant institutional reform, or be abolished. A small number of states have non-uniformly enacted revised Articles 3 and 4, which evidences the commercial law community's reception of these criticisms. *Id.* at 645.

- Based on what you learned in Chapter 1, Part A about the process by which the UCC is drafted and revised, what challenges do the drafters face in seeking to balance the interests of commercial entities and consumers?

International Perspective: Payment Systems

Read 3-102 Comment 5. The landscape of international payment-systems law is more complex than the body of international sales law presented in this textbook, in that no single body of uniform payment-systems law dominates international transactions to the extent that the CISG does in the area of sales of goods. The United Nations Convention on International Bills of Exchange and International Promissory Notes (CIBN) is an attempt by UNCITRAL to create a more universally acceptable compromise instrument where none has succeeded thus far.   The following excerpt from Gerold Herrmann, *Background and Salient Features of the United States Convention on International Bills of Exchange and International Promissory Notes*, 10 U. Pa. J. Intl. Bus. L. 517 (1988), provides an overview of the motivation for the CIBN and describes some of the most influential bodies of payment-systems law in the world market:

> The text of the CIBN can be found online at www.jus.uio.no/ lm/un.bills.of. exchange.and. promissory.notes. convention.1988/doc. html.

In the law of negotiable instruments, as in other traditional branches of commercial law, the history of the unification effort goes back much farther than the twenty years of UNCITRAL's existence. In fact, legislative actions with unifying effects in a particular region or legal system began in the early nineteenth century with a view towards regaining the harmony which had characterized medieval commercial usage of international bills of exchange and which had been lost by "departmentalization" through national law barriers.

French and German laws were used as models in a number of civil-law countries. In the first half of the twentieth century, however, more organized efforts towards unification, such as the Conferences at the Hague in 1910 and 1912 and at Geneva, under the auspices of the League of Nations, in 1930 and 1931, led to a considerable degree of harmonization in the civil-law world, with more than forty countries either adopting or closely following the Geneva Uniform Laws on bills of exchange, promissory notes, and checks (GUL).

In the common-law world, the source of unification was provided by English law, specifically, the Bills of Exchange Act of 1882 (BEA). It has essentially shaped the laws still in force in the member States of the Commonwealth and inspired the Uniform Instruments Law, the predecessor of the current article 3 of the Uniform Commercial Code. Looking at this situation, one might well conclude that UNCITRAL's task was "simply" to bridge the gap between the two main systems of negotiable instruments law, the Geneva and the Anglo-American system. However, such a view would be overly narrow for two reasons.

First, if one looks more closely at each of these two systems, one detects considerable disparities within the system, both in the details of the legal régime and, in some respects, even in principal issues. On the common-law side, the English Bills of Exchange Act and its derivative enactments in Commonwealth countries are by no means identical to the Uniform Commercial Code, and divergences in case law as well as commercial practice contribute to further disparity. On the civil-law side, the apparent uniformity is punctured in at least four respects. As indicated earlier, not all States following the civil-law tradition have adopted the Geneva Uniform Laws. . . . Second, even the member States to the Geneva Conventions diverge by virtue of having made a number of different reservations to the Uniform Law without always making clear the positive rule that was to prevail. Third, case law differs considerably; nations fail to agree on crucial provisions such as those concerning claims and defenses available against the holder [of a negotiable instrument]. Finally, banking and trading circles feel the need to adjust to modern commercial practices not envisaged at Geneva more than half a century ago. As a consequence of all these factors, there have been repeated calls for a revision of the Geneva Uniform Laws.

> Defenses available against holders and holders in due course are discussed in Chapter 9, Part C.

The second aspect of UNCITRAL's task is that, in addition to these two major legal systems, there still exist other national laws and legal systems with different traditions and concepts. It seems only fair to respect the wishes of these States to have a voice in shaping a new legal régime for worldwide use in international payment and credit transactions. Moreover, these States have economic interests at stake which may lead to positions not necessarily taken by other States, even if they are members of the same legal family. Such divergent interests and wishes must be taken into account in any serious unification effort at the global level, for the benefit of the countries of the world irrespective of their location and their legal, economic, or political systems.

The Convention's truly global orientation, and the prospect of worldwide acceptability, became a first in the history of the unification of the law of negotiable instruments and has become a focal point of UNCITRAL's activities. *Id.* at 519-520.

- As a matter of law, policy, and politics, what are the advantages and disadvantages of introducing yet another body of law such as the CIBN, rather than attempting to rally the countries of the world around an existing body of law such as the BEA or the GUL?

- Are there reasons why it might be more difficult to develop a generally-accepted international convention governing negotiable instruments than a similar instrument governing sales of goods?

One characteristic of the CIBN is the drafters' decision to create two new negotiable instruments to be used only in international transactions, rather than adapting instruments from other law. In *The U.N. Convention on International Bills and Notes: A Primer for Attorneys and International Bankers*, 25 U.C.C. J. 99 (1992), Professor John A. Spanogle explains the new instruments:

> CIBN creates two negotiable instruments: the international bill of exchange and the international promissory note. It does not, however, include "cheques." CIBN will provide the parties to an international commercial transaction with a choice. They may allow their negotiable instruments to be governed by the different domestic negotiable instrument laws selected by the different choice-of-law concepts of whatever nation those instruments pass through on their international route of circulation. Or they may have their instrument governed by the single legal regime of CIBN as it circulates from nation to nation. However, in order to choose the second alternative, the parties will have to deliberately and expressly "opt in" to the Convention and its legal regime. *Id.* at 100.

> A draft convention on international cheques was circulated by UNCITRAL in 1982, but the project was suspended in 1984. See Donald J. Guiney, Student Comment, *Forged Indorsements Under the UNCITRAL Draft Convention on International Cheques*, 21 Colum. J. Transnat'l L. 585 (1982).

For the CIBN to come into force as an instrument of international law, ten nations must ratify the Convention. As of the publication of this textbook, the CIBN had not yet come into force. Thus, domestic payment-systems law dominates even international payment transactions involving negotiable instruments. In *Bills of Exchange: A Guide to Legislation in European Countries, Asia & Oceania* (International Chamber of Commerce 1999), Dr. Uwe Jahn presents a summary of the current payment-systems law of many major countries. The payment-systems law of each of the ten countries identified by the United States Department of Commerce as the top trading partners with the United States is as follows, as classified by Dr. Jahn and other sources:

Payment Systems Law: U.S. Top Trading Partners

Canada	Canada's Bills of Exchange Act, based on the British Bills of Exchange Act
China	Law of the People's Republic of China on Negotiable Instruments
France	French Commercial Code, based on the Geneva Uniform Laws for Bills of Exchange and Promissory Notes
Germany	Germany's Wechselgesetz, adopting the Geneva Uniform Laws for Bills of Exchange and Promissory Notes
Japan	Japan's Bills of Exchange Law, adopting the Geneva Uniform Laws for Bills of Exchange and Promissory Notes
Malaysia	The Bills of Exchange Ordinance, based on the British Bills of Exchange Act
Mexico	Mexico's General Law of Negotiable Instruments and Credit Operations
South Korea	Korean Bills Act, adopting (without ratifying) the Geneva Uniform Laws for Bills of Exchange and Promissory Notes
Taiwan	The Chinese Law on Negotiable Instruments, similar to the Geneva Uniform Laws for Bills of Exchange and Promissory Notes
United Kingdom	The British Bills of Exchange Act

Relevant provisions of the GUL and BEA are reproduced in the text as needed.

To present the laws U.S. commercial lawyers are most likely to face in international transactions, this textbook's chapters on payment-systems law make reference to the Geneva Uniform Laws, the English Bills of Exchange Act and, on occasion, the laws of other major U.S. trade partners, in addition to relevant CIBN provisions.

B. The Scope of Articles 3 and 4

This section introduces the parts of (and parties to) basic promissory notes and basic drafts such as checks, highlighting the distinction between two-party and three-party paper and the way in which this difference affects the parties' rights. This section also introduces the concept of conditional payment and its effect on the underlying transaction, showing how an Article

2 sale can also implicate Articles 3 and 4 when payment for goods is tendered by negotiable instrument.

Read 3-102 (a), together with 1-201 (b) (24) and Comment 24. Taken together, these provisions describe the scope of Article 3. Reading Chapter 8 will make it easier to understand why "money" is not a "negotiable instrument" within the meaning of Articles 3 and 4.

- Could "currency" be used as a synonym for "money," as the latter term is used in the Code?

Read 3-102 (c) and Comment 4. Negotiable instruments to which the United States is a party are governed by federal law as a matter of supremacy, rather than falling within the jurisdiction of state law such as the UCC. Nevertheless, federal policy may call for the application of the UCC.

- What other matters of supremacy are raised in 3-102 (c) and how are they resolved?

Merger and Conditional Payment

Read 3-310. This provision shows the relationship between a negotiable instrument and the underlying transaction motivating its issuance. *Harper v. K & W Trucking Co.*, 725 P.2d 1066, 2 U.C.C. Rep. Serv. 2d 556 (Alaska 1986), explains the statutory language as follows, as it relates to an ordinary, uncertified check:

> The statute strikes a balance between two possible approaches. Under one approach, the mere acceptance of the instrument would discharge the obligation. Under a second approach, acceptance of the instrument would have no effect, and the underlying obligation would remain in force until cash actually changed hands. The statute effectuates a compromise between these two approaches by suspending the obligation, but only until it is satisfied. *Id.* at 1068.

One odd result of the first approach would have been that the payee could accept a check in payment of a debt, then separately sue the drawer of the check on that debt, without first seeking to enforce the check.

- Why does payment with a cashier's check operate like payment with currency, eliminating the paid portion of the debt immediately, while payment with an ordinary check is "conditional payment" that suspends the underlying debt until the check is either (1) honored, eliminating the debt to the extent of the payment, or

As *Morgan v. Farmers & Merchants Bank*, 856 So. 2d 811 (Ala. 2003), shows, non-negotiable instruments such as the money-market certificate at issue in that case, fall outside Article 3 but may constitute "instruments" that can serve as collateral for an Article 9 transaction. Various kinds of Article 9 collateral are discussed in Chapter 13, Part B.

Certified checks are introduced in Part D of this chapter.

Cashier's checks are introduced in Part D of this Chapter.

Negotiable instruments can also be issued gratuitously. As Chapter 9 shows, a person who obtains a negotiable instrument without giving value for it cannot qualify as a "holder in due course."

(2) dishonored, reviving the underlying debt as its own cause of action?

3-310 illustrates a concept called "merger," which describes how a negotiable instrument and the underlying transaction motivating its issuance are fused, together representing a single right to payment. Because the negotiable instrument comes to symbolize the entire obligation, possession of the instrument becomes exceedingly important. Disputes can arise when the instrument falls into the hands of someone other than the person to whom the obligation is owed.

As 3-309 and 3-312 show, it is sometimes possible to enforce a lost, stolen, or destroyed item.

In *Lambert v. Barker*, 232 Va. 21, 348 S.E.2d 214 (1986), the court addressed such a situation. Barbara and William Barker purchased a parcel of real estate from Robert Davis, executing a promissory note to Davis in payment for the property. The Barkers then sold the property to David Beloff, who sold the property to Charles and Ann Harwood, each of whom, in turn, expressly agreed to pay the promissory note to Davis. Some time later, Davis transferred his right to receive payment on the note to Katherine Lambert, to secure a loan that Lambert's company made to him. When the Harwoods sold the property to Bryce and Nancy Bugg, Davis appeared at the closing with an affidavit in which he falsely represented that he was the noteholder but had lost the note. He was paid out of the closing proceeds. Ms. Lambert subsequently sued both the Harwoods and the Barkers to recover payment, presumably because Davis was either judgment-proof or unavailable for suit. The defendants claimed their obligations had already been satisfied through payment to Davis. The court ultimately held in favor of Ms. Lambert, noting that "[p]ayment or satisfaction discharges the liability of a party only if made to the holder of the instrument. . . . [T]he payor may protect himself by demanding production of the instrument and refusing payment to any party not in possession unless in an action on the obligation the owner proves his ownership."

Accord and satisfaction, and other forms of discharge by payment, are presented in Chapter 9, Part C.

3-309 may provide some guidance on this matter.

- Keeping the *Lambert* holding in mind, what specific advice would you give to a party in the position of the Harwoods who is in receipt of an affidavit such as the one presented by Davis?

Investment Service Co. v. Martin Bros. Container & Timber Products Corp., 255 Or. 192, 465 P.2d 868, 7 U.C.C. Rep. Serv. 373 (1970), includes further explanation of the importance of physical possession to the enforcement of a negotiable instrument. In that case, a depositary bank brought suit against the drawer of a check, seeking to recover funds the bank had paid to its customer who had deposited the check. The customer had withdrawn the funds before the deposited check was returned unpaid as the result of a stop-payment order. The facts were complicated by the fact that the depositary bank had released the check to its customer the payee. Consider the following excerpt from the court's holding in favor of the drawer, on the grounds of the bank's lack of possession:

> Two reasons are the probable basis for the requirement of possession. The most important is the danger of exposing the drawer to double liability if the drawer is required to pay one who does not have physical possession of the note. *Id.* at 201.
>
> * * *
>
> The other reason for the requirement of physical possession as a prerequisite to recovery on a negotiable instrument is the necessity for simplicity and clarity in the law of commercial paper in order to facilitate commercial dealings. The basic principle of commercial dealings in negotiable instruments is that one who presents an instrument which on its front and back establishes the right of payment is entitled to be paid and one who cannot make such a showing is not entitled to be paid. Exceptions to this should be rare. *Id.* at 204.

- How would the utility of negotiable instruments as currency substitutes be undermined if possession were not a prerequisite for enforcement?

Problem: Patrick Newell sought to purchase certain real property. Thorsen Realtors represented the seller and acted as the escrow agent for the transaction. Third party Gail Russie, as part of a separate agreement with Newell, agreed to provide a portion of the earnest money for the purchase. In satisfaction of this obligation, she provided North Towne Bank with a check drawn on her business account with that bank, which then issued a cashier's check for the same sum, payable to Thorsen Realtors. After the check was delivered to Thorsen Realtors, the Russie check used to pay for the cashier's check was dishonored, and North Towne Bank decided to stop payment on the cashier's check. Newell paid the earnest money himself from other funds. Newell then assigned his interest in the cashier's check to his attorney David Locks, to whom he owed money for legal services. Assume the cashier's check is still in Thorsen's possession.

- Applying the *Lambert* holding, as between Locks and the bank, who should bear the loss and why?

- Why does Newell believe he has an interest in the cashier's check, and is he correct?

The rights and obligations of a depositary bank and its customer with respect to an unpaid check are presented in Chapter 10, Part B. A depositary bank normally does not release to its customers checks it has credited to an account.

Chapter 8, Part E, builds on the concept suggested here of a negotiable instrument as a courier without baggage that is normally evaluated only on the basis of information contained within its own "four corners."

The right of stop payment is covered in Chapter 10, Part B. As those materials show, the bank erred by failing to secure the funds before issuing the cashier's check.

Based on *Locks v. North Towne National Bank of Rockford*, 115
Ill. App. 3d 729, 451 N.E.2d 19, 36 U.C.C. Rep. Serv. 1251
(1983).

An Introduction to Notes and Drafts

Read 3-104 (e), together with 3-103 (a) (8) and (12).
Article 3 is concerned with two primary types of negotiable
instruments: notes and drafts. A note is an unconditional
written promise by one party to pay money to another. A note
is usually an instrument of credit to be repaid at a designated
future date rather than a "demand" item payable at the time of
issuance. Notes are two-party paper, the two parties being (1)
the promisor, or maker, and (2) the promisee, or payee. **Read
3-103 (a) (7)** for the Code's definition of "maker."

> The distinction
> between "demand"
> notes and notes
> payable at a later
> date is presented in
> Chapter 8, Part G.

- In a loan transaction, which party (the bank or
  borrower) is the maker and which is the payee?

The following is a graphic representation of a simple
promissory note:

PROMISSORY NOTE

For value received, I do hereby promise to pay to
Payee of Note or order, one hundred fifty thousand
and no/100 dollars ($150,000.00) The terms and
conditions of such note are as follows: . . .

Maker of Note

> As 3-103 Comment 2
> suggests, with
> respect to checks,
> the drawee is always
> a bank. With
> respect to other
> kinds of drafts, the
> drawee need not be a
> bank.

Read 3-103 (a) (4) and (5). Drafts are three-party paper, the
three parties being (1) the drawer, who orders payment to be
made, (2) the drawee, which is the party that receives the order
and, if it accepts the order, makes payment accordingly, and (3)
the payee, to whom the draft is payable.

Read 3-104 (f). As this provision shows, a check is a type of
draft.

- For a check, which of the three parties is the bank
  customer and which is the bank?

The following is a graphic representation of a check:

```
Drawer's Name
123 Main Street          Date of Check _____
Detroit, MI 76543

Pay to the
Order of    Payee _____    $ amount

Amount of check and no/100 ------------------------

Drawee National Bank
                         Drawer of Check
MEMO _____              _____
```

Read 3-104 Comment 4. "Bill of exchange," although not used in the Code, is a term for a draft that comes up occasionally in the case law and is used in some other contexts, including the BEA and the CIBN.

As Chapter 10, Part A shows, for a drawee to be required to pay the amount of a draft, the drawee must (1) owe the drawer money and (2) accept the draft.

- In the case of a check, when does a drawee owe a drawer money?

Another type of draft that may be less familiar is the trade acceptance draft.

```
Trade Acceptance Draft    No _____    Due Date:_____

for value received issued by and

PAYABLE TO THE ORDER OF: _____(Seller's Name)_____

_____

Bank        (Buyer's Name)       Accepted: _____
Address:    _____      Company Name: (Buyer's Name)
City, State: _____     Authorized Signature:_____
```

A trade acceptance draft has the same parties as a check and is often used as an instrument of credit rather than being payable on demand like a check. To understand the illustration shown above, assume the seller prepared a trade acceptance draft that was delivered to the buyer together with the invoice and the goods ordered, as a means of securing payment. If the buyer agrees to make payment on the terms contained in the draft, the buyer will sign the draft, ordering its bank to make payment to the seller according to the terms of the draft. The seller, as payee, might then sell the draft to another party who will pay some amount less than the face value of the draft. The discounted amount takes into consideration both the time value of money and the risk of nonpayment. This process allows the seller to generate immediate cash that may be used to cover expenses associated with this transaction – or others.

- In this illustration, which party is the drawer, which is the drawee, and which is the payee?

- How would a trade acceptance note be different from a trade acceptance draft?

- What are the advantages of a trade acceptance draft over an ordinary check?

Note: Even though drafts and notes commonly take familiar forms, and seldom vary significantly from the simple graphic illustrations in this textbook, it is important to realize that the UCC permits variation in the form of a negotiable instrument, so long as the requisites presented in Chapter 8 are satisfied. In *United Milk Products Co. v. Lawndale National Bank of Chicago*, 392 F.2d 876, 5 U.C.C. Rep. Serv. 143 (1968), the court upheld the transfer of funds pursuant to a letter and, later, also a telegram in which two officers of a company directed the company's bank to transfer company funds to an identified entity. Rejecting the company's claim that the bank was negligent in honoring requests made in this fashion, the court held as follows:

> We see no merit in the claim that the Bank was negligent in transferring [the company's funds] pursuant to a letter and telegram rather than pursuant to a "check. . . ." The signed letter and telegram satisfy the requirements for a check in the Uniform Commercial Code. Moreover, it cannot be said that the Bank's failure to insist on a formal check caused any loss to [the company]. It is clear that, had the Bank insisted on a formal check, [the company officers] would have supplied it. *Id.* at 879.

- Can this holding be explained by reference to the concept of the "cheapest cost avoider" introduced in Chapter 3, Part B?

- Cases involving a negotiable instrument of unusual form are rare. Regardless of whether the UCC will recognize a nontraditional document as a negotiable instrument, what reasons exist for choosing a traditional form?

Problem: Find the error in the following paragraph, taken verbatim from *New Jersey Steel Corp. v. Warburton*, 139 N.J. 536, 655 A.2d 1382, 26 U.C.C. Rep. Serv. 2d 14 (1995):

> This appeal concerns the allocation of check-fraud losses under specific provisions of Articles 3 and 4 of the Uniform Commercial Code, adopted in New Jersey. . . . The Court must allocate those losses between a corporation whose negligence allowed the defalcation to occur and a depositary-payor bank that accepted checks for deposit without following its own procedures for inspecting the [i]ndorsements on those checks. Defendant Midlantic National Bank failed to discern [i]ndorsements that did not correspond to the payees as well as forged maker signatures, thus violating its duty to pay an instrument "in accordance with reasonable commercial standards" and to exercise "ordinary care." Plaintiff, New Jersey Steel Corporation, failed to examine its monthly statements, thus violating its statutory and contractual duty "to exercise reasonable care and promptness to examine the statements and items to discover . . . unauthorized signature or any alteration on an item." *Id.* at 538.

> The rights and obligations of banks and their customers with regard to the discovery of forgery are discussed in Chapter 10, Part B.

International Perspective: The CIBN's Scope

Read CIBN Articles 1, 2, and 3. As the Spanogle excerpt in Part A explains, the CIBN applies only to specific drafts and notes that fall within the definitions of "international bill of exchange" and "international promissory note" set forth in CIBN Article 2. As CIBN Article 1 reiterates, checks are not within the scope of the CIBN. Consistent with the UCC, CIBN Article 3 defines "bills of exchange" as orders to a third party to pay money on behalf of the party making the order, and "promissory notes" as promises to pay money. Chapter 8 explores CIBN Article 3's requirements for both kinds of negotiable instruments.

- Why, as a practical matter, would the CIBN's drafters have chosen to adopt such a limited scope?

C. The Concept of Negotiability

This section introduces the idea of negotiable instruments as "couriers without luggage" and highlights the distinction between assignment and negotiation. Doing so illuminates the scope of Articles 3 and 4.

> *Overton v. Tyler*, the case that first used this language to describe a negotiable instrument, is presented and discussed in Chapter 8, Part E.

Read 3-104. This section, which is the primary focus of Chapter 8, provides an overview of the features that make a

For an examination of the historical development of the concept of negotiability from the early eighteenth century, see James Steven Rogers, *The Myth of Negotiability*, 31 B.C. L. Rev. 265 (1990).

As Chapter 18, Part C shows, the analogue of a holder in due course for negotiable warehouse receipts and bills of lading is called a "holder by due negotiation."

payment instrument negotiable. Negotiability is a characteristic of negotiable instruments and certain other commercial documents within the purview of other Articles of the UCC, such as negotiable warehouse receipts and bills of lading. "Negotiability" describes the way in which these instruments pass through the commercial marketplace without burdening purchasers with research to determine the worth of, and risks associated with, each item. Instead, purchasers can rely on the information found on the face of such instruments to disclose any defects or risks that affect their value. In addition, as Chapter 9 shows, only negotiable commercial paper can be transferred in such a way that a transferee can be deemed a "holder in due course," a denomination that carries superior rights of enforcement under some circumstances.

Third-Party Rights in Goods

In illustrating the importance of negotiability, it may be useful to begin with a contrasting example from Article 2 involving theft of goods.

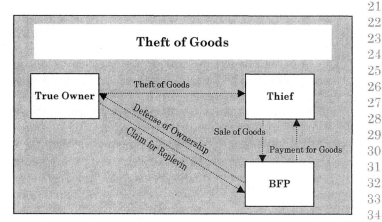

As Chapter 6 shows, it is impossible for a purchaser of stolen goods, even a "bona fide purchaser for value" within the definition of 2-403, to obtain good title. Instead, because the thief had void title (which is no title at all) to those goods, by definition the thief had nothing of value that could be conveyed. Under these circumstances, if the true owner and the BFP were to assert competing claims to the goods, the true owner's claim would prevail.

Third-Party Rights in a Check

The opposite result can be reached in some cases under Articles 3 and 4, if what is stolen is a negotiable instrument rather than goods. First, consider the possibility of a stolen check.

As Chapters 8 and 9 show, if (1) what is transferred is a "negotiable instrument" within the meaning of 3-104, if (2) it is transferred in such a way as to constitute a "negotiation" as defined in 3-201 rather than a simple assignment, and if (3) the final possessor of the instrument qualifies as a "holder in due course," as defined in 3-302, then the holder in due course may be entitled to enforce even a stolen check.

For an argument that negotiability "may operate unfairly and harmfully at the expense of some, while giving to others windfalls that serve no significant social or commercial need," see Albert J. Rosenthal, *Negotiability – Who Needs It?*, 71 Colum. L. Rev. 375 (1971).

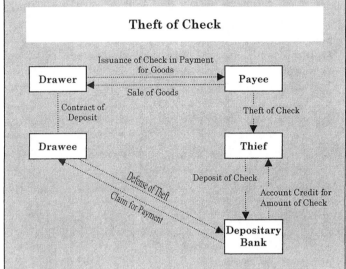

In the graphic illustrations in this textbook, double-sided or double arrows indicate an exchange for value, a line without arrows indicates that a contractual relationship governs the parties' interests in the item, and a single-sided or single arrow indicates a theft or gift. As you will understand after studying Chapter 8, Part C, this graphic assumes that the thief steals "bearer paper," rather than "order paper."

The above illustration shows a post-issuance theft of a check from its payee. Because a depositary bank is often a holder in due course, it may be able to enforce the check despite the theft. As Chapter 9, Part C shows, a depositary bank that qualifies as a holder in due course can enforce this check because theft is a "personal defense" that does not affect the rights of a holder in due course. This can be contrasted with a "real defense," a concept also covered in Chapter 9, Part C, which affects the rights of any holder, even a holder in due course.

Chapter 9, Part B shows how the payee could, through "special indorsement," have protected itself and prevented the thief from being able to negotiate the check.

Favors v. Yaffe, 605 S.W.2d 342, 31 U.C.C. Rep. Serv. 154 (Tex. Civ. App. 1980), highlights the importance of negotiability by showing that a holder in due course can have better rights than the original payee. In 1971, Mr. and Mrs. Favors were in New Orleans and were approached by a salesman selling land in Arizona. He represented that the land purchase was backed by a six-month money-back guarantee. Mr. and Mrs. Favors knew, even on the front end, that there were some limitations attached to the guarantee. They could get their money back only if, "upon their on-site inspection of the property in Arizona, they wished to back out." Thus, they understood they would have to expend money to go and see the property if they desired to cancel the transaction. In addition, they were told at the

outset that the transaction could be cancelled only if the
mortgage promissory note they executed for the property were
not in default. Following these disclosures, Mr. and Mrs.
Favors purchased the property sight-unseen.

Approximately six months later, Mr. and Mrs. Favors traveled
to Arizona for the purpose of exercising the refund option.
When they arrived in Arizona, a company representative
offered to extend the guarantee for another year, during which
time the company would try to sell the Favors' land to another
person, and would then split the profit with Mr. and Mrs.
Favors. Mr. and Mrs. Favors agreed and continued to make
payments on the property for some time. Later, they decided to
make a second attempt to exercise their refund option.

In the meantime, and unbeknownst to the Favors family,
twelve days after they purchased the property, the land-sales
company sold the mortgage to a third party. Testimony
indicated that the third party knew nothing about the
guarantee, which did not appear on the face of the promissory
note, but was instead contained in a separate document. The
third party further testified that it would not have purchased
the note had it known of the guarantee. Thus, the third party
refused to honor the guarantee and sought to enforce the note,
and Mr. and Mrs. Favors claimed they had been defrauded.

Because the court found the third party was a holder in due
course, and because Mr. and Mrs. Favors' defense of fraudulent
inducement is a personal defense that does not bind a holder in
due course, the third party was entitled to enforce the
promissory note.

- Against whom, if anyone, do Mr. and Mrs. Favors have
  a remedy?

- As between the Favors family and the third-party
  purchaser of the note, does the concept of the cheapest
  cost avoider help to explain why the third party
  prevails in this fact pattern?

Could these facts have been important in the court's ultimate decision against Mr. and Mrs. Favors?

1
2
Third-Party Rights in a Note
3
When a note is stolen instead of a draft, the names of the
4 parties change:
5
6
7
8
9
10

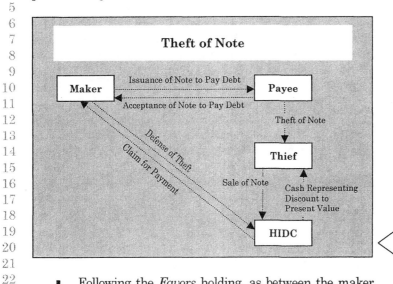

Theft of Note

Maker — Issuance of Note to Pay Debt → Payee
Acceptance of Note to Pay Debt
Theft of Note
Thief
Defense of Theft
Claim for Payment
Sale of Note — Cash Representing Discount to Present Value
HIDC

Make sure you understand why the holder in due course pays a discounted amount.

22
23   •   Following the *Favors* holding, as between the maker
24   and the holder in due course, who should prevail and
25   why?

26
27
Third Party Rights in an Assigned Debt
28
29 Compare the outcome in the three previous hypotheticals to
30 that in a case involving the assignment of a creditor's right to
31 payment based upon a simple debt. In addition, this time,
32 assume there is no theft involved; instead, the defense raised
33 relates to the quality of the services giving rise to the debt:
34

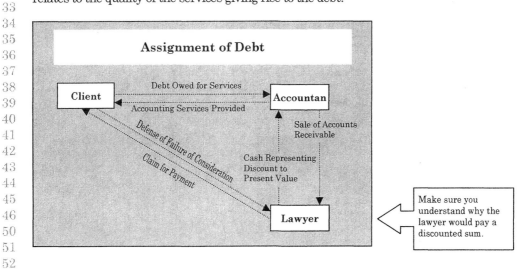

Assignment of Debt

Client — Debt Owed for Services → Accountan
Accounting Services Provided
Defense of Failure of Consideration
Claim for Payment
Sale of Accounts Receivable
Cash Representing Discount to Present Value
Lawyer

Make sure you understand why the lawyer would pay a discounted sum.

50
51
52
53

When the accountant assigns his or her accounts receivable, including this client's debt, to an attorney for collection, the attorney's right to collect on the debt will be subject to any defenses the client could have raised against the accountant, even a personal defense such as failure of consideration.

A review of the materials in Chapter 6, Parts A and B may assist you in answering this question.

- Now that you have studied each example, how is Article 3 different from Article 2 with regard to its treatment of third-party rights?

- How do third-party holders of negotiable instruments such as the draft and note in the examples above have greater rights than a third party who acquired a non-negotiable payment right through assignment?

International Perspective: Negotiability

Read CIBN Articles 3 and 30. CIBN Article 3, which is covered in Chapter 8, sets forth the requirements for a bill of exchange and a promissory note under the CIBN. Article 30, which is covered in Chapter 9, shows that a protected holder (the CIBN's equivalent of the UCC's holder in due course) has the right to take an international bill of exchange or promissory note free from many of the defenses that bound the transferor and that would bind a party who is not a protected holder. Thus, and as will become clearer in the next two chapters, the CIBN and UCC provisions on negotiability are fairly similar to one another.

Traveler's checks and certificates of deposit, are covered in 3-104 (i) and (j), respectively. For security reasons, a traveler might wish to avoid traveling with large amounts of currency; rather than hoping that merchants will accept a personal check drawn on a bank far away, the traveler might purchase traveler's checks. A bank customer might purchase a certificate of deposit as a savings device that may earn a higher interest rate than a regular savings account.

D. Specialized Instruments

This chapter has already introduced the basic forms for drafts and promissory notes. This section builds upon that preliminary material by introducing teller's and cashier's checks, certified checks, and money orders.

Read 3-104 (f), (g), and (h) and 3-409. Sometimes, an ordinary draft (such as a check) or promissory note is ill-suited to the parties' needs for one of a variety of reasons, and a different negotiable instrument is employed instead. Out of concern that a purchaser's personal check may be dishonored for insufficient funds, a seller might insist that the purchaser provide a cashier's check, teller's check, or certified personal check. If a purchaser lacks a personal checking account, he or she might choose to make payment with a money order

1   purchased with cash, especially if payment is to be sent by
2   mail. Each instrument is defined and governed by the Uniform
3   Commercial Code.
4
5   **Read 3-104 (g).** A cashier's check is purchased by a remitter
6   who is often, but not always, a customer of the issuing bank.
7   Having received funds from the remitter, the issuing bank
8   draws the cashier's check on its own funds.
9
10   ▪ Is the remitter a party to the cashier's check?
11

> Looking at the following graphic may assist you in answering this question.

12
13
14
15   **Drawer National Bank Cashier's Check**   **No. 1234567**
16
17
18   Pay to the
     Order of   *Payee* $ amount

     Amount of check and no/100 --------------------

     Drawer's Agent Signature
     MEMO _____

22   ▪ Why would a cashier's check be deemed more secure,
23   from the payee's point of view, than a personal check?
24

> Although this issue is more fully discussed in Chapter 10, Part A, you should have a sense of this already.

26   ▪ Should an issuing bank accept an uncertified personal
27   check drawn on another bank as payment for the
28   cashier's check?

> Certified personal checks are introduced later in this section.

29
30   **Read 3-104 (h).** To avoid drawing on its own funds, a bank
31   may issue a teller's check instead of a cashier's check. As 3-104
32   Comment 4 indicates, a teller's check is like a cashier's check in
33   that it is drawn at the request of a remitter, after receipt of
34   funds from the remitter. A teller's check is drawn, however,
35   not on the bank's own funds like a cashier's check, but on
36   another bank or, occasionally, a nonbank drawee. Like an
37   ordinary personal check, a teller's check requires a pre-existing
38   deposit or credit relationship between the drawer and drawee.
39   The following graphic represents a teller's check:
40
41   **Drawer National Bank Teller's Check**   **No. 1234567**
42
43   *Date of Check*
44   Pay to the
     Order of   *Payee* $ amount

46   *Amount of check and no/100 --------------------*

50   Drawn On
51   **Drawee National Bank**
52   *Drawer's Agent Signature*
     MEMO _____
53

- To which entity does the purchaser remit payment for a teller's check – to the drawer bank or to the drawee bank?

- Would you expect a teller's check to be considered substantially less secure than a cashier's check?

- Would you expect a teller's check to be considered substantially more secure than a personal check?

> "Unbanked" persons, and the options available to them in the financial-services industry, are discussed in Chapter 12, Part C.

Read 3-104 (f) and Comment 4. A money order may be used when the purchaser does not have access to, or does not wish to use, a personal checking account. As Comment 4 explains, money orders vary in form, depending on how and by whom they are issued.

MONEY ORDER		
Serial No.	**Year/Month/Day**	**Issuing Office**
_____	_____	_____
Amount of check and no/100 ----------------------		**$ amount**
Name of Purchaser		Name of Payee
Address of Purchaser		Address of Payee
	Debt Being Paid	

- To quote the language of Comment 4, why should "their form determine[ ] how [money orders] are treated in Article 3"?

> Reading Comment 4 may assist you in answering these questions.

- Does the fact that a money order is equated with a check in 3-104 (f) suggest it is more or less secure than a personal check?

- Would you expect a money order to be considered more or less secure than a cashier's check or teller's check?

Read 3-409 (d). Chapter 10, Part A introduces a process called drawee acceptance which, for a normal, uncertified personal check, does not occur until the check has been issued to the payee, perhaps transferred to one or more holders, and presented to the drawee bank for payment. At the time of acceptance, the drawee bank determines whether the check is properly payable and makes a decision whether to pay the check. A certified check is different in that the acceptance decision is made prior to the check's issuance. In the case of a certified check, the drawer presents the check to his or her bank for acceptance prior to delivering the check to the payee.

> "Properly payable" is a term of art presented in Chapter 10, Part A.

```
┌─────────────────────────────────────────────────────────────┐
│ Drawer's Name                                               │
│ 123 Main Street                    Date of Check            │
│ Detroit, MI 76543              ACCEPTED                      │
│                              Bank Representative            │
│ Pay to the      Payee                           $ amount   │
│ Order of                                                    │
│ Amount of check and no/100 ------------------               │
│                                                             │
│ Drawee National Bank                                        │
│                                  Drawer of Check            │
│ MEMO _____                 _____        │
└─────────────────────────────────────────────────────────────┘
```

- What steps would you expect the bank representative to take before deciding whether to accept an unissued check?

- Why might it make sense to equate a certified personal check with a cashier's check?

The following case explains why negotiability is so important to the commercial-paper marketplace. In reading this case, think about why the court's opinion compares cashier's checks and money orders to currency.

Transamerica Insurance Co. v. Long,
318 F. Supp. 156 (D.C. Pa. 1970).

Marsh, Chief Judge.

The plaintiff, Transamerica Insurance Company, brought this action against the present District Director of Internal Revenue, a former District Director, and the United States of America. The action against the United States of America has been withdrawn by the plaintiff.

* * *

From the pleadings, it appears to be undisputed that on April 22, 1964, the plaintiff was surety on a bond in favor of Punxsutawney National Bank Dayton, Pennsylvania; that on that date William Hanzl, acting in conspiracy with others, robbed the bank of the sum of $18,500 for which crime he was later apprehended and convicted. The plaintiff reimbursed the bank for the loss incurred in the robbery, and the bank assigned to plaintiff all its rights to the robbery proceeds.

> This is an example of subrogation.

It appears from the affidavits and answers to interrogatories that on April 24, 1964, two days after the robbery, Hanzl paid in excess of $4,500 to Revenue Officer Francis Klaus in satisfaction of his tax liability for the years 1960 and 1962. Of this payment, $565.54 was in cash, and on the same day with that cash Klaus purchased a cashier's check payable to the Internal Revenue Service in that amount from Mellon National Bank. The remainder of the amount received by Klaus was in the form of a cashier's check and money orders which were deposited by him in an IRS account in the People's Union Bank, McKeesport, Pennsylvania, on April 28, 1964.

Hanzl was arrested on April 29, 1964. Shortly after his arrest on that date, he stated to agents of the Federal Bureau of investigation "that he had been given $2,000 as proceeds of the robbery and that he had paid this money to the Internal Revenue Service."

Thereafter, "agent Klaus was told that Mr. Hanzl might have robbed a bank to pay tax obligations," and that "Mr. Hanzl might have been involved in a robbery of the Dayton Branch of the Punxsutawney National Bank on April 22, 1964, and that this robbery might have made possible his April payments to the Internal Revenue Service."

* * *

Since the United States has been dropped as a party, this action is being pursued against the District Directors of Internal Revenue Service in their individual capacities and any recovery must be based upon their wrongful seizure and appropriation of the bank's money to apply on Hanzl's taxes. A District Director who wrongfully seizes and applies property to tax payments is subject to an adverse judgment against him even though he paid the proceeds into the Treasury of the United States.

It is important to recognize that actions against a District Director are limited to claims showing that the Director has been guilty of wrongful conduct in the collection or exaction of taxes. Before this court can continue to exercise jurisdiction in this case, there must be an issue of fact which, if resolved in favor of the plaintiff, would establish wrongdoing on the part of one or both of the District Directors resulting in a judgment to recover the money. There is no such issue, hence no jurisdiction.

* * *

But even if jurisdiction existed, the plaintiff would not be entitled to recover. Assuming that the money Hanzl stole provided the means for him to pay his income taxes, most of it had been deposited and exchanged for a cashier's check and money orders, and all the funds had been deposited in bank accounts by the revenue officer before any revenue official knew of the robbery. It seems established that after stolen money has been negotiated, the victim-owner, or one standing in his shoes, cannot recover a like amount from a third-party recipient unless it can be proved that the recipient had prior knowledge that the money was stolen.

It is a rule of law that title to currency passes with delivery to the person who receives it in good faith and for valuable consideration. It seems clear that an obligation to pay income taxes constitutes a valid preexisting debt, and the transfer of currency in payment of that debt is for value. Thus, we hold that Hanzl's obligation to pay income taxes constituted a valid debt, and his transfer of currency in payment of those taxes was for value.

Likewise, it has become a general rule of the commercial world that one who takes a cashier's check or money order in good faith for a valuable consideration holds good title to its proceeds against all the world. Nothing short of actual or constructive notice that the instrument was purchased with money that was not the property of the person who offers to sell it – that is, nothing short of mala fides, will defeat the holder's title to the proceeds. Thus, any revenue official who receives cashier's checks or money orders without notice that the money represented thereby was stolen may apply them without recourse in payment of the taxes of the person who gave them to the revenue official.

It is absolutely necessary for commerce and business to continue that one who receives money, cashier's checks, or money orders is not put on inquiry as to the source from which the funds have been derived. It is generally impossible or impractical to discover the source of money, and for this reason one who receives money in good faith for valuable consideration prevails over the victim. Moreover, in the case sub judice, the claimants of the allegedly stolen funds are equally innocent parties, i.e., Transamerica on one side and the Directors of Internal Revenue on the other. The law has traditionally refused to lend its support where the equities are equal. In summary, this cause of action will be dismissed for lack of jurisdiction. There was no wrongful conduct on the part of either Director or their employee in receiving Hanzl's voluntary payments of his taxes which would confer jurisdiction on this federal court. But, if jurisdiction should exist, nevertheless, the defendants' motion for summary judgment would have to be granted because of the strong public policy behind the free negotiability of money, cashier's checks, and money orders.

An appropriate order will be entered.

- Compare currency, cashier's checks, and money orders, with regard to the reasonable expectations of a holder as to whether there is reason to be concerned about competing claims of third parties.

- Is the holding of this case consistent with the fraud and theft examples presented in the previous section? Explain your answer.

Note 1: In both *Laurel Bank & Trust Co. v. City National Bank of Connecticut*, 33 Conn. Sup. 641, 365 A.2d 1222, 20 U.C.C. Rep. Serv. 685 (1976), and *Kerr Steamship Co., Inc. v. Chartered Bank of India, Australia, and China*, 292 N.Y. 253, 54 N.E.2d 813 (1944), a cashier's check is compared to a promissory note. The *Laurel Bank* court uses the following language: "The proper approach is to view the issuing bank, acting in its dual role as drawer and drawee, as the equivalent of a maker of a negotiable promissory note payable on demand."

- Is this a reasonable comparison? Why or why not?

4-106 provides additional coverage of this concept.	

Note 2:　Comment 4 to 3-104 makes reference to insurance checks, which nearly every litigator will encounter as a means of settlement.　Insurance checks typically are not "checks" within the definition of Article 3 because they are "payable through" the bank on which they are drawn, rather than being drawn on the bank in the usual sense.　*Harper v. K & W Trucking Co.*, 725 P.2d 1066, 2 U.C.C. Rep. Serv. 2d 556 (1986), which was introduced in Part B's discussion of the concept of merger, includes language that explains why insurance companies might choose this form of payment:

> A "payable through" draft is similar to an ordinary check, but it is different in that a check is drawn on a bank, whereas a "payable through" draft is actually drawn on the drafter itself. . . . The upshot is that the bank named on the draft has no authority to make payment, but must present the draft to the drafter for payment.　The "payable through" draft is used for a variety of reasons, e.g. to control the float.　It provides the drawer with greater control over payment than ordinary checks.　*Id.* at 1068.

The bank collection process and resultant "float" are introduced in Chapter 10, Part A.

The following graphic represents an insurance settlement check:

```
Citizens Insurance Co.
123 Main Street
Detroit, MI 76543                        September 8, 1977

Pay to the Order of   Ann Insured                    $4,450.00

    Four thousand four hundred fifty and no/100 -------------

Payable through First National Bank of Howell

         Claim 1234 Stolen Car            Mr. Herbert Citizen
  MEMO
         8/15/77, Policy No. 6789        President, Citizens Insurance
```

- Based on *Harper*, what steps would you expect First National Bank to take when Ann Insured presents this check for payment?

E. Stages in a Negotiable Instrument's Life

This section introduces the concepts of issuance, transfer, and presentment, setting up the later discussions of transfer and presentment warranties, as well as property rights in the instrument.

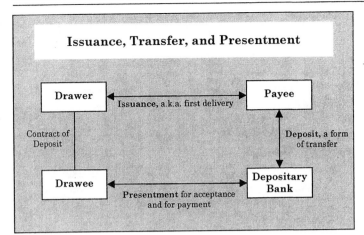

Read 3-105 (a) and 1-201 (b) (15). Issuance is the first stage in the life of a negotiable instrument, when the item is voluntarily transferred from the maker or drawer to the payee. There can be only one issuance of a negotiable instrument.

Read 3-203 (a). Transfer is the second stage in a negotiable instrument's life. A negotiable instrument can go through an unlimited number of transfers during its lifetime. As Chapter 9, Part C shows, some transfers are negotiations, and the distinction between negotiations and other transfers will lead to a study of holders and holders in due course, illuminating the protected status of holders in due course.

Read 3-501 (a). Presentment is the third and final stage in the life of a negotiable instrument. As Chapter 10, Part A shows, there are two kinds of presentment: presentment for acceptance and presentment for payment. In the case of an uncertified personal check, both occur at the same time, when the check reaches the drawee bank after having been in the hands of the payee and perhaps also a number of holders. In the case of a certified personal check, however, as is shown in Part D, the check is presented for acceptance before it is issued to the payee. In such a case, presentment for payment is made when the payee or holder seeks to enforce the check against the drawee. In each circumstance, presentment is made only to the drawee.

- Applying the language of 3-203 (a), why is a payee or other holder's presentation of a check for payment not a transfer?

- How many transfers, issuances, and presentments are illustrated in the following graphic?

Issuance, Transfer, and Presentment

```
    Drawer  ◄──────────►  Payee
      │                     ▲
      │                     │
      ▼                     ▼
  Drawee Bank            Holder 1
      ▲                     ▲
      │                     │
      ▼                     ▼
 Intermediary            Holder 2
    Bank
        ╲                 ╱
         ╲               ╱
          ▼             ▼
          Depositary
             Bank
```

International Perspective: Stages in the Life of a Negotiable Instrument

Read CIBN Articles 13, 15, 51, and 55. In language much like the UCC, the CIBN defines "issue" as the "first transfer of an instrument to a person who takes it as a holder." It also defines transfer and presentment. Article 13 defines transfer and, when read in conjunction with Article 15, differentiates between negotiations and other transfers in the same way that the UCC does. Articles 51 and 55, likewise, define presentment for acceptance and presentment for payment in ways that are consistent with the UCC.

Chapter Conclusion: In leaving this chapter, you should be comfortable with the basic forms of drafts and promissory notes, as well as the specialized instruments presented herein. You should also have a sense of the lifespan of a negotiable instrument and should begin to understand the significance of negotiability and, ultimately, the way in which a holder in due course can secure broader rights than the transferor from whom the instrument was received.

Chapter 8:
Requirements for Negotiability

Read 3-104 and Comment 1. 3-104 is the primary focus of this chapter. Comment 1 provides an introduction to the seven requirements for negotiability introduced throughout the balance of the chapter. The test for whether an item qualifies as a negotiable instrument is formal rather than functional. Article 3 provides the exclusive mechanism by which an item may be deemed negotiable; it is not possible for a non-negotiable instrument to be made negotiable by custom.

- How would a functional test differ from 3-104?

- Is the parties' intent to be considered in determining whether an item is negotiable?

A. The Requirement of a Writing

A negotiable instrument must be a writing. This section shows the writing requirement is fairly flexible and introduces the "permanent and portable" test used to determine whether an item complies with the requirement.

Read 1-201 (b) (43) and 3-103 (a) (8) and (12).

- Where do you find the requirement of a writing?

Whether an item meets the "writing" requirement is generally judged on the basis of whether the item is both "permanent" and "portable," neither of which are defined in the Code. Both concepts are relative: a writing in sand is not permanent, while a writing on paper is; likewise, a brick wall is not portable, while a cow is. The following graphics, which were introduced in Chapter 7 and appear in various modified forms throughout this chapter, represent typical negotiable instruments that would meet the "permanent and portable" test.

> The apocryphal "Case of the Negotiable Cow" is introduced below.

```
Drawer's Name
123 Main Street
Detroit, MI 76543                Date of Check _____

Pay to the
Order of    Payee _____    $ amount

   Amount of check and no/100 -----------------------

Drawee National Bank
                              Drawer of Check
   MEMO _____
```

> # PROMISSORY NOTE
>
> For value received, I do hereby promise to pay to Payee of Note or order, one hundred fifty thousand and no/100 dollars ($150,000.00). The terms and conditions of such note are as follows: . . .
>
> *Maker of Note*

In addition, an item can qualify as a "writing" even if it takes an uncommon – even bizarre – form. The following description of the famous fictitious "Case of the Negotiable Cow," an English story by A.P. Herbert, comes from F. H. Buckley's article *Machine Law*, in the Summer 2003 issue of the magazine *Green Bag*.

> There is a great store of harmless nonsense in the common law, to one who knows how to extract it. A.P. Herbert's satires were masterpieces of the genre. Herbert wrote up mock accounts of court decisions, recounting the efforts of an obstreperous layman, Alfred Haddock, to exercise an Englishman's rights and privileges just as often as he could. In *R. v. Haddock*, the accused was charged with leading "a large white cow of malevolent aspect" through the City of London to the offices of the Collector of Taxes. In his defense, Haddock argued that the cow was tendered as delivery of his taxes, since he had signed the cow and endorsed it "Pay to the Collector of Taxes, who is no gentleman, or Order, the sum of fifty-seven pounds (and may he rot!)." The court held that the personal comments were simply an honest man's understandable reaction to paying taxes, and did not deprive the cow of its status as an unconditional promise of payment, as required by the [British] Bills of Exchange Act. The method of payment was somewhat unconventional, to be sure, but nothing in the statute required promissory notes to be written on paper. The charge was therefore dismissed, since the accused had lawfully paid his taxes with a negotiable cow.

■ Since the Code allows leeway with regard to the "writing" requirement, why do most parties use negotiable instruments similar to the traditional forms shown above, rather than creating a different format and crafting a note or draft on a cocktail napkin, sticky note, or other material that might be convenient at the time?

> After you have finished this chapter, return to this example and consider whether the "negotiable cow" meets each of the seven requirements of negotiability. In addition, make sure you know why the cow is called a promissory note and not a check.

1
2
3
4
5
6
7
8
9
10
11
12
13
14
15
16
17
18
19
20
21
22
23
24
25
26
27
28
29
30
31
32
33
34
35
36
37
38
39
40
41
42
43
44
45
46
50
51
52
53

International Perspective: What Is a Writing?

Read CIBN Article 3 and UCC 3-104 Comment 5. CIBN Article 3 sets forth the basic requirements of a negotiable instrument under the Convention. UCC 3-104 Comment 5 compares the UCC and CIBN standards for negotiability in general terms. Similarly, in his article *The Draft Convention on International Bills of Exchange and International Promissory Notes: Formal Requisites*, 27 Am. J. Comp. Law 515 (1979), Norman Penney compares the UCC and CIBN with regard to the formal requirements for a negotiable instrument. With respect to the writing requirement, Penney states as follows:

> The [CIBN] does not contain a definition of the word "written" or the term "a writing," but the commentary to the initial Secretariat draft stated that the term "written," in the context of the statute, "would include any mode of representing or reproducing words in visible form, and is sufficiently flexible to permit the law to apply to long-distance electronic transmission or reproduction of a writing. . . ." *Id.* at 517.

- How does the CIBN standard compare to the UCC "permanent and portable" test?

Penney continues as follows:

> The Working Group has not clearly decided whether electronic transmissions would, or ought to be covered by the [CIBN]. *Id.* at 517.

Chapter 10, Part A introduces Check 21 and explains its relationship to electronic transmissions.

- Does Article 3 apply to electronic transmissions? Where do you find the answer to this question?

Section 3 of the English Bills of Exchange Act of 1882 provides as follows:

Reference is made to Section 3 throughout this chapter, in making comparisons between the UCC, CIBN, and BEA. To refresh your recollection as to which countries follow the BEA, or some form thereof, see the international materials in Chapter 7, Part A.

> (1) A bill of exchange is an unconditional order in writing, addressed by one person to another, signed by the person giving it, requiring the person to whom it is addressed to pay on demand or at a fixed or determinable future time a sum certain in money or to the order of a specified person, or to bearer.
>
> (2) An instrument which does not comply with these conditions, or which orders any act to be done in addition to the payment of money, is not a bill of exchange.
>
> (3) An order to pay out of a particular fund is not unconditional within the meaning of this section; but an unqualified order to pay, coupled with (a) an indication of a particular fund out of

which the drawee is to reimburse himself or a particular account to be debited with the amount, or (b) a statement of the transaction which gives rise to the bill, is unconditional.

(4) A bill is not invalid by reason –
    (a) That it is not dated.
    (b) That it does not specify the value given, or that any value has been given therefore.
    (c) That it does not specify the place where it is drawn or the place where it is payable.

According to the English treatise *Byles on Bills of Exchange* (27th ed., Sweet & Maxwell 2002), the BEA employs a narrower construction of the word "writing" than the UCC does, permitting "any convenient substitute for paper" and generally allowing "printing, lithography, etc." but not extending so far as the more liberal UCC "permanent and portable" test.

- Is the UCC "permanent and portable" test unnecessarily liberal, given how few attempts are made to negotiate items of nonstandard format?

> After completing this chapter, return to this subsection and make sure you know whether each of these statements in Section 3 (4) is consistent with the UCC.

B. Signature Requirement

A negotiable instrument must be signed. This section demonstrates the flexible nature of this requirement, showing some nontraditional forms a signature might take under the Code. This section discusses how a party may sign an instrument on its own behalf. Signatures by representatives are discussed in Chapter 9, Part B.

> The drawer's signature is commonly found in the bottom right corner of a check.

Drawer's Name
123 Main Street
Detroit, MI 76543

Date of Check _____

Pay to the Order Of _Payee_____ $ _____

Amount of check and no/100 --------------------------- amount

Drawee National Bank

MEMO_____   **Drawer of Check**

PROMISSORY NOTE

For value received, I do hereby promise to pay to Payee of Note or order, one hundred fifty thousand and no/100 dollars ($150,000.00). The terms and conditions of such note are as follows: . . .

Maker of Note

The maker's signature is typically found at the bottom of a note.

Read 1-201 (b) (37) and Comment 37, 3-103 (a) (8) and (12), and 3-401 (b) and Comment 2.

- Where do you find the signature requirement?

Revised Article 1, which requires that a signature be made "with present intention to adopt or accept a writing," differs from prior Article 1, which required "present intention to authenticate a writing."

- How are these two standards different from one another?

Note that the pre-revision language still appears in 3-401 (b).

- Which definition should be applied to determine whether an item has been signed within the meaning of 3-103?

3-401(b) allows a party to sign with an assumed name.

- Could this action constitute fraud, forgery, or both?

- When an illiterate person marks an "X" to sign a document, how can this symbol be a signature since many persons use the same mark?
- How would one establish whose signature an "X" is?

- If a party inadvertently misspells his own name in signing an instrument, is the signature still valid?

- What is the result if the aforementioned misspelling is, as a matter of coincidence, the legal name of a third person who knows nothing of the instrument?

International Perspective: Signatures

To refresh your recollection of which countries follow the GUL and BEA, see the international materials in Chapter 7, Part A.

Read CIBN Article 5 (k) and BEA Section 3 from Part A of this chapter. The BEA, GUL, CIBN, and UCC all contain a signature requirement. In *The Draft Convention on International Bills of Exchange and International Promissory Notes: Formal Requisites*, 27 Am. J. Comp. Law 515 (1979), Norman Penney notes that only the CIBN and UCC define "signature." Penney continues as follows:

> [A] major issue under the heading of "signature and writing" is the desirability of relaxing the requirement that signatures on negotiable instruments be handwritten. The opinion of bankers and lawyers around the world is still divided on this question. France and the U.S. are among the leading countries which have long recognized facsimile signatures, particularly for endorsements. Of course, facsimile signatures of drawers on checks are quite commonplace in the U.S. The [CIBN] Working Group chose to favor the argument supporting the validity of such signatures, generally.

As the context suggests, seals and marks are means of authentication. Mary L. Riley, *China: Negotiable Instruments: Signatures and Seals*, J.I.B.L. 1996, 11 (6), N113-N114, provides an introduction to the related issue of signature by seal in Chinese negotiable-instrument practice.

> A similar debate occurred at the time the [GUL] was being considered. The countries that then urged recognition of more than handwritten signatures were Japan and India, who were concerned that this requirement might interfere with the use of seals in Japan and marks in India. In the recent work, it was the countries interested in adapting to new technology and bill-handling procedures that argued for the liberalization of the requirement. The concern of the opponents was not such much the abandonment of customary practices as the possible facilitation of forgery. The proponents of "liberalization" prevailed, at least in the Working Group, although a proposal was accepted to permit ratifying and acceding states to make special declarations respecting signatures on instruments signed in such states. *Id.* at 519.

The materials in Chapter 1, Part A may be of assistance in answering this question.

- What are the benefits and risks of allowing countries to make "reservations" to certain provisions of the CIBN?

According to *Byles on Bills of Exchange* 2-05 (27th ed., Sweet & Maxwell 2002), the BEA allows a bill of exchange to be signed by an "X" if the signer is illiterate, but whether signature by a rubber stamp or initials is permissible has been questioned.

- How would the UCC resolve each of these issues?

- Can a reasoned distinction be made between the "X," on the one hand, and the initials and rubber stamp, on the other?

C. "Magic" Words of Negotiability

As this section shows, certain kinds of negotiable instruments must contain words indicating the issuer's intention that the instrument be negotiable.

Drawer's Name
123 Main Street
Detroit, MI 76543   Date of Check
_____

Pay to the   Payee $ amount
Order of   _____

  Amount of check and no/100 ------------------------

Drawee National Bank
                              Drawer of Check
MEMO _____   _____

> On a check, the "magic" words of negotiability are typically present, although not required, and usually precede the payee's name.

PROMISSORY NOTE

For value received, I do hereby promise to **pay to Payee of Note or order**, one hundred fifty thousand and no/100 dollars ($150,000.00). The terms and conditions of such note are as follows: . . .

Maker of Note

> How does the phrasing "pay to Payee of Note or order" suggest negotiability?

Read 3-104 (a) (1) and (c) and Comment 2, and 3-109 and Comments 1 and 2.

- Where do you find the "magic words" requirement?

- What are the "magic words"?

- What negotiable instruments do not require this wording?

The language "pay to the order of [name of payee]" denotes negotiability by indicating the named payee may choose to enforce the instrument personally or may choose to transfer the item to another named party, who should also be permitted to enforce the item. The language "pay to bearer" indicates that whomever is in possession of the item – even if not named in the item – should be permitted to enforce it. The former language creates what is called "order paper," while the latter denotes "bearer paper."

> Chapter 10 and 3-109 (c) show that an instrument issued as order paper can, through indorsement, be changed to bearer paper, and vice versa.

- **Read 3-104 and Comment 3.** Is it possible to keep a check from being negotiable?

- Which are order paper and which are bearer paper?

As Chapter 10 shows, 3-115 indicates how the instrument will be treated if the blank is filled in after issuance.

- A promissory note that reads, "Pay to the order of _____," where the blank has not been filled in.

- A check that reads, "Pay to Merry Christmas."

Section 3-404 (b) may assist you in answering this question.

- A trade acceptance draft that reads, "Pay to Uniform Commercial Code Corporation," where no such corporation is in existence.

- A promissory note that reads, "Pay to [payee's name] or bearer."

- A trade acceptance draft that reads, "Pay to [payee's name]."

- A check that reads, "Pay to the order of bearer."

International Perspective: "Magic" Words

The text of BEA Section 3 can be found in Part A of this chapter.

Read CIBN Articles 1 and 3, and BEA Section 3.

- What are the similarities and differences between the BEA, CIBN, and UCC with regard to the "magic" words of negotiability presented in this section?

- Does each recognize both bearer paper and order paper?

In *The Proposed Uniform Law on International Bills of Exchange and Promissory Notes: A Discussion of Some Special and General Problems Reflected in the Form and Content, Choice of Law, and Judicial Interpretation of Articles*, 9 Cal. W. Intl. L. Rev. 30 (1979), Robert F. Blomquist addresses the CIBN as follows:

> Conflicting arguments can be put forth regarding the [CIBN's] lack of a requirement of specific words of negotiability. On the one hand, since an instrument must be expressly designated as an "International Bill of Exchange" or as an "International Promissory Note" to be subject to the [CIBN], it has been suggested that such additional words of negotiability would be mere "surplusage." Such an argument is based on the assumption

that the terms "bill" and "note" universally connote negotiability. *Id.* at 55-56.

- What distinction is Blomquist drawing between the wording of the relevant provisions in the CIBN and the UCC, in concluding the CIBN does not require specific words of negotiability?

- Is the easy answer to this issue to replace the heading required by CIBN Article 1 with the phrase "Negotiable International Bill of Exchange" or "Negotiable International Promissory Note," as Blomquist suggests later in his article?

It may be appropriate to characterize the headings required by CIBN Article 1 as the CIBN's own "magic words" that will be new and unfamiliar to U.S. attorneys. In his article *Draft Uniform Law on International Bills of Exchange and International Promissory Notes*, 21 Am J. Comp. L. 474 (1973), Jürgen Dohm addresses this potential stumbling block, as follows:

> [T]he deviation of the [CIBN] from the common-law liberality is necessary to manifest clearly the choice of the uniform law. Also, the requirement of the designation clause in the text of the international instrument makes it impossible for a holder of an instrument not submitted to the [CIBN] to add, without the agreement of the prior parties, a clause stating that the paper is governed by the uniform law. Hence the formalism of the [CIBN] is necessary and justified. *Id.* at 481.

- Would it otherwise be possible, absent CIBN Article 1's requirement of a heading, for a later holder to change the document in such a way as to bind the original parties to the CIBN?

Although Chapter 10 provides more specific guidance regarding the liability of parties to negotiable instruments, you should have an instinctual sense of the answer to this question already.

The excerpt continues with the following:

> The result that a [CIBN] instrument cannot be made payable "to bearer" is somewhat questionable. The rationale for this legal proscription was strong pressure from certain European central banks to bar instruments made payable "to bearer," in order to protect against the use of such instruments as a currency substitute or as a device to avoid exchange-control laws. *Id.* at 481.

As Blomquist later states, and as Chapter 9, Part B shows, it is possible to get around this proscription by indorsing an instrument originally made payable to an identified payee, in blank. Doing so will make the negotiable instrument payable to bearer.

The CIBN proscription mirrors similar restrictions in the GUL.

- Why might a government or central bank be concerned with the use of bearer paper as a "currency substitute or . . . a device to avoid exchange-control laws"?

- Are there other ways such concerns might be addressed?

D. The "Unconditional" Requirement

This section explains the "unconditional" requirement, showing how it can be violated and also clarifying that acceleration clauses, clauses addressing collateral, and certain other language will not violate this rule.

Read 3-104 (a) and 3-106 and Comments.

- Where do you find the "unconditional" requirement?

As the commentary suggests, the purpose of the "unconditional" requirement is to ensure negotiable-instrument holders are not saddled with the burden of research to determine whether a condition stated in the item has been satisfied.

- What is the difference between "express conditions" that render an item non-negotiable and "implied conditions" that do not?

- Since 3-106 is intended to ensure holders are not required to do research to determine their rights and responsibilities, why can an instrument make reference to another record "for a statement of rights with respect to collateral, prepayment, or acceleration" without losing its negotiable status?

- Can a holder elect not to do such research?

- Consider the following graphics. Why is the emphasized language in the first item impermissible, while that in the second is acceptable?

1
2
3
4
5
6
7
8
9
10
11
12
13
14
15
16
17
18
19
20
21
22
23
24
25
26
27
28
29
30
31
32
33
34
35
36
37
38
39
40
41
42
43
44
45
46
50
51
52
53

Drawer's Name
123 Main Street
Detroit, MI 76543   Date of Check _____

Pay to the
Order Of   Payee _____ $ _____
                                            amount

Amount of check and no/100 --------------------

Drawee National Bank
MEMO Subject to the terms of the contract dated August 4   Drawer of Check

> "Subject to" signals an impermissible condition.

PROMISSORY NOTE

For value received, I do hereby promise to pay to
Payee of Note or order, one hundred fifty thousand
and no/100 dollars ($150,000.00) **as per the
contract dated August 4**. The terms and
conditions of such note are as follows: . . .

Maker of Note

> The language "as per" normally does not affect negotiability.

The following case explains that a non-negotiable instrument is not wholly worthless – although it is probably worth less than a negotiable instrument of the same face value. The case also demonstrates the difference between the rights and responsibilities of immediate parties to an item and those of transferees. In addition, the case explains the policy underlying the "unconditional" requirement.

First State Bank v. Clark,
91 N.M. 117, 570 P.2d 1144, 22 U.C.C. Rep. Serv. 1186 (1977).

Easley, Justice.

First State Bank of Gallup sued M. S. Horne on a promissory note. The trial court granted summary judgment against [Horne], and we affirm.

Horne had executed a $100,000 note in favor of R. C. Clark, which contained a restriction that the note could not be transferred, pledged, or assigned without the written consent of Horne. As part of the transaction between Horne and Clark, Horne gave Clark a separate letter authorizing Clark to pledge the note as collateral for a loan of $50,000, which Clark anticipated making with First State. Clark did make the loan and pledged the note, which was accompanied by Horne's letter authorizing the note to be used as collateral. First State also called Horne to verify that he was in agreement that his note could be accepted as collateral. First State attempted to collect from Horne on Horne's note to Clark which had been pledged as collateral. Horne refused to pay, and this suit resulted.

> The last sentence of the opinion explains Horne's refusal to pay.

The issues raised on appeal include (1) whether the note was a negotiable instrument for purposes of Article 3 of the Uniform Commercial Code; (2) if it is, whether First State qualifies as a holder in due course under the UCC; (3) whether, if Article 3 does not apply to the instrument, the note was nevertheless negotiable as between the parties under ordinary contract principles; and (4) whether, under ordinary contract law, Horne is estopped to deny the note's validity.

* * *

In order to be a "negotiable instrument" for Article 3 purposes, the paper must precisely meet the definition set out in 3-104, since 3-104 itself states that, to be a negotiable instrument, a writing "must" meet the definition therein set out. Moreover, it is clear that, in order to determine whether an instrument meets that definition, only the instrument itself may be looked to, not other documents, even when other documents are referred to in the instrument.

* * *

The note in question here failed to meet the requirements of 3-104, since the promise to pay contained in the note was not unconditional. Moreover, the note was expressly drafted to be non-negotiable since it stated:

> This note may not be transferred, pledged, or otherwise assigned without the written consent of M. S. Horne.

Can you explain the presence of the words "Pay to the order of" on the face of a note the court believes was intended to be non-negotiable?

These words, even though they appeared on the back of the note, effectively cancelled any implication of negotiability provided by the words "Pay to the order of" on the face of the note. Notations and terms on the back of a note, made contemporaneously with the execution of the note and intended to be part of the note's contract of payment, constitute as much a part of the note as if they were incorporated on its face.

* * *

The whole purpose of the concept of a negotiable instrument under Article 3 is to declare that transferees in the ordinary course of business are only to be held liable for information appearing in the instrument itself and will not be expected to know of any limitations on negotiability or changes in terms, etc., contained in any separate documents. The whole idea of the facilitation of easy transfer of notes and instruments requires that a transferee be able to trust what the instrument says, and be able to determine the validity of the note and its negotiability from the language in the note itself. . . .

Since the note in question is not negotiable for Article 3 purposes, First State cannot be a holder in due course under Article 3, and we need not discuss that issue.

What distinction is the court making here? Does the language of the UCC support this distinction?

Even though a note or instrument is not a "negotiable instrument" for Article 3 purposes, it may nevertheless be negotiable between the parties involved under ordinary contract law. . . . [E]ven where an instrument is negotiable for Article 3 purposes, the parties in any transaction are always bound by the totality of documents which are intended to form a contract between them, not just the terms set forth in one which happens to be a negotiable instrument. The same is true when the instrument does not meet Article 3 requirements.

As between Clark and Horne, Clark had a contract right to pledge Horne's note to Clark as security. Clark had a contract right to negotiate the note. Thus, the note was negotiable for Clark's limited purposes, even though it was not an Article 3 negotiable instrument. Before accepting Clark's pledge, First State verified by direct conversation with Horne that Clark had Horne's authority to pledge the note as the letter permitted. Horne in no way suggested that he had any offsetting defense to the validity of the note. Horne failed to notify First State that Clark had given him an offsetting note which was intended to nullify the effect of Horne's note to Clark, should Clark default on his loan obligation secured by that note.

- Why is the use of parol evidence, or reference to other documents incorporated by reference, inappropriate in determining whether an item is negotiable?

To ensure you understand of the significance of the court's decision that the item was non-negotiable, consider what the rights and obligations of the parties would have been if the note had been transferred to a third party.

- Would a third party have been able to enforce the note against Horne, or would Horne have been successful in asserting the defense of the offsetting note?

> In addressing this question, it will be helpful to know that Horne's defense would be considered a "personal defense" under 3-305, rather than a "real defense." This distinction will be further explored in Chapter 9.

Note 1: Read 3-106 (b) (ii) and Comment 1. Under former law, an item was conditional (and therefore not negotiable) if it stated it was to be paid out of a particular fund. Such instruments are sometimes called "warrants." As Comment 1 states, this result has now been reversed, the rationale being that market forces will value such instruments appropriately, such that there is no need to make them non-negotiable. Former law created an exception for government warrants, deeming them negotiable even though payment was to be made from a particular fund or source. Some states, however, chose to treat these items differently. Florida law, for example, continues to characterize government warrants as non-negotiable.

> As Chapter 1, Part A shows, states can alter the UCC by other state law or by nonuniform enactment.

- In the case of a government warrant, what is the "particular fund" from which payment might be made?

In *State of Florida v. Family Bank of Hallandale, Inc.,* 623 So.2d 474, 20 U.C.C. Rep. Serv. 2d 1273 (Fla. 1993), the court considered a dispute arising from the Florida Department of

Transportation's contract with Ted's Sheds, Inc. for several metal buildings to be used at various service plazas on the Florida Turnpike.   Ted's Sheds, Inc. provided a Fort Lauderdale, Florida address during the bidding process, but then sent an invoice with an address of Bonita Springs, Florida. In response, the DOT issued a warrant for $16,392 payable to the order of Ted's Sheds, Inc. and sent it to the Fort Lauderdale address. There were actually two companies – Ted's Sheds of Broward, Inc., in Fort Lauderdale, and Ted's Sheds, Inc, in Bonita Springs. The latter company was the contracting party, but the former company received and deposited the warrant through its account with Seminole National Bank.   Ted's Sheds, Inc. contacted the State Comptroller, not having received payment, so the State Comptroller placed a stop-payment order on the first warrant and issued a duplicate to the Bonita Springs entity.

> **The right of stop payment is discussed in Chapter 10, Part B.**

The Family Bank of Hallandale, successor in interest to Seminole National Bank, then brought suit because it had already allowed its depositor, Ted's Sheds of Broward, Inc., to withdraw the proceeds of the warrant.   Its depositor, Ted's Sheds of Broward, Inc., had been administratively dissolved in the meantime, so the bank could not recover its money from the company through the chargeback process.   The bank's theory of recovery was that it was a holder in due course and should be allowed to enforce the item against the State, notwithstanding the erroneous issuance of the warrant. Because the court found the item non-negotiable as a matter of Florida law, this argument failed.   In so holding, the court stated as follows:

> **The depositary bank's right of chargeback is discussed in Chapter 10, Part A.**

> Warrants are devices, prescribed by law, for drawing money from the state treasury. They are orders issued by the official whose duty it is to pass on claims to the treasurer to pay a specified sum from the treasury for the persons and purposes specified.   A warrant is not an order to pay absolutely, rather it is generally prima facie evidence of indebtedness payable out of a particular fund or appropriation. *Id.* at 476.

- Why might a state make government warrants non-negotiable?

> **The materials in Chapter 9, Part A may assist you in answering this question.**

- Was Ted's Sheds of Broward, Inc. a holder of the warrant?

Note 2: As the questions introducing this section indicated, the precise language chosen by the parties can affect whether an item is negotiable, or conditional and thus non-negotiable. In *First Federal Savings & Loan Association v. Gump & Ayers Real Estate, Inc.*, 771 P.2d 1096, 8 U.C.C. Rep. Serv. 2d 720

(Utah App. 1989), the court considered a promissory note with the following language:

> This Note is secured by that certain Purchase and Security Agreement dated June ___, 1984. Reference is made to the Purchase and Security Agreement for additional rights of the holder thereof. *Id.* at 1096.

In finding the note negotiable, the court held the quoted language was a "mere reference" to another document that did not affect its negotiability.

- Can you explain the court's decision?

> Reading 3-106 (a) and (b) and Comment 1 may assist you in answering this question.

Problem 1: Philip Farrington was a wealthy young man with little business experience, just out of college. He secured employment with Davis Aircraft Engineering, Inc., and was given an opportunity to purchase most of its preferred stock. Daniel Davis and Donald Atkinson owned the common stock. Some time after joining the company, Farrington was asked to sign a series of promissory notes of which the company was the maker and a local bank was the payee. He asked Davis why he was being asked to sign, and Davis responded that the notes were being prepared in connection with a loan and the only reason his signature was required was to show the bank that the shareholders were aware of the transaction. The notes, which Farrington signed but did not read, stated as follows:

> This note evidences a borrowing made under, and is subject to, the terms of a loan agreement dated January 3, 1952, between the undersigned and the payee thereof . . . .

The notes included signature lines for Davis, Atkinson, and Farrington. The loan agreement, a separate document that Farrington never saw and did not sign, established a revolving line of credit for the company and included the following language:

> All borrowings under this credit are to be personally endorsed or guaranteed by Daniel E. Davis, Donald T. Atkinson, and Phillip Farrington.

The line of credit was much larger than Farrington's investment in the company. The company became insolvent, and the bank sued Farrington on the note.

- Is the note a negotiable instrument?

- Will Farrington be liable to the bank?

Based on *United States v. Farrington,* 172 F. Supp. 797, 1
U.C.C. Rep. Serv. 207 (D. Mass. 1959).

Problem 2: Consider the following excerpt from a divorce
settlement:

> For value received, I, Koyt Woodworth Everhart, Jr., do hereby
> promise to pay to Jane Carter Everhart or her order, One
> hundred fifty thousand and no/100 dollars ($150,000.00) in lieu of
> a property settlement supplementing that certain Deed of
> Separation and Property Settlement, dated May 1, 1972, the
> terms of which are incorporated herein by reference. As of the
> signing of said document, Jane Carter Everhart was not aware of
> the extent of property interests of Koyt Woodworth Everhart, Jr.,
> nor was she represented by counsel at said time. In order to
> prevent involvement in litigation and dissolution of assets, Koyt
> Woodworth Everhart, Jr. does hereby promise to pay to Jane
> Carter Everhart or her order, the sum of one hundred fifty
> thousand and no/100 dollars ($150,000.00); the terms and
> conditions of such note are as follows: . . .
>
> *Koyt Woodworth Everhart, Jr.*

- Is this document a negotiable instrument?

- Does the negotiability of this item depend on whether
  it was supported by consideration?

Based on *Booker v. Everhart,* 294 N.C. 146, 240 S.E.2d 360, 24
U.C.C. Rep. 165 (1978).

Problem 3: On December 1, 1928, Power Equipment
Company of Des Moines, Iowa executed and delivered to
Turner Manufacturing Company of Statesville, North Carolina
a trade acceptance draft with the following language:

> No. 394, Statesville, N.C. 12/1/1928
>
> To Power Equipment Company, Des Moines, Iowa
>
> On March 1, 1929, Pay to the Order of Turner Manufacturing
> Company Twelve Hundred Eighty-Five and 34/100 dollars
> (1,285.34).
>
> The obligation of the acceptor hereof arises out of the purchase of
> goods from the drawer, maturity being in conformity with the
> original terms of the purchase.
>
> Accepted at Des Moines, Iowa on December 1, 1928.
> Payable at Des Moines National Bank

See 4-106 to
understand the
"payable at"
language.

1
2
3
4
5
6
7
8
9
10
11
12
13
14
15
16
17
18
19
20
21
22
23
24
25
26
27
28
29
30
31
32
33
34
35
36
37
38
39
40
41
42
43
44
45
46
50
51
52
53

Signature lines for Power Equipment Company and Turner Manufacturing Company appeared on the front of the item, and both signed.

- Who is the drawer and who is the drawee?

- Who presumably owed money to whom when the instrument was executed and delivered?

- Is this draft unconditional within the meaning of Article 3?

Based on *First National Bank v. Power Equipment Co.*, 211 Iowa 153, 233 N.W. 103 (1930).

> Preparing a graphic similar to that of the trade acceptance draft in Chapter 7, Part A may be useful in answering this portion of the question.

International Perspective: Unconditionality

Read CIBN Article 3 and BEA Section 3. Both the BEA and the CIBN require that the promise or order to pay be unconditional. In *The Proposed Uniform Law on International Bills of Exchange and Promissory Notes: A Discussion of Some Special and General Problems Reflected in the Form and Content, Choice of Law, and Judicial Interpretation of Articles,* 9 Cal. W. Intl. L. Rev. 30 (1979), Robert F. Blomquist critiques this portion of the CIBN as follows:

> The text of BEA Section 3 can be found in Part A of this chapter.

> [W]hen international sellers and their financial intermediaries use negotiable instruments, they expect certainty and clarity in their fundamental right to be paid. Acknowledging this truth, the [CIBN] Working Group adopted the traditional notion of existing local negotiable-instrument laws that, for an instrument to come within the ambit of the Convention, it must contain certain language which amounts to an order (in the case of a bill) or a promise (in the case of a promissory note).

> * * *

> Similarly, in conformity with existing negotiable-instrument codes, the [CIBN] requires the order or promise to pay to be "unconditional." [T]he [CIBN] engenders uncertainty by not defining the term "unconditional," apparently on the belief that this word of art has a universal meaning. This, however, is an erroneous assumption. *Id.* at 46-47.

The CIBN has no official commentary analogous to the UCC Comments, so many terms are unexplained.

- What are the risks and benefits of this decision?

In addition, consider the following excerpt from BEA Article 11:

> An instrument, expressed to be payable on a contingency, is not a bill, and the happening of the event does not cure the defect.

- Is this language consistent with the UCC?

- Why does "the happening of the event . . . not cure the default?"

E. Additional Promises and Negotiability

Students often confuse the "unconditional" requirement with the "no additional promise" requirement. Sections D and E of this chapter explain the difference between the two.

Read 3-104 (a) (3).

- Using the language of 3-104 (a) (3), why is the language in the first item permissible, while the language in the second is not?

The language on the memo line is permissible.

> Drawer's Name
> 123 Main Street
> Detroit, MI 76543
>
> Date of Check _____
>
> Pay to the Order Of   Payee _____ $ amount _____
>
> Amount of check and no/100 ----------------------------
>
> Drawee National Bank
>
> MEMO Drawer will also agree to supply collateral in the amount of the check, to be disposed of by the payee if the check is returned NSF.   Drawer of Check _____

The bold language renders this item non-negotiable.

PROMISSORY NOTE

For value received, I do hereby promise to pay to Payee of Note or order, one hundred fifty thousand and no/100 dollars ($150,000.00). ~~I also agree to convey real estate to Payee of Note with a market value of at least $25,000.~~ The terms and conditions of such note are as follows: . . .

Maker of Note

- Refer to Part D, Note 1. Why does the same reasoning that permits a warrant to be negotiable even though it is to be paid from a particular fund or source, not apply to a note containing a promise to pay $1,000 and deliver 10 cords of wood?

> As Part D, Note 1 explains, warrants are permitted as negotiable instruments under Article 3, on the theory that the market will value the items appropriately.

The following pre-UCC case is the origin of the phrase "courier without luggage," which is the famous description of the requirement that a negotiable instrument be capable of being fully understood, and fully appraised, without reference to other sources.

Overton v. Tyler,
3 Pa. 346 (1846).

Gibson, C.J.

L. Smith drew a promissory note, falling due June 30th, 1845, for discount at bank, which was endorsed for him by Tyler et al., as sureties. While this note was maturing, he gave to Tyler the following instrument:

> Suretyship by indorsement is discussed in Chapter 11, Part A.

"1,000. Athens, February 15, 1845.

For value received, I promise to pay Francis Tyler and Levi Westbrook, or bearer, one thousand dollars, with interest, by the first day of June next. And I do hereby authorize any attorney of any court of record in Pennsylvania, to appear for me and confess judgment for the above sum to the holder of this single bill, with costs of suit, hereby releasing all errors and waiving stay of execution and the right of inquisition on real estate; also waiving the right of having any of my property appraised which may be levied upon, by virtue of any execution issued for the above sum.

L. SMITH.

> After you have studied the entire chapter, return to these facts to examine whether this item meets the UCC's "sum certain" and "date certain" requirements.

* * *

. . . The note is for the payment of money; it is payable to bearer; and it is payable absolutely: yet it is obvious that it was not intended to be negotiable in a commercial sense. . . . The debt is still between the original parties; and the contract by which it was created is to be interpreted, like any other, by their actual meaning. If they meant to make, not a promissory note, . . . but a special agreement with power to enter up judgment on it, they are bound by the result as they themselves viewed it. . . . Nor would a subsequent holder take the paper on any other terms than those expressed in it. It has in it all the parts of a promissory note; but it has more: it contains not only a warrant to confess judgment with a release of errors, but an agreement to waive appraisement and stay of execution. But a negotiable bill or note is a courier without luggage. It is a requisite that it be framed in the fewest possible words, and those importing the most certain and precise contract; and though this requisite be a minor one, it is entitled to weight in determining a question of intention. To be within the statute, it must be free from contingencies or conditions that would embarrass it in its course; for a memorandum to control it, though endorsed on it, would be incorporated with it and destroy it. But a memorandum which is merely directory or collateral, will not affect it. ... A warrant to confess judgment, not being a mercantile instrument, or a legitimate part of one, but a thing collateral, would not pass by endorsement or delivery to a subsequent holder; and a curious question would be, whether it would survive as an accessory separated from its principal, in the hands of the payee for the benefit of his transferee. I am unable to see how it could authorize him to enter up judgment, for the use of another, on a note with which he had parted. But it may be said that his transfer would be a waiver of the warrant as a security for himself or any one else; and that subsequent holders would take the note without it. The principle is certainly applicable to a memorandum endorsed after signing, or one written on a separate paper. But the appearance of paper with such unusual stipulations incorporated with it, would be apt to startle commercial men as to their effect on the contract of endorsement, and make them reluctant to touch it. All this shows that these parties could not have intended to impress a commercial character on the note, dragging after it, as it would, a train of special provisions which would materially impede its circulation.

> According to this court, why would a clause allowing confession of judgment not create rights passing to a subsequent holder?

> 3-104 (3) (ii) may assist you in answering this question.

- Why is the item described in this case non-negotiable?

- Setting aside its famous language, is this case still good law?

Note: Read 3-104 (a) (3) (i) and (ii) and 3-106 (b). Creditors may require borrowers to agree to supply additional collateral or agree to the acceleration of the indebtedness, upon the happening of some specified event. The portions of 3-104 that relate to collateral are subject to the Article 1 good-faith requirement found in 1-309, which incorporates by reference the definition of good faith in 1-304 and Comment 1. *State National Bank of El Paso v. Farah Manufacturing Co., Inc.,* 678 S.W.2d 661, 40 U.C.C. Rep. Serv. 764 (1984), shows how acceleration clauses may be used in good faith:

> Even where an insecurity clause is drafted in the broadest possible terms, the primary question is whether the creditor's attempt to accelerate stemmed from a reasonable, good-faith belief that its security was about to become impaired. Acceleration clauses are not to be used offensively such as for the commercial advantage of the creditor. They do not permit acceleration when the facts make its use unjust or oppressive. *Id.* at 685.

- Precisely how does an acceleration clause protect a creditor?

Problem: The Richmond Indiana Venture Partnership added Mr. Woodworth as a new partner and loaned him the money to buy into the partnership. His share was to be just over $650,000, and the loan was memorialized with a promissory note. The partnership negotiated the note to Signet Bank, so it could receive a discounted sum immediately rather than waiting for Woodworth to make payment in full over time. The note contained the following clause:

> The undersigned agrees that, in the event any payment due pursuant to the terms of this note not be timely made, at the option of the Partnership, the undersigned shall retroactively lose any interest in the Partnership from the date hereof and the Partnership shall have no obligation to account for any payments theretofore made by the undersigned, and that this remedy is in addition to other remedies afforded by the Partnership Agreement.

- Does the note satisfy the "no additional promise" requirement?

Based on *Woodworth v. The Richmond Indiana Venture*, 13 U.C.C. Rep. 2d 1149 (1990).

International Perspective: Additional Terms

Read CIBN Article 3 and BEA Section 3.

BEA Section 3 can be found in Part A of this chapter.

- What are the similarities and differences between the BEA, CIBN, and UCC with regard to the "no additional promise" requirement?

Problem: This language was part of a Canadian promissory note:

> The undersigned . . . agrees to pay to Province of Alberta Treasury Branches all costs, including without limitation solicitor/client fees incurred by it in enforcing payment in the event of default hereunder, together with interest . . . on all costs until paid by the undersigned.

Solicitors (as distinguished from barristers) prepare cases for trial but do not litigate them.

The Alberta Court of Appeal found the note non-negotiable under Canada's Bills of Exchange Act, holding as follows:

Canada's Bills of Exchange Act of 1890 was based upon the British Bills of Exchange Act of 1882. The Canadian Act was most recently revised in 1985.

> The existence of this obligation in the note affects the valuation of the note for negotiation and therefore affects the currency of the note. Because possible future collection expenses are not readily ascertainable, to permit such a term in a note is to undermine the principles of bills of exchange. . . . The lesson is that if, for whatever reason, it is important to maintain the essential nature

> After you have read Part F, consider whether the note also violates the "fixed amount of money" requirement.

of the instrument as a promissory note, extreme caution should be exercised if additional terms are being inserted into the note.

- Would this language be permissible under the BEA, CIBN, and UCC, or is it an impermissible additional promise?

Based on *Province of Alberta Treasury Branches v. D & L Insulation*, an unreported case from the Alberta Court of Appeal, described in Edwin Cook's Case Comment found at J.I.B.L. 1992, 7(1), N8-9.

F. The Requirement of a Sum Certain

This section explains the "fixed amount of money" requirement, showing why variable interest rates and certain other seeming exceptions to the rule are permissible.

Read 1-201 (b) (24), 3-104 (a) and Comment 1, 3-107, and 3-112 and Comments.

- Where do you find the "fixed amount of money" requirement?

> On a check, the amount to be paid is usually indicated numerically and also spelled out.

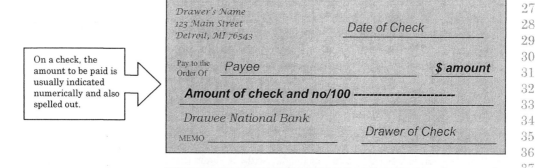

> The format for promissory notes is often similar to that used for checks.

The following case introduces concepts that are revisited in Chapter 15's coverage of various methods for the perfection of

Article 9 security interests. For current purposes, this case is useful for its analysis of Article 3's nonapplication to "payment in kind certificates" issued by the United States government to farmers. Watch for application of the "fixed amount of money" requirement.

In re George,

85 B.R. 133, 5 U.C.C. Rep. Serv. 2d 1117 (D. Kan. 1988).

John K. Pearson, Bankruptcy Judge.

The Santa Fe Credit Union furnished operating funds under an open-end credit plan to the debtors to finance their farming operation. In January 1980, Dannell Joe and Bernita Mae George (debtors), signed a security agreement giving Santa Fe a security interest in all crops planted or to be planted in consideration for the funds advanced under the open-end credit plan. On April 14, 1986, debtors signed a new security agreement and a financing statement giving Santa Fe a security interest in a "growing wheat crop" on specifically described real property and "all debtors' rights in any ASCS or other state or federal government payments pertaining" to the wheat crop. Santa Fe's financing statements covering the government payments were filed April 21, 1986, with the Kansas Secretary of State. Dannell Joe George was issued three generic PIK certificates. The first was issued May 22, 1986, and the last two were issued June 12, 1986. The PIK certificates were issued for debtors' participation in the PIK acreage-reduction and land-diversion program. After receiving the three PIK certificates, the debtors filed their Chapter 7 [bankruptcy] petition on October 20, 1986. After filing, the debtors delivered the three generic PIK certificates to Lynn D. Allison, ([bankruptcy] trustee). The trustee sold the certificates for $2,075.39, and has deposited the proceeds in the bankruptcy estate's account.

The trustees challenge the validity of the creditors' security interests on the ground that the applicable FDA/CCC regulations preempt state law and prohibit the attachment of any security interest in PIK certificates. They further assert, should the Court find state law to be applicable, that a PIK certificate is negotiable and therefore possession is required to perfect a security interest in it.

Over the last several years, Congress has adopted various programs under which eligible farmers receive a variety of price-support and other payments from the government. Around the basic programs authorized by Congress, the Department of Agriculture (USDA) has erected a veritable briar patch of regulations. The programs and regulations change from year to year. Generally, the USDA handles the various programs through the Commodity Credit Corporation, (CCC) a quasi-governmental corporation established under 15 USC §§ 714, et seq. The CCC promulgates regulations governing the administration of the programs.

Prior to 1986, the programs involved direct payment to the farmer by check. However, in the Food Security Act of 1985, Congress authorized the Secretary of Agriculture to use government-owned commodities

---

After completing Chapter 13, Part B, identify the Article 9 classification for this collateral.

ASCS is the Agricultural Stabilization and Conservation Service of the U.S. Department of Agriculture.

PIK certificates are defined on the following page.

CCC is defined below. As Chapter 15 shows, perfection of a security interest in a negotiable instrument under the 1999 revisions to Article 9 can be effectuated by possession, as the court indicates, but can also be accomplished by public filing of a financing statement. UCC 9-312 (a) and 9-313 (a) supply the relevant law.

and "negotiable" certificates redeemable in a commodity owned by the
CCC for payments under the programs. Under prior programs, the
certificates became known as PIK certificates, and the name has
continued in use even though the certificates are now generic and do
not entitle the holder to delivery of a specific commodity. They may
still, however, be redeemed in a commodity. The CCC promulgated
regulations to implement the 1986 and 1987 PIK programs. While
earlier PIK programs and cash-deficiency-payment programs
permitted assignment of the farmer's right to the payment, the final
regulations issued by the CCC for 1986 and 1987 provide: "Commodity
certificates shall not be subject to any lien, encumbrance, or other claim
or security interest, except that of an agency of the U.S. Government
arising specifically under Federal statute." 7 CFR § 770.4 (b) (2),
published October 16, 1986. . . .

The actual certificates issued to the debtors in these cases and sold by
the trustees contained the following language:

> This Certificate shall not be subject to any State law or
> regulation, including but not limited to State statutory and
> regulatory provisions with respect to commercial paper, security
> interests, and negotiable instruments. This certificate shall not be
> encumbered by any lien or other claim, except that of an agency
> of the United States Government.

The issue presented is one of law: does the federal regulation "preempt"
the state law of secured transactions, thus vitiating the creditors'
claimed security interests?

It is a fundamental precept that, to the extent a conflict exists between
state and federal law, state law must yield.

* * *

[A]lthough it is true that federal regulations may preempt state law, a
federal agency's power to do so through regulation is severely limited.
Congress' delegation of preemption power to the federal agency must
be clearly manifested. Neither the general corporate authority of the
CCC nor the Food Security Act enabling language is sufficient to
support the preemption of state commercial law attempted in the
regulations. The Court therefore holds that the antiassignment
provision of the regulation may not be used by a trustee in bankruptcy
or a debtor in possession to avoid a properly perfected security interest.
The preemptive provisions of the regulation purporting to invalidate
state-law security interests are simply unenforceable here.

. . . The sole remaining issue is how a "negotiable" certificate fits within
the scheme of the UCC. . . .

The enabling legislation authorizes the CCC to issue "negotiable
certificates" and fails to specify the nature of the farmer's rights in the
entitlement prior to the issuance of the actual certificate. Further, it
fails to define the nature of the "negotiability" of the piece of paper so
uttered.

"PIK" stands for "payment in kind."

As a matter of policy, why might this limitation make sense?

Under the PIK program, producers who plant one or more program crops (wheat, corn, grain sorghum, barley, or oats), and participate in and comply with the acreage-reduction and land-diversion program for crops, are eligible for program benefits. Under the pre-1986 program, producers became entitled to receive a quantity (in pounds or bushels) of the same commodity by reducing the acreage of the planted crops or by withdrawing the entire crop acreage base from production and devoting this acreage to conservation usage.

As of February 1, 1986, under the farm programs the CCC began issuing a "generic PIK" certificate. The U.S. Department of Agriculture issues the PIK certificates in lieu of cash to pay producers who are participating in various crop programs. The certificates are not crop-specific. They carry an expiration date. The certificates can be sold for cash, often in excess of their face value. They may also be redeemed for a specific quantity of CCC-owned commodities. Commercial organizations buy the PIK certificates and then redeem them for CCC-owned commodities by a certain date.

Upon receipt of the certificate, the farmer may and usually does transfer the certificate to a purchaser for cash or to the CCC to redeem a quantity of grain. The only requirements are that the transfer must be for the full amount of the certificate and be made by restrictive endorsement, signed by the transferor showing the name of the transferee and the date of the transfer.

> **Read UCC 3-203 (d).** Is this requirement consistent with Article 3? Restrictive indorsement is defined in 3-206 and discussed in Chapter 9, Part B.

* * *

The concept of negotiability is not a simple label; it is rather a specific legal doctrine which may not be adopted in a purblind manner. It has evolved over a period of time in commercial usage and is now generally a matter of statute. The Food Securities Act neither specially defines nor imports negotiability from some other statute. That failure makes the definition of a farmer's rights virtually impossible. In the absence of an appropriate federal definition, the Court will look to the UCC for guidance on negotiability.

* * *

. . . Since the issued generic PIK certificates are redeemable in either money *or commodities,* the right to redeem the appropriate payment in commodities does not meet the UCC's definition requiring that instruments may only be payable in money. Thus the negotiable-instrument status of the certificates is destroyed.

* * *

Simply labeling the certificate "negotiable" does not make them legally negotiable in any applicable definition of the term. PIK certificates are not negotiable documents, instruments, or securities for purposes of creating and perfecting a state-law security interest, and possession is not required to protect a lender.

The better analysis (and indeed the accepted analysis under prior PIK regulations) is that the contractual right to an unissued PIK certificate

As Chapter 13 shows, "general intangible" is one category of Article 9 collateral. Chapter 15 confirms the filing requirement referenced here.

and the certificate itself is a contract right or a general intangible requiring the creditor to file to protect its security interest.

* * *

The trustees' challenges to the validity of the creditors' security interests, therefore, are overruled, and a separate order will be entered directing the trustee in each case to turn over to the creditor the proceeds of the PIK certificates in issue.

- How must the PIK-certificate program be changed for the items to be negotiable?

Note 1: Read 3-104 (a), 3-112, and Comments 1 and 2. Comment 2 prohibits negotiable instruments from containing interest provisions that violate other law.

- What "other law" could be implicated in this context?

As *Taylor v. Roeder*, 234 Va. 99, 360 S.E.2d 191, 4 U.C.C. Rep. Serv. 2d 652 (Va. 1987), shows, variable interest rates were not expressly addressed by former Article 3, and some courts assumed instruments containing such rates were not negotiable. The *Taylor* holding illustrates the competing concerns courts faced at that time:

> [V]ariable-interest loans have become a familiar device in the mortgage lending industry. Their popularity arose when lending institutions, committed to long-term loans at fixed rates of interest to their borrowers, were in turn required to borrow short-term funds at high rates during periods of rapid inflation. Variable rates protected lenders when rates rose and benefited borrowers when rates declined. They suffer, however, from the disadvantage that the amount required to satisfy the debt cannot be ascertained without reference to an extrinsic source . . . Although that rate may readily be ascertained from published sources, it cannot be found within the "four corners" of the note.
>
> * * *
>
> The UCC introduced a degree of clarity into the law of commercial transactions which permits it to be applied by laymen daily to countless transactions without resort to judicial interpretation. The relative predictability of results made possible by that clarity constitutes the overriding benefit arising from its adoption. In our view, that factor makes it imperative that, when change is thought desirable, the change should be made by statutory amendment, not through litigation and judicial interpretation. Accordingly, we decline . . . to create an exception, by judicial interpretation, in favor of instruments providing for a variable rate of interest not ascertainable from the instrument itself. *Id.* at 104-105.

Later in its opinion, the court rejects the argument that the items should be enforced as "symbolic instruments," even if they are not negotiable.

- Where else in this chapter have you encountered a similar argument, and what was the result then?

Amberboy v. Societe de Banque Privee, 831 S.W.2d 793, 17 U.C.C. Rep. Serv. 2d 145 (Tex. 1992), in which the court takes the opposite approach from *Taylor*, includes the following language in support of the court's holding that variable interest rates are consistent with the "sum certain" requirement of Article 3:

> [T]he drafters of the UCC expressly contemplated that the courts would advance the basic purpose of the Code by construing the UCC's provisions "in the light of unforeseen and new circumstances and practices." [Citing 1-102, Comment 1.]
>
> * * *
>
> Section 3-106 lists several instances in which reference to sources outside the instrument are necessary to determine the sum payable under the instrument.
>
> Section 3-106 does not explicitly mention variable rate notes ("VRNs") because, when the UCC was developed in the 1950s and adopted in the 1960s, VRNs were virtually unknown. *Id.* at 794.

In what other instances does 3-106 permit "reference to sources outside the instrument?" Should variable interest rates be treated differently?

- Before the drafters expressly authorized VRNs as 3-112 (b) now indicates, could other courts have used the fact that 3-106 does not mention VRNs to argue for the opposite result?

The court's holding continues as follows:

> A VRN which contains provison for interest to be paid at a variable rate that is readily ascertainable by reference to a bank's published prime rate is compatible with the Code's objective of "commercial certainty." The Code does not require "mathematical certainty" but only "commercial certainty." *Id.* at 796.

- What is the distinction between "mathematical" and "commercial" certainty?

The dissenting judge in *Taylor* suggests that VRNs with specific interest-rate references such as "interest payable at three percent above the prime rate established by the Chase Manhattan Bank of New York City" should be permissible, but language such as "interest payable at the current rate" should not be.

- Can you articulate this distinction?

- From what you have read, would the *Amberboy* court recognize this distinction?

- What do the *Taylor* and *Amberboy* opinions suggest about the varying viewpoints of each court with regard to the balance of law-making power between courts and legislatures?

- Which approach is more attractive to you and why?

Note 2: Read 3-114. Other disputes over the "sum certain" requirement arise when an instrument includes numeric and textual descriptions of the sum to be paid that are in conflict with one another.

- What assumptions have the drafters of 3-114 made as to which kinds of terms (written versus numerical, and handwritten versus typed) are most likely to capture the parties' intentions?

Problem: In the following examples, which amount term prevails?

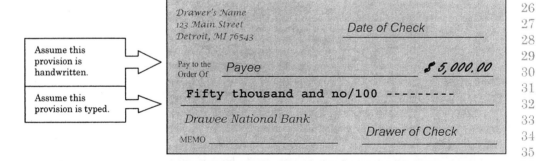

International Perspective: A Sum Certain

Read Articles 7 and 8 of the CIBN, and Section 3 of the BEA. Also consider Section 9 of the BEA, which reads as follows:

Section 3 of the BEA can be found in Part A of this chapter.

> (1) The sum payable by a bill is a sum certain within the meaning of this Act, although it is required to be paid –
>
> (a) With interest
> (b) By stated instalments
> (c) By stated instalments, with a provision that upon default in payment of any instalment the whole shall become due
> (d) According to an indicated rate of exchange or according to a rate of exchange to be ascertained as directed by the bill.
>
> (2) Where the sum payable is expressed in words and also in figures, and there is a discrepancy between the two, the sum denoted by the words is the amount payable.
>
> (3) Where a bill is expressed to be payable with interest, unless the instrument otherwise provides, interest runs from the date of the bill, and if the bill is undated from the issue thereof.

Both the BEA and the CIBN require that a negotiable instrument specify a determinate amount of money to be paid. In *The Proposed Uniform Law on International Bills of Exchange and Promissory Notes: A Discussion of Some Special and General Problems Reflected in the Form and Content, Choice of Law, and Judicial Interpretation of Articles*, 9 Cal. W. Intl. L. Rev. 30 (1979), Robert F. Blomquist critiques this portion of the CIBN, as follows:

> Among the major legal systems, definiteness of monetary obligation on the face of a commercial instrument has been a traditional requirement of negotiability. Under the Anglo-American tradition, absolute sum certainty has not been required because of the recognition of other competing business needs. For example, since commercial paper is a form of credit in addition to a mode of payment, common business practice has indulged the inclusion of interest provisions and/or installment agreements relating to the principal sum. Further, to encourage creditors to lend, the UCC allows an instrument to provide for payment with the cost of collection and/or attorney's fees upon default without destroying negotiability.
>
> The civil-law experience, reflected in [the GUL], has been less accommodating to other business needs. This tradition reflects a preference for structuring terms of credit by requiring the drawer or maker to include interest in the principal sum. The [CIBN] attempts a compromise between the Anglo-American and civil-law

How would an item "include interest in the principal sum"?

traditions by permitting a modest range of additions to a principal sum denominated on an instrument, without destroying the certainty of the sum. *Id.* at 48.

- What "additions to a principal sum" are permitted by the UCC but not the CIBN?

As Professor Kenneth C. Randall and attorney John E. Norris show in *A New Paradigm for International Business Transactions*, 71 Wash U. L.Q. 599 (1993), the CIBN allowed variable interest rates and permitted payment by installments even before the UCC was revised to allow both. Randall and Norris contextualize this decision by the CIBN drafters, as follows: "Installment and variable-interest-rate terms are . . . important modern provisions frequently desired in international transactions, particularly because, unlike checks, most negotiable instruments are instruments of credit rather than merely of payment." In *Background and Salient Features of the United Nations Convention on International Bills of Exchange and International Promissory Notes*, 10 U. Pa. J. Intl. Bus. L. 517 (1988), Gerold Herrmann provides the following additional information about the decision on the part of the CIBN drafters to permit variable interest rates:

> This insight comes from Herrmann's experience as Senior Legal Officer in the International Trade Branch of the Office of Legal Affairs for the United Nations.

> The drafters overcame the traditional objection, based on principle, that a variable rate of interest was contrary to the requirement that the sum payable be "definite." In response to concerns that the new facility might operate unfairly to the detriment of debtors, they introduced certain safeguards. Apart from the possibility of setting a certain limit to the permissible degree of variation in the interest rate, each reference rate . . . must be published (or publicly available) and must not be subject, directly or indirectly, to unilateral determination by a person named in the instrument at the time of issue, unless the person is named only in the reference-rate provisions. *Id.* at 535.

- Are these safeguards also contained in the UCC?

G. The "Time Certain" Requirement

This section highlights the distinction between "demand" (or "sight") and "time" drafts and notes, and illustrates the definiteness in timing that is required when an instrument is issued. The "time certain" requirement is important for at least two reasons: (1) for a "time" instrument to be discounted to present value, it is necessary to know its due date with certainty; and (2) as Chapter 9, Part D shows, for a holder to be a holder in due course, he or she must take the item "before maturity," which requires that the due date of the instrument be readily apparent.

Read 3-104 (a) (2), and 3-108 and Comments.

- Where do you find the "time certain" requirement?

- Which of the following graphic illustrations represents an item "payable at a definite time"?

- Which represents an item "payable on demand"?

Drawer's Name
123 Main Street
Detroit, MI 76543

December 13, 2001

Pay to the
Order Of   Payee $ amount

Amount of check and no/100 ----------------------

Drawee National Bank

                        Drawer of Check
MEMO _____

> What date is typically written in the upper right corner of a check? The answer may assist you in responding to the question above.

PROMISSORY NOTE

For value received, **forty-five days after sight**, I do hereby promise to pay to Payee of Note or order, one hundred fifty thousand and no/100 dollars ($150,000.00). The terms and conditions of such note are as follows: . . .

Maker of Note

> Is it necessary that this note include the date of issuance?

- Which of the following are "payable on demand" and which are "payable at a definite time"?

  - A promissory note, payable on "Leap Day 2008."

  - A promissory note with no due date listed.

  - A trade acceptance draft "payable at the will of the holder."

  - A trade acceptance draft "payable on April 21, 2018, or at such later date as the drawer may determine."

- A promissory note "payable on April 21, 2018, or on demand."

- A promissory note "payable on April 21, 2018, or at such later date as the holder may determine."

The following case applies the parol-evidence rule to determine whether the item in question meets the "date certain" requirement.

Ferri v. Sylvia,
100 R.I. 270, 214 A.2d 470, 3 U.C.C. Rep. Serv. 52 (1965).

Joslin, Justice.

This action of assumpsit based upon a promissory note was tried before a justice of the superior court sitting without a jury, and resulted in a decision for the plaintiff of $2,600. The defendants prosecute their exceptions to evidentiary rulings and to the decision.

The note, which is dated May 25, 1963, obligates defendants to pay to plaintiff or her order $3,000 "within ten (10) years after date." The trial justice determined that the maturity of the note was uncertain, admitted testimony of the parties as to both their intention and prior agreements, and premised upon such extrinsic evidence found that plaintiff "could have the balance that may be due at any time she needed it and that she could call for and demand the full payment of any balance that may be due or owing her at the time of her demand."

The question is whether the note is payable at a fixed or determinable future time. If the phrase "within ten (10) years after date" lacks explicitness or is ambiguous, then clearly parol evidence was admissible for the purpose of ascertaining the intention of the parties. Moreover, if it was apparent from an inspection of the note that it did not include the entire agreement of the parties, then it was permissible to accept extrinsic evidence of their prior agreements relative to its due date in supplementation and explanation of the writing; provided, however, that the collateral terms are consistent therewith and such as would normally have been excluded by the parties from the note. While the trial justice in admitting and accepting the extrinsic evidence apparently relied on these principles, neither is applicable because the payment provisions of the note are not uncertain nor are they incomplete.

> The law merchant is introduced in Chapter 1, Part A.

At the law merchant, it was generally settled that a promissory note or a bill of exchange payable "on or before" a specified date fixed with certainty the time of payment. The same rule has been fixed by statute, first under the Negotiable Instruments Law, and now pursuant to the Uniform Commercial Code. . . .

The courts in the cases we cite were primarily concerned with whether a provision for payment "on or before" a specified date impaired the negotiability of an instrument. Collaterally, of course, they necessarily considered whether such an instrument was payable at a fixed or determinable future time for, unless it was, an essential prerequisite to negotiability was lacking.

They said that the legal rights of the holder of an "on or before" instrument were clearly fixed and entitled him to payment upon an event that was certain to come, even though the maker might be privileged to pay sooner if he so elected. They held, therefore, that the due date of such an instrument was fixed with certainty and that its negotiability was unaffected by the privilege given the maker to accelerate payment. . . .

We . . . equate the word "within" with the phrase "on or before." So construed, it fixes both the beginning and the end of a period and, insofar as it means the former, it is applicable to the right of a maker to prepay, and insofar as it means the latter, it is referable to the date the instrument matures. We hold that the payment provision of a negotiable instrument payable "within" a stated period is certain as well as complete on its face and that such an instrument does not mature until the time fixed arrives.

For the foregoing reasons, it is clear that the parties unequivocally agreed that the plaintiff could not demand payment of the note until the expiration of the ten-year period. It is likewise clear that any prior or contemporaneous oral agreements of the parties relevant to its due date were so merged and integrated with the writing as to prevent its being explained or supplemented by parol evidence.

- Would the proposed parol evidence be used for explanation of, addition to, or contradiction of the item?

Refer back to Chapter 2, Part B as needed to answer this question.

- Why did the court not consider parol evidence?

Problem 1: James T. Balkus died intestate. Shortly thereafter, his sister Ann was examining his personal belongings and found six deposit slips from his savings account. On each deposit slip was written the following language: "Payable to Ann Balkus Vesely on POD. The full amount and other deposits." She sued his estate for the money. The parties agreed that POD meant payable on death.

Because savings deposit slips themselves are usually expressly marked "non-negotiable," the important issue here is what is written *on* the deposit slip, not the slip itself.

- Why are these items non-negotiable?

- How could the fact that Balkus died without a will have been important to the court in finding the items non-negotiable?

- What language could have been used to accomplish the desired result (payment at death) more effectively?

Based on *In re Estate of Balkus*, 128 Wis. 2d 246, 381 N.W.2d 593, 42 U.C.C. Rep. Serv. 877 (1985).

Problem 2:   Mickey Michael executed a promissory note to Charles Donner for $8,000 with the due date left blank. The note was assigned to Nathan Schekter, who demanded payment. Michael defended on the grounds that the note was not to become due until an indefinite date upon which the parties had agreed orally when the note was made. The court held that persons were assumed conclusively to know the legal effect of their actions, and that, "[i]f a person executes and delivers a promissory note in which no time for payment is expressed, he is charged with knowledge that it is payable on demand."

- **Read 3-108 (a).**   When someone sues on a note in which no date for payment is given, alleging it is a "demand" item payable at any time, should the other party be able to introduce a parol agreement suggesting the parties had agreed upon a specific due date?

- Should it matter whether these assertions are made by the payee rather than an assignee or holder in due course?

Based on *Schekter v. Michael*, 184 So.2d 641 (Fla. 1966).

International Perspective: Due Dates

Both the BEA and the CIBN require that payment be made at a definite time or on demand.

Read Article 9 of the CIBN. Also read Articles 10 and 11 of the BEA, which provide as follows:

Bill payable on demand
10. —(1) A bill is payable on demand —
(a) which is expressed to be payable on demand, or at sight, or on presentation; or
(b) in which no time for payment is expressed.
(2) Where a bill is accepted or indorsed when it is overdue, it shall, as regards the acceptor who so accepts it, or any indorser who so indorses it, be deemed a bill payable on demand.

Bill payable at future time
11. —(1) A bill is payable at a determinable future time within the meaning of this Act which is expressed to be payable —
(a) at a fixed period after date or sight; or

(b) on or at a fixed period after the occurrence of a specified event which is certain to happen, though the time of happening may be uncertain.

(2) An instrument expressed to be payable on a contingency is not a bill, and the happening of the event does not cure the defect.

In *The U.N. Convention on International Bills and Notes (CIBN): A Primer for Attorneys and International Bankers*, 25 U.C.C. L.J. 99 (1992), Professor John A. Spanogle states that the CIBN is different from the UCC in requiring "that the instrument be dated," which the UCC does not expressly do.

> In *The Draft Convention on International Bills of Exchange and International Promissory Notes: Formal Requisites*, 27 Am. J. Comp. Law 515 (1979), Norman Penney shows that the CIBN follows the lead of GUL Article 1 (7), which also "includes the date of issuance as an essential element among its formal requisites."

- Where does Professor Spanogle find the relevant language in both instruments?

- What distinction is he making?

The CIBN is more restrictive than the UCC with regard to the acceleration of payment, allowing acceleration only upon default in an installment. As Norman Penney shows in *The Draft Convention on International Bills of Exchange and International Promissory Notes: Formal Requisites*, 27 Am. J. Comp. Law 515 (1979), the CIBN drafters were concerned that provisions allowing acceleration "when the holder deems himself insecure" or "at will," as UCC 3-109 permits, could result in abuse.

- Is the "good faith" limitation in UCC 1-208 sufficient to prevent abuse in the use of acceleration clauses?

- Alternatively, does the CIBN provision represent a more balanced approach?

Chapter Conclusion: In leaving behind this chapter, you should be comfortable with the seven elements of negotiability these materials have presented. One way to test your comfort level with these materials is to answer one or more of the following questions:

> Those with a strong knowledge of history can make this inquiry more interesting by examining whether the answer would have been different when the United States was subject to the Gold Standard in its issuance of currency.

- Is a "Federal Reserve Note" such as a dollar bill a promissory note within the meaning of Article 3? If not, which element or elements of negotiability fail?

- Consider the following language from the pre-UCC case of *Carnwright v. Gray*, 127 N.Y. 92, 27 N.E. 835 (1891):

A promissory note is defined to be a written engagement by one person to pay absolutely and unconditionally to another person therein named, or to the bearer, a certain sum of money at a specified time or on demand. *Id.* at 99.

- Is this an accurate and complete description of the standards for negotiability under the Uniform Commercial Code?

Lawyers sometimes encounter cases in which one party to a note or draft claims the item should be deemed non-negotiable because it was issued gratuitously – in other words, without consideration. Chapter 9, Part D shows that this fact is relevant in determining whether a holder is a holder in due course. Based upon what you have learned in this chapter, is this fact also relevant to the issue of whether the item is a negotiable instrument?

Chapter 9:
Holders in Due Course

A. The Concept of a Holder

This section explains what it means to be a "holder" of a negotiable instrument, as well as how this status sets the stage for the concept of a holder in due course.

Read 1-201 (b) (15) and (21) (A), 3-105 (a) and (c), 3-201, and 3-203 (a). This material requires a brief review of some of the concepts in Chapter 7, Part B. A maker of a promissory note or drawer of a draft *issues* the instrument to the payee. Issuance is also called "first delivery." Then, the payee *transfers* the note or draft to another person for the purpose of giving that other person the right to enforce the instrument. This process can be repeated an unlimited number of times. When *transfers* are done in such a way as to be called *negotiations*, the person to whom the instrument is transferred becomes a *holder*. If the transfer does not qualify as a negotiation, it is an *assignment*, and the transferee is known as an *assignee*. As Chapter 7, Part C shows, the distinction between negotiation and assignment is important because, although a holder in due course sometimes has greater rights than his or her transferor did, an assignee can never have greater rights than his or her assignor.

> Is the payee also a holder? How do you know?

- Why does issuance require a voluntary transfer of possession, while negotiation can be voluntary or involuntary?

- Can a thief be the holder of a negotiable instrument?

> Reading 3-201, Comment 1 may assist you in answering this question.

Along the same lines, as *Holly Hill Acres, Ltd. v. Charter Bank of Gainesville*, 314 So. 2d 209, 17 U.C.C. Rep. Serv. 144 (1975), shows, the assignee of a non-negotiable instrument can never be a holder, even if the assignee is a bona-fide purchaser of the instrument for value. In that case, the court held a bank that purchased a non-negotiable mortgage promissory note would be bound by the borrower's personal defense of fraudulent inducement to the contract, to the same extent as the original payee would have been. Thus, the qualifications of a holder in due course introduced in Part D of this chapter include the initial requirements of (1) a negotiable instrument that is (2) transferred in such a way as to constitute negotiation.

> Part C of this chapter discusses the difference between personal defenses, which bind transferees who are not holders in due course, and real defenses, which bind all transferees.

- Consider the following graphic. Who can be a holder?

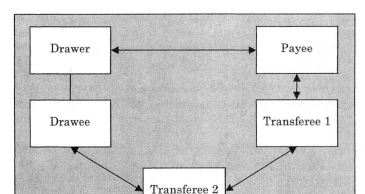

In studying these materials, note that ownership of a negotiable instrument and the right to enforce the instrument are not the same thing. Instead, ownership of an instrument is determined by property law, while rights of enforcement are covered by UCC Article 3.

- How is it possible to own an instrument without having the right to enforce it?

Note: Revisit the facts of *In re Estate of Balkus*, 128 Wis. 2d 246, 381 N.W.2d 593, 42 U.C.C. Rep. Serv. 877 (1985), introduced in Chapter 8, Part G. This chapter's treatment of the case will focus on the two promissory notes found at the brother's home along with the deposit slips that were previously discussed. The sister claimed the promissory notes had been constructively delivered to her through a letter she received from her brother in August 1974, prior to his death in December 1983. The letter included the following language:

Is "delivery" a correct word in this context? Is it the most precise word that could be used in this context? Explain your answer.

> I will bequeath to you all my other junk in my apartment, such as tools, radios, TV sets, clothing, clothes, and also the money I owe you. I have $6,000 in government bonds made out in your name, and the banker told me nobody could take it away from you. I also have two judgment notes made out to you for the amount of money I borrowed from you in 1961 and 1962. That should take care of the interest I was supposed to pay you but I didn't. *Id.* at 253.

In rejecting the sister's argument, the court held constructive delivery "occurs only when the maker indicates an intention to make the instrument an enforceable obligation against him or her by surrendering control over it and intentionally placing it under the power of the payee or a third person." Because the promissory notes remained in the brother's home at his death, the court concluded constructive delivery had not occurred.

- How could the facts be changed to show constructive delivery?

Problem: An agent of a business called the business's bank to request that a cashier's check be issued telephonically to the order of a certain payee. The bank's vice president prepared the check, together with a debit slip securing the funds from the business's account. Later that day, and before coming to pick up the check, the same agent called to say the company was being placed involuntarily in bankruptcy. Upon hearing this news, the bank vice president prepared a credit slip to balance the debit slip, and cancelled the check.

- If the payee learns of the check's creation and seeks to enforce it, can the bank successfully argue the check was never issued?

- Would the result be different if the item in question were a certified check instead of a cashier's check?

Based on *Rex Smith Propane, Inc. v. National Bank of Commerce*, 372 F. Supp. 499, 14 U.C.C. Rep. Serv. 978 (N.D. Tex. 1974).

International Perspective: Holders

Read CIBN Articles 13 and 15. The CIBN's concept of a holder is consistent with the UCC. There is, however, an important difference in terminology, as Professor John A. Spanogle points out in *The U.N. Convention on International Bills and Notes (CIBN): A Primer for Attorneys and International Bankers*, 25 U.C.C. L.J. 99 (1992):

> The concept of "transfer of an assignment" under CIBN Article 13 means the same thing as "negotiation of an instrument" does under . . . 3-201. There is no conceptual change, only a linguistic one, but "transfer" under the Convention does have a different meaning from the UCC meaning of "transfer." *Id.* at 109-110.

- How can an attorney make sure he or she understands how vocabulary such as "transfer" is being used in an international transaction involving a promissory note?

B. Indorsement

Note the Code's spelling of the word "indorsement."

This section introduces blank and special indorsements, showing how such indorsements can be used to create "bearer" or "order" paper, respectively, and how a single instrument can be both bearer paper and order paper at different points in the negotiation process. These concepts are connected with the "holder" status addressed in Part A. This section also explains the concept of agency in the negotiable-instrument context, discussing the liability of principals and agents when an agent purports to sign on a principal's behalf.

Read 3-204 (a) and (b) and Comment 1.

- To what extent does intent determine whether a signature on a negotiable instrument is an indorsement?

3-205 (d) and Comment 3 may assist you in answering this question.

- How is the purpose of an anomalous indorsement different from that of an ordinary indorsement?

The way an item is indorsed is important in determining whether the item has been negotiated, such that the transferee is a holder and might be a holder in due course.

Read 3-205 (a), (b), and (c). These subsections introduce special and blank indorsements. Negotiation of a specially indorsed item is impossible without the signature of the named party, while an item indorsed in blank can be negotiated by mere transfer of possession.

- When would a holder employ a special indorsement in choosing to negotiate an instrument to another party?

- When and how would a holder convert a blank indorsement to a special indorsement, or a special indorsement to a blank indorsement?

Read 3-206 (a), (c), and (e), and Comment 3. These subsections introduce restrictive indorsement, which is another means by which a holder may seek to control the funds an instrument represents.

- Does a holder have a greater, lesser, or equivalent ability to make an item non-negotiable than the maker or drawer does?

- Why is it fair, in the example in Comment 3, for the grocery store and bank to be liable in conversion if they cash a check, marked "for deposit only," that turns out to be stolen?

- What should an indorser do upon deciding to cash a check he or she had previously marked "for deposit only"?

- Would a restrictive, special, or blank indorsement be useful in the following circumstances? If so, which kind of indorsement would you use and why?

  - An individual doing business with an out-of-state bank wishes to mail a deposit consisting of several large checks made payable to him or her.

  - A bank customer wishes to cash a check made payable to him or her.

  - A parent wishes to sign over a rebate check to his or her child, because the child purchased the goods for which the rebate was issued, with his or her own money.

Read 3-110. Chapter 8 illustrates various ways a payee may be identified. Once the payee's identity is determined, the item must be appropriately indorsed before it can be negotiated.

- What policy preferences can you discern from each of the following circumstances addressed in 3-110?

  - An instrument is presumed to be payable to two persons alternatively, rather than jointly, when the language of the instrument is ambiguous.

  - The intent of the maker or drawer controls to whom an instrument is payable, even if the name on the instrument is not the true name of the payee.

  - When an instrument is made payable to an account number represented as being associated with an identified person, the instrument is payable to the identified person rather than the holder of the account, if the account is not held by the identified person.

  - If an instrument is made payable to an office or to a person described as holding an office, the

instrument is payable to the named person, the
incumbent, or the successor of the incumbent.

Read 3-201 (b). The form of the last indorsement controls
what is required for the further negotiation of an instrument.
Blank indorsement creates bearer paper, while special
indorsement creates order paper. If the last indorsement
renders an item bearer paper, then negotiation of the item
requires only transfer of possession. If the last indorsement
creates order paper, then negotiation requires not only transfer
of possession, but also indorsement by the named person.
Consider the following language from *Peacock v. Rhodes*, 2
Dougl. 634 (1781), a famous English case:

> A bill indorsed by the payee, is to be considered to all intents as
> cash, unless he chooses to restrain its currency, which he may do
> by a special indorsement, as "Pay the contents to William Fisher."
> The very object in view, in making negotiable [instruments], is
> that they may serve the purposes of cash . . . Here, the bill was
> indorsed in blank, but that was the same thing in effect, as if it
> had been made payable to the bearer. A blank indorsement is an
> indorsement to all the world; to anybody who shall happen to be
> the bearer. *Id.* at 634.

- Would a bill of exchange bearing the language "pay the
  contents to William Fisher" satisfy 3-104 (a) (1)?

Read 3-203 (c) and 4-205. The UCC provides special
protection to depositary banks: they are automatically deemed
holders of negotiable instruments their customers neglected to
indorse before deposit, so long as the customers were holders at
the time of deposit. In addition, as 3-203 (c) shows, the bank
has a specifically enforceable right to require the customer to
indorse the item, so long as the bank has given value for the
item. The cases in Part D of this chapter show how a bank
gives value in the context of a deposit.

- Does 4-205 offer banks more protection than 3-203 (c)
  does?

The following case illustrates the relationship between
indorsement and negotiation with regard to items payable
jointly or in the alternative. This case also shows the
importance of paying attention to the precise words used in
indorsement, to determine whether the item has been
negotiated. The case alludes to the matter of signatures by
agents, which is discussed later in this section.

These concepts are sometimes difficult to understand in the abstract. Creating mock drafts and notes may be useful.

This portion of the court's holding may bring to mind the discussion in Chapter 7, Part A, in which the purpose of negotiable instruments was introduced.

Review Chapter 8, Part C as needed to answer this question.

What is the difference between an item payable to two persons jointly and one payable to those same two persons in the alternative?

Kenerson v. Federal Deposit Insurance Corp.,
44 F.3d 19, 25 U.C.C. Rep. Serv. 2d 401 (1995).

Keeton, District Judge.

This case arises from the fraudulent conduct of an attorney who forged check indorsements and absconded with a widow's money. The attorney, however, is not a party. Rather, the widow, appellant Jean Kenerson, suing in her capacity as administratrix of her deceased husband's estate, seeks to recoup her losses from the institution that wrote the checks and the banks on which they were drawn. . . .

One week after the death of Vaughan H. Kenerson in July 1981, the Sullivan County Probate Court appointed Jean R. Kenerson and [attorney] John C. Fairbanks as co-administrators of his Estate. Mrs. Kenerson, having limited experience in financial matters, including estate administration and investments, relied on Fairbanks' legal and investment counsel. She took little, if any, role in the Estate administration.

In August 1981, Fairbanks opened an Estate checking account at First Citizens National Bank, listing himself as the sole authorized signatory. He also maintained a trust account for his law offices at the same bank.

In November 1981, Fairbanks opened an account for the Estate with Dean Witter Reynolds, Inc., into which he placed stock holdings of the Estate valued at $248,660.87. Fairbanks did not inform Mrs. Kenerson of the existence of the Dean Witter account or of his withdrawals from it, totaling $255,978.38 between November 1981 and the closing of the account in October 1984. Fairbanks received the withdrawals in the form of checks that were mailed to him. Most of the checks were issued in the following manner:

> Pay to the order of
> Estate of Vaughan H. Kenerson
> Jean R. Kenerson &
> John C. Fairbanks, Administrators

. . . The checks were drawn on Dean Witter's accounts at Morgan Guaranty Trust Company and Bank of California.

Fairbanks deposited one of the Dean Witter checks, in the amount of $150,000, in his own account at First Citizens National Bank. He deposited the other checks in the Estate checking account that he had opened at First Citizens National Bank. Fairbanks indorsed these checks by writing first his own name (without any description of his role), followed by the name of Mrs. Kenerson. No evidence was offered at trial that Mrs. Kenerson had ever affirmatively authorized Fairbanks to indorse any checks in her name.

In each instance, First Citizens National Bank, the depository bank, accepted the check and transmitted it to the drawee bank – Morgan Guaranty Trust or Bank of California – and the drawee bank paid the check. Though the record is not explicit, the parties appear to have

assumed, and we take it to be undisputed, that in each instance the
drawee bank charged Dean Witter's account.

Fairbanks withdrew from the Estate bank account, for his own benefit,
all but a small portion of the funds in that account. Mrs. Kenerson
acknowledged receiving only $20,000. In any event, appellees do not
contend that she received any more than $66,000. Beyond this sum,
little if any of the remaining funds from the Estate account with First
Citizens National Bank were disbursed in any way that inured to Mrs.
Kenerson's benefit, either individually or in her capacity as co-
administrator.

Plaintiff did not sue the most obvious target, Fairbanks; he had
disappeared. Instead she sued Dean Witter, drawer of the checks, and
Morgan Guaranty Trust and Bank of California, drawees (or payors) of
the checks. (Plaintiff initially sued the depositor bank, too, but claims
against the F.D.I.C., as that bank's successor in interest, were
dismissed by stipulation.)

Plaintiff sued Dean Witter on the theory that it was still liable to her on
the checks because she had received only a small portion of their value
and, in her capacity as co-administrator and later sole administratrix,
was entitled to recover a sum equal to the remainder of the full value.
She sued the drawee Banks on the theory that they had converted the
proceeds of the checks when they paid them over the forged
indorsements of her name.

> Plaintiff sued Dean Witter on the negotiable-instrument contract and the drawee banks on a tort theory of conversion. Both causes of action are discussed in Chapter 11.

* * *

The trial court read the checks as payable to the Estate. Based on this
reading, the court concluded that Fairbanks' negotiation of the checks –
by his own indorsement and the forged indorsement in plaintiff's name
– absolved defendants of liability to plaintiff. We conclude that the trial
court's reasoning rested on an impermissible reading of the checks and
that the rules of law invoked by the trial court do not apply to the
checks at issue in this case.

> How is this court's determination different from that of the trial court?

. . . Contrary to the determination of the trial court, . . . we conclude
that the only reasonable construction of the checks at issue in this case
is that they were payable to plaintiff and Fairbanks together (that is,
collectively) as payees, in their capacities as administrators of the
Estate.

* * *

> **Read UCC 3-309.** Current law on point is found in this provision. Which part (if any) covers the facts of this case?

Plaintiff sued Dean Witter, drawer of the checks, on the ground that
Dean Witter was liable to her on the instruments themselves. She
brought her suit against Dean Witter under New Hampshire R.S.A.
382-A:3-804, which provides in relevant part:

> The owner of an instrument which is lost, whether by destruction,
> theft, or otherwise, may maintain an action in his own name and
> recover from any party liable thereon upon due proof of his
> ownership, the facts which prevent his production of the
> instrument and its terms.

* * *

Dean Witter asserted that it was discharged from liability to plaintiff under R.S.A. 382-A:3-603 (1), which provides in relevant part:

> The liability of any party is discharged to the extent of his payment or satisfaction to the holder even though it is made with knowledge of a claim of another person to the instrument. . . .

* * *

We conclude, in light of various provisions of the statute taken together, that payment to Fairbanks was not "payment . . . to the holder" for purposes of § 3-603. Nonetheless, Fairbanks was an agent of plaintiff for some purposes, and was authorized to receive the checks on her behalf; therefore, under a rule of the common law that was not abrogated by enactment of the UCC in New Hampshire, Dean Witter's delivery of the checks to Fairbanks, followed by the payment of the checks through the Banks, absolved Dean Witter of liability on the instruments.

* * *

The New Hampshire statute, as well as the Uniform Commercial Code on which it is based, defines a "holder" as a person who is in possession of an instrument drawn, issued, or indorsed to him or to his order. A holder of an instrument has the power to negotiate or transfer it, or to discharge the instrument or enforce payment on it in his own name. Negotiation is the transfer of an instrument in such form that the transferee becomes a holder. Negotiation of an instrument that is payable to the order of specific persons is accomplished by delivery of the instrument with all the necessary indorsements.

It is undisputed that Fairbanks was in possession of the checks, and that the checks were drawn to him in his capacity as administrator. They were not drawn to him alone, however, but to him and plaintiff together in their capacities as administrators. Neither co-administrator, acting on his or her own, could negotiate the checks. Rather, the indorsements of both administrators were necessary . . . to "negotiate[ ]" the checks as that term is used in § 3-116 (b), according to which an instrument payable to two or more persons, if not in the alternative, is payable to all of them together and may be "negotiated" only by all of them. Plaintiff never indorsed the checks. Thus, Fairbanks did not properly negotiate the checks when he signed his indorsement, forged the indorsement of plaintiff, and delivered the checks to the depository bank. Consequently, Dean Witter's payment to Fairbanks on those checks did not constitute the "payment . . . to the holder" that results in discharge of a drawer's liability under § 3-603. To conclude otherwise would be entirely inconsistent with § 3- 116 (b), under which, as stated in a comment, "the rights of one [co-payee] are not discharged without his consent by the act of the other [co-payee]."

* * *

Margin notes:

Read 3-602 (c), which contains the current UCC rule on point.

As between Mrs. Kenerson and Dean Witter, which party was in the best position to avoid the loss?

This rule is now found in UCC 3-110 (d).

Similarly, because the checks were not properly negotiated by Fairbanks, the depository bank did not become a holder of the checks when Fairbanks delivered them to the bank. Thus, Dean Witter's payment to the depository bank, through the drawee banks, also did not constitute payment to a holder under § 3-603.

[The portion of the court's opinion relating to the allocation of loss between the banks and Mrs. Kenerson based upon the attorney's forgery has been omitted and is revisited in Chapter 10, Part B.]

- How could Dean Witter prevent losses like Mrs. Kenerson's?

Problem 1: Price, Miller, Evans & Flowers was a law firm representing clients involved in construction contracts to be performed by Leo Proctor Construction Company. Proctor was to construct four Pizza Hut restaurants and receive progress payments for doing so. On January 3, 1979, the law firm made a payment on behalf of its clients in the amount of about $37,000. The payment was made via two checks payable to Proctor, drawn on the law firm's trust account with First National Bank of Jamestown.

On January 4, an employee of Proctor presented the checks to Marine Midland Bank, where Proctor did not maintain an account. The employee requested the funds be wire-transferred to Proctor's account with the First National Bank of Bethany. Proctor did not indorse the checks, but the bank employee to whom they were presented stamped the checks "credited to the account of the payee herein named/Marine Midland National Bank" and carried out the requested wire transfer.

> What was the apparent purpose of this stamp?

After Proctor had been given the checks, one of the law firm's clients informed it Proctor was in default of its obligations under the construction contracts and, at the client's request, the law firm stopped payment on the checks. First National Bank of Jamestown returned the checks unpaid. Marine Midland Bank sought to recover the funds from Proctor and, upon learning the company had filed for bankruptcy, demanded payment from the law firm. Marine Midland Bank had no knowledge of Proctor's default.

In seeking to recover from the law firm, Marine Midland Bank introduced evidence that six prior progress payments had been successfully paid in exactly the manner these two checks had been processed. The bank also showed it had cashed many payroll checks for Proctor employees without incident, except that two checks were returned for insufficient funds. In processing these checks, the bank had made several telephone calls to Proctor's bank to check its credit or ensure that sufficient funds were on deposit. Assume the evidence of Proctor's default under the construction contracts is uncontroverted.

- Who should prevail and why?

Based on *Marine Midland Bank, N.A. v. Price, Miller, Evans & Flowers*, 57 N.Y.2d 220, 441 N.E.2d 1083, 34 U.C.C. Rep. Serv. 1207 (1982).

Problem 2: Cathay Trading Corporation delivered to Asian International, Ltd. a check for $200,000 for ten separators. The President and Treasurer of Asian International indorsed the check to the order of Ben F. Fort, Jr., a third party, in repayment of a loan from Fort to Asian International. Fort deposited the check in his Merrill Lynch bank account, and Merrill Lynch credited his account and received payment from the drawee bank.

> A separator is defined as "a device for separating liquids of different specific gravities (as cream from milk) or liquids from solids. *Merriam-Webster Collegiate Dictionary* (11th ed.).

- For Merrill Lynch to be a holder of the check, must each of the following have indorsed the check at the time of the deposit?

  - Ben F. Fort, Jr.
  - An authorized agent of Asian International, Ltd.
  - An authorized agent of Merrill Lynch

Based on *Asian International, Ltd. v. Merrill Lynch, Pierce, Fenner and Smith, Inc.*, 435 So. 2d 1058, 37 U.C.C. Rep. Serv. 171 (La. Ct. App. 1983).

Signatures by Agents

Read 3-401 and Comment 1, 3-402 and Commentary, and 3-403. Signature is a legally important event under the Code, making the signer liable for the amount of the negotiable instrument. When a purported agent signs an instrument on behalf of some principal, two issues are raised: (1) whether the principal is bound by the agent's signature, and (2) whether the agent is personally bound.

- Which part of 3-402 addresses whether an agent is bound when he or she signs an instrument on behalf of a principal?

- Which part of 3-402 addresses whether a principal is bound when an agent signs on its behalf?

- What role, if any, does parol evidence have in establishing an agent's liability on a negotiable instrument?

- What role, if any, does it have in establishing the liability of a principal when an agent signs on its behalf?

- How and why is the rule in 3-402 (c) for checks different from the rules in the rest of 3-402 for notes and non-check drafts?

- Who is liable on a negotiable instrument signed by an alleged agent without actual, implied, or express authority to do so?

- Can a principal be liable on a note on which its name does not appear?

Note 1: *Security Pacific National Bank v. Chess*, 58 Cal. App. 3d 555, 19 U.C.C. Rep. Serv. 544 (1976), involved a series of promissory notes payable to Petroleum Equipment Leasing Company of Tulsa, Oklahoma (PELCO). The notes were properly indorsed by PELCO and transferred to Equipment Leasing Company of California (ELC). Once in ELC's possession, some of the notes were indorsed "Richard L. Burns" or "Richard L. Burns, Pres.," and the validity of these indorsements as ELC's signature was questioned. In finding Burns' signature would bind ELC, the court held as follows:

> Burns was at the time the president of ELC, and there is no question of his authority, or any reason to doubt his intention thereby to effect a transfer of the notes to [a third party now seeking to enforce them]. His handwriting therefore constitutes the signature of the corporation, under the principle that a party may adopt any form or symbol as its signature for a particular transaction. *Id.* at 561.

- Under 3-402, would Burns be personally liable on the notes?

Note 2: *Pollin v. Mindy Manufacturing Co.*, 211 Pa. Super. 87, 236 A.2d 542, 4 U.C.C. Rep. Serv. 827 (1967), addresses checks signed in a representative capacity. Benjamin and Arthur Pollin owned the Girard Check Exchange, where employees of Mindy Manufacturing Company brought payroll checks drawn on Continental Bank and Trust to be cashed. The Pollins cashed the checks and then indorsed and deposited them in Girard Check Exchange's account with Provident National Bank of Philadelphia. After going through the collection process dictated by Article 4 and described in Chapter 10, Part A, the checks were presented to Continental, which refused to pay because insufficient funds remained in Mindy Manufacturing's account after the bank had exercised its right of set-off to satisfy a pre-existing debt. The Pollins contacted Mindy Manufacturing, which refused to reimburse Girard Check Exchange for the bad checks. The Pollins then sought to recover from Robert F. Apfelbaum, president of Mindy Manufacturing, on a theory of personal liability. The checks were pre-printed with the name of the corporation, and Apfelbaum signed the checks with only his signature, providing no indication he was signing in a representative capacity.

> The right of set-off is described in Chapter 10, Part B.

In finding Mr. Apfelbaum was not personally liable, the court noted the checks clearly showed on their face that they were drawn on a corporate payroll account over which Apfelbaum had no control as an individual. The court found (1) the check, when completed, was clearly that of a corporation and not of any individual, (2) the corporation could not be liable on any pre-printed check unless it was signed by an authorized individual, and (3) because corporations act only through individuals, it is natural (and necessary) that an individual sign a corporate check. Since Apfelbaum was authorized to sign checks for Mindy Manufacturing, the court held he was not personally liable for the payroll checks in issue.

- Would the result differ for a trade acceptance draft?

Problem: Oliver Martin was the president and sole shareholder of Elliott Bay Investment Company, and Nancy Christopherson was the company's salesperson and real-estate broker. Richard and Josie Zeldenrust owed Elliott Bay several commissions as a result of real-estate transactions, and executed several promissory notes payable to Elliott Bay in payment of these commissions. Martin transferred and delivered the notes to Christopherson in payment of certain salary obligations. Martin signed the back of the notes, as follows:

> Pay to the order of Nancy Christopherson
> Oliver H. Martin

> What, if any, additional information do you need to answer this question?

- Is Christoperson a holder of these notes?

- How does the previous question relate to the concept of signatures by agents?

Based on *Wesche v. Martin*, 64 Wash. App. 1, 822 P.2d 812, 17 U.C.C. Rep. Serv. 2d 510 (1992).

As Chapter 8, Part C shows, the CIBN does not permit instruments to be issued as bearer paper, but an item issued as order paper becomes bearer paper by indorsement in blank.

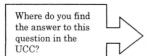

International Perspective: Indorsement

Read CIBN Articles 14 and 16. The CIBN is consistent with the UCC in recognizing special and blank indorsements, and in making it possible for such indorsements to convert a single instrument from order paper to bearer paper and vice versa.

Consider the following excerpt from the BEA:

Article 32: Requisites of a valid indorsement

(3). Where a bill is payable to the order of two or more payees or indorsees who are not partners, all must indorse, unless the one indorsing has authority to indorse for the others.

- Is this provision consistent with the UCC?

Where do you find the answer to this question in the UCC?

C. Real and Personal Defenses

The following material illuminates the significance of holder-in-due-course status.   A holder in due course escapes any "personal defenses" an obligor might raise but is bound by any "real defenses"; other transferees are bound by both real and personal defenses. Real defenses generally involve problems with mutual assent that are sufficiently serious to render the underlying obligation void, while personal defenses generally involve less severe circumstances that render the transaction voidable.

Read 3-305 (a) and (b) and Comment 1.

- Which portion of 3-305 sets forth real defenses?

- Which portion of 3-305 sets forth personal defenses?

- Which are real defenses and which are personal defenses?

  - Fraud in the factum
  - Fraudulent inducement
  - Failure of consideration
  - Discharge by payment
  - Discharge in bankruptcy
  - Economic duress
  - Physical duress
  - Illegality

1
2
3
4
5
6
7
8
9
10
11
12
13
14
15
16
17
18
19
20
21
22
23
24
25
26
27
28
29
30
31
32
33
34
35
36
37
38
39
40
41
42
43
44
45
46
50
51
52
53

■ What real defense normally renders contracts voidable rather than void as a matter of state law?

The following case discusses the interplay between a promissory-note payee's fraud and the maker's duty to read, in the context of determining whether a later holder is a holder in due course.

Roberts v. Agricredit Acceptance Corp.,
764 N.E.2d 776 (2002).

Mathias, Judge.

[Leland] Roberts was in the farming-and-construction business. It is unclear from the record whether he continues these endeavors. During his operation of these businesses, Roberts purchased and traded farm-and-construction equipment, tools, and supplies from and with Sulphur Implement Corporation. In 1996, Roberts and Sulphur executed a Lease Agreement, an Additional Terms and Conditions sheet, a Leased Equipment Addendum, and a Leased Agreement Purchase Option Supplement (hereafter known collectively as "the Lease Agreement"). Although Roberts acknowledges his signature on each of the documents, Roberts executed all of these documents in blank.

As part of its business practices, Sulphur would sell its commercial paper, which included commercial paper involved in its transactions with Roberts, to Agricredit [Acceptance Corporation], a commercial-lending institution with its principal place of business in Des Moines, Iowa. . . . On July 19, 1996, Sulphur assigned the Lease Agreement to Agricredit for value. Subsequent to the assignment, Agricredit received Lease Agreement payments, pursuant to the terms and conditions of its recourse agreement with Sulphur. However, Agricredit did not receive its January 1, 1999, payment, and instituted default proceedings.

According to the terms of the Lease Agreement, Roberts agreed to pay the rental price in four equal annual installments payable in advance on the first day of January, commencing January 1, 1997. Roberts disputes that he made any of these payments to either Sulphur or Agricredit.

Also in accordance with its recourse agreement with Sulphur, Agricredit sought to recover against Sulphur for the missed payment, but discovered that Sulphur had filed a petition for relief under Chapter 11 of the United States Bankruptcy Code. As a result of the bankruptcy proceeding, Agricredit could not collect under its recourse agreement with Sulphur, and proceeded against Roberts for default. Roberts disputed liability, forcing Agricredit to file suit against Roberts.

Under Chapter 11, a debtor-in-possession may seek reorganization pursuant to a court-confirmed plan. The "automatic stay" found in 11 USC § 362 generally prevents creditors from proceeding against a debtor who has filed a bankruptcy petition, while the stay is in effect.

On July 31, 2000, Agricredit filed a Motion for Summary Judgment asserting holder-in-due-course status under a valid assignment. Roberts responded to Agricredit's Motion on September 18, 2000, asserting a defense of fraud under Indiana Code section 26-1-3.1-305. After hearing oral argument, the trial court determined that Roberts' fraud defense failed as a matter of law, that there were no genuine issues of material fact, and that Agricredit was entitled to judgment as a matter of law. Roberts now appeals. Additional facts will be provided as necessary.

* * *

While Roberts does not deny the execution of the Lease Agreement, he argues that he executed the Lease Agreement upon the express condition that its subject would be new farm-and-construction equipment. Specifically, Roberts claims that the farm-and-construction equipment listed in the Lease Agreement was of such poor quality and age that, had he known it was to be the subject of the Lease Agreement, he never would have executed the Lease Agreement in blank. Roberts argues that he never granted Sulphur the authority to complete the Lease Agreement to apply to the equipment Roberts received, and that, because Sulphur acted without his authority, its actions amounted to fraud.

> **What kind of fraud must Roberts prove for him to escape liability to a holder in due course? Do the facts support such a defense?**

Roberts does not dispute the assignment of the Lease Agreement to Agricredit or that Agricredit was a holder in due course; he merely asserts that, as a holder in due course, Agricredit is subject to the defenses of Indiana Code section 26-1-3.1-305, in the instant case 26-1-3.1-305 (a), and is therefore precluded from enforcing Roberts' obligation under the Lease Agreement because of Sulphur's fraudulent actions.

* * *

> **What distinction is the court drawing, and what is the legal effect of the distinction?**

When considering the issue of fraud, we focus on the element of the obligor's reliance, in two distinct parts: the *fact* of reliance and the *right* of reliance. Regarding the fact of reliance, our supreme court has previously stated:

> [w]hen both parties are dealing at arm's length and one party, in spite of the facts well known to him, deliberately ignores such facts and chooses to believe statements to the contrary, he closes his eyes to the truth and deliberately takes a chance. It then cannot be said that he was injured in law. All that can be said is that he gambled and lost.

Plymale v. Upright, 419 N.E.2d 756, 761 (Ind. Ct. App. 1981), *citing Security Trust Co. v. O'Hair*, 103 Ind. App. 56, 61, 197 N.E.2d 694 (1935). The Lease Agreement at issue was executed in 1996. According to Roberts' testimony, he only had the right to use the leased equipment, which was stored on Sulphur's site, pursuant to the Lease Agreement, following its execution. He alleges that he contested the condition of the equipment, but he did not seek to modify the contract terms, or rescind the contract and enter into a new one. The dispute did not arise until Agricredit sought recourse against Roberts.

The *right* of reliance is far more difficult to determine, as it is bound up in the duty of individuals to be diligent in safeguarding their interests. It is well settled that "[a] man who can read and does not read an instrument which he signs is, as a general rule, guilty of negligence."

Robinson v. Glass, 94 Ind. 211, 212, 1884 WL 5217 (1883). Moreover, it is also settled that where persons stand mentally on equal footing, and in no fiduciary relation, the law will not protect one who fails to exercise common sense and judgment. Common sense dictates, and our system of jurisprudence requires, the application of a principle that parties engaged in the negotiation of a contract or the sale and purchase of property be obligated to protect their interest by reading the attendant documents before signing.

> How are the reasonable expectations of parties different when a fiduciary is involved?

Based on the record before us on appeal, it is clear that, although Roberts may have initially relied on the alleged representations of Sulphur, Roberts had no right to rely on them, and failed to clearly contest Sulphur's provision of equipment at issue pursuant to the Lease Agreement. Therefore, Roberts' fraud claim must fail as a matter of law.

Roberts and Sulphur enjoyed an extensive working relationship, beginning sometime prior to 1990, for the purchase and sale of farm-and-construction equipment. According to the testimony of the parties, this mutually beneficial relationship continued for years without incident. Presumably, each transaction between Roberts and Sulphur involved the signing of lease documents and, although the current appeal involves signatures in blank, Roberts argues that there is no history of signing documents in such a manner. Roberts simply failed to read the Lease Agreement prior to signing, and the law will not protect him for his failure to exercise his own common sense and judgment. Also, because this is not the first transaction involving these parties, Roberts could not have been totally ignorant of the Lease Agreement's contents. After a six-year business relationship with Sulphur, Roberts was certainly not without knowledge and had a reasonable opportunity to learn of the character or essential terms of the Lease Agreement. Therefore, his fraud claim must fail as a matter of law.

Because Agricredit was a holder in due course not subject to any valid defense in Indiana Code section 26-1-3.1-305 (a), we find that the trial court did not err in granting Agricredit's motion for summary judgment.

- Does Roberts have a valid cause of action against anyone?

Note: *Bankers Trust Co. v. Litton Systems, Inc.*, 599 F.2d 488, 26 U.C.C. Rep. Serv. 513 (C.A.N.Y. 1979), demonstrates a layer of complexity in the law of illegality that can be a trap for the unwary. Litton Systems, Inc., decided to purchase photocopiers to be used in the branch offices of its private telephone business. Royal Typewriter Company was a subsidiary of Litton, and a Royal salesperson recommended that Litton purchase photocopiers from Regent Leasing Corporation. As it turned out, this salesperson was receiving kickbacks from Regent for making this recommendation. Regent purchased the equipment from Royal and leased it to Litton.

After reading the materials contained in Chapter 13, make sure you can identify the appropriate classification for this collateral.

To finance the purchase of the machines, Regent borrowed money from Bankers Trust Company and assigned the Litton leases as security. Litton later defaulted on the leases. In defending against the lender's suit for collection, Litton claimed the kickbacks rendered Litton's obligations void and therefore served as a defense, even as against a holder in due course such as Bankers Trust.

The court noted, as a preliminary matter, that there is nothing illegal about leasing photocopiers. Only the bribery contract between the Royal salesperson and Regent was illegal. Because there was a direct connection between the bribery contract and the leasing contract, Regent would not be permitted to enforce the lease contracts. The more difficult question was whether Bankers Trust would be subject to the same defense. Thus, the critical question was whether the bribery rendered the obligation between Litton and Regent void or simply voidable. Making an analogy to the personal defense of fraud in the inducement, the court concluded the lender should be able to enforce the contract despite the salesperson's illegal conduct.

A second important case in understanding the illegality defense is *Kedzie and 103rd Currency Exchange, Inc. v. Hodge,* 156 Ill. 2d 112, 619 N.E.2d 732, 21 U.C.C. Rep. Serv. 2d 682 (1993). As that case shows, for illegality to prevent enforcement of a negotiable instrument, there must be a clear connection in existing law between the illegal conduct and the enforceability of the negotiable instrument.

Fred Fentress agreed to install a flood-control system at the Chicago home of Eric and Beulah Hodge for $900. In partial payment, Mrs. Hodge wrote a $500 check payable to "Fred Fentress – A-OK Plumbing," drawn on the Hodges' joint account at Citicorp. Fentress never performed the promised work for the Hodges, so Eric Hodge called Fentress to tell him the contract was cancelled. The same day, Hodge placed a stop-payment order with Citicorp.

Stop payment is covered in Chapter 10, Part B.

Fentress took the check to the Kedzie and 103rd Currency Exchange, a check-cashing company, endorsed it as sole owner of A-OK Plumbing, and obtained payment. Currency Exchange presented the check to Citicorp, which returned the check unpaid in accordance with the stop-payment order. Currency Exchange sued Mrs. Hodge for the value of the check. In the ensuing litigation, Mrs. Hodge admitted Currency Exchange was a holder in due course, but claimed the check was void under a theory of illegality. Illinois Plumbing Law required that all plumbing be performed by licensed plumbers and made noncompliance a misdemeanor. Currency Exchange admitted Fentress was not a licensed plumber, but argued it should be able to enforce the check anyway.

In holding for Currency Exchange, the court distinguished between an illegal transaction and the unenforceability of an instrument issued in connection with the transaction: "Unless the instrument arising from a contract or transaction is itself made void by statute, the illegality defense under Section 3-305 is not available to bar the claim of a holder in due course." The court noted, by way of comparison, that usury is illegal, but usurious negotiable instruments are not usually deemed void. Instead, courts typically grant relief targeted at the usury alone – such as reducing the interest to be paid.

> Make sure you can articulate the court's distinction.

- Consider the following language from the dissent, which claimed Currency Exchange did not prove it was a holder in due course and probably was not one:

It can hardly be doubted that any currency exchange would question whether it would be able to collect on an uncertified personal check. Further, the check in this case was made payable to "Fred Fentress—A-OK Plumbing. . . ." Any currency exchange presented with such a check and indorsement would have to question whether the named individual was indeed the sole owner of the named business and entitled to the proceeds of the check.

Also, this personal check was made payable to the order of a business. It is reasonable to assume that a businessperson would have a business bank account where the check could be negotiated without a fee. Why would such a person choose to pay a fee to a currency exchange? *Id.* at 126.

- Should check-cashing companies take on a higher burden than banks in proving holder-in-due-course status?

- What could Mr. and Mrs. Hodge have done to avoid this loss?

> After reading Chapter 12, return to this question and consider whether payment by credit or debit card would have offered more protection.

Problem 1: Several partners associated with a law firm executed a promissory note to a bank in return for the bank's loan to the firm. Later, the law firm declared bankruptcy, the partners defaulted on the note, and the FDIC sought to collect as successor in interest to the bank, which had become insolvent. The partners responded by raising a claim of duress, claiming they signed the note only because of the threat that their wages and standing in the firm would decrease if they refused.

> The special holder-in-due-course status of the FDIC is presented in Part E of this chapter.

- If the partners proved their duress claim, could the FDIC, as a holder in due course, enforce the note anyway?

Based on *Federal Deposit Insurance Corp. v. Meyer*, 755 F. Supp. 10, 13 U.C.C. Rep. Serv. 2d 1154 (D.D.C. 1991).

Problem 2: Jim and Marie Estepp sought to consolidate their debt through United Bank and Trust Co., which was unwilling to loan money to them without the signature of a third party who owned property locally. Mr. Estepp therefore approached Marvin O. Schaeffer, who worked under Estepp as a groundskeeper at the Tantallon Country Club and owned real estate in the area. Schaeffer had known Estepp for eight years at the time and later testified, "I thought he was a wonderful guy," adding that Estepp had assisted him in making funeral arrangements when his wife died. Upon Estepp's request, Schaeffer signed the note as a surety.

Consider the following exchange between Schaeffer, who completed third grade, had a limited ability to read, and suffered loss of vision earlier in his life due to a bottle explosion, and the attorney for United Bank, which sought to recover from Schaeffer after the Estepps defaulted.

Q: Well, Mr. Schaeffer, will you please tell us why you do not feel apparently that you should pay this debt?

A: Because Jim Estepp when he told me to sign that paper it wasn't for paying a debt.

Q: Well now, you are saying Jim Estepp. You are not saying United Bank and Trust Company; is that correct?

A: No. Jim told me that when I filled the application out to sign and I signed it. He said it was a character witness.

Q: Are you stating nobody explained to you that this was a note?

A: No, sir.

- Who should prevail?

- What facts are most important in your analysis?

Based on *Schaeffer v. United Bank & Trust Co. of Maryland*, 32 Md. App. 339, 360 A.2d 461, 20 U.C.C. Rep. Serv. 125 (1976).

International Perspective: Defenses

Read CIBN Articles 28, 29, and 30. The CIBN refers to a
"protected holder," whereas the UCC refers to a "holder in due
course." The two are similar but not identical. Both provide
special rights to these classes of holders. As Gerold
Herrmann's article *Background and Salient Features of the
United Nations Convention on International Bills of Exchange
and International Promissory Notes*, 10 U. Pa. J. Intl Bus. L.
517 (1988), shows, the CIBN represents a compromise between
the common-law and civil-law traditions on this point:

> With regard to the right of the holder of an instrument and its
> limitation by the rights or defenses that others may invoke against
> him, a sharp contrast between the Geneva system and the
> common-law system had to be reconciled. The cornerstones of the
> Geneva system in this respect are GUL Article 16, which subjects
> the lawful holder to the right of a dispossessed person, provided
> that the holder had acquired the instrument in bad faith or with
> gross negligence, and GUL Article 17, which opens the door for
> certain personal defenses only if the holder, in acquiring the
> instrument, knowingly acted to the detriment of the debtor. These
> provisions, apart from the fact that they have given rise to
> considerable divergences in the case law of Geneva States, do not
> provide a complete list of the defenses which may actually be
> raised. . . .

> The common-law system, which combines the rights to an
> instrument and the defenses against liability on the instrument,
> uses a two-tiered system distinguishing between a normal holder
> and a holder in due course. While the normal holder is less
> protected than the lawful holder under the Geneva system, the
> holder in due course is accorded special protection. However, it is
> far from easy to acquire the status of holder in due course,
> particularly because of the requirement that one be without
> knowledge of any claim to or defense upon the instrument,
> whether the claim or defense might be relied upon by the
> respective debtor or a third person.

> It was this all-or-nothing approach which proved especially
> unacceptable to representatives of the Geneva States, who
> preferred a more individualized approach sensitive to the
> individual creditor-debtor relationship. The final consensus, as
> reflected in [CIBN] Articles 28 to 30, was facilitated by a
> concession of common-law representatives . . . .

> The framework of the Convention as finally agreed to is, in short,
> a two-tiered system that distinguishes between a protected holder
> (reminiscent of the "holder in due course") and a mere holder (who
> is not a "protected holder"). This latter holder is not, however,
> completely unprotected. He derives a considerable degree of

protection from the rules in [CIBN] Article 28, subsections (1) (b), (1) (c), and (2), indicating that claims and certain defenses – in line with the above individualized approach – may be raised against him only if he knew of them or was involved in a fraud or theft concerning the instrument. *Id.* at 526-527.

- What is the GUL equivalent of the UCC's "holder in due course" and the CIBN's "protected holder"?

In *The U.N. Convention on International Bills and Notes (CIBN): A Primer for Attorneys and International Bankers*, 25 U.C.C. L.J. 99 (1992), Professor John A. Spangole adds some additional context:

Under the CIBN, the protected holder cuts off all defenses against remote parties except incapacity, fraud in the factum, forgery, alteration, nonpresentment, and the statute of limitations, and also any fraud defenses that arise in an underlying transaction to which the holder and the defendant were both parties. This list of defenses is longer than the comparable list of defenses available against a holder under the Geneva system, but much shorter than the list of "real defenses" available against a "holder in due course" in all common-law systems. The U.S. Department of State's Study Group on CIBN recommended that duress, illegality, and insolvency proceedings not be included in the list of real defenses under the Convention because such defenses would depend upon the local law of a wide range of legal systems, and foreseeably could be the subject of abuse under some of those other legal systems. *Id.* at 117.

- Based on what you have read, compare and contrast the UCC, GUL, and CIBN approaches with one another.

D. Proving Holder-in-Due-Course Status

This section introduces the basic requirements for proving holder-in-due-course status. The holder in due course is compared with and contrasted to the Article 2 bona-fide purchaser for value.

Read 3-302 (a). 3-302 (a) identifies five elements that must be satisfied for a holder to be a holder in due course:

(1) The holder must take the item for value;

(2) The item must not show signs of being overdue or having been dishonored;

1
2
3
4
5
6
7
8
9
10
11
12
13
14
15
16
17
18
19
20
21
22
23
24
25
26
27
28
29
30
31
32
33
34
35
36
37
38
39
40
41
42
43
44
45
46
50
51
52
53

(3) The item must bear no indicia of suspicious irregularity or incompleteness;

(4) The holder must act in good faith; and

(5) The holder must have no notice of any defense to the enforcement of the item.

As is the modern trend, this section will deal with elements (3), (4), and (5) as a single requirement.

- What do elements (3), (4), and (5) have in common that would justify treating them as one?

- The parallels between a holder in due course and a bona-fide purchaser for value are obvious. Why do you suppose the UCC does not use the same term to describe both?

As *Peoria Savings and Loan Association v. Jefferson Trust and Savings Bank*, 81 Ill. 2d 461, 410 N.E.2d 845, 29 U.C.C. Rep. Serv. 1305 (1980), shows, holder-in-due-course status is determined when the holder acquires the item. That case involved a check-kiting scheme. The kiter obtained a cashier's check from Peoria Savings and Loan Association by supplying a personal check drawn on an account with Northern Trust Company. Peoria Savings issued the check without first verifying the personal check. The kiter then indorsed and delivered the Peoria Savings check to Jefferson Trust and Savings Bank, where he had an account. Jefferson Trust and Peoria Savings were located next door to one another. After the check was delivered to Jefferson Trust, but before it was processed by a teller, representatives of Peoria Savings contacted Jefferson Trust suggesting its depositor was involved in a kiting scheme and the Northern Trust check would be dishonored for insufficient funds, causing Peoria Savings to suffer a loss if Jefferson Trust chose to deposit the check. Jefferson Trust chose to process the cashier's check, and Peoria Savings sued to recover its lost funds. In finding for Jefferson Trust, the court held the bank was a holder in due course when the cashier's check was delivered to it, and this status did not change as a result of the information the bank received thereafter.

> Check kiting is discussed in Chapter 10, Part A.

> After you have completed the materials in Chapter 10, Part A, return to this case and make sure you understand why Peoria Savings would suffer a loss under these facts.

- Can you explain the court's holding by reference to the concept of the cheapest cost avoider presented in Chapter 3, Part B?

Similarly, in *Lynnwood Sand and Gravel, Inc. v. Bank of Everett*, 29 Wash. App. 686, 630 P.2d 489, 33 U.C.C. Rep. Serv.

1703 (1981), the court held that "[s]ubsequent notice of infirmities in the instrument has no effect upon the rights of a holder in due course, absent a showing of bad faith."

Where do you find the relevant definition of good faith in your jurisdiction? The Legislative Note to 3-103 may assist you in answering this question.

- Did Jefferson Trust act in bad faith by depositing the check?

When a Holder Gives Value

Read 3-303 and Comment 1, 4-210 (a) and (b) and Comment 1, and 4-211 and Comments. It is obvious that a holder gives value when it receives a promissory note in exchange for credit, or a check in exchange for goods. More complex situations arise when performance has been promised in return for an instrument but not yet given, or when a depositary bank credits a check to the account of the holder.

- Is an executory promise "consideration" under contract law?

- Is an executory promise "value" under Article 3?

4-205 (1) may assist you in answering this question.

- Is a depositary bank a holder of a deposited item?

4-201 (a) may assist you in answering this question.

- Is a depository bank an owner of a deposited item?

Determining when a bank gives value requires an understanding of how banks credit depositors' accounts.

- **Read 4-210 (b)** and consider which of the following is the more accurate description of how banks manage deposit accounts.

The "shelf" analogy: Like cartons of milk in a grocery store, the newest cash is "loaded from the back of the shelf," pushing older cash forward to be spent first.

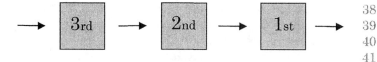

The "stack" analogy: Like dishes in a cabinet, the newest cash is "lifted from the top, used, and replaced" with even newer cash. The oldest cash is used only when the account is exhausted entirely.

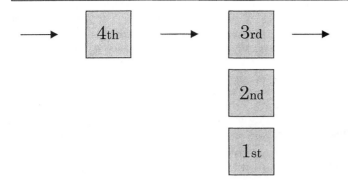

The following case reviews how Article 3 resolves conflicting numerical and written amounts and explores the concepts of value, irregularity, and notice insofar as they relate to holder-in-due-course status.

This concept is introduced in Chapter 8, Part E.

St. Paul Fire and Marine Insurance Co. v. State Bank of Salem,
    412 N.E.2d 103, 30 U.C.C. Rep. Serv. 557 (Ind. App. 1980).

Neal, Judge.

On November 26, 1975, [Mr.] Stephens, a farmer, delivered and sold 184 bushels of corn to Aubrey[, Inc.] for $478.23. Aubrey was engaged at the time in the sale and distribution of feed and grain in Louisville, Kentucky, under the name of Aubrey Feed Mills, Inc. The following day, Aubrey prepared its check payable to Stephens in payment for the corn and mailed it to Stephens. The check was prepared in the following fashion: the amount "478.23" was typewritten upon the line customarily used to express the amount of the check in numbers, abutting the printed dollar sign. On the line customarily used to express the amount in words there appeared "The sum of $100478 and 23 cts," which was imprinted [and perforated] in red by a checkwriting machine; the line ended with the printed word "Dollars."

On December 9, 1975, Stephens appeared at the [State Bank of Salem] branch in Hardinsburg, Indiana, and presented the Aubrey check and two other items totaling $5,604.51 to the branch manager, Charles Anderson. Stephens told Anderson that he wished to apply these funds to the amount of his indebtedness to the Bank, to withdraw $2,000.00 in cash, and to deposit the balance in his checking account. During the interval between November 27, 1975, and December 9, 1975, someone had typed on the check the figures "100" immediately before the typed figures "478.23." This was rather crudely done, and involved typing the "100" in an uneven line; the second "0" was typed directly over the printed dollar sign on the check.

Anderson questioned Stephens about the Aubrey check, since Stephens's prior dealings with the Bank had not involved transactions in the amount represented by the Aubrey check. Anderson also knew that Stephens had filed a voluntary petition in bankruptcy several months prior, but had subsequently reaffirmed his obligations to the Bank. Stephens explained that he had purchased a large quantity of corn in northern Indiana and had sold it in Kentucky at a higher price.

Evidently satisfied with his explanation, Anderson stamped nine promissory notes, of which Stephens was maker, "paid" and returned them to Stephens. Anderson then directed a teller at the Bank to fill out a deposit slip for the transaction. At that point, neither Anderson nor the teller noticed the typewritten modification on the check. The transaction consisted of applying the funds represented by the three items in the deposit ($106,082.74) to Stephens's debt represented by the nine promissory notes ($31,851.81), an installment payment, of which Stephens was a joint obligor, of $27,559.27, accrued interest owed the Bank by Stephens in the amount of $5,265.65, and the $2,000 cash given to Stephens. The balance was credited to Stephens's account. Stephens then left the Bank.

Later that afternoon, Anderson began thinking about the transaction and examined the items in the deposit. He noted that Aubrey's check bore signs of possible tampering and contacted Aubrey's office in Louisville to inquire about the validity of the check. An Aubrey representative told Anderson that a check in that amount was suspicious, and Anderson then "froze" the transaction. The next day, Aubrey stopped payment on the check.

What does it mean for a depositary bank to "freeze" a transaction? The answer to this question will become clearer after you have studied the materials in Chapter 10, Part A.

Thereafter, the Bank attempted to recover possession of the nine promissory notes from Stephens but was unsuccessful. Stephens subsequently left Hardinsburg, and his present whereabouts are unknown.

After freezing Stephens's account, the Bank reversed the December 9, 1979, transaction by applying the $5,604.51 then on deposit in Stephens's account (said sum representing the amount of the two checks deposited on December 9, 1979, with Aubrey's check) against the $2,000 paid to Stephens in cash on December 9, 1979, and crediting the remaining $3,604.51 against the aggregate principal balance of the nine promissory notes delivered to Stephens on that date. As a result, the Bank claimed a loss of $28,193.91 and made demand therefore upon Aubrey . . . . Such demands were refused, and this action followed.

* * *

We think the only issue dispositive of Aubrey's appeal is whether the trial court could rightfully have found on the evidence that the Bank was a holder in due course of the Aubrey check under the Uniform Commercial Code as adopted in Indiana.

* * *

Make sure you know why this statement is true.

The Bank's right to recover on the check is conditioned upon its status as a holder in due course of the check. . . .

There is no contention on appeal, and there was none at trial, that the Bank did not take the Aubrey check in good faith. . . . There is also no question that the Bank was a holder of the instrument, as it was in possession of the check indorsed by the payee Stephens in blank.

* * *

We are of the opinion that the Bank took the check for value. The issue is most readily resolved by 3-303 (b) which states in part:

> A holder takes the instrument for value (b) when he takes the instrument in payment of or as security for an antecedent claim against any person whether or not the claim is due; ...

> This language is now found in UCC 3-303 (a) (3).

The statute plainly states that value is given for an instrument when the instrument is taken in payment for an antecedent debt not yet due. The statute contains no provision precluding application of the rule when fraud is exercised by the presenter of the instrument, as Aubrey would have us find.

While this section has not been construed in Indiana, an examination of authorities from other jurisdictions lends support to the Bank's position that the application of funds made available by the Aubrey check to Stephens's indebtedness and the surrender of the notes constituted taking the instrument for value.

* * *

Further, we believe that the Bank gave value for the check under 4-208 (1) and 4-209, in that it acquired a security interest in the check to the extent funds represented thereby were applied to Stephens's debt.

> The relevant provisions in current Article 4 are 4-210 and 4-211.

* * *

We find no support for Aubrey's argument that the Bank did not give value since it did not change its position vis-á-vis Stephens and made a bookkeeping entry only of the credit given Stephens. Aubrey appears to liken the transaction under review to the situation arising when a bank provisionally credits a depositor's account pending final settlement of a deposited item. It is true that the giving of provisional credit, which has not ripened into credit available for withdrawal as a matter of right, and nothing more, does not constitute the giving of value for deposited item. ... When the credit is drawn upon, however, value is given to that extent. Further, if the depositor's account is overdrawn at the time the check is taken, and funds represented thereby are applied to the overdraft by way of set-off, value is given to that extent if the check is later dishonored.

> The concept of provisional credit is discussed in Chapter 10, Part A.

* * *

Aubrey vigorously contends the Bank was not a holder in due course of the check because, under the objective standard imposed upon the Bank by 3-304 (1), the Bank took the check with notice of a defense to the check on the part of Aubrey. Aubrey argues the evidence of alteration on the face of the check and the irregular circumstances attending the transaction were such as to put a reasonably prudent banker, exercising normal commercial standards, on notice. The circumstances alleged to have imparted notice to Bank include the small size of Stephens's farming operations, Stephens's banking history including frequent indebtedness and overdrafts, the Bank's knowledge of Stephens's petition in bankruptcy, the size of the Aubrey check in relation to typical transactions undertaken by the Bank, and the

> The referenced language is now found in 3-302 (a) (2).

implausibility of Stephens's explanation to Anderson, himself familiar
with farming, of the transaction underlying Stephens's receipt of the
check. The Bank concedes the UCC imposed an objective standard of
conduct upon it in the transaction. The essence of the Bank's
contention is that the matter of the Bank's notice is a question of fact,
and the trial court's implicit finding that the Bank took the check
without notice of Aubrey's defense was not erroneous.

* * *

The gist of Aubrey's argument is that the alleged "alteration" on the
face of the check, i.e. the typed figure "100," was "such visible evidence"
of alteration as to call into question its validity or terms.

We do not think that the trial court erred as a matter of law in finding
that the Bank took the Aubrey check without notice of a defense.

The Bank's branch manager, Anderson, with whom Stephens dealt in
the transaction, admitted that he took the check without comparing
the amount expressed by the checkwriting machine with the amount
expressed in typewritten figures; indeed, he testified that he did not
even look at the figures. He relied, instead, upon the amount expressed
by the checkwriter that was entered upon the line generally used to
express the amount of a check in words.

* * *

The holder is . . . able to take an instrument confident that he will be
able to enforce the instrument according to the written terms without
having to bring in the original parties to the instrument to ascertain
the intended amount.

As the section makes clear, in the event of an ambiguity between
printed terms and typewritten terms, the latter would control. We do
not consider the impressions made by the check imprinter to be
"printed" terms under this section.

This language is
now found in 3-114.

A conflict between the two amounts on a check would be resolved by
3-118 (c) which states that words control figures. Arguably, the
amount imprinted by the checkwriting machine upon the line
customarily expressing the amount in words, is expressed in figures.
(Recall that the entry reads: "The sum of $100478 and 23 cts.") We
think, however, that the purposes of the UCC are best served by
considering an amount imprinted by a checkwriting machine as
"words" for the purpose of resolving an ambiguity between that amount
and an amount entered upon the line usually used to express the
amount in figures.

* * *

Aubrey further argues that the circumstances surrounding the
transaction were so irregular as to put a reasonably prudent banker on
notice of a defense to Aubrey's check. Aubrey directs us to no cases in
which a holder was denied holder in due course status because of its
knowledge of the questionable general financial position of the

presenter of the instrument. Our research reveals that such knowledge is not sufficient in itself to defeat holder in due course status.

* * *

We therefore hold that the evidence supports the trial court's determination that the Bank was a holder in due course of the Aubrey check. Since Aubrey has not shown a "real defense" under 3-305 (2), the Bank may enforce the check against Aubrey to the extent it gave value therefore, and we shall not disturb the trial court's award of that amount.

- Whose action probably resulted in the check being imprinted "The sum of 100478 and 23 cts."?

- How might this fact have affected the court's holding?

- In what way did the bank satisfy the "value" requirement?

Note 1: Several cases addressing the "value" requirement involve attorneys as parties. *Koerner & Lambert v. Allstate Insurance Co.*, 374 So. 2d 179, 27 U.C.C. Rep. Serv. 478 (1979), involved a dispute arising from marine-insurance claims. Burnell Robinson and George Driscoll each owned boats damaged in unrelated incidents. Both were insured by Allstate Insurance Company, and both chose to have their boats repaired at Marina-Rama, which was owned by Paul H. Boucher. Boucher prepared estimates for each repair.

Without notifying either insured party, Allstate mailed checks representing the full value of the repairs directly to Boucher. Each check was payable to the insured party and Marina-Rama. Boucher forged the insured's signature on each check and presented the checks to his attorney, Louis R. Koerner, Jr., for payment to his creditors in his bankruptcy proceeding. Koerner deposited the checks in his client account and used the funds to pay Boucher's creditors and legal bills. Koerner knew nothing of Boucher's fraud. Robinson and Driscoll were each issued an additional check by Allstate, which sought to recover the expense from Koerner. The court held that, since the funds were received with the expectation that part of the monies were to be used to pay Boucher's legal fees, Koerner was a holder in due course.

- Based on these facts, in what way did Koerner give value?

Note 2: Courts disagree whether a bank's application of a check to an overdrawn bank account constitutes giving value within the meaning of 3-302 and 3-303. *Marine Midland*

Banks–New York v. Graybar Electric Co., Inc., 41 N.Y.2d 703, 363 N.E.2d 1139, 21 U.C.C. Rep. Serv. 1094 (1977), stands for the proposition that no value is given under these circumstances. In so holding, the court stated as follows:

> The clearest instance of giving value in this sort of case is where a bank actually extinguishes a debt by, for example, parting with a note in exchange for a check and seeking to collect on the check. With respect to [4-211], however, one text has suggested that its purpose was to give "the bank protection in any case in which it is not clear that the bank purchased the item outright, but in which it is clear that the bank has done something, of advantage to the depositor, more than giving the depositor a mere credit on the bank's books. . . ."

> To say that the bank was doing something of advantage . . . by applying the credit to that debtor's indebtedness [in the form of an overdraft] is to ignore what actually happened. The bank was merely seeking to protect itself and not giving value, in any traditional sense. *Id.* at 713.

- To give value, why must the bank do "something of advantage" for the depositor?

In *Laurel Bank & Trust Co. v. City National Bank of Connecticut*, 33 Conn. Super. 641, 365 A.2d 1222, 20 U.C.C. Rep. Serv. 685 (1976), the court found value had been given when a deposited check was applied to an overdraft, holding as follows:

> It is clear that, if a depositor's account is not overdrawn and he deposits a check which is credited to his account but not drawn on, then no value is given. It is clear . . . that a bank has given value and is a holder in due course to the extent that a depositor actually draws against a check given for collection, even if the check is later dishonored. It is immaterial that the bank takes the check for collection only and can charge back against the depositor's account the amount of the uncollected item.

The bank's right of chargeback is discussed in Chapter 10, Part A.

> The reason for that rule is to prevent the hindrance to commercial transactions which would result if depositary banks refused to permit withdrawal prior to clearance of funds. . . .

> * * *

> In the present case, the [bank's] actions in provisionally crediting a . . . deposit to the antecedent debt of the depositor [which was the overdraft] was an exercise of its common-law right of setoff and also gave the [bank] a security interest sufficient to constitute value. *Id.* at 646-648.

The right of setoff is discussed in Chapter 10, Part B.

- How is an overdraft a debt that a customer owes to a bank?

Note 3: Issues arise in the "value" context when a holder agrees to buy an item at a discount and does not pay the full sum promised.

- Which addresses this issue: 3-203 (d) or 3-302 (d)?

There are two ways of calculating the extent to which the holder can be a holder in due course under these facts, assuming he or she otherwise qualifies. Under the *amount* test, he or she is a holder in due course only for the amount actually paid. Under the *percentage* test, the following formula is applied:

$$\text{Amount for which H is HIDC} = \frac{\text{amount paid}}{\text{amount promised}} \times \text{face value of item}$$

- Does Article 3 require one approach rather than the other?

- Assume a holder has promised to pay $800 for a promissory note with a face value of $1,000, but has paid only $400 so far. To what extent has the holder given value under each test?

Although paying a discounted sum for an instrument constitutes giving value within the meaning of the UCC, at some point the discount can be so high that the holder is deemed to have notice of a problem with the item's enforceability.

Problem: On November 13, 1919, the National Hay Company deposited a check in the sum of about $450 in its account with the National Bank of Commerce. At the close of business on that day, the company's account balance was about $21,700. By November 18, 1919, the bank had paid checks from the account totaling about $21,800 and, by November 24, 1919, the bank had paid checks from the account totaling about $66,200. Due to additional deposits, the account was never overdrawn.

- Under the "shelf" rule, did the bank give value for the check?

- What would be the result if the "stack" rule were applied?

Based on *National Bank of Commerce v. Morgan*, 92 So. 10, 207 Ala. 65 (1921).

Determining Whether the Item is Overdue

Read 3-304 and Comment 2. If the face of an item shows it is overdue, a subsequent holder will have reason to doubt the enforceability of the item and therefore will not be a holder in due course.

- Does 3-304 apply to a check dishonored for insufficient funds?

- How does 3-304 distinguish installment notes from single-payment notes?

- How does 3-304 distinguish interest from principal?

The following case elucidates the difference between an "overdue" note and one that is "in default."

Richardson v. Girner,
282 Ark. 302, 668 S.W.2d 523, U.C.C. Rep. Serv. 1294 (1984).

Purtle, Justice.

[Mr. and Mrs. Girner] executed a $5,000 promissory note to First Realty Corporation on September 25, 1980. Monthly payments on the note were to commence on January 15, 1981. A schedule was printed on the back of the note. The note was assigned by First Realty to Imran Bohra in exchange for property. On July 27, 1981, Bohra transferred the note to his attorney, F. Eugene Richardson, in payment for legal services rendered by Richardson. Prior to this assignment, [the Girners] filed suit against Bohra for an accounting and for default on the purchase of certain properties. The chancery court entered a decree against Bohra in favor of the [Girners] on April 26, 1982. On July 27, 1981, when [Richardson] took the promissory note in assignment for legal services, there was no entry of any payment on the back of the note.

The primary issue before us is whether [Richardson] took the note without notice that it was overdue or was otherwise subject to defense on the part of any holder prior to [Richardson]. . . . Six payments should have been made at the time of the transfer to [Richardson]. [Richardson] found out during the meeting with Bohra, at the time of the assignment, that the note was past due. [Richardson] argues that the note was not declared to be in default until after he contacted the maker. It is not necessary to have the holder of the note declare that it is in default when this fact is obvious in other ways. . . .

[T]ransfer of an instrument vests in the transferee such rights as a transferor possesses. In the present case, Bohra knew that the Girners had claims against him far in excess of the amount of the note here in question. From the record, there is an indication that Bohra had been told by the Girners, prior to assignment of the note to Richardson, that he should consider the note paid. He was given credit in the amount of the note by the Girners on their claim against him.

In view of the fact that [Richardson] had notice that payments on the note were overdue at the time he took the note, he was not a holder in due course.

- What, if anything, should the Girners have done differently?

- What is the difference between "overdue" and "in default"?

Determining the Holder's Good or Bad Faith

Read 3-103 (a) (6) and 3-302 (a). *Branch Banking & Trust Co. v. Gill,* 293 N.C. 164, 237 S.E.2d 21, 22 U.C.C. Rep. Serv. 1026 (1977), describes the relationship between good faith and notice of irregularity or defenses to the enforcement of an item in a way that shows why the three elements are often covered together, as in these materials. In that case, which involved the issuance of negotiable warehouse receipts as part of a fraudulent scheme by a grain elevator, the court held as follows in considering whether the bank that accepted the receipts had acted in good faith and without notice of any problem with the underlying transaction, so as to be a holder in due course:

> Negotiable warehouse receipts are discussed in Chapter 18, Part C.

> Good faith . . . and notice, although not synonymous, are inherently intertwined. Therefore, the relation between the two cannot be ignored. "The same facts which call a party's 'good faith' into question may also give him 'notice of a defense.'" *Id.* at 183.

The following case illustrates the kind of willful indifference that violates the "good faith and without notice of any irregularity or defense" requirement.

Northwestern National Insurance Co. v. Maggio,
976 F.2d 320, 18 U.C.C. Rep. Serv. 2d 808 (7th Cir. 1992).

Posner, Circuit Judge.

This diversity suit on a promissory note was brought by Northwestern National Insurance Company against the note's maker, Anthony Maggio. The district court, holding that Northwestern was a holder in due course and had therefore taken the note free of any defenses Maggio might have had to a suit by the promisee, gave judgment for Northwestern on the latter's motion for summary judgment.

In 1981, Maggio had purchased a limited partnership in a new venture created by a former astronaut to develop an optoelectronic scanner designed to provide perimeter security for sprawling properties such as airfields, oil fields, and pipelines. As consideration for his partnership interest, Maggio gave the partnership a noninterest-bearing note for $55,000, maturing October 31, 1990. The partnership negotiated the note to a venture-capital company that in turn negotiated it to Goldman Sachs, which in 1988 negotiated it to Northwestern, along with other notes of the limited partners, at a 50-percent discount. When the note matured on October 31, 1990, Northwestern demanded payment from Maggio of the full face amount. He refused.

Maggio claims that he was induced to purchase the limited partnership by fraud. If so, he has of course a claim against the partnership itself and perhaps the general partner and others, but he has no claim against Northwestern if the latter is a holder in due course. It is not if it did not take the note "in good faith" . . . .

* * *

The . . . substantial issue is whether the 50-percent discount at which Northwestern bought the note should have made Northwestern inquire into the possible existence of defenses. Maggio does not argue that the discount itself established bad faith – only that it was a sufficiently suspicious circumstance to make Northwestern guilty of ostrich conduct, or more precisely to raise a jury issue and thus forestall summary judgment. Bad faith is a conscious state, but it includes the deliberate avoidance of inquiry by one who fears what inquiry would bring to light.

Northwestern reminds us that a noninterest-bearing note at fixed maturity *must* sell at a discount. No one will pay $1,000 today for the right to receive $1,000 in two years, and Northwestern bought Maggio's note from Goldman Sachs two years before it was to mature. But a 50-percent discount on a note bought two years before maturity implies an interest rate of about 40 percent a year, and Maggio asks us to infer that no one would compensate the buyer of a note at such a rate unless the promisor had defenses. . . . But this overlooks an obvious reason for the discount besides compensation for the time value of Northwestern's money – the risk that Maggio, even if he had no defenses to a suit for collection brought by the original promisee, would raise some anyway, as he has done, or wouldn't have the assets to pay the note when it matured. A bird in the hand is said to be worth two in the bush. Goldman Sachs got the bird in the hand; Northwestern got the two birds in the bush.

The fact that a note is sold at a discount is thus not in itself a suspicious circumstance that triggers a duty of inquiry by the buyer.

- What evidence should Maggio gather to support its claim that such a high discount rate suggests bad faith?

- Does Posner seem to believe that a high discount rate should ever be prima facie evidence of bad faith?

Note 1: *Funding Consultants, Inc. v. Aetna Casualty and Surety Co.*, 187 Conn. 637, 447 A.2d. 1163, 34 U.C.C. Rep. Serv.

591 (1982), shows it is sometimes appropriate to introduce
expert testimony challenging the good faith of a holder. That
case involved a promissory note that Benjamin C. Preisner
executed as maker and delivered to Paul King, Jr., as payee, in
the process of purchasing King's insurance business. Aetna
signed the note as a surety for Preisner. The note was for
$68,000, to be paid in four equal annual installments. King
discounted the note to Funding Consultants, Inc., which gave
King $5,000 cash and a promissory note for $35,000, to be paid
in four equal bi-monthly installments.

> Suretyship is discussed in Chapter 11, Part A.

After Preisner refused to make payment on the note, alleging it
was procured fraudulently, Funding Consultants invoked the
note's acceleration clause and sued Aetna. Aetna impleaded
Preisner as the primary obligor on the note. As part of its
defense, Aetna wished to introduce expert testimony that
Funding paid such a steep discount for the note that it clearly
knew or must have known there would be trouble enforcing the
item.

> Aetna was invoking its equitable right of exoneration as a surety. This right is discussed in Chapter 11, Part A.

- What element of good faith is Aetna presumably
  challenging here: honesty in fact, commercial
  reasonableness, or both?

- Computing present values is a crucial component of
  determining whether the amount a party pays for a
  promissory note or time draft is reasonable. The
  formula is as follows:

> Why is "time draft" specified here?

$$PV=FV/(1 + r)^n$$

FV is the future value (often also the face value) of the item, *r* is
the interest rate compounded annually, expressed as a decimal,
and *n* is the number of years until the item reaches maturity.

- Applying this formula, what is the present value of the
  $68,000 promissory note, assuming a six-percent
  annual interest rate?

Note 2: A number of cases address how much information a
holder must have about the transaction, or a party's financial
condition, before it will be deemed to have acted in bad faith.
In *Citizens National Bank of Englewood v. Fort Lee Savings &
Loan Association*, 89 N.J. Super 43, 213 A.2d 315, 2 U.C.C.
Rep. Serv. 1029 (1965), the court addressed whether allowing a
customer to draw on uncollected funds when its account was
either very low or overdrawn was an exercise in bad faith. In
that case, the remitter of a cashier's check alleged that the
payee, Mr. Winter, procured issuance of the check by fraud. In

finding the bank had not acted in bad faith in allowing the
payee to withdraw the uncollected proceeds of the check, the
court held as follows:

> Winter's account was low in funds. However, this fact, or the fact
> that Winter's account was overdrawn, currently or in the past, if
> true, would not constitute notice to the collecting bank of an
> infirmity in the underlying transaction or instrument and is not
> evidence of bad faith chargeable to the bank at the time it allowed
> withdrawal against the deposited check.

The court is referring here to 4-401 (a), which is discussed in Chapter 10, Part B.

> Moreover, a depositary bank may properly charge an account by
> honoring a check drawn by a depositor even though it creates an
> overdraft. It would be anomalous for a bank to lose its status as a
> holder in due course merely because it has notice that the account
> of its depositor is overdrawn. *Id.* at 48-49.

- Why does the bank prevail?

By contrast, *Farmers & Merchants State Bank v. Western
Bank*, 841 F.2d 1433, 5 U.C.C. Rep. Serv. 2d 372 (9th Cir.
1987), illustrates the kind of knowledge that can support a
claim for bad faith. That case addressed a check-kiting scheme
between OK Livestock and Fred Currey that involved accounts
at two banks over a period of more than a year. Farmers &
Merchants State Bank was aware that the account of its
customer, OK, was almost continuously overdrawn as against
collected funds. However, because F&M allowed OK to
withdraw uncollected funds, it was able to operate its account
continuously. Most of the deposited checks were from Currey's
Western Bank account. (Currey, meanwhile, was depositing a
large number of OK checks drawn on its account with F&M.)
After almost two years, a representative of F&M met with OK's
principal, Ken Troutt, and confronted him directly about the
bank's suspicions of check kiting, which he denied. Troutt was
told he would not be allowed to keep operating his account in a
state of overdraft, but he continued to do so.

The language "overdrawn as against collected funds" will make more sense after you have studied Chapter 10, Part A's materials on Regulation CC.

F&M finally decided to close OK's account due to these ongoing
issues. In preparation for closing the account, F&M adopted a
policy of requiring that Western supply F&M with cashier's
checks in exchange for any checks drawn on Currey's Western
account that OK wished to deposit. In this way, F&M sought
to guarantee that the funds would be available. F&M also
decided to dishonor any Western checks drawn by OK that
were not backed by collected funds. After F&M obtained and
deposited a cashier's check totaling over $700,000 from
Western, in exchange for thirteen Currey checks drawn on his
account with Western (which turned out to be drawn on
insufficient funds), Western brought suit seeking to recover the
funds and alleging F&M had tried to shift to Western the loss

from a kiting operation it knew was underway, without notifying Western. The allegation was that F&M had superior knowledge because it knew Currey's Western account, while appearing to hold sufficient funds, was funded almost entirely with OK checks drawn on F&M that F&M had already decided to dishonor. The court ultimately held in favor of Western, rejecting F&M's contention that "Western was responsible for knowing the state of Currey's account." The court concluded as follows:

> [W]e find inescapable the conclusion that F&M's actions were consciously calculated to shift to someone else the probable loss resulting from F&M's longstanding acquiescence and assistance in OK's operation on uncollected funds. When [F&M's representative] went to Western . . . to obtain the cashier's check, F&M knew that Currey's account balance would reflect the . . . OK checks that F&M had dishonored the evening before . . . . F&M knew Western issued its cashier's check in reliance on Currey's account – an account that F&M had itself already seriously impaired by its own acts of dishonorment and that F&M knew reflected millions of dollars in additional OK checks which F&M did not intend to honor. . . . We do not believe that a bank engaging in such conduct has exhibited the "honesty in fact" required of a holder in due course. *Id.* at 1445.

- In your own words, what was the effect of F&M's exchanging the Western checks for a cashier's check?

- Why is there strong disincentive for banks to communicate with one another in discovering a kite?

Note 3: The issue of notice has additional layers of complexity when a fiduciary relationship is involved. In *Smith v. Olympic Bank*, 103 Wash. 2d 418, 693 P.2d 92, 40 U.C.C. Rep. Serv. 519 (1985), the court addressed a dispute arising from a guardian's misuse and personal appropriation of funds intended for the support of a minor. The child's father, Charles Alcombrack, had wrongfully deposited in his personal account a check made payable to "Charles Alcombrack, Guardian of the Estate of Chad Stephen Alcombrack, a Minor." The minor's representative brought suit against the bank that accepted the deposit. Because the check clearly indicated on its face that it was to be paid in a guardianship capacity and should therefore have been deposited in a guardianship account, and because the attorney for the child had communicated with the bank regarding the requirements for setting up such an account, the court concluded the bank had acted in bad faith in accepting the check as presented.

Chapter 10, Part A includes a chart showing how a check-kiting operation works. If you are unfamiliar with this concept, the chart may provide a useful introduction. The court's opinion includes five signs of kiting:

1) Regular or frequent deposits of checks drawn by the same maker.
2) Deposits consistently increasing in size.
3) Frequent requests for balance of account.
4) Statement showing large debits and credits, but small balance.
5) Continuous drawing against uncollected funds.

After you have studied Chapter 10, Part A's materials on check kiting, you should have a sense of why each is a red flag.

- Explain the court's holding by applying the doctrine of the cheapest cost avoider, introduced in Chapter 3, Part B.

Note 4: When an item is facially incomplete, a holder may be deemed to have notice of potential enforcement problems that may prevent him or her from being a holder in due course. In *Winter & Hirsch, Inc. v. Passarelli*, 122 Ill. App. 2d 372, 259 N.E.2d 312, 7 U.C.C. Rep. Serv. 1210 (1970), Mr. and Mrs. Passarelli borrowed money through Equitable Mortgage, a brokerage firm that arranged for them to borrow money from Winter & Hirsch, Inc. at a usurious interest rate. Equitable sold the note for $11,000 to Winter & Hirsch. The Passarellis defaulted, and Winter & Hirsch sued them to enforce the note. The Passarellis counterclaimed, seeking to recover a penalty under state law based on usury.

After reading the materials in Part E of this chapter on the FTC Holder in Due Course Rule, return to these materials and consider whether the FTC rule, if it had been in existence, would have prevented Winter & Hirsch from being a holder in due course, assuming the note was drafted in compliance with the rule.

The usurious interest rate did not appear on the face of the promissory note, which simply recited a total amount (including interest) of $16,260 as being given for "value received." Because Winter & Hirsch gave Equitable the money before the note was executed, the court found Winter & Hirsch knew or should have known the note's terms. Even if Winter & Hirsch had not paid Equitable until it saw the note, the court found Winter & Hirsch knew a usurious interest rate was being charged, because otherwise it would make no sense that Equitable was willing to sell a note with a face value of $16,260 for only $11,000. Under such facts, the court found the discounter had a duty to ask more questions. One lesson of this case is that, even though the Code interposes no general duty to inquire into the transaction underlying the issuance of commercial paper, a holder may not choose to remain ignorant when the item itself raises suspicions.

- In what way can the note be deemed "facially incomplete"?

Problem: The following promissory note was issued in conjunction with the purchase of aluminum siding by Mr. and Mrs. Ingel from Allied Aluminum Associates, Inc.:

> This Is a Negotiable Promissory Note
> $1890.00 (Total Amount of Note)
>
> Fitchburg, Mass.
>
> June 22, 1959
>
> I/WE JOINTLY AND SEVERALLY PROMISE TO PAY TO
> ALLIED ALUMINUM ASSOCIATES, INC. OR ORDER THE

> SUM OF EIGHTEEN HUNDRED NINETY DOLLARS IN 60
> SUCCESSIVE MONTHLY INSTALLMENTS OF $31.50
> EACH, EXCEPT THAT THE FINAL INSTALLMENT SHALL
> BE THE BALANCE THEN DUE ON THIS NOTE.
> COMMENCING THE 25 DAY OF JULY 1959, AND THE
> SAME DATE OF EACH MONTH THEREAFTER UNTIL
> PAID, with interest after maturity at the highest lawful rate, and
> a reasonable sum (15% if permitted by law) as attorney's fees, if
> this note is placed in the hands of any attorney for collection after
> maturity. Upon nonpayment of any installment at its maturity,
> all remaining installments shall at the option of the holder
> become due and payable forthwith. Charges for handling late
> payments, of 5¢ per $1 (maximum $5), are payable on any
> installment more than 10 days in arrears.
>
> Customer acknowledges receipt of a completed copy of this
> promissory note.
>
> ALBERT T. INGEL
> DORA INGEL

After issuance, the note was transferred to Universal C.I.T. Credit Corporation, which had received the following report regarding Allied Aluminum Associates before it purchased the note:

> The subject firm is engaged in the sale of storm windows, doors, roofing, siding, and bathroom and kitchen remodeling work. The firm engages a crew of commission salesmen, and it is reported they have been doing a good volume of business. They are reported to employ high-pressure sales methods for the most part. They have done considerable advertising in newspapers, on radio, and have done soliciting by telephone. They have been criticized for their advertising methods and have been accused of using bait advertising, and using false and misleading statements. The Boston Better Business Bureau has had numerous complaints regarding their advertising methods and have reported same to the Attorney General.

A few months after signing the contract, Mr. and Mrs. Ingel contacted Universal C.I.T. Corporation, seeking to avoid their obligations under the note on the grounds of fraudulent inducement.

- Is the following letter an appropriate description of the financing company's responsibility for the alleged fraud?

October 27, 1959

Mr. Albert Ingel
115 Belmont
Fitchburg, Massachusetts

Re: 200-12-51767

Dear Sir.

We are sorry to learn that the Aluminum Siding on which we hold your promissory note is giving you cause for complaint. Our part in the transactions consisted of extending the credit which you desired, and arranging to accept prepayment of the advance on terms convenient to you. We did not perform any of the work, and any questions in connection with materials and workmanship should be adjusted with the dealer from whom you made your purchase. Therefore, we have passed your report along to Allied Aluminum, and we are confident that everything reasonably possible will be done to correct any faulty conditions which may exist.

In the meantime, we shall appreciate your continuing to make payments on your note as they fall due so that your account may be kept in current condition.

Very truly yours,

UNIVERSAL C. I. T. CREDIT CORPORATION
C. KEVENY
Collection Man

Based on *Universal C.I.T. Credit Corp. v. Ingel*, 347 Mass. 119, 196 N.E.2d 847, 2 U.C.C. Rep. Serv. 82 (1964).

International Perspective: Protected Holders

Read CIBN Article 29 and UCC 3-302 Comment 8. One major distinction between the UCC and CIBN is that the CIBN does not require that a protected holder – its equivalent of a holder in due course – have given value. The following excerpt from Jürgen Dohm, *Draft Uniform Law on International Bills of Exchange and International Promissory Notes*, 21 Am J. Comp. L. 474 (1973), provides some context for this decision:

This approach, which differs from the UCC and BEA but conforms with the [GUL], was selected because of the problems of unifying the various views on "value" (or consideration) among divergent legal systems. Dispensing with the requirement of consideration or value certainly constitutes a "simplification" and is therefore appropriate for a law establishing compromise solutions. It should be the more easily acceptable for the Anglo-American countries, since international instruments are almost always given for value or consideration. *Id.* at 496.

- What are the relative benefits and risks of the CIBN/GUL and UCC/BEA approaches?

In contrast to the CIBN, the Bills of Exchange Act defines "holder in due course" in language similar to that in the UCC:

Article 29 (1): A holder in due course is a holder who has taken a bill, complete and regular on the face of it, under the following conditions; namely,

(a) That he became the holder of it before it was overdue, and without notice that it had been previously dishonoured, if such was the fact.

(b) That he took the bill in good faith and for value, and that at the time the bill was negotiated to him he had no notice of any defect in the title of the person who negotiated it.

Central Bank of Yemen v. Cardinal Financial Investments Corp. (Case No. A3/2000/0433 in the Supreme Court of Judicature Court of Appeal in London), explains, in language that should be familiar to U.S.-trained lawyers, why notice that a bill is overdue prevents a holder from being a holder in due course under the BEA:

[A] person to whom an overdue bill or note is offered is put on inquiry. He knows that the bill or note ought to have been paid, and he takes it with the knowledge that there may be some defect of title in the holder which prevented the holder from enforcing payment.

- When might a holder choose to purchase an overdue item?

E. Special Problems Involving Holders

This section introduces the close-connectedness doctrine, the shelter doctrine, and the ways in which consumer law prevents some holders of consumer paper from being holders in due course. This section also discusses why a payee normally is too

close to the transaction to be as a holder in due course (but may
sometimes qualify), and the federal estoppel, or *D'Oench*,
doctrine, which gives the Federal Deposit Insurance
Corporation preferred status as a holder in due course.

The Doctrine of Close Connectedness

The following case, which pre-dates the Federal Trade
Commission's Holder in Due Course Rule introduced below,
explains some of the policy reasons behind the rule and
illustrates how the common-law doctrine of close connectedness
attempted to address some situations now covered by the FTC
rule.

Unico v. Owen,
50 N.J. 101, 232 A.2d 405, 4 U.C.C. Rep. Serv. 542 (1967).

Francis, J.

Defendant's wife, Jean Owen, answered an advertisement in a
Newark, N.J. newspaper in which Universal Stereo Corporation of
Hillside, N.J., offered for sale 140 albums of stereophonic records for
$698. This amount could be financed and paid on an installment basis.
In addition the buyer would receive "without separate charge" (as
plaintiff puts it) a Motorola stereo record player. The plain implication
was that, on agreement to purchase 140 albums, the record player
would be given free. A representative of Universal called at the Owens'
home and discussed the matter with Mr. and Mrs. Owen. As a result,
on November 6, 1962, they signed a "retail installment contract" for the
purchase of 140 albums on the time-payment plan proposed by
Universal.

* * *

The contract provided:

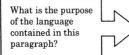
What is the purpose
of the language
contained in this
paragraph?

> If the Buyer executed a promissory note of even date herewith in
> the amount of the time balance indicated, said note is not in
> payment thereof, but is a negotiable instrument separate and
> apart from this contract, even though at the time of execution it
> may be temporarily attached hereto by perforation or otherwise.

* * *

Universal contemplated assigning the contract forthwith to Unico, and
it was so assigned. Of course, it was a bilateral executory contract, and,
. . . the reasonable and normal expectation by Owen would be that
performance of the delivery obligation was a condition precedent to his
undertaking to make installment payments. . . .

[As the facts below show,] Universal sought under paragraph 5 [of the
contract] to deprive Owen of his right to plead failure of consideration
against its intended assignee, Unico. The paragraph provides:

1
2
3
4
5
6
7
8
9
10
11
12
13
14
15
16
17
18
19
20
21
22
23
24
25
26
27
28
29
30
31
32
33
34
35
36
37
38
39
40
41
42
43
44
45
46
50
51
52
53

Buyer hereby acknowledges notice that the contract may be assigned and that assignees will rely upon the agreements contained in this paragraph, and agrees that the liability of the Buyer to any assignee shall be immediate and absolute and not affected by any default whatsoever of the Seller signing this contract; and in order to induce assignees to purchase this contract, the Buyer further agrees not to set up any claim against such Seller as a defense, counterclaim, or offset to any action by any assignee for the unpaid balance of the purchase price or for possession of the property.

* * *

At this point the hyper-executory character of the performance agreed to by Universal in return for the installment payment stipulation by Owen must be noted. Owen's time balance of $819.72 was required to be paid by 36 monthly installments of $22.77 each. Universal's undertaking was to deliver 24 record albums a year until 140 albums had been delivered. Completion by the seller therefore would require 5⅓ years. Thus, although Owen would have fully paid for 140 albums at the end of three years, Universal's delivery obligation did not have to be completed until 2⅓ years thereafter. This means that 40% of the albums, although fully paid for, would still be in the hands of the seller. It means also that for 2⅓ years Universal would have the use of 40% of Owen's money on which he had been charged the high time-price differential rate. In contrast, since Universal discounted the note immediately with Unico on the strength of Owen's credit-and-purchase contract, the transaction, so far as the seller is concerned, can fairly be considered as one for cash. In this posture, Universal had its sale price almost contemporaneously with Owen's execution of the contract, in return for an executory performance to extend over 5⅓ years. And Unico acquired Owen's note which, on its face and considered apart from the remainder of the transaction, appeared to be an unqualifiedly negotiable instrument. On the other hand, on the face of things, by virtue of the ostensibly negotiable note and the waiver or estoppel clause quoted above which was intended to bar any defense against an assignee for the seller's default, Owen had no recourse and no protection if Universal defaulted on its obligation and was financially worthless.

> What does the court mean in describing the contract as "hyper-executory"?

> Based on what you may have learned in a contracts course, is Owen likely to prevail on a theory of unconscionability or a claim that the agreement is a contract of adhesion?

* * *

Owen received from Universal the stereo record player and the original 12 albums called for by the contract. Although he continued to pay the monthly installments on the note for the 12 succeeding months, he never received another album. During that period, Mrs. Owen endeavored unsuccessfully to communicate with Universal, and finally ceased making payments when the albums were not delivered. Nothing further was heard about the matter until July 1964, when the attorney for Unico, who was also one of its partners, advised Mrs. Owen that Unico held the note and that payments should be made to it. She told him the payments would be resumed if the albums were delivered. No further deliveries were made because Universal had become insolvent. Up to this time, Owen had paid the deposit of $30 and 12 installments of $22.77 each, for a total of $303.24. Unico brought this suit for the balance due on the note plus penalties and a 20% attorney's fee.

Owen defended on the ground that Unico was not a holder in due course of the note, that the payment of $303.24 adequately satisfied any obligation for Universal's partial performance, and that Universal's default and the consequent failure of consideration barred recovery by Unico. . . .

* * *

In the field of negotiable instruments, good faith is a broad concept. The basic philosophy of the holder-in-due-course status is to encourage free negotiability of commercial paper by removing certain anxieties of one who takes the paper as an innocent purchaser knowing no reason why the paper is not as sound as its face would indicate. It would seem to follow, therefore, that the more the holder knows about the underlying transaction, and particularly the more he controls or participates or becomes involved in it, the less he fits the role of a good-faith purchaser for value; the closer his relationship to the underlying agreement which is the source of the note, the less need there is for giving him the tension-free rights considered necessary in a fast-moving, credit-extending commercial world.

We are concerned here with a problem of consumer-goods financing. Such goods are defined in the Uniform Commercial Code as those used or bought for use primarily for personal, family, or household purposes. . . . And it is fair to say also that in today's society, sale of such goods and arrangements for consumer-credit financing of the sale are problems of increasing state and national concern. The consumer-credit market is essentially a process of exchange, the general nature of which is shaped by the objectives and relative bargaining power of each of the parties. In consumer-goods transactions, there is almost always a substantial differential in bargaining power between the seller and his financer, on the one side, and the householder on the other. That difference exists because generally there is a substantial inequality of economic resources between them, and of course, that balance in the great mass of cases favors the seller and gives him and his financer the power to shape the exchange to their advantage. Their greater economic resources permit them to obtain the advice of experts; moreover, they have more time to reflect about the specific terms of the exchange prior to the negotiations with the consumer; they know from experience how to strengthen their own position in consumer-credit arrangements; and the financer-creditor is better able to absorb the impact of a single imprudent or unfair exchange.

This portion of the court's opinion may bring to mind the concept of the Repeat Player, discussed in Chapter 4, Part D.

The courts have recognized that the basic problem in consumer-goods sales and financing is that of balancing the interest of the commercial community in unrestricted negotiability of commercial paper against the interest of installment buyers of such goods in the preservation of their normal remedy of withholding payment when, as in this case, the seller fails to deliver as agreed, and thus the consideration for his obligation fails. Many courts have solved the problem by denying to the holder of the paper the status of holder in due course where the financer maintains a close relationship with the dealer whose paper he buys; where the financer is closely connected with the dealer's business operations or with the particular credit transaction; or where the financer furnishes the form of sale contract and note for use by the dealer, the buyer signs the contract and note concurrently, and the dealer endorses the note and assigns the contract immediately thereafter or within the period prescribed by the financer. Other courts have said that, when the financer supplies or prescribes or approves the form of sales contract, or conditional sale agreement, or chattel mortgage as well as the installment-payment note (particularly if it has the financer's name printed on the face or in the endorsement), and all the documents are executed by the buyer at one time and the contract assigned and note endorsed to the financer and delivered to the financer together (whether or not attached or part of a single instrument), the holder takes subject to the rights and obligations of the seller. The transaction is looked upon as a species of tripartite proceeding, and the tenor of the cases is that the financer should not be permitted "to isolate itself behind the fictional fence" of the Negotiable Instruments Law, and thereby achieve an unfair advantage over the buyer.

Before looking at the particular circumstances of the above cases, it seems advisable to examine into the relationship between Universal and the financer Unico.

Unico is a partnership formed expressly for the purpose of financing Universal Stereo Corporation, and Universal agreed to pay all costs up to a fixed amount in connection with Unico's formation. . . . As collateral security for the loans, Universal agreed to negotiate "to the lender" all customers' notes listed in a monthly schedule of new sales contracts, and to assign all conditional sale contracts connected with the notes, as well as the right to any monies due from customers.

* * *

For purposes of consumer-goods transactions, we hold that, where the seller's performance is executory in character and, when it appears from the totality of the arrangements between dealer and financer that the financer has had a substantial voice in setting standards for the underlying transaction, or has approved the standards established by the dealer, and has agreed to take all or a predetermined or substantial quantity of the negotiable paper which is backed by such standards, the financer should be considered a participant in the original transaction and therefore not entitled to holder-in-due-course status. . .
.

Plaintiff argues that, even if it cannot be considered a holder in due course of Owen's note, it is entitled to recover regardless of the failure of consideration on the part of Universal, because of the so-called waiver-of-defenses or estoppel clause contained in the sale contract.

* * *

The plain attempt and purpose of the waiver is to invest the sale agreement with the type of negotiability which, under the Negotiable Instruments Law, would have made the holder of a negotiable promissory note a holder in due course and entitled to recover regardless of the seller-payee's default.

In our judgment, such a clause in consumer-goods conditional-sale contracts, chattel mortgages, and other instruments of like character is void as against public policy.

* * *

Accordingly, the judgment for the defendant is affirmed.

Note: *Kaw Valley State Bank & Trust Co. v. Riddle,* 219 Kan. 550, 549 P.2d 927, 19 U.C.C. Rep. Serv. 869 (1976), provides guidance as to when the doctrine of close connectedness may keep a holder from being a holder in due course. In addition, this case contextualizes the materials on notice in Part C of this chapter. The case involved John Riddle's purchase of construction equipment from Co-Mac, Inc. Originally, Riddle decided to purchase a certain set of machinery, and he executed a promissory note to this effect. Before the machinery was delivered, he changed his mind, chose a more expensive set of machinery, and executed a second promissory note, having been assured the first note would be destroyed. The dispute arose because the first note was not destroyed, but was negotiated to Kaw Valley State Bank and Trust Co., which sought to enforce the note as a holder in due course notwithstanding the complete failure of consideration. The court found for Riddle based on the doctrine of close connectedness. In so holding, the court stated as follows:

> The cases dealing with the question of "reason to know a defense exists" seem to fall into four categories.
>
> The first includes those cases where it is established the holder had information from the transferor or the obligor which established the existence of a defense. . . .
>
> The second group of cases are those in which the defense appears in an accompanying document delivered to the holder with the note. For example, when a security agreement is executed concurrently with a note evidencing an indebtedness incurred for machinery to be delivered in the future. In such case, the instrument may under certain circumstances disclose a defense to the note, such as nondelivery of the machinery purchased . . . .
>
> A third group of cases are those in which information appears in the written instrument indicating the existence of a defense, such as when the note on its face shows that the due date has passed or bears visible evidence of alteration and forgery or the note is clearly incomplete. . . .
>
> In the fourth category of cases, it has been held that the holder of a negotiable instrument may be prevented from assuming holder-

in-due-course status because of knowledge of the business practices of his transferor or when he is so closely aligned with the transferor that the transferor may be considered an agent of the holder and the transferee is charged with the actions and knowledge of the transferor. *Id.* at 557-558.

- Into which category does the *Unico* case fit best?

Problem: Ken Hessler raised hogs for the John Smith Grain Company. The company supplied him with hogs and, each time it did so, required him to execute a promissory note to cover the replacement cost of the hogs and the cost of their feed. The company would then, without Hessler's knowledge or consent, sell each note to Arcanum National Bank. The bank and the company had several officers and directors in common, and the bank bought the company's commercial paper as a matter of course. Unbeknownst to Hesseler, the bank also opened a commercial loan account in his name, into which it placed the payments he made on the notes. When the hogs were sold, Hessler would get a flat fee and a share of the proceeds and would pay off the promissory note.

> Why would the company require him to cover the replacement of the hogs?

On January 4, 1977, the company delivered a shipment of hogs and had Hessler sign a promissory note. Because the company also required the signature of his wife Carla, Hessler signed for her as well. She was left-handed, and his facsimile of her signature was a poor one. Because Mr. and Mrs. Hessler had a checking account with Arcanum National Bank, the bank had signature cards on file for both of them. Hessler did not know at the time that the company had already mortgaged the hogs to the Producer's Livestock Association, such that there was no consideration to support the note. A few months later, the Association came and took the hogs from Hessler because the company, which was in the process of bankruptcy, had failed to make its mortgage payments. Hessler thus had no hogs to sell to make the money he would need to pay off his note to the company. The bank sued him on the note, claiming holder-in-due-course status.

> Why was there no consideration to support the note?

- What are Hessler's strongest arguments against the bank?

- Which facts should he emphasize?

Based on *Arcanum National Bank v. Hessler*, 69 Ohio St. 2d 549, 433 N.E.2d 204, 33 U.C.C. Rep. Serv. 604 (1982).

The FTC Holder in
Due Course Rule
and other federal
regulations can be
found at www.
gpoaccess.gov/cfr/
retrieve.html.

The FTC Holder in Due Course Rule

Read 3-106 (d) and Comment 3, 3-302 (g) and Comment 7, and 16 CFR Part 433. Under the Federal Trade Commission Holder in Due Course Rule, found at 16 CFR Part 433, consumers receive special protections when they execute negotiable promissory notes for the purpose of purchasing or leasing consumer goods. This rule addresses the typical transaction in which a consumer executes a negotiable promissory note payable to a dealer and gives a security interest to the dealer in the purchased or leased item. The dealer normally does not finance the transaction itself, but instead negotiates the commercial paper to a third-party financing agency. The agency would like to enforce the debt free of any personal defenses the consumer could raise against the dealer. To do so, the agency must be a holder in due course.

A policy decision has been made that, in the commercial setting, it is appropriate for a holder in due course to escape the personal defenses of a commercial purchaser or lessee. In the consumer context, however, the decision was that consumers should have an opportunity to assert personal defenses against any holder in an action for payment on a negotiable credit instrument. This result is accomplished by way of a required notice, contained within the text of 16 CFR 433.2, which warns any holder of a consumer-credit contract that it cannot be a holder in due course, but will instead be subject to any defenses the consumer borrower could have raised against the original payee. Professor Kurt Eggert's article *Held Up in Due Course: Codification and the Victory of Form over Intent in Negotiable Instrument Law*, 35 Creighton L. Rev. 363 (2002), provides context for the development of the FTC Rule:

What is meant by
the language of this
paragraph?

> The FTC's Holder in Due Course Rule, which took effect May 14, 1976, does not, by itself, create any additional rights or remedies for a consumer, but instead merely preserves those rights or defenses the consumer has, regardless of who holds the credit instrument.
>
> The FTC . . . stepped in after concluding that unethical merchants were cheating thousands of consumers, while the merchants and their financiers relied on the holder-in-due-course doctrine to force the consumers to pay the lenders, despite the fraud committed by the sellers.
>
> . . . [T]he FTC's stated goal in promulgating the Holder in Due Course Rule was to place the risk of loss caused by unscrupulous merchants onto the lenders, rather than the consumers. In this way, the FTC hoped to force the lenders to police the merchants they dealt with, and relied on the lenders' greater ability to obtain information regarding the practices of merchants and to return

1
2
3
4
5
6
7
8
9
10
11
12
13
14
15
16
17
18
19
20
21
22
23
24
25
26
27
28
29
30
31
32
33
34
35
36
37
38
39
40
41
42
43
44
45
46
50
51
52
53

the loss to the merchants who caused the loss. The FTC's rule not only abolishes the holder-in-due-course rule, it reverses it in an iron-clad manner. Not only does the FTC's rule assign the risk of loss to the assignees of credit instruments, it makes the assignment of loss unwaivable by consumers, preventing merchants from circumventing the rule merely by including language in their contracts undoing the FTC's action. Once assigned this loss, lenders could seek recovery from the dishonest merchants or, at least, be given a reason to stop buying consumer papers from those merchants. Unethical merchants would find their business's income stream drying up when they could no longer sell their credit instruments and instead were forced to try to collect their income from angry customers who retained their defenses to those instruments. *Id.* at 426-428.

Eachen v. Scott Housing Systems, Inc., 630 F. Supp. 162 (M.D. Ala. 1986), addressed whether a consumer should be permitted to raise violations of the FTC Holder in Due Course Rule offensively when the lender has not sued the consumer for the balance due. The following excerpt from the court's opinion shows why it believed providing the consumer with an affirmative right of action was appropriate:

> This regulation was specifically intended, according to the FTC, to provide that "a consumer can . . . maintain an *affirmative action* against a creditor who has received payments for a return of monies paid on account." The FTC expressly rejected amendments to the regulation that would limit the consumer to a "defense" or "setoff." The FTC stated,
>
>> Many industry representatives suggested that the rule be amended so that the consumer may assert his rights only as a matter of defense or setoff against a claim by the assignee or holder. Industry representatives argued that such a limitation would prevent the financer from becoming a guarantor and that any limitation in the extent of a third party's liability was desirable.
>>
>> The practical and policy considerations which militate against such a limitation on affirmative actions by consumers are far more persuasive.
>
> The FTC observed, among other things, that if the consumer is limited to a purely defensive position, the assignee-creditor may elect not to sue for the balance due when the consumer's defenses seem to have merit and the seller is judgment proof. The FTC observed that
>
>> . . . [a] consumer may stop payment after unsuccessfully attempting resolution of a complaint with the seller, or he may have finally discovered that the seller has moved, gone out of business or reincorporated as a different entity. During this period, the consumer may have been making payments

to the financer in good faith, notwithstanding the prior existence of defenses against the seller.

If the consumer stops payment, he may be sued for the balance due by the third-party financer. The financer may, however, elect not to bring suit, especially if he knows that he would be unable to implead the seller and he knows the consumer's defenses may be meritorious. Under such circumstances, the financer may elect to not sue in the hopes that the threat of an unfavorable credit report may move the consumer to pay. *Id.* at 164-165.

In *Courtesy Financial Services, Inc. v. Hughes*, 424 So. 2d 1172, 35 U.C.C. Rep. Serv. 1551 (La. App. 1st Cir. 1982), the court addressed what happens when the required FTC legend does not appear on the note:

An FTC regulation requires that notice be given that the holder of a consumer credit contract is subject to all claims and defenses which the debtor could assert against the seller. However, it is the inclusion of the required language that prevents a subsequent holder from becoming a holder in due course. *Id.* at 1175.

Thus, if the required language is omitted, a holder can be a holder in due course, but the payee may be subjected to a fine of up to $10,000 as a matter of federal law. States can add additional penalties if they so choose.

- Why is the fine levied on the payee rather than the holder?

The FDIC and the *D'Oench* Doctrine

As a matter of common law, the Federal Deposit Insurance Corporation receives preferred status as a holder in due course, in many instances without being required to satisfy the requirements introduced in Part D of this chapter. This principle is captured in what is called the *D'Oench* doctrine.

Some good, basic information about the FDIC can be found online at www.fdic.gov/about/learn/symbol/index.html.

The following case describes the purposes of the *D'Oench* doctrine and addresses one argument against it – namely, that the doctrine constitutes a taking of property without just compensation, in violation of the due process guaranteed by the Constitution.

Campbell Leasing, Inc. v. Federal Deposit Insurance Corp.,
901 F.2d 1244, 12 U.C.C. Rep. Serv. 2d 138 (5th Cir. 1990).

Clark, Chief Judge.

On February 16, 1984, Campbell Leasing, Inc. executed a promissory note in the amount of $136,804.24, plus interest, payable to RepublicBank Brownwood. To secure payment of the note, Campbell Leasing granted RepublicBank a security interest in a 1979 Piper airplane. RepublicBank also obtained the personal guarantee of George A. Day.

> Suretyship is covered in Chapter 11, Part A.

In May of 1986, Campbell Leasing defaulted on the note. RepublicBank accelerated the maturity of the note after Campbell Leasing failed to cure its default. On June 12, 1986, RepublicBank seized the airplane.... The seizure prompted [Campbell Leasing and Day] to file this lawsuit. RepublicBank counterclaimed for payment of the note, plus interest, costs, and attorneys' fees.

> Repossession is discussed in Chapter 17, Part A.

On July 29, 1988, the successor to RepublicBank, First RepublicBank Brownwood, N.A., was declared insolvent and closed. The Comptroller of Currency appointed the FDIC as receiver. The FDIC entered into a purchase-and-assumption agreement with a federally established bridge bank, which purchased the promissory note, security agreement, and guarantee at issue in this case. The bridge bank became NCNB Texas National Bank.

The district court granted summary judgment for NCNB and the FDIC, concluding that all of the appellants' claims and affirmative defenses were barred by the federal common-law doctrine announced in *D'Oench, Duhme & Co. v. Federal Deposit Insurance Corp.*, 315 U.S. 447, 62 S.Ct. 676, 86 L.Ed. 956 (1942).... The court entered judgment against Campbell Leasing and Day jointly and severally for the amount due on the note, plus interest, and awarded the FDIC and NCNB costs and attorneys' fees. The court also foreclosed the lien on the plane and its attachments, and directed the appellants to deliver the maintenance records and log books to the FDIC and NCNB. Finally, the court ordered the airplane sold and the amount of the judgment reduced by the proceeds.

The appellants now challenge the district court's entry of summary judgment....

The appellants concede that the *D'Oench, Duhme* doctrine bars their claim that the promissory note was extinguished in a transaction involving Tex-Star [Airlines, Inc., whereby Tex-Star had agreed to purchase the aircraft and Republic Bank had agreed to a novation in favor of Campbell Leasing and Day in return for Tex-Star's promissory note to Republic Bank], because the transaction was not documented in RepublicBank's records. They argue instead that the *D'Oench, Duhme* doctrine violates their rights under the Fifth Amendment by depriving them of valuable property – their defense to liability on the note – without just compensation or due process of law. We disagree.

The *D'Oench, Duhme* doctrine is "a common law rule of estoppel precluding a borrower from asserting against the FDIC defenses based upon secret or unrecorded "side agreements" that alter[ ] the terms of facially unqualified obligations." Even borrowers who are innocent of any intent to mislead banking authorities are covered by the doctrine if they lend themselves to an arrangement which is likely to do so. The doctrine thus "favors the interests of depositors and creditors of a failed bank, who cannot protect themselves from secret agreements, over the interests of borrowers, who can."

In this case, the appellants were in a position to protect themselves by ensuring that the alleged Tex-Star transaction was adequately documented in RepublicBank's records. They failed to do so. Because the absence of documentation was likely to mislead banking authorities as to the value of the Campbell Leasing note, the appellants are estopped from asserting against the FDIC and NCNB any claims relating to the Tex-Star transaction.

The *D'Oench, Duhme* doctrine does not deprive the appellants of property without just compensation. The appellants have simply deprived themselves of certain defenses to liability by failing to protect themselves in the manner required by the *D'Oench, Duhme* doctrine. The government has never been required "to compensate [property owners] for the consequences of [their] own neglect."

Nor have the appellants been denied due process. The *D'Oench, Duhme* doctrine is a federal common-law rule of general applicability that was established long before the appellants' claims arose. Because the appellants had "a reasonable opportunity both to familiarize themselves with [its] general requirements and to comply with those requirements," due process has been satisfied. We conclude that the *D'Oench, Duhme* doctrine does not violate the Takings Clause or the Due Process Clause of the Fifth Amendment.

The Federal Holder in Due Course Doctrine bars the makers of promissory notes from asserting various "personal" defenses against the FDIC in connection with purchase-and-assumption transactions involving insolvent banks. The protection extends to subsequent holders of the notes.

This doctrine is grounded in the federal policy of "bringing to depositors sound, effective, and uninterrupted operation of the [nation's] banking system with resulting safety and liquidity of bank deposits." The most effective way for the FDIC to implement this policy when a bank becomes insolvent is by arranging a purchase-and-assumption transaction rather than by liquidating the bank. If the FDIC were required to determine the value of the bank's notes in light of all possible "personal" defenses, a purchase-and-assumption transaction could not take place in the timely fashion necessary to ensure "uninterrupted operation" of the bank and the "safety and liquidity of deposits." Thus, the FDIC as a matter of federal common law enjoys holder-in-due-course status in order to effectively perform its congressionally mandated function.

In this case, the appellants assert various defenses and counterclaims to liability on the note. They contend that RepublicBank tortiously interfered with their efforts to lease the Piper airplane to a third party and delayed too long after the plane's seizure before attempting to sell it. They maintain that the note could have been completely discharged absent RepublicBank's wrongful actions. They also claim that RepublicBank elected to keep the airplane in full satisfaction of the note and caused Day to suffer mental and emotional distress. Because these are "personal" rather than "real" defenses to liability on the note, the FDIC and NCNB as holders in due course acquired the note free of these claims.

Retention of collateral as an Article 9 self-help remedy is discussed in Chapter 17, Part B.

[The balance of the court's opinion, which addressed claims (1) that the FDIC had notice of the defenses and therefore should . . . not be protected, (2) that the FDIC was acting in a receivership capacity that should not receive protection, and (3) that the sale of the aircraft was not commercially reasonable, has been omitted.]

- Why is the *D'Oench* doctrine sometimes also called the "federal estoppel doctrine"?

Note 1: *Desmond v. Federal Deposit Insurance Corp.*, 798 F. Supp. 829, 20 U.C.C. Rep. Serv. 2d 196 (D. Mass. 1992), illustrates the application of the federal estoppel doctrine to a situation in which the FDIC sought to liquidate, rather than purchase and assume control of, the failed bank. Robert Desmond was general partner of a partnership developing a subdivision called Round Hill. He guaranteed some Round Hill promissory notes payable to Eliot Bank and also executed some personal notes to the bank. His combined debt to Eliot Bank was almost 13 million dollars.

Over a year later, Desmond (through Philip Notopolous, his attorney) and the bank began negotiations to restructure the debt. At a critical point in negotiations, the bank forced Notopolous to withdraw for an alleged conflict of interest, citing Notopolous' representation of the bank in unrelated matters, of which it had known for years. After forcing this withdrawal and before Desmond had time to secure substitute counsel, the Bank forced him to sign a forbearance agreement which added additional collateral and required Desmond to waive all defenses to the notes' enforcement. Part of the additional collateral was Strawberry Hill Farm, where Desmond's 87-year-old mother lived.

In less than another year, Desmond and Round Hill were in default under the restructured arrangement. Even though the bank promised to take no action so long as the parties were attempting to resolve the matter, bank agents entered Strawberry Hill Farm and took some paintings, rugs, furniture, and light fixtures. While doing so, one agent remarked to

Desmond's mother, "If you have a problem, lady, just remember your son did this to you." In addition, after the bank had agreed to accept $4 million in full settlement of Desmond's debts, when Desmond stood ready to perform the bank demanded $4.5 million instead.

Around that time, the bank was failing, and the FDIC took over for purposes of liquidation. The FDIC sought to recover on the notes, claiming rights under the federal estoppel doctrine, which would have protected the FDIC by allowing it to rely on the book description of the bank's assets. The bank's records valued the Desmond/Round Hill debt at $13 million; the promise to accept $4 million was unrecorded. The FDIC also argued that, as a holder in due course, it should escape Desmond's other claims of wrongdoing. In considering these competing arguments, the court acknowledged that the FDIC has traditionally been given broad protection to facilitate purchase-and-assumption transactions. Since this was a liquidation transaction, however, the court found this policy did not apply.

- As a matter of policy, why does a different standard apply to the FDIC when it is liquidating a failed bank, rather than purchasing it for the purpose of assumption?

- If this had been a purchase-and-assumption transaction, would Desmond's defenses be barred by the federal estoppel doctrine, or has Desmond alleged real defenses that would bind even a holder in due course?

Note 2: *Sunbelt Savings, FSB Dallas, Texas v. Montross*, 923 F.2d 353, 13 U.C.C. Rep. Serv. 2d 792 (1991), illustrates an additional limit on the federal estoppel doctrine: protection of the FDIC does not extend to non-negotiable instruments. The court held as follows, in deciding not to extend the protection of the *D'Oench* doctrine:

> At first blush, [the] policy justifications [supporting the *D'Oench* doctrine] seem to apply with equal force to non-negotiable instruments. On closer examination, however, we conclude that applying the doctrine to non-negotiable instruments is fundamentally different from the earlier protections that we have afforded the FDIC. *D'Oench* [acts] to prevent the FDIC from being disadvantaged when it is forced to assume control of a troubled financial institution. [T]he FDIC is protected from the disadvantages attendant upon its role, but the nature of the assets the FDIC receives from the institutions remains unchanged. Conversely, extending federal holder-in-due-course protection to

non-negotiable instruments would bestow a benefit on the FDIC by changing the assets' nature – actually enhancing their value.

We do not view negotiability as a technical requirement. Negotiability is the foundation underlying all of Article 3 and of holder-in-due-course status in particular....

Extending holder-in-due-course status to the FDIC and its successors respecting non-negotiable instruments is both unnecessary and undesirable. When the FDIC assumes control of an institution, the assets are what they are – negotiable instruments, contracts, real property, and so on. We agree that the FDIC should not be disadvantaged by the circumstances of its assumption of control, but this policy does not require giving the FDIC the ability to transmute lead into gold. Alchemy is the province of Congress; therefore, we decline to extend [the federal estoppel doctrine] to non-negotiable instruments. *Id.* at 356-357.

- Why is it reasonable to refuse federal estoppel protection to the FDIC on non-negotiable instruments but not reasonable to require the FDIC to be bound by secret agreements of the kind explored in *Campbell Leasing?*

Payees as Holders in Due Course

Read 3-302 Comment 4. It is possible, but not common, for a payee of a negotiable instrument to be a holder in due course. Examples of this phenomenon typically involve an isolated payee dealing with the maker or drawer through an intermediary. Whatever the specific facts, the payee must prove it lacked notice of any irregularity with the transaction or the instrument.

First, consider Comment 4, Case #4, which could be titled "The Case of the Sneaky Secretary." An employer gave a blank, signed check to the corporate secretary to type in the name of A Corporation, to which the employer owed money. Instead, the secretary typed in the name of B Corporation, to which the secretary owed money personally, and delivered the check to B Corporation. B Corporation, as the payee, could be a holder in due course if it had no reason to know of the secretary's deceit. Note the "information wall" between the drawer and payee in the following graphic:

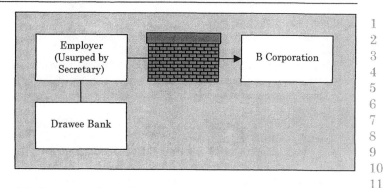

Another example in Comment 4 is Case No. 3, which could be called "The Case of the Sneaky Corporate Officer." The corporation drew a check payable to Bank. A corporate officer was given the check to deliver to Bank in payment of the debt the corporation owed Bank. The corporate officer also had a personal account at Bank and, instead of giving Bank the check for purposes of paying the corporate debt, the officer deposited the check in his personal account. If Bank had no reason to know of the fiduciary capacity in which the officer was given the check, Bank could be a holder in due course.

Notice of breach of fiduciary duty is covered in 3-307.

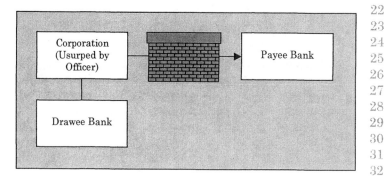

- Can you explain the outcome in these cases by application of the doctrine of the cheapest cost avoider in Chapter 3, Part B?

Problem: John and Teresa Hughes purchased a used 1976 Plymouth Fury station wagon from Security Motors. The salesperson was also a loan officer for Courtesy Financial Services, to which the Hugheses executed a promissory note for the car. Mr. and Mrs. Hughes drove the car for a year and a half, during which time they experienced a number of problems with the vehicle. They stopped paying for the car one month after they stopped driving it. By that time, they had paid more than two-thirds of the financed amount, having continued to make payments even though they both were unemployed. At one point, they borrowed an additional $600 from Courtesy for repairs on the vehicle. When Courtesy sued Mr. and Mrs.

1
2
3
4
5
6
7
8
9
10
11
12
13
14
15
16
17
18
19
20
21
22
23
24
25
26
27
28
29
30
31
32
33
34
35
36
37
38
39
40
41
42
43
44
45
46
50
51
52
53

Hughes for the balance due under the note, they counterclaimed on a theory of failure of consideration.

- How, if at all, should the facts in the last three sentences of this paragraph affect the court's holding?

- Assuming Courtesy is unable to rebut the Hugheses' testimony regarding the poor quality of the vehicle, should Courtesy be successful in claiming it is a holder in due course?

Based on *Courtesy Financial Services, Inc. v. Hughes*, 424 So. 2d 1172, 35 U.C.C. Rep. Serv. 1551 (La. App. 1st Cir. 1982).

The Shelter Doctrine

Read 3-203 (b) and Comment 2. Pursuant to the shelter rule, a transferee of a negotiable instrument generally will acquire all rights of the transferor; in fact, the transferee of a holder in due course obtains all of the rights of the holder in due course (even if the transferee would not otherwise qualify) unless the transferee was personally involved in fraud or illegality or the transferee was a prior holder with knowledge of a defense or claim against the instrument. Note the specific language used here: 3-203 (b) does not state that the transferee of a holder in due course will *be* a holder in due course, but that the transferee will have *the rights of* a holder in due course.

- What is the distinction being made here?

- How does the shelter doctrine benefit a transferee?

Comment 2 may assist you in answering this question.

International Perspective: Special Problems Involving Holders in Due Course

Read CIBN Article 31. Like the UCC, the CIBN provides a shelter doctrine. In addition, like the UCC, the CIBN's shelter-doctrine protection will not apply to a transferee who has reason to know of a defense to the enforcement of the instrument. Unlike the UCC, the CIBN's shelter doctrine appears to apply only to assignees of protected holders, rather than to all assignees.

The Canadian case of *Federal Discount Corp., Ltd. v. St. Pierre and St. Pierre*, O.R. 310, 32 D.L.R. (2d) 86, shows that Canadian courts recognize a doctrine of close connectedness

much like that applied in United States courts.   Note the
following language from the court's opinion:

> It is not necessary for the support of ordinary commercial
> transactions that the holder of a bill of exchange should under all
> circumstances be permitted to shield himself behind the guise of a
> holder in due course and attempt to separate his character as
> holder in due course from the debilitating effect of facts and
> circumstances actually known to him at the time he acquired the
> bill or which were reasonably inferable from facts and
> circumstances which were brought to his knowledge.

> In the examination of any transfer to decide if it constituted the
> transferee a holder in due course, the [transferee's] actual
> involvement with the transferor will be a major factor; on this
> account, the whole relationship between the [transferee] and its
> transferor must be examined and considered.

- What are the benefits and risks of regulating
  consumer contracts by application of the doctrine of
  close connectedness, as opposed to the FTC Holder in
  Due Course Rule?

Chapter Conclusion: In leaving this chapter, you should be
familiar with the differences between negotiation and
assignment and between holders in due course and other
holders and assignees.   You should know how to prove each
element of holder-in-due-course status and should be able to
recognize payees as holders in due course, entities that are
closely connected with one another, consumer credit contracts,
FDIC assumption or liquidation of banks, and transferees
claiming rights through their transferors.

Chapter 10:
The Collection Process

A. Introducing the Collection Process

This section introduces the concepts of final payment and dishonor and also discusses the midnight deadline rule and Regulation CC, showing how interplay between the two gives rise to the possibility of check kiting. In addition, this section discusses MICR encoding, electronic presentment, and other means of expediting the collection process.

Relationship between Articles 3 and 4

As the following excerpt from NCCUSL's introduction to the 1990 amendments to Article 4 shows, Articles 3 and 4 are closely related:

> Articles 3 and 4 are companion Articles. Article 3 provides for all negotiable instruments, including checks and certificates of deposit. Article 4 is entitled "Bank Deposits and Collections." Most checks are drawn upon bank accounts, and certificates of deposit are banking instruments. Banks, also, conduct transactions in other types of negotiable instruments, as well, and are the central institutions for conducting business in instruments. The close relationship between Articles 3 and 4 is, therefore, quite clear.
>
> Article 4 establishes the basic rules by which banks handle checks and other "items" in the process of obtaining payment when presented for that purpose by any holder entitled to such payment. The operative term is "item," a term which covers checks or any instrument handled by a bank for collection or payment. . . ."

"Item" is defined in 4-104 (a) (9).

> Much of Article 4 concerns the obligations of banks in their varying roles in handling "items." Banks act as "depositary" banks, "payor" banks, "intermediary" banks, "collecting" banks, and "presenting" banks. Much of the transactional environment involves banks dealing with each other in obtaining collection and payment of an "item," and Article 4 reflects this fact.

This vocabulary comes from 4-105 and will be further explored and applied later in this section.

> A "depositary" bank is the bank in which an "item" first appears in the process of obtaining collection and payment. When any person deposits a check, for example, in an account, that person's bank is a "depositary" bank.
>
> It is also a "collecting" bank, because its role is to send the "item" on its way to the "payor" bank for payment. It is collecting the value of the check deposited in its customer's account. The last "collecting" bank becomes a "presenting" bank, because it is the bank that delivers the instrument (or its representation) to the "payor" bank for payment.

Electronic presentment, discussed below, allows presentment of a "representation" of an instrument.

The "payor" bank is the bank in which the person who wrote the check has an account, and against whose account payment will be debited. Any bank in any given situation may perform one or more of these prescribed roles.

The fundamental task is, always, to get the "item" presented by somebody's customer to the right bank in a timely manner, so that it can be paid and all participants' books appropriately debited and credited in the process. Article 4, also, deals with the situation in which an "item" is entered into this payment system, and is dishonored. Who carries the loss in such a situation? Who warrants what in the process of transferring an "item" from one person or institution to another person or institution? These are the matters that Article 4 addresses.

Read 4-101 Comment 3. The commentary states that Article 4 "does not regulate the terms of the bank-customer agreement."

- What body of law regulates this agreement?

Read 4-102 (a) and Comment 1. Most cases and examples in this chapter involve bank collection of checks.

Comment 8 to 4-104 may assist you in answering this question.

- What other items are processed by banks?

The Federal Reserve is introduced later in this section.

Read 4-103 (a), (b), and (c) and Comment 3. These subsections and commentary describe the relationship between Federal Reserve regulations, operating circulars, clearing-house rules, and the UCC.

- Do Federal Reserve regulations and operating circulars and/or clearing-house rules pre-empt the UCC?

- Can parties opt out of Federal Reserve regulations and operating circulars and/or clearing-house rules?

- **Read 4-103 and Comment 2.** To what extent can parties contract out of provisions of Article 4?

Electronic Presentment

Read 4-101, Comment 2. Technological changes have helped banks cope with the increase in check usage since Article 4 was drafted in 1950. The 1990 amendments to Article 4 were intended to facilitate expedited check processing. *First National Bank of Boston v. Fidelity Bank, National Association,* 724 F. Supp. 1168, 10 U.C.C. Rep. Serv. 2d 1 (E.D. Pa. 1989), describes how the technology has developed:

The method of processing checks now in universal use in the United States, Magnetic Ink Character Recognition (MICR), was first adopted by the American Bankers Association in 1956, and has been in common use since the mid-1960s. The form of each bank check is preprinted with magnetic characters, along the bottom of the check, toward the left-hand side. These characters designate the bank upon which the check is drawn, and the account number of the maker. When a check is presented to another bank (the "depositary bank"), that bank adds additional magnetic encoding, at the lower right-hand side of the check, specifying the amount of the check. From that point on, the check works its way through the bank-clearing system to the bank on which the check is drawn and is charged against the maker's account – all without further human intervention. Thus, the role of the encoder at the depositary bank is crucial, since all subsequent steps in the processing of the check for payment depend upon the accuracy of the encoded information; ordinarily, no other human being actually examines the check from that point on. The development of this method of processing checks, it is generally agreed, has enabled the banking system to meet the needs of our ever-expanding economy. *Id.* at 1168-1169.

> The characters designating the drawee are called "routing and transit" numbers.

In *First National Bank of Boston*, a check written for the amount of $100,000 was encoded by the depository bank, accepted by the drawee bank, and paid as if the amount were $10,000. The depository bank, having credited the payee's account with the face value of $100,000, sought to recover the additional $90,000 from the drawee. The drawee refused on the grounds that the account had insufficient funds to pay a $100,000 check at all relevant times. Part of its defense was that the "amount of the item" for the purposes of Article 4 was the encoded $10,000, rather than the $100,000 face value. The court held as follows:

> The encoding bank is required to warrant the accuracy of its encoding. Encoding warranties are governed by 4-209 and discussed in Chapter 11, Part C.

I reject the argument that the "amount of the item" for § 4-213 (1) purposes is the encoded amount, rather than the face amount, of the check. Stated that broadly, the argument is manifestly unacceptable, for if the encoded amount were greater than the face amount of the check, the error would produce a windfall for the collecting bank, and patently unjustifiable increases in the potential liability of the payor bank, the maker, or both. Any such rule would have chaotic repercussions, and would be totally inconsistent with the scheme of the UCC.

> This language is now found in 4-215 (d).

A more narrowly stated rule – that the "amount of the item" for purposes of § 4-213 (1) is the face amount of the check or the encoded amount, whichever is less – is merely another way of stating what I conceive to be the true thrust of defendant's argument in this case, namely, that as between the encoding bank and all other banks in the collecting process, including the payor bank, the encoder is estopped from claiming more than the encoded amount of the check. *Id.* at 1172.

- How does the court's holding differ from the drawee's argument?

- Because the drawer's account never contained funds sufficient to cover a $100,000 check, is it possible that the depositary bank actually benefited from its own error?

The *First National Bank of Boston* case suggests how a depositor might take advantage of a bank's error in over-encoding a check. In addition, sometimes drawers try to take advantage of a bank's error in under-encoding a check. In *Georgia Railroad Bank & Trust Co. v. First National Bank & Trust Co of Augusta*, 139 Ga. App. 683, 229 S.E.2d 482, 20 U.C.C. Rep. Serv. 262 (1976), the court considered the under-encoding and processing of a $25,000 check for $2,500. When the depositor discovered the error, his bank credited his account for the additional $22,500, then sought to recover from the drawee bank. When the drawee contacted the drawer, he "told the [bank] not to 'bother' his account," refusing to pay the additional sum although his account contained sufficient funds to cover it. The court held that, by paying the incorrect, smaller amount, the drawee had accepted liability for the check pursuant to the doctrine of final payment introduced later in this chapter. The drawer would, of course, be liable for the full sum as well.

> After you have covered the materials contained in Part B of this chapter regarding stop-payment, make sure you understand why the court rejected the argument, found elsewhere in the opinion, that the drawer effectively stopped payment on the check by making this statement.

- What theory or theories of liability might the court employ to establish the liability of the drawer for the full amount?

Encoding technology has created opportunities for new kinds of fraud. In *United States Fidelity and Guaranty Co. v. Federal Reserve Bank*, 620 F. Supp. 361, 41 U.C.C. Rep. Serv. 1153 (S.D. N.Y. 1985), the court considered the proper allocation of loss among banks victimized by a check-fraud scheme that utilized MICR technology. The fraudfeasor had created and deposited a series of worthless checks drawn on a non-existent account. By manipulation of the routing and transit numbers to be read by a MICR-processing machine, the wrongdoer was able to ensure the check would be routed among a number of different banks before the fraud was discovered. In the meantime, the fraudfeasor withdrew the funds and disappeared. The court's opinion explains various measures banks employ to protect against fraud and shows how failing to follow these practices can result in significant loss. *Northpark National Bank v. Bankers Trust Co.*, 572 F. Supp. 524, 37 U.C.C. Rep. Serv. 385 (S.D. N.Y. 1983), provides insight into how such a scheme might operate:

[I]t is clear how a fraud of this type is accomplished. Its object is to cause a worthless check deposited for collection to take a sufficiently long detour in its progress to the drawee bank, to insure that the notice of non-payment will not arrive at the depositary bank until after the expiration of the hold which it placed on the availability of the proceeds from transit items. Having received no such notice before the expiration of the hold, the depositary bank supposes the items to have been paid and allows its proceeds to be withdrawn. By the time notice arrives the malefactor has, of course, absconded with the spoils. The crucial detour is caused by imprinting the fraudulent check with the wrong MICR routing number – *i.e.,* one that does not correspond to the bank designated on the face of the check as the drawee bank, but to a different bank, preferably one that is distant from the institution designated as the drawee bank on the face of the check. The fraudulent check in our case bore the MICR routing number of Bankers Trust Co. in New York and identified the "Bank of Detroit" – a fictitious institution – as the drawee bank. *Id.* at 526.

> The reference here is to Regulation CC holds, discussed later in this section. One way in which a check kiter maximizes the chance of success is to convince banks to exempt the kiter's account from Regulation CC holds and other measures intended to prevent loss through fraud.

The court noted the fraud would have been equally effective if "the account on which [the check] is drawn at a (real) bank does not exist, or because the (real) account on which it is drawn at a (real) drawee bank is without funds."

- Do you agree?

The Federal Reserve System

The Federal Reserve is the central bank for the United States. It was established in 1913 by President Woodrow Wilson and bears primary responsibility for the country's monetary policy. Twelve regional Federal Reserve Banks are located in major cities around the country. *Greater Buffalo Press, Inc. v. Federal Reserve Bank of New York*, 866 F.2d 38, 7 U.C.C. Rep. Serv. 2d 956 (2d Cir. 1989), provides a description of the Federal Reserve System's role in the Article 4 collection process:

> For more information about the Federal Reserve System and a map of the 12 districts, visit www.federalreserve.gov.

> When payment is made by means of a check, a payor draws the check against an account at his or her bank, the payor bank. Upon receiving the check, the payee will often deposit it in his or her own bank, the depositary bank. At this point, two processes must occur. First, the check itself must be physically transported from the depositary bank to the payor bank. Second, payment must be made from the payor bank back to the depositary bank.

> One option available to the depositary bank is to utilize the check-clearing services of the Federal Reserve System. In order to do so, the depositary bank must send the check to the Federal Reserve Bank for its district. If the payor bank is in the same district, then the Federal Reserve Bank can present the check directly to the payor bank. If the payor bank is located in a different district, the Federal Reserve Bank receiving the check will forward it to the

Federal Reserve Bank for the payor bank's district. That Federal
Reserve Bank will then present the check to the payor bank.

In addition to effecting the physical delivery of the check, the
Federal Reserve System also serves to facilitate payment between
the payor and depositary banks. After sending a check to its
Federal Reserve Bank for processing, the depositary bank will
receive credit for the check in its reserves account with the Federal
Reserve. This credit will be given usually within one or two days,
depending on how long it is expected to take the check to reach the
payor bank for payment. After the check reaches the payor bank,
the Federal Reserve System uses transfers of credit through an
Interdistrict Settlement Fund to achieve payment.

* * *

In 1980, . . . Congress enacted the Monetary Control Act of 1980.
This Act provided, *inter alia,* that all banks in the United States
would be required to maintain reserves with the Federal Reserve.
Additionally, check-clearing services were . . . to be made available
to all banks, regardless of whether or not they were member
banks, but all banks would . . . have to pay for the service. *Id.* at
40.

> Section 9 of the Federal Reserve Act describes how state banks can apply for membership.

- What purpose is served by requiring banks to
  maintain reserves with the Federal Reserve?

Read 4-105 and Comments 1 and 3. 4-105 includes some of
the most important vocabulary in this chapter: the labels for
the various banks involved in the Article 4 collection process.
These labels were briefly introduced in the NCCUSL excerpt at
the beginning of this chapter. Comment 1 states that "the
definition of 'depositary bank' does not include the bank to
which a check is made payable if a check is given in payment of
a mortgage."

- What would be a more appropriate label for such a
  bank?

- Consider the following illustration of a collection
  process involving two Federal Reserve Banks serving
  different regions.

1
2
3
4
5
6
7
8
9
10
11
12
13
14
15
16
17
18
19
20
21
22
23
24
25
26
27
28
29
30
31
32
33
34
35
36
37
38
39
40
41
42
43
44
45
46
50
51
52
53

Hint: the Interdistrict Settlement Fund is not a bank.

- Which party or parties fits each of the following labels?

  - collecting bank
  - depositary bank
  - intermediary bank
  - payor bank
  - presenting bank

Check Kiting

Check clearing is accomplished through a precisely timed series of events. The fact that depositary banks frequently release uncollected funds creates the possibility of check kiting. *National State Bank v. Federal Reserve Bank of New York*, 979 F.2d 1579, 19 U.C.C. Rep. Serv. 2d 209 (3d Cir. 1992), explains how a kite works:

The materials on Regulation CC later in this section show why uncollected funds are often made available for withdrawal.

> A check kiter is a person who first draws a check on a fictitious account or on an account with insufficient funds to cover the amount of the check. The bank in which the account is supposedly located is the payor bank. The kiter then deposits the check in an account in a second bank, the depositary bank. The depositary bank does not learn that the check cannot be covered by funds in the account in the payor bank until after the kiter, or the kiter's accomplice, has withdrawn the money from the depositary bank.
>
> In order to understand why the depositary bank may not learn that the check has been dishonored until after the funds have been withdrawn, we must take a look at the check-collection system in the United States. . . . While checks are in transit, the collecting banks extend provisional credit to the depositary banks

and make provisional debits to the accounts of the payor banks. If, when a payor bank physically receives a check, there are insufficient funds in the account on which it is drawn to cover it, the payor bank will notify the depositary bank that the check has been dishonored. This usually will occur within a matter of a day or two. However, if the transaction has proceeded normally and there are funds in the payor bank to cover the check, the payor bank will not generally advise the depositary bank that final payment has been made on a particular check.

It is on the occasions when there is a delay in transmitting a check or in giving notice of its dishonor that a check kiter may create an opportunity to withdraw funds from an account in the depositary bank even though there are insufficient funds in the account in the payor bank. *Id.* at 1580.

- How is the check kiting described here different from the encoding fraud discussed earlier in this section?

> **Make sure you can explain how the operation in the graphic below works.**

The following illustration shows how a kite might operate. Repeating this cycle over a period of time creates the illusion of considerable wealth.

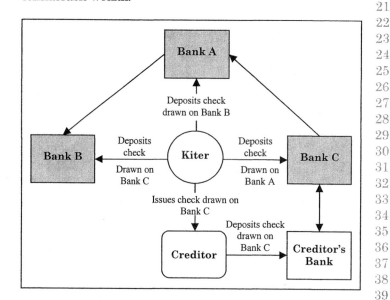

As the court states in *First National Bank in Harvey v. Colonial Bank*, 898 F. Supp. 1220, 28 U.C.C. Rep. Serv. 2d 290 (N.D. Ill. 1995), "A really successful defrauder will have numerous accounts in fictitious names at banks in widely separated states."

- Why is this statement true?

The *First National Bank in Harvey* court goes on to state as follows:

> There is. . . no duty between competing institutions [such as depositary and drawee banks] to inform one another of the existence of a check-kiting scheme because these institutions deal at arms' length, have their own means of detecting check kiting, and, realistically, need no protection from other institutions. *Id.* at 1231.

- What are the risks and benefits of this rule?

- What "means of detecting check kiting" do banks have at their disposal?

Regulation CC

Skim 12 USC §§ 4002, 4003, and 4004, which are pertinent provisions of the Expedited Funds Availability Act (EFAA), the implementation of which is described in Regulation CC. The EFAA provides a schedule with which depository banks are required to comply in making funds available to their depositors.

> For a discussion of the EFAA, see Edward L. Rubin, *Uniformity Regulation, and the Federalization of State Law: Some Lessons from the Payment System,* 49 Ohio St. L.J. 1251 (1989). The EFFA is online at www. gpoaccess.gov/uscode /index. html.

Skim 12 CFR 229.10, 229.12, and 229.13. Taken together, these subparts provide an overview of Regulation CC, which often requires depositary banks to release uncollected funds to their customers. The check-collection process can thus be described as a race in which depositary banks seek to secure payment from drawee banks for deposited checks before releasing those checks for their customers' use. The following information, circulated to banks by the Federal Reserve Board in its publication entitled *A Guide to Regulation CC Compliance* summarizes the relevant deadlines:

> To ensure that you understand how Regulation CC works, consider working through the sample problems presented (and answered) by the Federal Reserve Board at http://www.federalre serve.gov/pubs/RegC C/examples.htm.

> Regulation CC states when deposits of various types must be made available to your customers, measured in business days following the banking day on which the deposit is made. Business days are defined as Mondays through Fridays except most federal holidays. A banking day is any business day (up to the bank's cut-off hour) when your institution is open for substantially all of its banking activities. All references to the number of days to funds availability in this guide indicate maximum time limits for making funds available; your institution may provide earlier availability of funds if it chooses and may extend the time when funds are available up to periods set by Regulation CC on a case-by-case basis.

> The concept of a "banking day" is explored in the section that follows on the midnight rule and midnight deadline.

- When might a bank choose to make funds available earlier?

The following types of deposits must be made available on the first business day following the banking day of deposit ("next-day availability"):

1. **Cash** deposited in person to one of your employees.

2. **Electronic payments** received by your institution for deposit in an account. . . .

3. **U.S. Treasury checks** deposited in an account held by a payee of the check – Unlike deposit types listed in 4 through 8 below, which pertain to deposits made in person, Treasury checks deposited at an ATM owned by your institution (a "proprietary" ATM) must be accorded next-day availability.

4. **U.S. Postal Service money orders** deposited in person to one of your employees and into an account held by a payee of the check.

5. **Federal Reserve Bank and Federal Home Loan Bank checks** deposited in person to one of your employees and into an account held by a payee of the check.

6. **State or local government checks** deposited in person to one of your employees and into an account held by a payee of the check, if your institution is in the same state as the payor of the check. . . .

7. **Cashier's, certified, or teller's checks** deposited in person to one of your employees and into an account held by a payee of the check. . . .

8. **Checks drawn on an account held by your institution** ("on-us checks") deposited in person to one of your employees or at on-premises ATMs or night depositories, if the branch or branches involved are in the same state or check-processing region.

9. Deposits that include some checks of types not listed above – **The first $100** (or the total amount of the deposit if it is less than $100) of **non-"next-day" checks must be made available the next day.**

- What do the first 8 types of deposits have in common?

- What is the apparent policy reason for the last item?

The publication continues as follows:

Exceptions: When deposits of types 1, 4, 5, 6, and 7 are not made in person (for example, when they are made at one of your ATMs), the funds must be made available by the second business day. Deposits, cash or check, made at an ATM that you do not own (a "nonproprietary" ATM) must be made available by the fifth business day.

For checks of types not discussed above, funds generally must be made available in accordance with a schedule specified in Regulation CC. That schedule varies depending on whether the check is considered "local" or "nonlocal."

> What kinds of checks would be governed by this paragraph?

A check is considered "local" if your institution is located in the same check-processing region as the paying institution. Funds from local checks must be made available by the second business day following the day of deposit.

A check is considered "nonlocal" if your institution is not located in the same check-processing region as the paying institution. Funds from nonlocal checks must be made available by the fifth business day following the day of deposit.

> A "check-processing region," as defined in the EFAA, 12 USC § 4001 (9), is the geographical region served by each of the 12 Federal Reserve banks. For a map showing the regional boundaries, see www.federalreserve.gov/otherfrb.htm.

There are several minor exceptions to the two- and five-day availability rules. They involve, for example, certain checks deposited outside the continental United States and cash withdrawals from certain checks. A detailed explanation can be found in section 229.12 of Regulation CC.

But remember – no matter whether the check is local or nonlocal, the first $100 of a deposit that is not already subject to next-day availability must be made available by the first business day following the day of deposit. This does not apply to deposits at nonproprietary ATMs and to deposits subject to certain exception holds. . . .

Delaying Funds Availability

For certain types of deposits, Regulation CC permits financial institutions to delay, for a "reasonable period of time," the availability of funds. A "reasonable" time period is generally defined as one additional business day (making a total of two business days) for on-us checks, five additional business days (total of seven) for local checks, and six additional business days (total of eleven) for nonlocal checks; your institution may impose longer exception holds, but you may have the burden of proving that they are "reasonable."

If you decide to hold funds beyond the period specified in your institution's general availability policy, you must give the customer a notice at the time of the deposit explaining why the funds are being held and when they will be available. If the deposit is not made in person to an employee of your institution or if you decide to extend the time when deposited funds will be made available after the deposit has been made, you must mail or deliver the notice to the customer not later than the first business day after the banking day on which the deposit is made.

Deposits of cash and electronic payments are not eligible for exception holds. The six types of deposits that are eligible are

1. **Large deposits** (greater than $5,000) – Any amount exceeding $5,000 may be held. Your institution must make the first $5,000 of the deposit available for withdrawal according to your availability policy and the remainder within the "reasonable" time frames discussed above.

> Why should checks that are postdated or missing an endorsement be treated differently?

2. **Redeposited checks** – May be held unless the check was returned because an endorsement was missing or because the check was postdated. In such a case, if the deficiency has been corrected, the check may not be held as a redeposited check.

3. Deposits to accounts that are **repeatedly overdrawn** – An account may be considered repeatedly overdrawn and items may be held if

    a. On six or more banking days during the previous six months the account had a negative balance, or would have had a negative balance had checks and charges been paid, or

    b. On two or more banking days during the previous six months the account balance was negative in the amount of $5,000 or more, or would have been had checks and charges been paid.

4. **Reasonable cause to doubt the collectibility** of a check – Doubtful collectibility may exist for postdated checks, checks dated more than six months earlier, and checks that the paying institution has said it will not honor. The general criterion for doubting collectibility is "the existence of facts that would cause a well-grounded belief in the mind of a reasonable person" that the check is uncollectible. The reason for your belief that the check is uncollectible must be included in your notice to the customer.

5. Checks deposited during **emergency conditions** that are beyond the control of your institution – Such checks may be held until conditions permit you to provide availability of the funds. Examples of emergency conditions are natural disasters, communications malfunctions, and other situations that prevent your institution from processing checks as it normally does.

6. Deposits into accounts of **new customers** (open for less than 30 days) – Next-day availability applies only to cash, electronic payments, and the first $5,000 of any other next-day items; the remaining amount from next-day items must be available by the ninth business day. You may choose any availability schedule for deposits of local, nonlocal, and on-us checks into the accounts of these new customers.

▪   What do these 6 categories of deposits have in common that would justify eligibility for an exception hold?

1
2
3
4
5
6
7
8
9
10
11
12
13
14
15
16
17
18
19
20
21
22
23
24
25
26
27
28
29
30
31
32
33
34
35
36
37
38
39
40
41
42
43
44
45
46
50
51
52
53

1   ▪   Why would a kiter seek to manipulate Regulation CC
2   holds and releases?
3
4   As the materials later in this section show, each bank in the
5   collection   process,   from   the   depositary   bank   to   the
6   drawee/payor bank, must adhere to a strict schedule in moving
7   the check forward. Once the check reaches the payor/drawee
8   bank, that bank decides whether to honor the check, thus
9   effectuating final payment, or dishonor the check, returning it
10   unpaid. *USAA Investment Management Co. v. Federal Reserve*
11   *Bank of Boston*, 906 F. Supp. 770, 28 U.C.C. Rep. Serv. 2d 959
12   (D. Conn. 1995), explains how each bank in the collection
13   process indorses each item, creating a map of where the check
14   has been and where it must be sent back if returned unpaid:
15
16   The Expedited Funds Availability Act requires each depositary
17   institution and Federal Reserve bank to place its endorsement
18   and other notations specified in the regulations of the Board on
19   checks in positions specified in such regulations. Regulation CC
20   then requires all banks, other than paying banks, that handle a
21   check during the forward collection process or that handle a
22   returned check, to legibly endorse the check. . . . Thus, Regulation
23   CC creates a chain of endorsements extending from the bank of
24   first deposit through all collecting banks to the paying bank. And,
25   should a check be returned for any reason, this chain extends back
26   through all of the returning banks to the depositary bank.
27
28   Moreover, because of the importance of identifying the depositary
29   bank in the case of a returned check, Regulation CC imposes
30   special requirements on the depositary bank's endorsement. . . .
31   [N]ot only is the depositary bank's routing number set off by
32   arrows, it is also located in an area specially reserved for its
33   endorsement and none others.
34
35   Each subsequent collecting-bank endorser is required to protect
36   the   identifiability   and   legibility   of   the   depositary-bank
37   endorsement. . . .
38
39   This sensible system ensures that the depositary's bank's routing
40   number will not be overwritten or obscured by any of the collecting
41   or returning banks' endorsements, and thus dishonored checks
42   can be easily returned to the depositary bank. *Id.* at 777-778.

> This requirement is found in 12 USC 4008 (b) (5).

> This provision is found at 12 CFR 229.35 and Appendix D.

In the *USAA Investment Management* case, the depositary
bank failed to indorse the deposited check as required by
Regulation CC. Instead, the indorsement was in the wrong
part of the check, thus rendering other bank indorsements
illegible. This illegibility created delay and caused loss to the
depositary bank when the check was returned unpaid after the
bank had already released the funds to its customer. The court
allocated the loss between the depositary bank and a collecting
Federal   Reserve   Bank   that   neglected   to   research   the

indorsements as thoroughly as it could have, so as to prevent at least some of the delay. In so holding, the court applied a fact-specific "ordinary care" standard to the conduct of each bank.

Read 12 CFR 229.31 (b), which describes a returning bank's obligations when it cannot identify the depository bank.

- What research would you expect a returning bank to undertake?

The Midnight Rule and Midnight Deadline

Read 4-104 (a) (10), which defines the "midnight deadline" with which every bank in the Article 4 cycle must comply in moving a check forward or returning it unpaid.

> "Banking day" is defined in 4-104 (a) (3).

- Assume a bank provides notice that its banking day ends at 2 p.m. If this bank receives a check at 3 p.m. on a Monday, when will its midnight deadline expire?

Read 4-301 and Comments 1 and 3. This section explains the "deferred posting" process that allows payor banks to make provisional settlement on the banking day of receipt and then have until the midnight deadline to make final payment or dishonor the item.

> "Settle" is defined in 4-104 (a) (11).

- What is the advantage of deferred posting?

Read 4-302. In addition to the "midnight deadline" each bank must meet, the drawee bank is required to meet a separate deadline called the "midnight rule" in making the provisional settlement referenced in the previous paragraph. *Hanna v. First National Bank of Rochester*, 87 N.Y.2d 107, 661 N.E.2d 683, 28 U.C.C. Rep. Serv. 2d 417 (1995), explains how both deadlines relate to one another:

> The midnight rule – the requirement that the payor bank must settle for the item on the day of receipt – is addressed primarily to the payor bank's prompt treatment of demand items. It maintains the preexisting legal requirement that payor banks "pay" for demand items on the day of receipt, notwithstanding the extension by one day of the payor bank's right to dishonor or return the items. The payor bank's settlement for the item, whether provisional or final, is necessary and important because it establishes the pivotal link between the upstream flow of provisional credits and the downstream flow of final payment from the payor bank through collecting banks to payee. It also ensures that use of the funds represented by the item is available to the party immediately entitled to it.

* * *

The midnight deadline – requiring dishonor or return of the item by the payor bank by midnight of the next day – results in final payment of the item "simply with the lapse of time." The deadline, which presupposes a prior settlement for the item, was adopted to save banking institutions the effort and expense of sending confirmation of final payment of items.

* * *

Section 4-302 is intended to sanction institutions failing to meet the requirements for posting and dishonoring items contained in UCC 4-301. It does so by imposing liability for the amount of the item as a penalty upon a payor bank that fails to comply with either of the midnight requirements. The separate force of the two requirements is recognized in the statute. *Id.* at 108-117.

- Why sanction a bank that meets the midnight deadline but not the midnight rule, or vice versa?

> As stated in *Blake v. Woodford Bank and Trust Co.*, 555 S.W.2d 589 (Ky. App. 1977), the precursor to 4-302 was passed in the World War II era in which "the increasingly large number of checks processed each day and the shortage of qualified bank personnel [made it] impossible for banks to determine whether a check was 'good' in only 24 hours," as former law required.

Acceptance and Final Payment

Read 3-409 (a) and 4-215 (a).   These subsections define acceptance and final payment, two closely related processes that take place at the drawee/payor bank. Simply stated, once an item is accepted, the bank is obligated to make final payment on it.   *Flournoy v. First National Bank of Jeffersonville, Indiana*, 78 Ga. 222, 2 S.E. 547 (1887), explains the concept of acceptance:

The effect of accepting a bill is to acknowledge that the drawer has funds in the hands of the acceptor applicable to its payment, and the payee is entitled to repose with absolute trust and confidence upon that admission, and is under no duty to inquire further. If the admission proves injurious, he who made it must take the consequences. What has the payee to do . . . with the state of the accounts between drawer and acceptor? Nothing whatever. The acceptor is the party primarily liable, and his dealings about consideration for acceptance are with the acceptor. The payee's dealings are with the drawer. If the payee gives value to the drawer and acquires the bill in due course of trade before maturity, he is entitled to all the protection which commercial law can afford to the most favored class of creditors. *Id.* at 549.

> The concepts of primary and secondary liability are explored in Chapter 11, Part A.

- What does this excerpt suggest about a payee's reliance on final payment?

Problem: In *Sabin Meyer Regional Sales Corp. v. Citizens Bank*, 502 F. Supp. 557 (N.D. Ga. 1980), a payee claimed a drawee bank had wrongfully refused to make final payment after verbally indicating the drawer's account contained sufficient funds to pay the checks. Assume the checks were returned because they were drawn on insufficient funds, and further assume the payee claimed the verbal promise constituted either acceptance or certification.

- Based on these facts, who should prevail?

Read 4-215 and Comments 1, 2, 8, and 10. Normally, a drawee/payor bank may revoke a provisional settlement on the next banking day following receipt of the item, and thereby avoid final payment. A clearing-house rule or other local rule may, however, provide for additional time.

- What distinction does Comment 2 recognize between movement of the item, movement of the proceeds, and final settlement?

- What is the relationship between final settlement and final payment?

- When a check is cashed by the payee's bank (not the drawee/payor bank), has final payment occurred?

How does this comport with Regulation CC as presented above?

- Why is a collecting bank accountable to its customer only for items on which it has received final settlement?

As the court explains in *First National Bank in Harvey v. Colonial Bank*, 898 F. Supp. 1220, 28 U.C.C. Rep. Serv. 2d 290 (N.D. Ill. 1995), the drawee/payor bank is normally strictly liable when it misses its midnight deadline, thus effectuating final payment through lapse of time:

How does the midnight deadline impose "liability regardless of negligence"?

> [T]he special role of the payor bank in the check-collection system justifies the imposition of liability regardless of negligence. The midnight deadline requires the payor bank – the bank in the best position to know whether there are funds available to cover the check – to decide whether to pay or return the check. *Id.* at 1226.

- What would be the negative consequences of allowing a drawee bank to reverse final payment as a matter of course?

Presentment warranties are discussed in Chapter 11, Part B.

As 4-215 (b) shows, the payor bank may escape liability notwithstanding its failure to meet the midnight deadline or midnight rule if another party breached its presentment warranty to the payor bank or engaged in conduct intended to defraud the payor bank.

Read 3-418 and Comments 2 and 3. This section describes when a drawee may, as a matter of fairness, be permitted to recover from a payee or other person receiving payment made by mistake. 3-418 (d) and Comment 4 describe the interplay between this section and 4-215.

- From whom will a payee seek to recover if acceptance is revoked pursuant to 3-418 (d)?

Drawee banks may reverse final payment only in exceptional circumstances, such as when the payee has actual knowledge that it received payment in error. *Morgan Guaranty Trust Co. of New York v. American Savings and Loan Association*, 804 F.2d 1487, 2 U.C.C. Rep. Serv. 2d 785 (9th Cir. 1986), illustrates such a situation. In that case, the court considered the relative rights and obligations of a payor bank and a payee that received payment on two bearer notes after it learned the maker had filed for bankruptcy. After the bank realized its error, it sought to recover the funds from the payee, which refused. In finding the payee was required to restore the funds, the court held as follows:

> The payee who receives payment aware that he is not entitled to it does not have the same expectation of finality as an innocent payee, and the payor bank in this circumstance does not have superior knowledge. A party who accepts payment on an instrument knowing that the payor was entitled to dishonor it justifiably receives less favorable treatment by a court of equity than a payee ignorant of any problem. *Id.* at 1496.

- When is it fair to allow a drawee/payor bank to recover under 3-418 notwithstanding its own failure to exercise reasonable care?

Read 4-109 (b) and Comment 3. Sometimes, due to factors outside a bank's control, normal processing channels are unavailable. Under such circumstances, 4-109 (b) may relieve the bank from liability for delay. *First Wyoming Bank v. Cabinet Craft Distributors*, 624 P.2d 227, 30 U.C.C. Rep. Serv. 1194 (Wyo. 1981), addressed a payor bank's claim that it should be permitted to make a late dishonor of a check drawn on insufficient funds. The relevant facts are as follows:

> The untimely dishonor of the check was due to delay in delivering checks from a computer center in Billings, Montana, to the [drawee] bank in Sheridan [, Wyoming]. Normally, the same courier delivering the checks to the Montana computer center from Sheridan would have driven them back to Sheridan after the center had processed them. However, after the check in issue had been taken to Billings, the main road between Billings and Sheridan became flooded. Although the courier could have taken an alternate route back to Sheridan, the check was instead given to Western Airlines[, a local carrier,] by the computer center to be placed on the next morning's flight to Sheridan. For unknown

reasons, Western Airlines failed to deliver the check to Sheridan, although it made its usual flight. Western Airlines' failure to deliver the check to Sheridan as planned caused the bank to miss its Uniform Commercial Code deadline for dishonoring the check. *Id.* at 229.

In finding the bank strictly liable for the amount of the check, notwithstanding the payee's failure to show it was harmed by the delay, the court applied 4-109 (b):

> It is obvious that the flooded road between Billings and Sheridan which disrupted the normal procedure for delivery of the check was a "circumstance beyond the control of the bank". . . . Our inquiry is whether the bank used "such diligence as the circumstances required." . . . In answering this question, we must consider that the stipulated facts show that the bank had an alternative to using Western Airlines: its courier could have taken a different route. We are also somewhat handicapped by a lack of information. For example, although we know that the bank had previously used the airline's delivery service, we do not know what the airline's previous record for timely deliveries had been. We do not know if the computer center in turning the check over to the airline emphasized the need for a timely delivery. We do not know if the bank could have traced the checks which failed to arrive on the Western Airlines flight and gotten them sooner. *Id.* at 232.

- What advice would you give to a bank to ensure its processes would protect it in the event of an unforeseen delay?

Problem 1:   Park Corporation agreed to sell used mining equipment to DAI International Investment Corporation. For part of its down payment, DAI provided Garland Caribbean Corporation, the agent for the sale, with a check for $75,000. The equipment was not to be delivered until the purchase price was fully paid.   Before indorsing the check to Park, a representative of Garland called the drawee bank to find out whether DAI had sufficient funds in its account to cover the check. After learning that it did not, and without relating this information to Park, Garland transferred the check to Park, which sought to enforce the check. The check was paid by mistake, and Park refused the drawee's demand for repayment of the check proceeds.

- Is Park Corporation, a holder in due course, entitled to enforce the check notwithstanding the erroneous payment?

Based on *National Savings and Trust Co. v. Park Corp.*, 722 F.2d 1303, 37 U.C.C. Rep. Serv. 817 (6th Cir. 1983).

Problem 2: On December 6 and December 19, 1973, Wayne Blake deposited two checks made payable to him. The depositary bank was Morristown Bank and the drawee bank was Woodford Bank and Trust Company. The amounts of the two checks were approximately $16,500 and $11,000, respectively. Woodford Bank received the checks on the morning of Monday, December 24 and was closed for Christmas, reopening the following day. According to Woodford Bank's president, approximately 4,500 checks were processed on a normal day, but almost 7,000 checks were processed on December 26 because of the holiday the previous day. The president also testified that two of the bank's four posting machines were inoperable on December 26 and one of the bank's four bookkeepers charged with operating the machines was absent due to illness that day. The bank processed the checks, found them to be drawn on insufficient funds, and returned them to the regional Federal Reserve Bank on Thursday, December 27.

- Applying *First Wyoming Bank*, should Woodford Bank be liable for late return of the items?

Based on *Blake v. Woodford Bank and Trust Co.*, 555 S.W.2d 589, 21 U.C.C. Rep. Serv. 383 (Ky. App. 1977).

Notice of Dishonor

Read 3-503. When a bank returns an item unpaid, it must provide notice of its decision. If it fails to do so, it may not be able to enforce the dishonored instrument as against any indorser and some drawers.

- Which drawers are entitled to notice of dishonor?

- Must banks provide one another with notice of dishonor?

Comment 1 may assist you in answering this question.

Skim 3-504 and 3-505. 3-504 (b) and (c) state when a failure or delay in giving notice of dishonor is excused, and 3-505 indicates how to prove dishonor.

As Chapter 11, Part A shows, dishonor triggers the secondary liability of the drawer and indorsers and revives the underlying obligation. Thus, proving dishonor can be important.

- What is protest and when might it be desirable?

The following case describes how a court might allocate the loss arising from a failure to provide timely notice of dishonor.

Wells Fargo Bank v. Hartford National Bank and Trust Co.,
484 F. Supp. 817, 28 U.C.C. Rep. Serv. 446 (D. Conn. 1980).

Blumenfeld, Senior District Judge.

This is a suit commenced by Wells Fargo Bank, National Association to recover $25,000 from the Hartford National Bank and Trust Company. Wells Fargo is seeking to reverse the credit it gave to HNBT in the course of handling a check which it had received for collection on which it was later unable to collect. HNBT, in turn, seeks indemnification from the depositary bank, Lincoln First Bank-Central, National Association. . . .

Unlike many bank-collection cases, this case does not involve the liability of the payor bank, First National Bank of Nevada, which has not been sued, nor does it involve the liability of the now-bankrupt drawer of the check. The sole question presented by this action is which of these three banks in the chain of collection will have to absorb the loss occasioned by the "bad" check. . . .

* * *

On November 22, 1971, John D. Porter, as agent for Great Western Industries, Inc., opened a checking account [in New York] with Lincoln by depositing a check for $25,000 payable to the order of Lincoln. The check was drawn on the Great Western account with the Reno branch of the Nevada bank. After it received the check and opened the account for Great Western, Lincoln forwarded the check on for collection.

> What is the "normal" Regulation CC hold for such a check? What, if any, "exception hold" would Regulation CC permit?

Instead of utilizing the Federal Reserve Bank clearing-house system, Lincoln chose instead to use private collection channels, which promised an earlier availability of funds. In this particular case, Lincoln indorsed the check and sent it to HNBT with the understanding that HNBT would promptly forward the check on for collection.

HNBT received the check on November 22, the same day on which it had initially been deposited. After crediting Lincoln's account for $25,000, HNBT indorsed the check and mailed it to its California correspondent bank, Wells Fargo. On November 23, Wells Fargo received and indorsed the check, credited HNBT's account, and then mailed the check to the Las Vegas branch of the Nevada bank.

During this last transfer, a substantial delay was encountered. According to the Las Vegas branch bank records, the check inexplicably was not received in the mail until December 8, 1971, 15 days after Wells Fargo sent it. Moreover, an additional one-day delay followed because the check was not drawn on the Las Vegas branch but rather on the Reno branch of the Nevada bank. Since Las Vegas records did not reflect the extent of funds in Great Western's Reno account, it was necessary for the Las Vegas branch to forward the check to the Reno branch before the Nevada bank could establish whether there were sufficient funds to cover

> For guidance on how the UCC addresses branches of a single bank, see 4-107 and its comments.

the check. When the check finally arrived at Reno, the Nevada bank promptly discovered that there were insufficient funds in Great Western's account.

At 4:45 p.m. on December 10, 1971, Nevada bank personnel sought to inform Wells Fargo by telephone that the check had been dishonored. The call was made to a bank officer in Wells Fargo's San Francisco branch, but it was apparently "rejected" because it was not accompanied by sufficient identifying information. The Nevada bank made a second call, this time to Wells Fargo's Los Angeles Branch. At 5:30 p.m., this call was "accepted."

> Why do you suppose "rejected" and "accepted" are in quotation marks?

Since December 10, 1971, was a Friday, the next banking day was Monday, December 13, 1971. On Monday, the Nevada bank posted the dishonored check to Wells Fargo, which did not receive it until Friday, December 17. Nevada also reversed the credit which it had given to Wells Fargo.

Upon receiving the check, Wells Fargo immediately wired notice of the dishonor to HNBT. On the same day, Wells Fargo also returned the dishonored item by mail to HNBT and reversed the credit it had previously given. HNBT claims not to have received the telegram on the 17th but admits that it received the check in the mail on Monday, December 21. On that same day, HNBT notified Lincoln by telegram that the check had been dishonored. This notice, however, did not indicate the name of the drawer of the check and therefore failed to give Lincoln effective notice. Lincoln's first opportunity accurately to identify the dishonored item came when it received the check on December 27, 1971. HNBT had mailed the check to Lincoln on December 21 and had at the same time reversed the credit it had given earlier.

> Is this sentence consistent with 3-503 (b)?

For the purpose of ruling on these motions, it is not necessary to detail the remaining transfers of the check. Suffice it to say that, on December 28, 1971, Lincoln declined to accept the check, claiming that the notice of dishonor had arrived too late. The item was sent back through the chain of collection and ultimately Wells Fargo ended up with both the check and the $25,000 loss. After several unsuccessful efforts at working out repayment from Great Western, Wells Fargo commenced this action.

Wells Fargo now moves for summary judgment against HNBT on three separate counts. It claims a right to proceed on HNBT's indorsement pursuant to UCC 3-414 (1), a right to proceed on HNBT's breach of an implied warranty pursuant to UCC 4-207 (2), and a right to "charge-back" to HNBT pursuant to UCC 4-212 (1). As a necessary prerequisite to recovery under any of these theories, Wells Fargo must first establish that it gave HNBT timely notice of Nevada's dishonor of the check. If Wells Fargo, with all the disputed facts resolved in its favor, cannot establish that it gave a notice of dishonor when due, HNBT and Lincoln are entitled to prevail on their cross-motions for summary judgment.

> Indorser liability is now covered in 3-415 (a) and is discussed in Chapter 11, Part A; transfer warranties are introduced in Chapter 11, Part B; and charge-back is now addressed in 4-214 (a) and presented later in this section.

<table>
<tr><td>

The court is quoting the definition of "midnight deadline" in 4-104 (a) (10).

</td><td>

. . . [I]n order to determine whether Wells Fargo gave HNBT a timely notice of Nevada's dishonor, it is first necessary to establish "the banking day on which (Wells Fargo received) the relevant item or notice. . . ."

As indicated above, Wells Fargo received a notice of Nevada's dishonor by telephone on Friday afternoon, December 10, 1971. It sent no notice to HNBT before the midnight deadline on its next banking day, Monday, December 13. Wells Fargo first received written notice from Nevada on Friday, December 17, when the dishonored check arrived in the mail. Notice of dishonor was then sent to HNBT prior to midnight on Monday, December 21, the next banking day following receipt of the written notice. Therefore, the first question this court must decide is whether oral notice from the payor bank, Nevada, can trigger the obligation of the collecting bank, Wells Fargo, to give notice to its customer, HNBT.

</td></tr>
</table>

Review 4-103 (b) for a reminder of how Federal Reserve operating circulars should be read in conjunction with Articles 3 and 4.

In its affidavits, Lincoln established that the transaction in question was governed by the terms of the Federal Reserve Operating Circular No. 6. At the time of the transaction, this operating circular provided that payor banks can, in fact, must give notice by "wire" when they dishonor items with values in excess of $1,000. "Wire" is expressly defined to include "telephonic" notices. Thus, since this operating circular governed the transaction here in dispute, it is clear that Nevada's telephonic notice was an adequate notice of dishonor, and Wells Fargo was not entitled to wait for written notice.

As is indicated above, Wells Fargo's failure to give timely notice essentially precludes it from prevailing under any of the three counts in its complaint. Nonetheless, it has argued that it is entitled to relief under section 4-103 (5), which provides in pertinent part: "The measure of damages . . . is the amount of the item reduced by an amount which could not have been realized by the use of ordinary care . . . ."

The current citation is 4-103 (e).

Wells Fargo argues that, even if it had exercised "ordinary care," it would not have been able to protect Lincoln from a loss on the bad check. Lincoln had allowed Great Western to withdraw $23,000 of the $25,000 initially deposited by Mr. Porter within four banking days after the deposit. Wells Fargo argues that this is an unreasonably short time and that no amount of "care" on its part could have avoided the loss. In fact, even as of the first time that Wells Fargo received oral notice from Nevada, December 10, 1971, the funds had already been long since withdrawn from Lincoln's account. Thus, under section 4-103 (5), Wells Fargo argues that it should not be saddled with the loss.

This argument misconceives the nature of the statute. By its terms, the statute is only applicable to "(t)he measure of damages for failure to exercise ordinary care in handling an item . . . ." In other words, the statute is designed to act as a shield in the hands of a negligent defendant. No cases have been cited to this court nor have any been found where the statute was allowed to act as a sword in the hands of a plaintiff. Consequently, in this case, where no one has filed a complaint against Wells Fargo alleging a lack of ordinary care, the statute is inapplicable.

> Make sure you follow why Wells Fargo has not been sued.

* * *

For the foregoing reasons, Wells Fargo's motion for summary judgment against HNBT and HNBT's motion for summary judgment against Lincoln are denied. HNBT's motion for summary judgment against Wells Fargo and Lincoln's motion for summary judgment against HNBT are granted.

- In your own words, why does Wells Fargo's claim fail?

Note: *Alioto v. United States*, 593 F. Supp. 1402 (N.D. Cal. 1984), addresses when a bank will be liable for mishandling an item:

> [T]o recover from a bank for the mishandling of a check, the claimant must show two things: first, that the bank mishandled the check, and, second, that the claimant would have had a reasonable chance of collecting the amount owed if not for the bank's mishandling.

- What fact patterns generally support a mishandling claim?

Problem: Essex Construction Corporation deposited a check for about $120,000 into its account with Industrial Bank on March 31, 1995. The check was drawn on East Side Manor Cooperative Association's account with Signet Bank. Industrial Bank provisionally credited Essex's account for the amount of the check, but notified it that only $100 of the deposit would be available until April 6.

- Is Industrial's behavior consonant with Regulation CC?

> What, if any, additional facts are needed to answer this question?

On April 6, Signet Bank informed Industrial Bank that East Side had stopped payment on the check, and Industrial Bank revoked the provisional credit to Essex's account. On April 7, Industrial Bank mailed a notice to Essex, informing it that the check had been returned and enclosing the checks so Essex could pursue a cause of action on the check personally if desired. That same day, Essex wrote two checks totaling approximately $40,000 against the East Side check funds, which it expected to be in its account at that time. Essex received notice of dishonor on April 11 and brought suit against Industrial Bank, claiming that "it is entitled to recover because Industrial Bank failed either to provide notice of dishonor or to make the funds available by April 6, the date specified in the notice it provided."

> After you have studied the materials in Chapter 11, Part A, return to these facts and consider against whom Essex could enforce the check.

- What is the legal flaw in Essex's argument?

Based on *Essex Construction Corp. v. Industrial Bank of Washington, Inc.*, 913 F. Supp. 416, 29 U.C.C. Rep. Serv. 2d 281 (D. Md. 1995).

Charge-Back

> Who is the immediate customer of a collecting bank that is not also a depositary bank?

Read 4-214 and Comment 3. 4-214 describes a collecting bank's right to charge back the account of its customer for the amount of a check for which it does not receive final settlement from the drawee.

- Is it ever too late for a collecting bank to charge back an uncollected check?

The following case illustrates the interplay between a depositary bank's right of charge-back and the concept of final payment, showing how the question of whether cash or checks were deposited can make a difference in whether final payment has occurred.

Kirby v. First & Merchants National Bank,
168 S.E.2d 273, 6 U.C.C. Rep. Serv. 694 (Va. 1969).

Gordon, Justice.

> Note that this was an "on us" check insofar as the bank was concerned. What is the maximum hold Regulation CC would permit on such a check?

On December 30, 1966, defendant Margaret Kirby handed the following check to a teller at a branch of plaintiff First & Merchants National Bank:

NEUSE ENG. AND DREDGING CO.
Number _____

                                                       12-29-1966

Pay to the
order of   William J. Kirby & Margaret Kirby
 $ 2,500.00

    Twenty-Five Hundred -------------------- Dollars

FIRST & MERCHANTS
NATIONAL BANK
NEUSE ENG. & DREDGING CO.
Virginia Beach, Virginia
6-28-728-514   /s/ W.R. Wood

> What kind of indorsement have the Kirbys apparently given? Refer back to Chapter 9, Part B as needed to answer this question.

The back of the check bore the signatures of the payees, Mr. and Mrs. Kirby. Mrs. Kirby, who also had an account with the Bank, gave the teller the following deposit ticket:[FN1]

FN1. The handwriting in the upper-left portion of the deposit ticket corresponds with Mrs. Kirby's handwriting on the back of the check. The record does not indicate what persons added the other handwritten information on the ticket.

* * *

DEPOSIT TICKET		CURRENCY	2,300	00
NAME *Mrs. William J. Kirby*		COIN		
ADDRESS *324 Lillian Ave*		CHECKS LIST SINGLY BE SURE EACH ITEM IS ENDORSED	*6-28-728-514 (partial)*	
Va. Beach, VA				
ACCOUNT NUMBER		TOTAL FROM OTHER SIDE		
		TOTAL	2,300	00
DATE *Dec. 30, 1966*				

Checks and other items accepted for deposit subject to the terms and conditions of the banks's deposit agreement.

FIRST & MERCHANTS NATIONAL BANK

27 PL

2,500.00
2,300.00
200.00

The teller handed $200 in cash to Mrs. Kirby, and the Bank credited her account with $2,300 on the next business day, January 3, 1967. The teller or another Bank employee made the notation "Cash for Dep." under Mr. and Mrs. Kirby's signatures on the back of the Neuse check.

On January 4, the Bank discovered that the Neuse check was drawn against insufficient funds. Instead of giving written notice, a Bank officer called Mr. and Mrs. Kirby on January 5 to advise that the Bank had dishonored the check and to request reimbursement. Mr. and Mrs. Kirby said they would come to the Bank to cover the check, but they did not. On January 10, the Bank charged Mrs. Kirby's account with $2,500, creating an overdraft of $543.47.

On January 18, the Bank instituted this action to recover $543.47 from Mr. and Mrs. Kirby. At the trial, a Bank officer, the only witness in the case, testified:

Q. Did you cash the check (the Neuse check for $2,500) before you credited this deposit (the deposit of $2,300 to Mrs. Kirby's account)?

A. Yes, sir.

Q. So the bank, in effect, cashed the check for $2,500.00 and then gave the defendant a credit of $2,300.00 to their (sic) account and gave them (sic) $200.00 in cash?

A. Correct.

* * *

Q. So you cashed the check for $2,500.00?

A. Yes, sir.

> Is the Bank the depositary bank, the payor bank, both, or neither? See 4-105 as needed to answer this question.

The trial court, sitting without a jury, entered judgment for the plaintiff First & Merchants, and the defendants, Mr. and Mrs. Kirby, appeal. The question is whether the Bank had the right to charge Mrs. Kirby's account with $2,500 on January 10 and to recover from Mr. and Mrs. Kirby the overdraft created by that charge ($543.47). [If] First & Merchants paid the Neuse check in cash on December 30, it then made final payment and could not sue Mr. or Mrs. Kirby on the check except for breach of warranty.

* * *

When Mrs. Kirby presented the $2,500 Neuse check to the Bank on December 30, the Bank paid her $200 in cash and accepted a deposit of $2,300. The Bank officer said that the Bank cashed the check for $2,500, which could mean only that Mrs. Kirby deposited $2,300 in cash. And the documentary evidence shows that cash was deposited. The deposit of cash is evidenced by the word "currency" before "2,300.00" on the deposit ticket and by the words "Cash for Dep" on the back of the check.[FN5] The Bank's ledger, which shows a credit of $2,300 to Mrs. Kirby's account rather than a credit of $2,500 and a debit of $200, is consistent with a cashing of the Neuse check and a depositing of part of the proceeds. We must conclude that First & Merchants paid the Neuse check in cash on December 30 and, therefore, had no right thereafter to charge Mrs. Kirby's account with the amount of the check.

> FN5. Since no dollar amount was inserted after "checks" on the deposit ticket, the notation "6-28-728-514 partial" was apparently inserted to identify the source of the currency being deposited.

> Indorser liability is now found in 3-415. After you have read Chapter 11, Part B, consider whether Mrs. Neuse breached any warranties to the Bank.

The trial court apparently decided that Mr. and Mrs. Kirby were liable to the Bank because they had indorsed the Neuse check. But under UCC 3-414 (1) an indorser contracts to pay an instrument only if the instrument is dishonored. And, as we have pointed out, the Bank did not dishonor the Neuse check, but paid the check in cash when Mrs. Kirby presented it.

> Make sure you understand the logic of this paragraph.

As a practical matter, the contract of an indorser under UCC 3-414 (1) does not run to a drawee bank. That contract can be enforced by a drawee bank only if it dishonors a check; and if the bank dishonors the check, it has suffered no loss.

The rule that a drawee who mistakenly pays a check has recourse only against the drawer was firmly established before adoption of the Uniform Commercial Code. . . .

* * *

Nevertheless, First & Merchants contends that, under the terms of its deposit contract with Mrs. Kirby, the settlement was provisional and therefore subject to revocation whether or not the Neuse check was paid in cash on December 30. It contends that in this regard the deposit contract changes the rule set forth in the Uniform Commercial Code. But in providing that "all items are credited subject to final payment," the contract recognizes that settlement for an item is provisional only until the item is finally paid. Since the deposit contract does not change the applicable rule as set forth in the Uniform Commercial Code, we do not decide whether a bank can provide by deposit contract that payment of a check in cash is provisional.

Even if the Bank's settlement for the Neuse check had been provisional, . . . the Bank concedes that it neither sent written notice of dishonor nor returned the Neuse check before the "midnight deadline." So the Bank had no right to charge the item back to Mrs. Kirby's account.

For the reasons set forth, the trial court erred in entering judgment for First & Merchants against Mr. and Mrs. Kirby.

[The dissenting opinion of Justice Harrison has been omitted.]

- ▪ What advice would you give the bank to avoid similar liability in the future?

Note: A bank may, by contract, broaden its right of charge-back beyond what is provided in 4-214. *Lema v. Bank of America, N.A.*, 375 Md. 625, 826 A.2d 504 (2003), addressed the effect of the following language in a customer deposit agreement:

> Unless prohibited by applicable law or regulation, we . . . reserve the right to charge back to your account the amount of any item deposited to your account or cashed for you which was initially payed by the payor bank and which is later returned to us due to an allegedly forged, unauthorized, or missing indorsement, claim of alteration, encoding error, or other problem which in our judgment justifies reversal of credit. *Id.* at 632.

- ▪ How does this language depart from what 4-214 would otherwise permit?

In *Lema*, a friend of the accountholder deposited a check for $63,000 which turned out to be altered, having been issued in the amount of $3,000. After Bank of America, the depositary bank, discovered the fraud, it charged back the account, citing the contractual language quoted above. In finding for the bank, the court emphasized the contractual nature of the customer-bank relationship and cited 4-103, which permits the parties to vary the effect of many provisions of Article 4 by contract.

- ▪ What limitations would 4-103 place upon the parties' ability to modify the bank's right of charge-back?

Responsibilities of Collecting Banks

Read 4-201 (a) and Comments 1, 2, and 4. A collecting bank acts as an agent of the owner of an item presented for collection. Comment 4 explains some practical implications of such a bank's agency status.

- How does the collecting bank's status as an agent affect its rights and responsibilities with regard to checks it collects for its customers' accounts?

Read 4-202 and Comments 2 and 4. 4-202 describes the duty of ordinary care insofar as it relates to collecting banks.

- How are the duties of ordinary care different for presenting banks than for other collecting banks?

- What are the relative benefits and risks of the Massachusetts and New York rules described in Comment 4?

> Note that part (b) adopts the "First In, First Out" rule introduced in Chapter 9, Part D.

Read 4-210 and Comments 1 and 3. 4-210 describes a collecting bank's security interest in items being collected.

> Reading 4-211 may assist you in answering this question.

- How is the security interest in 4-210 necessary so that otherwise qualified collecting banks can be deemed holders in due course?

> Alternatively, you may find these provisions listed as Check 21 Act §§ 2 (b), 3 (16), 4, and 5. The text of Check 21, together with resources for applying it, is available online at www.federalreserve.gov/paymentsystems/truncation/.

- What does Comment 3 mean by describing the security interest as "self-liquidating"?

Introduction to Check 21

Read 12 USC §§ 5001 (b), 5002 (16), 5003, and 5004. These sections provide an overview of Check 21, which is federal legislation that facilitates electronic check presentment but does not require it.

Read 4-110 and its commentary, which describes electronic presentment and how parties may agree to it.

The following excerpts from the Federal Reserve Board publication *Check Clearing for the 21st Century Act* explain Check 21:

> What does "truncation" mean in this context?

The Check Clearing for the 21st Century Act (Check 21) was signed into law on October 28, 2003, and became effective on October 28, 2004. Check 21 is designed to foster innovation in the payments system and to enhance its efficiency by reducing some of the legal impediments to check truncation. The law facilitates check truncation by creating a new negotiable instrument called a substitute check, which permits banks to truncate original checks, to process check information electronically, and to deliver substitute checks to banks that want to continue receiving paper checks. A substitute check is the legal equivalent of the original check and includes all the information contained on the original check. The law does not require banks to accept checks in electronic form, nor does it require banks to use the new authority granted by the Act to create substitute checks.

- What does it mean for a substitute check to be the "legal equivalent of the original check"?

The following graphics and text from the same Federal Reserve Board publication illustrate a substitute check and describe its function:

A substitute check is a special paper copy of the front and back of an original check. The substitute check may be slightly larger than the original check. Substitute checks are specially formatted so they can be processed as if they were original checks. The front of a substitute check should state: "This is a legal copy of your check. You can use it the same way you would use the original check." The following sample shows what a substitute check looks like.

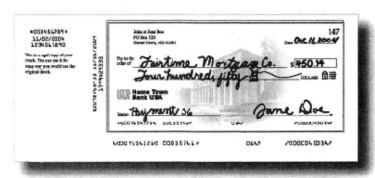

Front of a substitute check

Back of a substitute check

- How does the creation of a new "substitute check," itself a piece of paper, facilitate development of electronic check processing?

International Perspective: Notice of Dishonor

Read CIBN Article 1 (3). Because the CIBN does not apply to checks, much of what is discussed in this chapter is outside the purview of the Convention. However, just as banks might process promissory notes and non-check drafts in addition to checks, they may also process the International Bills of Exchange and International Promissory Notes that are the subject of the CIBN. To the extent that they do so, certain other articles of the CIBN may come into play.

Read Articles 64 through 68 of the CIBN. These Articles describe the obligations of the holder with regard to notice of dishonor.

- What are the similarities and differences between the UCC and the CIBN with regard to notice of dishonor?

> Note the different spelling for "dishonour" and "cheque."

In *Dishonoured Cheques: A Comparative Analysis*, J.I.B.L. 2001, 16 (3), 77, Neil Kibble and Andrew Campbell describe what they term the "standard practice" in the United Kingdom for merchants to accept cheques only from those customers who produce a "cheque guarantee card." So long as the merchant complies with the conditions set forth in the "Standard Cheque Card Scheme," the bank promises to pay the item on presentment. The required conditions include the following:

> After you have read the materials in Chapter 12 on credit and debit cards, you might consider how the United Kingdom's system compares to the protections currently in place in the United States for users of credit and debit cards.

(1) Payment will be guaranteed only up to the sum indicated on the card (typically 50 or 100 pounds, but sometimes as much as 250).

(2) The cheque must bear the same name and number as the card.

(3) The cheque must be signed in the presence of the payee, so that person can compare the signature on the cheque with that on the card.

(4) The payee must write the card number on the cheque.

(5) The card must not be defaced or altered.

The effect of such a card is that, "for relatively small transactions, the bank [assumes] the risk of customer default." The authors indicate that the availability of these cards "has led to the virtual universal acceptance of cheques by shopkeepers and other traders."

- Would you support a similar system in the United States?

B. Banks and Their Customers

This section introduces the "properly payable" rule and the concept of wrongful dishonor. This section also discusses the customer-deposit contract, the bank-statement rule, postdated checks, and checks drawn on insufficient funds. Finally, this section presents circumstances that terminate a bank's authority to pay items on behalf of its customer, including legal process, stop-payment, death or incompetence, staleness, and bankruptcy.

A Bank's Right to Debit a Customer Account

Read 4-401. This provision, which is called the "properly payable" rule, often becomes relevant when a drawee bank chooses to pay an item drawn on insufficient funds, a postdated item, or an altered item, and its customer – the drawer – disputes its decision to do so. In each circumstance, the key to a bank's right to debit a customer's account is that the item must be "properly payable."

- What does it mean for an item to be properly payable?

- Why is it fair for a drawee to have the option to pay a check drawn on insufficient funds (or not), while the drawer has no right either to insist that such a check be paid or to object if the drawee pays the check?

> Re-reading the materials on MICR encoding and expedited check processing contained earlier in this chapter may assist you in answering this question.

- Why will a bank normally be permitted to accept postdated checks prior to the date of the check, unless notice is given as described in 4-401 (c)?

- How does the Code allocate responsibility for altered items?

The following case illustrates the interplay between incapacity, setoff, and a bank's right to pay checks drawn on insufficient funds.

> Incapacity and setoff are discussed in Part B of this chapter.

Lincoln National Bank and Trust Co. v. Peoples Trust Bank,
177 Ind. App. 312, 379 N.E.2d 527,
24 U.C.C. Rep. Serv. 1229 (1978).

Staton, Judge.

The action below was brought by the co-administrators of the Estate of
William S. Wyss, deceased. The Estate recovered a sum of money
which Lincoln National Bank and Trust Company of Fort Wayne had
set off against a certificate of deposit which Wyss held in the Bank. We
reverse in part.

This case raises the question of whether the Bank properly cashed
checks which created overdrafts on a depositor's account, thereby
entitling the Bank to set off such amounts against other deposits held
by the depositor in the Bank.

> **What effect, if any, will the check's lack of a date have on its legal status? Review UCC 3-113 (b) as needed to answer this question.**

Wyss had a checking account at Lincoln National Bank and also owned
a $50,000 certificate of deposit at the Bank, payable on February 18,
1974. Apparently, during the latter years of his life, Wyss' mind was
somewhat unstable. Near the end of his life, he wrote three checks for
which his account's funds were insufficient. The first, drawn on his
Lincoln account and dated December 3, 1973 (# 2223), was in the
amount of $8,981.83. It was delivered by Wyss to Harold F. Allen and
was payable to Rudisill Motors. A second check, drawn on the Lincoln
account and dated December 10, 1973 (# 2397), was in the amount of
$300. In the record it bears the legend, "account closed." The third
check, drawn on Indiana Bank and undated (# 1015), was in the
amount of $300. It was presented to Lincoln and was honored by
cashing.

The main controversy involves the sequence of events culminating in
the cashing of check # 2223 for $8,981.83. On December 3, 1973,
Harold F. Allen attempted to cash check # 2223 at a Lincoln branch
office. The Bank refused to cash the check, for a reason not evident in
the record. Later the same day, after banking hours, Allen presented

> **Bank Americard changed its name to Visa in 1976.**

the check to a BankAmericard teller at Lincoln's main office. He
endorsed the check with his name, followed by "Rudisill Motors." The
teller accepted the check, credited part of the amount to Allen's
BankAmericard account, and issued the remainder in the form of a
cashier's check made out to Allen. The teller failed to abide by an
internal bank rule, which required a manager's approval before a teller

> **Stop-payment, including stop-payment on a cashier's check, is covered in Part B of this chapter.**

cashed or certified a check for over $500. Allen cashed the cashier's
check at a savings and loan association the same day. Lincoln
subsequently attempted to stop payment on the check, but later made
payment.

The record shows that two "holds" (in other words, no check would be
paid without the express authority of the Bank's officers), dated
December 5 and December 6, 1973, were entered on Wyss' checking
account at the request of someone other than Wyss himself.

> **The common-law right of setoff is referenced in UCC 4-215 (e), 4-210 (a), and 4-303 (a) and exists where created by other law.**

Wyss died on January 29, 1974. Lincoln effected a setoff in the amount
of $9,581.83 (the sum of the three checks) against Wyss' certificate of
deposit. His estate sought to recover that amount.

Trial was brief. The evidence presented concerned the circumstances of the cashing of check # 2223 and the Bank's knowledge of Wyss' mental instability. . . .

The trial court concluded that the law was with the Estate and granted the Estate judgment against Lincoln in the amount of $9,581.83 plus interest in the amount of $1,725.00.

Lincoln failed to take issue with the trial court's findings . . . which involved the propriety of the Bank's handling of checks # 2397 and # 1015, each drawn for $300. In addition, Lincoln failed to address any argument against the Estate's recovery of the amount of these two checks, totaling $600. Therefore, Lincoln has waived any issue it may have raised concerning that portion of the trial court's judgment. . . .

The only issue we must resolve, then, is whether Lincoln properly cashed check # 2223 and became entitled to set off $8,981.83 against Wyss' certificate of deposit. . . .

* * *

Check # 2223 was properly payable on its face. The check was completed and signed by the depositor and was not altered in any way. Thus, unless the check was not "properly payable" for some other reason, the trial court erred in finding . . . that the check was not properly payable.

The Estate argues that check # 2223 was not properly payable for several reasons: it was cashed without sufficient funds to cover it; it was cashed without a manager's approval; it had been dishonored previously; and no evidence was presented establishing the relationship between Allen and Rudisill Motors.

The Estate's objections fail to establish that the check was not properly payable. IC 1971, 26-1-4-401, supra, clearly authorizes a bank to cash a check which creates an overdraft. The requirement of a manager's approval before cashing certain checks is an internal banking rule, the violation of which in this instance cannot be invoked for the benefit of the Estate. . . . The evidence itself fails to establish that the teller's violation of the internal banking rule was the direct cause of harm to the Estate; even if the teller had adhered to the rule, a manager still had the option of approving the transaction which created an overdraft on Wyss' account, under IC 1971, 26-1-4-401, supra. Likewise, a previous dishonor of check # 2223, whatever the reason, did not affect Lincoln's right to decide to pay the check upon a later presentment, again under IC 1971, 26-1-4-401, supra. Further, as Lincoln points out, the Estate in no way relied on the earlier dishonor to its detriment. Finally, the relationship (or lack of it) between Allen and Rudisill Motors is not at issue in this case. The Estate presented no evidence at trial tending to establish that someone other than the proper payee had received the proceeds from check # 2223. Both parties seemed to presume, as we will, that Allen was acting in a representative capacity in cashing a check made out to Rudisill Motors.

We hold that check # 2223 was properly payable as a matter of law.

In its brief, the Estate claimed that the trial court's judgment for the
Estate could be sustained on an alternative ground, that is, that
Lincoln failed to exercise reasonable care in cashing check # 2223. The
grounds for charging negligence include those which we have already
discounted. However, the Estate also argues that Lincoln, which was
"monitoring" Wyss' account, was negligent in cashing a check when its
officers knew of Wyss' mental instability.

The trial court's finding . . . that the Bank had been notified not to
honor Wyss' checks before check # 2223 was presented on December 3,
1973, would appear to support such an argument. However, the finding
is not supported by any evidence in the record. While Bank officers had
been requested to "monitor" Wyss' account before presentment of check
2223, the record shows that an actual "hold" was not placed on Wyss'
account until December 5, 1973. A bank's duty to "monitor" an account
cannot give rise to an action for negligence when a teller cashes a
properly payable check.

Finally, it is not at all clear under what authority the bank would have
stopped payment of checks drawn on Wyss' account. IC 1971, 26-1-4-
403 concerns the manner in which the "customer" may order a bank to
stop-payment on checks. In the case at hand, Wyss never requested
that a "hold" be placed on his account. He continued to write checks
drawn on his account. The "hold" was ordered by his attorney, who
claimed that Wyss was mentally incompetent. . . .

The record contains no evidence that Wyss was ever adjudicated to be
incompetent. Lincoln could not be held negligent in cashing a properly
payable check authorized by Wyss, simply because Wyss' attorney
communicated to the Bank that Wyss was mentally unsound and in
need of having his account monitored.

When Lincoln cashed check # 2223, an overdraft on Wyss' account
resulted. Wyss became indebted to Lincoln for the amount of the check.
Lincoln had the right to charge the amount to Wyss' other deposits in
the Bank. Therefore, Lincoln had the right to set off the amount of
$8,981.83 against the $50,000 certificate of deposit Wyss owned in the
Bank.

With regard to check # 2223, the trial court erred in concluding that the
law was with the Estate and in granting the Estate judgment in the
amount of $8,981.83. We reverse the award of $8,981.83 plus interest
and remand to the trial court with instructions to enter judgment for
Lincoln. We affirm the portion of the judgment granting the Estate
recovery of $600.00 plus interest.

- **Read 4-401 and 4-405 in conjunction with one
  another.** Does mental incapacity prevent items
  issued by an incompetent person from being properly
  payable?

Note: When a bank decides to pay an item into overdraft, it
will not normally be able to pass any resultant loss to another
party. The assumption is that the bank, having taken the

After you have read
the materials on
incapacity later in
this section, consider
whether this portion
of the court's holding
comports with 4-405,
which provides the
relevant rule on
point.

1   chance that its customer would not deposit sufficient funds to
2   cover the check, is in the best position to avoid the loss. *Demos*
3   *v. Lyons*, 151 N.J. Super. 489, 376 A.2d 1352, 22 U.C.C. Rep.
4   Serv. 754 (1977), addressed a drawee bank's claim that it
5   should be able to recover from the payee for a check drawn on
6   insufficient funds, based on a theory of restitution. The bank
7   had decided to honor the check, "[s]o as not to embarrass their
8   customer in [what the bank deemed to be an] important
9   transaction" giving rise to the issuance of the check.   In
10 rejecting this argument, the court held as follows:

> The bank was presumably basing its claim on UCC 3-418.

12   As a rule of law, "payment is final" refers to the common law
13   principle that one cannot recover back money paid, simply because
14   of a change of mind. Its rationale is repose. Establishing the
15   finality of a payment tends to assure stability in people's affairs.
16   However, the law may compel restitution where there are
17   competing considerations such as fraud, duress, and mistake
18   favoring the payor. When these considerations are raised, the
19   evidence must be examined and equities balanced. Under some
20   circumstances the payor's equities are insufficient to overcome
21   those of the payee or others who may have relied in good faith on
22   the payment. But even where no one has relied on the payment,
23   the policy of repose may nevertheless prevail where the payor's
24   asserted equity is based on facts he knew before payment and
25   freely chose to disregard. Where the payor is denied restitution
26   because others relied in good faith on the payment, he is said to be
27   estopped. Where no one relied upon the payment but restitution is
28   denied because the payor voluntarily paid knowing he had reason
29   not to, he is said to have waived his right to restitution based on
        that reason. *Id.* at 496.

30   ▪ **Read 3-418 and Comment 3.** Does the holding
31   comport with 3-418?

Wrongful Dishonor

Read 4-402 and Comments 1 and 5. As 4-402 shows, banks
are normally liable to their customers for actual damages
caused by wrongful dishonor.

    ▪ Will a payor bank be liable to the holder of a
       dishonored item?

    ▪ May wrongful dishonor justify punitive damages?

In *Maryott v. First National Bank of Eden, South Dakota*, 2001
S.D. 43, 624 N.W.2d 96, 44 U.C.C. Rep. Serv. 2d 240 (2001),
drawer Ned Maryott was able to show he sustained damages
based on the drawee bank's decision to dishonor three checks
drawn on his account despite the fact that sufficient funds
existed in his account. He had done business with the bank for

almost twenty years and had never incurred an overdraft or
made a late loan payment. The bank's decision to dishonor the
checks was a result of its incorrect suspicion that Maryott, a
livestock dealer, was involved in a check-kiting scheme. At the
same time, and based on the same suspicions, the bank
exercised its right of setoff and appropriated a significant
portion of Maryott's account to pay off almost the entire balance
of several loans Maryott owned to it. These loans were not
overdue at that time. Based on the bank's actions, two of the
payees made claims on the bond Maryott was required to
maintain as part of his business. Because these claims
exceeded the amount of the bond, Maryott forfeited his state
license for selling livestock and lost his livelihood.

- What damages would you expect to see awarded in
  Maryott?

The following case elaborates on concepts introduced in the
Maryott excerpt, illustrating how banks can be liable to their
customers when, acting on their own suspicions, they dishonor
checks drawn on sufficient funds. Keep cases like this one in
mind when tempted to criticize a bank for responding too
slowly to a check-kiting scheme.

Wallick v. First State Bank of Farmington,
532 S.W.2d 520, 18 U.C.C. Rep. Serv. 1272 (Mo. App. 1976).

Smith, Chief Judge.

Defendant [First State Bank of Farmington] appeals from a judgment
against it in accord with the verdict of a jury in a suit in two counts
premised upon wrongful dishonor and breach of contract. The
judgment was for $770.87 on Count I, the wrongful dishonor, and for
$508.42 actual damages and $2,500 punitive damages on Count II, the
breach of contract.

> How would the
> parties' rights and
> obligations be
> different if this were
> an escrow account or
> the bank had a
> security interest in
> the account?
> Consult a legal
> dictionary as
> necessary to answer
> this question.

Plaintiff Harold Wallick made arrangements for the building of a
residence in St. Francois County through a general contractor, Clay
Wideman. Plaintiff borrowed $26,500 from defendant which was
placed in a "special account" in defendant bank. The account was not
an escrow account, and the bank had no security interest in the
account itself. Checks on the account required the signatures of two of
three persons, plaintiff, Wideman, or Jack Sebastian, an officer of the
bank. Originally, plaintiff would approve invoices and transmit them
from the St. Louis area to the bank and checks would be issued, signed
by Wideman and Sebastian. Certain difficulties arose with
subcontractors and some lack of faith in Wideman arose, so it was
agreed that plaintiff would make out the checks which would then be
presented by the contractor or subcontractor to Sebastian for signature.
In every circumstance except one, checks on the account payable to the
contractor or a subcontractor were either signed by plaintiff or were
supported by invoices approved by him. The one exception was a check

to Jennings Lumber Company for $508.42, signed only by Sebastian and which was unsupported by any invoice, bill, or other record in the bank files. The president of the defendant was also the president of Jennings Lumber Company. Sebastian "thought" that plaintiff had orally approved such payment; plaintiff stated that he had not and knew nothing about the check until he received a bank statement some 5 months after the check was issued.

Approximately a year later, on August 26, 1969, the house was largely finished although there were still some items to be corrected. No liens were pending, and no money was owed by plaintiff to any contractor or subcontractor. Plaintiff, accompanied by his lawyer, attempted to withdraw from the account the remaining balance, some $1,447. The bank refused to turn over the funds. Plaintiff then issued a check to his wife for that balance; she presented the check to Sebastian for his signature; Sebastian refused to sign the check, stating that the money in the account did not belong to the Wallicks. At trial, Sebastian stated that he was trying to be a "good Samaritan" to protect any subcontractors who might have claims against Wideman, who by this time was insolvent. He admitted the money in the account belonged to Wallick and the bank had no interest or claim against it. The heating-and-air-conditioning subcontractor had filed a lien and suit against the Wallicks and Wideman but, on August 13, 1969, that suit and the lien were dismissed with prejudice as to the Wallicks. Judgment was entered against Wideman and, in October 1969, a writ of garnishment in execution of the judgment against Wideman was served on the defendant apparently naming the Wallicks as judgment debtors. Without notifying Wallick, the bank, on November 14, 1969, paid over to the Circuit Court $770.87 from Wallick's account. Subsequently, the bank paid to Wallick the amount left in the account after the payment under the garnishment.

> Was Wallick wrong in attempting to obtain the funds this way?

Plaintiff's petition was in two counts. Count I sought recovery of the $1447.86 from defendant under a theory of wrongful dishonor. Count II sought recovery of the $770.87 for breach of contract plus punitive damages. . . . [O]ver defendant's objection, plaintiff was allowed to amend his petition by adding to Count II the allegations concerning the Jennings Lumber payment. Defendant then requested a mistrial and a continuance to conduct additional discovery. These requests were denied. . . .

> Can Wallick recover the face amount of both checks, or is recovery limited to one or the other?

* * *

Whether plaintiff owed Jennings Lumber Company money or not was a matter solely between plaintiff and Jennings. The bank's function is to honor its contract with plaintiff; it is not the bank's function to determine which creditors should or should not be paid.

* * *

When the bank made payment to Jennings, it did so as a volunteer or intermeddler, and it cannot recover or set off that payment against plaintiff's claim. . . .

As to Count I, defendant contends that no wrongful dishonor occurred because the check issued to Mrs. Wallick did not carry two signatures. We do not agree. The missing signature was that of the bank officer. By that officer's testimony, it is clear that the bank had no interest in the money on deposit. Its loan was secured by a deed of trust, and payment of checks was in no way dependent upon any security interest of the bank in the funds. The money was Wallick's. [The UCC] does not define wrongful dishonor. Taking the transaction as a whole, including Sebastian's explanation of his reasons for refusal to sign, which were legally insufficient, we find the evidence sufficient to support recovery for wrongful dishonor. Nor do we accept defendant's contention that the wrongful garnishment was the proximate cause of plaintiff's loss. Obviously, if the check to Wallick's wife had been honored, as it should have been, there would have been no funds to which the garnishment could attach and no loss to plaintiff.

We are unable to approve the award of punitive damages on Count II. Punitive damages are not allowed for breach of contract. The exceptions to this rule occur where the breach amounts to an independent, willful tort and there are proper allegations of malice, wantonness, or oppression. We are not advised by respondent what independent tort is established by the evidence nor do we find one. The award of punitive damages was improper.

- What facts most strongly support the court's holding?

- What act constituted wrongful dishonor?

Note: As *Wallick* affirms, punitive damages are not normally available for a bank's wrongful dishonor of its customer's checks. Punitive damages may, however, be awarded in exceptional circumstances such as those presented in *Northshore Bank v. Palmer*, 525 S.W.2d 718, 17 U.C.C. Rep. Serv. 488 (Tex. 1975).

An unknown fraudfeasor obtained some of Mr. Marvel Fikes' blank checks and made one of those checks payable to James T. Palmer in the amount of $275. The wrongdoer then took the check to Northshore Bank, where Palmer had an account, and requested that the bank cash the check. The teller did so without verifying the identify of the person presenting the check. Four or five days later, the drawee bank returned the check to Northshore Bank, having noted the forged signature of Mr. Fikes. Northshore charged the returned check against the account of Mr. Palmer, who had no knowledge of the forgery and asserted his innocence. The bank also closed Mr. Palmer's account and recalled several valid checks written by Mr. Palmer to various payees, on which it had already made final payment, stamping those checks "paid in error" or "account closed." Mr. Palmer was charged an "insufficient funds" fee for each check thus recalled, and the bank placed the matter with a collection agency when he refused to pay these charges.

When Mr. Palmer went to the bank to attempt to clear up the matter in person, a bank employee called over an armed guard to escort Mr. Palmer from the premises. Mr. Palmer reported the forgery to the police, personally contacted Mr. Fikes and his bank, and telephoned the payee of each check Northshore Bank had recalled. The bank never repaid Mr. Palmer the funds it had taken from his account. The court upheld the jury's award of punitive damages of $3,500, coupled with actual damages of $2,000.

- Which party could most easily have avoided the loss and how?

- What aggravating factors distinguish this case from *Wallick*?

Problem: On Sunday, May 13, 1979, Kenneth and Vicki Isaacs noticed their checkbook was missing and reported this fact to their bank, Twin City Bank, on Monday. Soon after, they learned two forged checks totaling about $2,000 had been cashed against their account on May 11 and 12. On Monday morning, after the Isaacs notified the bank of the loss, the bank "froze" the account, which contained a balance of about $2,000. Because Mr. Isaacs had been convicted of burglary some years before, the bank was initially concerned that he might be involved in some kind of wrongdoing but, by May 30, the police had apprehended the forger and notified Twin City Bank that the Isaacs were in no way involved. The police repeated this information to the bank in mid-June, but the bank continued to keep the account "frozen" for approximately four years, even though the Isaacs' credit with Twin City Bank was "impeccable." During this four-year period, not only was the Isaacs' credit impaired with Twin City Bank, but they were unable to obtain credit elsewhere as well and were forced to borrow from relatives and friends. A check they wrote as "earnest money" for a house they planned to purchase shortly before the account was frozen was dishonored, and the sale therefore fell through. At one point during this period, one spouse filed for divorce; although the petition was dropped, the Isaacs testified to the considerable strain the matter had placed upon their marriage. In addition, Twin City Bank repossessed two vehicles because the Isaacs did not have access to the funds in their account to make car payments. One vehicle was repossessed before the parties' contractual five-day grace period had expired.

- Are punitive damages appropriate?

Based on *Twin City Bank v. Isaacs*, 283 Ark. 127, 672 S.W.2d 651, 39 U.C.C. Rep. Serv. 35 (1984).

Stop-Payment

Read 4-303 and Comments 1, 2, and 6, and 4-403. These sections describe a customer's right to stop payment and the period during which a customer can exercise that right. Because the drawer-drawee relationship is contractual, the drawer can revoke the instruction to pay an item, up until the drawee accepts the item or makes an irrevocable settlement for the item. The right of stop-payment is commonly raised in cases involving checks but can also be implicated in a fact pattern involving a promissory note or non-check draft.

- **Read 4-403 Comment 3.** When is it possible to stop payment on a note?

> This is often called payment "over" a stop-payment order.

The following case illustrates how courts determine whether a drawer has suffered a loss when a drawee pays an item despite a valid stop-payment order. The drawee is liable only if the drawer proves a loss.

Dunnigan v. First National Bank,
217 Conn. 205, 585 A.2d 659, 13 U.C.C. Rep. Serv. 2d 1196
(1991).

> The trustee seeks to maximize the funds available to unsecured creditors by bringing funds within the estate.

Borden, Associate Justice.

The [trustee in bankruptcy of Cohn Precious Metals, Inc.] brought this action against the bank for wrongfully paying a check issued by Cohn over Cohn's valid stop-payment order. The trial court . . . rendered judgment for the amount of the check. This appeal followed.

* * *

The parties stipulated to the following facts. On November 8, 1978, pursuant to purchase order 1142, Lamphere Coin, Inc., a trader in coins and precious metals, delivered to Cohn certain silver dollars with a unit price of $1.71 and with a total value of $27,492.07. Cohn's bookkeeper incorrectly recorded the unit price of those coins, however, as $17.10, resulting in an erroneous total value of $47,098.93. On November 9, 1978, Cohn paid Lamphere $47,098.93 by wire transfer to Lamphere's bank account, resulting in an overpayment to Lamphere by Cohn of $19,606.86. On November 10, 1978, Lamphere delivered three and one-half bags of silver dollars to Cohn pursuant to Cohn's purchase order 1145. The value of the silver dollars was $21,175. On the same day, Cohn issued two checks drawn on its account at the bank to Lamphere, one in the amount of $12,175 and one in the amount of $9,000, totaling $21,175.

Between November 10 and November 15, Cohn discovered its bookkeeper's error and, on November 14, 1978, directed the bank to stop payment on the two checks totaling $21,175 that had been issued on November 10, 1978. The bank stopped payment on the $9,000 check but, on or about November 20, 1978, the bank inadvertently honored the $12,175 check over the valid stop-payment order. Cohn retained the three and one-half bags of silver dollars, but never recovered its overpayment from Lamphere. . . .

. . . The bank argues that, where there is good consideration for a particular check, or where the check was given as payment on a binding contract, the bank that paid the check over a valid stop-payment order is not liable to its customer, because there was no "loss resulting from [its] payment." Thus, in the bank's view a customer cannot establish a loss under this provision of the code by relying on the loss of credits due the customer from prior, unrelated transactions between the customer and the payee of the check. The plaintiff argues, as the trial court concluded, that whether a customer has incurred a "loss" . . . cannot be determined solely by focusing on the transaction underlying the particular check involved, but must be determined by focusing on the entire relationship between the customer and the payee of the check. The plaintiff contends that it is unreasonable to disregard the relative positions of the parties, especially where they have demonstrated a continuing course of business dealings, where there are likely to be such credits. Under such circumstances, the plaintiff claims that focusing on a single transaction is contrary to the intent of the Code. Thus, in the plaintiff's view, Cohn would have had a good "defense" to a claim by Lamphere on the check because of the overpayment, and by paying the check the bank caused Cohn a loss. . . .

> The court's language is taken from UCC 4-403 (c).

* * *

[A] bank customer has the right to order his bank to stop-payment on a check, so long as he does so in a timely and reasonable manner, and, . . . an oral stop-payment order is binding on the bank for a limited period of time. The fact that the bank has paid the check over the customer's valid stop-payment order does not mean, however, that the customer is automatically entitled to repayment of the amount of the check. Under § 4-403 (3), the customer must also establish "the fact and amount of loss resulting from" the bank's improper payment.

> **Read UCC 4-403 (b).** How long is an oral stop-payment order valid?

> The current citation is to UCC 4-403 (c).

[W]e conclude that, as a matter of law, Cohn suffered no "loss" within the meaning of § 42a-4-403 (3). The check was supported by good consideration because it was issued in payment for the silver coins that Lamphere delivered to Cohn. Furthermore, on the basis of that underlying transaction, Lamphere had enforceable rights to payment by Cohn for those coins. . . .

. . . [T]he language of § 42-4-403 (3) suggests a narrower reading than would be required by the plaintiff's position. Section 42a-4-403 (3) places on the bank's customer the "burden of establishing the *fact and amount of loss resulting from the payment* of an item contrary to a binding stop-payment order. . . ." (Emphasis added.) By contrast, § 42a-4-402, which deals with a bank's liability to its customer for a wrongful *dishonor,* as opposed to a wrongful payment, provides as follows: "A payor bank is liable to its customer for *damages proximately caused by the wrongful dishonor* of an item. When the dishonor occurs through mistake, liability is limited to actual damages proved. If so, proximately caused and proved damages may include damages for an arrest or

The current version
of UCC 4-402
includes minor
changes to the
quoted language.

prosecution of the customer or other consequential damages. Whether any consequential damages are proximately caused by the wrongful dishonor is a question of fact to be determined in each case." (Emphasis added.) Thus, pursuant to § 42a-4-402, the wrongfully dishonoring bank may be liable for all consequential damages proximately caused by its wrongful conduct, including damages resulting from arrest or prosecution of the customer, whereas there is a conspicuous absence from § 42a-4-403 (3) of language indicating such a broad scope of liability for wrongful payment.

* * *

A factual finding must be reversed as clearly erroneous if it was based on an incorrect rule of law. The trial court's finding in this case that the plaintiff had established a loss within the meaning of § 42a-4-403 (3) was so based.

[The dissenting opinion has been omitted].

- ■   What distinction does the court make between 4-402 and 4-403, and how does this distinction affect the court's holding?

Note 1:   Read 4-407 and Comments 1, 2, and 3.   4-407 provides a drawee with subrogation rights in the event of a dispute involving a stop-payment order.   Each of the following circumstances illustrated in the Comments implicates the drawee's right of subrogation:

Make sure you know
the difference
between a "valid"
and a "rightful" stop-
payment order.

1)   A drawer might sue the drawee after an item is charged against its account over a valid stop-payment order.   Because the drawee has already paid the item, the payee will have no reason to participate voluntarily in litigation regarding payment of the item.   The drawee, wishing to avoid double liability, may assert against the drawer any defenses the payee could have raised.   For example, if the payee could have shown stop-payment was unwarranted as a matter of contract law because the drawer received valuable goods or services from the payee for which the disputed item represented payment, the drawee could assert such facts in defending against the drawer's claim, thus proving the drawer suffered no harm from payment of the item.

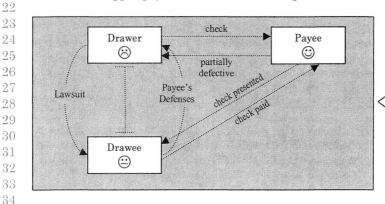

The emoticons represent the parties' pre-litigation posture: the payee is satisfied because it has been paid for the goods it delivered; the drawer is dissatisfied because its stop-payment order was not followed; the drawee's status is less certain because it faces the threat of double payment (and thus loss) if a court requires it to recredit the drawer's account due to its error.

2) Assume the drawer purchased goods from the payee, paying with a check on which the drawer later attempted unsuccessfully to stop payment. Further assume the drawer has now sued the drawee under 4-403. If the goods were partially defective such that the payee was not entitled to the full contract price but was owed some amount, the drawee can assert this defense against the drawer. The drawer would have gotten a windfall by receiving the goods free of charge if the drawee had stopped payment on the check as requested.

The emoticons represent pre-litigation postures analogous to the first case.

3) The drawee, having paid a check over a valid stop-payment order, might re-credit the account of the drawer immediately to avoid rancor. The drawer would therefore have no reason to participate voluntarily in litigation involving payment of the item. The bank, having already paid twice the value of the item, might then seek to recoup its loss. To do so, the bank might sue the payee, asserting any rights the drawer could have asserted. For example, if the payee engaged in fraud that prompted the issuance of the item, the bank could sue the payee to recover the value of the item and, in so doing, could raise the fraud claim that originally belonged to the drawer.

Guaranty Bank and Trust v. Smith, 952 S.W.2d 787 (Mo. App. 1997), provides an example of a bank's use of subrogation against a payee.

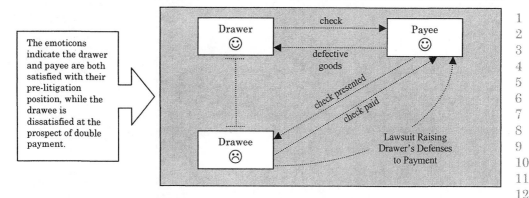

The emoticons indicate the drawer and payee are both satisfied with their pre-litigation position, while the drawee is dissatisfied at the prospect of double payment.

Note 2: Read 4-403 Comment 4 and 3-411. A bank may be liable if it wrongfully refuses to pay a cashier's check. In *State ex rel. Chan Siew Lai v. Powell*, 536 S.W.2d 14, 19 U.C.C. Rep. Serv. 626 (Mo. 1976), the court considered a remitter's request to enjoin enforcement of a cashier's check he had purchased and delivered to the payee, and on which he had sought (without success) to stop payment through the bank's ordinary channels. The remitter contended the payee had procured the issuance of the check by fraud, having misrepresented the business transaction in which he had promised to engage with the remitter. In finding no grounds on which the bank could appropriately refuse payment, the court held as follows, denying injunctive relief:

> The nature and usage of cashier's checks in the commercial world is such that public policy does not favor a rule that would permit stopping payment of them. It is aptly stated in *National Newark & Essex Bank v. Giordano*, 111 N.J. Super. 347, 268 A.2d 327 (1970): "A cashier's check circulates in the commercial world as the equivalent of cash. . . . People accept a cashier's check as a substitute for cash because the bank stands behind it, rather than an individual. In effect, the bank becomes a guarantor of the value of the check and pledges its resources to the payment of the amount represented upon presentation. To allow the bank to stop payment on such an instrument would be inconsistent with the representation it makes in issuing the check. Such a rule would undermine the public confidence in the bank and its checks and thereby deprive the cashier's check of the essential incident which makes it useful. People would no longer be willing to accept it as a substitute for cash if they could not be sure that there would be no difficulty in converting it into cash." *Id.* at 16.

- **Read 3-411 (c) and Comment 3.** Would the result be different if the bank stopped payment because it, rather than its customer, was defrauded?

Teller's checks are sometimes compared with personal checks and sometimes with cashier's checks. For an examination of how each approach would affect the right of stop-payment, see *Meritor v. Duke*, 1993 WL 946108 (Va. Cir. Ct. 1993).

Note 3: The application of stop-payment principles to money orders is explored in *Garden Check Cashing Service, Inc. v. First National City Bank*, 25 A.D.2d 137, 267 N.Y.S.2d 698, 3 U.C.C. Rep. Serv. 355 (N.Y. App. Div. 1st Dept. 1966). On April 13, 1962, Mr. Higgins purchased a money order from Garden Check Cashing Service, Inc. in the amount of $130.37. He did not fill in the name of the payee. Later that day, Mr. Higgins reported the money order lost and requested stop-payment. The same day, Mr. Walker – a stranger to Mr. Higgins – found and presented the money order to First National City Bank, having filled in his own name as payee. First National paid him the face value of the money order, minus a small fee. Upon presentment of the money order for payment, the item was returned unpaid due to Mr. Higgins' stop-payment order.

- Applying 3-407, did Mr. Walker alter the money order?

- Was Mr. Higgins negligent within the meaning of 3-406?

In upholding the stop-payment order, the court held as follows:

> We see small difference between the present transaction and one where a person deposits with the bank a sum of money and receives a quantity of blank checks. The obvious difference [with a money order] is that a single deposit was made and a single blank check received with the amount of the deposit inserted therein. *Id.* at 141.

- Is this holding consistent with 4-403 and its commentary?

In *Sequoyah State Bank v. Union National Bank of Little Rock*, 274 Ark. 1, 621 S.W.2d 683 (1981), the court addressed an issuing bank's attempt to stop payment on a money order of its own accord after it found that the check it had accepted in payment for the money order was drawn on insufficient funds. In finding such action inappropriate, the court held as follows:

> The personal money order constituted an obligation of Union [National Bank, the issuer,] from the moment of its sale and issuance. The fact that Union was frustrated in retaining the funds because instead of cash it accepted a check drawn on insufficient funds is no reason to hold otherwise.... We note by analogy that the Uniform Commercial Code on Sales ... provides [in 2-403 (1) (b)] that a purchaser of goods, who takes delivery in

exchange for a check which is later dishonored, transfers good title to the goods. *Id.* at 4.

- In your own words, explain the court's analogy to 2-403 (1) (b).

Note 4: Considerable litigation has addressed the issue of when a stop-payment order, although incorrect in some way, nevertheless provides a bank with information sufficient to act on the order. One such case is *Staff Service Associates, Inc. v. Midlantic National Bank*, 207 N.J. Super. 327, 504 A.2d 148, 42 U.C.C. Rep. Serv. 968 (1985). Staff Service Associates, Inc. maintained an account with Midlantic National Bank. On July 2, 1982, a representative of Staff Service, Raymond Nelson, issued a check drawn on the Midlantic account to Lynn Gross for $4,117.12. On July 7, John Tracy, the president of Staff Service, contacted the bank to stop payment on the check. In writing the stop-payment order, Tracy incorrectly wrote that the amount of the check was $4,117.72, thus making an error in one digit. At the bottom of the stop-payment form, which Tracy admits he read, was the following statement:

> IMPORTANT: The information on this Stop-payment Order must be correct, including the exact amount of the check to the penny, or the Bank will not be able to stop payment and this Stop-payment Order will be void. *Id.* at 329.

Because of the error, Midlantic's computers were not able to stop payment on the check, and Staff Service brought suit. In finding the bank liable for any damages Staff Service could prove it suffered, the court held as follows:

> Staff Service's representative did not know that Midlantic utilized a computer to effect stop payment of a check. In addition, Midlantic never informed Staff Service that the exact amount of the check is necessary for the computer to pull the check. It chose a computerized system which searches for stopped checks by amount alone. By electing this system, Midlantic assumed the risk that it would not be able to stop payment of a check despite the customer's accurate description of the account number, the payee's name, the number and date of the check, and a *de minimis* error in the check amount. Midlantic should not be permitted to relieve itself of this risk unless it calls attention to its computerized system and the necessity for the exact check amount to meet computer requirements.
>
> The court is not persuaded by the clause in the stop-payment order which states that Midlantic cannot stop payment unless the information provided by the customer is correct, including the exact amount of the check to the penny. Indeed this clause is inaccurate since, as Midlantic's representative explained in his certification, "if the amount of the check is correct, the check will

be stopped, although a discrepancy may exist in the remaining elements of the stop-payment order, unless and until the customer instructs otherwise." *Id.* at 151-152.

- How should the bank revise the notice it provides to its customers regarding stop-payment orders?

Problem 1: Francis A. Dziurak had a savings account with Chase Manhattan Bank containing about $18,000. Mario Staveris convinced him to enter a business relationship whereby Dziurak would acquire a one-third interest in a restaurant for about $22,000. Pursuant to the parties' oral contract, Dziurak paid $5,000 down and requested that his bank issue a check for the balance, payable to the order of Staveris. Mr. Monaco, an officer of the bank, advised Dziurak to have the check made payable to himself as payee, rather than to Staveris, and further advised him to seek the advice of an attorney, who would instruct him in how to indorse the check to Staveris. Dziurak assented, and a check for $17,000 was issued in his name. His savings account was debited for the amount of the check.

> Would the Statute of Frauds require a writing? Review the materials in Chapter 2, Part B as needed.

- What do you think Mr. Monaco was trying to accomplish?

- Was this an appropriate practice?

Ignoring the advice of Mr. Monaco that he seek the advice of an attorney, Dziurak wrote on the back of the check, "Francis Dziurak. Pay to order Mario Staveris" and delivered the item to Staveris. Instead of depositing the check in the restaurant account as promised, Staveris appropriated the check for his own personal use.

- Would a different indorsement have been more protective of Dziurak's interests?

> Review Chapter 9, Part B as needed to answer this question.

In the meantime, before the check had cleared, Dziurak sought the advice of counsel. The attorney advised him to try to get the bank to stop payment on the check. The bank refused to do so, believing it could not do so absent a court order.

- Did the attorney give Dziurak good advice, given what you have learned about stopping payment on cashier's checks?

Assume Dziurak declined to get a court order, and the check was paid. Further assume the bank could have stopped payment without liability.

- Does Dziurak have any cause of action against the bank, in his capacity as remitter or as payee of the cashier's check?

Based on *Dziurak v. Chase Manhattan Bank*, 58 A.D.2d 103, 396 N.Y.S.2d 414, 21 U.C.C. Rep. Serv. 1130 (N.Y. App. Div. 2d Dept. 1977).

Problem 2: In May 1998, Linda Kressler, also known as Madam Linda, the "spiritual advisor" to Benito Dalessio's girlfriend Jennifer Lopez, informed Dalessio that Lopez could not marry her unless he paid Lopez's debts first. On Monday, November 9 of that year, Dalessio went to his bank, Republic National Bank of New York, and asked the bank to certify a personal check for $107,000 made payable to Kressler for the purpose of paying Lopez's debts. The following day, November 10, Dalessio returned to cash a check for $15,000. Noting Dalessio appeared nervous, the teller referred him to the branch manager. In the conversation that ensued, Dalessio informed the branch manager that Lopez and Kressler had visited Dalessio in his home to tell him that Lopez "would only be free to marry him if he paid her the funds requested." The branch manager notified Dalessio's sister, who was the co-owner of the account, and recommended she employ the services of an attorney to get a court order to stop payment on the certified check. On November 11, the courts and banks were closed for Veteran's Day. On November 12, Justice Irving S. Aronin signed a temporary restraining order directed to the bank, enjoining payment of the check. The bank received the court order prior to paying the check and paid the check without responding to the order or appearing in court to contest the order, based on its assumption that it was legally required to pay the check, having certified it.

Although a bank's obligations when it receives notice of legal process are discussed later in this section, you should be able to formulate an instinctual response already.

- Should this case be handled differently from *Chan Siew Lai*?

Based on *Dalessio v. Kressler*, 6 A.D.3d 57, 773 N.Y.S.2d 434, 52 U.C.C. Rep. Serv. 2d 805 (N.Y. App. Div. 2d Dept. 2004):

Stale Checks

Read 4-404 and Comment. Read and compare 3-414 (f) and Comment 6 with 3-415 (e).

- 4-404 refers to a bank's obligation "to a customer having a checking account." What items are excluded?

4-404, which generally allows (but does not require) banks to honor checks more than six months old, is consistent with other provisions of the UCC that lessen certain parties' obligations over time. Although a drawer is not normally excused from liability on a check once issued, even if the item has not been presented for a long period of time, 3-415 (e) automatically discharges an indorser from liability after 30 days.

> This provision is discussed in Chapter 11, Part A.

- When is a drawer excused from liability under 3-414 (f)?

- Why is the liability of an indorser excused after 30 days, while most drawers remain liable indefinitely?

- Why are certified checks excluded from the provisions of 4-404?

- Do cashier's checks and teller's checks fall within 4-404?

> The answer to this question will become clearer after you have studied the materials in Chapter 11, Part A, but you should have a general sense of the answer at this point.

- From whom, if anyone, can a holder recover if the drawee refuses to pay a stale check?

Problem: In *IBP, Inc. v. Mercantile Bank of Topeka*, 6 F. Supp. 2d 1258, 36 U.C.C. Rep. Serv. 2d 270 (D. Kan. 1998), the court considered a bank's payment of an exceedingly stale check. On July 15, 1986, IBP, Inc. issued a check to Meyer Land & Cattle Company in the amount of approximately $135,000 for the purchase of cattle. The check was drawn on IBP's account with Mercantile Bank of Topeka. Representatives of Meyer lost the check, and Tim Meyer found the check behind a desk drawer some time in the fall of 1995. Although he noticed the check was 9 years old, he assumed correctly that it represented payment for a sale of cattle, and he sought to enforce the check. To this end, he indorsed the check and deposited it in his account at Sylvan State Bank. Sylvan accepted the check for deposit, as Meyer frequently presented checks of similar amount. The check was routed to Mercantile Bank via an automated clearing-house. Mercantile Bank paid the check and debited IBP's account. That month, IBP issued almost 15,000 checks, many of which were in excess of $100,000. IBP brought suit against Mercantile Bank, claiming it had improperly honored the stale check.

- Can IBP sue Mercantile Bank in conversion?

- IBP claimed Mercantile Bank had a duty to ascertain for itself whether IBP still owed money to Meyer before it paid this stale check. Does 4-404 support such a duty?

- Can a drawer protect itself against payment of a stale check?

Legal Process

Read 4-303, Comment 1. Receipt of legal process terminates a bank's authority to pay items drawn on its customer's account, so long as the bank receives notice of the proceedings within the period specified in 4-303. *W&D Acquisition, LLC v. First Union National Bank,* 262 Conn. 704, 817 A.2d 91 (2003), addressed the issue of how quickly a bank must comply with an order of garnishment, in determining whether "a reasonable time for the bank to act" within the meaning of 4-303 (a) had expired. Garnishment papers were served on the bank holding the account in question some time around noon. On that same day, the accountholder entered the bank around 3:30 p.m. and withdrew almost the entire balance of the account, leaving virtually no funds to which the garnishment could attach. The garnishor brought suit, alleging the garnishee bank had sufficient time to secure the funds prior to the withdrawal and seeking to recover the amount of money it contended it should have received pursuant to the order of garnishment. The court quoted 1-205 for the proposition that a "reasonable time" within the meaning of 4-303 would be a fact-specific inquiry and would not necessarily be synonymous, as the lower court had assumed, with the "midnight deadline" in 4-104 (a) (10). Because the lower court had inappropriately applied the "midnight deadline" to the facts at bar, the court reversed and remanded the case for further proceedings.

> Such a claim is called a "writ of scire facias."

- On remand, what evidence should the bank present to show it responded to the garnishment order within a "reasonable time"?

Death or Incompetence of Customer

Read 4-405 and Comments. A customer's death or adjudicated incompetence will terminate a bank's authority with regard to that customer's accounts, but only after notice is received.

- Why is there a ten-day window after a bank receives notice of death, during which it may continue to pay checks so long as no person claiming an interest in the account orders otherwise?

- Is the bank required to pay checks during this window?

1
2
3
4
5
6
7
8
9
10
11
12
13
14
15
16
17
18
19
20
21
22
23
24
25
26
27
28
29
30
31
32
33
34
35
36
37
38
39
40
41
42
43
44
45
46
50
51
52
53

- Why should the same window not exist when a bank receives notice that a customer has been adjudicated incompetent?

- Must a bank research the validity of an order to stop payment, given by a person claiming an interest in the account pursuant to 4-405 (b)?

As the following case shows, items issued at or near death can raise issues of estate-planning law, especially when the court believes an item was intended to function as a will substitute.

> The reference to issuance "at death" should make more sense after you have read the *DeLuca* opinion.

DeLuca v. BancOhio National Bank, Inc.,
74 Ohio App. 3d 233, 598 N.E.2d 781,
19 U.C.C. Rep. Serv. 2d 216 (1991).

Petree, Judge.

This case involves a dispute over a $75,000 check allegedly given to Carolyn DeLuca on Friday, January 27, 1989, by decedent Joseph G. Rotondo. At the time, decedent was a seventy-eight-year-old practicing attorney and Carolyn DeLuca was his secretary.

On Friday, January 27, 1989, decedent, who for years had suffered from emphysema, heart problems, and other ailments, felt very ill. He called Carolyn in the morning to take him to the hospital. They stopped first at his office. Despite his discomfort, he signed several blank payroll checks that were on his desk. Before they left for the hospital, decedent told Carolyn, who usually did the payroll banking, that he had one check for her in his desk.

At the hospital, decedent was treated in the emergency room. Carolyn remained with him, and eventually her daughter Jacqueline arrived as well. Further, decedent's son, Eric P. Rotondo, also visited. Eric is an attorney practicing law in the same office as his father. Earlier that morning, Eric had seen the blank checks on his father's desk and had overheard his father's comment about a check left for Carolyn.

Carolyn was at decedent's side in his hospital room. At one point, she maintained that decedent told her that he wanted to pay her debts and asked her how much she needed. She told him that her debts were $75,000. So, decedent told her that if anything happened to him, she was to take the blank check in his desk and fill it in for that amount. No one else was present to hear this conversation.

Carolyn remained at the hospital until decedent died at 4:46 p.m. . . .

After decedent died, Carolyn returned to decedent's office to pick up some personal items, finish the payroll, and pick up her check. Subsequently, she went home.

Eric remained at the hospital to make funeral arrangements. When he returned to the law office, he noticed that the payroll checks were properly in their envelopes, except that one was missing.

Eventually, Carolyn filled in the blank check as decedent had instructed. She filled in her name as payee, the amount of $75,000, and the date. She then went to the Bexley branch of BancOhio [National Bank, Inc.] with Jacqueline on Saturday, January 28, 1989. She presented the check to the next available teller, Kathleen R. Miller, who in fact was head teller. Carolyn indicated that she needed the funds deposited in her BancOhio account. After some discussion about the availability of the funds to pay bills, Miller told Carolyn that the funds would be available on the next banking day. Miller then deposited $75,000 into plaintiffs' account.

Thereafter, Eric, who is co-executor of his father's estate, learned about the transaction at BancOhio. He consulted an attorney who filed for an *ex parte* temporary restraining order on Monday, January 30, 1989, to stop-payment on the check and the transfer of any funds. After the trial court granted this relief, the TRO was presented to BancOhio on Monday afternoon.

> Does Carolyn have any cause of action, other than her lawsuit against the bank, following dishonor of the check?

The bank then dishonored the check, removed a provisional credit from plaintiffs' account, recredited decedent's account, and returned the check to Carolyn with a stamp on it and an explanation that the check had been dishonored due to the TRO. Decedent's estate was then able to withdraw the $75,000 for the benefit of the estate.

Plaintiffs filed suit on March 22, 1989, alleging that BancOhio removed $75,000 from their joint bank account without authority to do so and refused to repay the funds. Both parties filed motions for summary judgment, but the trial court overruled them. At trial, at the close of plaintiffs' case, BancOhio orally moved for a directed verdict and the trial court granted it.

In findings of fact and conclusions of law, the court wrote that BancOhio obeyed the TRO and dishonored the check. The court acknowledged that Carolyn ". . . took the check to defendant's Bexley branch to deposit the funds in plaintiffs' savings account. . . . " But the court found that Carolyn did not inform the bank that the maker of the check was dead nor that she had completed the check ". . . by naming herself as payee and by inserting the amount of $75,000." The court concluded that the check was ". . . invalid, payment was properly denied, and the account of plaintiffs' was properly debited."

In their assignments of error, plaintiffs argue that BancOhio cashed the $75,000 check on Saturday and could not thereafter undo such final payment.

* * *

. . . By contrast, BancOhio submitted affidavits and other evidence to establish that Carolyn only deposited the check, which allowed the bank to revoke any provisional credit granted prior to its so-called midnight deadline. . . .

[This portion of the court's opinion addressing whether the check was cashed before deposit, which brings to mind the *Kirby* opinion in Part A, has been omitted. The court held for Carolyn on this point. The portion of the court's opinion addressing the bank's response to the son's TRO has also been omitted.]

BancOhio's last line of defense is based on the theory that plaintiffs breached their presentment warranty to the payor bank and therefore, it has a cause of action for the amount of the check which negates any recovery by plaintiffs. . . .

> Presentment warranties are discussed in Chapter 11, Part B. The Article 4 presentment warranty is now found in 4-208.

4-207, like 3-417, establishes certain presentment warranties given to good faith payors by customers obtaining payment on items. . . .

Here, BancOhio argues that Carolyn had no authority to fill in the incomplete check after decedent's death. On this score, we are compelled to agree.

In her deposition, Carolyn squarely admitted that the subject check was intended as a gift to her. As is evident from the deposition, it is at least arguable that decedent attempted to effectuate a gift *causa mortis* of the check in question. However, the law as it stands cannot permit this on these facts.

Lord Chancellor Ashbourne once said that: ". . . , I do not look with particular favor on these death-bed gifts." The same sentiment applies in Ohio.

> The reference here is to Edward Gibson, the first Baron Ashbourne, who held the position of Lord Chancellor of Ireland between 1885 and 1905.

Although such gifts are enforceable in Ohio, gifts by check pose a special problem. The almost uniform rule at common law was that a donor's own check not paid or accepted prior to death could not establish a gift *inter vivos* or *causa mortis*. The same effect was said to obtain under the Negotiable Instruments Law.

The theoretical underpinning for this rule is that a check is not an assignment of funds and therefore, any intended gift could not be complete because the donor retains the power to stop payment on his order. The Code today also provides that a check is not an assignment of funds.

* * *

On the evidence presented, Carolyn's authority to fill in the check was revoked by decedent's death. Consequently, she breached the presentment warranty against material alterations. For this reason, the court should have directed a verdict for BancOhio.

> Answering this question requires a careful examination of the decedent's and the plaintiff's relationships with BancOhio as revealed by the facts of the case.

- ▪ Would Regulation CC have permitted BancOhio to place a hold on the funds in questions?

- ▪ **Read 3-115 and Comments 2 and 3.** Did Carolyn act wrongfully in completing the check?

- Was the trial court correct that the check was "invalid"?

Note: As a result of exploitation by a third party, 76-year-old Maria Johnson depleted her savings before she was adjudicated incompetent. Her legal guardian sued her bank, asserting that red flags such as the rapid withdrawal of large sums from a personal checking account using starter checks and counter checks should have put the bank on notice of a problem. The court held that the UCC relieves the bank of liability because it had no notice of Ms. Johnson's mental incapacity and because she had not yet been adjudicated incompetent. After this litigation, Florida adopted legislation requiring banks to report suspected financial abuse of elders.

> Why would the use of starter checks and counter checks arguably raise a red flag?

> This legislation can be found at F.S.A. § 415.1034, available online at www. flsenate.gov/statutes.

- How do credit-card issuers deal with suspicious transactions?

- Would such a system be appropriate for checking accounts?

In *Can Bank Tellers Tell? Legal Issues Related to Banks Reporting Financial Abuse of the Elderly*, 58 Consumer Fin. L.Q. Rep. 293 (2004), Sandra L. Hughes catalogues state and federal legislation addressing elder financial abuse and lists the following indicia of potential financial abuse:

An unusual volume of banking activity.

Banking activity inconsistent with a customer's usual habits.

Sudden increases in incurred debt when the elder appears unaware of transactions.

Withdrawal of funds by a fiduciary or someone else handling the elder's affairs, with no apparent benefit to the elder.

Implausible reasons for banking activity are given either by the elder or by the person accompanying him or her. *Id.* at 294.

- What are the risks and benefits of a bank's intervening when it observes conduct of the kind referenced by Ms. Hughes?

Based on *Republic National Bank of Miami v. Johnson*, 622 So. 2d 1015, 20 U.C.C. Rep. Serv. 2d 1300 (Fla. 3d Dist. App. 1993).

The Bank-Statement Rule

Read 4-406 and Commentary. This Code section sets forth the bank-statement rule, which allows banks to shift responsibility to their customers for certain losses.

- Does 4-406 require banks to provide statements of account?

- Does 4-406 permit banks to charge for the service of providing copies of checks to customers who do not receive cancelled checks with their bank statements?

- Upon receiving a bank statement, is the customer required to discover unauthorized indorsements? Alterations in amount? Forgeries of his or her own signature?

Read 4-103 and Comment 4. The following case illustrates the bank-statement rule and the same-wrongdoer rule, showing how the duty of ordinary care referenced in 4-103 applies to the relationship between a bank and its customer. The case also illuminates some pertinent provisions of a typical deposit contract.

Spacemakers of America, Inc. v. Suntrust Bank,
271 Ga. App. 335, 55 U.C.C. Rep. Serv. 2d 893 (2005).

Ellington, Judge.

Spacemakers of America, Inc. sued SunTrust Bank after the bank processed approximately 65 checks that had been forged by the company's bookkeeper. The trial court granted the bank's motion for summary judgment on Spacemakers' claims for negligence, conversion, and unauthorized payment of forged items. Spacemakers appeals, claiming the trial court erred when it misapplied the law, granted summary judgment on its tort claims, and found the bank was not negligent as a matter of law. Because summary judgment was properly granted in this case, we affirm.

* * *

. . . Jenny Triplett applied with Spacemakers of America, Inc. for a bookkeeping position in November 1999. Triplett listed no prior employment on her application, and the application did not inquire about her criminal history. Prior to hiring Triplett, employees of Spacemakers did not ask her about her criminal history or conduct a criminal background check. Had it done so, Spacemakers would have learned that Triplett was on probation from a 1997 conviction for thirteen counts of forgery in the first degree, as well as from convictions for theft by taking and theft by deception in March 1999, just eight months before she applied for the Spacemakers job. All of these convictions were the result of Triplett forging the checks of previous employers.

Spacemakers hired Triplett as a bookkeeper on December 1, 1999, delegating to her the sole responsibility for maintaining the company's checkbook, reconciling it with the monthly bank statements, and preparing financial reports. According to Dennis Rose, Spacemakers' president, Triplett also handled the company's accounts payable and regularly presented him with invoices from vendors and payroll records for employees. Rose stated that he spent several hours reviewing the vendor invoices each month before giving Triplett specific directions about which ones should be paid. After Triplett wrote the checks, she gave them to Rose so he could sign them. No other Spacemakers' employee, . . . looked at the company's checkbook register to ensure that Triplett wrote only authorized checks on the company's account. Further, Rose admitted that no other employee checked the accuracy of Triplett's financial reports and that he simply relied on Triplett's representations regarding how much money was in the bank account at any given time.

On January 3, 2000, just weeks after starting her job at Spacemakers, Triplett forged Rose's signature on a check for $3,000. She made the check payable to her husband's company, "Triple M Entertainment Group," which was not a vendor for Spacemakers. By the end of her first full month of employment, Triplett had forged five more checks totaling $22,320.30, all payable to Triple M. Then, over the next nine months, Triplett forged fifty-nine more checks totaling approximately $475,000. Triplett made all of these checks payable to Triple M. Most of the checks were for amounts between $5,000 and $10,000, and only two of the checks were for an amount over $20,000: a check for $24,500 dated September 1, 2000, and a check for $30,670 dated October 5, 2000. There is no evidence that anyone at Spacemakers other than Triplett reviewed the company's bank statements between January and October 2000 or that Spacemakers ever notified SunTrust that there had been any unauthorized transactions during that period.

On October 13, 2000, a SunTrust loss-prevention employee visually inspected the $30,670 check. She became suspicious of the signature and immediately contacted Rose. The SunTrust employee faxed Rose a copy of the check, which was made payable to "Triple M." Rose knew that Triple M was not one of the company's vendors and that he had not authorized the check. During the phone conversation, a Spacemakers' employee reminded Rose that Triplett's husband owned Triple M. Rose's wife immediately called the police, and Triplett was arrested.

On November 9, 2000, Spacemakers sent a letter to SunTrust demanding that the bank credit $523,106.03 to its account for the forged checks. The bank refused, contending that Spacemakers' failure to provide the bank with timely notice of the forgeries barred its claim under the notice provisions of the account agreement between the bank and Spacemakers, as well as under the notice provisions of the Georgia Commercial Code, specifically OCGA § 11-4- 406. The bank also contended that Spacemakers' negligence in hiring and failing to supervise Triplett, a convicted felon, barred the company's claim under

OCGA §§ 11-3-406 and 11-4-406. Spacemakers subsequently sued the bank for negligence, conversion, and unauthorized payment of forged items.

> **Read UCC 3-406**, which addresses forged signatures and alterations made possible by another party's contributory negligence coupled with the actions of a wrongdoer.

* * *

Spacemakers claims the trial court erred in applying OCGA § 11-4-406 to the facts of this case.

* * *

[T]his rule imposes upon a bank customer the duty to promptly examine its monthly statements and notify the bank of any unauthorized transaction. If the customer fails to report the first forged item within 30 days, it is precluded from recovering for that transaction *and for any additional items forged by the same wrongdoer.* . . . The underlying justification for this provision is simple: one of the most serious consequences of the failure of a customer to timely examine its statement is that it gives the wrongdoer the opportunity to repeat his misdeeds. Clearly, the customer "is in the best position to discover and report small forgeries before the [same] wrongdoer is emboldened and attempts a larger misdeed."

In this case, . . . [t]here is every reason to believe that, if Spacemakers had simply reviewed its bank statement for January 2000, it would have discovered the forgeries. More importantly, it would have been able to timely notify the bank of its discovery and avoided its subsequent losses of almost $475,000. Clearly, Spacemakers' extensive and unnecessary loss due to forgery is precisely the scenario that the duties created by OCGA § 11-4-406 were designed to prevent. Accordingly, we find that Spacemakers is precluded as a matter of law from asserting claims based upon the forgeries in this case. The trial court did not err in granting summary judgment to the bank.

> UCC 4-406 (d), to which the court makes reference here, is sometimes called the "same wrongdoer rule."

Spacemakers also contends the trial court erred in finding that there was no evidence that the bank failed to use ordinary care in processing customers' checks. Specifically, Spacemakers claims a jury issue existed as to whether the bank was negligent because it did "absolutely nothing" to verify signatures on commercial checks written for less than $20,000. Further, Spacemakers argues that, if *both* the customer and the bank are negligent, then the loss from the forged checks is allocated between the two parties according to the extent each party's negligence contributed to the loss. See OCGA §§ 11-3-406; 11-4-406 (e). Therefore, according to Spacemakers, the bank should be liable for at least part of the company's losses from the forged checks. . . .

Under OCGA § 11-3-103 (a) (7), . . . [o]rdinary care in this context is comparable to a "professional negligence" standard of care and does not refer to what a "reasonable person" would do under the circumstances.

> The relevant rule is now found in UCC 3-103 (9) (a) and has been changed slightly from the quoted language.

The bank . . . presented a prima facie showing that it exercised ordinary care in this case. According to the affidavit of Jeffrey Dalrymple, a SunTrust Senior Vice-President, the bank's regional operations center handles between 650,000 and 1,200,000 checks per day, and its fraud-detection software, ASI/16, is "an industry standard and one of the most sophisticated rules-based fraud detection software systems available." This fraud-detection software program reviews every check written for $250 and over and looks for certain suspicious characteristics which may indicate fraud on an account. These characteristics include, but are not limited to, the following: check numbers that are out of sequence; checks that have duplicate, missing, or out-of-range serial numbers; checks for high dollar amounts; checks for an amount greater than average for the account; and checks for an amount which exceeds the largest found in the account's history. If a check meets any of these characteristics, it is "outsorted" and visually inspected by SunTrust employees. Further, commercial checks for $20,000 or greater are automatically reviewed and verified by SunTrust employees. Dalrymple's affidavit also stated that he has personal knowledge of commercial standards in the banking industry in general and in the Atlanta area, as well as SunTrust's policies and procedures regarding the processing of checks. According to Dalrymple,

> SunTrust's standards with respect to thresholds for sight inspection of checks drawn on commercial accounts not only meet, but are in fact more stringent than, the standards for sight inspection of such checks among other banks in the Atlanta, Georgia area and are in observance and in fact exceed reasonable commercial standards.

Finally, Dalrymple's affidavit stated that SunTrust followed its standard procedures when it processed checks drawn on Spacemakers' account.

. . . The only evidence Spacemakers presented to refute SunTrust's showing was an expert witness, who testified that he had never analyzed fraud-detection systems in any national bank in the Atlanta area. He also admitted that he did not know what fraud-detection procedures SunTrust actually performs on commercial checks under $20,000. Even so, the witness deposed that, in his opinion, the bank was negligent because it did not visually inspect the signature on every check it processes, regardless of the check's amount. The expert witness later abandoned that position, however, and admitted that he did not think that reasonable commercial standards for national banks in the Atlanta area required banks to visually inspect every check. The witness had no opinion as to how large a check amount would have to be for the bank to be required to visually inspect it for fraud in order to comply with reasonable commercial standards in the Atlanta area. He also deposed that he was not aware of any provision in the Georgia Commercial Code which requires a bank to visually examine every check it processes. Further, although the expert witness claimed SunTrust was negligent for failing to notify its customers of its fraud detection policies and procedures, he admitted that he did not know what SunTrust told its customers, or what other banks in the area tell their customers, regarding their fraud detection program.

Accordingly, we find the record supports the trial court's conclusion that Spacemakers failed to create a jury issue as to whether the bank exercised ordinary care under the circumstances.

We also find that, even if OCGA § 11-4-406 did not preclude Spacemakers from recovering from the bank, there was a second basis for granting summary judgment on the company's claims. The evidence showed that Spacemakers' commercial account with SunTrust was subject to certain terms, which were documented in a booklet entitled "Rules and Regulations [for] Non-Personal Deposit Accounts." The booklet expressly notified commercial customers that the bank does not verify the signatures on every check paid against their account and instructed customers to promptly examine their monthly statements to verify that only authorized checks have been paid. In fact, a second provision specifically detailed the customer's duty with regard to recognizing account discrepancies and its liability to fulfill this duty:

> You should carefully examine the statement and canceled checks (including the face and back), if included in the statement, when you receive the statement. The Bank will not be liable for any unauthorized signature, alteration, misencoding, or other error on the face of any item in your statement, or for any incorrect amount or other error on the statement itself . . . unless you notify the Bank with thirty (30) calendar days from the date the Bank . . . makes your statement available to you or anyone to whom you request it be sent. . . . Moreover, because you are in the best position to discover an unauthorized signature . . . , you agree that the Bank will not be liable for paying such items if . . . you did not examine the statement and the canceled checks (if included) or you have not reported the unauthorized signatures . . . to us within the time period set forth above.

Most importantly, the booklet contained the following provision: "Bookkeepers. In the event you authorize any third person . . . to retain possession of or prepare items for [your company], you agree to assume full responsibility for any errors or wrongdoing by such third person . . . if the Bank should pay such items." Therefore, under these express provisions, Spacemakers cannot recover from the bank for the payments on the forged checks.

* * *

Accordingly, summary judgment was appropriate and there was no error.

What effect does a deposit contract have on the parties' Article 3/Article 4 obligations? Review UCC 4-103 and Comment 2 as needed to answer this question.

- Does this case involve a forged signature, an altered instrument, both, or neither?

3-405 Comment 3, cases #2 and #4 may be useful by analogy in helping you to answer this question.

Note: Both Professor James Steven Rogers and Professor Benjamin Geva have suggested, in the words of Professor Rogers, that the UCC has adopted a policy "that the burden of unpreventable loss should rest with the providers of the payment system rather than the users of the payment system." James Steven Rogers, *The Basic Principle of Loss Allocation for Unauthorized Checks*, 39 Wake Forest L. Rev. 453 (2004); Benjamin Geva, *Allocation of Forged Cheque Losses – Comparative Aspects, Policies and a Model for Reform*, L.Q.R.

1998, 114 (APR), 250-291 (1998). Geva describes some of the advantages of the current rule, as follows:

> Obviously, compared to the customer, the bank is the better risk bearer who is able to distribute losses among all customers, whether in the form of bank charges, or the availability of insurance. Conversely, a customer on whom forgery loss is allocated is unable to distribute losses. . . . [B]esides loss allocation, the allocation of forgery losses to banks will encourage forgery detection as well as promote higher investment in technologies directed to that end. *Id.* at 285.

- How, if at all, does this rule apply to the *Spacemakers* case?

Problem 1: By negligent failure of supervision, New Jersey Steel Corporation made it possible for consultant Rupert Warburton to forge checks drawn on the company through an elaborate scheme. Warburton created a separate business entity for himself and prepared checks drawn on New Jersey Steel Corporation and made payable to fictitious payees with names similar to that of his business. He then indorsed the checks only with the account number of his business and deposited the checks into an account at Midland National Bank, which was both the drawee and the depository bank. The bank had an internal directive for tellers to examine individually the indorsements of all deposits with 5 checks or fewer, but did not follow this procedure in Warburton's case. Had it followed this directive, the examining teller would have rejected every such check Warburton deposited, on the grounds that the indorsed account number did not match that of the payee. Warburton continued this scheme for eleven months, making fourteen deposits totaling more than $570,000.

> Is this a proper signature? Review Chapter 9, Part B as necessary to answer this question. Is it a forgery?

- Applying a standard of comparative negligence, how should the loss be allocated in this case?

Based on *New Jersey Steel Corp. v. Warburton*, 655 A.2d 1382, 26 U.C.C. Rep. Serv. 2d 14 (N.J. 1995).

Problem 2: Neal and Helen Rogers were in their eighties, and Neal was bedridden. Helen hired Jackie Reese to help care for her husband and to run errands and do chores. Over the course of about a year, Jackie wrote unauthorized checks on four checking accounts the Rogerses maintained with Union Planters Bank, totaling more than $58,000. Some were written to "Helen Rogers," some to "cash," and some to "Jackie Reese." Jackie hid or disposed of the statements from Union Planters Bank during this time period. After Neal died, his son Neal, Jr., worked with Helen to straighten out the family finances, and the two discovered the forgeries. The last forged checks were written about a month before the forgeries were discovered.

- ▪ Does the bank-statement rule, coupled with the "same-wrongdoer rule" found in 4-406 (d) (2), protect Union Planters Bank from liability to Helen Rogers?

Based on *Union Planters Bank, National Association v. Rogers*, 912 So. 2d 116, 57 U.C.C. Rep. Serv. 2d 236 (Miss. 2005).

International Perspective: Forgery and Loss

The allocation of loss for forged indorsements is a topic about which the international community has significant disagreement. GUL Article 16, to which reference is made below, provides as follows:

> The possessor of a bill of exchange is deemed to be its lawful holder if he establishes his title to the bill through an uninterrupted series of endorsements, even if the last endorsement is in blank. In this connection, cancelled endorsements are deemed not to be written (*non écrits*). When an endorsement in blank is followed by another endorsement, the person who signed this last endorsement is deemed to have acquired the bill by the endorsement in blank.
>
> Where a person has been dispossessed of a bill of exchange, in any manner whatsoever, the holder who establishes his right thereto in the manner mentioned in the preceding paragraph is not bound to give up the bill unless he has acquired it in bad faith, or unless in acquiring it he has been guilty of gross negligence.

In his article *Forged Indorsements*, 27 Am. J. Comp. L. 547 (1979), Willem Vis describes the GUL approach to the issue, as follows:

> [U]nder the [GUL], a forged indorsement is, with respect to the rights of the taker from the forger, a valid indorsement provided that the taker meets the conditions set forth in Art. 16. It is also a valid indorsement with respect to the rights of subsequent indorsees if they knew about the earlier forgery. The dispossessed owner may claim the bill from the person who took it from the forger, but if such person is a lawful holder he will succeed only if he proves bad faith or gross negligence. . . . The risk of a forged indorsement falls on the person who lost the bill or from whom it was stolen: on the drawer if the bill was stolen before it reached the payee; on the payee or indorsee from which the bill was stolen and whose indorsement was forged. *Id.* at 552.

> The Vis article contains a more comprehensive analysis of this issue than can be included here, including problems that compare the BEA, GUL, UCC, and CIBN approaches to the issue of forged indorsements.

> "Lawful holder" is a term of art discussed in Chapter 9, Part C's international materials.

- In your own words, how is the GUL approach different from that of the UCC?

Read CIBN Article 25. Vis describes the CIBN approach to the issue, as follows:

> The approach of the [CIBN] is basically that of the [GUL], but additional rules are proposed in order to achieve results corresponding to the rationale of the common-law rules. . . . Under this rule, a forged indorsement . . . is considered to be effective as an indorsement if it is part of "what appears on the face of the instrument" to be an "uninterrupted series of indorsements." Consequently, the person who so acquires the instrument becomes a "holder" and as such has all the rights conferred on him by this Convention against the parties to the instrument. *Id.* at 554-555.

This language is from CIBN Article 15 (1) (b).

In *A New Paradigm for International Business Transactions,* 71 Wash. U. L.Q. 599 (1993), Professor Kenneth C. Randall and attorney John E. Norris described the conflict and resultant compromise during the CIBN drafting process regarding liability for forged indorsements:

> As with the CISG, . . . nations' jealousy over the sanctity of their own laws played a part in the negotiation of the CIBN. Compromises between different legal traditions became necessary, particularly between the civil-law nations and those with a common-law tradition. . . . The common-law tradition breaks the chain of negotiability if a forgery occurs, while civil law protects a bona-fide taker of a forged instrument. Thus, the common law puts the risk of a forgery upon the taker from the forger, while the civil law puts the risk upon the person whose signature is forged. Both positions are reasonable, and both seek to resolve tension between valid public policy concerns. In attempting to reconcile these positions, the CIBN, rather than choosing one of the traditional positions, attempted somewhat unsuccessfully to find compromise between them, resulting in a confusing risk-of-loss scheme. *Id.* at 621.

- In what way can the CIBN approach be described as a compromise between the UCC and GUL on this point?

Chapter Conclusion: This chapter should have given you a clear picture of each bank's role in the Article 4 collection process, from the depositary bank to the payor bank. Leaving these materials, you should also understand the allocation of rights and responsibilities between banks and their customers.

Chapter 11:
Liability under Articles 3 and 4

There are four common ways to incur liability in a transaction involving a negotiable instrument:

(1)   Contract liability on the negotiable instrument;
(2)   Warranty liability;
(3)   Tort liability; and
(4)   Contract liability on the underlying transaction.

When a "transaction in goods" is involved, contract liability on the underlying transaction implicates the principles introduced in Chapters 2 through 6. This chapter discusses the three remaining sources of liability.

> The relationship between the goods contract and the negotiable-instrument contract is introduced in Chapter 7, Part A.

A. Contract Liability under Articles 3 and 4

This section follows up on the discussion in Chapter 9, Part B regarding the importance of signature in establishing contract liability in the Article 3/Article 4 context. These materials describe the contract-law obligations of makers and drawers, indorsers, drawees, and accommodation parties. This section also covers accrual of the contract-law cause of action, the statute of limitations, discharge, and accord and satisfaction.

> Professor Barry Zaretsky's article *Contract Liability of Parties to Negotiable Instruments*, 42 Ala. L. Rev. 627 (1991), provides a comprehensive overview of the principles of contract liability under Article 3.

Primary and Secondary Liability

Tepper v. Citizens Federal Savings & Loan Association, 448 So. 2d 1138, 38 U.C.C. Rep. Serv. 528 (Fla. 3d Dist. App. 1984), explains the concepts of primary and secondary liability, insofar as three-party paper such as a draft is concerned:

> The act of accepting the instrument renders the drawee primarily liable as an acceptor. Because there are no conditions precedent to its liability, a cause of action accrues against an acceptor in the case of a demand instrument on the date of the instrument or date of issue.
>
> The drawer, on the other hand, is only secondarily liable on the instrument, in that there are conditions precedent to liability. The normal conditions precedent include presentment to the drawee, dishonor, and notice of dishonor. Therefore, a cause of action against the drawer of a draft accrues only upon demand following dishonor of the instrument. Notice of dishonor constitutes a demand. *Id.* at 1140.

> What is meant by the phrase, "Notice of dishonor constitutes a demand"?

As you work through this section, consider the following chart:

- Who has primary liability and who has secondary liability?

- How would the chart differ if a note were involved?

- How would you describe the relative liability of the drawer, collecting banks and other indorsers, and drawee?

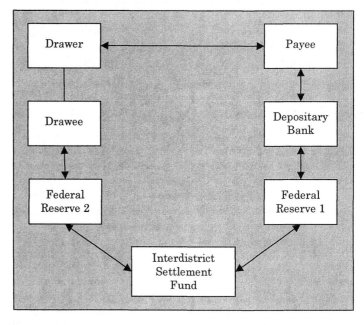

Read 3-414 and Comments 2 and 4. This Code section establishes the secondary liability of drawers.

- Explain this language from Comment 2: "The liability of the drawer of an unaccepted draft is treated as a primary liability."

- Explain the difference between 3-414 (c) and (d).

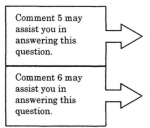

- Why is it impermissible for checks to be drawn "without recourse," although other drafts may be drawn this way?

- When is a drawer's liability discharged under 3-414 (f)?

Read 3-412 and Comment 1. 3-412 establishes the primary liability of makers of notes, as well as those drawers of drafts who are also drawees.

Comment 5 may assist you in answering this question.

Comment 6 may assist you in answering this question.

- Why does it make sense to group these parties together?

- Why is the maker of a note primarily liable at issuance, while the drawer of a draft is secondarily liable?

Read 3-601 (b). A party to a negotiable instrument will sometimes claim discharge from liability on the grounds that he or she has already paid the debt the item represents. Discharge by payment is a personal defense that is ineffective against a holder in due course. The party thus may face double liability if he or she makes payment to a person who is not the holder of the item and who is not entitled to payment. In *Groover v. Peters*, 231 Ga. 531, 202 S.E.2d 413 (1973), the court addressed a maker's potential double liability, as follows:

> The maker of a negotiable note . . . must determine at the time of payment whether the payee is the holder of the instrument or the authorized agent of the holder in order to protect himself against liability for double payment. If the original grantee has assigned the instrument to another, who is a holder in due course, the burden rests with the maker to determine same and pay only the holder or his authorized agent. . . .

> The long and short of the matter is that the borrower must be as careful in repaying the debt as the lender presumptively was in making the loan. *Id.* at 532.

- How can a party protect itself against double liability?

Liability of Indorsers

Read 3-204 (a) and Comment 1. Under the Code, signatures on negotiable instruments are presumptively for the purpose of indorsement.

- For what other purposes may an instrument be signed?

- What is an example of an indorsement made for each of the three purposes described in 3-204 (a)?

Read 3-415 and Comment 5. This Code section describes the secondary liability of indorsers, which is more limited than that of drawers.

Comment 5 is relevant to the discussion of accommodation parties below.

- Compare indorsers and drawers with regard to the following:

  - Discharge by passage of time.
  - Discharge by failure to give notice of dishonor.
  - Ability to sign "without recourse."
  - Parties to whom liability is owed.

Brannons Number Seven, Inc. v. Phelps, 665 P.2d 860, 36 U.C.C. Rep. Serv. 225 (Okla. Civ. App. 1983), illustrates indorser liability. Robert Phelps was employed by Jet Service Company, which issued payroll checks to Phelps totaling just under $800. Brannons Number Seven, a grocery store, cashed the checks after Phelps indorsed them. When Brannons Number Seven presented the checks to the drawee, they were dishonored for lack of funds. Brannons Number Seven therefore sought to recover the amount of the checks from Phelps. In finding Phelps would not become liable unless and until he was given notice of dishonor, the court held as follows:

> An indorser's liability is contingent and does not become fixed unless and until the holder complies with the requirement of notice of dishonor. This notice is an element of Brannons' cause of action, and Brannons thus has the burden of proving that it gave notice. *Id.* at 861-862.

- Rather than presenting the checks to the drawee bank for cash, assume Brannons Number Seven deposited the checks in an account with a bank other than the drawee. Would the depositary bank have rights of charge-back and/or a cause of action under 3-415 against the store upon dishonor?

[box: Review the materials in Chapter 10, Part A as needed to answer this question.]

- **Read 3-503 and 3-504 (b).** Who must give notice of dishonor?

Although indorser liability can be discharged by a failure to give notice of dishonor, under some circumstances a failure to give notice may be excused or an indorser may be deemed to have notice of the dishonor. *Hane v. Exten,* 255 Md. 668, 259 A.2d 290, 7 U.C.C. Rep. Serv. 35 (1969), addresses the latter issue. In that case, the holder of a note that had been dishonored by the maker sought to recover from an indorser based on 3-415. The indorser defended on the grounds that it had not received notice of dishonor. The holder claimed its failure to provide notice should be excused because the indorser knew the maker was insolvent and therefore "ha[d] no reason to expect . . . that the instrument [would] be paid." In rejecting this argument, the court held that "[a]n indorser's knowledge of the maker's insolvency, standing alone, will not excuse the

[box: This language is taken from 3-504 (a).]

giving of notice of dishonor" and does not establish that the indorser "knew or should have known that the note would not be paid."

- How must the facts be changed for the holder to prevail on this point?

Read 3-502. Dishonor triggers secondary liability. The following chart shows when various items are deemed dishonored.

Make sure you can reason your way through the information presented in this chart.

TYPE OF ITEM	DETAILS	DISHONORED WHEN?
Notes	Demand Note	If not paid on the day of presentment
	Time Note	If not paid on the day of presentment, or the day on which it becomes payable, whichever is later
Unaccepted Drafts	Check presented over the counter	If not paid on the day of presentment
	Check presented through Article 4's check-collection process	If timely return or timely notice of dishonor is given under 4-301 or 4-302
	Demand draft	If not paid on the day of presentment
	Time draft	If not paid on the day of presentment or the date on which it becomes payable, whichever is later, or if not accepted when presented for acceptance before it becomes payable
Accepted Drafts	Demand draft	If not paid on the day of presentment
	Time draft	If not paid on the day of presentment or the date on which it becomes payable, whichever is later

Note: As 3-415 (b) shows, indorsement without recourse is a means by which indorsers can avoid contract liability for items they transfer to others. In *Boyles Brothers Drilling Co. v. Orion Industries, Ltd.*, 761 P.2d 278, 6 U.C.C. Rep. Serv. 2d 1164 (Colo. App. 1988), the court considered an indorser's claim that the negotiable instrument it had signed should be reformed to reflect the parties' agreement that indorsement would be

without recourse.   In allowing parol evidence to prove
reformation was appropriate, the court held as follows:

> As between the immediate parties, a negotiable instrument or an
> indorsement thereof is merely a contract. While parol evidence is
> not admissible to vary or contradict the terms of a promissory note
> or a blank indorsement of the note, nevertheless, parol evidence of
> a contemporaneous oral agreement or transaction may be
> admissible if its effect its to prove a defense to payment of the
> instrument according to its terms. Thus, in an action to reform an
> instrument that does not reflect the intent of the parties because of
> fraud or mistake, parol evidence is admissible. *Id.* at 280-281.

- What distinction is made between "immediate parties"
  and others?

- How is the item not "merely a contract" when the
  rights of third parties are involved?

Although indorsement without recourse allows an indorser to
escape contractual exposure, such indorsement will not entirely
insulate a party from liability.   Instead, it is important to
consider other potential sources of liability, such as warranty
and tort, discussed later in this chapter.   *Hartford Life
Insurance Co. v. Title Guarantee Co.*, 520 F.2d 1170 (D.C.
1975), explains how contractual liability can be disclaimed, yet
warranty liability may remain:

> A "without recourse" endorsement is a qualified endorsement; it
> does not eliminate all obligations owed by the transferor of an
> instrument to his transferee. By endorsing the note "without
> recourse," [the payee] still warranted to [its transferee] that it had
> no knowledge of any fact which would establish the existence of a
> good defense against the note. *Id.* at 1174-1175.

Problem: Is this transfer made with or without recourse?

FOR VALUE RECEIVED, the undersigned TWIN CITY STATE
BANK, hereby sells, transfers, sets over, and assigns to the
ANDERSON LOAN ASSOCIATION its entire right, title, and
interest in and to each and all of the following described bona-fide
mortgages executed to or held by the undersigned, all prior
mortgages held by the undersigned, all prior mortgages held by
the assignor having been fully paid and released, together with
all of the promissory notes and any other indebtedness thereby
secured which said mortgages are hereinafter described and
identified by the names of the mortgagors, the dates of execution,
and the amounts of the original loans, the book and page of
recordings in Grant County, Indiana, and the exact principal
balances due on each at this transfer date as follows: (a list then
followed)

We hereby assign the within note to First Savings & Loan Ass'n.

(Date)
Twin City State Bank
/s/ Donald F. Hundley
/s/ Donald F. Hundley, Pres.

> What is the apparent meaning of Mr. Hundley's two signatures on the item?

Based on *First Valley Bank v. First Savings & Loan Association of Central Indiana*, 412 N.E.2d 1237 (Ind. App. 1980).

Read 3-603. This Code section describes how tender of payment affects negotiable-instrument liability. Whether tender has occurred will be determined as a matter of state law outside the UCC. In *Davis v. Dillard National Bank*, 50 UCC. Rep. Serv. 2d 877 (M.D. N.C. 2003), for example, the court applied North Carolina law and held that "[m]erely offering to produce payment or showing a readiness to perform is insufficient to establish tender; actual production of payment is necessary."

- How is tender of payment different from payment?

- Compare the effect of tender of payment on the liability of an accommodation party or indorser, as opposed to a drawer.

> "Accommodation party" is introduced and defined in 3-419 and Comment 1. This concept is explored later in this section.

- Why would a holder ever want to refuse tender of payment?

As the earlier materials in this section show, the contract liability of drawers and indorsers does not come into play until the item is dishonored. Dishonor occurs when an item is presented for acceptance and/or payment, and is not accepted and/or paid. Thus, it is important to understand the rules for presentment.

Read 3-501. This Code section explains presentment. Until a proper presentment is made, a drawer's refusal to pay an item is not dishonor.

- What is the difference between presentment for acceptance and presentment for payment?

Accord and Satisfaction

Read 3-311 and Comment 1. A common way of settling contract disputes and discharging the parties' negotiable-instrument liability is through the accord-and-satisfaction doctrine found in 3-311. As the court held in *McMahon Food Corp. v. Burger Dairy Co.*, 103 F.3d 1307 (7th Cir. 1996), "[t]he purpose of 3-311 is to encourage informal dispute resolution by full-satisfaction checks. Its drafters intended to codify the common law of accord and satisfaction with some minor variations to reflect modern business conditions."

> Comments 5 and 6 may assist you in answering this question.

- How does 3-311 "reflect modern business conditions"?

Solomon v. American National Bank, 243 Ill. App. 3d 132, 612 N.E.2d 3 (Ill. App. 1st Dist. 1993), shows how carefully a drawer must act in preparing and tendering a check in satisfaction of a disputed debt, to ensure acceptance of the check will have the desired effect. In that case, a landlord tendered a check to his former tenants for $452.33 bearing the legend, "Security deposit pd. in full." The tenants' original security deposit had been $1,350. The tenants crossed out the legend and cashed the check, then sought to recover the balance of the deposit as well as certain state statutory damages for the landlord's delay in refunding the full deposit owed. When the landlord defended on the grounds that cashing the check had extinguished the tenants' claim, the court held as follows in rejecting this argument, insofar as the state statutory damages were concerned:

> Where do you find each of these 5 elements reflected in the text of 3-311?

> To constitute an accord and satisfaction there must be: (1) a *bona-fide* dispute; (2) an unliquidated sum; (3) consideration; (4) a shared and mutual intent to compromise the claim; and (5) execution of the agreement. An accord and satisfaction is contractual in nature; thus, the intent of the parties is of central importance. The debtor must show that the creditor intended to accept the payment of less than what is claimed as full satisfaction; otherwise, the payment operates only as a discharge of the amount paid. To determine the intent of the parties, it is necessary to examine the language of the relevant documents.
>
> The language of the checks the landlord sent to the tenants clearly refers to plaintiffs' security deposits being paid in full. However, this language does not establish that the landlord intended that cashing the checks would extinguish the plaintiffs' claims for landlord's failure to refund the security deposit within the time prescribed by law. *Id.* at 1134-1135.

- Is the court's holding consistent with 3-311?

- Upon receipt of a check such as the one in this case, how can a payee protect its interest in the entire disputed sum?

- What should the drawer have done differently?

Crossing out the "full satisfaction" language can backfire on a payee. In *Morgan v. Crawford*, 106 S.W.3d 480, 50 UCC. Rep.

Serv. 2d 373 (Ky. App. 2003), the court found that doing so conclusively established the payee knew the check was tendered in full satisfaction of the parties' disputed claim, such that the claim was discharged when the payee cashed the check.

- Explain the court's logic in your own words.

Obligation of Drawee as Acceptor

Read 3-408, 3-413, and 3-410. A drawee takes on primary liability for any draft it accepts. Unless and until it accepts the draft, it will have no contract liability for the item, although it may face liability to the drawer for wrongful dishonor.

> Wrongful dishonor is discussed in Chapter 10, Part B and is a cause of action belonging only to the drawer.

- What is the effect of a drawee's acceptance on the liability of a drawer or indorser for the item accepted?

> Review 3-414 (c) and (d) and 3-415 (d) as needed to answer this question.

- How could an acceptance vary from the terms of a draft, and why might the holder choose to treat such an item as dishonored?

The following case illustrates how a drawee's signature proves its acceptance of, and resultant contract liability on, a negotiable instrument.

First National Bank of Alamosa v. Ford Motor Credit Co., 748 F. Supp. 1464, 13 U.C.C. Rep. Serv. 2d 810 (D. Colo. 1990).

Nottingham, District Judge.

Plaintiff First National Bank in Alamosa's lawsuit against Ford Motor Credit Company is based on Ford's refusal to honor nine sight drafts presented to Ford, as acceptor or drawee, and directing it to pay a total of $93,144.86. The drafts were drawn on Ford by Clark/Cravens Alamosa Motors, Inc. (the Bank's customer and a car dealer associated with Ford Motor Company), and delivered to the Bank for collection through the commercial banking system. Alamosa Motors initiated the collection process by depositing the nine drafts into its account at the Bank between March 3, 1986, and March 10, 1986. The Bank treated the drafts as "cash items" – that is, it credited Alamosa Motors' account and permitted Alamosa Motors to have immediate use of the funds represented by that credit, as had been its practice when Alamosa Motors deposited similar drafts on prior occasions. Unfortunately, the principals of Alamosa Motors left town, literally in the middle of the night, around March 12, 1986. By the time the sight drafts (1) had been presented through the interbank-collection system, (2) were dishonored, and (3) came back to the Bank, Alamosa Motors' account at the Bank was overdrawn by $64,543.28. Unable to recover from Alamosa Motors, the Bank initiated this lawsuit against Ford.

> What is a sight draft? Review the materials contained in Chapter 7, Part B, as needed to answer this question.

> What type of sight draft is this?

* * *

Ford provides blank, pre-printed drafts such as the nine at issue here
to approved dealers of Ford Motor Company. The drafts are among the
numerous documents used in the system by which Ford finances
automobile sales to consumers. The customer who wants to buy a car
on credit from a Ford Motor Company dealer enters into a retail-
installment-sales agreement with the dealer, promising to pay the
amount financed and giving the dealer a security interest in the
automobile. Since dealers do not typically want to finance the sale
themselves, Ford's system provides a means by which Ford assumes
responsibility for financing the consumer's purchase, and the dealer
receives the amount financed. To use this system, a dealer does two
things. First, after the consumer signs the retail-installment-sales
agreement, the dealer assigns the agreement to Ford and sends the
agreement and related documents to Ford for approval. Second, the
dealer completes one of the pre-printed drafts (by paying itself or its
bank the amount financed) and presents the draft for payment through
the commercial banking system. Assuming that the documents are in
order and that Ford agrees to finance the transaction, Ford transfers
the amount financed to the dealer by honoring the sight draft.
According to Ford's evidence (undisputed by the Bank), sight drafts are
commonly used in the automobile industry. Their purpose is to
facilitate and expedite payment to the dealer.

> Transactions such as these implicate the FTC Holder in Due Course Rule discussed in Chapter 9, Part E.

The nine sight drafts also contain the language "payable through . . .
The First National Bank, Colorado Springs, Colorado," which is printed
in the lower left-hand side of each draft. To understand how the drafts
were used, this provision must be explained. Ford employed The First
National Bank of Colorado Springs as its "collecting bank." After a
collecting bank such as the First National Bank of Colorado Springs
receives a sight draft from a depositary bank, it contacts Ford to ask
Ford if it is prepared to pay the draft. If Ford disapproves the
transaction, it instructs its collecting bank to dishonor the sight draft. If
it wants to pay the draft, Ford instructs the collecting bank to pay the
draft and mails the collecting bank a Ford check in the amount of the
draft. The collecting bank, in turn, pays depositary banks, such as First
National Bank in Alamosa, the amount of the sight draft, by means of
inter-bank credits provided through the Federal Reserve system.

> What are the benefits of Ford's use of "payable through" drafts? Review 4-106 as needed to answer this question.

Dealers often execute and deposit the pre-printed Ford sight draft with
their local bank as soon as the consumer sale is made. This can create
problems. If the sight draft reaches Ford's collecting bank through the
bank-collection system before the retail-installment-sales agreement
reaches Ford through the mails, Ford will instruct its bank not to honor
the dealer's sight draft. More importantly, Ford will not honor a sight
draft if the agreement and related documents are not in order, or if the
dealer has failed to pay Ford the wholesale price for the car which the
dealer has sold and proposes to finance through Ford.

> Why would Ford instruct its bank to dishonor any draft not accompanied by sales documentation?

The nine drafts in question here were used in the commercial setting
described above. Each sight draft represents a separate retail
consumer-financing transaction. Ford dishonored seven of the drafts
because Alamosa Motors had not paid Ford the wholesale price of the
car which it was seeking to have Ford finance. It rejected an eighth
because Alamosa Motors had not submitted to Ford the retail-
installment-sales agreement. It rejected the ninth because the

automobile in question had previously been leased, and Alamosa Motors had not paid off the retail lease account on the vehicle.

* * *

Ford is not liable on these nine instruments for the simple reason that it did not "accept" the sight drafts. Under the UCC, a drawee who refuses acceptance is generally not liable *on the instrument*. Plaintiffs remedy on the instruments is against the drawer of the drafts, Alamosa Motors.

> Why is the language "on the instrument" emphasized here?

The Bank seeks to avoid the conclusion that Ford is not liable on the instruments. . . . [I]t asserts that the name "Ford Motor Credit Company" is prominently pre-printed on the drafts in two places – once in the upper left-hand corner (next to the Ford logo) and once in the middle of the draft, on the left-hand side, in the form, "To Ford Motor Credit Company." The Bank notes that Ford supplied these forms to its dealers as a means of facilitating payment to the dealers. It concludes that Ford has thus "signed." . . .

* * *

Here, the nine drafts themselves sufficiently demonstrate, on their face, that the words "Ford Motor Credit Company" were not placed thereon with a "present intention" to authenticate the drafts. . . .

The point concerning the significance of the pre-printed words "Ford Motor Credit Company" on these drafts can be made by comparing them to a more common form of draft – the ordinary check. Checks are commonly pre-printed with the name of the drawee bank in the place where Ford's name appears as drawee on the drafts here, and the name of the account holder and prospective drawer at the top of the check. . . . The pre-printed Ford sight drafts with the Ford name and corporate logo are no more a "signature" than are any individual's pre-printed personal checks, which do not ordinarily constitute the signature of either the individual or the drawee bank.

* * *

In claiming that Ford is liable on a negligence theory, the Bank asserts that Ford has carelessly designed form instruments with the words "Ford Motor Credit Company" and "SIGHT DRAFT" prominently displayed thereon and allowed those instruments to circulate in the commercial banking system. Thus, argues the Bank, Ford has confused depositary banks and misled them into thinking that the instruments were backed up by Ford and would always be honored by Ford. Ford never told the Bank "that the drafts might not be honored by" Ford or that Ford "did not consider the drafts to be drawn by [Ford] or against [Ford] funds."

The Bank's negligence claim must fail, because Ford did not owe the Bank or anyone else a general duty to refrain from preparing and using instruments such as the nine at issue here. There is nothing confusing or misleading about the words "SIGHT DRAFT." "Sight drafts" and

drafts "payable through" collecting banks are expressly recognized by
the UCC, discussed in numerous court decisions, and used regularly in
commerce. . . . Ford's evidence demonstrates (and the Bank does not
dispute) that the sight-draft system is widely used in the automobile
industry. The reported cases also suggest that sight drafts are
commonly used in other industries.

Similarly, the use of Ford's name on the drafts is not confusing or
misleading; indeed, it would have been confusing had Ford's name not
appeared on the drafts. The words, "To Ford Motor Credit Company,"
clearly name Ford as the drawee and thus identify for holders of the
drafts the person to whom they must be presented. As previously
noted, there is no general drawee liability where the drawee has
neither accepted nor signed the instrument. If the Bank was confused
or misled by the drafts, it was because of its own misunderstanding of
the nature of these instruments.

[The portion of the opinion relating to promissory estoppel is omitted.]

- How could the bank have avoided the loss in this case?

Liability of Accommodation Parties

Read 3-419 and Comments 1, 3, 4, and 5. This Code section
describes the rights and responsibilities of accommodation
parties.   An   accommodation   relationship   requires   three
contracts:

(1) An underlying contract between the accommodated
    party and the creditor. This is the central contract
    motivating the transaction.

(2) The contract of guaranty between the accommodation
    party and the creditor. This is the contract by which
    the accommodation party takes on contractual liability
    to the accommodated party's creditor.

(3) The   contract   for   reimbursement   between   the
    accommodation party and the accommodated party.
    This contract allows the accommodation party to
    recover from the accommodated party if it is required
    to pay that party's debt.

- Why is each contract necessary?

Comment 3 may
assist you in
answering this
question.

- What is the difference between "accommodation party"
  and "surety"?

- Explain the following language from 3-419 (b), using
  the labels *primary liability* and *secondary liability*: "An
  accommodation party may sign the instrument as

maker, drawer, acceptor, or indorser and, subject to
subsection (d), is obliged to pay the instrument in the
capacity in which the accommodation party signs."

- What is the difference between "guaranteeing
  collection" and "guaranteeing payment" within the
  meaning of 3-419 (d)?

Read 3-305 (d) and Comment 5. If an accommodation party
pays an item, he or she has the right to be reimbursed by the
accommodated party. In addition, he or she has the right to
assert many of the accommodated party's rights against the
creditor, as well as the creditor's rights against the
accommodated party. This right is called subrogation.

- What claims can the accommodation party *not* raise by
  subrogation?

Read 3-601 and 3-605. 3-601 defines "discharge," and 3-605
addresses discharge of indorsers, accommodation parties, and
other secondary obligors. As 3-605 (f) shows, although the Code
provides that secondary obligors will be discharged under the
circumstances described in 3-605, it is common for secondary
obligors to waive these rights by contract.

- **Read 3-103 (a) (17).** What is the difference between a
  "secondary obligor" under 3-605 and a party with
  "secondary liability" as described earlier in this
  chapter?

3-605 (a) states that a creditor's release of a principal obligor
will generally also release a secondary obligor.

- What are the risks and benefits of this rule?

3-605 (b) addresses how an extension of time to the primary
obligor will affect the liability of a secondary obligor, and 3-605
(c) addresses the effect that other modifications to the
agreement between the primary obligor and the creditor will
have on the secondary obligor.

- Why is a secondary obligor normally *not* discharged by
  an extension of time, but generally is discharged when
  the agreement is modified in other ways?

> Comments 5 and 6
> may assist you in
> answering this
> question.

Read 3-605 (d) and Comment 7. Accommodation parties
are released from liability when the creditor impairs the
collateral held as security for the obligation. *Langeveld v.
L.R.Z.H. Corp.*, 74 N.J. 45, 376 A.2d 931, 22 U.C.C. Rep. Serv.
106 (1977), explains the policy behind this means of release:

The doctrine is an equitable one, designed to protect the surety's right of subrogation. Upon paying the debt, the surety is, as a matter of law, subrogated to all the creditor's rights against the principal debtor and is entitled to all benefits derivable from any security of the principal debtor that may be in the creditor's hands. The rule forbidding impairment of collateral has as its chief aim the protection of these potential benefits made available through subrogation. *Id.* at 51.

The following is a typical form of guaranty, taken from *Langeveld*:

Read 3-419 and Comment 2. Is consideration for the sureties' signatures required? If so, is sufficient consideration given?

> To induce the said JOHN P. LANGEVELD to accept the above note, the undersigned hereby guaranty performance of all obligations of the obligors under the note and under the mortgage securing the indebtedness described in the note. The said undersigned guarantors agree to be principally liable on the indebtedness jointly and severally, and further agree to their obligation jointly and severally without the necessity of presentment, demand, or notice of dishonor.
>
> The undersigned guarantors agree to pay the tenor of this instrument notwithstanding that [the primary obligor] may effectuate an assignment for the benefit of creditors, be declared a bankrupt, be discharged from bankruptcy, or otherwise be excused, except by payment, of the debt.
>
> /s/ Joseph A. Higgins, Sr.
> /s/ Albin H. Rothe
> /s/ Louis J. Zoghby L.S.

The guaranty also contained the following language:

> The undersigned and all other parties who at any time may be liable hereon in any capacity, jointly and severally waive presentment, demand for payment, protest, and notice of protest of this note, and authorize the holder hereof, without notice, to grant extensions in the time of payment and reductions in the rate of interest on any moneys owing on this note. *Id.* at 52.

- What protections have the guarantors waived in this note?

Guarantors who waive their Article 3 defenses may later regret doing so. In *Agribank, FCB v. Whitlock*, 251 Ill. App. 3d 299, 621 N.E.2d 967 (Ill. App. 4th Dist. 1993), the court rejected an argument that a common waiver provision allowing the lender to pursue the accommodation parties even if it released the accommodated party from liability, was in contravention of the good-faith provisions of the UCC. The accommodation parties claimed the waiver constituted bad faith because the lender knew the parties intended that the accommodated party, rather than the accommodation party, would repay the loan obligation. In upholding the waiver language, the court held as follows:

> 3-605 (a) and Comment 4 set forth the default rule, which releases secondary obligors when the principal obligor is released.

> We do not believe we can construe the duty of good faith imposed by the Code to prevent the lender from inserting a provision in the instrument or accompanying documents, when the use of such a provision has been expressly sanctioned by the Code. Rather, we believe the effect of the good-faith obligation in the context of the advance consent to release the accommodated party, is to place the obligation upon the lender to act in good faith when releasing the accommodated party.

> What distinction is the court making here?

> As a practical matter in most accommodation situations, the accommodation party intends only to lend his credit so the accommodated party may obtain a loan. Both the accommodated party and accommodation maker intend, at the time of the signing of the contract, that the accommodated party will make the payments of the loan. The lender who is aware one individual is an accommodation maker may be cognizant that the accommodation maker merely intends to help the accommodated party obtain a loan, but has no expectation that he (the accommodation maker) will be called upon to satisfy the indebtedness . . . .

> While many accommodation parties may be surprised to learn the consent provisions in the instrument or accompanying documents essentially preclude them from asserting suretyship defenses and render little difference between their liability and the liability of the accommodated party, such consent provisions are sanctioned by the Code and routinely utilized by lenders. *Id.* at 311-312.

- How would you advise a client who has expressed interest in serving as an accommodation party for a child, friend, or business partner?

> Proverbs 6:1-5 and 11:15 may assist you in answering this question.

Read 3-116 and Comment 2. As 3-116 shows, parties signing in the same capacity are generally jointly and severally liable with one another. A holder can recover the full amount of the item from any party who shares joint and several liability, but the party required to pay can then seek contribution from the others sharing liability, requiring each to pay a proportional share.

- How are reimbursement and contribution different?

Accommodation parties and ordinary indorsers are treated differently, insofar as joint and several liability is concerned. Consider the following language from Comment 2:

> An "ordinary" indorser is distinguished from an anomalous indorser, who signs for the purpose of accommodation.

> Indorsers normally do not have joint and several liability. Rather, an earlier indorser has liability to a later indorser. . . . [However], [i]f more than one accommodation party indorses a note as an

accommodation to the maker, the indorsers have joint and several liability.

- Why are accommodation parties treated differently from ordinary indorsers, insofar as 3-116 is concerned?

Read 3-205 (d) and Comment 3 and 3-419 (b) and (e). An accommodation party usually signs as a co-maker or an anomalous indorser. Because an accommodation party can sign in any capacity, however, it is sometimes not clear when a party is signing for the purpose of accommodation.

- How is an accommodation co-maker different from other co-makers, with regard to rights of reimbursement, contribution, and subrogation?

While the plain language of the UCC generally allows a creditor to recover from an accommodation party before pursuing the principal obligor, some jurisdictions that adopted the doctrine of *Pain v. Packard*, 13 Johns. 174, 7 Am. Dec. 369 (N.Y. Sup. 1816), may allow an accommodation party, after default has occurred, to insist that the creditor obtain a judgment and return of execution against the principal obligor before the accommodation party's liability will come into play. The doctrine is described in *Amick v. Baugh*, 402 P.2d 342 (Wash. 1965).

Article 10 of the UCC, entitled "Effective Date and Repealer," is not included in some modern statutory supplements. It can be found on Westlaw by searching for "Article 10" within the database "UCC-TEXT."

- **Read UCC Article 10.** What guidance does it provide as to whether the UCC repealed the doctrine of *Pain v. Packard*?

Note 1: Read 3-419 (a) Comment 1 and note the words "direct beneficiary." When a putative accommodation party receives some benefit from a transaction, but is not the primary beneficiary, it can be difficult to determine whether that party is in fact an accommodation party. *In re Robinson Brothers Drilling, Inc.*, 9 F.3d 871 (10th Cir. 1993), provides some guidance on this issue.

> Although a party lending his or her name to another on an instrument is still an accommodation maker despite being paid for rendering such service, [the UCC] does not declare that one may remain an accommodation maker despite being a direct beneficiary of the instrument itself. Receiving the direct benefit of the instrument itself is contrary to the basic principle of lending one's name or credit to another (rather than using it for oneself), while accepting payment for assuming the role of surety is, by its own terms, obviously consistent with surety status. *Id.* at 874.

- What distinction is the court drawing?

Note 2: Determining whether a signer intended to serve as an accommodation party can present a challenge. *Transamerica Commercial Finance Corp. v. Naef*, 842 P.2d 539, 21 U.C.C. Rep. Serv. 2d 704 (Wyo. 1992), addresses this issue. Transamerica Commercial Finance Corporation sought to recover from Linda Naef under a promissory note she had signed as an accommodation party for her husband's business. The business and the husband had filed for bankruptcy protection, and Transamerica pursued payment from Mrs. Naef under 3-305 (d), which provides that an accommodation party cannot raise the principal obligor's insolvency to avoid liability. The court rejected Transamerica's claim against Mrs. Naef because the evidence showed Mrs. Naef owned no interest in the business and expressly lacked the intent to be a party to the note; in fact, when she was asked to sign the note, she informed the bank she would not sign because she could not guarantee her husband's obligation. The bank officer assured her that her signature was not important.

> As a matter of policy, why does it make sense that an accommodation party cannot raise the principal obligor's insolvency as a defense?

- Why might a court be reluctant to find a person is an accommodation party in a close case?

- Would Mrs. Naef escape liability if the note were transferred to a holder in due course?

> A careful reading of 3-419 (a) may provide a clue to the proper answer.

Problem 1: Jerry Iguess executed a promissory note to Calcasieu Marine Bank for approximately $7,000. On the reverse side of the note were the signatures of Alvin Daigle, his wife Marlene, and David Chaisson, along with the word "indorser" under each. The three signatures appeared horizontally across the back of the note, coupled with the following language: "The undersigned hereby jointly and severally guarantee to the bank . . ." Before the note came due, Iguess filed for bankruptcy and received discharge on the note. After the note became past due, the bank demanded payment from the indorsers. Daigle paid and then sued Iguess and Chaisson.

Consider this language from the court's opinion: "Plaintiff, Alvin Daigle, an indorser and presently the holder of the note, seeks indemnity or, in the alternative, contribution from the defendant, David Chaisson, a co-indorser."

> Make sure you understand how Daigle became holder of the note.

- Based on this language, what status is Alvin Daigle claiming?

- Is the "guarantee" language dispositive in establishing this status?

- On what theory could Daigle sue Chaisson?

- On what theory could Daigle sue Iguess?

Based on *Daigle v. Chaisson*, 396 So. 2d 573, 31 U.C.C. Rep. Serv. 1032 (La. App. 3d Cir. 1981).

Problem 2: Donald F. Boyer executed two promissory notes payable to People's National Bank of Mora. His parents, Donald E. and Dorothy Boyer, signed as accommodation parties. Their contract of guaranty with the bank included a provision whereby they consented to any extension of time or renewal of the loans. In accordance with this provision, each loan was renewed several times. In August 1981, the two loans were consolidated. Mr. and Mrs. Boyer never signed the renewed notes, nor did they sign the consolidated note, even though the bank contacted them three times, asking them to do so. The consolidated note bore a higher rate of interest than the two initial promissory notes did. In addition, the credit-life-insurance policies issued in conjunction with the two original notes were cancelled and new insurance was issued, with the new premiums added to the consolidated balance. In March 1982, the son filed for bankruptcy, and the bank sought to recover from the parents.

- Should the bank prevail in arguing that the renewals and consolidation represent a mere "extension of time" that will not discharge the liability of Mr. and Mrs. Boyer?

Based on *People's National Bank of Mora v. Boyer*, 354 N.W.2d 559 (Minn. 1984).

Problem 3: Walter Fithian and Richard Jamar formed a business partnership and applied to the People's Bank of Chestertown, Maryland for a loan of $11,000 to purchase some equipment for their new business. The bank was willing to extend credit only if Walter's wife Connie, Richard's wife Janet, and Walter's parents Bill and Mildred would co-sign the promissory note. When Walter and Richard asked why the co-signatures were required, the bank's Vice President replied, "They will make the bank more secure." Each of the six parties signed the promissory note in the bottom right-hand corner.

> Is this an accurate response on the part of the bank?

- In what capacity did each party sign?

After the partnership failed, Walter and Richard defaulted on the note, and the bank demanded payment from Bill and Mildred. After paying, they demanded payment from Richard.

- Who had primary liability on the note, at issuance?

- Who had secondary liability?

- What rights do each of the following parties have as against the others? Explain any factual assumptions you made.

  - Richard v. Connie
  - Janet v. Connie
  - Richard v. Walter
  - Janet v. Walter

Based on *Fithian v. Jamar*, 286 Md. 161, 410 A.2d 569, 27 U.C.C. Rep. Serv. 481 (1979).

Articles 3 and 4 Statutes of Limitations

Read 3-118 and 4-111. The usual limitations period for Article 3 contract actions on a negotiable instrument is 6 years, and the Article 3 limitations period for tort and warranty claims is 3 years. The Article 4 limitations period is three years for each kind of claim. The following chart provides detailed information regarding enforcement of items under Article 3.

> Sections 3-416 (d), 3-417 (f), 4-207 (e), and 4-208 (f) provide guidance as to when warranty actions accrue under each Article.

TYPE OF INSTRUMENT	MUST COMMENCE ACTION TO ENFORCE
Note payable at a definite date	Within 6 years after due date on note or accelerated due date
Unaccepted demand note	Within 10 years of date of note or 6 years from dishonor, whichever is first
Unaccepted draft	Within 10 years of date of draft or 3 years from dishonor, whichever is first
Certified, teller's, cashier's, and traveler's checks	No time limit to make demand Must sue within 3 years, once dishonored
Certificates of deposit	Within 6 years after demand, and no more than 6 years after due date appearing on face of item
Other accepted drafts	Within 6 years of due date if payable at a definite time Within 6 years of date of acceptance if payable on demand

Tepper v. Citizens Federal Savings & Loan Association, 448 So. 2d 1138, 38 U.C.C. Rep. Serv. 528 (Fla. 3d Dist. App. 1984), addresses when a cause of action accrues for wrongful dishonor. Rose Tepper was adjudicated incompetent in December 1982. Shortly thereafter, her personal representative found a large 8-year-old check among her belongings. Ms. Tepper was the payee. The drawer was

Citizens Federal Savings & Loan Association and the drawee
was Jefferson National Bank.

- What kind of negotiable instrument is this?

The representative immediately presented the check to the
drawee, which refused payment.   Next, the representative
approached the drawer, which also declined to honor the check.

- Why would it make sense to approach the parties in
  this order?

The representative then brought suit.   Addressing the
limitations period, the court held as follows:

> A cashier's check is a check on which the issuing bank acts as both
> the drawer and the drawee. Its own act of issuance renders the
> bank a drawee who has accepted the draft; thus the issuing bank
> becomes primarily liable as an acceptor. Presentment of a
> negotiable instrument is not necessary in order to establish
> liability against parties who are primarily liable. In such a case,
> the statute of limitations begins to run on a demand instrument at
> the moment of issuance.
>
> As to parties secondarily liable, however, such as the drawer
> herein, there is no instant liability and thus no cause of action
> until demand following presentment and dishonor. *Id.* at 1140.

- What distinction does the court draw between
  cashier's checks and instruments such as the one Mrs.
  Tepper's representative presented?

- Is the court's dicta regarding cashier's checks
  consonant with 3-118?

- Under what circumstances, if any, will the statute of
  limitations never begin to run and thus never expire?

Problem: Carlisle Distributing Co. delivered a check for
$10,000 to William Paladino, who pledged the check to a third
party, Wildman Stores, Inc., as security for a loan of $8,000,
which he later paid in full.   After having the check for
seventeen months, Wildman Stores, Inc. sought to enforce it,
and the payor bank dishonored it.   Wildman Stores, Inc. then
sued Carlisle Distributing Co. on a theory of secondary liability.

- What apparent reason exists for the bank to dishonor
  the check?

- Was the bank required to dishonor the check?

- Is Carlisle Distributing Co. still liable on the check?

- If so, when would its liability expire?

- Assume Paladino indorsed the check before delivering it to Wildman Stores, Inc. Is he still liable on the check?

- If so, when would his liability expire?

Based on *Wildman Stores, Inc. v. Carlisle Distributing Co., Inc.,* 15 Ark. App. 11, 688 S.W.2d 748, 40 U.C.C. Rep. Serv. 1766 (Ark. App. Div. 1 1985).

International Perspective: Contract Liability

Read CIBN Articles 38, 39, 40, and 44, together with UCC 3-414 Comment 7, 3-412 Comment 4, 3-413 Comment, and 3-415 Comment 6. These provisions set forth the basic obligations of drawers, makers, drawees, and endorsers, in language that should be familiar to a student of the UCC.

Note the CIBN spelling of "endorser."

Read CIBN Article 47. There is a significant difference between the common-law and civil-law approaches to guarantors' negotiable-instrument contract liability. The CIBN, attempting to respond to both, incorporates the concept of the *aval,* a civil-law form of suretyship that may be unfamiliar to those trained in common law. The following excerpt from Gerold Herrmann, *Background and Salient Features of the United Nations Convention on International Bills of Exchange and International Promissory Notes,* 10 U. Pa. Intl. Bus. L. 517 (1988), introduces this concept:

> The civil-law system has created a concept of guarantee in which the guarantor's rights and liabilities are governed solely by the law of negotiable instruments. As a rule, the giver of an *aval* may not raise the defenses that a surety may raise under the general law of suretyship. . . .
>
> * * *
>
> [W]ith regard to the defenses that a guarantor may invoke, his liability is independent of that of the person whose liability is guaranteed, provided that that person's undertaking is formally valid. The independence of the guarantor's liability is perhaps most dramatically demonstrated by the rule that, in the event the guarantor has guaranteed the liability of, say, a drawer whose signature appears on the bill but who is a fictitious person, the

guarantor is nevertheless liable even though the purported
drawer is not liable since he does not exist. *Id.* at 532-533.

The excerpt uses language from GUL Articles 30 and 32, which
provide as follows:

> Article 30: Payment of a bill of exchange may be guaranteed by an
> "aval" as to the whole or part of its amount.
>
> This guarantee may be given by a third person or even by a person
> who has signed as a party to the bill.
>
> Article 32: The giver of an "aval" is bound in the same manner as
> the person for whom he has become guarantor.
>
> His undertaking is valid even when the liability which he has
> guaranteed is inoperative for any reason other than defect of form.
>
> He has, when he pays a bill of exchange, the rights arising out of
> the bill of exchange against the person guaranteed and against
> those who are liable to the latter on the bill of exchange.

- How do the GUL and UCC approaches to suretyship
  differ?

- How does the CIBN attempt to deal with the
  competing common-law and civil-law traditions,
  insofar as suretyship is concerned?

B. Warranty Liability under Articles 3 and 4

This section covers Article 3 and Article 4 transfer and
presentment warranties, explaining the similarities and
differences between the two and showing when each is
implicated. In addition, this section discusses the encoding and
retention warranties that have been created as a result of
attempts to expedite the collection process through electronic
presentment. As you study these materials, begin to make
notes on the following chart.

- Who owes presentment warranties to whom?

- Who owes transfer warranties to whom when bearer
  paper is negotiated?

- How would your answer change for order paper?

- Who owes encoding warranties to whom, assuming
  the depositary bank transmits an electronic image of

the item and all banks in the collection chain are willing and able to receive an image rather than the item?

- Applying the assumptions presented in the previous question, who owes retention warranties to whom?

- How would your answers change if a note were involved?

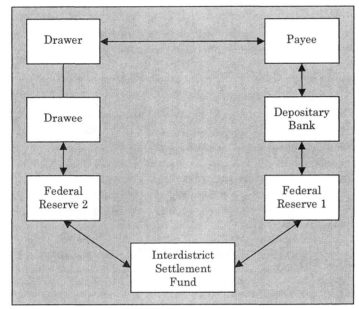

As Chapter 7, Part E shows, there are three periods in the life of a negotiable instrument: Issuance, Transfer, and Presentment. Remembering these will be useful in determining when the warranties in this section are applicable.

Transfer Warranties

Read 3-416 and Comments 3, 5, 6, and 8, and 4-207 and Comment 1.

- Compare and contrast the Article 3 and Article 4 transfer warranties.

- What is a "remotely-created consumer item," and how might its issuance implicate a transfer warranty?

- How are damages for breach of transfer warranty different from damages for breach of the negotiable-instrument contract?

Presentment Warranties

Read 3-417 and Comments 2, 3, 4, and 5, and 4-208 and Comment 1.

- How are presentment warranties different from transfer warranties, with regard to what is warranted?

- Compare and contrast the Article 3 and Article 4 presentment warranties.

- Explain the difference between the warranties in 3-417 (a) and 4-208 (a), on one hand, and 3-417 (d) and 4-208 (d), on the other.

The following case involves transfer and presentment warranties. As this case shows, the drawee and depositary banks may use these warranties in combination to shift the loss caused by a forged indorsement.

Girard Bank v. Mount Holly State Bank,
474 F. Supp. 1225, 26 U.C.C. Rep. Serv. 1210 (D.N.J. 1979).

Brotman, District Judge.

On August 4, 1977, . . . Penn Mutual Life Insurance Company issued its check numbered 377406, dated August 4, for $28,269.54 to a Morris Lefkowitz of New York City, as a return of a policy premium. The check was drawn on Penn Mutual's account at plaintiff Girard Bank in Philadelphia. The check, prepared and signed in Philadelphia, was to be sent by mail to Penn Mutual's agency in New York for distribution to Mr. Lefkowitz.

On August 5, . . . Darlene Payung deposited the check in her account at Mount Holly State Bank of Mount Holly, New Jersey, the defendant and third-party plaintiff. The check bore a forgery of Mr. Lefkowitz's signature as an indorsement; the origin of the forgery is disputed. Ms. Payung also added her signature as an indorsement when she deposited the check. Mount Holly transferred the check through normal banking channels to Central Penn National Bank of Philadelphia, which then presented it for payment to the drawee and payor, Girard. Mount Holly, the depository and a collecting bank, recovered the full amount of the check from Central Penn.

> Assuming that Ms. Payung was the forger, was the addition of her own signature necessary for her to be liable on the instrument?

. . . According to a Penn Mutual official, its New York agency first alerted the Philadelphia office that the check had not been received by a telephone call on August 19; the agency had become aware about August 11 that the check might be missing. . . . [B]oth Girard and Mount Holly were notified that the check was missing on the 19th.

. . . [Mount Holly was able] to freeze the remaining $5,600 in Ms. Payung's account. Most of the proceeds had already been withdrawn by

Ms. Payung. . . . Penn Mutual also discussed the check with a Girard Bank officer on August 25, the same day that Mr. Lefkowitz signed an affidavit swearing that the indorsement was forged. That telephone conversation was confirmed by letter dated August 26 from Penn Mutual to Girard.

It is not certain how the check was stolen and forged. Mount Holly maintains that several checks had been stolen by Penn Mutual employees prior to August 4, and that the company knew of the problem and unreasonably failed to take proper security measures. The defendant further contends that it can prove at trial that the Lefkowitz check, which was deposited at Mount Holly the day after it was drawn, was stolen by a Penn Mutual employee. Girard has sued Mount Holly to recover on the latter's presentment warranty, which it alleges was breached by the forged check. . . .

* * *

The forged indorsement prevented Mount Holly, the depository and collecting bank, from obtaining good title to the check, and Mount Holly therefore breached its warranty. [FN2] The overriding scheme of the Code is to place liability on the person who takes from the forger, which is often the depository bank. The rationale is that this party is normally in the best position to detect the forgery and prevent the fraud. This has long been the policy of negotiable-instruments law.

> FN2. The forged indorsement of Mr. Lefkowitz's name in blank does not convert the check into a valid bearer instrument which could allow Ms. Payung to pass good title.

This policy is reflected throughout Articles 3 and 4 of the Code. Various sections indicate that a check bearing a forged indorsement is not "properly payable" within the terms of 4-401 (1). That section indicates that, absent cognizable negligence on the part of the drawer, the drawee bank may not charge the drawer for a check that is not "properly payable." However, the drawee which has paid the check may seek recovery against prior banks in the collection chain for breach of presentment warranty under 4-207. The depository bank may also sue the prior transferring party under a similar warranty provided in 3-417. In the instant case, Mount Holly, if found liable to Girard, may be able to shift the loss back to the prior transferor, Ms. Payung. However, it is often the case that a depository bank will be unable to recover from a prior party and will ultimately bear the loss.

* * *

Mount Holly argues that there is a genuine issue of material fact precluding summary judgment as to whether Girard asserted its claim [for breach of presentment warranty] within a reasonable time.

While reasonableness has been held to present a fact question, the court finds there is nothing in the record to show that Mount Holly suffered a loss as the result of any delay by Girard in making its claim against Mount Holly. . . . [A]ny delay in Girard's noticing Mount Holly could not possibly have caused any loss since all proceeds of the check

Margin notes:

Which portion of 4-208 is implicated?

Make sure you know why this statement is true. Review the materials in Chapter 9, Part B as necessary.

The current reference is 4-208.

The current reference is 3-416.

were frozen the same day Girard first learned it had a claim against Mount Holly.

- Where should liability rest for a forged indorsement?

- Which party most frequently bears the loss and why?

> 4-208 (c) and 4-406 Comment 5 may assist you in answering this question.

- If Penn Mutual engaged in negligent supervision within the meaning of 3-406 that contributed to the loss, can Girard simply ignore Penn Mutual's negligence, recredit its account, and sue Mount Holly pursuant to 4-208?

> 3-403 and Comment 1 may assist you in answering this question.

- Is an agent's abuse of authority in signing as a putative representative tantamount to a forgery of the principal's signature?

Note 1: To recover for a breach of presentment warranty, a drawee must show it is a "payor in good faith" within the meaning of 4-208. In *Savings Banks Trust Co. v. Federal Reserve Bank of New York*, 577 F. Supp. 964, 37 U.C.C. Rep. Serv. 1638 (S.D.N.Y. 1984), the court held a drawee bank is not a "payor in good faith" if it pays an item over a valid stop-payment order or is aware of any defense or claim against it. By contrast, as the court held in *Wachovia Bank, N.A. v. Federal Reserve Bank of Richmond*, 338 F.3d 318 (4th Cir. 2003), a drawee bank does not act in bad faith merely by failing to implement a system to review high-dollar checks manually before they are paid. The court found that, even if the bank's conduct were negligent, it would not constitute the kind of "unfair or dishonest" behavior contemplated as bad-faith by the drafters. In so holding, the court distinguished between "reasonable commercial standards" and "reasonable commercial standards of fair dealing" within the ambit of Revised 1-304.

- Where do you find "good faith" language in 4-208?

- Does 3-417 include similar language?

Note 2: *Aetna Life and Casualty Co. v. Hampton State Bank*, 497 S.W.2d 80, 13 UCC Rep. Serv. 876 (Tex. Civ. App. 1973), involved a transfer-warranty claim based upon a stolen check bearing a fictitious payee and a forged drawer's signature. The depositary bank credited the check to a customer's account and, after the drawee bank returned the check unpaid, sought to recover the loss from its own insurance company. (The customer was presumably unavailable for suit or judgment-proof.) One of the issues before the court was the possibility of warranties owed to and owed by the depositary bank. The court acknowledged, "It may seem odd to speak of a warranty of title to a forged check, but that is exactly what we have here." The court explained its holding as follows:

> Title to a check does not necessarily mean the right to collect it from the drawer, since the drawer may have a good defense. A person (other than the drawee bank) who has paid value for a forged check has title to the spurious instrument which enables him to recover against his transferor under 3-417 (b) (2) and against prior indorsers under 3-414. A warranty of title is nothing more than an assurance that no one has better title to the check than the warrantor, and therefore, that no one is in a position to claim title as against the warrantee, as the payee or other owner of a genuine check could do if his indorsement were forged. *Id.* at 84.

> The current references should be to 3-416 and 3-415, respectively.

- The court uses the expression "warranty of title." How do the transfer and presentment warranties in Articles 3 and 4 compare with the warranty of title in 2-312?

Problem 1: An individual in Africa contacted Impact Computers and Electronics, Inc., claiming to be associated with Westgate Fabrics, Inc., a Texas corporation. Impact agreed to sell computers to this individual that were worth about $63,000. After Impact received a check from this individual, it deposited the check in its account with Bank of America and, once the bank indicated the check had cleared, shipped the computers to Africa. A bank representative ostensibly informed Impact that "nothing could affect the funds" after the check cleared. The bank subsequently learned that the check had been altered as to both its amount and the identity of the payee. After notifying Impact, the bank debited the amount of the check from its account, which created an overdraft of approximately $22,000.

> Is this a correct statement on the part of the bank representative?

- Based upon these facts, are any warranties owed?

- Have any warranties been breached?

Based on *Impact Computers and Electronics, Inc. v. Bank of America, N.A.*, 852 So. 2d 946 (Fla. 3d Dist. App. 2003).

Problem 2: Theresa Piotrowski defaulted on a promissory note for a 1957 Ford automobile. She refused to pay because she claimed she had neither purchased the car nor signed the note. The bank holding the note then sought to recover the balance due from the Ford dealer, the original payee that indorsed and transferred the note to the bank. The bank acknowledged Ms. Piotrowski never signed the note, but claimed an authorized agent, Edward Rogalia, signed on her behalf.

> This problem includes elements of Article 3 contract liability as well as warranty liability.

Review the materials in Chapter 9, Part B, as needed to answer this portion of the problem.

- What facts are needed for a court to determine whether Piotrowski and/or Rogalia are liable on the note?

- On what theories can the bank sue the car dealer?

- Can the dealer escape liability if it indorsed the note "without recourse?"

Based on *Union Bank v. Mobilla*, 43 Erie Co. Leg. J. 45 (1959).

Problem 3: Interamerican Business Institute owner Diego Aguirre perpetrated a scam involving student-loan proceeds. Great Lakes Higher Education Corporation issued 224 student-loan checks drawn against its account with First Wisconsin Bank and delivered the checks to Interamerican, where the students named as payees on those checks were presumably enrolled. The students' indorsements were forged, and the checks were deposited at Austin Bank of Chicago, where Interamerican banked. First Wisconsin paid the checks. The following excerpts from a Department of Education report describe the scam:

> Investigation showed that most of the students for whom the checks were issued had canceled their enrollment and never attended IBI, or only attended the school for a short time. Aguirre . . . converted the funds for his own use. Aguirre also destroyed the files for these students before he closed the school in 1992, thereby hindering the investigation.

- Have any warranties been made?

- Have any warranties been breached?

Based on *Great Lakes Higher Education Corp. v. Austin Bank of Chicago*, 837 F. Supp. 892, 22 U.C.C. Rep. Serv. 2d 858 (N.D. Ill. 1993).

Problem 4: Read 3-203 (a). Is each a transfer?

- Depositing a check with a bank other than the drawee.

- Presenting a check to the drawee for cashing.

- Presenting a check to a drawee who is also a payee, to make payment on a mortgage held by the drawee.

Encoding and Retention Warranties

Read 4-209 and Comments 1 and 2. Encoding and retention warranties are necessitated by electronic presentment, which makes it possible for banks to process checks as digital information without ever being in possession of them.

> Electronic presentment is introduced in Chapter 10, Part A's discussion of Check 21.

- How does each of these two warranties facilitate the electronic-presentment process?

- Why hold a bank liable for breach of an encoding warranty if its customer encodes checks before delivering them to the bank?

- How should such a bank protect itself from liability?

- Is the customer also liable?

Applying the language of Comment 2, if the drawer writes a check for $25,000, and the depositary bank encodes it for $2,500, the payor bank is liable for the full amount of the check. Because the incorrect encoding is not an alteration, the check is still valid for the full amount.

- When will an error in encoding result in a loss to the payor bank, causing it to proceed against the depositary bank for breach of an encoding warranty?

Problem: Harold France financed the purchase of a tractor and decided to pay off the note early by writing two checks for the remaining balance. Due to an encoding error by the creditor's agent, the first check was encoded and debited from his account as $506 rather than the correct amount of $8,506. Due to an error by France's wife, the amount of the second check was written in numbers as $8,000 and in words as "eight dollars." The creditor's agent made a second error, encoding this check for $800. Once again, the payor bank debited France's account for only the encoded amount. Upon demand for the balance due, Mr. France refused to make further payment, claiming his obligations were eliminated by these repeated errors.

> What was the amount of this second check, applying 3-114?

- Will he prevail?

> Reading 3-602 (a) in conjunction with 4-209 may assist you in answering this question.

Based on *France v. Ford Motor Credit Co.*, 323 Ark. 167, 913 S.W.2d 770, 29 U.C.C. Rep. Serv. 2d 249 (1996).

International Perspective: Warranty Liability

Read CIBN Article 45 and UCC 3-416 Comment 9. As Professor John A. Spanogle states in *The U.N. Convention on International Bills and Notes (CIBN): A Primer for Attorneys and International Bankers*, 25 U.C.C. L.J. 99 (1992), the GUL does not recognize transfer warranties as a cause of action, and the CIBN drafters were therefore faced with the problem of how to reconcile the competing traditions on this point. The resultant compromise is reflected in the language of CIBN Article 45.

- How is the CIBN warranty narrower than the UCC warranty?

C. Tort Liability under Articles 3 and 4

This section discusses the torts of conversion, forgery of drawer and indorser signatures, and alteration. The discussion of forgery also addresses comparative negligence, validation of a forgery, and the same-wrongdoer rule.

Read 3-420 and Comment 1. 3-420 explains the application of the common law of conversion in the context of negotiable instruments.

- Why does a drawer have no conversion action against a depositary bank for payment over a forged indorsement?

- Compare the damages contemplated under 3-420 with the damages awarded pursuant to a breach-of-contract or warranty claim under Article 3.

Read 3-206 (c) and Comment 3. 3-206 (c) ties together restrictive indorsement and conversion. The rightful holder of an instrument has a cause of action in conversion against a bank or other party that cashes the item for a wrongdoer claiming entitlement to enforce the item. In addition, when a holder indorses a check or other item with a restrictive indorsement such as "for deposit only," a bank may be liable in conversion if it handles the item in a manner inconsistent with these instructions – such as paying the item in cash.

> Restrictive indorsement is discussed in Chapter 9, Part B.

- How does a bank engage in conversion when it pays an item in disregard of a restrictive indorsement?

- What distinction does 3-206 (c) recognize between the liability of depositary banks and other banks within the collection process, with regard to liability for conversion?

In studying these materials, begin to make notes on the following chart.

- What parties face liability in conversion when a check or other draft is paid over a forged indorsement?

- What parties can bring suit for conversion under these circumstances?

- How can the combination of tort and warranty liability best serve to place liability on the party who should bear the loss?

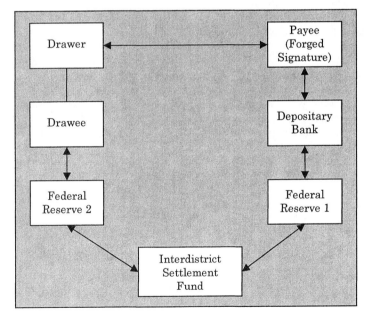

Read 3-307. The following case shows when a bank is deemed to have notice that a depositor is acting in a fiduciary capacity, thus rendering the bank liable for conversion when it allows a deposit to a non-fiduciary account. The case also shows that making payment in compliance with a restrictive indorsement will not always shield the bank from liability for conversion.

Crick v. HSBC Bank USA,
775 N.Y.S.2d 497, 53 U.C.C. Rep. Serv. 2d 271 (2004).

Jack M. Battaglia, J.

In two separate actions, Bertram V. Crick and Elsa V. Webb are seeking to recover from HSBC Bank USA the face amounts of four checks, totaling $31,500.00, that they delivered to Daniel Stern, an attorney, and that Mr. Stern deposited with the Bank. . . .

The four checks were issued in connection with the contemplated purchase and sale of several parcels of real property owned by sellers represented by Mr. Stern. [Crick and Webb were each seeking to purchase some of this property.] One of the checks was drawn on an account maintained by "Val Crick's Real Estate" with the Chase Manhattan Bank, was payable to the order of "Slovak and Stern Esq.," and shows an address on the "memo" line. The other three checks were drawn on one of the two accounts maintained by Ms. Webb with the Dime Savings Bank of New York, were payable to "Slovak and Stern Esq.," or "[unintelligible] Slovak-Stern Attorney," and also show addresses on the "memo" line. One of the checks that is payable to "[unintelligible] Slovak-Stern Attorney" contains the words "Down Payment" above the address.

On the back of each of the checks, there is a handwritten signature, apparently made by the same person, that the parties treat as the signature of Daniel Stern. Under the signatures, there are stamped indorsements that read: "Pay to the order of HSBC Bank USA / For Deposit Only / Madison Importing, Inc." Numbers appear below the Madison name, which, presumably, represent one or more accounts maintained with the Bank. The Bank presented the checks for payment to the respective drawee banks, which paid them, and the Bank then made the funds available to Mr. Stern through the Madison account(s). Mr. Stern obtained the funds, but did not apply them to the contemplated real-estate transactions or deliver them to Plaintiffs.

The Bank now moves for summary judgment in both actions, contending that "the only issues presented in the Complaint are those of law i.e., whether the actions of HSBC in these matters was (*sic*) commercially reasonable or otherwise violated the New York Uniform Commercial Code," and arguing that since "HSBC followed the instructions provided to it in the endorsements (*sic*) on the subject checks . . . , it is not liable for the Plaintiffs' losses." . . . Plaintiffs' position, in any event, is that the Bank "acted in bad faith and departed from the reasonable commercial standards set by the UCC," in that "the checks were issued to a law firm and therefore should have been deposited in the firm's escrow account" and that the Bank was required "to inquire about checks being deposited in account (*sic*) that belong to someone other than the payee."

* * *

As to Plaintiffs' claim for "misappropriation of funds," the drawer of a check cannot sue a depositary bank when the check is paid by the drawee / payor bank even though the check is not "properly payable," as in the case of a check containing a forged indorsement, and the proceeds then made available by the depositary bank to its customer, the theory being that the drawee/payor bank has given its own funds to the depositary bank, so that the drawer has no interest in their disposition. The rationale applies whenever the check is not "properly payable," as in the case of missing indorsements.

> Make sure you can explain the distinction the court is making in this paragraph and the next, in your own words.

When, however, any irregularity in the check is nonetheless effective against the drawer so as to render the check "properly payable," then the drawer's funds are "in play," and the drawer may sue the depositary bank that has acted wrongfully. A depositary bank acts wrongfully when it disregards a restrictive indorsement.

* * *

Here, there is no dispute that the Bank followed the instructions of the restrictive indorsement; indeed, that is precisely what Plaintiffs are complaining about. The Bank apparently is of the view that, having complied with the indorsement, there can be no basis for liability to Plaintiffs, or, put differently, that the only wrongdoing of a depositary bank that would permit an action by a drawer is failure to comply with a restrictive indorsement. But there is nothing in the caselaw that requires that conclusion, and applicable provisions of Article 3 of the Uniform Commercial Code point elsewhere.

> Why are the plaintiffs complaining about compliance with the restrictive indorsements?

* * *

[I]t seems clear that payment in accordance with a restrictive endorsement does not insulate a depositary bank from liability when it handles a check with knowledge of a breach of fiduciary duty, although establishing that knowledge may be difficult. . . .

* * *

None of the checks here was made payable to an attorney "as attorney for" the drawer or any third party. Although Plaintiffs insist that "[t]he notation on the checks clearly and unequivocally states for down payment of the respective properties with their addresses" in fact only one of the four checks contains on the "memo" line the words "down payment" with an address.

Whatever standard is applied, including one of "should have known" that would be very favorable to Plaintiffs, three of the checks at issue do not sufficiently identify the payees as a fiduciary, so as to engage any particular duty of care or vigilance on the part of the depositary bank. A check payable to an attorney is more likely to be intended for non-fiduciary purposes, such as payment of the attorney's fee, than pursuant to a special relationship, and the addition of an address on the "memo" line adds little, even assuming that a bank will be charged with seeing it. At least when a depositary bank otherwise handles the check properly, paying the named payee in accordance with any restrictive indorsement, the check on its face establishes *prima facie* the bank's freedom from fault. Plaintiffs point to no other evidence that the Bank here would have had sufficient awareness of a fiduciary relationship or purpose.

The remaining check at issue, containing the additional words "down payment," cannot be as easily set aside. Such a notation might well be understood as indicating a fiduciary relationship. Assuming, now, the standard most favorable to the Bank, one of "actual knowledge," it cannot be said that such a check on its face establishes *prima facie* the absence of sufficient awareness of a fiduciary relationship or purpose. That which appears on the face of a check can provide sufficient notice for purposes of determining holder-in-due-course status. . . .

And the same applies to the ultimate issues concerning any wrongdoing on the part of the Bank in handling the "down payment" check. In light of . . . the little discovery that has been conducted so far, . . . the serious and complex questions concerning the nature of any potential liability and its proof, and the importance of those questions to the banking system and all who rely upon it, the Court determines that the resolution of the claim with respect to the one check should await further proceedings.

> ▪ **Read 3-307 Comment 2.** What specific facts must be proven on remand for the plaintiffs to prevail against the bank?

Note 1: *First National Bank of Commerce v. Anderson Ford Lincoln-Mercury, Inc.*, 704 S.W.2d 83, 42 U.C.C. Rep. Serv. 1684 (Tex. App. 5th Dist. 1985), elucidates the practical difference between contract and tort liability, in the context of a negotiable instrument. A vice president of First National Bank of Commerce, presumably acting as the bank's agent, orally told an employee of Anderson Ford Lincoln Mercury, Inc., "Draft on me for $13,000" which was the price of the new truck that Anderson Ford customer Jerry McKnight wished to purchase. This was a common, informal way of securing financing. Based upon the bank's representation, the dealership sold McKnight the truck and gave him a rebate of about $1,600. The bank refused to sign the written draft when it was presented, claiming it had changed its mind and did not wish to finance the purchase. The dealership sued, and the court held the bank could not be liable in contract because it never signed the draft, but could be liable in tort for failing to exercise ordinary care toward the dealership.

> This case is introduced in Part B of this chapter.

Note 2: Review the facts of *Great Lakes Higher Education Corp. v. Austin Bank of Chicago*, 837 F. Supp. 892, 22 U.C.C. Rep. Serv. 2d 858 (N.D. Ill. 1993). Both plaintiffs – Great Lakes Higher Education Corporation and First Wisconsin Bank – raised a common-law negligence claim against Austin Bank. The court held as follows, in rejecting this claim:

> Plaintiffs invoke the law of common-law negligence against Austin. . . . When only economic loss is incurred, the plaintiff may only raise contract theories, even if the defendant's alleged conduct constituted a tort as well as a breach of contract."

. . . Here, First Wisconsin and Great Lakes have other remedies under the UCC which they have alternatively plead in their complaint, thus showing that a common-law action for negligence is unnecessary and may not be alleged here. *Id.* at 896.

- What purpose does the economic-loss rule serve?

- What other claims can First Wisconsin make against Austin?

Note 3: Read 3-404 (a) and (d) and Comments 1 and 3. 3-404 sets forth the "imposter rule," which can limit drawee liability by shifting the loss to another party in a better position to avoid the loss. *Covington v. Penn Square National Bank,* 545 P.2d 824 (Okla. Civ. App. 1975), illustrates the interplay between conversion and the imposter rule.

- Who is an "imposter" as the word is used in 3-404 (a)?

In November 1972, James F. Beaird, Jr. contacted Mr. A.M. Covington, offering to sell him an oil lease and claiming to work for Western Geophysical Company of Houston, Texas. He showed Covington maps of test holes and logs indicating oil sand had been discovered in each test area. Mr. Covington contacted Western Geophysical Company and, upon asking whether "James Beaird" was an employee, was told that "James Baird" was in charge of the data processing department. When Mr. Covington sought to clarify with Mr. Beaird the spelling of his name, he responded "that his name was spelled with an 'I.'"

On November 16, Covington purchased a cashier's check from Boulder Bank in the amount of $6,400, made payable to "James Baird." On November 17, James Beaird cashed the check at Penn Square National Bank, where he had banked for five years. He informed the teller that his name had been misspelled and, at the teller's request, indorsed the check twice, once using each spelling.

> 3-204 (d) indicates that either spelling could effectuate indorsement, but a bank might choose to require both.

On November 18 and 19, Covington began to investigate Beaird more carefully, having become suspicious. He found that James Beaird was not the "James Baird" employed by Western Geophysical and that no exploration had taken place on the land he had agreed to lease. On November 20, he requested that Boulder Bank stop payment on the cashier's check, and the bank agreed to do so in return for Covington's agreement to indemnify the bank for any losses it suffered by doing so. When Penn Square National Bank presented the check for payment, Boulder Bank initially returned the item

stamped "payment stopped," but relented and paid the check
when Penn Square demanded it do so.

Covington sought to recover from Boulder Bank and Penn
Square National Bank, claiming Boulder was liable for its
failure to stop payment and Penn Square was liable because it
indorsed the check "with all prior indorsements guaranteed."
In rejecting both claims, the court held as follows:

> Statutory language and case law unmistakably place the burden
> of loss from a forged instrument on the party who deals with the
> forger.
>
> * * *
>
> The policy underlying this rule is that the person who is taken in
> by an imposter or a dishonest employee should bear the burden of
> loss rather than a collecting bank. This is so despite the fact that
> the transaction with the collecting bank is based on a forgery. *Id.*
> at 826.

Review the
materials in Chapter
10, Part B as needed
to answer this
question.

- Can the plaintiff recover from Boulder Bank for paying
  the check despite its request for stop payment?

- What facts must the plaintiff prove to recover from
  Penn Square Bank under 3-404?

Problem 1: Jeff Messing was the holder of a check for about
$1,000, drawn on the account of Toyson J. Burruss, d/b/a
Prestige Auto Detail Center. On August 3, 2000, Messing
presented the check for payment at Bank of America, the
drawee. The teller confirmed that sufficient funds were in the
drawer's account and stamped the check with the date, time,
check amount, account number, and teller number. At the
same time, the teller placed a hold on Burruss' account for the
amount of the check. Upon the teller's request, Messing
produced two forms of identification and signed the back of the
check. The teller counted out cash equal to the value of the
check and inquired as to whether Messing was a customer of
Bank of America. Upon learning that he was not, she informed
him that, pursuant to bank policy, he would be required to
place a thumbprint on the check before it would be cashed.
Messing refused and, following a conversation in which the
branch manager refused to waive the thumbprint requirement,
left the bank with the check. At that time, the teller released
the hold on Burruss' account, returned the cash to her drawer,
and voided the transaction on her computer terminal. Messing
brought suit against Bank of America, claiming conversion and
wrongful dishonor. The allegations of conversion are based
upon the following claim:

Petitioner's position is that the Bank exercised unauthorized dominion and control over the proceeds of the check to the complete exclusion of the Petitioner after the Bank accepted the check and refused to distribute the proceeds, counted out by the teller, to him.

- Does any cause of action in conversion exist under these facts?

- How will the bank respond to the claim of wrongful dishonor?

- How do you respond to the following paragraph from the dissent? (The majority found the fingerprint program consistent with Article 3, which permits banks to require reasonable identification at presentment):

  Today, honest citizens attempting to cope in this world are constantly being required to show or give drivers' licenses, photo identification cards, social security numbers, the last four digits of social security numbers, mothers' "maiden names," 16 digit account numbers, etc. Now, the majority takes the position that it is "reasonable" for banks and other establishments to require, in addition, thumbprints and fingerprints. Enough is enough. The most reasonable thing in this case was petitioner's "irritation with the Bank of America's Thumbprint Signature Program."

Based on *Messing v. Bank of America, N.A.*, 373 Md. 672, 691, 704, 821 A.2d 22, 34, 40, 50 U.C.C. Rep. Serv. 2d 1 (2003).

Problem 2: James Henderson owned and operated a Ramada Inn in Augusta, Georgia. Beginning in the fall of 1984, he employed Thomas Muia as general manager. As general manager, Muia was responsible for all personnel and purchasing matters, as well as daily supervising of all operations. These responsibilities included indorsing checks made payable to the Inn with a rubber stamp or with the hotel computer, and depositing the checks into one of two corporate accounts, a "regular" account or a "special" account for specific kinds of expenses such as liquor and entertainment. He was authorized to write checks only on the "special" account. Henderson introduced Muia to the manager at Henderson's bank and, as a result of these introductions, Muia opened a personal account with the bank.

In February of 1985, Muia indorsed three checks made payable to Ramada Inn and deposited those checks, bearing his handwritten indorsement both on behalf of the Inn and on his own behalf, in his personal account. Between June and

November of that year, he deposited to his personal account checks made payable to the Inn from American Express Travel Related Services Company. He indorsed these checks in blank on behalf of the Inn and sometimes added his personal indorsement and/or personal account number. Henderson sued the bank, seeking to recover the amount of each check Muia had converted for his personal use. The majority held in relevant part as follows:

> In the case at bar, Muia's endorsements on the checks deposited into his personal account were "forged" because, with intent to defraud, he knowingly signed and presented the checks so as to give the appearance of authority from appellee, which he did not have.

> By accepting the checks for deposit into Muia's personal account, the bank converted appellee's funds. . . .

> In the case at bar, the endorsements were unusual for checks made out to the Ramada Inn, in that the customary rubber stamp, containing a restrictive endorsement, was not present, nor had the checks been run through the Ramada Inn's cash register, which also provided a restrictive endorsement. This was an "irregularity" such as the jury could have concluded should have put the bank on notice and activated the bank's duty to make inquiry, particularly because . . . the checks were being deposited into the depositor's personal account. In fact, this irregularity *was* brought to the bank's attention when one of its tellers questioned the propriety of depositing a check made out to the Ramada Inn, and endorsed in blank by Muia, to Muia's personal account.

The dissent stated in relevant part as follows:

> In the case sub judice, in my view plaintiff's statement to the bank's branch manager that Mr. Muia was the "new general manager of the Ramada Inn . . .," combined with plaintiff's authorization allowing Mr. Muia to endorse checks and deposit funds into Ramada Inn's regular checking account and withdraw funds from Ramada Inn's special checking account, was sufficient to support the bank's conclusion that Mr. Muia had wide authority to conduct Ramada Inn's financial transactions. This conclusion is further supported by evidence indicating that Mr. Muia had authority to bind plaintiff for services rendered and products supplied to Ramada Inn by vendors and service personnel. . . .

> Consequently, in the case sub judice, with the bank's specific denial that it had knowledge of the misappropriation by Muia of funds belonging to plaintiff, this court should conclude that the facts and circumstances relied upon by plaintiff to show knowledge by the bank of conversion of funds by Mr. Muia do not make an issue of fact for the jury.

- ▪ Which argument is stronger and why?

Based on *Trust Co. Bank of Augusta, N.A. v. Henderson*, 364
S.E.2d 289, 291, 295-296, 185 Ga. App. 367, 370, 376, 6 U.C.C.
Rep. Serv. 2d 167, 171, 175 (1987):

Chapter Review Problem: You received the following letter
and enclosed check at your home address. Assume your legal
name is Winifred Robins, you have never heard of Tony Davis
or James Powell, and you know nothing of the transaction to
which the letter makes allusion. Further assume you are
experiencing urgent financial need at this time and $2,500
would make an appreciable difference in your fiscal situation.
Several friends have urged you to "just deposit the check and
see what happens, hoping for the best."

- What is the mysterious sender of this letter seeking to
  accomplish?

*Sorry for the delay in getting the check, I will like you to deduct your charges for
the item and send the remaining balance to the shipper via Western Union Money
Transfer TODAY so that they can schedule a date for the shipment and come for
the pickup in your base. Here is the information you are to use for the transfer of
the funds via Western Union.*

NAME: TONY DAVIS

ADDRESS   50 SCRIVEN STREET
*   HACKNEY*
*   LONDON*
*   E8 4HY*
*   UNITED KINGDOM.*

*After the transfer of the funds you are to get back to me with the below
information which I am to give to the shipper to get the money today and
schedule a time for the pickup.*

AMOUNT SENT AFTER WESTERN UNION CHARGES

SENDERS NAME AND ADDRESS

MTCN (MONEY TRANSFER CONTROL NUMBER)

- What possible liability (if any) could you face if you
  deposit the check, and to whom might you be liable?

International Perspective: Tort Liability

The following quotation from *Byles on Bills of Exchange* 26-11 (27th ed., Sweet & Maxwell 2002), describes conversion in a way that should be familiar to students of the UCC: "A bill, note, or cheque is treated as any other piece of moveable property, and the true owner may bring an action in conversion against any person dealing wrongfully with it."

A similar approach can be found in the following case decided by the Supreme Court of Canada and applying Canada's Bills of Exchange Act, based upon the United Kingdom's B.E.A.

Boma Manufacturing Ltd. v. Canadian Imperial Bank of Commerce,
3 S.C.R. 727 (1996).

The appellants, two small, family-owned companies whose only shareholders and officers are M and his wife, were defrauded by their bookkeeper A through a series of fraudulent cheques issued over a five-year period. A, along with the two principals, was a duly authorized signing officer on the bank accounts maintained by the companies. Cheques drawn on these accounts required only one authorized signature. A used the appellants' pre-printed cheque forms to create some 155 cheques totalling $91,289.54, payable to a number of persons connected with the appellants, including the principals, several employees, and one of the subcontractors, Van Sang Lam (all but one of the cheques payable to Lam were made to "J. Lam" or "J. R. Lam," the initials and the last name mimicking the name of A's first husband). A signed 146 of the cheques on behalf of the appellants, and fraudulently obtained M's signature on the other nine. She deposited all the cheques into one of her accounts at the respondent bank. The respondent bank's policy with respect to a customer wishing to deposit a third party cheque to her account was to require that the cheque be endorsed by the payee. However, the bank accepted 107 of the cheques payable to "J. Lam" or "J. R. Lam" for deposit without endorsement. The tellers apparently assumed that the payee was A's first husband. A forged endorsements on some of the Lam cheques, and on all of the cheques payable to other third parties. The appellants brought an action in negligence, and in the alternative, conversion, against their own bank and against the respondent. They were successful at trial, and the respondent was ordered to pay $91,289.54. A majority of the Court of Appeal allowed the respondent's appeal, reducing the judgment so as to reflect only the amount of the nine cheques bearing M's signature.

* * *

Per Lamer C.J. and L'Heureux-Dubé, Sopinka, Gonthier, Cory, Iacobucci and Major JJ.: A bill of exchange is a chattel that can be negotiated from party to party. Title to a bill, such as a cheque, is obtained through negotiation. Once an individual has obtained title, that individual has the right to present the bill to the drawee for payment, as well as a right of recovery against the drawer if the bill is dishonoured by the drawee. If a bank pays to its customer the amount of a cheque to which that customer is not entitled, the bank will be strictly liable to the owner of the cheque for conversion. As a matter of principle, contributory negligence is not available in the context of a strict-liability tort. If the contributory negligence approach is to be introduced into this area of the law, it must be at the instance of the legislative branch.

The respondent is prima facie liable to the drawer for conversion in this case. The general rule is that a forged or unauthorized endorsement is wholly inoperative, and no right to retain the bill or to enforce payment thereof can be acquired through or under such a signature. An exception to this rule appears in 20 (5) of the Bills of Exchange Act, which provides that a bill payable to a fictitious or non-existing person may be treated as payable to bearer. A cheque payable to bearer can be negotiated by simple "delivery" to the bank; endorsement is not required. If the cheques in question were payable to fictitious persons, and could accordingly be treated as bearer cheques, the bank would become a "holder in due course" . . . despite the forged and missing endorsements and would consequently have a defence against liability for conversion. The policy underlying the fictitious-person rule seems to be that a drawer who has drawn a cheque payable to order, not intending that the payee receive payment, loses, by his or her conduct, the right to the protections afforded to a bill payable to order.

> The analogue in the B.E.A. is Article 7 (3), which provides, "Where the payee is fictitious or non-existing, the bill may be treated as payable to bearer."

> A similar provision can be found in UCC 3-404 (b).

Many of the cheques in question were payable to "real" persons, albeit persons to whom no money was owed by the companies. Because A, the writer of the cheques, did not intend these payees to receive the proceeds of the cheques, the Court of Appeal concluded that the drawer of the cheques intended them to be payable to bearer. The Court of Appeal erred in focussing on A's intention. It is the intention of the drawer that is significant for the purpose of 20 (5), not the intention of the signatory of the cheque. A is not the drawer because she cannot be said to be the guiding mind of the corporate appellants; she simply had signing authority within limited circumstances. The relevant intention in this case is that of the appellant companies, as expressed by their guiding mind.

> 3-110 addresses this issue, insofar as the Code is concerned.

Where a drawer is fraudulently induced by another person into issuing a cheque for the benefit of a real person to whom no obligation is owed, the cheque is to be considered payable to the payee and not to a fictitious person. Here the cheques payable to actual persons associated with the appellants were not payable to fictitious persons, and could not be treated by the respondent bank as payable to bearer. While many of the cheques were made payable not to actual persons associated with the companies, but to "J. Lam" and "J. R. Lam," M was reasonably mistaken in thinking that the payee was an individual associated with his companies. These cheques thus could not be treated by the respondent bank as payable to bearer. While the cheques certainly were "delivered" by A to the respondent bank, . . . for negotiation to be effected, endorsement by the payee was required.

. . . A was not the payee or a legitimate endorsee of the cheques in question. . . . Absent valid endorsements, the cheques were not validly negotiated to the bank. As a result, the respondent bank took the cheques subject to the equities of the situation. A was not entitled to the cheques, but the respondent bank credited her with the amount of those cheques. This constitutes conversion, for which the bank is strictly liable.

[The dissenting opinion is omitted.]

- ▪ What distinction does the court recognize between the intent of the fraudfeasor that the named payees have no interest in the checks, and the intent of the company to pay the named payees, and how does this difference affect the outcome of the case?

- ▪ Does a similar distinction exist under the Code?

3-110 (a) may assist you in answering this question.

- ▪ Would the Code recognize a distinction between the items A signed and those on which she fraudulently obtained M's signature?

Chapter Conclusion: As you leave this chapter, you should be comfortable with each of the three major sources of liability under Articles 3 and 4: contract, warranty, and tort. You should feel confident that you could dissect a fact pattern and advise a potential client as to each cause of action that it could raise, and each cause of action that it should anticipate being raised against it. You should also be ready to assess the costs and benefits of choosing among various causes of action when several are available.

Chapter 12:
Credit Cards, Debit Cards, Electronic Payments, and Nonbank Systems

A. Credit Cards

This section presents the provisions of the Truth in Lending Act (TILA), governing the unauthorized use of credit cards, as well as those addressing consumer disputes regarding goods purchased with a credit card. As you read these materials, compare and contrast the credit-card accountholder with a holder in due course of a negotiable instrument, noting how federal law has given special protection to consumers in this context. This section also describes the relationship between merchants and credit-card issuers.

Consumers and Credit Cards

Consumers' use of credit cards is governed, not by the UCC, but by TILA and other federal statutes, together with the contract between the cardholder and the credit-card issuer. *Ratner v. Chemical Bank New York Trust Co.*, 329 F. Supp. 270 (S.D.N.Y. 1971), describes TILA's purpose in general terms:

> The Truth in Lending Act is [subchapter] I, 15 USC §§ 1601 et seq. of the Consumer Credit Protection Act of May 29, 1968. Under the Act, an "open-end credit plan" is one "prescribing the terms of credit transactions which may be made thereunder from time to time, and under the terms of which a finance charge may be computed on the outstanding unpaid balance from time to time thereunder." As everyone knows who has not sojourned lately in a cave, plans of this kind have proliferated widely in the last few years. . . . *Id.* at 272.

How does a credit card involve an "open-end credit plan"?

> * * *

> The Act imposes an array of disclosure requirements to further the objective of "truth in lending" – "so that the consumer will be able to compare more readily the various credit terms available to him and avoid the uninformed use of credit." Among other things, the creditor under an open-end plan, before opening an account, must disclose to the prospective obligor, "to the extent applicable," the conditions for imposing finance charges, the length of any freeride period, the method of determining finance charges, the periodic rate for computing finance charges, and "the corresponding nominal annual percentage rate determined by multiplying the periodic rate by the number of periods in a year." *Id.* at 273.

- How do these disclosures "avoid the uninformed use of credit"?

Unauthorized Use of Credit Cards

Read 15 USC § 1643 (§ 133 of TILA). TILA provides powerful protection for consumers against liability for unauthorized credit-card use.

> TILA and other provisions of the U.S. Code are available online at www.gpoaccess.gov/uscode/index.html.

- Must the card issuer prove use of the card was authorized, or must the cardholder prove the use was unauthorized?

- What is the minimum and maximum liability a cardholder will face for purchases made by an unauthorized user *after* the cardholder has notified the card issuer that the card has been lost or stolen?

- What is the minimum and maximum liability a cardholder will face for purchases made by an unauthorized user *before* the cardholder has notified the card issuer that the card has been lost or stolen?

- **Read 15 USC §§ 1603 and 1645 (§§ 104 and 135 of TILA).** To what extent are businesses protected by § 1643?

Authorization of use is determined by the credit-card contract, interpreted in the context of state agency law. The following case illustrates express, implied, and apparent authority, as they relate to credit-card use. The case also illustrates some risks inherent in a cardholder's decision to allow a third person to use his or her card.

Towers World Airways, Inc. v. PHH Aviation Systems, Inc.,
933 F.2d 174 (2d Cir. 1991)

In February 1988, PHH [Aviation Systems, Inc.] issued a credit card to Towers [World Airways, Inc.] to purchase fuel and other aircraft-related goods and services for a corporate jet leased by Towers from PHH. World Jet Corporation, a subsidiary of United Air Fleet, was responsible for maintaining the aircraft. An officer of Towers designated Fred Jay Schley, an employee of World Jet, as the chief pilot of the leased jet and gave him permission to make purchases with the PHH credit card, at least in connection with non-charter flights, which were used exclusively by Towers executives. Notwithstanding United Air Fleet's agreement to pay the cost of fuel on chartered flights, which provided service for other clients, Schley used the credit card to charge $89,025.87 to Towers in connection with such flights, prior to the cancellation of the card in August 1988.

1 * * *

2

3 The issues on appeal are whether Schley's use of the card to incur the
4 $89,025.97 in connection with chartered flights was "unauthorized"
5 within the meaning of the Truth in Lending Act, and whether that
   question was properly decided on summary judgment.
6

7 Congress enacted the 1970 Amendments to the Truth in Lending Act,
8 in large measure to protect credit cardholders from unauthorized use
9 perpetrated by those able to obtain possession of a card from its original
10 owner. In addition to imposing criminal sanctions for the most
11 egregious cases, those involving fraud, the amendments enacted a
12 scheme for limiting the liability of cardholders for all charges by third
13 parties made without "actual, implied, or apparent authority" and
14 "from which the cardholder receives no benefit." Where an
   unauthorized use has occurred, the cardholder can be held liable only
15 up to a limit of $50 for the amount charged on the card, if certain
16 conditions are satisfied. Except as provided in section 1643, "a
17 cardholder incurs no liability from the unauthorized use of a credit
18 card."

19

20 By defining "unauthorized use" as that lacking in "actual, implied, or
21 apparent authority," Congress apparently contemplated, and courts
22 have accepted, primary reliance on background principles of agency
23 law in determining the liability of cardholders for charges incurred by
24 third-party card bearers. Under the parameters established by
25 Congress, the inquiry into "unauthorized use" properly focuses on
26 whether the user acted as the cardholder's agent in incurring the debt
27 in dispute. A cardholder, as principal, can create express and implied
28 authority only through manifestations to the user of consent to the
   particular transactions into which the user has entered.

29

30 In the pending case, there remains an unresolved issue of fact as to
31 whether Steven Hoffenberg, the Towers officer who dealt with Schley,
32 expressly or impliedly authorized Schley to purchase fuel on chartered
33 flights. Hoffenberg's testimony that he instructed Schley to limit his
34 use of the card to purchases "benefit[ing] . . . Towers' use of the
35 airplane" supports the inference that Schley lacked both express and
36 implied authority to make the disputed purchases. Whether Schley's
37 testimony to the contrary should be credited can be resolved only by a
38 factfinder. Accordingly, we cannot affirm the grant of summary
39 judgment on the theory that Schley possessed express or implied
   authority.

40

41 Unlike express or implied authority, however, apparent authority
42 exists entirely apart from the principal's manifestations of consent to
43 the agent. Rather, the cardholder, as principal, creates apparent
44 authority through words or conduct that, reasonably interpreted by a
45 third party from whom the card bearer makes purchases, indicate that
46 the card user acts with the cardholder's consent. Though a cardholder's
50 relinquishment of possession may create in another the appearance of
51 authority to use the card, the statute clearly precludes a finding of
52 apparent authority where the transfer of the card was without the
   cardholder's consent, as in cases involving theft, loss, or fraud. However
53 elastic the principle of apparent authority may be in theory, the

15 USC § 1643 became effective on October 29, 1970.

Why will a cardholder avoid liability only when the third party lacked authority of any kind *and* the cardholder received no benefit from the third party's card usage?

15 USC § 1602 (o)
(§ 103 (o) of TILA)
defines the term
"unauthorized use."

language of the 1970 Amendments demonstrates Congress's intent
that the category of cases involving charges incurred as a result of
involuntary card transfers are to be regarded as unauthorized under
sections 1602 (o) and 1643. The description in section 1643 of the
conditions precedent to an issuer's recovery of up to $50 from the
cardholder for unauthorized uses clearly assumes that cases of loss or
theft fall within the definition of unauthorized uses.

Because the statute provides no guidance as to uses arising from the
voluntary transfer of credit cards, the general principles of agency law,
incorporated by reference in section 1602 (o), govern disputes over
whether a resulting use was unauthorized. These disputes frequently
involve, as in this case, a cardholder's claim that the card bearer was
given permission to use a card for only a limited purpose and that
subsequent charges exceeded the consent originally given by the
cardholder. Acknowledging the absence of express or implied authority
for the additional charges, several state courts have . . . declined to
apply the Truth in Lending Act to limit the cardholder's liability,
reasoning that the cardholder's voluntary relinquishment of the card
for one purpose gives the bearer apparent authority to make additional
charges.

Though we agree that a cardholder, in lending or giving his card for one
purpose, acts in a way that significantly contributes to the appearance
of authority, at least as perceived by the third-party merchant, to make
other purchases, we need not decide whether voluntary relinquishment
for one purpose creates in every case apparent authority to incur other
charges. In the pending case, the appearance of authority for Schley to
purchase fuel on chartered flights was established not only by Towers'
consent to Schley's unrestricted access to the PHH card but by other
conduct and circumstances as well.

Nothing about the PHH card or the circumstances surrounding the
purchases gave fuel sellers reason to distinguish the clearly authorized
fuel purchases made in connection with non-charter flights from the
purchases for chartered flights. It was the industry custom to entrust
credit cards used to make airplane-related purchases to the pilot of the
plane. By designating Schley as the pilot and subsequently giving him
the card, Towers thereby imbued him with more apparent authority
than might arise from voluntary relinquishment of a credit card in
other contexts. In addition, with Towers' blessing, Schley had used the
card, which was inscribed with the registration number of the
Gulfstream jet, to purchase fuel on non-charter flights for the same
plane. The only difference between these uses expressly authorized and
those now claimed to be unauthorized – the identity of the passengers –
was insufficient to provide notice to those who sold the fuel that Schley
lacked authority for the charter-flight purchases.

Towers contends that, despite its own failure to have the card
cancelled, once PHH, as the card issuer, learned, either through
Towers or a third party, that Schley lacked authority to make certain
charges, any such transaction that Schley entered into becomes an
unauthorized use, even if fuel sellers reasonably perceived that Schley
had apparent authority to charge fuel purchases. Whether notifying

the card issuer that some uses (or users) of a card are unauthorized makes them so has divided those courts that have considered the issue.

* * *

The rule of agency law contained in section 166 of the Restatement would permit the principal to qualify the authority of an agent to make purchases from a merchant by giving the merchant notice of the limitation. The limitation would surely be effective in an ordinary three-party arrangement in which an agent charges purchases on a principal's running account with a merchant. It is more doubtful whether a principal can similarly avoid liability by notifying the merchant of limitations on an agent's authority when an agent makes purchases using a credit card. Both cardholders and merchants normally regard anyone voluntarily entrusted with a credit card as having the right to make any purchases within the card's contractually specified limits. But, to whatever extent a cardholder can limit the authority of a card user by giving notice to a merchant, we do not believe he can accomplish a similar limitation by giving notice to a card issuer. In four-party arrangements of this sort, it is totally unrealistic to burden the card issuer with the obligation to convey to numerous merchants whatever limitations the cardholder has placed on the card user's authority.

> The reference here is to *Restatement (Second) of Agency* § 166 (1958).

. . . In many cases, the cardholder can avoid unwanted charges simply by repossessing the card. Where a card issuer permits a cardholder to cancel the card, and thereby any contractual obligation to pay, a cardholder can limit his liability even if unable to regain possession by cancelling his card. Even where the card issuer also requires return of the card prior to cancellation of the agreement, a cardholder who has tried and failed to recover a card from an "estranged spouse, a dishonest employee, or a disappeared 'friend,'" likely can prevail on the claim that the card user has stolen the card and that any subsequent charges are for that reason unauthorized. . . .

Because the disputed charges were not unauthorized . . . , PHH was entitled to recover their full value from Towers under their credit agreement.

- After this case, what limitations, if any, remain on Schley's apparent authority to use the credit card in question?

- In addition to cancelling or repossessing the card, how else could Towers have limited Schley's authority?

Note 1: Courts take varying approaches to the issue of one spouse's liability for the other's use of his or her separate credit card. *Society National Bank v. Kienzle*, 11 Ohio App. 3d 178, 463 N.E.2d 1261 (1983), involved an estranged wife's credit-card spree with her husband's card. The husband, Richard Kienzle, was sued by the credit-card issuer, and the suit proceeded to a judgment against him, from which he appealed,

> Why does one spouse's abuse of a card issued from a jointly-owned account not raise similar issues?

claiming the charges were unauthorized. The card issuer admitted Mr. Kienzle had called in a timely manner to report his card stolen by his spouse, but claimed the wife's use of the card was authorized as a matter of spousal liability. In finding the issuer failed to prove the wife's use of the card was authorized, the court held as follows:

> In Ohio, a husband is not answerable for the acts of his wife unless the wife acts as his agent or he subsequently ratifies her acts. In this case, there was no evidence introduced that defendant's wife acted as his agent, or that he ratified her conduct. Indeed, the transcript reveals that defendant notified plaintiff immediately after his discovery of someone else using his credit card. The transcript is devoid of any other evidence of agency or ratification. *Id.* at 182.

Some other jurisdictions focus on whether the cardholder benefited from the spouse's purchase, regardless of whether the purchase was authorized or ratified.

Note 2: When a cardholder's friend – rather than a spouse – uses his or her credit card, the court's analysis may be different. In *Universal Bank v. McCafferty*, 88 Ohio App. 3d 556, 624 N.E.2d 358 (1993), the court considered a dispute arising from James McCafferty's decision to apply for a Universal Bank credit card, which he subsequently received. His wife, concerned about the large number of cards the family already had, returned the card to the bank. Mr. McCafferty telephoned Universal Bank and asked that the card be reissued to a different address, where a friend lived. The bank assented, sending the card and PIN to the friend's address. The friend used the card for purchases and cash advances totaling around $3,800, without notifying Mr. McCafferty or reimbursing him for the charges. Universal Bank sought to recover from Mr. McCafferty on a theory of apparent authority. In finding the charges were unauthorized and Mr. McCafferty's liability was therefore limited to $50, the court held as follows:

> Universal contends that McCafferty and his friend had an agency relationship based on apparent authority. Apparent authority is not established by the conduct of the agent, but by acts of the principal which cloak the agent with apparent power to bind the principal. Universal claims that McCafferty's act of requesting that the credit card be sent to his friend's address clothed his friend with apparent authority. We disagree. While McCafferty authorized Universal to send the card to his friend's address, that did not authorize use of the card by the addressee. The mere authorization to mail a credit card to a certain address cannot be expanded to encompass the apparent authorization to charge on that credit card. *Id.* at 558.

- How can spouses' unauthorized use of credit cards be distinguished from similar conduct by friends?

- How can a card issuer avoid disputes like *Society National Bank* and *Universal Bank*?

Note 3. For a cardholder alleging unauthorized use to be liable for the maximum of $50 as provided by TILA, the card must be "an accepted credit card." *Transamerica Insurance Co. v. Standard Oil Co.*, 325 N.W.2d 210 (N.D. 1982), defines this term.

> An "accepted credit card" is any credit card which the cardholder has requested, signed, used, or authorized another to use for the purpose of obtaining money, property, labor, or services on credit. *Id.* at 214.

Transamerica Insurance involved the alleged authorized use of an Amoco Torch Club card. Because Minot Builders Supply Association, the cardholder, never signed, used, or authorized use of this credit card – instead, Minot's agent Robert Smith obtained the card without the company's consent – the card was not "an accepted credit card."

- How can the issuer ensure a card is "accepted"?

Transamerica also illustrates allocation of liability. Even though the card was not "an accepted credit card," the court found Minot Builders Supply should have discovered Smith's fraud after it received the first statement from Amoco on the new account:

> Because the Torch Club card issued to Smith was not an accepted card, MBS [is] not liable for the initial fraudulent charges made by Smith. However, the trial court erred in not looking beyond Amoco's negligence in issuing Smith the card. After receiving the first statement from Amoco containing the fraudulent charges, MBS was negligent in not finding and reporting the fraud. . . .

> . . . We believe that MBS's negligence in not examining its monthly statements from Amoco removes this case from the statutory limit on cardholder liability.

> A bank customer has a duty to examine his bank statement promptly, using reasonable care to discover unauthorized signatures or alterations. If the bank uses reasonable care in making the statement and if the bank customer fails to examine his statement, the customer is precluded from asserting his unauthorized signature against the bank after a certain time. This commercial-paper situation parallels the facts at hand. Amoco was not negligent in billing MBS. If someone at MBS other than Smith had examined its statements from Amoco, he would have

What UCC section is the court applying by analogy here?

discovered Smith's fraud. It was the responsibility of MBS to institute internal procedures for the examination of the statements from Amoco. The failure of MBS to institute such procedures is the cause of that portion of the defalcation which occurred following the billing from Amoco which contained the first evidence of Smith's fraud.

Because of MBS's negligence, we will reexamine whether or not Smith acquired ostensible authority in his use of the Torch Club card after MBS became negligent. . . . *Id.* at 214-215.

* * *

. . . Smith embezzled money from MBS for three years through his fraudulent use of the Torch Club credit card. During this lengthy period of embezzlement, MBS always paid its monthly bill to Amoco. MBS contends that it is not proper for the court to consider the fact that MBS paid all the Amoco credit card charges. That contention is without merit. As a result of MBS's acts of paying for the charges and its failure to examine its statements so that it could notify Amoco of the fraud, MBS allowed Amoco to reasonably believe that Smith was authorized to use the credit card.

MBS claims that it relied upon its accountants to find fraud during annual audits. MBS made the decision to hire and rely upon accountants. This decision does not protect MBS from the inability of these accountants to discover the fraud.

We conclude that Amoco is liable for Smith's fraudulent purchases from the time the credit card was issued until MBS received the first statement from Amoco containing Smith's fraudulent charges plus a reasonable time to examine that statement. After that time, [MBS] is liable for the remaining fraudulent charges. We reverse the judgment and remand this case for a determination of when MBS should have examined its statements and discovered Smith's fraud, and, consistent with this opinion, for a new calculation of the damages. *Id.* at 216.

- How and when did Smith acquire ostensible authority to use the card?

- What opportunities did MBS have to avoid this loss?

Problem 1: Daniel Calvin and Karen Horton lived together in New Jersey in a romantic relationship from January through March 1987. In March, Calvin stole Horton's car, created a bill of sale showing his ownership of it, and left for Mississippi. He returned later that month, and the two continued to cohabitate, although their personal relationship did not continue. While Calvin was in Mississippi, Horton discovered he had stolen a gasoline credit card and a briefcase from her and had obtained a sum of money from her by misrepresentation. She cooperated with authorities in a criminal prosecution to which he later pled guilty.

In August, Horton realized her American Express card was missing when she sought to use it to pay for gasoline. The station attendant told her he had seen Calvin with the card earlier in the day. Horton immediately called American Express and reported the card missing. By that time, Calvin had used the card to purchase merchandise costing approximately $5,250. Approximately $925 was spent at Blaisdell Lumber Company during seven separate transactions. On at least one occasion, Calvin was accompanied by an unidentified female. Neither Calvin nor his companion were asked for identification. Calvin signed each charge slip in his own name.

Assume Horton and Calvin were still cohabitating at the time of the August purchases, and Horton denied knowing of the purchases.

- Were the Blaisdell Lumber Company purchases authorized?

- How, if at all, would your answer change if Horton and Calvin were married?

Based on *Blaisdell Lumber Co. v. Horton*, 242 N.J. Super. 98, 575 A.2d 1386 (1990).

Problem 2: Read 15 USC Section 1602 (o) and (m) (§ 103 (o) and (m) of TILA). Consider the following facts:

In July 1979, [Gloria] Harlan, who was prior to that time a VISA cardholder at [Walker Bank & Trust Co.] requested that her husband, John Harlan, be added to the account as an authorized user. The Bank honored this request and issued a card to Mr. Harlan. Shortly thereafter, at some point between July and the end of 1979, the Harlans separated and [Mrs.] Harlan informed the Bank by letter that she either wanted the account closed or wanted the Bank to deny further extensions of credit to her husband.

Notwithstanding the explicit requirement in the account agreement that all outstanding credit cards be returned to the Bank in order to close the account, [Mrs.] Harlan did not tender either her card or her husband's at the time she made the aforementioned request. As to her card, she informed the Bank that she could not return it because it had been destroyed in the Bank's automated teller. Notwithstanding, however, she returned the card to the Bank some three months later [in March 1980].

In the interim period, . . . several charges were made (purportedly
by Mr. Harlan) on the account for which the Bank now seeks
recovery. The Bank has sued only Mrs. Harlan.

- Is Mr. Harlan a cardholder within the meaning of 15
  USC § 1602 (m)?

- Is he an unauthorized user within the meaning of 15
  USC § 1602 (o)?

- Distinguish the facts of this case from those in
  Problem 1.

Based on *Walker Bank & Trust Co. v. Jones*, 672 P.2d 73 (Utah
1983).

Credit-Card Dispute Resolution

Read 15 USC § 1666i (§ 170 of TILA). TILA provides
protection to cardholders who are dissatisfied with goods or
services purchased with a credit card and are unsuccessful in
resolving the dispute directly with the seller.

- Courts and commentators sometimes describe § 1666i
  as providing cardholders with holder-in-due-course
  status. What does this expression mean, and how does
  this phenomenon encourage cardholders to use credit
  cards for large, important, or risky purchases?

- What circumstances would implicate the geographic
  and purchase-amount limitations in 1666i (a)?

- As a practical matter, what steps should a cardholder
  take to protect himself or herself from losing the
  protections in 1666i when paying a credit-card bill that
  includes disputed charges?

TILA dispute-resolution provisions are available only when the
cardholder has already tried, and failed, to obtain a reasonable
resolution from the seller. As *Izraelewitz v. Manufacturers
Hanover Trust Co.*, 120 Misc. 2d 125, 465 N.Y.S. 2d 486 (1983),
shows, whether the merchant has acted reasonably is a fact-
specific inquiry.   George Izraelewitz ordered electronic
diagrams from Don Britton Enterprises, a Hawaiian company
that also sold rooftop-mounted listening devices and other
surveillance- and counter-surveillance equipment.   He then
sought to return the merchandise. As a part of this process,
Izraelewitz contacted Manufacturers Hanover Trust Company,
his credit-card issuer, indicating the diagrams were unsuitable
for his needs. He provided Manufacturers Hanover with a

receipt showing he had returned the merchandise. The card issuer credited his account and waived the finance charges relating to the purchase. Manufacturers Hanover then charged the purchase price back to the merchant. The merchant refused the charge-back, citing its strict "no refund policy" and emphasizing that Izraelewitz had admitted he was aware of the policy. The merchant produced evidence that the consumer had acted dishonestly by attempting to ensure the return would be accepted by labeling the package without a return address, repacking the merchandise, and delivering the returned package through indirect means rather than shipping it directly to the company. The merchant also indicated the diagrams appeared to have been photocopied. The card issuer then informed Izraelewitz that it would redebit his account and, when he objected, the entire cycle of charge-back and refusal of the charge-back was repeated.

The charge-back process is described later in this section.

In finding the "no refund" policy was not unreasonable and that TILA's dispute-resolution process was therefore unavailable to Izraelewitz, the court held as follows:

> "No Refund" policies, per se, are not unconscionable or offensive to public policy in any manner. [The] Truth in Lending Law "(n)either requires refunds for returns nor does it prohibit refunds in kind." Bank-merchant agreements, however, usually do contain a requirement that the merchant establish a fair policy for exchange and return of merchandise.
>
> To establish the fairness in Don Britton's policy, the strength of the reasons behind the policy and the measures taken to inform the consumer of it must necessarily be considered. Don Britton's rationale for its policy is compelling. It contends that printing is a very small part of its business, which is selling original designs, and "once a customer has seen the designs, he possesses what we have to sell." Britton's policy is clearly written in its catalog directly on the page which explains how to order merchandise. To compensate for not having a refund policy, which would be impractical considering the nature of the product, Britton offers well-advertised backup plans with free engineering assistance and an exchange procedure, as well, if [the] original plans are beyond the customer's capabilities. *Id.* at 127-128.

- What is meant by the statement, "once a consumer has seen the designs, he possesses what we have to sell"?

The court's opinion begins with the following language:

> As the texture of the American economy evolves from paper to plastic, the disgruntled customer is spewing its wrath upon the purveyor of the plastic rather than upon the merchant.

- How and why does TILA permit a consumer to "spew[]
  its wrath upon the purveyor of the plastic rather than
  upon the merchant?"

Note: TILA rights may accrue before the cardholder's
application for credit has been approved. In *Bryson v. Bank of
New York*, 584 F. Supp. 1306 (S.D.N.Y. 1984), the court
addressed when these rights first arise:

> Both sides agree that "consummation" of a transaction is required
> before a consumer's right of action attaches under the Truth in
> Lending Act. This is the general consensus among courts which
> have considered the question. However, it is not entirely clear
> what "consummation" means. . . .
>
> Defendant claims that "consummation" occurs only when a legally
> binding contract is created between both parties. I cannot agree.
> . . . [T]he Act was designed to facilitate informed shopping for
> credit as well as informed purchase of credit. Toward that end, it
> requires disclosure before, as well as when, credit is extended.
> Accordingly, the time of attachment of a right of action under the
> Act should be fixed with a view toward protecting the interests of
> those shopping for credit as well as those actually purchasing
> credit. Imposing the requirement that a binding contract be
> created on both sides before a right of action attaches would
> needlessly limit the plaintiff class while inhibiting enforcement of
> the former purpose. A more appropriate time of attachment is that
> point at which the consumer, on the basis of the information his
> "comparison shopping" has generated, makes a choice and
> commits himself or herself to the purchase of credit, without
> regard for the degree of commitment of the lender. This marks the
> end of the consumer's shopping. It is at this time that the
> consumer becomes vulnerable to actual damage from the lender's
> inadequate or deceptive disclosures, for at this time he or she can
> be contractually bound to the terms of the lending contract at the
> option of the lender. The rule insures that all plaintiffs are
> seriously-intentioned consumers of credit, for it requires them to
> incur some risk in return for a right of action under the Act. At the
> same time, it prevents the lender from binding his potential
> debtors with inadequate disclosure and then selecting as
> customers those whom he thinks are least likely to pursue their
> rights under the Act. Instead, it impresses upon the lender the
> importance of full compliance with the Act before the customer is
> committed. *Id.* at 1316-1317.

- What are the risks and benefits of a rule granting
  consumers TILA rights at the time of their
  commitment rather than earlier or later?

Problem: Critique the following advice given by a newspaper
columnist to a consumer who had written to inquire about his
or her rights relating to unsatisfactory goods for which the
consumer had paid with a credit card:

| When does a consumer "commit himself or herself to the purchase or credit without regard for the degree of commitment of the lender? |

| Is the court's holding consonant with the principles of mutual assent? |

First, using a credit card is not like writing a check. You can put a stop payment on a check. With credit cards, unless fraud or theft is involved, you have to wait until the charge appears on your statement before you can dispute it. At that point, you have 60 days to do so. Once you dispute a charge, you are issued a temporary credit. However, if the originator of the charge . . . can prove that the charge is legitimate, it will be put back on the account.

The correct procedure if you have a problem with merchandise you have purchased is to attempt to resolve it with the seller first. This will generally involve returning the merchandise. Keep in mind that retailers are free to establish their own return policies, which must be posted in the store. This includes how much time customers have to return merchandise. Receipts are generally required for any returns. Unless payment was made by cash, copies of receipts or checks can be obtained from the financial institution.

At this point, [since more than 60 days have passed since the statement date on which the charge appeared], your best bet is to accept the fact that the refund is gone.

Based on Nancy Paradis, *Action*, St. Petersburg Times 2E (June 9, 2005).

Account Cancellation and Billing Errors

Cardholders sometimes sue issuers for wrongful account cancellation. In *Novack v. Cities Service Oil Co.*, 149 N.J. Super. 542, 374 A.2d 89 (1977), the court considered claims of defamation and breach of contract based on allegations of wrongful card revocation. The facts of the case are as follows:

Plaintiff applied for and obtained a Cities Service [Oil Company] credit card in September 1972. Included with the card, when mailed to plaintiff, was a pamphlet describing generally the terms of the account. One such term was that the account could be cancelled at any time and that, upon written request, the card was to be returned to Cities Service. On February 4, 1974, plaintiff's account had a substantial balance which was then more than 40 days past due. On that same date, defendant mailed a notice to the operator of one of its service stations which plaintiff had used on a regular basis. The notice informed the operator that plaintiff's card was no longer to be honored and that a reward would be paid for its return. *Id.* at 546.

The operator seized the card, and the cardholder brought suit. In rejecting the cardholder's contract claim, the court held as follows:

What argument could be made that a credit-card issuer does in fact receive consideration for its issuance of a new card?

The issuance of a credit card is but an offer to extend a line of open-account credit. It is unilateral and supported by no consideration. The offer may be withdrawn at any time, without prior notice, for any reason or, indeed, for no reason at all, and its withdrawal breaches no duty – for there is no duty to continue it – and violates no rights. Acceptance or use of the card by the offeree makes a contract between the parties according to its terms, but we have seen none which prevents a termination of the arrangement at any time by either party. As a rule, there is no requirement of prior notice for termination by the issuer. A request to the person holding the card that it be surrendered upon termination of the extension of credit by the issuer is reasonable, and if he has the card it should be surrendered. *Id.* at 548.

* * *

Basically, . . . a credit card is nothing more than an indication to sellers of commodities that the person who has received a credit card from the issuer thereof has a satisfactory credit rating and that if credit is extended, the issuer of the credit card will pay (or see to it that the seller of the commodity receives payment) for the merchandise delivered. *Id.*

What is meant by the phrase "if credit is extended"?

In other cases, issuers have been found liable for wrongful account cancellation. In *Gray v. American Express Co.*, 743 F.2d 10 (D.C. Cir. 1984), the court addressed the following facts:

> [Oscar] Gray had been a[n American Express] cardholder since 1964. In 1981, following some complicated billings arising out of deferred travel charges incurred by Gray, disputes arose about the amount due American Express. After considerable correspondence, . . . American Express decided to cancel Gray's card. No notification of this cancellation was communicated to Gray until the night of April 8, 1982, when he offered his American Express card to pay for a wedding-anniversary dinner he and his wife already had consumed in a Washington restaurant. The restaurant informed Gray that American Express had refused to accept the charges for the meal and had instructed the restaurant to confiscate and destroy his card. Gray spoke to the American Express employee on the telephone at the restaurant who informed him, "Your account is cancelled as of now." *Id.* at 13.

The portion of TILA including 15 USC §§ 1666-1666i (§§ 161-171 of TILA) is also known as the Fair Credit Billing Act.

Based on these facts, Mr. Gray brought suit pursuant to the Fair Credit Billing Act, alleging American Express had handled the parties' billing dispute improperly by cancelling the account. **Read 15 USC § 1666 (§ 161 of TILA)**, which describes the procedure for billing disputes. In finding a cause of action under the Fair Credit Billing Act sufficient to withstand summary judgment, the court held as follows:

[The] Fair Credit Billing Act seeks to prescribe an orderly procedure for identifying and resolving disputes between a cardholder and a card issuer as to the amount due at any given time. . . .

If the [cardholder] believes that the statement contains a billing error, . . . he then may send the creditor a written notice setting forth that belief, indicating the amount of the error and the reasons supporting his belief that it is an error. If the creditor receives this notice within 60 days of transmitting the statement of account, [the Act] imposes two separate obligations upon the creditor. Within 30 days, it must send a written acknowledgment that it has received the notice. And, within 90 days or two complete billing cycles, whichever is shorter, the creditor must investigate the matter and either make appropriate corrections in the [cardholder's] account or send a written explanation of its belief that the original statement sent to the [cardholder] was correct. The creditor must send its explanation before making any attempt to collect the disputed amount.

A creditor that fails to comply with [the Act] forfeits its right to collect the first $50 of the disputed amount including finance charges.   In addition, [the Act] provides that, pursuant to regulations of the Federal Reserve Board, a creditor operating an "open-end consumer credit plan" may not restrict or close an account due to a [cardholder's] failure to pay a disputed amount until the creditor has sent the written explanation required by [the Act]. *Id.* at 13-14.

* * *

. . . American Express . . . urges that, even if the Act is otherwise pertinent, Gray was bound by the terms of the Cardmember Agreement, which empowered American Express to cancel the credit card without notice and without cause.

The contract between Gray and American Express provides:

> [W]e can revoke your right to use [the card] at any time. We can do this with or without cause and without giving you notice.

American Express seems to argue that . . . it can exercise its right to cancellation for cause unrelated to the disputed amount, or for *no* cause, thus bringing itself out from under the statute. At the very least, the argument is audacious. American Express would restrict the efficacy of the statute to those situations where the parties had not agreed to a "without cause, without notice" cancellation clause, or to those cases where the cardholder can prove that the sole reason for cancellation was the amount in dispute. We doubt that Congress painted with such a faint brush. *Id.* at 15.

In allowing Gray's suit to continue past summary judgment, the court held as follows:

Gray stated . . . a contract claim, in which he alleged that American Express violated the Cardmember Agreement by wrongfully canceling it. *Id.* at 16.

* * *

. . . Within the limits of state and federal statutes, credit cards can still be cancelled without cause and without notice. But the cancellation can affect only transactions which have not occurred before the cancellation is communicated to the cardholder. In practical terms, American Express will have to make an effort to communicate its cancellation decision to the cardholder. The effort may be as informal as a phone call or a telegram. . . .

. . . If a cardholder seeks to use his American Express card to buy a car, for example, we think that a communication, through the car dealer, that the card has been cancelled prior to title passing to the cardholder may effect notice in reasonable fashion. But where the meal has been consumed, or the hotel room has been slept in, or the service rendered, the communication through the merchant comes too late to void the credit for that transaction.

> What is meant by the language, "Even contracts of adhesion are contracts"? The discussion of "blanket assent" in Chapter 2, Part A may assist you in answering this question.

Even contracts of adhesion are contracts. To allow cancellation without any communication of the decision is to turn the contract into a snare and deceit. *Id.* at 19.

■ What advice would you give to a credit-card issuer seeking to terminate a cardholder's account privileges?

■ How would your advice differ if the affected cardholder were engaged in a billing dispute with the issuer?

> BAPCA is Pub. L. No. 109-8, §§ 1 et seq., 119 Stat. 23 (2005).

Note: The Bankruptcy Abuse Prevention and Consumer Protection Act of 2005 (BAPCA), which became federal law on April 20, 2005, includes the following language:

1301. ENHANCED DISCLOSURES UNDER AN OPEN-END CREDIT PLAN.

(a) MINIMUM PAYMENT DISCLOSURES. – Section 127 (b) of the
Truth in Lending Act (15 USC 1637 (b)) is amended by adding at the end the following:

"(11) (A) In the case of an open-end-credit plan that requires a minimum monthly payment of not more than 4 percent of the balance on which finance charges are accruing, the following statement, located on the front of the billing statement, disclosed clearly and conspicuously: 'Minimum Payment Warning: Making only the minimum payment will increase the interest you pay and the time it takes to repay your balance. For example, making only the typical 2% minimum monthly payment on a balance of $1,000 at an interest rate of 17% would take 88 months to repay the balance in full. For an estimate of the time it would take to repay your balance, making only minimum payments, call this toll-free number: lllll.' (the blank space to be filled in by the creditor)."

In addition, under pressure from the U.S. Office of the Comptroller of the Currency, some issuers have raised the minimum monthly credit-card payment from 2% to 4%.

- What is the apparent purpose of each initiative?

- What are the risks and benefits of each?

Problem: Glen Wood was an executive vice president of SAR Manufacturing Company. He checked into a Holiday Inn in Phenix City, Alabama on business on February 1, 1972, and, pursuant to an arrangement between Gulf Oil Company and Holiday Inn Hotels & Resorts, tendered his Gulf credit card as payment for his room. The desk attendant made an imprint of the card and returned it to him.

As part of its normal practices, Gulf evaluated Wood's account regularly and provided information regarding the account to National Data Corporation. As part of this same process, Holiday Inn was authorized to contact National Data Corporation to inquire about the creditworthiness of Wood or any other Gulf cardholder. Gulf's credit manager had reviewed Wood's credit account on January 17, 1972, and had become concerned about the account, although payment was current at the time. The credit manager's concern related to the increasing charges being made in relation to Wood's income. Gulf therefore directed National Data Corporation to give the following message to any person seeking credit approval on Wood's account: "Pick up travel card. Do not extend further credit. Send card to billing office for reward."

During the middle of the night, after Wood had checked in, Phenix City Holiday Inn night auditor Jessie Goynes contacted National Data Corporation for an authorization on Wood's account and received the message Gulf had directed National Data Corporation to give. Accordingly, Goynes telephoned Wood's room around 5:00 a.m. and advised him that he needed to make another imprint of the card, since the first one was not readable. Wood assented, and Goynes came to the room to get the card. When the card had not been returned within half an hour, Wood became concerned that Goynes had stolen it. He dressed, went to the hotel's front desk, and was informed that Goynes had seized the card "upon the authority of National Data." Goynes demanded payment in cash and refused Wood's request to call Gulf.

When Wood returned home, he contacted Gulf to complain about its refusal to authorize the room charge. Gulf confirmed his account was current and immediately reinstated his charging privileges. Three days later, while Wood was relating the story to a friend, still angry about the events, he suffered a heart attack.

- Do these facts support a cause of action for wrongful cancellation?

Based on *Wood v. Holiday Inns, Inc.*, 508 F.2d 167 (5th Cir. 1975).

Merchants and Credit Cards

Merchants and credit-card companies have ongoing relationships, just as cardholders and card issuers do. Certain characteristics of credit-card transactions that enable a merchant to accept credit cards are a matter of common experience. For example, customers may use credit cards only when purchasing goods or services from merchants equipped to accept the card tendered, meaning that the merchant must have a pre-existing relationship with the credit-card company, be it Visa, MasterCard, American Express, Discover, or some other brand. In addition, when a customer makes a purchase by credit card, a credit-card sales slip is generated. *First United Bank v. Philmont Corp.*, 533 So. 2d 449, 7 U.C.C. Rep. Serv. 2d 1550 (Miss. 1988), explains these and other features of a typical credit-card transaction involving Visa or MasterCard, from the point of view of the merchant:

> At the center of the credit-card-collection system is the "member bank." These are the banks which are authorized by Visa/MasterCard to issue credit cards. At the same time, these member banks also act as clearinghouses for the collection of credit-card-sales slips within a defined geographic area. The member banks in turn recruit "non-member banks" to act as local agents and as points of collection for credit-card-sales slips.

> The non-member banks enter into agreements with local merchants whereby the merchants honor the Visa and/or MasterCard credit cards at their places of business, and the bank agrees to accept an "assignment" of all sales slips. Frequently, the merchant will open an account at a local participating bank for the purpose of posting and processing these credit-card-sales slips, although this is not required by the merchant agreement.

> If the merchant chooses *not* to maintain an account at any participating bank, the member bank agrees to pay the merchant by check no later than thirty days after presentation of the sales slips. If, however, the merchant has such an account with the non-

These slips represent "accounts" within the meaning of 9-102 (a) (2). As 9-109 shows, assignment of such accounts for collection does not implicate Article 9, but sales of such accounts do.

member bank, the merchant's deposit of these credit-card-sales slips is very similar to a deposit of personal checks.

. . . Once these sales slips are deposited, the local participating bank provisionally credits the merchant's account and forwards the batch to the local member bank. The member bank then . . . processes the batch by sending each sales slip to the bank which issued the credit card used in the sales transaction. Each member bank can then assemble a monthly statement for each of its customers. *Id.* at 454.

- The *First United Bank* court describes a deposit of credit-card slips as "very similar to a deposit of personal checks." Are credit-card slips "instruments" within the meaning of Article 3 or "items" within the meaning of Article 4?

> Reviewing 3-104 and 4-104 (a) (9) may assist you in answering this question.

When cardholders invoke the dispute-resolution process described earlier in this section, the merchant's account will be "charged back" if it is determined that the cardholder was justified in disputing the charge. As *Izraelewitz* demonstrated, merchants can dispute charge-backs. High levels of charge-backs – which can result from a customer's unauthorized use of a card, a merchant's failure to obtain the cardholder's signature on the credit slip, a merchant's acceptance of an expired card, or processing errors, as well as disputes regarding the goods or services delivered – can lead to cancellation of the merchant's account.

Note 1: The following businesses are sometimes characterized as tending to have difficulty obtaining or sustaining a merchant credit-card account.

- Adult bookstores	- Dating services
- Airlines	- Gambling facilities
- Auto rentals	- Health clubs
- Bail bondsmen	- Infomercial merchants
- Bars without a restaurant	- Insurance businesses
	- Limousine services
- Businesses with no storefront	- Pawn shops
	- Real-estate-related businesses
- Check-cashing businesses	- Sellers of self-improvement courses
- Collection agencies	
- Credit unions	- Tour companies

- What traits do the businesses on this list have in common?

Note 2: Merchant credit-card accounts are susceptible to a variety of fraudulent schemes. *Broadway National Bank v.*

Barton-Russell Corp., 585 N.Y.S. 2d 933, 154 Misc. 2d 181, 19
U.C.C. Rep. Serv. 2d 228 (1992), describes one:

> The fraud is best coined an "illusory authorization hoax."
> Defendant Barton-Russell Corporation had a merchant credit-
> card account. Barton omitted preauthorization numbers or
> assigned improper preauthorization numbers on credit-card
> charge slips for the purported purchase of merchandise or services,
> creating the illusion that the charges had been duly
> preauthorized. The slips were deposited into a merchant account
> at Broadway National Bank, and the account was credited with
> cash the next day. [A]n illusory authorization number does not
> come to the active attention of processing banks until the charge to
> the customer's account is rejected and the slip is returned to the
> network member bank initiating the processing. . . . As the charge
> is being processed, which takes a goodly period of time, more
> charge slips can be generated, converted to cash, and cash
> withdrawn. *Id.* at 935.

The court's opinion provides guidance in detecting fraud:
"Among recognized 'red flags' of credit-card fraud. . . are a large
number of charges on a single credit card, numerous
handwritten slips, and improperly completed slips."

- To what kind of Article 3/Article 4 fraud is Barton's
  scheme similar, and how do the "red flags" compare for
  each?

International Perspective: Credit Cards

In *Credit Cards and Debit Cards in the United States and
Japan*, 55 Vand. L. Rev. 1055 (2002). Professor Ronald J.
Mann compares U.S. and Japanese use of credit cards:

> In the market for retail purchases in the United States, the credit
> card is a massive success: it was used in 1999 for 14 billion
> transactions worth almost $1.1 trillion, about $76 per transaction.
> U.S. Department of Commerce statistics indicate that, in the same
> year, credit cards were used in about eighteen percent of all
> transactions, for about twenty-three percent of the value paid in
> all American consumer-payment transactions. For the most part,
> those transactions were conducted as revolving-credit
> transactions. Under American practices, that means that the
> cardholder decides each month what share of the total account
> balance it will pay back; the cardholder is required to make only a
> tiny minimal payment, in an amount that often would not
> amortize the entire balance for several years. In practice,
> somewhat more than half of American cardholders take
> advantage of that option to defer payment of some or all of their
> credit-card-account balance each month. The payments that they

do make are made for the most part by writing a check and mailing it to the issuer.

The contrast with Japan is considerable. First, Japanese consumers plainly do not use cards as frequently as American consumers: one recent study, for example, indicated that, even excluding cash transactions (by all accounts the dominant method of point-of-sale payment in Japan), credit cards accounted for only ten percent of the value of payment transactions. Industry statistics indicate only 21.58 trillion yen ($195 billion) of credit-card transactions in 2000, about six percent of Japanese consumer spending that year. That reflects purchases of about $1,650 per capita, as compared to about $3,500 per capita in the United States. The data also show that the average credit-card transaction is about three times as large in Japan as it is in the United States, in the range of 25,000 yen ($225).

> Why might Japanese consumers make fewer credit-card purchases, but with a higher average cost?

Perhaps the most striking feature of the Japanese transactions is the limited extent to which they involve credit. The overwhelming majority – about eighty-five percent – of Japanese credit-card transactions are settled by "ikkai barai" (which means something like "payment in one cycle"). Under ikkai barai, the consumer agrees that the transaction will be paid to the issuer in full on the next monthly-payment date. Also different from American practice is the timing of the payment decision: where American cardholders typically decide their repayment schedule when they receive their monthly bills, the Japanese cardholder typically makes that decision at the cash register at the time of the sale.

The full implications of ikkai barai for the credit-card system come from its interaction with the general absence of the check from the Japanese consumer-payment system. The ordinary Japanese consumer pays bills by a credit transfer or a prearranged debit transfer (similar to the automated-clearinghouse transactions American consumers often use to pay mortgages or other regularly recurring bills). Thus, in the credit-card transaction, the customer's consent to ikkai barai amounts to a general commitment to pay in one month – analogous to the American cardholder's general commitment when it signs a credit-card slip that it will repay "in accordance with the agreement with the card issuer." The consent to ikkai barai also includes an authorization for a transfer out of the customer's account to pay the transaction shortly after the last day of the payment cycle. Because the cardholder at the point of purchase already has given the issuer access to a specified amount of funds in a specified account, the transaction resembles much more closely an American debit-card transaction than an American credit-card transaction.

After the end of each payment cycle, the issuer sends the cardholder a statement summarizing the charges. Absent an affirmative and timely objection by the cardholder, the issuer causes the funds to be transferred from the cardholder's bank account to the issuer's account on the designated date. When the cardholder uses ikkai barai, there typically is no interest or other charge for the deferral of payment from the date of the transaction to the monthly payment date. Thus, the roughly eighty-five-percent share of transactions processed by ikkai barai involves no significant extension of credit by the issuer. When credit is extended, the rates are relatively modest by American standards, in the range of twelve percent per annum. *Id.* at 1072-1075.

The following is one possible explanation Professor Mann provides for the differing credit-card usage patterns in the United States and Japan:

> [T]he limited success of the credit card may derive from the relatively limited protection Japanese law provides Japanese credit-card holders. Most obviously, Japan has no analogue to section 170 of the Truth-in-Lending Act, which generally preserves the right of American cardholders to present against the issuer any defense to payment that they would have against the merchant. The parallel Japanese statute at first glance seems to provide the same protection, but it is limited to transactions that involve extended borrowing (kappu). Because those transactions are a relatively small share of the Japanese credit-card industry,

> This is an alternative citation for 15 USC § 1666i.

- To what extent are consumers motivated by legislation such as TILA in making financial decisions?

- Compare ikkai barai to the federal reforms introduced earlier in this section, aimed at addressing U.S. consumer debt.

B. Electronic Fund Transfers

Read 15 USC §§ 1693f and 1693g, and 12 CFR 205.6 and 205.11. ATM and debit-card transactions are governed by the Federal Electronic Fund Transfer Act (EFTA), 15 USC §§ 1693 et seq., which is part of the Consumer Credit Protection Act, 15 USC §§ 1601 et seq. Regulation E, which is 12 CFR Part 205, was promulgated to effectuate EFTA.

> EFTA is subchapter VI of the CCPA; TILA is subchapter I of the same Act.

- Are business accounts within the protection of EFTA?

- How does EFTA's protection for unauthorized ATM or debit-card use compare to TILA's protection for consumer credit-card purchases?

- **Skim EFTA and Regulation E.** Does EFTA contain a dispute-resolution provision analogous to TILA?

- What advice would you give a consumer who has both a credit card and a debit card and is trying to decide which to use for a given purchase?

When a customer alleges an electronic-funds-transfer error has occurred, EFTA requires the bank that made the transfer to investigate the allegations and report the outcome to the consumer. In *Bisbey v. D.C. National Bank*, 793 F.2d 315 (D.C. Cir. 1986), the court considered a suit based on a bank's alleged failure to follow-up on its investigation by providing its customer with notice of the outcome. The bank conducted an investigation and concluded no error had occurred, but notified its customer of these results only telephonically, rather than in writing. In finding the customer had stated a cause of action under EFTA, the court held as follows:

> This section imposed a duty upon the Bank to "deliver or mail" the results of its investigation to [its customer who had requested the transfer] and to advise her of her right to request reproductions of all documents which it relied upon to conclude that no error occurred. The oral notice given to appellant was insufficient. *Id.* at 317.

This language comes from 15 USC § 1693f (d) (§ 908 (d) of EFTA).

Because the court found the customer had suffered no damage due to the bank's failure of notice, it awarded only nominal damages.

15 USC § 1693m (§ 915 of EFTA) provides the appropriate measure of damages.

Read 15 USC Section 1693a (6) (§ 903 (6) of EFTA). Determining when EFTA applies is not always simple. *Wachter v. Denver National Bank*, 751 F. Supp. 906 (D. Colo. 1990), provides the following test:

> [T]wo requirements must be met to qualify a transaction as an electronic-fund transfer: (1) it must be initiated through an electronic terminal, telephonic instrument, or computer or magnetic tape, and (2) it must order, instruct, or authorize a financial institution to debit or credit an account.

The language in this paragraph is taken directly from the statute.

> Whether the first requirement is satisfied depends in part on who initiated the transfer, the financial institution or the consumer. A bank's use of an electronic device merely to process a transaction internally does not constitute an electronic-funds transfer within the Act's meaning. Rather, the Act's focus is upon consumer-initiated or consumer-authorized transfers where electronic devices are utilized in place of face-to-face banking transactions. *Id.* at 908.

In *Kashanchi v. Texas Commerce Medical Bank*, 703 F.2d 936 (5th Cir. 1983), a bank customer sought to recover from her bank for an unauthorized withdrawal from her savings account. The withdrawal was initiated by a telephone call from someone other than the customer or her sister, who were the two owners of the account. The other party to the call was the bank employee who, upon receipt of the call, made the requested transfer of about $4,900. The bank refused to recredit the account, and one sister brought suit under EFTA. In finding EFTA did not apply, the court held as follows:

> The plaintiff ignores the essential difference between electronic-fund-transfer systems and personal transfers by phone or by check. When the bank employee allegedly agreed to withdraw funds from the plaintiff's account, he or she presumably could have asked some questions to ascertain whether the caller was one of the account holders. The failure to attempt to make a positive identification of the caller might be considered negligence or a breach of the deposit agreement under state law. When someone makes an unauthorized use of an electronic-fund-transfer system, however, the financial institution often has no way of knowing that the transfer is unauthorized. For example, in order to make a transfer at an automatic teller machine, a person need only possess the machine card and know the correct personal identification number. The computer cannot determine whether the person who has inserted the card and typed in the magic number is authorized to use the system. *Id.* at 941-942.

- Applying the *Wachter* holding, why does EFTA not apply?

- What is "the essential difference between electronic-fund-transfer systems and personal transfers by phone or by check"?

Problem: On December 1, 1988, June Elga Wachter entered a branch of Denver National Bank and presented $153.42 in cash, which was used to effectuate a wire transfer of $143.42 to a recipient in California and to pay a $10 wire-transfer fee. Bank personnel initiated the transfer and provided Ms. Wachter with confirmation of the transaction.

- Is this an electronic-fund transfer?

Based on *Wachter v. Denver National Bank*, 751 F. Supp. 906 (D. Colo. 1990).

Automated Teller Machines

Read 15 USC Section 1693g (§ 909 of EFTA). This U.S. Code section describes the allocation of responsibility for unauthorized electronic-fund transfers. Unauthorized withdrawals from automated teller machines can raise issues of customers' and banks' shared liability analogous to those presented in Chapter 10, Part B's discussion of the bank-statement rule. The following case shows how one court resolved the issue.

Kruser v. Bank of America NT & SA,
230 Cal. App. 3d 741 (1991)

Stone (W. A.), J.

Appellants Lawrence Kruser and Georgene Kruser filed a complaint against Bank of America, claiming damages for unauthorized electronic withdrawals from their account by someone using Mr. Kruser's "Versatel" [ATM] card. The trial court entered summary judgment in favor of the Bank because it determined appellants had failed to comply with the notice-and-reporting requirements of the Electronic Fund Transfer Act.

. . . The Krusers maintained a joint checking account with the Bank, and the Bank issued each of them a "Versatel" card and separate personal identification numbers which would allow access to funds in their account from automatic teller machines.
. . .

The Krusers believed Mr. Kruser's card had been destroyed in September 1986. The December 1986 account statement mailed to the Krusers by the bank reflected a $20 unauthorized withdrawal of funds by someone using Mr. Kruser's card at an automatic teller machine. The Krusers reported this unauthorized transaction to the Bank when they discovered it in August or September 1987.

* * *

In September 1987, the Krusers received bank statements for July and August 1987 which reflected 47 unauthorized withdrawals, totaling $9,020, made from an automatic teller machine, again by someone using Mr. Kruser's card. They notified the bank of these withdrawals within a few days of receiving the statements. The Bank refused to credit the Krusers' account with the amount of the unauthorized withdrawals.

* * *

The ultimate issue we address is whether, as a matter of law, the failure to report the unauthorized $20 withdrawal which appeared on the December 1986 statement barred appellants from recovery for the losses incurred in July and August 1987. . . .

* * *

The trial court concluded the Bank was entitled to judgment as a matter of law because the unauthorized withdrawals of July and August 1987 occurred more than 60 days after appellants received a statement which reflected an unauthorized transfer in December 1986. . . .

Appellants contend the December withdrawal of $20 was so isolated in time and minimal in amount that it cannot be considered in connection with the July and August withdrawals. . . . They argue that, if a consumer receives a bank statement which reflects an unauthorized minimal electronic transfer and fails to report the transaction to the bank within 60 days of transmission of the bank statement, unauthorized transfers many years later, perhaps totaling thousands of dollars, would remain the responsibility of the consumer.

The result appellants fear is avoided by the requirement that the bank establish the subsequent unauthorized transfers could have been prevented had the consumer notified the bank of the first unauthorized transfer. Here, although the unauthorized transfer of $20 occurred approximately seven months before the unauthorized transfers totaling $9,020, it is undisputed that all transfers were made by someone using Mr. Kruser's card which the Krusers believed had been destroyed prior to December 1986. According to the declaration of Yvonne Maloon, the Bank's Versatel risk manager, the Bank could have and would have cancelled Mr. Kruser's card had it been timely notified of the December unauthorized transfer. In that event, Mr. Kruser's card could not have been used to accomplish the unauthorized transactions in July and August. . . .

* * *

[N]othing in the record reflects any extenuating circumstances which would have prevented Mr. Kruser from reviewing the bank statements. The understanding he had with Mrs. Kruser that she would review the bank statements did not excuse him from his obligation to notify the bank of any unauthorized electronic transfers.

Appellants cite no authority which supports their claim that the consumer must not only receive the statement provided by the bank, but must acquire actual knowledge of an unauthorized transfer from the statement. Such a construction of the law would reward consumers who choose to remain ignorant of the nature of transactions on their account by purposely failing to review periodic statements. Consumers must play an active and responsible role in protecting against losses which might result from unauthorized transfers. A banking institution cannot know of an unauthorized electronic transfer unless the consumer reports it.

The Bank has established that the losses incurred in July and August 1987 as a result of the unauthorized electronic transfers by someone using Mr. Kruser's Versatel card could have been prevented had appellants reported the unauthorized use of Mr. Kruser's card as reflected on the December 1986 statement. The Bank is entitled to judgment as a matter of law.

- ▪ What facts would support a holding that subsequent unauthorized transfers could *not* have been prevented by the customer's notification of an earlier unauthorized transfer?

- ▪ How would the parties' rights and obligations have been different if this case had involved a credit card?

Note 1: In cases involving a bank customer's allegations that he or she attempted to make an ATM withdrawal and the funds were deducted from the customer's account but never dispensed from the machine, courts face difficult questions of fact and policy. *Porter v. Citibank, N.A.*, 123 Misc. 2d 28, 472 N.Y.S.2d 582 (1984), which involved such a claim by Citibank customer Robert Porter, makes a comparison to the circumstance in which a customer and bank dispute whether a night deposit was made:

> [A] minority of the few courts in the Nation that have considered the question have declined to grant a recovery against a bank solely on the testimony of a customer that a deposit was made. This reluctance is based on the fear of fraudulent suits against these public institutions. . . .

> However, the preferable majority view is to permit recovery where the court is convinced that the deposit was in fact made, and the bank could not explain its absence. Although the bailment presumptions applicable to night-deposit cases cannot be said to be applicable to the opposite situation at bar where the claim is that the withdrawal was not received, the cases are pertinent in their holdings that a court may give credence to testimony of an undocumented deposit. Similar to the night-depository customer, who is not in a position to produce any documentary evidence to establish that he made the deposit, the cash-machine customer can produce nothing to show that the money was not dispensed to him. *Id.* at 29-30.

To what "bailment presumptions" might the court be referring?

In electing to allow Porter to recover, the court held as follows:

> Here we are dealing with machines which [Citibank's] witnesses acknowledged were out of balance one or two nights a week. Such witnesses also stated their belief that at times a subsequent machine customer received money properly belonging to the prior user of the machine. [Porter] was a rather credible witness who had no record of banking problems although he had used the machines numerous times.

> Under the circumstances, the court holds that [Porter] established by a fair preponderance of the evidence that he did not receive the money for which he was charged as a result of the above-mentioned transactions. . . .

> In so deciding, the court is not unmindful of the possibility of fraudulent suits. However, this fear exists in many areas of the law and the history of jurisprudence has not indicated that courts have been unable to competently (although certainly not perfectly) deal with such challenges. *Id.* at 30.

The court found without elaboration that the plaintiff had
proven his case by "a fair preponderance of the evidence."
Porter's only evidence in support of his claim was his own
testimony.

- Should such evidence be sufficient?

Note 2: *Judd v. Citibank*, 107 Misc. 2d 526, 435 N.Y.S.2d 210
(1980), elaborates upon the evidentiary problem to which
Porter alludes, in the slightly different context of an alleged
unauthorized use of an ATM card. Dorothy Judd and her
husband had a joint checking account with Citibank and were
each issued an automated teller card. Each was responsible for
choosing a PIN that would be known only to him or her and
could not be retrieved by any third person, not even a bank
representative. On February 26, 1980, between 2:13 and 2:14
p.m. and on March 28, 1980, between 2:30 and 2:32 p.m., funds
totaling $800 were withdrawn from the Judd account, by
automated-teller-machine transactions. Mrs. Judd sought to
recover those funds from Citibank, claiming neither she nor her
husband, nor any person authorized by either, had withdrawn
the funds. She produced a letter from her employer showing
she had been at work when both withdrawals were made. She
testified that she had never written down her personal
identification number or shared the number with any person.
Citibank, which produced computer records showing the
withdrawals, responded that one of the Judds, or some person
authorized by one of them, must have completed the
transactions. The court described the factual quandary before
it as follows:

> In this case we are met with a credible witness on the one hand,
> and a computer printout on the other. It is evident that there was
> no opportunity to cross-examine the computer or the printout it
> produced. However, the court was benefitted to some extent by the
> testimony of the Citibank branch manager. . . . Although not
> qualified as an expert in computer systems, he was familiar with
> the read-outs provided by the Citibank cash machines. The
> question then becomes, who (or what) to believe, the person or the
> machine? *Id.* at 527-528.

In holding for Mrs. Judd, the court quoted with approval the
following language from the 1977 Final Report of the National
Commission of Electronic Fund Transfers, which represented
the culmination of a federal government study of EFT matters:

> An EFT account holder should have no liability for an
> unauthorized use of his account unless the depository institution
> can prove, without benefit of inference or presumption, that the
> account holder's negligence substantially contributed to the
> unauthorized use and that the depository institution exercised

12 USC § 2401 established the Commission that prepared the Report, dated October 28, 1977, as mandated by 12 USC § 2403 (b) as part of its duty under 12 USC § 2403 (a) to "conduct a thorough study and investigation and recommend appropriate administrative action and legislation necessary in connection with the possible development of public or private electronic-fund-transfer systems."

reasonable care to prevent the loss. Negligence in this instance should be limited to writing the PIN on the card, keeping the PIN with the card, or voluntarily permitting the account-accessing devices, such as the PIN and the card, to come into the possession of a person who makes or causes to be made an unauthorized use. *Id.* at 528.

The court ended its opinion as follows:

[T]his court is not prepared to go so far as to rule that, where a credible witness is faced with the adverse "testimony" of a machine, he is as a matter of law faced also with an unmeetable burden of proof. It is too commonplace in our society that, when faced with the choice of man or machine, we readily accept the "word" of the machine every time. This, despite the tales of computer malfunctions that we hear daily. *Id.* at 529-530.

- Describe the risks and benefits of the *Judd* court's approach.

Note 3: *Feldman v. Citibank*, 110 Misc. 2d 838, 443 N.Y.S. 2d 43 (1981), and *Ognibene v. Citibank*, 112 Misc. 2d 219, 446 N.Y.S. 2d 845 (1981), address a fraudulent scheme involving automated teller machines. The *Ognibene* facts explain how the scheme unfolds:

A customer enters the automated-teller-machine area for the purpose of using a machine for the transaction of business with the bank. At the time that he enters, a person is using the customer-service telephone located between the two automated teller machines and appears to be telling customer service that one of the machines is malfunctioning. This person is the perpetrator of the scam, and his conversation with customer service is only simulated. He observes the customer press his personal identification code into one of the two machines. Having learned the code, the perpetrator then tells the customer that customer service has advised him to ask the customer to insert his [ATM card] into the allegedly malfunctioning machine to check whether it will work with a card other than the perpetrator's. When a good-samaritan customer accedes to the request, the other machine is activated. The perpetrator then presses a code into the machine, which the customer does not realize is his own code which the perpetrator has just observed. After continuing the simulated conversation on the telephone, the perpetrator advises the customer that customer service has asked if he would try his [ATM card] in the allegedly malfunctioning machine once more. A second insertion of the card permits cash to be released by the machine, and if the customer does as requested, the thief has effectuated a cash withdrawal from the unwary customer's account. *Id.* at 220.

The two courts came to different conclusions about where liability should rest, as between the bank and the customer.

The *Ognibene* court held as follows, noting that Citibank had received information that scams of this kind were taking place and therefore deciding the bank should bear the loss for a fraudulent $400 withdrawal:

This language is taken from 15 USC § 1693g (a) (§ 909 (a) of EFTA).

> [EFTA] requires that the consumer have furnished to a person initiating the transfer the "card, code, or other means of access" to his account to be ineligible for the limitations on liability afforded by the act when transfers are "unauthorized." The evidence establishes that, in order to obtain access to an account via an automated teller machine, both the card and the personal identification code must be used. Thus, by merely giving his card to the person initiating the transfer, a consumer does not furnish the "means of access" to his account. To do so, he would have to furnish the personal identification code as well.
>
> The court finds that plaintiff did not furnish his personal identification code to the person initiating the $400 transfer, within the meaning of [EFTA]. There is no evidence that he deliberately or even negligently did so. On the contrary, the unauthorized person was able to obtain the code because of defendant's own negligence. Since the bank had knowledge of the scam and its operational details (including the central role of the customer-service telephone), it was negligent in failing to provide [the] plaintiff customer with information sufficient to alert him to the danger when he found himself in the position of a potential victim. . . .   Since a customer of defendant's electronic-fund-transfer service must employ both the card and the personal identification code in order to withdraw money from his account, the danger of loaning his card briefly for the purpose of checking the functioning of an adjoining automated teller machine would not be immediately apparent to one who has not divulged his personal identification number and who is unaware that it has been revealed merely by virtue of his own transaction with the machine. *Id.* at 222-223.

- How does the *Ognibene* court come to the conclusion that the bank customer "did not furnish his personal identification code" to the fraudfeasor "even negligently"?

The *Feldman* court applied similar standards to similar facts, but determined the customer had "unwittingly allowed an unauthorized use of his account" such that EFTA mandated judgment in favor of the bank.

- Which approach do you find more compelling, and why?

Wholesale Wire Transfers

Read 4A-104 (a) and 4A-108, and skim the Prefatory Note to Article 4A, focusing on the section entitled, "Description of transaction covered by Article 4A." Article 4A addresses wholesale wire transfers, which primarily utilize two payment systems: Fedwire, which is the Federal Reserve wire-transfer network, and CHIPS, the New York Clearing House Interbank Payments Systems. As 4A-108 shows, any electronic-fund transfer within the scope of EFTA is outside the purview of Article 4A. "CHIPS" is a means by which funds are transferred electronically among the member banks that own the system. *Delbrueck & Co. v. Manufacturers Hanover Trust Co.*, 464 F. Supp. 989 (S.D.N.Y. 1979), describes the process:

> The mechanics of effecting an interbank payment under the CHIPS system are as follows: When the paying or sending bank receives a telex from one of its customers instructing it to make a payment to a receiving bank, another member of the CHIPS system, for the account of one of the receiving bank's customers, the paying bank first tests and verifies the telex. Thereafter, the tested and verified telex is sent to one of the CHIPS computer-terminal operators, and the payment order contained in the telex is programmed into the terminal by typing into the computer the relevant information i.e., the identifying codes for the party originating the transfer, the remitting bank, the receiving bank, the party for whom the receiving bank is receiving the transfer and the amount of the transfer. This information is then transmitted to the central computer located at the Clearing House, which, based upon the identifying codes, searches out all the necessary clerical information, stores the message, and causes a sending form to be automatically typed at the sending bank. *Id.* at 1049.

Read 4A-103. This Section defines the parties to a wholesale wire transfer as follows: The party requesting the wire transfer is the "sender"; the bank making the transfer at the sender's request is the "receiving bank"; the bank to which the transfer is sent for the account of one of its customers is the "beneficiary's bank"; and the customer to whose account the transfer is made is the "beneficiary." 4A-103 (a) (1) refers to this process as the transmission of a "payment order."

- How do the Article 4A labels match up with the parties as identified in the following paragraphs from the *Delbrueck* opinion?

> Once the programming of the computer has been completed, the send form is sent to the appropriate area at the sending bank for approval. When a determination is made at the sending bank to make the payment, the form is returned to one of the computer-

terminal operators, reinserted in the computer, and the release
key is depressed. At that moment, the central computer at the
Clearing House causes a credit ticket to be printed automatically
at the terminal of the receiving bank and a debit ticket to be
printed at the terminal of the sending bank. Further, the central
computer automatically makes a permanent record of the
transaction and debits the Clearing House account of the sending
bank and credits the Clearing House account of the receiving
bank. . . .

The funds received by a receiving bank for the account of one of its
customers via the receipt of a CHIPS credit message are made
available to the customer and can be drawn upon by the customer
in the discharge of its obligations that same day, as soon as the
receiving bank is aware of the fact that the funds have been
received. *Id.*

- Another means of transferring funds among banks is
  by cashier's check. What are the benefits and risks of
  the CHIPS system?

The following case shows how consequential damages are
calculated in the Article 4A context, by way of analogy to the
famous contracts case, *Hadley v. Baxendale.*

Evra Corp. v. Swiss Bank Corp.,
673 F.2d 951, 1982 A.M.C. 2665, 33 Fed.R.Serv.2d 1666,
34 U.C.C. Rep. Serv. 227 (7th Cir. 1982).

Posner, Circuit Judge.

The question – one of first impression – in this diversity case is the
extent of a bank's liability for failure to make a transfer of funds when
requested by wire to do so. The essential facts are undisputed. In
1972, Hyman-Michaels Company, a large Chicago dealer in scrap
metal, entered into a two-year contract to supply steel scrap to a
Brazilian corporation. Hyman-Michaels chartered a ship, the Pandora,
to carry the scrap to Brazil. The charter was for one year, with an
option to extend the charter for a second year; specified a fixed daily
rate of pay for the hire of the ship during both the initial and the option
period, payable semi-monthly "in advance"; and provided that, if
payment was not made on time, the Pandora's owner could cancel the
charter. Payment was to be made by deposit to the owner's account in
the Banque de Paris et des Pays-Bas (Suisse) in Geneva, Switzerland.

The usual method by which Hyman-Michaels, in Chicago, got the
payments to the Banque de Paris in Geneva was to request the
Continental Illinois National Bank and Trust Company of Chicago,
where it had an account, to make a wire transfer of funds. Continental
would debit Hyman-Michaels' account by the amount of the payment
and then send a telex to its London office for retransmission to its
correspondent bank in Geneva-Swiss Bank Corporation-asking Swiss
Bank to deposit this amount in the Banque de Paris account of the

Using the
terminology in UCC
4A-103, what label
would you give each
party?

Pandora's owner. The transaction was completed by the crediting of
Swiss Bank's account at Continental by the same amount.

When Hyman-Michaels chartered the Pandora in June 1972, market
charter rates were very low, and it was these rates that were fixed in
the charter for its entire term – two years if Hyman-Michaels exercised
its option. Shortly after the agreement was signed, however, charter
rates began to climb and, by October 1972, they were much higher
than they had been in June. The Pandora's owners were eager to get
out of the charter if they could. At the end of October, they thought they
had found a way, for the payment that was due in the Banque de Paris
on October 26 had not arrived by October 30, and on that day the
Pandora's owner notified Hyman-Michaels that it was canceling the
charter because of the breach of the payment term. Hyman-Michaels
had mailed a check for the October 26 installment to the Banque de
Paris rather than use the wire-transfer method of payment. It had
done this in order to have the use of its money for the period that it
would take the check to clear, about two weeks. But the check had not
been mailed in Chicago until October 25, and of course did not reach
Geneva on the twenty-sixth.

> What effect, if any, should the Pandora's owners' desire to end the contract have on the rights and obligations of the parties?

> What effect, if any, should Hyman-Michaels' attempt to use the "float" afforded by payment via check have on the rights and obligations of the parties?

When Hyman-Michaels received notification that the charter was
being cancelled, it immediately wired payment to the Banque de Paris,
but the Pandora's owner refused to accept it and insisted that the
charter was indeed cancelled. The matter was referred to arbitration
in accordance with the charter. On December 5, 1972, the arbitration
panel ruled in favor of Hyman-Michaels.   The panel noted that
previous arbitration panels had "shown varying degrees of latitude to
Charterers"; "In all cases, a pattern of obligation on Owners' part to
protest, complain, or warn of intended withdrawal was expressed as an
essential prerequisite to withdrawal, in spite of the clear wording of the
operative clause. No such advance notice was given by Owners of M/V
Pandora."   One of the three members of the panel dissented; he
thought the Pandora's owner was entitled to cancel.

> "M/V" stands for "merchant vessel." What kind of evidence is the arbitration panel apparently considering in this paragraph? Review UCC 1-303 as needed to answer this question.

Hyman-Michaels went back to making the charter payments by wire
transfer. On the morning of April 25, 1973, it telephoned Continental
Bank and requested it to transfer $27,000 to the Banque de Paris
account of the Pandora's owner in payment for the charter hire period
from April 27 to May 11, 1973. Since the charter provided for payment
"in advance," this payment arguably was due by the close of business
on April 26. The requested telex went out to Continental's London
office on the afternoon of April 25, which was nighttime in England.
Early the next morning, a telex operator in Continental's London office
dialed, as Continental's Chicago office had instructed him to do, Swiss
Bank's general telex number, which rings in the bank's cable
department.   But that number was busy and, after trying
unsuccessfully for an hour to engage it, the Continental telex operator
dialed another number, that of a machine in Swiss Bank's foreign-
exchange department which he had used in the past when the general
number was engaged. We know this machine received the telexed
message, because it signaled the sending machine at both the
beginning and end of the transmission that the telex was being
received. Yet Swiss Bank failed to comply with the payment order, and

no transfer of funds was made to the account of the Pandora's owner in
the Banque de Paris.

No one knows exactly what went wrong. One possibility is that the
receiving telex machine had simply run out of paper, in which event it
would not print the message although it had received it. Another is
that whoever took the message out of the machine after it was printed
failed to deliver it to the banking department. Unlike the machine in
the cable department that the Continental telex operator had originally
tried to reach, the machines in the foreign-exchange department were
operated by junior foreign-exchange dealers rather than by professional
telex operators, although Swiss Bank knew that messages intended for
other departments were sometimes diverted to the telex machines in
the foreign-exchange department.

At 8:30 a.m. the next day, April 27, Hyman-Michaels in Chicago
received a telex from the Pandora's owner stating that the charter was
cancelled because payment for the April 27 – May 11 charter period
had not been made. Hyman-Michaels called over to Continental and
told them to keep trying to effect payment through Swiss Bank even if
the Pandora's owner rejected it. This instruction was confirmed in a
letter to Continental dated April 28, in which Hyman-Michaels stated:
"please instruct your London branch to advise their correspondents to
persist in attempting to make this payment. This should be done even
in the face of a rejection on the part of Banque de Paris to receive this
payment. It is paramount, in order to strengthen our position in an
arbitration, that these funds continue to be readily available." Hyman-
Michaels did not attempt to wire the money directly to the Banque de
Paris as it had done on the occasion of its previous default. Days
passed while the missing telex message was hunted unsuccessfully.
Finally, Swiss Bank suggested to Continental that it retransmit the
telex message to the machine in the cable department, and this was
done on May 1. The next day, Swiss Bank attempted to deposit the
$27,000 in the account of the Pandora's owner at the Banque de Paris,
but the payment was refused.

> Why does Hyman-
> Michaels believe it is
> important for
> payment efforts to
> be continued?

Again the arbitrators were convened and rendered a decision. In it,
they ruled that Hyman-Michaels had been "blameless" up until the
morning of April 27, when it first learned that the Banque de Paris had
not received payment on April 26, but that, "being faced with this
situation," Hyman-Michaels had "failed to do everything in (its) power
to remedy it. The action taken was immediate but did not prove to be
adequate, in that (Continental) Bank and its correspondent required
some 5/6 days to trace and effect the lost instruction to remit. (Hyman-
Michaels) could have ordered an immediate duplicate payment – or
even sent a Banker's check by hand or special messengers, so that the
funds could have reached owner's Bank, not later than April 28th." By
failing to do any of these things, Hyman-Michaels had "created the
opening" that the Pandora's owner was seeking in order to be able to
cancel the charter. It had "acted imprudently." The arbitration panel
concluded, reluctantly but unanimously, that this time the Pandora's
owner was entitled to cancel the agreement. The arbitration decision
was confirmed by a federal district court in New York.

Hyman-Michaels then brought this diversity action against Swiss Bank, seeking to recover its expenses in the second arbitration proceeding plus the profits that it lost because of the cancellation of the charter. The contract by which Hyman-Michaels had agreed to ship scrap steel to Brazil had been terminated by the buyer in March 1973, and Hyman-Michaels had promptly subchartered the Pandora at market rates, which by April 1973 were double the rates fixed in the charter. Its lost profits are based on the difference between the charter and subcharter rates.

The case comes to us on Swiss Bank's appeal from the judgment in favor of Hyman-Michaels. . . .

* * *

When a bank fails to make a requested transfer of funds, this can cause two kinds of loss. First, the funds themselves or interest on them may be lost, and of course the fee paid for the transfer, having bought nothing, becomes a loss item. These are "direct" (sometimes called "general") damages. Hyman-Michaels is not seeking any direct damages in this case and apparently sustained none. It did not lose any part of the $27,000; although its account with Continental Bank was debited by this amount prematurely, it was not an interest-bearing account, so Hyman-Michaels lost no interest; and Hyman-Michaels paid no fee either to Continental or to Swiss Bank for the aborted transfer. A second type of loss, which either the payor or the payee may suffer, is a dislocation in one's business triggered by the failure to pay. Swiss Bank's failure to transfer funds to the Banque de Paris when requested to do so by Continental Bank set off a chain reaction which resulted in an arbitration proceeding that was costly to Hyman-Michaels and in the cancellation of a highly profitable contract. It is those costs and lost profits – "consequential" or, as they are sometimes called, "special" damages – that Hyman-Michaels seeks in this lawsuit, and recovered below. It is conceded that, if Hyman-Michaels was entitled to consequential damages, the district court measured them correctly. The only issue is whether it was entitled to consequential damages.

. . . *Hadley v. Baxendale*, 9 Ex. 341, 156 Eng. Rep. 145 (1854), is the leading common-law case on liability for consequential damages caused by failure or delay in carrying out a commercial undertaking. The engine shaft in plaintiffs' corn mill had broken, and they hired the defendants, a common carrier, to transport the shaft to the manufacturer, who was to make a new one using the broken shaft as a model. The carrier failed to deliver the shaft within the time promised. With the engine shaft out of service the mill was shut down. The plaintiffs sued the defendants for the lost profits of the mill during the additional period that it was shut down because of the defendants' breach of their promise. The court held that the lost profits were not a proper item of damages, because "in the great multitude of cases of millers sending off broken shafts to third persons by a carrier under ordinary circumstances, such consequences (the stoppage of the mill and resulting loss of profits) would not, in all probability, have occurred; and these special circumstances were here never communicated by the plaintiffs to the defendants." 9 Ex. at 356, 156 Eng. Rep. at 151.

The rule of *Hadley v. Baxendale* – that consequential damages will not be awarded unless the defendant was put on notice of the special circumstances giving rise to them – has been applied in many Illinois cases, and *Hadley* cited approvingly.   *See, e.g., Underground Construction Co. v. Sanitary District of Chicago*, 367 Ill. 360, 369, 11 N.E.2d 361, 365 (1937); *Western Union Telephone Co. v. Martin*, 9 Ill. App. 587, 591-93 (1882); *Siegel v. Western Union Telephone Co.*, 312 Ill. App. 86, 92-93, 37 N.E.2d 868, 871 (1941); *Spangler v. Holthusen*, 61 Ill. App.3d 74, 80-82, 18 Ill. Dec. 840, 378 N.E.2d 304, 309-10 (1978). In *Siegel*, the plaintiff had delivered $200 to Western Union with instructions to transmit it to a friend of the plaintiff's. The money was to be bet (legally) on a horse, but this was not disclosed in the instructions. Western Union misdirected the money order, and it did not reach the friend until several hours after the race had taken place. The horse that the plaintiff had intended to bet on won and would have paid $1,650 on the plaintiff's $200 bet if the bet had been placed. He sued Western Union for his $1,450 lost profit, but the court held that, under the rule of *Hadley v. Baxendale*, Western Union was not liable, because it "had no notice or knowledge of the purpose for which the money was being transmitted." 312 Ill. App. at 93, 37 N.E.2d at 871.

The present case is similar, though Swiss Bank knew more than Western Union knew in *Siegel*; it knew or should have known, from Continental Bank's previous telexes, that Hyman-Michaels was paying the Pandora Shipping Company for the hire of a motor vessel named Pandora. But it did not know when payment was due, what the terms of the charter were, or that they had turned out to be extremely favorable to Hyman-Michaels. And it did not know that Hyman-Michaels knew the Pandora's owner would try to cancel the charter, and probably would succeed, if Hyman-Michaels was ever again late in making payment, or that despite this peril Hyman-Michaels would not try to pay until the last possible moment and, in the event of a delay in transmission, would not do everything in its power to minimize the consequences of the delay. Electronic-funds transfers are not so unusual as to automatically place a bank on notice of extraordinary consequences if such a transfer goes awry. Swiss Bank did not have enough information to infer that, if it lost a $27,000 payment order, it would face a liability in excess of $2 million.

* * *

Siegel, we conclude, is authority for holding that Swiss Bank is not liable for the consequences of negligently failing to transfer Hyman-Michaels' funds to Banque de Paris; reason for such a holding is found in the animating principle of *Hadley v. Baxendale*, which is that the costs of the untoward consequence of a course of dealings should be borne by that party who was able to avert the consequence at least cost and failed to do so. In *Hadley*, the untoward consequence was the shutting down of the mill. The carrier could have avoided it by delivering the engine shaft on time. But the mill owners, as the court noted, could have avoided it simply by having a spare shaft. Prudence required that they have a spare shaft anyway, since a replacement could not be obtained at once even if there was no undue delay in carting the broken shaft to and the replacement shaft from the manufacturer. The court refused to imply a duty on the part of the carrier to guarantee the mill owners against the consequences of their own lack of prudence, though of course, if the parties had stipulated for such a guarantee, the court would have enforced it. The notice requirement of *Hadley v. Baxendale* is designed to assure that such an improbable guarantee really is intended.

> How would the parties' contract presumptively have changed "if the parties had stipulated for such a guarantee"?

This case is much the same, though it arises in a tort – rather than a contract – setting. Hyman-Michaels showed a lack of prudence throughout. It was imprudent for it to mail in Chicago a letter that, unless received the next day in Geneva, would put Hyman-Michaels in breach of a contract that was very profitable to it and that the other party to the contract had every interest in canceling. It was imprudent thereafter for Hyman-Michaels, having narrowly avoided cancellation and having (in the words of its appeal brief in this court) been "put . . . on notice that the payment provision of the Charter would be strictly enforced thereafter," to wait till arguably the last day before payment was due to instruct its bank to transfer the necessary funds overseas. And it was imprudent in the last degree for Hyman-Michaels, when it received notice of cancellation on the last possible day payment was due, to fail to pull out all the stops to get payment to the Banque de Paris on that day, and instead to dither while Continental and Swiss Bank wasted five days looking for the lost telex message. Judging from the obvious reluctance with which the arbitration panel finally decided to allow the Pandora's owner to cancel the charter, it might have made all the difference if Hyman-Michaels had gotten payment to the Banque de Paris by April 27 or even by Monday, April 30, rather than allowed things to slide until May 2.

This is not to condone the sloppy handling of incoming telex messages in Swiss Bank's foreign department. But Hyman-Michaels is a sophisticated business enterprise. It knew or should have known that even the Swiss are not infallible; that messages sometimes get lost or delayed in transit among three banks, two of them located 5,000 miles apart, even when all the banks are using reasonable care; and that therefore it should take its own precautions against the consequences – best known to itself – of a mishap that might not be due to anyone's negligence.

We are not the first to remark on the affinity between the rule of *Hadley v. Baxendale* and the doctrine, which is one of tort as well as contract law and is a settled part of the common law of Illinois, of avoidable consequences. If you are hurt in an automobile accident and unreasonably fail to seek medical treatment, the injurer, even if negligent, will not be held liable for the aggravation of the injury due to your own unreasonable behavior after the accident. If in addition you failed to fasten your seat belt, you may be barred from collecting the tort damages that would have been prevented if you had done so. Hyman-Michaels' behavior in steering close to the wind prior to April 27 was like not fastening one's seat belt; its failure on April 27 to wire a duplicate payment immediately after disaster struck was like refusing to seek medical attention after a serious accident. The seat-belt cases show that the doctrine of avoidable consequences applies whether the tort victim acts imprudently before or after the tort is committed. Hyman-Michaels did both.

The rule of *Hadley v. Baxendale* links up with tort concepts in another way. The rule is sometimes stated in the form that only foreseeable damages are recoverable in a breach of contract action. So expressed, it corresponds to the tort principle that limits liability to the foreseeable consequence of the defendant's carelessness. The amount of care that a person ought to take is a function of the probability and magnitude of the harm that may occur if he does not take care. If he does not know what that probability and magnitude are, he cannot determine how much care to take. That would be Swiss Bank's dilemma if it were liable for consequential damages from failing to carry out payment orders in a timely fashion. To estimate the extent of its probable liability in order to know how many and how elaborate fail-safe features to install in its telex rooms or how much insurance to buy against the inevitable failures, Swiss Bank would have to collect reams of information about firms that are not even its regular customers. It had no banking relationship with Hyman-Michaels. It did not know or have reason to know how at once precious and fragile Hyman-Michaels' contract with the Pandora's owner was. These were circumstances too remote from Swiss Bank's practical range of knowledge to have affected its decisions as to who should man the telex machines in the foreign department or whether it should have more intelligent machines or should install more machines in the cable department, any more than the falling of a platform scale because a conductor jostled a passenger who was carrying fireworks was a prospect that could have influenced the amount of care taken by the Long Island Railroad. *See Palsgraf v. Long Island Railroad*, 248 N.Y. 339, 162 N.E. 99 (1928).

In short, Swiss Bank was not required in the absence of a contractual undertaking to take precautions or insure against a harm that it could not measure but that was known with precision to Hyman-Michaels, which could by the exercise of common prudence have averted it completely. . . .

* * *

The legal principles that we have said are applicable to this case were not applied below. Although the district judge's opinion is not entirely clear, he apparently thought the rule of *Hadley v. Baxendale* inapplicable and the imprudence of Hyman-Michaels irrelevant. He did state that the damages to Hyman-Michaels were foreseeable because "a major international bank" should know that a failure to act promptly on a telexed request to transfer funds could cause substantial damage; but *Siegel* . . . make[s] clear that that kind of general foreseeability, which is present in virtually every case, does not justify an award of consequential damages.

We could remand for new findings based on the proper legal standard, but it is unnecessary to do so. The undisputed facts, recited in this opinion, show as a matter of law that Hyman-Michaels is not entitled to recover consequential damages from Swiss Bank.

- After this case, how would you advise Hyman-Michaels to alter its business practices to prevent similar loss in the future?

- Why does this case not create a windfall for the bank?

International Perspective: Debit Cards

In *Credit Cards and Debit Cards in the United States and Japan*, 55 Vand. L. Rev. 1055 (2002), Professor Ronald J. Mann compares U.S. and Japanese use of debit cards, as follows:

In the United States, debit cards are used for about six percent of all retail payment transactions. Because the data from which that figure is derived include payments sent through the mail (or made electronically) – payments for which debit-card usage is quite rare – it substantially understates the debit card's share of payments made at the point of sale. Looking solely to retail-purchase transactions, the debit card in 1999 was used in about thirty-two percent of all card-based transactions. Even though the debit-card transactions tend to be relatively small (about $36, as opposed to $76 for the average retail credit-card transaction), they still accounted for fifteen percent of the total transaction volume at the point of sale (with industry sources estimating that they will account for one-third of that volume by 2010).

In contrast, the Japanese debit-card system (J-Debit) is used much more rarely. Specifically, J-Debit cards were used in December 2000 for just over 500,000 transactions, significantly less than one percent of all card-based transactions. It is interesting that the average debit-card transaction – contrary to usage in the United States – is significantly larger than the average credit-card transaction: about 45,000 yen for the debit-card transaction (about $400), as compared to 25,000 yen for the average credit-card transaction (about $230).

The 45,000 yen figure is somewhat misleading, however, because it reflects a relatively small number of large securities transactions. Another large component of the transactions are relatively large transactions at electronics stores, doubtless driven by merchant desire to save money on credit-card-transaction fees as well as their desire to mitigate the risk of fraud. But even putting those unusually large transactions to one side, the average transaction would be in the range of 24,000 yen (about $220), much larger than the average American debit-card transaction. *Id.* at 1101.

Professor Mann explains the differences, as follows:

The first point must be that the American debit card, albeit successful, has not itself been in use for very long. Although they

first were designed in the 1960s, debit cards gained a significant
market share only in the mid 1990s. The key event was a fall in
the cost of PIN-pad point-of-sale terminals that made it
practicable for merchants to purchase the terminals. So what the
evidence suggests for now is a delay in mass introduction of just a
few years – not decades of differences [between U.S. and Japanese
use], as in the credit-card system.

Having said that, it remains unclear whether the debit card in
Japan will ever develop as successfully as the debit card in the
United States. The basic problem is that neither of the two main
market functions that the debit card serves in the United States
are as promising in Japan as they are in the United States. First,
speaking as an American debit cardholder, one of the primary
roles of the American debit card is to accommodate the relatively
limited willingness of American consumers to carry cash. . . .
Japanese consumers, however, tend to carry more cash than
American consumers and also can obtain much larger amounts of
cash at each trip to an automated teller. Thus, their need to use a
card for small-dollar purchases is much smaller. Hence, that
market niche for the debit card is much smaller in Japan.
A second market role that the debit card plays in the United
States is that it allows cardholders the quasi-rational convenience
of paying with a card without having to resist the risky temptation
of overextending themselves with credit purchases. But Japanese
consumers do not need a debit card to have that comfort. They get
it by accepting ikkai barai as the method of payment with
standard Japanese credit-card transactions. *Id.* at 1102-1103.

Ikkai barai is
discussed in the
international
materials in Part A,
drawing from
another part of
Professor Mann's
article.

- How is the Japanese concept of ikkai barai similar to
  and different from the debit-card system of payment?

C. Non-Bank Financial Services

Between 10 and 20 million households – or approximately 10%
of United States households, 90% of them low-income, conduct
their financial transactions through non-bank providers of
financial services. The following text and chart were part of an
American Bar Association Business Law Section program
entitled *Banking on the Unbanked – The Last Consumer
Financial Services Frontier?*

In recent years, a proliferation of alternative services and products
have emerged to serve the financial needs of a significant portion
of the consumer population, often referred to as the "unbanked."
These services and products include, among others, money
transmitting, prepaid debit cards, check cashing, auto pawn, and
rent-to-own. These services and products each have an analogue
in the traditional consumer-financial-services marketplace:

TRADITIONAL PRODUCT	SERVICE ALTERNATIVE EQUIVALENT
Deposit Accounts	Check Cashing; Wire Transfers
Checks	Money Orders
Retail Installment Contracts	Rent-to-Own Agreements
Home Equity Loans	Pawn; Title Pawn
Credit Card Cash Advances	Payday Loans
Credit Cards	Prepaid Cards; Payroll Cards

- As you explore this section, consider the extent to which each comparison in this chart represents a true analogue.

EBT and Basic Banking

The following excerpt from Professor Mark E. Budnitz's article *The Revision of UCC Articles Three and Four: A Process Which Excluded Consumer Protection Requires Federal Action*, 43 Mercer L. Rev. 827 (1992), describes a different side of the banking world from that which has dominated this text's coverage so far. As you read this excerpt, consider the "basic banking" and EBT options presented, together with the risks and benefits of each. Marginal notes show how the ideas and government policies he discusses have evolved since his article was published.

Millions of government-benefits recipients who do not have bank accounts currently receive their benefits checks in the mail. These checks often are lost or stolen. If the recipient is fortunate enough to escape this misfortune, then the recipient must find someone to cash the check. Check-cashing services are happy to oblige, because these largely unregulated companies often charge exorbitant fees. Converting a government-benefits check to cash presents the recipient with many problems. For example, cash can be easily lost or stolen, and recipients are ill-advised to pay bills by sending cash through the mail. Therefore, recipients must either convert the cash into something else or go to each creditor or vendor of goods and services individually to pay their bills. This process may necessitate the further expense of transportation to each obligor. In addition, by using cash, recipients cannot take advantage of safeguards available to those using checks.

From your study of Articles 3 and 4, what "safeguards" are available to drawers of checks?

Rather than walking around with cash that must last for an entire month and paying rent, utilities, and other bills in cash, many recipients buy money orders. The cost of money orders is high in many instances, and the recipient using them loses many of the advantages associated with using checks.

To what advantages of using checks might Professor Budnitz be referring?

The recipient can purchase several money orders in one stop soon after the benefits check arrives to pay for recurring bills of the same amount, such as rent. However, unanticipated bills, and bills whose exact amount depends on usage (such as utilities) require additional trips to the store that sells money orders. This results in further expense and considerable hardship for many recipients, including those who live in rural areas and those who are disabled.

The fact that the poorest, most vulnerable people in the country, the ones who need the safest payment system, lack a system with even minimal legal safeguards, has caused many to advocate "basic banking," or "lifeline banking," in which financial institutions would be required to offer banking services to all. . . . Because of the cost to the government of mailing benefits checks to recipients and the disadvantages to recipients, state governments and the federal government are planning to establish a new electronic delivery system, EBT. . . .

> EBT delivery is now well underway.

The federal and state governments have conducted various pilot EBT projects in order to experiment with different approaches to electronic delivery of benefits. The federal government currently is developing plans to implement EBT nationwide. In an EBT system, recipients of certain government benefits such as Aid to Families With Dependent Children [AFDC] and Supplemental Security Income (which includes disability benefits) are issued a card which accesses automated teller machines and point-of-sale terminals at retail establishments. When the recipient wishes to obtain cash, he or she may use the card at either an ATM or POS terminal to receive it. Recipients of food-stamp benefits use their cards at grocery stores much the way they use credit and debit cards to buy goods. *Id.* at 828-830.

> By June 2004, all federal food-stamp payments were made by EBT.

* * *

Congress is considering federal legislation requiring banks to offer a basic banking service. Although the details vary from one bill to another, the legislation generally would mandate a bank account with no required balance or a low minimum required balance and a small number of free checks per month. . . . A 1983 study sponsored by the Federal Reserve Board and other government agencies found that families without bank accounts were disproportionately low income, high school dropouts, headed by a female, and nonwhite. . . . A . . . study by the Financial Management Service of the Department of the Treasury identified seven reasons why people do not have checking accounts. *Id.* at 843-844.

> The more recent versions of this triennial Survey of Consumer Finances by the Federal Reserve Board are consistent in their findings as to the reasons some consumers are "unbanked."

The seven reasons listed in the referenced study are as follows: "1) inaccessibility to and inconvenient hours of banks; 2) distance to, or lack of familiarity with banks; 3) previous negative experience with banks; 4) preferring to use cash; 5) lacking funds to meet minimum-balance requirement or justify maintaining an account; 6) illiteracy; and 7) inadequate math-and-reading skills."

- Which program – EBT or "basic banking" – would best address each enumerated reason that many persons lack checking accounts?

The article continues as follows:

> Most bankers oppose basic banking. In addition to the banks' concerns about the profitability of such accounts and the details of the legislation, basic banking represents substantial government interference with the free-market system. It a step toward turning the bank into an institution like a public utility. Nevertheless, the problematic features of EBT lead to the conclusion that basic banking may be a more attractive alternative.

> Through EBT, the government hopes to switch to a system that is less expensive than the present system. Whether EBT will be less expensive to the government is, however, unclear, because much depends upon who bears certain costs of EBT. For example, the federal government acknowledges that training programs that teach recipients how to use EBT are "absolutely critical." Special training programs must also be devised for the disabled and the non-English speaking recipients.

> In addition to the cost of training, EBT may require substantial capital outlays for equipment. Who will pay for this is unclear. . . .

> EBT is costly in other respects. It is undecided who will pay the cost of issuing EBT access cards and personal identification numbers or who will pay for implementing error resolution procedures. Banks fear that they will be liable if EBT recipients are mugged at ATMs. . . .

> Some cost issues depend upon whether the government or the recipient owns the account. If the recipient owns the account, EFTA applies and, absent revisions to EFTA, the bank must supply ATM recipients with notices and periodic statements. Also, the bank is liable for losses due to unauthorized use beyond the amount for which the consumer is liable. If the government owns the account, the bank's obligations and costs are limited to those in the contract between the bank and the government.

> Electronic systems fail. Sometimes they fail because of natural disasters or technological reasons; at other times they fail because wrongdoers sneak into the system and steal or foul things up. Whatever the cause, system breakdowns cost money to fix and cause recipients distress when they cannot gain access to their funds. . . .

> Finally, EBT's fundamental problem is that it provides the recipient with cash. The government has not yet decided how many free withdrawals per month recipients will be allowed. If few are permitted, recipients must walk around with cash representing a considerable amount of their total monthly benefit. In that case, recipients are susceptible to mugging or losing their money. In the alternative, they may hide it in their often

Margin notes:

The Financial Services Act of 1998 dropped the "lifeline basic banking" provision from the version approved by the House of Representatives. The Act never became law. Several states adopted legislation requiring that such accounts be made available, including New York's 1995 Omnibus Consumer Protection and Banking Deregulation Act.

If you wish to see how the cost-allocation matters between the federal government and the administering states were decided after this article was published, you can find many of the answers in 7 CFR 274.12.

In January 1997, the Federal Reserve Board issued amendments to Regulation E exempting certain EBT programs from the requirements of EFTA. These can be found in the revised text of 12 CFR Part 205. The relevant U.S. Code provisions are referenced in the text following this excerpt.

States differ on this matter, generally permitting between zero and 4 free withdrawals per month and generally charging $1 or less per additional withdrawal. Many allow unlimited free balance inquiries, but some either limit or prohibit such inquiries. Most (but not all) allow unlimited withdrawals as part of point-of-sale transactions.

burglarized residences. To pay bills such as rent and utilities, they must take the money from the ATM to a store that sells money orders. . . .

* * *

Given the enormity of the issues confronted, the uncertainty of the ultimate cost of implementing EBT, and the problems associated with successfully linking the diverse recipient population to the most technologically (and perhaps most vulnerable) advanced payment system, the government must consider alternative systems that may be less problematic. The checking account is the alternative solution. *Id.* at 844-848.

Read 15 USC § 1693b (d) (2) (§ 904 (d) (2) of EFTA). This provision shows how EFTA has addressed EBT.

- Should EBT funds be exempted from EFTA?

- Do you agree with Professor Budnitz's description of the relevant costs and benefits of EBT and basic banking?

Since Professor Budnitz's article was written, AFDC has been greatly changed, and the new program has been named TANF (Temporary Aid for Needy Families). In addition, what he called EBT is now frequently referred to as ESD (Electronic Services Delivery) and encompasses many different kinds of governmental electronic payments, including Social Security, Supplemental Security Income, USDA's Special Supplemental Nutrition Program for Women, Infants and Children (WIC), child-care assistance, child-support payments, and unemployment compensation.

- If there should be rights of access to the financial system, what obligations should rest on those who desire to exercise such rights?

- If a right of access to the financial system is created, who should pay for the costs associated therewith?

Community Development Institutions

In *Banking, Finance, and Community Economic Empowerment: Structural Economic Theory, Procedural Civil Rights, and Substantive Racial Justice*, 107 Harv. L. Rev. 1463 (1994), Anthony D. Taibi describes some challenges that face the banking industry:

The structure of America's financial system necessarily has a profound effect on the social and economic conditions of our neighborhoods and communities. The current small-business-credit crunch increasingly stifles those businesses that provide the bulk of new jobs and give regular people a chance for entrepreneurial independence. The continuing discrimination and redlining in both mortgage and consumer credit hinder the ability of Black people to buy and improve their homes and therefore block asset accumulation, stakeholding, and revitalization in Black communities. The ongoing consolidation of the banking industry has had and will continue to have a profound negative impact in low- and moderate-income communities and in non-White communities. *Id.* at 1466.

He continues by describing a paradigm that he believes may hold the greatest promise for addressing some of these challenges:

[S]ome significant positive signs have appeared on the horizon. Quietly, over the past fifteen years, with little governmental support, a billion-dollar community development financial institution (CDFI) industry has emerged. Development banks, credit unions, and loan funds have collectively extended more than $2 billion in loans and are currently capitalized with more than $290 million – much of it raised from within the communities served. Although assisted by banks receiving CRA credit for investing in CDFIs, the emergence of the CDFI industry is largely a testament to what can be achieved by committed and visionary grassroots activism coupled with the support of small business.

"CRA" refers to the Community Reinvestment Act of 1977, 12 USC § 2901. Its implementing regulations are found at 12 CFR Parts 25, 228, 345, and 563e. The CDFI Fund supporting and promoting the mission of CDFIs was established by the Reigle Community Development and Regulatory Improvement Act of 1994.

CDFIs exist in a variety of forms: some are bank holding companies or other insured depository institutions; others are unregulated non-profit corporations. All CDFIs are responsible financial intermediaries primarily devoted to developing the community in which they operate. They are structured so as to encourage community input in making policy. Thus, CDFIs express the community-empowerment mindset: they transcend the liberal-conservative dichotomy, they are not entirely market driven but are not charities, and they are not bureaucratic government programs. Rather, they are responsible local businesses dedicated to helping their local community, institutions, and people to help themselves. *Id.* at 1520-1521.

* * *

There are a variety of traditional reasons to support the assistance of the CDFI industry. Developing credit in low-and moderate-income communities is vital to our nation's economic prospects. As corporate downsizing is expected to continue, small businesses will continue to provide the bulk of new job growth; as the conventional financial industry becomes more concentrated and increasingly neglects small business, and as the possibility of direct governmental aid becomes increasingly remote, the role of CDFIs becomes ever more crucial. In addition, CDFI lending programs encourage entrepreneurship, self-sufficiency, and

creative problem solving – essential qualities for national and
community economic prosperity, and for breaking the cycles of
poverty and welfare dependency. Notably, CDFls measure their
success, not only by institutional and client economic gains, but
also by their contributions to building the civic infrastructure of
businesses, professions, voluntary organizations, church groups,
families, and other community institutions. *Id.* at 1521-1522.

* * *

1. Community-Development Banks. – A community-development
bank – the most comprehensive of the CDFI models – provides for
development credit for its community through the vehicle of a
commercial bank, credit union, or savings and loan. It utilizes
proactive subsidiaries or affiliates to carry out its mission to
develop the community. A community-development bank
incorporates a broad range of services rather than specializing in a
product or credit service as do other CDFls. The depository-
institution subsidiaries of community-development banks are, of
course, legally identical to and bound by the same regulations as
their conventional insured depository counterparts. *Id.* at 1522.

* * *

2. Community-Development Credit Unions.–Community-
development credit unions (CDCUs) are regulated and federally
insured depository institutions that are cooperatively owned and
operated by their members on a one-person, one-vote system
regardless of the amount on deposit. As non-profit cooperative
institutions, credit unions are tax exempt. Although their services
vary depending on the credit union's size, age, level of
organization, and the desires of its members, most CDCUs offer
only a basic set of retail banking services. *Id.* at 1523-1524.

* * *

CDCUs serve as the only bank for many poor Americans.
Members are provided with basic financial services—bank
accounts; check cashing; financial planning; and personal, car,
tuition, and home-repair loans. By bringing people into the
financial mainstream, credit unions help members to develop
mainstream creditworthiness. Membership in the credit union
offers not only reduced costs for needed services like check cashing
and bill paying, but also encouragement to save through regular
deposits and payroll deductions. Most importantly, credit-union
membership encourages better attitudes toward sound personal
financial management.

Lending is, of course, central to the mission of most CDCUs. All
credit unions make loans to their members, but CDCUs strive to
make loans that will contribute to community development as
well as benefit individual members. CDCUs typically encourage
loans that enable members to get and keep jobs, start and expand
businesses, and improve members' property. Many CDCUs also
work with other community-development organizations to make

Community-
development banks
can operate
pursuant to state or
national charter.

For information
about CDCUs, visit
the National
Federation of
Community
Development Credit
Unions at
www.cdcu.coop.

loans for such development projects as the rehabilitation of multi-family apartment buildings.

3. Community-Development Loan Funds. – Community-development loan funds (CDLFs) are unregulated and uninsured financial intermediaries that aggregate capital raised from individual and institutional social investors at below-market interest rates. They lend this money primarily to nonprofit and cooperative housing and business developers in low-income rural and inner-city communities. CDLFs emphasize financing projects that provide new economic opportunities and resources in their communities. By providing low-income people with an economic stake, CDLFs encourage participation in community-business, social, and political affairs. . . .

The National Housing Trust Community Development Fund is one entity offering loans nationwide.

CDLFs provide credit that is neither affordable nor available from mainstream lenders. Frequently, CDLFs' borrowers cannot seek financing from mainstream institutions because they lack credit histories or require too much technical assistance. . . .

. . . Despite the absence of traditional risk-management policies, of the more than $100 million loaned by CDLFs, loan-default losses have amounted to less than one percent of all loans made.

4. Microloan Funds. – Microloan fund programs make very small, short-term loans from a revolving-loan fund to people who want to start up or expand very small . . . businesses that are often part-time, home-based, and minority-owned. Microloan funds most often appear as one component among many in micro-enterprise development programs that promote and teach entrepreneurship by integrating both economic and human development among low-income people. These micro-enterprise ventures include such businesses as home day care, tailoring, catering and food service, hair and nail styling, engine repair, trucking, and retail sales. Pioneered in the developing world by Accion International and Bangladesh's Grameen Bank, microloan funds are relatively new to the United States; the first such fund was established here in 1983. . . .

The United States Small Business Administration Microloan Program makes funds available to local nonprofit intermediaries to make microloans of up to $35,000, with an average loan of slightly less than half that amount.

Many microloan programs rely on a peer-group lending model, in which a small group of would-be entrepreneurs come together for the purpose of obtaining credit; after training and analyzing each other's business plans, the group selects a plan to receive the first loan. If payments on the first loan remain current for a certain length of time, other members of the group are eligible to borrow. In most programs, if one member defaults, no one else is eligible to borrow. Members meet regularly to evaluate business plans, track repayments, exchange information, and lend mutual support. Group borrowing creates tremendous peer pressure to repay loans, and by assuming administrative tasks, participants lower operating costs. *Id.* at 1524-1527.

▪ What are the similarities and differences in the programs proposed by Budnitz and Taibi?

In *Microfinance and Financial Development*, 26 Mich. J. Intl. L. 271 (2004), Professor Michael S. Barr addresses the potential role of microfinance in addressing the United Nations Millennium Development Goals, which include the eradication of poverty by 2015. He notes that, as part of this effort, the UN made 2005 the International Year of Microcredit. He sees microcredit as part of a larger program of financial development, "not simply as a marginal program to serve the poor." He describes the following as four possible sources of opportunity:

> First, financially sustainable microfinance programs can contribute directly, and at scale, to poverty alleviation, and promote market deepening that in turn advances financial development. Second, microfinance may be a useful strategy to consider in countries with bad governance where other development strategies face significant barriers. Third, microfinance can help financial markets in developing countries to mature, while playing more limited, but useful, roles in poverty alleviation in both financially undeveloped and financially developed countries. Fourth, microfinance can help to break down opposition to, and build support for, domestic financial reforms. *Id.* at 281.

▪ Based upon what you have read, what role (if any) do you envision for microfinance as a tool for addressing poverty in the United States, as opposed to developing countries?

Payroll Cards

Payroll cards are sometimes viewed as substitutes for credit cards for unbanked persons. In *Payroll Cards: Would You Like Your Pay With Those Fries*, 9 N.C. Banking Inst. 35 (2005), attorneys Beth S. Desimone and Carrie A. O'Brien describe some of the features of payroll cards:

> Payroll cards are a type of stored-value card, similar to a prepaid debit card, that operate on an "open loop" or universal system, which means that they can be accepted at any ATM, point-of-sale, or merchant location that accepts debit cards. The cards are typically offered by an employer through a bank issuer. The employer sets up a payroll-card account at the employer's bank and deposits funds representing the employees' wages (minus various federal and state taxes and other deductions) into the account. The bank then issues individual cards, embossed with the employee's name, to each employee that signs up for the card. Cards typically are branded with a Visa USA or MasterCard International, Inc. logo and are connected to an ATM network, thus allowing them to be used by employees at ATMs and POS terminals. The bank keeps track of the funds attributable to each card, typically through its back-office processor, and processes all

credits, debits, and fees relating to each card. On each payday, the payroll card is automatically reloaded with the amount of the employee's net pay, but an employee cannot otherwise load personal funds or deposits onto the card. *Id.* at 37-38.

. . . The attachment of a Visa or MasterCard logo to the card, a so-called "branded" card, creates a "signature-based" card that can be used like a credit card at merchants such as restaurants or department stores which do not have PIN-based systems. Unbranded cards, or cards without the Visa and MasterCard logo, still carry the logos of different ATM networks allowing them to be accepted at ATMs and POS terminals that accept PIN-based transactions. These unbranded cards may or may not have an employee's name embossed on them. Cards that do not have an employee's name embossed on them can be quickly issued to any employee for immediate use. Non-embossed cards, however, have higher security risks than embossed cards as they can be used by anyone, not just the person whose name is embossed on the card.

* * *

The numerous advantages to using payroll cards for employers and employees appear to far outweigh the disadvantages. The main benefit to employers offering payroll cards is to lower internal costs associated with payroll. It is estimated that, in 2003, employers using payroll cards saved approximately $114.4 million in payroll costs. Moreover, employers no longer have to pay the costs associated with checks, such as handling and distributing the checks and reprocessing lost or stolen checks. While the cost to an employer for a direct deposit transaction is about 20 cents, and the cost to issue a check is between $1.00 and $2.00, the cost to issue a payroll card falls between 20 cents and $1.00. In addition, it can cost employers up to $10.00 to replace a lost or stolen check. This replacement cost is eliminated almost completely when employees are paid with a payroll card or through direct deposit.

Employers also gain a convenient method to pay employees working in remote locations. Normally, payroll checks are processed where the employer is located and sent via an overnight service to the employee in time for payday. . . .

Payroll cards are also advantageous to employees, particularly those without deposit accounts who no longer need to use a check-cashing service to access their pay. . . . [I]f the fees that banks charge for use of the card are reasonable, consumers will pay less to use a payroll card than to use a check casher or to maintain a basic bank account. . . .

Payroll cards also eliminate the need to stand in line on payday to cash a paycheck and should discourage consumers from stashing large amounts of cash in their homes. In addition, if employees are on vacation or have the payday off from work, they no longer have to go to work to pick up their paychecks. . . . Some Visa or MasterCard payroll cards even allow cardholders to pay their bills online. These services would not be available to many nonbanked cardholders without the payroll-card program.

There are disadvantages of using a payroll card, of course, including the fees and other limits placed on ATM withdrawals and cash back at POS merchants. Critics of payroll cards also allege that the cards do not offer enough consumer protections. . . .

Consumer groups also complain that, while banks tout MasterCard and Visa's "zero liability" policy as a consumer protection measure, these policies are voluntary and do not replace the consumer protections enumerated in Regulation E. For example, the zero-liability policies of MasterCard and Visa may not apply if a card is used at an ATM or after a certain number of unauthorized uses on the card in a year.

Consumer groups are also concerned that the payroll-card product is being offered as a means of savings, and as such, is an inadequate savings vehicle. These critics complain that the payroll-card account may not help consumers accumulate capital or develop a credit history. Payroll-card accounts, however, are not designed to be savings vehicles, since deposits other than wage payments are normally not allowed and no interest is paid on the funds. Instead, payroll cards have been marketed as a safer way for employees to hold their money as an alternative to cash, not as a safer alternative to a deposit or a savings account. Instead of carrying around large amounts of cash or hiding cash in their home where it is susceptible to being stolen, cash is available to cardholders as needed through the card. If the payroll card is ever lost or stolen, it is protected with the secret PIN number and by the fact that the employee can report the card as lost or stolen and obtain a replacement card. The hope is that, once cardholders become comfortable using a payroll card, they will be more willing to open a traditional bank account where they are encouraged to save money. *Id.* at 39-43.

- Are you persuaded by the authors' positive presentation of payroll cards?

The following excerpt from Professor Mark E. Budnitz's article *Payment Systems Update 2005: Substitute Checks, Remotely-Created Items, Payroll Cards, and Other New-Fangled Products*, 59 Consumer Fin. L.Q. Rep. 3 (2005), describes some legal and regulatory issues raised by payroll cards despite the Federal Reserve Board action to bring them with Regulation E.

The employee may be permitted to access funds only from a limited number of ATMs that may not be in locations convenient to the employee. Employees may have to pay a fee every time they use an ATM to withdraw a portion of their wages or after a limited number of withdrawals. Employees may have to pay a monthly fee. If the fees are high, the costs may be as great as what employees pay to check cashers. There may be a POS fee every time employees use the card in connection with the purchase of

Visa's "zero liability" policy, adopted voluntarily, allows a consumer to escape even the maximum $50 liability for unauthorized credit-card use allowed by federal law. By interim final rule effective July 1, 2007, the Federal Reserve Board decided payroll cards fall within the purview of Regulation E.

goods. Inactivity fees may be imposed if an employee does not use the card for a certain period of time. There may be a fee every time new funds are loaded onto the card. If a card is lost, stolen, or defective, the employee may have to pay a fee to obtain a replacement card. *Id.* at 6-7.

- What are the risks and benefits of Visa and MasterCard branded payroll cards, insofar as consumer expectations, parity with credit cards, and functionality are concerned?

- How do the risks Budnitz describes and the benefits Desimone and O'Brien list compare with those for traditional banking accounts?

- How do the risks and benefits of payroll cards compare with those of the financial-services-industry products listed in the table at the beginning of this section?

International Perspective: Access to Banking

Dr. William Freund, formerly the chief economist for the New York Stock Exchange, and Mr. Clive Weil of Johannesburg, South Africa, a consultant for the banking industry, have written about the E Bank model developed by Standard Bank of South Africa Ltd. to reach "unbanked" persons. Their article, *A New Approach to Banking the Unbanked*, 116 Banking L.J. 271 (1999), suggests that South Africa's experience with the E Bank model may offer a useful perspective on providing banking services to needy persons. E Bank is "an independent electronic-card-based banking operation designed to serve the masses" through highly interactive, convenient electronic kiosks. In creating the E Bank program, Standard Bank engaged in extensive market research that "identified clearly and unambiguously the urgent need for greater convenience, superior user friendliness, faster speed of transaction, and a very high degree of safety and security for the transactor," both in attracting unbanked customers and making the program a financial success. Previous attempts to attract low-income customers with traditional banking services had been unsuccessful: the bank had realized negative returns on these accounts, and low-income customers "tended to swamp the branch network to the detriment of both higher margin private and corporate clients."

E-Bank was developed to address these concerns and to provide an alternative model. The model involves hundreds of electronic branches located in retail centers featuring "warm,

vibrant colors, ethnic music, and . . . a high level of personal
assistance designed to make customers feel 'at home' with card-
based electronic banking." Customers receive on-screen
assistance through graphic illustrations and can complete
transactions using any one of South Africa's 11 official
languages. Further support is provided by E Bank personnel.
Each customer receives an account-access card with biometric
security features, bearing the customer's photograph.
Customers can put funds, at their election, in a "cash purse" or
a "savings purse" that earns a modest rate of return so long as
a low minimum-balance requirement is met. The program has
been enormously successful, both in attracting new customers
and in creating positive financial returns for the bank.

- Compare South Africa's E Plan with the payroll-card
  program advocated by Desimone and O'Brien. Which
  better addresses the reasons for being "unbanked"?

- Which represents a better policy decision?

Chapter Conclusion: This is the final chapter covering the law
of payment systems. These materials should help you
understand when non-UCC bodies of law govern financial
transactions, including those involving debit and credit cards
and automated-teller-machine withdrawals. This chapter also
raised questions regarding access to banking services and
suggested some possible solutions.

PART IV:
SECURED TRANSACTIONS

Chapter 13 begins the final unit of this textbook, which is concerned with the law of secured transactions. First, this chapter introduces students to the scope of Article 9. Then, this chapter discusses and describes various categories of collateral so that students can readily determine whether a good constitutes consumer goods, equipment, farm products, or inventory, and can recognize varying kinds of quasi-tangible and intangible collateral. The chapter closes by describing the advantages of secured credit and the importance of priority.

Chapter 14 addresses the creation and attachment of security interests. The chapter introduces the security agreement and other means of creating a security interest, discussing when a security agreement is required and what constitutes a sufficient security agreement. The chapter closes with the concept of attachment, including (1) a signed security agreement or the secured party's possession or control of the collateral, (2) the necessity of "giving value," and (3) the requirement that the debtor have rights in the collateral.

> Attachment is the process by which a secured party obtains rights in the collateral.

Chapter 15 is concerned with perfection of security interests, including perfection by filing a financing statement and by other means including automatic perfection, perfection by possession or control, and temporary perfection. This chapter explores the requirements for a legally sufficient financing statement, the basic organizational system used by most filing offices, expiration and renewal of financing statements, and drafting or filing errors.

> Perfection is the process by which a secured party puts the outside world on notice of its security interest, thereby seeking to protect itself against competing claims to the collateral in which the creditor has a security interest.

Chapter 16 examines priorities among creditors. These materials show that an unperfected holder of an Article 9 security interest may have an advantage over certain other creditors, but also explain the relative disadvantage of unperfected creditors as compared to statutory or judicial lien creditors, certain buyers, and those holding perfected interests. In addition, these materials demonstrate that a secured creditor can go through each of the enumerated steps – creation, attachment, and perfection of a security interest – and still lose out to another secured creditor holding superior priority. Finally, this chapter addresses priority rules involving collateral that has been sold and transactions involving a statutory or judicial lien creditor.

Chapter 17 is concerned with default. These materials begin by addressing notice and the role of good faith in acceleration of payments, as well as the importance of contract law in

identifying an event of default. Next, this chapter examines   1
repossession and sale or other disposition of collateral. This   2
chapter closes by discussing the right of the debtor to redeem   3
the collateral before disposition has occurred.   4
                                                                     5
Chapter 13:   6
An Introduction to Article 9   7
                                                                     8
                                                                     9
A. The Purpose and Scope of Article 9   10
                                                                     11
This section introduces the purpose of Article 9 and the variety   12
of transactions within (and excluded from) its purview.   13
Consignments and leases are covered briefly within this   14
introductory material.   15
                                                                     16
Purpose of Article 9 and Basic Vocabulary   17
                                                                     18
> References to Article 9 are to the version as revised in 1999, unless otherwise noted.

Read 1-201 (b) (35) and Comment 35, and 9-102 (a) (12)   19
and (72) and Comments 2 (b) and 3 (a). These provisions   20
demonstrate the basic purpose behind Article 9 and introduce   21
three important concepts: the security interest, collateral, and   22
the secured party.   23
                                                                     24
The following excerpt from Professor Grant Gilmore's article   25
Article 9: What It Does for the Past, 26 La. L. Rev. 285 (1965),   26
provides background on the use of chattel (or non-real-estate)   27
mortgages, such as those now recognized by Article 9, to secure   28
debt. As Chapter 14 shows, security interests in chattel can be   29
created by the execution of a security agreement or by granting   30
possession or control of the property to the secured party. As   31
Professor Gilmore indicates, possession – also called pledge – is   32
the oldest means of creating a security interest in personal   33
property.   34
                                                                     35

The idea of using personal property as security for debt in any   36
other way than by its simple delivery in pledge is not an old one.   37
We need look no further back than the first half of the nineteenth   38
century for the filing statutes which authorized mortgages of   39
chattels with the mortgagor remaining in possession throughout   40
the loan period or until default. The only statutory contribution at 41
this point was the establishment of a filing or recording system   42
under which public notice of the mortgagee's interest through a   43
public record was substantiated, as a validating or perfecting   44
device, for the pledgee's traditional possession. The development   45
of the substantive content of the new law of nonpossessory   46
security interests in personal property was left to judicial   50
improvisation. No doubt it was assumed, to the extent that   51
anyone gave thought to the problem, that the law of real-property   52
mortgages and the law of pledge would provide the necessary   53
guides of helpful analogy. But a mortgage of Blackacre presents

problems quite different from those presented by a mortgage of a business enterprises's equipment, inventory, or receivables. And property safely in a pledgee's possession is not at all the same thing as the same property in the borrower's possession. The analogies drawn from the law of pledge and mortgage proved to be feeble reeds to lean on. *Id.* at 286.

- How do nonpossessory security interests in personal property raise different issues from pledges and real-estate mortgages?

- Why (and for whom) is it advantageous for the law to permit nonpossessory security interests to be created in personal property, as well as in real estate and by pledge?

Secured transactions frequently arise in situations that invoke other Articles of the UCC as well. An Article 2 sale of goods and an Article 3 promissory note may be part of the same transaction as an Article 9 security interest. Consider the following form, taken from *In re Shinault Lumber Products, Inc.*, 323 F. Supp. 1041 (N.D. Miss. 1970):

> Alternatively, rights in the security-interest collateral can arise from a previous transaction governed by Article 2 or 3.

		$60,000.00
$60,000.00 JACKSON, MISSISSIPPI, July 12, 1967		
TEN (10) YEARS after date _WE_ promise to pay to		
_____ _____ BANK OF JACKSON, or Bearer		
BEE KAY ASSOCIATES SIXTY THOUSAND		
AND NO/100 - - - - - DOLLARS for value received,		
with interest at the rate of _6 ½_ per centum per		
annum after _ * * *_ until paid. In case of default in		
the payment of this note and it is placed in the hands		
of an attorney for collection by suit or otherwise, the		
maker or makers hereof agree to pay 10% attorney's		
fee. Negotiable and payable at the _____ BANK,		
Jackson, Miss., the maker or makers hereof having		
deposited as collateral security for this note the		
following:		
* * *payable monthly starting Jan. 1, 1968, at the rate of $681.30 per month with privilege to prepay sooner without penalty.		
1 Walker Moulder Serial #1050		
1 Walker Moulder Serial #1028		
1 Walker Moulder Serial #717		
And list of machinery marked Schedule A attached herewith, and that title ownership of the above will be vested in Bee Kay Associates until paid.		

Approved by _____

In case this note shall not be paid at maturity, the holder of this note is hereby authorized to sell the said collateral, or any part thereof, at any time, thereafter, at public or private sale, without advertising the same or giving any notice and to apply the net proceeds after paying all expenses, to the payment of this note, and said holder is hereby authorized to purchase the whole or any part of said collateral at such sale, free from any right of redemption on the part of the maker or makers hereof, which is hereby waived and released. If, at any time before maturity of this note said collateral, or any part thereof, should depreciate below the present value, which is today estimated to be at least 5% greater than the amount of this note, the holder shall have the authority to demand additional security, either by oral demand or by notice left at the place of business or residence of the maker or makers hereof or by demand addressed to the last known post office address of the undersigned, and if such additional security be not furnished when part thereof, at any time thereafter, in the manner hereinabove stated. The holder of this note shall also have a lien on all of the above mentioned collateral for any other debt due or to become due by the maker or makers hereof to such holder. Should any money paid on such collateral, while so held, come into the hands of the maker or makers hereof, it shall be held in trust for the holder of this note, to be paid over and applied to this note.

The maker or makers and endorsers severally waive presentment for payment, protest and notice of protest, and non-payment of this note.

SHINAULT LUMBER PRODUCTS, INC.

Spain Shinault

SPAIN SHINAULT, PRESIDENT

Id. at 1043.

> *After you have finished the materials in Chapters 13 through 17, you might analyze the legal effect of the various clauses in this paragraph.*

Article 2 governs the sale of the machinery listed in the note, Articles 3 and 4 govern the enforcement of the promissory note evidencing the referenced loan, and Article 9 governs the security interest the bank holds until the debt is fully satisfied. Due to the connections between the various Articles, it makes sense to focus on the Code's recurring themes that show the drafters' concern with consistency among the Articles. In his article *Remote Control: Revised Article 9 and the Negotiability of Information*, 63 Ohio St. L.J. 1327 (2002), Professor Jonathan Lipson invites a comparison between Articles 3 and 4, on the one hand, and Article 9 on the other. Consider the following excerpt:

> Article 9 governs secured transactions – transactions in which personal property secures payment or performance of an obligation. Like the rest of the UCC, Article 9 attempts to strike a balance on negotiability. In general, property that is subject to a security interest (in technical terms, "collateral") remains subject to the security interest notwithstanding sale, exchange, or other disposition. Thus, in general, Article 9 collateral is not freely negotiable. So, for example, if a debtor granted a security interest in an electronic list of its customers, which was bought or licensed by another business, the security interest should follow the list into the computer of that buyer. At least in theory, the secured party would have the right to "take" the list from [the buyer] if [the debtor] failed to satisfy its obligations to the secured party.

> This general rule is, however, subject to an important exception: A party that acquires collateral "in ordinary course" takes its rights in the collateral free of the security interest. *Id.* at 1331.

> *This concept is discussed in Ch. 16, Part D.*

1
2
3
4
5
6
7
8
9
10
11
12
13
14
15
16
17
18
19
20
21
22
23
24
25
26
27
28
29
30
31
32
33
34
35
36
37
38
39
40
41
42
43
44
45
46
50
51
52
53

- To what negotiable-instrument concepts is Professor Lipson inviting a comparison?

Comparisons between Articles 2 and 9 are also common. In *Quest for Uncertainty: A Proposal for Flexible Resolution of Inherent Conflicts Between Article 2 and Article 9 of the Uniform Commercial Code*, 87 Yale L.J. 907 (1977), Professor Thomas Jackson and Professor (now Justice) Ellen Peters explore differences in orientation between the two Articles:

> One transaction that recurrently crosses Article lines is a contract for the sale of goods that can either become, or come into confrontation with, a security interest. Article 2, the sales Article, consistent with its historical antecedents and responsive to its applicability to conspicuously diverse commercial interactions, leans heavily to statements of principle and presumptive guidelines. Its pattern is to define a few core concepts with core consequences, which are then located in a broader network of open-ended constructs with multifaceted implications. It is, in sum, a rulemaking statute in the common law tradition. Article 9, the secured-transactions Article, consistent with its historical antecedents and responsive to the unitary but absolute requirement that security interests survive attack in bankruptcy, leans heavily to positivist prescriptions of rules that dictate outcomes. *Id.* at 908-909.

- What is the fundamental difference in orientation between Articles 2 and 9 and how do you expect this difference to affect the law contained in each?

- Using the language found in the Schwartz & Scott excerpt in Chapter 1, Part C, is each Article as characterized by Jackson & Peters dominated by "directives," risk allocations," "enabling provisions," or "vague admonitions"?

Read 9-602 and Comments 2 and 3. 9-602, which is explored in various parts of the remaining chapters on secured transactions, lists a number of rights and duties that cannot be varied or waived by the parties' agreement. The existence of such non-waivable rights, which has no equivalent in Articles 2, 3, and 4, other than the general limitations found in 1-302 (b), is an example of the difference in orientation to which the Jackson & Peters excerpt makes reference.

- What examples from Article 2 can you find tending to show it "is a rulemaking statute in the common law tradition"?

Read 9-101, Comment 1. Article 9 changed the landscape of secured-finance law by eliminating many of the mechanisms –

Under a conditional sale, the buyer would receive title to the goods only upon full performance of some obligation – usually payment for the goods.

such as the conditional sale – by which secured credit was [1] formerly given. Thus, attorneys researching in this area of law [2] should exercise caution, as cases decided before Article 9 was [3] enacted may include vocabulary that is no longer meaningful. [4] The following excerpt from *In re United Thrift Stores*, 363 F.2d [5] 11, 3 U.C.C. Rep. Serv. 460 (3d Cir. 1966), puts the transition [6] from prior law to Article 9 in perspective: [7]

[8]

As Chapter 1, Part A and the General Comment to the UCC indicate, the Uniform Conditional Sales Act and the Uniform Trust Receipts Act were promulgated by NCCUSL in 1918 and 1933, respectively. A trust receipt is a mechanism whereby goods are released to the buyer but title remains in the lender providing financing for the purchase.

> The Uniform Commercial Code was designed to bring the body of [9] commercial law into the contemporary world of business. It would [10] hardly be consistent with that design . . . to reestablish in new [11] form limitations which reflect a passion for legal technicality over [12] commercial reality. . . . [13]
>
> The Code has eliminated the older, technical, and restricted [14] categories of security agreements. Gone are the definitional [15] difficulties and transactional fictions of the chattel-mortgage, the [16] conditional sale, the trust receipt. In their stead is a general set of [17] rules for the creation of a security interest in the secured party. [18] *Id.* at 14. [19]

[20]

▪ Based on what you have read, how is an Article 9 [21] security interest different from a common-law [22] conditional sale? [23]

[24]

Earlier chapters describe various difficulties the Code drafters [25] have encountered in attempting to revise the UCC or [26] promulgate new uniform law, especially when consumer- [27] protection concerns are involved. Article 9 is no different, and [28] the following excerpt from Professor Marion Benfield's article [29] *Consumer Provisions in Revised Article 9*, 74 Chi.-Kent L. Rev. [30] 1255 (1999), describes some challenges during the most recent [31] revision process, which ended in 1999: [32]

[33]

Chapter 7, Part A makes reference to the kinds of concerns to which Professor Benfield alludes here.

> The question of how to deal with consumer transactions was one [34] of the major concerns in the revision of Article 9. The reasons for [35] the concern were both substantive and political. As a substantive [36] matter, many consumers are ill-equipped to understand, or to [37] bargain about, provisions in contracts, including security [38] agreements, that may adversely affect them. Similarly, defaulting [39] consumers may need more information and more protection from [40] possible . . . overreaching than commercial borrowers. Therefore, [41] as a policy matter, additional or different rules especially [42] protective of consumers may be justified. As a political matter, [43] recent experience . . . with Revised Articles 3 and 4 of the Uniform [44] Commercial Code indicates that significant consumer-group [45] opposition to proposed UCC changes may delay or prevent [46] enactment. At the same time, it was understood that securing [47] uniform adoption of a Revised Article 9 with substantial additional [48] special consumer provisions would be difficult. The initial report of [50] the Article 9 Consumer Subcommittee issued in 1996 put the [51] problem as follows: [52]

[53]

. . . [I]t is very difficult to reach a national consensus on consumer issues which is acceptable in the various states. The differences in social, economic, and political conditions in the states are sufficiently great that rules that in one state are seen as insufficiently protective of consumer interests are seen in another as unjustified interference with market forces. Therefore, the drafting participants must recognize that the question of coverage of consumer issues in Article 9 involves not only a judgment as to the best substantive rule, but also a judgment regarding whether there is sufficient consensus on the appropriate substantive rule outside the Conference and the American Law Institute that a decision made by the Conference and the ALI would be acceptable. Therefore, provisions which the sponsoring organizations believe substantively desirable might nevertheless not be included in Article 9 because of enactability concerns.

> Chapter 1, Part A shows some of the issues the drafters face in seeking to balance good policy with political realities.

* * *

The Consumer Subcommittee found that the consumer and creditor representatives were far apart in their views as to desirable consumer provisions in Article 9. Consumer representatives made a number of proposals for additional consumer protections in Article 9; particularly for additional consumer rights during the Article 9 foreclosure process, and for additional remedies when a creditor fails to comply with Article 9 foreclosure requirements. Among their major requests were (1) attorneys' fees for consumer plaintiffs who prevail on a claim that a creditor failed to comply with Article 9 foreclosure requirements, (2) an absolute-bar rule prohibiting recovery of any deficiency if the creditor fails to comply with the foreclosure requirements, (3) a right to reinstate the debt after repossession by making past-due payments, and (4) a post-sale notice of the debt, the proceeds of the sale, the costs of sale, and the resulting deficiency or surplus.

> As you work through these materials, you might look for how the drafters ultimately dealt with each concern raised.

At the same time, consumer-creditor representatives strongly argued against additional consumer rights or remedies in Article 9 and, to the contrary, argued that the present statutory damages provisions for creditor failures in the consumer-debtor foreclosure process had little relationship either to actual harm to the consumer or to reprehensibleness or willfulness of the creditor conduct. They suggested no, or reduced, statutory damages, and a good-faith defense to any statutory damages. *Id.* at 1255-1258.

- Why is uniform enactment of Article 9 an important goal?

- What, if any, harm could result from a body of law creating too much protection for consumers or, alternatively, for creditors?

Read 9-101 Comment 4 (j). This comment summarizes some of the consumer-protection features of Revised Article 9.

Scope of Article 9

Read 9-101 Comment 4 (a), and 9-109 and Comment 2.
Recognizing which transactions fall within Article 9 is a
significant challenge, especially because the Article's scope
expanded with the 1999 revisions. First, Article 9 includes
transactions creating security interests by contract. The
language "by contract" indicates these are consensual
transactions. Most liens arising by statute or operation of other
law are outside Article 9, with the exception of agricultural
liens, which are expressly included. Article 9 also applies to the
sale of accounts receivable and chattel paper, loans for which
accounts receivable and chattel paper are given as collateral,
various security interests created under other Articles, and
many consignments.

- Does Article 9 apply to real-estate transactions and/or
  the commercial paper they generate?

Read 9-505 (b) and Comment 2. Because it is sometimes
not clear whether the law will classify certain transactions as
being inside or outside the scope of Article 9, the Code protects
parties who file Article 9 papers in an abundance of caution,
even if not needed. A filing cannot be used as evidence that a
transaction implicates Article 9.

For an overview of
preemption, consider
the concise
explanation in the
book by Professors
John E. Nowak and
Ronald D. Rotunda,
*Principles of
Constitutional Law*
196-200 (2d ed.
2005), and the more
comprehensive
coverage found in
Erwin
Chemerinsky's book
*Constitutional Law:
Principles and
Policies* 376-401 (2d
ed. 2002).

Read 9-109 (c) (1). This subsection shows the relationship
between Article 9 and federal law: the UCC defers to federal
law where the rules of preemption require, but also frequently
supplements federal law. Common instances when federal law
is implicated include matters involving airplanes, railroads,
intellectual property, ships, or long-haul trucking.

Read 9-109 (a) (1) and (d) (1) and Comment 10. *Shurlow
v. Bonthius*, 456 Mich. 730, 576 N.W.2d 159 (Mich. 1997),
addresses whether Article 9 applies to a landlord's lien created
by a lease agreement rather than by statute. In deciding such
liens are within Article 9, the court held as follows:

> A landlord's lien is the right of a landlord to levy upon the goods of
> a tenant in satisfaction of unpaid rents or property damage.
> Although landlords' liens may arise by statute, common law, or
> contract, commonly these liens take the form of statutory liens
> that give the lessor the status of a preferred creditor. . . .

> * * *

> . . . Generally, security interests that are not consensual but that
> arise by operation of law are excluded under this article.
> Substance predominates over form in determining Article 9
> applicability. Thus, the determinative factor is not the form of the

transaction as much as it is the intent of the parties in entering into the transaction.

* * *

While a literal reading of subsection [9-104 (d) (1)] supports [the argument that all landlord's liens should be excluded], we cannot ignore the clear intent of Article 9, which is to bring all consensual transactions within the scope of UCC coverage. *Id.* at 734.

- Is it possible to square the *Shurlow* holding with the following language from *In re Zwagerman*, 115 B.R. 540, 12 U.C.C. Rep. Serv. 2d 365 (Bankr. W.D. Mich. 1990)?

A court should adhere strictly to the provisions of the Code in order to achieve stability, consistency, and predictability. And an "overly" liberal interpretation of the Code should be avoided as creating uncertainty among businessmen and their legal advisors who believe themselves to be entering into transactions on the basis that the Code means what it says. *Id.* at 554.

- In light of 9-505 (b), referenced above, what steps should a landlord take if he or she is uncertain as to whether a landlord's lien falls within Article 9?

Accounts and Rights to Payment

Read 9-109 (a) (3) and Comments 4 and 5. Article 9 applies to many outright sales of receivables such as accounts and chattel paper, as well as to transactions in which a security interest is given in this kind of collateral. As the Comments suggest, the inclusion within Article 9 of such sales, as well as security interests in such collateral, is intended to prevent confusion in close cases in which it is not clear which kind of transaction has taken place.

> "Account" and "chattel paper" are defined in 9-102 (a) (2) and (11), respectively.

Read 9-109 (d) (4) through (7) and Comment 12. Not all transactions involving interests in receivables, however, fall within Article 9's scope. Instead, as Comment 12 states, the drafters intended to exclude "certain sales and assignments of receivables that, by their nature, do not concern commercial financing transactions."

- What do the receivables enumerated in 9-109 (d) (4) through (7) have in common, justifying their exclusion from Article 9?

In *Marandola v. Marandola Mechanical, Inc.*, 2004 R.I. Super. Lexis 115, 53 U.C.C. Rep. Serv. 2d 1057 (R.I. 2004), the court addressed the assignment of a right to payment falling within

9-109 (d) (6), explaining why such rights were excluded from
Article 9:

> The quoted language is found in 9-109 (a) (1) and (3).

Subject to certain exceptions, Article 9 applies to, inter alia, "[a]
transaction, regardless of its form, that creates a security interest
in personal property or fixtures by contract" and "[a] sale of
accounts, chattel paper, payment intangibles, or promissory
notes." A "security interest," as defined by the UCC, includes "an
interest in personal property or fixtures which secures payment or
performance of an obligation" and "any interest of a consignor and
a buyer of accounts, chattel paper, a payment intangible, or a
promissory note in a transaction that is subject to Chapter 9."

> The quoted language is found in 1-201 (b) (35).

> The quoted language is found in 9-109 (d) (6).

Article 9 "does not apply to . . . an assignment of a right to
payment under a contract to an assignee that is also obligated to
perform under the contract . . . ." In other words, Chapter 9 does
not cover "the total assignment of a contract under which the
assignee is to take over performance and receive payment." 1
Grant Gilmore, *Security Interests in Personal Property* § 10.5
(1965). . . .

In effect, § 9-109 (d) (6) makes Article 9 "inapplicable to certain
transfers of accounts, contract rights and chattel paper which are
not made in anything that could reasonably be described as a
financing transaction." Gilmore, supra, § 19.6. *Id.* at 15-17.

- What would be an example of a "total assignment"
  such as that to which Gilmore makes reference?

- What is meant by the language in the excerpt that
  transactions within 9-109 (d) (6) "could [not]
  reasonably be described as . . . financing
  transaction[s]"?

Consignments

> A consignment is a business transaction in which the consignee acts as the selling agent for the consignor, who maintains title to the goods, controls the terms of the sale, and takes back any unsold goods.

**Read 9-102 (a) (20) and Comment 14, and 9-109
Comment 6.** Following the 1999 revisions, most
consignments are within Article 9, to give potential creditors of
the consignee notice that the consigned goods do not belong to it
and thus are not appropriate collateral for any debt of the
consignee. As the court states in *In re Valley Media*, 279 B.R.
105, 47 U.C.C. Rep. Serv. 2d 1178 (D. Del. 2002),

> The purpose of . . . 9-102 (a) (20) is to protect general creditors of
> the consignee from claims of consignors that have undisclosed
> consignment arrangements with the consignee that create secret
> liens on the inventory. Under these UCC provisions, the court is
> not concerned with the rights between the consignor and
> consignee, but rather solely with the rights of the third-party
> creditors of the consignee. Creditors of the consignee need not
> demonstrate actual reliance on the goods or the lack of a financing

statement in extending credit in order to benefit from the protections of these provisions. *Id.* at 125.

- Which consignments remain outside Article 9, following the 1999 revisions? How does Article 9's definition of "consignment" address the concern with secret liens referenced in the court's opinion?

> Students should be wary of pre-revision cases involving consignments, for two reasons: (1) whereas most consignments were formerly excluded from Article 9, most are now included, and (2) the definition of "consignment" has changed.

Read 2-326 and Comments 1 and 2, and 2-327. These provisions describe a "sale or return," sometimes confused with a consignment. The following case shows the distinction between the two kinds of transactions.

Bufkor, Inc. v. Star Jewelry Co., Inc.,
552 S.W.2d 522, 22 U.C.C. Rep. Serv. 388
(Tex. App. 9th Dist. 1977).

Dies, Chief Justice.

On February 20, 1975, plaintiff below, Star Jewelry Company, Inc., delivered certain items of jewelry to "Tavenier (sic) 1704 S. Post Oak Houstn (sic), Texas." The invoice contained these words: "Goods must be purchased or returned within 5 days of receipt or they may be automatically invoiced to your account." On January 15, 1975, defendant below, Bufkor, Inc., obtained a judgment against James T. Dolleslanger, individually, and doing business as Tavernier Jewelers. Thereafter, on April 2, 1975, Bufkor, Inc., levied execution upon jewelry which Star had placed in Tavernier's possession. On March 12, 1976, Star Jewelry, Inc., filed suit against Bufkor, Inc., . . . [on the grounds] that it owned the property because same had been delivered to Tavernier on consignment.

> Bufkor is a third party as to any transaction between Star and Tavernier.

. . . [J]udgment was entered in favor of Star Jewelry Company, Inc., from which Bufkor perfects this appeal. . . .

Tavernier has since gone into bankruptcy, and Bufkor, Inc., seeks preferred status relying on its judgment. Star Jewelry contends title did not pass to Tavernier because of a consignment arrangement.

> Bufkor claims the status of a lien creditor under 9-102 (a) (52). The priority of such creditors is discussed in Chapter 16, Part E.

It is true that the term "consignment" was used in the dealings of the parties, but it is also true that Tavernier maintained a place of business for the purpose of selling jewelry merchandise, had authority to sell this merchandise, and Star did not seek return of the merchandise.

> How does each factor tend to suggest a "sale or return" rather than a consignment?

Transactions which once might have been regarded as consignments are now regarded as sales by the Uniform Commercial Code. The purpose of this change was to permit people to deal with a debtor upon the assumption that all property in his possession is unencumbered, unless the contrary is indicated by their own knowledge or by public records.

Chapter 9 of the Texas Uniform Commercial Code provides a method by which Star could have given notice of its lien, i.e., by filing a

financing statement with the Secretary of State. Tavernier's president
Dolleslanger gave Star the form and suggested that such a statement
be filed. . . . The intention of the parties is no longer determinative of
the question of whether a transaction is a sale or a consignment.

Consequently, we hold that these goods should be held to have been
delivered for "sale or return," and thus, that neither the title nor the
right to possession of these goods was retained by plaintiff Star Jewelry
Company.

Star, having neither title nor right to possession, may not prevail in a
trial of right of property.

- In your own words, what is the difference between a
  consignment and a "sale or return"?

- What is the difference between a "sale or return" and
  an ordinary sale?

Leases

Read 1-203 and Commentary. Leases are outside Article 9
and are covered instead by Article 2A. As Chapter 2, Part A's
discussion of 1-203 shows, whether a transaction is a sale or a
lease is a fact-specific inquiry.

In re Aspen Impressions, Inc., 94 B.R. 861, 10 U.C.C. Rep. Serv.
2d 172 (E.D. Pa. 1989), explains the difference in purpose
between a lease and a security agreement:

> Generally, true leases cover the temporary lease of property for a
> price, and require the leased item's return to the lessor. Leases
> intended as security, however, are conditional sales of equipment
> with a reservation of title to provide security. . . If it is determined
> that [an] agreement is a true lease, then [the lessor] retains a
> reversionary interest in the [goods] and is entitled to the proceeds
> of the sale of that equipment. *Id.* at 864.

- To whom does a conditional sale provide security?

- How does a lease involve different issues than a sale
  pursuant to a security interest?

The court also cautions against making an assumption that a
transaction including no purchase option is necessarily a lease:

> [A]greements containing no option to purchase . . . might simply
> reflect an intent for title to pass with no additional consideration
> because the property is expected to have no market vale at the
> expiration of the lease term. . . . The salient factor, then, is the
> relationship of the amount paid towards the equipment over the

Refer back to those
materials as needed.

1
2
3
4
5
6
7
8
9
10
11
12
13
14
15
16
17
18
19
20
21
22
23
24
25
26
27
28
29
30
31
32
33
34
35
36
37
38
39
40
41
42
43
44
45
46
50
51
52
53

life of the agreement to the property's fair-market value at the end of the lease. *Id.* at 866.

In re International Plastics, Inc., 18 B.R. 583, 33 U.C.C. Rep. Serv. 1080 (Bankr. D. Kan. 1982), discusses when the consideration paid for an item at the end of a lease is nominal and when a lease extends for the full life of an asset, two characteristics of a disguised sale:

> Generally, the consideration is regarded as nominal and the transaction is a disguised installment sale if the option price is less than twenty-five percent of the original purchase price or such that the only sensible course of action for the lessee is to exercise the option. *Id.* at 586.

What is meant by the language "the only sensible course of action . . . is to exercise the option"?

- Does the text of the Code support such a bright-line rule?

- Why would parties choose to characterize a "sale" as a "lease"?

1-203 Comment 2 may assist you in answering this question.

The excerpt continues as follows:

> A lease extends for the useful life of the asset if the lessee is entitled to possess the leased property for a primary term and applicable renewal terms substantially corresponding to the estimated useful life of the property. *Id.* at 587.

- Which language is more precise: "entitled to possess" or "required to possess"?

In re Zaleha, 159 B.R. 581, 23 U.C.C. Rep. Serv. 2d 1035 (Bankr. D. Idaho 1993), presents considerations that may have led the Code drafters to abandon some of the factors formerly used in distinguishing a lease from a secured sale. This excerpt also addresses when the character of a transaction as a lease or secured sale is determined:

An extensive list of such factors is presented in the *International Plastics* decision in Problem 1, below.

> Costs such as taxes, insurance, and repairs are necessarily borne by one party or the other. They reflect less the true character of the transaction than the strength of the parties' respective bargaining positions.
>
> * * *
>
> . . . Parties make the agreement at the outset. It is only there that they have the common intention to create a lease or a security agreement, and it is at that time we should measure the economic realities to determine their true intention. *Id.* at 584, 586.

- Why would a lessee ever agree to pay for taxes, insurance, or repairs on goods it does not own?

The following case presents issues of public policy reminiscent of the *Williams v. Walker-Thomas Furniture Co.* unconscionability case mentioned in Chapter 2, Part B. As you read this case, note how whether the transaction is a lease or a sale will affect the daily life of the debtors.

In re Powers,
983 F.2d 88, 19 U.C.C. Rep. Serv. 2d 689 (7th Cir. 1993).

Cummings, Circuit Judge.

> The current reference would be to UCC 1-203.

Keith Alan Powers ("Debtor") and Royce, Inc., a rental company, dispute whether certain contracts are "true leases" or installment-sales contracts under Section 1-201 (37) of the Uniform Commercial Code. If the contracts are true leases, Royce will be able to repossess certain household goods from the bankrupt Debtor. If the contracts are installment sales, Debtor will retain possession of the goods and Royce will only receive partial payment for the goods' value. For reasons stated below, we find that the agreements are true leases.

On September 29, 1989, and July 7 and July 9, 1990, Debtor rented used household goods from Royce under three written contracts. The Agreements provide for an initial two-week rental period with a series of optional two-week rental periods thereafter. There is no obligation to rent the property beyond the initial two-week rental period. The option to rent the property for an additional two-week period is exercised by paying a designated rental payment to Royce. The Agreements are terminable at any time by the lessee Debtor without penalty or further obligation. . . . Under the Agreements, the Debtor could purchase the used household goods (1) immediately for cash, (2) for the cash price at any time within 90 days of taking possession, (3) for a sliding-scale price that may be exercised after 90 days, or (4) by making the total number of rental payments to acquire ownership with no additional consideration.

> Chapter 13 of the Bankruptcy Code, by its title, provides for "Adjustment of Debts of an Individual with Regular Income." Although a Chapter 13 debtor is required to pay the full value of each secured claim into the plan, the value is divided among secured and unsecured creditors.

Debtor filed a Chapter 13 bankruptcy proceeding on May 22, 1991. At the time of the bankruptcy filing, he had possession of the property under the Agreements and had been making rental payments. In the Chapter 13 proceedings, Debtor's schedules listed Royce as a secured creditor to the claim of $3,041–$1,000 of which was secured by the goods and $2,041 of which was unsecured. Under Debtor's plan, Royce was to be paid $1,000 secured, and the balance as unsecured, with unsecured creditors receiving approximately 30%. Royce filed an objection to the confirmation of the plan and sought return of the property leased to Debtor. Royce also filed a motion to lift the automatic stay and for judgment on the pleadings. The Debtor requested that the bankruptcy court permit him to retain possession of the property.

> The automatic stay in 11 USC § 362 prevents a creditor from pursuing collection against a debtor who has filed for bankruptcy.

Royce took the position that the Royce Agreements were true leases rather than disguised security agreements and were therefore subject to assumption or rejection under Section 365 of the Bankruptcy Code. Royce asserted that the purpose of Section 365 is that, in order to retain possession of the property, the Debtor was required to assume the leases under Section 365, cure existing rental defaults, and thereafter

> **Skim 11 USC § 365.** Why might a trustee choose to assume an unexpired lease or executory contract?

1
2
3
4
5
6
7
8
9
10
11
12
13
14
15
16
17
18
19
20
21
22
23
24
25
26
27
28
29
30
31
32
33
34
35
36
37
38
39
40
41
42
43
44
45
46
50
51
52
53

make the rental payments stated in the Agreements or exercise one of the purchase options. No such assumption occurred, and in its absence Royce asserted that under Section 365, the leases would be deemed rejected, the Debtor's right to possession would be terminated, and Royce would be entitled to have the property returned. The Debtor countered that the Agreements were disguised installment sales that gave Royce a security interest in the goods, and thus that the Debtor could keep the property without assuming the leases under Section 365 or without paying Royce the amounts necessary to purchase the property under the options provided in the Agreements.

* * *

This case is controlled by our decision in *In re Marhoefer Packing Co., Inc.,* 674 F.2d 1139, 33 U.C.C. Rep. Serv. 370 (1982), where we held that an agreement similar to the Royce Agreements that included two options to purchase the equipment in question was a true lease. Judge Pell concluded that, as here, where a lessee has the right to terminate the lease before the option arises to purchase the property for no additional or nominal consideration, the lease is a true lease and cannot be a conditional sale. . . . The Debtor in this case could terminate the Royce Agreements at any time after the initial two-week rental period, making the Agreements true leases under *Marhoefer.*

Marhoefer reviewed a contract between two companies for the lease of a commercial meat-processing machine. Like the Royce Agreements, the *Marhoefer* contract provided the lessee with more than one purchase option. The lessee in *Marhoefer* argued that, because his contract contained an option to acquire the goods for nominal consideration at the end of the lease's term, his contract was an installment sale under the conclusive presumption established by clause (b) of UCC § 1-201 (37). Although this contract did not involve the leasing of goods to unsophisticated consumers, as in the present case, the *Marhoefer* contract resembles the Royce Agreements in one critical respect: under both agreements, the lessee was under no obligation to make the installment payments that would ultimately allow the lessee to exercise or refuse the option to own the goods. This feature of the contract leads this Court to conclude that clause (b) of UCC § 1-201 (37) did not apply. In other words, because the lessee could terminate the lease at any time, the presence of an option to acquire the goods for a nominal price did not convert the leases into installment sales. The same conclusion applies to the Royce Agreements: even though the lessee can acquire the goods at the end of the lease's term, the lessee is under no obligation to make the payments that will allow him to exercise the option.

> Is it appropriate for the court to equate the facts of these two cases?

> This clause is now found in UCC 1-203 (b) (4).

As in *Marhoefer,* this conclusion does not end our inquiry. This Court must determine whether the rest of the agreement supports the conclusion that the parties intended it to be a true lease. . . . The Agreements are studded with terms like Renter, Lessor, Rental Period, and Rental Payments. They also state that Debtor will not own the property until "(1). . . [he] will have made the number of rental payments and the total amount of rental payments necessary to acquire ownership of the property; or (2). . . exercised the early-purchase option as provided in this agreement." In sum, the Debtor

Do you agree that
each factor suggests
a true lease?

was renting the goods and would never own them unless he fulfilled
either condition. Other factors outlined in *Marhoefer* indicate that the
Royce Agreements are leases. First, the initial rental period and each
optional rental period is short (two weeks) in relation to the length of
time that must elapse before a lessee who does not exercise an early-
purchase option will own the goods (two or more years). Second, the
amount of each rental period payment is small in relation to the
amount necessary to purchase the goods under any of the purchase
options. Finally, the purchase price in the Royce Agreements was much
less than the total amount of rental payments.

We recognize, of course, that for lessees who rent furniture intending
eventually to own it, these Agreements function as secured installment
sales (provided the lessee makes all the payments). But, unlike buyers
in standard installment sales, Royce's hybrid "rental-buyers" are not
obligated to make payments, and they can change their minds and
return their furniture at any time. This flexibility is not worthless, and
in return Royce earns the benefits of a lease when some of its renter-
buyers become insolvent. . . .

* * *

On the facts of this case, . . . we adhere to *Marhoefer* and conclude that
the Royce Agreements were true leases. Therefore, the district court's
judgment is affirmed with directions to order the return of the goods to
Royce.

- What equities did the court balance in reaching its
  decision?

Problem 1: The following excerpt is from *In re International
Plastics, Inc.*, 18 B.R. 583, 33 U.C.C. Rep. Serv. 1080 (Bankr. D.
Kan. 1982), decided under former Article 9:

> The following factors have been held indicative of a true lease: (1)
> the purchase price of the property at the end of the lease term is
> approximately equal to the market value; (2) rentals are intended
> to compensate the lessor for loss of value over the lease term due
> to aging or wear and tear; (3) rentals are reasonable, and the
> purchase-option price at the end of the lease term is not too low; (4)
> lessee is not acquiring any equity in the goods during the term of
> the lease. Factors indicative of a disguised secured transaction
> include: (1) lessee pays taxes, insurance, and bears risk of loss; (2)
> the lease contains default provisions governing acceleration and
> resale; (3) a substantial non-refundable deposit is required; (4)
> goods are to be selected from a third party by the lessee; (5) rental
> payments approximately equal the cost of the property plus
> interest; (6) the lessor lacks the facilities to store or retake the
> goods; (7) the lease is discounted with a bank; (8) warranties are
> disclaimed; [and] (9) lessee pays sales tax incident to acquiring the
> property. *Id.* at 586.

- Under 1-203, which factors remain relevant to whether a transaction is a lease or a disguised security interest?

Problem 2: Consider these facts: The lease at issue is for a 1991 Toyota 4WD Deluxe ExtraCab Pickup. The lease has a term of five years and calls for 60 monthly payments of $323.82. The debtor could become the owner of the vehicle at the end of the lease term for $5,390.00, which the lease defines as both the "Purchase Option Price" and the "Estimated Residual Value." The debtor contends this amount undervalues the vehicle. The debtor presented copies of the current Blue Book, which indicates a five-year-old Toyota pickup with comparable options and mileage has an average retail value of $8,275.00. Based on this, debtor argues the vehicle will have an expected value at lease termination of at least $8,275.00.

- Is this most likely a secured sale or a lease?

- Does your answer change if the debtor maintained the truck particularly well, such that it is worth more than $5,390 at the end of the lease term?

Based on *In re Zaleha*, 159 B.R. 581, 23 U.C.C. Rep. Serv. 1035 (Bankr. D. Idaho 1993).

Efficiency and Justice Concerns

This textbook raises issues of efficiency and justice in its materials on sales and negotiable instruments. The law of secured transactions raises its own such concerns. The following excerpt from Professor Steven Schwarcz, *The Easy Case for the Priority of Secured Claims in Bankruptcy*, 47 Duke L.J. 425 (1997), describes some pertinent efficiency concerns:

> The secured-credit controversy started when law-and-economics scholars applied the classic Modigliani-Miller hypothesis to secured lending. The Modigliani-Miller hypothesis maintains that, in a perfect universe, every savings achieved by a change in one part of a company's capital structure will result in an offsetting of costs to other parts of the capital structure. A logical corollary of that hypothesis is that, unless the universe is imperfect, changes made to a debtor-company's capital structure to benefit the debtor and a particular class of holders of claims or interests in the debtor could take value away from other classes of holders of such claims or interests. Applying this hypothesis to secured lending, law-and-economics scholars initially assumed that unsecured creditors would raise their rates in response to the debtor's granting of collateral to others.

The hypothesis is named for Franco Modigliani and Merton Miller, both economists.

[The assumption was that] secured creditors will charge lower interest rates because security reduces their risks, but unsecured creditors will raise their interest rates in response because security reduces the assets on which they can levy, and so increases their risks. The interest-rate reductions are precisely matched by interest-rate increases; hence, the firm makes no net gain from granting security. However, those scholars later realized that, outside of a perfect universe, many creditors are nonadjusting and cannot raise their rates to compensate for the increased risk. Secured credit then benefits the debtor by lowering the risk and therefore the interest rate that the debtor must pay on secured credit; but that saving to the debtor can result in an uncompensated increase in risk to nonadjusting creditors.

> What factors might explain why "many creditors are nonadjusting"?

. . . [T]he . . . scholarly works addressing the secured-debt controversy are incomplete because they fail to recognize that the most important form of secured debt, where lenders offer new money in return for collateral ("new-money secured credit"), tends to create value for unsecured creditors as well as for the debtor. New-money secured credit . . . must be distinguished from situations where the debtor grants security for existing debt. In the latter case, "the granting of security reduces the assets on which the remaining unsecured creditors can levy and thereby increases the risk for such unsecured creditors." New-money secured credit, in contrast, does not necessarily reduce the assets on which unsecured creditors can levy because the debtor receives the loan proceeds. More importantly, the availability of new-money secured credit reduces the risk that the debtor will go bankrupt by increasing a debtor's liquidity, and therefore increases the expected value of unsecured claims.

Commentators have missed this last point because they have failed also to realize that, in an imperfect universe, there is a difference between the use of secured credit and the availability (and use only if needed) of secured credit. As a result, previous models of secured debt assume that a debtor that can borrow on an unsecured basis would prefer to borrow on a secured basis to reduce interest cost. However, that assumption is inconsistent with the expected behavior of an economically rational debtor, as well as the experience of actual debtors. *Id.* at 429-431.

- What distinction is the author drawing between "new money" and other secured credit?

- When does a debtor not receive "new money" in a secured-credit transaction?

- Why might a debtor prefer to borrow on an unsecured basis?

The following excerpt from Robert E. Scott, *The Truth About Secured Financing*, 82 Cornell L. Rev. 1436 (1997), introduces some justice concerns, insofar as they relate to the rights of creditors:

[The secured-financing] debate reflects two separate normative claims. The first is a fairness concern stimulated by the evidence of significant redistribution in debt financing. This objection rests on the claim that secured debt redistributes wealth in the wrong direction. Sophisticated lenders, such as banks and finance companies, will know of the existence of security. These creditors can (and do) protect themselves against the issuance of secured debt through the interest rates they charge, or they share in the gains that security generates by forcing the debtor to split the pie. Creditors who are unlikely to know of the existence of security or unable to protect themselves against it include employees with wage claims, consumer purchasers who have warranty contracts with the debtor, actual and potential tort claimants, and small suppliers. The existence of secured debt may disadvantage all of these creditors. Hence, to the extent that the distributional story holds, security tends to redistribute wealth from the relatively poor and uninformed to the rich and sophisticated. Shifting wealth in this direction is contrary to prevailing redistributional theories.

> What is meant by this paragraph's descriptions of how creditors protect themselves?

Concerns about regressive redistribution are influenced largely by the degree to which unsophisticated creditors are adequately informed of these additional risks through the Article 9 filing system, Article 9's chief vehicle for overcoming information asymmetries. *Id.* at 1463.

- How might secured credit raise social-justice concerns?

- How does a filing system "overcom[e] information asymmetries"?

International Perspective: Current Initiatives

International secured-transactions law has been somewhat less successful than efforts in the area of international sales, and somewhat more successful than efforts involving international payment systems. One United Nations convention is currently in force, and two others may join its ranks at a future date. The United Nations Convention on International Interests in Mobile Equipment was adopted on November 16, 2001, and entered into force on April 1, 2004. The Protocol to the Convention on International Interests in Mobile Equipment on Matters Specific to Aircraft Equipment was adopted the same day and came into force on March 1, 2006. The United Nations Convention on the Assignment of Receivables in International Trade was adopted on December 12, 2001, and has not entered into force.

> The Convention can be found online at www.unidroit.org/english/conventions/mobile-equipment/main.htm. "Mobile equipment," as defined in Article 2 (3) of the Convention, includes "airframes, aircraft engines, and helicopters," "railway rolling stock," and "space assets." What do these kinds of collateral have in common?

The United Nations Convention on International Interests in Mobile Equipment, also called the "Cape Town Convention," has a different mission from some other instruments of

international law, as illustrated by the following excerpt from
Professor Iwan Davies, *The New Lex Mercatoria: International
Interests in Mobile Equipment*, 52 Intl. & Comp. L.Q. 151
(2003):

> The Cape Town Convention . . . is not "ecumenical" in the sense
> that it represents a harmonization of laws of different legal
> systems and jurisdictions.   Harmonization as a model for law
> reform embraces diversity in that what is sought in the process of
> harmonization is the making of regulatory requirements of
> different jurisdictions similar.   Essentially, it is a normative
> assertion that the differences in the laws and policies of (at least)
> two jurisdictions should be reduced. The main characteristic of
> harmonization is that it eschews uniformity and preserves the
> diversity of the laws harmonized. What is seen in the Cape Town
> Convention is not a type of harmonization process, but rather a
> unification-of-laws process. The significance of the Cape Town
> Convention is that it cuts new ground in international commercial
> law by establishing a substantive legal regime of international
> secured-credit law. As such, it is not concerned with promoting
> merely an international commercial standard or practice . . .
> Neither is the Convention concerned with a sui generis form of
> commercial instrument. *Id.* at 153.

- How is the word "ecumenical" used in this excerpt, and
  how is the Cape Town Convention "not ecumenical,"
  according to Professor Davies?

- According to this excerpt, how is the Cape Town
  Convention different from an initiative that seeks to
  establish "merely an international commercial
  standard or practice"?

- What international convention presented in this
  textbook is "concerned with a sui generis form of
  commercial instrument"?

The international community has also developed regional
instruments.   The European Bank for Reconstruction and
Development (EBRD) published a Model Law on Secured
Transactions in 1994, based upon research into the practices of
26 countries served by the EBRD. The Asian Development
Bank (ADB) completed a similar project in 2001, based on
research exploring the law of 5 Asian countries. The Model
Inter-American Law on Secured Transactions, based on
research that began in 1992, compared and harmonized
Mexican, Central American, and South American law and
practices in secured transactions with those of the United
States and Canada.   The Organization of American States
(OAS) approved the draft Model Law in 2002.

B. Types of Collateral

The Code recognizes three categories of collateral, each with several subparts: goods, quasi-tangible property, and intangible property.

Read 9-102 (a) (23), (33), (34), (44), (48), and Comment 4 (a). "Goods" includes consumer goods, equipment, farm products, and inventory.

- Which of the four subcategories is the catch-all classification for goods not within one of the other three?

- What is the distinction between equipment and inventory?

Read 9-102 (a) (41), and 9-334 and Comments 3 and 4. One common source of litigation is whether personal property has become a "fixture" such that it is part of real property. Even when the property has become a fixture, a security interest may be created and perfected as provided in 9-334. When property becomes a fixture is governed by other law. *In re Cliff's Ridge Skiing Corp.*, 123 B.R. 753, 13 U.C.C. Rep. Serv. 2d 1309 (Bankr. N.D. Mich. 1991), demonstrates how one state has addressed the matter:

> In Michigan, whether personal property becomes a fixture and thereby part of realty is determined by a three-part test: (1) is the property annexed or attached to the realty, (2) is the attached property adapted or applied to the use of the realty, and (3) is it intended that the property will be permanently attached to the realty? *Id.* at 759.

- What peculiar problems arise with fixtures that justify the Code's addressing this type of collateral with particularity?

Students sometimes struggle to differentiate the various types of collateral. In *The Language of the Uniform Commercial Code*, 77 Yale L.J. 185 (1967), Professor David Mellinkoff minces no words in stating his perception of the Code's definition of one category of goods collateral, "farm products":

> [T]he UCC definition of *farm products* distorts the common understanding of the language, as distinguished from merely giving special application to words of variable content. Goods are classified as *farm products*, for example, if they are "supplies *used* or *produced* in farming operations." Thus, something may be a UCC *farm product* even though it is *used*, rather than *produced*, in "farming operations"; indeed, even though it is an English

language *product* of an oil well or a salt mine rather than a *farm*. For purposes of classifying security for a loan, it may be desirable to treat gasoline or salt used in farming operations in the same category with anything else that a farmer can borrow on, but it is not necessary to scuttle the English language in order to do so. When we run out of words or imagination, it will be better to join the telephone company in the candid confusion of digits than to pretend it is still English we are writing. *Id.* at 199.

- Would a different label address Professor Mellinkoff's concerns?

Read 9-102 (a) (11), (30), (47), (49), (51), and Comment 5 (b), (c), and (e). Quasi-tangible property includes chattel paper, documents, instruments, investment property, and letter-of-credit rights.

- What is the difference between tangible and quasi-tangible property?

- What other Articles govern quasi-tangible collateral?

Read 3-104 (b) as needed to answer this question.

- What is the distinction between an Article 9 "instrument" and an Article 3 "instrument"?

Read 9-102 (a) (2), (13), (29), (42), and Comment 5 (a), (d), and (g). Intangible property includes accounts, commercial tort claims, deposit accounts, and general intangibles.

- What is the distinction between quasi-tangible and intangible property?

As 9-109 (d) (12) and Comment 15 indicate, some tort claims are excluded from Article 9 entirely.

- What claims would be included in and excluded from the category "commercial tort claims"?

- How would you classify a trademark for Article 9 purposes?

To figure out the nature of collateral, look at how the user says he or she will use it. Generally, the creditor can take the user at his word, even if the user lies – unless the creditor has reason to know about the user's dishonesty. Also, even if the use changes, collateral will be classified according to the use declared when the security interest in the collateral attached. Farm products can change into inventory when they go through a manufacturing process. Except for farm products, collateral will not change from one category to another while in the hands of a single user.

The fact that there is not necessarily an "inherent" classification for a given kind of collateral is illustrated in *Morgan County Feeders, Inc. v. McCormick*, 836 P.2d 1051, 18 UCC Rep. Serv. 2d 632 (Colo. App. Div. 3, 1992), in which the court considered the appropriate classification for cattle that were used for "recreational cattle drives" and would thus be used for a longer period of time than cows purchased as "feeders." For this reason, the court held the cattle were "equipment," rather than "inventory," which would be the classification for cattle used for most ranching purposes. The court acknowledged this classification of cattle was unusual, but decided the unique circumstances of the case militated in favor of classifying the cattle as equipment.

■ How would you categorize an automobile in each situation?

- In pieces in a manufacturer's factory, awaiting assembly;
- On a dealer's showroom floor, awaiting sale;
- In a consumer's possession, driven as a company car;
- In a consumer's possession, driven for household purposes.

■ How would you categorize an egg in each situation?

- Freshly laid, ready to be gathered;
- On a grocer's shelf, awaiting sale;
- In a restaurant refrigerator, ready to become an omelet;
- In a consumer's refrigerator, ready to become an omelet.

The following case illustrates the detailed analysis a court may undertake to determine the nature of collateral. The case also shows how classification of collateral may affect the parties' legal rights by affecting how a security interest in such collateral is to be perfected.

> Perfection, which is covered in depth in Chapter 15, is the process by which a secured creditor seeks to establish its rights against third parties claiming an interest in the same property.

In re Newman,
993 F.2d 90, 20 U.C.C. Rep. Serv. 2d 1377 (5th Cir. 1993).

Reynaldo G. Garza, Circuit Judge.

West Loop [Savings Association] is a creditor in [Bobby Lynn] Newman's bankruptcy. West Loop had loaned Newman an amount in excess of $166,000. As security for the loan, West Loop received an assignment of an annuity contract issued by Manufacturers Life

Insurance Company. However, West Loop neglected to file a financing statement with the Texas Secretary of State.

Read 11 USC § 544. What was the trustee seeking to accomplish?

This action started when appellee Knostman, the trustee, filed an adversary proceeding in the bankruptcy court under Section 544 of the Bankruptcy Code. While it was undisputed that West Loop held a security interest in the annuity, it was disputed as to whether West Loop had perfected its security interest in the annuity.

* * *

The only issue to be confronted on appeal is: did West Loop perfect its security interest in the annuity contract it received from the debtor, Newman. This issue reduces to the classification of the annuity contract. If the contract is an instrument, then West Loop perfected its security interest in the annuity [by possession]; however, if the contract is a general intangible, then West Loop did not perfect its security interest. We find that the contract is a general intangible and, thus, West Loop had to file a financing statement with the secretary of state in order to perfect its security interest. As a result of West Loop's failure to file a financing statement, they now hold an unsecured interest in the annuity.

Read UCC 9-102 (a) (42) to see how this description comports with the Code definition.

* * *

The UCC defines a general intangible merely by stating what is not a general intangible. A general intangible is essentially a bundle of rights such as those inherent in a franchise, a chose in action, a copyright, or an annuity.

The term "general intangibles" brings under this Article miscellaneous types of contractual rights and other personal property which are used or may become customarily used as commercial security. Note that this catch-all definition does not apply to money or other types of intangibles that are specifically excluded from the coverage of the Article under Section 9-104.

The current reference is to UCC 9-109 (d).

... Uniform Commercial Code provision 9-104 excludes twelve types of transactions from the scope of Article 9. Section 9-104's exclusions fall generally under three main categories: (i) transactions that are subject to overriding governmental interests; (ii) transactions that are nonconsensual; and (iii) transactions that are out of the mainstream of commercial financing.

Read 9-102 Comment 5 (a) and (d). What is the difference between an account and a general intangible such as a payment intangible?

There is a dearth of case law on the classification of general intangibles. In fact, most of the cases focus on the difference between an account and a general intangible.

Perhaps the only substantive confrontation with the instrument versus general intangible classification occurred in [*In re*] *Coral Petroleum*, [*Inc.*] 50 B.R. [830, 42 U.C.C. Rep. Serv. 1001 (Bankr. D. Tex. 1985)]. In *Coral Petroleum*, Bankruptcy Judge Manuel Leal concluded that a promissory note was an instrument. Interestingly, the creditor in *Coral Petroleum* sought to have the note classified as a general intangible in order to have a perfected security interest because it did not possess the note, but had filed a financing statement. Conversely, herein West

Loop seeks to have the annuity classified as an instrument because it has possession, but did not file a financing statement. [FN7]

> FN7. If collateral is classified as an instrument, then the only way to perfect is to take possession via a pledge. On the other hand, if collateral is classified as a general intangible, then the only way to perfect is to file a financing statement. This case painfully illustrates the problems that creditors encounter when they fail to account for Article 9 problems. The best practice in cases where a precise categorization is elusive, would be to comply with both requirements. . . .

Why do creditors not always simply comply with all potential requirements when classification is uncertain?

Coral Petroleum approached the problem in a pragmatic manner. The court concluded that the test for determining whether a writing is transferable in the ordinary course of business [and is thus an instrument rather than a general intangible] hinges on what professionals would ordinarily do to transfer such an interest. The court reasoned that, if professionals would attach significance to possession of the writing and treat certain collateral as an instrument, then the law should likewise treat the collateral similarly.

After carefully reviewing the record, we find no indication that this or any other annuity is transferred in the regular course of business by endorsement. In an instance such as this, where precise categorization is unclear, it seems to this court that a finding of general intangible is warranted. The cases indicate that collateral such as certificates of deposit and promissory notes are instruments because professionals attach significance to their possession. However, interests such as Keogh Plans and the contractual right to receive insurance are treated as general intangibles because they are not customarily transferred by delivery with endorsement. These annuities are general intangibles because based upon the "reasonable professional standard" outlined in *Coral Petroleum* there is no indication that they are regularly traded by delivery or that possession of the annuity certificate confers the right to payment.

How does your study of Articles 3 and 4 inform your understanding of this paragraph? **Read 9-102 Comment 5 (c)** *to see where it addresses this matter.*

Keogh Plans are retirement-savings plans for self-employed persons.

In a vacuum, if left to formulate our own test for distinguishing between a general intangible and an instrument, our benchmark would begin with the definition of an instrument. Section 9-105 (a) (9) defines an "instrument" as "any other writing which evidences a right to the payment of money and is not itself a security agreement or lease and is of a type of which is in the ordinary course of business transferred by delivery with any necessary indorsement or assignment." Because the annuity contract in question: (i) does not evidence a right to payment on its face; and (ii) is not ordinarily transferred by delivery, it is not an instrument.

The current reference is to 9-102 (a) (47) and has been slightly modified from the language quoted here.

Further, it appears from the face of the contract that possession alone is not enough to confer the right to payment. The Certificate reads:

> Protection of Payments. If you choose someone other than yourself to receive payments, that payee cannot commute, assign, or encumber the payments unless that right was granted when the payee was chosen. The same is true if the beneficiary chooses someone else to receive the payments.

The trustee contends, and we agree, that based upon this language, possession is irrelevant to the right to receive payments. The trustee also asserts that the certificate expressly contemplates that persons other than the owner of the annuity contract, or the possessor of the certificate, may receive payments. This contention is buttressed by reading the provision entitled "currency and place of payment," which conspicuously omits any requirement of possession. We agree with the lower court and conclude that possession of the certificate alone does not convey the right to receive payments.

* * *

The annuity contract that Newman assigned to West Loop was a general intangible. The annuity contract is a general intangible principally because, after applying the reasonable-professional test outlined in *Coral Petroleum*, we conclude that professionals do not attach significance to the possession of the annuity certificate itself. Moreover, the language of the annuity contract does not contemplate that the annuity is an instrument. Consequently, we find that West Loop holds an unperfected security interest in the annuity contract, and we affirm the district court's summary judgment in favor of the trustee.

▪   What are each of the court's justifications for its holding?

Note 1: Read 9-102 Comment 4 (a). *In re Ripley Oil Co., Inc.*, 71 B.R. 631, 3 U.C.C. Rep. Serv. 2d 1126 (Bankr. S.D. Ohio 1987), illustrates how one court determined whether collateral was equipment or inventory:

> The debtor was a retail distributor of petroleum products located in a rural area of southern Ohio. The goods which are the subject of this dispute are some 520 oil tanks and pumps which [the] debtor loaned to its farm customers as storage facilities for the fuel [the] debtor sold them. In order to obtain a storage tank, the customer was usually required to sign an "equipment agreement" which in essence stated that the tank was being loaned to the "borrower," that the tank remained the personal property of the debtor, and that it could be removed by the debtor upon termination of the agreement or at any other time the debtor saw fit.
>
> On September 14, 1983, Citizens National loaned the debtor $60,000 and obtained a security interest on "all accounts receivable and inventory" of the debtor. Citizens National asserts that the oil tanks constitute "inventory" and accordingly that the trustee should abandon them under 11 USC § 554. The trustee counters that they are equipment, and thus not subject to Citizens National's security interest.

Read 11 USC § 554. Why might abandonment be a practical decision?

* * *

1
2
3
4
5
6
7
8
9
10
11
12
13
14
15
16
17
18
19
20
21
22
23
24
25
26
27
28
29
30
31
32
33
34
35
36
37
38
39
40
41
42
43
44
45
46
50
51
52
53

Our review of the facts and the essential elements of the statute leads us to conclude that the tanks fall within the category of equipment, not inventory. The debtor never held these goods for sale, either in the ordinary course of business or otherwise, since no title was passed from a seller to a buyer for a price. To the contrary, both the debtor and the customers intended that title to the tanks would remain in the debtor. *Id.* at 631.

This case also provides a review of the lease principles introduced in Part A of this chapter:

> [T]he arrangement between the debtor and its customers did not have the essential attributes of a lease. The customer did not have exclusive rights to dominion and control of the tanks, there was no definite term of possession, and there was no rental or other cash payment made by the customers in exchange for use and possession.
>
> The relationship between the debtor and its customers is most properly characterized as a bailment for the mutual benefit of the parties. The customer obviously benefitted from having the tank loaned to him by the debtor, because it obviated the need to buy one; the benefit to the debtor was equally obvious, because it facilitated the sale of oil. *Id.* at 632.

Note 2: The term "securitization" is commonly found in Article 9 literature. In *The Impact on Securitization of Revised UCC Article 9*, 74 Chi.-Kent L. Rev. 947 (1999), Professor Steven Schwarcz describes securitization as follows:

> Asset securitization is "by far the most rapidly growing segment of the U.S. credit markets" and increasingly is becoming a major part of foreign credit markets. In a typical securitization, a company (usually referred to as the "originator") sells rights in income-producing or financial assets – such as accounts, instruments, lease rentals, franchise and license fees, and other intangible rights to payment – to a special purpose vehicle ("SPV"). The SPV, in turn, issues securities to capital-market investors and uses the proceeds of the issuance to pay for the assets. The investors, who are repaid from collections of the assets, buy the securities based on their assessment of the value of the assets. Because the SPV (and no longer the originator) owns the assets, their investment decision often can be made without concern for the originator's financial condition. Thus, viable companies that otherwise cannot obtain financing because of a weakened financial condition now can do so. Even companies that otherwise could obtain financing now will be able to obtain lower-cost capital-market financing.

> "Bankruptcy-remoteness" is a key attribute of the SPV; that is, if the company becomes insolvent, the SPV will not be part of the estate administered in bankruptcy.

> * * *

> . . . Revised Article 9 will apply to securitization transactions so long as the financial assets being sold consist of accounts (including credit-card, health-care-insurance, license, and

franchise-fee receivables), chattel paper, promissory notes, or payment intangibles. *Id.* at 948, 950.

- How does securitization help the originator obtain financing?

International Perspective: Types of Collateral

Article 9 includes no express limitation on the collateral that may support a secured transaction. Instead, parties may fashion for themselves transactions involving collateral not contemplated by the drafters. As the following excerpt from Professor Jonathan Lipson's article *Secrets and Liens: The End of Notice in Commercial Finance Law*, 21 Emory Bankr. Dev. J. 421 (2005), shows, the civil-law tradition takes a different approach, called *numerus clausus*, that limits the classes of collateral to those provided by statute:

Professor Lipson refers, throughout the excerpt, to the work of Professors Thomas W. Merrill and Henry E. Smith. Merrill and Smith have explored in depth the principle of numerus clausus, from the standpoint of economic efficiency. One influential article of theirs is *Optimal Standardization in the Laws of Property: The Numerus Clausus Principle*, 110 Yale L.J. 1 (2000).

> Neoclassical views about the notice function of property are rooted in the "numerus clausus," the idea that property rights come in a fixed and closed number of forms.
>
> The numerus clausus appears to be a well-articulated feature of many civil-law jurisdictions. In the common law, however, its role is more opaque. Although courts and lawyers are characterized as hostile to the numerus clausus, [Professors Thomas W.] Merrill and [Henry E.] Smith contend they "routinely abide by the principle, even if they are unaware of its existence." For example, as to estates in land, "courts enforce the numerus clausus principle strictly. . . . The menu of forms is regarded as complete and not subject to additions." . . .
>
> The principal explanation for the sub rosa vitality of the numerus clausus is economic, oriented around the inefficiency that stems from the excessive fragmentation of rights or rights holders. Merrill and Smith take the economic explanation one step further, arguing that we restrict property forms not out of concerns about fragmentation, per se, but about information costs associated with the creation of excessively idiosyncratic property rights ("fancies"). Thus, Merrill and Smith believe that the need for the numerus clausus "stems from an externality involving measurement costs: Parties who create new property rights will not take into account the full magnitude of the measurement costs they impose on strangers to the title."
>
> The information costs of idiosyncratic property forms explain for Merrill and Smith the underlying basis of the numerus clausus. "One way to control the external costs of measurement to third parties is through compulsory standardization of property rights." . . . Limiting the number of basic property forms allows a market participant or a potential violator to limit his or her inquiry to

whether the interest does or does not have the features of the forms on the menu. Fancies not on the closed list need not be considered because they will not be enforced. When it comes to the basic legal dimensions of property, limiting the number of forms thus makes the determination of their nature less costly. The "good" in question here might be considered to be the prevention of error in ascertaining the attributes of property rights. Standardization means less measurement is required to achieve a given amount of error prevention. Alternatively, one can say that standardization increases the productivity of any given level of measurement efforts. There is, on this view, an "optimal" number of property forms, and this number is determined by the information costs associated with excessively idiosyncratic forms of property. On the one hand, costs in error and measurement would be lowest . . . in a highly regimented system, which recognizes only a single, simple form of property, such as the fee simple absolute. However, frustration costs arising from stymied creativity would be quite high. On the other hand, a system of unfettered customization of property forms – pure contract – may have low frustration costs – it is difficult to be frustrated if the law recognizes anything you do – but high costs of verification and measurement. Both the parties that created the fancy, and others who might try to discover what it is and what rights are held in it, will expend large sums in ascertaining and managing these rights. The social cost of limitless customization of property rights is simply too great. The optimal level of customization – the number and type of fancies permitted by the numerus clausus – is somewhere in between and should result in the lowest information cost. *Id.* at 493-496.

- In Professor Lipson's view, what is the relative influence of the concept of "numerus clausus" on common-law and civil-law secured transactions?

- What are some risks and benefits of a "closed list" system?

C. Types of Creditors

This section introduces the concepts of secured and unsecured creditors and the importance of priority. This section also explains the basic relationship between Article 9 and the law of bankruptcy.

The advantages of secured credit become clear when the debtor faces bankruptcy, and creditors are competing for satisfaction of their claims. 11 USC § 544 gives the bankruptcy trustee the status of a lien creditor, capable of exercising the power of general levy over the debtor's entire estate. The trustee exercises this power for the benefit of all unsecured creditors.

Pursuant to 9-317 (a) (2), this power gives the trustee (and thus the unsecured creditors) priority over any security interest perfected after the date of the bankruptcy petition. A secured creditor with a high-priority claim is much more likely than an unsecured creditor, or a secured creditor with a lower-priority claim, to recover most or all of the amount owed from a debtor with limited resources. Under 11 USC § 544, the bankruptcy trustee also has the power to set aside certain pre-bankruptcy-petition transfers if the debtor has given a preference to one creditor while disadvantaging others in a way that is inconsistent with bankruptcy law's goal of equitable distribution of assets.

Knox v. Phoenix Leasing, Inc., 35 Cal. Rptr. 2d 141, 24 U.C.C. Rep. Serv. 2d 1049 (Cal. App. 1st Dist. 1994), explains some advantages of secured credit from the point of view of the creditor, together with some principles that operate to protect the debtor. As Chapter 16 shows and the previous paragraph suggested, some secured parties enjoy priority over others. One creditor with preferential status who will feature prominently in these materials is a secured party holding a purchase-money security interest or "PMSI."

The concepts presented will be discussed comprehensively in Chapter 16, Priorities.

A secured creditor which has complied with all relevant code requirements to perfect its security interest, . . . [starts] with something like a presumption in its favor. The whole point of Article 9 is to establish a comprehensive scheme affording maximum protection to the secured creditor who has followed its provisions. This does not, of course, guarantee payment in full. Even a secured creditor which has perfected its security interest may be subordinated to another of like status which is chronologically senior, or to other specified classes of creditors, the most prominent of which are those having a purchase-money security interest. But, having taken the trouble to satisfy all statutory requirements for protecting its interest, a secured creditor is entitled to a rebuttable preference for payment as against a creditor who has not demonstrated a similar compliance.

This preference would be reinforced by the failure of the unsecured creditor to use various nonstatutory protections. As courts and commentators have noted, the unsecured creditor could have (1) demanded cash payment on delivery, (2) perfected a purchase-money security interest, (3) checked with the appropriate governmental office to determine if the debtor had already granted a security interest posing a possible threat to repayment, or (4) obtained a secured creditor's agreement to subordinate its priority. *Id.* at 1364.

Read 9-339 and Comment 2, which address subordination agreements. This concept is found in Chapter 16, Part C.

- ▪ **Read 9-103 (b) and Comment 3.** Why, as a matter of policy, would it make sense that a "PMSI" creditor would normally enjoy priority of interest over other secured creditors?

Professor Ronald Mann's article *Explaining the Pattern of Secured Credit*, 110 Harv. L. Rev. 625 (1997), describes some of the benefits and burdens of secured credit, insofar as the borrower is concerned:

> Granting collateral lowers the aggregate costs of a lending transaction by lowering the pre-loan perception of the risk of default. Secured credit can do this not only by increasing the lender's ability to collect the debt forcibly through liquidation of the collateral, but also in less direct ways: by decreasing the borrower's ability to obtain subsequent loans; by increasing the lender's leverage over the borrower's activities; and by repairing the loan-induced differentiation of the incentives of the borrower and the lender. Conversely, a grant of collateral can increase the costs of a lending transaction by increasing the costs of entering the transaction as well as the costs of administering the loan. *Id.* at 626.

- How does secured credit both increase and decrease the costs of a loan transaction?

Given the advantages of secured credit for both borrowers and lenders, this kind of financing has become an important part of commercial transactions in this country for businesses and consumers alike. Even so, in his article *The Role of Secured Credit in Small-Business Lending*, 86 Geo. L.J. 1 (1997), Professor Ronald Mann predicts that the secured lending will become less dominant in the business context:

> Professor Mann's article was published before Revised Article 9 became effective. It may be interesting to consider whether the revisions have reduced Article 9 transaction costs sufficiently to respond to some of the concerns he raises.

> All things must pass. Economic and legal institutions – including secured credit and the institutions that make it useful – are no exception. Good reasons justified the broad acceptance of secured lending during the last half of this century. The simplification and unification of the legal rules by Article 9 of the UCC facilitated that acceptance. But there is nothing inevitable about the widespread use of secured credit. Like all other law-supported institutions, it will become less useful if the businesses that use it can devise other transactions that work more cheaply than the law-supported transaction. And the ability of businesses to devise new transactional forms accelerates whenever new technology limits the comparative advantage of the law-supported transaction. In the secured-credit area, the widespread use of the guaranty and the tremendous advances in the technology for acquiring and evaluating information have undermined the traditional advantages of secured credit.

> The accommodation parties addressed in 3-419 and discussed in Chapter 11, Part A, provide one form of "guaranty."

> To put it all together, I see the pattern of secured and unsecured credit dividing the market for business loans into three segments. The first segment is the small-business segment. . . . That segment will be characterized increasingly by unsecured lending, with pockets of secured lending for particularly liquid or stable collateral like motor vehicles and real estate. The upper boundary

of that segment will be the lower boundary of the second, middle-market segment.

The middle-market segment will be characterized by predominantly secured lending. The boundary between those segments will be defined by transaction-cost concerns related to size: the point at which the economies of scale of larger transactions justify the more time-intensive practices that make secured credit useful. It is difficult to predict how that boundary will move over time. The boundary might fall if technological advances decrease the costs of the more time-intensive practices. Conversely, the boundary might rise as . . . technologies . . . increase in efficiency and thus decrease the relative attractiveness of secured credit even more than they have already.

The final segment is the large-company segment, which is characterized by unsecured lending, with pockets of secured lending by large companies that have less impressive credit strength. . . . [T]he boundary between the middle-market and large-company segments is defined not by the kinds of transaction-cost concerns that separate the first two segments. Rather, it is defined by a different type of economy of scale – the point in size of firms at which firms generally exhibit the credit strength that makes secured credit a futile exercise. Although I have no empirical support for my view, I expect that boundary to fall over time, as increasing sophistication in underwriting enhances the ability of ever-smaller firms to gain access to public debt and equity markets. With access to public capital markets, firms can more quickly exhibit the strong reputation for financial strength that leads to predominantly unsecured lending. *Id.* at 44.

- What social, economic, or other factors, if proven, would tend to support Professor Mann's thesis? What factors would tend to refute his thesis?

- How do rising and falling interest rates affect Professor Mann's thesis?

- Why is secured credit arguably a "futile exercise" for the large companies Professor Mann describes?

International Perspective: Security Interests

In *Secured Transactions in Poland: Practicable Rules, Unworkable Monstrosities, and Pending Reforms,* 17 Hastings Intl. & Comp. L. Rev. 389 (Winter 1994), Lech Choroszucha describes various classifications of security interests under Roman law and shows how these have influenced the civil tradition. This excerpt also ties in the concept of *numerus clausus*, introduced in Part B of this chapter.

The civilian concept of real security is that the debtor grants the creditor ownership, possession, or a limited right (*ius in re aliena*) in the debtor's property, which serves as security for the debt. Real security differs from personal security, such as suretyship or guarantee, which is based on a purely contractual obligation of the debtor to repay the loan. A security interest gives the creditor, as a secured party, priority over the debtor's personal creditors. The creditor may seek satisfaction for a credit up to the amount of the value of the property encumbered.

> "Ius in re aliena" describes a right in property owned by another person.

* * *

Roman law classified the limited rights in re into personal servitudes, real servitudes, and security interests. Taking security for a loan was common in ancient Rome, and three types of real security were developed. The first to develop was *fiducia*. Fiducia required the transfer of ownership to the creditor. This transfer had important consequences for the relative positions of the creditor and the debtor, with the former enjoying a significant level of protection, including a right to sell the collateral upon default. The position of the debtor, on the other hand, was weak; since he relinquished his ownership, the debtor could not establish a second encumbrance on the property and had to rely on retransfer when the debt was paid. However, the debtor was usually allowed to retain possession of the collateral.

Fiducia was eventually replaced by *pignus*, which gave the creditor actual possession of the collateral but not its ownership. Upon repayment of the debt, the pledgor's interest was protected by *rei vindicatio*, an action available to the owner to reclaim his ownership. In case of default, the creditor could sell the collateral, but only if the contract between the parties so provided. Since the creditor's limited property right was conceptualized as ius in re aliena, the secured party could not dispose of the collateral short of a specific contractual proviso.

Hypotheca was the final and most advanced type of a real security interest developed by the Romans. It gave the debtor both ownership and possession of the collateral and authorized the creditor to take possession only upon default. For the debtor, it was the most advantageous form of limited property right. It gave him both the use of the collateral and the ability to encumber it with additional limited property rights. In case of default, the prior creditor had priority over the later creditor in satisfying his loans.

Roman real-security concepts permeate the laws on real security in civil law countries. The common characteristic of these laws is that a catalog of limited rights in re is strictly defined by statutes. The statutes contain an exhaustive enumeration of rights in re and generally prohibit parties from contractually expanding the scope of rights as provided for by the legislatures (*numerus clausus*). Also, the statutes define the scope of each right and determine its nature and content. Although the specific content of the limited property right can be modified, parties may do so only to the extent permitted by statute.

The pledge is the most prominent real security among the
numerus clausus of limited property rights in movable property.
Its roots are in the Roman pignus. The pledge requires a contract
between the owner and the creditor and a delivery of possession to
the creditor. The delivery requirement is a serious obstacle in
commercial secured transactions because debtors often need to use
the collateral in order to generate income required to repay the
loan. The French legislature has solved this problem by passing
statutes providing for nonpossessory security interests in the form
of equipment liens. The German law followed a different path. It
developed a fiduciary transfer of title under which the debtor may
remain in the actual possession of the collateral.

The civilian concept of a security interest in real property is based
on Roman hypotheca. Consequently, debtors retain ownership
and possession of the property but grant creditors a limited
property right that gives the creditors, upon default, a priority in
recovering their credits from the proceeds of the sale of the
charged real property. . . . *Id.* at 392-395.

- Does Article 9 generally provide a creditor with
  "ownership, possession, or a limited right . . . in the
  debtor's property"?

- What is the difference between real security and
  personal security?

- What is an example of personal security covered in
  this book?

Chapter Conclusion: This chapter provided a general
introduction to the law of secured transactions, discussing the
purposes, advantages, and challenges of secured credit, as well
as the scope of Article 9 and the various classifications of
collateral to which it applies. Leaving this chapter, you should
be comfortable with the basic Article 9 vocabulary and the
general structure of a secured transaction.

Chapter 14:
The Rights of Debtors and Secured Parties Vis-à-vis One Another

A. Creating a Security Interest

This section will discuss when a security agreement is required to create a security interest, what constitutes a sufficient security agreement, and the treatment of after-acquired collateral and future advances. A secured transaction typically involves two forms – the security agreement and the financing statement. The security agreement creates and describes the rights and obligations of a secured creditor and a debtor vis-à-vis one another. This document is a principal focus of this chapter. The financing statement, which is filed publicly to give third parties information about the security interest, is discussed in Chapter 15.

Read 9-203 and Comments 3 and 4. 9-203 describes the means by which a security interest is created and attaches under Article 9.

> Attachment of a security interest is discussed in Part B of this chapter.

- Under what circumstances can a security interest be created without an authenticated security agreement?

- **Read 9-102 (a) (7) and Comment 9 (b).** What is the difference between authentication and signature?

- What does it mean to give value within the meaning of 9-203?

- Where is "value" defined for the purposes of 9-203?

Read 9-108 and Comments 2 and 5, and 9-504 and Comment 2. 9-108 and 9-504 provide the standards for description of collateral in security agreements and financing statements, respectively.

- Compare the requirements found in each.

- What is a supergeneric description and why might it be used?

- Is such a description permissible in a security agreement?

> For each, you might also ask yourself, "Why or why not?"

- Is such a description permitted in a financing statement?

- When does description by type of collateral not suffice, and what policy motivates this limitation?

In *Thorp Commercial Corp. v. Northgate Industries, Inc.*, 654 F.2d 1245, 31 U.C.C. Rep. Serv. 801 (8th Cir. 1981), the court described the relative functions of the security agreement and financing statement:

What should a potential creditor do, upon finding a previously-filed financing statement referencing its would-be debtor, with a supergeneric collateral description, to find out what collateral is actually covered by the prior creditor's filing?

> The security agreement defines what the collateral is so that, if necessary, the creditor can identify and claim it, and the debtor or other interested parties can limit the creditor's rights in the collateral given as security. The security agreement must therefore describe the collateral. The financing statement, on the other hand, serves the purpose of putting subsequent creditors on notice that the debtor's property is encumbered. The description of collateral in the financing statement does not function to identify the collateral and define property which the creditor may claim, but rather to warn other subsequent creditors of the prior interest. The financing statement, which limits the prior creditor's rights vis-á-vis subsequent creditors, must therefore contain a description only of the type of collateral. *Id.* at 1249.

- How are the differing purposes of security agreements and financing statements reflected in the formal requirements found in 9-108 and 9-504?

Intent of the Parties

An eponymous security agreement clearly shows the parties' intent to create a secured transaction. Sometimes, intent is less clear. The following case shows how a court would analyze the parties' intent if no security agreement existed, but other documents suggested the parties intended to engage in secured financing.

In re Bollinger Corp.,
614 F.2d 924, 28 U.C.C. Rep. Serv. 289 (3d Cir. 1980)

Rosenn, Circuit Judge.

This appeal from a district-court review of an order in bankruptcy presents a question that has troubled courts since the enactment of Article 9 of the Uniform Commercial Code governing secured transactions. Can a creditor assert a secured claim against the debtor when no formal security agreement was ever signed, but where various documents executed in connection with a loan evince an intent to create a security interest? The district court answered this question in the affirmative and permitted the creditor, Zimmerman & Jansen, to assert a secured claim against the debtor, bankrupt Bollinger Corporation, in the amount of $150,000. We affirm.

The facts of this case are not in dispute. Industrial Credit Company made a loan to Bollinger Corporation on January 13, 1972, in the amount of $150,000. As evidence of the loan, Bollinger executed a promissory note in the sum of $150,000 and signed a security agreement with ICC giving it a security interest in certain machinery and equipment. ICC in due course perfected its security interest in the collateral by filing a financing statement. . . .

Bollinger faithfully met its obligations under the note and, by December 4, 1974, had repaid $85,000 of the loan, leaving $65,000 in unpaid principal. Bollinger, however, required additional capital and, on December 5, 1974, entered into a loan agreement with Zimmerman & Jansen, Inc., by which Z&J agreed to lend Bollinger $150,000. Z&J undertook as part of this transaction to pay off the $65,000 still owed to ICC in return for an assignment by ICC to Z&J of the original note and security agreement between Bollinger and ICC. Bollinger executed a promissory note to Z&J, evidencing the agreement, containing the following provision:

> Security. This Promissory Note is secured by security interests in a certain Security Agreement between Bollinger and Industrial Credit Company . . . and in a Financing Statement filed by ICC . . . and is further secured by security interests in a certain security agreement to be delivered by Bollinger to Z & J with this Promissory Note covering the identical machinery and equipment as identified in the ICC Agreement and with identical schedule attached in the principal amount of Eighty-Five Thousand Dollars ($85,000).

No formal security agreement was ever executed between Bollinger and Z&J. Z&J did, however, in connection with the promissory note, record a new financing statement signed by Bollinger containing a detailed list of the machinery and equipment originally taken as collateral by ICC for its loan to Bollinger.

Bollinger filed a petition for an arrangement under Chapter XI ['Reorganization'] of the Bankruptcy Act in March 1975 and was adjudicated bankrupt one year later. In administrating the bankrupt's estate, the receiver sold some of Bollinger's equipment but agreed that Z&J would receive a $10,000 credit on its secured claim.

Z&J asserted a secured claim against the bankrupt in the amount of $150,000, arguing that, although it never signed a security agreement with Bollinger, the parties had intended that a security interest in the sum of $150,000 be created to protect the loan. The trustee in bankruptcy conceded that the assignment to Z&J of ICC's original security agreement with Bollinger gave Z&J a secured claim in the amount of $65,000, the balance owed by Bollinger to ICC at the time of the assignment. The trustee, however, refused to recognize Z&J's asserted claim of an additional secured claim of $85,000 because of the absence of a security agreement between Bollinger and Z&J. The bankruptcy court agreed and entered judgment for Z&J in the amount of $55,000, representing a secured claim in the amount of $65,000 less $10,000 credit received by Z&J.

Applying your knowledge of Articles 3 and 4, what purpose would this assignment serve?

This case was decided under the Bankruptcy Act, which predated the Bankruptcy Code. In modern parlance, the "receiver" is called the "trustee." **Skim 11 USC § 363 (b) and (c).** Who would normally receive the proceeds of a trustee's sale?

* * *

Despite the minimal formal requirements set forth in section 9-203 for the creation of a security agreement, the commercial world has frequently neglected to comply with this simple Code provision. Soon after Article 9's enactment, creditors who had failed to obtain formal security agreements, but who nevertheless had obtained and filed financing statements, sought to enforce secured claims. Under section 9-402, a security agreement may serve as a financing statement if it is signed by both parties. The question arises whether the converse is true: Can a signed financing statement operate as a security agreement? The earliest case to consider this question was *American Card Co. v. H.M.H. Co.*, 97 R.I. 59, 196 A.2d 150, 152 (R.I. 1963), which held that a financing statement could not operate as a security agreement because there was no language granting a security interest to a creditor. Although section 9-203 (1) (b) makes no mention of such a grant-language requirement, the court in *American Card* thought that implicit in the definition of "security agreement" under section 9-105 (1) (h) was such a requirement; some grant language was necessary to "create or provide security. . . ."

> **Read UCC 9-502 Comment 4.** Is this statement still good law?

> The current reference is UCC 9-203 (b).

> The current reference is UCC 9-102 (a) (73).

The Ninth Circuit in *In re Amex-Protein Development Corp.*, 504 F.2d 1056, 15 U.C.C. Rep. Serv. 286 (9th Cir. 1974), echoed criticism by commentators of the *American Card* rule. The court wrote: "There is no support in legislative history or grammatical logic for the substitution of the word 'grant' for the phrase 'creates or provides for.'" It concluded that, as long as the financing statement contains a description of the collateral signed by the debtor, the financing statement may serve as the security agreement and the formal requirements of section 9-203 (1) (b) are met. . . .

Some courts have declined to follow the Ninth Circuit's liberal rule allowing the financing statement alone to stand as the security agreement, but have permitted the financing statement, when read in conjunction with other documents executed by the parties, to satisfy the requirements of section 9-203 (1) (b). The court in *In re Numeric Corp.*, 485 F.2d 1328, 13 U.C.C. Rep. Serv. 416 (1st Cir. 1973), held that a financing statement coupled with a board of directors' resolution revealing an intent to create a security interest were sufficient to act as a security agreement. The court concluded from its reading of the Code that there appears no need to insist upon a separate document entitled "security agreement" as a prerequisite for an otherwise valid security interest.

> This is sometimes called the "composite document" test.

A writing or writings, regardless of label, which adequately describes the collateral, carries the signature of the debtor, and establishes that in fact a security interest was agreed upon, would satisfy both the formal requirements of the statute and the policies behind it.

The court went on to hold that, "although a standard form financing statement by itself cannot be considered a security agreement, an adequate agreement can be found when a financing statement is considered together with other documents."

> **Read UCC 9-521's Uniform Form of Written Financing Statement.** Why can it not be considered a security agreement, standing alone?

More recently, the Supreme Court of Maine in *Casco Bank & Trust Co. v. Cloutier*, 398 A.2d 1224, 26 U.C.C. Rep. Serv. 499 (Me. 1979), considered the question of whether composite documents were sufficient to create a security interest within the terms of the Code. Writing for the court, Justice Wernick allowed a financing statement to be joined with a promissory note for purposes of determining whether the note contained an adequate description of the collateral to create a security agreement. The court indicated that the evidentiary and Statute-of-Frauds policies behind section 9-203 (1) (b) were satisfied by reading the note and financing statement together as the security agreement.

In the case before us, the district court went a step further and held that the promissory note executed by Bollinger in favor of Z&J, standing alone, was sufficient to act as the security agreement between the parties. In so doing, the court implicitly rejected the *American Card* rule requiring grant language before a security agreement arises under section 9-203 (1) (b). The parties have not referred to any Pennsylvania state cases on the question, and our independent research has failed to uncover any. But, although we agree that no formal grant of a security interest need exist before a security agreement arises, we do not think that the promissory note, standing alone, would be sufficient under Pennsylvania law to act as the security agreement. We believe, however, that the promissory note, read in conjunction with the financing statement duly filed and supported, as it is here, by correspondence during the course of the transaction between the parties, would be sufficient under Pennsylvania law to establish a valid security agreement.

. . . When the parties have neglected to sign a separate security agreement, it would appear that the better and more practical view is to look at the transaction as a whole in order to determine if there is a writing, or writings, signed by the debtor describing the collateral which demonstrates an intent to create a security interest in the collateral. In connection with Z&J's loan of $150,000 to Bollinger, the relevant writings to be considered are: (1) the promissory note; (2) the financing statement; [and] (3) a group of letters constituting the course of dealing between the parties. The district court focused solely on the promissory note, finding it sufficient to constitute the security agreement. Reference, however, to the language in the note reveals that the note standing alone cannot serve as the security agreement. The note recites that, along with the assigned 1972 security agreement between Bollinger and ICC, the Z&J loan is "further secured by security interests in a certain Security Agreement to be delivered by Bollinger to Z&J with this Promissory Note. . . ." The bankruptcy judge correctly reasoned that "(t)he intention to create a separate security agreement negates any inference that the debtor intended that the promissory note constitute the security agreement." At best, the note is some evidence that a security agreement was contemplated by the parties, but by its own terms, plainly indicates that it is not the security agreement.

Looking beyond the promissory note, Z&J did file a financing statement signed by Bollinger containing a detailed list of all the collateral intended to secure the $150,000 loan to Bollinger. The

> How does the court use each document to support its holding?

financing statement alone meets the basic section 9-203 (1) (b) requirements of a writing, signed by the debtor, describing the collateral. However, the financing statement provides only an inferential basis for concluding that the parties intended a security agreement. There would be little reason to file such a detailed financing statement unless the parties intended to create a security interest. The intention of the parties to create a security interest may be gleaned from the expression of future intent to create one in the promissory note and the intention of the parties as expressed in letters constituting their course of dealing.

The promissory note was executed by Bollinger in favor of Z&J in December 1974. Prior to the consummation of the loan, Z&J sent a letter to Bollinger on May 30, 1974, indicating that the loan would be made, "provided" Bollinger secured the loan by a mortgage on its machinery and equipment. Bollinger sent a letter to Z&J on September 19, 1974, indicating [as follows]:

> With your (Z&J's) stated desire to obtain security for material and funds advanced, it would appear that the use of the note would answer both our problems. Since the draft forwarded to you offers full collateralization for the funds to be advanced under it and bears normal interest during its term, it should offer you maximum security.

Subsequent to the execution of the promissory note, Bollinger sent to Z&J a list of the equipment and machinery intended as collateral under the security agreement which was to be, but never was, delivered to Z&J. In November 1975, the parties exchanged letters clarifying whether Bollinger could substitute or replace equipment in the ordinary course of business without Z&J's consent. Such a clarification would not have been necessary had a security interest not been intended by the parties. Finally, a letter of November 18, 1975, from Bollinger to Z&J indicated that "any attempted impairment of the collateral would constitute an event of default."

From the course of dealing between Z&J and Bollinger, we conclude there is sufficient evidence that the parties intended a security agreement to be created separate from the assigned ICC agreement with Bollinger. All the evidence points towards the intended creation of such an agreement and since the financing statement contains a detailed list of the collateral, signed by Bollinger, we hold that a valid Article 9 security agreement existed . . . between the parties which secured Z&J in the full amount of the loan to Bollinger.

- ■ What advice would you give to a client, insofar as 9-203 (b) is concerned, who wished to protect its interests as a secured creditor at minimal cost?

- ■ Under Revised Article 9, a financing statement need not be signed by the creditor, and a debtor who has signed a security agreement need not also sign the financing statement. How can mutual assent be established under these circumstances?

Note 1: Read 9-203, Comments 1, 3, and 5. *In re Ace Lumber Supply, Inc.*, 105 B.R. 964, 10 U.C.C. Rep. Serv. 2d 989 (Bankr. D. Mont. 1989), shows that, despite the liberalization reflected in *Bollinger*, the writing requirement endures. Ace Lumber Supply, Inc. operated a retail building supply company and purchased products from Minot Builders Supply at wholesale. By April of 1988, Ace owed Minot about $160,000, and its account was in default. On April 26, two representatives of Minot spoke with Chuck Taylor, the president of Ace, about the account. Richard Winje, Minot's vice president, took notes on the conversation, during which the parties agreed Ace could purchase from Minot only on a cash basis and would resolve the delinquencies within a few weeks.

On May 25, another conversation between the parties took place, and Winje once again took notes. This time, the parties agreed Ace would pay $35,000 per month, the account would accrue interest at 1% over the prime rate, and future purchases would be capped at $10,000 per month, with a cash discount in the event of timely payment. The parties further agreed both the delinquencies and any future purchases would be secured by the inventory, equipment, and accounts receivable of Ace. Taylor indicated no creditor had a pre-existing security interest in this collateral, and Minot's credit manager prepared a financing statement, which Taylor and a Minot representative signed. Ace made only one payment of $35,000 before filing for bankruptcy. No other documents (such as a security agreement) were executed. The evidence was clear that the parties intended to create a security interest and believed the execution of the financing statement was sufficient to do so. The referenced notes and UCC-1 financing statement are represented by the following graphics:

ACE LUMBER & SUPPLY   415PM   5-25-88

✓ UCC 1   Acct #

✓ $35,000/Month   ✓ Start $164,000

✓ 1% over prime 9 ³/⁴

✓ Cash Discount on New Purchases. We will allow if _timely_.

✓ No NSF Checks!!

✓ 3 Accounts: ACE Lbr, Remodeling CTR, VLS Mach. Staining

✓ $10,000 Combined limit over limit COD

✓ Current Fin. Stat.? Will fax Concerns – Volume, Expenses

   Chuck Comments:
   No other UCC1 @ check
   Internal problem – non profit 03 15 70
   Looking to move: affected by inventory, shrinkage no details
   _____ UCC 1 lifted after debt paid "ok"

   John, Chuck & me

"UCC-1" is a common name for a financing statement of the type found in 9-521.

This FINANCING STATEMENT is presented to a filing officer for filing pursuant to the Uniform Commercial Code		For Filing Officer (Date, Time, Number and Filing Officer)
Debtor(s) Legal (last name, first name, middle initial, and mailing address): **Ace Lumber Supply** **P.O. Box 1915** **Billings, Mt. 59103** **(Yellowstone County)** SOCIAL SECURITY NO.	Secured Party(ies) Name and address **Minot Builders Supply Assoc.** **P.O. Bos 1288** **Minot, MD 58702**	292737 SECRETARY OF STATE MONTANA 1983 July -2 AM 10-17

The financing statement covers the following types (or items) of collateral (if collateral is crops growing or to be grown which are or are to become fixtures. Describe real estate concerned and add name and address of record owner or record lessee of real estate.

All inventory now owned or hereinafter acquired

All Accounts Receivable now outstanding or hereinafter arising

All equipment now owned or hereinafter acquired

Name and Address of Assignee of Secured Party

Name and address of record owner or lessee of real estate concerned

Check [x] if covered   [xx] Proceeds of collateral are also covered   [xx] Products of collateral are also covered

Filed with

TERMINATION STATEMENT No Filing Fee

This statement of Termination of Financing is presented to a filing officer for filing pursuant to the Uniform Commercial Code. The Secured Party certifies that the Secured Party no longer claims a security interest under the Financing Statement bearing the File Number shown above.

Dated: .... 19 ....

....……..……..

By

Signature of Secured Party or Assignee of Record—Not Valid Until Signed

3) Filing Officer—Acknowledgment—Filing Officer endorse filing data on this copy and return it to the person filing as an acknowledgment.

The court addressed the legal effect of these documents as follows:

> The current UCC reference is to 9-203 (b) (3) (A).

I conclude that, under Montana law, the composite-document rule is available to provide evidentiary support to create a security interest in collateral. That rule, however, does not allow only a financing statement signed by the debtor to satisfy § 30-9-203 (1). ... Other than the financing statement signed by the Debtor, the only other writings presented by the creditor were handwritten telephone notes attached to this Order. The combination of the financing agreement and the telephone notes do not satisfy the requirements of Article 9 in that none of them contain any language creating a security interest in the collateral. As [*In re Amex-Protein Development Corp.*, 504 F.2d 1056, 15 U.C.C. Rep. Serv. 286 (9th Cir. 1974)], states:

> While there are no magic words which create a security interest there *must be language in the instrument* which "leads to the logical conclusion that it was the intention of the parties that a security interest be created." *Id.* at 1059.

> 9-203 Comment 3 may assist you in answering this question.

- How can 9-203 (b) (3) be compared to a statute of frauds?

- Is this case consistent with *Bollinger*?

Note 2: Sometimes parties become confused as to which law supplies the relevant procedures for secured financing. In *Baystate Drywall, Inc. v. Chicopee Savings Bank*, 385 Mass. 17,

429 N.E. 2d 1138 (Mass. 1982), a bank that loaned funds for the purchase of an automobile followed the recording procedures in the state certificate-of-title statute, rather than Article 9, and failed to have the debtor authenticate a security agreement as 9-203 requires. Instead, an agent signed the security agreement on the debtor's behalf. In analyzing whether the parties might nevertheless have sufficiently demonstrated an intention to create a security interest, the court held as follows:

> As Chapter 15, Part A shows, the state certificate-of-title statute would supply the relevant procedures for *perfection* of a security interest in this automobile, but not for *creation* of the interest.

> We accept the view, generally held, that a security interest in a motor vehicle cannot be created just by completing the process prescribed by a "certificate of title" statute, nor does a reference to a lien stated on a title certificate alone constitute a security agreement. A debtor need not, however, sign a document designated "security agreement" in order to satisfy the Code requirement that the debtor sign a security agreement. A combination of documents may meet that requirement.

> On the basis of these principles, we conclude that the combination of (1) the security agreement signed by [the debtor's agent with his] authority and (2) his written acknowledgment of the existence of the security interest, stated in his application for a title certificate to the motor vehicle, constituted a security agreement signed by the debtor for the purposes of permitting enforcement of the security interest in favor of the bank. There was a clear indication of the security interest both on the security agreement and on the title certificate, and the application for the title certificate was a document signed by [the debtor] acknowledging the existence of the security interest. No creditor or other third party could reasonably have been misled. Although the procedures followed by the bank are hardly recommended practices, the bank's security interest did attach and was perfected before the plaintiff acquired any rights in the motor vehicle. *Id.* at 23.

- What does this case add to *Bollinger* and *In re Ace Lumber*?

Note 3: The preceding principal case and notes showed how courts may find intent to engage in secured financing when the documentation is unclear. As a counterpoint, courts may also look beyond an apparent expression of intent to enter a security agreement and find no actual intent. *Expeditors International v. Official Creditors Committee*, 166 F.3d 1012, 37 U.C.C. Rep. Serv. 2d 475 (9th Cir. 1999), is one example. In August 1991, Expeditors International of Washington began providing freight-forwarding and other transportation-related services for Everex Systems, Inc. For 17 months before Everex filed for bankruptcy, Expeditors provided these services and was therefore in continuous possession of goods owned by Everex. Expeditors used a standard-form invoice to bill Everex for these services. During the course of the parties' business

relationship, Expeditors sent Everex about 330 invoices
containing the following fine-print language under the heading,
"Terms and Conditions of Service":

> 15. General Lien on Any Property. The Company shall have a
> general lien on any and all property (and documents relating
> thereto) of the Customer, in its possession, custody, or control, or
> en route, for all claims for charges, expenses, or advances
> incurred by the company in connection with any shipments of the
> Customer and, if such claim remains unsatisfied for thirty (30)
> days after demand for its payment is made, the Company may
> sell *at public auction or private sale, upon ten (10) days written
> notice,* sent certified or registered mail with return receipt
> requested to the Customer, the goods, wares, and/or
> merchandise, or so much thereof as may be necessary to satisfy
> such lien, and apply the net proceeds of such sale to the payment
> of the amount due to the Company. Any surplus from such sale
> shall be transmitted to the Customer, and the Customer shall be
> liable for any deficiency in the sale.
>
> 16. In any referral for collection or action against the Customer
> for monies due to the Company, upon recovery by the Company,
> the Customer shall pay the expenses of collection and/or
> litigation, including a reasonable attorney fee. *Id.* at 1014.

Everex never signed these invoices, or any other agreement
with Expeditors. The parties never discussed the fine-print
provisions of the invoices. Only within the 90 days before
Everex filed for bankruptcy did Expeditors indicate it would
enforce Sections 15 and 16 of the invoice terms. Expeditors
claimed the invoices created an enforceable security interest in
Everex's property, either under a theory of mutual assent or
based on the course of dealing between the parties. In rejecting
these arguments, the court held as follows:

> Although Expeditors appears to have met the . . . requirements
> delineated in the UCC, the transactions lack the intent to create a
> security interest. No documents were executed by Everex
> manifesting its intention to give Expeditors a security interest.
> The terms for a security interest appear only on the creditor's
> forms. The parties stipulated that they never discussed these
> terms and that Everex never signed the invoices or any other
> agreement containing these terms. The invoices alone are
> insufficient to form a security interest because pre-printed
> agreements used by a creditor do not create a security interest if
> the debtor never intended the collateral to be used for this
> purpose. . . .

> * * *

Why does the court
point out the reason
for Expeditors'
possession of
Everex's property?
Reading 9-313 may
provide a hint.

Expeditors possessed Everex's property because it was providing
freight-forwarding services, not because Expeditors was securing
Everex's obligation through a general lien. On these facts, the

requirement that both parties demonstrate an intent to create a security interest has not been met. The pre-printed invoice terms did not explicitly create a security interest.

* * *

Course-of-dealing analysis requires a determination whether there exists "an indication of the common knowledge and understanding of the parties." Course-of-dealing evidence may supplement the agreement by providing evidence of the parties' intentions, but it should not be used to create an agreement. The bankruptcy court noted this distinction in its ruling: "Course of dealing usually refers to previous dealings between parties which indicate the parties previously agreed on a specific issue that is now in dispute."

Course-of-dealing analysis is not proper in an instance where the only action taken has been the repeated delivery of a particular form by one of the parties. . . .

. . . Although Expeditors' desire to have a security interest in the goods that it shipped for Everex is evident in the invoice terms, Expeditors did not obtain a negotiated agreement signed by Everex that reflected these terms. This case is the first dispute between the parties. Neither party has taken any action with respect to the creation of a security interest beyond the repeated sending of a particular form. No mutual agreement existed as to the creation of a security agreement. Course-of-dealing analysis is inappropriate under these circumstances. *Id.* at 1016-1018.

- What advice would you give to Expeditors if the company indicated it wished to continue using the invoices as its means of claiming a security interest, even after this litigation?

- Why wasn't Expeditors' possession of the collateral sufficient to establish a security interest?

Problem 1: On December 13, 1982, Joseph and Maryanne Modafferi executed a promissory note to Peg-Leg Productions in return for a loan of $10,000. Under the terms of the note, they were to repay the principal plus interest at ten percent per annum, with payments to be made quarterly. The note mentioned no collateral. About a month later, Peg-Leg filed a financing statement signed by Joseph Modafferi and the president of Peg-Leg. The form listed the office equipment, accounts payable, and furniture of Joseph Modafferi, CPA. No other documents were executed. A year later, the Modafferis filed for bankruptcy, and Peg-Leg sought to proceed against the listed collateral as a secured creditor, to recover the unpaid balance.

- Applying *Bollinger*, does a security interest exist?

Based on *In re Modafferi*, 45 B.R. 370, 40 U.C.C. Rep. Serv. 268 (Bankr. S.D.N.Y. 1985).

Problem 2: Does the following language, taken from various documents signed by the debtor, establish a security agreement? The first three documents memorialize the loan transaction between the debtor and secured party, while the last relates to a lease by the debtor from a third party.

> "Hypothecation" was a term of art under prior Article 9 referring to collateralization.

PROMISSORY NOTE

The Collateral, and each part thereof, shall secure the indebtedness and each part thereof. The covenants and conditions set forth or referred to in any and all instruments of hypothecation constituting the Collateral are hereby incorporated in this Note as covenants and conditions of the undersigned with the same force and effect as though such covenants and conditions were fully set forth herein.

Upon the non-payment of the indebtedness, or any part thereof, when due, whether by acceleration or otherwise, Holder is empowered to sell, assign, and deliver the whole or any part of the Collateral at public or private sale.... [continues with extensive list of holder's rights with regard to the collateral].

LOAN AGREEMENT

3. Terms of Loan
   c. Collateral:
      1. First lien evidenced by Security Agreement(s) and UCC-1 filing(s) on all
         a. equipment (excluding titled motor vehicles);
         b. inventory; and
         c. accounts receivable now owned and hereafter acquired.
      2. Prior to first disbursement, the appropriate UCC lien searches must be made to determine Lender's priority of lien.

UCC-1

Describes parties as "debtor" and "secured party." Contains a complete description of all collateral.

LESSOR'S SUBORDINATION AGREEMENT

Lessor subordinates to all liens securing the note, until payment in full, every lien or claim against any or all of the property hypothecated as collateral for the indebtedness in favor of [the secured party] hereinabove referred to.

Based on *Maddox v. Federal Deposit Insurance Corp.*, 92 B.R. 707, 9 U.C.C. Rep. Serv. 2d 333 (Bankr. W.D. Tex. 1988).

Description of the Collateral

The following case shows how a court may interpret a security agreement that contains a schedule of collateral, coupled with an "omnibus" clause.

Citizens Bank and Trust v. Gibson Lumber Co., 96 B.R. 751, 8 U.C.C. Rep. Serv. 2d 496 (Bankr. W.D. Ky. 1989)

Boyce F. Martin, Jr., Circuit Judge, Sitting by Designation.

On December 31, 1982, Gibson Lumber Company granted a security interest in its property to Citizens Bank and Trust Company. A security agreement was signed by the parties and perfected by a proper filing on January 3, 1983. The agreement described the collateral in which Citizens took a security interest as "[a]ll inventory of lumber and logs, accounts receivable, all saw mill equipment, and all rolling stock, including, but not limited to...." It then went on to list some twenty-one separate items in varying degrees of specificity. For example, item "1" is described as "Fulghum debarker, decks, conveyers, motors, controls," whereas item "20" is described as "Lumber grading shed, rips, gangs, saws, decks, & misc. equipment."

What was not specifically listed in this schedule of collateral was Gibson Lumber's Corley gang saw, Delta feeder mechanism, and a Detroit Allison diesel generator. This equipment constituted an integral part of the operation of the Gibson sawmill, and was substantial enough to be housed in its own building. These items were sold at auction by the trustee in bankruptcy on October 16, 1985. Citizens claims that, as the senior secured creditor, it is entitled to the proceeds from this sale.

> How, if at all, should the facts in this sentence affect the court's analysis?

The question before the bankruptcy court was the effective scope of the security agreement, specifically, whether either the phrase "all sawmill equipment" or "saws" was sufficient to create a security interest in the Corley gang saw, the Delta feeder mechanism, and the Detroit Allison diesel generator....

In reaching its decision, the bankruptcy court reviewed Kentucky law regarding the effect of omnibus clauses...

The bankruptcy court held that, under *Mammoth Cave Production Credit Association v. York*, 429 S.W.2d 26, 5 U.C.C. Rep. Serv. 11 (Ky. App. 1968), omnibus clauses are not effective in Kentucky because they fail to identify in a reasonable manner the collateral they are designed to encumber....

In resolving the question of whether Citizens' description of collateral was sufficient to encumber the property in question, the bankruptcy court applied an "inquiry test." It found authority for this test in numerous cases decided by Kentucky courts. Under this test, "a

How might one critique this test as a matter of policy insofar as it refers to security agreements? Refer to the *Thorp Commercial Corp.'s* description of each document as needed.

description of collateral is sufficient for either a security agreement or a financing statement if it puts subsequent creditors on notice so that, aided by inquiry, they may reasonably identify the collateral involved."

In applying this test to the present case, the bankruptcy court stated in its original opinion that "[a] fair reading of the enumerated items would lead a third party to the logical conclusion that Citizens did not intend to obtain, and that Gibson Lumber did not intend to grant, any security interest in any equipment not specifically listed in the security agreement." The court again reached the same conclusion following rehearing and reconsideration of the case. The court asserted that "[i]t would stretch credibility to hold that these large and expensive items of equipment were intended as collateral when other similar items were so specifically enumerated." In reiterating its position, the court was careful to note that it did not rely upon *York* as the basis of its decision.

The bankruptcy court was wise to shy away from *York* because that opinion has been the subject of criticism. More importantly, it now appears that *York* is no longer the law of Kentucky. In *Nolin Production Credit Association v. Canmer Deposit Bank*, 726 S.W.2d 693, 2 U.C.C. Rep. Serv. 2d 636 (Ky. App. 1986), the Kentucky Court of Appeals effectively rendered *York* meaningless. . . .

* * *

. . . Because the use of an omnibus clause in a security agreement is consistent with the purpose of the Uniform Commercial Code, we find that Citizens' omnibus clause "all equipment" is effective to cover the Corley gang saw, Delta feeder, and the [Detroit] Allison diesel generator.

Given that such a clause is effective, the question then becomes, does it provide a description of collateral sufficient to include specific collateral not listed on a schedule of specific collateral which is part of the same security agreement? This is precisely the same issue addressed by the Second Circuit in *In re Laminated Veneers Co. Inc.*, 471 F.2d 1124, 11 U.C.C. Rep. Serv. 911 (2d Cir. 1973). That case involved a security agreement with a schedule of specific items of collateral, including among other things, a truck. The security agreement also contained an omnibus clause which ostensibly created a security interest in all equipment of the debtor. The question before the court was whether this omnibus clause was sufficient to grant a security interest in two automobiles not listed on the schedule of collateral. These automobiles did constitute "equipment" as defined by the Code with regard to the debtor.

The current reference is to UCC 9-108.

The court in *Laminated Veneers* found that, under UCC § 9-110, a description of personal property in a security agreement must "reasonably identify" what is described. It then asked a question similar to the "inquiry test" in *Nolin Production Credit:* "What would a potential creditor find upon examination of the security agreement in this case?" The Court concluded that "[a]ny examining creditor would conclude that the truck as the only vehicle mentioned was the only one intended to be covered." This seems illogical. An examining creditor could just as easily conclude that "all equipment" included the cars not specifically listed on the schedule. A potential creditor could reasonably conclude that the parties intended "all equipment" to include equipment not listed on the schedule, and that this equipment was to be covered by the security agreement.

It appears the bankruptcy court in the present case committed the same error in reasoning as the Second Circuit did in *Laminated Veneers*. It found that "[a] fair reading of the enumerated items would lead a third party to the logical conclusion that Citizens did not intend to obtain, and that Gibson Lumber did not intend to grant, any security interest in any equipment not specifically listed in the security agreement." This, however, is only one fair reading of the security agreement. It does not constitute the only logical conclusion which can be drawn. An examining creditor could just as easily conclude that Gibson Lumber intended to grant, and Citizens intended to obtain, a security interest in all of Gibson's equipment. A subsequent creditor could reasonably and logically conclude that the parties inadvertently forgot to list the Corley gang saw, Delta feeder mechanism, and Detroit Allison diesel generator on the schedule, but did intend for this equipment to be covered.

> Who should bear the risk of uncertainty under these facts — the filing creditor or a subsequent examining creditor?

The problem in each of these cases is that the intent of the parties is ambiguous. The use of both a schedule listing specific items of collateral and an omnibus clause describing a general type of collateral creates ambiguity when a specific item fails to appear on the schedule but is ostensibly covered by the omnibus clause.

Because this ambiguity concerns the intent of the parties, it may be subject to resolution by further factual inquiry. . . Accordingly, we remand this case to the bankruptcy court to resolve the ambiguity in this case. . . . In the absence of clear and convincing evidence that the parties did intend the property in question to be encumbered by a security interest, the ambiguity shall be resolved against the creditor, in this case Citizens.

> This maxim of contract interpretation may be familiar to you from a first-year course in contract law.

The justification for allocating the burden of ambiguity in such a situation is found in the purpose and underlying scheme of the Uniform Commercial Code. A major purpose of Article 9 of the UCC is to protect those creditors who obtain security interests and who provide adequate notice to subsequent potential creditors that certain property is encumbered. If such notice is properly completed, the creditor perfects his or her security interest and receives a priority interest in the collateral over competing third parties. If a security agreement contains an omnibus clause as well as a schedule of specific collateral which does not list all that the omnibus clause ostensibly describes, then the initial creditor has failed to provide adequate notice to subsequent creditors. Where an inquiry into the intent of the parties fails to show by clear and convincing evidence that certain specific collateral not listed on the schedule was encumbered, then the ambiguity shall be construed against the initial creditor.

- ▪ Is an omnibus clause the same as a supergeneric description?

- ▪ How could Citizens better protect its interests?

Note: Not all courts agree with the language of 9-108 (c) prohibiting supergeneric descriptions in security agreements. *In re Legal Data Systems, Inc.*, 135 B.R. 199, 16 U.C.C. Rep. Serv. 2d 519 (Bankr. E.D. Mass. 1991), which was decided under pre-1999 Article 9, provides another approach. On February 18, 1986, Legal Data Systems, Inc. and some individuals borrowed $500,000 from Olympic International Bank and Trust Company. The parties executed a promissory note, security agreement, and financing statement. The security agreement indicated the collateral was "all of the Debtor's properties, assets, and rights of every kind and nature, wherever located, whether now owned or hereafter acquired or arising, and all proceeds and products thereof, including, without limiting the generality of the foregoing, [an itemized list of subgroups, as follows]":

[1] all inventory;

[2] all accounts receivable;

[3] all contract rights;

[4] all other rights to the payment of money, including without limitation amounts due from affiliates, tax refunds, and insurance proceeds;

[5] all interest in goods as to which an account receivable shall have arisen;

[6] all files, records (including without limitation computer programs, tapes, and related electronic data-processing software), and related writings;

[7] all goods, instruments, documents of title, policies and certificates of insurance, securities, chattel paper, deposits, cash, or other property which are now or may hereafter be in the possession of Olympic;

[8] all general intangibles (including without limitation any rights to retrieval from third parties of electronically processed and recorded information pertaining to any of the foregoing types of collateral); and

[9] any property, real or personal, tangible or intangible, in which Olympic now has or hereafter acquires a security interest.

The documents on file included language very similar to the security agreement, together with an additional six-page schedule of specific items of collateral. In the ensuing bankruptcy action, another creditor, Digital Equipment Corporation, claimed the omission of the word "equipment" from the itemized list of subgroups meant no equipment was

within the collateral given to Olympic. Although items of
equipment were listed in the six-page schedule, Digital claimed
the schedule was not part of the security agreement.

In considering Digital's competing claim to the equipment, the
court noted Digital was correct that a financing statement
cannot extend the reach of a security agreement. In addition,
although equipment is a kind of "good" within the meaning of
subgroup 7, the court found no evidence that Olympic had ever
been in possession of any Legal Data Systems equipment. The
court therefore held that only the general introductory
language regarding "all of the Debtor's properties . . ." could
address equipment. Noting such "supergeneric" phrases are
often deemed insufficient, the court addressed this matter as
follows:

> Why does this assertion make sense, as a matter of policy?

> The Court has never understood the majority view. The statutory
> requirement is that a security agreement contain a description of
> the collateral which reasonably identifies what is described. A
> financing statement must indicate the types, or describe the items,
> of collateral.
>
> One of the basic words in English is "all." It is actually easier to
> understand "all" than a compilation of all of the UCC generics.
> Why must a security document state 1 + 1 + 1 when 3 is easily
> understood?
> The Court finds that "all of the Debtor's properties, assets and
> rights of every kind and nature" includes equipment, even if the
> specific generic is not used. *Id.* at 201.

> As UCC 9-108 Comment 2 indicates, Article 9 as revised in 1999 adopted the majority rule refusing to enforce such language in security agreements.

- What arguments exist for and against the court's
  holding?

Problem 1: The following language is from a security
agreement:

> In order to secure the payment of the indebtedness as defined in
> [the referenced] Note, . . . Debtor hereby grants, transfers, and
> conveys to Secured Party a security interest in all machinery,
> equipment, furniture, and fixtures now owned and hereafter
> acquired by Debtor for use in Debtor's business, including,
> without limitation, the items described on Schedule "A" attached
> hereto, together with all replacements thereof and all
> attachments, accessories, and equipment now or hereafter
> installed therein or affixed thereto (all of the aforesaid hereinafter
> called the "Goods").

"Schedule A" was attached and specifically described various
types of machinery, equipment, furniture, and fixtures. On
December 5, 1977, the defendant filed a financing statement
with the Illinois Secretary of State. The financing statement
described the property covered as follows:

> All accounts receivable . . . evidencing any obligation to Debtor for payment for goods sold . . . and all inventory of Debtor of every description . . .

- Are inventory and accounts receivable within the security agreement?

Based on *Forest Park National Bank v. Martin Grinding & Machine Works*, 42 B.R. 888, 39 U.C.C. Rep. Serv. 1462 (Bankr. N.D. Ill. 1984).

Problem 2: Consider the following excerpt from a security agreement between a car dealership and the bank financing its inventory:

> (a) "Inventory" means new and used motor vehicles now owned or hereafter acquired by Dealer which are held for sale or lease, . . ., together with all of the proceeds thereof, including, but not limited to, cash or its equivalent, accounts receivable, factory receivables, and contract rights.
>
> * * *
>
> (c) "Collateral" means all Inventory, property described in paragraph 5 (e) of this Agreement, and other property from time to time subject to the security interest herein provided for, including but not limited to all proceeds of every kind of any such Inventory and property.
>
> * * *
>
> 5 (e) Dealer grants to Bank a security interest in, and agrees and acknowledges that Bank shall continue to have a security interest in, all of the furniture, fixtures, equipment, tools, machinery, accessories, appliances, accounts receivable (including, but not limited to, factory receivables), contract rights, and any other personal property of Dealer now owned or hereafter acquired, and in all of the proceeds thereof.

- Are "parts" included in the collateral thus described?

Based on *NBD Park Ridge Bank v. SRJ Enterprises, Inc.*, 151 B.R. 198, 22 U.C.C. Rep. Serv. 2d 1181 (Bankr. N.D. Ill. 1993).

After-Acquired Collateral

Read 9-204 (a) and (b) and Comments 2, 3, 4, and 7. A floating lien is an encumbrance of collateral acquired in the future, as well as that which is owned when the security interest is created.

- What are the reasons for (1) the court's general allowance of such liens and (2) the limitations in the consumer context?

- How are after-acquired-collateral clauses treated differently in security agreements and financing statements?

A careful lawyer will make sure the language in the security agreement refers to "now-owned and after-acquired collateral" if both are desired. This is particularly important when dealing with inventory, because the intention is that it be sold and replaced continually. So as to keep the creditor from having to prepare new documents each time the debtor's inventory changes, it is crucial to include after-acquired inventory up front.

In the following case, the court describes a split of authority with regard to the presumptive inclusion of after-acquired inventory and receivables when the security agreement is silent, developing the arguments on both sides of the dispute. The court also explains how a presumption of inclusion can be rebutted.

Paulman v. Gateway Venture Partners III, L.P.,
163 F.3d 570, 37 U.C.C. Rep. Serv. 2d 799 (9th Cir. 1998).

Filtercorp, Inc. was a Washington corporation which developed and distributed carbonated pads used in the food-service industry to filter cooking oils. Beginning in November 1991, the company took out a series of loans from [Henry] Paulman, an individual salesman, to help fund further development and meet large orders. The loans were short term, ranging from two to three months, and memorialized by promissory notes drafted by Paulman's attorney. The final note – the subject of this litigation – was a three-month note, executed on June 30, 1992, and due September 30, 1992.

The June 1992 note provided for the following security:

> This note is secured by 75,000 shares of Filter Corp. [sic] stock owned by Robin Bernard, the accounts receivable and inventory of Filter Corp. [sic] (see UCC-1 filing and attached inventory listing), and John Gardner personally.

The parties never executed a separate security agreement. However, Paulman perfected his security interest by filing a UCC-1 financing statement on October 5, 1992. The UCC-1 statement identified the collateral as (1) accounts receivable and (2) materials inventory. Despite the note's reference to an inventory listing, none was ever attached to the note or the financing statement.

There is no contemporaneous evidence shedding light on whether the
parties intended to secure after-acquired inventory or accounts
receivable with the June 1992 note. In the course of this litigation, the
parties presented conflicting versions of their intent. Paulman claimed
that he and Filtercorp, Inc. understood the security interest to attach to
future rather than presently-held inventory and accounts receivable, so
as not to interfere with the company's ability to raise additional capital.
Hence, he did not attach the inventory listing. In contrast, Robin
Bernard, President of Filtercorp, Inc., stated that, in light of the short,
three-month term of the loan, he did not contemplate an ongoing
security interest.

* * *

The bankruptcy court [held] that Paulman had no security interest in
any of Filtercorp's assets because his liens did not attach to after-
acquired property and none of the remaining assets could be traced to
the assets in existence at the time that his security interest was
created. In particular, the court ruled that there was no security
interest in after-acquired inventory or accounts receivable because the
note did not expressly grant such an interest. The court also found that
it could not determine the intent of the parties when they signed the
note because the conflicting declarations of Paulman and Filtercorp,
Inc.'s President lacked any evidentiary support. . . .

* * *

Courts disagree over what terms are required in a security agreement
to cover after-acquired inventory and accounts receivable. A minority
of jurisdictions require express language evidencing the parties' intent
to cover after-acquired inventory or accounts receivable. These courts
view the Uniform Commercial Code provision concerning after-
acquired property as contemplating express after-acquired-property
clauses. They reason that it is "neither onerous nor unreasonable to
require a security agreement to make clear its intended collateral." To
do so simplifies the interpretation of security agreements and provides
more precise notice to third parties of the extent of a perfected security
interest in the debtor's property. In these jurisdictions, a grant of a
security interest in "inventory" or "accounts receivable," without more,
is insufficient to include after-acquired property.

However, we find more persuasive the contrary position, adopted by
the majority of jurisdictions, that a security interest in inventory or
accounts receivables presumptively includes an interest in after-
acquired inventory or accounts receivable, respectively. The rationale
for this position rests on the unique nature of inventory and accounts
receivable as "cyclically depleted and replenished assets." Because
inventory and accounts receivable are constantly turning over, "no
creditor could reasonably agree to be secured by an asset that would
vanish in a short time in the normal course of business." Essentially, a
floating lien on inventory and accounts receivable is presumed because
the collateral is viewed in aggregate as a shifting body of assets.

* * *

What does each party stand to gain from the testimony?

How does this portion of the court's opinion comport with the *Citizens Bank* holding?

The presumption that a grant of a security interest in inventory or accounts receivable includes after-acquired property is, of course, rebuttable. For example, the presumption would be overcome where the security-agreement language itself manifests an intent to limit the collateral to specific identified property, where a party presents clear evidence of contemporaneous intent to limit the collateral, or where the debtor can demonstrate that it was engaged in a type of business where the named collateral, whether inventory or receivables, does not regularly turn over so that the rationale for the presumption does not apply.

We conclude that, were the issue to come before the Washington Supreme Court, it would hold that after-acquired collateral is presumptively covered by a security agreement referencing "inventory" or "accounts receivable." . . .

Applying the foregoing analysis to the security agreement between Paulman and Filtercorp, we reach different results with respect to accounts receivable and inventory. The note (which serves as the security agreement) states that it was secured by "the accounts receivable and inventory of Filter Corp. [sic] (see UCC-1 filing and attached inventory listing.)." While the presumption that after-acquired property is included stands unrebutted as to accounts receivable, it is rebutted for inventory by the reference to the attached inventory listing.

Under the approach we adopt, the reference to "accounts receivable" presumptively includes after-acquired accounts receivable. The bankruptcy court found the opposing declarations of Paulman and Filtercorp, Inc.'s President as to their contemporaneous intent to be inconclusive. That finding of fact is not clearly erroneous. There is no other evidence of intent in the record. Therefore, we hold that Paulman has a security interest in after-acquired accounts receivable of Filtercorp. That security interest was perfected when Paulman filed a UCC-1 financing statement before other creditors, and before Filtercorp filed for bankruptcy.

With respect to the security interest in inventory, the note referenced an "attached inventory listing" which, however, was never attached to either the note or the financing statement. Paulman claims that he did not attach the listing because he agreed with Filtercorp, Inc.'s President Bernard to create a security interest in inventory in general, including after-acquired inventory. Bernard, in contrast, claims that after-acquired inventory was never discussed by the parties prior to entering into the loan agreement and that he did not intend to attach after-acquired property given the short term nature of the loans. The bankruptcy court's finding that this conflicting evidence is inconclusive is not clearly erroneous. Thus, we are left with the language of the note itself.

When, as in this case, a security interest in inventory is described by reference to a list, it suggests an intent to limit the collateral rather than cover inventory as a floating mass including after-acquired inventory. Yet, reference to an attached list does not preclude securing after-acquired collateral when the agreement or the listing demonstrate an intent to do so.

Here, the Paulman-Filtercorp note referenced an inventory listing, which rebuts the presumption that after-acquired inventory is attached, and failed to demonstrate any particular intent to cover after-acquired inventory. The note's ambiguity regarding the security interest in inventory must be construed against Paulman, the drafter of the note. We conclude that Paulman does not have a security interest in after-acquired inventory of Filtercorp.

- How did the court decide after-acquired accounts receivable – but not inventory – were within the security agreement?

Note: *In re Gary & Connie Jones Drugs, Inc.,* 35 B.R. 608, 37 U.C.C. Rep. Serv. 563 (Bankr. D. Kan. 1983), shows how courts can use a "reasonable person" test to find after-acquired inventory is included in the collateral for a security agreement. On July 24, 1979, Jack and Linda Simons sold a drugstore and its assets to Gary and Connie Jones Drugs, Inc. for about $110,000. The assets included about $20,000 in inventory. The transaction was memorialized with a promissory note and security agreement granting Mr. and Mrs. Simons a security interest in the assets of the store, including "equipment and trade fixtures and merchandise inventory described in Exhibit A attached hereto and included herein by reference, presently owned and located at the property . . . ." The security agreement included a covenant whereby the debtor promised to keep the inventory-stock level at the same approximate value as at the date of sale, to notify the secured parties of any significant drop in stock level, and to allow inspection of the inventory. The major issue before the court was whether Mr. and Mrs. Simons obtained a perfected security interest in after-acquired inventory; this matter was critical to Mr. and Mrs. Simon's recovery because the inventory in the store at the time of sale was long gone by the time the debtors filed for bankruptcy. In addressing this issue, the court held as follows:

> The majority view appears to be to determine the parties' intent, applying a reasonable-man test to the facts and circumstances; that is, if a reasonable man looking at the entire security agreement and financing statement would recognize that the parties intended to secure after-acquired inventory. . . .

> * * *

> Applying the "reasonable man" test to the instant facts, the Court finds that the debtor intended to give the Simons a security interest in present and after-acquired inventory. This intent is evidenced by the covenant to keep a stable level of inventory and the Simons' right to periodic inspection of the inventory. If the

Simons were not secured by after-acquired inventory, such provisions would be unnecessary and meaningless. Therefore, this Court finds that the Simons have a perfected security interest in the after-acquired inventory. *Id.* at 611-612.

- Could the "reasonable person" test militate against including after-acquired inventory under these facts?

Dragnet Clauses

Read 9-204 (c) and Comment 5. In *Pride Hyundai, Inc. v. Chrysler Financial Co., L.L.C.*, 369 F.3d 603, 53 U.C.C. Rep. Serv. 2d 423 (1st Cir. 2004), the court defined "dragnet clause" as follows:

> This is also called a future-advances clause.

> Dragnet clauses purport to secure all of a debtor's obligations to a creditor, regardless of whether those obligations arise prior to, concurrent with, or after the instrument containing the dragnet clause itself. *Id.* at 606.

The following case illustrates the application of a dragnet clause. As you read this case, make sure you can articulate the differences between a dragnet clause and an after-acquired-collateral clause.

> If you have difficulty differentiating between the two, you might read Judge Posner's opinion in *In re Kazmierczak*, 24 F.3d 1020, 23 U.C.C. Rep. Serv. 2d 915 (7th Cir. 1994).

Stannish v. Community Bank of Homewood-Flossmoor,
24 B.R. 761, 35 U.C.C. Rep. Serv. 235 (Bankr. N.D. Ill. 1982)

Community Bank [of Homewood-Flossmoor] holds three separate debt instruments signed by [Debtors Michael and Margaret Stannish]. The first instrument, entitled a "Check Credit Account Agreement," was dated May 1, 1976. It created a line of credit which could be drawn upon by the debtors with special checks. The line of credit also provided coverage for checking-account overdrafts. The balance due on this agreement was $1,454.20 on January 4, 1982, the date on which the debtors filed their Chapter 7 [bankruptcy] petition.

The second instrument is a note and security agreement, dated July 21, 1980. This instrument reflects a purchase-money loan of $3,600.00, plus credit-insurance premiums. The instrument is also a security agreement, identifying a new 1980 Pontiac Phoenix as collateral. The agreement contains the following relevant language in number three of its terms and conditions:

> Debtor(s) agrees that Holder shall have, and there is hereby created in favor of Holder, a security interest in the Collateral described herein to secure (i) the payment of the debt evidenced hereby . . . and (iv) all other past, present and future, direct or contingent liabilities of Debtor(s) to Holder. The Holder shall have the right of setoff against any deposits and other sums which may now or in the future be owing by the Holder to the Debtor(s).

As part of the explanatory language on the first page of the agreement, the following is found after the words "Security Interest":

> This loan is secured by a security interest created under this Security Agreement in the property described above which security interest may attach to any accessions thereto. In addition to the foregoing security, the Holder has a security interest for the payment of all obligations due it in all property and assets of Debtor(s) which are in the possession or control of Holder and a right of setoff or lien on any deposit or sums now or hereafter owed by Holder to Debtor(s). Holder has a Security Interest in the proceeds and the unearned premiums in any insurance required or purchased. This Security Agreement will secure future or other indebtedness.

It appears the trustee assumed this contract under 11 USC § 365.

The title to the Phoenix is in the possession of Community Bank, which is listed as the first lienholder on the face of the title. The balance at the time of the bankruptcy filing was $2,768.39. Debtors continued to make monthly payments of $112.23 as of the time the motion for summary judgment was filed on June 8, 1982, and therefore, the balance due was decreasing each month.

The third instrument is an installment note, dated August 9, 1980, for a $1,000.00 loan to debtors. The balance due on this note at the time of the petition was $654.46.

On November 24, 1980, General Finance Corporation loaned the debtors $2,233.87 which was also secured by the Phoenix automobile. General Finance is listed on the car's title as the second lienholder.

Who is likely to object to the proposed setoff and why?

The issue before the court is whether Community Bank may use the value of the car in excess of the amount owed the bank on the purchase-money loan to setoff unpaid amounts remaining on other loans extended from Community Bank to the debtor.

The note and security agreement for the purchase-money loan on the car contains language as quoted above, which secures prior amounts owned and future advances with the collateral securing the purchase-money loan. This clause, referred to as a "dragnet" clause, is commonly found in security agreements and is not favored under Illinois law. Dragnet clauses will be upheld, however, where no ambiguity exists and will be interpreted according to the language used. The law presumes the parties intended the agreement to mean what the language clearly imports.

The Uniform Commercial Code provides that a secured agreement may cover future advances without an additional agreement. Code Section 9-201 states that, "Except as otherwise provided by this Act, a security agreement is effective according to its terms between the parties, against purchasers of the collateral, and against creditors." Section 9-204 provides that such a security agreement may secure "future advances or other value, whether or not the advances or value are given pursuant to commitment."

* * *

It is well established that clear and unambiguous security-agreement clauses extending the collateral to secure past and future advances are valid under common law and the Uniform Commercial Code. Clearly, the clause in question here was clear and unambiguous and provided sufficient notice to the subsequent creditor, General Finance, that their security interest in the 1980 Pontiac Phoenix was secondary to any other obligations the debtor owed to Community Bank.

- What are the differences in the purpose of, and court's attitude toward, dragnet clauses and after-acquired-property clauses?

Note: Read 9-201 and Comment 2. *Pride Hyundai, Inc. v. Chrysler Financial Co., L.L.C.*, 369 F.3d 603, 53 U.C.C. Rep. Serv. 2d 423 (1st Cir. 2004), shows that courts generally will recognize unusual arrangements between secured parties and borrowers, especially in the commercial context. Price Hyundai, Pride Dodge, Blackstone Subaru, and Pride Chrysler-Plymouth were four car dealerships owned by Alfredo Dos Anjos. In early 1987, Pride Chrysler-Plymouth entered into a retail financing agreement with Chrysler Financing Company. Such an agreement allowed the dealership to provide installment financing to its customers. Simply put, Chrysler Financing Company would purchase the dealership's commercial paper. The agreement provided that, if a customer either defaulted or paid off the contract before maturity, either of which would lessen the financing company's expected profits, the dealership would be liable for some portion of the lost profit. These payments were called charge-backs. The dealership was required to maintain a certain minimum balance in an account maintained for the benefit of the financing company, for the purpose of covering these charge-backs.

> An analogy can be made to the charge-backs provided for in UCC 4-214 and discussed in Chapter 10, Part A.

In 1994, Chrysler Financing Company entered retail financing relationships with the other dealerships owned by Dos Anjos and also began to provide wholesale inventory financing (also known as floor-plan financing) for the dealerships. Wholesale inventory financing provides funds to dealerships to finance their purchase of automobiles as inventory. The retail financing agreement with each dealership contained the charge-back provisions referenced above, but the minimum-account-balance requirement was not enforced until 2000. Each wholesale-inventory-financing agreement contained a dragnet clause not in the retail financing contracts, providing as follows:

> 3.0 *Security* – Debtor hereby grants to Secured Party a first and prior security interest in and to each and every Vehicle financed hereunder. . . . The security interest hereby granted shall secure the prompt, timely, and full payment of (1) all Advances, (2) all interest accrued thereon in accordance with the terms of this Agreement and the Promissory Notes, (3) all other indebtedness and obligations of Debtor under the Promissory Notes, (4) all costs and expenses incurred by Secured Party in the collection or enforcement of the Promissory Notes or of the obligations of the Debtor under this Agreement, (5) all monies advanced by Secured Party on behalf of Debtor for taxes, levies, insurance, and repairs to and maintenance of any Vehicle or other collateral, and *(6) each and every other indebtedness or obligation now or hereafter owing by Debtor to Secured Party including any collection or enforcement costs and expenses or monies advanced on behalf of Debtor in connection with any such other indebtedness or obligations* (emphasis added). *Id.* at 606.

Thus, the dragnet clause provided that all of the dealerships' past and future obligations to the financing company (not just the wholesale inventory contracts, but also the retail financing contracts) would be secured by almost all of the dealerships' assets. Because the financing company provided retail (as well as wholesale) financing to the dealerships, the effect was to give the financing company an additional security interest not contained in those retail contracts. Thus, the new wholesale agreements changed the terms of the parties' relationship as memorialized in the retail contracts. Having a security interest in dealership assets for retail financing contracts is not common in the automobile industry. In rejecting the dealerships' argument that such terms should not be enforceable insofar as the retail contracts were considered, the court held as follows:

In what other ways does Article 9 distinguish between consumer and commercial transactions?

> The parties in transactions involving dragnet clauses are typically sophisticated market actors. Commercial parties on both sides of a transaction may have good reasons to enter into a security agreement that secures not only present liabilities, but also future liabilities of a different class or type. Such an arrangement allows future credit to be extended between the parties on a secured basis without the additional transaction costs that would accompany the execution of a new agreement for each such transaction.
>
> * * *
>
> Given the clear and unambiguous language of the dragnet clause in the wholesale financing agreements, the lack of any evidence of a violation of the duty of good faith, and the absence of other special circumstances rendering such an interpretation unreasonable or against public policy, we hold that the dragnet clause did apply to the contingent debt arising out of the retail financing agreements. *Id.* at 615-618.

- How do wholesale and retail financing agreements differ?

- What is unusual about the parties' credit relationship, and why does the court enforce the agreement as written?

International Perspective: Secret Liens

The following excerpt from Swiss attorney Hans Kuhn's article *Multi-State and International Secured Transactions under Revised Article 9 of the Uniform Commercial Code*, 40 Va. J. Intl. L. 1009, 1054 (2000), describes the basic system of secured transactions in Germany:

> Secrecy of secured transactions is a distinct feature of German secured-transaction law. The sole statutory device for creating security interests in personal property is the pledge, which requires transfer of possession of the collateral and therefore is possessory in nature. "However, the pledge is hardly of any relevance in the practice of modern business financing." It was replaced by non-statutory, nonpossessory security devices developed by the marketplace and recognized by the judiciary, including reservation of ownership (Eigentumsvorbehalt), "security ownership" (Sicherungsübereignung), and the assignment of receivables for security purposes (Sicherungsabtretung). Reservation of ownership is the supplier's primary security device in order to secure the purchase price. The seller may condition the transfer of full ownership upon full payment. The buyer then receives actual possession of the good, while the seller retains constructive possession until the payment is completed.   If the purchaser is in default, the seller is legally entitled to rescind the contract and to repossess the goods. This right prevails over the rights of other creditors that seize the collateral. Moreover, practice has developed a number of devices that extend the retention of title.   For example, it is common practice for buyers to assign to suppliers all receivables arising from the future sale of the goods covered by a retention of title. The reservation of ownership does not require any kind of publicity; it is secret in nature.
>
> To secure a bank's loan, the most common device is the transfer of "security ownership" in chattels. Creation of a security ownership requires (1) an agreement between the creditor and the debtor that need not be in writing and (2) the transfer of ownership. . . . Whether or not the transfer must be accompanied by some public act is controversial, and recent judgments do not require a public act to execute the transfer of security ownership. Therefore the parties may keep the security transaction entirely secret.

The quoted language here comes from Jens Hausmann, *The Value of Public-Notice Filing Under Uniform Commercial Code Article 9: A Comparison with the German Legal System of Securities in Personal Property*, 25 Ga. J. Intl. & Comp. L. 427, 474 (1996).

The assignment of receivables for security purposes ("security assignment") has become an important security device in German credit. As in the transfer of security ownership, the assignment of claims for security purposes requires both the transfer of [the receivable by way of assignment] and a security agreement. . . . Notice to the account debtor is advisable because, if the debtor pays in good faith to the initial creditor (the secured party's debtor), the creditor loses his security interest. However, there is no public-notice requirement, and the assignment is fully effective without such notice. Priority among subsequent assignees is established by the first-in-time rule, without regard to any kind of notice or publicity. *Id.* at 1055-1057.

- How are German nonpossessory security interests inherently secret in nature?

- What provisions would you add to a security agreement covering foreign collateral or involving a foreign debtor?

The following case shows how the inherent secrecy of German nonpossessory security interests may make a U.S. court hesitant to apply German law in a close case. Note how the court determines public policy militates against application of German law, given the court's concern with third-party interests. Make sure you understand how and why the court's analysis would have been different if the secured party and the borrower were the only parties affected by the matter.

The Hong Kong and Shanghai Banking Corp., Ltd.
v. HFH USA Corp.,
805 F. Supp. 133, 19 U.C.C. Rep. Serv. 2d 885 (W.D.N.Y. 1992).

Skretny, District Judge.

> As a condition of the sale, Eli and Finkenrath agreed that German law would govern the parties' rights and obligations.

[Hong Kong and Shanghai Banking Corp., Ltd.] alleges that it loaned funds to Eli Industries (USA), Inc., secured by a perfected first-lien security interest in Eli's present and future inventory. Hugo Finkenrath OHG sold goods to Eli that were included as inventory under HSBC's security agreement with Eli. Plaintiff [HSBC] never received notice of any security interest in these goods claimed by Finkenrath. [Eli never paid for the goods. Thus,] [o]n behalf of Finkenrath, HFH [USA Corp.] took possession of the goods and returned them to Finkenrath in Germany. HSBC notified HFH of its prior perfected security interest in the inventory and demanded either return of the goods or payment of their value to HSBC. The inventory was never returned to HSBC, nor was any payment made. Therefore, HSBC claims that HFH converted these goods, in which HSBC had a superior interest.

As defenses, HFH asserts that it was acting as an agent for Finkenrath. HFH alleges that Finkenrath had rights in the goods that were superior to those of HSBC, under a title-retention agreement between Finkenrath and Eli that was included in the sales contract and that is governed by German law. . . .

* * *

Under normal circumstances, contracting parties are free to stipulate what state's or nation's law will govern their contractual rights and duties, provided that the state or nation has a reasonable relationship with the transaction, and the law chosen does not violate a fundamental public policy of the forum state. Nonetheless, the parties' stipulation will not be regarded where it would operate to the detriment of strangers to the agreement, such as creditors or lienholders. Where the rights of third parties are implicated, the court should be governed by the ordinary rule that the federal district courts apply the choice-of-law rules of the state in which they sit. The district court must apply the law it believes the state's highest court would apply.

In this case, the agreement between Finkenrath and Eli provided that German law was to govern the interests and relationships created under the agreement. Under German law [and the parties' agreement, until Eli made full payment,] Finkenrath would have title to the goods, instead of a mere security interest. If this dispute involved only Eli and Finkenrath (or its agent HFH), this Court would respect the parties' stipulation of German law in the agreement. Nevertheless, because the stipulation would work to the detriment of HSBC – a third party and a stranger to the agreement – this Court must disregard the stipulation and look to the forum state's choice-of-law rules to determine the interests of the parties.

* * *

Therefore, regardless of the parties' stipulation of German law, this Court must look to Article 9 of the UCC to identify and prioritize the interests held by HSBC and HFH.

- What policies does the court weigh in reaching its decision?

B. Attachment of a Security Interest

Creation of a security interest is a prerequisite to attachment. In discussing attachment, this section examines the concept of "giving value" and the requirement that the debtor have rights in the collateral.

Read 9-203 (a) and (b) and Comment 2. Attachment is the final step in establishing rights between the debtor and secured party.

> Once you have completed the materials in Chapter 15, make sure you understand why perfection is not a step in establishing rights between a debtor and a secured party.

Read 9-502 (d) and Comment 2. 9-502 (d) addresses
financing statements filed before a security interest has
attached.

- Will early filing of the financing statement cause a
  security interest to attach before it otherwise would?

- When might the parties choose early filing?

Read 9-102 (a) (64) and 9-203 (f). These provisions address
attachment of a security interest in proceeds. Article 9's
treatment of proceeds will be a recurrent theme throughout
this textbook's discussion of secured transactions.

- What are proceeds?

> 9-315 (a) (2) governs
> perfection of an
> interest in proceeds.

- When does a security interest in proceeds attach?

> You may wish to
> review the facts in
> Part A to refresh
> your recollection of
> the parties and their
> theories.

The following case was introduced in the international
materials in Part A. The portion of the holding excerpted
below, which applies Article 9, illustrates how and when a
security interest attaches.

The Hong Kong and Shanghai Banking Corp., Ltd.
v. HFH USA Corp.,
805 F. Supp. 133, 19 U.C.C. Rep. Serv. 2d 885 (W.D.N.Y. 1992).

> The current
> reference is to 9-203
> (a) and (b).

Under UCC § 9-203 (1), a security interest attaches when:

   (a)   the collateral is in the possession of the secured party
       pursuant to agreement, or the debtor has signed a security
       agreement which contains a description of the collateral . . .;
       and

   (b)   value has been given; and

   (c)   the debtor has rights in the collateral.

In the present case, HFH argues that HSBC did not acquire a security
interest in the goods contained in the first shipment because Eli never
acquired rights in the goods. HFH maintains that, because Eli never
paid the customs duty on the goods or took physical possession of them,
no rights were acquired. This argument of HFH is unpersuasive. This
Court finds that Eli did possess sufficient rights in the goods for HSBC
to acquire a security interest in them pursuant to its security
agreement.

> Why is 2-401 useful
> by analogy? Why is
> it not literally
> applicable here?

Although the UCC does not define the term "rights in the collateral,"
other courts have found assistance in UCC § 2-401, which deals with
the passage of title to goods. . . .

Two things in this section are worthy of note. First, title-retention
contracts are construed as creating only security interests under the
UCC . . . § 9-102 brings such interests within the scope of Article 9. . . .

Second, title to goods passes when the seller fulfills his obligation to
deliver the goods to the place identified in the contract. Although title is
not the precise equivalent of "rights in the collateral," title is indicative
of certain rights that the debtor has to dispose of the goods. . . .

> 9-202 Comment 1 may explain this paragraph. The scope of Article 9 is now in 9-109 rather than 9-102.

There is nothing in the agreement between Finkenrath and Eli
indicating that title did not pass upon delivery to the FTZ. Although
the agreement assumes the application of German law, this Court is
bound to construe the title-retention clause as a security interest under
New York's UCC. Under this construction, title to the goods passed to
Eli upon delivery to the FTZ. Pursuant to the agreement, Finkenrath
shipped the goods ordered by Eli from Antwerp to the FTZ in Buffalo.
Finkenrath billed Eli for this shipment, and the parties agreed that
payment of the applicable customs duty would be Eli's responsibility.
The goods remained in the FTZ because Eli did not pay the duty
required to remove the goods for import into the United States. Thus
Finkenrath complied with the delivery terms indicated in the
agreement. Title passed to Eli in the FTZ, although Eli failed to
remove the goods by its failure to pay the required duty. Although title
is not the equivalent of "rights in the collateral," a determination of
which party has title to the goods can be a critical step in finding
whether the debtor has such rights. . . .

> "FTZ" is the foreign trade zone in Buffalo, New York.

* * *

The case of *Chartered Bank of London v. Chrysler Corp.,* 115 Cal. App.
3d 755, 171 Cal. Rptr. 748 (Cal. App. 2d Dist. 1981), is instructive.
Chrysler involves the delivery of a boat by a manufacturer to a
warehouse. The manufacturer instructed the warehouse that
possession of the boat was not to be relinquished to the dealer until the
dealer paid the full price for the boat. Meanwhile, the dealer entered
into a contract with the buyer to sell the boat, under which the dealer
purported to retain a security interest in the boat to secure payment of
the balance due by the buyer. This security interest was then assigned
by the dealer to a bank. Despite the purported sale, the dealer made no
payment to the warehouse for the boat, the warehouse never delivered
the boat to the dealer, and the buyer never received possession of the
boat. The manufacturer reclaimed the boat from the warehouse and,
shortly thereafter, the buyer defaulted. The bank sued the
manufacturer for conversion, asserting its alleged security interest in
the boat.

Addressing the issue of whether the buyer had sufficient rights in the
collateral, the court explained that, because the manufacturer did not
intend to relinquish possession of the boat to the dealer until the dealer
paid the purchase price to the warehouse, the dealer never possessed
the boat. Therefore, the buyer never took possession and did not
acquire sufficient rights in the boat to create a security interest.

In the present case, Eli had a far greater interest in the goods in the
foreign trade zone than the dealer in *Chrysler*. Under § 2-401 of the
UCC, title is considered to have passed to Eli upon delivery of the goods
to the FTZ. Finkenrath did not make delivery or possession of the
goods contingent upon payment of the full purchase price by Eli. . . .
The only thing preventing Eli from taking the goods in the first

shipment into the United States was its failure to pay the customs duty.

Furthermore, although Eli could not transport the goods to its place of business in Buffalo without payment of the duty, Eli could have disposed of the goods while they remained in the FTZ. . . . In view of the fact that title to the goods passed to Eli upon delivery at the FTZ under the UCC, Eli could have manipulated and disposed of the goods in a host of ways without having to pay duty on them. Eli had a considerable degree of control or authority over the goods even while they remained in the FTZ.

. . . Therefore, Eli possessed sufficient "rights in the collateral" to give HSBC a security interest under UCC § 9-203.

- How does "passage of title" relate to "rights in the collateral"?

- How did Eli have "a far greater interest in the goods" than the dealer in *Chrysler*?

This question and the next one may require you to review the materials in Chapter 3, Parts A and B.

- Did Eli have an insurable interest in the goods under 2-501?

- Had risk of loss passed to Eli under 2-509 and 2-510?

Note 1: *Littwiller Machine & Manufacturing, Inc. v. NPB Alpena Bank*, 184 Mich. App. 369, 457 N.W.2d 163 (Mich. App. 1990), describes another context for attachment of a security interest. Littwiller Machine and Manufacturing, Inc. was in the business of steel fabrication. It was awarded a government contract for the production of 39 boom assemblies for the United States Department of Defense. Koss Industries had been awarded a similar contract earlier, and thus Littwiller contacted Koss to arrange for Koss to fabricate the boom assemblies Littwiller was under contract to produce. By agreement, Littwiller was to purchase the necessary components and have them shipped by the supplier directly to Koss for Koss to fabricate the boom assemblies. After fabrication, Koss would ship the assemblies directly to the Defense Department.

Before fabrication was complete, Koss defaulted on a loan from NPB Alpena Bank. Because the loan had been secured by a perfected security interest in all of Koss's inventory, raw materials, work in progress, and supplies, the bank sought to foreclose upon this interest. Although Littwiller informed the bank that it, not Koss, owned the components to be used in satisfying Littwiller's government contract, the bank seized these components and sold them at public sale. Littwiller sued the bank in conversion, contending the bank's security interest in Koss's after-acquired inventory could not attach to these components; the bank defended on the grounds that Koss had sufficient rights in the components to support the bank's security interest. The court addressed these competing claims, as follows:

> The question whether components which have been supplied to a manufacturer for fabrication constitute inventory of the manufacturer was addressed in *Morton Booth Co. v. Tiara Furniture, Inc.,* 1977 Okla. 45, 564 P.2d 210 (Okla., 1977). . . .
>
> [W]e conclude that plaintiff's components were a part of Koss' inventory, and thus were described in the security agreement between Koss and defendant. The first requirement for defendant's security interest to attach to the components is satisfied.
>
> We next consider the third requirement for attachment of defendant's security interest to the components, that the debtor (Koss) must have sufficient "rights in the collateral." Plaintiff contends that Koss was a mere bailee of plaintiff's components. Defendant contends that Koss had a greater interest in them.

> The second requirement, that value be given, was not disputed.

> The phrase "rights in the collateral" is not defined in the UCC. The UCC, however, does not require that a debtor have full ownership rights. Indeed, title to goods is of little relative consequence under the UCC. A deliberate effort was made by the drafters of the UCC to avoid defining the rights of the parties to goods in terms of who has title.

> 9-202 and its commentary reflects this policy as characterized by the court.

> The *Booth* court described "rights in the collateral" as follows:
>
>> [M]ere possession of goods is not enough under the Code to demonstrate that the debtor had "rights" in the collateral. . . . The provisions of Article 9 were never intended to give rise to a security interest where the debtor was, for example, a mere gratuitous bailee. The cases generally hold, however, that where a debtor gains possession of collateral pursuant to an agreement endowing him with any interest other than naked possession, the debtor has acquired such rights as would allow the security interest to attach.
>
> * * *
>
> In this case, we conclude that Koss had sufficient rights in the components supplied by plaintiff so that defendant's security interest attached to those components. . . . Koss had contract rights to the goods to the extent of the amount due for its work and could impose a lien on the goods to enforce that right. . . . Koss had the right to use and incorporate the components for what must be characterized as a sale of the completed assemblies to plaintiff. This amounts to more than "naked possession" of the components. *Id.* at 373-379.

- Following this case, how would you describe the point at which sufficient "rights in the collateral" exist to support attachment?

Note 2: Under some circumstances, the parties may agree to delay attachment of a security interest. In *Barton v. Chemical Bank*, 577 F.2d 1329, 24 U.C.C. Rep. Serv. 497 (5th Cir. 1978), the court addresses an allegation that the parties did so. Chemical Realty Corp. loaned Charles Barton $8 million for real-estate development on July 19, 1973. Barton executed a document entitled, "Deed to Secure Debt and Security Agreement." This document included a clause whereby Chemical Realty Corp. would withhold approximately $2.3 million from the loan proceeds to cover interest and other costs associated with the property. The parties also agreed in this document that Barton would supply additional reserves to supplement the retained funds as necessary. At closing, the lender determined the $2.3 million reserve might be insufficient and requested that Barton purchase a $200,000 certificate of deposit using some of the loan proceeds and pledge the certificate of deposit to the lender to supplement the reserve. Therefore, by letter dated the same day as the closing, Barton directed Chemical Bank, which was affiliated with the lender, to purchase a certificate of deposit in the requested amount and to deliver it to the lender "to hold under a pledge agreement which is being prepared by counsel for Chemical Realty Corp." Chemical Bank followed these instructions, and the mortgage-loan administrator for the lender sent Barton a receipt when she received the certificate of deposit. No written pledge agreement was ever executed. Barton's letter to Chemical Bank of July 19, 1973, read in relevant part as follows:

> Reference is made to the $8,000,000 mortgage loan being closed today. We hereby authorize that $5,175,500 in loan funds being advanced today be deposited by Chemical Realty Corporation into my account # 006-385915 to be withdrawn as follows:
>
> 1. Withdraw from my said account the sum of two hundred thousand dollars ($200,000.00) and purchase a one-year Certificate of Deposit at 9% per annum issued by Chemical Bank. Please deliver this Certificate to Mr. Wechsler at Chemical Realty Corporation to hold under a pledge agreement which is being prepared by counsel for Chemical Realty Corporation.

Once a year for the next three years, each time the certificate of deposit matured, the lender delivered the certificate to Chemical Bank with directions to deposit the interest in Barton's account, purchase a new certificate, and deliver it to the lender. Barton received correspondence memorializing each of these transactions.

The third year, when the certificate matured, the lender noted the reserves had become insufficient and requested the proceeds of the certificate be deposited in the lender's account with Chemical Bank rather than used to repurchase another certificate. Chemical Bank followed these instructions. That same afternoon, Barton and his attorney appeared at the bank to demand delivery of the proceeds from the certificate of deposit. After confirming with the lender that these funds had been continuously pledged to it, Chemical Bank refused Barton's demands, and Barton filed suit. The major issue in the case was whether the lender's security interest in the certificate of deposit had attached. The court held as follows:

> We conclude . . . that the effectiveness of the agreement reached by Barton and Chemical Realty Corporation was not actually conditioned on the execution of a written agreement. A security interest attaches as soon as the parties reach an agreement, the creditor gives value, and the debtor has rights in the collateral "unless explicit agreement postpones the time of attaching." Barton views the July 19, 1973, letter to defendant Chemical Bank as an explicit instruction postponing attachment. However, the statement that "a pledge agreement . . . is being prepared" is not an explicit instruction that the security interest is not to attach until the oral agreement of the parties is placed in written form. Further, the security agreement had to be reached between Barton and Chemical Realty Corporation, not between Barton and Chemical Bank. Thus, a letter to Chemical Bank cannot postpone the time when Chemical Realty Corporation's security interest in the collateral would attach. *Id.* at 1336.

- What facts would you assume were most important to the court in finding attachment had occurred?

- Why might parties delay attachment of a security interest?

International Perspective: Attachment

The Cape Town Convention, also known as the Convention on International Interests in Mobile Equipment, was briefly introduced in Chapter 13. The Convention was intended to facilitate secured interests in very expensive, highly mobile equipment including "airframes, aircraft engines and helicopters, railway rolling stock, and space assets." Chapter 15 considers some unique issues relating to the perfection of security interests in such assets; for the purposes of the current

chapter, we will focus on the attachment of such interests. The
following excerpt from Professor Charles W. Mooney's article
The Cape Town Convention: A New Era for Aircraft Financing,
18 Air & Space L. 4 (2003), describes how attachment works in
this context:

> The formal requirements for creating an international interest
> closely resemble the requirements for attachment of a security
> interest under UCC Article 9. An international interest is created
> pursuant to an "agreement," which is defined to include a "security
> agreement," "title reservation agreement," or "leasing agreement."
> First, an agreement must be in "writing," which is defined to
> include records other than traditional paper-and-ink records.
> Second, the agreement must relate to an object to "which the
> chargor, conditional seller, or lessor has power to dispose." Third, a
> security agreement must "enable the secured obligations to be
> determined" but it need not "state a sum or maximum sum
> secured." *Id.* at 5.

■   How do these requirements compare to those found in
      Article 9 for the creation and attachment of a security
      interest?

Chapter Conclusion: This chapter should leave you with a
clear sense of when a security interest has been created, as
between a secured party and a debtor. You should be able to
describe the kind of demonstrated intent and description of
collateral that is necessary to prove a security interest, as well
as whether such an interest will include a dragnet clause or
after-acquired collateral.   You should also have a solid
understanding of when a security interest will attach, so as to
set the stage for Chapter 15's discussion of perfection and
Chapter 16's coverage of priority of claims.

Chapter 15:
Perfection of Security Interests

Chapters 13 and 14 describe the advantages of secured credit, classify the most common collateral that may be used to support a debt, and explain how a security interest is created in, and attaches to, the collateral in question. While creation and attachment of a security interest fix the rights of the debtor and secured party vis-à-vis one another, perfection of the interest establishes the rights of the secured party against third parties by putting them on notice of the secured claim.

This chapter begins by addressing perfection by filing, including the requirements for a legally sufficient financing statement; the logistics of filing; errors in filing, indexing, and searching; and when filing is required. Next, the chapter introduces other means of perfecting a security interest, including automatic perfection for PMSI creditors and for some accounts receivable; perfection by possession or control; and temporary perfection.

Read 9-308 (a) and Comment 2. 9-308 is the most important provision regarding perfection, and 9-308 (a) and Comment 2 describe the concept of perfection in general terms.

- What is the purpose and effect of perfection?

Read 9-308 (c) and Comment 4. 9-308 (c) and Comment 4 address the possibility of continuous perfection, first by one means (such as possession of the collateral) and then by another (such as filing).

- What is the purpose of continuous perfection and when is it a useful device?

A. Perfection by Filing

Read 9-310 (a) and (b) and Comments 2 and 3. These subsections introduce perfection by filing, the dominant means of perfection. As this chapter shows, sometimes perfection is possible only by filing, sometimes perfection can be accomplished by filing or some alternative means, such as possession or control, and sometimes filing is ineffective to accomplish perfection and, instead, an alternative means of perfection is required. The appropriate means of perfection will depend on the type of collateral and the nature of the transaction.

- In general terms, when is filing required for perfection?

The Financing Statement

Read 9-502 and Comments 2 and 3. When perfection is effectuated through filing, the document that must be filed is a financing statement. The logistics of filing and the proper identification of the debtor in a financing statement are covered later in this chapter. First, these materials examine the purpose of a financing statement and how the collateral is to be identified.

- In what way does a financing statement constitute "notice filing," and what does this expression mean?

Read 9-504 and Comment 2. 9-504 describes how collateral is to be identified in a financing statement.

- How is an "indication of collateral," as that term is used in 9-504, different from the "description of the collateral" required by 9-108?

- What do these differing standards tell you about the different purposes of the security agreement and the financing statement?

> Many states provide standard forms, as well.

Read 9-521 and Comment 2. 9-521 provides a standard-form financing statement.

- What is the advantage of using this form?

- Are there any disadvantages of doing so?

In re Robert Bogetti & Sons, 162 B.R. 289 (Bankr. E.D. Cal. 1993), describes the purpose of a financing statement, as compared with a security agreement:

> A security agreement is an agreement describing the property in which the debtor has conveyed a security interest to the creditor. The Code comments emphasize that it is in the nature of a statute of frauds designed to establish whether a security interest in fact exists, and its scope or extent. By contrast, a financing statement is not designed to define or create contractual rights and is merely a notice-and-perfection tool. A financing statement is publicly filed. It perfects a creditor's interest vis-à-vis subsequent lien creditors and allows interested parties to obtain fuller information before entering into transactions with the debtor. The description of collateral in a financing statement may be, and is often, more expansive than the security agreement to ensure that perfection and notice is unquestioned in the collateral specifically described

in the security agreement. Accordingly, where disputes arise as to what collateral is covered by a security interest, courts limit their inquiry to what is described in the security agreement even though the financing statement may describe additional collateral. *Id.* at 296.

- Why can the description of collateral in a financing statement not be used to enlarge the scope of collateral as reflected in the security agreement?

Thorp Commercial Corp. v. Northgate Industries, Inc., 654 F.2d 1245, 31 U.C.C. Rep. Serv. 801 (8th Cir. 1981), presents two competing theories as to when a financing statement sufficiently identifies the collateral securing the referenced debt:

> Under one view, a financing statement adequately covers collateral if it reasonably puts a subsequent creditor on notice of a need for further inquiry about the possibility that the collateral is subject to a prior security interest. The reasonableness of the notice would depend on balancing such factors as the difficulty of making further inquiry against factors such as the likelihood the type of collateral described in the financing statement might include the collateral which interests the subsequent creditor.
>
> Under the second view of Article 9, a financing statement suffices to perfect a security interest in collateral if the financing statement itself contains a reasonable description of the collateral. The determination of reasonableness involves balancing such factors as the ease with which the prior creditor could make the description of the collateral more precise or clearer against factors like the danger that a subsequent creditor might fail to recognize that the collateral is covered. *Id.* at 1250.

- What are the differences between the two approaches?

The court held as follows, in accepting the first approach:

> Article 9 simply does not require that the financing statement describe anything more than the type of collateral, and leaves to interested parties the burden of seeking more information. Ultimately, such a requirement for a description of the collateral itself in a financing statement would eliminate the distinction between the financing statement and the security agreement, because the only way for a creditor to make sure that the financing statement describes the collateral would be to use the same description which identified the collateral in the security agreement setting up the security interest. Indeed, the district court suggested in the instant case that the "optimum practice" is for the creditor "to describe the collateral in the financing statement exactly as it appears in the security agreement." Such a requirement was rejected by the drafters of the UCC who specifically commented,

> [T]he financing statement is effective to encompass transactions under a security agreement not in existence and not contemplated at the time the notice was filed, if the description of collateral in the financing statement is broad enough to encompass them. Similarly, the financing statement is valid to cover after-acquired property . . . whether or not mentioned in the financing statement.

<blockquote style="border:1px solid black;">Very similar language is now found in UCC 9-502 Comment 2.</blockquote>

UCC § 9-402, official comment 2 (Official Draft 1972). One central purpose of allowing a broad financing statement is to allow a creditor that envisions an ongoing financing arrangement to protect the priority of its interest by filing at an early date a notice to third parties which will cover the existing arrangement and broad range of potential future modifications. By requiring a description of the collateral in the financing statement itself, courts would destroy this flexibility. *Id.* at 1251.

- Why else might parties desire that the financing statement describe the collateral in a manner different from the description in the security agreement?

<blockquote style="border:1px solid black;">9-204 Comment 7 may assist you in answering this question.</blockquote>

- Compare and contrast the discussion of after-acquired property and future advances in 9-502 Comment 2 with that contained in 9-204. How can the two be understood in conjunction with one another?

Even though it adopted the more liberal approach, the *Thorp Commercial Corporation* court was careful to indicate that it did not intend to eliminate the "collateral description" requirement entirely:

> [W]e do not overlook the district court's concern that a creditor should not benefit from use of a misleading or overreaching financing statement. The notice-filing concept has a primary purpose of facilitating ongoing financing arrangements, not merely by the first creditor on the scene, but also subsequent creditors. The requirement for filing a financing statement provides notice, at least theoretically, to subsequent creditors of what assets may already be encumbered by prior creditors. The financing statement would not provide notice where the description of collateral is misleading, for example, if the description were simply wrong or if the description seemingly would not cover the collateral but contained coverage under some hidden ambiguity that could not be considered reasonable notice. *Id.* at 1252.

- What advice would you give to a debtor regarding the description of collateral in a financing statement?

- How, if at all, would your advice to a future secured party reviewing the financing statement differ?

The following case illustrates why a secured creditor might be wise to draft a relatively nonspecific description of collateral.

In re Value-Added Communications, Inc.,
139 F.3d 543, 35 U.C.C. Rep. Serv. 2d 1047 (5th Cir. 1998)

Per Curiam.

The CLC Equipment Company leased a telephone-processing system to Value-Added Communications, Inc. VAC used that system to service the Minnesota state prisons under VAC's contract with the state to operate a telephone system for the inmates. VAC granted CLC a security interest in VAC's contract with Minnesota (the Site Leases), including the proceeds and revenues earned under that contract. In 1995, VAC filed a voluntary bankruptcy petition under Chapter 11. The bankruptcy court avoided CLC's security interest, finding that the financing statements were insufficient to perfect CLC's security interests in the revenues and proceeds of the Site Leases. The district court affirmed that judgment on appeal. Now, we affirm.

> As 11 USC § 546 (b) (1) (A) indicates, the trustee would not have been permitted to avoid the security interest if it were perfected before the bankruptcy petition was filed.

On March 14, 1994, VAC and CLC entered into an Equipment Lease Agreement (the Equipment Lease) under which CLC leased to VAC a System 20 inmate-call-processing system including coin-operated pay telephones. VAC installed this telephone system at five Minnesota state correctional facilities under VAC's Site Leases with the state. The Minnesota prison officials collected the money from the inmates for their use of the system.

The collateral at issue in this dispute is approximately $181,000 from inmates who used the telephone system VAC leased from CLC. The parties agree that there was a valid security agreement covering these funds. That security agreement states:

> [VAC] hereby grants, transfers, and conveys to CLC all of its right, title, and interest in and to each location Equipment Lease ("Site Lease") identified in Schedule "A" and in and to all revenues, rents, income, and profits arising from each of said Site Leases and in and to each and every right lessee as to said Site Leases.
>
> [VAC] hereby grants to CLC a security interest in (i) all of Lessee's contract rights in said Site Leases, (ii) all of Lessee's rights to receipts pursuant to said Site Leases, and (iii) the proceeds, products, additions, replacements, substitutions, and extensions of said Site Leases.

On April 18, 1994, and April 20, 1994, CLC filed financing statements with the Texas Secretary of State and the Minnesota Secretary of State. Those financing statements described the collateral as follows:

> All equipment and other personal property and all modifications and additions thereto and replacements and substitutions therefore, in whole or in part, now or hereafter covered by that Equipment Lease Agreement dated 3/14/94 and all schedules now or hereafter referencing said lease between Secured Party,

Review the
materials in Chapter
13, Part A as needed
to make sure you
understand why this
was a
"precautionary filing
only"

as lessor, and Debtor, as lessee. Secured Party and Debtor have
entered into a valid lessor-lessee relationship and this is a
precautionary filing only. Proceeds of collateral are also covered
but without power of sale.

The financing statements did not refer to VAC's contract with
Minnesota.

After VAC filed its Chapter 11 bankruptcy petition, CLC claimed a
security interest in the $181,000 collected by Minnesota under its
contract with VAC. The Trustee of VAC's bankruptcy estate attacked
that security interest, arguing that the financing statements were
inadequate to cover the money collected under the Site Leases. The
bankruptcy court agreed. The financing statements covered the
equipment described in the Equipment Lease as well as the proceeds of
that equipment, but the financing statements made no reference to the
Site Leases or the revenues and proceeds of those Site Leases. The
funds at issue here were revenues from the Site Leases. On appeal, the
district court affirmed.

. . . A financing statement must reasonably describe the collateral that
is covered by the security interest. "A collateral description in a
financing statement should be held adequate to perfect a security
interest in an item of property if the description reasonably provides
prospective creditors with inquiry notice regarding the type of property
at issue." Collateral descriptions are liberally construed, and the
identification of a particular type of collateral is usually sufficient.

The quoted language
is from *Production
Credit Assoc. v.
Bartos*, 430 N.W.2d
238, 241 (Minn. Ct.
App. 1988).

Our first step in evaluating these financing statements is to determine
whether these statements provide adequate notice "so that a
subsequent creditor would reasonably make further inquiry." The
financing statements refer to equipment and personal property covered
by the Equipment Lease as well as proceeds of that collateral. A
creditor making a reasonable inquiry would consult the Equipment
Lease. The express language of the financing statements covers no

Does a "reasonable
inquiry" include
looking at the
security agreement?

more than the items in the Equipment Lease. A reasonable inquiry,
then, would be limited to that agreement because, to perfect a security
interest, the financing statement must describe the collateral. These
financing statements do not describe collateral beyond that in the
Equipment Lease.

The theory of notice filing is that a reasonably diligent searcher will be
put on notice, not only of a security interest, but also of what collateral
is covered by the security agreement. Thus, no reported case upholds
total omission of a description from the financing statement. Such a
financing statement fails in one of its fundamental notice functions. . . .
[T]he reasonable searcher may safely conclude that collateral not
described in the financing statement is not encumbered, at least not by
this creditor.

CLC drafted the financing statement and chose to describe the
collateral in more detail than was required. CLC's narrow description
excluded the Site Leases and the revenues and proceeds from the Site
Leases from its coverage. CLC must live with the consequences of the
collateral description it drafted.

The funds at issue here are not described in the Equipment Lease, nor are they proceeds of the items described. . . . The funds collected from the prisoners were the product of the use of the equipment. Use is not a disposition of the collateral within the meaning of the definition of "proceeds." If fruits and products from the use of collateral were treated as proceeds, every creditor with a security interest in equipment would have a security interest in all items produced from the equipment as well as the revenues earned by the equipment. The revenues earned from the inmates' use of the equipment were the proceeds of the Site Leases. CLC's financing statements do not cover those leases.

> **Read UCC 9-102 (a) (64) and Comment 13.** Why are the described funds not proceeds of the Equipment Lease?

For the foregoing reasons, the judgment is affirmed.

- What was the apparent purpose of the financing statements CLC filed, and why are the Site Lease revenues not included?

- How could the collateral description be changed to cover the proceeds of the Site Leases?

Note 1: *In re S&J Holding Corp.*, 42 B.R. 249, 39 U.C.C. Rep. Serv. 668 (Bankr. S. D. Fla. 1984), shows how a court might analyze the distinction between "proceeds" and "products" of other collateral, an issue to which the *CLC Equipment Co.* court also made reference. The case involved the following facts:

> The debtor's business [Shazamm Enterprises, Inc.] is primarily in operating video games. . . . The debtor executed a security agreement covering "[a]ll of the assets of Shazamm Enterprises, Inc., including without limitation all . . . equipment, . . . inventory, . . . accounts receivable, contract rights, intangibles, video games, cigarette machines, coin changes (sic), and any and all other personal property or assets owned and used by the debtor in its business wherever located as well as any and all personal property hereinafter acquired." The same items were listed on the financing statement which was filed with the Secretary of State, and the debtor also checked the box which provides, "Products of collateral are covered." *Id.* at 250.

In finding no perfected security interest in the cash revenues generated by the video-game machines, the court held as follows:

> [T]he cash obtained through the machines is not proceeds of other collateral which might have automatic perfection under Florida Statute § 679.306. . . . The video-game equipment is collateral under the security agreement in question. But the cash which is generated through that equipment is not received from the sale of the collateral, but rather, through the use of it. It is more analogous to income generated through the use of, for example, construction equipment, which is given as collateral. The fact that

> In Revised UCC Article 9, see 9-315 (a) (1).

the money was earned through the use of the collateral does not make it "proceeds" subject to the protection of § 679.306.

The fact that the financing statement stated that "products" of collateral are also covered is of no significance at all. Only the property specifically defined in § 679.306 is given any unique protection, and the money here does not fit within the definition.

Although the money in question is not "proceeds," it might have been included as collateral standing on its own. However, the only item which might apply to it is "intangibles." The court concludes that this is an insufficient description to cover the revenue from the machines. *Id.*

- Is the court's holding consistent with *CLC Equipment Co.?*

- How should the financing statement be altered to cover the revenues?

Note 2: *Farmers & Merchants State Bank v. Teveldal*, 524 N.W. 2d 874, 27 U.C.C. Rep. Serv. 2d 643 (1994), shows how federal requirements can affect a party's Article 9 obligations in preparing a financing statement. In this case, which involved the interplay between UCC Article 9 and the federal Food Security Act of 1985, the court considered the following facts:

Farmers & Merchants State Bank and Kevin Teveldal d/b/a Kevin's Livestock Management Service claim priority of competing security interests in hogs owned by Gary Haiar and in the proceeds of sale. On January 7, 1991, Bank filed a financing statement with the South Dakota Secretary of State and perfected a security interest in Haiar's farm products, including beef cattle, dairy cattle, and hogs.

Teveldal provided Haiar with hog feed in the amount of $24,358.96 from September 3, 1991, to May 24, 1992. Bank claims it released $32,710.00 to Haiar, from August 9, 1991, to June 12, 1992, so that Teveldal could be paid for supplying feed. When Haiar did not pay for the feed, Teveldal telephoned the Secretary of State's office to inquire whether any security interest existed in Haiar's hogs. He was told that the Bank had a security interest in beef and dairy cattle under the farm-products section of the Effective Financing Statement list (EFS), which Congress required in the Food Security Act (FSA). Teveldal filed a Financing Statement with the Secretary of State on August 4, 1992, perfecting a security interest in 600 head of Haiar's hogs to secure payment of debt of $26,852.04.

* * *

In addition to the written description of the collateral on form UCC-1, the holder of a security interest in farm products is to designate the products by a code number for EFS purposes under

The Food Security Act of 1985 is found at 16 USC §§ 3801-3862.

9 CFR 205.206 lists the codes to be used.

the FSA. Bank provided the codes for beef and dairy cattle but not for hogs. . . .

* * *

Each party claims a superior perfected security interest in Haiar's hogs. Under SDCL 57A-9-312 (5) (a), the first security interest perfected is superior to all competing claims. Since Bank perfected first, we must determine whether Bank's failure to list the EFS code for hogs destroyed perfection of its security interest and whether the FSA protects Teveldal.

This rule is now found in UCC 9-322 (a) (1).

* * *

. . . Here, Bank's financing statement provided general notice that Bank held a security interest in Haiar's hogs. Teveldal should have conducted a search more thorough than a mere EFS code inquiry. The omission of the code number in the EFS section did not render Bank's financing statement insufficient. The formal requirements for a financing statement were met, and the Bank's filing constituted perfection of its security interest in Haiar's hogs. *Id.* at 876-878.

- Why did the omission of the EFS Code for hogs not render the financing statement "seriously misleading"?

Problem: Does this description sufficiently identify the listed collateral for purposes of a financing statement, or is it necessary to classify each item according to the Article 9 collateral classifications introduced in Chapter 13, Part B?

> all nursery stock
> all tractors
> all farm equipment
> all nursery equipment
> one 1979 pickup 4-speed vehicle
> one 530 Case backhoe
> one trailer to haul backhoe
> one tractor plow
> one row cultivator
> one 24 disc

- Where do you find the answer to this problem?

Based on *In re Frazier*, 16 B.R. 674, 33 U.C.C. Rep. Serv. 1150 (Bankr. M.D. Tenn. 1981).

Logistics of Filing and Errors in Filing

The UCC indicates where and by whom Article 9 filings may be made, as well as describing how the debtor is to be identified and the effect of errors. For many of the other logistics for filing

and searching under Article 9, most states follow the
recommendations of the International Association of
Commercial Administrators Secured Transactions Section.
The IACA website (www.iaca.org) is a good resource for IACA-
sanctioned forms and also provides links to the filing-and-
searching procedures for 48 U.S. jurisdictions.

**Read 9-509 and Comments 3 and 4, together with 9-502
Comment 3.** Together, these provisions describe who may file
a financing statement.

- Who is authorized to file a financing statement?

- How is this authorization commonly expressed?

Read 9-518 and Comments 2 and 3. 9-518 describes the
availability of correction statements.

- Who may file a correction statement?

- What is the legal effect of a correction statement?

- **Read 9-513 and Comments 2, 3, and 5.** How is a
  correction statement different from a termination
  statement?

- **Read 9-512.** How is a correction statement different
  from an amendment?

- What information may be corrected?

**Read 9-510 (c) and Comment 4, and 9-515 and
Comments 2, 3, and 5.** These provisions address the
effectiveness of financing statements and continuation
statements.

- When does a financing statement become effective,
  and how long does it remain effective?

- When must a continuation statement be filed?

- What is the effect of a lapsed financing statement?

- Once lapse has occurred, can a secured party re-perfect
  its security interest and regain its position of priority?

Read 9-506 and Comment 2. This provision addresses the
effect of certain errors on the effectiveness of a financing
statement and introduces the "seriously misleading" test.

- How does 9-506 distinguish between errors as to the debtor's name and other errors?

Errors as to the name of the debtor are addressed later in this chapter. First, these materials discuss other errors that may render a filing seriously misleading.

- What is the effect of a financing statement's being deemed "seriously misleading"?

The following case should inform your understanding of what kinds of errors will render a financing statement "seriously misleading." As you read this case, pay attention to the specific error alleged and make sure you can articulate why the court holds as it does.

In re Grabowski,
277 B.R. 388, 47 U.C.C. Rep. Serv. 2d (Bankr. S.D. Ill. 2002).

Kenneth J. Meyers, Bankruptcy Judge.

This case involves a priority dispute between defendants Bank of America and South Pointe Bank regarding their security interests in three items of farm equipment owned by the debtors. Both lenders filed financing statements perfecting their interests. Bank of America, the first to file, described its collateral in general terms and listed the debtors' business address, rather than their home address where the collateral was located. South Pointe, by contrast, described the collateral more specifically and included the debtors' home address. South Pointe contends that Bank of America's description was ineffective to perfect the Bank's security interest in the equipment and that South Pointe has a superior interest by reason of its subsequently filed financing statement.

The facts are undisputed. In April 2001, debtors Ronald and Trenna Grabowski of Dubois, Illinois, filed this Chapter 11 proceeding to reorganize their farming operation in Washington and Perry counties, Illinois. The debtors have been engaged in farming at this location for the past 30 years. Beginning in 1993, the debtors also owned and operated a John Deere farm-equipment business, Grabowski Tractor-Benton, Inc., at 12047 Highway 37, Benton, Illinois. During this time, debtor Trenna Grabowski, a certified public accountant, moved her accounting practice to the Benton dealership. Although the dealership was sold in 1999, Trenna Grabowski continues to conduct her accounting practice from the Benton location.

The debtors' schedules include a list of items of equipment used in their farming operation. The debtors filed the present proceeding to determine the validity, priority, and extent of liens held by various lenders in this equipment. . . . [T]he items . . . as to which a dispute remains between Bank of America and South Pointe, consist of a John Deere 925 flex platform, a John Deere 4630 tractor, and a John Deere 630 disk.

Bank of America claims a prior security interest in this equipment by virtue of a security agreement signed by the debtors in December 1998. The Bank's financing statement, filed on December 31, 1998, identifies the debtors as "Ronald and Trenna Grabowski" and lists their address as "12047 State Highway # 37, Benton, Illinois 62812." The financing statement describes the Bank's collateral as:

> All Inventory, Chattel Paper, Accounts, *Equipment*, and General Intangibles (emphasis added)[.]

South Pointe subsequently obtained a lien on the debtors' equipment in January 2000. South Pointe's financing statement, filed January 18, 2000, identifies the debtors as "Ronald and Trenna Grabowski" at "P.O. Box 38, Dubois, Illinois 62831" and describes South Pointe's collateral as:

> JD 1995 9600 combine . . ., *JD 925 FLEX PLATFORM . . ., JD 4630 TRACTOR . . ., JD 630 DISK 28' 1998. . . .* (emphasis added).

* * *

South Pointe asserts that Bank of America's financing statement, although prior in time, was insufficient to perfect the Bank's interest because it failed to place other lenders on notice of Bank of America's interest in the subject equipment. Specifically, South Pointe notes that the Bank's financing statement contained the address of the debtors' farm-equipment business rather than that of the debtors' home where their farming operation is located and, further, that it failed to mention any specific items of equipment or even make reference to "farm equipment" or "farm machinery." South Pointe argues that, based on this description, a subsequent lender would reasonably conclude that Bank of America's intended security was the personal property of the debtors' business rather than equipment used in the debtors' farming operation. South Pointe maintains, therefore, that the Bank's financing statement did not reasonably identify the Bank's collateral as required to fulfill the notice function of a financing statement under Illinois' Uniform Commercial Code.

> Is there such a classification as "farm equipment" or "farm machinery"? Why isn't this collateral a "farm product"?

* * *

South Pointe asserts . . . that it was misled by the incorrect address contained in Bank of America's financing statement and "reasonably concluded" that the only equipment subject to the Bank's lien was that located at the debtors' farm-equipment dealership. The Court disagrees that such conclusion was "reasonable." The debtors' business address was not part of the Bank's description of its collateral and, thus, did not serve to limit the collateral subject to the Bank's lien as South Pointe argues. In fact, Bank of America's financing statement indicated the Bank had a lien on the debtors' "equipment," with no indication that its interest was confined to equipment located in a particular place. Rather than serving to describe the Bank's collateral, therefore, the debtors' address merely provided a means by which subsequent lenders could contact the debtors to inquire concerning the Bank's lien.

While a subsequent creditor should not be imposed upon to be a "super-detective" in investigating prior secured transactions, the debtors' address in this case was an accurate and ready means of contacting the debtors. The Court notes, moreover, that even though the mailing address on the Bank's financing statement was that of the debtors' business, the debtors' names were listed as "Ronald and Trenna Grabowski," not "Grabowski Tractor-Benton, Inc.," the name of the debtors' business. Accordingly, the Court finds that a reasonably prudent lender would not be misled into believing that the collateral listed was property of the debtors' business, rather than that of the debtors individually.

For the reasons stated, the Court concludes that Bank of America's financing statement was sufficient to perfect its security interest in the subject farm equipment and that the Bank's interest, being prior in time, is superior to that of South Pointe.

- Does Article 9 require the debtor's address to be included in the financing statement?

- How, if at all, should this fact affect the outcome of the case?

Note 1: Read 9-516 (a). *Peoples National Bank v. Weiner*, 129 A.D.2d 782, 3 U.C.C. Rep. Serv. 2d 1615 (N.Y. App. Div. 2d Dept. 1987), addresses whether a filing statement mailed, but not received by the filing office, should nevertheless be deemed effective. In answering this question in the negative, the court held as follows:

> UCC 9-403 (1) states that "[p]resentation for filing of a financing statement and tender of the filing fee or acceptance of the statement by the filing officer constitutes filing under this Article." The defendants erroneously equate "acceptance" with "receipt" and argue that receipt is not required because either presentation *or* receipt constitutes filing. The defendants confuse the filing officer's performance of duty, i.e., acceptance, with receipt of the document. Acceptance is not the equivalent of receipt. Acceptance is not necessary to filing, while receipt is. "[T]he contemplation of the UCC is that filing be effective regardless of whether the officer receiving the *controlling* documents makes the right gestures of *acceptance.*" *(Matter of Flagstaff Food-Service Corp.*, 16 Bankr. 132, 135; emphasis supplied). The *Flagstaff* rule reflects the proposition that the party presenting the financing statement shall not bear the risk that the filing officer will not properly perform his duty. It is self-evident that the filing officer cannot carry out the duty to record or index a financing statement if the statement is not received. *Id.* at 784.

> With minor changes, this language is now found in 9-516 (a).

- What is meant by the statement, "Acceptance is not necessary to filing while receipt is"?

- At what point in time does responsibility shift from the
  secured party to the filing officer?

Read 9-102 (a) (18) and Comment 9 (b). Revised Article 9
uses the term "communication" rather than "presentation."

- Do you think this change in terminology would alter
  the holding of the *Peoples National Bank* court?

The *Peoples National Bank* court also showed how its decision
relates to Article 9's provisions on priority, which are the
subject of Chapter 16:

> We reject the defendants' further contention that the presumption
> of mail delivery can satisfy the evidentiary requirement of receipt.
> The presumption is inadequate in two respects. First, in order to
> establish priorities, the time, as well as the fact of receipt, must be
> established. The purpose of UCC 9-403 (1) is not only to absolve
> the secured party of responsibility for errors or omissions by the
> filing officer in matters such as indexing, but also "'to render
> certain the time when filing will be deemed to have occurred.'" *In
> re Brawn*, U.C.C. Rep. Serv. 1031, 1037).

- How does the court's holding help to "render certain
  the time when filing will be deemed to have occurred"?

Note 2: Some states have adopted filing requirements that
differ from the provisions of Article 9 on point. *In re Pipes*, 116
B.R. 154, 12 U.C.C. Rep. Serv. 2d 579 (Bankr. W.D. Mo. 1990),
illustrates such a wrinkle in Missouri law:

> [In] 1963, . . . the Missouri legislature, in its collective and infinite
> wisdom, adopted the so-called dual-filing system for financing
> statements pertaining to business property. Such a system, while
> in the distinct minority, requires filing both with the Secretary of
> State and the Recorder of Deeds of the obligor's county of business
> location, if business property is the claimed collateral. On the
> other hand, if the claimed collateral is consumer goods, farm
> products, or farm equipment, the filing is required in the county of
> the obligor's residence only. *Id.* at 155.

- What is the best way to determine whether a given
  jurisdiction imposes unique filing requirements?

Perfected Interests in Proceeds

The *CLC Equipment Co.* case above alluded to the importance
of determining whether assets are proceeds or products of
secured collateral. This section further explores issues of
perfection involving proceeds.

Would certified mail
or return receipt
work?

Read 9-315 and Comments 2, 3, and 4. As Comment 2 indicates, although a security interest often continues in collateral after it has been sold, when a "buyer in the ordinary course of business" under 9-320 (a) takes the collateral free from the security interest, it will be important for the secured party to establish rights in the proceeds of the sale since he or she will no longer be able to repossess the collateral in the event of default. As 9-315 (a) (2) indicates, the security interest will attach to "any identifiable proceeds of collateral."

> What is the difference between a security interest in collateral and a security interest in the proceeds of the collateral?

- Under what circumstances must a secured party file a financing statement to maintain perfection of a security interest in the proceeds of collateral that has been sold?

A number of cases explore whether certain collateral should be deemed the proceeds of other collateral. In *In re McDougall*, 60 B.R. 635 (Bankr. W.D. Pa. 1986), the court found that the cattle that ate the grain in which the secured party had a perfected interest should not be deemed proceeds of the grain.

In *Chemical Bank v. Miller Yacht Sales*, 173 N.J. Super. 90, 413 A.2d 619 (N.J. Super. App. Div. 1980), the court considered a transaction involving the trade-in of a 32-foot Luhrs motorboat on a $47,500 Marine Trader motorboat. The seller's original purchase of the Luhrs for $29,000 had been financed through Chemical Bank. The seller received a trade-in allowance of $22,500 for the Luhrs when the Marine Trader was purchased. After the seller defaulted on his payments for the Luhrs (which he had already traded in by that time), Chemical Bank sought to enforce its security interest in the Luhrs. Chemical Bank also sought to enforce its security interest in the Marine Trader as proceeds of the Luhrs. The court found that the buyer of the Luhrs was not a buyer in ordinary course of business and therefore took the Luhrs subject to Chemical Bank's security interest. The court rejected Chemical Bank's other theory of recovery, however, holding the Marine Trader was not proceeds of the Luhrs. Instead, the court found the relationship of the Luhrs to the Marine Trader too "tenuous and remote" for the latter to constitute proceeds of the former.

> The competing claims of secured creditors and buyers in ordinary course of business are discussed in Chapter 16, Part D.

In *In re Kingsley*, 865 F.2d 975, 7 U.C.C. Rep. Serv. 2d 1252 (8th Cir. 1989), the court considered whether government payments for the diversion of farmland for conservation purposes should be considered proceeds of the crops that would otherwise have been grown on the land. In rejecting this theory, the court found that "[t]here is simply no sense in which the Kingsleys[, the farmers in question,] received the diversion

payments "upon the sale, exchange, collection, or other
disposition" of their crops, as the Article 9 definition of proceeds
would require.   The court also found that the deficiency
payments the Kingsleys received when "the target price for the
crop [as set by the United States Department of Agriculture]
exceed[ed] the higher of the national weighted average market
price received by farmers for the crop during the first five
months of the marketing year, or the national average loan
rate for the crop before reduction to maintain the crop's
competitive market position" were not proceeds of their crops,
although the court acknowledged this was a closer call. The
court rejected the argument that deficiency payments should
be deemed proceeds because they are "part of the minimum
return the Kingsleys expected on their crops," although noting
the argument had "significant appeal," concluding that "[a]
study of the documents upon which the payments are made
convincingly demonstrates that the payments are based on
contract rights having origin in the statutory and regulatory
fabric of the farm-support program, rather than upon
marketing the crop."

- In your own words, why are the diversion payments
  not proceeds of the crops the Kingsleys would
  otherwise have grown?

- What distinction does the court draw between
  payments "based on contract rights" and based "upon
  marketing the crop"?

In *In re Tower Air, Inc.*, 397 F.3d 191, 56 U.C.C. Rep. Serv. 2d
71 (3d Cir. 2005), by contrast, the court found that a secured
party with a perfected interest in an airplane engine could also
claim an interest in the insurance check the debtor received
when the engine was damaged. The cost of the repair to the
engine was approximately $2.2 million.   The subsequent
insurance payment was for approximately $950,000, with the
shortfall being due to the policy's $1 million deductible. The
court found that the payment constituted proceeds for the
engine, even though the payment did not fully cover the
damage to the engine. The court added that the secured party
could not, of course, both recover the insurance money and
retain the engine itself, if the combined value of the two
exceeded the balance due under the secured debt.

- What guidance do you draw from the *McDougal,
  Chemical Bank, Kingsley,* and *Tower Air* cases,
  considered together?

The following case analyzes whether proceeds remain
identifiable after they have been deposited into an account with

other funds, applying 9-315 (b) (2) and the "lowest intermediate balance rule" referenced in Comment 3.

Universal CIT Credit Corp. v. Farmers Bank,
358 F. Supp. 317, 13 U.C.C. Rep. Serv. 109 (E.D. Mo. 1973)

Gerald W. Ryan, doing business as Ryan-Chevrolet & Olds Co., a proprietorship, operated an automobile dealership in Portageville, Missouri. On or about June 18, 1968, Ryan entered into an agreement with plaintiff [Universal CIT Credit Corporation] for wholesale financing, commonly known as floor-plan financing. Under the terms of this agreement, plaintiff from time to time advanced funds to pay the manufacturer's invoice on new automobiles, acquiring a security in such automobiles. As each automobile was sold by Ryan, he was required to remit plaintiff's advance. These remittances were in the form of checks drawn on Ryan's checking account at [Defendant Farmers Bank of Portageville.] The financing statements filed in New Madrid County reflect the security interest in the proceeds of the sale of the automobiles. Proper filing is not disputed.

> Has a purchase-money security interest been created?

Toward the end of 1969, plaintiff decided . . . to terminate the floor-plan arrangement.   Ryan was notified that the floor plan would be terminated December 31, 1969.

Sometime after 3:00 p.m. on January 15, 1970, Ryan had a conversation with Richard L. Saalwaechter, President of defendant bank. Ryan told Saalwaechter that he was being put out of business by plaintiff since plaintiff had revoked the floor plan, and that he wanted to be sure that the bank got paid. He said "let CIT be last – they put me out of business." Ryan discussed his debt to the bank on a demand promissory note. He told Saalwaechter that he wanted the bank to be safe on its loan. Ryan asked Saalwaechter to debit his account and credit the bank with $12,000 from his checking account. Saalwaechter then verified Ryan's checking account and determined that there was a balance of $16,340.00. When Saalwaechter suggested that Ryan write a check to the bank, Ryan told him that he preferred that the bank run a debit against the account because CIT was after him and he didn't know what they could do to him. Ryan further told Saalwaechter that CIT had checks out, and that he wanted to make a cash withdrawal to keep CIT from getting its checks. Thereupon, although the bank's business day had closed at 3:00 p.m., Saalwaechter debited Ryan's account in the amount of $12,000.00. The next morning, January 16th, Ryan came to the bank and made a cash withdrawal of $3,100.00. Saalwaechter testified that he had no knowledge that any of Ryan's checks to CIT [had already arrived] in the bank [for processing according to the bank's role as drawee] until after the debit and the withdrawal.

> As UCC 4-108 and its commentary indicate, a bank may, with proper notice, adopt a policy that items received after some specified time of day not prior to 2 p.m. will be treated as having been received the following business day. The "midnight rule" described in 4-301 (a) would require the bank to settle for the item before midnight on the banking day of receipt, but the "midnight deadline" defined in 4-104 (a) (10) would allow it until midnight of the next banking day to revoke this settlement and return the item unpaid.

The funds in dispute derive from the sale by Ryan of six motor vehicles. In some cases, a trade-in was involved with which we are not concerned. In each case, Ryan received a check from the purchaser in payment of the cash portion of the deal. Each check was deposited in Ryan's account with defendant bank, and he received full credit therefore. Each automobile sold, and the proceeds thereof, were subject

to plaintiff's security interest. The checks representing the proceeds of
the six automobiles sold by Ryan were all deposited on or prior to
January 15, 1970, and aggregate $18,112.44.

* * *

It is not disputed that plaintiff had a continuously perfected security
interest in six automobiles and their proceeds. Ryan sold separately
each of these automobiles and deposited the amount received on each
sale in his checking account at the defendant bank. Funds from other
sources were deposited in the checking account prior to and
contemporaneously with such deposits. Numerous checks were issued
on the account between the time of the first and last sale. Plaintiff
contends that the defendant bank was not entitled to debit Ryan's
checking account in the amount of $12,000 on January 15, 1970,
relying upon Section 400.9-306 (2). . . .

This material is now found at UCC 9-315 (a).

Defendant contends that the proceeds from the sales of the six
automobiles were not "identifiable" within the meaning of § 400.9-306
(2). Defendant argues that, when the proceeds were deposited and
thereby commingled with other funds in Ryan's account and thereafter
substantial withdrawals were made exceeding the amount of the
deposited proceeds, the proceeds completely lost their identity. No
Missouri case defines the term "identifiable" as used in this section. It
is provided in § 400.1-103 that all supplemental bodies of law continue
to apply to commercial contracts except insofar as displaced by the
particular provisions of the Uniform Commercial Code. Applying
§ 400.1-103, this court concludes that proceeds are "identifiable" if they
can be traced in accordance with the state law governing the
transaction. . . . The mere fact that the proceeds from the sales of the
six automobiles were commingled with other funds and subsequent
withdrawals were made from the commingled account does not render
the proceeds unidentifiable under Missouri law. . . .

* * *

This court's . . . task is to trace the proceeds of the sales of the six
automobiles to determine if they were taken by the bank when it
debited Ryan's account after the close of business on January 15, 1970.
. . . [I]n tracing commingled funds, it is presumed that any payments
made were from other than the funds in which another had a legally
recognized interest. This is commonly referred to as the "lowest
intermediate balance" rule. *Restatement of Trusts, Second*, § 202,
Comment *j* provides in pertinent part:

> *j. Effect of withdrawals and subsequent additions.* Where the
> trustee deposits, in a single account in a bank, trust funds and his
> individual funds, and makes withdrawals from the deposit and
> dissipates the money so withdrawn, and subsequently makes
> additional deposits of his individual funds in the account, the
> beneficiary cannot ordinarily enforce an equitable lien upon the
> deposit for a sum greater than the lowest intermediate balance of
> the deposit.

Illustration 20 to Comment *j* is as follows:

> A is trustee for B of $1,000. He deposits this money together with $1,000 of his own in a bank. He draws out $1,500 and dissipates it. He later deposits $1,000 of his own in the account. He is entitled to a lien on the account for $500, the lowest intermediate balance.

* * *

It was stipulated at trial that the following deposits were received by Ryan from the sale of the six automobiles and their proceeds in which plaintiff held a continuously perfected security interest:

Vehicle	Serial No.	Purchaser	Date of Deposit	Amount
1. 1969 Chev.	866578	Campbell	12-19-69	$5,700.00
2. 1970 Olds.	217371	Faulkner	12-20-69	4,125.00
3. 1969 Chev.	890453	Hunter	1-09-70	1,599.94
4. 1970 Chev.	138013	Carlisle	1-12-70	2,237.50
5. 1970 Olds.	160314	Rone	1-15-70	2,700.00
6. 1970 Chev.	141638	Hendricks	1-15-70	1,750.00

The court has examined the banking records of the Ryan account and finds that the identifiable proceeds in which plaintiff held a continuously perfected security interest on January 15, 1970, prior to the bank's $12,000 debit entry was $11,429.11. This amount may be traced according to the following summarization:

Date	"Proceeds" Deposited	End Balance	"Proceeds" Remaining in Account
12-18-69		$ 710.74	
12-19-69	(1) $5,700.00	9,100.58	$ 5,700.00
12-20-69	(2) 4,125.00	9,709.90	*9,709.90
12-24-69		6,201.41	*6,201.41
1-02-70		4,715.30	*4,715.30
1-09-70	(3) 1,599.94	11,987.65	6,315.24
1-12-70	(4) 2,237.50	15,426.72	8,552.74
1-14-70		6,979.11	*6,979.11
1-15-70	(5) 2,700.00		
	(6) 1,750.00	16,340.00	11,429.11

* Lowest Intermediate Balance

On January 15, 1970, the bank debited against the Ryan account checks aggregating $516.65 and in addition made the $12,000.00 debit entry in its favor. The $12,000.00 debit entry was made at 3:00 p.m. after the close of business. It may, therefore, be inferred that the

From this chart, together with the textual explanation, can you follow how the court calculated the amount of proceeds remaining in the account?

checks aggregating $516.65 were received prior thereto in the ordinary course on January 15, 1970, during banking hours. The pro forma balance prior to the $12,000.00 debit entry was, therefore, $15,823.35. Subtracting from this amount the "proceeds" remaining in the account ($11,429.11), the amount which the bank was entitled to debit was $4,394.24. Accordingly, plaintiff is entitled to recover from the bank the excess amount debited, or $7,605.76. That amount is identified as proceeds in which plaintiff had a perfected security interest, and plaintiff is entitled to recover this amount, together with interest at 6% from October 26, 1970, the filing date of the complaint.

Based on your knowledge of Articles 3 and 4, answer the following questions:

- When Ryan was seeking to protect the funds in his account from CIT's claim, why might he prefer a debit to a check?

- Why did he withdraw cash?

- What is the significance of the fact that the transaction at Farmer's Bank took place "[s]ometime after 3:00 p.m."?

Responsibilities of the Filing Party

- **Read 9-102 (a) (28) and Comment 2 (a) Examples 1 through 4.** When the party owing a secured debt is not the same as the party supplying the collateral, which is termed the "debtor" for Article 9 purposes?

Read 9-503 and Comment 2. This section establishes the requirements for proper identification of the debtor in the financing statement. One of the most important duties of a party preparing a financing statement is to ensure that the debtor is properly identified.

The following well-known case explains why an accurate indication of the debtor's name is of such importance to the Article 9 filing system.

In re Kinderknecht,
308 B.R. 71, 53 U.C.C. Rep. Serv. 2d 167
(Bankr. 10th Cir. 2004)

Thurman, Bankruptcy Judge.

The Chapter 7 trustee timely appeals a final judgment of the United States Bankruptcy Court for the District of Kansas in favor of Deere and Company and Deere Credit Services, Inc. (collectively, "Deere"), refusing to avoid Deere's interests in the debtor's property pursuant to 11 USC § 544 (a) (1). . . .

It is undisputed that the debtor's legal name is "Terrance Joseph Kinderknecht." In addition, it is undisputed that the debtor is informally known as "Terry."

The debtor granted Deere security interests in two farm implements. Deere promptly filed financing statements in the appropriate place, listing the debtor as "Terry J. Kinderknecht."

Subsequently, the debtor filed a Chapter 7 petition. His petition, while signed by "Terry Kinderknecht," is filed under his legal name, "Terrance J. Kinderknecht."

. . . According to the trustee, Deere's interests in the property were avoidable because they were not perfected under the Kansas Uniform Commercial Code inasmuch as its financing statements, listing the debtor by his nickname as opposed to his legal name, were "seriously misleading" and ineffective. Deere argued that providing the debtor's commonly used nickname in its financing statements was sufficient, and that its interests in the debtor's property were perfected under Kansas law. . . .

* * *

. . . For the reasons stated below, we conclude that the bankruptcy court erred in holding that Deere's financing statements were sufficient and served to perfect its interests in the debtor's property. For a financing statement to be sufficient under Kansas law, the secured creditor must list an individual debtor by his or her legal name, not a nickname.

* * *

Section 84-9-502 (a) of the Kansas Statutes Annotated states that "a financing statement is sufficient only if it: (1) Provides the name of the debtor[.]" This requirement is to facilitate "a system of notice filing" under which security-interest documents need not be filed, but rather only a single document notifying parties in interest that a creditor may have an interest in certain property owned by the named debtor. Because notice of a secured interest in property is accomplished by searching the debtor's name, "[t]he requirement that a financing statement provide the debtor's name is particularly important." Accordingly, pursuant to § 84-9-506 (b), if a financing statement "fails sufficiently to provide the name of the debtor" it is "seriously misleading."

The "name of the debtor" required in § 84-9-502 (a) (1) and its "sufficiency" for purposes of § 84-9-506 (b) is defined in § 84-9-503 (a).

. . .

* * *

> **Read 11 USC § 544 (a) (1).** When could the trustee "avoid Deere's interests in the debtor's property"?

> The quoted language is taken from UCC 9-502 Comment 2.

> What is meant by "Security-interest documents need not be filed"?

> The quoted language is taken from UCC 9-503 Comment 2.

Review UCC 9-521. What guidance does it provide regarding the appropriate indication of the debtor's name?

Although § 84-9-503 specifically sets parameters for listing a debtor's name in a financing statement when the debtor is an entity, it does not provide any detail as to the name that must be provided for an individual debtor – it simply states that the "name of the debtor" should be used. This could be construed, as it was by the bankruptcy court, as allowing a debtor to be listed in a financing statement by his or her commonly used nickname. But we do not agree with that interpretation because the purpose of § 84-9-503, as well as a reading of that section as a whole, leads us to conclude that an individual debtor's legal name must be used in the financing statement to make it sufficient under § 84-9-502 (a) (1).

As discussed above, § 84-9-503 . . . was enacted to clarify the sufficiency of a debtor's name in financing statements. The intent to clarify when a debtor's name is sufficient shows a desire to foreclose fact-intensive tests, such as those that existed under the former Article 9 of the UCC, inquiring into whether a person conducting a search would discover a filing under any given name. Requiring a financing statement to provide a debtor's legal name is a clear-cut test that is in accord with that intent.

If the debtor's legal name is required, why might a creditor list other names as well?

Furthermore, § 84-9-503, read as a whole, indicates that a legal name should be used for an individual debtor. In the case of debtor-entities, § 84-9-503 (a) states that legal names must be used to render them sufficient under § 84-9-502 (a). Trade names or other names may be listed, but it is insufficient to list a debtor by such names alone. A different standard should not apply to individual debtors. The more specific provisions applicable to entities, together with the importance of naming the debtor in the financing statement to facilitate the notice-filing system and increase commercial certainty, indicates that an individual debtor must be listed on a financing statement by his or her legal name, not by a nickname.

Our conclusion that a legal name is necessary to sufficiently provide the name of an individual debtor within the meaning of § 84-9-503 (a) is also supported by four practical considerations. First, mandating the debtor's legal name sets a clear test so as simplify the drafting of financing statements. Second, setting a clear test simplifies the parameters of UCC searches. Persons searching UCC filings will know that they need the debtor's legal name to conduct a search, they will not be penalized if they do not know that a debtor has a nickname, and they will not have to guess any number of nicknames that could exist to conduct a search. Third, requiring the debtor's legal name will avoid litigation as to the commonality or appropriateness of a debtor's nickname, and as to whether a reasonable searcher would have or should have known to use the name. Finally, obtaining a debtor's legal name is not difficult or burdensome for the creditor taking a secured interest in a debtor's property. Indeed, knowing the individual's legal name will assure the accuracy of any search that creditor conducts prior to taking its secured interest in property.

* * *

By using the debtor's nickname in its financing statements, Deere failed to provide the name of the debtor within the meaning of § 84-9-

503 (a), and its financing statements are not sufficient under § 84-9-502 (a). Because the financing statements do not "sufficiently . . . provide the name of the debtor" under § 84-9-503 (a), they are "seriously misleading" as a matter of law pursuant to § 84-9-506 (b). Furthermore, the undisputed facts in this case show that § 84-9-506 (c) does not apply in this case. That section saves a financing statement from being "seriously misleading" if a search of UCC filings "under the debtor's correct name, using the filing office's standard search logic, . . . would disclose a financing statement that fails sufficiently to provide the name of the debtor" in accordance with § 84-9-503 (a). Included in the record before us are the results of a UCC search conducted by Deere's counsel in Kansas's official and unofficial UCC search systems. Under both systems, she found no matches for the debtor's legal name "Terrance," but numerous matches for his nickname "Terry" and the initial "T." Thus, a search of the debtor's "correct name" did not disclose a financing statement, and therefore, § 84-9-506 (c) does not apply. The result of Deere's UCC searches underscores the need for a clear-cut method of searching a debtor's name in UCC filings. The logical starting point for a person searching records would be to use the debtor's legal name. When a UCC search of the debtor's legal name does not provide any matches, parties in interest should be able to presume that the debtor's property is not encumbered, and they should not be charged with guessing what to do next if the legal-name search does not result in any matches. Deere's financing statements, being seriously misleading, do not perfect its interest in the debtor's property and, therefore, the bankruptcy court erred in refusing to avoid its interests as against the trustee as a hypothetical lien creditor under 11 USC § 544 (a) (1).

- How could the facts of the case be changed to satisfy 9-506 (c)?

- Should the searching party be required to search, at least, for common nicknames close to the debtor's legal name, such as "Charlie" for "Charles"?

- What would be the risks and benefits of such a rule?

- How can a debtor's legal name be determined with certainty?

Responsibilities of the Searching Party

Just as an attorney who prepares a financing statement on behalf of a secured creditor has a duty to follow Article 9's requirements in doing so, an attorney representing a potential lender who is considering advancing funds to a borrower has a duty to assist the lender in ensuring that any prior security interests are identified before the transaction is finalized.

The following case shows how a potential lender might protect its interests when searching for prior filings against the

collateral of its would-be debtor. This case also demonstrates
that some lien creditors (such as the United States
government) are subject to different standards from those
imposed by Article 9, with regard to preparing a legally
sufficient financing statement:

In re Spearing Tool & Manufacturing Co., Inc.,
412 F.3d 653, 56 U.C.C. Rep. Serv. 2d 807 (6th Cir. 2005)

Cook, Circuit Judge.

In April 1998, Spearing Tool and Manufacturing Co. and appellee[s]
Crestmark [Bank and Crestmark Financial Corporation] entered into a
lending agreement which granted Crestmark a security interest in all
of Spearing's assets. The bank perfected its security interest by filing a
financing statement under the Uniform Commercial Code, identifying
Spearing as "Spearing Tool and Manufacturing Co.," its precise name
registered with the Michigan Secretary of State.
In April 2001, Spearing entered into a secured-financing arrangement
with Crestmark, under which Crestmark agreed to purchase accounts
receivable from Spearing, and Spearing granted Crestmark a security
interest in all its assets. Crestmark perfected its security interest by
filing a UCC financing statement, again using Spearing's precise name
registered with the Michigan Secretary of State.

Meanwhile, Spearing fell behind in its federal employment-tax
payments. On October 15, 2001, the IRS filed two notices of federal tax
lien against Spearing with the Michigan Secretary of State. Each lien
identified Spearing as "SPEARING TOOL & MFG. COMPANY INC.,"
which varied from Spearing's precise Michigan-registered name,
because it used an ampersand in place of "and," abbreviated
"Manufacturing" as "Mfg.," and spelled out "Company" rather than use
the abbreviation "Co." But the name on the IRS lien notices was the
precise name Spearing gave on its quarterly federal tax return for the
third quarter of 2001, as well as its return for fourth-quarter 1994, the
first quarter for which it was delinquent. For most of the relevant tax
periods, however, Spearing filed returns as "Spearing Tool &
Manufacturing" – neither its precise Michigan-registered name, nor
the name on the IRS tax liens.

Crestmark periodically submitted lien-search requests to the Michigan
Secretary of State, using Spearing's exact registered name. Because
Michigan has limited electronic-search technology, searches disclose
only liens matching the precise name searched – not liens such as the
IRS's, filed under slightly different or abbreviated names. Crestmark's
February 2002 search results came back from the Secretary of State's
office with a handwritten note stating: "You may wish to search using
Spearing Tool & Mfg. Company Inc." But Crestmark did not search for
that name at the time, and its exact-registered-name searches thus did
not reveal the IRS liens. So Crestmark, unaware of the tax liens,
advanced more funds to Spearing between October 2001 and April
2002.

How, if at all, should
this fact affect the
court's holding?

On April 16, 2002, Spearing filed a Chapter 11 bankruptcy petition. Only afterward did Crestmark finally search for "Spearing Tool & Mfg. Company Inc." and discover the tax-lien notices. Crestmark then filed the complaint in this case to determine lien priority. The bankruptcy court determined the government had priority; the district court reversed. The questions now before us are whether state or federal law determines the sufficiency of the IRS's tax-lien notices, and whether the IRS notices sufficed to give the IRS liens priority.

Crestmark argues Michigan law should control the form and content of the IRS's tax lien with respect to taxpayer identification. The district court, though it decided in favor of Crestmark on other grounds, rightly disagreed. [Instead, this is a matter of federal law.]

* * *

An IRS tax lien need not perfectly identify the taxpayer. The question before us is whether the IRS's identification of Spearing was sufficient. We conclude it was.

The critical issue in determining whether an abbreviated or erroneous name sufficiently identifies a taxpayer is whether a "reasonable and diligent search would have revealed the existence of the notices of the federal tax liens under these names." *Tony Thornton Auction Service, Inc. v. United States,* 791 F.2d 635, 639 (8th Cir. 1986). In *Tony Thornton,* for example, liens identifying the taxpayer as "Davis's Restaurant" and "Daviss (sic) Restaurant" sufficed to identify a business correctly known as "Davis Family Restaurant." In *Hudgins v. IRS (In re Hudgins),* 967 F.2d 973, 976 (4th Cir. 1992), the IRS lien identified the taxpayer as "Hudgins Masonry, Inc." instead of by the taxpayer's personal name, Michael Steven Hudgins. This notice nonetheless sufficed, given that both names would be listed on the same page of the state's lien index.

Crestmark argues, and we agree, that those cases mean little here because in each, creditors could search a physical index and were likely to notice similar entries listed next to or near one another – an option which no longer exists under Michigan's electronic-search system. So the question for this case becomes whether Crestmark conducted a reasonable and diligent electronic search. It did not.

Crestmark should have searched here for "Spearing Tool & Mfg." as well as "Spearing Tool and Manufacturing." "Mfg." and the ampersand are, of course, most common abbreviations – so common that, for example, we use them as a rule in our case citations. Crestmark had notice that Spearing sometimes used these abbreviations, and the Michigan Secretary of State's office *recommended* a search using the abbreviations. Combined, these factors indicate that a reasonable, diligent search by Crestmark of the Michigan lien filings for this business would have disclosed Spearing's IRS tax liens.

Crestmark argues for the unreasonableness of requiring multiple searches by offering the extreme example of a name it claims could be abbreviated 288 different ways ("ABCD Christian Brothers Construction and Development Company of Michigan, Inc."). Here, however, only two relevant words could be, and commonly are, abbreviated: "Manufacturing" and "and" – and the Secretary of State specifically recommended searching for those abbreviations. We express no opinion about whether creditors have a general obligation to search name variations. Our holding is limited to these facts.

Finally, we note that policy considerations also support the IRS's position. A requirement that tax liens identify a taxpayer with absolute precision would be unduly burdensome to the government's tax-collection efforts. Indeed, such a requirement might burden the government at least as much as Crestmark claims it would be burdened by having to perform multiple lien searches. . . .

Crestmark urges us to require IRS liens to meet the same precise-identification requirement other lien notices now must meet under Uniform Commercial Code Article 9. We decline to do so. The UCC applies to transactions "that create[ ] a security interest in personal property or fixtures *by contract.*" Mich. Comp. Laws § 440.9109 (1) (a) (emphasis added). Thus, the IRS would be exempt from UCC requirements even without the strong federal policy favoring unfettered tax collection.

More importantly, the Supreme Court has noted that the United States, as an involuntary creditor of delinquent taxpayers, is entitled to special priority over voluntary creditors. Thus, while we understand that a requirement that the IRS comply with UCC Article 9 would spare banks considerable inconvenience, we conclude from Supreme Court precedent that the federal government's interest in prompt, effective tax collection trumps the banks' convenience in loan collection.

We reverse the district court and affirm the bankruptcy court's grant of summary judgment for the government.

- Is this court's opinion consistent with *In re Kinderknecht*?

- Which is easier to determine with certainty: the legal name of an individual or that of a corporation?

- Following this case, how would you describe the allocation of responsibility between a searching party and a filing party, with regard to conducting a diligent search of the filed records, on the one hand, and preparing a sufficient financing statement, on the other?

- How, if at all, does your answer to the previous question change if the financing statement is prepared by the U.S. government?

Note 1: *ITT Commercial Finance Corp. v. Bank of the West,* 166 F.3d 295, 37 U.C.C. Rep. Serv. 2d 855 (5th Cir. 1999)

Margin notes:

Do you agree with this assertion? Why or why not?

The issue of tax-lien priority is further discussed in Chapter 16, Part E.

addresses how changes in technology have affected the analysis of what constitutes a "seriously misleading" filing:

> Before the advent of computerization, debtors were indexed alphabetically in an index book that contained all of the financing statements on file. A search in response to a request from a prospective creditor required an employee of the Secretary of State to look manually through the index book, much as someone would page through a telephone book. A benefit of manual searching is that the searcher can retrieve and list not only those financing statements that exactly match the requested name, but also those statements that are similar enough to the requested name to fall in close proximity in the index.
>
> Ironically, computerized searching can be less flexible than manual searching; because of the search parameters used by many computers, computerized searching often retrieves only names that exactly match the requested name. The Secretary of State's computer software has some built-in mechanisms to retrieve filings that do not match exactly, but are similar to, the requested name. For example, the system retrieves financing statements matching two or three words in the requested name. It does not, however, retrieve similar prefixes, suffixes, or alternative spellings of the debtor's name. . . . [W]hen searching for a hyphenated word, the search program ignores the hyphen and leaves a space in its place, with the result that the system treats a hyphenated name as two separate words. It searches under each of those separate words, but does not search under the combination of the two. *Id.* at 301.

- This portion of the court's opinion identifies several disadvantages of computerized filing. What are some of the advantages of computerized filing?

Note 2: In *Lory v. Parsoff*, 296 A.D.2d 535, 745 N.Y.S.2d 218 (N.Y. App. Div. 2d Dept. 2002), the court held that an attorney's "failure to file a UCC financing statement in the manner necessary to perfect his client's security interest constitutes malpractice as a matter of law." In *Barnes v. Turner*, 278 Ga. 788, 606 S.E.2d 849 (Ga. 2004), the court took this analysis a step further. In that case, an attorney filed a UCC financing statement on behalf of his client, to perfect the client's interest in a promissory note with a ten-year repayment term. The promissory note represented payment for the client's business, which he had sold to the maker of the note. The attorney neglected either to renew the financing statement or to advise the client that it must be renewed, and the court held that the attorney's omissions supported a claim of legal malpractice sufficient to withstand a motion for dismissal. The court rejected the attorney's claim "that he was not retained to file renewal statements," holding as follows:

As 9-515 (a) indicates, a financing statement is generally effective for five years.

An attorney has the duty to act with ordinary care, skill, and diligence in representing his client. In sales of business transactions where the purchase price is to be paid over time and collateralized, it is paramount that the seller's attorney prepare and file UCC financing statements to perfect his client's security interest. We further hold . . . that if the financing statements require renewal before full payment is made to the seller, then the attorney has some duty regarding the renewal. Otherwise the unpaid portion of the purchase price becomes unsecured, and the seller did not receive the protection he bargained for.

* * *

Safeguarding a security interest is not some unexpected duty imposed upon the unwitting lawyer; it goes to the very heart of why [this attorney] was retained: to sell [his client's] business in exchange for payment. *Id.* at 790.

- What steps should an attorney take to protect himself or herself from the kind of potential liability this case raises?

Problem: Is a financing statement for a debtor named "Silverline Building and Maintenance Company" "seriously misleading" if it incorrectly lists the debtor as "Silvermine Building Maintenance Co."?

Based on *District of Columbia v. Thomas Funding Corp.*, 593 A.2d 1030, 15 U.C.C. Rep. Serv. 2d 242 (D.C. Cir. 1991).

When Filing is Required

Read 9-310 and 9-313. Lawyers representing secured parties must become familiar with Article 9's provisions on perfection to ensure that their clients' security interests are properly perfected. A secured party who takes possession of collateral, only to find that perfection can be accomplished only by filing — or vice versa — can lose the benefits of secured status to others with perfected interests that will enjoy priority in the event of default.

The following case shows that perfection of a security interest in general intangibles such as computer information requires filing. This case also illustrates, in more general terms, how the type of collateral affects the appropriate means of perfection.

In re Information Exchange,
98 B.R. 603, 8 U.C.C. Rep. Serv. 2d 823 (Bankr. N.D. Ga. 1989).

W. Homer Drake, Jr., Bankruptcy Judge.

This case is before the Court on a motion for relief from the automatic stay filed by John C. Dabney, Jr. on February 16, 1989. At the hearing on the motion on March 14, 1989, the Court took the matter under advisement, and the parties have submitted letter briefs and a stipulation of facts which can be summarized as follows.

The debtor was in the business of collecting, sorting, storing, and reselling public legal-record information by use of a computer program and database.

Dabney is an attorney who was hired to represent the debtor in a suit by the previous owner of the debtor's business, who sought to recover the balance of the purchase price called for in the transaction for the sale of the business assets. During the course of the representation, Dabney was provided with magnetic computer tapes which included a copy of the debtor's program and database. The trustee concedes for present purposes that the debtor gave Dabney an oral security interest in the magnetic tapes to secure the payment of attorney's fees.

> If Dabney were representing the debtor in the bankruptcy action, he would file a statement of compensation under 11 USC § 329 to be approved by the court. Because, however, his claim relates to earlier representation of the debtor in a matter unrelated to the bankruptcy, he must seek relief from the automatic stay imposed by 11 USC § 352.

The trustee holds another copy of the program and database which is subject to a first-priority security interest held by Capital South Group, Ltd., to secure a claim in excess of $83,000.00. The trustee opposes Dabney's motion because the return to the secured creditor and the benefit to the estate from the sale of the database would be reduced if Dabney is also able to sell a copy.

Dabney asserts that he holds a valid attorney's lien. . . .

* * *

[A]s to Dabney's assertion that he holds an oral security interest perfected by possession of the collateral, it is true that O.C.G.A. § 11-9-203 (1) (a) permits the *creation* of a security interest to arise by possession rather than by a signed security agreement. However, *perfection* of the security interest is a different matter. A security interest in letters of credit, goods, instruments, money, negotiable documents, or chattel paper may be perfected by possession of the collateral pursuant to O.C.G.A. § 11-9-305. As to security interests which cannot be perfected by possession pursuant to § 11-9-305, a financing statement must be filed in order to perfect the security interest as required by § 11-9-302 (1) (a).

> See Revised UCC 9-203 (b) (3).

> See Revised UCC 9-313.

> See Revised UCC 9-310.

The Court is of the opinion that the collateral in which Dabney claims a security interest is a "general intangible" as defined by § 11-9-106, which is not included within the listed types of collateral in which security interests can be perfected by possession pursuant to § 11-9-305. Although security interests in "goods" or tangible personal property may be perfected by possession, it is not the computer tape itself which is actually in issue here, but the information and

> **Read revised UCC 9-102 (a) (42) and Comment 5 (d).** Which portion of the definition best covers the collateral in this case?

programming which is recorded on the tape. That is, the tape in and of itself is of little value; it is the information copied on the tape which is claimed as collateral. Because such information is a general intangible, Dabney can only perfect his security interest in the collateral by filing a financing statement.

This conclusion is buttressed by the consideration of the rationale behind permitting perfection by possession for some types of property. If a secured party has possession of a tangible item of collateral belonging to a debtor, this possession serves as a substitute for a filed financing statement by giving third parties notice of the likely existence of a security interest. Here, Dabney's mere possession of a *copy* of the debtor's program provides no notice to third parties that Dabney holds a security interest in the program itself or in all existing copies. Therefore, Dabney's oral security interest could not be perfected by possession and is unperfected. The security interest is therefore subject to avoidance by the trustee under 11 USC § 544.

- What Code section would you cite as authority for the proposition that filing is required for perfection of a security interest in general intangibles?

- As a general rule, why is possession or control insufficient to perfect a security interest in general intangibles?

When Filing is Permissive

Read 9-312 (a) and Comments 2, 3, 4, and 9. As 9-312 (a) suggests, when read in conjunction with 9-313, there is more than one means of perfecting a security interest in some types of collateral.

- For what kinds of collateral can a security interest be perfected by either filing or possession?

Problem: How could a security interest have been perfected under the following facts?

Plaintiff bankruptcy trustee filed this action seeking a determination that defendant does not hold a perfected security interest in certain assets of the debtor. The Court finds for the plaintiff. On January 14, 1987, the debtor, Dr. Roger Harold Schoenfeld, borrowed $4,000.00 from his father, defendant, Roger P. Schoenfeld. In exchange, the debtor signed a promissory note as well as a security agreement granting defendant a security interest in the debtor's gun collection. The determination of the perfection of the security interest in this case is complicated by the fact that the city of Joplin, Missouri[, where the debtor lives and works], is located within two counties – Jasper County and Newton County. The father attempted to perfect such security interest by filing UCC-1 financing statements with the Secretary of State and with the Recorder of Deeds of Jasper County, Missouri. The UCC-1 filed by the father lists an address for the debtor which was his office in Newton County, Missouri. The security agreement states that the guns will be kept at such address.

Based on *In re Schoenfeld*, 111 B.R. 832, 12 U.C.C. Rep. Serv. 2d 574 (Bankr. W.D. Mo. 1990).

Compliance with Other Law

Read 9-311 (a) and (b) and Comments 2 and 3, taking note of the phrase "not necessary or effective" in (a). 9-311 addresses the interplay between Article 9 and other state and federal law dealing with security interests.

- What are some examples of security interests falling within the purview of other bodies of law?

- What is the significance of the reference to "obtaining priority over the rights of a lien creditor" in (b)?

> 11 USC § 544 may assist you in answering this question.

When more than one body of law seems to govern how a security interest is to be perfected, confusion can result. *In re Hurst*, 308 B.R. 298, 53 U.C.C. Rep. Serv. 2d 342 (Bankr. S.D. Ohio 2004), consistent with 9-311 (d), stands for the proposition that a notation on the title of a motor vehicle that is being held as inventory for sale or lease is not sufficient for perfection under Article 9; instead, filing is required:

> [C]urrent Article 9 in Ohio . . . mandates the filing of financing statements to perfect motor vehicles held in inventory. . . .
>
> * * *
>
> Although there do not appear to be any reported decisions in Ohio on this specific issue, in reported decisions, interpreting statutes similar to the applicable Ohio statutes, other courts have consistently ruled vehicles held as inventory must be perfected by filing financing statements and, when necessary to continue their perfected status, appropriate continuation statements. *Id.* at 304.

However, if one of those automobiles had been sold to a consumer, 9-311 (a) (2) indicates that only the state certificate-of-title statute must be followed for perfection; in such a case, Article 9 does not impose additional requirements. *In re Psalto*, 225 B.R. 753 (Bankr. D. Idaho 1998), is illustrative:

> In most instances, the Uniform Commercial Code allows perfection of a creditor's security interest in goods by the filing of a financing statement with the Secretary of State. One important

exception to this general rule applies to property subject to Title 5 of Title 49 of the Idaho Code, the Idaho motor-vehicle-title statutes. For motor vehicles, issuance of a certificate of title and *the notation of the creditor's lien on that certificate is the exclusive* method of perfection. *Id.* at 754.

- Why does it make sense for the Code to treat the same automobile differently, depending on whether it is inventory held for sale or a consumer good?

Read 9-501 (a). As this provision shows, fixture filings and financing statements perfecting interests in standing timber or as-extracted collateral must be filed in the office where the related real-property mortgage is recorded, while other financing statements are filed in the office designated by the legislature in (a) (2).

The following case involves a lease-purchase of real estate, furnishings, and equipment. Because the transaction was recorded only in the county land records, not in the personal-property records as designated in 9-501 (a) (2), the security interest in the leased property was deemed unperfected. The case also reviews the distinction between a true lease and a secured sale, a concept addressed by 1-203 and covered in Chapter 2, Part A and Chapter 13, Part A.

In re 20th Century Enterprises, Inc.,
152 B.R. 119, 20 U.C.C. Rep. Serv. 2d 589
(Bankr. N.D. Miss. 1992).

David W. Houston, III, Bankruptcy Judge.

The items of equipment that are the subject of this adversary proceeding are more particularly described in a bill of sale from Jimmy Timms to [the] Tishomingo County [Board of Supervisors], . . . which equipment is currently in the possession of Tishomingo County.

20th Century Enterprises, Inc., hereinafter referred to as 20th Century, on or about April 12, 1990, executed and delivered to [the] Peoples Bank [and Trust Company] a promissory note and security agreement, . . . whereby 20th Century promised to pay Peoples Bank the sum of $200,081.00, with interest thereon at the rate of 12% per annum and reasonable attorneys fees necessary for collection.

In connection with the above described promissory note and security agreement, Peoples Bank caused to be filed with the Chancery Clerks of Chickasaw and Tishomingo Counties and the Mississippi Secretary of State, Uniform Commercial Code financing statements. . . .

On August 18, 1989, Tishomingo County and 20th Century entered into a memorandum agreement. . . . Under the terms of the said memorandum agreement, Tishomingo County proposed to purchase from Jimmy Timms a manufacturing facility, consisting of certain real property, buildings, and equipment for a total price of $850,000.00. In return for Tishomingo County's purchase of the said facility, 20th Century agreed to lease the facility, including the equipment, at an annual rental sufficient to repay Tishomingo County's acquisition costs over a fifteen-year period plus 4% interest. At the end of the fifteen-year period, Tishomingo County agreed to sell the facility, including the equipment, to 20th Century for $100.00.

Pursuant to the aforementioned memorandum agreement, Tishomingo County purchased the facility and equipment from Jimmy Timms on August 18, 1989, and on the same date entered into a lease-purchase agreement with 20th Century on the terms described in the memorandum agreement. . . .

The lease-purchase agreement was filed of record in the land records of Tishomingo County, Mississippi, on October 25, 1989, and is recorded in Book B-134, Page 680.

. . . Subsequent to the execution of the lease-purchase agreement, 20th Century entered into possession of the premises and utilized the equipment in its manufacturing operation and continued to do so up and through the filing of its bankruptcy petition.

Tishomingo County did not file a Uniform Commercial Code financing statement with either the Chancery Clerk of Tishomingo County, the Chancery Clerk of Chickasaw County, or the Mississippi Secretary of State, prior to the bankruptcy filing by 20th Century.

* * *

The transaction documentation is, for all practical purposes, silent as to its applicability to the equipment, but, as set forth in the stipulation, the parties have unequivocally agreed that the transaction did include the equipment. . . . As such, if the lease-purchase agreement is a true lease, Tishomingo County is the owner of the equipment and would not be required to file any additional documentation to perfect its ownership. On the other hand, if the lease-purchase agreement is a lease intended for security, Tishomingo County would be required by law to file appropriate Uniform Commercial Code financing statements to perfect its security interest.

> What is the difference between a "true lease" and a "lease intended for security"?

The total consideration paid by Tishomingo County for the real estate, furnishings, and equipment that were leased to 20th Century was $850,000.00. The lease-purchase agreement provided that 20th Century would pay 180 monthly installments in the sum of $6,287.75 each for a total consideration of $1,131,795.00. . . . [T]he agreement granted 20th Century an option to purchase the entire leased premises, including the land, buildings, fixtures, furnishings, and equipment, for only $100.00 after all of the 180 monthly installments were paid.

The court is of the opinion that § 75-1-201 (37), Miss. Code Ann., is dispositive of this entire proceeding. A lease agreement which provides the lessee, upon compliance with the terms of the lease, with an option to purchase the entire leased premises for a nominal consideration

> The referenced language is now found in UCC 1-203 (b) (3).

makes the lease one intended for security. In this case, the option-purchase price of $100.00 is obviously nominal.

* * *

In order to perfect its security interest in the equipment, Tishomingo County, therefore, was obligated to file financing statements with the Chancery Clerk of Tishomingo County and the Secretary of State of the State of Mississippi in keeping with § 75-9-401, Miss. Code Ann. As stipulated, it did not do either.

> The requirement is now found in UCC 9-501.

To the contrary, Peoples Bank filed appropriate financing statements as required by law perfecting its security interest in the subject equipment. As such, its perfected security interest has priority over the unperfected security interest of Tishomingo County.

* * *

Tishomingo County also argues that the recordation of the lease-purchase agreement afforded constructive notice of its interest in the equipment. This argument fails for three reasons:

A. Although the parties candidly agree that the lease-purchase agreement is applicable to the subject equipment, there is no mention of the equipment in the recorded agreement.

B. The lease-purchase agreement is recorded in the *land* records of Tishomingo County, Mississippi, not in the appropriate Uniform Commercial Code *personal* property records which is necessary to perfect a security interest in equipment. Section 75-9-401 (2), Miss. Code Ann., cannot be stretched to the extent that the recordation of the lease-purchase agreement in the real-property records is effectively a recordation in the Uniform Commercial Code records.

C. Nowhere in the factual stipulation, the motions for summary judgment, or the respective memoranda of law is there any factual indication that Peoples Bank had any notice, constructive or otherwise, that Tishomingo County had an ownership or security interest in the subject equipment.

. . . In this proceeding, the parties have agreed that there are no material factual disputes, and the court has determined that, as a matter of law, the perfected security interest of Peoples Bank has priority over the unperfected security interest of Tishomingo County. Therefore, the motion for summary judgment filed by Peoples Bank is well taken and must be granted. The motion for summary judgment filed by Tishomingo County is not well taken and will be overruled.

> 9-501 (a) (1) (B) and Comment 4 may assist you in answering this question.

- Assuming that the "furnishings" referenced in this case were "fixtures" within the meaning of 9-102 (a) (41), was the recordation in this case sufficient to perfect an interest in them?

- What additional facts, if any, would you need to find conclusively – as the court did – that the $100.00 option price is nominal?

International Perspective: Filing

Professor Ronald Cuming, in *Article 9 North of 49#: The Canadian PPS Acts and the Quebec Civil Code*, 29 Loy. L.A. L. Rev. 971 (1996), provides a summary of Canadian law as it relates to the perfection of a security interest by filing, explaining what is filed and where:

> [T]he [Canadian Personal Property Security] Act . . . provides for perfection by registration of security interests in all types of collateral, including money and negotiable securities. A financing statement, either written or electronic, may be registered before an agreement is executed and may relate to any number of separate security agreements between the parties. . . .
>
> When registering a financing statement, the registering party can choose the period of registration between one and twenty-five years, or the party can choose infinity registration. The registration fees in Saskatchewan are five dollars per year or $400 for infinity registration.
>
> Long before PPSAs were adopted in Canada, it was recognized that a system that uses only the name of the debtor as the registration-search criterion has a fundamental weakness. Such a system works well where the collateral is present or future inventory or accounts. It works less well, however, where the collateral is a specific item that is easily identifiable. The problem with a debtor-name registration-search system is that it does not give protection to a searching party who is not in the position to obtain a search of the registry based on the debtor's name because the existence or identity of the debtor is unknown to the searching party. If a unique identifier, such as the serial number of the machine, is available as a search criterion, a remote party will get the protection of the registry system.
>
> The need for a system which offers collateral-description registration-search criteria is particularly acute where collateral is property for which there is an active resale market. Motor vehicles are the most important items of collateral falling within this category. Since no province in Canada has enacted a certificate-of-title system for goods which provides for the issue of paper titles, it was necessary for Canadian legislators to address the problem of remote-party protection through the use of collateral-description registration-search criteria. Regulations to the Act provide that, where the collateral is a motor vehicle, boat, aircraft, or trailer held as consumer goods, the collateral must be described by serial number. For motor vehicles, this is the vehicle

identification number provided by the manufacturer. For boats and aircraft, it is the Ministry of Transport designation. When these types of collateral are held as equipment, a generic description may be used, but such a description provides protection only against the trustee in bankruptcy and execution creditors. If full protection is sought, the serial number must be provided. When the collateral is held by the debtor as inventory, there is no requirement that specific items of collateral be described on the financing statement. *Id.* at 980-982.

- When might a secured party choose infinity registration?

- Why would it ever choose registration for a shorter period?

- What are the relative benefits and risks of debtor-name and collateral-description registration-search systems?

The Freshfields publication *Doing Business in China* (Freshfields, Bruckhaus & Deringer eds., Juris Publg. 1996), discusses the "Security Law" of the People's Republic of China, which allows mortgages in the following assets: "buildings and other fixtures owned by the mortgagor; machinery, transportation equipment, and other property owned by the mortgagor; land-use rights; state-owned machinery, transportation equipment, and other property over which the mortgagor has the right of disposition in accordance with the law...." Consider the following excerpt:

> Pursuant to the Security Law, some kinds of mortgages must be registered, whilst for others registration is voluntary. Mandatory registration applies, broadly speaking, to mortgages over real property, woodlands, vessels, equipment, and other movables of an enterprise. If mandatory registration is required, the mortgage contract will become effective only upon registration, whereas if registration is voluntary, the mortgage contract will take effect as from the date of signing but will not bind any third parties unless it has been registered with the notarial authority of the place where the mortgage is located. *Id.* at 15-26.

Read 9-307 (c) and Comment 2. U.S. law recognizes foreign law governing perfection of security interests in collateral supplied by non-U.S. debtors, so long as the law of the debtor's home jurisdiction "require[s] notice in a filing or recording system as a condition of perfecting nonpossessory security interests."

- Would China's Security Law satisfy 9-307 (c)?

- What would be the implications of finding that a jurisdiction's law does not satisfy 9-307 (c)?

B. Other Means of Perfection

This section discusses several alternatives to perfection of a security interest by filing: automatic perfection, perfection by possession, perfection by control, and temporary perfection.

Automatic Perfection for PMSI Creditors

Read 9-309 (1) and Comment 3. As 9-309 (1) shows, most purchase-money security interests in consumer goods are automatically perfected as soon as the interest "attaches" within the meaning of 9-203.

> "Purchase-money security interest" is defined in 9-103.

- Why are consumer goods treated differently?

- When must a financing statement be filed for a security interest in consumer goods to be perfected, or to preserve the lender's priority?

- When might a creditor choose to file a financing statement to protect its purchase-money security interest, even when doing so is not required?

The following case answers the question of how to determine whether a purchase-money security interest has been created. This case also addresses how to determine whether the collateral in question is "consumer goods" within the purview of 9-309 (1).

In re Lockovich,
124 B.R. 660, 14 U.C.C. Rep. Serv. 2d 605 (W.D. Pa. 1991)

Lee, District Judge.

On or about August 20, 1986, John J. Lockovich and Clara Lockovich, his wife (Debtors), purchased a 22-foot 1986 Chapparel Villian III boat from the Greene County Yacht Club for $32,500.00. Debtors paid $6,000.00 to Greene County Yacht Club and executed a "Security Agreement/Lien Contract" which set forth the purchase-and-finance terms. In the Contract, Debtors granted a security interest in the boat to the holder of the Contract. Gallatin paid to the Yacht Club the sum of $26,757.14 on Debtor's behalf, and the Contract was assigned to Gallatin [National Bank].

Some states use the term "prothonotary" to describe the chief clerk of court.

Gallatin filed financing statements in the Greene County Prothonotary's Office and with the Secretary of the Commonwealth of Pennsylvania. Greene County was the county in which Gallatin was located, but Debtors were residents of Allegheny County. The filing of the financing statements, therefore, was ineffective to perfect the security interest in the boat.

The Debtors defaulted under the terms of the Security Agreement to Gallatin by failing to remit payments as required. Before Gallatin could take action, Debtors filed for relief under Chapter 11 of the Bankruptcy Code. Gallatin filed a Motion for Relief from the Automatic Stay, seeking to enforce their rights pursuant to the Security Agreement.

11 USC § 362, which provides for the "automatic stay," also provides a list of circumstances, in part (d), in which relief from the stay may be granted. Pursuant to 11 USC § 1107, a debtor-in-possession in a Chapter 11 proceeding has many of the rights that are afforded to the bankruptcy trustee in other kinds of bankruptcy cases, including the "hypothetical lienholder" status described in 11 USC § 544.

On October 2, 1989, the Bankruptcy Court denied Gallatin's Motion for Relief from the Automatic Stay, holding that Gallatin failed to perfect its security interest in the boat and, therefore, was an unsecured creditor in the Chapter 11 bankruptcy. As a holder of an unperfected security interest, Gallatin's right to the boat was inferior to that of the debtor-in-possession, a hypothetical lienholder pursuant to 11 USC § 544.

The issue on appeal is whether Gallatin must file a financing statement to perfect its purchase-money security interest in the boat. Gallatin's position is that the boat is a consumer good as defined by the Pennsylvania Uniform Commercial Code. Because the boat was a consumer good subject to a purchase-money security interest, Gallatin contends it was not required to file a financing statement in order to perfect its security interest. . . . [The Bankruptcy Court rejected this argument.]

* * *

After you finish reading this case, make sure you can articulate the court's response to each of these questions.

There are three significant problems in determining automatic perfection of purchase-money interests in consumer goods. First, what is a purchase-money security interest? Second, what are "consumer goods"? Third, can massive and expensive items qualify as consumer goods?

A purchase-money security interest is defined as one: (1) taken or retained by the seller of the collateral to secure all or part of its price or (2) taken by a person who, by making advances or incurring an obligation, gives value to enable the debtor to acquire rights in or the use of collateral if such value is in fact so used. It is undisputed in the instant case that the security interest held by Gallatin was a purchase-money security interest; therefore, the first hurdle has been cleared.

. . . "Goods" are defined as "consumer goods" if they are used or bought for use primarily for personal, family, or household purposes. The goods are not classified according to design or intrinsic nature, but according to the use to which the owner puts them. Debtors have never maintained that the boat was used for anything other than for their personal use.

The question remaining for this Court is whether a $32,500.00 watercraft can be properly classified as consumer goods. . . .

It is apparent from the opinion of the Bankruptcy Court, and from the opinion of the court in *Union National Bank of Pittsburgh v. Northwest Marine, Inc.,* 62 Erie Co. L.J. at 90, that those courts perceive a void in the Code which does not address the problem of secret liens on valuable motorboats. The court in *Northwest Marine* stated that this void was "best filled by interstitial law-making by the court" until the Legislature acts to bridge the gap.

> If the court had determined that the boat was not a consumer good, what other classification for the goods would be most reasonable?

We disagree. Determining what is a consumer good on an *ad hoc* basis leaves creditors with little or no guidelines for their conduct. Under the clear mandate of the Code, a consumer good subject to exception from the filing of financing statements is determined by the use or intended use of the good; design, size, weight, shape, and cost are irrelevant. Should a millionaire decide to purchase the Queen Mary for his personal or family luxury on the high seas, . . . the great Queen is nothing but a common consumer good. There need be no debate as to cost, size, or life expectancy. Creditors must be confident that, when they enter into a commercial transaction, they will play by the rules as written in the Code.

> The ship "Queen Mary" was built in 1933 with a 1500-person capacity.

* * *

The Bankruptcy Court was also interested in protecting the reasonable expectations of subsequent creditors and purchasers.   . . . [A] subsequent purchaser who intends to use the goods for personal, family, or household purposes is protected by § 9307 (b). A subsequent purchaser with resale as its intent, . . . or a subsequent creditor, [is], or should be, sophisticated in commercial dealings. They are charged with the knowledge of the contents of the Code, and should conduct themselves accordingly. A boat dealer is certainly aware when dealing with a consumer on the trade-in of a boat, that such boat could conceivably be subject to a purchase-money security interest capable of perfection without filing. Likewise, a subsequent creditor is aware of the perils associated with accepting collateral which can clearly be subject to a secret lien.

> The current citation is to UCC 9-320. This section is discussed in Chapter 16, Part C.

* * *

This Court, therefore, holds that Chapparel Villian III is a consumer good, and . . . a financing statement was not required to be filed by Gallatin to perfect the security interest in the boat. Gallatin has a valid security interest in the boat and under 11 USC § 362 (d), is entitled to relief from the automatic stay.

An appropriate order shall follow.

- ▪ How could the court's holding arguably exacerbate "the problem of secret liens on valuable motorboats"?

- What kind of "interstitial law-making by the court" did the lower court and the *Northwest Marine* court presumably intend?

Note 1: *In re Norrell*, 426 F. Supp. 435 (M.D. Ga. 1977), explores how the existence of an "add-on clause" affects the creditor's claim of a purchase-money security interest.

> The debtors . . . purchased from [W.S. Badcock Corporation], on credit, a variety of household appliances and goods in the amount of $977.15. In connection with this transaction, they granted a security interest to the creditor, . . . as follows:

> > "I hereby grant to Seller a security interest in the above described property and in all other items purchased from the seller . . . to secure the payment of my account balance, such security to remain in such property until the total cash price, and all finance charges, and insurance charges, if any, applicable thereto, and any subsequent purchases (plus any charges applicable thereto) added to this contract while there is a balance due thereon, have been paid in full."

> One month later, the debtors purchased a vacuum cleaner in the total amount of $92.65 and added it to their account, signing another financing agreement. The bankruptcy judge, relying on *In re Manuel*, 507 F.2d 990 (5th Cir. 1975), held that the creditor had a valid security interest in the vacuum cleaner, but not in the other property.

> *In re Manuel* involved an add-on clause in a security agreement under which the credit purchaser who never completely paid off his indebtedness before purchasing another item on credit and adding it to that indebtedness never gained title to anything until the entire debt was paid, and the creditor thus retained a security interest in all of the property so purchased to secure only the more recent purchases. The creditor in *In re Manuel*, not having filed a financing statement, nevertheless argued that his security interest in the household furniture the bankrupt had purchased from him under such an arrangement was perfected pursuant to Ga. Code Ann. 109A-9-302, which provides that filing is not required for perfection of "a purchase-money security interest in consumer goods." The court rejected this argument, stating that because the security agreement had purported to make collateral secure debt other than its own price, it was not a purchase-money interest entitled to be perfected without filing.

The current reference is to UCC 9-309 (1).

> That holding is directly applicable here: the security agreement clearly provides that, so long as any indebtedness is outstanding, property stands as collateral, not only for its price, but also for the price of property subsequently acquired on credit. Thus, Badcock does not have a purchase-money interest in the property purchased on the first sale and, therefore, the exception from the filing requirement provided for purchase-money security interests in consumer goods does not apply. Having failed to file a financing

statement, therefore, the creditor does not have a perfected security interest. *Id.* at 435-436.

- Does the add-on clause in this case differ from an after-acquired-property or future-advances clause within the meaning of 9-204?

- Why does the creditor lack a perfected security interest?

- What policy considerations support this decision?

Note 2: *Thorp Finance Corp. v. Ken Hodgins & Sons,* 73 Mich. App. 428, 251 N.W.2d 614 (Mich. App. 1977), addresses the availability of automatic perfection for future advances.

On November 2, 1971, [Ken] Hodgins purchased [a] payloader from Bark River Culvert Equipment Company for $38,125. Thereafter, Hodgins executed a note for $24,789.24 and a security agreementcovering the payloader, which Bark River subsequently assigned to State Bank [of Escanaba] on November 8, 1971. On November 10, 1971, State Bank filed a financing statement covering the payloader with the Secretary of State.

* * *

On March 20, 1974, Hodgins gave Bark River a note which was subsequently assigned to State Bank in the amount of $23,070.31, which included the balance then owing on the payloader. The note of March 20, 1974, contained specific reference to the November 2, 1971, security agreement on the payloader, and the original note was marked "renewed." State Bank did not file a new financing statement as to this loan.

> What is meant by the language "included the balance"?

* * *

. . . The issue is whether a secured party's perfected status continues as to a later advance without a new filing.

* * *

The majority view on this subject has been recently summarized as follows:

* * *

The better view holds that, where originally a security agreement is executed, an indebtedness created, and a financing statement describing the collateral filed, followed at a later date by another advance made pursuant to a subsequent security agreement covering the same collateral, the lender has a perfected security interest in the collateral not only for the original debt but also for the later advance.

... *James Talcott, Inc. v. Franklin National Bank of Minneapolis*, 292 Minn. 277, 291-292, 194 N.W.2d 775, 784 (1972).

. . . State Bank acquired a perfected security interest in the payloader when the original financing statement was filed in 1971. . . . In 1974, State Bank advanced an additional sum including the amount owing on the original loan. The requirements of attachment were satisfied, and the March 20, 1974, note incorporated by reference the 1971 security agreement into the 1974 loan. As soon as the 1974 security interest attached, it became perfected automatically by the previously filed financing statement of November 10, 1971.

The policy of the Uniform Commercial Code is merely to put potential lenders on notice of possible security interests. A potential creditor of Hodgins, the debtor, would have discovered the 1971 financing statement upon examination of the recordings in the proper place. Once the prior filing was discovered, the creditor could have requested the filing of a termination statement as to the filed financing statement, or entered into a subordination agreement with the first lender to apportion the priorities in the collateral in question. By following either procedure, an intervening creditor could protect himself against a subsequent advance by the first secured creditor. *Id.* at 430-437.

- Why does the court believe it is not unfair to other creditors to allow automatic perfection of a prior secured party's future advance?

Automatic Perfection for Some Accounts Receivable

Read 9-309 (2) and Comment 4. Filing is required to perfect a security interest in an assignment of accounts receivable, unless the assignment amounts to something less than a "significant part of the outstanding accounts" of the party making the assignment. In *Black, Robertshaw, Frederick, Copple & Wright, P.C. v. United States*, 130 Ariz. 110, 634 P.2d 398 (Ariz. App. 1st Div. 1981), the court introduced three tests for determining the significance of assigned accounts:

They are, (1) a "percentage of accounts" test, (2) a "casual and isolated transaction" test, and (3) a combination of both (1) and (2). *Id.* at 113.

In adopting the "percentage of accounts" test, the court held as follows:

This seems to us an appropriate place to exercise our bias in favor of certainty. If the courts define "significant" in terms of a percentage of the total accounts of the assignor, we can hope for the cases to produce a comparatively certain and reliable rule on which creditors and debtors can rely. If, on the other hand, we leave it to the courts to determine which sales are casual and isolated and which are not, we suspect that the process could go on for the rest of this century and part of the next without ever producing a rule on which a lawyer could rely. Since we see no powerful policy at work other than the desire to have the law certain, we hope the courts will . . . define "significant" in terms of a percentage of the assignor's accounts or contract rights. *Id.*

The court in *In re Tri-County Materials, Inc.*, 114 B.R. 160, 12 U.C.C. Rep. Serv. 2d 869 (C.D. Ill. 1990), took a different approach, holding that a party attempting to escape the filing requirement for an assignment of accounts receivable must satisfy both the "percentage" test and the "casual and isolated" test. The court justified its holding as follows:

The statutory language specifically requires that the assignment be an insignificant part of the outstanding account. Thus, at the very least, this test must be met in every instance. A showing of a casual or isolated assignment of a significant part of outstanding accounts would not be entitled to the exemption given this clear statutory requirement. On the other hand, given the comments to the UCC regarding the purpose of this exemption, in a case involving the transfer of an insignificant part of outstanding accounts to a creditor whose regular business is financing, such accounts should not fall within this exemption. Thus it is a logical result of the language and purpose of this section to require that both tests be met. *Id.* at 164.

- What are the benefits and risks of each test?

- What other tests could be considered?

Problem: Consider the following facts.

On or about May 7, 1982, Fort Dodge Roofing Co. assigned seven accounts receivable to Stetson Building Products Corp. with a total value, as per the face of the assignments, of $52,702.51. At that time, Fort Dodge Roofing Co. owed Stetson Building Products Corp. in excess of $170,000.00 on open account. Stetson Building Products Corp. provided materials to Fort Dodge Roofing Co. for use in its various contracting jobs. These were provided to Fort Dodge Roofing Co. on an open-account basis.

The total accounts receivable of Fort Dodge Roofing Co. at the time the assignment was made totalled $842,762.18. In addition, Fort Dodge Roofing Co. had work in progress on numerous jobs for which it had contract rights of $831,610.30.

On only one previous occasion, approximately two years prior to taking the assignment from Fort Dodge Roofing Co., had Stetson Building Products Corp. been involved in an assignment of accounts receivable with one of its customers. The President of Stetson testified that, in general, Stetson only does business with its customers on open account and does not take a secured position with its customers.

- Applying the tests from the *Black* case, is filing required to perfect an interest in these accounts receivable?

Based on *In re Fort Dodge Roofing Co.*, 50 B.R. 666, 41 U.C.C. Rep. Serv. 1839 (N.D. Iowa 1985).

Perfection by Possession

Read 9-313 (a) and Comment 2. As this subsection shows, perfection by possession is possible only for certain kinds of collateral. For some of these, either filing or possession is an effective means of perfection. For others, possession is the only way to perfect a security interest.

- **Read 9-313 (a) in conjunction with 9-312 (a) and Comments 2 and 3.** For which collateral is more than one means of perfection available and for which is possession the sole method of perfection?

9-312 Comment 2 may assist you in answering this question.

- When filing is not required, why might a secured party nevertheless choose to do so?

- Why should possession of the collateral listed in 9-313 (a) effectuate perfection without filing, and why are other kinds of collateral excluded from this list?

- **Read 9-313 (c).** Why might the parties choose to put the collateral in the possession of a third party rather than in the possession of the secured creditor?

In re Viscount Furniture Corp., 133 B.R. 360, 15 U.C.C. Rep. Serv. 2d 1315 (Bankr. N.D. Miss. 1991), shows one application of the Article 9 rule that a security interest in money can be perfected only by possession. The case involved a law firm that had secured a retainer from its client, which subsequently filed for bankruptcy. The court found that the firm's continuous possession of the funds satisfied the Code's requirement of perfection. The law firm was therefore permitted to apply the money toward satisfaction of the client's unpaid legal fees, rather than being required to surrender the funds to the bankruptcy trustee.

- In what other circumstances – other than a retainer – might a party take a security interest in money?

- When did the firm's security interest in the money become perfected, and how long would it remain perfected?

As 9-313 (a) indicates, possession is also a means of perfecting an interest in certificated securities.

- What is a certificated security, and where do you find this definition?

> 9-313 (d) may assist you in answering this question.

Read 9-313 Comments 3 and 4. When collateral is delivered to a third party, rather than to the secured party, other bodies of state law such as bailment and agency can affect the rights and obligations of the parties. These other bodies of law can be important factors in a court's determination as to whether the third party's possession of the collateral serves to perfect the secured party's interest.

In re Copeland,
531 F.2d 1195, 18 U.C.C. Rep. Serv. 833 (3d. Cir. 1976)

Seitz, Chief Judge.

This is a consolidated appeal from two separate orders of the district court in a Chapter XI bankruptcy proceeding instituted by Lammot duPont Copeland, Jr. The appeals are united by a common factual basis. In July of 1967, Copeland personally guaranteed payment on a $2,700,000 loan by Pension Benefit Fund, Inc. to two corporations and entered into an agreement which required him to pledge as collateral security 18,187 shares of Christiana Securities Co. stock. An "escrow agreement" was simultaneously executed between Copeland, Pension Benefit, and Wilmington Trust Company which designated Wilmington Trust as escrow holder of the pledged stock.

> The reference to "Chapter XI" indicates that this case was decided under the Bankruptcy Act that preceded the Bankruptcy Code. "Chapter 11" is now used. Chapter 11 of the Bankruptcy Code provides for reorganization of a debtor's estate pursuant to a court-confirmed plan.

Nearly three years later, in April 1970, there was a default on the loan. Following written demand upon the principal corporations for payment, Pension Benefit notified Copeland and Wilmington Trust by letter of September 11, 1970, of the uncured default and of its intention to demand the surrender of the escrowed stock in accordance with the pledge agreement. Copeland did not respond to this letter, but on October 20, 1970, filed a petition for an arrangement under Chapter XI of the Bankruptcy Act, and an application to stay enforcement of Pension Benefit's lien on the Christiana stock. Thereafter, Copeland withdrew his objection to the delivery of the stock to Pension Benefit, and the stock was turned over by Wilmington Trust on December 1, 1970. . . .

> Copeland appears to have been an "accommodation party" within the meaning of 3-419.

* * *

. . . [O]n October 19, 1973, debtor filed an independent application for an order requiring Pension Benefit to surrender the stock itself and dividends received with respect thereto. Debtor's application was

11 USC § 1102
creates creditors'
committees, which
normally consist of
the seven persons
holding the largest
unsecured claims.

The current
references to the
sections referenced
here as 9-105 (1) (g),
9-304 (1), and 9-305
are to UCC 9-102 (a)
(47), 9-312, and
9-313, respectively.

denied by the district court, sitting as a bankruptcy court, by order dated February 3, 1975.   Debtor and the Statutory Creditors' Committee appealed.

* * *

Relying on 9-304 (1) and 9-305, Copeland . . . argues that, even assuming the security interest had attached, it was not properly perfected on the date of bankruptcy.   Section 9-304 provides that a security interest in instruments, defined in 9-105 (1) (g) and 8-102 to include corporate securities such as the Christiana stock, can only be perfected by the secured party's taking possession.   Section 9-305 modifies this rule by permitting a secured party to perfect his security interest through the possession of his bailee. . . .

Debtor maintains that Pension Benefit's security interest was not perfected by Wilmington Trust's possession of the stock because Wilmington Trust was the agent of both parties. . . .

* * *

. . . [W]e believe that the language and policy underlying 9-305 support the district court's conclusion that Pension Benefit's security interest was perfected upon delivery of the stock to Wilmington Trust in July 1967. . . .

. . . Historically and prior to the Code, possession of collateral by a creditor or third party has served to impart notice to prospective creditors of the possessor's possible interest therein. The Code carries forward the notice function which the creditor's possession formerly provided.   Notice to future lenders is furnished under the Code by a filed financing statement, or by the possession of the property subject to the security interest by a secured party or his agent, depending upon the nature of the collateral.

Where the Code requires perfection by possession of the secured party or his bailee, it is clear that possession by the debtor or an individual closely associated with the debtor is not sufficient to alert prospective creditors of the possibility that the debtor's property is encumbered. . . .

It does not follow from this statement or from the policy underlying 9-305, however, that possession of the collateral must be by an individual under the sole dominion and control of the secured party, as debtor urges us to hold. Rather, we believe that possession by a third-party bailee, who is not controlled by the debtor, which adequately informs potential lenders of the possible existence of a perfected security interest satisfies the notice function . . . .

In the case presently before us, the collateral was held by Wilmington Trust pursuant to the terms of both the pledge and escrow agreements. Regardless of whether Wilmington Trust retained the stock as an escrow agent or as a pledge holder, its possession and the debtor's lack of possession clearly signaled future creditors that debtor's ownership of and interest in the stock were not unrestricted. As an independent, institutional entity, Wilmington Trust could not be regarded automatically as an instrumentality or agent of the debtor alone. There was consequently no danger that creditors would be misled by its possession.

* * *

Having found that Wilmington Trust's possession of the stock afforded the requisite notice to prospective creditors, we conclude that . . . its possession therefore perfected Pension Benefit's security interest. Hence, perfection occurred in July 1967, more than three years in advance of bankruptcy, on the date the stock was delivered to Wilmington Trust with notification of Pension Benefit's interest therein. For this reason, the district court correctly concluded that debtor's interest in the stock as debtor-in-possession was subordinate to that of Pension Benefit and properly denied debtor's application for a turnover order.

> The court's reference here is to a debtor-in-possession's rights under 11 USC § 1107.

- Read 9-313 Comment 3, focusing on its reference to escrow relationships. Is the court's holding consistent with the commentary?

Perfection by Control

Read 9-314 and Comment 2 in conjunction with 9-312 (b).

- For what kinds of collateral can a security interest be perfected only by control?

Read 9-104 through 9-107, 7-106, and 8-106. These provisions define "control."

- How is control different from possession?

The following case discusses perfection by control, illustrating how a secured party who relies on filing to perfect an interest in collateral, when that interest actually can be perfected only by control, may lose his priority position when, in the event of default, creditors seek to foreclose upon their security interests.

Counceller v. Ecenbarger, Inc.,
834 N.E.2d 1018,
59 U.C.C. Rep. Serv. 2d 524 (Ind. App. 5th Dist. 2005)

Bailey, Judge.

Appellant-Intervenor John Counceller appeals the small-claims court's judgment . . . in favor of Appellee-Plaintiff Ecenbarger, Inc. d/b/a Applied Metal and Machine Works. We affirm.

Counceller raises three issues, which we consolidate and restate as whether the filing of the financing statement perfected his security interest in the deposit accounts at issue – i.e., accounts that belong to Defendant First Metals and Plastics Technologies, Inc. – such that Counceller's interest enjoys priority over Applied Metal's judgment lien.

Counceller is the president and majority shareholder of Defendant and has individually loaned Defendant funds in excess of $200,000.00, which have not been repaid. On December 30, 2002, Counceller filed a financing statement with the Indiana Secretary of State, listing Defendant as the "Debtor." The financing statement gives Counceller an interest in "[a]ll Debtor's presently owned or hereafter acquired assets, including, without limitation, . . . deposit accounts . . . and all products and proceeds of the foregoing." At all times pertinent to this action, however, Defendant remained in control of the bank accounts at issue.

On June 15, 2004, Applied Metal received a default judgment against Defendant [in an unrelated matter] in the amount of $5,270.25, plus costs. Defendant has not moved for relief from this default judgment, and its validity is not at issue in the present controversy. On July 26, 2004, Applied Metal filed a verified motion . . . to collect the unpaid portion of the judgment, i.e., $5,411.28, wherein it named National City Bank ("Bank") as a garnishee defendant. In its response to Applied Metal's request for interrogatories, Bank disclosed that Defendant maintains two checking accounts at its facility, with a combined balance, at that time, of $5,411.28.

On September 7, 2004, Counceller filed a Verified Petition to Intervene and Assert Claim, wherein he alleged that his filing of the financing statement gave him a security interest in the accounts at issue, which is superior to any subsequent creditors of Defendant, including Applied Metal. Counceller's petition provided:

> 5. That on August 13, 2004, counsel for [Applied Metal] was given notice of the lien of [Counceller] and a request was made that [Applied Metal] "unfreeze" the sum of $5,411.28 held by [Bank] . . . as a result of [Applied Metal's] collection action. . . .

> 6. That [Applied Metal] has failed and refused to take action to "unfreeze" the National City Bank account and, as a result, the intervenor has found it necessary to employ counsel, incur costs and expenses, and take action to intervene in this case to assert his rights.

> 8. That [Applied Metal's] lien on [D]efendant's bank account with [Bank] . . . should be lifted.

As relief, Counceller requested that the small-claims court "grant him the right to intervene in this cause to assert his claim, [and] order the lien on [D]efendant's bank account . . . lifted." On September 16, 2004, the small-claims court granted Counceller's request to intervene, but denied his prayer for relief as follows:

5. [Counceller's] request for the hold on the Defendant's bank account to be lifted is now *DENIED.* The intervenor is seeking declaratory and/or injunctive relief from this Court by requesting that his security interest be deemed to have priority over [Applied Metal's] judgment lien and requested garnishment order thereon. Further, the intervenor is not seeking a monetary judgment for collection of any amounts owed pursuant to his lien. His prayer for relief and argument presented at hearing simply assert that the bank accounts should be released to the Defendant. This Court does not have jurisdiction to issue such relief.

That same day, the small-claims court ordered Bank to garnish Defendant's account and pay $5,411.28 to the Clerk of the Court. The small-claims court further permitted Counceller to "file any appropriate action, noticing *all* parties, to seek the enforcement of his lien through judgment in this Court (within jurisdictional limits)." In so doing, the court gave Counceller ten days to file such action and cautioned that, "[s]hould the intervenor fail to file said pleadings by September 27, 2004, the monies being held by the Clerk of this Court shall be released to [Applied Metal]."

On September 28, 2004, Counceller filed his "Intervenor's Claim," alleging that his security interest in the bank accounts at issue was perfected upon the filing of the financing statement and, thus, is superior to Applied Metal's judgment lien. This time, Counceller sought payment of the $5,411.28, which was being held by the Clerk of the Court, as partial satisfaction of his claim against Defendant. The small-claims court conducted a hearing on Counceller's claim, at which the evidence apparently demonstrated that the monetary balance of the Defendant's accounts with Bank totaled $38,000.00. On November 22, 2004, the small-claims court denied Counceller's claim because he does not "control" the accounts at issue pursuant to Indiana Code Section 26-1-9.1-312 (b) (1). In particular, the small-claims court reasoned:

> In the case at hand the Court is inclined to deny the Intervenor's claim for payment of the garnished funds. The evidence is clear that the Defendant remains in control of the accounts and continued to pay its day-to-day expenses from said accounts. Further, the Intervenor has not sought to gain control or assert his security interest over the entire account in a Court of appropriate jurisdiction. Rather, the Intervenor, if allowed to assert his security interest, post judgment and post garnishment, would simply be circumventing the payment of this judgment.

On December 1, 2004, after receiving the garnished funds from the Clerk, Applied Metal filed a release of judgment with the small-claims court. Thereafter, on December 17, 2004, Counceller filed his motion to correct error, which the small-claims court denied. Counceller now appeals the November 22, 2004, order.

* * *

On appeal, Counceller argues that the small-claims court's judgment in favor of Applied Metal is clearly erroneous because his interest in the accounts at issue has priority over Applied Metal's judgment lien. In

particular, Counceller contends that the financing statement served to
perfect his security interest in the deposit accounts in dispute,
regardless of his lack of control over such accounts. . . .

. . . [T]he parties do not contest that Counceller's security interest has
attached to the collateral, including Defendant's deposit accounts and
the proceeds of such accounts. Indeed, the parties agree that the only
issue presently before this Court is whether Counceller has a perfected
security interest in the deposit accounts in question, such that his
interest is superior to Applied Metal's subsequently obtained judgment
lien. Put another way, the sole issue presented is whether Counceller's
interest was perfected upon the filing of the financing statement or
whether, to perfect his interest in the bank accounts, he was required
to maintain control over the accounts. To determine whether a valid
security interest in the deposit accounts has been perfected, we look to
the statutory provisions of the Uniform Commercial Code, which are
controlling.

* * *

Pursuant to these statutory provisions, the only way to perfect a
security interest in a deposit account is by control under Indiana Code
26-1-9.1-312 (b), unless the security interest is in proceeds and the
original collateral – from which the proceeds derived – was perfected.

In the present case, the undisputed evidence reveals that Counceller
did not control the deposit accounts at issue under Indiana Code
Section 26-1-9.1-312 (b). Nevertheless, Counceller maintains that the
filing of the financing statement perfected his interest in the bank
accounts, which contained proceeds from Defendant's inventory. The
record is devoid of any evidence, however, demonstrating that the
funds comprising the two accounts in dispute were the proceeds from
Defendant's inventory. Rather, the evidence merely shows that such
funds were used in the operation of Defendant's business, i.e., to pay
the daily operating expenses of the business. Because Counceller has
failed to prove that Defendant's deposit accounts were composed of
inventory proceeds such that inventory was the original collateral, the
exception to perfection by control provided in Indiana Code Section 26-
1-9.1-315 does not apply.

Moreover, to the extent that the funds in question were proceeds from
Defendant's original bank accounts, we note that the filing of the
financing statement, alone, was still insufficient to perfect the security
interest in proceeds because it was insufficient to perfect the original
deposit accounts. As previously mentioned, pursuant to Indiana Code
Section 26-1-9.1-315, a security interest in proceeds is a perfected
security interest only if the security interest in the original collateral
was perfected.

Here, because Counceller never controlled the bank accounts at issue
pursuant to Indiana Code Section 26-1-9.1-312 (b), his interest in such
accounts was never perfected. Accordingly, Counceller's interest in
Defendant's bank accounts is not entitled to priority over Applied
Metal's judgment lien, because Counceller had never perfected his

interest. Therefore, the trial court did not err by denying Counceller's claim.

- Why were the deposit accounts not proceeds of the inventory in which Counceller claimed a security interest?

- Why would Counceller still not have prevailed on his claim, even if he had been able to prove the inventory constituted proceeds of the accounts?

- What should Counceller have done differently?

Note: An American Bar Association task force has completed a Model Deposit Account Control Agreement, which can be downloaded free of charge from the ABA Business Law Section website at http://www.abanet.org/dch/committee.cfm?com= CL710060. The Initial Report of the Joint Task Force on Deposit Account Control Agreement, dated February 13, 2006, contextualizes this project as follows:

> Control of a deposit account under Article 9 is achieved in one of three ways. Two are very straightforward. Under one method, if the secured party is the depositary bank, the secured party automatically has control. Under a second method, if the secured party is the depositary bank's customer with respect to the deposit account, the secured party has control.
>
> There is also a third method for a secured party to achieve control. Under that method, the debtor, the secured party, and the depositary bank must have "agreed in an authenticated record that the bank will comply with instructions originated by the secured party directing the disposition of the funds in the deposit account without further consent of the debtor." Accordingly, when the secured party is not the depositary bank and it is not desirable or practical for the secured party to become the bank's customer with respect to the deposit account, the secured party must, to have control over the deposit account, obtain a tri-partite agreement in a signed writing or other authenticated record that the depositary bank will follow the secured party's instructions directing the disposition of the funds in the deposit account without the debtor's further consent. This tri-partite agreement is commonly referred to as a "deposit account control agreement."
>
> The method for a secured party to achieve control by entering into a control agreement with the debtor and the depositary bank has in some cases become problematic in practice. Secured parties and depositary banks have developed their own forms of control agreements that largely focus on their own needs and concerns. On the one hand, secured parties generally seek, in control agreements, not only to achieve control for purposes of perfection, but also to obtain assurance of the priority of the security interest, as well as ongoing monitoring, enforcement, and other rights, all

without undue exposure to themselves. On the other hand, depositary banks view the control-agreement structure largely as an administrative accommodation to their customers that exposes them to potential liability to a third party that they would not otherwise have. As a result, depositary banks desire that the control agreement provide them with appropriate exculpatory and indemnification protections against liability for operational and other risks.

The result has been a classic "battle of the forms," with each secured party and depositary bank insisting on using its own form. Financing transactions sometimes are delayed while deposit account control agreements are negotiated. Alternatively, the negotiations continue post-closing with debtors facing impending events of default in their loan documents with secured parties unless the deposit account control agreements are finalized and executed by certain dates set forth in the post-closing arrangements. Depositary banks suffer as well. In-house lawyers at major financial institutions acting as depositary banks often have the task of negotiating numerous control agreements under the pressures of closings or impending post-closing customer defaults. Generally, practitioners and clients complain of delays, costs, and the use of resources that could be better employed elsewhere.

With this background, the Business Law Section of the American Bar Association organized an ad hoc task force to attempt to develop a standard form of deposit account control agreement that could gain wide acceptance in the industry and which could be implemented with no or minimal negotiation.

■   As an attorney, what factors will you consider in deciding whether to use the ABA Model Deposit Account Control Agreement – or any other standard-form document?

Temporary Perfection

Read 9-312 (e), (f), (g), and (h) and Comments 8 and 9.

■   What is the purpose behind the concept of temporary perfection?

■   When the temporary-perfection period ends, how can the secured party maintain perfection?

■   When might a creditor release a negotiable instrument from its possession to the debtor, thereby implicating 9-312 (f)?

- If the debtor sells the negotiable instrument to a bona fide purchaser for value, can the creditor recover the instrument?

- How, if at all, can the creditor protect its interests under these circumstances?

- What is the distinction between the transactions covered by part (e) and those covered by (f) and (g)?

As the following case shows, two major risks of temporary perfection are that the debtor will convey the collateral to a buyer in ordinary course of business and that the debtor will file for bankruptcy before the collateral is returned or the interest is perfected by another means.

In re Schwinn Cycling and Fitness, Inc.,
313 B.R. 473, 54 U.C.C. Rep. Serv. 2d 645 (D. Colo. 2004).

Nottingham, District Judge.

This is an appeal from the bankruptcy court. Appellant Expeditors International of Washington, Inc. appeals from the bankruptcy court's order that appellant's security interest in goods and proceeds thereof did not remain indefinitely perfected after the debtor's bankruptcy filing. . . .

The parties have stipulated to the following undisputed facts. Appellant is a shipping company that shipped goods belonging to Debtor Schwinn Cycling and Fitness. The contract between appellant and debtor provided that appellant had a general lien and security interest in all of debtor's property in its possession, custody, or control.

On July 16, 2001, debtor filed a voluntary petition of bankruptcy under Chapter 11 of the United States Bankruptcy Code. Within the twenty-day time period proceeding the petition date, appellant had in its possession some of debtor's goods. During this twenty-day time frame, appellant transferred possession of these goods to the debtor, who thereafter sold the goods. Thus, either shortly before or shortly after the petition date, debtor/debtor's bankruptcy estate had possession of the cash proceeds from the goods.

The parties agree that, on and prior to the petition date, appellant held a perfected security interest in the goods and the proceeds from the goods. Appellant perfected its security interest by way of its actual or constructive possession of the goods. Appellant did not file a financing statement with respect to the goods within twenty days after it relinquished custody of the goods to the debtor. . . .

* * *

At some point prior to the debtor's bankruptcy filing, appellant had a perfected security interest in the goods by possession. Appellant lost the

perfected security interest by possession when it gave possession of the
goods to debtor. After it relinquished possession of the goods to the
debtor, appellant had a temporarily perfected security interest in the
goods under Colorado Revised Statute section 4-9-312 (1). . . . At the
conclusion of this twenty-day period, in order to still be perfected, the
Uniform Commercial Code requires the secured party to perfect in
another way, such as by filing or possession. Appellant did not do so.

Appellant argues, however, that it did not need to perfect the security
interest after this time because the debtor's decision to file for Chapter
11 protection during the interim resulted in its security interest being
rendered permanently perfected. The Tenth Circuit comprehensively
addressed this argument in the case of *In re Reliance Equities, Inc.*, 966
F.2d 1338, 1341-45 (10th Cir. 1992), and this decision controls the
result of this case . . . .

The issue before the Tenth Circuit in *Reliance* was whether the
appellant held a perfected security interest in the proceeds from the
sale of promissory notes under the former version of Colorado's
codification of the Uniform Commercial Code. The *Reliance* appellant
had a temporarily perfected security interest in the proceeds pursuant
to Colorado Revised Statute sections 4-9-304 (4) and 4-9-306 (3) (1992),
the precursors in relevant part to the current Colorado Revised Statute
section 4-9-312 (f-h). This temporary perfection expired before the
Reliance appellant filed a financing statement. The *Reliance* debtor,
however, filed for bankruptcy while the *Reliance* appellant's security
interest was temporarily perfected. The *Reliance* appellant,
accordingly, raised the identical argument that appellant raises here,
arguing "that the perfected status of its security interest in proceeds
continued indefinitely once bankruptcy proceedings began because the
bankruptcy petition was filed during the ten-day period during which .
. . it [had] an automatic perfected interest in the proceeds."

The Tenth Circuit rejected this argument, explaining that,

> [i]n this case, [appellant] did not file a financing statement.
> Rather, [appellant] relies upon temporary perfection under Colo.
> Rev. Stat. § 4-9-306 (3). To freeze priorities upon the initiation of
> insolvency proceedings in an automatic perfection situation would
> contravene one of the principal purposes of the Bankruptcy
> Reform Act: to strike down secret liens.

> The automatic perfection provisions of sections 4-9-304 (4) and 4-9-
> 306 (3) were designed to address particular short-term exigencies
> where creditors could not always be expected to perfect their
> security interests otherwise. The motivating reasons behind these
> sections do not logically extend throughout the duration of a
> potentially lengthy bankruptcy proceeding. The short and precise
> durations explicitly provided for by the automatic security
> provisions in sections 4-9-304 (4) and 4-9-306 (3) are inconsistent
> with the concept urged upon us by [appellant] that a bankruptcy
> filing by the debtor should extend such security interests
> indefinitely . . . .

11 USC § 362 (b) (3)
allows continuation
of perfection despite
the automatic stay,
which ordinarily
prohibits new
perfections.

[Moreover, w]e find it especially significant that Colo. Rev. Stat. §§ 4-9-304 (4) and 4-9-306 (3), which address short-term automatically perfected security interests, make no mention of an extension of the perfection period in the event insolvency proceedings are commenced.

This reasoning applies with the same force to the new temporary-perfection rules found in Colorado Revised Statute sections 4-9-312 (f) and 4-9-313 (d). Therefore, *Reliance* controls the outcome of this case.

* * *

Appellant . . . contends that this case is distinguishable from *Reliance* because other creditors should have been aware of its security interest. This argument . . . fails because appellant's lien was unrecorded, so once it gave up possession, other creditors would not be aware of its security interest.

"The moral of this story," as one set of legal commentators explained, "is that temporary perfection is indeed temporary." Barkley Clark & Barbara Clark, 02-04 *Clarks' Secured Transactions Monthly* 5 (Feb. 2004). For the foregoing reasons, I affirm the well reasoned opinion of the bankruptcy court regarding its conclusion that appellant lost its perfected status in the goods because it failed to file a financing statement.

[The portion of the opinion addressing appellant's claim of a security interest in the proceeds of the collateral has been omitted.]

- Why does the appellant's argument fail, and what should it have done differently?

Problem: Consider the following facts:

In September 1964, Mr. Carney became indebted to Mr. Watson and executed a note for $2,500. Watson delivered the note to appellee, First National Bank, as one of several items of security for a substantial loan. A security agreement and financing statement were executed, and the note was listed therein. The note was a negotiable instrument; there was nothing on the face of the note which might give notice to anyone that it was security for a debt owed First National.

In August 1969, First National permitted Watson to withdraw the note from its files, presumably for the purpose of collection. A little over a year later, Watson obtained judgment against Carney on the note. McIlroy Bank[, to which Watson owed money as the result of a separate transaction,] learned of the judgment and forthwith initiated garnishment proceedings against the judgment because Watson was delinquent in a large debt to McIlroy. First National intervened in the garnishment proceedings, asserting its secured interest in the note which was the basis of the Carney judgment.

- How would permitting Watson to have temporary possession of the note advance "the purpose of collection"?

- Is First National's interest in the note perfected?

Based on *McIlroy Bank v. First National Bank*, 252 Ark. 558, 480 S.W.2d 127 (1972).

International Perspective: The Availability of Other Means of Perfection

> The text of the Convention can be found at www.unidroit.org/ english/conventions/ mobile-equipment/ main.htp if it is not in your statutory supplement.

Read Article 29 of the Convention on International Interests in Mobile Equipment. This chapter has addressed several ways, other than filing, in which the UCC allows parties to perfect a security interest in various kinds of collateral. As Article 29 suggests, the Convention allows for no such variety; instead, registration is the sole means of perfection. One of the major implications of the Convention's insistence on only one method of perfection is that the priority rules reflected in Article 29 of the Convention are remarkably simple. Simply stated, earlier-registered interests prevail over later-registered interests, and buyers take mobile equipment subject only to those interests that have been registered.

- "Mobile equipment" is more analogous to "goods" as defined by Article 9 of the UCC than to any other classification of collateral.   Under the UCC, what means of perfection – other than filing – are permissible for goods?

- Why should such additional means of perfection not also be available under the Convention?

Chapter Conclusion: This chapter introduced perfection by filing, automatic perfection, perfection by possession or control, and temporary perfection. Having studied these materials, you should know when each type of perfection is indicated and, when more than one method of perfection is available, the risks and benefits of each alternative.

Chapter 16:
Priorities Among Creditors

This chapter begins by introducing the concept of priority, describing its importance in the process of valuing a secured claim. As these materials show, even a secured party who has taken care to ensure that his or her security interest has satisfied each of the three steps presented so far – creation, attachment, and perfection – may nonetheless end up empty-handed if the debtor becomes insolvent and higher-priority claims of other secured creditors exhaust the collateral securing the debt. The balance of the chapter explores some of the most important rules by which priority of claims is determined.

A. Introduction to Priority

The following excerpt from the United Nations Commission on International Trade Law's *September 2003 Draft Legislative Guide on Secured Transactions Report of the Secretary General* describes the role of priority, as follows:

> This document is
> Appendix F to
> *International*
> *Secured*
> *Transactions*
> (Oceana
> Publications 2004).
> These remarks are
> found in Section VII
> (A) (1) of that
> document.

> The concept of priority is at the core of every successful legal regime governing security rights. It is widely recognized that a priority rule is necessary to promote the availability of many forms of low-cost secured credit. Priority makes it possible for grantors to create more than one security right in their assets, thus utilizing the full value of their assets to obtain more credit, which is one of the key objective factors of any effective and efficient secured-transactions regime. In addition, to the extent that priority rules are clear and lead to predictable outcomes, creditors, even unsecured creditors, are able to assess their positions in advance of extending credit and to take steps to protect their rights, which reduces the risks to creditors and thereby has a positive impact on the availability and the cost of credit.

> A creditor will normally extend credit on the basis of the value of specific property only if the creditor is able to determine, with a high degree of certainty at the time it extends the credit, the extent to which other claims will rank ahead of its security right in the property. The most critical issue for the creditor in this analysis is what its priority will be in the event of the grantor's insolvency, especially where the encumbered asset is expected to be the creditor's primary or only source of repayment. To the extent that the creditor has any uncertainty with respect to its priority at the time it is evaluating whether to extend credit, the creditor will place less reliance on the encumbered asset. This uncertainty may increase the cost of the credit to reflect the diminished value of the encumbered asset to the creditor, and may even cause the creditor to refuse to extend the credit altogether.

> To minimize this uncertainty, is important that secured-transaction laws include clear priority rules that lead to

predictable outcomes. The existence of such rules, together with
efficient mechanisms for ascertaining and establishing priority at
the time credit is advanced, may be as important to creditors as
the particulars of the priority rules themselves. It often will be
acceptable to a creditor that certain competing claimants have a
higher priority, as long as the creditor can determine that it will
ultimately be able to realize a sufficient value from the
encumbered assets to repay its claim in the event of nonpayment
by the grantor. For example, a creditor may be willing to extend
credit to a grantor based upon the value of the grantor's existing
and future inventory, even though the inventory may be subject to
the prior claims of the vendor who sold the inventory to the
grantor, or of the warehouseman who stored the inventory for the
grantor, as long as the creditor can determine that, even after
paying such claims, the inventory may be sold or otherwise
disposed of for an amount sufficient to repay its secured obligation
in full. *International Secured Transactions* (Oceana Publications
2004), App-F-45-46.

- How does priority "make it possible for grantors . . . [to
  utilize] the full value of their assets to obtain more
  credit"?

- What is it called when a debtor borrows from multiple
  lenders against the same collateral, in the real-estate
  context?

> Priority rules
> involving lien
> creditors are
> described more
> generally in Part E
> of this chapter.

The following case describes the relationship between the
Code's priority rules and the federal bankruptcy trustee's
power as a "hypothetical lien creditor" to avoid certain
transactions by asserting priority over them. In so doing, the
case demonstrates the importance of priority rules to the
bankruptcy process. The case also involves the first Chapter 13
bankruptcy proceeding that has been covered in these
materials. In reading this case, note how the Chapter 13
context affects the rights and obligations of the parties.

In re Bell,
194 B.R. 192 (Bankr. S. D. Ill. 1996)

Kenneth J. Meyers, Bankruptcy Judge.

> 9-311 (a) (2) and
> Comment 3 explain
> the relationship
> between state
> certificate-of-title
> statutes and Article
> 9, insofar as
> perfection is
> concerned. This
> relationship is
> discussed in Chapter
> 15, Part A.

The Chapter 13 [bankruptcy] cases under consideration present a
common factual scenario. In each case, the debtor borrowed money
prior to bankruptcy to purchase a vehicle and granted the creditor a
security interest in the vehicle. The creditor's lien, however, was never
recorded on the vehicle's certificate of title. The debtor then filed for
relief under Chapter 13 of the Bankruptcy Code, and the Chapter 13
trustee brought an action under 11 USC § 544 (a) (1) to avoid the lien
as an unperfected security interest.

While the defendant creditors raise various issues in arguing that their
liens should not be avoided, the Court's focus in this opinion is on the

effect of such avoidance in a Chapter 13 case in which the subject property is not liquidated by the trustee, but is retained by the debtor upon completion of the Chapter 13 proceeding. Specifically, the Court will address what rights, if any, a creditor possesses after avoidance of its lien and whether such avoidance results in a windfall to the debtor, who will obtain a vehicle free and clear of liens after paying a percentage of the creditor's claim as unsecured under the Chapter 13 plan.

> Chapter 13 provides for "adjustment of debts of an individual with regular income."

* * *

Section 544 (a) (1) provides that a bankruptcy trustee acquires, as of the commencement of a case, the status of a hypothetical judicial lien creditor and "may avoid" any lien or encumbrance on property of the debtor that is voidable by such a creditor under state law. Under this provision, federal and state law work in tandem. First, the substance of the trustee's rights as judicial lien creditor – primarily the priority of his claim in relation to other interests in the property – is determined by reference to state law. If the trustee has priority over a third party's interest under state law, federal law prescribes the consequence. Under § 544 (a) (1), the trustee may entirely avoid the inferior third-party interest in the property, and the third party is left with only an unsecured claim against the debtor's estate.

> The "state law" to which the court refers here is Article 9. Note how the trustee's avoidance rights allow it essentially to convert an attached claim with lower priority than the trustee has, to an unsecured claim.

This result obtains even if state law provides that the competing interest is subordinate, rather than void, as to a judicial lienholder. State law generally ranks interests in priority so that a subordinate junior interest is not voided, but survives and is paid from any surplus value that remains after senior claims are paid. Nevertheless, and notwithstanding the literal language of § 544 (a) (1), an interest that is merely subordinate to the claim of a judicial lienholder under state law is completely eliminated in bankruptcy as a matter of federal law.

In the cases before the Court, applicable Illinois law provides that an unperfected security interest in a motor vehicle is subordinate to a judgment lien such as that held by the trustee under § 544 (a). The Illinois Vehicle Code sets forth the requirements for perfection of a security interest in a motor vehicle and provides that an unperfected security interest in a vehicle "is not valid against subsequent transferees or lienholders of the vehicle. . . ." 625 ILCS 5/3-202 (a). The Uniform Commercial Code further provides, regarding the priority of competing interests in a vehicle, that "an unperfected security interest is subordinate to the rights of . . . (b) a person who becomes a lien creditor before the security interest is perfected." 810 ILCS 5/9-301 (1) (b). Since, in these cases, the trustee as of the date of filing had the rights of a lien creditor with priority over the unperfected security interests of the defendant creditors, these interests may be entirely avoided by the trustee under 11 USC § 544 (a) (1). Accordingly, the creditors' interests are eliminated as to the subject vehicles, and their claims survive only as unsecured claims against the debtors' estates.

> The current reference is to UCC 9-317 (a) (2).

The creditors, in an effort to avoid this unfavorable result, argue that the Court should exercise its equitable powers and deem their security interests perfected by way of equitable liens because the parties intended the creditors' interests to be secured, and it was due to the

> Equitable subordination is discussed below in Part C.

debtors' inaction or failure to cooperate that the creditors' liens were not
properly recorded on the vehicles' titles.   The Court rejects this
argument, as it has previously ruled that equitable liens arising under
state law are contrary to the letter and purpose of the Bankruptcy Code
and are, therefore, ineffective against a trustee's § 544 (a) avoiding
powers.

> The role of a
> Chapter 13 trustee
> is described in 11
> USC § 1302 and is
> more limited than in
> other kinds of
> bankruptcy cases.

The creditors additionally assert that the trustee is without standing to
bring these lien-avoidance actions because a Chapter 13 trustee serves
only a limited administrative function of objecting to claims and
ensuring compliance with confirmation requirements and plan
provisions. . . . Since . . . avoidance of the creditors' liens would increase
the proportion of the debtors' income to be paid to other unsecured
creditors under their Chapter 13 plans, the trustee may properly
exercise his avoidance power, and the creditors' standing argument is
without merit.

The creditors further contend that, despite the superiority of the
trustee's claim as hypothetical lien creditor in the context of these
bankruptcy proceedings, their unperfected security interests remain
enforceable as between the debtors and themselves, and thus survive
as effective liens when property of the Chapter 13 estate revests in the
debtors upon confirmation. The creditors cite the rule that "failure to
perfect a lien as to third parties does not invalidate a lender's security
interest as against the original borrowers," *First Galesburg National
Bank & Trust Co. v. Martin*, 58 Ill. App. 3d 113, 15 Ill. Dec. 603, 604,
373 N.E.2d 1075, 1076 (1978), and also invoke the maxim that a
bankruptcy discharge, being personal to the debtor, does not discharge
in rem liability or release liens or security interests in the debtor's
property. The creditors reason that, although they may be treated as
unsecured creditors in the debtors' Chapter 13 cases, they are still
entitled to enforce their liens against the debtors' property and thus
seek recovery of the subject vehicles upon completion of the bankruptcy
proceedings.

The creditors' argument is misplaced in that it overlooks the
consequences of a trustee's avoidance of liens under federal bankruptcy
law. A lien is avoided under § 544 (a) as a transfer of the debtor's
interest in property, and the consequence of such avoidance is
nullification of the transfer. This nullification means that the transfer
is retroactively ineffective and that the transferee – here, the defendant
creditors – legally acquired nothing through it. In the present cases,
the trustee's avoidance of the creditors' liens results in nullification of
the transfer of property represented by those liens, and the security
transactions are ineffective not only as to the trustee, but also as to the
debtor and creditor themselves as the immediate parties to the
transactions.

* * *

> **Read 11 USC § 551.**
> What is the effect of
> this provision?

While lien avoidance under § 544 (a) renders a security transaction
ineffective as between the parties, the avoided lien does not simply
vanish but is preserved for the benefit of the estate pursuant to 11 USC
§ 551.   The former lienholder's interest in the debtor's property
automatically becomes property of the estate and merges with any

1
2
3
4
5
6
7
8
9
10
11
12
13
14
15
16
17
18
19
20
21
22
23
24
25
26
27
28
29
30
31
32
33
34
35
36
37
38
39
40
41
42
43
44
45
46
50
51
52
53

residual interest in the debtor which passed to the estate when the bankruptcy case commenced. Thus, in a Chapter 13 case, when property of the estate subsequently vests in the debtor upon confirmation of the Chapter 13 plan, the debtor acquires his previously encumbered asset free and clear of the avoided lien – subject only to reinstatement of the lien if the case is dismissed prior to the debtor's discharge.

> Dismissal and confirmation are discussed in 11 USC §§ 1307 and 1327, respectively.

Application of these principles in each of the present cases results in the debtor obtaining a vehicle free of the lien granted to secure its purchase price, while paying the creditor only a portion of its claim as an unsecured creditor under the debtor's Chapter 13 plan. The creditors term this result an "abuse" of the bankruptcy process. The Court notes, however, that the creditors could have easily prevented this alleged "abuse" by tightening their procedures for ensuring that the liens were properly recorded on the vehicle titles. Nevertheless, the Bankruptcy Code does not leave these creditors without protection. Rather, as one of the provisions designed to safeguard the rights of Chapter 13 creditors, the Code assures that unsecured creditors in a Chapter 13 case will receive at least as much as they would have received if the estate were liquidated under Chapter 7. This provision, known as the "best interests of creditors" test, essentially requires the debtor to pay for his non-exempt assets over the term of the plan. Thus, although the debtors in these Chapter 13 cases will retain the subject vehicles following bankruptcy, they will have "purchased" them by paying into the plan an amount of money equal to their value as of the effective date of the plan. This amount will be distributed among unsecured creditors of the estate, including the defendant creditors who will receive a substantial portion of their now-unsecured claims. While the creditors in these cases, by not perfecting their liens, have forfeited their preferred position in the distribution of plan payments, no windfall results to the debtors, who must pay into the plan as much as if the subject vehicles were liquidated for the benefit of estate creditors in a Chapter 7 case.

> Discharge of debts is discussed in 11 USC § 1328.

> This provision is found in 11 USC § 1325 (a) (4).

For the reasons stated in this opinion, the Court finds that judgment should enter for the Chapter 13 trustee and against the defendant creditors in the trustee's lien avoidance actions under § 544 (a) (1). In order to protect the creditors' interests in the event their liens are reinstated upon dismissal of the debtors' cases prior to discharge, the Court finds that the debtors should be prohibited from transferring the subject vehicles until further order of the Court or until their Chapter 13 plans have been completed and their orders of discharge entered.

- How does priority affect the value of the secured claims referenced in this case?

- Why are the creditors unsuccessful in arguing that their liens survive, as between the debtors and themselves, notwithstanding the trustee's exercise of avoidance power?

B. Priority Rules for Unperfected Interests

Read 9-322 (a) (2) and (3) and Comment 3. Although perfected security interests prevail over unperfected ones, an unperfected holder of an Article 9 security interest may still have an advantage over other unperfected creditors whose interests attached or became effective later. These unperfected creditors have a relative disadvantage, however, as compared to lien creditors, and certain buyers, among others. 9-320, which is discussed later in this chapter, shows that certain buyers who qualify as "buyers in ordinary course of business" acquire goods free from most security interests, even those that are perfected.

The following case shows how priority would be determined as between a lien creditor and the holder of an unperfected security interest. This case also illustrates the interplay between automobile title law and Article 9.

Keep Fresh Filters, Inc. v. Reguli,
888 S.W.2d 437, 25 U.C.C. Rep Serv. 2d 599 (Tenn. App. 1994).

Koch, Judge.

Connie L. Reguli purchased a 1986 BMW on April 7, 1990, using money she had borrowed from her daughter, Iona Senecal. On June 11, 1990, the Davidson County Clerk, acting on Ms. Reguli's behalf, submitted an application for certificate of title and registration to the Motor Vehicle Division of the Tennessee Department of Revenue. The application did not identify any lienholders and certified there were no liens on the automobile other than those listed on the application. On July 20, 1990, the Motor Vehicle Division issued a certificate of title showing Ms. Reguli as the automobile's owner and indicating that there were no outstanding liens.

> The referenced note was entirely separate from the automotive-purchase transaction.

On January 9, 1991, Keep Fresh Filters, Inc. filed suit against Ms. Reguli to enforce a note. Ms. Reguli received service of a copy of the summons and complaint on January 12, 1991. On January 29, 1991, Ms. Reguli and Ms. Senecal requested the Motor Vehicle Division to issue a new certificate of title showing that Ms. Senecal had a lien on the automobile. The Motor Vehicle Division notified Ms. Senecal on February 7, 1991 that it had disapproved the application "due to improper documentation" and that it would not process the application "until [its] objections are removed."

Keep Fresh Filters obtained a default judgment against Ms. Reguli for $12,460.39, plus post-judgment interest on March 15, 1991. The trial court filed its judgment on March 27, 1991, and Keep Fresh Filters recorded a copy of the judgment in the register's office on May 7, 1991. The clerk and master issued a writ of execution on May 8, 1991, directing the Davidson County Sheriff to take possession of Ms. Reguli's automobile. On May 15, 1991, the sheriff's office took possession of the automobile and issued a notice of a sheriff's sale to be held on June 6, 1991.

On May 28, 1991, approximately two weeks after the sheriff took possession of the automobile, Ms. Reguli and Ms. Senecal took copies of Ms. Senecal's cancelled check and the document certifying the existence of Ms. Reguli's promissory note to the Motor Vehicle Division. The Motor Vehicle Division issued a new certificate of title on May 28, 1991, showing Ms. Senecal as the first lienholder and January 29, 1991, as the date of her security interest.

Ms. Reguli and Ms. Senecal immediately took the new certificate of title to the sheriff's department. Notwithstanding the valid levy of execution, the sheriff's department returned the automobile to Ms. Reguli and cancelled the sheriff's sale without consulting Keep Fresh Filters or the trial court. Keep Fresh Filters did not discover what the sheriff's department had done until Ms. Reguli had already obtained the automobile.

* * *

Three bodies of law govern the respective rights that Keep Fresh Filters and Ms. Senecal have in Ms. Reguli's automobile. They include Article 9 of the Uniform Commercial Code, the statutes governing motor-vehicle certificates of title, and the statutes governing judgment liens and executions. Construed together, these statutes provide the principles for fixing the priorities among competing lien claimants and secured parties.

* * *

Even though the motor-vehicle title-and-registration statutes control the filing requirements for perfecting security interests in automobiles, the Uniform Commercial Code still provides the rules for determining priorities among persons claiming an interest in the same automobile. Secured parties, even unperfected secured parties, have greater rights in collateral than any other creditor unless Article 9 provides otherwise. While Tenn. Code Ann. § 47-9-312 (1992) governs the priorities among competing security interests in the same collateral, Tenn. Code Ann. § 47-9-301 (1992) governs the priorities among unperfected security interests and other types of claims.

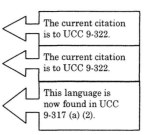

The current citation is to UCC 9-322.

The current citation is to UCC 9-322.

This language is now found in UCC 9-317 (a) (2).

Tenn. Code Ann. § 47-9-301 (1) (b) specifically provides that an unperfected security interest is subordinate to the rights of "a person who becomes a lien creditor before the security interest is perfected." This provision controls the outcome of this appeal. Thus, sorting out the competing claims of Keep Fresh Filters, Ms. Reguli, and Ms. Senecal requires the consideration of four questions: (1) Is Keep Fresh Filters a lien creditor? (2) If Keep Fresh Filters is a lien creditor, when did it become a lien creditor? (3) Was Ms. Senecal's security interest unperfected when Keep Fresh Filters became a lien creditor? and (4) What effect, if any, did Ms. Senecal's later perfection of her security interest have on the priority of her claim?

The current citation is to UCC 9-102 (a) (52).

The current citation is to UCC 1-201 (b) (13).

A "lien creditor" according to Tenn. Code Ann. § 47-9-301 (3), is a "creditor who has acquired a lien on the property involved by attachment, levy, or the like." Determining whether a particular creditor is a lien creditor requires consideration of state law distinct from the Uniform Commercial Code. We must first determine whether the claimant is a creditor under Tenn. Code Ann. § 47-1-201 (12) (Supp.1994). Then we must determine whether the claimant has a lien recognized by state law and whether the lien attaches to property subject to a conflicting claim. Finally, we must determine whether the lien arises from an "attachment, levy, or the like."

The record leaves little room for doubt that Keep Fresh Filters is Ms. Reguli's creditor, and that both Keep Fresh Filters and Ms. Senecal are asserting conflicting claims regarding the same property. Keep Fresh Filters is Ms. Reguli's judgment creditor by virtue of its valid $12,460 judgment against her, and both parties are claiming an interest in Ms. Reguli's automobile. The remaining two issues concerning whether Keep Fresh Filters has a lien on the automobile and, if it does, whether Keep Fresh Filters obtained the lien by "attachment, levy, or the like" are not as straightforward.

A lien, in its broadest sense, is a legal claim or charge on real or personal property used as security for the payment of some debt or obligation. Persons who obtain a judgment become judgment creditors and may obtain . . . [an] execution lien authorized by Tenn. Code Ann. § 25-5-103 (1980) that attaches to the judgment debtor's personal property. This lien requires the registration of the judgment within sixty days after it is rendered, and issuance and levy of a writ of execution.

A writ of execution is now the customary vehicle for enforcing money judgments. It is simply an order directing the sheriff to levy upon and sell the judgment debtor's property identified in the writ that is not statutorily exempt. Clerks of the courts of record must issue writs of execution thirty days after the entry of a judgment as a matter of course, or sooner if requested by the judgment creditor.

A levy of execution is the officer's act of appropriating or singling-out the debtor's property for the satisfaction of a debt. It is accomplished by the officer's asserting dominion over the property by actually taking possession of it or doing something that amounts to the same thing. A levy on personal property results in the actual divestiture of the judgment debtor's title. It places the debtor's personal property in the custody of the law, and the sheriff acquires a special interest in the property.

A judgment creditor's execution lien is thus inextricably linked to the sheriff's levy of execution. Since judgment creditors such as Keep Fresh Filters have acquired their liens by execution and levy, they are lien creditors for the purpose of Tenn. Code Ann. § 47-9-301 (3).

The existence and efficacy of an execution lien depends only upon strict compliance with the statutes governing execution liens and writs of execution. As long as these statutory requirements are observed, persons claiming an execution lien need not comply with Article 9's

1
2
3
4
5
6
7
8
9
10
11
12
13
14
15
16
17
18
19
20
21
22
23
24
25
26
27
28
29
30
31
32
33
34
35
36
37
38
39
40
41
42
43
44
45
46
50
51
52
53

filing requirements because execution liens are not consensual security interests created by contract. Likewise, they need not comply with the motor-vehicle title-and-registration statutes since execution liens depend on possession.

* * *

The clerk and master issued the writ of execution directing the sheriff to levy on Ms. Reguli's automobile on May 8, 1991. In accordance with Tenn. Code Ann. § 26-1-109, the writ's teste date was May 8, 1991. Therefore, Keep Fresh Filters' execution lien on Ms. Reguli's automobile arose on May 8, 1991.

> A writ's "teste date" is its date of issuance.

* * *

Ms. Senecal's security interest in Ms. Reguli's automobile was unperfected on May 8, 1991. Her lien did not appear on the automobile's certificate of title issued on July 20, 1990, and the Motor Vehicle Division had disapproved her January 29, 1991 application to note her lien on the title. In accordance with Tenn. Code Ann. § 47-9-301 (1) (b), Ms. Senecal's lien was, therefore, subordinate to Keep Fresh Filters' execution lien.

- In your own words, why did Ms. Senecal's theory fail and how could she more effectively have protected her interest?

- Why was Keep Fresh Filters allowed to proceed against the automobile, despite the fact that it had no recorded interest in the vehicle?

International Perspective: Enforcement of Interests that are Unperfected

The following is a brief excerpt from *England*, by Richard Bethell-Jones, in *Bank Security and Other Credit Enhancement Models: A Practical Guide on Security Devices Available to Banks in Thirty Countries Throughout the World* (Winnibald E. Moojen & Matthieu Ph. Van Sint Truiden eds., Kluwer Law International 1995). This paragraph introduces the concept of "legal and equitable mortgages" as they exist in English law:

> In England, there is a fundamental distinction between a legal and an equitable mortgage or charge. Essentially, a legal mortgage or charge over an asset is created when everything necessary has been done to transfer legal title to the asset to the mortgagee, or to enable the mortgagee to transfer legal title to a purchaser on exercise of its power of sale. In other words, a legal mortgage, once all registrations and formalities have been

completed, will be a "perfect" security. An equitable mortgage or
charge is a more informal kind of security. For example, an
agreement to create a legal mortgage gives rise to an immediate
equitable mortgage. There must be a clear intention by the owner
of the relevant property to appropriate that property to satisfy
defined indebtedness or obligations. An equitable mortgage will,
subject to any necessary registrations, protect the mortgagee in
the event of the insolvency of the owner of the property. However,
an equitable security interest is "imperfect"; in the sense that third
parties can acquire an interest in the asset which will rank ahead
of the holder of the equitable mortgage or charge. . . . It is even
possible to create an equitable charge . . . over property which will
be acquired or come into existence at a future time. *Id.* at 133.

- Compare and contrast an English equitable mortgage
  with an Article 9 security interest that has been
  created and has attached, but is unperfected.

In *The Law of Secured Finance: An International Survey of
Security Interests over Personal Property* (Oxford University
Press 2002), Author P.A.U. Ali describes the priority of
unperfected security interests in Malaysia – as contrasted with
England – as follows:

> In contrast to England . . . , an unperfected but attached security
> interest (that is, a registrable charge which has not been
> registered within the time prescribed by the companies legislation)
> is void against a liquidator and any creditor of the security
> provider, in . . . Malaysia. . . . The holder of such a security interest
> will thus be in a position no different from that of the security
> provider's unsecured creditors. *Id.* at 49.

The reference to a "liquidator" presupposes an insolvency proceeding.

- What practical and policy reasons might exist for a
  jurisdiction to deny enforcement of unperfected-but-
  attached security interests?

- What reasons militate in favor of enforcement?

C. Priority Rules Among Secured Creditors

Read 9-322 (a) (1) and Comments 3 and 4. These materials
show that a secured creditor can go through each of the
enumerated steps: creation, attachment, and perfection of a
security interest – and still lose out to another secured creditor
holding a perfected interest with superior priority. This section
emphasizes the "first-to-file-or-perfect" rule and the competitive
advantage of PMSI creditors. *Ag Services of America, Inc. v.
Empfield,* 255 Neb. 957, 587 N.W.2d 871 (Neb. 1999),

illustrates the policy behind the first-to-file-or-otherwise-perfect rule:

> Section 9-312 (5) is a "pure race" type statute. Under 9-312 (5), the secured party who is first to perfect or file his or her security interest will have priority over all unperfected security interests, even though such party had actual or constructive knowledge of a prior unperfected security interest. Section 9-312 (5) was adopted to promote certainty in commercial transactions by placing reliance on the filing records. It requires a secured party to take diligence to perfect his or her security interest. If a party fails to perfect, then the party runs the risk of having his or her interest subordinated. *Id.* at 960.

> The current citation is to UCC 9-322 (a) (2).

- 9-322 (a) (1) is sometimes called the "first-to-file" rule. Why is this label imprecise?

- What is the difference between a "pure race" rule and a "notice-race" rule?

- What are the advantages of each kind of rule?

Future Advances

Read 9-323 and Comment 3. As Comment 3 indicates, "a secured party takes subject to all advances [including future advances] secured by a competing security interest having priority" under 9-322 (a) (1)'s "first-to-file-or-otherwise-perfect" rule.

The following case illustrates how a court might analyze priorities among creditors where future advances are involved. The case also emphasizes the duty of careful drafting in creating a security interest.

Coin-O-Matic Service Co. v. Rhode Island Hospital Trust Co.,
3 U.C.C. Rep. Serv. 1112 (1966).

Light, J.

On July 11, 1963, Munroe Doroff purchased a motor vehicle from Warwick Motors, Inc. on a time-payment basis. The security agreement representing the purchase was assigned to the [defendant,] Rhode Island Hospital Trust Company. The security agreement did not have any provision for after-acquired property or future advances. It described the collateral as one Chevrolet Greenbrier Station Wagon 1963. The financing statement filed July 16, 1963, contained a reference to the same Chevrolet Greenbrier Station Wagon.

On October 2, 1964, Doroff became indebted to [the plaintiff,] Coin-O-Matic Service Company, in the sum of $5,600.00, represented by a promissory note and secured by a security agreement. A financing

agreement was filed October 23, 1964. On November 13, 1964, Doroff
owed the Hospital Trust Company $302.77 on the security agreement
of July 11, 1963, and on that date Rhode Island Hospital Trust
Company loaned Doroff the sum of $1,000.00, from which sum he paid
to Rhode Island Hospital Trust Company $302.77 in full satisfaction of
his July 11, 1963, obligation. Rhode Island Hospital Trust Company
thereupon cancelled the old agreement. Doroff executed a new
promissory note secured by a security agreement. A new financing
statement was filed on November 17, 1964. On December 7, 1964,
Doroff went into bankruptcy. It was stipulated that the value of the
motor vehicle at the time it came into Rhode Island Hospital Trust
Company's possession was $1,200.00. It was further stipulated that
the automobile was used in Doroff's business, and there is no question
that the automobile was part of the collateral given to Coin-O-Matic
Service Company, the plaintiff.

* * *

[In the resultant litigation, the plaintiff sought to prove it had a
superior claim to the automobile.]

The defendant contends that its original financing statement was
sufficient to protect not only the original conditional sales agreement,
but also the subsequent agreement, despite the fact that there
intervened a security agreement between Doroff and Coin-O-Matic and
a filed financing statement in connection therewith.

* * *

The defendant [claims that,] . . . having entered into a security
transaction which covered the 1963 Chevrolet Greenbrier Station
Wagon and having filed a financing statement, it comes ahead of the
plaintiff who had a security interest in the same collateral but whose
filing of a financing statement was subsequent in time to the original
filing and ahead of defendant's second filing. Obviously, with respect to
the original transaction there is no dispute that the prior filing of the
financial statement would govern. But the defendant carries its
argument a step further and contends that the original financing
statement is an umbrella which gives the defendant a priority with
respect to its second security transaction, notwithstanding that the
plaintiff's security interest was established in point of time prior to
defendant's second security transaction.

The defendant contends that, as long as there is a financing statement
on file, the whole world is given notice that the debtor is obligated; that
there is a security interest in the particular collateral; and that the
debtor may at any time after the original transaction become further
indebted and enter into an additional security agreement with respect
to the collateral.

* * *

The current citation
is to UCC 9-210.

Section 9-208 provides that a debtor may request information from the
lender as to the amount due on the obligation and the collateral
covered by the security agreement. If the secured party, without

reasonable excuse, fails to comply with the request, he is liable for any loss caused to the debtor thereby, and if the debtor has properly included in his request a good-faith statement of the obligation, or a list of the collateral, or both, the secured party may claim a security interest only as shown in the statement against persons misled by his failure to comply.

If the Code gives the lender an interest in the collateral for future advances even though no provision is made for such future advances, then the information secured by the debtor and given to a subsequent lender is of little value because the second creditor surely could not rely upon the information. If the defendant's interpretation of the Code is correct, there seems to be hardly any substantive reason why the original lender should be bound to comply with the borrower's request for information concerning a correct statement of the outstanding balance and the collateral covered under the security agreement.

> Why could the second creditor not rely upon an accounting given by the first creditor, if the court were to adopt the defendant's theory?

It should be observed that the defendant and the original debtor believed that the original conditional sales transaction was a single transaction and did not provide for future advances by virtue of the original financing statement. This is clear from an examination of the agreed statement and the exhibits attached thereto. When, on November 15th, Doroff's balance with the Hospital Trust was $302.77 on the security agreement of July 11, 1963, and when, on that date, the defendant loaned Doroff $1,000.00, which paid off the original balance and the old agreement was cancelled, Doroff executed a new promissory note secured by new security agreement, and a new financing statement was filed with the Secretary of State on November 17, 1964.

It would seem to this court that, without a consideration of the meaning of § 9-312 (5), this case might properly be decided on what the parties themselves did and what the parties themselves intended. Insofar as Doroff and the Rhode Island Hospital Trust Company were concerned, these parties intended an entirely new transaction when the additional loan was made and they considered the original transaction as terminated. They did not intend to affect an intervening creditor.   Certainly Doroff, although he subsequently went into bankruptcy, might well have not agreed to a new transaction if such new transaction was to have the effect of cutting out the intervening creditor.   What these parties intended was a completely separate transaction, and the claim now that the defendant is entitled to the protection of the original financing statement comes, in the judgment of this court, as an afterthought.

> The current citation is to UCC 9-322 (a).

> Why might Doroff have been concerned about the status of the intervening creditor?

It is the considered judgment of the court, after a careful consideration of the agreed statement of facts and the applicable provisions of the Commercial Code, that, particularly in this case, the defendant is not entitled to rely upon the original financing statement in order to bring its subsequent loan ahead of that of the intervening creditor. This is said, not because of the application of the principles of estoppel or waiver, but because the parties surely are not prohibited under the Code from treating their transactions as separate and unrelated transactions.

> What is meant by this sentence?

Section 6A-9-312 (5) deals with priority between conflicting security interests in the same collateral and gives a priority in the order of the filing, but that obviously does not relate to separate and distinct security transactions. Moreover, a careful examination of 6A-9-312 and the other applicable provisions of the Code lead to the conclusion that the reasonable interpretation of 6A-9-312 is that a security agreement which does not provide for future advances is a single transaction and, in the case of subsequent security agreements, there is required a new financing statement. That is to say, a single financing statement in connection with a security agreement when no provision is made for future advances is not an umbrella for future advances based upon new security agreements, notwithstanding the fact that involved is the same collateral.

- Why does Rhode Island Hospital Trust Company lose the priority of its claim, and what should it have done differently in this transaction?

Note 1: Read 9-339 and Comment 2. Parties may agree to a different order of priority than would otherwise be recognized under Article 9. The following excerpt from *ITT Diversified Credit Corporation v. First City Capital Corp.*, 737 S.W.2d 803, 4 U.C.C. Rep. Serv. 2d 927 (Tex. 1987), demonstrates how such a subordination agreement might work:

> The current citation is to 1-302.

[N]othing in Article 9 prevents subordination by agreement by any person entitled to priority. . . . Section 1-102 of the Code specifically allows provisions of the Code to be varied by agreement. . . . Moreover, a subordination agreement is nothing more than a contractual modification of lien priorities and must be construed according to the expressed intention of the parties and its terms.

. . . In a non-real-property situation, the third lienholder should be able to succeed to that part of the interest that was subordinated by the first lienholder, so long as the second lienholder is neither burdened nor benefitted by the subordination agreement. For example, A, B, and C have claims against the debtor which are entitled to priority in alphabetical order. "A" subordinates his claim to "C." After foreclosure of the secured interest, the resulting fund is insufficient to satisfy all three claims. The proper distribution of the fund is as follows.

1. Set aside from the fund the amount of "A's" claim.

2. Out of the money set aside, pay "C" the amount of its claim, pay "A" to the extent of any balance remaining after "C's" claim is satisfied.

3. Pay "B" the amount of the fund remaining after "A's" claim has been set aside.

4. If any balance remains in the fund after "A's" claim has been set aside and "B's" claim has been satisfied, distribute the balance to "C" and "A."

Thus, "C," by virtue of the subordination agreement, is paid first, but only to the amount of "A's" claim, to which "B" was in any event junior. "B" receives what it had expected to receive, the fund less "A's" prior claim. If "A's" claim is smaller than "C's," "C" will collect the balance of its claim, in its own right, only after "B" has been paid in full. "A," the subordinator, receives nothing until "B" and "C" have been paid except to the extent that its claim, entitled to first priority, exceeds the amount of "C's" claim, which, under its agreement, is to be first paid. *Id.* at 804.

- Who must agree to the subordination agreement for it to be valid?

9-339 Comment 2 may assist you in answering this question.

- Why and when would a party with a superior priority agree to subordinate its interest?

- Explain, in your own words, how the court would allocate funds between A, B, and C.

Note 2: Just as the parties can enter into a subordination agreement, the court can institute what is called "equitable subordination," changing the priorities of the parties based on considerations of fairness. Consider the following excerpt from *In re ASI Reactivation, Inc.*, 934 F.2d 1315 (4th Cir. 1991):

Generally, equitable subordination involves a number of inquiries: 1) whether the claimant engaged in fraudulent conduct, 2) whether the conduct resulted in injury to creditors, and 3) whether subordination would be consistent with other bankruptcy law. *Id.* at 1321.

In *Kham & Nate's Shoes No. 2, Inc. v. First Bank of Whiting*, 908 F.2d 1351 (7th Cir. 1990), the court described the appropriate application of equitable subordination as follows, applying standards similar to those set forth in *EEE Commercial Corp. v. Holmes*:

Equitable subordination usually is a response to efforts by corporate insiders to convert their equity interests into secured debt in anticipation of bankruptcy. Courts require the insiders to return to their position at the end of the line. . . .

Cases subordinating the claims of creditors that dealt at arm's length with the debtor are few and far between. *Benjamin v. Diamond*, 563 F.2d 692 (5th Cir. 1977), suggests that subordination depends on a combination of inequitable conduct, unfair advantage to the creditor, and injury to other creditors. Debtor [in this case] submits that conduct may be "unfair" and "inequitable" for this purpose even though the creditor complies with all contractual requirements, but we are not willing to embrace a rule that requires participants in commercial transactions not only to keep their contracts but also do "more" – just how much more resting in the discretion of a bankruptcy

judge assessing the situation years later. Contracts specify the
duties of the parties to each other, and each may exercise the
privileges it obtained. . . . Courts may not convert one form of
contract into the other after the fact, without raising the cost of
credit or jeopardizing its availability. Unless pacts are enforced
according to their terms, the institution of contract, with all the
advantages private negotiation and agreement brings, is
jeopardized.

"Inequitable conduct" in commercial life means breach plus some
advantage-taking, such as the star who agrees to act in a motion
picture and then, after $20 million has been spent, sulks in his
dressing room until the contract has been renegotiated. Firms that
have negotiated contracts are entitled to enforce them to the letter,
even to the great discomfort of their trading partners, without
being mulcted for lack of "good faith." Although courts often refer
to the obligation of good faith that exists in every contractual
relation, this is not an invitation to the court to decide whether one
party ought to have exercised privileges expressly reserved in the
document. . . .

> A "mulct" is an arbitrary fine.

We do not doubt the force of the proverb that the letter killeth,
while the spirit giveth life. Literal implementation of unadorned
language may destroy the essence of the venture. Few people pass
out of childhood without learning fables about genies, whose
wickedly literal interpretation of their "masters'" wishes always
leads to calamity. Yet knowledge that literal enforcement means
some mismatch between the parties' expectation and the outcome
does not imply a general duty of "kindness" in performance, or of
judicial oversight into whether a party had "good cause" to act as it
did. Parties to a contract are not each others' fiduciaries; they are
not bound to treat customers with the same consideration
reserved for their families. Any attempt to add an overlay of "just
cause" . . . to the exercise of contractual privileges would reduce
commercial certainty and breed costly litigation. . . . "[I]n
commercial transactions, it does not in the end promote justice to
seek strained interpretations in aid of those who do not protect
themselves" ([quoting from] *James Baird Co. v. Gimbel Bros., Inc.*,
64 F.2d 344, 346 (2d Cir.1933) (L. Hand, J.)). *Kham & Nate's
Shoes*, 908 F.2d at 1356-1357.

- After reading this excerpt, how would you describe the
  appropriate parameters for application of the concept
  of equitable subordination?

- How would you describe the relationship between
  equitable subordination and good faith?

International Perspective: Priority Rules

Professor Hwang Hyun Suk's article *International Secured Transactions: South Korea*, in *International Secured Transactions* (Oceana Publications 2005), describes the filing system and priority rules of South Korea as one in which, apart from a registration-system that is available to record security interests involving a few specified kinds of "registrable assets such as automobiles, aircraft, construction machinery, and ships, a notice-filing system does not exist at all." For these "registrable" assets, perfection by filing is the appropriate means of establishing priority of a security interest, and priority is given to the first-recorded interest. For non-registrable movable assets, a secured party perfects its interest by possession of the collateral. Priority of pledge is determined based on the date on which the secured party comes into possession of the collateral. For receivables, the third-party obligor must be notified of the secured party's interest for that interest to be perfected. Priority of claims involving receivables is based upon the date of notice to the third-party obligor.

- How would you counsel a client who is considering expanding his or her business to South Korea, if that business has historically engaged in secured financing?

Purchase-Money Security Interests

Read 9-103 (a) and (b) (1) and Comments 2, 3, and 7. 9-103 defines "Purchase-Money Security Interest," which is commonly abbreviated, "PMSI."

- What is meant by the phrase, "if the value is in fact so used," and how can a lender best ensure this requirement is met?

This language is taken from 9-103 (a) (2).

- In what kinds of collateral can a PMSI be created?

- What is the "dual status" rule and when does it apply?

Comment 7 (a) may assist you in answering this question. In addition, you might consider how this concept relates to after-acquired collateral, discussed in the prior chapter.

Read 9-324 and Comments 3 and 4. This Code Section establishes the basic rules of priority with regard to PMSIs.

- Compare 9-324's provisions on inventory and livestock. How are the policy considerations similar for each?

> A more comprehensive explication of this topic can be found in Professor Timothy R. Zinnecker's article *Pimzy Whimsy in the Eleventh Circuit: Reflections on* In re Alphatech Systems, Inc., 40 Gonz. L. Rev. 379 (2004-2005).

- Why does it make sense to treat these two kinds of collateral differently from others?

In *United States v. Dailey*, 749 F. Supp. 218 (D. Arizona 1990), the court explained the policy behind the preferred status of PMSI creditors as compared with judgment-lien creditors, as follows:

> The policy behind allowing priority to purchase-money-mortgage liens is reliance. [Unlike purchase-money security interest creditors], simple judgment creditors [do] not extend their credit relying on repayment from specific property. . . .
>
> Equity and justice justify the protection afforded a vendor who parts with his property on the faith that his mortgage or trust deed securing purchase monies loaned to the vendee is entitled to priority over any preexisting claims which may be asserted against the vendee mortgagor. To grant a preexisting judgment-lien creditor a preference over a vendor's purchase-money mortgage would be to bestow on that judgment-lien creditor a pure windfall at the expense of a vendor. *Id.* at 220.

> Here the court is quoting from *Nelson v. Stoker*, 669 P.2d 390, 394 (Utah 1983).

- What is meant by the language indicating that providing priority to judgment-lien creditors over PMSI creditors would "bestow . . . a pure windfall at the expense of a vendor"?

Read 9-324 (c) and (e) and Comments 5 and 6. A PMSI creditor with an interest in inventory or livestock must provide notice to any holder of a pre-existing secured claim in the same collateral, if the pre-existent claim was perfected by filing.

The following case illustrates the application of the notice requirement in a case involving inventory.

In re Daniels,
35 B.R. 247, 37 U.C.C. Rep. Serv. 967
(Bankr. W.D. Okla. 1983).

Richard L. Bohanon, Bankruptcy Judge.

The matter for determination arises from a motion made by ITT Diversified Credit Corporation for a decision as to its priority status regarding conflicting security interests. The matter has been fully briefed by all parties, and the facts are not controverted. Due to a thorough stipulation of facts, there remains only the sole question of whether a letter of notification sent by American Bank of Commerce to ITT complied with 12A O.S.1981 § 9-312.

> The current citation is to UCC 9-324.

In January 1982, the debtor entered into two wholesale financing-and-security agreements with ITT Diversified Credit Corporation for the purpose of purchasing boats, motors, and related accessories for his business operation known as Daniels Marine, Inc. ITT was granted a security interest in several items listed as exhibits and made a part of the record. ITT properly perfected its security interest in these items by filing the necessary financing statements.

The Small Business Administration, through the American Bank of Commerce, subsequently loaned Daniels Marine, Inc., certain sums of money and, in return, was granted a security interest in the inventory and equipment. In July 1981, the American Bank of Commerce forwarded to all known creditors of Daniels Marine, Inc., a letter regarding their security interest in said inventory and equipment. That letter provides in pertinent part:

> Gentleman:
>
> The American Bank of Commerce has taken, or plans to take, a security interest in the following equipment located at the customer's place of business at Longtown, Oklahoma, mailing address Highway # 9, Eufaula, Oklahoma: All machinery & equipment; inventory; accounts receivable; automotive equipment, furniture & fixtures now owned or hereafter acquired; all used boats and motors now owned or hereafter acquired including but not limited to: [listing numerous items with specific descriptions and serial numbers].
>
> /s/ John Freeman

ITT admits that it received the subject letter and raises no question regarding time of receipt, description of the collateral, or other points beyond the issue raised by this proceeding.

[Daniels became insolvent.] In April 1982, pursuant to an order of this Court, the Small Business Administration conducted a foreclosure sale of property in which it claimed a security interest pursuant to agreements with the debtor as previously set forth. Among the property sold at the foreclosure sale were certain items in which both ITT and the Small Business Administration, through the American Bank of Commerce, claimed a security interest.

This proceeding raises a novel and interesting question regarding the perfection of a purchase-money security interest in inventory, and is a case of first impression. We are asked to decide the priority among conflicting security interests in the same collateral. . . .

In the instant case the notification letter from American Bank of Commerce to ITT did not literally track the specific language of 12A O.S.1981 § 9-312 (3) (d) in that it only states, "[The bank] has taken, or plans to take, a security interest . . ." and makes no mention of a "purchase-money security interest." ITT urges that failure of the bank to state the taking of a purchase-money security interest in the notification is insufficient to meet the standards prescribed by law, and therefore the bank may not be afforded priority status which it otherwise would acquire. On the other hand, the bank argues the letter was sufficient to put ITT on notice even though it did not contain the words "purchase money" since there could have been no other

> The recommended language referenced here is now found in UCC 9-324 (b) (4).

reason for sending the notice, nor did the letter contain any misleading information.

* * *

Some recognition must be given to the policy and commercial reasons why purchase-money security interests receive special priority. The drafters of the Code realized the impact upon commercial flow which would result, should a debtor be strangled by a prior secured creditor. Such a creditor, by not providing additional funds, could cripple a debtor's commercial operation. The debtor, on the other hand, would be hamstrung in receiving other financing since another creditor would have no collateral protection. The purchase-money security interest rescued the debtor from this commercial impasse. . . .

Consequently, there is a strong policy statement which supports the operation of the purchase-money interest which should not be interrupted for the sake of mere technical conformity. Moreover, it is generally accepted that the UCC provisions should be liberally construed in order to promote the underlying policies and purposes of the Code. Conversely, we are unable to identify any policy or purpose which would be served by a literalist statutory reading of 12A O.S.1981 § 9-312.

* * *

[T]he notice provision was for the protection of the prior secured creditor. The first creditor would be alerted not to make further advances, since another inventory financer could usurp his prior secured position. If this written notice requirement is essentially accomplished, the linguistical technique of how it is accomplished becomes of little importance. Indeed, the drafters of section 9-312 specifically direct the reader to the definitional cross-references of "give notice" and "knowledge" found in section 1-201. These sections clearly provide that:

Both definitions are now found in 1-202.

This language is now found in 1-202 (a).

(25) A person has "notice" of a fact when
(a) he has actual knowledge of it; or
(b) he has received a notice or notification of it; or
(c) from all the facts and circumstances known to him at the time in question he has reason to know that it exists.

This language is now found in 1-202 (d).

(26) A person "notifies" or "gives" a notice or notification to another by taking such steps as may be reasonably required to inform the other in ordinary course whether or not such other actually comes to know of it.

We do not feel that the reference to the section 1-201 definitions in 9-312 are to be discarded as mere surplusage. Rather, we think these definitional terms are to be equally applied to 9-312 when the circumstances so demand in order to promote the underlying policies of the UCC. We think this is one such circumstance. Here we are not dealing with simple garden-variety consumers untrained in the commercial world. These parties are sophisticated commercial entities in the business of commercial lending and financing. The letter received by ITT, although not containing the magic words "purchase money," did contain terms which clearly indicate a purchase-money interest. The use of the terms "furniture or fixtures now owned or hereafter acquired" and "boats and motors now owned or hereafter acquired" should be clear indicators to a sophisticated commercial entity that a purchase-money transaction is at hand. This conclusion is buttressed by the fact that in no other situation excepting a purchase-money interest is another creditor required to forward any notice to the prior secured party. This is not to say that, as a matter of commercial courtesy or for communication purposes, creditors may not provide such notices to each other. However, such practices should not confuse the issue at hand in view of the totality of circumstances which exist here.

In light of what we have stated, we do not see how ITT could have been misled or confused by the notification letter not having stated "purchase money" among its terms. To reach any other conclusion would be contrary to reason and militate against the very policy of having purchase-money security transactions. Moreover, a literal reading of 9-312, while serving no policy interest or purpose, would ignore the referenced definitional terms of notice and the liberal construction of the Code. Therefore, in light of all the facts and circumstances known to ITT we find the absence of the terms "purchase money" in the notice forwarded to ITT to be de minimus.

- How many arguments does the court provide in support of its holding, and what are they?

- How does the availability of, and priority afforded to, purchase-money security interests protect a debtor from being "hamstrung" by a prior secured creditor who refuses to advance additional funds?

Note: Read 9-309 (1) and 9-322 Comment 5. As 9-309 (1) shows, a PMSI in consumer goods is generally perfected at attachment, while non-consumer-goods PMSIs do not enjoy the same automatic perfection. *Citizens National Bank v. Cockrell*, 850 S.W.2d 462, 19 U.C.C. Rep. Serv. 2d. 1205 (1993), shows how a court might analyze priority as between a non-consumer-goods PMSI creditor and a secured creditor claiming an interest pursuant to an after-acquired-property clause:

Refer back to Chapter 15, Part B as needed.

> Respondent John H. Cockrell, Jr. owned a mini-blind manufacturing business in Dallas, Texas. On August 1, 1985, he executed a written agreement for the immediate sale, assignment, and transfer of the business and its assets, including merchandise, leases, and fixtures, to Kevin and Richard Sydnor. Cockrell promised to pay all business debts incurred prior to August 1, but he was to be paid all accounts receivable that had accrued as of that date. The Sydnors paid Cockrell $5,000 cash and signed a promissory note in the principal amount of $130,000. To secure payment of the note, the Sydnors agreed to grant Cockrell a security interest in the transferred assets.

The Sydnors began operating the mini-blind business on August 1, assuming the lease on the warehouse where the equipment was located on that date. However, Cockrell also participated in the day-to-day operations and had access to the equipment until early October. . . .

> What is the significance of the events on or about October 3?

. . . On October 3, Cockrell turned over to the Sydnors his set of keys to the warehouse. On or about the same day, Cockrell testified, he and the Sydnors executed the security agreement and signed the financing statement.   Cockrell filed the financing statement with the Secretary of State on October 7, 1985.

Prior to making this agreement, the Sydnors had become indebted to Provident Bank of Denton on a promissory note in the original amount of $40,000, backed by a security interest in all equipment then owned or thereafter acquired by the Sydnors. Provident Bank had filed a financing statement covering this security interest on May 9, 1985. When the Sydnors acquired rights in the mini-blind equipment by purchasing the business from Cockrell, Provident Bank's security interest attached to the collateral and became perfected.   The note and security interest were subsequently purchased by Petitioner Citizens National Bank of Denton (the Bank).

After assuming complete control of the mini-blind business on October 3, the Sydnors defaulted in their obligations to the Bank. The Bank foreclosed on the equipment and sold it to a third party. Cockrell then brought this suit against the Bank, claiming that, since his security interest had priority, the Bank's foreclosure and sale amounted to conversion of the property. Although Cockrell concedes that the Bank's security interest attached and became perfected prior to perfection of his security interest on October 7, 1985, he asserts the priority accorded to a purchase-money security interest.   Section 9-312 (d) gives a purchase-money security interest priority over a conflicting security interest "if the purchase-money security interest is perfected at the time the debtor receives possession of the collateral or within 20 days thereafter." The decisive question in this case is whether the perfection of Cockrell's security interest on October 7, 1985, was within 20 days after the Sydnors "received possession" of the equipment.

> This language is now found in UCC 9-324 (a).

* * *

The term "possession" is not defined in the Uniform Commercial Code, and we have found no decision specifically addressing whether "possession" under section 9-312 (d) must be exclusive. . . .

> As 9-324 Comment 3 indicates, pre-1999 Article 9 included a ten-day grace period. The current grace period is twenty days. The Bankruptcy Code, 11 USC § 547 (c) (3) (B), provides a thirty-day grace period.

* * *

The purpose of the twenty-day grace period (which in most states is only ten days) is to enable the financer to keep its priority even when the debtor-purchaser demands immediate delivery of the goods. That purpose is not thwarted by requiring the financer to file within twenty days of delivery even if, as here, the nature of the transaction requires the financer to maintain some control over the collateral beyond that twenty-day period.

* * *

[W]e think that the court of appeals erred in limiting "possession" in section 9.312 (d) to a power over property exercisable to the exclusion of all other persons. . . . That the equipment was in the Sydnors' place of business beginning on August 1, 1985 was undisputed. It was similarly uncontested that the equipment was used in the Sydnors' business during the succeeding months, and Cockrell presented no evidence to suggest that the equipment was in some manner set aside or specially labeled to denote his purchase-money interest in it. . . . [T]his undisputed evidence establishes the Sydnors' "possession" under section 9-312 (d) as we conclude that section must be read. *Id.* at 462-466.

- **Read 9-324 Comment 3.** Is the Court's holding consistent with the illustrations in the commentary?

Problem: Consider the following facts:

In 1959, Brodie [Hotel Supply, Inc.] sold [certain] restaurant equipment to Standard Management Company, Inc., for use in a restaurant at Anchorage, Alaska. Standard Management went bankrupt. Brodie repossessed the equipment but left it in the restaurant. With the consent of Brodie, [a third party named] James Lyon took possession of the restaurant and began operating it on June 1, 1964. Throughout the summer of 1964, Brodie and Lyon negotiated over the price and terms under which Lyon was to purchase the equipment.

> How might equipment be repossessed but left in the restaurant, and why would a party do this? 9-609 (a) (2) and Comment 6 may assist you with this question.

On November 2, 1964, Lyon borrowed seventeen thousand dollars from the National Bank of Alaska and, as security for the loan, which was evidenced by a promissory note, executed a chattel mortgage covering the restaurant equipment. This equipment consisted of 159 separate types of items, including a refrigerator, a dishwasher, an ice-cream cabinet, spoons, forks, cups, ladles, pots, pans, and assorted glassware and chinaware. The bank assigned its mortgage to the Small Business Administration. . . . On November 4, 1964, the bank filed a financing statement, showing the SBA as assignee.

On November 12, Brodie delivered to Lyon a bill of sale covering the equipment. On the same day, Lyon executed a chattel mortgage on the equipment, naming Brodie as mortgagee. This mortgage was given to secure the unpaid purchase price of the equipment. Brodie filed a financing statement on November 23, 1964.

- Based on these facts, when did Lyon's interest in the equipment attach, within the meaning of 9-203?

- Which party has priority and why?

Based on *Brodie Hotel Supply, Inc. v. United States*, 431 F.2d 1316, 8 U.C.C. Rep. Serv. 113 (9th Cir. 1970).

D. Priority Rules When Collateral is Sold

This section addresses how the sale of collateral affects priorities in a subsequent insolvency proceeding. These materials focus especially on the preferred status of a "buyer in ordinary course of business."

Read 1-201 (b) (9) and Comment 9 and 9-320 and Comments 2, 3, and 5. 1-201 (b) (9) defines "buyer in ordinary course of business," and 9-320 describes the priority rights of such a buyer under Article 9.

- What distinction is recognized between 9-320 (a) and (b)?

- Why might the buyer in part (b) be called a "specialized BFP"?

9-320 Comment 6 may assist you in answering this question.

- How does the secured party's consent to the sale affect the buyer's rights?

- When might a PMSI creditor wish to file a financing statement to protect his or her interest in consumer goods?

- What kind of collateral is ordinarily involved in a sale "in ordinary course of business"?

The following case illustrates "ordinary course of business." As the court holds, "relatively infrequent" sales can be within the "ordinary course of business," so long as they are "customary" and even if "only incidental to the predominant business purpose." Although, as 9-320 (e) and Comment 8 indicate, Revised Article 9 changes the outcome of this case, it remains a useful explication of the concept of "buyer in ordinary course of business."

Tanbro Fabrics Corp. v. Deering Milliken, Inc.,
39 N.Y.2d 632, 350 N.E.2d 590 (N.Y. 1976).

The term "greige goods," which denotes unbleached, undyed textiles, can be pronounced "gray" or pronounced as if it rhymes with "beige."

Breitel, Chief Judge.

In an action for the tortious conversion of unfinished textile fabrics (greige goods), plaintiff Tanbro sought damages from Deering Milliken, a textile manufacturer. Tanbro, known in the trade as a "converter," finishes textile into dyed and patterned fabrics. The goods in question had been manufactured by Deering and sold on a "bill-and-hold" basis to Mill Fabrics, also a converter, now insolvent. Mill Fabrics resold the goods, while still in Deering's warehouse, also on a bill-and-hold basis, to Tanbro.

Sales of goods stored in warehouses often involve Article 7 warehouse receipts, covered in Chapter 18, Part C.

Deering refused to deliver the goods to Tanbro on Tanbro's instruction because, although these goods had been paid for, there was an open account balance due Deering from Mill Fabrics. Deering, under its sales agreements with Mill Fabrics, claimed a perfected security interest in the goods.

At Supreme Court, Tanbro recovered a verdict and judgment of $87,451.68 for compensatory . . . damages. . . .

The issue is whether Tanbro's purchase of the goods was in the ordinary course of Mill Fabrics' business, and hence free of Deering's perfected security interest.

There should be an affirmance. Mill Fabrics' sale to Tanbro was in the ordinary course of business, even though its predominant business purpose was, like Tanbro's, the converting of greige goods into finished fabrics. All the Uniform Commercial Code requires is that the sale be in ordinary course associated with the seller's business. The record established that converters buy greige goods in propitious markets and often in excess of their requirements as they eventuate. On the occasion of excess purchases, converters at times enter the market to sell the excess through brokers to other converters, and converters buy such goods if the price is satisfactory or the particular goods are not available from manufacturers. Both conditions obtained here.

Tanbro and Mill Fabrics were customers of Deering for many years. Goods would be purchased in scale on a "bill and hold" basis, that is, the goods would be paid for and delivered as the buyers instructed. When the goods were needed, they were delivered directly where they were to be converted, at the buyers' plants or the plants of others if that would be appropriate. Pending instructions, the sold-and-paid-for goods were stored in the warehouses of the manufacturer, both because the buyers lacked warehousing space and retransportation of the goods to be processed would be minimized.

Mill Fabrics, like many converters, purchased greige goods from Deering on credit as well as on short-term payment. Under the sales notes or agreements, all the goods on hand in the seller's warehouse stood as security for the balance owed on the account. Tanbro was familiar with this practice. It was immaterial whether or not particular goods had been paid for. If the goods were resold by Deering's customers, Deering obtained for a period a perfected security interest in the proceeds of resale for the indebtedness on the open account.

Deering's sales executives advised Tanbro that it had discontinued production of a certain blended fabric. Upon Tanbro's inquiry, the Deering sales executives recommended to Tanbro that it try purchasing the blended fabric from Mill Fabrics, which Deering knew had an excess supply. Ultimately, Tanbro purchased from Mill Fabrics through a broker 267,000 yards at 26 cents per yard. Tanbro paid Mill Fabrics in full.

During October and November of 1969, approximately 57,000 yards of
the blended fabric was released by Deering on Mill Fabrics' instructions
and delivered to a Tanbro affiliate. There remained some 203,376
yards at the Deering warehouse.

In early January of 1970, Tanbro ordered the remaining fabric
delivered to meet its own contractual obligation to deliver the blended
fabric in finished state at 60 cents per yard. Deering refused.

By this time, Mill Fabrics was in financial trouble and its account-debit
balance with Deering at an unprecedented high. In mid-January of
1970, a meeting of its creditors was called and its insolvency confirmed.

As noted earlier, under the terms of the Deering sales agreements with
Mill Fabrics, Deering retained a security interest in Mill Fabrics'
"property" on a bill-and-hold basis, whether paid for or not. This
security interest was perfected by Deering's continued possession of the
goods. Tanbro argued that, if it had title by purchase, its goods were
excluded from the security arrangement which was literally restricted
to the "property of the buyer," that is, Mill Fabrics. In any event, unless
prevented by other provisions of the code, or the sale was not
unauthorized, Tanbro took title subject to Deering's security interest.

Read 9-320 Comment 6. How would the analysis be different if the sale were authorized?

Under the Code, a buyer in the ordinary course of the seller's business
takes goods free of even a known security interest, so long as the buyer
does not know that the purchase violates the terms of the security
agreement. . . . Critical to Tanbro's claim is that it purchased the goods
in the ordinary course of Mill Fabrics' business and that it did not
purchase the goods in knowing violation of Deering's security interest.

Can anything other than inventory be sold "in ordinary course of business"?

Under the Code, whether a purchase was made from a person in the
business of selling goods of that kind turns primarily on whether that
person holds the goods for sale. Such goods are a person's selling
inventory. Note, however, that not all purchases of goods held as
inventory qualify as purchases from a person in the business of selling
goods of that kind. . . . [A] qualifying purchase is one made from a
seller who is a dealer in such goods.

A former Mill Fabrics' employee testified that there were times when
Mill Fabrics, like all converters, found itself with excess goods. When it
was to their business advantage, they sold the excess fabrics to other
converters. Although these sales were relatively infrequent, they were
nevertheless part of, and in the ordinary course of, Mill Fabrics'
business, even if only incidental to the predominant business purpose.
Examples of a nonqualifying sale might be a bulk sale, a sale in
distress at an obvious loss price, a sale in liquidation, a sale of a
commodity never dealt with before by the seller and wholly unlike its
usual inventory, or the like.

Bulk sales are discussed in Chapter 3, Part C.

The combination of stored, paid-for goods, on a hold basis, and the
retention of a security interest by Deering, makes commercial sense.
Mill Fabrics' capacity to discharge its obligation to Deering was in part
made possible because it sold off or converted the goods held at the
Deering warehouse. Mill Fabrics, as an honest customer, was supposed
to remit the proceeds from resale or conversion to Deering and thus

reduce, and eventually discharge its responsibility to Deering. Thus, so long as it was customary for Mill Fabrics, and in the trade for converters, to sell off excess goods, the sale was in the ordinary course of business. Moreover, on an alternative analysis, such a sale by Mill Fabrics was therefore impliedly authorized under the code if its indebtedness to Deering was to be liquidated.

All subdivision (1) of section 9-307 requires is that the sale be of the variety reasonably to be expected in the regular course of an on-going business. This was such a case.

> The current reference is to 9-320 (a).

- What facts support the court's statement that the sale was "impliedly authorized"?

- Does this case help to clarify why the Code uses the phrase "buyer in ordinary course of business," not "buyer in *the* ordinary course of business"?

- How would revised 9-320 (e) change the outcome of this case, and what policy supports treating possessory security interests differently from nonpossessory ones, insofar as the rights of a "buyer in ordinary course of business" are concerned?

> Comment 8 may assist you in answering this question.

Note: Read 2-403 (2) and Comment 2. *Sears Consumer Financial Corp. v. Thunderbird Products*, 166 Ariz. 333, 12 U.C.C. Rep. Serv. 2d 675 (Ariz. App. 1st Div. 1990), connects the materials in this section with those in Chapter 6, Part B. This case involves the wrongful sale of entrusted goods, and the effect of this sale on a pre-existing security interest. The facts and excerpted holding of the case are as follows:

Thunderbird Products . . . manufactures and sells motor boats. In late 1985, Thunderbird sold a 1986 Formula F 25PC 25-foot cabin cruiser to Glen Canyon Marine, a boat dealer in Page, Arizona, for it to sell at retail. ITT Commercial Finance financed the sale to Glen Canyon Marine. ITT filed a blanket UCC financing statement signed by Glen Canyon Marine as debtor.

When Glen Canyon Marine went out of business in 1986, Thunderbird bought ITT's interest in the secured debt on the boat. Thunderbird thereafter engaged D & J Marine and RV Services, also in the business of selling new and used boats in Page, to repossess the boat from Glen Canyon Marine and temporarily store it on Thunderbird's behalf. While Thunderbird knew that D & J was in the boat-sales business, Thunderbird did not authorize D & J to sell the boat, but only to store it.

> Repossession is addressed in Chapter 17, Part A.

D & J nonetheless displayed the boat for public sale. On September 12, 1986, it entered into an agreement to sell it to Eugene Abernathy for $57,240.00. Sears [Consumer Financial Corporation] agreed to lend Abernathy $40,000.00 to complete his purchase of the boat. Neither Abernathy nor Sears had knowledge of Thunderbird's claim to the boat. Abernathy created

Why would any documents need to be filed to perfect Sears' PMSI rights in these consumer goods? Review 9-309 (1), 9-320, and the materials on PMSI rights earlier in this chapter as needed.

a purchase-money security interest in the boat in favor of Sears. ... Although Sears paid the $40,000.00 loan proceeds to D & J, the documents necessary to perfect Sears' purchase-money security interest in the boat were never filed. D & J delivered neither the boat nor a certificate of title to Abernathy. D & J paid none of the sales proceeds to Thunderbird.

The boat continued to sit in storage at Page. Unaware of the transactions between D & J and Abernathy and assuming continued ownership of the boat, Thunderbird took possession of it from D & J in October 1986 and stored it elsewhere in Page until February 1987. Thunderbird then transported the boat back to its factory in Indiana and resold it to Renton Marine Center in Trenton, New Jersey. Abernathy subsequently defaulted on his Sears loan. Sears then looked to the boat for its security. Only then did it discover that Thunderbird had previously repossessed it.

In January 1988, Sears brought this action against Thunderbird for conversion. ...

* * *

The authorities are split on whether UCC § 2-403 (2) operates to extinguish an Article 9 security interest. ...

With respect to entrustment by secured parties, ... [i]t is certainly true that, when a secured party is not in control of the collateral and does not acquiesce in its entrustment to a merchant who deals in goods of that kind, the sale to a buyer in the ordinary course of the merchant's business should not affect the secured party's rights in the collateral. However, where the secured party itself entrusts the collateral, or acquiesces in its entrustment as occurred here, § 2-403 (2) governs. "Where one of two innocent parties must suffer through the act or negligence of a third person, the loss should fall upon the one who by his conduct created the circumstances which enabled the third party to perpetuate the wrong or cause the loss." *Al's Auto Sales v. Moskowitz*, 203 Okl. 611, 224 P.2d 588, 591 (1950).

What doctrine, prevalent in this textbook, is the *Al's Auto Sales* court referencing?

* * *

Our conclusion is consistent with the basic goal of the UCC to protect good faith purchasers. A major aim of the UCC is to facilitate the merchantability of property. In this case, Thunderbird, as a secured party, entrusted possession of the boat to D & J, a merchant dealing in this kind of goods. Under the explicit language of § 2-403 (2), Thunderbird unwittingly thereby gave D & J the power to transfer all Thunderbird's rights in the boat to Abernathy. D & J exercised that power by selling the boat to Abernathy in the ordinary course of its business. The sale by D & J to Abernathy extinguished Thunderbird's perfected security interest in the boat. Accordingly, Thunderbird at that point lost any legal right to repossess it . . . . Sears acquired the right to possession of the boat under its purchase-money security interest with Abernathy. Thunderbird's repossession of the boat constituted conversion of Sears' interest even though Thunderbird acted without knowledge of Sears' interest. As between these two innocent parties, UCC § 2-403 (2) places liability on the party whose conduct first allowed this boat to set sail on this uncharted voyage. *Sears*, 166 Ariz. at 334.

- In your own words, why does Article 2 rather than Article 9 control the outcome of this dispute?

- How could Thunderbird have better protected its interests?

- Against whom, if anyone, does Thunderbird have a cause of action?

Problem: Read 9-337 and Comment 2, and consider the following facts:

On or about October 1, 2002, Americredit [Financial Services, Inc.] repossessed a 1997 Ford Taurus from [Theresa] Metzger, who had purchased the vehicle from a used car dealership in March of 2002. Metzger did not realize that Americredit had a prior lien on the vehicle or that it had been repossessed. As a result, she reported the vehicle as stolen to the police.

Metzger later learned that Americredit had obtained a security interest in the vehicle in 1998, when the company financed James Strong's purchase of the vehicle in the State of New York. The New York certificate of title issued to Strong reflected Americredit's security interest in the vehicle.

Strong later moved from New York to Georgia and submitted a[n] application form, along with the existing title and the required fee, to the Cobb County tag agent for the Georgia Department of Motor Vehicles in order to convert the existing New York certificate of title to a Georgia one. The DMV processed the application, but as a result of a clerical data-entry error, the DMV issued a Georgia certificate of title that did not reflect Americredit's security interest in the vehicle.

Strong later transferred the vehicle to an automobile dealer owner, and the vehicle thereafter passed through a non-dealer owner and additional dealer owners before Metzger purchased it in March of 2002. None of the subsequent Georgia certificates of title issued for the vehicle in connection with these transfers reflected Americredit's security interest.

After Metzger purchased the vehicle and registered it with the DMV, Americredit, having finally located the vehicle, repossessed it from Metzger's residence and sold it at auction. Once she learned from the police department that her vehicle had been repossessed rather than stolen, Metzger filed suit against Americredit in the Superior Court of Clayton County.

- Which party has priority and why?

- Why does 9-337, rather than 9-320 (b), best address this fact pattern, and how could the facts be changed to implicate 9-320 (b)?

- Why does 9-320 (a) not allow the buyer to prevail?

Based on *Metzger v. Americredit Financial Services, Inc.*, 273 Ga. App. 453, 453-454, 56 U.C.C. Rep. Serv. 825 (Ga. App. 2005).

> Paying close attention to the language "created by the buyer's seller" and Comment 3, Example 1 may assist you in answering this question.

> It would be a mistake, however, to conclude that Canada's Personal Property Security Act is identical to Article 9. In *When the Creditor is Across the Border*, 14 Bus. L. Today 41 (2005), attorney Martin Fingerhut points out some of the most important differences between the two bodies of law.

International Perspective: Sales of Collateral to Buyers in Ordinary Course of Business

The following case shows how Canadian law addresses a sale to a "buyer in ordinary course of business." In reading this case, note how Article 9 has influenced the development of Canadian law on security interests.

Spittlehouse v. Northshore Marine, Inc.,
1994 CanLII 1295 (ON C.A.)

Grange J.A.

[P]laintiffs [Mr. and Mrs. Spittlehouse] entered into a contract with the defendant Northshore Marine for a Grand Banks 46-foot classic boat for the selling price of $555,000. They have paid 90% of the purchase price and are more than willing to pay the balance upon delivery of the boat as provided in the contract of sale "in the water at Port Credit, Ontario."

The difficulty is two-fold. First, the defendant Transamerica Commercial Finance Corporation has a perfected security interest in all the assets of Northshore including this boat and secondly, the contract of sale provided that "title to the above described equipment shall be transferred to the buyer when the buyer has made payment in full for the equipment."

> When does title ordinarily pass under Article 2? Review 2-401 and the materials in Chapter 3, Part A as needed to answer this question.

At some time in the course of delivery of the boat, an official of Northshore Marine advised Transamerica of certain defalcations on its (Northshore's) part including its failure to pass on trust moneys. As a result of this information and a general default on payments by Northshore to Transamerica, the latter . . . seized the boat in question. This action resulted. [Northshore is now insolvent.]

The claim of the defendants is simply stated. Transamerica has a perfected security against the boat. The plaintiffs have no title to the boat, having a contractual – not a property – interest, and can rank only as unsecured creditors against the estate of Northshore. It is conceded that there will be little recovery for those unsecured creditors.

The judge of first instance recognized that the result claimed by the defendants would "produce a result that is manifestly unjust." He accepted "with great reluctance" that the Sale of Goods Act rules for ascertaining the passing of title could not be invoked in the plaintiffs' favour, but found the plaintiffs to have an equitable interest in the boat which was not defeated by the reservation of title. He considered, but felt he did not have to decide, whether the plaintiffs were the beneficiaries of a resulting trust of the boat.

> As the name suggests, the Sale of Goods Act is the Canadian equivalent of UCC Article 2.

In my view, the whole issue is readily resolved by the provisions of § 28 (1) of the Personal Property Securities Act, S.O. 1989, which provides as follows:

> 28. (1) A buyer of goods from a seller who sells the goods in the ordinary course of business takes them free from any security interest therein given by the seller even though it is perfected and the buyer knows of it, unless the buyer also knew that the sale constituted a breach of the security agreement.

> Compare this language to UCC 9-320 (a).

There is no question that in the contract between the plaintiffs and Northshore the latter was acting in the ordinary course of business. It was a dealer in boats, and its business was to sell them. The plaintiffs were seeking to buy a boat, indeed the very boat that was the subject of the contract. They had no knowledge of the security agreement between Northshore and Transamerica, much less of any breach of that agreement (if indeed there was a breach). The only possible problems are whether the plaintiffs were buyers of the boat and Northshore was the seller. In my opinion they indubitably were.

> Where are "buyer" and "seller" defined in the UCC, and would the Spittlehouses and Northshore fall within those definitions?

There is no definition of "buyer" or "seller" in the Personal Property Security Act, but the transaction between the plaintiffs and Northshore was in common parlance clearly a sale. It is what used to be called a conditional sale and was governed by what was called the Conditional Sales Act, replaced by the Personal Property Security Act of 1976, the forerunner of the present Act. The Act is replete with reference to "sales," "purchasers," and "sellers" in reference to the transaction between the conditional vendor and the conditional purchaser. This transaction is a sale with title withheld until the purchase price is fully paid. It is a device to protect the seller until full payment is made and no more. It is valid to the extent that the purchasers cannot demand the transfer of title until all of the purchase price is paid.

> Does Article 9 recognize a transaction called a "conditional sale"? 9-202 Comment 2 may assist you in answering this question.

This conclusion might seem contrary to that reached by the Saskatchewan Court of Appeal in *Royal Bank of Canada v. 216200 Alberta Ltd.* 33 D.L.R. (4th) 80, the only Canadian case on the subject I can find. The Court was concerned with the priorities between a secured-interest holder and certain customers of an insolvent furniture dealer. Saskatchewan had a section of their PPSA almost identical with ours. When dealing with the status of the claims of persons who have paid part of the purchase price for personal property in the possession of the seller, the court stated:

I am of the opinion that before a buyer can take property free of the security interest of the appellant, he must establish that there has been a sale and that he is a buyer in the ordinary course of business. The application of the provisions of the Sale of Goods Act, while not being specifically referred to in Section 30, must be referred to to determine whether or not there has been a sale. Section 3 (4) of the Sale of Goods Act defines "sale" as follows:

> 3. (4) Where, under a contract of sale, the property in the goods is transferred from the seller to the buyer, the contract is called a sale; but where the transfer of the property in the goods is to take place at a future time or is subject to some condition thereafter to be fulfilled, the contract is called an agreement to sell.

Goods are sold when title passes to the buyer and §§ 18, 19, and 20 are relevant for the determination of that issue. The import of those sections is that no title passes to the buyer in unascertained goods until the goods are ascertained and appropriated to the sale.

The court reached its conclusion after examining two lines of cases in the United States under Article 9-307 (1) of the Uniform Commercial Code (similar to our § 28 (1) of the PPSA and § 30 of the Saskatchewan Act) and specifically approved the case of *Chrysler Corp. v. Adamatic, Inc.*, 208 N.W. 2d 97 (1973), a decision of the Wisconsin Supreme Court which held that a "buyer" was not a "buyer" within the meaning of the Code until title had passed. That decision was in effect reversed by the very court that pronounced it in *Daniel v. Bank of Hayward*, 425 N.W. 2d 416 (1988), in which it was said at pp. 420-21 in words equally appropriate, in my view, to the case at bar:

> . . . The cases and commentaries that have considered the issue since *Chrysler* have generally been critical of the reasoning the court employed in *Chrysler*. . . . We conclude that we erred in relying on the date of transfer of title as the date on which a purchaser becomes a buyer in ordinary course of business. Reliance on the concept of title is contrary to the thrust of the Uniform Commercial Code and the commentary. The drafters of the Uniform Commercial Code tried to avoid giving technical rules of title a central role in furthering the policies of the Uniform Commercial Code. Although title issues may be of significance in determining some issues under the Code, we conclude that reliance on title to interpret 409.307 (1) is an unduly narrow and technical interpretation.

In my opinion, the Sale of Goods Act is not relevant or material to the resolution of our problem. Here, there was a sale with a seller and a purchaser who between them agreed that title in the goods would not pass until all purchase money was paid. The agreement between them states, "the dealer agrees to sell and the buyer agrees to purchase" and refers "to the equipment being purchased" and that such equipment "is being sold." It cannot be regarded as anything but a sale. The Sale of Goods Act may affect the time when property in the goods passes but it cannot change what is clearly a sale in another Act into something it is not.

Margin notes:

The current reference is to 9-320.

See the official comment to 2-101 and the text of and commentary to 9-202 for language expressing the drafters' intent to downplay the importance of title.

For these reasons, I would not follow the *Royal Bank* case. The plaintiff may take advantage of § 28 (1) of our Act upon tendering the balance of the purchase price, and I would dismiss the appeal accordingly.

- What distinction does Transamerica attempt to draw between "contractual" and "property" interests and how would this argument, if accepted, allow it to prevail?

E. Priority Rules for Lien Creditors

This section shows the interplay between the Uniform Commercial Code and the varying laws of the states that have enacted the Code, in the area of liens and their priority. These materials also address federal tax liens. The federal bankruptcy trustee's status as a "hypothetical lien creditor" under 11 USC § 544 (a) (1) lends particular significance to these materials. Because other cases, including the *McRoberts* case in Part A of this chapter, have illustrated how the trustee's special status affects the determination of Article 9 priorities, this section focuses on providing some other examples of lienholder interests.

Read 9-317 and 9-333 and Comment 2.

- Which liens are governed by 9-317 and which are governed by 9-333?

- How do consensual and nonconsensual liens rank in relative priority to one another?

- What law governs the creation of the liens addressed by 9-333?

> 9-109 (d) (2) and Comment 10 may assist you in answering this question.

Metropolitan National Bank v. United States, 901 F.2d 1297 (5th Cir. 1990), provides an introduction to federal tax liens as established by the Federal Tax Lien Act, 26 USC §§ 6321-6323:

> Under 26 USC § 6321, the amount of a delinquent taxpayer's liability constitutes a lien in favor of the United States upon all of the taxpayer's property and rights to property, whether real or personal. The lien imposed by § 6321 is effective from the date of assessment of the tax, and continues until the liability is satisfied or becomes unenforceable by reason of lapse of time. The question whether and to what extent a taxpayer has "property" or "rights to property" to which the tax lien attaches is determined under the applicable state law. . . .

Once it has been determined under state law that the taxpayer owns property or rights to property, federal law controls for the purpose of determining whether an attached tax lien has priority over competing liens asserted against the taxpayer's property. "When a third party also claims a lien interest in the taxpayer's property, the basic priority rule of 'first in time, first in right' controls, unless Congress has created a different priority rule to govern the particular situation." *Texas Commerce Bank-Fort Worth, N.A. v. United States*, 896 F.2d 152 (5th Cir.1990). Section 6323 of the Internal Revenue Code, as amended by the Federal Tax Lien Act of 1966, governs the validity and priority of federal tax liens imposed by § 6321 against "certain persons." . . . Thus, the respective priorities with respect to federal tax liens and competing claims that are protected under § 6323 (a) are dependent upon which claim is perfected "first in time." *Id.* at 1300.

The following case defines "judgment lien" and illustrates how the priority of federal tax liens is analyzed under the Federal Tax Lien Act.

- ▪ Why is the priority of federal tax liens not governed by Article 9? 9-109 (c) (1) and Comment 8 may assist you in answering this question.

Litton Industrial Automation Systems, Inc.
v. Nationwide Power Corp.,
106 F.3d 366, 31 U.C.C. Rep. Serv. 2d 1175 (11th Cir. 1997).

Birch, Circuit Judge.

The facts in this appeal are essentially undisputed. Plaintiff Litton Industrial Automation Systems, Inc., filed this interpleader action in the United States District Court for the Eastern District of Michigan, from which it was transferred to the United States District Court for the Middle District of Florida. Litton deposited in the registry of the court $572,627.46, which it owed to Nationwide Power Corporation pursuant to a judgment obtained by Nationwide on August 15, 1989. The real parties in interest are Highlander International Corporation and the United States.

> Cash collateral is normally cash or a cash equivalent in which the secured creditor has a security interest as proceeds. How else, if at all, could Highlander have perfected its interest in these funds?

Highlander's interest in the interpleaded funds stems from an agreement between Nationwide and Highlander, pursuant to which Nationwide sought to secure a debt it owed to Highlander. In this agreement, Nationwide granted to Highlander a security interest in certain "cash collateral," including Nationwide's cause of action against Litton, which eventually resulted in the money judgment here in dispute. This interest arose on the date of the agreement, April 15, 1986. Highlander did not file a UCC-1 statement until August 1989, however. The Government's interest in the interpleaded funds arose from a tax assessment on June 9, 1986, of tax penalties exceeding $700,000 against Nationwide. On July 3, 1986, the Internal Revenue Service filed a notice of federal tax lien in Broward County, Florida, in which Nationwide had its principal executive office.

On July 27, 1989, the IRS served a notice of levy on Litton's attorney, directing him to deliver to the IRS any monies owed to Nationwide. After judgment was entered in favor of Nationwide in its suit against Litton, Litton initiated the instant interpleader action to determine which party is entitled to the funds. The district court granted summary judgment to the Government, holding that the federal tax lien was entitled to priority over Highlander's security interest. This appeal followed.

. . . This case involves a pure question of law: Is Highlander the "holder of a security interest" which is entitled to priority over the Government's federal tax lien under the Federal Tax Lien Act of 1966?

* * *

It is undisputed in this appeal that a tax lien arose upon all Nationwide's property on June 9, 1986, the first date of the tax penalty assessments against Nationwide. It is also undisputed that the IRS properly filed a notice of this tax lien in Nationwide's county of residence, as required by 26 USC § 6323 (f) (2) (B), on July 3, 1986. Therefore, for Highlander's interest to take priority over the tax lien, Highlander must have been the holder of a "security interest," as that term is defined in the FTLA, on July 3, 1986. To do so, Highlander must establish that its interest satisfies four conditions:

> This definition is found in 26 USC § 6323 (h) (1).

> (1) that the security interest was acquired by contract for the purpose of securing payment or performance of an obligation or indemnifying against loss; (2) that the property to which the security interest was to attach was in existence at the time the tax lien was filed; (3) that the security interest was, at the time of the tax lien filing, protected under state law against a judgment lien arising out of an unsecured obligation; and (4) that the holder of the security interest parted with money or money's worth.

> How is the second condition satisfied under the facts of this case?

Haas v. Internal Revenue Service (In re Haas), 31 F.3d 1081, 1085 (11th Cir.1994), cert. denied, 515 U.S. 1142, 115 S.Ct. 2578, 132 L.Ed.2d 828 (1995). As in *Haas*, the only issue on appeal in this case is whether the third condition is satisfied. In other words, this case turns on whether Highlander's interest was protected under Florida law – the applicable local law – against a judgment lien arising out of an unsecured obligation on July 3, 1986.

> The tax lien was a "judgment lien arising out of an unsecured obligation" and became effective on July 3, 1986.

Relying on the "hypothetical judgment-lien-creditor test" adopted by this court in *Haas*, the district court held that Highlander's interest was not protected under Florida law against a judgment lien.

> [T]he hypothetical judgment-lien-creditor test operates to put the IRS in the shoes of any subsequent judgment creditor, including the most favorable shoes. Thus, if any subsequent judgment creditor could prevail over [Highlander], then the IRS prevails.

Haas, 31 F.3d at 1089 (footnote omitted). The district court reasoned that a class of judgment creditors, those who qualify as "lien creditors" as defined in UCC § 9-301 (3) and who have no notice of Highlander's previous unperfected interest, could have prevailed over Highlander's

> This definition is now found in 9-102 (a) (52).

interest under Florida law. The court concluded that the Government prevails here.

* * *

Highlander contends, however, that under Florida law a "judgment lien" does not attach to intangible assets, such as the funds at issue in this case, until the judgment creditor has taken further judicial action – by way of garnishment or an independent suit to enforce the debt. Highlander concludes that the holder of a simple "judgment lien" on intangibles does not qualify as a UCC "lien creditor" under Florida law. Thus, Highlander's security interest, though unperfected, prevails over the judgment lien because Highlander's interest was the first to attach.

* * *

. . . The FTLA does not define the phrase "judgment lien." Highlander . . . argue[s] that the plain meaning of the phrase "judgment lien" is a "simple unperfected judgment lien." The gist of this argument is that, under Florida law, a simple money judgment against a defendant creates a "lien" on all of its property. Such a lien, "a simple judgment lien," . . . does not attach to the defendant's intangible personal property until further judicial action is taken. Highlander's argument is unconvincing.

Federal law, not state law, governs a priority contest between a security interest and a federal tax lien. Thus, although the FTLA resolves such a contest by comparing the security interest to a judgment lien under state priority rules, what constitutes a "judgment lien" within the meaning of section 6323 (h) (1) is a matter of federal law. We are concerned with what Congress intended that phrase to mean, not with what state law labels as a judgment lien.

The phrase "judgment lien" does not have a generally understood meaning. For example, in contrast to Florida, there appears to be no such thing as a "judgment lien," whether labeled "simple" or not, on personal property in some states. In other states, a simple judgment creates no lien at all on personal property, and a judgment lien does not arise until certain additional action is taken by the judgment creditor.

* * *

We conclude that the phrase "judgment lien" has no ordinary meaning so as to compel Highlander's interpretation of the phrase within the context of the FTLA. The Government argues that "judgment lien," as used in the FTLA, is equivalent to the interest of a UCC lien creditor. This interpretation is one that has been adopted almost unanimously by the commentators. The rationale for adopting this interpretation is that one of Congress's main goals in enacting the FTLA was "to conform the lien provisions of the internal revenue laws to the concepts developed in [the] Uniform Commercial Code." H.R. Rep. No. 89-1884, at 1-2 (1966), reprinted in Committee on Ways and Means, 89th Cong., Legislative History of H.R. 11256: Federal Tax Lien Act of 1966, at 443-44 (1966) [hereinafter Legislative History]. The only way in which the UCC gives effect to the interest of a judgment creditor is the "lien creditor" concept embodied in section 9-301 (3) of the UCC. The logical conclusion, though by no means an inevitable one, is that Congress intended the phrase "judgment lien" to mean the interest, arising from a judgment (as opposed to assignment, for example), that a lien creditor has in a given property. This conclusion is further supported by the fact that it gives effect to Congress's "specific legislative intent . . . to enable creditors to protect certain types of security interests against subsequent federal tax liens, and to do so by taking the same steps already necessary under state law to protect their interests against various other types of competing claims."

In short, we are faced with two possible interpretations of an ambiguous phrase that Congress used in the FTLA. Although we believe that the interpretation offered by the Government is the better one, we need not resolve this case solely on the basis of the statutory analysis described above. Congress has entrusted the administration of the Internal Revenue Code, which includes the FTLA, to the United States Department of Treasury and the IRS. In construing an administrative (or regulatory) statute, we are guided by the framework of analysis set out by the Supreme Court in *Chevron, U.S.A., Inc. v. Natural Resources Defense Council, Inc.*, 467 U.S. 837, 104 S.Ct. 2778, 81 L.Ed.2d 694 (1984). "First, always, is the question whether Congress has directly spoken to the precise question at issue. If the intent of Congress is clear, that is the end of the matter; for the court, as well as the agency, must give effect to the unambiguously expressed intent of Congress." If Congress did not express its intent unambiguously, we defer to the agency's interpretation if it "is based on a permissible construction of the statute."

As we have already stated, we believe that Congress did not express its intent unambiguously when it used the phrase "judgment lien" in section 6323 (h) (1). Department of Treasury regulations, however, define "judgment lien" as "a lien held by a judgment lien creditor." Treas. Reg. § 301.6323 (h)-1 (a) (2).

> The term "judgment lien creditor" means a person who has obtained a valid judgment, in a court of record and of competent jurisdiction, for the recovery of specifically designated property or for a certain sum of money. In the case of a judgment for the recovery of a certain sum of money, a judgment lien creditor is a person who has perfected a lien under the judgment on the property involved. . . . If recording or docketing is necessary under local law before a judgment becomes effective against third parties acquiring liens on real property, a judgment lien under such local law is not perfected . . . until the time of such recordation or docketing. If under local law levy or seizure is necessary before a judgment lien becomes effective against third parties acquiring liens on personal property, then a judgment lien under such local law is not perfected until levy or seizure of the personal property involved.

Treas. Reg. § 301.6323 (h)-1 (g). In short, the regulation codifies the interpretation of "judgment lien" that the Government advocates in this case and that we have already determined is not only permissible, but also is the better interpretation. This interpretation holds that a judgment lien is equivalent to the interest of a UCC lien creditor.

Under the second step of *Chevron*, we must defer to the Department's interpretation.

Because Highlander's interest in the interpleaded funds was unperfected under Florida law on July 3, 1986, it was subordinate to that of a UCC lien creditor. See Fl. Stat. ch. 679.301 (1) (b). Highlander's interest, therefore, was not protected under local law against a judgment lien arising on that date; it was not a "security interest" within the meaning of 26 USC § 6323 (h) (1). The Government's tax lien is entitled to priority.

> The current reference is to UCC 9-317 (a) (2) (A).

- How and why did the proper definition of "judgment lien" affect the court's holding?

- Is the result in this case consistent with the priority that is generally afforded to liens created by operation of law under 9-333?

Problem: Consider the following facts:

[Harry and Linda McCord] owned and operated two Petland pet stores in Maryland, initially as a sole proprietorship, and later as a corporation owned wholly by the McCords. The two stores were located in Lavale and in Hagerstown. Harry McCord obtained the Lavale store by assignment from a previous franchisee on June 1, 1992, and obtained the Hagerstown store by franchise agreement on February 4, 1993. On December 15, 1997, Harry McCord filed Articles of Incorporation of Brandywine Pets, Inc. The McCords transferred the assets and liabilities of the pet stores to Brandywine sometime in 1998.

Prior to the incorporation, Petland obtained two liens on the McCords' pet stores. On December 4, 1997, the McCords executed two promissory notes in favor of the defendant Petland, Inc. in the amounts of $95,000 and $60,646.73. The notes were secured by a lien on all accounts, leasehold items, fixtures, inventory, equipment, proceeds, and after acquired collateral of the Hagerstown and Lavale stores, respectively. Petland filed a UCC-1 financing statement for the interest in the Lavale store with the Maryland Department of Assessments and Taxation on January 31, 1997, and filed a financing statement for the interest in the Hagerstown store on May 15, 1997.

Subsequent to Petland's filing of its UCC financing statements, the IRS filed two Notices of Federal Tax Liens in Berkeley County, West Virginia, the McCords' county of residence. These liens arose from unpaid federal Insurance Contribution Act taxes. The notices were filed on November 13, 1998, and on April 15, 1998.

The debtors filed a petition under Chapter 13 of the Bankruptcy Code on May 25, 1999. In their schedules, the McCords claimed to have $60,000 assets in real property and $91,803.05 in personal property. The McCords claim a personal-property interest of $1,000 in fixtures and $10,000 in actual liquidation value of inventory in the two stores. During discovery, the McCords admitted that essentially all of the inventory on hand on the date of the bankruptcy filing came into existence after April 14, 1998, (the day before the first tax lien was filed); that there were no accounts receivable on April 14, 1998; and that all leasehold items, fixtures, and equipment were purchased prior to April 14, 1998. The McCords further stated that the fair-market value of the leasehold items, fixtures, and equipment was $39,808 but could probably be sold for only $1,000 to $2,000.

Petland maintains that its liens have priority over those of the IRS by virtue of the fact that it perfected its liens before the IRS filed its notices of liens. The IRS contends that Petland's liens attached to property acquired by the McCords after the IRS filed its notices and that the IRS liens have priority.

- Based on these facts, does Petland's lien cover after-acquired inventory? Review 9-204 and the materials in Chapter 14, Part A as needed to answer this question.

- Which party has priority and why? In answering this question, **read 9-508 (a) and Comment 2**, which addresses how the incorporation should be figured into your analysis.

Based on *In re McCord*, 264 B.R. 814, 815-816 (Bankr. N.D. W. Va. 2001).

=====

International Perspective: Lienholders

Professor Hwang Hyun Suk's article *International Secured Transactions: South Korea*, in *International Secured Transactions* (Oceana Publications 2005), describes the rights of lienholders in South Korea as follows:

> In many legal systems, once general unsecured creditors have acquired a court judgment based on their claims and have taken certain steps set forth by law, such as seizing specific property or registering the judgment, such creditors are given the equivalent of a security right in that property. However, Korean law does not recognize any security rights arising from a court judgment and ensuring enforcement measures.
>
> * * *
>
> Under the Civil Code, creditors who improve or fix encumbered assets, such as equipment repairers, have a right to retain the encumbered assets until the claims of the creditors have been paid in full. *Id.* at 20-21.

- What incentives are created by this approach?

- On balance, does the South Korean system provide more or less security to repairpersons than U.S. law generally does, with regard to ensuring that they receive payment for services rendered?

Review 9-333 and Comment 2 as needed to answer this question.

Rights of a Secured Party

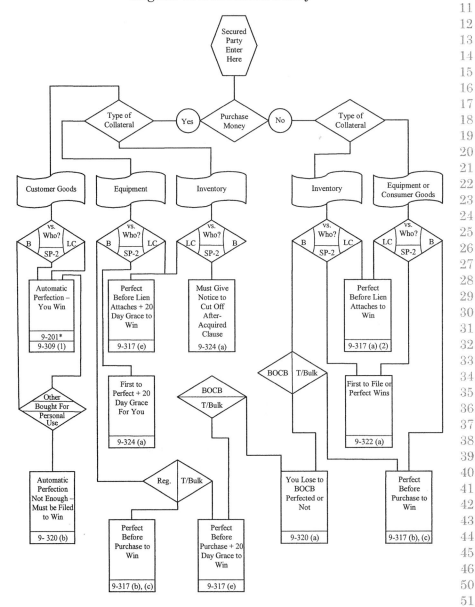

*See 9-317 (a) (2) and 9-324 (a).

- To review many of the important concepts introduced in this chapter, make sure you can reason your way through this flowchart, adapted from the original by attorney Gerald P. Nehra. This chart shows how the interests of a secured party (SP-1) fare in priority competitions with buyers (B), lien creditors (LC), and other secured creditors (SP-2), insofar as interests in certain common collateral are concerned. "BOCB" is "Buyer in ordinary course of business" and "T/Bulk" refers to "Taker from a bulk sale."

Chapter Conclusion: This chapter has provided a general introduction to Article 9's most common priority rules.   In leaving these materials, you should be familiar with the basic contours of Article 9's priority rules involving competitions between secured and unsecured creditors, two secured creditors, lien creditors, and buyers of collateral that is subject to a security interest.

Chapter 17: Default

This chapter puts into context the materials in Chapters 13 through 16. **Read 9-601 and Comments 2 through 4.** Secured parties, specifically those who have first priority, have a significant advantage when an insolvent debtor defaults, because they can proceed against the collateral to satisfy the remaining debt. The UCC does not define default; instead, this is a matter of contract law.

- What document in a secured transaction typically defines the term "default"?

- Other than a failure to pay sums when due, what else might constitute an event of default?

- Why might parties choose to define default broadly?

- **Read 9-601 (g) and Comment 9.** What distinction is drawn between consignors and the enumerated buyers, on the one hand, and other secured parties, on the other?

A. The Right of Repossession

This section discusses the possibility of self-help through repossession, the requirement that a secured party refrain from breaching the peace in exercising the right of repossession, and the possibility that the secured party may obtain assistance from the sheriff or other third party in carrying out the repossession.

Read 9-609 and Comment 3. This Code section sets forth a creditor's right to repossess the collateral in the event of default.

- In the context of repossession, what does it mean for a secured party to proceed "pursuant to judicial process," as opposed to "without judicial process"?

- When might a secured party choose each option?

When a debtor files for bankruptcy, the automatic stay found in 11 USC § 362 prevents a secured party from proceeding against the collateral during the period after the bankruptcy petition is filed, unless and until the petition is dismissed or relief from the stay is granted. Because there may be significant delay between the bankruptcy filing and the ultimate disposition of the collateral, during which time the

11 USC § 361 addresses the issue of "adequate protection" against depreciation.

As the name suggests, an "undersecured creditor" is one whose security interest is worth less than the remaining debt owed to him or her.

The "state-law remedies" referenced here include those found in Article 9.

collateral may depreciate significantly, a secured party may be entitled to "protection payments" to minimize its potential depreciation loss. *In re Deico Electronics, Inc.*, 139 B.R. 945 (Bankr. App. 9th Cir. 1992), discusses protection payments, as follows:

> In *United Savings Association v. Timbers of Inwood Forest*, 484 U.S. 365, 108 S.Ct. 626, 98 L.Ed.2d 740 (1988), the Supreme Court held that undersecured creditors are entitled to adequate protection to compensate them for the depreciation in their collateral. Adequate protection prevents creditors from becoming more undersecured because of the delay that bankruptcy works on the exercise of their state-law remedies.
>
> Accordingly, adequate-protection analysis requires the bankruptcy court to first determine when the creditor would have obtained its state-law remedies had bankruptcy not intervened. Presumably, that will be after the creditor first seeks relief. The court must then determine the value of the collateral as of that date. . . .
>
> The amount by which the collateral depreciates from that valuation is the amount of protection adequate to compensate the creditor for the loss occasioned by bankruptcy. But collateral may not always depreciate according to a precise monthly schedule. Moreover, requiring a lump sum of past-due protection could suffocate a debtor otherwise able to reorganize.
>
> Therefore, while the amount of adequate protection to which an undersecured creditor is entitled is equal to the amount of depreciation its collateral suffers after it would have exercised its state-law remedies, neither that determination nor the schedule for its tender are appropriate for application of a rigid formula. Instead, the bankruptcy court must have discretion to fix any initial lump-sum amount, the amount payable periodically, the frequency of payments, and the beginning date, all as dictated by the circumstances of the case and the sound exercise of that discretion. *Id.* at 947.

- ▪ Why should protection payments not be calculated from the date on which the secured party perfects its interest in the collateral, so long as the interest has been continuously perfected since that time?

"Repossession title" describes a secured party's post-default rights in the collateral. Such title vests in the secured creditor the power to dispose of the collateral, but nevertheless falls short of full ownership rights. In *In re Estis*, 311 B.R. 592, 54 U.C.C. Rep. Serv. 2d 198 (Bankr. D. Kan. 2004), the court addressed whether a secured party had violated the automatic stay by selling a repossessed vehicle after receiving notice of the debtor's bankruptcy filing. In holding the creditor had violated the stay, the court elaborated as follows:

A "repossession title" provides nothing more than a mechanism by which a creditor may pass legal or record title to a transferee upon exercising its remedies under the UCC. Because the plaintiff [debtor] retained legal and equitable title in the repossessed vehicle on the date of her Chapter 13 petition, and the [defendant secured creditor's] "repossession title" was merely a mechanism for passing legal title upon exercising remedies under the UCC, the Court concludes that the repossessed vehicle became part of the plaintiff's bankruptcy estate pursuant to section 541, and that the defendant needed relief from the automatic stay prior to any disposition of the repossessed vehicle. *Id.* at 598.

> 9-619 describes how a secured party can transfer legal or record title to collateral it has repossessed.

> 11 USC § 541 (a) (1) provides that "all legal or equitable interests of the debtor in property [at] commencement of the case" become part of the estate.

In *Motors Acceptance Corp. v. Rozier*, 278 Ga. 52, 597 S.E.2d 367 (Ga. 2004), the court explored the concept of repossession title further:

> The UCC's statutory framework makes clear that repossession alone is not enough to extinguish the debtor's ownership in the collateral, but that a creditor must go through additional steps after repossession to obtain ownership. For example, [9-610 to 9-614] provide the procedure by which a creditor may dispose of collateral after default, and [9-610 (c)] specifically provides that the "secured party may purchase [the] collateral." The creditor would not need to purchase the collateral if it already owned it. Also, [9-620 to 9-622] allow a creditor to accept the collateral in full or partial satisfaction of the debt, with the debtor's consent. These provisions would also be meaningless if the creditor already owned the collateral. . . .
>
> [The creditor in this case] argues that a debtor has only one right after repossession, the right of redemption under [9-623], and that this right is insufficient to constitute ownership. The right of redemption is an important right, but [the creditor] is incorrect that it is a debtor's only right after repossession. Under the UCC, a debtor's rights also include: to demand that the creditor act with due care to preserve the collateral [9-207 (a)]; to be notified before the creditor disposes of the collateral [9-611 to 9-614]; to remittance of any surplus from sale of the collateral [9-615 (d) (1)]; and to damages for the creditor's failure to comply with the UCC's provisions [9-625]. *Id.* at 53.

- In your own words, describe the relative rights of a debtor and a secured party in the collateral, after default.

- How are these rights different from the rights that each party held before default?

Wrongful Repossession

Read 9-625 (a) and (b) and Comment 2. As Comment 2 indicates, a secured party must act in good faith and must exercise commercial reasonableness when proceeding against

collateral after an event of default. In addition, the secured 1
party must ordinarily provide reasonable advance notification 2
of its intended conduct to the debtor. 3

4

The following case addresses the issue of wrongful 5
repossession, which can arise in the context of allegations that 6
the secured creditor has acted in bad faith in exercising its 7
rights of repossession pursuant to an acceleration clause. 8

9

As 1-309 indicates, a creditor's rights under an acceleration clause must always be exercised in good faith.

Clayton v. Crossroads Equipment Co., 10
655 P.2d 1125, 34 U.C.C. Rep. Serv. 1448 (Utah 1982). 11

12

Howe, Justice. 13

14

The plaintiff, David D. Clayton, brought this action against the 15
defendants Crossroads Equipment Company and John Deere 16
Company seeking damages and possession of two John Deere 17
combines, which he alleged they wrongfully repossessed from him. The 18
trial court, sitting without a jury, awarded the plaintiff $27,400 19
representing the amount he had paid on the combines, and $100 20
nominal damages for "unlawful detention." Plaintiff was also awarded 21
$20,000 punitive damages against Deere. Crossroads and Deere were 22
awarded the combines . . . and Crossroads was awarded a set-off 23
against the plaintiff in the amount of $1,413 and attorney's fees of $750 24
for money he owed to Crossroads on an open account. Defendants 25
appeal. 26

On October 7, 1977, the plaintiff purchased a John Deere combine from 27
Crossroads for $47,250. Plaintiff signed a contract marked "Retail 28
Installment Contract, Security Agreement," which provided for a down 29
payment of $18,900, an initial installment payment of $4,352 due on 30
July 1, 1978, and equal payments of $3,793 every six months 31
thereafter, commencing January 1, 1979, until the balance was paid. 32
Crossroads assigned this contract to Deere's branch office in Portland, 33
Oregon for financing, and it was accepted. 34

On May 15, 1978, plaintiff purchased a second combine on terms 35
similar to those of the first purchase. The total purchase price was 36
$54,470 minus a discount of $10,000. Plaintiff paid down $8,500 cash 37
and gave a promissory note for $3,000 for the balance of the required 38
down payment of $11,500. The first installment of $4,880 was due on 39
July 1, 1978, and payments thereafter were to be made at six-month 40
intervals. This contract was also submitted for assignment to Deere at 41
Portland for financing, but Deere refused to accept it. [Obtaining 42
financing was an express condition of the parties' contract. The 43
evidence showed that the parties attempted to secure financing from 44
May to September.] 45

Plaintiff used both combines to harvest crops for farmers. He traveled 46
from state to state to work and had 14 years of experience as a contract 50
harvester. In early August of 1978, he brought both combines back to 51
Utah in search of harvesting work. He had hoped to harvest barley for 52
Ivan Barlow, president of Crossroads. When plaintiff arrived in Utah, 53

however, he discovered that Barlow's barley crop was overrun with weeds and was not yet ready for harvest.

Plaintiff then had the combines serviced by Crossroads together with some warranty work. On September 21, 1978, he commenced leaving with them intending to travel to Illinois where he had arranged to harvest corn. [The plaintiff had spent several hours on the telephone that morning in a failed attempt to raise money, since Crossroads had indicated it would need to add $10,000 to the purchase price due to the failure of financing if the plaintiff would not agree to leave the combines on the Crossroads lot.] Crossroads had earlier informed the plaintiff that he could not take the second combine from the Crossroads lot since Deere had refused to accept the contract for financing, which left the combine without insurance coverage. When Ivan Barlow discovered that the plaintiff had taken both combines and was leaving town, he attempted to overtake him. On his way, he stopped to enlist the help of Deputy Sheriff Wayne Holt. When Deputy Holt and Barlow caught up with plaintiff, he had already been stopped by Barlow's son, Les. Les Barlow had observed the plaintiff leaving and had pulled his pickup across the path of the 1978 combine, which was being driven by Bill Miles, an assistant of the plaintiff. After a roadside discussion between the men, the officer took temporary possession of the keys to the two trucks on which the combines were loaded. Later that day, Deere requested Crossroads' assistance in further detaining the 1977 combine. The two combines were moved to Crossroads' lot. Plaintiff did not pursue obtaining their possession at that time, but later brought this action.

Plaintiff was awarded damages of $27,400 against both defendants, plus punitive damages of $20,000 against Deere because of its improper repossession. He also recovered nominal damages of $100 for slander, false arrest, or "unlawful detention." Possession of the combines was given to the defendants. Crossroads was awarded a set-off of $1,413, which plaintiff owed to it on his open account, together with reasonable attorney's fees of $750.00 for collection services.

* * *

The . . . question presented is whether the 1977 combine was wrongfully repossessed. In the sales contract, there is a provision that:

> In the event of the default (as defined on the reverse side hereof), holder may take possession of the goods and exercise any other remedies provided by law.

The event of default with which we are here concerned is recited on the back of the agreement as follows:

> This note shall be in default . . . if for any reason the holder of this note deems the debt or security unsafe, and in any such event the holder may immediately and without notice declare the entire balance of this note due and payable, together with all expenses of collection by suit or otherwise, including reasonable attorney's fees.

This language is
now found in UCC
1-309.

The validity of such a contractual provision is not in dispute. Section
70A-1-208, U.C.A. (1953), provides that such provisions shall be
construed to mean that the secured party shall have the power to
exercise the remedies provided for "only if he in good faith believes that
the prospect of payment or performance is impaired." The defendants
could, therefore, accelerate the contract (note) and repossess the
combine only in a good-faith belief that the debt or their security was
about to become impaired.

. . . The obvious purpose of requiring that a secured party act in good
faith is to impose the basic obligation of fair dealing, and to protect the
purchaser from the mere whim or caprice of the secured party. In the
instant case, the trial court found that no cause or reason existed on
September 21, 1978, the date of the repossession, for Deere to feel any
less secure than it did at the time the 1977 (first) contract was entered
into between the parties. The court further found that nothing had
occurred during the interim to make the plaintiff less credit-worthy
and concluded that Deere had acted in bad faith in repossessing the
combine, particularly because the plaintiff was then current with his
payments.

Deere assails this finding and conclusion primarily on the ground that,
when it investigated the plaintiff's credit at the time the second
contract was submitted to it for acceptance of financing, it obtained
information from its branch office in Dallas, Texas ([with which] the
plaintiff had formerly dealt) that he was a poor credit risk. The
difficulty with Deere's position is that the record fails to establish that
the transactions and events which formed the basis for the derogatory
credit report from the Dallas office occurred after October 1977, when
Deere accepted the first contract. Deere, without much investigation,
had accepted the plaintiff as a credit risk on the 1977 contract. It
would be highly inequitable to allow Deere to change its mind once it
had accepted that contract, simply because it subsequently conducted a
more thorough investigation; it is unfair to put the buyer in default
based upon information which was apparently available in one of
Deere's own branch offices at the time that it had accepted plaintiff.
Under pre-UCC law, it was held that "insecurity" clauses contained in
chattel mortgages and other security agreements were meant to apply
to possible changes in conditions or circumstances, or new
developments affecting the mortgagee's security. Facts that would
justify the mortgagee's taking possession "must arise from the acts of
the parties or changes in values occurring subsequent to the execution
of the mortgage." *Watson v. Cudney*, 144 Ill. App. 624, 627 (1908).
Neither has Deere cited, nor have we found, any cases which have been
decided under the UCC on this point, but no reason is apparent why
the law should be any different now.

This is not a case where the plaintiff's credit had deteriorated after the
contract had been accepted by Deere. On the contrary, the plaintiff had
made all required payments to date on the 1977 combine.
Furthermore, a representative of Deere had met in June 1978 with the
plaintiff to collect an overdue payment, which plaintiff made to him.
He indicated to the plaintiff that he would use his effort to induce
Deere to accept the second contract. We therefore affirm the trial
court's finding that Deere failed to act in good faith, based upon its

finding that there was no substantial change in his credit standing
between the time of the execution of the 1977 sales agreement and the
time the defendants repossessed the combine.

[The court therefore affirmed the lower court's holding awarding
possession of the equipment to the defendants, based on the plaintiff's
failure to meet the contractual condition of obtaining financing, but
awarding damages to the plaintiff for wrongful repossession, including
punitive damages based in part upon the fact that repossession
occurred during harvest season.]

- What event of default do the defendants allege?

- Why was the repossession in this case wrongful?

- Since the repossession was wrongful, why were the
  defendants allowed to retain the combines?

- How did the secured creditor use the acceleration
  clause to support its claim that it had the right to
  repossess the collateral?

- If you represented Crossroads Equipment Co., how
  would you advise it to avoid a similar loss in the
  future?

Note 1: As the *Clayton* case demonstrates, cases involving
repossession also may raise the issue of acceleration of debt. In
Dunn v. General Equities, 319 N.W.2d 515, 33 U.C.C. Rep.
Serv. 1615 (Iowa 1982), the court considered the debtor's
argument that the creditor had waived its right to accelerate
the debt by having accepted late payments on prior occasions.
In agreeing that waiver had occurred, the court held as follows:

> Contract rights, of course, can be waived, and an option to
> accelerate a debt is one such waivable right. Acceleration
> provisions are not self-executing, and "the holder of an instrument
> . . . must take some positive action to exercise his option to declare
> payments due under an acceleration clause. . . ." *Weinrich v.
> Hawley*, 236 Iowa 652, 656, 19 N.W.2d 665, 667 (1945). A failure
> to exercise the option or an acceptance of late payment will
> establish waiver.

> * * *

> Moreover, this court has recognized that one way to prove waiver
> of contract provisions is "by evidence of a general course of dealing
> between the parties." *Livingston v. Stevens*, 122 Iowa 62, 69, 94
> N.W. 925, 927 (1903). The court has held, for example, that a prior
> "course of dealing," as defined in the Uniform Commercial Code,
> "may overcome express terms in [a] security agreement and
> translate into an authorization for sale free of lien." *Citizens*

"Course of dealing"
is defined in UCC
1-303.

Savings Bank v. Sac City State Bank, 315 N.W.2d 20, 26 (Iowa 1982). *Id.* at 516.

9-315 (a) (1) and 9-320 Comment 6 may assist you in answering this question.

- What is the legal effect of finding "an authorization for sale free of lien"?

Mercedes-Benz Credit Corp. v. Morgan, 312 Ark. 225, 850 S.W.2d 297 (1993), suggests that a creditor who has accepted late payments on prior occasions should be required to notify a debtor that the creditor intends to enforce the contract strictly on a going-forward basis, or risk being barred from doing so as a matter of estoppel.

- Precisely how should such a notice be worded?

- What liability does a creditor risk if it declines to give such notice and later chooses to repossess the collateral?

Notification is not, however, always required. As the court held in *Williams v. Ford Motor Credit Co.*, 435 So. 2d 66, 36 U.C.C. Rep. Serv. 1799 (Ala. 1983), a creditor may not be required to notify a debtor before repossession, even though it has accepted late payments previously, if the parties have agreed contractually to both a "nonwaiver" provision and a "nonmodification" clause. The *Williams* court held as follows:

[I]n *Hale v. Ford Motor Credit Co.*, 374 So. 2d 849 (Ala. 1979), . . . this Court delineated the rights and obligations of the parties under the terms of a security agreement containing both a non-waiver acceleration clause and a non-modification clause . . . [T]his Court ruled that the secured party is not required to give notice to the debtor prior to repossession, even though past-due payments have been accepted on previous occasions. Further, this Court concluded that a security agreement is effective according to the terms expressed in the agreement and that the inadvertence of the debtor in failing to make timely payments cannot raise an estoppel against the contractual interest of the creditor under the express terms of the security agreement, when there has been no written modification as required by the terms of the agreement. *Id.* at 68.

- What is the difference between a "non-waiver" clause and a "non-modification" clause?

- How does the combined operation of these two clauses support the court's holding?

Note 2: As 1-309 states, a creditor normally is required to exercise good faith in acting pursuant to an acceleration clause, even one that, on its face, provides the creditor with unfettered discretion to accelerate an indebtedness whenever it "deems itself insecure" or "at will." *Greenberg v. Service Business Forms Industries, Inc.*, 882 F.2d 1538, 9 U.C.C. Rep. Serv. 2d 841 (10th Cir. 1989), suggests, however, that the good-faith requirement does not necessarily apply to a clause that permits the creditor to accelerate upon an event of default.

- What policy distinction can be made between an ordinary acceleration clause, to which the good-faith requirement applies, and a clause allowing acceleration only upon default, to which some courts have held the good-faith requirement does not apply?

- Which kind of clause did the *Clayton* case involve?

Problem 1: Ted Moe purchased a John Deere tractor for approximately $120,000. To finance the purchase, he traded in two old tractors and agreed to pay approximately $12,000 every year on October 1st for the next five years. The first year, Moe made his payment two months late, but added interest to the payment. The second year, Moe paid half the agreed payment amount, more than three months late. John Deere agreed to accept the second installment on March 1 and then, once he had missed this deadline, on March 20. He failed to meet the extended deadline, as well. No further correspondence occurred until a John Deere representative contacted Moe in early June. The Deere representative offered to let Moe pay $2,000 (with no precise due date specified), with the balance – including interest – to be due when Moe began to harvest the year's crop. No payment was forthcoming, and Deere repossessed the tractor on July 30, before Moe's harvest.

- Based upon these facts, was the repossession rightful?

- What advice would you give to the John Deere Company if it were your client, assuming a company representative told you John Deere wished to balance the interests of fairness and good customer relations, on the one hand, and preserving its contractual rights, on the other?

Based on *Moe v. John Deere Co.*, 516 N.W.2d 332, 25 U.C.C. Rep. Serv. 2d 997 (S.D. 1994).

Problem 2: J.R. Hale Contracting Company executed a promissory note for $400,000 to United New Mexico Bank. There was to be a single interest payment five months after the note was signed, and the balance was due eight months after signing. At the time at which the note was executed, the company had done business with the bank for approximately

11 years. During this time, the company had a number of
revolving-credit accounts with the bank with balances that
increased steadily over time. The company made a number of
late payments on these various accounts, ranging from a few
days late to a number of weeks late. The bank renewed each
note when it came due, regardless of these occasional
delinquencies. The bank sometimes contacted the company
regarding its late payments; in response, the company would
send a check or the bank would simply deduct the delinquent
payment from one of the company's accounts, sending a notice
indicating it had done so.

The $400,000 note, which was twice the amount of any
previous note between the parties, included the following
language:

Waiver of
presentment and
notice of dishonor
are addressed in
UCC 3-504 (b).
Protest, which is the
term used to
describe a document
evidencing dishonor,
is covered in 3-505.

> If ANY installment of principal and/or interest on this note is not
> paid when due . . . or if Bank in good faith deems itself insecure or
> believes that the prospect of receiving payment required by this
> note is impaired; thereupon, at the option of Bank, this note and
> any and all other indebtedness of Maker to Bank shall become
> and be due and payable forthwith without demand, notice of
> nonpayment, presentment, protest, or notice of dishonor, all of
> which are hereby expressly waived by Maker. . . .

Approximately one week before the interest payment was due,
the company began to negotiate with the bank to borrow
additional funds. The negotiations continued past the interest
due date, and the interest remained unpaid. The company
president carried a blank check to these meetings, intending to
make the interest payment, but repeatedly forgot to do so. On
at least one occasion, he asked a bank officer to provide him
with the precise amount due, including all accrued interest, but
the officer did not do so. No further correspondence between
the parties took place with regard to this matter. Three weeks
after the interest payment came due, the bank summoned the
company president to a meeting, at which time he was
informed that the entire balance of the note was due and
payable immediately. The company president drew a blank
check from his pocket and offered to pay the delinquent interest
immediately, but the bank refused to reconsider its position.

- Did the bank act in good faith when it accelerated
  payment on the debt pursuant to the "insecurity
  clause" in the parties' contract?

- How, if at all, would you recommend that the bank
  change its lending practices and/or its loan documents?

Based on *J.R. Hale Contracting Co., Inc. v. United New Mexico Bank*, 110 N.M. 712, 799 P.2d 581 (N.M. 1990).

Breach of Peace

Read 9-609 (b) (2) and Comments 3 and 4. A secured party may engage in self-help, repossessing collateral without judicial process, so long as it can do so without breaching the peace.

- Why, as a matter of efficiency and policy, does it make sense to allow repossession without judicial process, so long as it can be accomplished without a breach of the peace?

Comment 3 and the following case illustrate how a court might analyze whether a breach of peace has taken place.

Davenport v. Chrysler Credit Corp.,
818 S.W.2d 23, 15 U.C.C. Rep. Serv. 2d 324 (Tenn. App. 1991).

Koch, Judge.

Larry and Debbie Davenport purchased a new 1987 Chrysler LeBaron from Gary Mathews Motors on October 28, 1987. They obtained financing through Chrysler Credit Corporation and signed a retail-installment contract requiring them to make the first of sixty monthly payments on or before December 8, 1987.

The automobile developed mechanical problems before the Davenports could drive it off the dealer's lot. Even before their first payment was due, the Davenports had returned the automobile to the dealer seven times for repair. They were extremely dissatisfied and, after consulting a lawyer, decided to withhold their monthly payments until the matter was resolved.

Chrysler Credit sent the Davenports a standard delinquency notice when their first payment was ten days late. The Davenports did not respond to the notice, and on December 23, 1987, Chrysler Credit telephoned the Davenports to request payment. Mrs. Davenport recounted the problems with the automobile and told Chrysler Credit that she would consult her lawyer and "would let them know about the payment." After consulting the dealer, Chrysler Credit informed Mrs. Davenport that it would repossess the automobile if she did not make the payment.

Chrysler Credit telephoned the Davenports on December 30, 1987, because their first payment was three weeks late. Mr. Davenport told Chrysler Credit that he had turned the matter over to his lawyer and that he was not going to make the payment. Chrysler Credit telephoned again on January 7, 1988. On this occasion, Mrs. Davenport stated that their lawyer had instructed them to make the payment, and Chrysler Credit requested her to send the payment to its Brentwood office.

Chrysler Credit telephoned the Davenports one last time on January 13, 1988. It had still not received their first payment, and their second payment was five days past due. Mrs. Davenport insisted that she had mailed one payment and added that she "was not responsible for the mail." Before hanging up abruptly, she also stated that she did not intend to make any more payments "on the advice of her attorney." At this point, Chrysler Credit determined that the Davenports were in default and requested American Lender Service Company to repossess the car.

> If the Davenports had sought to invoke the doctrine of shaken faith as described in Chapter 5, Part C, what (if anything) would they have needed to do differently?

Employees of American Lender Service arrived at the Davenports' home on the evening of January 14, 1988. They informed the Davenports that they were "two payments in default" and requested the automobile. The Davenports insisted that they were not in default and, after a telephone call to their lawyer, refused to turn over the automobile until Chrysler Credit obtained the "proper paperwork." The American Lender Service employees left without the car.

> To what "proper paperwork" could the Davenports be referring?

Before leaving for work the next morning, Mr. Davenport parked the automobile in their enclosed garage and chained its rear end to a post using a logging chain and two padlocks. He also closed the canvas flaps covering the entrance to the garage and secured the flaps with cinder blocks. When the Davenports returned from work, they discovered that someone had entered the garage, cut one of the padlocks, and removed the automobile.

> The debtor's right of redemption is found in 9-623 and addressed in Part C of this chapter.

American Lender Service informed Chrysler Credit on January 18, 1988, that it had repossessed the automobile. On the same day, Chrysler Credit notified the Davenports that they could redeem the car before it was offered for sale. The Davenports never responded to the notice. Instead of selling the automobile immediately, Chrysler Credit held it for more than a year because of the Davenports' allegations that the automobile was defective. In July 1989, Chrysler Credit informed the Davenports that the automobile had been sold and requested payment of the $6,774 deficiency.

* * *

> The current reference is to UCC 9-609.

We now consider whether the repossession of the Davenports' automobile was consistent with Tenn. Code Ann. § 47-9-503 (1979). The trial court determined that it was, relying on *Harris Truck & Trailer Sales v. Foote*, 58 Tenn. App. 710, 436 S.W.2d 460 (1968). We disagree, but only because *Harris Truck & Trailer Sales v. Foote* improperly restricts the scope of the protection Tenn. Code Ann. § 47-9-503 affords to buyers of consumer goods.

Tennessee has long recognized that secured parties have a legitimate interest in obtaining their collateral from a defaulting debtor. Prior to the Uniform Commercial Code, secured parties could repossess collateral either with or without the assistance of the courts. If they chose to proceed without judicial assistance, they were required to obtain the debtor's consent and to proceed without a breach of the peace.

The General Assembly preserved the secured parties' self-help remedies when it enacted the Uniform Commercial Code in 1963. It also preserved the requirement that repossessions must be accomplished without a breach of the peace. . . .

Tennessee's version of the Uniform Commercial Code does not define "breach of the peace." Like the UCC's drafters, the General Assembly decided that this task should be left to the courts. Thus, it falls to us to determine what types of conduct the General Assembly intended to proscribe when it decided in 1963 that repossessions must be accomplished without a breach of the peace.

* * *

There is a dearth of Tennessee authority concerning the meaning of "breach of the peace" as it appears in Tenn. Code Ann. § 47-9-503. The only reported case, decided over twenty years ago, involved the repossession of an unoccupied truck that the owner had left in a third-party's open parking lot. This court held:

> We think the legislative intent in the enactment of T.C.A. section 47-9-503, in using the words "if this can be done without breach of the peace," contemplated that the breach of the peace there referred to must involve some violence, or at least threat of violence. *Harris Truck & Trailer Sales v. Foote*, 58 Tenn. App. at 718, 436 S.W.2d at 464.

We have determined that the *Harris* court improperly narrowed the scope of Tenn. Code Ann. § 47-9-503 by requiring that a repossession must be accompanied by violence or a threat of violence in order to be considered a breach of the peace. Its interpretation of "breach of the peace" is inconsistent with the common law and with the Supreme Court's earlier interpretations of the term.

The term "breach of the peace" is a generic term that includes all violations or potential violations of the public peace and order.

While breaches of the peace frequently involve offenses against individuals, they also include offenses against the public at large or the State.

* * *

Secured parties may repossess their collateral at a reasonable time and in a reasonable manner. Thus, determining whether a particular secured creditor's conduct amounts to a breach of the peace requires a review of the reasonableness of the secured party's conduct in light of the facts of the case.

Professors White and Summers have recommended that the inquiry should take into consideration (1) where the repossession took place, (2) the debtor's express or constructive consent, (3) the reactions of third parties, (4) the type of premises entered, and (5) the creditor's use of deception. *See White & Summers* § 27-6, at 575-76.

How does each factor generally tend to support – or militate against – a finding of breach of peace?

Public policy favors peaceful, non-trespassory repossessions when the
secured party has a free right of entry. However, forced entries onto
the debtor's property or into the debtor's premises are viewed as
seriously detrimental to the ordinary conduct of human affairs.
Accordingly, courts have consistently found that repossessions
accomplished by breaking locks or cutting chains are inconsistent with
the Uniform Commercial Code.

The courts have also disapproved of repossessions in which the secured
party or its agent entered the debtor's closed premises without
permission, and repossessions causing damage to the debtor's property.
These decisions, and others like them, have prompted Professors White
and Summers to observe that "a breach of the peace is almost certain to
be found if the repossession is accompanied by the unauthorized entry
into a closed or locked garage." *See White & Summers* § 27-6, at 577 n.
11.

Self-help procedures such as repossession are the product of a careful
balancing of the interests of secured parties and debtors. On one hand,
secured creditors have a legitimate interest in obtaining possession of
collateral without resorting to expensive and sometimes cumbersome
judicial procedures. On the other hand, debtors have a legitimate
interest in being free from unwarranted invasions of their property and
privacy interests.

Repossession is a harsh procedure and is, essentially, a delegation of
the State's exclusive prerogative to resolve disputes. Accordingly, the
statutes governing the repossession of collateral should be construed in
a way that prevents abuse and discourages illegal conduct which might
otherwise go unchallenged because of the debtor's lack of knowledge of
legally proper repossession techniques.

American Lender Service's repossession of the Davenports' automobile
was not accompanied by violence or the threat of violence, because the
Davenports were not at home at the time. However, Chrysler Credit
and American Lender Service do not dispute that they obtained the
automobile by entering a closed garage and by cutting a lock on a chain
that would have prevented them from removing the automobile.
Despite the absence of violence or physical confrontation, entering the
closed garage and cutting the lock amounted to a breach of the peace.
Thus, unlike the trial court, we find that the manner in which the
Davenports' automobile was repossessed was inconsistent with the
requirements Tenn. Code Ann. § 47-9-503 places on secured parties
who are repossessing collateral from defaulting debtors.

* * *

The Davenports have never challenged the commercial reasonableness
of Chrysler Credit's disposition of their automobile, and we have
already concurred with the trial court's finding that Chrysler Credit
was justified in repossessing the automobile and accelerating the debt
because the Davenports were in default. Accordingly, the Davenports
are only entitled to recover their damages stemming directly from the
manner in which American Lender Service repossessed their
automobile.

The Davenports' only proof concerning these damages is a broken lock and minor, cosmetic damage to their driveway. They are not entitled to recover for damage to their credit reputation because Chrysler Credit did not wrongfully accelerate their debt and because the proof showed that they had other credit problems. Thus, the Davenports are entitled to recover only Tenn. Code Ann. § 47-9-507 (1)'s minimum penalty.

> The minimum penalty to which consumers are entitled is now found in UCC 9-625 (c) (2) and explained in Comment 4.

- Did the Davenports have the right to stop making payments on the Chrysler?

- If not, what should they have done instead?

- Following this case, what conduct rises to the level of a "breach of peace"?

- In your opinion, does the definition of this term in the repossession context differ from what a layperson would expect to constitute a breach of peace?

> For those who are interested in exploring the topic further, the majority and dissenting opinions in *Willams v. Ford Motor Credit Co.*, 674 F.2d 717 (8th Cir. 1982), show how the same set of facts can be interpreted in markedly different ways, with one party strongly asserting – and the other strongly denying – a breach of the peace.

Note: Whether a breach of peace has occurred in the course of a repossession is a fact-specific inquiry. In *Wade v. Ford Motor Credit Co.*, 8 Kan. App. 2d 737, 668 P.2d 183 (1983), the court held that merely showing the debtor did not consent to repossession is not sufficient to prove a breach of peace. The court held this was true even though the debtor had threatened, on a previous occasion, to use deadly force if repossession were attempted. The court explained its holding as follows:

> We find it is clear from a survey of the cases dealing with self-help repossession that the consent of the debtor to the repossession is not required. K.S.A. 16a-5-112[, a state non-UCC statute discussing repossession] even presupposes the lack of consent: "Upon default by a consumer, unless the consumer voluntarily surrenders possession. . . ." . . . Repossession, without the consent of the debtor, absent more, does not constitute a breach of the peace by the creditor.

> The trial court also emphasized the potential for violence brought on by [the debtor's] threats made during the first repossession attempt [in this case]. A breach of the peace may be caused by an act likely to produce violence. The facts presented in this case do not, however, rise to that level. A period of one month elapsed between the [first and second] repossession attempts. [The second attempt was successful.] During that period, [the creditor and debtor] were in communication, and two payments were made. We find the potential for violence was substantially reduced by the passage of this time. Moreover, the actual repossession was effected without incident. The time of the repossession [during the middle of the night] was such that, in all likelihood, no confrontation would materialize. In fact, [the debtor] was totally unaware of the repossession until after [the creditor's agent] had

successfully left the premises with the car. We therefore find that as a matter of law there was no breach of the peace. *Id.* at 745.

- What does this case add to your understanding of when a breach of peace has taken place?

> What does it mean for the parties to term this transaction a "conditional sale"? Review 9-202 as needed to answer this question.

Problem 1: Stone Machinery sold a D-9 Caterpillar tractor to Frank Kessler pursuant to a conditional sales contract. The purchase price was $23,500, including a $6,000 down payment. The balance of $17,500 was to be paid through a series of monthly payments. The defendant made several late payments, but eventually brought the account current again each time. After this pattern had occurred several times, when another payment was approximately one month late, Stone's credit manager contacted Mr. Kessler and demanded either payment of the full balance due, or immediate possession of the tractor. At this time, approximately $6,000 was left unpaid. Mr. Kessler indicated that he could not afford to make payment in full – or, indeed, to make any payment – at that time, but that he anticipated being awarded a contract in the near future that would allow him to do so. He also refused to relinquish the tractor and warned the credit manager that "someone would get hurt" if a repossession attempt were made by anyone "without proper papers."

Mr. Stone was awarded the contract he had mentioned, and he took the tractor to another state to perform the job he had been awarded. While he was there, Stone's credit manager located the tractor by use of an airplane, then contacted the local sheriff to accompany him in repossessing the tractor. The sheriff drove to the location of the tractor, in his official vehicle, together with the credit manager, in his private car; a Stone truck driver, in a company-owned lo-boy truck; and a Stone mechanic, in a company-owned pick-up truck.

After arriving, the sheriff and the credit manager saw Mr. Kessler working in a river with the tractor. They motioned for him to bring the equipment to shore. The sheriff was in his uniform and was wearing his badge and sidearms. The sheriff stated, "We come to pick up the tractor." The defendant asked the sheriff if he had "proper papers to take the tractor," and the sheriff replied, "No." Kessler protested but offered no physical resistance as the tractor was loaded on the lo-boy.

- Was the repossession rightful?

- Was the peace breached?

> 9-609 Comment 3 may be of assistance.

- What is the effect of the local sheriff's involvement?

Based on *Stone Machinery Co. v. Kessler*, 1 Wash. App. 750, 463 P.2d 651 (Div. III 1970).

Problem 2: While he was living in Denver, Trey Salisbury borrowed $13,000 from Colorado Central Credit Union, pledging five vehicles as collateral for the loan. He then moved to Slater, Colorado, where he lived very close to the property owned by the family corporation, Salisbury Livestock Company. His father and mother lived on land owned by the corporation. Trey subsequently defaulted on the note. After mailing notice of its intended repossession of the vehicles, Colorado Central hired a repossession company, CARS-USA. The owner of CARS-USA called Trey's home and received directions from a female who did not identify herself.

The next morning, at 5 a.m., the CARS-USA crew arrived at Trey's house and found one of the vehicles, a conversion van, in the driveway with a key in the ignition. The crew took the van but did not see any of the other vehicles constituting collateral for the note. The crew then drove back down the road on which they had arrived. After driving a short distance, they saw a sign bearing the single word, "Salisbury," which the woman had identified as a landmark when she provided directions. Although they did not see any vehicles from the road, the crew turned down the driveway and, after traveling approximately fifty yards, spotted several vehicles, including two that had been identified as part of the collateral to be repossessed. The crew pushed both vehicles, a Corvette and a second conversion van, onto a tow truck and removed them from the property. In the process, the crew broke a two-by-four that was on the ground near the vehicles. By that time, it was daylight, and the crew heard (but did not see) persons in a nearby building. They did not ask for permission to enter the land or remove the vehicles, and they did not encounter any people during the repossession. As it turns out, the land on which these final repossessions took place belonged to Salisbury Livestock Company and was the home of Trey's parents.

- What arguments would you make in favor of, and against, the proposition that a breach of peace has occurred?

Based on *Salisbury Livestock Co. v. Colorado Central Credit Union*, 793 P.2d 470, 12 U.C.C. Rep. Serv. 2d 894 (1990).

International Perspective: Default

The following excerpt from P.A.U. Ali, *The Law of Secured Finance: An International Survey of Security Interests over Personal Property* (Oxford University Press 2002), shows how the Cape Town Convention addresses a creditor's rights with regard to large, expensive collateral such as aircraft, railway rolling stock, and space property:

> The secured party is entitled, on the security provider's default, to take possession or control of the mobile equipment [that is] the subject of the security interest, sell or lease the mobile equipment, and collect or receive any income arising from the management of the mobile equipment. Any moneys received by the secured party on the exercise of these remedies may then be applied towards the discharge of the secured obligations.
>
> The parties may also agree that, on a default, the mobile equipment will vest in the secured party, in or towards satisfaction of the secured obligations.
>
> Further, . . . the secured party may:
>
> - Procure the de-registration of an aircraft.
> - Procure the export and physical transfer of aircraft frames, aircraft engines, or helicopters from the State in which they are situated.
> - Procure the export and physical transfer of railway rolling stock from the State in which it is situated via the use of a transnational railway network.
> - Alter the access and command codes required to access, command, control, or operate the space property. *Id.* at 305.

- How does the unique nature of the collateral governed by the Cape Town Convention influence the remedies provided to a secured party thereunder?

B. Sale or Other Disposition of the Collateral

Notice

Read 9-611 and Comments 2, 3, and 4. A secured party is ordinarily required to provide reasonable notification to the debtor, any secondary obligors, and certain other secured parties, before disposition of the collateral. If the secured party fails to give the notice required by 9-611, courts apply several different standards in determining the appropriate penalty to be imposed. Some courts apply what is called an "absolute bar" rule, while others apply the "rebuttable presumption" or the "set-off" test. As the name suggests, the "absolute bar" standard totally prevents a creditor who has failed to provide notice of sale from recovering any deficiency that remains after the sale. The court in *First State Bank v. Hallet*, 291 Ark. 37, 722 S.W.2d 555 (1987), described the rationale for the "absolute bar" rule as follows, quoting *Atlas Thrift Co. v. Horan*, 27 Cal. App. 3d 999, 104 Cal. Rptr. 315 (1972):

> "[I]t was never contemplated that a secured party could recover [a deficiency] judgment after violating the statutory command as to notice . . . The rule and requirement are simple. If the secured party wishes a deficiency judgment, he must obey the law" . . . When the Code provisions have delineated the guidelines and procedures governing statutorily-created liability, then those requirements must be consistently adhered to when that liability is determined. *First St. Bank*, 291 Ark. at 41.

In *Emmons v. Burkett*, 256 Ga. 855, 353 S.E.2d 908 (1987), the court described the "rebuttable presumption" test as follows:

> Under the rebuttable-presumption test, if a creditor fails to give notice or conducts an unreasonable sale, the presumption is raised that the value of the collateral is equal to the indebtedness. To overcome this presumption, the creditor must present evidence of the fair and reasonable value of the collateral, and the evidence must show that such value was less than the debt. If the creditor rebuts the presumption, he may maintain an action against the debtor or guarantor for the deficiency. Any loss suffered by the debtor as a consequence of the failure to give notice or to conduct a commercially reasonable sale is recoverable under [9-507] and may be set off against the deficiency. For example, if a creditor has conducted a commercially unreasonable sale, the debtor may suffer a loss, in that he will not receive as much of a credit from the sale of the collateral as he should have. In such an instance, the debtor is entitled to be awarded an additional credit equaling the difference between the fair-market value of the collateral and the amount for which the collateral was sold. *Id.* at 857.

> ▪ In what two ways may a creditor be punished for its failure of notice, under the "rebuttable presumption" test?

The third approach, the "set-off" test, allows the secured creditor to recover the deficiency, subject to a set-off for the amount of damages suffered by the debtor due to the creditor's failure of notice. Unlike the "rebuttable presumption" test, the "set-off" test places upon the debtor the burden of proving the fair-market value of the collateral. In considering, and ultimately rejecting, this test, the court in *Ruden v. Citizens*

Bank & Trust Co., 99 Md. App. 605, 638 A.2d 1225 (Md. Spec. App. 1994), held as follows, quoting *Bank of Chapmanville v. Workman*, 185 W.Va. 161, 406 S.E.2d 58 (1991):

> The main problem with this rule is that the debtor . . . will usually have a hard time proving that the fair-market value was higher than what the collateral actually sold for at the repossession sale. In many cases, the secured creditor's commercially unreasonable behavior (*e.g.*, lack of adequate notice to the debtor) will have greatly hindered the debtor's ability to prove his damages. *Ruden*, 99 Md. App. At 617.

- In your own words, how do the three approaches differ?

- **Read 9-626 and Comments 3 and 4.** Does the Code suggest one approach in lieu of the others?

- How could "the secured creditor's commercially unreasonable behavior . . . greatly hinder [ ] the debtor's ability to prove his damages"?

- **Read 1-305.** How should the appropriate test be determined for whether a secured creditor may obtain a deficiency judgment following a commercially unreasonable sale, in light of the Code's rejection of penal damages as part of an award of damages unless specifically authorized by the Code or other law?

As the court held in *Ford Motor Credit Co. v. Welch*, 2004 Vt. 94, 177 Vt. 563 (2004), the fact that the debtor has voluntarily surrendered the collateral does not constitute waiver of the debtor's right to notice. The court held, "Such a construction would merely discourage voluntary surrender and frustrate the state's interest in promoting peaceful repossessions."

- Does the Code permit the debtor to waive his or her right to notice?

- If so, how and when would this be accomplished?

- Why should the debtor be entitled to receive notice of a private sale since, by definition, the debtor is not permitted to bid at such a sale?

Read 9-613 and 9-614. These Code sections provide standard forms for providing notice to debtors before a sale or other disposition of collateral.

- **Read 9-611 (c) and Comment 4.** Are unsecured creditors entitled to notice?

- Which other secured creditors, if any, are entitled to notice?

Commercial Reasonableness

This section discusses the requirement that a secured party arrange a commercially reasonable sale if it chooses to dispose of the collateral by a sale. These materials also discuss the penalties for failing to comply with this requirement. In addition, this section addresses the possibility that the creditor will accept the collateral in satisfaction of the debt, instead of selling it; as well as the rights of junior creditors and the debtor's general liability for any deficiency remaining after disposition of the collateral.

Read 9-610 (a) and (b) and Comment 2, together with 9-627. Taken together, these provisions describe the creditor's duty to dispose of collateral in a way that is commercially reasonable.

Read 9-602, which describes some rights that are so important that the Code drafters determined they should not be capable of being waived by contract. Some provisions in 9-602 relate to a secured party's obligations with regard to the disposition of collateral.

- Can a debtor waive the requirement of a commercially reasonable disposition? Why or why not?

- What do the non-waiver provisions have in common, and what does that tell you about how the UCC drafters see the interaction between debtors and creditors when default has occurred?

Read 9-624. 9-624 is important in putting 9-602 in context. As 9-624 indicates, certain Article 9 protections, though they cannot be waived by a debtor earlier, can be waived after the debtor's default. This concept is sometimes explained by reference to the so-called "mirage of hope," which is the idea that most debtors believe they will never default – and thus cannot make reasoned decisions about what should happen after default – unless and until default actually occurs. Once that happens, the "mirage" has evaporated, and a debtor may waive certain rights that were not waivable before.

- Does 9-624 address waiver of the "commercially reasonable sale" requirement?

9-610, introduced above, describes the standards of "commercial reasonableness" with which a disposition of collateral must comply. The section addresses both private and public sales. *Benton v. General Mobile Homes, Inc.*, 13 Ark. App. 8, 678 S.W.2d 774 (Div. II 1984), defines a public sale as "one made at auction to the highest bidder."

- **Read Comment 7.** What is a private sale, and when is it permissible?

- Why are private sales treated as being somewhat suspect?

Read 9-625, which provides the remedies available when a secured party fails to follow the "commercially reasonable disposition" requirements of 9-610.

- **Read 9-625 Comment 3.** Do unsecured creditors have standing to challenge the commercial reasonableness of a sale?

- Does a junior secured creditor have standing to do so? Why or why not?

Read 9-615 and Comments 2, 4, and 6. This section addresses how the proceeds of a sale of collateral are to be distributed and specifically addresses the rights and obligations of the parties if there is a surplus – or a deficiency – remaining after the sale.

9-102 (a) (59) may assist you in answering this question.

- If the debtor and the party supplying the collateral are not the same, which is liable for any deficiency remaining after disposition of the collateral?

- Which is entitled to any surplus?

- If there is a low-value sale of collateral to an insider, such as the secured party itself, how will the court determine the amount of credit the debtor should receive from the sale?

The following case illustrates how a court might analyze whether a disposition of collateral was commercially reasonable, specifically examining the secured party's pre-sale advertising and the decision to have a private sale instead of a public sale.

1 *General Electric Capital Corp. v. Stelmach Construction Co.,*
2   45 U.C.C. Rep. Serv. 2d 675 (D. Kan. 2001).
3
4 Murguia, District Court.
5
6 Plaintiff [General Electric Capital Corporation] and defendant
7 Stelmach Construction entered into a promissory note, a master
8 security agreement, and several related agreements, on or about June
9 30, 1998. Defendant Stelmach Construction signed the Agreements.
10 Pursuant to the Agreements, defendant Stelmach Construction agreed
11 to repay to plaintiff the principal sum of $400,000.00, plus interest at
12 9.32% in forty-two consecutive monthly installments to begin August
13 25, 1998. The Agreements also provide for interest at the rate of 18%
14 per annum upon default and a 5% late payment charge on delinquent
15 payments. Also, on or about June 30, 1998, defendant Christopher
16 Stelmach executed an individual guaranty of the amount loaned to
17 defendant Stelmach Construction.

> Now that you have studied both promissory notes and security agreements, how is the purpose of each different?

18 As the term of the note progressed, Stelmach Construction failed to
19 make the required principal and interest payments due under the
20 Agreements. Accordingly, plaintiff and defendant Stelmach
21 Construction entered into a modification agreement, thereby modifying
22 the terms of payment. Defendant Stelmach Construction executed the
23 modification agreement. Although defendants waived notice,
24 presentment, and other defenses in the Agreements and the guaranty,
25 on April 7 and June 9, 1999, plaintiff sent both defendants notices of
26 default with respect to payments due by defendant Stelmach
27 Construction.

> 3-504 governs waiver of presentment and notice of dishonor.

28 Subsequently, on or about June 24, 1999, plaintiff and defendants
29 entered into a voluntary-surrender agreement, wherein defendant
30 Stelmach Construction retained all of its rights as a debtor, including
31 but not limited to the right to challenge the commercial reasonableness
32 of the sale of the collateral. [The collateral in this case consisted of
33 multiple pieces of heavy equipment used in construction.]

* * *

35 Pursuant to [the] voluntary-surrender agreement, defendants
36 voluntarily surrendered the collateral with the understanding that
37 plaintiff would sell it. Plaintiff notified defendants that the sale of the
38 collateral would occur on or after August 6, 1999.

40 Plaintiff hired Elcor, Inc. to repossess, appraise, and sell the collateral.
41 Elcor inspected and evaluated the condition of each piece, and prepared
42 a condition report and approximate value for each piece of equipment.
43 When analyzing the collateral piece by piece, Elcor's approximate
44 values totaled $258,200.00. In contrast, defendants present the report
45 of Kenneth Fowler – their designated expert in the area of construction
46 appraisal – who opines that the value of the collateral as of August 6,
   1999, was $457,400.

51 Plaintiff advertised the sale through publications in two nationally
52 recognized trade magazines, and on two internet sites known by the
53 trade. The advertisements gave a complete description of the make,

model, and year of each piece of collateral, and identified where the collateral could be viewed. None of the advertisements specified whether the collateral would be sold by the lot or individually. GECC also advertised the sale of collateral through mass mailing, targeting potential purchasers.

The collateral was stored in the Lee's Summit, Missouri area during the advertisement period and was available for inspection by interested bidders. Plaintiff received six (6) bids for the collateral from third-party bidders. All of the bids were made for the entire lot. The bids ranged in price from $225,000.00 to $311,000.00.

Plaintiff accepted the highest bid, selling the collateral for $311,000.00, with costs to plaintiff of $6,800.00 for obtaining possession of the collateral, evaluating the collateral, and properly preparing the collateral for sale, and costs of $31,100.00 for commission expenses with respect to the sale. When the collateral was sold on August 24, 1999, the principal amount due by defendants was $389,710.68. Interest and delinquency charges at that time totaled $31,355.56. Additional interest accrued after August 24, 1999, at the contract rate of $54.91 per diem. Pursuant to the terms of the Agreements, defendants agreed to pay plaintiff's attorneys fees and costs incurred in collecting under the Agreements.

As of August 24, 1999, (the sale date of the collateral), the amount due and owing to plaintiff, after crediting all payments made and the proceeds from the sale of collateral, totaled:

> Remaining principal balance after sale of collateral ($389,710.68 (principal) less $311,000.00 (proceeds from sale of collateral)) $78,710.68

> Interest and delinquency charges (Additional interest accrued after August 24, 1999, at the contract rate of $54.91 per diem) $31,355.56

> Costs to repossess/recondition collateral $6,800.00
> Commission expenses on sale $31,100.00

> Amount due and owing by defendants (attorneys' fees obligations not included) $147,966.24

The parties dispute the total amount due by defendants to plaintiff as a result of the breach. Plaintiff asserts the sale of the collateral was conducted in accordance with the Agreements between the parties and in accordance with Article 9 of the Uniform Commercial Code. Defendants, however, argue that the sale of collateral conducted by plaintiff was not commercially reasonable.

* * *

Plaintiff, as the secured creditor, has the burden to establish that the sale of the collateral at issue was conducted in a commercially reasonable manner. . . .

The Kansas Uniform Commercial Code provides that "every aspect of the disposition [of collateral] including the method, manner, time, place, and other terms must be commercially reasonable." When determining whether the sale of collateral was conducted in a commercially reasonable manner, "the trial court should consider all of the relevant factors together as part of a single transaction." *Westgate [State Bank v. Clark*, 231 Kan. 81, 91, 642 P.2d 961, 969 (1982)]. In *Westgate*, the Kansas Supreme Court identified nine factors relevant to determining whether a sale has been conducted in a commercially reasonable manner, including: (1) the duty to clean, fix up, and paint the collateral; (2) public or private disposition; (3) wholesale or retail disposition; (4) disposition by unit or in parcels; (5) the duty to publicize the sale; (6) length of time collateral held prior to sale; (7) duty to give notice of the sale to the debtor and competing secured parties; (8) the actual price received at the sale; and (9) other methods, including the number of bids received and the method employed in soliciting bids, the time and place of the sale. This list of factors is not exclusive, and a court should consider other factors, where relevant in a particular case.

> The quoted language is found in UCC 9-610 (b).

> UCC 9-610 Comments 3, 4, 7, and 10 may help you to understand how each factor affects reasonableness.

Defendants assert three separate arguments contending that the sale was not conducted in a commercially reasonable manner. First, defendants contend plaintiff did not provide proper notice of the sale. Prior to a sale or other disposition of repossessed collateral, a secured creditor is required to give the debtor notice of any proposed disposition. Generally, it is the secured party's decision whether to dispose of the collateral by public or private sale. . . .

The parties do not seem to dispute that the sale of the collateral here was by private sale, as it was not conducted by auction. Instead, defendants contend plaintiff did not properly notice the private sale. Pursuant to the Kansas UCC, any notice of sale must state the time and place of any public sale or the time after which any private sale or other intended disposition of the collateral will take place.

> This requirement is found in UCC 9-613 (1) (E).

The court finds plaintiff's notice of the private sale was sufficient under the Kansas UCC. The uncontroverted facts demonstrate that plaintiff notified defendants that the sale of the collateral would occur on or after August 6, 1999. The heading of plaintiff's notice indicated, "NOTICE OF PRIVATE SALE OF COLLATERAL UNDER SECTION 9-504 OF THE UNIFORM COMMERCIAL CODE." The text of the notice provided, "NOTICE is hereby given that on or after August 6, 1999, General Electric Capital Corporation will sell at a public or private sale the following property" . . . The notice then listed each item of property to be sold.

> The current reference would be to UCC 9-610.

. . . [O]ne of the primary reasons for the notice requirement is to allow the interest holder the opportunity to redeem the security by paying off the debt. Here, the court finds the notice provided by plaintiff allowed defendants this opportunity, as the defendants were notified that the sale of the collateral would take place "on or after August 6, 1999." Accordingly, the court finds plaintiff's notice is compliant with the Kansas UCC and therefore, such notice does not render the sale of the collateral commercially unreasonable.

Second, defendants contend that, in order for the sale to have been commercially reasonable, the collateral should have been disposed of on a piecemeal basis, rather than in bulk. Specifically, defendants argue the plaintiff's advertisements for the collateral implied that the collateral was offered only in bulk.

> **The quoted language is found in UCC 9-610 (b).**

As noted above, the Kansas UCC allows that the "sale or other disposition [of repossessed collateral] may be as a unit or in parcels. . . ." However, the linchpin remains commercial reasonableness.

* * *

Reviewing plaintiff's advertisements, the court does not find that a reasonable factfinder could conclude that potential bidders were misled into believing that the collateral was available only as a lot, rather than individually. Plaintiff's advertisements for the sale of the collateral list each item of collateral and indicate that they are "accepting bids." The advertisements do not indicate the collateral may be purchased only in its entirety.

Defendants emphasize that each of the six bids received for the collateral was for the entire lot, rather than for a single item. However, an examination of the bids reveals that, although each bidder did seek to purchase the entire lot, they did not use identical language, as may have been done where the advertisements limited purchase to the "entire lot." For example, the bidders placed bids on "your schedule of equipment," "entire package of equipment (16 pieces)," the "entire lot," the "total package," and the "package of equipment."

> **Must a seller always allow either a bulk sale or a piecemeal sale, in the interet of reasonableness?**

Moreover, although defendants' expert report places the fair-market value of the collateral as a whole at $457,400, compared to the $311,000 received for the collateral by plaintiff, the expert did not opine that selling the collateral individually, rather than in bulk, would have been more likely to generate the fair-market value of the collateral.

Accordingly, the court finds the plaintiff's advertisements and the plaintiff's acceptance of one of six bids for the entire lot, did not render the sale commercially unreasonable.

Finally, defendants contend that the price received for the collateral indicates the sale was commercially unreasonable. Specifically, defendants argue the difference between defendants' expert's assessment of the fair-market value of the collateral ($457,400) and the price plaintiff obtained from the sale ($311,000) demonstrates the commercial unreasonableness of the sale. That is, defendants argue the $146,400 difference makes the sale presumptively commercially unreasonable.

> **The quoted language is found in UCC 9-627 (a).**

Although the court must examine the price obtained for the collateral in determining the commercial reasonableness of a sale, "[t]he fact that a better price could have been obtained by a sale at a different time or in a different method from that selected by the secured party is not of itself sufficient to establish that the sale was not made in a commercially reasonable manner." "If the secured party either sells the collateral in the usual manner in any recognized market therefor or if he sells at the price current in such market at the time of his sale, or if he has otherwise sold in conformity with reasonable commercial practices among dealers in the type of property sold, he has sold in a commercially reasonable manner."

> The quoted language is found in UCC 9-627 (b).

Defendants do not argue that the collateral was not sold in a recognized market for the equipment or that the collateral was not sold in the usual manner for the sale of such equipment. Nor do defendants contend that plaintiff did not follow reasonable commercial practices among dealers in the type of equipment sold when selling the collateral. Instead, defendants contend the price obtained for the collateral was not the current price in the market at the time of the sale.

. . . The difference between the price obtained and the presumptively correct valuation of the collateral by defendants' expert is large. However, as noted in the Kansas UCC and in Kansas case law, simply because a higher price could have been obtained does not establish a sale was not commercially reasonable. As noted herein, the court finds that each of the remaining factors regarding commercial reasonableness weigh in favor of plaintiff. Therefore, even though a low price was obtained from the sale, because the court has found all procedures regarding the sale of the collateral were handled in line with section 84-9-504 of the Kansas UCC, the court finds the low price, on its own, does not render the sale of the collateral commercially unreasonable.

> What might account for this discrepancy?

> The current citation is to UCC 9-610.

Plaintiff argues that, in addition to the three factors discussed above, the five additional relevant factors set forth in Westgate demonstrate the commercial reasonableness of the sale of the collateral. First, plaintiff contends it satisfied its duty to prepare the collateral for sale by hiring Elcor, Inc. to assess, prepare and clean each piece of collateral prior to the sale. Plaintiff invested $6,800 preparing the collateral in order to maximize the ultimate sale price. Second, plaintiff contends it chose the method of disposition – a private sale – most likely to result in a higher return. Third, plaintiff advertised the sale in multiple national trade publications and on several internet sites commonly used by the construction industry. Plaintiff also conducted direct-mail solicitations all over the country to likely purchasers. Plaintiff made the collateral available for inspection prior to any sale. Fourth, plaintiff held the collateral for approximately one month prior to agreeing to a sales price. And fifth, plaintiff received six bids from third party bidders prior to accepting the highest bid.

Defendants do not dispute the facts set forth by plaintiff supporting these five factors. Accordingly, the court finds plaintiff has set forth evidence sufficient to establish no genuine issue of material fact exists as to these five factors.

Accordingly, given the above analysis, the court finds plaintiff has met its burden to establish entitlement to judgment as a matter of law on its damages claim. That is, plaintiff has met its burden to establish the commercial reasonableness of the sale of the collateral at issue. Therefore, plaintiff's motion for summary judgment on damages is granted. Plaintiff is granted judgment in the amount of $147,966.24, for principal and interest through August 24, 1999, plus pre-judgment and post-judgment interest accruing after that time at a per diem rate of $54.91, plus reasonable attorneys' fees and costs in an amount to be approved by the court.

- ▪ What are the defendants' arguments in support of their claim that the sale was not commercially reasonable, and how does the court respond to each?

Note 1: The court held in *Ford & Vlahos v. ITT Commercial Finance Corp.*, 8 Cal. 4th 1220, 885 P.2d 877 (1994), that satisfaction of the notice requirement in 9-611 does not create a safe harbor shielding the creditor from challenges to the reasonableness of the sale. Instead, the court held, "[N]otice, on the one hand, and publicity or advertising, on the other, are separate but related concepts under the California Uniform Commercial Code." The court's analysis continued as follows:

> We cannot conclude that the Legislature meant to provide that a sale's advertising is commercially reasonable as long as the bare requirements of formal notice are met, even if, to sell the type of collateral involved, a responsible dealer would employ more extensive advertising than placing a legal notice in agate type in an obscure newspaper. Publicity is much too important to a proper sale of foreclosed collateral for such a hypothesis to be commercially viable. *Id.* at 1230.

The word "agate" is used here to denote 5-1/2-point type. By way of comparison, the excerpts in this book employ 9-point type and the principal text uses 10-point type.

- ▪ In your own words, how can notice and commercial reasonableness be distinguished from one another?

Note 2: In *Ford Motor Credit Co. v. Jackson*, 126 Ill. App. 3d 124, 466 N.E.2d 1330 (3d Dist. 1984), the court addressed the question of how to compute a debtor's damages resulting from a commercially unreasonable sale. The court discussed the issue in the context of deciding whether a creditor who has made a commercially unreasonable sale may nevertheless exercise its right, under 9-615, to recover any post-sale deficiency from the debtor. The specific question before the court was whether it should apply one of the recognized tests for whether a deficiency judgment should be permitted despite a secured party's failure to give notice of the impending disposition, as described earlier in this chapter – or some other standard. The court analyzed the issue as follows:

The current reference is to UCC 9-625.

> The only remedy provided a debtor under the Code is an action for damages under Section 9-507. Every Illinois court which has found a commercially unreasonable sale has also found inadequate notice. Thus, the question of a debtor's remedy in an action by a creditor for a deficiency judgment where commercial unreasonableness only is shown is one of first impression in Illinois.

In resolving this question, we first consider whether the remedy for commercial unreasonableness should be the same as the remedy for inadequate notice. The courts of Illinois are split as to the proper remedy where a creditor seeking a deficiency judgment fails to show adequate notice. Several courts follow the "rebuttable presumption" approach, in which the failure to provide adequate notice raises the presumption that the value of the collateral is equal to the remaining debt. This court, on the other hand, recently held that a failure to provide notice results in an absolute bar to recovery of the deficiency judgment.

Thus, by analogy to lack of notice, one remedy for failure to conduct a commercially reasonable sale would be a bar to the creditor's recovery of the deficiency. However, . . . the lack of notice necessitates an absolute bar because it places a debtor in the position of challenging the creditor's evidence of commercial reasonableness of the sale without ever attending the sale.

The same dilemma is not created where the creditor fails to conduct a commercially reasonable sale. A debtor who knows of the sale has the opportunity to observe the sale, thereby enabling the debtor to challenge its reasonableness in an action for the deficiency. We conclude, therefore, that where a sale of collateral is found commercially unreasonable, a better result follows from the "rebuttable presumption" approach. Under this approach, a creditor's failure to conduct a commercially reasonable sale creates a rebuttable presumption that the value of the collateral is equal to the amount of the debt which the creditor seeks to recover in the deficiency action. A creditor is then required to prove that the value of the collateral is equivalent to its sale price before the creditor may recover damages. A debtor may present evidence demonstrating that the value of the collateral is equal to the debt he still owes and that, but for the commercial unreasonableness of the sale, the proceeds from the collateral would have satisfied the debt remaining after the sale. *Id.* at 127-128.

- Are you convinced by the court's assertion that damages resulting from a commercially unreasonable sale should be determined according to the "rebuttable presumption" test, even though a creditor's failure to provide notice was to be analyzed in this particular jurisdiction according to the "absolute bar" rule?

Note 3: Read 9-615 (d) and (e). After collateral has been sold, 9-615 (d) requires a secured party to account to the debtor for any surplus. The court held in *Major's Furniture Mart, Inc. v. Castle Credit Corp., Inc.*, 602 F.2d 538, 26 U.C.C. Rep. Serv. 1319 (3d Cir. 1979), that the debtor cannot waive its right to the surplus, even by express agreement.

- What distinction does 9-615 recognize between a security agreement securing an indebtedness, on the one hand, and a sale of accounts, contract rights, or chattel paper, on the other?

- What policy considerations support such a distinction?

Problem 1: Based on the following notice, will the creditor be entitled to recover a deficiency judgment from the debtor if the referenced sale does not generate funds sufficient to satisfy the entire debt, including fees and costs?

April 4, 2002

To: Debtor Steven L. Downing

Re: 1999 BMW 528i, WBADP5340XBR95304

This letter confirms you have rejected and/or terminated your loan due to the filing of bankruptcy. BMW Financial Services NA, LLC has taken possession of the Vehicle.

You are notified that BMW Financial Services NA, LLC intends to sell the vehicle as allowed under state law, but no sooner than 10 days after the date of this letter.

This letter is not being sent in violation of the discharge injunction of 11 USC §§ 727 and/or 1328 (e), if any, but is merely an attempt to comply with requisite notice requirements under the contract/lease and applicable law. If you have received a discharge in bankruptcy, this letter is an attempt to collect a debt solely from the vehicle pledged to secure payment of the contract/lease and not from you personally, and any information obtained will be used for that purpose.

Should you have any questions, call us at the number referenced below, Monday through Friday, 9:00 a.m. to 5:00 p.m. ET or at either address listed below.

/s/
BMW Financial Services NA, LLC

> **Read the two referenced statutes.** What would need to be true of the letter for it to be in violation of these provisions?

Based on *In re Downing*, 286 B.R. 900, 49 U.C.C. Rep. Serv. 2d 697 (Bankr. W.D. Mo. 2002).

Problem 2: Sometimes, a debtor challenges a secured party's failure to accept a bid offered for collateral being sold.

- What arguments would you make in favor of, and against, the commercial reasonableness of the secured party's decision not to accept the bid described in the following fact pattern?

1   Debtors defaulted on their $350,000 loan from Wainwright
2   Bank & Trust Co., which they had used for the purchase and
3   operation of a restaurant called the Golden Manor. The default
4   occurred after the restaurant had been in operation for only a
5   few months. After default, the business was repossessed and
6   appraised at approximately $450,000. Prior to the public sale
7   of the collateral, businessman Dr. Fred Spottsville, Jr., offered
8   $415,000 conditioned on the creditor's allowing him to assume
9   the debtors' loan, but the creditor refused to allow him to do so.
10 Thereafter, the collateral was sold at public sale for
11 approximately $245,000.

13 Dr. Spottsville, a young cardiologist with an existing practice,
14 had a net worth of $9,500 at the time of his offer. Of the
15 $41,000 that would have been due at the closing of the loan, he
16 had $3,500 cash on hand. He owned no stocks, bonds, or real
17 property. His annual income at the time was $43,000, and his
18 annual obligations totaled approximately $18,500. His debt-to-
19 net-worth ratio was 9 to 1, and that of his personal corporation
20 was 4.7 to 1.

22 Based on *Wainwright Bank & Trust Co. v. Railroadmens*
23 *Federal Savings & Loan Association*, 806 F.2d 146, 4 U.C.C.
24 Rep. Serv. 2d 1295 (7th Cir. 1986).

26 **Problem 3: Read 9-611 (d).** This provision exempts creditors
27 from the notice requirement when the collateral is perishable
28 or when a "recognized market" sets sales prices that can be
29 deemed presumptively reasonable. Consider the following fact
30 pattern, with this provision in mind:

32 The debtors were in the business of importing, distributing,
33 and selling exclusive alpine ski equipment and accessories.
34 After the debtors defaulted on loans totaling $800,000, the
35 secured party obtained a writ of attachment allowing it to
36 repossess the debtors' inventory, among other collateral.
37 Eleven months later, in November of 1987, the creditor began
38 to sell the collateral without notifying the debtor.

40   ▪   What are the arguments that notice should be
41   required?

43   ▪   What are the arguments in favor of exempting the
44   secured party from the notice requirement?

46   ▪   What is the purpose of the "recognized market"
50   exception and what are the most appropriate cases for
51   its application?

Based on *Chittenden Trust Co. v. Andre Noel Sports*, 159 Vt. 387, 621 A.2d 215 (1992).

Exercise of Reasonable Care Toward the Collateral

Read 9-207 and Comment 2. The following case describes the secured party's duty of reasonable care toward the collateral, providing specific examples of what is required – and what is not required – as part of this duty.

Layne v. Bank One,
395 F.3d 271, 55 U.C.C. Rep. Serv. 2d 704 (6th Cir. 2005).

Moore, Circuit Judge.

This case arises out of two loan transactions made by [Bank One, Kentucky, N.A. and Banc One Securities Corporation (collectively, "Bank One")] to plaintiffs [Charles E.] Johnson and Geoff Layne. Johnson was the founder and CEO of PurchasePro.com, Inc.; Layne served as the national marketing director of the company. Following a successful initial public offering, both Johnson and Layne had considerable net worth, though their PurchasePro shares were subject to securities laws restricting their sale. To increase their liquidity, Johnson and Layne entered into separate loan agreements with Bank One for an approximately $2.8 million and $3.25 million line of credit respectively, secured by their shares of PurchasePro stock. The loan agreements included a Loan-to-Value ratio, which conditioned default on the market value of the collateral stock. The LTV ratio was calculated as the outstanding balance on the line of credit over the market value of the collateral stock. Specifically, Layne's loan agreement had a 50% LTV ratio, which meant that the market value of the collateral stock must be at least twice the outstanding balance on the line; Johnson's loan agreement had a 40% LTV ratio, which meant that the market value must remain two and a half times the outstanding balance. The credit agreements provided that, if the LTV ratio exceeded those specified percentages, Johnson and Layne had five days to notify Bank One and either increase the collateral or reduce the outstanding balance such that the target LTV ratios were met. Failure to remedy the situation would be an immediate default, and [the credit agreement specified that] Bank One "may exercise any and all rights and remedies" including, "at Lender's discretion," selling the shares. If Bank One intended to sell the shares, it had to give Johnson written notice ten days prior to the sale. Pursuant to these agreements, Johnson and Layne entered into trade-authorization agreements that enabled Bank One to sell the shares without their consent. Though Bank One had the option of selling the collateral shares if the LTV ratios were not met, nothing in the loan agreements obligated it to do so.

In February 2001, along with the rest of the Internet sector, the stock price of PurchasePro fell considerably, such that both loans exceeded their respective LTV ratios. Rather than selling the collateral stock,

Bank One entered into discussions with Johnson and Layne to pledge more collateral. The record reveals that Layne and Johnson repeatedly stated their intentions to pledge additional collateral to meet the LTV requirements. On March 6, 2001, Layne wrote that he had "been able to hold [Bank One] off from calling [the loan] in because of additional collateral that I have pledged." On March 19, 2001, Johnson sent an email to Layne inquiring about whether Bank One was "hanging in there." On March 22, 2001, Bank One sent a letter to Layne informing him that the loan was in default. That same day, in a conversation with Bank One, Layne stated that "[you] guys have been great . . . holding on for this long," but he indicated he would like to begin selling some of the collateral stock. After this conversation, Bank One began taking steps to liquidate the collateral stock for both loans. Later that same day, however, Johnson sent an email to Layne under the subject heading, "Bank 1," which stated "they want to sell our shares and I want to stop it with additional collateral – pls call." Later that night, Layne sent an email to Burr Holton, Bank One's loan officer, under the heading, "Hold off on selling," which stated that "[Johnson] is putting together a collateral package (real estate, additional shares, etc.) to secure the note at acceptable levels." Early the next morning, Layne left a voicemail for Doug Thompson, Bank One's senior trader, stating, "It's a possibility that . . . [Johnson]'s gonna put up some additional securities to secure his note and my note and maybe we don't sell right now. So I just wanna put a hold on any . . . trading activity until [Johnson] talks with [the loan officer]." On April 3, 2001, Layne called Holton and stated that "he was ready to sell his [collateral] stock as soon as possible" and that "he has decided not [to work] with Mr. Johnson on combining their loans and adding additional collateral, which would have cured their default." The next day, April 4, 2001, Layne faxed a letter to Holton which stated that he would not be able to provide additional collateral to satisfy the loan agreement. The following day, however, Layne changed his mind again and faxed Holton a letter which stated:

> [Johnson] and myself are putting together a collateral package to secure our notes with Bank One. I DO NOT wish for the bank to proceed with any liquidation whatsoever of my PurchasePro stock at this time. I believe we have a strong company and that market conditions will improve, thus enabling the stock to recover to a price that allows me to pay my debt to Bank One in it's [sic] entirety. And that is certainly in everybody's best interest.

The same day, Layne sent an email to Holton which stated, "[Johnson] will be back this afternoon and we will firm up the plan then. I would like to have time to discuss this [sic] him before we start liquidation." The record reveals that Johnson and Bank One were involved in discussions in the end of April and May to pay down the balance or pledge additional collateral, including his house in Las Vegas. At the end of May, the proposed deal fell through and Bank One sent letters to Johnson notifying him of his continued default on the loans. Throughout the entire time from February to May 2001, Layne and Johnson continued to make principal and interest payments under the terms of the agreement, but both loans significantly exceeded their respective LTV ratios. Bank One finally sold Johnson's PurchasePro shares over four days in July, recovering $524,757.39 in net proceeds to pay down his debt, leaving approximately a $2.2 million unpaid balance.

Layne and Johnson separately filed suit against Bank One in the United States District Court for the Eastern District of Kentucky on a number of counts. On January 30, 2002, the cases were consolidated. Bank One filed counterclaims against Johnson and Layne, seeking payment for the deficiencies on the loans. On November 1, 2002, Bank One filed a motion for summary judgment on all counts as well as its counterclaims. On March 26, 2003, the district court granted Bank One's motion. Johnson appeals from that ruling.

* * *

We first consider Johnson's argument that Bank One violated a duty under Kentucky law to preserve the value of the collateral held in its possession. With respect to the regulation of secured transactions, Kentucky has adopted the Uniform Commercial Code, which states that "a secured party shall use reasonable care in the custody and preservation of collateral in the secured party's possession. In the case of chattel paper or an instrument, reasonable care includes taking necessary steps to preserve rights against prior parties unless otherwise agreed." Whether a secured party's duty to preserve collateral applies to pledged shares is an issue of first impression in Kentucky. . . .

> *The quoted language is found in UCC 9-207 (a).*

The comment to § 9-207 states that the provision "imposes a duty of care, similar to that imposed on a pledgee at common law, on a secured party in possession of collateral," and cites to §§ 17-18 of the *Restatement* of *Security*. Section 17 of the *Restatement* is essentially identical to the first sentence of § 9-207, and its accompanying explanatory comment states that "[t]he rule of reasonable care expressed in this Section is confined to the physical care of the chattel, whether an object such as a horse or piece of jewelry, or a negotiable instrument or document of title." Section 18 of the Restatement mirrors the second sentence of § 9-207 and addresses "instruments representing claims of the pledgor against third persons." Though it deals with negotiable instruments rather than equity investments, § 18 sheds light on the topic of preserving collateral value. Specifically, the explanatory comment accompanying the section states, "The pledgee is not liable for a decline in the value of pledged instruments, even if timely action could have prevented such decline." In the context of pledged stock, courts have used this language from the Restatement to hold that "a bank has no duty to its borrower to sell collateral stock of declining value." *Capos v. Mid-America National Bank*, 581 F.2d 676, 680 (7th Cir.1978). As the Seventh Circuit stated, "It is the borrower who makes the investment decision to purchase stock. A lender in these situations merely accepts the stock as collateral, and does not thereby itself invest in the issuing firm." . . .

> *The quoted language is from UCC 9-207 Comment 2.*

> *The quoted language is from § 17 cmt. a of the Restatement.*

> *The quoted language is from § 18 cmt. a of the Restatement.*

We agree with the reasoning of these courts and believe that the Kentucky Supreme Court would adopt a similar approach with regards to Ky. Rev. Stat. Ann. § 355.9-207. Specifically, we conclude that, under Kentucky law, a lender has no obligation to sell pledged stock held as collateral merely because of a market decline. If the borrower is concerned with the decline in the share value, it is his responsibility, rather than that of the lender, to take appropriate remedial steps, such as paying off the loan in return for the collateral, substituting the pledged stock with other equally valued assets, or selling the pledged stock himself and paying off the loan.

* * *

. . . Therefore, the district court's grant of summary judgment on this issue is affirmed.

- Based on what you have read, what kind of facts would have supported a finding that Bank One had breached its duty of care under 9-207 with regard to the stock held as collateral?

Note: *City National Bank v. Unique Structures, Inc.*, 49 F.3d 1330, 26 U.C.C. Rep. Serv.2d 268 (8th Cir. 1995), provides some clarification regarding a secured creditor's duty to protect collateral.   That case involved City National Bank's repossession of 27 mobile homes. By the time the mobile homes were sold, they were in poor condition. Appliances and other fixtures had been removed from the homes, windows had been broken, and the plumbing had frozen, causing additional damage. The bank had not cleaned or repaired the homes prior to sale, and the evidence suggested the bank had failed to pursue possible insurance claims for damage to the homes. The proceeds from the repossession sale fell far short of the owed amount and, when the bank sued for the amount of the deficiency, the debtor counterclaimed, alleging the bank had violated its duties with regard to the collateral. In affirming the lower court's finding that the bank had breached its duty of care with regard to the collateral, the court qualified its holding as follows:

> CNB did not have a duty to preserve the mobile homes immediately upon the default of the individual debtors [who originally owned the homes]. This duty to preserve arose only after the mobile homes were in CNB's possession. [FN5]
>
> > FN5 . . . Contrary to the holding of the district court, "possession" requires more than the bare right to repossess the collateral. Possession involves some level of physical control over the collateral. *Id.* at 1333.

- What kinds of facts would demonstrate "physical control" over a mobile home sufficient to constitute "possession"?

Retention of the Collateral

Read 9-620 (a) and Comment 2. Under certain circumstances, a secured creditor may elect to retain the collateral in full or partial satisfaction of the debt. As Comment 1 indicates, such retention of collateral is called "strict foreclosure."

- In what kinds of cases might it be unclear whether the secured party has elected to retain the collateral?

The following case introduces three tests for determining whether a secured creditor has elected to keep collateral in satisfaction of the debt.

Schmode's, Inc. v. Wilkinson,
219 Neb. 209, 361 N.W.2d 557 (1985).

Caporale, Justice.

Schmode's[, Inc.] entered into a business transaction with Harco Leasing Company, Inc., whereby Schmode's sold to Harco a 1978 International tractor truck and a 1978 Hobbs trailer. Harco and [Mary and Ronald] Wilkinson[ ] then, on April 27, 1978, executed a conditional sales agreement, entitled "LEASING AGREEMENT," with respect to the truck, which obligated the Wilkinsons to pay Harco a principal amount, plus amortized interest and other charges, in 60 equal monthly installments and a larger 61st payment representing the truck's "residual value." On May 19, 1978, Harco and the Wilkinsons entered into a similar agreement with respect to the trailer, obligating the Wilkinsons to pay Harco a principal amount, plus amortized interest and other charges, in 60 equal monthly installments and a larger 61st payment representing the trailer's "residual value." Schmode's guaranteed Harco that, if the Wilkinsons defaulted on their obligation such as to result in Harco's reclaiming the truck and trailer from the Wilkinsons, Schmode's would repurchase them from Harco.

The Wilkinsons defaulted, and on December 19, 1979, they delivered possession of the truck and trailer, collectively the collateral, to Schmode's.

The collateral was in need of repair, and Schmode's restored it to sound mechanical condition, the restoration work being completed by May 3, 1980. The collateral was then placed on Schmode's lot in an attempt to sell it. As the collateral did not sell, Schmode's used it by leasing it to others through about mid-April of 1983, during which time it was operated a minimum of 204,000 miles.

Schmode's honored its agreement with Harco and paid the sums due Harco from the Wilkinsons. The parties do not dispute that Schmode's had a security interest in the collateral.

The collateral was publicly sold on April 28, 1983, pursuant to the trial judge's order. At the trial on the merits, the trial judge found that the April 28 sale had not been commercially reasonable "because of the lapse of nearly three years and the use of said vehicles before the sale." The trial judge accordingly ruled that the Wilkinsons were entitled to setoffs for the damages they suffered due to the commercially unreasonable sale.

The Wilkinsons argue that Schmode's elected to retain the collateral in satisfaction of the obligation by keeping and leasing it for a period of almost 3 years after restoration and causing it to be operated for at least 204,000 miles, and therefore cannot obtain a deficiency judgment. . . .

Although we have not had occasion to deal with whether acts by a secured party other than the sending of notice may result in a § 9-505 (2) election, other states with statutes virtually identical to ours have. There appear to be three different approaches.

> The current reference is to UCC 9-620 (a).

One approach holds that an election under § 9-505 (2) is impossible absent the service of notice on the debtor of the secured party's intent to retain the collateral in payment of the debt. *Flickinger v. Genesee Corp.*, 71 A.D.2d 382, 423 N.Y.S.2d 73 (1979), typifies this view, which seems to be premised on the notion that, since the Code provides a specific method for indicating that the secured party has elected to retain the collateral to satisfy the obligation, such an election cannot be implied from conduct not specified by the Code. We reject this view on the ground that a secured party ought not be allowed to penalize a debtor by asserting the secured party's own failure to give the notice contemplated by § 9-505 (2).

> How would the *Flickinger* approach allow a secured party to penalize the debtor by the secured party's own failure to act?

A second approach is that an election can be implied from an unreasonably prolonged retention of the collateral by the secured party, and that the determination of what constitutes an unreasonable period of time is a question for the trier of fact. This view appears to rest on the theory that to allow the secured party to retain the collateral for an unreasonably long time and then elect to sue the debtor on the underlying obligation would be unfair to the debtor.

The third approach requires that the secured party manifest an intent to accept the collateral in satisfaction of the obligation by some conduct other than an undue delay in disposing of the collateral. This view rests, at least in part, on the notion that, since the debtor is protected by other provisions in the Code and because, at common law, the analogous concept of accord and satisfaction requires proof of the creditor's assent, in the absence of notice a clear manifestation of an election on the part of the creditor is required.

> What other protections does the Code provide to a debtor that would protect it under these circumstances?

Under the circumstances of this case we need not choose at this time between the second and third approaches. Although we consider the question to be one of fact, we hold that in this case there is but one reasonable conclusion, and, therefore, as a matter of law, Schmode's, by using the collateral for a period of nearly 3 years after restoration by leasing and causing it to be operated for at least 204,000 miles, elected to retain the collateral in satisfaction of the Wilkinsons' obligation. The trial court was clearly wrong in not so holding.

We leave to another day and another case the question of whether, under some circumstances, the mere retention of collateral for an unreasonably long time may in and of itself imply a § 9-505 (2) election.

- Which test do you find most compelling and why?

Note: In *Munao v. Lagattuta*, 294 Ill. App. 3d 976, 691 N.E.2d 818 (1st Dist. 1998), in determining that the secured party had not retained the collateral – which consisted of certain restaurant fixtures and other food-service equipment that the secured party had repossessed from the debtors' restaurant – in full satisfaction of the debt, the court considered, among other factors, the fact that "[t]he disparity between the value of the collateral and the debt was so great that [the creditors'] acceptance of the collateral in full satisfaction of the debt would have made little economic sense."

- What arguments can be made in favor of the court's decision to consider this evidence?

- What arguments can be made against the court's decision to do so?

Problem: Douglas and Gayle Reed sold a restaurant and bar called the Palomino Room to Ralph and Beverly Crosby, retaining a security interest in the business until the promissory note the Crosbys had executed to the Reeds for the purchase price was fully paid. The Crosbys defaulted on their obligations under the note, and the Reeds foreclosed on the collateral. They re-opened and began to operate the restaurant for a period of about nine months. The local newspaper published an article stating that the Reeds were "back at the helm" of the restaurant. During this period, the Reeds made improvements to the restaurant facilities and applied for a liquor license. At the close of the first month, the Reeds had the property appraised; at the close of the ninth month, they published a notice indicating the property would be sold at public auction. The Reeds were the only bidders at the auction, which was conducted by a licensed auctioneer. They purchased all of the assets for the appraised value.

- Does this fact pattern establish the creditor's retention of the collateral in satisfaction of the debt?

- Do these facts establish a commercially reasonable sale?

Based on *In re Crosby*, 176 B.R. 189, 25 U.C.C. Rep. Serv. 2d 1032 (Bankr. App. 9th Cir. 1994).

International Perspective: A Reasonable Sale

The following excerpt is taken from Tibor Tajti, *Comparative Secured Transactions Law* (Akadémiai Kiadó 2002):

> Canadian legislators were not convinced that the general standard of commercial reasonableness, without a more detailed guidance as a mechanism for balancing the interests of the secured party and the debtor, is the adequate solution. Instead, detailed enforcement rules have been provided, and courts were given broad discretionary power of relief from these rules. *Id.* at 226.

- What are the relative benefits and risks of applying general standards of reasonableness, as opposed to detailed criteria?

C. The Right of Redemption

This section will discuss the debtor's right to redeem the collateral by paying the debt and other fees and costs associated with default and repossession. This right may be exercised after default and repossession, but before disposition of the collateral has occurred.

Read 9-623. This provision gives the debtor the power to redeem the collateral, under certain circumstances, upon full payment of the defaulted amount or the collateral's value, together with certain costs and penalties.

- When does the debtor's power to redeem the collateral expire?

The following case shows the importance of the debtor's right of redemption. As you read this case, note the court's discussion of the debtor's agreement not to exercise its right of redemption, made before, as opposed to after, the event of default giving rise to repossession of the collateral.

Lewis Broadcasting Corp. v. Phoenix Broadcasting Partners,
232 Ga. App. 94, 502 S.E.2d 254 (1998).

Blackburn, Judge.

Lewis Broadcasting Corporation appeals the trial court's grant of
summary judgment to Phoenix Broadcasting Partners on Lewis' suit
for specific performance of an option agreement. For the reasons
discussed below, we affirm.

In January 1994, Phoenix's predecessor-in-interest, Gulf Atlantic
Media of Georgia, Inc., borrowed $650,000 from Lewis. The purpose of
the loan was to enable Gulf to finance a settlement with its lender and
to avoid a forced sale of its two Savannah radio stations, for which a
receiver had been appointed. All parties were represented by counsel
in the negotiation and execution of the loan documents. Gulf executed
a $650,000 promissory note in favor of Lewis, which note was to
mature one year after the assignment from the receiver to Gulf of the
FCC licenses to operate the stations, but no later than July 1, 1995.
Gulf executed a security agreement granting Lewis a security interest
in all of the operating assets of the two stations except their FCC
licenses, which under the rules of the FCC could not be transferred or
assigned without FCC approval. The agreement provided that the
licenses would become part of the collateral in the event of any rule
change by the FCC allowing a security interest to be given in such
licenses.

As part of the transaction, Gulf also executed an option agreement,
giving Lewis the option to purchase the radio stations' assets, including
the FCC licenses (subject to FCC approval), upon the occurrence of a
default under the loan. The option price was $650,000, less any
amount outstanding on the loan. Phoenix also agreed to pay a
$100,000 consultation or noncompetition fee to Gulf's principal, Carl
Marcocci, and his wife upon exercise of the option. This option
agreement was executed on January 19, 1994, the same day as the
security agreement.

Phoenix subsequently acquired all of Gulf's assets and assumed its
obligations under the loan documents. After Phoenix defaulted on the
loan, Lewis gave notice of its intent to exercise the option to purchase
the radio stations. When Phoenix refused to perform under the option
agreement, Lewis filed this action seeking payment of the loan and
specific performance of the option agreement. The trial court granted
Phoenix's motion for summary judgment on the specific performance
claim, finding that the option agreement was an impermissible
restraint on the debtor's right to redeem its collateral upon default.

Lewis contends that the trial court erred in finding the option
agreement void and granting summary judgment to Phoenix on Lewis'
claim for specific performance of such agreement.

The facts of this case are similar to *Bromley v. Bromley,* 106 Ga. App.
606, 611, 127 S.E.2d 836 (1962), where a borrower assigned to the
lender as security for a loan certain shares of stock owned by the
borrower. The assignment agreement also contained a provision

allowing the lender, upon default by the buyer, to purchase the stock by crediting a set amount against the outstanding indebtedness. In holding such a provision invalid, we stated as follows: "The common law has jealously guarded the mortgagor's equity of redemption which may not be 'fettered' or 'clogged.' [Citation omitted]. In general, any provision in the mortgage at its inception which takes away the right of the mortgagor to exercise his equity of redemption is void. The mortgagor cannot, by the initial agreement, bind himself not to exercise his equity to redeem the property. A direct agreement, part of the original transaction, whereby a chattel mortgagor, a pledgor, or a mortgagor of personal property forfeits, or clogs, or fetters his equity of redemption, is void. [Citations omitted]. The mortgagor cannot enter into a contract with a mortgagee at the time of the loan for purchase of the equity of redemption at a fixed sum.... Pledges, chattel mortgages, and bills of sale to secure debt are treated similarly by the law and equity; certainly this is true insofar as any forfeiture of the equity or right of redemption is asserted or may be involved." *Id.* at 611.

Bromley thus stands for the proposition that an option to purchase collateral for a fixed price upon default, entered into at the time of the original loan transaction granting a security interest in such collateral, constitutes an impermissible attempt to defeat the debtor's right to redeem the collateral. This proposition is consistent with the Uniform Commercial Code....

* * *

For the above reasons, the trial court did not err in granting summary judgment to Phoenix on Lewis' claim for specific performance of the option agreement.

- In your own words, why does the court strike down an agreement not to redeem, executed before the debtor's default? [9-602 (11) may assist you in answering this question.]

- **Read 9-624 (c).** Would such an agreement have been enforceable if it had been executed after default?

- How is the concept of a "mirage of hope," described earlier in this chapter, relevant to an understanding of the court's holding?

Note: *Task Enterprises, Inc. v. Pratt Adjustment Co.*, 695 P.2d 762, 39 U.C.C. Rep. Serv. 1167 (Colo. App. 1984), provides guidance as to how a court may interpret 9-623's requirement that a debtor tender all funds required, as a precondition to exercising his or her right of redemption. In that case, the debtor "deposited funds sufficient to redeem the [repossessed] vehicle in a bank account and offered to send such funds to the Bank on condition that he be allowed to examine the vehicle." In holding the debtor had not satisfied the "tender" requirement, the court analyzed the issue as follows:

"Tendering fulfillment requires an actual, present, unconditional, physical production of payment, and a mere willingness, readiness, or proposition to pay is not enough."

- Why might a debtor insist on examining the collateral before releasing funds to redeem the collateral?

- Why might the creditor insist that such a conditional tender is insufficient to exercise the debtor's right of redemption?

Problem: Does the following notice, sent by a secured party after the debtor's default, accurately reflect the debtor's rights and obligations with regard to redemption of collateral under 9-623?

> You are entitled to redeem the said goods provided that, within fifteen days from the date of delivery of this notice, you pay [the secured party] the sum of $650.39, which is the aggregate amount in default under the Agreement . . . , together with any other amount that may become due prior to redemption.
>
> If you do not redeem as aforesaid, the goods will thereafter be sold at private sale and, if a deficiency arises, you will be liable for such deficiency.

Based on *First National Bank v. DiDomenico*, 302 Md. 290, 487 A.2d 646 (1985).

International Perspective: The Rights of Creditors and Debtors upon Default

Consider the following excerpt from *Taiwan*, by Lawrence S. Liu & Catherine I.C. Ken, in *Bank Security and Other Credit Enhancement Methods: A Practical Guide on Security Devices Available to Banks in Thirty Countries Throughout the World* 405 (Winnibald E. Moojen & Matthieu Ph. Van Sint Truiden eds., Kluwer Law International 1995):

> If the debtor defaults on his obligation, the creditor may seize and sell the object without prior judicial decision through an auction. Notification is necessary before seizure. If the object is sold at auction, the proceeds will go first towards the cost of collecting on the object (i.e. auction fee), then [towards] the interest on the debt, and finally [towards] the principal debt. Excess proceeds derived from the sale of the object are returned to the debtor. . . . The creditor may not take title of the . . . property. *Id.* at 406.

- From what you have read, how is Taiwanese practice different from, and similar to, Article 9 on point?

The same source includes an essay entitled *Korea*, by Eui Jae Kim. The following excerpt summarizes Korean law regarding sales of collateral, insofar as the rights and obligations of both the creditor and the debtor are concerned:

> A *yangdo-dambo* is created through a simple agreement between the parties, whereby a loan contract is first concluded and, thereafter, the parties agree to transfer ownership of the property or property right from the debtor to the creditor for purposes of securing the creditor's claim to the principal and interest arising out of the loan contract. Generally, in practice, the property subject to *yangdo-dambo* is a movable. In the case of movables, a mere declaration by the transferor that he will thereafter hold the movables for the transferee allows the transferor to retain use of the movables though the creditor holds the ownership thereof. Generally, if the debtor fails to make the repayment of the debt in time, the creditor satisfies his claim to the principal and interest of the loan by having the property appraised and sold. The creditor must return any excess proceeds from the sale to the debtor even though, in principle, the creditor acquires absolute ownership over the property. Furthermore, even if the debtor fails to make a timely repayment, the creditor is obligated to return the property if the debtor tenders the full amount before the creditor can appraise the property. Despite this general rule, the parties can agree to enable the creditor to foreclose on the property as soon as the repayment period has expired. It should be noted that the creditor "owns" the property only for the purposes of security. . . . Further, if the creditor damages or transfers the property to a third party, he or she is liable to the debtor for breach of contract. However, from a *bona-fide* third-party perspective, after the completion of a *yangdo-dambo* transaction, the property has been perfectly and completely transferred to the creditor. For example, the creditors of the *yangdo-dambo* creditor can levy execution against the *yangdo-dambo* creditor. *Id.* at 254.

- Based upon this excerpt, what are the differences and similarities between Korean law and Article 9 as to the rights and obligations of debtors and creditors?

_____

Chapter Conclusion: As you complete this Chapter, you should not only be comfortable with the various rights and responsibilities of the debtor and creditor after an event of default, but should also have an understanding of how the contents of the previous four chapters, which described the scope of Article 9, the creation, attachment, and perfection of a security interest, and the system of priorities under Article 9, affect the parties' rights after default has occurred.

PART V:
DOCUMENTARY TRANSACTIONS

Chapter 18 provides a general introduction to documentary transactions involving letters of credit and documents of title. As the last chapter in this book, a primary purpose of Chapter 18 is to show how a single transaction may implicate not only Articles 5 and 7, the principal sources of law for letters of credit and documents of title, respectively, but also the other Articles covered in this book.

Chapter 18: Documentary Sales

A. An Introduction to Documentary Sales

This section briefly introduces letters of credit and documents of title, both of which are covered in somewhat greater detail later in this chapter, and shows how the two are often used in a single transaction called a documentary sale to minimize risk to buyers and sellers who may be located far from one another and may not be willing to rely upon one another's creditworthiness. The following language from *Bank of Cochin Ltd. v. Manufacturers Hanover Trust Co.*, 612 F. Supp. 1533, 41 U.C.C. Rep. Serv. 920 (S.D.N.Y. 1985), describes a letter-of-credit transaction in general terms:

> A letter of credit is a financing mechanism designed to allocate commercial-credit risks whereby a bank or other issuer pays an amount of money to a beneficiary upon presentment of documents complying with specified conditions set forth in the letter. The beneficiary, typically the seller of goods to a buyer-customer, uses the letter to substitute the credit of the issuer for the credit of its customer. The customer applies for the letter of credit, specifies the terms of the letter, and promises to reimburse the issuer upon honor of the beneficiary's draft. The letter of credit is thus an engagement by the issuer to the beneficiary to cover the customer's agreement to pay money under the customer-beneficiary contract. The reliability and fluidity of the letter of credit are maintained because the issuing bank is concerned exclusively with the documents, not the performance obligations created by the customer-beneficiary contract. *Id.* at 1537.

> This party is the "applicant" or "account party" in Article 5 terminology.

> Reference is made here to the Independence Principle, which is presented below in Part B.

- How does a letter of credit "substitute the credit of the issuer for the credit of the applicant"?

The following language, taken from the disputed letter of credit in *Intraworld Industries, Inc. v. Girard Trust Bank*, 461 Pa. 343, 336 A.2d 316 (1975), shows how a standby letter of credit — that is, a letter of credit to be drawn upon only in the event of

> A standby letter of credit is distinguished from a commercial letter of credit, which is drawn upon without any requirement of default.

default – might read. This letter of credit was used to ensure
payment of all rental amounts due to Paulette Cymbalista, the
lessor of certain hotel property, by Intraworld Industries, Inc.,
the lessee.

> IRREVOCABLE LETTER OF CREDIT NO. 35798
> Date: September 5, 1972
> Amount: $100,000.00
> Beneficiary: Paulette Cymbalista
> C/o Carlton Hotel
> St. Moritz, Switzerland
>
> For account of: Intraworld Industries, Inc.
> 116 South Main Street
> Wilkes Barre, PA 18701
>
> Madam:
>
> You are hereby authorized to draw on us at sight the sum of One
> Hundred Thousand and 00/100 Dollars United States Currency
> ($100,000.00) due on November 10, 1973, under a lease, a copy of
> which is attached to both Beneficiary's copy and Bank's copy of
> this letter of credit as Exhibit 1, available by your draft for said
> amount, accompanied by:
>
> 1. Simple receipt for amount drawn.
>
> 2. A signed statement of the drawer of the draft to the effect that
> the drawer is the lessor under said lease and that the lessee
> thereunder has not paid the installment of rent due under said
> lease on November 10, 1973, within 10 days after said
> installment was due and payable.
>
> This credit expires on November 30, 1973.
>
> Drafts under this credit must contain the clause "drawn under
> Credit No. 35798 of Girard Trust Bank, dated September 5,
> 1972."
>
> Girard Trust Bank hereby agrees with the drawers, endorsers
> and bona-fide owners of the bills drawn strictly in compliance
> with the terms of this credit that the same will be duly honored
> upon presentation.
>
> Except so far as otherwise expressly stated, this credit is subject
> to the Uniform Customs and Practices for Documentary Credits
> (1962 revision), International Chamber of Commerce Brochure
> No. 222. *Id.* at 349.

> As this paragraph shows, the lessee's default is the trigger for payment.

> The doctrine of Strict Compliance is discussed below in Part B.

> This important resource, commonly called the UCP, is introduced in this section's international materials.

- ▪ What language indicates that this document is a
  standby – rather than commercial – letter of credit?

A commercial letter of credit would differ from the standby
letter of credit above in that a commercial letter of credit does

not require the applicant's default as a precondition to
payment. While a commercial letter of credit ensures payment
is made for delivered goods, a document of title controls the
right to possession of the goods. As the *BII Finance Co., Ltd.*
case below shows, a document of title may be negotiable or non-
negotiable. This chapter introduces two kinds of documents of
title: warehouse receipts and bills of lading. These are the
most common documents of title. Others, however, can also
exist. As 1-201 Comment 16 indicates, "the definition is left
open so that new types of documents may be included." *Bank
of New York v. Amoco Oil Co.*, 35 F.3d 643, 24 U.C.C. Rep.
Serv. 2d 209 (2d. Cir. 1994), a case arising pursuant to a
negotiable document of title that the parties called a "holding
certificate," involved Amoco Oil Company's leasing of platinum
from Drexel Burnham Lambert Trading Corporation. The
platinum was to be combined with aluminum and used to
create catalysts for the gasoline-refining process. After each
catalyst was used for about six months, it was deemed "spent"
and returned to Drexel Burnham, where the platinum was
separated from the aluminum and prepared for re-use. The
following document-of-title language, taken from the case,
memorializes the parties' transaction:

This is to certify that as of [date], we are holding for the account
or order of:

Drexel Burnham Lambert Trading Corporation
60 Broad Street
New York, New York 10004

The following material: [number of] troy ounces of platinum
sponge metal 99.95% catalytic grade.

This material is free of all liens and encumbrances.

Material is to be released on surrender of this Certificate properly
endorsed.

Company Name: Amoco Oil Company

By: [Signature]

Date: [Date]
Id. at 651.

After you have
completed this
chapter, return to
this language and
make sure you
understand why this
document of title is
negotiable.

The following graphic illustrates a typical documentary sale.
Note how many Articles of the UCC can be implicated in a
single transaction: The sale of goods between the buyer and
seller will be governed by Article 2 or, alternatively, if the goods
were leased, by Article 2A. If the letter of credit is what is
called a "standby" letter of credit to be drawn upon only in the

event of default, payment might be expected from the buyer in
the form of a draft or promissory note governed by Article 3 or a
wholesale wire transfer governed by Article 4A. If payment
were made by check or other item collected through a bank,
Article 4 would govern the collection process. The letter of
credit itself is governed by Article 5, and the document of title
representing the right to the goods is governed by Article 7.
Article 9 would govern any security interest the seller retained
in the goods.

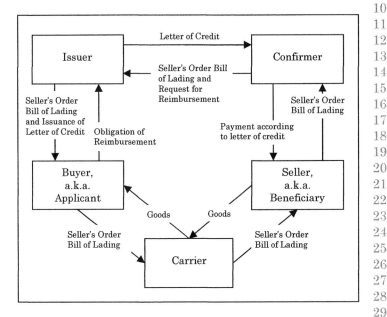

The applicant first opens a letter of credit with the issuer,
which is typically a bank. The issuer might then communicate
the letter of credit to another bank (or other entity), called a
correspondent, with which it has a contractual relationship.

- **Read 5-102 Comment 3.** What body of law governs
  the contractual relationship between the applicant and
  beneficiary, pursuant to which the letter of credit is
  issued?

Read 5-102 (a) (4) and (a) (11) and Comment 1, and 5-107.
As these provisions indicate, the correspondent is called a
nominated person unless and until it accepts the obligation to
pay the beneficiary pursuant to the letter of credit, at which
time it will be called a *confirmer*.

Review 3-408 and
the materials
contained in
Chapter 10, Part B
as needed to answer
this question.

- Compare the concept of a nominated person's choosing
  to become a confirmer (or not) with the concept of
  drawee acceptance (or dishonor) of a draft under
  Articles 3 and 4.

1   ▪ Applying the language of 5-107 Comment 1, how can a
2   confirmer have greater rights against the issuer than
3   the beneficiary does, and how can the confirmer's
4   rights be compared with those of a holder in due
5   course under Articles 3 and 4?

> Review 3-302 and the materials contained in Chapter 9, Part D as needed to answer this question.

6
7   ▪ What is the difference between the role of an adviser
8   and that of a confirmer?
9
10   **Read 5-108 (b) and Comment 2.** Upon receiving notice
11   advising it that a letter of credit has been opened for its benefit,
12   a beneficiary must gather and present the documents specified
13   in the letter of credit to obtain payment. An issuer or confirmer
14   receiving the presented documents has a reasonable time not to
15   exceed seven days in which to examine them for compliance
16   with the letter of credit and determine whether payment will
17   be made. As Comment 2 indicates, the seven-day period is not
18   a "safe harbor"; a court may find the issuer or confirmer should
19   have acted more quickly.
20
21   One of the documents often specified in a letter of credit is a bill
22   of lading. A bill of lading functions as both a document of title
23   and a contract of carriage. A carrier delivering goods to a buyer
24   issues a document of title to the seller when it receives the
25   goods. When the seller receives the bill of lading, it takes the
26   bill, together with any other documents specified in the letter of
27   credit, and makes presentation to the designated issuer or

> "Presentation" is defined in 5-102 (a) (12).

28   confirmer, which examines the documents and, if they conform
29   with the requirements of the letter of credit, makes payment.
30   The applicant must reimburse the issuer for payment, and the
31   issuer must reimburse the confirmer. In the meantime, the bill
32   of lading is sent to the buyer, which surrenders it to the carrier
33   in return for the goods.
34
35   ▪ **Read 5-104 and Comment 1.** What information
36   does a letter of credit normally contain, and how does
37   this list of information compare with the requirements
38   for creating a negotiable instrument under Article 3?

> Review 3-104 and the materials contained in Chapter 8 as needed to answer this question.

39
40   An issuer, confirmer, or adviser typically charges a service fee.
41   As 5-106 indicates, letters of credit are presumptively
42   irrevocable and expire one year after the stated date of
43   issuance, except "perpetual" letters of credit, which expire five
44   years after the date of issuance.
45
46   The letter of credit protects the seller, ensuring it will receive
50   payment. The issuer or confirmer must pay the seller
51   according to the terms of the letter of credit if the seller
52   produces documents that comply with the letter of credit,
53   notwithstanding any potential nonconformity in the delivered

goods. The buyer can protect itself against any nonconforming tender by specifying that inspection and insurance certificates supporting the quality of the goods be among the documents required by the letter of credit. Such certificates are not required for a documentary sale; instead, the buyer must negotiate this requirement into the contract if it so desires. The following language, based on *Banco Espanol de Credito v. State Street Bank and Trust Co.*, 385 F.2d 230, 4 U.C.C. Rep. Serv. 862 (1st Cir. 1967), is typical of a certificate of inspection for garments:

> COATS or JACKETS (Garments)
>
> A sample inspected in Spain.
>
> As required by the letter of credit, we do hereby certify that the goods are in conformity with the order, that a ten-percent random sample has been taken, and that the whole has been found conforming to the conditions stipulated in the order.

The following case shows how letters of credit and documents of title such as bills of lading work together in a documentary transaction. This case distinguishes between negotiable and non-negotiable bills of lading and alludes to the respective coverage of UCC Article 7 and the Federal Bills of Lading Act found at 49 USC §§ 80101 et seq.

The Federal Bills of Lading Act is not otherwise covered in these materials.

BII Finance Co., Ltd. v. U-States Forwarding Services Corp., 95 Cal. App. 4th 111, 115 Cal. Rptr. 2d 312 (2d Dist. 2002).

Mosk, J.

On June 5 and 6, 1997, Primaline, [Inc.], a shipping company that acted as agent for U-States [Forwarding Services Corp.], issued four bills of lading in favor of Shineworld Industrial Limited, a Hong Kong manufacturer and exporter of garments. Although the goods covered by the bills of lading (cartons of jackets) were to be shipped to the buyer, Jacobs & Turner, Ltd. in Glasgow, Scotland, the goods were consigned simply "To Order," without specifying any name or person.

As 7-102 (a) (3) and (4) and the discussion in Part C show, the term "consignment" is used in this context to describe delivery of goods to a carrier.

Jacobs & Turner agreed to pay by letter of credit approximately US $200,000 for the goods covered by the bills of lading. . . . Shineworld assigned each bill of lading to BII [Finance Co. Ltd.], a commercial Hong Kong bank, for a loan of approximately US $200,000.

The goods were placed on a vessel in early June 1997 and arrived in the United Kingdom in July 1997. While the goods were in transit, BII sent the shipping documents (including the bills of lading) to Jacobs & Turner's bank, Clydesdale Bank PLC, in Glasgow, Scotland, and requested payment under the letter of credit. On June 25, 1997, Clydesdale Bank gave notice to BII that, because the bank had found discrepancies between the letter of credit and the shipping documents sent to it by BII, the bank would not release the funds to BII until the buyer, Jacobs & Turner, consented to a waiver of the discrepancies. BII then notified Shineworld of the claimed discrepancies, and Shineworld responded that it would contact Jacobs & Turner about the matter.

> As discussed below in Part B, 5-108 (a) allows an applicant to waive noncompliance with the strict terms of a letter of credit.

Shineworld apparently did not have any further communications with BII about the shipment. Sometime later, in September 1997, BII learned that the goods had been released to Jacobs & Turner at Shineworld's direction, even though BII had not been paid for the goods. In fact, on July 15, 1997, Shineworld had inexplicably sent a letter to Primaline requesting that it release the goods to Jacobs & Turner without requiring surrender of the original bills of lading. This request or instruction was not noted on the bills of lading because Shineworld had already transferred them to BII.

As a result of the communication from Shineworld, U-States (by its agent, Primaline) released the goods to Jacobs & Turner on July 15, 1997, without the surrender of the original bills of lading. There is no indication that Jacobs & Turner had waived the claimed discrepancies under the letter of credit or had paid for the goods.

U-States had no knowledge that Shineworld had assigned the original bills of lading to BII at the time U-States released the goods to Jacobs & Turner. BII did not know of Shineworld's letter instructing U-States to release the goods to Jacobs & Turner until September 1997, after the goods had been released, and had not authorized the release of the goods.

BII could not recover from Shineworld because Shineworld had no ascertainable assets. BII claimed against Jacobs & Turner, which party asserted that the goods were defective, although there was a certificate from the inspector of the goods at the place of delivery that the goods were not defective. BII and Jacobs & Turner agreed that, as a settlement between them, Jacobs & Turner would pay to BII 65 percent of the goods' total agreed price, and that amount was paid.

. . . BII then sought the unpaid amount of the original contract price from U-States in this case.

Alleging causes of action for breach of contract and conversion, BII asserted that U-States' delivery of the goods to Jacobs & Turner without the surrender of the original bills of lading was a misdelivery for which U-States is liable in damages to BII. BII relied on the bills of lading that were consigned "To Order" and on what it deemed to be the applicable law. U-States contended that the bills of lading should be read to have permitted the delivery it made. . . .

Bills of lading have long been used in international sales transactions as one means to protect the interests of sellers, who want assurance of being paid for goods shipped by a carrier, and buyers, who do not want to pay for goods until they arrive. They also are used as a means to facilitate credit arrangements and to reflect title in goods being shipped by a carrier.

The bill of lading constitutes a receipt for the goods shipped, a contract for their carriage, and a document of title. It describes the goods shipped, identifies the shipper (or consignor) and the buyer (consignee), and directs the carrier to deliver the goods to a specified location or person. As a contract of carriage drafted by the carrier, a bill of lading is strictly construed against the carrier.

A negotiable bill of lading, in effect, requires delivery to the bearer of the bill or, if to the order of a named person, to that person. A non-negotiable bill of lading is one in which the consignee is specified. If the bill of lading is negotiable, the holder of the original bill can negotiate it by indorsing and delivering it to another or, when it is indorsed in blank or to bearer, by delivery alone. An indorsee is the holder and, in effect, holds title to the goods covered by the bill.

In a typical international transaction, once the buyer and seller have agreed on terms, the buyer (in this case, Jacobs & Turner) obtains a letter of credit with its bank (here, Clydesdale Bank in Scotland) in favor of the seller (here, Shineworld). The seller (generally referred to as the shipper) delivers the goods to a carrier (here, U-States through its agent Primaline). The carrier issues a bill of lading, usually in duplicate sets, and gives the original bill of lading to the shipper.

The shipper issues a draft or other document directing the buyer to pay the purchase price to the shipper or the shipper's nominee. The shipper or its nominee then presents the draft and the bill of lading (made to the order of or indorsed to the buyer) to the buyer's bank for payment.

The buyer's bank compares the draft and bill of lading against the letter of credit to ensure there are no discrepancies between them. If none is found, the bank pays the shipper or its nominee and forwards the original bill of lading to the buyer, who presents it to the carrier to obtain delivery of the goods. If the bank finds discrepancies between the letter of credit and the shipper's documents, as it did here, the bank notifies the shipper, who may ask the buyer to waive the discrepancies. If the buyer agrees to such a waiver, the bank pays the shipper and forwards the bill of lading to the buyer, who presents it to the carrier for delivery of the goods. If there is no waiver, the original bill of lading is returned to the shipper, and the transaction is cancelled.

The transaction at issue in this case essentially was initiated as we describe, in that Jacobs & Turner obtained a letter of credit to purchase goods from Shineworld, Shineworld delivered the goods to U-States' agent for shipment to Jacobs & Turner, and U-States (through its agent, Primaline) issued bills of lading and gave them to Shineworld. Shineworld then indorsed the bills of lading to BII in exchange for a loan by BII to Shineworld in the amount that was covered by the amount owed by the buyer, Jacobs & Turner. Therefore, BII, rather than Shineworld, presented the original bills of lading to Clydesdale Bank for payment. When the bank found discrepancies that Jacobs & Turner did not waive, the bank returned the original bills of lading to BII.

With regard to issues concerning the bills of lading at issue in this case, we apply (as do the parties) California law, in accordance with the terms of the bills of lading that were issued by U-States, a California corporation. . . .

Although the Federal Bills of Lading Act (49 USC §§ 80101-80116), when applicable, preempts much of the application of division 7 of the California Uniform Commercial Code, the Act applies only to interstate and foreign commerce in which the goods travel through one of the states of the United States. Because the goods in this case did not travel through the United States, the Federal Bills of Lading Act does not supersede California law here.

California Uniform Commercial Code section 7104 governs whether a document of title, such as a bill of lading, is negotiable or non-negotiable. . . .

> The negotiability of documents of title is further discussed in Part C of this chapter.

The bills of lading in this case were consigned "To Order." They were not to the order of any specific person or entity; nor did they specifically provide for delivery of the goods to the bearer. Therefore, the bills of lading do not appear to fall within the scope of subdivision (1) as negotiable.

* * *

Subdivision (3) is a California addition to the Uniform Commercial Code. As noted above, that section provides that, if a non-negotiable bill of lading is not conspicuously marked "non-negotiable," a holder who purchased the bill of lading for value "supposing it to be negotiable" may treat the bill of lading as imposing upon the bailee (in this case, U-States) the same liabilities it would have incurred had the document been negotiable. Therefore, even if the bills of lading in this case were not negotiable under subdivision (1), they may be treated as negotiable if BII purchased them for value supposing them to be negotiable, because the bills of lading were not marked "non-negotiable."

U-States asserts that BII did not purchase the bills of lading for value because it says that the transaction was a "post-shipment financing." Yet BII advanced moneys to the shipper, Shineworld, against the shipping documents, thereby, in effect, purchasing the bills of lading for value. The evidence is that the parties considered the bills of lading to be negotiable, and BII has elected to treat the bills of lading as negotiable. Accordingly, under California Uniform Commercial Code section 7104, subdivision (3), if the bills of lading are not actually negotiable, U-States has the same liabilities by virtue of the documents it would have incurred had the bills of lading been negotiable.

> As the final paragraph of the excerpted opinion indicates, whether BII has purchased the bills of lading for value is relevant to a determination of whether it qualifies as a holder by due negotiation, a status comparable to that of a holder in due course within the meaning of Articles 3 and 4.

The parties do not dispute that U-States delivered the goods to someone who did not surrender the original bills of lading. . . .

* * *

U-States chose to comply with Shineworld's instruction without determining whether Shineworld was the proper holder of the bills of lading and whether Jacobs & Turner was the party with the right of possession of the goods. Thus, U-States, without requiring the original bills of lading, assumed the risk that neither party had the right to possession and that it would be liable to the holder of the bills of lading by due negotiation. The trial court correctly determined that, because BII was the holder of the bills of lading by due negotiation, U-States'

misdelivery of the goods to Jacobs & Turner renders U-States liable to
BII.

> 7-403 (a) and 7-102
> (a) (8) may assist
> you in answering
> this question.

- How does whether the bills of lading are negotiable affect the outcome of this case?

- What are the risks and benefits of California's nonuniform enactment of 7-104?

International Perspective: The Various Laws Affecting Documentary Sales

Read 5-103 Comment 2, and 5-116 (c) and Comment 3. In addition to Article 5, commercial-law practitioners – particularly those who engage in international practice – need to be familiar with the Uniform Customs and Practice for Documentary Credits, known as the UCP, promulgated by the International Chamber of Commerce. The current version of the UCP is known as "UCP 500," in recognition of the fact that it is the 500th publication of the ICC. Although the UCP is not law, where the parties have expressly agreed to follow its provisions (as many do), Article 5 generally defers to its terms in the event of conflict. As 5-103 Comment 2 indicates, the provisions of the UCP are particularly important in determining compliance with the performance standards for issuers set forth in 5-108.

> The role of the UCP
> is further described
> in the Prefatory
> Note to Article 5.

> The ICC, like the
> ALI and NCCUSL,
> has no law-making
> authority of its own.

In addition to the UCP, there are three other international resources to be considered – the ICC's Uniform Rules for Demand Guarantees (URDG) and International Standby Practices ISP 98 (ISP 98) – and the UNCITRAL Convention on Independent Guarantees and Stand-By Letters of Credit. The Convention entered into force on January 1, 2000. The United States signed the Convention on December 11, 1997, but has not ratified it. The following excerpt from David Barru, *How to Guarantee Contractor Performance on International Construction Projects: Comparing Surety Bonds with Bank Guarantees and Standby Letters of Credit*, 37 Geo. Wash. Intl. L. Rev. 51 (2005), describes the UCP, URDG, ISP 98, and UNCITRAL Convention in general terms:

> The Convention can
> be found online at
> www.uncitral.org/
> pdf/english/texts/
> payments/
> guarantees/
> guarantees.pdf

> There are currently three major sets of rules governing credit transactions, all of which have been adopted by the International Chamber of Commerce: (1) Uniform Customs and Practice for Documentary Credits; (2) Uniform Rules for Demand Guarantees; and (3) International Standby Practices ISP98. The ICC adopted three separate sets of rules to govern three distinct situations: the UCP 500 to govern commercial letters of credit; the URDG to

govern independent demand guarantees; and the ISP 98 to govern standby letters of credit. In practice, however, the UCP 500 enjoys widespread use, while the other two sets of rules are infrequently used. In addition to these three sets of rules, there is also the United Nations Commission on International Trade Law Convention on Independent Guarantees and Standby Letters of Credit. The Convention is a treaty and has the force of law for those countries that adopt it.

These ICC rules purport to codify existing international banking practice, and they become part of an individual letter of credit or bank guarantee only if the instrument incorporates the specific set of rules by reference. Rules of practice incorporated into the credit are considered to be explicit terms of the credit. If the credit is silent on the issue and does not expressly incorporate any rules of practice, the laws of the applicable local jurisdiction will govern. This is normally the law of the jurisdiction in which the credit was issued. Even when rules of practice are expressly incorporated into the credit, they may not preempt local law in its entirety.

The ICC rules of practice address many issues that are fundamental to credit transactions, such as the amount of time the bank has to honor a demand, treatment of non-documentary conditions, standards for examination of documentation, and liability of the bank. Accordingly, when a letter of credit or bank guarantee incorporates rules of practice by reference, the credit instrument need only recite the most basic terms, such as the names of the parties, the amount of the credit, the date of expiry, and the specific conditions for presentment and honor. The rules of practice fill in the gaps in the instruments.

The UCP 500 is by far the most common and widely used of these sets of rules, and is routinely utilized in both domestic and international letter of credit and bank guarantee transactions. It is intended to deal with documentary credits used in the sale-of-goods context, but specifically includes standby letters of credit within its scope. One common criticism of the UCP 500 is that it has a number of provisions that are simply inapplicable to standby letters of credit and bank guarantees. It is, nevertheless, commonly incorporated into these instruments. . . . In jurisdictions that do not have well-developed law to address bank guarantees or standby credits, a court may look to the UCP 500 to resolve a credit dispute, even though it has not been specifically incorporated into the instrument at issue.

The URDG is intended to apply to independent guarantees, but standby letters of credit are also included within its scope. In practice, very few demand guarantees have been issued subject to the URDG.

The ISP 98 is the latest set of rules adopted by the ICC. It specifically addresses international standby letters of credit; however, it is not limited by its terms to international usage. . . . It is intended to govern standby letters of credit, but is broad enough that it may also be incorporated into any independent

As the text below indicates, parties often choose to apply the UCP to standby letters of credit, rather than the ISP 98 drafted for that purpose. For purposes of this text, an "independent demand guarantee" covered by the URDG can be considered the functional equivalent of a standby letter of credit; in fact, as a later portion of this excerpt indicates, the UNCITRAL Convention includes both within the single term, "undertaking."

A revision to be called UCP 600 is underway, but the promulgation date remains uncertain.

undertaking, including demand guarantees. The ISP 98 has been subject to some stinging academic criticism.

The UNCITRAL Convention was adopted by the U.N. General Assembly in 1995. . . .   It applies only to international undertakings, which pursuant to Article 2 of the Convention are "known in international practice as an independent guarantee or as a standby letter of credit." An American Bar Association working group stated that "[t]he Convention would bridge the difference between standby letters of credit—like those typically issued by United States banks—and international bank guaranties issued by banks in certain foreign countries." Unlike the ICC rules of practice, which apply only if the credit instrument specifically incorporates them by reference, the Convention, if adopted by the United States, would become federal law that automatically applies to all international undertakings issued in the United States. The parties to a credit, however, may opt out of the Convention. When the parties do not opt out and the Convention applies, it contemplates that the credit may be supplemented with rules of custom and practice, such as the UCP 500, URDG, and ISP 98. *Id.* at 62-72.

- How will you determine which body of rules – the UCP 500, URDG, ISP 98, Article 5, or the UNCITRAL Convention – governs a given letter-of-credit transaction?

B. Letters of Credit

As the Prefatory Note to Article 5 indicates, unlike many other bodies of law codified in the UCC, there was no pre-existing uniform law governing letters of credit; instead, prior to the UCC, this area was governed by common law. As the commentary to 5-101 states, Article 5 thus adopted a more limited scope than might otherwise have been chosen.

Read 5-101 Official Comment. This Comment describes the history behind Article 5 and provides context for this material.

- How is a letter of credit an "idiosyncratic form of undertaking"?

- What other rules, in addition to the UCC and the resources mentioned in the international materials above, may govern a letter-of-credit transaction?

> As Chapters 13 through 17 show, this power is lessened somewhat in Article 9.

Read 5-103 (c) and Comment 2.   1-302 allows parties significant freedom to fashion their commercial transactions in ways that depart from many of the "default rules" contained in the Code.

- Can parties vary Article 5's rules by agreement?

- Can parties agree to remove a letter-of-credit transaction entirely from the purview of Article 5?

The Doctrine of Strict Compliance

Read 5-108 (a) and Comment 1. This subsection sets forth the "strict compliance" test that an issuer (or confirmer) must follow in determining whether to make payment pursuant to a letter of credit upon the beneficiary's presentation of documents. Comment 1 provides guidance as to how the test is to be interpreted and applied.

- After reading Comment 1, what is the difference between "strict compliance," "substantial compliance," and "slavish conformity to the terms of the letter of credit"?

- **Read 5-108 Comment 7.** To whom does the obligation to honor a conforming presentation run and how can this concept be compared and contrasted with the notion of wrongful dishonor under Articles 3 and 4?

> Review 4-402 and the materials contained in Chapter 10, Part B as needed to answer this question.

- **Read 5-108 (e),** which describes the practices issuers and confirmers must follow. What resources can an attorney use in identifying standard practices of the kind referenced in 5-108 (e)?

> 5-108 Comment 8 may assist you in answering this question.

- **Read 5-108 (g) and Comment 9.** How can Article 5's treatment of "nondocumentary conditions" be compared and contrasted with Article 3's notion of a negotiable instrument as a "courier without baggage"?

> Review the materials contained in Chapter 7, Part A as needed to answer this question.

The following case describes those kinds of nonconformities that will – and will not – justify dishonor according to the UCP. The case also demonstrates the requirement, found in both the UCC and the UCP, that an issuer or confirmer provide proper notice of any nonconformity in the documents presented.

Voest-Alpine Trading USA Corp. v. Bank of China,
167 F. Supp. 2d 940, 46 U.C.C. Rep. Serv. 2d 808
(S.D. Tex. 2000).

Gilmore, District Judge.

On June 23, 1995, Plaintiff Voest-Alpine Trading USA Corporation entered into a contract with Jiangyin Foreign Trade Corporation to sell JFTC 1,000 metric tons of styrene monomer at a total price of $1.2 million. To finance the transaction, JFTC applied for a letter of credit through Defendant Bank of China. The letter of credit provided for payment to Voest-Alpine once the goods had been shipped to Zhangjiagang, China and Voest-Alpine had presented the requisite paperwork to the Bank of China as described in the letter of credit. The letter of credit was issued by the Bank of China on July 6, 1995, and assigned the number LC9521033/95. In addition to numerous other typographical errors, Voest-Alpine's name was listed as "Voest-Alpine USA Trading Corp." instead of "Voest-Alpine Trading USA Corp" with the "Trading USA" portion inverted. The destination port was also misspelled in one place as "Zhangjiagng," missing the third "a." The letter of credit did indicate, however, that the transaction would be subject to the 1993 Uniform Customs and Practice, International Chamber of Commerce Publication Number 500.

> **How, if at all, does the decline in market price influence the parties' subsequent behavior?**

By the time the product was ready to ship, the market price of styrene monomer had dropped significantly from the original contract price between Voest-Alpine and JFTC. Although JFTC asked for a price concession in light of the decrease in market price, Voest-Alpine declined and, through its agents, shipped the styrene monomer on July 18, 1995. All required inspection and documentation was completed. On August 1, 1995, Voest-Alpine presented the documents specified in the letter of credit to Texas Commerce Bank, the presenting bank. Texas Commerce Bank found discrepancies between the presentation documents and the letter of credit, which it related to Voest-Alpine. Because Voest-Alpine did not believe that any of the noted discrepancies would warrant refusal to pay, it instructed Texas Commerce Bank to forward the presentation documents to the Bank of China.

> **Make sure you can identify the applicant, issuer, beneficiary, and confirmer in this transaction.**

Texas Commerce Bank sent the documents via DHL courier to the Bank of China on August 3, 1995. According to the letter of credit, Voest-Alpine, the beneficiary, was required to present the documents within fifteen days of the shipping date, by August 2, 1995. As the documents were presented on August 1, 1995, they were presented timely under the letter of credit. Bank of China received the documents on August 9, 1995.

On August 11, 1995, the Bank of China sent a telex to Texas Commerce Bank, informing them of seven alleged discrepancies between the letter of credit and the documents Voest-Alpine presented, six of which are the subject of this action. The Bank of China claimed that 1) the beneficiary's name differed from the name listed in the letter of credit, as noted by the presenting bank; 2) Voest-Alpine had submitted bills of lading marked "duplicate" and "triplicate" instead of "original"; 3) the invoice, packing list and the certificate of origin were not marked "original"; 4) the date of the survey report was later than that of the bill of lading; 5) the letter-of-credit number in the beneficiary's certified copy of the fax was incorrect, as noted by the presenting bank; and 6) the destination was not listed correctly in the certificate of origin and the beneficiary's certificate, as noted by the presenting bank. The telex further stated, "We are contacting the applicant of the relative discrepancy [sic]. Holding documents at your risks and disposal."

On August 15, Texas Commerce Bank faxed the Bank of China, stating that the discrepancies were not an adequate basis to refuse to pay the letter of credit and requested that the bank honor the letter of credit and pay Voest-Alpine accordingly. The telex identified Voest-Alpine as the beneficiary in the transaction. Voest-Alpine also contacted JFTC directly in an effort to secure a waiver of the discrepancies but was unsuccessful.

On August 19, 1995, the Bank of China sent another telex to Texas Commerce Bank further explaining what it believed to be discrepancies between the letter of credit and the documentation presented by Voest-Alpine according to the UCP 500. In relevant part, the telex provided:

> You cannot say [the discrepancies] are of no consequence. The fact is that our bank must examine all documents stipulated in the credit with reasonable care, to ascertain whether or not they appear, on their face, to be incompliance [sic] with the terms and conditions of the credit. According to Article 13 of UCP 500. An irrevocable credit constitutes a definite undertaking of the issuing bank, providing that the stipulated documents are complied with the terms and conditions of the credit according to Article UCP 500. Now the discrepant documents may have us refuse to take up the documents according to article 14(B) of UCP 500.

The Bank of China returned the documents to Voest-Alpine and did not honor the letter of credit.

* * *

. . . The current statutory law requires an issuer to honor a presentation that, as determined by standard practice of financial institutions that regularly issue letters of credit, "appears on its face strictly to comply with the terms and conditions of the letter of credit." Determination of what constitutes standard practice of financial institutions is a "matter of interpretation for the court."

> The quoted language is found in UCC 5-108 (a).

> The quoted language is found in UCC 5-108 (e).

* * *

In this case, the parties expressly adopted the UCP 500 as the governing authority in the letter of credit. Where parties explicitly refer to the UCP 500 in their contracts, the UCP has been interpreted to apply to the transaction. Accordingly, the Court will look to the UCP for guidance in analyzing whether the actions of the Bank of China were in conformity with "standard practice" of financial institutions.

The Bank of China claims that its August 11, 1995, telex to Texas Commerce Bank constituted notice of refusal under the UCP 500 because it contained the required elements listed in Article 14 (d). Voest-Alpine argues that the telex did not constitute notice of refusal because there is no clear statement of refusal and because the portion of the telex that indicated that the Bank of China was contacting JFTC to seek a waiver rendered the communication ambiguous.

> The Article 5 equivalent to this provision is 5-108 (b).

Article 14 (d) of the UCP 500 provides:

> i. If the Issuing Bank . . . decides to refuse the [presentation] documents, it must give notice to that effect by telecommunication or, if that is not possible, by other expeditious means, without delay but no later than the close of the seventh banking day following the day of receipt of the documents. Such notice shall be given to the bank from which it received the documents, or to the Beneficiary, if it received the documents directly from him.

> ii. Such notice must state all discrepancies in respect of which the bank refuses the documents and must also state whether it is holding the documents at the disposal of, or is returning them to, the presenter.

According to Article 14 (d), if the issuing bank elects not to honor the presentation documents, it must provide a notice of refusal within seven banking days of receipt of the documents and the notice must contain any and all discrepancies and state the disposition of the rejected documents. The section requires that if a bank wishes to reject a presentation of documents, it *"must give notice to that effect."* (emphasis supplied).

Here, the Bank of China's notice is deficient because nowhere does it state that it is actually rejecting the documents or refusing to honor the letter of credit or any words to that effect. While it is true that, under the UCP 500, the notice must contain a list of discrepancies and the disposition of the documents and the Bank of China's telex of August 11, 1995, does indeed contain these elements, this only addresses the requirements of Article 14 (d) (ii). A notice of refusal, by its own terms must actually convey refusal, as specified in Article 14 (d) (i). This omission is only compounded by the statement that the Bank of China would contact the applicant to determine if it would waive the discrepancies. . . . [T]his additional piece of information holds open the possibility of acceptance upon waiver of the discrepancies by JFTC and indicates that the Bank of China has not refused the documents.

In the August 19, 1995, telex, the Bank of China stated, *"Now the discrepant documents may have us refuse to take up the documents according to article 14 (B) of UCP 500"* (emphasis supplied). This is the bank's first mention of refusal, and it is tentative at best. The use of "now" further indicates that the documents were not previously refused in the August 11, 1995, telex. Even if this second telex was sent as a notice of refusal, it came too late. The Court finds that the evidence establishes that the telex was sent on August 19, 1995. Seven banking days, the refusal period allotted by the UCP 500 Article 14 (d), would have expired on August 18, 1995.

Accordingly, the Court finds that the Bank of China did not provide a notice of refusal within seven banking days of receipt of the presentation documents as required by Article 14 (d) of the UCP 500. The Bank of China's failure to formally refuse the documents before the deadline precludes the bank from claiming that the documents are not in compliance with the terms and conditions of the credit, according to Article 14 (e) of the UCP 500. Although the Court could properly conclude its analysis here, the Court will analyze the discrepancies listed by the Bank of China in the August 11, 1995, telex.

> How does the result in this portion of the court's holding comport with the notion of holding a drawee bank liable for a draft it has failed to dishonor and return in a timely fashion, as addressed in 4-215, 4-302, and Chapter 10, Part A?

Voest-Alpine claims that the six remaining discrepancies cited by the Bank of China are mere technicalities and typographical errors that do not warrant the rejection of the documents. Voest-Alpine argues for a "functional standard" of compliance, contending that if the whole of the documents obviously relate to the transaction covered by the credit, the issuing bank must honor the letter of credit. The Bank of China argues that the discrepancies were significant and that if the documents contain discrepancies on their face, it is justified in rejecting them and is not required to look beyond the papers themselves.

Section 13 (a) of the UCP 500 provides:

> Banks must examine all documents stipulated in the Credit with reasonable care, to ascertain whether or not they appear, on their face, to be in compliance with the terms and conditions of the Credit. Compliance of the stipulated documents on their face with the terms and conditions of the Credit shall be determined by international standard banking practice as reflected in these Articles. Documents which appear on their face to be inconsistent with one another will be considered as not appearing on their face to be in compliance with the terms and conditions of the Credit.

The UCP 500 does not provide guidance on what inconsistencies would justify a conclusion on the part of a bank that the documents are not in compliance with the terms and conditions of the letter of credit or what discrepancies are not a reasonable basis for such a conclusion. The UCP 500 does not mandate that the documents be a mirror image of the requirements or use the term "strict compliance."

The Court notes the wide range of interpretations on what standard banks should employ in examining letter-of-credit document presentations for compliance. Even where courts claim to uphold strict compliance, the standard is hardly uniform. The first and most restrictive approach is to require that the presentation documents be a mirror image of the requirements.

Second, there are also cases claiming to follow the strict-compliance standard but support rejection only where the discrepancies are such that would create risks for the issuer if the bank were to accept the presentation documents. A third standard, without much support in case law, is to analyze the documents for risk to the applicant.

The mirror-image approach is problematic because it absolves the bank reviewing the documents of any responsibility to use common sense to determine if the documents, on their face, are related to the transaction or even to review an entire document in the context of the others presented to the bank. On the other hand, the second and third approaches employ a determination-of-harm standard that is too unwieldy. Such an analysis would improperly require the bank to evaluate risks that it might suffer or that might be suffered by the applicant and could undermine the independence of the three contracts that underlie the letter-of-credit payment scheme by forcing the bank to look beyond the face of the presentation documents.

The Court finds that a moderate, more appropriate standard lies within the UCP 500 itself and the opinions issued by the International Chamber of Commerce Banking Commission. One of the Banking Commission opinions defined the term "consistency" between the letter of credit and the documents presented to the issuing bank as used in Article 13 (a) of the UCP to mean that "the whole of the documents must obviously relate to the same transaction, that is to say, that each should bear a relation (link) with the others on its face . . . ." The Banking Commission rejected the notion that "all of the documents should be *exactly* consistent in their wording."

A common sense, case-by-case approach would permit minor deviations of a typographical nature because such a letter-for-letter correspondence between the letter of credit and the presentation documents is virtually impossible. While the end result of such an analysis may bear a strong resemblance to the relaxed strict-compliance standard, the actual calculus used by the issuing bank is not the risk it or the applicant faces, but rather, whether the documents bear a rational link to one another. In this way, the issuing bank is required to examine a particular document in light of all documents presented and use common sense but is not required to evaluate risks or go beyond the face of the documents. The Court finds that, in this case, the Bank of China's listed discrepancies should be analyzed under this standard by determining whether the whole of the documents obviously relate to the transaction on their face.

First, the Bank of China claimed that the beneficiary's name in the presentation documents, Voest-Alpine *Trading USA,* differed from the letter of credit, which listed the beneficiary as Voest-Alpine *USA Trading.* While it is true that the letter of credit inverted Voest-Alpine's geographic locator, all the documents Voest-Alpine presented that obviously related to this transaction placed the geographic locator behind "Trading," not in front of it. Furthermore, the addresses corresponded to that listed in the letter of credit and Texas Commerce Bank's cover letter to the Bank of China identified Voest-Alpine Trading USA as the beneficiary in the transaction with JFTC. The letter of credit with the inverted name bore obvious links to the documents presented by Voest-Alpine Trading USA. This is in contrast to a misspelling or outright omission. In contrast with these cases, the inversion of the geographic locator here does not signify a different corporate entity. . . .

Second, the Bank of China pointed out that the set of originals of the bill of lading should have all been stamped "original" rather than "original," "duplicate," and "triplicate." It should be noted that neither the letter of credit nor any provision in the UCP 500 requires such stamping. [Moreover, it] is clear from the face of the documents that

> The Banking Commission opinions, which are published by the ICC and often relied upon by courts, are considered the ICC's official analysis of the UCP.

these documents are three originals rather than one original and two copies. The documents have signatures in blue ink, vary slightly, bear original stamps oriented differently on each page, and clearly state on their face that the preparer made three original bills. Further, one possible definition of duplicate is "[t]o make or execute again" and one definition of triplicate is "[o]ne of a set of three identical things." *Webster's II New Riverside University Dictionary* 410, 1237 (1994). While the "duplicate" and "triplicate" stamps may have been confusing, stamps do not make obviously original documents into copies.

> In your own words, what point is being made here?

Third, the Bank of China claimed that the failure to stamp the packing list documents as "original" was a discrepancy. Again, these documents are clearly originals on their face, as they have three slightly differing signatures in blue ink. There was no requirement in the letter of credit or the UCP 500 that original documents be marked as such. . . . The failure to mark obvious originals is not a discrepancy.

Fourth, the Bank of China argues that the date of the survey report is after the bill of lading and is therefore discrepant. A careful examination of the survey report reveals that the survey took place "immediately before/after loading" and that the sample of cargo "to be loaded" was taken. The plain language of the report reveals that the report may have been issued after the bill of lading but the survey itself was conducted before the ship departed. The date does not pose a discrepancy.

Fifth, the Bank of China claims that the letter-of-credit number listed in the beneficiary's certified copy of fax is wrong. The letter-of-credit number was listed as "LC95231033/95" on the copy of fax instead of "LC9521033/95" as in the letter of credit itself, adding an extra "3" after "LC952." However, adding the letter-of-credit number to this document was gratuitous and, in the numerous other places in the documents that the letter of credit was referenced by number, it was incorrect only in one place. Moreover, the seven other pieces of information contained in the document were correct. The document checker could have easily looked to any other document to verify the letter-of-credit number, or looked to the balance of the information within the document and found that the document as a whole bears an obvious relationship to the transaction. Madame Gao, the document checker who reviewed Voest-Alpine's presentation documents for the Bank of China, testified that she did not look beyond the face of this particular document in assessing the discrepancy. The cover letter from Texas Commerce Bank, for example, had the correct number.

Finally, the Bank of China claims that the wrong destination is listed in the certificate of origin and the beneficiary's certificate. The certificate of origin spelled Zhangjiagang as "Zhangjiagng" missing an "a" as it is misspelled once in the letter of credit, making it consistent. The beneficiary's certificate, however, spelled it "Zhanjiagng," missing a "g" in addition to the "a", a third spelling that did not appear in the letter of credit. Madame Gao first considered the discrepancy a "misspelling" rather than an indication of the wrong port, according to her notes. There is no port in China called "Zhangjiagng" or "Zhanjiagng." "Gng" is a combination of letters not found in Romanized Chinese, whereas "gang" means "port" in Chinese. The other

information contained in the document was correct, such as the letter
of credit number and the contract number, and even contained the
distinctive phrase "by courie lukdt within 3 days after shipment,"
presumably meaning by courier within three days after shipment, as in
the letter of credit. The document as a whole bears an obvious
relationship with the transaction. The misspelling of the destination is
not a basis for dishonor of the letter of credit where the rest of the
document has demonstrated linkage to the transaction on its face.

Based on the foregoing, the Court finds in favor of the plaintiff, Voest-
Alpine.

- What standard does the court apply, and does this
  standard differ from the "strict compliance" mandated
  by 5-108 (a)?

- How should the Bank of China's communications with
  Texas Commerce Bank have been changed to satisfy
  the requirement that the bank provide notice of its
  intended dishonor?

Note: Numerous cases have explored the concept of strict
compliance under the UCC. In *Middlesex Bank & Trust Co. v.
Mark Equipment Corp.*, 19 Mass. L. Rep. 122, 56 U.C.C. Rep.
Serv. 2d 443 (Mass. Super. 2005), the court found a bank acted
properly in honoring a draft made pursuant to a letter of credit,
even though the beneficiary's presentation erroneously
referenced the issuance date of a previous, expired letter of
credit that had been issued to it, rather than the issuance date
of the then-current letter of credit pursuant to which it was
seeking payment. Because the issuance date was not a
required component of the beneficiary's presentation, the court
found no reason for the bank to dishonor the presentation. In
so holding, the court stated, "[t]he strict compliance rule . . . is
not absolute, as a bank may not reject a demand for payment
on the basis of a hypertechnical reading of a letter of credit.
Rather, a variance between documents specified and
documents submitted is not fatal if there is no possibility that
the documents could mislead the paying bank to its detriment."

By contrast, as the court found in *Courtaulds N.A., Inc. v.
North Carolina National Bank*, 528 F.2d 802, 18 U.C.C. Rep.
Serv. 467 (4th Cir. 1975), where a letter of credit required that
"the draft be accompanied by a 'commercial invoice in triplicate
stating (inter alia) that it covers 100% acrylic yarn,'"
presentation of an invoice indicating the goods consisted of
"imported acrylic yarn" did not satisfy the "strict compliance"
test. The court noted that the issuer had contacted the
applicant to inquire whether it would waive the discrepancies,
and the applicant indicated it was not in a position to do so.
The court explained its holding as follows, showing how the

"independence principle" and "strict compliance" test work together:

> [T]he drawee bank is not to be embroiled in disputes between the buyer and the seller, the beneficiary of the credit. The drawee is involved only with documents, not with merchandise. Its involvement is altogether separate and apart from the transaction between the buyer and seller; its duties and liability are governed exclusively by the terms of the letter, not the terms of the parties' contract with one another. Moreover, as the predominant authorities unequivocally declare, the beneficiary must meet the terms of the credit – and precisely – if it is to exact performance of the issuer. Failing such compliance, there can be no recovery from the drawee. *Id.* at 806.

> The "drawee" referenced here is the issuer.

The court also rejected the beneficiary's argument that the issuer should have looked beyond the language of the invoices and should have noticed that the attached packing slips used the correct terminology: "100% acrylic yarn." In approving the correctness of the issuer's conduct, the court held as follows:

> This is not a pharisaical or doctrinaire persistence in the principle, but is altogether realistic in the environs of this case; it is plainly the fair and equitable measure. (The defect in description was not superficial, but occurred in the statement of the quality of the yarn, not a frivolous concern.) The obligation of the drawee bank was graven in the credit. Indeed, there could be no departure from its words. [The issuer] was not expected to scrutinize the collateral papers, such as the packing lists. Nor was it permitted to read into the instrument the contemplation or intention of the seller and buyer. *Id.*

- What concerns must an issuer balance in determining whether to make payment when the documents exhibit discrepancies?

- What distinction, if any, do you find between the UCC and UCP compliance standards?

Problem: After reading the Note above and the *Voest-Alpine* case, what is the probable outcome in each of the following cases?

1. A standby letter of credit was given to ensure performance of a construction project according to a contract the applicant had made with the beneficiary, a county in Florida. The letter of credit required presentation of a certificate by the County's Public Works Director declaring the applicant to be in default under the contract, as a precondition to payment. In seeking payment pursuant to the letter of credit, the County presented two documents: (1) an internal

office memorandum from the Director requesting that
another county official seek payment pursuant to the
letter of credit because the applicant-contractor had
defaulted, and (2) a certificate by the Director's
subordinate declaring the applicant to be in default.

Based on *Fidelity National Bank v. Dade County*, 371 So. 2d
545 (1979).

> This case includes some colorful language that may help you to remember the strict-compliance test: "Compliance with the terms of a letter of credit is not like pitching horseshoes. No points are awarded for being close."

2. A commercial letter of credit was issued at the request
   of an applicant named Mohammed Sofan, a resident of
   the Yemen Arab Republic, to facilitate his purchase of
   two prefabricated houses from a seller in the U.S.,
   Dessaleng Beyene. The letter of credit required the
   beneficiary, Beyene, to submit, among other
   documents, a bill of lading to provide Mr. Sofan with
   assurance that he would receive the houses. The bill of
   lading Beyene presented identified the purchaser as
   "Mr. Mohammed Soran" and indicated that Mr.
   "Soran" was to be notified upon the goods' arrival in
   Yemen.

Based on *Beyene v. Irving Trust Co.*, 762 F.2d 4, 40 U.C.C. Rep.
Serv. 1811 (7th Cir. 1985).

3. Change the applicant's name in #2 to "Mohammed
   Smith" and assume the bill of lading bears the name
   "Mohammed Smithh."

Based on dicta to *Beyene v. Irving Trust Co.*, 762 F.2d 4, 40
U.C.C. Rep. Serv. 1811 (7th Cir. 1985).

The Independence Principle

Read 5-103 (d) and Comment 1, and 5-108 (f) (1).
Together, these provisions set forth the "independence
principle" that describes an issuer's relationship (or, more
precisely, lack thereof) to the transaction motivating the
issuance of the letter of credit.

> For a more thorough analysis of the issue of fraud, you might read Professor Stephen Laycock's article *Fraud in the International Transaction: Enjoining Payment of Letters of Credit in International Transactions*, 17 Vand. J. Transnat'l L. 885 (1984).

- In your own words, what is the independence principle
  and how is it essential to letter-of-credit law?

The following case explains the independence principle and its
importance to the efficacy of letter-of-credit transactions. The
case also sets forth a limited exception for certain kinds of fraud
that may vitiate an issuer or confirmer's payment obligations.

Mennen v. J.P. Morgan & Co., Inc.,
91 N.Y.2d 13, 689 N.E.2d 869, 666 N.Y.S.2d 975,
34 U.C.C. Rep. Serv. 2d 162 (1997).

Bellacosa, J.

This case arises from a 1991 stock buy-out of Mennen Medical, Inc., in which plaintiffs were major shareholders. Plaintiffs sold their shares to a group of investors, including an entity named Odyssey Partners, L.P. To finance the transaction, Mennen executed and delivered a five-year promissory note to each plaintiff. The notes were identical except for the names of the shareholders and the amount of the note. Each note called for five equal annual payments of principal commencing September 1991, with monthly interest payments the first year, followed by annual interest payments on subsequent anniversary dates. The notes also contained an acceleration clause to cover defaults.

To secure the notes for payment to bought-out shareholders, Mennen obtained standby irrevocable letters of credit from defendant Morgan Guaranty Trust Company. Each letter of credit is identical in form, except for the named beneficiary and face amounts. The letters of credit provide for payment within 10 days after presentation of a draft accompanied by a notarized statement that the draw represents an unpaid note installment or that the outstanding balance is due as a consequence of default. The letters of credit also include a standard merger clause to the effect that they reflect the full contractual undertaking and that "such undertaking shall not in any way be modified, amplified or amended by reference to any document, instrument, agreement or note referred to herein and any such reference shall not be deemed to be incorporated herein by reference to any such document, instrument, agreement or note." The letters of credit also expressly provide that they are subject to the Uniform Customs and Practice for Documentary Credits.

> As 2-202 and Chapter 2, Part B indicate, merger clauses can affect the admission of parol evidence.

Mennen Medical, the obligor, timely paid the first two installments due under the promissory notes. Eventually, Odyssey took financial control of the group of investors who had purchased the Mennen stock. Prior to the third due payment, Odyssey defaulted on its obligations, and plaintiffs accelerated the notes and drew upon the maximum payment provided under the letters of credit.

> As 1-309 indicates and Chapter 5, Part A discusses, the right of acceleration is subject to a good-faith limitation, even when the contract purports to allow acceleration at will.

Morgan promptly paid the respective draws to the beneficiaries of the letters of credit. Several months later, however, Morgan concluded that the amounts it had paid exceeded the amounts due under the promissory notes themselves. Morgan demanded reimbursement from plaintiffs for the alleged overpayments, totaling approximately $230,000. Morgan alleged misstatements of the amounts declared to have been owing in the notarized draw statements. The beneficiaries retorted that the "overpayments" represented a premium above the face amounts of the notes, orally negotiated at the time of the purchase. They added that the premiums were designed to compensate them for increased tax liabilities upon acceleration and for the loss of future interest.

A defeasance agreement thus eliminates the applicant's obligation of reimbursement as found in 5-108 (i) (1).

Notably, Morgan had contractually relinquished the right to seek reimbursement from its customer Odyssey through a defeasance agreement between those two parties. Under the defeasance device, Morgan, in exchange for an up-front, lump-sum payment, released Odyssey from any subsequent obligation to reimburse Morgan for any amounts Morgan paid to the beneficiaries pursuant to the letters of credit.

The beneficiaries preemptively sued for a declaration that their draws under the letters of credit were correct in amount and that Morgan enjoyed no separate rights over against them. Morgan counterclaimed for alleged overpayments under theories of money had and received, breach of contract, payment by mistake, unjust enrichment, negligent misrepresentation, and fraud. It moved for summary judgment, and plaintiffs cross-moved for similar relief and for dismissal of the counterclaims.

[The Supreme Court and Appellate Division held against Morgan.]

In your own words, what fraudulent acts does Morgan allege on the part of the beneficiaries and what is their response?

On this appeal, appellant Morgan argues that it should be entitled to recover overpayments made to plaintiffs . . . , notwithstanding that plaintiffs' allegedly false documentation facially complied with the terms of the instrument. Morgan contends that it did not learn until after making payments that the documents fraudulently (as it perceives and alleges the circumstance) specified the amounts owing and, as such, it should be permitted to assert a claim against the payee-beneficiaries subsequent to satisfaction pursuant to the letters of credit.

* * *

Letters of credit typically involve three separate contractual relationships and undertakings: the underlying contract between the customer and the beneficiary; the agreement between the bank and its customer, by which the letter of credit is issued in exchange for the customer's promise to reimburse the bank; and, the letter of credit itself, which represents the financial institution's commitment to honor drafts presented by the intended beneficiary upon compliance with the terms and conditions specified in the instrument.

"[A] fundamental principle governing these transactions is the doctrine of independent contracts," which "provides that the issuing bank's obligation to honor drafts drawn on a letter of credit by the beneficiary is separate and independent from any obligation of its customer to the beneficiary under the . . . contract and separate as well from any obligation of the issuer to its customer under their agreement." *First Commercial Bank v Gotham Originals, supra,* 64 NY2d 287, 289 (1985). "Stated another way, this principle stands for 'the fundamental proposition . . . that all parties [to a letter of credit transaction] *deal in documents rather than with the facts the documents purport to reflect.*'" *Id.* at 294 (emphasis added). Therefore, "the issuer's obligation to pay is fixed upon presentation of the drafts and the documents specified in the letter of credit. It is not required to resolve disputes or questions of fact concerning the underlying transaction." *Id.* at 295.

1
2
3
4
5
6
7
8
9
10
11
12
13
14
15
16
17
18
19
20
21
22
23
24
25
26
27
28
29
30
31
32
33
34
35
36
37
38
39
40
41
42
43
44
45
46
50
51
52
53

The twist presented by this case requires the Court to determine first whether an issuer has violated this principle when it promptly pays a draw and only subsequently challenges the validity of the documentation on fraud grounds. A leading authority on the letters-of-credit-type negotiable instruments has stated that, "[i]n the event the documents comply on their face with the terms of the credit, the issuer should have a cause of action against the beneficiary if the issuer honors the conforming demand and then learns that, for some reason, the documents do not comply." Dolan, *Letters of Credit: Commercial and Standby Credits* ¶ 9.04, at 9-48 [2d ed]. Therefore, the issuer's initial, timely payment sufficiently satisfies the independence principle and, "[a]fter payment . . . the independence principle should not bar the issuer's claim against a beneficiary." *Id.* at 9-48.

This is so because the independence doctrine realistically reflects "[t]he exigencies of credit law," which necessitate that the issuer honor presentations that comply on their face without looking beneath the documents Dolan, *op. cit.,* at 9-48. . . . The underlying purpose of the rule, however, should not "permit a beneficiary to say, after payment, that [its] false, fraudulent, or inaccurate documents satisfied the conditions of the credit." Dolan, *Letters of Credit: Commercial and Standby Credits* ¶ 9.04, at 9-48 [2d ed].

The above precedents and authorities persuade us that Morgan, by timely paying the letters of credit upon presentation, did not violate the independence principle. The underlying purpose of the doctrine to insure that promptness of payment was and is fulfilled by requiring the issuer to pay up front, even though it would also recognize the issuer subsequently pursuing recovery against a beneficiary based on alleged fraud.

We, thus, conclude that the Appellate Division's holding that the independence principle was violated by Morgan in the instant case is not well founded. . . .

[The portion of the court's opinion relating to the application of UCP principles and ultimately affirming the lower court's holding against Morgan on grounds not relevant to this textbook's coverage has been omitted, as has Justice Titone's dissent.]

- Following this case, what kind of fraud will vitiate an issuer or confirmer's obligation to pay pursuant to a letter of credit?

- Why did the bank's conduct not violate the independence principle?

International Perspective: Letters of Credit

The following excerpt from *Doing Business in Mexico*, in *Mexican Law of Secured Transactions* (Philip von Mehren ed.,

Transnational Publications 2000), by Professor Dale Beck
Furnish shows how a letter of credit may provide a valuable
alternative when secured credit is prohibitively expensive or
unavailable. This excerpt follows an introduction in which
Professor Furnish describes the difficulties created by the fact
that "Mexico has not yet harmonized its law of secured
transactions with that of the United States and Canada."
Instead, as the author indicates, "Mexico . . . remain[s] tethered
to a system of secured transactions that dates back to Roman
law, when real property was the major source of wealth and the
virtually exclusive form of collateral for loans."

> Suppose that a U.S. or Canadian seller of heavy mining
> machinery wishes to sell millions of dollars of mining machinery to
> a mine in Mexico, on credit terms providing three years to
> complete payment. One could secure the debt by taking a
> collateral interest in the equipment itself, by one or more of several
> methods . . . , and should do so. Greater security, however, could
> be attained by using a standby letter of credit for the amount of
> the sale and any accruing interest, to the benefit of the seller-
> exporter. *Id.* at 1-7.

As Professor Furnish notes, a standby-letter-of-credit
arrangement will allow the creditor to demand immediate
payment pursuant to the terms of the letter of credit, simply by
producing conforming documents upon an event of default.
Doing so gives the creditor cash collateral to be applied to the
debt, which can be simpler than proceeding against collateral
as a secured party. To accomplish such a result, the buyer
should arrange for a standby letter of credit to be issued in the
contract amount with the seller as beneficiary. The letter of
credit should require the beneficiary to produce certification of
default, together with documentation proving the equipment
was shipped and received.

Furnish acknowledges that an arrangement like this one
requires a long-term commitment by the issuer and substantial
monitoring of the buyer, but suggests the parties may be able
to agree to an "evergreen" arrangement by which a letter of
credit in the amount of each installment will be issued and
automatically renewed unless notification of termination is
given. Doing so will make it unnecessary for the applicant to
secure a single, large letter of credit for the full contract sum.
Alternatively, if a single, large letter of credit is issued, the total
amount of the issuer's obligation may be reduced each time the
applicant makes timely payment of an installment.

- According to Professor Furnish, what advantages are
  there of a letter-of-credit transaction over a secured
  transaction, under Mexico's current legal system?

Sidebar notes:

The Roman-law approach to secured transactions is discussed in Chapter 13, Part C's international materials.

How would the procedures described in this paragraph limit the risk, and thus presumably also the cost, of a letter-of-credit transaction?

Review the materials found in Chapter 13, Part C as needed to answer this question.

Line numbers: 1–21, 22–46, 50–53

Another example of how letters of credit have assisted in the development of law can be found in the genesis of standby letters of credit. These payment instruments were developed in the United States to serve as a substitute for performance bonds, which U.S. banks could not issue due to the legal prohibition against banks' engaging in the business of insurance. This topic is explored in Peter S. O'Driscoll, *Performance Bonds, Bankers' Guarantees, and the Mareva Injunction*, 7 Nw. J. Intl. L. & Bus. 380, 384-385 (1985).

C. Documents of Title

Read 7-101 Official Comment. This commentary describes the history of Article 7 and how it can be understood in conjunction with tort law and other state, federal, and international law that may govern a transaction involving a document of title.

- How does deletion of the criminal provisions found in earlier law addressing documents of title comport with Karl Llewellyn's intended tone and purpose of the UCC?

> Review the materials found in Chapter 1, Part 1 as needed to answer this question.

Note the structure of Article 5: Parts 1, 4, 5, 6, and 7 are applicable to all documents of title, while Parts 2 and 3 address only warehouse receipts and bills of lading, respectively.

Read 1-201 (b) (6) and Comment 6. As the name suggests and the graphic in Part A of this chapter indicates, a bill of lading is a document of title evidencing a carrier's receipt of goods for the purpose of shipment.

> "Carrier" is defined in 7-102 (a) (2).

Read 1-201 (b) (42). A warehouse receipt is a document of title issued by a person who has accepted goods for storage.

Read 1-201 (b) (16) and Comment 16, together with 7-104. Both bills of lading and warehouse receipts are "documents of title" within the meaning of 1-201 (b) (16). As 1-201 Comment 16 indicates, documents of title may be electronic or tangible. In addition, as 7-104 states, documents of title may be negotiable or non-negotiable.

- Compare the requirements for negotiability of an Article 7 document of title with the requirements for negotiability of an instrument within the meaning of Articles 3 and 4.

> 7-104 Comment 1 may assist you in answering this question. In addition, review 3-104 and the materials contained in Chapter 8 as needed to formulate your answer.

- **Read 7-104 Comment 2, and 3-104 (d).** Why is it possible to render a document of title non-negotiable by labeling it as such, while such labeling is ineffective to render a check non-negotiable?

- Does labeling a document of title "negotiable" make it so?

Read 7-102 (a) (3), (4), and (5). Much vocabulary applies to both kinds of documents of title, but there are some differences. For example, as 7-102 (a) (3) and (4) indicate, the person delivering goods to a carrier is called the consignor, and the person to whom the goods are delivered is called a consignee. The Code provides no such labels for the person delivering goods to a warehouse and the person to whom the warehouse releases the goods; instead, drawing from the definition of "delivery order" in 7-102 (a) (5), these parties are commonly called "deliveror" and "deliveree."

Read 7-102 (a) (1) and Comment 1. Because parties must be able to rely upon documents of title, Article 5 defines a bailee as a person who "acknowledges possession of goods" rather than a person who is *in possession of goods* and has agreed by contract to deliver them. Thus, if a putative bailee issues a document of title indicating receipt of goods, he or she is held to the delivery obligations required of a bailee even if he or she never actually obtained possession of those goods.

Read 7-104 Comment 1. Because documents of title represent rights to goods, while negotiable instruments and security certificates represent rights to payment and rights to securities respectively, it is easy to make comparisons between Articles 7, 3 and 4, and 8.

- What is the difference between Article 7 "commodity paper," Articles 3 and 4 "money paper," and Article 8 "investment paper"?

Read 7-102 (a) (9), 7-204, 7-309, and 7-403. Bailees are charged with a nondelegable duty of care with regard to the goods accepted for storage or for carriage; these rights are set forth in 7-204 and 7-309 for warehouses and carriers, respectively. In addition, as 7-403 indicates, bailees have an obligation to deliver goods to a "person entitled under a document of title." "Person entitled under the document" is defined in 7-102 (a) (9) as the holder of a negotiable document of title or the person designated in a non-negotiable document of title.

Read 7-501 (a). A document of title may pass through the hands of a wrongdoer and end up in the hands of an innocent party who has purchased it "in good faith, without notice or any defense or claim to it on the part of any person, and for value." If (1) the document of title is negotiable and (2) the document of title has been transferred in such a way as to constitute a negotiation rather than a simple assignment, then (3) the innocent party may claim rights as a "holder by due negotiation" that may exceed the rights of the wrongdoer who held the document at an earlier time.   A document of title payable "to bearer" is negotiated by mere transfer of possession, while a document of title payable "to the order of" a named person must be indorsed and delivered to another for negotiation to take place.

Students who have studied Articles 3 and 4 will recognize a clear analogy here to an Article 3/Article 4 "holder in due course." Students who have not studied these materials should consider skimming Chapter 7 for a basic orientation to the concepts of negotiability vs. assignment and "order paper" vs. "bearer paper."

The following case provides an overview of some important bailment concepts in an Article 7 transaction. This case also shows how carriers and warehouses can interact with one another in a transaction that may generate both bills of lading and warehouse receipts.

Soto v. Sea-Road International, Inc.,
942 S.W.2d 67, 34 U.C.C. Rep. Serv. 2d 484
(Tex. App. 13th Dist. 1997).

Rodriguez, Justice.

Luciano S. Soto, defendant below, appeals from an adverse judgment in a suit brought by Sea-Road International, Inc. Sea-Road, a transportation-service company, sued Soto for conversion resulting from a breach of implied contract for bailment. Following a bench trial, the court rendered judgment for Sea-Road and ordered that it recover $85,000 in damages with prejudgment interest and costs. . . . Soto challenges the legal and factual sufficiency of the trial court's findings of fact and conclusions of law. We affirm.

This lawsuit arises from the sale of 100,500 yards of fabric by Dae Uk Trading Co., Ltd., a South Korean company, to The Textile Corporation. Textile never received the fabric, and Dae Uk was never paid. Result: Dae Uk sued its shipping/transportation provider, Sea-Road International, forcing it to pay back 70% of the freight's value ($82,750 plus attorney's fees and interest). Sea-Road, in turn, sought restitution from Soto, the customs agent working on behalf of Textile.

The fabric was first transported from Seoul to Los Angeles pursuant to a "Combined Transport Bill of Lading" issued by Sea-Road to Dae Uk Trading. According to the bill of lading, the fabric was consigned to the order of The Textile Corporation. The fabric was accepted in Los Angeles by Sea-Road International, Inc., the "stateside" transportation-service company, which then arranged, at the oral request of Textile, to forward the fabric to Luciano Soto's warehouse in Brownsville, Texas. The fabric was transported to Soto pursuant to a "Delivery Order" indicating that the shipment of goods was from Sea-Road to Soto "C/O SEA ROAD INTL/TEXTILE CORP." The order instructed the destination warehouse (Soto) as follows: "YOU MUST CHECK WITH SEA ROAD INT'L BEFORE RELEASING ANY MERCHANDISE." Both parties acknowledge that the fabric was received and stored by Soto. The parties also agree that Soto subsequently released the fabric to a third-party trucking company without first notifying Sea-Road. After its release, the fabric disappeared.

The dispute focused on the storage and release of the fabric while in Soto's possession. K.W. Kim, Sea-Road's general manager, testified that Sea-Road had not released the cargo to Soto, but rather, had merely transferred it to Soto's warehouse for storage. This transfer was documented in the delivery order that specifically required Soto to notify Sea-Road before releasing the fabric. Kim conceded that they transferred the cargo without first receiving the bill of lading, which would have been the preferred document by which to transfer possession of the fabric, but since Textile wanted the fabric stored at Soto's warehouse, the release restrictions were put on the delivery order as a "guarantee to [them that] the cargo [would] remain at the warehouse of L.S. Soto." After the fabric had been stored with Soto for three months, Sea-Road sent Soto an inventory request to which Soto did not respond. Five months later, Sea-Road sent letters and faxes to Soto inquiring about the fabric and demanding entry into Soto's warehouse to inventory the cargo. Sea-Road later learned that Soto had released the goods to Textile but that Textile never received them.

Soto acknowledges that the goods were received by Santiago Trevino, his employee and attorney-in-fact. He also confirms that Trevino signed the delivery order executed by Sea-Road and initialed by the special instructions on the order. Nevertheless, he testified that he did not have to notify Sea-Road or get its release before surrendering the goods because the instructions merely said to "check with Sea-Road." Soto testified that after the goods arrived at his warehouse, he presented them to customs under an immediate export document and then released the goods to Armando Mireles. Soto testified that he did not know who Mireles worked for but that he could only assume that either Sea-Road or Textile instructed him to release the goods to Mireles. He conceded that he had never received any documentation by way of a power of attorney or representation letter showing that Mireles was Textile's agent, but that, with respect to "the goods," "[w]ho they went to or who they belonged to was not [his] concern."

In finding for Sea-Road, the trial court made the following findings of fact:

1. Plaintiff, Sea-Road International, Inc., delivered certain property that are the subject of this suit to the warehouse of Defendant, Luciano S. Soto, doing business as L.S. Soto Customs Broker, in Brownsville, Texas on October 14, 1988.

2. Defendant's employee signed the Delivery Order covering and pertaining to the Goods and assumed possession of the Goods. The Delivery Order signed by Defendant's employee contained the following instruction:

Why is it important that Sea-Road had not released the goods to Soto?

Note that Soto denies he has any obligations as a bailee with regard to these goods.

> TO: DESTINATION WAREHOUSE. YOU MUST CHECK
> WITH SEA ROAD INTERNATIONAL BEFORE RELEASING
> ANY MERCHANDISE 370 S. CRENSHAW BLVD. # E-205
> TORRANCE, CA 90503 SOPHIA SONG-YANG.

3. Defendant knowingly and voluntarily accepted delivery and assumed possession of the Goods subject to Plaintiff's instructions as shown on Plaintiff's Delivery Order.

4. Plaintiff Sea-Road International, Inc. delivered the Goods to Defendant's warehouse with the intention and expectation that Defendant would not release the Goods without its authorization as per instructions at the time of delivery to Defendant's warehouse.

5. After accepting the Goods, Defendant assumed possession, dominion, and control of the goods thereby creating a contract of bailment, and Defendant subsequently converted the Goods to his own use & purpose by delivering the Goods to a third party without prior notice to Plaintiff and without Plaintiff's authorization and consent.

6. Defendant has failed to return the Goods to Plaintiff upon Plaintiff's demand for return of said Goods.

7. Plaintiff did not discover and could not reasonably have discovered that Defendant had released the Goods to said third party, without its authorization, until May 11, 1989, [seven months after delivery to Defendant].

8. Defendant's actions were the proximate cause of Plaintiff's actual damages of $85,000, which is the sum of money the Plaintiff had to pay to the owner of the Goods as compensation for the loss of the Goods.

* * *

Soto contends that several factors weigh against the court's finding of a bailment contract. First, he argues that since he and Sea-Road had no communications concerning the shipment, there can be no implied contract of bailment. Citing a case out of the Washington Supreme Court, Soto argues that he never gave Sea-Road any indication that he would act on its behalf, and thus, no contract of bailment was created. Second, he argues that his duties ran only to the buyer, Textile, the named consignee on the bill of lading. Thus, as customs broker working on behalf of Textile, he had no contractual relationship or duty to Sea-Road.

The basic elements of bailment are: (1) the delivery of personal property by one person to another in trust for a specific purpose; (2) acceptance of such delivery; (3) an express or implied contract that the trust will be carried out; and (4) an understanding under the terms of the contract that the property will be returned to the transferor or dealt with as the transferor directs. Soto contests only the third element requiring the formation of a contract.

A bailment contract may arise by implication of law if, through the
proof of sufficient circumstances, the implied relationship of bailor and
bailee is shown to rest upon substantive foundation.

Here, Sea-Road presented evidence that it transferred the fabric to
Soto's warehouse for customs clearance and storage with specific
instructions concerning the cargo's release. Sea-Road also presented
evidence that Soto's agent received and signed for the delivery and
initialed by the special instructions showing an understanding of Sea-
Road's directions. Soto's argument that he is not bound because he had
no formal contact with Sea-Road is unpersuasive. Formal
communication and negotiation was not necessary. Both Sea-Road's
and Soto's experts in customs-house brokerage testified that
instructions on delivery orders are understood by the industry as
obligatory and are usually adhered to when cargo arrives at their
facilities. By signing and initialing the delivery order, Soto expressly
indicated that he could accept the goods under the conditions attached
and in that regard, that the trust or specific purpose of the agreement
would be carried out. We conclude that there was legally and factually
sufficient evidence of a bailment contract. We overrule Soto's . . . point
of error.

Conversion is any distinct act of dominion wrongfully exerted over
another person's personal property in denial of, or inconsistent with,
that other person's right in the property, either permanently or for
indefinite time. The failure to return bailment property at the end of
the bailment period constitutes, in law, a conversion of the bailment
entitling the bailor to recover its value. A plaintiff must prove that at
the time of the conversion, he or she was the owner of the property, had
legal possession of it, or was entitled to possession. Thus, conversion
can take place even when the person in possession does not have title
to property, so long as he has a right of possession.

Soto's principal arguments here concern possession—Sea-Road's right
to possession and the surrender of that possession. Soto first argues
that there was no conversion because Sea-Road was neither the owner
of the goods nor entitled to possession of the goods after it surrendered
possession of the goods to Border To Border Trucking Company for
delivery to Soto. He contends that once the seller, Dae Uk vis-a-vis Sea-
Road, delivered the goods to Border To Border, Sea-Road no longer had
a right to control possession because title passed to Textile, the named
consignee on the bill of lading.

Soto's argument, however, does not apply to international documentary
sales transactions. Under the terms of an international documentary
sales transaction involving a bill-of-lading contract, a carrier such as
Sea-Road, in return for payment of freight charges, will promise to
deliver the goods in one of two ways depending upon the type of bill of
lading: (1) directly to the named consignee when under a "straight"
(non-negotiable) bill of lading, or (2) to the person in possession of an
"order" bill of lading (i.e., the holder of a negotiable bill of lading). When
a negotiable bill of lading is used in international documentary sales
transactions (also known as letter-of-credit transactions), a buyer such
as Textile can obtain delivery of the goods only if it has physical
possession of the original bill of lading. The bill of lading is thus a

document of title because it controls access to and delivery of the goods. Dae Uk Trading is assured payment by a promise, in the form of a letter of credit, from a bank to pay Dae Uk the amount of the purchase price, and the bank's promise is conditioned upon Dae Uk presenting evidence that the goods have been shipped, via Sea-Road, to Textile's port or destination. The bill of lading is evidence that Dae Uk has shipped the goods. After the bank has paid Dae Uk and in return received the bill of lading, the bank can obtain payment from Textile. Only when Textile pays the bank does it obtain the bill of lading and, consequently, title to the goods.

In the present case, Textile never paid Dae Uk (via the bank) and therefore never obtained legal title to the goods. The bank eventually returned the bill of lading to Dae Uk, again making Dae Uk the legal owner of the goods; Textile was never the legal owner. Therefore, unlike a "straight" bill of lading transaction where delivery is made and ownership is conferred when the seller transfers possession to the carrier, here delivery was never made because title at all times remained with the holders of the negotiable bill of lading—Dae Uk and the bank. Consequently, while Sea-Road never had title to the goods, at all times once it received the goods from Dae Uk, it had a superior right to possess and control the goods as intended by the bill of lading and thus satisfied the "possession" element of conversion.

[The discussion of the appropriateness of damages and the relevant limitations period has been omitted.]

- How did Sea-Road have a right to control possession of the goods after it surrendered them for delivery to Soto – and thus a conversion claim?

- How did Soto convert the goods in question?

- To whom did Soto owe a duty to deliver the warehoused goods?

International Perspective: Documents of Title

The following excerpt from Richard LaCroix and Panos Varangis, *Using Warehouse Receipts in Developing and Transition Economies*, 33 Fin. & Dev. 36 (Sept. 1996), shows how strong markets in documents of title can assist in a country's economic development. As you read this excerpt, note the relationship between secured credit and the use of documents of title in the fashion the authors describe.

> Warehouse receipts provide farmers with an instrument that will allow them to extend the sales period of modestly perishable products well beyond the harvesting season. When delivering the product to an accredited warehouse, the farmer obtains a

warehouse receipt that can be used as collateral for short-term borrowing to obtain working capital. That way, the farmer does not need to sell the product immediately to ease cash constraints. Of course, this option will be attractive only if the farmer expects that seasonal price increases will make it worthwhile to store the product and sell it later.

Unfortunately, governmental price supports are often structured in such a way that these expectations are not met. Rather, owing to governments' efforts to decrease price volatility and "stabilize markets," support prices are frequently fixed for most of the period between harvests and, on top of that, are set uniformly for the entire country. Moreover, real interest rates are often very high in developing and transition countries, making borrowing against inventories infeasible. This occurs because it is unlikely that borrowing costs can be recouped through seasonal price increases, even in the absence of other price-dampening measures.

The availability of secure warehouse receipts may, however, allow owners of inventories to borrow abroad in currencies for which real interest rates are lower, particularly if loans are made against inventories of an export commodity, thereby hedging against the foreign exchange risk of foreign borrowing. This practice is followed in Kenya and Uganda, where coffee stocks are often financed in pounds sterling. Also, since high real interest rates are often linked to perceived risks, particularly when it concerns agriculture, secure warehouse receipts may reduce risk and lead to lower lending rates.

Correctly structured warehouse receipts provide secure collateral for banks by assuring holders of the existence and condition of agricultural inventories "sight unseen." Warehouse receipts can be used by farmers to finance their production, and by processors to finance their inventories. If there is a default on any obligation guaranteed with the warehouse receipt – for instance, a bank loan – the holder has first call on the underlying goods or their monetary equivalent. Collateralizing agricultural inventories will lead to an increase in the availability of credit, reduce its cost, and mobilize external financial resources for the sector.

Warehouse receipts contribute to the creation of cash and forward markets and thus enhance competition. They can form the basis for trading commodities, since they provide all the essential information needed to complete a transaction between a seller and a buyer. Their availability will thus both increase the volume of trade and reduce transaction costs. Since buyers need not see the goods, transactions need not take place at either the storage or the inspection location. Indeed, with a functioning warehouse-receipt system, commodities are rarely, if ever, sold at the warehouse proper. A transaction can take place informally or on an organized market or exchange. In either case, the warehouse receipt forms the basis for the creation of a spot, or cash, market. If transactions involve the delivery of goods on a future date, warehouse receipts can form the basis for the creation of a forward market and for the delivery system in a commodity futures exchange. A broader benefit of warehouse receipts is that they increase the confidence of participants, particularly those in the private sector, in market transactions. *Id.* at 36-37.

- Based upon this excerpt, how can a strong market in documents of title improve the secured-lending environment?

Chapter Conclusion: As you leave this chapter and complete your study of Commercial Transactions in this survey course, you should have a sense of how each UCC Article that has been presented – primarily Articles 2, 3, 4, 5, 7, and 9 – can work together in a single transaction to govern the rights and responsibilities of the parties in various aspects of their business relationships with one another. You should also have a sense of when other Articles – such as 2A and 4A – might be implicated, requiring study that goes beyond the scope of this textbook, or when other bodies of law – state, federal, or international – or private agreement may interpose rights and responsibilities additional to or different from those in the Code. It is my hope that this book has given you a basic understanding of the commercial law of the United States, as well as some perspective on international and transnational law, that will serve as a foundation for your continued study of this area and will assist you in your future practice of law.

INDEX

ABA Business Law Section........ 1-10, 15-51
Absolute bar rule 17-19, 17-29
Acceleration clause.....8-10, 8-20, 8-35, 9-35, 13-1, 17-4, 17-7, 17-8
Acceptance2-1, 5-17, 5-19, 10-15, 11-5, 11-7, 11-9
Accepted credit card................................12-7
Accommodated party............................ 11-14
Accommodation party 11-1, 11-7, 11-12, 11-13, 11-16, 11-17
Accord and satisfaction 11-1, 11-7
Account cancellation.................. 12-13, 12-14
Accounts 13-22
Accounts receivable.......... 13-8, 14-21, 15-42
Accrual...11-1
Add-on clause 15-40
Adjudicated incompetence....... 10-50, 10-51, 10-54, 11-20
Adviser...18-5
After-acquired collateral 14-1, 14-18, 14-20, 14-21, 14-23, 14-25, 15-4, 15-41
After-acquired inventory 14-19, 14-21, 14-23
Agency 9-4, 9-6, 9-11, 10-27, 12-2, 12-3, 12-5, 15-45
Agreement 1-4, 1-8, 2-24
Agricultural lien 13-8
Aid to Families With Dependent Children (AFDC) 12-42
Alces, Peter 1-8
Ali, P.A.U. 16-10
Alteration 9-22, 9-27, 9-28, 11-30
Amendment.. 15-10
American Bar Association.......... 1-10, 15-51
American Law Institute (ALI). 1-1, 1-3, 1-9, 1-10, 1-12, 7-6
American Legal Realism 1-5
Amount test...9-31
Anomalous indorsement.................9-4, 11-16
Anticipatory repudiation 5-13, 5-15, 5-45, 5-46
Applicant..18-4, 18-5
Article 1 – General Provisions 1-16
Article 2 – Sales 1-16
Article 2A – Leases 1-17
Article 3 – Negotiable Instruments 1-17
Article 4 – Bank Deposits and Collections 1-17
Article 4A – Funds Transfers 1-17
Article 5 – Letters of Credit....................1-17
Article 6 – Bulk Sales 1-18
Article 7 – Documents of Title 1-18

Article 8 – Investment Securities...........1-18
Article 9 – Secured Transactions 1-18
As-extracted collateral 15-32
Assignment................................ 7-1, 7-19, 9-1
Assurance of performance......................5-13
Attachment of security interest.............13-1, 14-30, 14-32, 14-34, 14-35, 15-1, 16-1
Attorney 9-29
Australia 3-8
Authentication..14-1
Auto pawn 12-40
Automated-teller-machine transactions 12-22, 12-24, 12-27, 12-28, 12-43
Automatic perfection 13-1, 15-1, 15-37, 15-41, 15-42
Automatic stay....................15-39, 17-1, 17-2
Automobile title law 16-6
Aval 11-21, 11-22
Ayres, Ian..5-5
Bad faith ...4-34, 9-21, 9-24, 9-33, 9-35, 17-4
Bailment 6-9, 15-45, 18-28, 18-29, 18-31
Baird, Douglas G. 1-6
Bank-collection processes 7-1
Bank-customer agreement......................10-2
Banking day 10-14, 10-22
Bankruptcy............. 6-19, 10-31, 13-29, 17-1
Bankruptcy Abuse Prevention and Consumer Protection Act............... 12-16
Bankruptcy trustee.................. 13-30, 16-33
Bank-statement rule 10-31, 10-55
BAPCA.. 12-16
Barnes, Richard.......................................2-2
Barr, Michael S.................................... 12-48
Barru, David 18-10
Basic banking............................ 12-41, 12-43
Battle of the forms..........................2-24, 2-31
Baxter, Thomas C. Jr. 7-5
Bearer paper 8-7, 8-8, 8-9, 9-4, 9-6, 9-14
Before maturity 8-31
Beneficiary....................12-31, 18-1, 18-5
Beneficiary's bank 12-31
Benfield, Marion......................................13-6
Benjamin, Judah......................................1-11
Bernstein, Lisa............................... 1-7, 3-13
Bethell-Jones, Richard............................16-9
Bill of lading 18-3, 18-5, 18-6, 18-7, 18-9, 18-27, 18-29
Billing errors 12-13, 12-16
Bills of Exchange Act........7-4, 7-8, 7-9, 7-10, 7-15, 8-2, 8-3, 8-4, 8-6, 8-8, 8-17, 8-18, 8-21, 8-22, 8-29, 8-34, 9-14, 9-41, 11-40
Blank indorsement 9-4, 9-6, 9-14

Blanket assent 2-41

Blomquist, Robert F. 8-8, 8-17, 8-29

Blue-Pencil Rule 2-34

Boghossian, Nayiri 5-52

Boilerplate 2-26, 2-35, 2-40

Bona-fide purchaser for value........1-19, 2-2, 6-3, 6-5, 6-9, 6-21, 7-18, 9-1, 9-22, 9-23
See also Good-faith purchaser for value

Breach of peace 17-1, 17-11, 17-13, 17-14, 17-15

Breach of warranty 2-1, 4-9, 7-2

Browsewrap 2-38, 2-39

Buckley, F. H. 8-2

Budnitz, Mark E. 12-41, 12-50

Bulk sale ...6-17, 6-19, 6-20, 6-21, 6-22, 6-23

Buyer in ordinary course of business ...6-10, 6-12, 6-14, 6-16, 15-15, 16-6, 16-24, 16-26, 16-27, 16-30

Campbell, Andrew 10-30

Canada 1-15, 2-21, 7-10, 8-21, 8-22, 9-57, 11-40, 11-41, 15-35, 16-30, 16-31, 16-32, 18-26

Cape Town Convention............. 13-19, 14-35

Card issuer 12-1, 12-5, 12-7

Cardholder.........12-1, 12-2, 12-3, 12-4, 12-5, 12-6, 12-10

Carrier 18-29

Case of the Negotiable Cow 8-2

Cash 10-10, 10-11, 10-24

Cashier's check 7-11, 7-13, 7-22, 7-24, 7-27, 10-44, 10-49, 11-20

Casual and isolated transaction test. 15-42, 15-43

Caveat emptor 4-1, 4-10

CCC..8-23

CDCU 12-46

CDLF 12-47

Certificate of inspection............................18-6

Certificate of origin 18-19

Certificated securities........................... 15-45

Certificate-of-title statute 14-9, 15-31, 16-2, 16-6, 16-7, 16-9

Certified check 7-22, 10-49

Charge-back 10-21, 10-24, 10-27, 12-19

Chattel..13-2

Chattel paper 13-8, 13-22

Chattel-mortgage 13-6

Cheapest cost avoider...............................6-5

Check 7-9, 7-10, 7-14

Check Clearing for the 21st Century Act..... 10-28

Check kiting 9-36, 10-1, 10-7, 10-9, 10-36

Check truncation................................... 10-28

Check-cashing companies 9-19, 12-40

Check-processing region 10-11

Checkwriting machine..............................9-28

Cheque guarantee card............................ 10-30

Child-care assistance 12-44

Child-support payments 12-44

China 1-15, 2-21, 7-10

CHIPS 12-31, 12-32

Choice of law 1-23, 2-21, 2-23

Choroszucha, Lech 13-32

CIF 3-19

Cigarettes....................................4-15, 4-34

Civil Aeronautics Act...............................2-37

Clearing houses 7-4, 10-2, 10-16

Clickwrap....................................2-38, 2-39

Coase theorem 3-14, 3-16

Coase, Ronald H. 3-14

Collateral 8-10, 8-20, 11-13, 13-1, 13-2, 13-4, 13-21, 13-22, 13-26, 13-28

Collateral description 15-4

Collateral-description registration search 15-35, 15-36

Collected funds 9-36

Collecting bank 10-1, 10-13, 10-14, 10-24, 10-27

Co-maker 11-16

Commercial letter of credit.....................18-2

Commercial realty 1-14

Commercial reasonableness ... 17-21, 17-22, 17-23, 17-25, 17-26, 17-27, 17-29

Commercial tort claim 13-22

Commercial units.....................................5-17

Community development bank (CDB)......... 12-46

Community development bank credit union (CDCU) 12-46

Community development financial institution (CDFI).......................... 12-45

Community development loan funds (CDLF)... 12-47

Comparative negligence 11-30

Composite documents 14-5

Computer information 2-14, 2-16, 15-28

Computerized searching...................... 15-27

Conditional payment................................7-11

Conditional sale 13-6, 13-12

Confirmation 2-24, 2-31

Confirmer..18-4, 18-5

Consequential damages......4-33, 4-46, 4-47, 5-19, 5-40, 5-41, 5-43, 5-52, 10-42, 12-32, 12-35, 12-36, 12-38

Consideration...9-24

Consignee... 18-28

Consignment........... 13-2, 13-8, 13-10, 13-12

Consignor... 18-28

Constructive delivery 9-2

Consumer Credit Protection Act 12-1, 12-22

Consumer goods 9-48, 13-1, 13-21, 15-37, 15-38, 15-39

Consumer protection 1-8, 9-41, 9-58

Continuous perfection 15-1

Contract liability. 7-2, 11-1, 11-5, 11-7, 11-9, 11-21

Contract of carriage 18-5

Contract of guaranty 11-12

Contribution..11-15

Convention on International Interests in Mobile Equipment ... 13-19, 14-35, 15-56

Conversion.. 9-4, 10-49, 11-30, 11-31, 11-40, 11-41, 18-32

Cooter, Robert...................................4-48, 5-12

Correction statement.............................. 15-10

Correspondent 18-4

Courier without luggage 7-1, 7-17, 8-19

Course of dealing......1-14, 2-32, 4-11, 14-10, 17-7

Cover......................................5-40, 5-43, 5-44

Creation of security interest 13-1, 15-1, 16-1

Credit...7-2

Credit card.. 12-20

Credit-card fraud...................................... 12-20

Credit-card sales slip 12-18

Cuming, Ronald.. 15-35

Cure ... 1-7, 5-28, 5-32, 5-34, 5-35, 5-38, 5-41

Currency 7-25, 7-27

Currency substitute...................................8-10

Custom 1-14, 2-32, 3-12, 5-22, 5-23, 8-1

Custom goods...5-51

Customer-deposit contract 10-31

Customs 3-13

D'Oench, Duhme doctrine 9-42, 9-50, 9-52, 9-54

Dallas, Lynne L. 5-10

Damages for breach of warranty 4-42

Date certain requirement.......................8-32

Davies, Iwan... 13-20

Death 10-31, 10-50

Debit cards..........................7-2, 12-22, 12-39

Debtor.. 15-20

Debtor-name registration-search system..... 15-35

Default...... 1-14, 9-32, 13-1, 13-2, 17-1, 17-4, 17-5, 17-9, 18-3, 18-4

Default terms...1-4

Deferred posting 10-14

Deficiency........................ 17-19, 17-22, 17-29

Deliveree 18-28

Deliveror 18-28

Delivery order 18-28, 18-30

Demand draft..11-5

Demand note..11-5

Deposit account................................... 13-22

Depositary bank 9-6, 9-24, 10-1, 10-5, 10-6, 10-7, 10-9, 10-13, 11-29

Description of collateral 14-1, 14-13, 15-2, 15-3

Desimone, Beth S................................... 12-48

Determination-of-harm standard....... 18-18

Directives...1-20

Discharge 11-1, 11-13

Discharge by payment 9-14, 11-3

Discharge in bankruptcy 9-14

Disclaimer.. 2-1, 3-22, 4-25, 4-26, 4-28, 4-29, 4-30, 4-31

Discount 9-31, 9-34

Disguised sale 13-13

Dishonor...... 10-1, 10-8, 10-13, 10-15, 10-19, 10-33, 10-35, 10-36, 11-1, 11-5, 11-7, 11-20

Disposition of collateral... 13-2, 17-20, 17-22

Doctrine of close connectedness...9-41, 9-42, 9-46, 9-57

Doctrine of independent contract........ 18-24

Doctrine of shaken faith.................5-29, 5-32

Doctrine of strict compliance... 18-13, 18-17, 18-20

Document of title......18-5, 18-6, 18-7, 18-27, 18-33

Documentary transaction.... 18-1, 18-3, 18-6

Documents....................................13-22, 18-3

Documents of title 18-1, 18-3

Dohm, Jürgen 8-9, 9-40

Dolan, John F..2-18

Double liability..11-3

Draft... 7-1, 7-10, 7-14

Dragnet clause............... 14-23, 14-24, 14-26

Drawee 7-14, 7-15, 11-1, 11-9

Drawer 7-14, 7-15, 7-29, 11-1, 11-2, 11-7

Dual-filing system 15-14

Due Process Clause 9-50, 9-52

Duress...9-14, 9-22

Duty to preserve collateral 17-35

Duty to read a contract 9-15

EBT 12-41, 12-42, 12-43

Economic-loss rule 11-35

Eggert, Kurt 9-48

Eigentumsvorbehalt.............................. 14-27

Elder financial abuse............................. 10-54

Electronic contracts 2-38

Electronic Fund Transfer Act (EFTA) 12-22, 12-23, 12-24, 12-30, 12-31, 12-43, 12-44

Electronic presentment....7-2, 7-3, 8-3, 10-1, 10-2, 10-10, 10-11, 10-28, 10-29, 11-29

E-mail 2-53

Emergency conditions 10-12

Enabling provisions 1-20

Encoding fraud 10-8
Encoding warranty 11-23, 11-29
Entrustment.......... 2-1, 6-9, 6-13, 6-14, 6-16,
    16-27, 16-28
Equipment............. 13-1, 13-21, 13-23, 13-26
Equitable mortgage 16-9, 16-10
Equitable subordination 16-15
Errors in filing...............................15-1, 15-9
Escrow account 10-36, 11-32
ESD (Electronic Services Delivery) 12-44
Estoppel...17-8
European Bank for Reconstruction and
    Development (EBRD)...................... 13-20
Execution lien 16-8
Executory promise 9-24
Expedited check processing 10-2
Expedited Funds Availability Act (EFAA) ..
    10-9, 10-13
Expert testimony.....................................9-35
Express conditions 8-10
Express warranty........ 4-1, 4-3, 4-4, 4-5, 4-6,
    4-11, 4-13, 4-14, 4-24, 4-26, 4-29, 4-30,
    4-37, 4-38
Extension of time.................................. 11-13
Extrinsic evidence 8-32
Facsimile signature 8-6
Failure of a contract remedy's essential
    purpose 4-29
Failure of consideration 9-14
Fair Credit Billing Act.......................... 12-14
Farm products 13-1, 13-21, 13-22
Federal Bills of Lading Act.. 1-14, 18-6, 18-9
Federal Deposit Insurance Corporation
    (FDIC)..............................9-50, 9-53, 9-54
Federal estoppel doctrine...............9-53, 9-54
Federal Home Loan Bank check......... 10-10
Federal regulatory law...........................1-15
Federal Reserve Note 8-35
Federal Reserve System 7-4, 7-6, 10-2, 10-5,
    10-6, 10-9, 10-10, 10-13
Federal tax lien.............. 16-33, 16-35, 16-37
Federal Tax Lien Act................. 16-33, 16-35
Federal Trade Commission.....................9-42
Federalism..1-11
Fedwire... 12-31
Felemegas, John...5-9
Fiducia.. 13-33
Fiduciary relationship..... 9-37, 11-32, 11-33
Final payment...... 10-1, 10-13, 10-15, 10-16,
    10-24
Final Report of the National Commission
    of Electronic Fund Transfers 12-28
Final settlement 10-16, 10-24
Financial abuse.. 10-54

Financial Management Service of the
    Department of the Treasury 12-42
Financing statement . 13-1, 14-1, 14-2, 14-3,
    14-4, 14-5, 14-6, 14-8, 15-1, 15-2, 15-3,
    15-8, 15-10
First-Shot Rule 2-34
First-to-file-or-otherwise-perfect rule...........
    16-10, 16-11
Fixed amount of money requirement ....
    8-22, 8-23
Fixtures 13-21, 15-32
FOB..3-19
Food and Drug Act...............................1-15
Food Security Act...........................8-24, 15-8
Forced acceptance 5-17, 5-19
Foreign-natural test 4-19
Forged indorsement............. 8-6, 9-22, 10-61,
    10-62, 11-24, 11-26, 11-30, 11-31
France............................ 1-15, 2-21, 7-8, 7-10
Fraud 1-8, 9-57
Fraud in the factum......... 6-1, 6-2, 9-14, 9-22
Fraud in the inducement................. 6-2, 9-14
Free-ride..5-13
Frisch, David...1-8
FTC Holder in Due Course Rule. 9-42, 9-48,
    9-49, 9-50, 9-52
FTLA 16-35, 16-36
Full satisfaction language 11-8
Fundamental breach............5-19, 5-30, 5-31
Furnish, Dale Beck 18-26
Future-advances clause 14-1, 15-4, 15-41,
    16-11, 16-13, 16-14
Galanter, Marc 4-47
Gaps 1-14
Garnishment.. 10-50
General Comment 1-3, 1-19
General contract for sale of goods 2-22
General intangible 13-22, 13-24, 13-25,
    13-26, 15-28, 15-29
General levy 13-29
Geneva Uniform Laws (GUL) 7-8, 7-10, 8-6,
    8-29, 9-21, 9-22, 9-41, 10-61, 11-22,
    11-30
Gerdes, Geoffrey R. 7-2
Germany 1-15, 2-21, 3-8, 4-36, 5-30, 5-31,
    7-8, 7-10, 14-27, 14-28, 14-29
Geva, Benjamin.................................. 10-59
Gilmore, Grant 1-4, 6-7, 13-2
Good faith 1-4, 1-6, 5-1, 5-3, 5-4, 5-5, 5-8,
    5-32, 5-40, 5-44, 6-6, 6-7, 6-12, 6-14,
    8-20, 8-35, 9-23, 9-26, 9-33, 9-35, 11-15,
    13-1, 17-3, 17-8
Good title... 6-1, 6-2

Good-faith purchaser for value........ 2-1, 6-2,
    6-3, 6-4, 6-6, 6-7, 16-28
    See also Bona-fide purchaser for value
Goods 2-1, 2-6, 13-21, 15-38
Goods and services...2-1, 2-6, 2-7, 2-12, 2-22
Government check 10-10
Government warrant 8-13
Gravamen of the complaint test..............2-9
Gross negligence...................................9-21
Guaranteeing collection 11-13
Guaranteeing payment........................ 11-13
Guaranty..................................... 11-14, 13-33
Guardian...9-37
Hardwick, Abby.....................................2-16
Harmonization..................................... 13-20
Herrmann, Gerold 7-7, 8-30, 9-21, 11-21
Hillinger, Ingrid Michelsen 2-19
Hillman, Robert....................2-38, 2-40, 2-41
Holder........ 7-1, 7-29, 9-1, 9-3, 9-4, 9-6, 9-15,
    9-21, 9-23, 9-24, 9-32, 9-33, 9-41, 9-42,
    9-44, 9-46
Holder by due negotiation 1-19
Holder in due course.... 1-19, 7-1, 7-18, 7-19,
    7-29, 9-1, 9-4, 9-14, 9-15, 9-16, 9-17,
    9-18, 9-21, 9-22, 9-23, 9-25, 9-26, 9-29,
    9-32, 9-33, 9-38, 9-40, 9-41, 9-42, 9-44,
    9-45, 9-46, 9-47, 9-48, 9-50, 9-55, 9-57,
    10-28, 12-1, 12-10
Holding certificate 18-3
Horizontal privity....................................4-37
Hughes, Sandra L. 10-54
Hypotheca................................... 13-33, 13-34
Hypothetical lien creditor 15-38, 16-2, 16-33
IACA 15-10
ICC 18-10, 18-11
ICC's Uniform Rules for Demand
    Guarantees (URDG)........................ 18-10
Identification to the contract.....................2-6
Ikkai barai 12-21, 12-22, 12-40
Illegality 9-14, 9-17, 9-18, 9-22, 9-57
Implied conditions....................................8-10
Implied warranty 4-10, 4-17, 4-26
Implied warranty of fitness for a particular
    purpose 4-11, 4-21, 4-23, 4-24, 4-26,
    5-42
Implied warranty of merchantability ....
    4-11, 4-13, 4-15, 4-16, 4-19, 4-23, 4-24,
    4-26, 5-42
Imposter rule.............................. 11-35, 11-36
Incapacity........................... 9-22, 10-31, 10-50
Incidental damages...................................5-40
INCOTERMS 3-19
Independence principle 18-22, 18-25
India...8-6
Indorsement. 7-1, 9-4, 9-6, 9-14, 10-13, 11-3

Indorser 11-1, 11-3, 11-4, 11-5, 11-7
Ineffective rejection...............5-20, 5-47, 5-50
Infancy...6-2
Infinity registration 15-35
Insecurity clause...........................8-20, 17-6
Insolvency 9-22, 11-17, 16-1
Inspection............. 2-1, 2-23, 5-20, 5-23, 18-6
Installment contract 2-1, 5-10, 5-13, 5-16,
    5-19, 5-20
Installment notes 9-32
Instrument 13-22, 13-25, 13-26
Insufficient funds 9-32, 10-31, 10-35
Insurable interest.......2-1, 3-1, 3-6, 3-9, 3-12
Insurance certificate 18-6
Insurance check.......................................7-28
Insurance contracts 1-14
Intangible property 13-21, 13-22
Interbank payment............................... 12-31
Interdistrict Settlement Fund 10-6
Interest..9-32
Interest groups...1-12
Intermediary bank..................................10-1
International Association of Commercial
    Administrators Secured Transactions
    Section (IACA) 15-10
International Bill of Exchange 7-9, 7-17,
    7-22, 8-8, 10-30
International Chamber of Commerce 18-10
International Promissory Note 7-9, 7-17,
    8-8, 10-30
International sources of commercial law
    1-15
International Standby Practices ISP 98
    (ISP 98).. 18-10
Inventory.... 13-1, 13-21, 13-22, 13-26, 14-19
Inventory swaps 6-22
Investment property............................. 13-22
Invoice..2-24
Irrational cooperation...............................5-13
Irregularity 9-23, 9-25, 9-33
ISP 98 .... 18-11, 18-12
Issuance 7-1, 7-28, 7-29, 9-1, 11-3, 11-23
Issuer 18-1, 18-4
Ius in re aliena 13-33
Jackson, Thomas....................................13-5
Japan 1-15, 2-21, 7-10, 8-6, 12-20, 12-21,
    12-22, 12-39, 12-40
J-Debit.. 12-39
Joint and several liability 11-15
Judgment lien 16-18, 16-34, 16-36, 16-37
Kappu 12-22
Ken, Catherine I.C. 17-42
Kenya.. 18-34
Kibble, Neil... 10-30
Kim, Eui Jae 17-43

King, Donald B. 2-22

Knight, W. H. Jr. 2-22

Knock-Out Rule...........................2-33

Korea 5-9, 17-43

Kuenzel, Calvin A. 2-22

Kuhn, Hans.............................. 14-27

LaCroix, Richard 18-33

Landlords' lien 13-8

Lapsed financing statement 15-10

Late dishonor 10-17

Law merchant............................ 1-6, 7-4

Lawrence, Lary...........................7-4

Lease .. 2-1, 13-2, 13-12, 13-14, 13-15, 13-16, 13-27

Legal malpractice................... 15-27

Legal mortgage 16-10

Legal process............................. 10-31, 10-50

Legal tender 1-14

Letter of credit......... 18-1, 18-8, 18-12, 18-25

Letter-of-credit rights 13-22

Levy of execution.......................16-8

Lien creditor .. 15-24, 16-6, 16-7, 16-8, 16-33

Lipson, Jonathan.......................... 13-4, 13-28

Liu, Lawrence S....................... 17-42

Llewellyn, Karl 1-5, 2-18, 2-41, 3-13

Logistics of filing...........................15-2, 15-9

Lookofsky, Joseph 5-52

Lost volume sales...........................5-44, 5-50

Lousin, Ann 2-15

Lowest intermediate balance rule 15-17, 15-18, 15-19

Lump-concept approach 3-3

Maggs, Gregory 2-55

Magic words 8-7, 8-8

Magnetic Ink Character Recognition (MICR)...........................10-1, 10-3, 10-4

Magnuson-Moss Warranty Act...4-42, 4-43, 4-44

Maker 7-14, 7-29, 11-1, 11-2

Malaysia...........................1-15, 2-21, 7-10

Malpractice........................... 15-27

Mann, Ronald J. 12-20, 12-39, 13-31

Material alteration..........................2-32

McDonnell, Julian B........................1-5, 1-11

Mellinkoff, David................... 13-21

Member bank........................... 12-18, 12-19

Mental incapacity..........................6-2, 10-34

Merchant...2-18, 2-19, 2-25, 4-11, 6-15, 6-16

Merchant's exception to the statute of frauds...........................2-19, 2-48, 2-51

Merchantability.....................4-11, 4-17, 4-18

Mere reference 8-15

Merger 4-39, 7-11, 7-28

Mexico.................. 1-15, 2-21, 5-8, 7-10, 18-25

Microfinance................... 12-47, 12-48

Midnight deadline rule .. 10-1, 10-14, 10-15, 10-16, 10-50, 10-52

Miller, Fred H. 1-9, 7-6

Minimum monthly credit-card payment 12-17

Minor 9-37

Mirage of hope 17-21

Mirror-image rule 18-17

Misrepresentation.....................3-12, 6-2

Mobile equipment 15-56

Model Deposit Account Control Agreement 15-51

Model Inter-American Law on Secured Transactions.................... 13-20

Modigliani-Miller hypothesis............. 13-17

Monetary Control Act of 1980 10-6

Money........................7-11

Money order .. 7-22, 7-24, 7-27, 10-45, 12-41

Mooney, Charles W..................... 14-36

Motor-vehicle-title statutes 15-32

Mutual assent..... 2-1, 2-35, 2-38, 9-14, 14-6, 14-10

Nachfrist........................5-39

Name of the debtor 15-2, 15-11, 15-20, 15-21, 15-23

Narrow-issue thinking 3-3

National Conference of Commissioners on Uniform State Laws (NCCUSL)1-1, 1-2, 1-10, 1-12, 1-13, 7-4, 7-6

Negligence 4-6

Negotiability 7-1, 7-18, 7-19, 8-1, 8-3, 8-7, 8-8, 8-9, 8-12, 8-25, 8-29, 13-4

Negotiable bill of lading 18-8

Negotiable document of title 18-3

Negotiable instrument.. 2-1, 7-1, 7-11, 7-19, 7-29, 8-1, 8-2, 8-3, 8-11, 8-12

Negotiable Instruments Law (NIL) 7-4

Negotiable warehouse receipt 9-33

Negotiation 7-19, 9-1, 9-3, 9-4, 9-6

Netherlands............................4-36

New customer account........................ 10-12

No additional promise requirement.....8-18, 8-21

No refund policy 12-11

Nominated person..........................18-4

Noncash payment 7-2, 7-3

Nonconforming goods..........................5-32

Non-consumer-goods PMSI creditor .. 16-21

Nondocumentary conditions............... 18-13

Nonmerchant..........................2-18, 2-25

Non-modification clause 17-8

Non-negotiable bill of lading 18-9

Non-negotiable instrument.. 8-1, 8-11, 8-12, 8-13, 8-14, 8-21, 9-1, 9-54

Nonpossessory security interest.13-3, 15-36

Nonpresentment 9-22
Non-uniform enactment 1-4, 1-12
Non-waivable rights 13-5
Non-waiver acceleration clause.............17-8
Non-waiver provision 17-8
Norms... 1-6, 5-13
Norris, John E............................. 8-30, 10-62
Notice 4-31, 4-32, 4-34, 4-35, 4-36, 4-40,
    5-25, 5-27, 5-32, 9-23, 9-25, 9-27, 9-33,
    9-37, 9-38, 9-41, 10-50, 16-18, 16-19,
    16-20, 16-21
Notice filing..15-2
Notice of dishonor 10-19, 10-21, 10-30, 11-1,
    11-4, 11-5
Notice of nonconformity 18-13, 18-16
Nuisance suit 4-48
Numerus clausus 13-28, 13-32, 13-33
O'Brien, Carrie A.................................. 12-48
O'Driscoll, Peter S. 18-27
Official commentary 8-17
Omnibus clause 14-13, 14-14, 14-15
On-us check 10-10
Open-end credit plan 12-1
Operating circulars 10-2
Option to purchase............................... 13-12
Order bill of lading 18-32
Order paper 8-7, 8-8, 9-4, 9-6, 9-14
Ordinary care 10-22, 10-28, 10-55, 10-57,
    11-34, 15-28
Ordinary use 4-11, 4-21, 4-24
Organization of American States (OAS) ......
    13-20
Overby, A. Brooke 7-6
Overdraft...... 9-30, 9-36, 10-33, 10-34, 10-36
Overdue.................................9-22, 9-32, 9-41
Over-encoding...10-4
Overview of the UCC...............................1-16
Ownership of a negotiable instrument ...9-2
Pain v. Packard doctrine...................... 11-16
Parol evidence rule....... 2-1, 2-42, 2-47, 2-53,
    4-29, 8-32, 8-33, 9-12, 11-6
Parsons, Theophilus 1-11
Part of the basis of the bargain. 4-1, 4-2, 4-5
Passage of title 3-1, 3-5, 3-8, 5-17
Pay to bearer 8-7
Pay to the order of.....................................8-7
Payable at a definite time........................8-31
Payable on demand 8-31
Payable through 7-28, 11-10
Payday loan 12-41
Payee......................................7-14, 7-29, 9-5
Payment in kind certificate....................8-23
Payment order 12-31
Payment systems 7-1
Payor bank .. 10-1, 10-5, 10-14, 10-16, 11-29

Payor in good faith 11-26
Payroll card 12-41, 12-48, 12-49, 12-50
Penney, Norman 8-3, 8-6, 8-35
Percentage of accounts test........9-31, 15-42,
    15-43
Perfect Tender Rule..... 1-8, 5-10, 5-16, 5-20,
    5-32, 5-36
Perfection 13-1, 15-1, 15-28, 16-1
Perfection by control 15-37, 15-47
Perfection by filing 15-1
Perfection by possession . 13-1, 15-37, 15-44
Performance 2-1, 4-1
Permanent and portable test............ 8-1, 8-3
Permanent Editorial Board 1-9
Permissive filing................................... 15-30
Perpetual letter of credit.........................18-5
Person entitled under the document.. 18-28
Personal check 7-22, 7-24
Personal defense..........7-19, 9-14, 9-18, 11-3
Personal Property Security Act........... 15-35
Personal Property Security Act (PPSA) ....
    16-31, 16-32
Personal security........................ 13-33, 13-34
Peters, Ellen 13-5
Physical duress................................6-1, 9-14
Physical possession.................................7-13
Pignus 13-33, 13-34
Pledge 13-2, 13-3, 13-34, 14-27
PMSI
    See Purchase-money security interest
Politicization...1-12
Possession of an instrument 9-1
Postdated check.................................... 10-31
Predominant purpose test...2-10, 2-12, 2-16
Preemption 13-8
Prefatory note 6-18
Prepaid debit cards 12-40
Prepayment of a debt 8-10
Pre-sale advertising 17-22
Present value 9-35
Presentation 18-5
Presenting bank 10-1, 10-28
Presentment........ 7-1, 7-28, 7-29, 11-1, 11-5,
    11-7, 11-20, 11-23
Presentment for acceptance..........7-29, 11-7
Presentment for payment 7-29, 11-7
Presentment warranty . 11-22, 11-24, 11-27
Previous Uniform Acts............................. 1-3
Primary liability 11-2, 11-9, 11-12
Principal..9-4, 9-11
Principal obligor 11-13, 11-16
Priority 13-1, 13-29, 13-30, 16-1
Private sale................................. 17-22, 17-25
Privity 1-8, 2-1, 4-36, 4-37, 4-38, 4-39,
    4-40, 4-41

Proceeds 14-30, 15-7, 15-14, 15-15, 15-16, 15-18, 15-19, 15-50
Products 15-7, 15-14
Promisee..7-14
Promisor...7-14
Promissory note 7-1, 7-10, 7-14, 7-22
Properly payable rule ... 10-31, 10-33, 10-34, 11-25, 11-33
Property law.....................................9-2
Prosser, William 4-40
Protected holder...........7-22, 9-21, 9-40, 9-57
Protected purchaser.................................1-19
Protection payments...............................17-2
Protest 10-19
Provisional credit.... 9-27, 10-7, 10-14, 10-52
Provisional settlement 10-14, 10-16
Public goods......................................5-13
Public sale 17-22
Puffing 4-1, 4-4
Punitive damages. 10-35, 10-37, 10-38, 17-7
Purchase option 13-12
Purchase order...................................2-24
Purchase-and-assumption transaction.9-54
Purchase-money security interest (PMSI)... 13-30, 15-37, 15-38, 15-40, 16-18, 16-19, 16-20, 16-21, 16-24
Purposive interpretation............................1-5
Quasi-tangible property 13-21, 13-22
Rachlinski, Jeffrey 2-38, 2-40
Randall, Kenneth C. 8-30, 10-62
Real defense 7-19, 9-14, 9-22, 9-29
Real security................................ 13-33, 13-34
Reasonable care............. 10-34, 17-32, 17-34
Reasonable expectations test.................4-19
Rebuttable presumption test ... 17-19, 17-29
Receiving bank....................................... 12-31
Recognized market 17-31
Redemption 17-39, 17-40, 17-41
Redeposited check................................... 10-12
Reformation...11-6
Registration.. 15-56
Regressive redistribution....................... 13-19
Regulation CC......... 10-1, 10-9, 10-11, 10-13
Regulation E............................... 12-22, 12-50
Rei vindicatio... 13-33
Reimbursement.......................... 11-12, 11-15
Rejection.....................................2-1, 5-19, 5-20
Relationship-preserving norms................1-7
Relativity of title 3-6
Remedies.................................2-1, 2-23, 5-39
Remedies available to the buyer 5-41
Remedies available to the seller............5-47
Remitter 7-23, 10-44
Remitting bank....................................... 12-31
Remotely-created consumer item 11-24

Rent-to-own 12-40
Repeat player 4-47, 4-48
Repossession ...13-2, 17-1, 17-3, 17-7, 17-11, 17-13, 17-14, 17-15
Repossession title 17-2
Reservation of title 3-8
Restatements of the Law 1-2
Restitution 10-35
Restrictive indorsement....9-4, 11-31, 11-32, 11-33
Retail financing 14-25, 14-26
Retail Installment Sales Acts 1-14
Retention of the collateral 17-36
Retention warranty 11-23
Returning bank 10-14
Revisions.................................. 1-4, 1-12, 2-54
Revocation of acceptance 2-1, 5-19, 5-25, 5-28
Rightful rejection...5-20
Rights in the collateral............................ 14-34
Risk of loss 2-1, 2-23, 3-1, 3-8, 3-9, 3-11, 3-14, 3-19, 3-20
Robinson-Patman Act 1-15
Rogers, James Steven 10-59
Rolling contract................................2-35, 2-38
Rusch, Linda J..1-12
Sale or return 13-11, 13-12
Sales and leases. 2-1, 2-2, 2-21, 15-32, 15-33
Sales contract...2-1
Sales in ordinary course of business......6-22
Sales of receivables 13-9
Same-wrongdoer rule 11-30
Schlechtreim, Peter 5-32
Schwarcz, Steven 13-17, 13-27
Schwartz, Alan 1-20
Scope of Article 1 1-22
Scope of Article 9 .... 13-1, 13-2, 13-8
Scott, Robert..................1-20, 2-55, 13-18
Sebert, John 5-39
Secondary liability 11-2, 11-3, 11-5, 11-12
Secondary obligor 11-13
Secret liens 13-11, 14-27, 15-39
Secured party... 13-2
Secured transaction 13-1, 15-32
Securitization 13-27, 13-28
Security agreement.... 13-1, 14-1, 14-2, 14-3, 14-4, 14-5, 14-6, 15-2, 15-3
Security interest 5-20, 6-18, 13-2, 14-1
Self-help 5-19, 17-1, 17-14
Sender.. 12-31
Sending bank 12-31
Seriously misleading test......... 15-10, 15-21, 15-23, 15-27, 15-28
Set-off.................... 10-31, 10-34, 10-36
Set-off test.. 17-19

Shaken faith 5-30
Shelf analogy 9-24
Shelter doctrine 9-57
Sheriff 17-1
Shrinkwrap 2-35
Sicherungsabtretung 14-27
Sicherungsübereignung 14-27
Sight draft 11-10
Signature .. 8-4, 8-5, 8-6, 9-4, 9-6, 9-11, 11-3,
    11-9, 11-30, 14-1
Single-delivery sale 2-1, 5-9, 5-10, 5-13,
    5-16, 5-19, 5-20, 5-31
Single-payment notes 9-32
Skilton, Robert 1-21
Social Security, Supplemental Security
    Income 12-44
Socioeconomics 5-10
South Korea 1-15, 2-21, 7-10
Spanogle, John A. 7-9, 8-35, 9-3, 9-22, 11-30
Special circumstances clause 4-44, 4-45
Special indorsement 9-4, 9-6
Specific performance 5-52
Speidel, Richard E. 1-14, 2-54
Spousal liability 12-6
Stack analogy 9-24
Stale check 10-31, 10-48, 10-50
Standard-form document 2-24
Standby letter of credit 18-1, 18-3, 18-27
Standing timber 15-32
Statute of frauds 2-1, 2-47, 2-48, 2-50,
    2-52, 2-53, 14-8
Statute of limitations 9-22, 11-1, 11-19,
    11-20
Statutory estoppel 6-12, 6-13
Stolen goods 7-18
Stone, Bradford 2-22
Stop-payment 10-31, 10-40, 10-42, 10-43,
    10-45, 10-46, 10-51
Story, Justice Joseph 1-11
Straight (non-negotiable) bill of lading
    18-32
Strict foreclosure 17-36
Strict liability 4-6
Subordination agreement 16-14
Subrogation 10-42, 11-14, 11-16
Substantial compliance 18-13
Substantial impairment to the buyer ....
    5-13, 5-15, 5-25, 5-26, 5-27, 5-28, 5-29
Substantial performance doctrine 5-10,
    5-20, 5-36
Substitute check 10-28, 10-29
Suk, Hwang Hyun 16-17, 16-39
Sum certain 8-27, 8-28, 8-29
Summers, Robert S. 1-14
Supergeneric description 14-1, 14-15, 14-17

Supremacy 7-11
Suretyship 11-12, 11-16, 13-33
Surplus 17-22, 17-29
Switzerland 3-8, 4-36
Symbolic instruments 8-27
Taibi, Anthony D. 12-44
Taiwan 1-15, 2-21, 7-10, 17-42
Tajti, Tibor 17-39
Taking delivery 5-19
Takings Clause 9-52
Tape recording 2-52
Teller's check 7-22, 7-24, 10-44, 10-49
Temporary Aid for Needy Families
    (TANF) 12-44
Temporary perfection 13-1, 15-1, 15-37,
    15-52, 15-54
Tender 5-9, 11-7, 17-41
Termination statement 15-10
Thaler, Richard 5-13
Theft 6-1, 9-1
Things in action 2-6
Threat of violence 17-13, 17-14
Three-party paper 7-14
Time certain requirement 8-30
Time draft 11-5
Time note 11-5
Title 2-1, 2-23, 3-1
Title certificate 3-1, 6-13, 6-14
Title pawn 12-41
Tort liability 7-2, 11-1, 11-34, 11-40
Total negation test 2-46
Trade acceptance draft 7-15
Trade usage 2-32, 2-46, 3-12, 4-6, 4-11
Transaction costs 3-17
Transfer of possession ... 7-1, 7-28, 7-29, 9-1,
    9-3, 9-4, 9-6, 11-23
Transfer warranty 11-23, 11-30
Transferee 9-1, 9-57
Transferor 9-1, 9-57
Trust receipt 13-6
Truth in Lending Act (TILA) 12-1, 12-2,
    12-3, 12-4, 12-7, 12-9, 12-10, 12-12,
    12-14, 12-22
Two-party paper 7-14
U.S. Office of the Comptroller of the
    Currency 12-17
U.S. Postal Service money order 10-10
U.S. Treasury check 10-10
UCITA 2-15, 7-6
UCP 500 .. 18-10, 18-11, 18-12, 18-15, 18-16,
    18-17, 18-18, 18-19
Uganda 18-34
Ulen, Thomas 4-48, 5-12
Unaccepted draft 11-2
Unauthorized use 12-1, 12-3, 12-7, 12-10

Unauthorized withdrawal........ 12-23, 12-24
Unbanked person...................... 12-40, 12-48
Uncertified personal check.....................9-19
UNCITRAL...7-7
UNCITRAL Convention on Independent
    Bank Guarantees and Stand-By Letters
    of Credit.................................. 1-16, 18-10
UNCITRAL Model Law on International
    Credit Transfers 1-16
Uncollected funds............................10-7, 10-9
Unconditional requirement..........8-10, 8-11,
    8-12, 8-17, 8-18
Unconscionability.....5-1, 5-3, 5-4, 5-5, 13-14
Under-encoding 10-4
Underlying transaction..................7-1, 11-12
Undersecured creditor..............................17-2
Undue influence 6-2
Unemployment compensation 12-44
UNIDROIT Convention on International
    Financial Leasing................................1-16
UNIDROIT Convention on International
    Interests in Mobile Equipment 1-16
Uniform Bills of Lading Act 1-3
Uniform Conditional Sales Act................1-3
Uniform International Law 1-16
Uniform Negotiable Instruments Law ... 1-3
Uniform Sales Act......................................1-3
Uniform Stock Transfer Act.....................1-3
Uniform Trust Receipts Act.....................1-3
Uniform Warehouse Receipts Act 1-3
United Kingdom. 1-15, 2-21, 7-8, 7-10, 9-41,
    10-30, 11-40, 16-9, 16-10
United Nations Commission on
    International Trade Law Convention on
    Independent Guarantees and Standby
    Letters of Credit............................... 18-11
United Nations Convention on Contracts
    for the International Sale of Goods
    (CISG).1-16, 2-20, 2-21, 2-22, 2-34, 2-47,
    2-53, 3-8, 3-19, 4-9, 4-30, 4-35, 4-36,
    4-41, 4-50, 5-8, 5-19, 5-30, 5-31, 5-39,
    5-52, 6-9, 6-17, 6-23, 7-7
United Nations Convention on
    International Bills of Exchange and
    Promissory Notes (CIBN). 1-16, 7-7, 7-9,
    7-10, 7-15, 7-17, 7-22, 8-6, 8-8, 8-9, 8-17,
    8-21, 8-29, 8-34, 8-35, 9-3, 9-14, 9-21,
    9-22, 9-40, 9-41, 9-57, 10-30, 10-62,
    11-22, 11-30
United Nations Convention on
    International Interests in Mobile
    Equipment... 13-19
United Nations Convention on the
    Assignment of Receivables in
    International Trade 13-19

Unlawful detention..........................17-4, 17-5
Unperfected creditor...........13-1, 16-6, 16-10
Unsecured creditor................................ 13-29
URDG.. 18-11, 18-12
Usages of trade 3-13
USDA 8-23
USDA's Special Supplemental Nutrition
    Program for Women, Infants and
    Children (WIC) 12-44
Used goods...............................4-13, 4-18
Usury laws...........................1-14, 9-19, 9-38
Vague Admonitions 1-21
Validation 11-30
Value.........6-10, 9-22, 9-24, 9-25, 9-27, 9-29,
    9-30, 9-31, 9-40, 9-41, 14-1
Varangis, Panos...................................... 18-33
Variable interest rates 8-22, 8-26, 8-27
Vertical privity...4-37
Violence 17-13, 17-14, 17-15
Vis, Willem 10-61
Void title.2-1, 6-1, 6-2, 7-18, 9-14, 9-18, 9-19
Voidable title 2-1, 6-1, 6-2, 6-6, 6-9, 9-14,
    9-18
Voluntary surrender............................. 17-20
Waiver 4-5, 17-7, 17-21
Walton, Jack K. II 7-2
Warehouse 18-29
Warehouse receipt ...3-9, 18-3, 18-27, 18-29,
    18-33, 18-34
Warrant...................................8-13, 8-14, 8-19
Warranty 2-1, 2-22
Warranty damages...................................4-50
Warranty liability 11-1, 11-6, 11-30
Warranty of quality 2-1, 4-1
Warranty of title..........2-1, 3-20, 3-25, 11-27
White, James J. 1-14
Whitman, James.....................................3-13
Wholesale inventory financing 14-25, 14-26
Wholesale wire transfer.......7-2, 12-31, 18-4
Will substitute 10-51
Willful indifference...................................9-33
Williston, Samuel W................................1-11
Windfall.. 10-43
Wire transfers....................................... 12-41
Without recourse.................. 11-2, 11-5, 11-6
Woodward, William J. Jr........................1-23
Writ of execution 16-8
Writing 8-1, 8-2, 8-3, 8-6
Wrongful dishonor 10-31, 10-35, 10-36,
    10-37, 10-38, 10-41, 11-20
Wrongful garnishment.......................... 10-38
Wrongful rejection....................................5-50
Wrongful repossession17-3, 17-4, 17-5, 17-7
Wrongful-but-effective rejection...5-20, 5-47